"Each language alters, either by occasion
  Of trade, which, causing mutuall commutation
  Of th'earths and Oceans wares, with hardy luck
  Doth words for words barter, exchange, and truck:
  Or else, because Fame-thirsting wits, that toyle,
  In golden termes to trick their gracious stile,
  With new-found beauties prank each circumstance,
  Or (at the least) doe new-coyned words inhaunce
  With currant freedome, and againe restore
  Th'old, rusty, mouldy, worme-gnawne words of yore."

(SYLVESTER, *Babylon*)

An Etymological Dictionary of MODERN ENGLISH

By

Ernest Weekley

With a new biographical memoir of the author by
MONTAGUE WEEKLEY

IN TWO VOLUMES:
Volume I.   A - K

Dover Publications, Inc., New York

Published in Canada by General Publishing Company, Ltd., 30 Lesmill Road, Don Mills, Toronto, Ontario.
Published in the United Kingdom by Constable and Company, Ltd.

This Dover edition, first published in 1967, is an unabridged and unaltered republication of the work originally published in London by John Murray in 1921. The work was originally published in one volume and is now published in two volumes. A new biographical memoir of the author was written by Montague Weekley especially for this Dover edition.

Standard Book Number: 486-21873-2
Library of Congress Catalog Card Number: 67-26968

Manufactured in the United States of America
Dover Publications, Inc.
180 Varick Street
New York, N. Y. 10014

ERNEST WEEKLEY

1865–1954

MY FATHER, Ernest Weekley, was born at Hampstead, which stands upon London's northwestern heights, on April 27, 1865.

Punch's issue of April 27, 1921, printed a fortuitous birthday greeting by C. L. Graves (1856–1944), for over thirty years on the staff of *Punch*, entitled: "The Merry Lexicographer: Lines inspired by Professor ERNEST WEEKLEY's *Etymological Dictionary of Modern English*." Graves made ingenious play with "Weekley" rhymes, and in his concluding stanza further play on the title of Oscar Wilde's classic farcical comedy *The Importance of Being Earnest*:

> In fine, these humble rhymes to close,
> His dictionary quite uniquely
> The paramount "importance" shows,
> And proves, "of being Ernest"—
> WEEKLEY.

Something will be said later in this biographical outline about what Graves also called "the learned levity of Weekley."

His father, Charles Weekley, a most handsomely distinguished-looking man, was from 1863 until 1906 in the service of the Hampstead Board of Guardians as relieving officer, administering the now extinct Poor Law. Ernest Weekley's mother, nee Agnes McCowen, was the daughter of a venerable figure in the life of Uxbridge, Middlesex, where George McCowen combined the functions in that quaint old township of schoolmaster and parish clerk. To his mother, Ernest Weekley owed encouragement and sacrifices which helped him up the arduous steep that was to culminate in international fame as a scholar. From his mother's side, also, he probably inherited his brains. Her uncle, Edward Farr, beginning life as a humble type of schoolteacher, established himself as a man of letters in the Buckinghamshire village of Iver, near Uxbridge, and had the distinction of being invited to complete the *History of England* begun by David Hume and Tobias Smollett.

The Hampstead of my father's childhood was a small country town, the population of which increased from about 19,000 in 1865 to 80,000 by the turn of the century. He could recall the alarm inspired in a small boy by a gipsy encampment which he passed on his way to school down Platt's Lane. It is a very long time since that part of Hampstead could be associated with such a scene. From 1898 to 1912, Weekley's parents rented number 40, Well Walk, once the Hampstead home of the painter John Constable.

Nine Weekley children survived their birth, Ernest being the second child. He became the eldest of the family on the death, at the age of eighteen, of his brother Montague, a promising mathematician. Here, then, was a struggling lower-middle-class family, typically Victorian in size, and offering in that era no encouraging prospect to a brilliant youngster of passing from some famous school to Oxford or Cambridge. Whereas, however, Weekley appears to have owed his intellectual endowment to his mother's family, it was to relatives of his father that he owed a schooling sufficient to enable him to graduate finally at two universities—the hard way. The Reverend Alfred Boulden, a cousin of Charles Weekley, had inherited a successful private boarding school at Margate, which lies on a bracing stretch of Kent's coastline. Boulden—who afterwards became an honorary canon of Rochester Cathedral—had graduated from Corpus Christi College, Cambridge, and was a good classical scholar. He generously accepted three Weekley boys as pupils without fees, although in the case of Ernest he obtained a splendid advertisement for the school, Dane Hill House, in the shape of spectacular examination successes. There were then, and for many years later, local examinations conducted by the Universities of Oxford and Cambridge. In these regional trials of scholastic strength, Ernest Weekley was Dane Hill's doughty champion. I recall the substantial library, with its many gilt calf bindings, won by my father's prowess as an examinee.

After a short apprenticeship to schoolmastering, begun at Colchester when he was only seventeen, Weekley returned to join Dane Hill's teaching staff. Thenceforward, he used his scanty leisure and school holidays for intensive study. His true bent was always towards languages and philology, but he also excelled at mathematics, and was thus able to offer it among the group of subjects in which he passed the examination for London University's ordinary bachelor of arts degree, a valuable teaching qualification at that time.

I can't now ascertain precisely when Weekley's mother contrived to find him financial help towards the cost of a year at the University of Bern, where, apart from other German studies, he learnt to speak the language fluently.

Finally came the momentous day of 1892 when he obtained a London master of arts degree in French and German. This crowning success as an external examinee of London University brought the prospect of a Cambridge career.

William Briggs, the dynamic founder, principal, and publisher of the University Tutorial Correspondence College, located at Cambridge, offered my father a post on his staff, to which H. G. Wells had also belonged in his earlier days. This meant that Weekley could combine part-time work for Briggs with reading for the Mediaeval and Modern Languages Tripos (*see* "tripos" in Volume II of this work). He entered Trinity College in the autumn of 1893. In 1896, as well as securing a major scholarship at his famous college, Weekley obtained an outstandingly brilliant first-class rating, with special distinctions in both French and German, and a mark indicating "proficiency in the pronunciation of modern German," a somewhat odd-sounding commendation.

Not content with such an impressive record as a student, Weekley spent the next year in Paris and the following one in Germany, at Freiburg-im-Breisgau. In the Paris of Toulouse-Lautrec, Yvette Guilbert, Aristide Bruant, and Anatole France, he attended the brilliant lectures at the Sorbonne of Gaston Paris (1839–1903), "le beau Gaston," famed among students of French for his *Littérature Française au moyen âge*, and incidentally, a philologist. During this year in Paris, Weekley supported himself narrowly by writing one of his series of textbooks for Briggs and by private tutoring. At Freiburg during 1897–98, he held the university post of lektor in English, his free time being devoted to study under the great Friedrich Kluge (1856–1926), author of the monumental *Etymologisches Wörterbuch der deutschen Sprache*, to whose vast erudition and personal charm Weekley was ever happy to pay tribute. Such, in brief, is the earlier life story of a man who, faced in youth with a most unhopeful outlook, contrived, so largely by his own efforts, to go from one famous seat of learning to another, like some wandering scholar of the Middle Ages. As a schoolboy, and in the course of working for his London bachelor of arts degree, my father had acquired more than Shakespeare's "small Latin and less Greek," although he always regretted not being an accomplished classical scholar. A profound knowledge, however, of French and German formed a foundation on which to base studies of Romance and Teutonic philology.

In 1898 Weekley became Professor of French and head of the modern languages department at University College, Nottingham, which half a century later secured university status. In 1951 the three-year-old university celebrated Weekley's eighty-sixth birthday by conferring on him an honorary doctorate of letters. The three others similarly honoured on that occasion were Dame Laura Knight, a Nottinghamian who had been elected a Royal Academician as a painter; E. M. Forster, the celebrated novelist; and Sir Frank Stenton, formerly Vice-Chancellor of Reading University. In a message read at the degree ceremony, Weekley recalled that it was more than fifty-three years since he had begun work at the old college in Shakespeare Street. "I am," he wrote, "the only survivor of what contemporary English would call 'the old gang,' and as such might have figured on this occasion as a quaint antique among my comparatively young and agile fellow doctors, but the years forbid."

The prestige of the pre-university college owed much, in its advance towards university status, to the widespread recognition attained by two members of the professorial staff: Weekley and his close friend for half a century, Frederic Stanley Kipping (1863–1949), Jesse Boot Professor of Chemistry, who coined the name "silicone" in the course of his researches into silicon compounds, which now belong to the history of science during the first half of our century. It is Kipping whom Weekley has largely in mind when, in the preface to this dictionary, he writes: "Practically all my scientific confrères at Nottingham have been occasionally pestered by me with inquiries as to the words specifically associated with their barbarous pursuits."

In 1899 Weekley had married Frieda, second daughter of Baron Friedrich von Richthofen, by whom he had a son and two daughters. He was ultimately fated to be remembered too much as the first husband of Frieda Lawrence, a circumstance often conflicting with just appreciation of his own achievement as a scholar and gifted popularizer of English etymology. D. H. Lawrence (1885–1930), a Nottinghamshire miner's son, entered the teachers' training department at the college in

1906. His American biographer, Harry T. Moore, quotes from Lawrence's novel *The Rainbow* its description of that Gothic pile (now the free municipal library): "The big college built of stone, standing in the quiet street with a rim of grass and limetrees, all so peaceful." Lawrence attended Weekley's French classes as part of his training course. Mr Moore also remarks: "So obviously a gentleman himself, Weekley was, Lawrence felt, merely sarcastic when he addressed the provincial students as 'gentlemen.'" Lawrence's elopement with Frieda Weekley in 1912 belongs now far more to *his* biography than to Weekley's.

The latter's parents insisted that he bring his three children to London and make his home with them. Their Hampstead house could not comfortably accommodate the grandparents, a housekeeping spinster aunt, a bachelor uncle, Ernest Weekley, and the children. The amalgamated households moved during September 1912 into a spacious and hideous Victorian house in the west London suburb of Chiswick, conveniently situated for St Paul's School and for St Paul's Girls' School, at which the boy and the two girls were educated. Many years later, whenever any question of a change of residence arose, Weekley was always ready to insist that he would leave 49, Harvard Road, Chiswick, "feet first." In 1938, however, the house was compulsorily acquired for demolition in order to open the way for a great road extension towards London Airport.

During those Chiswick years Weekley travelled between London and Nottingham, having quaintly old-fashioned, gaslit rooms at 30, Clarendon Street, near the College, for his nights in Nottingham. A large room on the ground floor of the Chiswick house, with big windows at both ends, could accommodate the considerable library he had accumulated. During the Edwardian years at Nottingham my father bought a number of rare etymological books, including several old dictionaries, from a second-hand bookseller close to Nottingham's picturesquely ancient market place, long since transformed by rebuilding.

Before and between the World Wars, Chiswick was a stolidly quiet region of London, congenial to elderly and distinguished neighbours such as Charles Pendlebury, long an assistant master at St Paul's, and author of very successful mathematical textbooks; Judge Crawford; Christopher Whall, an eminent craftsman in stained glass; and James Penderel-Brodhurst, an experienced newspaperman of the old school. As a descendant of the Penderels of Boscobel who concealed Charles II in the oak tree after his flight from the battle of Worcester, Penderel-Brodhurst enjoyed the royal annuity bestowed on successive generations of Penderels. My father's few interludes of leisure at home could therefore sometimes be spent with interesting people, but he lived laborious days, for his chair at Nottingham was not lucrative. A great part of his income, throughout a long career, was earned by severe toil as an examiner. Only unusual powers of swift and sustained concentration enabled him also to get through so much writing and editing. Apart from French textbooks for Briggs's University Tutorial Press, the first of Weekley's series of books on etymology appeared in 1912. This was *The Romance of Words*, which has remained in print and was reissued in the United States in 1960 by the publisher of this dictionary. Among Weekley's editions of French classics, he himself took a particular pride in his selection from the works of Paul Louis Courier (1772–1825), whom Anatole France and other famous French writers have so much admired as a *prosateur*.

A linguistic scholar must, *ipso facto*, possess a good memory. My father's was phenomenal. His humour, which will, I hope, be sufficiently apparent in his preface to these volumes, was that of a witty savant, a light and dry wine. I recall, for instance, his comment on somebody who struck him as having an unfortunate resemblance to a relative my father abhorred: "More like X—— Y—— than any professing Christian has a right to be." Weekley had the scholar's enjoyment of an apt quotation. I venture to mention one of my own that delighted him, perhaps because it enjoyed the advantage of brightening grim days. When the heavy bombing of London began in 1940, we agreed that we would not get up at night after a warning until we had heard actual firing from antiaircraft batteries. I said, "I shall call out: 'Oh father! I hear the sound of guns'" (Longfellow's "The Wreck of the Hesperus").

A move in 1938 from Chiswick to Richmond, Surrey, was too soon followed by the war. In the autumn of 1940 Weekley was bombed out of the house he rented at Richmond and ultimately spent most of the war years at Criccieth in North Wales, renting a flat near his friends the Kippings, who had acquired a holiday residence there before the Second World War began. The war thus brought them together again at an age when a few years tend to loom large in the passage of time.

After Criccieth, my father resumed his London life with his elder daughter, her husband and two boys, in a house at Putney, where his last years were passed pleasantly and peacefully. Within three days of taking to his bed, Ernest Weekley died on May 7, 1954, in his ninetieth year.

As a young man, he was athletic, fond of various outdoor games, and a good forward at hockey. A generous tribute appeared in the (then Manchester) *Guardian* of May 10, 1954, from the pen of a younger Nottingham colleague, Professor A. C. Wood, which I gratefully substitute at this point for my filial pen:

> Weekley was a man of distinguished presence and natural dignity of bearing: one glance at his fine face and figure convinced that he was not of the common ruck, yet he was always approachable, considerate, and ready to help even the most junior of his colleagues. With his students he had a real gift for friendship which lasted long after they had left the college. Only recently, as an old man well over eighty, he wrote: "I find nothing more pleasantly stimulating than the letters and visits of old students." Few can have spent forty years in academic life and evoked so much affection, and so little criticism as he did. . . . Domestic misfortune which might have embittered or broken a lesser man he accepted with reticent dignity, and never allowed it to warp his reaction to his fellow-men.

Announcing in London the death of "Professor Ernest Weekley, whose solid scholarship and work in popularizing etymology will long be remembered," *The Times* ventured on a prophecy which this republication of my father's magnum opus is helping to fulfil.

MONTAGUE WEEKLEY

CANONBURY, LONDON, 1967.

ELSIE, 'What's that, Daddy?' FATHER, 'A cow.' ELSIE, 'Why?'
(*Punch*, Jan. 17, 1906)

SPORTING OLD PARSON, 'I didn't ask you what a "yorker" was,—
(*with dignity*)—I know that as well as you do.   But why is it
called a "yorker"?'

PROFESSIONAL PLAYER, 'Well, I can't say, sir. I don't know what
else you could call it.'   (*ib*. Sept. 23, 1882)

PREFACE

THIS DICTIONARY is offered to those lovers of our language who, without wishing to stumble about in the dim regions which produce pre-historic roots and conjectural primitive-Teutonic word-forms, have an educated interest in words and an intelligent curiosity as to their origins and earlier senses. That is to say, it is meant for the class whose feeling for words is intermediate between the two extreme attitudes illustrated on the opposite page. It represents the results of etymological studies which may be said to have begun when the author, having reached the disyllabic stage of culture, acquired the habit of theorizing about words and worrying his elders with unanswerable questions. In form and scope it attempts to supply the help which many word-lovers, as distinct from philological experts, are still seeking. In the course of time it has gone through several metamorphoses. Conceived many years ago as a glossary of curious etymologies, an offshoot of which was the author's "Romance of Words" (1912), it has gradually grown, in the same unintentional way as Topsy, until it has become, from the point of view of vocabulary, the most complete Etymological Dictionary in existence. It may seem presumptuous for one who is by trade a student of foreign languages to essay the task of compiling a dictionary of his own; but the extenuating circumstance may be urged that the central Anglo-Saxon patch which is the nucleus of Modern English has been so long and so thoroughly worked by competent hands that not much remains to be done, at any rate from the unambitious point of view of the present writer. On the other hand, the huge and ever-growing foreign accretions can perhaps be not unprofitably investigated by one whose philological studies have been largely outside English.

Indeed, one of the forms through which this book has passed was that of an Etymological Glossary of the foreign elements in the language. This glossary was to have excluded not only the native element, but also all those words of Latin origin which, as Skinner says, "non obscure Romanam redolent prosapiam." But, reflecting that, after all, most people's Latin has a way of getting rusty, and that at no distant date a Soviet Board of Education may send Latin to join Greek in the limbo of "useless" studies, the author decided to rope in all the Latin words, as being likely to have at least an antiquarian interest for the rising generation. The difficult problem of demarcating strictly the native element from the early Scandinavian and Low German contributions was solved, or rather dodged, by the final decision to include everything, both native and foreign. The author thus finds that he has produced something much more ambitious than he originally intended. He can only plead, like Jo, that he "didn't go fur to do it."

The vocabulary dealt with is, roughly speaking, that of the "Concise Oxford

Vocabulary Dictionary" (1911), collated, during the printing of the book, with that of Cassell's "New English Dictionary" (1919). These two marvels of completeness and compression include, however, a great number of scientific and technical words which can hardly be regarded as forming part of the English language, while omitting, either by accident or design, others which, in my opinion, have acquired civic rights. As our language grows with the same majestic and unnoticed progress as our empire, it results that every dictionary is, strictly speaking, out of date within a month of its publication, and many words will be found here which are not recorded in either of the above compilations.

I have included the whole of the literary and colloquial vocabulary, so far as

Archaisms the former is not purely archaic and the latter not purely technical **and Slang** or local. In the matter of archaisms some clemency has been extended to Scott, whose picturesque, too often sham-antique, vocabulary made the author a word-hunter before his age had got into double figures. A certain number of Shakespearean words which still re-echo more or less unintelligibly in phrases to which Shakespeare gave currency are also included. Many slang words and expressions hitherto passed over by etymologists are here historically explained. In the past the slang of one generation has often become the literary language of the next, and the manners which distinguish contemporary life suggest that this will be still more frequently the case in the future.

In the matter of "scientific" terms, often coined with complete indifference

Scientific to linguistic laws and the real meanings of words, I have made it a **terms** rule to exclude everything which the "New English Dictionary" quotes only from technical treatises and dictionaries. But, as almost all the elements from which such terms are composed are found in more familiar words, the intelligent reader will have no difficulty in finding enlightenment; e.g. anyone who has not enough Greek to interpret *photomicrography* has only to look up *photo-*, *micro-*, *graph-*, and the search will do him no harm. Here again, it is impossible to predict what words may be promoted from Algebra to English in the course of the next few years. A European war may familiarize the public with unimagined lethal products of Kultur, just as a comic opera plot against a Prime Minister may turn the name of an obscure Indian poison into a temporary household word. On the whole it will be found that I have leaned rather towards inclusion than exclusion, though neologisms of Greek origin are bunched together as concisely as possible wherever the alphabetical order allows of this being done.

Foreign words are included, if, though still sufficiently "foreign" to be usually

Foreign printed in italics, they are likely to occur in reading and in educated **words.** conversation; and their etymology is traced as fully as that of the other words, i.e. just as far back as the ground seems firm and the author believes himself a competent guide. Among such foreign words are many neologisms due to the Great War, a certain number of which may successfully resist that demobilization of the war-words which is now actively proceeding. The more recondite foreign technicalities of war have been avoided, but the Anglo-Indian vocabulary of the British army, much of which is already to be found in the works of Mr Kipling and other Anglo-Indian writers, has been drawn upon freely. Purely Latin words and phrases are usually explained without comment, Latin etymology, except where it rests on quite sure foundations or shows interesting parallels with our own language, being outside the scope of this work.

As a rule the proper name is only admitted to the etymological dictionary **Proper names** when it has attained the small initial. This seems rather an artificial distinction and one not always easy to establish. My own interest in the etymology of personal names, and my conviction that the part they have played in the creation of our vocabulary is not yet realized by etymologists, have led me to include here a much larger proportion of them than is usually found in etymological dictionaries. The boundary-line between names and words is hardly real. It is constantly being crossed before our eyes, as it has been crossed throughout the history of language, and I cannot see why *Guy Fawkes* should be admitted to the dictionary as *guy*, while *Tommy Atkins* remains outside. It will be found that I have proposed personal-name origins for many of the hitherto unsolved problems of etymology, and that, in general, I have brought the two classes of words into closer connection than earlier etymologists. In the case of derivatives of proper names I have omitted the obvious (*Dantesque, Mosaic, Shakespearean,* etc.), but included the less familiar.

The word "etymology" is used here in a wider, if shallower, sense than in **Etymology** previous etymological dictionaries. These usually limit themselves to answering the question "Whence?" It has always seemed to the author that the living word is of more interest than its protoplasm, and that "Whence?" is only part of the problem, the real solution of which involves also answering the questions "How?" "When?" "Why?" and even, occasionally, "Who?" Few people, at least of those who care for words, need the help of a dictionary to elucidate *agnostic*[1] or *demarcation*, but many may be interested to learn that we owe the first to Huxley and the second to a Papal bull of 1493. Nor is it at first sight apparent why a large furniture van should bear a Greek name signifying a collection of all the arts.

In the matter of etymology, strictly speaking, the method has been as follows. **Aryan & Teutonic** For the small nucleus of Aryan words the parallel forms are given from the other languages, Teutonic and Romance, together with some indication of the existence of the word in Celtic and Slavonic, Persian and Sanskrit. It is in dealing with this small group that the author has felt most out of his depth and inclined to be apologetic, especially for inconsistencies in transliteration. Words of Common Teutonic origin are accompanied by the Dutch, German, Old Norse, and (if recorded) Gothic forms, while for West Germanic words the Dutch and German cognates are given. The classification of the Anglo-Saxon and

---

[1] Though the "etymology" from Latin *agnosco* has been ascribed to more than one eminent man.

Scandinavian element into these three groups (Aryan, Common Teutonic, West Germanic) is not a simple matter, and no doubt some errors will be found.

For words from Old or Modern French, or from the other Romance languages,
Romance element I give the Latin original[1], tracing this a little further back when it can be done with certainty. The parallel French, Italian and Spanish forms are usually given, and sometimes those of other Romance languages. It is well known that nouns and adjectives of these languages are usually derived from the Latin accusative case. It seemed unnecessary to repeat this information for every word, the more so as both cases would often give the same result, e.g. Old French *maistre* represents Latin *magister* as well as *magistrum*, while *pater* and *patrem* would both produce *père*. I have usually, for simplicity, given the nominative, showing the stem of imparisyllabics, e.g. *custom*, OF. *coustume* (*coutume*), L. *consuetudo, -tudin-*. For words adopted early from French the Modern French
French words form is given when it does not differ essentially from Old French. Where the citation of the Old French form seems desirable[2], its current representative is added in brackets, and the same course is followed for the other modern European languages. Everybody knows that our words of French origin are chiefly from Old French, and it is just as simple and true to say that English *dame* is French *dame* as to insist on the "Old."

In cases where it seems of interest the approximate date of appearance in the
Chronology language is given for foreign words, as also for many apparently native words which are not recorded until the Middle English period or later. But it must be understood that such dates, usually based on the quotations of the "New English Dictionary," are subject to revision. The actual written record of a word is largely a matter of accident, and the author's researches into the history of surnames have revealed the fact that hundreds of words and compounds are some centuries older than their first appearance in literature. Also, during the progress of the "New English Dictionary," numerous documents have been published which carry back the history of many words far beyond the dates which were known a few years ago. I have occasionally called attention to such cases. I have also tried to show how or why certain foreign words were introduced into the language, or what writers may be regarded as having coined, or given currency to, a new word or to an old word used in a new sense. Sometimes the honour belongs to a forgotten scribbler, but Shakespeare's share in such creations is enormous.

No definitions are given, except the brief indications which are needed to
Definitions distinguish homonyms or to suggest the region of ideas to which an unfamiliar word belongs. I learn from the "New English Dictionary" that to *kiss* is "to press or touch with the lips (at the same time compressing and

---

[1] Throughout the Dictionary the word "from" is used to indicate a connection which does not amount to exact phonetic equivalence, e.g. *poplar*, OF. *poplier* (*peuplier*), from L. *pōpulus*.

[2] Where the English word is identical with the Old French the latter is not repeated, e.g. *haste*, OF. (*hâte*).

then separating them), in token of affection or greeting, or as an act of reverence,"
and from Skeat that *twenty* is "twice ten." So much knowledge I assume every
Meanings reader to possess. On the other hand, I have tried to trace the
meanings of each word as well as its form, to account for, or at least
indicate, the various directions which the sense has taken, and to explain the
chief figurative uses and the process by which they have become part of the
living language, passing over of course all that is obvious to average intelligence.
Hence this Dictionary includes, in a way, a dictionary of phrases. This has involved a very rigid system of selection. To deal fully with the phraseology connected with any common verb would be an enormous task. This may be illustrated
by the fact that the "New English Dictionary" recognizes fifty different senses
for the locution to *take up*, which again is only an item in the mammoth article
devoted to the verb to *take*. But it seemed possible, within reasonable limits, to
supply an answer to a question addressed to the author much more frequently
than any of those mentioned on p. vii, viz. "Why do we say...?" I have seldom
touched on proverbs, the common inheritance of the nations, though expressed
in a notation which varies according to national history, tradition, pursuits and
characteristics. All of us constantly use phrases which, starting from some great,
or perhaps small, writer or orator, have become an inseparable element of colloquial
English, but which we often find it hard to localize. These reminiscences I have
tried to run to earth, without, however, aspiring to furnish a complete dictionary
of popular misquotations. It will be noticed that a very large number of such
expressions belong to the vocabulary of sport[1], and still more of them perhaps to
that of the sea, the Englishman's second language. Among my authorities (p. xx)
and sources for quotations (*ib.*) nautical literature accordingly holds a large
place. I am aware that all this is not usually regarded as etymology, but I see
no reason why it should not be. A reader who is left cold by the words *bean* and
feast may be interested in their collocation, most of us use habitually the expression
foregone conclusion in a sense remote from that intended by its coiner, and
the current sense of *psychological moment* is altogether different from its
original use.

It will be seen from what precedes that this Dictionary, whatever its defects or
merits, is something of a new departure. In some respects it accidentally resembles,
no doubt *longo intervallo*, the German edition of Falk and Torp's "Etymologisk
Ordbog over det Norske og det Danske Sprog," from which, however, it differs
by the modesty of its philological ambition and by the inclusion of quotations. It
Quotations has always seemed to the compiler that a dictionary without quotations is too unrelieved in its austerity. Those included here range
chronologically from the Venerable Bede to Mr Horatio Bottomley, and represent
the results of nearly fifty years omnivorous reading stored away in a rather
retentive memory. Some are given to prove the early occurrence of a word,

---

[1] United States metaphor is more often expressed in terms of the backwoods, the mine and the
railway.

others to illustrate an interesting phase of meaning or an obsolete pronunciation, others again as *loci classici* or for their historic interest, and a few no doubt because their quaintness appealed to the compiler. Some are given with only vague reference, having been noted for private satisfaction at a time when the project of a dictionary had not been formed. For many I am indebted to the "New English Dictionary," though coincidence does not by any means always **Sources of** indicate borrowing. On p. xx will be found a list of works specially **quotations** read or re-read for the purpose of the Dictionary, the reason for their selection being, I think, fairly obvious. I have made much use of the Bible translations, from the Anglo-Saxon Gospels to the Authorized Version, which have so strongly influenced the vocabulary and phrasing of modern English, and also of the medieval and 16–17 century Latin-English dictionaries, so valuable for the light they throw on the contemporary meanings of words. It did not seem desirable to add to the already too great bulk of the Dictionary by giving a list of all works quoted. Such a list would be almost a catalogue of English literature, with the addition of a very large number of non-literary sources, such as early collections of letters, private diaries, household accounts, wills and inventories, state papers, documents dealing with local administration, and most of the early travel records published by the Hakluyt Society. Matter of this kind, constantly published by antiquarian societies and by the Government, supplies a linguistic Tom Tiddler's Ground for the word-hunter. All quotations are given unaltered, except that *u* and *v*, *i* and *j* are distinguished, and *th*, *g* (or *y*) substituted for obsolete Anglo-Saxon and Middle English symbols[1]. From c. 1600 (Shakespeare and Authorized Version) modernized spelling is usual, but this depends usually on the edition consulted. Occasionally (e.g. *cozen*) the original Shakespearean spelling is given for etymological reasons.

    There are at present two schools of etymologists, the phonetic and the **Phonetics &** semantic. The former devote themselves to the mechanical explana- **Semantics** tion of speech-sounds and believe that "the laws of sound-change admit of no exceptions." The latter are guided in their investigations by the parallelisms and contrasts to be observed in sense-development in different languages. The present writer belongs, in his humble way, to the second school. He has every respect for the laws of phonetics, a science which has, within the last forty years, transformed the methods of the qualified etymologist; but he is at one with the greatest representative of the semantic school in declining to regard these laws as though they had been delivered to mankind on Mount Sinai. So it will be found that the minutiae of phonetics occupy little space in this Dictionary, and that occasionally, though with a caveat, etymologies are proposed which actually run counter to phonetic theory. A good many accidents happen to words in the course of their lives, and individual fancy is not without influence. Phonetics will explain general laws, but can hardly tell us by what

---

[1] Foreign symbols, other than Greek, are replaced throughout by transliteration into English italics. Such transliteration is necessarily sometimes of a rough-and-ready character.

process the schoolboy converts *swindle* into *swiz*, how *bicycle* becomes *bike*, or why the *Prince of Wales* should be known to his Oxford intimates as the *Pragger Wagger*. It is possible to recognize the great debt that etymology owes to the phonetician without necessarily regarding the study of the yelps and grunts of primitive man or his arboreal ancestors as the be-all and end-all of linguistic science.

The chief authority used in this compilation is, of course, the "New English Dictionary," the noblest monument ever reared to any language. But, in the nearly forty years that have elapsed since the inception of that great national work, and largely as a result of its inspiration, a great deal of good etymological work has been done and new sources of information have been opened. It will consequently be found that the etymologies given here sometimes differ from, or modify, those put forward by the "New English Dictionary" and uncritically repeated by other compilations. Besides the dictionaries recognized as more or less authoritative enumerated on p. xvii, I have had as mines of new knowledge many essays and monographs by eminent continental scholars, together with the numerous philological periodicals published in Europe and America. I have worked through all of these, so far as they touch, immediately or remotely, on English etymology, and venture to hope that not much of real importance has escaped me. Nor should I omit to mention, as a store-house of curious lore, our own "Notes and Queries." Considerations of space have limited the list of authorities (pp. xvii–xx) to the essential tools with which I have worked day by day, but no reputable source of information has remained unconsulted. As a rule authorities are not quoted, except for an occasional reference to the views of the "New English Dictionary," or, in disputed etymologies, of Skeat. In some few very ticklish cases I have sheltered myself behind the great name of Friedrich Kluge, my sometime chief and teacher, and, in dealing with the strange exotics which come to us from the barbarian fringe, I have now and then invoked the authority of my old schoolfellow James Platt, whose untimely death in 1910 deprived philology of the greatest linguistic genius of modern times.

The various preliminary drafts and the final shaping of this Dictionary having extended over many years, it is inevitable that there should be some unevenness, not to say inconsistency and needless repetition, in the final performance. There are moods in which conciseness seems most desirable, and others in which the temptation to be discursive gets the upper hand. My own impression is that the book improves as it goes on. The kind of shorthand which has to be used in compressing so vast a matter into one moderate-sized volume must lead to occasional obscurity, but I hope and believe that this has tended to diminish with the progress of the work. Scaliger compares the lexicographer with the convict—

> Si quem dira manet sententia judicis olim
>   Damnatum aerumnis suppliciisque caput,
> Hunc neque fabrili lassent ergastula massa
>   Nec rigidas vexent fossa metalla manus:
> Lexica contexat, nam cetera quid moror? Omnes
>   Poenarum facies hic labor unus habet.

Authorities

This is too gloomy a picture. There are, in dictionary-making, desolate patches, especially those that are overgrown with the pestilent weeds of pseudo-scientific neologism. There are also moments when the lexicographer, solemnly deriving words from Aztec, Maori or Telugu, languages of which he knows no more than the man in the moon, is more conscious than usual of being a fraud. But, as far as this book is concerned, the greater part of the work of compilation has been a labour of love, the end of which had in it as much of regret as of relief.

There remains to me the pleasant duty of expressing my thanks to the learned friends and confrères who have assisted me in watching over the Dictionary in its progress through the press. The compiler of a work of this kind must inevitably take much at second-hand and deal with many subjects of which his own knowledge is superficial or non-existent. Thus he is bound occasionally to give himself away badly unless his work is criticized by specialists in the various branches of linguistic science. It is not without a shudder that the author recalls certain precipices from which he was kindly but firmly pulled back by helpers more learned than himself. Professor Allen Mawer, of the Armstrong College, Newcastle, has most kindly read the whole work in proof and emended it from the point of view of the scientific Anglist. His assistance has been invaluable. My friend and Cambridge contemporary, the late Dr E. C. Quiggin, had undertaken to verify all Celtic forms and etymologies, but he had only read the first few sheets when his tragically sudden death robbed me of his help and the learned world of a scholar of rare attainments. Professor T. H. Parry-Williams, of Aberystwyth, at once responded to my invitation to replace Dr Quiggin and has untiringly given me the help of his specialist knowledge throughout. Professor Edward Bensly, formerly of Aberystwyth, has read the whole of the proofs. Readers of "Notes and Queries" will readily understand that no words can express what the Dictionary owes to his vast and curious erudition. My colleague, Mr E. P. Barker, has acted especially as classical corrector. He has called my attention to many points of Latin and Greek etymology, and, in collaboration with Professor Bensly and the reader of the Cambridge University Press, will, I trust, have gone far to create the illusion that the compiler of this Dictionary really knows something about Greek accents. In dealing with Slavonic words I have always had at my service the remarkable linguistic knowledge of my colleague, Mr Janko Lavrin. Practically all my scientific confrères at Nottingham have been occasionally pestered by me with inquiries as to the words specifically associated with their barbarous pursuits. Professor E. H. Parker, of Manchester, has enlightened me as to the origin of a few Chinese expressions, and Dr J. Rendel Harris has advised me on the transliteration of some Semitic words. It would no doubt have been better for the Dictionary if I had had the audacity to trouble these two high authorities more frequently. My especial thanks are due to my colleague, Mr R. M. Hewitt, who has not only given me his assistance in many languages of which I know little or nothing, but has also taken the keenest interest in my work from the beginning of its final shaping and has made to it contributions which amount to collaboration. The later sheets have had the advantage of being read by Professor Paul Barbier, of Leeds, whose authority on European fish-names is unique. To all these distinguished scholars, some of whom I have never seen in the flesh, and all of whom would probably regard an eight-hour day as approximating to the existence of the Lotus-eaters, I offer my most sincere thanks for the help so generously and untiringly given, together with my apologies for such blunders as may be due to my ineptitude in applying their learning. Finally I have to acknowledge the very great debt I owe to the care and accuracy of Mr W. H. Swift, reader to the Cambridge University Press.

Although this Dictionary is intended chiefly for the educated man (and woman) in the street, or, as Blount puts it, "for the more-knowing women and less-knowing men," it may also conceivably fall into the hands of scholars in this country or abroad. I need not say that criticisms and suggestions from such will be welcome to the author. If some of the more austere are scandalized by an occasional tone of levity, most unbecoming in such a work, I would remind them that its production has coincided with the sombre tragedy of the War and the sordid tragedy of the Peace, and that even a lexicographer may sometimes say, with Figaro, "Je me presse de rire de tout, de peur d'être obligé d'en pleurer."

ERNEST WEEKLEY

UNIVERSITY COLLEGE, NOTTINGHAM.
    September 1920.

ABBREVIATIONS

abbrev.: abbreviation
abl.: ablative
abstr.: abstract
acc.: accusative
act.: active
adj.: adjective
adv.: adverb-ial-ly
aeron.: aeronautics
AF.: Anglo-French
Afr.: Africa-n
agent.: agential
AL.: Anglo-Latin
alch.: alchemy
Alp.: Alpine
Amer.: America-n
anat.: anatomy
Anglo-Ind.: Anglo-Indian
Anglo-Ir.: Anglo-Irish
antiq.: antiquarian
aphet.: aphetic
app.: apparently
Arab.: Arabic
Aram.: Aramaic
arch.: architecture
archaeol.: archaeology
Armen.: Armenian
art.: article
AS.: Anglo-Saxon
AS. Gosp.: Anglo-Saxon Gospels (see p. xx)
assim.: assimilation
Assyr.: Assyrian
astrol.: astrology
astron.: astronomy
attrib.: attributive
augment.: augmentative
Austr.: Austrian
Austral.: Australia-n
auxil.: auxiliary
AV.: Authorized Version of Bible

Bav.: Bavarian
Bibl.: Biblical
bibl.: bibliography
biol.: biology
Boh.: Bohemian
bot.: botany
Bret.: Breton
Brit.: British
build.: building
Bulg.: Bulgarian
Byz.: Byzantine

c.: *circiter*=about
Camb.: Cambridge
Canad.: Canadian
carpent.: carpentry
Cath. Angl.: Catholicon Anglicum (see p. xviii)
Celt.: Celtic
cent.: century
cf.: *confer*=compare
Chauc.: Chaucer (see p. xx)
chem.: chemistry
Chin.: Chinese
Chron.: Chronicle
class.: classical
cogn.: cognate
collect.: collective

colloq.: colloquial-ly
commerc.: commercial
compar.: comparative
compd.: compound
Com. Teut.: Common Teutonic
conj.: conjunction
contemp.: contemporary
contr.: contraction
cook.: cookery
Coop.: Cooper (see p. xviii)
Corn.: Cornish
corrupt.: corruption
Cotg.: Cotgrave (see p. xix)
crim.: criminal
Croat.: Croatian
Coverd.: Coverdale (see p. xx)
Cumb.: Cumberland

Dan.: Danish
dat.: dative
def.: definite
demonstr.: demonstrative
Dev.: Devonshire
dial.: dialect
Dict.: Dictionary
Dict. Cant. Crew: Dictionary of the Canting
    Crew (see p. xx)
Dict. Gén.: Dictionnaire Général (see p. xvii)
dim.: diminutive
dissim.: dissimilation
Du.: Dutch
Duc.: Du Cange (see p. xviii)

E.: East
EAngl.: East Anglia-n
eccl.: ecclesiastical
econ.: economics
EDD.: English Dialect Dictionary (see p. xvii)
EFris.: East Frisian
e.g.: *exempli gratia*=for instance
Egypt.: Egyptian
EInd.: East India-n
electr.: electricity
ellipt.: elliptical-ly
eng.: engineering
entom.: entomology
equit.: equitation
erron.: erroneous-ly
esp.: especial-ly
Est.: Estienne (see p. xviii)
ethn.: ethnology
etym.: etymology, etymological-ly
euph.: euphemism, euphemistic
Europ.: European
exc.: except

F.: French
facet.: facetious
Falc.: Falconer (see p. xx)
falc.: falconry
f., fem.: feminine
fenc.: fencing
feud.: feudal-ism
fig.: figurative-ly
financ.: financial
fl.: *floruit*=flourished
Flem.: Flemish

Flor.: Florio (see p. xix)
folk-etym.: folk-etymology
fort.: fortification
frequent.: frequentative
Fris.: Frisian
fut.: future

G.: Greek
Gael.: Gaelic
gard.: gardening
gen.: general-ly
Gent. Dict.: Gentleman's Dictionary (see p. xx)
geog.: geography
geol.: geology
geom.: geometry
Ger.: German
gerund.: gerundive
Godef.: Godefroy (see p. xviii)
Goth.: Gothic
gram.: grammar

Hakl.: Hakluyt (see p. xx)
Hall.: Halliwell (see p. xviii)
Heb.: Hebrew
her.: heraldry
Hind.: Hindi
hist.: history, historical-ly
H. of C.: House of Commons
Hor.: Horace
hort.: horticulture
Hung.: Hungarian

Icel.: Icelandic
ident.: identical
i.e.: *id est*=that is
imit.: imitation, imitative
imper.: imperative
impers.: impersonal
improp.: improperly
incept.: inceptive
incorr.: incorrect-ly
Ind.: India-n
indef.: indefinite
infin.: infinitive
init.: initial
instrum.: instrumental
intens.: intensive
inter.: interrogative
interj.: interjection
intrans.: intransitive
Ir.: Irish
iron.: ironical
irreg.: irregular
It.: Italian

Jap.: Japanese
joc.: jocular
Johns.: Johnson (see p. xviii)

Kil.: Kilian (see p. xix)

L.: Latin
lang.: language
leg.: legal
legislat.: legislative
Lesc.: Lescallier (see p. xx)
Let.: Letters
LG.: Low German
ling.: linguistics
lit.: literal-ly
Litt.: Littleton (see p. xviii)
loc.: locative

log.: logic
Ludw.: Ludwig (see p. xix)
LXX.: Septuagint

m., masc.: masculine
Manip. Voc.: Manipulus Vocabulorum (see p. xviii)
masc.: masculine
math.: mathematics, mathematical
ME.: Middle English
mech.: mechanics, mechanical
med.: medicine, medical
MedL.: Medieval Latin
Merc.: Mercian
metall.: metallurgy
metaph.: metaphysics
metath.: metathesis
meteorol.: meteorology
metr.: metre, metrical
Mex.: Mexican
MHG.: Middle High German
mil.: military
Milt.: Milton
min.: mineralogy
Minsh.: Minsheu (see pp. xviii, xix)
mistransl.: mistranslation
MLG.: Middle Low German
Mod., mod.: modern
Mol.: Molière
MS(S).: manuscript(s)
mus.: music-al
myth.: mythology, mythical

N.: North.
NAmer.: North America-n
naut.: nautical
nav.: naval
Nav. Accts.: Naval Accounts (see p. xx)
NED.: New English Dictionary (see p. xvii)
neg.: negative
neol.: neologism
neut.: neuter
nom.: nominative
Norm.: Norman
north.: northern
Northumb.: Northumbrian
Norw.: Norwegian
NT : New Testament
numism.: numismatics

O: Old
obj.: objective
obs.: obsolete
occ.: occasional-ly
ODu.: Old Dutch
OF.: Old French
offic.: official
OFris.: Old Frisian
OHG.: Old High German
OIr.: Old Irish
OIt.: Old Italian
OL.: Old Latin
OLG.: Old Low German
ON.: Old Norse
ONF.: Old North French
onomat.: onomatopoetic
OPers.: Old Persian
OProv.: Old Provençal
OPruss.: Old Prussian
opt.: optics
orig.: original-ly
ornith.: ornithology
OSax.: Old Saxon

OSlav.: Old Slavonic
OSp.: Old Spanish
OSw.: Old Swedish
OT.: Old Testament
OTeut.: Old Teutonic
Oxf.: Oxford

paint.: painting
palaeont.: palaeontology
Palsg.: Palsgrave (see p. xviii)
part.: participle
pass.: passive
Paston Let.: Paston Letters (see p. xx)
path.: pathology
PB.: Prayer-Book
perf.: perfect
perh.: perhaps
Pers.: Persian
pers.: person-al
Peruv.: Peruvian
phil.: philology
philos.: philosophy
Phoen.: Phoenician
phon.: phonetics
phot.: photography
phys.: physics
physiol.: physiology
Pic.: Picard
Piers Plowm.: Piers Plowman (see p. xx)
pl.: plural
pleon.: pleonasm, pleonastic
poet.: poetical-ly
Pol.: Polish
pol.: political-ly
pop.: popular
Port.: Portuguese
posit.: positive
possess.: possessive
p.p.: past participle
prep.: preposition
pres.: present
pres. part.: present participle
pret.: preterite
print.: printing
prob.: probably
Prompt. Parv.: Promptorium Parvulorum (see p. xviii)
pron.: pronoun
pronunc.: pronunciation
prop.: properly
Prov.: Provençal
pugil.: pugilism
Purch.: Purchas (see p. xx)

quot.: quotation
q.v.: *quod vide*=which see

Rac.: Racine
R.C.: Roman Catholic
redupl.: reduplication
ref.: reference
reflex.: reflexive
reg.: regular
rel.: religion, religious
rhet.: rhetoric
Rom.: Romance, Romanic
Rum.: Rumanian
Russ.: Russian
RV.: Revised Version of the Bible

S.: South
SAfrDu.: South African Dutch

Sard.: Sardinian
Sc.: Scottish
sc.: *scilicet*=understand
Scand.: Scandinavian
scient.: scientific
sculpt.: sculpture
Semit.: Semitic
Serb.: Serbian
Shaks.: Shakespeare
Sic.: Sicilian
sing.: singular
Slav.: Slavonic
Slov.: Slovenian
Sp.: Spanish
spec.: special, specific-ally
Spens.: Spenser
subj.: subjunctive
superl.: superlative
surg.: surgery
s.v.: *sub voce*=under the word
Sw.: Swedish
swim.: swimming
Sylv.: Sylvester (see p. xx)
synon.: synonymous
Syr.: Syriac

Tasm.: Tasmanian
techn.: technical
temp.: *tempore*=in the time (of)
Teut.: Teutonic
theat.: theatre, theatrical
theol.: theology, theological
topogr.: topography
Torr.: Torriano (see p. xix)
trad.: traditional-ly
trans.: transitive
transl.: translation
Trev.: Trevisa (see p. xx)
Turk.: Turkish
Tynd.: Tyndale (see p. xx)
typ.: typography

ult.: ultimate-ly
univ.: university
US.: United States
usu.: usually

var.: variant
ven.: venery
Venet.: Venetian
vet.: veterinary
v.i.: *vide infra*=see below
Virg.: Virgil
viz.: *videlicet*=namely
VL.: Vulgar Latin
Voc.: Vocabularies (see p. xviii)
vol.: volume
v.s.: *vide supra*=see above
Vulg.: Vulgate
vulg.: vulgar

W.: West
Westm.: Westmorland
WGer.: West Germanic
Wyc.: Wyclif (see p. xx)

zool.: zoology

*: unrecorded form
†: died
×: combining with

BIBLIOGRAPHY

I. DICTIONARIES

A. MODERN ETYMOLOGICAL DICTIONARIES

New English Dictionary, ed. Murray, Bradley, Craigie, Onions (Oxford 1884...)   *NED.*
English Dialect Dictionary, ed. J. Wright (Oxford 1898–1905)   *EDD.*

Müller, E. Etymologisches Wörterbuch der Englischen Sprache, 2nd ed. (Cöthen 1878–9)
Kluge & Lutz. English Etymology (Strassburg 1898)
Skeat, W. W. Etymological Dictionary of the English Language, 4th ed. (Oxford 1910)
Holthausen, F. Etymologisches Wörterbuch der Englischen Sprache (Leipzig 1917)

Diez, F. Etymologisches Wörterbuch der Romanischen Sprachen, 5th ed., by Scheler (Bonn 1887)
Körting, G. Lateinisch-Romanisches Wörterbuch (Etymologisches Wörterbuch der Romanischen Hauptsprachen), 3rd ed. (Paderborn 1907)
Meyer-Lübke, W. Romanisches Etymologisches Wörterbuch (Heidelberg 1911–20)

Littré, E. Dictionnaire de la Langue Française (Paris 1878)
Scheler, A. Dictionnaire d'Étymologie Française (Brussels & Paris 1888)
Dictionnaire Général de la Langue Française, ed. Hatzfeld, Darmesteter,   *Dict. Gén.*
Thomas (Paris, n.d.)
Körting, G. Etymologisches Wörterbuch der französischen Sprache (Paderborn 1908)
Clédat, L. Dictionnaire Étymologique de la Langue Française, 4th ed. (Paris 1917)
Zambaldi, F. Vocabolario Etimologico Italiano (Città di Castello 1889)
Pianigiani, O. Vocabolario Etimologico della Lingua Italiana (Rome & Milan 1907)
Puşcariu, S. Etymologisches Wörterbuch der Rumänischen Sprache, I. Lateinisches Element (Heidelberg 1905)

Vercoullie, J. Beknopt Etymologisch Woordenboek der Nederlandsche Taal, 2nd ed. (Ghent & 's-Gravenhage 1898)
Franck, J. Etymologisch Woordenboek der Nederlandsche Taal, 2nd ed., by Van Wyk ('s-Gravenhage 1912)
Grimm, J. & W. Deutsches Wörterbuch (Leipzig 1854...)
Paul, H. Deutsches Wörterbuch, 2nd ed. (Halle a. S. 1908)
Weigand, F. L. K. Deutsches Wörterbuch, 5th ed., by Hirt (Giessen 1909)
Kluge, F. Etymologisches Wörterbuch der Deutschen Sprache, 8th ed. (Strassburg 1915)
Falk & Torp. Norwegisch-Dänisches Etymologisches Wörterbuch (Heidelberg 1910). The German edition of the same authors' Etymologisk Ordbog over det Norske og det Danske Sprog (Kristiania 1900–6)
Feist, S. Etymologisches Wörterbuch der Gotischen Sprache, 2nd ed. (Halle a. S. 1920...)

Walde, A. Lateinisches Etymologisches Wörterbuch, 2nd ed. (Heidelberg 1910)
Macbain, A. Etymological Dictionary of the Gaelic Language, 2nd ed. (Stirling 1911)
Yule & Burnell. Hobson-Jobson, a Glossary of Anglo-Indian Words and   Yule
Phrases, 2nd ed., by Crooke (London 1903)

B. DICTIONARIES OF THE MEDIEVAL OR ARCHAIC

Sweet, H. Student's Dictionary of Anglo-Saxon (Oxford 1897)
Clark Hall, J. R. Concise Anglo-Saxon Dictionary, 2nd ed. (Cambridge 1916)
Stratmann, F. H. Middle-English Dictionary, ed. Bradley (Oxford 1891)

White Kennett (†1728). Glossary (London 1816)
Nares, R. Glossary (esp. for Shakespeare and his contemporaries), new ed., by
    Halliwell & Wright (London 1872)
Halliwell, J. O. Dictionary of Archaic and Provincial Words, 10th ed. (Lon-   Hall.
    don 1887)
Schmidt, A. Shakespeare-Lexicon (Berlin & London 1874)
Onions, C. T. Shakespeare Glossary (Oxford 1911)
Skeat & Mayhew. Tudor and Stuart Glossary (Oxford 1914)

Godefroy, F. Dictionnaire de l'Ancienne Langue Française (Paris 1881–1902)   Godef.
Raynouard, M. Lexique Roman (Old Provençal) (Paris 1844), with supple-
    ment by Levy (1894...)
Schade, O. Altdeutsches Wörterbuch, 2nd ed. (Halle a. S. 1872–82)
Cleasby & Vigfusson. Icelandic-English Dictionary (Oxford 1874)
Du Cange. Glossarium Mediae et Infimae Latinitatis, ed. Henschel (Paris   Duc.
    1840)

C. EARLY DICTIONARIES QUOTED

i. ENGLISH

Minsheu, J. Guide into the Tongues (London 1617), 2nd ed. (1625)   Minsh.
Blount, T. Glossographia, or a Dictionary interpreting...Hard Words (Lon-
    don 1656)
Skinner, S. Etymologicon Linguae Anglicanae (London 1671)
Phillips, E. New World of Words (London 1678)
The same, 7th ed., by J(ohn) K(ersey) (London 1720)
Spelman, H. Glossarium Archaiologicum (London 1687)
Junius, F. (†1678). Etymologicum Anglicanum, ed. Lye (Oxford 1743)
Coles, E. English Dictionary (London 1708)
Bailey, N. English Dictionary (London 1721, 1727)
The same enlarged (London 1730)
Johnson, S. Dictionary of the English Language, 3rd ed. (London 1765)   Johns.
Ash, J. Dictionary of the English Language (London 1775)
Walker, J. Pronouncing Dictionary (London 1791)
Todd, H. J. New edition of Johnson's Dictionary (London 1827)

ii. LATIN—ENGLISH

Wright, T. Anglo-Saxon and Old English (=Middle English) Vocabularies,   *Voc.*
    2nd ed., by Wülcker (London 1884)
Promptorium Parvulorum (1440), ed. Way (Camden Soc. 1843–65)   *Prompt. Parv.*
The same, ed. Mayhew (EETS. 1908). This is the ed. usually quoted
Catholicon Anglicum (1483), ed. Herrtage (EETS. 1881)   *Cath. Angl.*
Levins, P. Manipulus Vocabulorum (1570), ed. Wheatley (EETS. 1867)   *Manip. Voc.*
Cooper, T. Thesaurus Linguae Romanae & Britannicae (London 1573)   Coop.
Morel, G. Latin-Greek-English Dictionary, ed. Hutton (London 1583)
Holyoak, F. Latin-English Dictionary, 2nd ed. (Oxford 1612)
Thomas, T. Latin-English Dictionary, 14th ed. (London 1644)
Littleton, A. Latin-English Dictionary (London 1677)   Litt.
Coles, E. Latin-English Dictionary, 5th ed. (London 1703)

iii. FOREIGN

Palsgrave, J. Lesclarcissement de la Langue Francoyse (1530). Reprint (Paris   Palsg.
    1852)
Du Guez, G. Introductorie for to lerne...French trewly (? 1532). Reprinted
    with Palsgrave
Estienne, R. Dictionarium Latinogallicum (Paris 1538)   Est.

Cotgrave, R. French-English Dictionary (London 1611)   Cotg.
The same, ed. Howell (1650), with English-French glossary by Sherwood.
   This is the ed. usually quoted, but the differences are inessential
Ménage, G. Origines de la Langue Françoise (Paris 1650)
The same enlarged, Dictionnaire Étymologique ou Origines de la Langue
   Françoise (1694)
Miège, G. New Dictionary French and English, with another, English and
   French (London 1679)
The same enlarged (1688)

Florio, J. Italian-English Dictionary (London 1598)   Flor.
The same, 2nd ed. (1611)
The same enlarged, ed. Torriano (1659)   Torr.
Duez, N. Dittionario Italiano & Francese (Leyden 1660)
Vocabolario de gli Accademici della Crusca (Venice 1686)

Percyvall, R. Dictionarie in Spanish, English, and Latine (London 1591)
Minsheu, J. Most copious Spanish Dictionarie, with Latine and English (Lon- Minsh.
   don 1599)
Oudin, C. Tesoro de las dos Lenguas, Española y Francesa (Brussels 1660)
Stevens, J. New Spanish and English Dictionary (London 1706)

Vieyra, A. Dictionary of the Portuguese and English Languages (London
   1794)

Trium Linguarum Dictionarium Teutonicae (Dutch) Latinae Gallicae (Frane-
   ker 1587)
Kilian, C. Etymologicum Teutonicae (Dutch) Linguae sive Dictionarium Teu- Kil.
   tonico-Latinum, ed. Potter (Amsterdam 1620)
The same enlarged, ed. Hasselt (1777)
Hexham, H. A copious English and Netherduytch Dictionarie (Rotterdam
   1648), also Woorden-boeck begrijpende den Schat der Nederlandtsche
   Tale, met de Engelsche Uytlegginge (1672)
Sewel, W. Large Dictionary English and Dutch (Amsterdam 1708)
The same, 3rd ed. (1727)
The same enlarged (1766)

Ludwig, M. C. Dictionary English, Germane and French (Leipzig 1706),   Ludw
   also Teutsch-Englisches Lexicon (1716)

Junius, A. Nomenclator Octilinguis, ed. Germberg (Frankfurt 1602)
Calepin, A. Dictionarium Octilingue (Lyon 1663)
Howell, J. Lexicon Tetraglotton (Eng. Fr. It. Sp.) (London 1665)

D. DICTIONARIES OF SPECIAL SUBJECTS

Dictionary of the Scottish Language (Edinburgh 1818)
Motherby, R. Taschen-Wörterbuch des Schottischen Dialekts (Königsberg
   1826)
Jamieson, J. Etymological Dictionary of the Scottish Language, ed. Lang-
   muir & Donaldson (Paisley 1879–87)
Francisque-Michel. Critical inquiry into the Scottish Language (Edinburgh
   & London 1882)
Morris, E. E. Austral English (London 1898)
Joyce, P. W. English as we speak it in Ireland (London & Dublin 1910)
Thornton, R. H. American Glossary (Philadelphia & London 1912)

Skene, J. The Exposition of the Termes and Difficill Wordes conteined in the
   Foure Buikes of Regiam Majestatem (Edinburgh 1599)
Cowell, J. Interpreter, or Booke containing the Signification of Words (Lon-
   don 1637). The first ed. (1607) was condemned by Parliament and burnt
   by the hangman
The same enlarged (1708)

Leigh, E. Philologicall Commentary (London 1658)
Blount, T. Law-Dictionary, 2nd ed. (London 1691)
Jacob, G. New Law-Dictionary (London 1729)

Sea-Dictionary of all the Terms of Navigation (London 1708)
Lescallier, D. Vocabulaire des Termes de Marine Anglois et François (Paris 1777) Lesc.
Falconer, W. Universal Dictionary of the Marine, 2nd ed. (London 1781) Falc.
Romme, C. Dictionnaire de la Marine Françoise (Rochelle & Paris 1792)
Vocabulary (English and French) of Sea Phrases and Terms of Art used in
 Seamanship and Naval Architecture. By a Captain of the British Navy
 (London 1799)
Jal, A. Glossaire Nautique, Répertoire Polyglotte des Termes de Marine
 Anciens et Modernes (Paris 1848)
Smyth & Belcher. Dictionary of Nautical Terms (Glasgow 1867)
Kluge, F. Seemannssprache (Halle a. S. 1911)

Gentleman's Dictionary, in Three Parts, viz. I. The Art of Riding the Great *Gent. Dict.*
 Horse. II. The Military Art. III. The Art of Navigation (London 1705)
Military Dictionary, 3rd ed. (London 1708). See also Sea-Dictionary
News-Readers Pocket-Book (London 1759). A later ed. of the above and of
 the Sea-Dictionary
Faesch, J. R. Kriegs-Ingenieur-Artillerie- und See-Lexicon (Dresden &
 Leipzig 1735)

Worlidge, J. Systema Agriculturae, 3rd ed. (London 1681)
Dictionarium Rusticum, Urbanicum & Botanicum, 2nd ed. (London 1717)

New Dictionary of the Canting Crew, by B. E., Gent. (London c. 1700) *Dict. Cant. Crew*
Grose, F. Classical Dictionary of the Vulgar Tongue (London 1785)
Hotten, J. C. Slang Dictionary (London 1864)

Davies, T. L. O. Supplementary English Glossary (London 1881)
Smythe-Palmer, A. Folk-Etymology (Dictionary) (London 1882)
Stanford Dictionary of Anglicized Words and Phrases, ed. Fennell (Cam-
 bridge 1892)

II. EARLY TEXTS MOST FREQUENTLY QUOTED*

Anglo-Saxon Gospels (c. 1000) AS. *Gosp.*
Piers Plowman (1362–93), ed. Skeat (Oxford 1886) *Piers Plowm.*
Wyclifite Bible Translations (c. 1380) Wyc.
Chaucer (Globe Edition 1910) Chauc.
Trevisa. Translation of Higden's Polychronicon (c. 1390) (Rolls Series, 1865– Trev.
 86)
Paston Letters (1422–1509), ed. Gairdner (Edinburgh 1910) *Paston Let.*
Naval Accounts and Inventories (1485–8, 1495–7), ed. Oppenheim (Navy *Nav. Accts*
 Records Society 1896)
Tyndale. New Testament (1525), Old Testament, incomplete (1529–31) Tynd.
Coverdale. Bible Translation (1535) Coverd.
Hakluyt. Principal Navigations Voyages Traffiques and Discoveries (1598– Hakl.
 1600). Reprint (Glasgow 1903–5)
Sylvester. Bartas his Devine Weekes and Workes translated (London 1605) Sylv.
Authorized Version of the Bible (1611) *AV.*
Shakespeare (†1616) Shaks.
Purchas. Hakluytus Posthumus or Purchas his Pilgrimes (1625). Reprint Purch.
 (Glasgow 1905–7)
Captain John Smith. Works (1608–31). Reprint (Edinburgh 1910)
Pepys. Diary (1659–69), ed. Wheatley (London & Cambridge 1893–6)
Milton (†1674) Milt.
Evelyn (†1706). Diary, ed. Bray (London 1879)

* See Preface, p. x.

ETYMOLOGICAL DICTIONARY

Malui brevius omnia persequi, et leviter attingere, quae nemini esse
ignota suspicari possint, quam quasi ῥαψωδεῖν, perque locos communes
identidem expatiari.

(Claud. Minos Divion. in praefat. commentar.
Alciat. Emblemat.)

a. See *an*.

a-. As E. prefix this generally represents AS.
an, on (*abed, asleep, twice-a-day*, etc.), less frequently ME. *of* (*anew*) and AS. *ge-* (*aware*).
In a few words it represents an AS. prefix
a-, orig. *ur-*, cogn. with Ger. *er-*, and having
intens. force (*arise, awake*). In words of F.
or L. origin it comes from *ad* (*achieve, arrive*) or *ab* (*avert*). Many scient. terms begin
with G. *ἀ-*, neg. (*amorphous*). Less common
origins are illustrated by the words *along,
ado, affray, alas*. The gerund preceded by
a- (= *on*), now dial., was literary E. in 17
cent.

Simon Peter saith unto them, I go a-fishing
(*John*, xxi. 3).

A 1. Symbol used in *Lloyd's Register* to describe a ship as first-class, the A referring
to the hull and the 1 to the stores. Cf. *first-rate* (see *rate*[1]).

A proper A 1 copper-bottom lie
(*Times*, Oct. 26, 1917).

aard-vark. SAfr. quadruped. Du. *aarde*,
earth, *vark*, pig (see *farrow*). Cf. *aard-wolf*.

aasvogel [*SAfr.*]. Vulture. Du., lit. carrion
fowl; cf. Ger. *aas*, carrion, prob. cogn. with
essen, to eat.

ab-. L., from, away; cogn. with *of* (q.v.).
Also *a-*, *abs-*.

aba. Substitute for sextant, invented by,
and named from, *Antoine d'Abbadie*.

aback. AS. *on bæc* (see *a-*), now reduced to
back, exc. in naut. lang. *Taken aback* is a
naut. metaphor from the sudden checking
of a ship through the square sails being
flattened back against the masts by a
change of wind or bad steering.

Gang thu sceocca on bæc
(*A.S. Gospels, Matt.* iv. 10).

abacot. Ghost-word which appears in most
dicts. from Spelman onward and defined as
"a cap of state, wrought up into the shape
of two crowns, worn formerly by English
kings." Orig. misprint for *a bicocquet*, an
OF. word (Sp. *bicoquete*, cap) of doubtful
origin.

abacus. Frame with balls on wires for mechanical calculation. L., G. ἄβαξ, ἀβακ-,
board, slab.

abaddon [*Bibl.*]. Heb. *ābaddōn*, destruction,
used in *Rev.* ix. 11 of the angel of the
bottomless pit, and by Milton (*Par. R.* iv.
624) of the pit itself (cf. *Job*, xxvi. 6, *RV.*).

The aungel of depnesse, to whom the name bi
Ebru Labadon [*var.* Abbadon], forsothe bi Greke
Appolion, and bi Latyn havynge the name Destrier
(Wyc. *Rev.* ix. 11).

abaft [*naut.*]. AS. *on bæft*, the latter for *bi
æftan*. See *aft*, and cf. *aback*.

abaisance [*archaic*]. OF. *abaissance*, humility, from *abaisser*, to abase (q.v.). Hence a
deep bow. Confused in E. with *obeisance*
(q.v.) by which it is now quite absorbed.

abaisance; a low conge, or bow (Bailey).

abandon. F. *abandonner*, from OF. adv. *à
bandon*, at will, at discretion (whence pleon.
ME. *at abandon*). *Bandon*, from *ban*[1] (q.v.),
had in OF. & ME. the meaning of control,
jurisdiction, etc. Current sense of adj.
abandoned is from earlier *abandoned to*,
given up to (not necessarily to wickedness,
etc. in ME.).

Trestute Espaigne iert hoi en lur bandun
(*Rol.* 2704).

The Scottis men dang on so fast,
And schot on thame at abandoune (Barbour).

abandon: bandon, free licence, full libertie for
others to use a thing (Cotg.).

abase. F. *abaisser*, VL. **ad-bassiare*. See
base[2].

abash. OF. *esbaïr*, *esbaïss-* (*ébahir*), to astound, make to gape, from L. *ex* and a
second element which may be *bah!* exclamation of astonishment (see *bay*[3]). The
-iss- of F. inchoative verbs regularly becomes *-ish* in E. (*cherish, flourish*, etc.), but
in ME. we find also forms in *-iss* (*cheriss,
fluriss*), so that *abash* has been confused in

form with *abase* (q.v.), in ME. also *abaiss*, and this confusion has influenced the sense of *abash*. Cf. *bashful*.

And thei weren abaischt [*Vulg.* obstupuerunt] with greet stoneying (Wyc. *Mark*, v. 42).

abate. F. *abattre*, lit. to beat off, from *battre*, to beat, VL. *battere for *battuere*. See *bate*[1]. Cf. to *knock something off* (the price).

abatis, abattis [*mil.*]. Defence made of felled trees. F. *abattis*, from *abattre*, to fell (v.s.). The ending *-is*, OF. *eïs*, represents L. *-aticius*, added to verb-stems.

abattoir. Slaughter-house. F., from *abattre*, to fell. See *abate*.

abba [*Bibl.*]. See *abbot*.

Abbassides [*hist.*]. Caliphs of Baghdad (749–1258), claiming descent from *Abbas*, uncle of Mohammed. Most famous was Haroun-al-Raschid.

abbé, abbess, abbey. See *abbot*.

abbot. AS. *abbod*, L. *abbas*, *abbat-*, G. ἀββᾶς, Syriac *abbā*, father (*Mark*, xiv. 36), applied in East to all monks and in West restricted to superior of monastery; cogn. with Arab. *abu*, father, so common in personal names. Ult. a word from baby lang.; cf. *papa*, *baby*, *babble*, and see *pope*. Other words of this group come via F., e.g. *abbé*, *abbess* (Late L. *abbatissa*), *abbey* (Late L. *abbatia*), or are of later and learned formation, e.g. *abbatial*, *abbatical*. Vague use of F. *abbé* for ecclesiastic, esp. one not holding Church office, dates from 16 cent.

abbreviate. From L. *abbreviare*, from *ad* and *brevis*, short. Cf. *abridge*.

abc. From 13 cent. Cf. *alphabet*, *abecedarian*.

Abderite. Democritus (q.v.), who was born at *Abdera* (Thrace). Cf. *Stagirite*.

abdicate. From L. *abdicare*, to proclaim off.

abdomen. L., from *abdere*, to hide away, from *ab* and *dare*, to give.

abduct. For earlier *abduce*. From L. *abducere*, *abduct-*, to lead away.

abeam [*naut.*]. Abreast, level with, i.e. neither ahead nor astern. The *beams* of a ship are at right-angles to the keel; cf. *beam-ends*.

abear [*dial.*]. AS. *āberan*, from *bear*[2]. Obs. from c. 1300, exc. in dial.

"Territorial" is a word that the dunderheads of the War Office "cannot abear"
(*Sunday Times*, Aug. 25, 1918).

abecedarian. Alphabetical, concerned with the alphabet. Still used in US. for begin-

ners at school. Cf. MedL. *abecedarium*, barbarously formed from ABC.

abecedarium: an absee (Coop.).

abed [*dial.*]. For *on bed*. See *a-*.

abele. White poplar. Du. *abeel*, OF. *aubel*, Late L. *albellus*, from *albus*, white.

aberglaube. Ger., superstition, from *glauben*, to believe, with pejorative prefix as in *abgott*, idol.

aberration. From L. *aberrare*, to wander off. See *err*.

aberuncator. Incorr. for *averruncator* (q.v.).

abet. OF. *abeter*, to egg on, from OF. *beter*, to bait, ON. *beita*, to cause to bite. See *bait*, *bet*. First in Shaks. (v.i.), but the noun *abetment* is found in ME.

Abetting him to thwart me in my mood
(*Com. of Errors*, ii. 2)

abeyance. OF. *abeance*, from *abeer*, to gape at, compd. of *bayer*, *béer*, to gape. Now usu. of a right or estate which is regarded with (gaping) expectancy. See *bay*[3].

abhor. L. *abhorrēre*, to shrink from, from *horrēre*, to bristle (see *horrid*). The *abhorrers* (hist.) expressed in various petitions to Charles II their *abhorrence* of Whig and Nonconformist views.

abide. AS. *ābīdan*, from *bīdan*, to bide (q.v.), remain. Followed by gen., it meant to wait for; hence, to endure, put up with, as still in dial. (*can't abide*). Shaks. use in the sense of pay for, expiate (v.i.) is due to confusion with obs. *abye*, AS. *abycgan*, to expiate, from *bycgan*, to buy, pay for.

If it be found so, some will dear abide it
(*Jul. Caes.* iii. 2).

abiet- [*chem.*]. From L. *abies*, *abiet-*, fir.

abigail. Waiting-maid. Name of character in Beaumont and Fletcher's *Scornful Lady* (1616), this perh. suggested by 1 *Sam.* xxv. 24 sqq.

ability. Re-fashioned, after ModF. *habileté*, from ME. & OF. *ableté*. See *able*. Often *hability* in 16–17 cents.

abiogenesis [*biol.*]. Generation of living organisms from dead matter. Coined (1870) by Huxley from G. ἀ-, neg., βίος, life. So also *biogenesis*, its opposite.

abject. From L. *abicere*, *abject-*, to cast away, from *jacere*.

abjure. L. *abjurare*, to swear off. See *jury*.

ablactation. Weaning. From L. *ablactare*, from *lac*, *lact-*, milk.

ablative. Lit. bearing away. F. *ablatif*, L. *ablativus*, from *ablat-* (*auferre*). Coined by Julius Caesar, there being no ablative in G.

ablaut [*ling.*]. Change of vowel. Ger., from *laut*, sound, with prefix cogn. with *off*. Cf. *umlaut*. Introduced by Jakob Grimm (1819).

ablaze. For *on blaze*. See *a-* and *blaze*¹, and cf. *aback*, *abed*, etc.

> They setten all on blase (Gower).

able. OF. (replaced by *habile*), L. *habilis*, fit, apt, from *habēre*, to have, hold. Cf. *capable* for sense-development.

ablution. From L. *abluere*, *ablut-*, to wash away. Orig. a chem. term (Chauc.), "the rinsing of chymical preparations in water, to dissolve and wash away any acrimonious particles" (Johns.).

abnegate. From L. *abnegare*, to deny off. Cf. *negative*.

abnormal. "Few words show such a series of pseudo-etymological perversions; G. ἀνόμαλος, L. *anomalus*, having been altered in Late L., after *norma*, to *anormalis*, whence F. *anormal* and E. *anormal*, the latter referred to L. *abnormis* and altered to *abnormal*. It has displaced the earlier *abnormous*" (*NED.*). See *normal*, *anomalous*.

aboard [*naut.*]. F. *à bord*, of Teut. origin (see *board*). With *to lay aboard* cf. orig. meaning of vb. *to board* (see *board*, *accost*).

abode. From *abide*; cf. *road* (*rode*) from *ride*.

abolish. F. *abolir*, *aboliss-* from L. *abolescere*, from *abolēre*, to destroy. Hence *abolitionism*, *-ist*, orig. coined by opponents of slave-trade (c. 1800). Some connect the L. word with G. ὄλλυμι, I destroy.

abominable. L. *abominabilis*, from *abominari*, to deprecate, shrink from the omen (cf. *absit omen*). Strong meaning is due to erron. medieval derivation from *ab homine*, as though inhuman, unnatural. Hence usual MedL., OF. & ME. spelling *abhomin-*. So Holofernes:

> This is abhominable, which he would call abominable (*Love's Lab. Lost*, v. i).

aborigines. L., from *ab origine*. First applied to original inhabitants of Greece and Italy.

abortion. From L. *aboriri*, *abort-*, to miscarry, from *oriri*, to appear.

abound. F. *abonder*, L. *abundare*, to overflow, from *unda*, wave. Cf. *superfluous*.

about. AS. *on-būtan*, for *on be ūtan*, on by outside, *ūtan* being adv. from prep. *ūt*. Cf. *above*. All senses spring from primitive meaning, e.g. a man *about fifty* is "in the neighbourhood" of fifty (cf. similar use of F. *environ*).

above. From AS. *bufan* for *be ufan*, by upward, from *uf*, up. First element added later by analogy with *abaft*, *about* (q.v.). Hence *above-board*, "a figurative expression, borrowed from gamesters, who, when they put their hands under the table, are changing their cards. It is used only in familiar language" (Johns.). Cf. F. *jouer cartes sur table*, to play fair.

abracadabra. Cabalistic word used as charm; first occurs in 3 cent. ?From G. ἀβραξάς, cabalistic word composed of letters whose numerical values give 365, the number of successive manifestations attributed to the Supreme Being by the gnostic Basilides.

abrade. L. *abradere*, to scrape off. See *razor*.

abram, to sham [*naut.*]. To feign sickness. Hotten's explanation is very doubtful.

> An Abraham-man is he that walketh bare-armed and bare-legged and faynyth hymselfe mad
>   (Awdeley, *Fraternytye of Vacaboundes*, 1561).
> It appears to have been the practice in former days to allow certain inmates of Bethlehem Hospital to have fixed days to go begging. Hence impostors were said to "sham Abraham" (the Abraham Ward in Bedlam having for its inmates these mendicant lunatics) when they pretended they were licensed beggars on behalf of the hospital (Hotten).

abranchiate [*biol.*]. Without gills. Cf. *branchiopod*. See *a-*.

abreast. Perh. orig. *of breast*; cf. F. *aller de front*. See *anew*.

abridge. F. *abréger*, L. *abbreviare*, from *ad* and *brevis*, short. Cf. F. *alléger*, to lighten, VL. **alleviare*, from *levis*, light.

abroach, to set [*archaic*]. Orig. to pierce a cask. See *broach*.

abroad. Altered, on adj. *broad*, from ME. *on brede*, on breadth, widely scattered, etc. Mod. sense of foreign travel is evolved from ME. meaning of out of doors. Cf. *travel*, *voyage*, for similar sense-development characteristic of sea-faring race.

abrogate. From L. *abrogare*, to call off. Cf. *repeal*.

abrupt. From L. *abrumpere*, *abrupt-*, to break off. See *rout*.

abscess. L. *abscessus*, from *abscedere*, *abscess-*, to go away, from *cedere*, to go.

abscissa [*math.*]. L. (sc. *linea*), from *abscindere*, *absciss-*, to cut off.

abscond. L. *abscondere*, to hide away. Orig. trans., mod. use being for earlier reflex.

> The poor man fled from place to place absconding himself (*NED.* 1721).

absent. F., L. *absens*, *absent-*, pres. part. of *abesse*, to be away (see *entity*). First records for *absentee* (Camden, Blount, Swift) refer to Ireland.

absentee: a word used commonly with regard to Irishmen living out of their country (Johns.).

absinthe. F., L. *absinthium*, G. ἀψίνθιον, the herb wormwood. In this sense used in E. in 1612, while the liqueur is first mentioned by Thackeray.

absit [*univ.*]. L., let him be absent. Cf. *exeat*.

absolve. L. *absolvere*, to set free, replacing from 16 cent. earlier *assoil* (q.v.). Hence *absolute*, freed from restraint or conditions. Much earlier (12 cent.) is *absolution*, in eccl. sense.

absorb. L. *absorbere*, to suck away, swallow up.

absquatulate [*US.*]. To make off, skedaddle. Facetious US. coinage, perh. suggested by *squat*, to settle.

Rumour has it that a gay bachelor, who has figured in Chicago for nearly a year, has skedaddled, absquatulated, vamosed, and cleared out.
(*Rocky Mountain News*, 1862).

abstain. From F. *abstenir*, VL. **abstenire* for *abstinēre*, to hold away. Orig. reflex. (cf. *abscond*).

Wryte unto them that they absteyne them selves from fylthynesse of idols (Coverd. *Acts*, xv. 20).

abstemious. From L. *abstemius*, from *temetum*, strong drink. Wider sense in E. partly due to association with *abstain*.

absterge. L. *abstergere*, to wipe away.

abstinence. F.; see *abstain*. *Total abstinence* in spec. sense dates from c. 1830.

The passionate Eastern character, like all weak ones, found total abstinence easier than temperance (Kingsley, *Hypatia*).

abstract. From L. *abstrahere*, *abstract-*, to draw away. As adj., withdrawn from matter, opposite of *concrete*.

abstruse. From L. *abstrudere*, *abstrus-*, to push away.

absurd. F. *absurde*, L. *absurdus*, from *surdus*, deaf, dull, dissonant.

abundance. See *abound*.

abuse. F. *abuser*, VL. **abusare*, from *abuti*, *abus-*, to misuse. Sense of reviling first in Shaks. (*Oth.* v. 1).

abut. Mixture of two F. verbs, viz. *abouter*, to join at the end (*bout*), and archaic *abuter*, to join exactly, reach the aim (*but*). But *bout* and *but* are ult. ident.

aby [*poet.*]. See *abide*. Revived by Scott.

abysm. OF. *abisme* (*abîme*), VL. **abismus*, altered, after words of G. origin in -*ismus*, from *abyssus*, G. ἄβυσσος, bottomless,

whence *abyss*. Mod. pronunc. is due to spelling, the -*s*- becoming mute in early OF.

Feele such a case, as one whom some abisme,
In the deep ocean kept had all his time
(Drummond of Hawthornden, 1616).

abyss. See *abysm*.

ac-. For *ad-* before *c-*.

acacia. L., G. ἀκακία, prob. from ἀκή, point.

academy. F. *académie*, L., G. ἀκαδήμεια. Orig. grove near Athens where Plato taught, named after a demi-god Ἀκάδημος. Sense of learned assembly after It. *accademia*.

Acadian. F. *acadien*, from *Acadie*, Nova Scotia (see *Evangeline*), from native name.

acanthus. L., G. ἄκανθος, from ἄκανθα, thorn, from ἀκή, point. Cf. *acacia*.

Accadian [*ling.*]. Lang. preserved in cuneiform inscriptions earlier than Assyr. and prob. obs. c. 2000 B.C. From *Accad* in Shinar (*Gen.* x. 10).

accede. L. *accedere*, to move towards. See *cede*.

accelerate. From L. *accelerare*, from *celer*, swift.

accent. F., L. *accentus*, from *ad cantus* (see *chant*), orig. translating G. προσῳδία, from πρός, to, ᾠδή, song, in sense of song added to instrumental music. Used in E. of diacritic signs from 16 cent.

accept. F., L. *acceptare*, frequent. of *accipere*, *accept-*, from *capere*, to take.

access. F. *accès* or L. *accessus*, from *accedere*, *access-*, to approach, come to. Cf. *accession*, coming to (the throne), *accessory*, coming as addition.

accidence. For *accidents*, pl. of *accident*, in sense of grammatical phenomenon. Cf. *occurrence*.

Not changing one word for another, by their accidents or cases
(Puttenham, *Art of English Poesie*, 1589).

accident. F., from pres. part. of L. *accidere*, to happen, befall, from *cadere*, to fall. Orig. chance, hap.

Moving accidents by flood and field (*Oth.* i. 3).

accipitral. From L. *accipiter*, hawk, associated with *accipere*, to take for oneself, but prob. for **acu-peter*, sharp winged, with second element cogn. with G. πτερόν.

acclaim. From L. *acclamare*, to shout to. See *claim*.

acclimatize. From F. *acclimater*. See *climate*.

acclivity. From L. *acclivitas*, upward slope, from *ad*, to, *clivus*, rising ground. Cf. *declivity*.

accolade [*hist.*]. F., It. *accollata*, from *accollare*, to embrace, from L. *collum*, neck.

accollade: a colling, clipping, imbracing about the necke; hence, the dubbing of a knight, or the ceremony used therein (Cotg.).

accommodate. From L. *accommodare*, to fit to. See *commodious*.

accompany. From F. *accompagner*. See *companion*.

accomplice. For earlier *complice*, F., L. *complex, complic-*, lit. woven together. Mod. form may be a mistake for *a complice* or be due to some fancied connection with *accomplish*.

Your brother, the booke-binder, and his accomplishes at Burie (Nashe, 1589).

accomplish. F. *accomplir, accompliss-*, from OF. *complir*, VL. **complire* for *complēre*, to fill. Current sense of *accomplishment* is "some study accomplished which accomplishes the student" (*NED.*).

accompt. Restored spelling of *account* (q.v.).

accord. F. *accorder*, VL. **accordare*, from *corda*, harp-string, but affected in sense by association with *cor, cord-*, heart. Cf. *concord, discord*. Hence *accordion*, invented at Vienna (1829), with ending imitated from *clarion*. *Of one's own accord*, i.e. consent, was in ME. *by one's own accord*.

accost. F. *accoster*, VL. **accostare*, from *ad* and *costa*, rib. Orig. to border on, come in contact with. Cf. F. *aborder*, "to approach, accoast, abboord; boord or lay aboord; come, or draw neer unto" (Cotg.). See *coast*.

accouchement. F., from *accoucher*, to bring to bed. See *couch*. Early 19 cent. euph.

account. OF. *aconter*, VL. **accomputare*, from *computare*, to reckon. See *count¹*. *Accountant* is from the OF. pres. part. For two groups of meanings (also in *recount*), now represented in F. by differentiated forms *conter, compter*, cf. those of *tell*.

accoutre. F. *accoutrer*, orig. to fit out, equip, in any way. For mod. restriction of meaning cf. *dress*. Of obscure origin. ?From F. *coutre*, ploughshare, L. *culter*, with orig. sense of equipping a plough, ? or from F. *couture*, seam, VL. **consutura*.

accredit. F. *accréditer*, from *crédit*, credit (q.v.).

accretion. L. *accretio-n-*, from *accrescere, accret-*, to grow to (v.i.).

accrue. Orig. p.p. fem. of F. *accroître*, to grow, L. *accrescere* (v.s.). Cf. *value, issue*, etc., and see *crew, recruit*.

accumulate. See *cumulate*.

accurate. From L. *accurare*, to give care to. See *cure¹*.

accursed. Perverted spelling of *acursed*, where the *a-* is intens. as in *awake*. See *curse*. For intrusive *-c-* cf. *acknowledge*.

accuse. F. *accuser*, L. *accusare*, to call to account, *causa*. Hence *accusative*, translating G. αἰτιατική, from αἰτία, cause.

ace. F. *as*, L. *as, ass-*, unity, said to be Tarentine ἄς for G. εἶς, one. Oldest sense is side of dice with one pip, the lowest throw. Hence *ambsace* (q.v.), *deuce ace* (see *deuce*), and *within an ace of*. With sense of crack airman, after ModF., cf. fig. use of *trump²*.

Your lordship is the most patient man in loss, the most coldest that ever turn'd up ace (*Cymb.* ii. 3).

Aceldama. G. Ἀκελδαμά, representing Aram. *h'qal d'mā*, field of blood (*Acts*, i. 19).

acephalous. From G. ἀ-, neg., κεφαλή, head.

acerbity. F. *acerbité*, L. *acerbitas*, from *acerbus*, harsh to the taste, from *acer*, keen.

acetic [*chem.*]. From L. *acetum*, vinegar, from *acēre*, to be sour (v.s.). Hence *acetylene*.

Achates. Faithful friend. L. *fidus Achates*, companion of Aeneas (Virg.).

ache. The verb, AS. *acan* (? cogn. with L. *agere*), was earlier, and correctly, *ake*, the noun was *ache* (*ch* as in *church*), whence dial. *eddage*, headache; cf. *bake, batch, speak, speech*, etc., and note pronunc. in quot. below. The noun was influenced by the verb and both became *ake*, while in the 18 cent. the spelling *ache* was introduced. "For this paradoxical result Dr Johnson is mainly responsible; ignorant of the history of the words, and erroneously deriving them from the Greek ἄχος (with which they have no connection), he declared them 'more grammatically written *ache*'" (*NED.*). The verb was orig. strong (past *ōc*).

I'll rack thee with old cramps,
Fill all thy bones with aches, make thee roar
(*Temp.* i. 2).

acherontic. Gloomy, moribund, from G. Ἀχέρων, river of Infernal Regions. Cf. *stygian*.

achieve. OF. *achiev-*, tonic stem of *achever*, VL. **accapare*, from *ad* and *caput*, head, or formed in F. from *à* and *chef*. Cf. F. *venir à chef de*, to succeed in.

Achilles tendon. Great tendon of the heel. Allusion to vulnerable heel of Achilles, by which his mother held him when dipping him in the Styx.

achromatic. Colourless. From G. ἀχρώματος. See *chrome*.

acid. F. *acide* or L. *acidus*, sharp, sour; cf. *acies*, edge, *acus*, needle.

ack emma. Mil. slang for A.M., letters easily confused on the telephone being perverted in the interests of clearness, e.g. *pip* for P, *tock* for T, etc.

> Not so much of your ac, ac, ac, and your O pip Emma. Wot's the blooming message?
> (Impatient Coastguard, in *Punch*).

acknowledge. Artificial spelling for *a-knowledge*. This is app. due to confusion between the ME. verbs *knowlechen* and *aknowen*, AS. *oncnāwan*, to perceive. See *know, knowledge*.

acme. G. ἀκμή, point. Usu. printed in G. letters up to 18 cent.

acne [*med.*]. ? From G. ἄχνη, small particle, e.g. froth, chaff, down on fruit.

acolyte. MedL. *acolitus* for G. ἀκόλουθος, following. For facet. sense cf. *myrmidon, satellite*.

aconite. Monkshood. L. *aconitum*, G. ἀκόνιτον. Origin unknown (see Pliny, *Hist. Nat.* 27. 10).

acorn. Mod. spelling is due to the word being regarded as *oak* (AS. *āc*) *corn*, but app. it is related to neither of these words. AS. *æcern*, Ger. *ecker*, Goth. *akran*, are supposed to be related to AS. *æcer*, field (see *acre*), and to have meant orig. wild fruit in general, then mast of forest trees, the meaning of the E. word becoming limited later to the most important kind of mast for feeding swine. Cf. OF. *aigrun*, collect. name for fruit and vegetables, from Teut.

acotyledon [*bot.*]. Without seed-lobes. See *cotyledon* and *a-*.

acoustic. F. *acoustique*, G. ἀκουστικός, from ἀκούειν, to hear.

acquaint. From Norm. form of OF. *acointier*, to make known, from *acoint*, Late L. *accognitus*. See *quaint*.

acquiesce. L. *acquiescere*, incept. formation from *quies*, quiet.

acquire. L. *acquirere*, from *quaerere*, to seek. *Acquisition* is L. *acquisitio-n-*, from *acquisit-*.

acquit. F. *acquitter*, VL. *adquitare, from *quitus, for *quietus*. Orig. to discharge a debt, obligation, etc. See *quit*.

acre. Earlier *aker*, AS. *æcer*, field, without ref. to dimension. Com. Teut.; cf. Du. *akker*, Ger. *acker*, ON. *akr*, Goth. *akrs*; cogn. with L. *ager*, field, G. ἀγρός. Mod. spelling is due to MedL. *acra*, OF. *acre*, but the more correct *aker* survives in some surnames, e.g.

Hardaker, Whittaker. As a measure of land it at first meant as much as a yoke of oxen could plough in a day, but was afterwards fixed by statute. *God's acre*, churchyard, is a mod. adaptation, due to Longfellow, of Ger. *Gottesacker*.

> I was jeered at [in 1880] as the apostle of "Three acres and a cow" (J. Collings).

acrid. From L. *acer, acr-*, sharp, sour. Irreg. formation due to analogy with *acid*.

acrimony. L. *acrimonia*, from *acer* (v.s.).

acroamatic. Of oral teaching, esoteric, esp. in ref. to Aristotle's intimate lectures. G. ἀκροαματικός, from ἀκρόαμα, from ἀκροᾶσθαι, to hear.

acrobat. F. *acrobate*, G. ἀκρόβατος, tip-toe walking, from ἄκρος, topmost (as in *Acropolis*), and *-βατος*, from βαίνειν, to go.

acropolis. G., from ἄκρος, highest, πόλις, city.

across. For *on cross*, or suggested by F. *en croix*, rendered *in crosse* by Caxton.

acrostic. Also earlier *acrostich*, F. *acrostiche* (cf. *distich*), from G. ἄκρος, extreme, and στίχος, a row, line of verse.

act. F. *acte* and L. *actus*, from *agere, act-*, to do. Verb is much later than noun. Theat. sense is in L.; legislat. sense appears in E. from 16 cent. In some senses partly superseded by later *action*.

actinia. Sea-anemone. Coined by Linnaeus from G. ἀκτίς, ἀκτῖν-, ray. Cf. *actinic* (phot.).

action. F., L. *actio-n-*, from *agere, act-*, to do. Leg. sense is earliest (c. 1300). Cf. *active*, F. *actif*, L. *activus*, and *activist* (neol.), app. from F.

acton [*hist.*]. Orig. quilted garment worn under armour; later, leather coat with plating. OF. *auqueton* (*hoqueton*), Sp. *alcoton*, Arab. *al-qūtun*, the cotton, in allusion to the padding. Revived by Scott (*Lay*, iii. 6).

actor. Orig. doer. L., from *agere, act-*, to do. In current sense from 16 cent.

actual. Late L. *actualis*, pertaining to *acts*. Mod. use of *actuality* in the sense of realism, contact with the contemporary, is due to F. *actualité*, from *actuel*, which does not mean actual, real, but now existing, up to date.

actuary. L. *actuarius*, recorder of items, proceedings, etc. Current sense is 19 cent.

actuate. From MedL. *actuare*, from *actus*, act.

acuity. From MedL. *acuitas*, from *acus*, needle.

aculeate. From L. *aculeatus*, furnished with a sting, from *aculeus*, dim. of *acus*, needle.

acumen. L., sharpness, from *acuere*, to sharpen.

acute. L. *acutus*, p.p. of *acuere*, to sharpen. See *acid*, and cf. *acacia*.

acushla [*Ir.*]. Darling. Short for *a chuisla mo chroidhe*, O pulse of my heart.

ad-. L. *ad*, to; cogn. with E. *at* (q.v.). Usu. assimilated to following consonant (*achieve, acquaint, affect, aggrandize, announce*, etc.). Often restored from earlier *a-* (*adventure, adjourn*, etc.), and sometimes wrongly substituted (*advance, admiral*).

adage. F., L. *adagium*, from *ad* and root of *aio*, I say.

adagio [*mus.*]. Slowly. It. *ad agio*, at ease. See *agio, ease*.

adamant. OF., L. *adamas, adamant-*, G. ἀδάμας, invincible, from ἀ-, neg., δαμάειν, to tame (q.v.). In earliest uses applied to very hard metals and stones, and later spec. to the loadstone or magnet, and the diamond. In the first of these meanings medieval scholars connected it with *ad-amare*, to attract (cf. F. *aimant*, magnet). Its popular form has given *diamond* (q.v.).

Adam's apple. Allusion to the forbidden fruit supposed to have stuck in Adam's throat. In most Europ. langs.

adapt. F., L. *adaptare*, from *aptus*, fit.

add. L. *addere*, to put to, from *ad* and *dare*, to give. Hence *addenda*, things to be added.

adder. AS. *nǣdre*, snake. Com. Teut.; cf. Du. *adder* (earlier *nadder*), Ger. *natter* (var. *otter*), ON. *nathr*, Goth. *nadrs*; cogn. with OIr. *nathair*, Welsh *nadyr*, and perh. with L. *natrix*, water-snake. Now limited to the common viper. The initial *n-* was lost in ME., *a nadder* being understood as *an adder*. Cf. *apron, auger*, and, for the converse, *newt. Nedder* is still in dial. use.

neddyr or *eddyr*: serpens (*Prompt. Parv.*).

addict. Orig. adj., L. *addictus*, adjudged, made over, p.p. of *addicere*, from *dicere*, to say, tell.

The number of drug addicts in the United States is estimated to be in excess of 1,000,000
(*Daily Herald*, June 25, 1919).

additament. L. *additamentum*, from *addere, addit-*, to add (q.v.). Cf. *addition*, F., L. *additio-n-*.

addle. AS. *ādela*, putrid mud, filth; cogn. with Dan. *aile*, urine of cattle. Now only in compds. *addle-egg, addle-pate*, etc. For later *addled* cf. *newfangled*.

address. Orig. to make straight. F. *adresser*, from *dresser*. See *dress* and cf. senses of *direct*. With *address*, skill, cf. *adroit* (q.v.).

Golf sense is a survival. To *address*, accost, is for earlier reflex. to *address oneself to*.

adduce. L. *adducere*, to bring to.

-ade. F. suffix in loan-words representing Prov. Sp. Port. *-ada*, It. *-ata*, L. *-ata*, which gave F. *-ée*. In 16–17 cent. often changed into pseudo-Sp. form, e.g. *ambuscado, palisado*, and the surviving *bastinado*.

ademption [*leg.*]. L. *ademptio-n-*, from *adimere, adempt-*, to take to oneself, take away.

adenoid [*med.*]. From G. ἀδήν, acorn, fig. gland (q.v.). See *-oid*.

adept. L. *adeptus*, p.p. of *adipisci*, to attain. Orig. used by medieval alchemists of those who had "attained" the great secret.

adequate. From L. *adaequare*, to make equal to.

ad eundem (sc. **gradum**) [*univ.*]. Admission of graduate "to the same (degree)" at another university.

adhere. L. *adhaerēre*, to stick to.

ad hoc. L., for this (specific purpose).

adiantum [*bot.*]. Fern. From G. ἀ-, neg., διαίνειν, to wet.

adieu. F., OF. *à Dieu*. Orig. said to the party left, as *farewell* was to the party setting forth.

adipose. From L. *adeps, adip-*, fat, unexplained alteration of G. ἄλειφαρ, unguent.

He never spoke of it as "fat,"
But adipose deposit (Gilbert).

adit. Approach to mine. L. *aditus*, from *adire*, to go to.

adjacent. From pres. part. of L. *adjacēre*, to lie by.

adjective. F. *adjectif*, L. *adjectivus*, from *adicere, adject-*, to add, from *jacere*, to throw.

adjourn. To put off, orig. fix a day for a person. F. *ajourner*, VL. **ad-diurnare*, from *diurnus*, adj. from *dies*, day; or possibly formed in OF. from *à* and *jorn* (*jour*), L. *diurnus*. To *adjourn sine die* is, strictly speaking, a bull.

adjourner: to cite, summon, warne to appeare; to serve a processe of appearance on (Cotg.).

adjudicate. From L. *adjudicare*, from *judex, judic-*, judge, from *jus*, law, *dicere*, to say.

adjunct. From L. *adjungere, adjunct-*, to join to.

adjure. From L. *adjurare*, to swear to.

adjust. Two F. verbs are included here, viz. OF. *ajoster* (*ajouter*), to add, put together, VL. **adjuxtare*, or formed in OF. from *à* and the prep. *joste* (L. *juxta*); and *ajuster*, formed from *à* and *juste*, or representing the above verb refashioned under the influence of *juste*, just, exact.

adjouster: to adde, adjoyne, set, or put unto; also, to increase, augment, eeke; also, as *adjuster*.
adjuster: to adjust, place justly, set aptly, couch evenly, joyne handsomely, match fitly, dispose orderly, severall things together (Cotg.).

adjutant. From pres. part. of L. *adjutare*, frequent. of *adjuvare*, to help. Prob. not straight from L., but a remodelled form of Sp. *ayudante*. Cf. Ger. *adjutant* (17 cent.), a Sp. loan-word from the Thirty Years War. The *adjutant-bird*, a gigantic Indian crane, is so named from his stiff military gait. Cf. *marabout*.

ad lib. Short for L. *ad libitum*, from *libēre*, to please.

adminicle. Auxiliary, corroboration. L. *adminiculum*, prop, from dim. of *manus*, hand.

administer. Orig. with province, estate, etc., as object. Hence to furnish, supply, e.g. castor oil or a thrashing. See *minister*.

admiral. Artificial spelling of *amiral*, F. Oldest sense in F. & E. is emir, Saracen chief. Arab. *amīr*, commander, is commonly followed by *al*, as in *amīr-al-bahr*, commander of the sea, and many other compds., from which a clipped noun *amiral* resulted. Mod. maritime sense is due to the office of *amīr-al-bahr* or *amīr-al-mā*, created by the Arabs in Spain and Sicily. Explained by a 16 cent. etymologist, with ref. to Columbus, as L. *admirans mare*, admiring the sea! From 16 cent. also applied to the admiral's ship or flag-ship, the admiral himself being called the general.

> Keepe the admiraltie,
> That wee be masters of the narrow see
> *(Libel of English Policie*, 1432).

admire. From L. *admirari*, to wonder at, from *mirus*, wonderful. Cf. *marvel*, *miracle*.

And I saw the woman drunken with the blood of the saints..and when I saw her I wondered with great admiration (*Rev.* xvii. 6).

admission. L. *admissio-n-*, from *admittere*, *admiss-* (v.i.).

admit. ME. *amit*, OF. *ametre* (*admettre*), remodelled on L. *admittere*, to send to.

admonish. ME. *amonest*, OF. *amonester* (*admonester*), VL. **admonestare*, an unexplained derivative of *admonēre*, from *monēre*, to advise. It has been assimilated to the large class of verbs in *-ish*. Cf. *astonish*, *distinguish*, etc.

ado. Orig. infin. *at do*, the prep. *at* being used in ON. with infin. like E. *to*. This usage

long survived in northern E. dial. Cf. *a great to do* and F. *affaire* (*à faire*), *avoir affaire à*.

-ado. See *-ade*.

adobe. Unburnt brick dried in the sun. US., from Mexico, often made into *'dobe*. From Sp. *adobar*, to plaster. Cf. F. *adouber*, to put in order, arrange. ? Same origin as *dub* q.v.); ? or Arab. *al-tub*, the brick.

adolescent. From pres. part. of L. *adolescere*, to grow up, from archaic L. *olēre*, to grow old. Cf. *adult*, from p.p.

Adonis. G. name from Phoenician *adōn*, lord. Cf. Bibl. name *Adoni-Bezek* (*Judges*, i. 5).

adopt. F. *adopter*, or L. *adoptare*, to choose for oneself. Cf. *option*.

adore. L. *adorare*, to pray to. Replaced ME. *aoure*, OF. *aorer*.

adorn. L. *adornare*. Replaced ME. *aorne*, OF. *aorner*.

adown [*archaic*]. For *of down*, AS. *of dūne*, lit. off hill. See *down*[1].

adrift. Prob. for *on drift*. See *a-*.

adroit. F., orig. adv., *à droit*, rightly. Cf. E. *to rights*. *Droit* is L. *directus*. See *dress*.

adscititious, ascititious. Supplemental, unsanctioned. Coined from L. *adscit-*, from *adsciscere*, to acknowledge, from *scire*, to know.

adscript, ascript. Chiefly in pedantic imit. of L. *adscriptus glebae*, enrolled to the soil, used of serfs.

Practically he [the working-man] is as firmly ascript to his trade as the mediæval serf was to the soil (*Fortnightly*, Aug. 1919).

adsum. L., I am here.

adulation. From L. *adulari*, to flatter, ? orig. to wag the tail, and ult. cogn. with Ger. *wedeln*, to wag the tail (see *wheedle*).

Adullamite [*hist.*]. Nickname given (1866) to group of M.P.s who seceded from Liberal party. Made current by a speech in which John Bright likened them to the discontented who rallied round David in the *Cave of Adullam* (1 *Sam.* xxii.), but recorded as pol. nickname for 1834. Cf. *cave*.

adult. See *adolescent*.

adulterate. From L. *adulterare*, to commit adultery, corrupt, from *alter*, other (*ad alterum convertere*).

adumbrate. From L. *adumbrare*, to foreshadow, from *umbra*, shadow. Almost obs. in 18 cent., but now overworked.

adust. L. *adustus*, p.p. of *adurere*, to burn, scorch. Parched, sunburnt; hence, gloomy in temperament.

advance. Bad spelling for earlier *avance*, F. *avancer*, to put forward, VL. *abantiare*, from *ab ante*, whence F. *avant*, before.

advantage. F. *avantage*, VL. *abantaticum* or formed in OF. from *avant* with suffix -*age*, L. -*aticum*. See *advance, vantage*.

advent. L. *adventus*, from *advenire*, to come to, arrive. Cf. F. *avent*.

adventitious. From L. *adventicius*, coming from abroad (v.s.).

adventure. For earlier *aventure, aunter*; respelt on L. *adventura*, from *advenire, advent-*, to happen. See *venture*.

adverb. F. *adverbe*, L. *adverbium*, "cujus significatio verbis adjicitur" (Priscian), translating G. ἐπίρρημα.

adverse. From L. *advertere, advers-*, to turn against. Hence *adversary*, in ME. esp. the Devil.

advert. Earlier *avert*, OF. *avertir*, VL. *advertire*, for *advertere*, to turn to. See *advertise*.

advertise. F. *avertiss-*, lengthened stem of *avertir*, to warn, from L. *advertere*, to turn to (v.s.). The *ad-* is a restoration, and the survival of the -*ise* form (cf. *advert, convert, revert*, etc.) is prob. due to noun *advertisement*, F. *avertissement* (cf. *aggrandize*). Mod. sense, developed from that of public announcement, is unknown in F.

Joachym king of Juda despraised the admonestementis, advertisementis, and the doctrines of God (*NED.* 1475).

My griefs cry louder than advertisement
(*Much Ado*, v. 1).

advice, advise Earlier *avice*, F. *avis*, counsel, opinion, warning. It. *avviso*, Sp. *aviso*, point to VL. *advisus*, from *ad* and *videre, vis-*, to see, but in OF. the two elements occur apart, as in the colloquial *Ce m'est avis* for *Ce m'est à vis* (*ad visum*). The differentiated spelling (cf. *prophesy, practise*) is artificial. The oldest meaning of the noun is opinion, of the verb to look at, or, reflex., to consider, F. *s'aviser*.

advocate. First as noun. ME. *avocat*, F., L. *advocatus*, called in. As leg. title now usu. Sc.

advowson. Right of presentation to a benefice. Earlier *avoueson*, OF. *avoëson*, L. *advocatio-n-*, from *advocare*, to call to, summon.

adytum. Sanctum. L., G. ἄδυτον, from ἀ-, neg., δύειν, to enter.

adze. Often spelt *addis, addice* as late as 17 cent. AS. *adesa*, of unknown origin.

aedile [*hist.*]. L. *aedilis*, commissioner of work, from *aedes*, building, cogn. with G.

αἴθειν, to burn (with suggestion of hearth as nucleus of home). Cf. *edify*.

aegis. L., G. αἰγίς, shield of Zeus or Pallas. From G. αἴξ, αἴγ-, goat, orig. applied to goat-skin shield-belt of Zeus.

aegrotat [*univ.*]. L., he is sick, *aeger*. Cf. *exit, affidavit*, etc.

Aeolian. (1) Mode of music; from *Aeolis* or *Aeolia*, Greek colony in Asia Minor. Cf. *Doric*. (2) Natural harp; from L. *Aeolus*, god of the winds (*Aen.* i. 52).

aeon. L., G. αἰών, age, cogn. with L. *aevum*. See *age*.

aerate. From L. *aer*, air, after F. *aérer*.

aerial. From L. *aer*, air, after *ethereal*. An "aerial ship," London to Paris, was advertised in 1835, but burst during inflation.

aero-. From G. ἀήρ, ἀέρ-, air. *Aerodrome* (neol.) is after earlier *hippodrome* (q.v.), *velodrome*. *Aerolite* is for *aerolith*, from G. λίθος, stone. *Aeronaut*, F. *aéronaute*, from ναύτης, sailor, pilot, *aerostat*, F. *aérostat*, from στατός, supported, both date from 1783 (cf. *Montgolfier*). *Aeroplane* (neol.) is F. *aéroplane*. *Aerobatics*, "stunts," is after *acrobatics*. *Aerobus* is mod. (Feb., 1919).

aeronautica: the pretended art of sailing in a vessel thro' the air or atmosphere
(Chambers' *Cyclopaedia*, 1753).
The *aeropark* (may I coin the word?) had many a lively time during the retreat
(Corbett-Smith, *Marne and after*).

aery, eyry. F. *aire*, "an airie, or nest of haukes" (Cotg.), dubiously connected with L. *ager*, field, which app. took the sense of home, place of origin, whence Prov. *agre*, nest. See *debonair*. Spelling *eyry* is app. due to Spelman's attempt to connect the word with ME. *ey*, egg. The spec. association of the word with the eagle suggests that it may rather be connected with the Teut. name for the bird (see *erne*), which has cognates in Celt. (Corn. Bret. *er*, Welsh *eryr*).

Aesculapian, Esculapian. Of *Aesculapius*, G. Ἀσκληπιός, god of medicine. Cf. *galenical*.

aesthete. G. αἰσθητής, from αἰσθέσθαι, to perceive. First recorded by *NED.* for 1881 (aesthetic craze), but *aesthetic* dates from 1798, having been introduced by Baumgarten into German philosophy (c. 1750) with the sense of criticism of taste. The word suffered (c. 1880) a temporary depreciation from which it has now recovered.

I am a broken-hearted troubadour,
Whose mind's aesthetic and whose tastes are pure
(Gilbert, *Patience*).

aestival, estival. Of summer. L. *aestivalis*, from *aestas*, summer. Cf. *aestivate*, opposite of *hibernate*.

aetiology, etiology. Study of causation. L. *aetiologia*, from G. αἰτία, cause.

afar. AS. *feor*, far, compd. with *of* and *on*. Both *of fer* (cf. F. *de loin*) and *on fer* (cf. F. *au loin*) became in 14 cent. *a fer*, whence *afar*. Thus *from afar*, *afar off* are sometimes pleon.

afeard [*dial.*]. Very common in Shaks., but now considered vulgar, having been supplanted by *afraid* (q.v.), with which it is quite unconnected. It is the p.p. of obs. *afear*, to terrify (see *fear*).

Fie, my lord, fie! a soldier and afear'd!
(*Macb.* v. 1).

affable. F., "easily spoken to by, willingly giving eare to, others" (Cotg.), L. *affabilis*, easy to be spoken to, from *adfari*, to address.

affair. F. *affaire*, OF. *afaire*, for *à faire*. Cf. *ado* (q.v.), *to do*.

affect. F. *affecter*, L. *affectare*, to aim at, frequent. of *afficere*, to apply (oneself) to, from *ad* and *facere*, to do. Hence *affection*, orig. (13 cent.) any mental state, the more mod. *affectation* preserving better the etym. sense. *Affect*, to influence, impress, etc., is rather directly from L. *afficere*, *affect-*.

affiance. OF. *afiance*, from *afier* (*affier*), VL. **affidare*, from *fidus*, faithful. Cf. *affidavit*. Or OF. *afiance* may be a compd. of OF. *fiance*, VL. **fidantia*. The oldest meaning was trust; then, pledging of troth; and finally the word was made into a verb.

affiche. F., from *afficher*, to affix, from *ficher*, to fix, ult. from L. *figere*.

affidavit. Lit. "he has pledged his faith," from VL. **affidare*, for which see *affiance*. Rogue Riderhood (*Our Mutual Friend*) makes it *Alfred David*, and it appears also in the vulgarism to *take one's davy*. In leg. lang. the deponent swears it and the judge takes it.

affiliate. From L. *affiliare*, to adopt as son, *filius*.

affinity. F. *affinité*, L. *affinitas*, from *affinis*, bordering on, from *finis*, end, boundary.

affirm. F. *affirmer*, L. *affirmare*, to make firm, *firmus*.

afflatus. L., from *afflare*, to inspire, from *ad* and *flare*, *flat-*, to blow.

afflict. From L. *affligere*, *afflict-*, from *fligere*, to strike.

affluence. F., L. *affluentia*, from *affluere*, to flow towards.

afflux. MedL. *affluxus* (v.s.). Cf. *influx*.

afford. Earlier *aforth*, AS. *ge-forthian*, from *forth*, forward. Orig. to "further," promote; then, supply, furnish. For prefix cf. *aware*; for consonant change cf. *burden*, *burthen*, *murder*, *murther*.

afforest. MedL. *afforestare*, from *ad* and *foresta*. See *forest*.

affray. First as verb, to frighten, OF. *esfreier* (*effrayer*), VL. **exfridare*, from OHG. *fridu* (*friede*), peace; thus a "breach of the peace." The noun is now aphetized to *fray*, and of the verb only the p.p. *afraid* (*affrayed*) survives, its success in supplanting the unrelated *afeard* being due to its regular use in the *AV*.

affright. Bad spelling of *afright*, from p.p. of AS. *āfyrhtan*, to terrify. See *fright*. Cf. *accursed*.

affront. F. *affronter*, VL. **affrontare*, to strike on the forehead, hence to insult, from *frons*, *front-*, forehead. In ModF. it means also confront, as *affront* does in Shaks.

That he, as 'twere by accident,
May there affront Ophelia (*Haml.* iii. 1).

afloat. AS. *on flote*. See *float*. So also *afield*, *afire*, *afoot*, etc. See *a-*.

afoot. For *on foot*. See *a-*. *The game's afoot*, i.e. on the move, is after 1 *Hen. IV*. i. 3.

afore. AS. *on foran* (see *fore* and *a-*) or *æt foran*. Now dial., but once literary equivalent of *before*. Cf. *pinafore*, *aforesaid*. Hence *aforethought*, in *malice aforethought*, transl. of *malice prepense*.

As I wrote afore in few words (*Eph.* iii. 3).

afraid. For *affrayed*, p.p. of *affray* (q.v.).

afreet, afrit. Evil demon of Mohammedan mythology. Arab. *'ifrit*. First in E. version of Beckford's *Vathek* (1786).

afresh. From *fresh*, after *anew* (q.v.).

Afrikander [*SAfr.*]. For Du. *Afrikaner* influenced by Du. *Englander*.

aft. AS. *æftan* (adv.), behind (cf. *abaft*). *After*, AS. *æfter* (adv. & prep.), was orig. compar. of a prep. cogn. with Goth. *af*, off, not of *aft*, though the words are related.

aftermath. After (the first) mowing. AS. *mǣth*, mowing, from *māwan*, to ·mow. *NED*. has no AS. or ME. record for the compd. It was also called *lattermath*. Cf. Ger. *grummet*, for *grün mahd*, green mowing, also called *nachheu*, after hay, and *spätheu*, late hay. Cogn. with *mead*². Now usu. fig.

aftermost. AS. *æftemest*, triple superl., -*te*-, -*me*-, -*est*, from prep. cogn. with Goth. *af*, off. But this seems to have died out, and *aftermost* was perh. refashioned from *after* on *foremost*, etc. See -*most*.

afterward. AS. *æftanweard*, which became *aftward* (naut.), current form being due to *after*. See -*ward*.

aga. Turk. *aghā*, master. Orig. mil. title.

again. AS. *ongegen*, *ongēan*, mod. *g*- being due to ON. influence; cf. Ger. *entgegen*. *Against* is for earlier *agains*, with spurious -*t* (cf. *amongst*, *betwixt*). It is a genitive formation in -*es* from *again*, which it has replaced as prep. Older use of *again* as prep. survives in *agen*, *agin* (*agin the government*), southern forms now considered vulgar. See also *gainsay*.

agamous [*biol.*]. Asexual, cryptogamous. From L., G. ἄγαμος, from ἀ-, neg., γάμος, marriage.

agapanthus. African lily. Coined from G. ἀγάπη, love, ἄνθος, flower.

agapé. Love-feast of early Christians. G. ἀγάπη, brotherly love. Hence *agapemone*, abode (G. μονή, stopping place) of free love, founded (1845) near Taunton by H. J. Prince and imitated in more recent times.

agaric. Fungus. L., G. ἀγαρικόν. Said to be from *Agaria* in Sarmatia.

agate¹. Stone. F., L. *achates*, G. ἀχάτης. In OF. we find also *acate* and in E. *achate*. Said to have been named from river *Achates* in Sicily.

Acate est ceste apelee
Por un eve [eau] u el est truvee
(Lapidaire de Marbod, 12 cent.).

agate² [*north. dial.*]. On the go. From *gate*², way.

agave. Plant. G. Ἀγαυή, myth. name, fem. of ἀγαυός, illustrious.

age. F. *âge*, OF. *aage*, *eage*, earlier *edage*, VL. **aetaticum*, from *aetas*, *aetat*-, for *aevitas*, from *aevum*, age, cogn. with G. αἰών. A good example of the expulsion of a native word (*eld*, q.v.) by one of F. origin.

-age. F., L. -*aticus*, -*aticum*; cf. It. -*aggio*.

agenda. Things to be done. L., neut. pl. of gerundive of *agere*, to do.

agent. From pres. part. of L. *agere*, to do, act.

agglomerate. From L. *agglomerare*, from *glomus*, *glomer*-, bunch, mass.

agglutinate. L. *agglutinare*, to glue together, from *gluten*, *glutin*-, glue. Applied to langs.

which stand midway between monosyllabic (e.g. Chinese) and inflexional (Aryan family). Cf. such tape-worm monstrosities of mod. chemistry as *trinitrobenzeneazo-chloronitrodiphenylhydrazine*.

Such words as *un-tru-th-ful-ly* preserve an agglutinative character (Whitney).

aggrandize. From F. *agrandir*, It. *aggrandire*, from L. *grandis*. For -*ize* cf. *advertise*.

aggravate. From L. *aggravare*, to make heavy, *gravis*. Cf. *aggrieve*.

aggregate. From L. *aggregare*, to form into a flock, *grex*, *greg*-. Cf. *egregious*, *gregarious*.

aggress. From L. *aggredi*, *aggress*-, to advance towards, from *gradus*, step.

aggrieve. See *grief*.

aghast. Earlier *agast*, p.p. of *agasten*, to frighten, from AS. *gæstan*, to terrify. Mod. spelling is due to association with *ghost* (q.v.). See also *ghastly*.

"Now, dere suster myn, what may it be
That me agasteth in my dreme?" quod she.
(Chauc. Leg. Good Women, 1170).

agile. F., L. *agilis*, from *agere*, to act.

agio [*financ.*]. Percentage charged on certain kinds of exchange. It. *agio*, ease, convenience. Hence *agiotage* (from F.), speculation, stock-jobbing. See *ease*.

agist. Orig. to admit cattle to pasture for a fixed period. Hence also *agistment*. OF. *agister*, from *à* and *giste* (*gîte*), resting-place, from archaic F. *gésir*, to lie, L. *jacēre*. Cf. *ci-gît*, seen on old tombstones. See also *gist*, *joist*.

agitate. From L. *agitare*, frequent. of *agere*, to do, in sense of drive. The earliest *agitators* were the delegates of the private soldiers in the Parliamentary army (1647 –9).

aglet, aiglet [*archaic*]. Orig. tag of a lace or "point"; then, ornamental tag or cord, esp. on uniform. In this sense now replaced by its F. original *aiguillette* (OF. *aguilette*), dim. of *aiguille* (OF. *aguille*), needle, VL. **acucula* (for *acicula*), dim. of *acus*, needle.

aglet: a little plate of any metal, a tag of a point
(Blount).

agley, agly [*Sc.*]. Askew. From ME. *glien*, to squint. Only in to *gang* (*go*) *agley*, after Burns.

to glee: limare (*Cath. Angl.*).

The best laid schemes o' mice and men
Gang aft agley (Burns).

The meetings of the plotters were orgies of talk, and, naturally, their best-laid plans went all agley
(Referee, Aug. 12, 1917).

agnail [*dial.*]. Orig. corn on the foot; later, painful swelling of any kind. Now used in dial. of loose skin or soreness at root of finger-nails. This meaning, like the corrupted forms *hang-nail* and *anger-nail*, is due to mistaken association with the finger-*nail*. The metal *nail* and the human *nail* are etym. ident., but in *agnail* the former is referred to. It is AS. *angnægl*, corn, where the first element means compressed, painful (cogn. with L. *angustus* and Ger. *eng*, narrow) and the second is AS. *nægl*, nail. Cf. F. *clou*, nail, also used of a swelling.

clou: a nayle, also, a corne (in a foot, or toe) (Cotg.).

agnate. Kin. F. *agnat*, L. *agnatus*, from *agnasci* (*ad gnasci*), to be born to.

agnomen. L., from *ad* and (*g*)*nomen*, name. Added to cognomen as result of some exploit, etc., e.g. Publius (praenomen) Cornelius (nomen) .Scipio (cognomen) Africanus (agnomen).

agnostic. Coined (1869) from G. ἄγνωστος, unknowing, unknown, unknowable, by Huxley, to whom it was suggested by *Acts*, xvii. 23 (ἀγνώστῳ θεῷ). From ἀ-, neg., γιγνώσκειν, to know.

Agnus Dei. L., Lamb of God.

ago. Earlier also *agone*, p.p. of AS. *āgān*, to pass (of time).

O he's drunk, sir Toby, an hour agone
(*Twelfth Night*, v. 1).

agog. Earlier also *on gog*. OF. *en gogues*, of unknown origin. Cf. *goguenard*, playful.

estre en ses gogues: to be frolicke, lustie, lively, wanton, gamesome, all-a-hoit, in a pleasant humour; in a veine of mirth, or in a merrie mood (Cotg.).

agony. Oldest in Bibl. sense (Wyc. *Luke*, xxii. 43). Prob. adopted from L. *agonia* (*Vulg.*), G. ἀγωνία, from ἀγών, assembly for the public games, from ἄγειν, to lead. F. *agonie* means throes of death. First *NED.* record of *agony column* is 1880.

agouti. Small rodent of guinea-pig tribe (SAmer. & WInd.). F., Sp. *aguti*, from native name.

agra, agrad [*Ir.*]. Darling. Voc. of Ir. *grádh*, love.

agraffe [*archaic*]. Clasp. F. *agrafe*, also OF. *agrappe*, from OHG. *krapfo* (*krapfen*), hook, via VL. **grappa*. Cf. *grape*.

agrail [*neol.*]. Portmanteau-word for *agricultural railway*.

A little while ago the Minister of Reconstruction invented "agrails" (*Observer*, Jan. 19, 1919).

agrarian. From L. *agrarius*, from *ager*, *agr-*, field. Hence spec. form of crime in Ireland, pol. party in Germany.

agree. F. *agréer*, VL. **adgratare*, from *gratus*, pleasing. Etym. sense survives best in *agreeable*.

agriculture. F., L. *agri cultura*, from *ager*, field, and *colere*, *cult-*, to cultivate. See *culture*. Cf. *agronomy*.

agrimony. Plant. L. *agrimonia*, corrupted (? by association with *ager*, field) from G. ἀργεμώνη. Some of the ME. forms are due to F. *aigremoine*. Perverted forms are found in other Europ. langs., e.g. Ger. *ackermennig*, Norw. Dan. *agermaane*.

aground. For *on ground*; cf. *afloat*, *ashore*. See *a-*.

ague. OF. *ague* (*aigue*), sharp, L. *acuta*, in *fièvre aigue*. In E. applied first to the burning or feverish stage of disease, then to the shivering stage, and finally to a spec. malarial fever.

ah. Natural ejaculation. Cf. F. *ah*, MHG. *ā*, ON. *æ*, also E. *ay*, *ey*, *ha*.

ahead. Orig. naut. Cf. *abeam*, *astern*.

ahem. Imit. of calling attention by clearing the throat. Cf. to *hem and ha*.

ahoy. ? From *hoy*, vessel. But cf. OF. *aoi*, interj. which ends each stanza of the *Chanson de Roland*.

Ahriman. Spirit of evil in OPers. mythology. F., L., G. Ἀρειμάνιος, Pers. *Ahirman*, Zend *anra-mainyu*, spirit that beats down.

Dark Ahriman, whom Irak still
Holds origin of woe and ill (*Talisman*, ch. iii).

ahungered. See *an-hungered*.

ai. Brazilian sloth. Native name, from cry.

aid. F. *aider*, L. *adjutare*, frequent. of *adjuvare*, *adjut-*, to help. Cf. *adjutant*.

aide-de-camp. F. In E. from 17 cent.

aigrette. Orig. lesser white heron, or *egret* (q.v.), then its crest, and later applied to various similar tufts.

aiguillette. See *aglet*.

ail. AS. *eglan*, to afflict, cogn. with Goth. *agljan*, and ult. with *awe*. Orig. trans. (cf. *What ails you?*), and in early ME. impers.

What ailed thee, o thou sea, that thou fleddest?
(*Ps.* cxiv. 5).

aileron [*aeron.*]. End of wing. F., from *aile*, wing, L. *ala*, for *axilla*. Orig. term of falconry.

aim. Earlier *eyme*. App. due to two OF. verbs, *esmer*, L. *aestimare*, *aesmer*, L. *adaestimare*. The oldest meaning is to esteem; then, to calculate with a view to action, while the sense of directing a missile or blow does not appear till 16 cent.

Or the sone of man, for thou eymest hym
(Wyc. *Ps.* cxliii. 3).

air. F., L. *aer*, G. ἀήρ, from ἄειν, to blow. Subsidiary sense of manner, taken from F., may have been developed from orig. sense in allusion to the "atmosphere" of a person or environment (cf. sense-development of L. *animus, spiritus*); but some regard it rather as belonging to a separate word (see *debonair*). For mus. sense, from It. *aere* (now replaced by *aria*), cf. Ger. *weise*, manner, tune, and mus. sense of *mode, mood*. In *airs and graces* there is prob. a secondary mus. allusion, a *grace* being an embellishment added to a tune. The numerous neologisms in *air-* (*aircraft, airman, airmanship, airworthy*, etc.) are modelled on the naut. vocabulary. *Air-raid* is of about the same date as *baby-killer*. *Airdrome* occurred in the published abstract of the peace terms (May, 1919).

aere: the aire. Also, an aspect, countenance, cheere, a look or appearance in the face of man or woman. Also, a tune or aire of a song or ditty
(Flor.).
As soon as our men got their air-legs (if there is such a thing), the reports they brought back were invaluable (Corbett-Smith, *Marne and after*).

airedale. Terrier from valley of the *Aire*, Bradford district of Yorks. Name registered by Kennel Club (1886), for earlier *Bingley* (where first bred), or *broken-haired* terrier.

airt [*Sc.*]. Direction, point of the compass. Gael. *aird*, Ir. *ard*, point, common in place-names. A late introduction in literary E., due to Burns:

Of a' the airts the wind can blaw,
I dearly like the west.

aisle. Orig. *ele*, OF. (*aile*), wing, L. *ala*, for *axilla*. Prop. a lateral division of a church, usually separated from the nave by rows of pillars. The curious spelling *aisle*, which Johns. attributes to Addison, is partly due to ModF. *aile*, but also to confusion with E. *isle*, ME. *ile*, island. This seems incredible, but is certified by the fact that *insula* was its usual rendering in MedL., while *island*, or rather its older and more correct form, actually occurs in the same sense. The word has also been confused with *alley*[1].

Orate pro animo Roberti Oxburgh...qui istud ele fieri fecit (*NED.* c. 1370).
In the portch in the south yland of the church
(*ib.* 1590).

ait. Small island, esp. in Thames. Now often spelt *eyet* or *eyot*. App. ...S. *iggath*, of obscure formation, related to AS. *īeg*, island. The ME. form is *eit, æit*, but the *NED.* has no record between 1205 and 1649. Cf. Anglese*y*, Sheppe*y*, and *Eig* (Hebrides).

aitch-bone. For *nache-* or *nage-*, the *n-* being lost as in *adder* (q.v.). ME. *nache, nage*, buttock, OF. *nache*, still used by F. butchers, VL. **natica* for *natis*. *Nachebone* occurs in Craven Gloss. (1828). The existing form is perh. due to a fancied resemblance of the bone to the letter H. Among other perversions in dial. use are *edge-bone, ice-bone*, etc. But some of these are rather connected with Du. *ijsbeen*, hip-bone, with which cf. LG. *īsbēn*, Ger. *eisbein* (from LG.), the first element of which may be G. ἰσχίον, hip-joint.

ajar. Formerly *on char*, on the turn. See *charwoman, chare*. Cf. synon. Du. *op een kier*, from *keeren*, to turn. Confused in quots. 3, 4, with *jar*[1] (q.v.).

The dure on char it stude (Gavin Douglas, c. 1513).
"On the what?" exclaimed the little judge.
"Partly open, my lord," said Serjeant Snubbin.
"She said on the *jar*," said the little judge with a cunning look (*Pickwick*).
Thou hast set my father and him at jares
(Lady Willoughby, 1595).
My temper was so thoroughly ajar
(H. Martineau).

akimbo. ME. *on kenebowe*. For *can bow*, the bow, or handle, of a *can*, or vessel. Cf. synon. L. *ansatus*, from *ansa*, handle, and F. *faire le pot à deux anses*, to stand with arms akimbo, lit. to play the pot with two handles. The same very natural metaphor is found in Du. Ger. Sp. and prob. other langs.

ansatus homo; one that in bragging manner strowteth up and down with his armes a-canne-bow
(Thomas, 1644).
jarra: a pot with a great belly and two handles
(Stevens).
andar en jarras: to set one's arms a-kimbo
(Seoane).

akin For *of kin*; cf. *next of kin*. Cf. *anew*.

Akkadian. See *Accadian*.

al-. In some words, chiefly of Sp. origin, represents Arab. def. art.

alabaster. OF. *alabastre* (*albâtre*), L. *alabaster*, G. ἀλάβαστρος. Said to come from *Alabastron* (Egypt).

alack. Prob. arbitrary alteration of *alas*, recorded two centuries earlier, by association with *lack*, in older sense of failure, shame.

Chiefly in *alack-the-day* or *alack-a-day*, whence *lack-a-day* and *lackadaisical*.

alacrity. From L. *alacritas*, from *alacer*, brisk. Cf. *allegro*.

alamode. Esp. in *alamode silk, beef.* F. *à la mode*, in the fashion.

alanna [*Ir.*]. Voc. of Ir. *leanbh*, child.

alar. L. *alaris*, from *ala*, wing.

alarm. F. *alarme*, OF. *à l'arme*, It. *all' arme*, a call "to (the) arms." With rolled -*r*- it has given *alarum*. With aphet. *larum* cf. Ger. *lärm*, "an alarm, alarum" (Ludw.). Cf. *alert*.

It was nothing but a false larum, given of purpose to see how every one would be found in a readinesse
(Purch.).
And so to bed, to be up by times by the helpe of a larum watch (Pepys, July 14, 1665).

alarum. See *alarm*.

alas. OF. *a las, he las* (*hélas*) or *lasse*, the adj. agreeing with the speaker. The first element is an interj., while *las*, weary, is L. *lassus*. Cf. It. *ahi lasso* or *lassa*.

alate. L. *alatus*, from *ala*, wing.

alb. Eccl. vestment. AS. *albe*, early loan from L. *alba* (sc. *vestis*). Cf. F. *aube*, alb, also found in ME.

albacore, albicore. Fish. Port. *albacor*, Arab. *al-bukr*, the young camel, from the size of the fish. In Hakl.

Albanian. Aryan lang. of *Albania*, allied to Greek, but containing much Slav. and L. admixture.

albatross. Corrupted from obs. *alcatras* (16 cent.), frigate-bird, under influence of *albus*, the name being extended from the frigate-bird, which is black, to a larger and white sea-bird (cf. *penguin*). Recorded in present form in 17 cent. *Alcatras* (Hawkins' *Voyage*, 1564) is Sp. Port. *alcatraz*, sea-fowl, pelican, orig. Port. *alcatruz*, bucket of a water-wheel, Arab. *al-qādūs*, borrowed from G. κάδος (L. *cadus*), jar. App. first applied to the pelican, from its storage capacity. Cf. Arab. *saqqā*, pelican, lit. water-carrier.

alcatraces: a kind of foule like a seamew that feedeth on fish (Percyvall).

albeit. For *all be it*, a survival of the ME. use of *all*, in sense of *although*, with a subjunctive.

albert (chain). Named after *Prince Albert*, Consort of Queen Victoria. Cf. *victoria*, and hundreds of words created in the same way.

albicore. See *albacore*.

Albigenses [*hist.*]. Southern F. protestants, orig. of *Albi* (Tarn), persecuted (13 cent.) at instigation of Innocent III.

albino. Sp. or Port., from L. *albus*, white. Orig. applied in Port. to "white negroes."

Albion. G. name for Great Britain; cf. L. *Albion* (Pliny), Gael. *Alba*, Scotland. Perh. "white land."

album. "A book in which foreigners have long been accustomed to insert the autographs of celebrated people" (Johns.). Neut. of L. *albus*, white, blank. Still in italics in *Ingoldsby*.

albumen. L., from *albus*, white.

alburnum. Sap-wood, L., from *albus*, white.

alcade, alcalde, alcayde. Magistrate. Sp., from Arab. *al-qādī*, the judge (see *cadi*). *Alcayde*, prison governor, is, strictly speaking, a different word, Arab. *qā'id*, leader (see *caid*), but the titles have been confused by E. writers.

alcalde: a sheriffe, or cunstable (Percyvall).

alcahest. See *alkahest*.

alcaic. Metre employed, e.g. by Horace, in imitation of Greek poet Ἀλκαῖος (fl. Mytilene, c. 600 B.C.). Cf. *Sapphic*.

alcazar. Palace, fortress. Sp., Arab. *al-qaçr*, from L. *castrum*.

alchemy. OF. *alchimie*, MedL. *alchimia*, Arab. *al-kīmīā*, G. χημεία, χειμεία, transmutation of metals (3 cent.). This has been connected with G. Χημία, Egypt (in Plutarch), and with G. χυμεία, pouring (χέειν, to pour), whence the archaic spellings *alcumy* (Shaks.), *alchymy, chymist*, etc. The medieval forms, due to folk-etym., are numerous. It seems clear that the word came from Alexandria via the Arabs into Europe.

alcohol. Arab. *al-koh'l*, the fine metallic powder used to darken the eyelids (see *kohl*). Later applied to fine chemical powders and then to subtle essences and quintessences. Current sense occurs first in *alcool of wine*.

It will be a consolation to Americans to know that there is one place where they may enjoy an alcoholiday (P. M. Murphy, June, 1919).

alcoran. F., Arab. *al-qorān*, the reading. Now usu. *koran*.

alcove. F. *alcôve*, Sp. *alcova, alcoba*, Arab. *al-qobbah*, the vault.

alcoba: a closet, a close roome for a bed (Percyvall).

alder. AS. *alr*, with intrusive -*d*-, as in *elder* (tree). Com. Teut.; cf. Du. *els*, Ger. *erle*

(OHG. *elira*), ON. *ölr*, Goth. **alisa* (whence Sp. *aliso*); cogn. with L. *alnus*. Earlier and dial. forms of *alder* appear in place- and surnames, e.g. *Alresford, Allerton, Ollerton, Oldershaw, Ollerenshaw, Lightowlers*, etc.

He advises that you plant willows or owlers about it [the fishpond] (*Compleat Angler*, ch. xx.).

alderman. AS. *ealdormann*. First element, though early confused with the compar. of *eald*, old, orig. meant patriarch, prince, formed from *eald* with the noun suffix *-or*. It is used in AS. to translate any title of high rank, but had also the spec. meaning now represented by *earl* (q.v.) which tended to displace it under the Dan. dynasty.

aldine [*typ.*]. From *Aldus Manutius*, Venetian printer (†1515). Cf. *elzevir*.

ale. AS. *ealu*; cf. ON. *öl*. See also *bridal*.

aleatory. Hazardous. L. *aleatorius*, from *alea*, die (dice).

alectryon. Cock. G. ἀλεκτρυών, youth changed into cock.

alegar [*dial.*]. Vinegar from ale. From *ale*, by analogy with *vinegar* (q.v.).

Alemannic. HG. tribe and dial. of Upper Rhine, now represented chiefly by Ger. Swiss. OHG. *alaman*, prob. "all man," whence F. *allemand*.

alembic. F. *alambic*, Sp. *alambique*, Arab. *al-anbīq*, the still, G. ἄμβιξ, ἀμβικ-, beaker. Aphet. form *limbeck* is obs.

Cucurbites and alambikes eek (Chauc. G. 794).

alambique: a limbecke, a stillitorie (Percyvall).

alerion, allerion [*her.*]. Small spread eagle without beak or claws. F. *alérion*, formed, with L. suffix *-io, -ion-*, from MHG. *adelar* (*adler*), eagle, orig. compd. *adel-ar*, noble eagle. Cf. MedL. *alario*.

alert. OF. *à l'erte* (*alerte*), It. *all' erta* for *alla erta*, to the height, L. *erecta*. Thus *on the alert* is pleon. Cf. *alarm*.

erta: a craggie place, an upright ascent, a high watch-tower (Flor.).

A l'erte et sur ses gardes (La Font. *Fab.* viii. 22).

Alexandrian, Alexandrine. Of the school of G. learning at *Alexandria* (B.C. 323–A.D. 640).

alexandrine [*metr.*]. Line of twelve syllables. Prob. from its use in a 13 cent. F. poem on *Alexandre le Grand*.

A needless alexandrine ends the song
That like a wounded snake drags its slow length
      along   (Pope, *Essay on Criticism*, 359).

alfalfa. Kind of clover. Sp., from Arab. *fachfacha*, lucerne.

al fresco. It., in the fresh (air). See *fresco*.

algarobba. Sp., Arab. *al-kharrūbah*, the carob tree.

algebra. It., Arab. *al-jebr*, the reunion of broken parts. In early use also in the sense of bone-setting.

algebra; the arte of figurative numbers or arithmetick. Also the art of bone-setting (Flor.).

-algia. From G. ἄλγος, pain.

algid. Cold. L. *algidus*, from *algēre*, to be cold.

Algonkin. Group of NAmer langs. F. *algonquin*, from native name.

algorism [*archaic*]. Arab., or decimal, system of notation; hence, arithmetic. OF. *algorisme*, MedL. *algorismus*, Arab. *al-Khowārazmī*, i.e. the man of *Khwārazm* (Khiva), famous Arab mathematician (fl. 9 cent.) through whose works the Arab. numerals became known in Europe. ModF. *algorithme*, refashioned on *logarithme*, also occurs in E. There was a ME. *augrime*, corresponding to OF. var. *augorime*.

His astrelabie, longynge for his art,
His augrym stones, layen faire apart
                    (Chauc. A. 3209)

alguazil. Sp. police officer. Sp. *alguazil* (*alguacil*), Arab. *al-wazīr*, the vizier (q.v.).

alguazil: shiriffe, bailiffe, chiefe executioner
                              (Percyvall).

The School Board and their alguazils
                         (*Daily Tel.* 1880).

algum [*Bibl.*]. Kind of tree (2 *Chron.* ii. 8). Incorr. *almug* (1 *Kings*, x. 11). Heb. *algūm*.

Alhambra. Short for Arab. *al-medīnat ul-hamrā*, the red city, palace.

alias. L., otherwise, from *alius*, other.

alibi. L. for *ali-ubi*, otherwhere.

alien. OF., L. *alienus*, of another country (see *deport²*). Sense of insanity in *alienation* is found in L.

Doth awey alyen goddis (Wyc. *Gen.* xxxv. 2).

alight¹. Verb. AS. *ālīhtan*, to spring down, orig. to lighten, from *līhtan*, to alight.

alight². Adj. Orig. p.p. of obs. verb *alight*, to set on fire, AS. *onliehtan*. Owing to influence of *ablaze, afire*, etc., it is used only predicatively.

align [*mil.*]. F. *aligner*, from *ligne*, line² (q.v.).

alike. ME. *yliche*, usu. for AS. *gelīc* (cf. Ger. *gleich*, OHG. *gelīh*) with prefix altered as in *aware*. But AS. also had the less common *anlīc, onlīc* and cogn. ON. *ālīkr*, which would give the same result. See *like*.

aliment. F., L. *alimentum*, from *alere*, to nourish. Cf. *alimony*, allowance for keep.

aliquot. L., from *alius* and *quot*, how many. See *quota*.

alive. ME. *on live*, AS. *on līfe*, dat. of *līf*, life.

alkahest [*alch.*]. Universal solvent. Prob. sham Arab. invented by Paracelsus.

alkali [*chem.*]. F. *alcali*, Arab. *al-qalīg*, the calcined ashes (of certain plants), from *qualay*, to roast. Occurs in Chauc. (G. 810).

alkanet. Plant and dye. Sp. *alcaneta*, dim. of *alcana*, Arab. *al-hennā*. See *henna*.

all. AS. *all, eall.* Com. Teut.; cf. Du. *al*, Ger. *all*, ON. *allr*, Goth. *alls. All in all* (*1 Cor.* xv. 28) is *Vulg. omnia in omnibus. All to brake* (*Judges*, ix. 53) would be more correctly *all to-brake*, i.e. quite shattered, *to* being an intens. particle, cogn. with Ger. *zer* (as in *zerbrechen*), prefixed to numerous verbs in AS. & ME. *All-fired* (US.) is euph. for *hell-fired*.

Al is to-brosten thilke regioun (Chauc. A. 2757).

Allah. Arab. *allāh*, for *al-ilāh*, the god; cf. Heb. *elōah* (*Matt.* xxvii. 46).

allay. AS. *ālecgan*, to put down, abate, from *lecgan*, to lay, e.g. to *allay* a tumult. But early confused with *allay*, a ME. form of *alloy* (q.v.), from OF. *aleiier*, and also with a ME. form of OF. *alegier* (*alléger*), to lighten, e.g. hunger or thirst, L. *alleviare*. Hence the gen. meaning, to moderate, temper.

When flowing cups run swiftly round
With no allaying Thames (Lovelace, *To Althea*).

allege. Represents in sense F. *alléguer*, learned formation from L. *allegare*, "to allege or bring forth, to name" (Coop.), but in form OF. *alegier*, var. of *eslegier*, to acquit, make free, etc. This was latinized as *adlegiare*, as though from *ad legem*, and gradually assumed the meaning of F. *alléguer*, though the process is not quite made out. OF. *eslegier* represents VL. **ex-ledig-are*, from Ger. *ledig*, free. See *allegiance* and *liege. Alléguer* would have given E. *alleague*.

allegiance. Corrupt. of ME. *legaunce*, OF. *ligeance*, from *lige*, whence E. *liege* (q.v.). This was latinized as *ligantia*, as though from *ligare*, to bind. Mod. form is due to confusion with another (obs.) leg. term, *allegeance* (from *allege*).

ligence: liegemanship, allegiance, faith, loyalty
(Cotg.).

allegory. L. *allegoria*, G. ἀλληγορία, from ἄλλος, other, ἀγορεύειν, to speak, from ἀγορά, place of assembly.

allegro. It., irreg. from L. *alacer*, "cherefull, quicke of sprite or witte" (Coop.).

alleluia. L., G. ἀλληλοῦϊα, LXX. transliteration of Heb. *hallēlū-yāh*, praise ye Jah, i.e. Jehovah.

alleviate. From L. *alleviare*, from *levis*, light. Cf. *aggravate*. Replaced (17 cent.) ME. *allege*, F. *alléger*. Cf. *abbreviate*, *abridge*.

allerion. See *alerion*.

alley[1]. Way, walk. F. *allée*, p.p. fem. of *aller*, to go.

alley[2]. Marble (18 cent.). Prob. short for *alabaster*, of which such are sometimes made. Cf. OF. *cassidoine*, chalcedony, similarly used, and *marble* itself.

alliaceous. Of garlic, L. *allium*.

alligator. Sp. *el lagarto*, the lizard, L. *lacertus*. Earlier forms *lagarto, alagarto*, etc. *Alligator* (also *avocado*) *pear* is corrupted from Aztec *ahuacatl*, via a Sp. form *alvacata*.

A fish called by the Spaniards lagarto, and by the Indians cayman, which is indeed a crocodile
(Hakl. x. 216).

alliteration. Coined from L. *ad* and *lit(t)era*, letter.

alliteration: a figure in rhetorick, repeating and playing on the same letter (Blount).

Apt alliteration's artful aid
(Churchill, *Prophecy of Famine*, 76).

allocate. From VL. *allocare*, from *locus*, place.

allocution. L. *allocutio-n-*, from *alloqui*, to address, from *loqui, locut-*, to speak.

allodial [*hist.*]. Of lands held in absolute ownership. MedL. *allodialis*, from *allodium* (in *Salic Law* and *Domesday Book*), OHG. *allōd*, all possession. Hence also F. *alleu*. OHG. *ōd* is cogn. with AS. *ēad*, wealth, bliss, etc., which is the first element in so many AS. names. Thus our *Edgar*, AS. *Eadgar*, corresponds to F. *Oger*, OHG. *Odgar*, now represented by the surname *Odgers*. It is uncertain whether Ger. *kleinod*, jewel, contains the same element. Cf. *udal*.

allopathy. Ger. *allopathie*, coined by Hahnemann (†1843) to express the opposite of *homoeopathy* (q.v.). From G. ἄλλος, other, πάθος, feeling.

allot. OF. *aloter*. See *lot*.

A vineyard and an allotment for olives and herbs
(*NED.* c. 1745).
The small greengrocer is up against the allotmenteer (*Ev. News*, June 8, 1918).

allotropy [*biol.*]. Variation of physical properties without change of substance. From G. ἄλλος, other, τρόπος, manner.

allow. F. *allouer*, representing both L. *allaudare* and VL. *allocare*. Cf. F. *louer*, to praise, L. *laudare*; and *louer*, to let, L. *locare*. From *allaudare* comes the notion of permission based on approval, from *allocare* that of "allocated" provision. The US. use of the word in the sense of granting, stating an opinion, still survives in E. dial.

alloy. F. *aloi*, from *aloyer*, L. *alligare*, to bind. In OF. also *alei* (whence obs. E. *allay*), from *aleiier*. The same word as *allier*, to unite (cf. F. *plier*, *ployer*, both from L. *plicare*). It has been suggested that the meaning of the word has been affected by some popular connection with *à loi*, OF. *lei*, thus, a mixture according to legal standard. See *allay*.

> For if that they were put to swiche assayes,
> The gold of hem hath now so badde alayes
> With bras, that thogh the coyne be fair at eye
> It wolde rather breste a-two than plye
> (Chauc. E. 1166).

allspice. So called because supposed to combine the flavour of cinnamon, nutmeg, and cloves.

allude. L. *alludere*, from *ludus*, play. Cf. to *play on* (a word).

allure. See *lure*.

alluvial. From L. *alluvius*, washed against, from *luere*, to wash. See *deluge*.

ally[1]. To unite. F. *allier*, L. *alligare*, from *ligare*, to bind (see *alloy*). The noun is from the verb, the latter being recorded for 13 cent.

ally[2]. Marble. See *alley*[2].

alma. Egyptian dancing-girl (Byron). Arab. *almah*, learned. Cf. F. *almée*.

almagest [*archaic*]. Orig. astrol. treatise by Ptolemy (fl. 2 cent.). OF. *almageste*, Arab. *al-majiste*, the greatest, borrowed from G. μεγίστη, greatest. See Scott, *Lay*, vi. 17.

> His Almageste and bookes grete and smale
> (Chauc. A. 3208).

Alma Mater. L., gracious mother, title of bountiful goddess (Ceres, Cybele), from *alere*, to nourish.

almanac. From 13 cent. in MedL. and Rom. langs. First in Roger Bacon. App. from Sp. Arab. *al-manākh*, but this is not an Arab. word. Eusebius (4 cent.) has G. ἀλμενιχιακά, calendars, perhaps from G. μηνιαῖος, monthly, but there is a great gap between this and the medieval forms. Probabilities would point to ult. connection with Aryan root of *moon* or *month*, but the

word, in spite of very numerous conjectures, remains a puzzle.

> In expositione tabularum, quae almanac vocantur
> (Roger Bacon, 1267).

almandine. Kind of garnet. Earlier *alabandine*, L. *alabandina*, from *Alabanda*, city of Caria. A poet. word (Beddoes, Tennyson, Browning) but app. never in general use.

> *almandine*: a certaine stone like a rubie (Cotg.).

almighty. AS. *eallmihtig*, applied to God (9 cent.) as rendering of L. *omnipotens*. See *all*, *might*.

almoign, almoin [*hist.*]. Alms. OF. *almosne* (*aumône*). See *alms*. Now only in archaic *frank almoin*, perpetual tenure by free gift of charity.

> Frank almoine (*libera eleemozyna*) in French (*frank ausmone*) signifieth in our common law, a tenure or title of lands (Cowel).

almond. OF. *alamande* (*amande*), from L. *amygdala*, G. ἀμυγδάλη. The forms are difficult to explain; but L. *amandula* (Pliny) is perh. altered on *mandere*, to chew. The *al-* is prob. due to confusion with numerous Arab. words in the Rom. langs. This is lost in It. *mandola* and Ger. *mandel*.

> An alemaunde tre (*Vulg.* amygdalus) schal floure
> (Wyc. *Eccles.* xii. 5).

almoner. See *alms*.

Almoravides. Arab. dynasty. See *marabout*.

almost. AS. *eallmǣst, mǣst eall*, most (nearly) all (cf. US. *most all*).

alms. AS. *ælmesse*, L. *eleemosyna*, G. ἐλεημοσύνη, from ἔλεος, compassion. Early Church word with numerous early compds. *Almoner* is later, through OF. *almosnier* (*aumônier*). To account for the forms of the word (OF. *almosne*, Ger. *almosen*) contact with L. *alimonia*, from *alere*, to support, feed, has been suggested. Sc. *almous*, *awmous*, is not a corrupt., but a separate introduction from ON. *almusa*. *Alms*, though sing. (*Acts*, iii. 3), has sometimes been wrongly regarded as a pl.

> For alms are but the vehicles of prayer
> (Dryden, *Hind and Panther*, iii. 106).
> "I thank you for your awmous," said Ochiltree
> (*Antiquary*, ch. xx.)

almug [*Bibl.*]. Corrupt. (1 *Kings*, x.) of *algum* (q.v.).

alnager [*hist.*]. Official measurer of cloth, abolished temp. Will. III. OF. *aulnageour*, from *aulnage* (*aunage*), measurement, from *au(l)ne*, ell (q.v.).

Alnaschar. As in *Alnaschar dreams*, castles in the air. From character, the "barber's fifth brother," in the *Arabian Nights*, lit. "the lawyer," who has visions like those of the milkmaid in the fable.

aloe. AS. *aluwe*, L., G. ἀλόη. Early med. word. Hence *lignaloes* (Chauc.), *lignum aloes*, aromatic wood, coined like *rosewood*.

aloft. ON. *ā lopt(i)*, in the air, on high, cogn. with AS. *lyft*, air (cf. Ger. *luft*). Naut. sense is later, but is combined with the original meaning by Dibdin.

There's a sweet little cherub that sits up aloft,
To keep watch for the life of poor Jack.

alone. Orig. *all one*, quite solitary (cf. Ger. *allein*). Hence *all alone* is pleon. By aphesis *lone*, whence *lonely*. *A lonely* occurs up to c. 1600.

[Athelstan] regned first al on in Engelond
(Trev. ii. 109).

along. AS. *andlang* (cf. Ger. *entlang*), first element cogn. with G. ἀντί, against (cf. *answer*). But in dial. *along of*, meaning on account of, owing to, it represents AS. *gelang*.

And when I lay in dungeon dark,
Of Naworth Castle, long months three,
Till ransom'd for a thousand mark,
Dark Musgrave it was long of thee
(Scott, *Lay*, v. 29).

aloof. Adapted from Du. *te loef*, to windward. Orig. naut., but no longer used by sailors. See *luff*.

The Dolphin lay a loofe off and durst not come nere (Hakl. vii. 37).

A coward, voide of valours proofe,
That for deaths feare hath fled, or fought a-loofe
(Sylv. i. 7).

aloud. From *loud*, after earlier *ahigh, alow*, etc. See *a-*.

Alp. L. *Alpes*, prob. Celt. Cf. Gael. *alp*, Ir. *ealp*, hill. In Switzerland used of a mountain pasture, as also in MHG. Hence *alpenstock* (Ger.).

alpaca. Peruv. llama, having long, fine, woolly hair. Sp. *alpaca*, or *alpacu*, from *el*, the, and *paco*, native name of animal, *al-* for *el-* being due to association with numerous words in *al-* from Arab. Cf. *alligator*.

alphabet. L. *alphabetum*, G. ἄλφα βῆτα, A B, Heb. *āleph*, ox, and *bēth*, house, from Phoenician symbols. First found in 16 cent., though *alpha* and *beta* both occur in ME. Cf. *abecedarian*.

Alphonsine tables [*astron.*]. Compiled (1252) by *Alphonso the Wise*, king of Castile.

already. Orig. adj., *all ready*, quite prepared.

Alsatia. Latinization of F. *Alsace*, Ger. *Elsass*, seat of strangers, cogn. with *else* and *sit*. Cant name for Whitefriars (Lond.), sanctuary for law-breakers. See *Fortunes of Nigel*, ch. xvi. Perh. from Alsace being regarded as a kind of No Man's Land.

All that neutral ground of character, which stood between vice and virtue; or which in fact was indifferent to neither, where neither properly was called in question; that happy breathing-place from the burthen of a perpetual moral questioning—the sanctuary and quiet Alsatia of hunted casuistry—is broken up and disfranchised (Lamb, *On the artificial Comedy of the last century*).

alsike. Kind of clover. From *Alsike* near Upsala.

Alsirat. Razor-like bridge over hell to Mohammedan paradise. Arab. *al-sirāt*, from L. *strata*, street.

Though on al-Sirat's arch I stood
Which totters o'er the fiery flood (*Giaour*).

also. For *all so*, AS. *eall-swā*. See *as*.

Altaic. Name of group of agglutinative langs., Ugro-Finnish, between *Altai Mountains* (Central Asia) and Arctic Ocean.

altar. L. *altare*. ME. has usually *awter*, OF. *auter* (*autel*). An early Church word in most Europ. langs., but AS. usu. has *wēofod*, for *wīg-bēod*, idol-table. Mod. spelling was fixed by rel. disputes of 16 cent., the Protestants preferring *Lord's table*.

altazimuth [*astron.*]. Instrument for determining *altitude* and *azimuth*. A portmanteau-word.

alter. F. *altérer*, MedL. *alterare*, from *alter*, other. The F. word now always implies degeneration.

alterer: to alter, change, vary, turne from what it was; also, to adulterate, falsifie, sophisticate
(Cotg.).

altercation. From L. *altercari*, to dispute, speak to each other (v.i.).

alternate. From L. *alternare*, to take turns, from *alternus*, from *alter*, other.

althaea. Mallow. L., G. ἀλθαία, cogn. with ἀλθαίνειν, to heal.

althing [*hist.*]. Icelandic parliament, abolished 1800. *All thing*, general assembly. Cf. *storthing* and see *thing*.

although. *All though*. Orig. more emphatic than *though*. Cf. *albeit*.

altitude. From L. *altitudo*, from *altus*, high.

alto. It. *alto*, L. *altus*. High (of male voices).

altogether. Three words in AS. See *together*. As equivalent for *in puris naturalibus* it dates from du Maurier's *Trilby* (1894).

altruism. F. *altruisme*, coined by Auguste Comte (*Philosophie positiviste*, i. 614) from It. *altrui*, to express the opposite of *egoism*. It. *altrui* and F. *autrui* are VL. *alterui, from *alter*, other, modelled on *cui*; cf. F. *lui*, from L. *illui. First used by Lewes (1853). See *comtism*.

alum. OF. *alum* (*alun*), L. *alumen*.

aluminium. Earlier *aluminum*. Discovered and named (c. 1812) by Davy, from *alum*.

alumnus [*univ.*]. L., nurseling, from *alere*.

alveolar. From L. *alveolus*, socket of tooth, dim. of *alveus*, channel, cogn. with G. αὐλός, flute, longitudinal cavity.

alway, always. From *all* and *way*. Must once have referred to space, but in earliest records to time alone. *Alway*, now poet., was the acc., and *always*, ME. *alles weis*, the gen. Cf. *once* (q.v.).

am. See *be*.

amadavat. See *avadavat*.

Amadis. Fantastic hero. From medieval Sp. and Port. romance of *Amadis of Gaul*.

amadou. German tinder. F., Prov. *amadou*, lit. lover, from quick kindling.

amain [*archaic*]. From *main*[1] (q.v.) by analogy with other words in *a-*.

amalgam. F. *amalgame*, MedL. *amalgama* (13 cent.), of obscure origin. The most probable conjecture, supported by the OF. var. *algame*, connects it, via Arab., with G. γάμος, marriage. The "marriage" of the metals is often referred to in alchemistic jargon, as in quot. 2, from Goethe, no doubt suggested by his study of Paracelsus.

algame: mixtion of gold, and quick-silver (Cotg.).

Da ward ein roter Leu (i.e. a red metal), ein kühner Freier,
Im lauen Bad der Lilie (i.e. a white metal) vermählt (*Faust*, i. 1043).

amanuensis. L. (Suetonius), from *a manu* (sc. *servus*), with ending *-ensis*, as in *atriensis*, steward, from *atrium*, hall.

amanuensis: a clarke or secretary alway attendyng; a scribe (Coop.).

amaranth. F. *amarante*, L., G. ἀμάραντος, everlasting, from ἀ-, neg., μαραίνειν, to wither. Final *-h* is due to influence of G. ἄνθος, flower, as in *polyanthus*.

Bid amaranthus all his beauty shed (*Lycidas*, 149).

amaryllis. Flower. Named by Linnaeus from G. Ἀμαρυλλίς, name of typical country-maiden. In latter sense used by Milton (*Lycidas*).

amateur. F., L. *amator-em*, from *amare*, to love. Orig. one who has an interest in, or a taste for, anything. This is still the usual meaning of F. *amateur*. In the sense of nonprofessional ModF. uses rather *dilettante* (q.v.). L. *amare* is prob. from a babysyllable *am* (see *aunt*).

amati. Violin by *Amati* family (Cremona, 16–17 cents.). Cf. *stradivarius*.

amaurosis [*med.*]. Disease of eye. G., from ἀμαυρός, dark.

amaze. Earlier *amase*. AS. *amasod*, confounded. Oldest sense, to put out of one's wits, stun, etc. *Maze* (q.v.) is of about the same date. Origin obscure; cf. Norw. dial. *masast*, to lose one's senses.

Amazon. L., G. Ἀμαζών, explained by the Greeks as from ἀ-, neg., and μαζός, breast, the Amazons being fabled to cut off the right breast for convenience in archery. This is prob. folk-etym. (cf. *butter* and *squirrel*). The river *Amazon* was named by Sp. travellers from female warriors encountered there.

ambassador. F. *ambassadeur*. But E. has many earlier forms due to those found in other Rom. langs. and in MedL. *Embassador* is the usual US. form; cf. *embassy*. L. *ambactus*, vassal, retainer, of a Gallic chief (Caes. *De Bello Gallico*, vi. 15), is said by Festus to be of Gaulish origin, "Ambactus apud Ennium lingua Gallica servus appellatur." The existence of Goth. *andbahti*, office, service, AS. *ambiht*, idem, OHG. *ambahti* (Ger. *amt*), all very common words, has suggested Teut. origin; but it is generally believed that these are very early loans from Celt., the origin being *amb-*, round about, and the root *ag-*, to go, cogn. with L. *amb-* and *agere* (see *ambiguous*).

amber. F. *ambre*, Arab. *anbar*, ambergris, a word brought home by Crusaders. E. *amber* is now replaced in this sense by *ambergris*, F. *ambre gris*, and is used only of fossil resin, F. *ambre jaune*. This has no connection at all with ambergris, but the two substances were confused, both being found by the seashore.

ambergris. See *amber*. The spellings *ambergrease* (Macaulay), *ambergreece* are due to folk-etym. For association with amber cf. Norw. Dan. *hvalrav*, ambergris, lit. whaleamber.

ambi-, amb-. L. *ambi-*, about, cogn. with G. ἀμφί, on both sides.

ambidexter. Late L., from *ambi* (v.s.) and *dexter*. See *dexterous*.

ambient. From pres. part. of L. *ambire*, to go about (v.s.).

ambiguous. From L. *ambiguus*, from *ambigere*, from *amb-* and *agere*, lit. to drive both ways. Cf. *desultory*, *prevaricate*.

ambit. L. *ambitus*, going round (v.i.).

ambition. F. *ambition*, L. *ambitio-n-*, lit. going about (for votes), from *ambire*, from *amb-* and *ire*, *it-*, to go.

> *ambire*: to goe about; to sue or stand for an office (Coop.).

> Agrippa and Bernyce camen with moche ambicioun [G. μετὰ πολλῆς φαντασίας] (Wyc. *Acts*, xxv. 23).

amble. F. *ambler*, L. *ambulare*, to walk.

ambo [*hist.*]. Reading-desk in early Christian churches. L., G. ἄμβων, from ἀναβαίνειν, to go up.

Amboyna wood. From *Amboyna*, one of the Moluccas.

ambrosia. L., G. ἀμβροσία, food of the immortals, from ἄμβροτος, immortal, from ἀ-, neg., βροτός (for μβροτός), cogn. with L. *mortuus*. Hence *ambrosial*, divine, often with reference to the fragrance associated with the gods.

ambry, aumbry [*dial.*]. Storehouse, cupboard. Earlier *armary*, *almery*, OF. *armarie*, *almarie*, L. *armarium*, "where bookes are layd or other stuffe of household" (Coop.), orig. place for arms and tools. The *-l-* of OF. *almarie* is due to dissim., but there has also been confusion with *almonry*. Cf. also Ger. dial. *almer*. ModF. *armoire*, cupboard, is the same word with change of suffix.

> *almoire*: an ambrie; cup-boord; box. Look *armoire* (Cotg.).

> The Eleemosinary, or Almonry, now corruptly the Ambry, for that the alms of the abbey were there distributed to the poor (Stow).

ambs-ace, ames-ace [*archaic*]. OF. *ambes-as* (L. *ambos asses*), two aces, lowest throw at dice. See *ace*. Still in gen. use in Munster in *within an aim's-ace of*.

ambulance. F. *ambulance*, earlier *hôpital ambulant*, from L. *ambulare*, to travel. Introduced into E. during Crimean War (1854 –5).

ambury. See *anbury*.

ambuscade. F. *embuscade*, It. *imboscata* or Sp. *emboscada*, p.p. fem. of *imboscare*, *emboscar*, to "enbush" (see *bosky*). The form *ambuscado* (*Rom. & Jul.* i. 4), common in 17 cent., is a specimen of the pseudo-Sp. words then popular. Cf. *camerado*, *camisado*, etc. See *ambush*.

ambush. OF. *embusche* (*embûche*), from *em-*

buscher, to hide in the woods, now replaced, under the influence of *embuscade*, by *embusquer*.

> *embuscher*: to belay, to lay in ambuscadoe for; to waylay (Cotg.).

âme damnée. F., familiar spirit; orig. soul damned by compact with controlling demon.

Ameer. Of Afghanistan. See *emir*.

ameliorate. From F. *améliorer*, OF. *ameillorer*, from *à* and *meilleur*, L. *melior-em*, better.

amen. L., G. ἀμήν, Heb. *ā-mēn*, certainty, truth, used as expression of consent, etc. In AS. transl. by *sōthlice*, soothly, or *swā hit sȳ*, so let it be. Cf. *sobeit* and F. *ainsi soit-il*.

amenable. Orig. liable to be brought before jurisdiction. AF., from F. *amener*, VL. **ad-minare*, from *minari*, to threaten, whence *mener*, *amener*, to lead. The transition in sense of the VL. word was prob. from cattle-driving.

amend. F. *amender*, VL. **amendare* for *emendare*, from *mendum*, fault. Hence aphet. *mend*, which has supplanted *amend* in most senses. *Amends*, as in *make amends*, is F. *amende*, from the verb. The earliest meaning in both langs. is pecuniary reparation, fine. The prevalence of the pl. form in E. is curious, but it is usu. treated as a sing.

> *amende*: a penalty, fine, mulct, amerciament; an amends made by an offendor to the law violated, or party wronged (Cotg.).

amenity. From L. *amoenitas*, from *amoenus*, pleasant. Orig. of places, as still in *loss of amenity* (as result of industrial operations).

amerce [*archaic*]. Earlier *amercy*, AF. *amercier*, to fine. Formed from *merci*, mercy, grace. The phrase *estre a merci*, to be at mercy, i.e. at the discretion of the tribunal, was corrupted to *estre amercié*, and thus a verb was evolved which, at first, in accordance with its origin, was used only in the passive. For a similar case of a verb formed from an adv. phrase see *abandon*.

> Frans hom ne seit amerciez pour petit forfet
> (*Magna Charta*).

American. In 16 cent. American Indian; current sense from end of 18 cent. *Americanism* (of speech) is recorded for 1794. The continent is named from *Amerigo Vespucci*, 15 cent. navigator.

> Another Italian, Americus Vesputius, carried the name away from them both [Columbus, Cabot] (Purch.).

ames-ace. See *ambs-ace*.

amethyst. Restored spelling of ME. *ametist*, OF. *ametiste* (*améthyste*), L., G. ἀμέθυστος, from ἀ-, neg., μεθύσκειν, to intoxicate, because supposed to act as a charm against intoxication.

> D'Inde nus vient iceste piere,
> Et est a entallier legiere.
> Ki l'a sur sei n'eniverra,
> Ne ja vins ne l'estordira
> (*Lapidaire de Marbod*, 12 cent.).

Amex [*neol.*]. Members of *A*merican *Ex*pedition in France (1917). Cf. *Anzac*.

amiable. Represents fusion of OF. *amable*, L. *amabilis*, from *amare*, to love, and *amiable*, L. *amicabilis*, from cogn. *amicus*, friend. The former has become in ModF. *aimable*, under influence of *aimer*. Not orig. differentiated from native *lovely*.

> How amiable are thy tabernacles, O Lord of Hosts
> (*Ps.* lxxiv. 1).

amianthus [*min.*]. For *amiantus*, L., G. ἀμίαντος, undefiled, from ἀ-, neg., μιαίνειν, to defile, because, being incombustible, it can be purified by fire.

amicable. Late L. *amicabilis*, from *amicus*, friend, from *amare*, to love.

amice [*archaic*]. Two different words have become confused here, both in form and meaning. In the sense of a square of white linen worn by the celebrant priest, *amice*, earlier *amit*, is OF. *amit*, L. *amictus*, from *amicere*, to cast round, from *ambi-* and *jacere*. The *amice gray*, a furred cape worn by religious orders, and variously described, is F. *aumusse*, with many medieval cognates (MedL. *almucia*) in the Rom. langs. Thence it appears to have passed into Du. (*almutse*) and Ger. (*almuz*), now reduced by aphesis to *muts* and *mütze*, a cap. From Du. comes Sc. *mutch*. The earlier history of the word is unknown, though the forms suggest Arab. origin. The confusion between the two appears in their earliest records, e.g. in Wyclif, who uses *amice* to translate both *amictus* and *capitium*, the latter corresponding rather to F. *aumusse*.

> The torch's glaring ray
> Show'd, in its red and flashing light,
> His wither'd cheek and amice white
> (*Lord of the Isles*, ii. 23).
> A palmer's amice wrapt him round,
> With a wrought Spanish baldric bound
> (*Lay*, ii. 19).

amid. AS. *on middan* (dat.), whence ME. *a-midde*. This became *a-middes*, with gen. *-s* added to many adv. expressions. The *-t* is excrescent. Cf. hist. of *against*, *amongst*. Hence also aphet. *'mid*, *'midst*. See *mid*.

amir. See *emir*.

amiss. From *miss*[1] (q.v.). To *take amiss* was orig. to misunderstand, "mis take" (v.i.). Cf. sense-development of *misunderstanding*.

> This dreem takun a mys turneth upsedoun the chirche (Wyc.).

amity. F. *amitié*, VL. *amicitas*, *-tat-*, for *amicitia*, from *amicus*, friend, from *amare*, to love.

ammonia. Mod. coinage (1782) from *sal ammoniac*, F. *ammoniac*, L., G. ἀμμωνιακόν, from *Ammonia*, region in Libya near shrine of *Jupiter Ammon*, where the salt is said to have been first obtained from camel's dung. Cf. *ammonite*.

> Arsenyk, sal armonyak, and brymstoon
> (Chauc. G. 798).

ammonite [*geol.*]. ModL. *ammonites* (18 cent.), for fossil called in MedL. *cornu Ammonis*, from its resemblance to the horns of *Jupiter Ammon*. Ἄμμων is G. form of Egypt. deity *Amūn*. See *ammonia*.

> The Libyc Hammon shrinks his horn
> (*Ode on Nativity*, xxii.).

ammunition. Colloq. F. *l'amunition* (16–17 cent.), for *la munition* (see *munition*), by wrong separation of def. art. Formerly applied to all mil. stores, e.g. *ammunition boots* (*bread*, etc.).

> Les soldats disent "pain d'amonition"; mais les officiers disent "pain de munition" (Ménage).

amnesia. G. ἀμνησία, forgetfulness (v.i.). Cf. *aphasia*.

amnesty. L., G. ἀμνηστία, oblivion, from ἀ-, neg., μνᾶσθαι, to remember. Cf. *mnemonic*.

amnion [*anat.*]. Membrane enclosing fetus. G. ἀμνίον, caul, dim. of ἀμνός, lamb.

amoeba. Microscopic animalcule perpetually changing. G. ἀμοιβή, change.

amok. See *amuck*.

among, amongst. AS. *on gemang*, the latter a noun, mingling, crowd, from *gemengan*, to mingle (q.v.). For spurious *-s-t* cf. *again*, *against*, *amid*, *amidst*.

amontillado. Sp., sherry having flavour of Montilla, dry sherry from hill district so named.

amoral [*neol.*]. Coined on *amorphous*, etc. to express absence of moral sense.

amorous. F. *amoureux*, Late L. *amorosus*, from *amor*, love, which is prob. from baby lang. (see *aunt*).

amorphous. From G. ἄμορφος, shapeless, from ἀ-, neg., μορφή, shape.

amortize. F. *amortir, amortiss-*, from *à* and *mort*, death. For form cf. *advertise* and MedL. *amortizare*. In ME. to alienate in mortmain. Sense of extinguishing a debt is quite mod. (*NED.* 1882) and is imitated from F. *amortir une dette*.

amount. First as verb. OF. *amonter*, to mount up, from *amont*, up hill, L. *ad montem*. Earlier used also in sense of *mount*.

> So up he rose, and thence amounted streight
> (*Faerie Queene*, i. ix. 54).

amour. F., L. *amor-em*. A common ME. word for love, later accented *ámour* (cf. *enamour*). Now with suggestion of intrigue and treated as a F. word.

> The amoors of Lotharius Learoyd
> (Private Ortheris).

ampère. Unit of electricity. Adopted by Paris Electric Congress (1881) from name of F. electrician (†1836). Cf. *ohm, volt*.

ampersand [*archaic*]. The sign &, formerly ℰ, ligature of *et*. This ended the "criss-cross row" of the hornbook, which was repeated aloud by children—"A per se A, B per se B, ... and per se and." Common in dial. with numerous vars.

> The pen commandeth only twenty-six letters, it can only range between A and Z; these are its limits—I had forgotten and-pussy-and (Southey). Tommy knew all about the work. Knew every letter in it from A to Emperzan (Pett Ridge).

amphi-. G. ἀμφί, on both sides, cogn. with L. *ambi-*. Hence, *amphibia*, L., G. ἀμφίβια, neut. pl., from βίος, life; *amphibology*, F. *amphibologie*, Late L., from G. ἀμφιβολία, ambiguity, from βάλλειν, to cast; *amphibrach*, metr. foot, e.g. ămātă, L., from G. βραχύς, short (on both sides); *amphictyonic*, orig. council of Greek States, G. ἀμφικτύονες, those dwelling around.

amphigouri, amphigory. Rigmarole. F. *amphigouri* (18 cent.). Origin obscure. ? Coined from G. ἀμφί and γῦρος, circle (cf. *roundabout, circumlocution*).

amphimacer. Metr. foot, e.g. cārĭtās. L., from G. μακρός, long (on both sides); cf. *amphibrach*.

amphisbaena. Fabled two-headed serpent. G. ἀμφίσβαινα, from ἀμφίς, both ways, βαίνειν, to go.

amphitryon. Host, entertainer. From Molière's *Amphitryon*, adapted from Plautus.

> Le véritable Amphitryon est l'Amphitryon où l'on dîne (iii. 5).

amphora. L., two-handled vessel, from G. ἀμφί, on both sides, φέρειν, to bear. In L. also *ampora*.

ample. F., L. *amplus*, from prefix *amb-, ambi-*, about, and *-plus* as in *duplus*, double.

ampulla. Globular vessel. L., dim. of *amphora* (q.v.).

amputate. From L. *amputare*, from *amb-*, about, and *putare*, to lop, prune. Thus, metaphor from gardening.

amuck, amok. Malay *amoq*, rushing in a state of frenzy to the commission of indiscriminate murder. First Europ. form (c. 1500) is Port. *amouco, amuco*, used of a frenzied Malay. Now only in to *run amuck*. Sometimes erron. understood as *a muck*.

> *amoucos*: a sort of rash people in India (Vieyra).
> Frontless and satire-proof, he scours the streets,
> And runs an Indian muck at all he meets
> (Dryden, *Hind and Panther*, iii. 1187).
> Thy cliffs, dear Dover, harbour and hotel,
> Thy custom-house, with all its delicate duties,
> Thy waiters running mucks at every bell
> (*Don Juan*, x. 69).
> The German submarines have been running amok among Norwegian trading-vessels
> (*Daily Chron.* Oct. 26, 1916).

amulet. F. *amulette*, L. *amuletum*, ? for *amolitum*, from *amoliri*, to avert; used to translate G. φυλακτήριον, from φύλαξ, φυλακ-, guard (see *phylactery*).

amuse. F. *amuser* (see *muse*). Not in Shaks. Orig. to make to muse, occupy the attention, and even trick, delude. So also *amusement*, distraction, orig. rather loss of time. The sense-development has been curious, and more of the orig. meaning is found in *bemuse*.

> *amuser*: to amuse; to make to muse, or think of, wonder, or gaze at; to put into a dumpe; to stay, hold, or delay from going forward by discourse, questions, or any other amusements (Cotg.).
> This...if well heeded, might save us a great deal of useless amusement and dispute (Locke).
> Le moindre amusement [delay] peut vous être fatal
> (*Tartufe*, v. 6).

amygdaloid [*geol.*]. Igneous rock. Lit. almond-shaped. See *almond*. *Amygd-* in med. terms refers to the tonsils, pop. called "almonds."

amyl- [*chem.*]. From G. ἄμυλον, starch.

an¹. Adj. Orig. ident. with *one* (q.v.), AS. *ān*. Cf. double use of F. *un*, Ger. *ein*. *An* was reduced early to *a* before a consonant. In Sc. *ane* has survived both as numeral and art.

an². Archaic conj. In *an it please you*, etc. See *and*.

an-. As G. prefix for *ana-* (q.v.) or for ἀ- neg. before vowel.

ana. Collection of sayings, gossip, etc. connected with any person, or (sometimes) place. Orig. neut. pl. of L. adj. ending *-anus*, as in *Virgiliana*, things relating to Virgil.

Boswell's Life of Johnson...is the ana of all anas
(Southey).

ana-, an-. G. *ἀνά*, of rather vague meaning, upon, up, back, again; cogn. with *on*.

anabaptist. From G. *ἀνά*, over again, *βαπτίζειν*, to baptise. Orig. Ger. sect of early 16 cent.

anabasis. Expedition. From Xenophon's *Anabasis* (of Cyrus). G. *ἀνάβασις*, going up, from *βαίνειν*, to go.

anachronism. F. *anachronisme*, L., G. *ἀναχρονισμός*, from *ἀνά*, backwards, *χρόνος*, time.

anacoluthon [*gram.*]. Failure in grammatical sequence. From G. *ἀνακόλουθος*, not following, inconsequent, from *ἀν-*, neg., *ἀκόλουθος*, following. Cf. *acolyte*.

anaconda. Orig. large serpent found in Ceylon, *anacandaia* (Ray). Now used vaguely of any boa or python. Not now known in Singhalese, but perh. orig. misapplication of Singhalese *henakandayā*, whip snake, lit. lightning-stem. It has been suggested that the mistake may have been due to a confusion of labels in the Leyden Museum, Ray's source for the word.

anacreontic. Lyric poetry suggesting metre or style of *Ἀνακρέων* (fl. 6 cent. B.C.).

anadem [*poet.*]. Wreath. L., G. *ἀνάδημα*, fillet, from *δέειν*, to bind.

anadromous. Fish ascending river to spawn (e.g. salmon). From G. *δραμεῖν*, to run.

anadyomene. Epithet of Venus. G., diving up, from *ἀναδύεσθαι*, to rise from the sea.

anaemia. G. *ἀναιμία*, from *ἀν-*, neg., *αἷμα*, blood.

anaesthetic. First employed (1848) in mod. sense by Sir J. Y. Simpson, who introduced use of chloroform. See *aesthetic*.

anaglyph [*arch.*]. Low relief ornament. G. *ἀναγλυφή*, from *γλύφειν*, to hollow out.

anagogic. G. *ἀναγωγικός*, mystical, from *ἀνάγειν*, to lead up, elevate.

anagram. F. *anagramme*, from G. *ἀναγραμματίζειν*, to transpose letters, from *γράμμα*, letter. A famous example is *Honor est a Nilo*, Horatio Nelson.

Anak. Giant. Usu. *son of Anak* (*Josh.*xiv. 15).

analects. Literary gleanings. G. *ἀνάλεκτα*, neut. pl., from *λέγειν*, to gather.

analogy. L., G. *ἀναλογία*, from *ἀνά*, up to, *λόγος*, ratio. Orig. math., but used in wider sense by Plato.

analysis. G. *ἀνάλυσις*, from *λύειν*, to loose.

ananas. Pine-apple. Guarani (Brazil) *anānā*. Early transported to Africa (Purch.).

anapaest. Metr. foot, e.g. *rĕmănēnt*. G. *ἀνάπαιστος*, struck back, reversed, because representing a reversed dactyl, from *ἀνά*, back, *παίειν*, to strike.

anarchy. F. *anarchie*, MedL., G. *ἀναρχία*, from *ἀν-*, neg., *ἀρχός*, chief (see *arch*[2]). *Anarchist* in mod. sense is one of the by-products of the French Revolution.

Ce nom d'anarchistes que depuis deux ans on affecte
de donner aux brigands (Laharpe, 1797).

anarthrous [*anat.*]. Jointless (see *arthritis*). In G. of nouns used without art.

anastatic [*typ.*]. From G. *ἀναστατός*, standing up. See *static*.

anastomosis. Intercommunication. G., from *ἀναστομόειν*, to furnish with a mouth, *στόμα*.

anathema. L., G. *ἀνάθεμα*, var. of *ἀνάθημα*, an offering, from *ἀνά*, up, *τιθέναι*, to set. Orig. an accursed thing, later applied to persons and to the Divine curse.

anatomy. F. *anatomie*, L., G. *ἀνατομία*, from *ἀνά*, up, *τέμνειν*, to cut (see *atom*). Vivisection was once called *live* (*quick*) *anatomy*. The meaning skeleton is common in 16–17 cent. and in mod. dial., aphet. *atomy* being often used in this sense.

anbury, ambury [*vet. & bot.*]. Spongy wart. Prob. for *angberry* (see *agnail*), confused with dial. *amper*, swelling, L. *ampulla*.

moro: a mulberie tree; also a wart in a horse called
an anburie (Flor.).

ancestor. OF. *ancestre* (*ancêtre*), L. *antecessor*, fore-goer. ME. had also *ancessour*, from OF. acc., L. *antecessor-em*; hence mod. ending *-or*. Cf. *forbear*[1].

For gentillesse nys but renommee
Of thyne auncestres, for hire heigh bountee
(Chauc. D. 1159).

anchor. AS. *ancor*, very early loan from L. *ancora*, G. *ἄγκυρα*, from *ἄγκος*, bend. App. the only L. naut. word adopted by the Teut. langs. (cf. Ger. *anker*, ON. *akkeri*). The spelling *anchor* is after corrupt L. form *anchora*. The *anchor watch* is set while the ship lies at anchor.

anchorite, anchoret. Earlier also *anachorete*, F. *anachorète*, L., G. *ἀναχωρητής*, from *ἀνά*, back, *χωρέειν*, to withdraw. Form has been influenced by the older *anchor, anker*, fem.

anchoress, representing the same word borrowed by AS., and surviving up to c. 1600. Cf. the 13th cent. *Ancren Riwle*, or Rule of Nuns, in which the name is pseudo-etym. explained as a metaphor, the nuns being "anchors" of Holy Church. Shaks. uses *anchor* (*Haml*. iii. 2).

anachorete: the hermet called an ankrosse, or anchorite (Cotg.).

anchovy. Earlier *anchove*, Sp. *anchova*. Forms of the word are found in all the Rom. langs., and F. *anchois*, app. a pl., is rather older than our word. Origin unknown.

anchylosis [*med.*]. Stiffness of joints. G., from ἀγκύλος, crooked, cogn. with *angle*[1, 2].

ancient. F. *ancien*, VL. **antianus*, from *ante*; cf. It. *anziano*, Sp. *anciano*. Often incorr. used formerly, e.g. by Shaks., for *ensign* in both senses (1 *Hen. IV*, iv. 2 ; 2 *Hen. IV*, ii. 4).

ancillary. Subordinate, from L. *ancilla*, handmaid, dim. of archaic L. *anca*.

Others are engaged in war-work or munitions work or on contracts ancillary thereto
(Lord Chief Justice, Nov. 15, 1916).

and. AS. *and*, *end*. Aryan; cf. Du. *en*, Ger. *und*, ON. *endr*, Goth. *and*, Sanskrit *ātha*; cogn. with L. *ante*, G. ἀντί, against, juxtaposed, and with *end*. See also *answer*. It was used not only as a simple copulative, but also to introduce a condition, in which sense it was often reduced to *an* and strengthened with a redundant *if*. This survives in the archaic *an it please you*, where older editions of Shaks. have *and*.

But and if that evil servant shall say in his heart
(*Matt*. xxiv. 48).

andante [*mus.*]. It., pres. part. of *andare*, to go, ? from L. *ad* and *nare*, to swim (cf. *arrive*). ? Or from L. *ambitare* (see *ambit*).

andiron. ME. *aundire*, etc., OF. *andier*, now *landier*, for *l'andier*. Ending is assimilated by folk-etym. to *brandiron*, a word of somewhat similar meaning. A further dial. corrupt. is *handiron*. See also *gridiron*. MedL. forms are numerous, *andena*, *anderius*, *anderus*, etc. ?From a Gaulish **andera*, young cow (cf. Welsh *anner*, heifer). Cf. synon. *fire-dog*, F. *chenet*, Ger. *feuerbock*, lit. fire-goat.

Andrea Ferrara [*hist.*]. Sc. broad-sword. *Andrea dei Ferrari*, i.e. Andrew of the armourers, was a famous 16 cent. swordsmith of Belluno, but it seems unlikely that any great number of his costly blades could have got to Scotland. According to some

Sc. authorities the native blades were made by *Andrew Ferrars* or *Ferrier* (? of Arbroath), who again, according to a popular legend, may have been the Italian in exile. See *Cornh. Mag.* Aug. 1865.

Andrew. Patron saint of Scotland ; hence *St Andrew's cross* on the national flag, supposed to be the shape of the cross (X) used at his martyrdom. *Merry Andrew*, quack's attendant, is from the common use of *Andrew* as name for a serving-man (cf. *abigail, zany, jack-pudding*). See also *dandy*.

androgynous [*anat.*]. Hermaphrodite. From G. ἀνδρόγυνος, from ἀνήρ, ἀνδρ-, man, γυνή, woman.

Andromeda [*astron.*]. G. maiden rescued from sea-monster by Perseus. Also used of a genus of shrubs.

anecdote. F., MedL., G. ἀνέκδοτα, neut. pl., things unpublished, from ἀν-, neg., ἐκδιδόναι, to give out. It thus corresponds exactly to F. *inédit*. Orig. private or secret details. *Anecdotage*, for garrulous old age, with a play on *dotage*, is a coinage attributed to John Wilkes.

Those who pretend to write anecdotes, or secret history (*Gulliver*).

anele [*archaic*]. To give extreme unction (*Haml*. i. 5). ME. *anelien*, from *ele*, oil, L. *oleum*.

anemone. L., G. ἀνεμώνη, wind-flower, lit. daughter of the wind, ἄνεμος.

anent. AS. *on efen*, on a level, with excrescent -*t*. Orig. side by side with, as still in dial.; cf. *fornent*, opposite, now esp. Ir. So also Ger. *neben*, near, beside, is for older *eneben*. In ME. *anentis*, *anenst* is the usu. form (cf. *against*). The word is very common in Sc. law, its use by ModE. writers being an affectation.

I cam to Jerusalem, for to se Petre, and dwellide anentis him [*Vulg.* apud eum] fifteene dayes
(Wyc. *Gal.* i. 18).

aneroid. F. *anéroïde*, coined from G. ἀ-, neg., νηρός, damp.

aneurism [*med.*]. Morbid dilatation of artery. From G. ἀνευρύνειν, from εὐρύνειν, to open.

anew. Earlier *of new*; cf. F. *de nouveau*.

Ther kan no man in humblesse hym acquite
As wommen kan, ne kan been half so trewe
As wommen been, but it be falle of newe
(Chauc. E. 936).

anfractuosity. F. *anfractuosité*, from L. *anfractuosus*, winding, roundabout, from *anfractus*, a breaking round, bending, from *ambi*- and *frangere*, *fract*-, to break.

angel. AS. *engel*, L., G. ἄγγελος, messenger, used by LXX. to translate Heb. *mal'āk*, messenger (of Jehovah). Orig. sense in *angel of death*. Adopted by all the converted nations. ModE. form is due to influence of L. and of OF. *angle, angele* (*ange*). The coin called an *angel* (15 cent.) was a new issue of the noble, stamped with St Michael and the Dragon. This was the coin always presented to patients touched for the "King's evil."

> visits
> Like those of angels, short and far between
> (Blair, *Grave*).
> Angel visits, few and far between
> (Campbell, *Pleasures of Hope*, ii. 386).

angelica. Herb. MedL. *herba angelica*, so named from reputed. med. qualities (16 cent.).

angelus. From init. word of devotional exercise repeated at the ringing of the angelus bell—*Angelus domini nuntiavit Mariae*... Mod. currency is due to Longfellow (*Evangeline*).

anger. ON. *angr*, cogn. with L. *angere* (see *anguish*). Orig. rather in passive sense of pain, affliction, etc. ? Influenced in later sense by OF. *engrès*, vehement, passionate, L. *ingressus*.

> To suffren al that God sente syknesses and angres
> (*Piers Plowm.* C. xxii. 291).

angina [*med.*]. L. *angina*, quinsy, from *angere* (v.s.), cogn. with G. ἀγχόνη. Usu. mispronounced *angīna*. See *anguish, quinsy*.

angio-. From G. ἀγγεῖον, dim. of ἄγγος, vessel, chest. ·

angle¹. Verb. From obs. *angle*, fish-hook, AS. *angel*, dim. of AS. *anga, onga*, prickle, goad, ult. cogn. with L. *uncus*, and also with *angle²*. So also the hist. *Angles* took their name from *Angul*, ON. *Öngull*, a hook-shaped district in Holstein.

> The fishers also shall mourn, and all they that cast angle [*Vulg.* hamus] into the brooks shall lament
> (*Is.* xix. 8).

angle². Noun. F., L. *angulus*, corner; cf. G. ἄγκος, bend. See *angle¹*.

Anglian [*ling.*]. Used to include Mercian and Northumbrian (see *angle¹*). *East Anglian* includes Norfolk and Suffolk.

Anglican. From 17 cent.; but MedL. form— *Anglicana ecclesia*—occurs in *Magna Charta* and earlier. App. modelled on *Gallicanus*. Becket couples the words in a letter to the Pope (1169).

Anglo-French [*ling.*]. French as spoken in England c. 1100–1400, chiefly from the Norman dial. of OF.

anglomania. First used in US. (18 cent.). Cf. later *anglophobia*, modelled on *hydrophobia*.

Anglo-Saxon. Sometimes understood as referring to mixture of *Angles* and *Saxons*, but orig. used to distinguish the English Saxons from the continental Saxons (cf. *Anglo-French*). It was applied esp. to the people of Wessex and the other -*sex* counties. The word fell out of use after the Conquest and does not reappear till c. 1600, when Camden, in his antiquarian and philological writings, adopted *Anglo-Saxonicus* or *English Saxon* as a name for the old English lang., which, like the race, had during the Middle Ages been known as *Saxon* only. *Anglo-Saxon* is now often replaced, e.g. in the *NED.*, by *Old English*, which serves to mystify the layman. At the same time *Anglo-Saxon* is a misnomer, as it strictly applies to only one of the three invading tribes.

angola. See *Angora*.

Angora. Mod. name of *Ancyra*, in Asia Minor, famous for breed of goats, and cats, · with long silky hair. Hence a material, often corrupted to *angola*.

angostura, angustura. A bark, used for making bitters, from a town on the Orinoco formerly so named. Now Ciudad Bolívar.

angry. See *anger*.

anguine [*biol.*]. Of the snake, L. *anguis*, *anguin-*.

anguish. OF. *anguisse* (*angoisse*), L. *angustia*, compression, from *angustus*, narrow; cogn. with *anger, anxious, quinsy*, and possibly with *pang*. Cf. Ger. *bange*, anxious, from OHG. *ango* (*enge*), narrow, with prefix *be-*.

anharmonic. Not harmonic. G. ἀν-, neg.

an-hungered [*Bibl.*]. For earlier *a-hungered*, with *a-* for earlier *of-* (cf. *anew*) with intens. force. Cf. Ger. *abgehungert*, starving, where the prefix is cogn. with E. *of*. See *athirst*.

anhydrous. G. ἄνυδρος, from ἀν-, neg., ὕδωρ, water.

anigh. Mod. sham antique, modelled on *afar*. A favourite word with William Morris.

> Mister Close expressed a wish that he could only get anigh to me;
> And Mister Martin Tupper sent the following reply to me (Gilbert, *Gentle Pieman*).

anile. L. *anilis*, imbecile, from *anus*, old woman.

aniline. Coined by Fritzsche (1841) from *anil*, indigo. F., Sp. *añil*, Arab. Pers. *annīl* for *al-nīl*, the indigo, orig. meaning (Sanskrit)

dark blue, as in the *Nilgherries*, or Blue
Hills. Cf. *nylghau*.

animadvert. L. *animadvertere*, for *animum
advertere*, to turn the mind to, take cognizance of. For sense-development cf. *twit*.

animal. L., for *animale*, neut. of *animalis*,
having breath of life, *anima*. Not in *AV*.
(see *beast*). *Animal spirits* orig. (16 cent.)
meant nerve force considered as centred in
the brain; contrasted with *vital* and *natural*
spirits. The earliest record in *NED*. for
mod. sense is 1813 (*Pride and Prejudice*).

The braine for the animall spirite, the heart for the
vitall, and the liver for the naturall (*NED*. 1594).

animalcule. L. dim. *animalculum*. A pl.
animalculae is often used by the ignorant.

animate. From L. *animare*, to give breath to
(see *animal*). Cf. G. ἄνεμος, wind.

animosity. F. *animosité*, Late L. *animositas*,
from *animus*, spirit. Not orig. hostile feeling.
Cf. *animus* (19 cent.) for similar sense-development.

anise. F. *anis*, L., G. ἄνισον. There is also
an obs. *anet*, L., G. ἄνηθον, dial. form of
above. *Aniseed* is for *anise seed*. F. *anisette*,
liqueur, is a dim. of *anis*.

That tithen mente, anese [*var.* anete] and comyn
                    (Wyc. *Matt.* xxiii. 23).

anker [*archaic*]. Cask. In most Teut. langs.,
earliest in Du. Older is MedL. *anceria*,
ancheria, a small vat. Origin obscure;
? OHG. *hant-kar*, hand tub.

ankle. AS. *anclēow*. The first element is
perh. related to *angle*[1], while the ending
suggests *claw*; cf. Du. *enclaauw*, OHG.
anchlāo, ON. *ökkla*. But this will not
explain ME. *ankyl*, mod. *ankle*, which
appears to represent a Fris. or Scand.
form; cf. Du. *enkel*, Dan., Sw. *ankel*, also
Ger. *enkel*, used in some dials. for the more
usual *knöchel* (see *knuckle*).

ankylosis. See *anchylosis*.

anlace [*hist.*]. Kind of dagger. Metath. of
OF. *alenas*, from *alène*, awl (cf. *cutlass*).
This suggests that it was not a blade, but
a kind of stiletto, used as a dagger of
mercy (quot. 2). See *awl*.

Genus cultelli, quod vulgariter anelacius dicitur
                    (Matthew Paris).

Un alenas en sa main
Cherche des armeures l'estre [joint]
Pour lui ocire et afiner (Duc. 1308).

An anlaas, and a gipser al of silk
Heeng at his girdel, whit as morne milk
                    (Chauc. A. 357).

His harp in silken scarf was slung,
And by his side an anlace hung (*Rokeby*, v. 15).

anna. Sixteenth part of a rupee. Hind.
ānā.

annals. F. *annales*, L. *annales* (sc. *libri*), year-
books, from *annus*, year.

annates [*hist.*]. First fruits, payment to
Rome of first year's income by newly
appointed ecclesiastics. F. *annate*, MedL.
annata (whence also F. *année*). Transferred
to the Crown at Reformation and later
used to establish the fund called Queen
Anne's Bounty.

anneal. AS. *on-ǣlan*, to set on fire, bake
(tiles, etc.), whence ME. *anele*. Perh. influenced by OF. *neeler* (*nieller*), It. *niellare*,
VL. **nigellare*, to blacken.

Up on the walles of anelid [*var.* bakun] tyil
                    (Wyc. *Is.* xvi. 7).

annelid [*zool.*]. ModL. *annelida* (Lamarck),
from F. *annelé*, ringed, from OF. *annel*
(*anneau*), L. *annellus*, dim. of *annulus*.

annex. Orig. to attach. F. *annexer*, from L.
annexus, from *ad*, to, *nectere*, *nex-*, to bind.
Cf. F. *annexe*, supplementary building.

annihilate. From Late L. *annihilare*, to reduce
to nothing, *nihil*. Cf. F. *anéantir*. See *nihilist*.

anniversary. L. *anniversarius* (adj.), returning yearly, from *annus*, year, *vertere*, *vers-*,
to turn.

Anno Domini. L., in the year of the Lord.

annotate. Elaborated from earlier *annote* (16
cent.), F. *annoter*, L. *annotare*. Occurs first
in Johns. as gloss to *comment*. See *note*.

announce. F. *annoncer*, L. *annuntiare*, from
ad and *nuntius*, messenger. Hence *annunciation*, earliest in ref. to Virgin Mary.

annoy. OF. *enoier*, VL. **in-odiare*, from the
phrase *in odio*, in hatred; cf. It. *annoiare*,
Sp. *enojar*. The E. word occurs first as a
noun, and its earlier sense was much
stronger than at present. *Ennui* is formed
from ModF. *ennuyer*, from tonic stem of
enoyer.

We licence our said cosyn [the Earl of Cumberland]
to anoye the Kinge of Spayne and his subjects, and
to burne, kill, and slaye, as just and needefull cause
shall require (Queen Elizabeth).

annual. Earlier *annuel*, F., Late L. *annualis*,
for *annalis*, from *annus*, year.

annuity. F. *annuité*, MedL. *annuitas*, from
L. *annuus*. An old word in both langs.

annul. F. *annuler*, L. *annullare*, to reduce to
naught, *nullum*; see *null* and cf. *annihilate*.

annular. L. *annularis*, from *annulus*, ring.

annunciation. See *announce*.

anode [*electr.*]. Positive pole. G. ἄνοδος, way
up, from ὁδός, way. Cf. *cathode*.

anodyne. L., G. ἀνώδυνος, painless, from ἀν-, neg., ὀδύνη, pain.

anoint. Orig. p.p. of OF. *enoindre*, Lat. *inungere*, from *in* and *ungere*, *unct-*, to anoint. The *Lord's Anointed* is used by Coverd. (1535) where Wyc. has the *Crist of the Lord*. Has replaced in rel. sense native *smear*.

Mīn heafod thū mid ele ne smȳredest; theos smȳrede mid sealfe mīne fēt (*Luke*, vii. 46).

anomalous. Earlier also *anomal*. L., G. ἀνώμαλος, from ἀν-, neg., ὁμαλός, even, from ὁμός, same. Cf. *homologous*.

anon. AS. *on ān*, into one, *on āne*, in one. Older sense, at once, forthwith, etc., but now used rather like *presently*, which has also changed its meaning; cf. Ger. *auf einmal*, pidgin *one time*. Dial. *anan*, meaning something like "What do you want?" is the same, originating from the stock reply of the summoned servant, common in Shaks., and corresponding to the modern waiter's "Coming, Sir." This may account for change of sense.

He that heareth the word and anon [G. εὐθύς, *Vulg.* continuo] with joy receiveth it (*Matt.* xiii. 20).

He shall presently [G. ἄρτι, *Vulg.* modo] give me more than twelve legions of angels (*Matt.* xxvi. 53).

anonymous. From G. ἀνώνυμος, from ἀν-, neg., ὄνομα, name.

another. For *an other*. In ME. often *a nother*.

anserine [*neol.*]. L. *anserinus*, belonging to the goose, f. *anser*, cogn. with G. χήν. See *goose*.

answer. AS. *andswarian*, to swear back, from noun *andswaru*. Cf. L. *respondēre*, to pledge in return. Orig. sense survives in to *answer an accusation*, to *answer for*, be *answerable*, etc. First element, surviving only in this word and partly in *along*, is cogn. with Ger. *ant-* (as in *antwort*), *ent-*, L. *ante*, G. ἀντί, etc. See *and*.

If it were so, it was a grievous fault;
And grievously hath Caesar answer'd it
(*Jul. Caes.* iii. 2).

ant. AS. *ǣmette*, whence ME. *amet*, *ampt* (cf. *Ampthill*, Beds.), *emet*. Archaic *emmet* is still in dial. use. Orig. cutter off; cf. ON. *meita*, to cut, Ger. *meissel*, chisel. Cf. Ger. *ameise*, ant, in Luther *emmeis*, whence prob. *emsig*, diligent. A more wide-spread Teut. name for the insect survives in *pismire* (q.v.).

Goe to the emmote ô sluggard
(*Douay Bible, Prov.* vi. 6).

ant-. For *anti-*, before vowel.

antagonist. L. *antagonista*, G. ἀνταγωνιστής, from ἀντί, against, ἀγωνίζεσθαι, to struggle. Cf. *agony*.

Antar. Hero of romance. From *Antar ibn Shaddād*, Eastern poet and warrior. Cf. *Amadis*, *Bayard*, etc.

Antarctic. See *Arctic*.

ante-. L. *ante*, before, cogn. with G. ἀντί, Ger. *ant-*, *ent-*, AS. *and-*, and ult. with *end*.

antecedent. From pres. part. of L. *antecedere*, to go before. Cf. *ancestor*.

antediluvian. Coined (17 cent.), ? by Sir T. Browne, from L. *ante* and *diluvium*, flood. See *deluge*.

antelope. OF. *antelop*, found in MedL. as *antalopus* and 4 cent. G. as ἀνθόλοψ, ἀνθόλοπ-. Orig. sense and lang. unknown. ModF. *antilope* is borrowed back from E. (Buffon). In ME. & OF. the antelope was a fabulous and formidable beast, like the unicorn, griffin, etc. Mod. sense dates from 17 cent.

The antelope and wolf both fierce and fell
(*Faerie Queene*, 1. vi. 26).

antennae [*biol.*]. Pl. of L. *antenna*, yard of a sail, used by Theodorus Gaza (15 cent.) to translate G. κεραῖαι, "horns" of insects, also ends of sail-yards, both being called *cornua* in L. F. *antenne* still has both senses.

anterior. L. compar. from prep. *ante*, before.

anthelion [*astron.*]. Late G., neut. of ἀνθήλιος, from ἀντί, opposite, ἥλιος, sun. Cf. *aphelion*, *perihelion*.

anthem. AS. *antefn*, L., G. ἀντίφωνα, neut. pl., from ἀντί, against, φωνή, sound. An early Church word, doublet of *antiphon*. The AS. form shows a VL. change of accent, *antíphona*, whence also F. *antienne*, "an antem, or supplication" (Cotg.). For the E. ending cf. *stem* (naut.), from AS. *stefn*. For Johnson's etym. (v. i.) cf. *ache*.

anthem: G. ἀνθύμνος, a hymn sung in alternate parts and should therefore be written *anthymn* (Johns.).

anther [*bot.*]. F. *anthère*, G. ἀνθηρά, fem. of ἀνθηρός, flowery (v. i.).

anthology. L., G. ἀνθολογία, from ἄνθος, flower, λέγειν, to gather.

Anthony, St. Patron saint of swineherds. Hence archaic *Anthony* (see *Tantony*), for the smallest pig in a litter. *St Anthony's fire* is an old name for erysipelas, for the cure of which the saint was invoked.

anthracite. From *anthrax* (q.v.).

anthrax. Malignant pustule. L., G. ἄνθραξ, coal, whence *anthracite*. Cf. *carbuncle* (q.v.).

"Antrax" is a postume....It is callyd also "carbunculus," for it brennyth as a cole (*NED.* 1398).

anthropo-. From G. ἄνθρωπος, man. Hence *anthropology*, orig. study of man in widest sense; *anthropophagi*, cannibals, L., G. ἀνθρωποφάγοι, from φαγεῖν, to eat.

And of the cannibals that each other eat,
The Anthropophagi (*Oth.* i. 3).

anti-, ant-. G. ἀντί, against, cogn. with L. *ante*, before. Hence a large and increasing number of compds. to indicate people who are "agin" something, e.g. *anti-conscriptionist* (1916).

antic. It. *antico*, antique, L. *antiquus*, used for *grotesque* (q.v.), this kind of work being ascribed to the ancients. In 16 cent. it was both noun and adj., of things and of persons; but its earliest recorded use (Foxe) is in the mod. sense of grotesque gambol.

grottesca; a kinde of rugged unpolished painters worke, anticke worke (Flor.).

All bar'd with golden bendes, which were entayled
With curious antickes, and full fayre aumayled
(*Faerie Queene*, II. iii. 27).

And there the antic [Death] sits,
Scoffing his state, and grinning at his pomp
(*Rich. II.* iii. 2).

Antichrist. Mysterious opponent of Christ whose advent was expected by the Middle Ages. Applied by early reformers to the Papal authority.

This false heresie and tyrantrie of Antichrist
(Wyc.).

anticipate. From L. *anticipare*, to take before, from *capere*, to take. *Intelligent anticipation*, for unfounded statement, is due to Lord Curzon.

antidote. F., L., G. ἀντίδοτον, given against, from διδόναι, to give.

Anti-Jacobin [*hist.*]. Opposed to the *Jacobins* (q.v.), esp. as name of an anti-democratic paper started in 1797.

antimacassar. Coined (c. 1850) as name of defence against the *macassar* oil with which people anointed their heads.

antimony. MedL. *antimonia*, first used by Constantinus Africanus of Salerno (11 cent.). Prob. a latinized form of some Arab. name, but origin very doubtful. Popularly understood as F. *anti-moine*, monk's bane, and explained by a ridiculous story concerning a 15 cent. chemist.

antinomian [*theol.*]. Opposed to law, G. νόμος. Esp. name of a Ger. sect (1535) which maintained that the moral law was not binding upon Christians.

Antinous. Handsome man. Page of Emperor Hadrian. Cf. *Adonis*.

antipathy. L., G. ἀντιπάθεια, from πάθος, feeling.

antiphon. See *anthem*.

antiphrasis. Late L., G. ἀντίφρασις, contradiction. See *phrase*.

antipodes. L., G. ἀντίποδες (pl.), from πούς, πόδ-, foot. Orig. the people on the other side of the earth. Prob. from OF., which has it rather earlier. Formerly pronounced to rime with *codes* and with a sing. *antipod* (cf. *decapod*).

Yonde in Ethiopia ben the Antipodes, men that have theyr fete ayenst our fete (*NED.* 1398).

antipyrin [*neol.*]. From *antipyretic*, from G. πυρετός, fever, from πῦρ, fire.

antique. F., L. *antiquus*. Now has F. pronunc., but formerly that of *antic* (q.v.), as still sometimes in verse. *Antiquary* in mod. sense is first recorded as offic. title conferred on John Leland by Henry VIII.

There stood the broad-wheeled wains and the antique ploughs and the harrows (*Evangeline*, I. i. 74).

antirrhinum [*bot.*]. Snapdragon. From G. ἀντί, against (counterfeiting), ῥίς, ῥιν-, nose. Cf. *rhinoceros*. The flower has, owing to its shape, a large number of dial. names in all langs. In Ger. it is usually *löwenmaul*, lion's mouth.

antiseptic. From 18 cent. From G. σηπτικός, putrefying, from σήπειν, to rot.

antithesis. L., G. ἀντίθεσις, from τιθέναι, to place. Cf. *contrast*.

antitoxin. Serum used against diphtheria. From G. τοξικόν, poison. See *intoxicate*.

antler. ME. *auntelere*, OF. *antoillier* (*andouiller*), VL. *ante-ocularis* (sc. *ramus*), branch before the eye. Cf. Ger. *augensprossen*, antlers, lit. eye-sprouts. Orig. the lowest forward directed branch of a stag's horn, now called *brow-antler*. The absence of the word from the other Rom. langs. makes this, otherwise convincing, etym. rather dubious.

antonomasia [*rhet.*]. Substitution of epithet. G., from ἀντί, instead, ὄνομα, name.

antonym. Opposite of *synonym* (q.v.).

anus [*anat.*]. L., lit. ring; cf. synon. G. δακτύλιος, lit. finger-ring.

anvil. Earlier *anvild*, AS. *anfilte*, from *an*, on, and an obscure second element prob. meaning to hammer, which appears also in *felt*; cf. L. *incus*, *incud-*, anvil, from *in* and *cudere*, to strike. Cogn. with *anvil* are OHG. *anafalz*, ODu. *aenvilte*. ModGer. has *amboss*, from OHG. *bōzan*, cogn. with *beat*, Du. has *aanbeld*, with which cf. Norw. Dan. *ambolt* (from LG.). In these the second element is cogn. with E. *bolt* and ult. with the *-filte*, *-falz* of the words above.

anxious. From L. *anxius*, from *angere*, to compress, choke. See *anguish*, *quinsy*.

any. AS. *ǣnig*, from *ān*, one; cf. Du. *eenig*, from *een*, Ger. *einig*, from *ein*.

anythingarian. Coined (early 18 cent.) on model of *trinitarian*, *unitarian*. Cf. slang F. *jemenfoutiste*.

Anzac [*hist.*]. Acrostic word coined during the Gallipoli campaign (1915) to denote collectively the Australasians—Australian New Zealand Army Corps. Cf. *Dora*, *Waac*, *Zarp*, etc.

aorist [*gram.*]. G. ἀόριστος, indefinite, from ἀ-, neg., ὁρίζειν, to define. See *horizon*.

aorta [*anat.*]. Great artery. G. ἀορτή, lit. what is hung up, from ἀείρειν, to raise.

Ap. Patronymic prefix in Welsh names, e.g. *Ap Rhys* (*Price*), *Ap Evan* (*Bevan*), etc. Earlier *map*, cogn. with Gael. *mac*.

apace. Orig. at a walk (F. *au pas*), but in early use associated with speed.

And forth she walketh esily a pas (Chauc. F. 388).

apache. Parisian desperado (late 19 cent.). From name of Red Ind. tribe. Cf. *mohock*.

apanage, appanage. Now used fig. of a perquisite, special possession, adjunct, etc., but orig. provision (territory, office, etc.) made for younger sons of royalty. F., from OF. *apaner*, MedL. *appanare*, to provide with bread, L. *panis*.

apart. F. *à part*, aside, L. *ad partem*.

apartment. F. *appartement*, It. *appartamento*, orig. division, separation, from *appartare*, from *a parte*, apart. MedL. *appartimentum* is directly from L. *partiri*, to divide, share. When first introduced, it meant, like F. *appartement*, a suite of rooms.

apathy. F. *apathie*, L., G. ἀπάθεια, from ἀ-, neg., πάθος, feeling.

ape. AS. *apa*. Com. Teut.; cf. Du. *aap*, Ger. *affe*, ON. *ape*. Prob. adopted in prehistoric times from some non-Aryan lang. With verb to *ape* cf. F. *singer*, Ger. *nachaffen*.

apeak [*naut.*]. Earlier (16 cent.) *a pike*, F. *à pic*, perpendicularly. Used of "anchor when the cable has been sufficiently hove in to bring the ship over it" (Smyth). Also *oars apeak*, held vertically, *yards apeak*, as sign of mourning. Cf. *peak*[2].

He's going, the land-crabs will have him; his anchor's apeak (*Roderick Random*).

apepsy [*med.*]. Lack of digestive power. From G. ἀ-, neg., and *-pepsy* (see *dyspepsy*).

aperçu. F., p.p. of *apercevoir*, to perceive (q.v.).

aperient. From pres. part. of L. *aperire*, to open.

aperture. L. *apertura*, from *aperire*, *apert-*, to open.

apex. L., summit.

aphaeresis [*ling.*]. L., G. ἀφαίρεσις, from ἀπό, off, αἱρέειν, to take. See *aphesis*.

aphasia [*med.*]. Coined by Trousseau (1864) for earlier *aphemia*, *alalia*, from G. ἀ-, neg., φάναι, to speak.

aphelion [*astron.*]. Coined by Kepler (16 cent.), after *apogee*, from G. ἀπό, off, ἥλιος, sun. Cf. *perihelion*.

aphesis [*ling.*]. G. ἄφεσις, letting go, from ἀπό, off, ἱέναι, to send. Suggested (1880) by the late Sir James Murray instead of the older *aphaeresis* (q.v.), for the loss of init. unaccented vowel so common in E., e.g. *prentice*, *gipsy*, *peal*, etc. Hence *aphetic*. It may conveniently be used also, as in this Dict., of the loss of a whole init. syllable, e.g. *drawing-room*, *tawdry*, etc.

aphetic. See *aphesis*.

aphis. Plant-louse. ModL., coined by Linnaeus. ? Back-formation from pl. *aphides*, suggested by G. ἀφειδής, unsparing.

aphorism. F. *aphorisme*, MedL., G. ἀφορισμός, a distinction, definition, from ἀφορίζειν, from ἀπό, from, ὅρος, boundary (see *aorist*). Cf. *definition*, from *finis*. Orig. the *Aphorisms of Hippocrates*, then extended to other statements of principles.

Aphrodite. Goddess of love, Venus. Trad. from G. ἀφρός, foam, but prob. ident. with *Ashtaroth*, *Astarte* of the Phoenicians, Assyr. *Ishtar*. Hence *aphrodisiac*.

apiary. L. *apiarium*, from *apis*, bee. Cf. *apiculture*.

Apician. From *Apicius*, famous Roman epicure, temp. Tiberius.

apiece. The prefix is the indef. art.

aplomb. F. adv. phrase *à plomb*, perpendicular, from *plomb*, lead, plummet, L. *plumbum*.

apo-, aph-, ap- G. ἀπό, off, from, cogn. with E. of(f).

Apocalypse. L., G. ἀποκάλυψις, from καλύπτειν, to cover. Cf. *revelation*, from *velare*, to veil. *Apocalypse* is the older word, *revelation* being used by Wyc. (v. i.) to explain it.

He hath techinge, he hath apocalips, or revelacioun, he hath tunge (Wyc. 1 *Cor.* xiv. 26).

apocope [*ling.*]. Loss of final syllable. L., G. ἀποκοπή, from ἀποκόπτειν, to cut off.

Apocrypha. L., neut. pl. (sc. *scripta*), from G. ἀπόκρυφος, hidden away, from κρύπτειν, to hide. Excluded from Bible at Reformation.

The other followynge, which are called *apocripha* (because they were wont to be reade, not openly and in common, but as it were in secrete and aparte) are neyther founde in the Hebrue nor in the Chalde (*Great Bible*, 1539).

apod [*biol.*]. Footless. G. ἄπους, ἀποδ-, from ἀ-, neg., πούς, ποδ-, foot. Cf. *apteryx*.

apodosis [*gram.*]. G., from ἀποδιδόναι, to give back. Cf. *protasis*.

apogee [*astron.*]. F. *apogée*, L., G. ἀπόγαιον, from γῆ, earth. Dates from Ptolemy the Alexandrian astronomer (2 cent.). Cf. the imitated *aphelion*.

apolaustic. G. ἀπολαυστικός, from ἀπολαύειν, to enjoy.

apollinaris. Vulg. "polly." Advertised in E. c. 1870. From *Apollinaris-brunnen* (spring) near Remagen, on the Rhine.

Apollo. Handsome man. L., G. Ἀπόλλων, the sun-god.

Apollyon. The destroyer. G. ἀπολλύων, pres. part., from ἀπό, from, λύειν, to loose. Used by Wyc. (see *Abaddon*).

apologue. F., "a pretty and significant fable, or tale, wherein bruit beasts, or dumbe things, are fained to speak" (Cotg.). L., G. ἀπόλογος, from λόγος, speech.

apology. F. *apologie*, L., G. ἀπολογία, a speaking away. Orig. formal defence or pleading, as in Plato's *Apology for Socrates*, and in *apologetics*.

Waistcoats edged with a narrow cord, which serves as an apology for lace (*NED.* 1752).

apophthegm. G. ἀπόφθεγμα, a terse saying, from φθέγγεσθαι, to utter. Prob. through F.

Jamais homme noble ne hait le bon vin, c'est un apophtegme monacal (Rabelais).

apoplexy. F. *apoplexie*, MedL., G. ἀποπληξία, disablement, from πλήσσειν, to strike. Cf. the vulgar "stroke."

aposiopesis [*rhet.*]. G. from G. ἀποσιωπάειν, to become silent.

Tantane vos generis tenuit fiducia vestri?
Jam caelum terramque meo sine numine, Venti,
Miscere, et tantas audetis tollere moles?
Quos ego...sed motos praestat componere fluctus
(*Aen.* i. 131).

He was in the act of stooping low to deposit the pantaloons in the grave which he had been digging for them, when Tom Ingoldsby came close behind him, and with the flat side of the spade——. The shock was effectual; never again was Lieutenant Seaforth known to act the part of a somnambulist (*Spectre of Tappington*).

apostate. F. *apostat*, L., G. ἀποστάτης, one who stands away, from ἵστασθαι, to stand.

apostille. Marginal note. F., from verb *apostiller*, from OF. *postille*, postil (q.v.).

apostle. AS. *apostol*, L., G. ἀπόστολος, messenger, from στελλειν, to send (cf. *emissary*). Influenced by OF. *apostle* (*apôtre*). In AS. & ME. used for messenger as well as in spec. sense. *Apostle spoons*, i.e. a set of twelve spoons of which the handles had figures of the apostles, were a usu. gift of sponsors.

apostrophe. L., G. ἀποστροφή, from στρέφειν, to turn. Orig. a turning aside of the orator's speech to address some individual, present or absent; hence to *apostrophize*. In the sense of sign of omission (') it comes later via F.

apostropher: to cut off (by an apostrophe) the last vowel of a word (Cotg.).

apothecary. F. *apothicaire*. VL. *apothecarius*, from G. ἀποθήκη, store-house, from τιθέναι, to put. Orig. keeper of a shop for what we should now call "colonial produce." Then esp. druggist. The London Apothecaries' Company was not separated from the Grocers' till 1617. Aphet. *potticary* (cf. *prentice*) was once usual and survives as a surname. Cf. F. *boutique*, Sp. *bodega*, both via L. from G. ἀποθήκη.

Ful redy hadde he [the Doctour of Physik] his apothecaries
To sende him drogges and his letuaries
(Chauc. A. 424).
Item to Goldring the potecary for marmalad and other things xs (*Rutland Papers*, 1551).

apotheosis. L., G. ἀποθέωσις, from ἀποθεοῦν, to make a god, θεός.

appal. OF. *apalir*, to make pale, also to become pale, the former the earlier sense. This suits the ME. meanings of *appal*, but the F. verb should have given *appale*, a word actually in use in 16 cent. The later meanings are, trans. to quell, frighten, intrans. to fade, become weak or tasteless, go flat, whence aphet. *pall²*. The pronunc. of the word is unexplained.

I appale ones colour: je appalis. *This sicknesse hath appaled hym very sore*: ceste maladie la appaly tres fort (Palsg.).

I appalle, as drinke doth or wyne, whan it leseth his colour or ale whan it hath stande longe: je appalys. *This wyne is appaled all redy, and it is nat yet an hour syth it was drawen out of the vessel*: ce vin est desja appaly, encore nest il pas ung heure quon la tiré du vaisseau (*ib.*).

appanage. See *apanage*.

apparatus. L., from *apparare*, to make ready, from *parare*, *parat-*, to prepare. See *pare*.

apparel. First as verb. F. *appareiller*, VL. **ad-pariculare*, with cognates in all Rom. langs. Orig. to put like things together, L. *par*, equal. Cf. F. *pareil*, like, VL. **pariculus*. In OF. & ME. to equip in any way. In ModF. to prepare to set sail. With the limitation of meaning in F. & E. cf. extension of *équiper*, *equip* in the same langs. See also *dress*. Aphet. forms were common in ME. and *parrel* survives as naut. term.

For his pore paraille and pylgrymes weedes
(*Piers Plowm.* B. xi. 228).

He sayde unto his contree moste he sayle,
For ther he wolde hire weddyng apparaylle
(Chauc. *Leg. Good Women*, 2472).

apparent. OF. *aparant*, pres. part. of *aparoir*, L. *apparēre*, to appear. Orig. plain, manifest, as still in *heir apparent*. Cf. *apparition*.

It is apparent foul play (*King John*, iv. 2).

apparitor [*hist.*]. Public servant of magistrate. L., one who appears.

appeal. F. *appeler*, L. *appellare* or *adpellare*, ? from *pellere*, to drive. The E. form represents the OF. tonic stem, now *appell-*. *Peal* is an aphet. form.

appear. OF. *apareir*, *aparoir*, L. *apparēre*. The F. verb has now been replaced by *apparaître*, VL. **ad-parescere*, exc. in some leg. phrases, e.g. *il appert*, which shows the tonic stem as in the E. word. The aphet. dial. *'pear* occurs in 17 cent. poetry and *peer³* (q.v.) is usu. the same verb, though it may also represent the simple OF. *paroir*.

assomar: to peere up, to appeere, to looke up; apparere, caput erigere (Percyvall).

How bloodily the sun begins to peer
Above yon busky hill (1 *Hen. IV.* v. 1).

paroir: to appeare, or be seene; to peepe out, as the day in a morning, or the sun over a mountain
(Cotg.).

appease. F. *apaiser*, from OF. *à pais* (*à paix*), at peace. For a somewhat similar formation see *atone*. ME. also had *apay*, OF. *apaier*, VL. **adpacare* (see *pay¹*).

appellation. See *appeal*.

append. F. *appendre*, L. *appendere*, to hang to, whence also *appendix* and *appendicitis* (late 19 cent.), inflammation of the vermiform appendix.

apperception. F. *aperception*, from *apercevoir*. See *perceive*.

appertain. From F. *appartenir*. See *appurtenance*.

appetite. F. *appétit*, L. *appetitus*, from *appetere*, to seek after, assail, from *ad* and *petere*, to seek.

applaud. L. *applaudere*, to clap. See *explode*.

apple. AS. *æppel*. North Europ. for L. *malum*, G. μῆλον. Com. Teut., with cognates also in some Celt. and Slav. langs.; cf. Du. *appel*, Ger. *appel*, ON. *epli*, Goth. **aplus*; also Ir. *aball*, OSlav. *abluko*, etc. Ult. origin unknown. In early use a general term for all kinds of fruits other than berries, including even nuts. In fact *apple* and *berry* (q.v.) are the only AS. fruit-names, the rest being of L. or exotic origin. Hence the common use of *apple*, as of F. *pomme*, in describing foreign fruits, e.g. *pine apple* (cf. *melon*, *pomegranate*). The *apple of Sodom*, a mythical fruit described by Josephus, is in Trevisa (1398). The *apple of discord*, inscribed "to the fairest," was thrown by Eris among the gods and goddesses and contended for by Juno, Venus and Minerva. The *apple of the eye*, i.e. pupil, occurs in AS. The *apple-john*, a kind of apple said to be in perfection when shrivelled, is ripe about St John's day (cf. *jenneting*). *Apple-pie bed* and *apple-pie order* are recorded only from 19 cent. and explanations of them are purely conjectural. I find no early example of to *upset the apple-cart*.

appliqué. F. (v. i.).

apply. OF. *aplier* (replaced by *appliquer*), L. *applicare*, lit. to bend to. Oldest meaning, to bring, or come, into contact. *Appliance*, instrument, is first in Shaks.

appoggiatura [*mus.*]. It., from *appoggiare*, to support, VL. **appodiare*, from *podium* elevation. See *appui*, *pew*.

appoint. F. *appointer*, from *à point*, duly, fitly, etc. (see *point*). Earlier sense, to settle, regulate, as in OF. A later ME. meaning, to fit out, equip, survives only in p.p., e.g. *well appointed*. Cf. *embonpoint*.

a poinct: aptly, fitly, conveniently, to purpose, in good time, in due season (Cotg.).

apposite. L. *appositus*, from *apponere*, *apposit-*, to put against.

apposition. In sense of 'Speech day' (St Paul's School) is a var. of *opposition*, in medieval sense of public disputation.

To Paul's school, it being Apposition-day there. I heard some of their speeches...but I think not so good as ours were in our time
(Pepys, Feb. 4, 1663).

appraise. F. *apprécier*, Late L. *appretiare*, from *pretium*, price. Replaced ME. *praise*, OF. *preisier*, Late L. *pretiare*, which developed the same double sense as *esteem*, *value*. L. *pretiare* gave OF. *preisier*, while *pretiat* gave OF. *prise*, whence a new F. infin. *priser*, to value. See *prize*[1].

appreciate. From Late L. *appretiare* (v.s.).

apprehend. L. *apprehendere*, to take hold of. The sense of fearing is ellipt. for the earlier one of understanding or anticipating any emotion.

Oh! let my lady apprehend no fear
(*Troil. & Cress.* iii. 2).

apprentice. OF. *aprentif* (*apprenti*), formed on *apprendre*, to learn (v.i.), with suffix from L. *-īvus*. The *-s* may represent the OF. nom. (cf. *Fitz*) or an orig. pl. (see *bodice*). It may even have been affected by the OF. fem. *aprentisse*. The usu. ME. form was the aphet. *prentice*, *prentis*, as still in *prentice-hand*.

apprise. F. *appris*, p.p. of *apprendre*, to learn, teach, L. *apprehendere*. The verb is formed from the p.p. fem. This is a common process in E. (cf. *comprise*, *value*, *issue*, etc.).

approach. F. *approcher*, Late L. *appropiare*, from *ad* and *propius*, nearer.

At ille: Ne appropies, inquit, huc (*Vulg. Ex.* iii. 5).

approbation. From L. *approbare*, to assent to. See *approve*.

appropriate. From Late L. *appropriare*, from *proprius*, own. See *proper*.

approve. F. *approuver*, L. *approbare*, from *probus*, honest, genuine. In some senses, esp. in the adj. *approved*, it represents rather F. *éprouver*, to test, VL. **ex-probare*. *Approver*, now meaning one who turns King's evidence, esp. in Ireland, was orig. one who offers to prove another guilty, hence informer. The older form is more

usu. *prover*, *provour*, and the *a-* may be artificial (cf. *accomplice*).

esprouvé: proved, tried; approved, experimented
(Cotg.).

approximate. From Late L. *approximare*, from *proximus*, nearest.

appui. In *point d'appui* (mil.), lit. fulcrum, point of support, from F. *appuyer*, VL. **appodiare*, from *podium*, support, etc. See *appoggiatura*, *pew*.

appurtenance. AF. *apurtenance*. Now used as noun from *appertain*, *pertain*, F. *appartenir*, compd. of OF. *partenir*, from L. *pertinēre*. But there was also an OF. *portenir*, from VL. **protinēre*, of which the Norm. form *purtenir* is responsible for the spelling of our word.

apricot. F. *abricot*, Port. *albricoque*, Arab. *al-burqūq*, where *al* is def. art., and *burqūq* is late G. πραικόκιον, from L. *praecoquum* (sc. *malum* or *pomum*), for *praecox*, early ripe, "precocious." The obs. *apricock* represents the Port. or Sp. form, while the spelling *apr-* is perhaps due to fancied connection with L. *apricus*, sunny. Thus Minsh. derives the word from *in aprico coctus*, ripened in a sunny place. Ger. *apricose*, from Du., was orig. pl. (cf. E. *quince*).

The other kindes are soner ripe, wherefore they be called abrecox or aprecox (Lyte's *Dodoens*, 1578).

abricot: the abricot, or apricock, plum (Cotg.).

April. L. *aprilis* (sc. *mensis*), ? a compar. formation from *ab*, *April* being the second month. Has supplanted earlier *avril*, *averil*, etc., from F. Both forms were orig. accented on second syllable. Replaced AS. *Eastermōnath*. With *April fool* cf. Sc. *April gowk* (cuckoo), F. *poisson d'avril*, Ger. *Aprilsnarr*. The origin of the custom is unknown. It is not old in England (17 cent.).

Whan that Aprille [*var.* Averylle], with his shoures soote,
The droghte of March hath perced to the roote
(Chauc. A. 1).

apron. ME. *naperon*, F. *napperon*, from *nappe*, cloth, L. *mappa*, whence *napery*, *napkin* (q.v.), F. *napperon* is now table-centre, *apron* being rendered by *tablier*. For loss of *n-*, *a naperon* becoming *an apron*, cf. *adder*, *auger*, etc. *Apron-string* was orig. leg., meaning tenure in right of one's wife, hence *tied to apron-strings*, under wife's control. Somewhat similar is F. use of *quenouille*, distaff. See also *spindle*.

> She made him to be dight
> In womans weedes, that is to manhood shame,
> And put before his lap a napron white
> (*Faerie Queene*, v. v. 20).

tenir de la quenouille: to hold of, or do homage to, the smocke; his wife to be his master (Cotg.).

apropos. Lit. to the purpose, F. *à propos*. See *purpose*.

apse. Earlier *apsis*, L., G. ἁψίς or ἀψίς, felloe of a wheel (from ἅπτειν, to fit), hence, wheel, vault, orbit. Earliest use is astron.

apt. L. *aptus*, p.p. of archaic *apere*, to fasten.

apteryx. New Zealand bird with rudimentary wings. From G. ἀ-, neg., πτέρυξ, wing. Earlier is *apterous*, wingless, as zool. term.

aqua fortis. Nitric acid. L., strong water. Cf. F. *eau-forte*, etching. *Aqua regia*, royal water, was named by the alchemists from its power of dissolving gold, the royal metal. *Aqua vitae*, alchemists' name for alcohol, was later used for brandy, etc. (cf. *whisky* and F. *eau-de-vie*).

aquamarine. Gem. L. *aqua marina*, sea water, from its colour. Earlier *agmarine*, F. *aigue marine*, "sea-water-greene colour" (Cotg.).

aquarelle. F., It. *acquerello*, water colour, from *acqua*, water.

Aquarius. L. water-bearer, from *aqua*, water. Cf. *aquarium*, introduced c. 1850, with meaning not found in L.; also *aquatic*, F. *aquatique*, L. *aquaticus*.

aquatint. F. *aquatinte*, It. *acqua tinta*, L. *aqua tincta*, from *tingere*, *tinct-*, to stain. Cf. *mezzotint*.

aqua Tofana [*hist.*]. Poison. It. *acqua Tofana*, from name of notorious poisoner (17 cent.).

aqueduct. L. *aquae ductus*, conduit of water, or perh. from obs. F. *aqueduct* (*aqueduc*).

aquiline. L. *aquilinus*, of the eagle, *aquila*. See *eagle*.

Arab. F. *Arabe*, L., G. Ἄραψ, Ἀραβ-. Owing to the great conquests of the Arabs in the East and in S. Europe, and to the medieval pre-eminence of the race in learning and science, Arabic is by far the greatest Semitic contributor to the Europ. langs. The *Arabian Nights* was translated from the *Mille et une nuits* of the F. Orientalist Galland (†1715). *City Arab*, now *street arab*, is recorded 1848 (v. i.).

> City Arabs...are like tribes of lawless freebooters
> (Lord Shaftesbury)

arabesque. F., It. *arabesco*. Earlier also *rebesk*, aphet. It. *rabesco*. The representation of living forms being forbidden by the Mohammedan religion, Moorish architecture uses interlacements and scroll-work as ornament.

arabesque: rebesk-worke; a small, and curious flourishing (Cotg.).

arabis. Plant. MedL., prob. from growing on stony or sandy soil suggesting Arabia.

arable. L. *arabilis*, from *arare*, to plough. See *ear*[2].

arachnid [*zool.*]. From G. ἀράχνη, spider. Cf. F. *araignée*.

Aramaic [*ling.*]. Branch of Semitic langs. which includes Syriac and Chaldee. From *Aram*, Heb. name for Syria. Lang. of Jews after Captivity.

araucaria [*bot.*]. From *Arauco*, province of Chili.

> The grass-plat, from whose centre rose one of the finest araucarias (its other name by the way is "monkey-puzzler"), that it has ever been my lot to see (Kipling, *Actions and Reactions*).

arbalest, arblast [*hist.*]. Cross-bow. OF. *arbaleste* (*arbalète*), Late L. *arcu-ballista*, bow-sling, from L. *arcus*, bow, G. βάλλειν, to throw. Early spellings very varied and influenced by folk-etym., e.g. *allblast*, *alablast*, *arowblast*. Hence surnames *Allblaster*, *Alabaster*.

> Petrone nor harquebuss shall ever put down Sir Arbalest (*Cloister & Hearth*, ch. xxiv.).

arbiter. L., judge, orig. to-comer (cf. *umpire*). Replaced ME. *arbitrour*, from OF. Current sense of *arbitrary* is evolved from the full powers assigned to the *arbiter*.

arblast. See *arbalest*.

arboreous. From L. *arboreus*, from *arbor*, tree. Cf. *arboretum*, L., collection of trees.

arbor vitae. L., tree of life.

arbour. Earliest form *erber*, AF. (*h*)*erber*, OF. *herbier*, L. *herbarium*. Orig. herb-garden, orchard, etc. Mod. spelling has been influenced by L. *arbor*, tree. Sense of shaded walk, bowered retreat, is the latest of all, and here there has been confusion with *harbour*, once a common spelling for *arbour*.

> And in a litel herber that I have,
> That benched was on turves fressh y-grave,
> I bad men sholde me my couche make
> (Chauc. *Leg. Good Women*, 203).

erbare: herbarium, viridarium (*Prompt. Parv.*).

arborata: an arbour or bowre, of boughs or trees (Flor.).

arbutus. L., "a tree growing in Italy, having thicke leaves like a bay" (Coop.). Origin unknown.

arc. F., L., *arcus*, bow.

arcade. F., It. *arcata*, "an arch of a bridge, a bending" (Flor.), from *arcare*, to bend, from L. *arcus*, bow.

Arcadian. From G. Ἀρκαδία, mountainous region in the Peloponnesus, regarded as ideally rural. Cf. *solecism*, *vandal*, etc. *Arcades ambo*, poets or musicians both (Virg. *Ecl.* vii. 4).

Each pull'd different ways with many an oath,
Arcades ambo, id est—blackguards both
(*Don Juan*, iv. 93).

arcana. L., secrets, lit. things enclosed in chests. See *ark*.

arch[1]. Noun. F., VL. *arca, for *arcus*, bow. The native and older word for *arch* is *bow*[1] (q.v.). Hence the church of *St Mary-le-Bow*, or *de Arcubus*, where the *Court of Arches*, or eccl. court of appeal for the province of Canterbury, was orig. held. With to *arch one's eyebrows*, cf. *supercilious*.

arch[2]. Adj. Orig. the prefix *arch-*, as in *archbishop*, used as a noun or adj. to mean principal. G. ἀρχι-, from ἀρχός, chief, from ἄρχειν, to begin; cf. F. *arch-*, *archi-*, It. Sp. *arce-*, Du. *aarts-*, Ger. *erz-*. From constant association with such words as *rogue*, *thief*, *knave*, etc., *arch* acquired the meaning of roguish, mischievous (cf. *arrant*), a meaning now softened down to pleasantly saucy. The oldest of the *arch-* words is *archbishop*. The prefix replaced AS. *hēah-*, high, in *hēah-biscop*, *hēah-engel*, etc.

The most arch deed of piteous massacre
(*Rich. III.* iv. 3).
Arch was her look and she had pleasant ways
(Crabbe).

archaeology. G. ἀρχαιολογία, from ἀρχαῖος, old. Cf. *archaic*.

archetype. See *arch*[2].

archer. F., VL. *arcarius, from *arcus*, bow, used for *sagittarius*, from *sagitta*, arrow.

archi-. See *arch*[2].

Archibald, Archie [*hist.*]. "It was at once noticed at Brooklands that in the vicinity of, or over, water or damp ground, there were disturbances in the air causing bumps or drops to these early pioneers. Some of these 'remous' were found to be permanent, one over the Wey river, and another at the corner of the aerodrome next to the sewage-farm. Youth being fond of giving proper names to inanimate objects, the bump near the sewage-farm was called by them *Archibald*. As subsequently, when war broke out, the effect of having shell bursting near an aeroplane was to produce a 'remous' reminding the Brookland trained pilots of their old friend *Archibald*, they called being shelled 'being *archied*' for short. Any flying-man who trained at Brooklands before the war will confirm the above statement" (Col. C. H. Joubert de la Ferté, I.M.S. ret.).

archil, orchil. Plant, dye. OF. *orchil*, It. *orcello*. Of unknown origin.

archimandrite. Abbot in Eastern Church. Late G. ἀρχιμανδρίτης, from μάνδρα, enclosure, monastery.

Archimedean. From *Archimedes*, mathematician and physicist of Syracuse (fl. 3 cent. B.C.). See *eureka*.

archipelago. Orig. Aegean sea. It. *arcipelago*, from G. ἀρχι- (see *arch*[2]) and πέλαγος, sea. Not a G. compound, but formed in It. (first record 1268) to render MedL. *Egeopelagus*, Aegean Sea. Hence any other sea studded with numerous small islands.

architect. F. *architecte*, L., G. ἀρχιτέκτων, chief builder or craftsman. See *arch*[2]. Orig. E. sense was master-builder.

architrave [*arch.*]. F., lit. chief beam, from G. ἀρχι-, arch[2], and OF. *trave*, L. *trabs*, *trab-*, beam. "A mungril compound" (Evelyn) used as a name for the epistyle.

archives. F., from MedL. *archivum*, G. ἀρχεῖον, public office, from ἀρχή, government (see *arch*[2]). Formerly used in sing. in F. & E., as still in Ger.

archivolt [*arch.*]. It. *archivolto*, *arcovolto*, first element from L. *arcus*, bow (hence not as in *architrave*). For second element see *vault*[1].

archon [*hist.*]. Athenian chief magistrate. G. ἄρχων, pres. part. of ἄρχειν, to rule.

-archy. From G. ἄρχειν, to begin, rule. See *arch*[2].

Arctic. F. *arctique*, L., G. ἀρκτικός, from ἄρκτος, bear, constellation of the Great Bear. Cf. *Antarctic*, opposite Arctic (see *anti-*).

Arcturus [*astron.*]. L., G. Ἀρκτοῦρος, from ἄρκτος, bear, οὖρος, guardian, from its situation at the tail of the Bear. ME. also *artour*, *arctour*, etc.

Canst thou bring forth Mazzaroth in his season? or canst thou guide Arcturus with his sons?
(*Job*, xxxviii. 32).

-ard. F., Ger. *-hart*, hard, strong, used as intens. suffix, becoming depreciatory in F.

& E. Cf. similar use of F. *-aud*, Ger. *-wald*, mighty.

ardent. From pres. part. of L. *ardēre*, to burn; cogn. with *arid*.

Arditi [*neol.*]. It. picked troops. Pl. of *ardito*, bold, hardy (q.v.).

arduous. From L. *arduus*, steep, difficult.

are[1]. Verb. See *be*.

are[2]. Measure. See *area*.

area. L., vacant piece of level ground in town. Arch. sense, with vulgar pronunc. "airy," dates from 17 cent. Hence also F. *are*, unit of extent in metric system.

areca. Port., from Tamil *aḍaikāy*, meaning closely clustered nut.

arefaction. From L. *arefacere*, to make dry. See *arid*.

arena. L., sand, prop. *harena*. Cf. F. *arène*, sand, also "a place to just in, strowed with gravell" (Cotg.).

Areopagite [*hist.*]. Member of the *Areopagus*, court that held its sittings on Mars' Hill, G. ἄρειος πάγος, from Ἄρης, Mars. Late L. *areopagus* (*Vulg.*).

Dionyse Ariopagite, or greet man of comun scole
(Wyc. *Acts*, xvii. 34).

arête [*Alp.*]. Sharp ridge. F., L. *arista*, beard of corn-ear, also fishbone. From OF. *areste* comes techn. *arris*, sharp edge.

areste: the small bone of a fish; also, the eyle, awne, or beard of an eare of corne; also, the edge, or outstanding ridge of a stone, or stone-wall
(Cotg.).

argali. Asiatic wild sheep. Mongol.

argand. Lamp. F., name of inventor (c. 1782).

argent. F., L. *argentum*, silver; cf. G. ἄργυρος, cogn. with ἀργός, white.

argillaceous. From L. *argilla*, clay; cf. G. ἄργιλος, white clay (v.s.).

argol [*chem.*]. Cream of Tartar. In Chauc. AF. *argoil*, of unknown origin.

argon [*chem.*]. Inert component of the atmosphere, discovered and named (1894), by Rayleigh and Ramsay, from G. ἀργός, idle, from ἀ-, neg., ἔργον, work.

Argonaut. Sailor, G. ναύτης, of the *Argo*, G. Ἀργώ, the ship of Jason, from ἀργός, swift, orig. shining. Also applied to a kind of nautilus. Martial connects it punningly with preceding word.

At vos tam placidas vagi per undas
Tuta luditis otium carina.
Non nautas puto vos, sed Argonautas
(*Epigrams*, iii. 67).

argosy [*hist.*]. Earlier *ragusye* (1577), It. *ragusea* (sc. *nave*), ship of *Ragusa*, in

Dalmatia. Chapman spells it *argosea*. The town also is called in 16 cent. E. *Arragouse*, *Aragosa*, etc. Used several times by Shaks. (*Merch. of Ven.*), but now only poet. Cf. *ship of Tarshish*.

argot. Slang. F., from 17 cent. Origin unknown.

argue. F. *arguer*, VL. *argutare* (Propertius), frequent. of *arguere*, to prove, chide, etc., ? orig. to make white and plain (see *argent*). Oldest sense, to bring evidence of, prove, as still in formal speech.

Argus, Argus-eyed. *Argus* had a hundred eyes and was appointed by Juno to watch Io, of whom she was jealous. After his death his eyes were transferred to the peacock's tail.

And full of Argus eyes their tayles dispredden wide
(*Faerie Queene*, i. iv. 17).

argute. Crafty. L. *argutus*, p.p. of *arguere*, to argue.

aria [*mus.*]. It., air (q.v.).

Arian [*theol.*]. Adherent of the heresy of *Arius* (Alexandria, 4 cent.), who denied that Christ was consubstantial with God. See *Athanasian*.

arid. L. *aridus*, from *arēre*, to be dry.

ariel. Gazelle. Arab. *aryil*, var. of *ayyil*, stag.

aright. Prob. for *on right* (see *a-*).

arise. AS. *ārīsan*, intens. of *rise*, by which it is now almost supplanted.

Aristarchus. Great critic. *Aristarchus* of Alexandria (†B.C. 157), critic of Homer.

aristocracy. F. *aristocratie*, OF. also *aristocracie*, from G. ἄριστος, best.

Aristotelian. Of *Aristotle*, G. Ἀριστοτέλης (fl. 4 cent. B.C.).

arithmetic. A restored form, borrowed from L. *arithmetica*, G. ἀριθμητική (sc. τέχνη, art), from ἀριθμός, number. OF. had *arismetique* (*s* for θ), whence ME. *arsmetrik*, understood as L. *ars metrica*. AS. used *tælcræft*, tell-craft, in this sense.

For in the lond ther was no crafty man
That geometrie or ars-metrik kan (Chauc. A. 1898).

ark. AS. *earc*, chest, Noah's ark, etc. An early pre-Christian loan in Teut. langs. from L. *arca*, chest or coffer, cogn. with *arcēre*, to keep off; cf. Du. *ark*, Ger. *arche*, ON. *örk*, Goth. *arka*. Still used in the north (hence name *Arkwright*). In sense of *Noah's ark* the F. form *arche* often occurs in ME. Luther has *Noahs kasten*, chest. The early and wide extension in the Teut. langs. of *ark*, box, chest, suggests that wooden receptacles, other than "dug-outs," were unknown to the early Teutons.

Fac tibi arcam de lignis laevigatis
(*Vulg. Gen.* vi. 14).

Make to thee an ark [*var.* schip] of planed trees
(Wyc. *ib.*).

arche: a cofer, chest; hutch, binne; also, an arke; whence *l'arche de Noë* (Cotg.).

arm¹. Limb. AS. *earm.* Com. Teut.; cf. Du. Ger. *arm*, ON. *armr*, Goth. *arms*; cogn. with G. ἁρμός, joint, Sanskrit *īrmá*, forequarter, and ult. with *art*.

arm². Weapon. F. *arme*, L. *arma*, neut. pl. taken as fem. sing.; cogn. with *arm¹*. Orig. applied to whole of warlike equipment, including device on shield, armorial bearings, as in *King-at-Arms*, herald.

armada. Sp., p.p. fem., L. *armata*, whence also *army* (q.v.). Incorr. *armado* is earlier (*Com. of Errors*, iii. 2).

armadillo. Sp., dim. of *armado*, L. *armatus*, man in armour.

Armageddon. In common use since beginning of the Great War. G. Ἁρ Μαγεδών (*Rev.* xvi. 16), app. *mount of Megiddo*, alluding to *Judges*, v. 19.

That plain of Esdraelon or Megiddo, which has been red with the blood of battles all through history
(*Daily Chron.* Nov. 29, 1917).

Our cavalry, traversing the field of Armageddon, had occupied Nazareth
(Sir E. Allenby, Sep. 22, 1918).

armament. L. *armamentum*, from *armare*, to arm. Of late esp. in *bloated armaments* (Disraeli).

Armenian. Lang. intermediate between the Aryan tongues of Asia and Europe. The survival of the race, in spite of periodical massacre, is remarkable.

Armida. Dangerous enchantress. From Tasso.

armiger. Esquire. L., arm-bearing.

armillary. Shaped like a bracelet, L. *armilla*.

Arminian [*theol.*]. From *Arminius*, latinization of *Harmensen*, Du. theologian (fl. 16 cent.) who opposed Calvin's doctrine of predestination.

armistice. F., ModL. *armistitium*, coined on *solstice* (q.v.). Cf. Ger. *waffenstillstand*.

armorial. From archaic *armory*, heraldry, F. *armoirie*, from *armoier*, to blazon, It. *armeggiare*. See *armoury*.

Armorican. Of Brittany. From L. *Armoricus* (Caesar), Gaulish, prob. "by the sea." See *mere¹*.

armour. Earlier *armure*, F., L. *armatura*. A word which would now have become anti-quarian but for the introduction of the "iron-clad" warship. In this sense *armoured* is recorded for 1862. See *iron-clad, monitor.* More mod. are *armoured train* (Egyptian war) and *armoured car.* Our soldiers at the front all now wear steel helmets, and in to-day's paper (*Daily Chron.* Nov. 9, 1916) is an article on the "Triumph of Armour."

armoury. F. *armurerie*, but gen. treated and felt as derived from E. *armour.* Earlier spellings also show confusion with the related *armory* (see *armorial*) and *ambry* (q.v.).

army. Earliest sense, armed expedition, then, naval force. F. *armée*, p.p. fem. of *armer* (cf. *armada*). The native word was *here* (as in *Hereford, harbour*, etc.; cf. Ger. *heer*). This was superseded by *host¹* (q.v.), and it is probable that *armée* orig. qualified this word, which it has now supplanted.

In the Grete See
At many a noble armee had he be (Chauc. A. 59).

arnica. ModL. (F. & E., 18 cent.). Origin unknown.

aroint [*archaic*]. In Shaks. (*Macb.* i. 3, *Lear*, iii. 4) and hence in Scott and the Brownings. Exact meaning and origin unknown. ? Connected with dial. *rointree*, rowan-tree, mountain-ash, efficacy of which against witches is often referred to in early folklore.

aroma. Restored spelling of ME. *aromat*, spice. F. *aromate*, L. neut. pl. *aromata*, from G. ἄρωμα, seasoning, spice.

aroon [*Ir.*]. Darling. Voc. of Ir. *rún*, secret, secret treasure. For voc. prefix cf. *asthore*. The Ir. word is cogn. with *rune*; cf. ON. *eyrarúna*, darling.

around. Perh. for F. *en rond.* Not in Shaks. or *AV*.

arouse. Formed from *rouse²* (q.v.) by analogy with *rise, arise; wake, awake.*

arpeggio [*mus.*]. It., from *arpeggiare*, to play the harp, *arpa.*

And little sweet arpeggios,
Like harps borne on the air
(Corney Grain, *Polka and Choir-boy*).

arquebus [*hist.*]. Also *harquebuss.* F. *arquebuse*, It. *archibuso.* This from MHG. *hakenbühse* or LG. *hakkebusse*, from Ger. *haken*, hook, *büchse*, gun, lit. box; cf. Du. *haakbus.* So called because orig. rested on a hook when fired. Cf. later F. *arquebuse à croc*, when the meaning was forgotten. The alteration of the first syllable was due to influence of It. *arco*, bow, and *arblast* (q.v.), which the *arquebus* replaced, while It. *buso*, hole, alludes to the barrel. The early vars. are very numerous and include the obs. *hackbut* (q.v.).

arquebuse: an harquebuse, caleever, or hand-gun (Cotg.).
arquebuse a croc: an harquebuse a-crock (somewhat bigger than a musket) (*ib.*).

arrack. Also *rack*[6]. Forms in most Europ. langs., borrowed from various Ind. vernaculars. Arab. *araq*, sweat, juice, as in *araq at-tamr*, (fermented) juice of the date.

arrah. Ir. expletive. In Farquhar (1705) who was of Ir. extraction.

arraign. For earlier *arayne*, with intrusive *-g-*, AF. *arainer*, OF. *araisnier*, VL. **adrationare*, orig. to address. ModF. *arraisonner* is from the OF. tonic stem.

arrange. F. *arranger*, from *à* and *rang* (see *rank*[2]). Orig. to draw up in line of battle, gen. sense first appearing c. 1800. Not in Shaks. or *A V*. See *range*.

There he araynged his men in the stretes (Berners' *Froissart*).

arrant. Var. of *errant* (q.v.). By constant association with *thief*, and later, with *rogue*, *vagabond*, etc., it lost its orig. meaning and came to be regarded as an intens. epithet (cf. *arch*[2]).

Right so bitwixe a titleless tiraunt
And an outlawe, or a theef erraunt,
The same I seye, ther is no difference (Chauc. H. 223).

arras. From *Arras* (Pas-de-Calais), place of manufacture. App. not known in F. in this sense. Cf. *cambric*, *lawn*, etc. *Arras* takes its name from the *Atrebates*.

array. OF. *areer*, *areier* (whence F. *arroi*), VL. **ad-red-are*, the root syllable being Teut. and cogn. with Goth. *garaids*, ready, prepared, E. *ready*, Ger. *rat*, supply, counsel; cf. It. *arredare*, Sp. *arrear*. With Goth. *garaidian*, to make ready, cf. Sc. *graith*, to make ready, from ON., whence also F. *gréer*, to rig (a ship), *agrès*, rigging. Oldest sense of *array* is usu. to marshal an army. See also *raiment*, *curry*[1]. ME. had also the opposite *deray*, *disray*, now replaced by *disarray*.

arrears. From adv. *arrear*, F. *arrière*, L. *ad retro*. Mod. sense (17 cent.) is evolved from the phrase *in arrear*, F. *en arrière*, behind-hand. ME. used *arrearage*, F. *arrérage*.

arrierage: an arrerage; the rest, or the remainder of a paiment; that which was unpaid, or behind (Cotg.).

arrect. L. *arrectus*, upright, from *arrigere*, from *ad* and *regere*.

arrest. OF. *arester* (*arrêter*), VL. **ad-restare*, to come to a halt. Orig. intrans., but had become trans. before adoption in E. See *rest*[2].

arride [*archaic*]. L. *arridēre*, to smile upon.

arrière-ban [*hist*.]. F., perversion of OHG. *hari-ban*, army summons. See *ban*[1], *harry*.

arris. See *arête*.

arrive. F. *arriver*, VL. **adripare*, from *ripa*, shore. Earliest meaning naut. Cf. *accost* and F. *aborder*. Oldest sense in E. is trans., to bring ashore, then, to land.

Iluec arrivet sainement la nacele [vessel] (*Vie de Saint-Alexis*, 11 cent.).

Let us go over unto the other side of the lake.... And they arrived at the country of the Gadarenes (*Luke*, viii. 22–26).

arrogate. From L. *arrogare*, to call to, claim, from *ad* and *rogare*, to ask. Hence *arrogant*, from pres. part.

arrow. AS. *arwe*, a rare word, cogn. with L. *arcus*, bow. More usual AS. words were *flā* and *stræl*. Cogn. with *arrow* are ON. *ör*, Goth. *arhwazna*. The broad arrow, "His Majesty's mark" (1661), is thought by some to have been orig. an anchor, used earlier (1609) on timber reserved for the Navy, but the use of the *broad arrow* as a distinguishing, though not royal, mark, goes back to the 16 cent. and prob. much further. *Arrow-root* (WInd.) is supposed to be so named from the use made of the tubers to absorb poison from wounds, especially those caused by poisoned arrows. But according to some it is from the native name *ara*.

arroyo [*US*.]. Water-course, gully. Sp. *arróyo*, MedL. *arrogium*, cogn. with L. *arrugia*, canal (Pliny).

'Arry. The *NED*. quotes *'Arry on 'Orseback*, from *Punch* (1874).

arse. AS. *ears*. Com. Teut.; cf. Du. *aars*, Ger. *arsch*, ON. *ars*; cogn. with G. *ὄρρος*, rump, where *ρρ* is for *ρσ*.

arsenal. Orig. (16 cent.) dock, wharf. Forms with numerous vars. in most Europ. langs. Immediate source is It. *arsenale*, earlier *arzenà* (Dante). Early It. var. is *darsena* (cf. Sp. *darsena*, Port. *tercena*, F. *darsine*, dock). First found at Venice, the *arsenal* of which is explained by Coryat (1611) as *quasi ars navalis*! The two groups of forms represent Arab. *aççināa'h*, for *al-çināa'h*, the work-shop, or the same preceded by *dār*, a house. For Arab. *dar-sinah* see Borrow's *Bible in Spain*, ch. lvi. For Arab. origin cf. *magazine*.

arsenale: a storehouse for munitions (Flor.).

arcenal: an arcenall; an armorie; a storehouse of armour, artillerie, shipping, or ships (Cotg.).

ataraçana: a docke for ships (Percyvall).

taracena, tarezena, or terecena: a store-house for shipping, or an arsenal (Vieyra).

arsenic. F., L., G. ἀρσενικόν (ἀρρενικόν), yellow orpiment, lit. male. For the fanciful name cf. the etym. suggested for *amalgam*. But the G. word is folk-etym. for Arab. *az-zirnikh*, Pers. *zarnĭkh*, orpiment, from *zar*, gold.

arsis [*metr*.]. G. ἄρσις, raising, from αἴρειν. Orig. of raising and beating time with the foot.

arson [*leg*.]. OF., VL. *arsio-n-*, burning, from *ardēre*, *ars-*. Law F.; cf. *larceny*, *barratry*, etc.

art. F., L. *ars*, *art-*, from a root meaning to fit together which appears also in *arm*[1, 2] and in *artus*, joint. In *Bachelor of Arts*, etc. orig. of the *trivium*, or three arts of medieval study, viz. grammar, logic, and rhetoric, and the *quadrivium*, arithmetic, geometry, music, and astronomy. Hence *artful* once meant learned, cultured, and later, dexterous. For its degeneration cf. *artificial*, *crafty*, *cunning*. So also *artless* was ignorant, clumsy. The *black art* is translated from *nigromancy*, perversion of *necromancy* (q.v.). The same misunderstanding has passed into most Europ. langs. and has led to the parallel adoption of *white* in *white magic*, etc. *Art and part* is prop. a Sc. leg. expression, the contriving and sharing in an act, hence accessory and principal, perh. orig. short for *artifex et particeps*.

artery. L., G. ἀρτηρία, perh. from αἴρειν, to raise. Earlier *arter*, OF. *artaire* (*artère*), used in the sense of windpipe.

artesian. F. *artésien*, of *Artois*, where such a well was first bored (18 cent.). *Artois* is L. adj. *Atrebatensis* (see *arras*).

arthritis [*med*.]. From G. ἄρθρον, joint, cogn. with L. *artus*.

artichoke. A word with, in all langs., an extraordinary number of early vars. due to folk-etym. Cf. F. *artichaut*, It. *carcioffo*, Du. *artisjok*, Ger. *artischoke*. Our form, like the Ger., represents North It. *articiocco*, influenced by *ciocco*, stump, for *arcicioffo*, from Sp. *alcarchove*, Sp. Arab. *alkharsõfa*, Arab. *al-kharshũf*, where *al* is def. art. and

the second part is the name of the plant, the cardoon. First used of the plant with edible flower, and later of the *Jerusalem artichoke* (v.i.), a species of sunflower with edible roots. The spelling is sometimes influenced by F. *chou*, cabbage (see quot. 2). *Jerusalem artichoke* is supposed to be a corrupt. of It. *girasóle*, turning to the sun, a name of the sunflower (cf. *heliotrope*). A further play of the popular imagination has resulted in *Palestine soup*, made of artichokes.

alcarhófa: an artochock (Percyvall).

In time of memory things have bene brought in that were not here before, as...the artichowe in time of Henry the eight (Hakl. 1599).

Error being like the Jerusalem-Artichoake; plant it where you will, it overrunnes the ground and choakes the heart (*NED.* 1641).

article. F., L. *articulus*, dim. of *artus*, joint. Earliest E. sense is rel. (*articles* of belief). As gram. term a direct translation of cogn. G. ἄρθρον, joint.

articulate. From L. *articulare*, to joint (v.s.). *Articulate speech* is intelligibly divided into words and syllables.

artifice. L. *artificium*, making by art. For degeneration of meaning cf. *artful*, *craft*, *cunning*.

Their canoas were as artificially made as any that ever we had seene (Purch.).

artillery. F. *artillerie*, from *artiller*, to equip, usu. connected with L. *ars*, *art-*, via VL. *articulare*; cf. It. *artiglieria*, Sp. *artillaria*. But OF. has also *atillier*, to equip, VL. *apticulare*, from *aptus*, fit, and in MedL. we find a group of words in *atil-* belonging to the same meaning. It seems therefore possible that the *art-* forms are altered by folk-etym. from the *at-* forms. Formerly used of warlike equipment of all kinds.

All maner of artelere, as drumes, flutes, trumpetes, gones, mores pykes, halbardes
      (*Diary of Henry Machyn*, 1550–63).
Jonathan gave his artillery [Wyc. aarmis, Coverd. wappens] unto his lad, and said unto him, Go, carry them to the city (1 *Sam.* xx. 40).

artisan. F., It. *artigiano* (cf. *partisan*[1]). Earlier sense in E. & F. also artist. Ult. form doubtful. ? VL. *artensianus*.

artist, artiste. The latter was introduced (19 cent.) in consequence of the gradual restriction of *artist*, F. *artiste*, It. *artista*, to painting.

arum. L., G. ἄρον. In dial. often *aaron*.

jarrus: wake-robin, starch-wort, rampe, aaron, calves-foot, cuckoe pint (Cotg.).

Aryan [*ling.*]. From Sanskrit *ārya*, noble. Hence also G. 'Αρεία, Eastern Persia, and Pers. *Irān*, Persia. Introduced by Max Müller, as generic name for inflected langs. (see *Caucasian, Japhetic*). Divided into West Aryan, i.e. most Europ. langs. (exc. Basque, Finnish, Hungarian, Turkish) and East Aryan, i.e. Persian, Sanskrit, and the Hindi vernaculars related to the latter. Armenian is regarded as intermediate between the two. Some use *Aryan* of the Asiatic group only.

as. AS. *ealswā, alswā,* i.e. *all so, also,* of which *as* is a worn-down form, the fuller *also* surviving in more emphatic position; cf. Ger. *als, also*. Our *as...as* was orig. *alswa...swa,* or *alswa...alswa,* and for some time the first term remained fuller than the second.

Also salt as ani se (*NED.* c. 1325).

asafoetida, assafoetida. Hybrid MedL. (14 cent.), from *asa*, Pers. *azā*, mastic, L. *fetida*, stinking.

asbestos. L., G. ἄσβεστος, unquenchable, from ἀ-, neg., σβεννύναι, to quench.

ascend. L. *ascendere*, to climb up, from *ad* and *scandere*. *In the ascendant* is from astrology, the *ascendant* being the degree of the zodiac rising above the eastern horizon at a particular moment, esp. at the birth of a child (cf. *jovial, mercurial, horoscope,* etc.). In the sense of superiority, control (over) now usu. replaced by *ascendancy* (18 cent.). The earliest word of the group is *ascension* in rel. sense.

Myn ascendent was Taur and Mars therinne
(Chauc. D. 613).

ascertain. Earlier *acertaine,* to assure or certify, OF. *acertener*, from *à* and *certain*. Later spelt *assertaine*, prob. by analogy with synon. *assure*. Mod. sense has been evolved from the reflex. use, to *ascertain oneself* of something.

ascetic. G. ἀσκητικός, from ἀσκητής, monk, hermit, from ἀσκέειν, to exercise, practise.

Ascètes, c'est-à-dire exercitants (Bossuet).

ascidium [*zool.*]. Mollusc with leathery casing. G. ἀσκίδιον, dim. of ἀσκός, wine-skin.

ascititious. See *adscititious*.

asclepiad [*metr.*]. From Ἀσκληπιάδης, G. poet of uncertain identity.

ascribe. Restored spelling of earlier *ascrive*, OF. *ascriv-,* stem of *ascrire*, L. *ascribere*, from *ad* and *scribere*, to write.

Lest...to my name the victorie be ascrived
(Wyc. 2 Sam. xii. 28).

ascript. See *adscript*.

aseptic. Not septic (q.v.). Prefix is G. ἀ-, neg.

Asgard [*myth.*]. Norse Olympus. ON. *āsgarthr*, home (garth) of the gods.

ash[1]. Tree. AS. *æsc*. Com. Teut.; cf. Du. *esch*, Ger. *esche*, ON. *askr*. Older and dial. forms survive in place-names and surnames, e.g. *Aske, Asquith, Ascham,* etc.

ash[2]. From fire. AS. *asce*. Com. Teut.; cf. Du. *asch*, Ger. *asche*, ON. *aska*, Goth. *azgō*; ult. cogn. with *arid*. *Ash Wednesday*, from penitents sprinkling ashes on their heads, is recorded for 13 cent. Cf. Ger. *aschermittwoch*, F. *jour (mercredi) des cendres*.

ashamed. Prefix may be *a-,· ge-,* or *of-,* all three forms occurring early. Cf. *athirst, aware*.

ashlar. Masonry constructed of flat squared stone, as opposed to *rubble* work. F. *aisselier*, boarding (cf. *aisseau*, wooden tile), from OF. *aissele*, plank, L. *axilla*, dim. of *axis*, whence F. *ais*, plank, board. Meaning has app. been transferred from woodwork to stonework.

Ashmolean Museum. At Oxford. Presented (1677) by Elias Ashmole.

ashore. For *on shore*. See *aboard.* Usual Elizabethan word is *aland*, *shore* (q.v.) not being a native word.

aside. Orig. *on side* (cf. *abed*, etc.), as still in to *put on one side*.

asinine. L. *asininus*, from *asinus*, ass.

as in praesenti. Latin rudiments. Opening words of mnemonic lines on conjugations in Lilley's *Lat. Gram.* (16 cent.).

We will sing to you the mystic numbers of *as in praesenti* under the arches of the Pons Asinorum
(Thackeray).

ask. AS. *āscian* or *ācsian*. WGer.; cf. Du. *eischen*, Ger. *heischen* (OHG. *eiscōn*). Mod. form should have become *ash, esh* (cf. *ash*[1]), forms found in ME. *Ask* is northern, while *ax*, from *ācsian* (v.s.) was literary E. till circa 1600, and is still in gen. dial. use in south and midlands.

Axe, and it shalbe geven you (Tynd. *Matt.* vii. 7).

askance. For *a sconce*. OF. *à esconse*, from an OF. p.p., hidden. Cf. F. *regarder quelqu'un à la dérobée,* from *dérober*, to steal, hide, and E. to *steal a glance*. *Askew* has a similar sense-history.

But let a soldier, that hath spent his bloud,
Is lam'd, diseas'd, or any way distrest,
Appeale for succour, then you looke a sconce
As if you knew him not (*Larum for London*, 1602).

askari. Arab., soldier, from *'askara*, to gather together.

A small warlike class, from whom their askaris, or soldiers, were selected
(D. Lloyd George, Jan. 5, 1917).

askew. See *skew*.

aslant. Very much older than *slant*, which is evolved from it. Earliest form *o-slant, on-slent, on-slont* (c. 1300), while *slant*, noun and verb, is not recorded till 16 cent. There is, however, a ME. verb *slenten*, app. of Scand. origin; cf. archaic Dan. *slente*, Sw. *slinta*, to glide, slip obliquely.

Towards the evening we had a slent of a northerly wind (Raleigh).

asleep. Earlier *on sleep*; cf. *abed, aside*, etc.

For David, after he had served his own generation by the will of God, fell on sleep (*Acts*, xiii. 36).

aslope. Much older than *slope*, adj., noun, and verb (16 cent.), which is evolved from it (cf. *aslant*). Prob. p.p. *āslopen* of AS. *āslūpan*, to slip away (cf. adj. *awake* from p.p. *awacen*). This is cogn. with *slip*.

Asmodeus. Evil spirit of Pers. legend corresponding to *Aeshmā Daēvā* of Iranian myth.

Daemonium nomine Asmodaeus occiderat eos, mox ut ingressi fuissent ad eam (*Vulg. Tobit*, iii. 8).

asp, aspic. OF. *aspe* and ModF. *aspic*, L., G. ἀσπίς, ἀσπίδ-. The form *aspic* (*Ant. & Cleop.* v. 2) is app. a F. alteration of Prov. *aspit*, from *aspid-em*.

aspide: an aspike or aspe (Flor. 1611).

asparagus. L., G. ἀσπάραγος for ἀσφάραγος. Earliest forms were aphet. and *sperage* was usual in 16–17 cents. Cf. F. *asperge*, Gɔr. *spargel*. The perverted *sparrow-grass* was the polite form till 19 cent.

asperge: the herb sparage or sparagus (Cotg.).
Brought home with me from Fenchurch St. a hundred of sparrowgrass, cost 18*d*.
(Pepys, Apr. 21, 1667).
Sparrow-grass is so general that *asparagus* has an air of stiffness and pedantry
(Walker, *Pronouncing Dict.* 1791).

Aspasia. Gifted and influential woman. Famous hetaira, mistress of Pericles. Cf. *Egeria*.

aspect. F., L. *aspectus*, from *aspicere*, to look at, from *ad* and *specere*. Earliest use is astron. (Chauc.).

aspen. Orig. an adj. (cf. *linden*), which has replaced the noun *asp*, though both *asp* and *aps* are still in dial. use. AS. *æspe* and *æps*. Com. Teut.; cf. Du. *esp*, Ger. *espe*, ON. *ösp*. The form *aspen* may be the gen., so common in the compd. *aspen-leaf*; cf. Ger. *zittern wie ein espenblatt*. For association with trembling cf. F. *tremble*, Ger. *zitterpappel*, lit. tremble-poplar. It is curious to note that one could once "quake like an aspen-leaf" with rage.

This Somonour in his styropes hye stood.
Upon this frere his herte was so wood [furious]
That lyk an aspen leef he quook for ire
(Chauc. D. 1665).

asperity. Remodelled on L. OF. *aspreté* (*âpreté*), from L. *asper*, rough, from *ab* and *spernere*, to repel, etc.

aspersion. Earlier used in its lit. sense of sprinkling, from L. *aspergere*, from *spargere*, *spars-*, to scatter. Now, bespattering, slandering, etc., usu. with *cast*.

By the aspersion of the bloud of Jesus Christ (Foxe).

asphalt. Mod. corrected form from F. *asphalte*. In ME. *aspaltoun, aspalt* (cf. It. *aspalto*) was used of "mineral pitch." G. ἄσφαλτος, but not a G. word. Rendered *bitumen* in *Vulg.* and *slime* in *AV*.

It [the Dead Sea] castethe out of the watre a thing that men clepen aspalt (Maundeville).

asphodel. F. *asphodèle*, L., G. ἀσφοδελός. Popular, and earlier, form was *affodil*, whence *daffodil* (q.v.).

asphyxia. G. ἀσφυξία, from ἀ-, neg., σφύξις, pulse.

asphyxia: a cessation of the pulse throughout the whole body; which is the highest degree of swooning and next to death (Phillips).

aspic[1]. Serpent. See *asp*.

aspic[2]. Or *aspic jelly*. F. (neol.). Littré suggests from *aspic*, asp, in allusion to the saying *froid comme un aspic*.

aspidistra. Plant. Coined 1822, app. from G. ἀσπίς, ἀσπίδ-, shield, ? and ἄστρον, star. Though a common word I find it in no mod. dict.

aspire. L. *aspirare*, to breathe towards, from *ad* and *spirare*. Hence *aspirate*, breathed sound.

aspirin. Drug. Ger., fancy trade-name.

asquint. Very much older (1230) than *squint* (16 cent.), which is evolved from it (cf. *aslant, aslope*). Origin obscure. It has been connected with Du. *schuin*, oblique, *schuinte*, obliquity, but these, of late appearance in Du. and of unknown origin, may be from E. The narrow window popularly called a leper's *squint* (hagioscope) is properly *squinch*, related to OF. *escoinson* (*écoinson*), from L. *ex* and *cuneum*, corner, explained by Cotg. as "a scunch; the back part of the jaumbe of a window." This suggests that *asquint* may belong to a Norman word of similar origin (L. *ex* and *cuneum*). Cf. obs. *askoyne*, sidelong, askance.

ass. AS. *assa* and *esol*. With the latter cf. Du. *ezel*, Ger. *esel*, ON. *asni*, Goth. *asilus*. Cogn. forms in Celt. and Slav. langs All from L. *asinus*, prob. of Semit. origin. The *Asses' Bridge* or *Pons Asinorum* (Euclid i. 5) is mentioned in 18 cent., but *bridge of asses* in gen. sense of crux is in Urquhart's *Rabelais*, ii. 26.

assafoetida. See *asafoetida*.

assagai, assegai. Became familiar in connection with the Zulu wars (19 cent.), but is found in Purch. in ref. to Guinea. From Africa, whither it was taken by the Portuguese (cf. *kraal*, *sjambok*). Ult. Arab. *az-zaghāyah*, *az* for *al*, the, and the Berber name of the weapon. Hence, through Sp., F. *zagaie*, formerly *azagaie*, *archegaie*. The latter is found in ME. and *l'archegaie* became by folk-etym. *lancegay*.

azagaya: a kind of a small Moorish spear (Vieyra).

And in his hand a launcegay,
    A long swerd by his side (Chauc. B. 1942).

They of Granade...fought ferseley with their bowes and archegayes (Berners' *Froissart*).

assail. Earlier *asale*, OF. *asalir* (*assaillir*), late VL. *adsalire* (Salic Law), to jump at, for L. *assilire*.

assart [*hist.*]. Cleared forest land. AF., OF. *essart*, from L. *ex-sarire*, *ex-sart-*, to root out, whence MedL. *assartare*.

assassin. F., It. *assassino*, Arab. *hashshāshīn*, eaters of *hashish*, an intoxicant made from hemp. For the pl. form cf. *Bedouin* (q.v.), *cherubim*. The orig. *assassins* were the emissaries of the Old Man of the Mountains, a famous sheikh at the time of the Crusades, who intoxicated themselves before attempting murder.

Hos tam Saraceni quam Christiani "Assisinos" appellant (Roger of Wendover, c. 1237).

assault. Earlier *assaut*, F., VL. **ad-saltus*; cf. *assail*. Mod. spelling is latinized (cf. *fault*). In *assault and battery* (Law F.) the second word is added to distinguish a real from a technical assault.

If one lifts up his cane, or his fist, in a threatning manner at another; or strikes at him, but misses him; this is an assault (Blackstone).

assay. Var. of *essay* (q.v.) which has survived in spec. sense of "trying" metals.

assegai. See *assagai*.

assemble. F. *assembler*, L. *adsimulare* (from *simul*, together), in its later sense of *simul cogere*. Cf. *dissemble*.

assent. OF. *assenter*, L. *assentare*, frequent. of *assentire* (*ad* and *sentire*, to feel), whence ModF. *assentir*.

assert. From L. *asserere*, *assert-*, from *serere*, to join; orig. to maintain a right, as in *self assertive*.

assess. OF. *assesser*, VL. **assessare*, frequent. of *assidēre*, to sit by (*ad sedēre*). Cf. F. *asseoir un impôt*. Aphet. *sess*, *cess*, was once common and the latter (q.v.) is still used in Sc. law. See also *assize*, *excise*.

asseoir: to set, settle, place, plant; also, to cesse, or tax (Cotg.).

assets. Late AF. *assets* (Littleton, 15 cent.), F. *assez*, enough, L. *ad satis*. Orig. in *to have assets*. The artificial sing. *asset* is quite mod. (1884 in *NED.*).

asseverate. For earlier *assever*, L. *asseverare*, to affirm solemnly, from *severus*.

assiduous. From L. *assiduus*, from *assidēre*, to sit down to (*ad* and *sedēre*, to sit).

assiento [*hist.*]. Contract with Spain for supplying slaves to Sp. colonies in America. Sp. *asiento*, as *assent* (q.v.).

assign. F. *assigner*, L. *assignare*, to allot by sign, *signum*. An *assignat*, paper money of first French Republic, was secured (*assigné*) on confiscated Church property.

assimilate. From L. *assimilare*, to make like, *similis*. In phonology *assimilation* is the tendency of a sound to imitate its neighbour, e.g. F. *chercher*, OF. *cercher* (cf. *search*), VL. **circare*. For a good E. example see *snicker-snee*.

assist. F. *assister*, L. *assistere*, to stand by. In the sense of to *be present* etym. meaning survives. Though now regarded as a F. idiom, this was once current E.

assize. Fem. p.p. of F. *asseoir*, VL. **ad-sedēre* for *assidēre*. Found in 12 cent. both of the "sitting," or session, of a court, and of the enactments passed. With the latter sense cf. AS. *gesetnes*, law, and Ger. *gesetz*. *Size* (q.v.) in all its senses is aphet. for *assize*.

associate. From L. *associare*, from *socius*, companion. *Association* football follows the rules of the *National Football Association*.

assoil [*archaic*]. OF. *asoile*, pres. subj. of *asoldre* (*absoudre*), L. *absolvere*, as in *que Dieus asoile*, whom may God absolve, in speaking of the dead, whence ME. *whom* (*whose soul*) *God asoile*, a stock phrase in

Past. Let. Now only poet.; but Sc. *assoilzie*, where *z* is a printer's substitution for an obsolete symbol representing F. *l mouillée* (cf. *tulzie*, *Dalziel*, *Mackenzie*, etc.), is still in leg. use.

L'abbes Adans de Saint Urbain, que Diex asoille, donna grant foison de biaus juiaus a moy
(Joinville).
I absolve, or assoyle from synne, or trespas: je assouls
(Palsg.).
And the holy man he assoil'd us, and sadly we sail'd away (Tennyson, *Voyage of Maeldune*).

assonance. Rudimentary rime consisting in agreement of tonic vowel. From L. *ad* and *sonare*, to sound.

Up and down the City Road,
In and out the Eagle.
That's the way the money goes.
Pop goes the weasel!

assort. OF. *'asorter* (replaced by *assortir*), from *à* and *sorte*. See *sort*.

assuage. OF. *asouagier*, VL. **adsuaviare*, from *suavis*, sweet; cf. Prov. *asuaviar*. For the -*g*- cf. *abridge*. ModF. has rejected it for *adoucir* (from *dulcis*).

addoucir: to sweeten; smooth; asswage (Cotg.).

assume. L. *assumere*, to take to oneself, from *ad* and *sumere*. Hence *assumption*, earliest (13 cent.) in lit. sense, "taking up" of the Virgin Mary.

assure. F. *assurer*, to make sure, from F. *sûr*, OF. *sëur*, L. *securus*.

aster. L., G. ἀστήρ, a star.

aster: a star; also the herb star-wort, spare-wort, or cod-wort (Phillips).

asterisk. L., G. ἀστερίσκος, dim. of ἀστήρ, star.

Wher ever ye seen asterichos...there wijte ye of Ebrue added, that in Latine bokis is not had
(Wyc. *Prol. 2 Chron.*).

astern. See *stern²*; cf. *ahead*, *afloat*, etc.

asthma. G. ἆσθμα, from ἄζειν, to breathe hard.

asthore [*Ir.*]. Darling. Voc. of Ir. *stór*, treasure (store), from E. Cf. *aroon*.

astigmatism [*med.*]. From G. ἀ-, neg., στίγμα, στίγματ-, point, spot.

astir. Not in E. dicts. before 1864. Adopted from Sc. *asteer*, for *on stir*. Cf. *aside*, etc.

astonish, **astony**, **astound.** OF. *estoner* (*étonner*), VL. **extonare*, to thunder-strike, became ME. *astone*, *astoun*, later *astound* (for spurious -*d* cf. *sound¹*, "*gownd*," etc.). From p.p. *astoned* was formed a new verb *astony* (cf. *levy*, *parry*, etc.), replaced after 1500 by *astonish*, a form influenced by verbs in -*ish* (cf. *extinguish*). *Stun* (q.v.)

is the same word, and Ger. *staunen*, *erstaunen* are borrowed from a Swiss-F. form of *estoner*. The meaning of *astonish* has weakened from that of stunning to that of surprising, but *astound* has kept more of orig. sense. F. *étonner* has weakened in the same way.

Si grant cop li dona que tot l'a estouné
(*Renaut de Montauban*).
I astonysshe with a stroke upon the head: jestourdis
(Palsg.).
Sir Edwarde...strake hym such a stroke on the helme with his swerde, that he was astonyed
(Berners' *Froissart*).
Nothing could stop that astonishing infantry
(Napier).

astound. See *astonish*.

Astraea. Goddess of justice in Golden Age, who left earth because of its wickedness and became the constellation Virgo. Cf. *Astræa Redux*, poem by which Dryden celebrated return of Stuarts.

astragal [*arch.*]. Moulding. L., G. ἀστράγαλος, knuckle-bone, in pl. dice.

astrakhan. Wool of very young lambs from *Astrakhan* on the Volga.

astral. Of a star, L. *astrum*, as in *astral spirit*, *astral lamp*. *Astral body*, as used in spiritualistic jargon, appears to be later than the first vol. of the *NED*.

astray. Found earlier as *on stray*, but this is perh. for *astray* by analogy with other E. phrases in *on*, *a*-. See *stray*.

astriction. From L. *astringere*, from *ad* and *stringere*, *strict*-, to tighten.

astride. Prefix is perh. from F. *à*; cf. *apace* and F. *à califourchon*, astride.

astringent. See *astriction*.

astrolabe. OF. *astrelabe*, MedL., G. ἀστρολάβον, from ἄστρον, star, and λαμβάνειν, to take. Used in desperation by Swinburne.

Love alone, with yearning
  Heart for astrolabe,
Takes the star's height, burning
  O'er the babe
(Swinburne, *Poems & Ballads*, 3rd series).

astrology. F. *astrologie*, L., G. ἀστρολογία, telling of the stars, from ἀστήρ, star. Orig. equivalent to *astronomy*, G. ἀστρονομία, arrangement of the stars, but gradually limited by 17 cent. to the supposed influence, etc. of the stars.

Assembled with astronomy
Is eke that ilke astrology,
The which in judgements accompteth
Theffect what every sterre amounteth (Gower).

astronomy. See *astrology*.

astute. L. *astutus*, from *astus*, craft.

asunder. AS. *on sundran*. See *sunder* and *a-*.

asylum. L., G. ἄσυλον, neut. of ἄσυλος, inviolable, from σύλη, right of seizure.

asymptote [*math.*]. G. ἀσύμπτωτος, from ἀ-, neg., σύν, together, πτωτός, apt to fall, from πίπτειν, to fall.

asyndeton [*rhet.*]. Omission of conjunctions, e.g. *veni, vidi, vici*. From G. ἀ-, neg., συνδεῖν, to bind together.

at. AS. *æt*. Com. Teut., but not now used in Du. & Ger.; cf. OSax. *at*, OHG. *az*, ON. Goth. *at*; cogn. with L. *ad*.

atabal [*hist.*]. Sp., Arab. *at-tabl*, for *al-tabl*, the drum. Cf. *tabor*.

ataghan. See *yataghan*.

ataman. See *hetman*.

ataunt [*naut.*]. With all sails set. Orig. of drinking as much as possible. F. *autant*, as much, in *boire d'autant*, *à autant*.

atavism. F. *atavisme*, coined from L. *atavus*, from *avus*, grandfather, with first element cogn. with Goth. *atta*, father (see *Attila*).

atavus: my great grandfathers grandfather
(Coop.).

ataxy. G. ἀταξία, from ἀ-, neg., τάξις, order; cf. *dis-order*. Chiefly in *locomotor ataxy*, loss of control over movements.

"They call ut Locomotus attacks us," he sez, "bekaze," sez he, "it attacks us like a locomotive" (*Private Mulvaney*).

atelier. F., workshop, OF. *astelier*, from *astele*, small plank, ? dim. of L. *hasta*, spear.

Athanasian. From *Athanasius*, a G. name, meaning "immortal" (cf. *ambrosia, tansy*), archbishop of Alexandria (temp. Constantine, 4 cent.), to whom has been attributed the compilation of the *Athanasian creed*.

atheism. F. *athéisme*, coined (16 cent.) from G. ἄθεος, from ἀ-, neg., θεός, god.

atheling [*hist.*]. Son of noble family. AS., from *æthel*, noble, and patronymic suffix *-ing*; cf. Du. Ger. *adel*, nobility, ON. *athal*. Perh. ult. cogn. with Goth. *atta*, father (see *Attila*).

athenaeum. G. Ἀθήναιον. Orig. temple of *Athene* (Minerva) in ancient Athens.

athirst. AS. *ofthyrst(ed)*, p.p. of *ofthyrstan*, where the prefix is intens. Cf. *an-hungered*.

Afyngered [a hungered] and athurst
(*Piers Plowm.* B. x. 59).

athlete. L., G. ἀθλητής, from ἆθλος, contest.

athwart. Formed from *thwart*[1] (q.v.) like *across* from *cross*. Esp. in *athwart hawse* (naut.), across the stem of another ship (see *hawse*), fig. of incommoding, provoking.

You lie, lubber! d—n your bones! what business have you to come always athwart my hause?
(*Peregrine Pickle*, Ch. i).

Atkins. See *Thomas, Tommy*.

Atlantic. L., G. Ἀτλαντικός, from Ἄτλας, Ἀτλαντ-. Orig. applied to that part of the sea near Mount Atlas in Libya (v.i.) on the west coast of Africa. Hence *Atlantis*, mythical island in ocean (Plato).

Atlas. Orig. one of the older G. gods, supposed to uphold the pillars of the world; later, Mount Atlas, regarded as supporting the firmament. The application to a map-book is said to be due to Mercator (q.v.) who used a figure of *Atlas* supporting the globe as a frontispiece (16 cent.).

Thou art no Atlas for so great a weight:
And, weakling, Warwick takes his gift again
(3 *Hen. VI.* v. 1).

atmosphere. L., G. ἀτμός, vapour, σφαῖρα, sphere. First used (1638) in connection with the moon, now believed to have no atmosphere. With mod. fig. senses cf. those of *air*.

atoll. Coral island with lagoon. Maldive *atollon, atol*, the Maldive islands being of such formation. Prob. of Malayalam origin. The word in its present form was popularized by Darwin (1842).

Every atollon is separated from others, and contaynes in itselfe a great multitude of small isles
(Purch.).

atom. F. *atome*, L., G. ἄτομος, indivisible, from ἀ-, neg., τέμνειν, to cut. Cf. *in-divid-ual*. The mod. *atomic theory* (chem.) is due to Dalton (1805).

atome: a moate in the sunne; a thing so small, that it cannot be divided (Cotg.).

atomy [*dial.*]. With mixed meaning from *atom* and *anatomy* (q.v.), the latter becoming colloq. *atomy*.

Thou atomy [i.e. skeleton], thou (2 *Hen. IV.* v. 4).
I suppose you have come here to laugh at us, you spiteful little atomy (*Water-Babies*).

atone. Orig. to reconcile, from adv. phrase *at one*, and preserving old pronunc. of the latter word, as in *only, alone*. In ME. *one, onement* were used in sense of *atone, atonement*. *Atonement* is in the *AV.*, but not *atone*. Cf., for the formation, OF. *aduner, aüner*, to unite, reconcile.

After this was God at one [*Vulg.* repropitiatus] with the londe (Coverd. 2 *Sam.* xxi. 14).

atonic. Unstressed. From G. ἀ-, neg. and *tonic* (q.v.).

atrabilious. From L. *atra*, black, *bilis*, bile, used orig. to translate G. μελαγχολία. See *melancholy*.

atrip [*naut.*]. Used of the anchor when it has just left the ground. Also of the sails, when ready for trimming. From *trip* (q.v.), in the sense of start. Cf. *apeak*.

atrocious. From L. *atrox, atroc-*, cogn. with *ater*, dark, treacherous.

atrophy. F. *atrophie*, L., G. ἀτροφία, from ἀ-, neg., τρέφειν, to nourish.

atropine. Poison. From *atropa*, botanical name of the night-shade, G. Ἄτροπος, inflexible, one of the Fates, from ἀ-, neg., τρέπειν, to turn.

attach. F. *attacher*; cf. It. *attaccare*, Sp. *atacar*. Ident. with *attack* (q.v.). Orig. to fasten to, tack on. The root syllable is of doubtful origin. ? Cf. *tag*[1].

attack. F. *attaquer*, It. *attaccare*. Not in Shaks. Borrowed by F. (16 cent.) to the indignation of Henri Estienne (v.i.). It. meaning is to join, F. & E. sense developing from *attaccare battaglia*, "to joyne battell" (Flor.).

Ce mot "attaquer" participe du françois "attacher" et de l'italien "attacar."…Les courtisans trouvent plus beau "attaquer" que "attacher"
(Estienne, *Nouveau françois italianisé*).

attain. F. *atteindre, atteign-*, L. *attingere*, from *ad* and *tangere*, to touch. See *attainder, attaint*. All of these may be rather from OF. *ataindre*, VL. **attangere*.

attainder. F. *atteindre* (v.s.), used as noun. Law F. Cf. *misnomer, rejoinder, remainder*, etc. See *attain, attaint*.

attaint. Orig. p.p. and so used in E. Then it became verb and noun, to condemn by *attainder* (q.v.), conviction by *attainder*. In sense of touching, infecting, etc., it has been supplanted by the aphet. form *taint* (q.v.). For the form (**attinctus* for *attactus*) and grammatical development, cf. *paint* (q.v.). In ME. *attain, attaint* are used indifferently in various senses.

Atteint they were by the lawe,
And demed for to hong and drawe (Gower).

attar. Earlier is the popular form *otto* (of roses). Pers. *atar-gul*, essence of roses, from Arab. *'itr*, perfume.

attempt. OF. *attempter*, latinized form of *attenter*, L. *attemptare*, to try.

attend. F. *attendre*, to wait, in OF. also in E. senses, L. *attendere*, lit. to stretch towards. Cf. *attention*. For development of current sense cf. *to wait on*.

attenuate. From L. *attenuare*, to make thin, *tenuis*.

attest. F. *attester*, from L. *attestari*, to bear witness, *testis*, to.

Attic, attic. Of *Attica*, Athens; hence, elegant, refined, etc. The architectural *attic*, orig. a small decorative order placed above a greater (usu. Attic) order, is the same word. An attic is upright, a garret is in a sloping roof.

Attico lepore tincti sales: sharpe and wittie sentences full of pleasauntnesse (Coop.).
Shall I, I say, suppress my Attic salt?
(Byron, *Hints from Horace*).

Attila. King of the Huns (†453), as type of devastating invader. The name (cf. OHG. *Etzel*) appears to have been given to him by the Goths and is dim. of Goth. *atta*, father; cf. Russ. title "little father." This *atta*, found in other Aryan langs., is of the type of *daddy*.

A rapid succession of Alarics and Attilas passed over the defenceless empire [of India] (Macaulay).

attire. Orig. to equip in any way. For mod. restriction cf. *apparel*. F. *attirer*, from *tirer*, to draw, etc. See *tire*[2].

attitude. F., It. *attitudine*, L. *aptitudo, aptitudin-*, from *aptus*, fit. Orig. (17 cent.) a techn. term of art. Hence to *strike an attitude*, like a statue, etc. Found also as *aptitude* (v.i.).

The several statues that we see with the same air, posture, and aptitudes (Addison).

attorney. From p.p. of OF. *atorner*, to appoint, constitute, from *à* and *tourner*, to turn. Orig. one duly appointed to act for another, as still in *power of attorney*. The title, often used contemptuously (pettifogger), was abolished in 1873 and absorbed in *solicitor*. It survives in *attorney general*, orig. an attorney with complete powers, as opposed to the obs. *attorney special*, but now only applied to the first law-officer of the crown.

Des attournez sount acuns generals, acuns especials
(Britton, 1292).
Orl. Then, in mine own person, I die.
Ros. No, faith, die by attorney
(*As you like it*, iv. 1).
Johnson observed, that "he did not care to speak ill of any man behind his back, but he believed the gentleman was an attorney" (Boswell).

attract. From L. *attrahere*, from *ad*, to, *trahere, tract-*, to draw.

attribute. The noun is the older. It is used in two senses in Portia's speech (*Merch. of Ven.* iv. 1). F. *attribut*, L. *attributum*, from *attribuere*, from *ad*, to, *tribuere*, to pay (tribute).

attrition. From L. *atterere*, from *terere*, *trit-*, to rub. In theol. sense an imperfect sorrow not amounting to *contrition*.

aubade. Morning music. F., Prov. *albada*, from *alba*, dawn. Cf. *serenade*.

auberge. Inn. F., from Prov., ult. ident. with *harbour* (q.v.).

aubergine. Fruit. F., Catalan *alberginera*, Arab. *al-bādindjān*; cf. Sp. *berengena*, *alberengena*.

auburn. OF. *auborne*, L. *alburnus*, whitish. ME. vars. *abrune*, *abroune* point to confusion with *brown* (v.i.), and this has affected the meaning of the word, formerly flaxen, now bright brown.

alburno: that whitish colour of womens haire which we call an alburne or aburne colour (Torr.).

The word probably is merely A *bron*, i.e. *brown* (Richardson).

auction. L. *auctio-n-*, from *augēre*, *auct-*, to increase. Cf. F. *vente aux enchères*, from *enchérir*, to make dearer, and Ger. *versteigerung*, lit. raising. In a *Dutch auction* goods are put up at a prohibitive price which is gradually lowered, app. from the practice of Dutch fishermen. With the north-country *sale by roup*, i.e. cry, cf. the, chiefly Irish, *sale by cant*, L. *cantus*.

auctio: open sale, or port sale, of private goods (Coop.).

enchere: a bidding, or out-bidding; the making or offering, the raising or enhauncing, of a price; any portsale, outrope, or bargaining, wherein he that bids most for a thing is to carry it (Cotg.).

audacious. From L. *audax*, *audac-*, from *audēre*, to dare, from **audus*, for *avidus*, greedy.

audience. F., L. *audientia*, from *audire*, to hear.

audit. L. *auditus*, a hearing, hence examination of accounts. *Audit ale*, specially strong brew at certain Oxf. and Camb. colleges, was orig. for the refreshment of college tenants who appeared on audit day.

Augean. Usu. with *stable*, from the cleansing of the stables of *Augeas*, king of Elis, one of the labours of Hercules.

auger. ME. *nauger*, AS. *nafugār*, from *nafu*, nave of a wheel, *gār*, borer, spear, with *n*-lost as in *adder*, *apron* (q.v.), as also in Du. *avegaar*, for older *navegaar*.

noger: that instrument of iron that we use to bore holes in the stone with (*Miners Dict.* 1747).

aught. AS. *āwiht*, from *ā*, ever, *wiht*, thing, creature, "whit," "wight," thus, e'er a whit. Hence ME. *oht*, *oght*, later *ought*, usual E. form up to c. 1550. Cf. *naught*,

AS. *nāwiht*, ne'er a whit, and Ger. *nicht*, not, OHG. *neowiht*, for *ni eo wiht*.

augment. F., L. *augmentare*, from *augēre*, to increase. See *eke*.

Augsburg, Confession of [*hist.*]. See *Augustan*.

augur. L., prob. from *avis*, bird (cf. *auspices*). The older form was *auger* and the second element is prob. from L. *gerere*, to manage, etc. Hence *inaugurate*, to take omens before action.

inaugurare: to gesse or divine by byrdes (Coop.).

August, august. Month (in Republican Rome *sextilis*) named after Emperor *Augustus*. Replaced native *wēod-mōnath*, weed month. In ME. also *aust*, OF. *aoust* (*août*). The name is L. *augustus*, venerable, from *augur* (q.v.), or perhaps from *augēre*, to increase. Hence *Augustan*, period of perfection in literature regarded as due to royal patronage. The *Augustan Confession* was drawn up (1530) by Luther and Melanchthon at Augsburg (*Augusti burgus*). The *Augustine*, or *Austin*, *Friars* took their name from *St Augustine*, bishop of Hippo (fl. 4 cent.).

Un Auguste aisément peut faire des Virgiles (Boileau).

auk. Sw. *alka* or Dan. *alke*, ON. *ālka*; cogn. with G. ἀλκυών, halcyon. Hence *great auk's egg*, rare curiosity.

auld lang syne. Sc., old long since. Popularized by Burns' song. Cf. *auld Reekie*, Edinburgh.

aulic [*hist.*]. Imperial Ger. council; later, Austrian war council. L. *aulicus*, from G. αὐλή, court.

aunt. OF. *ante*, L. *amita*, dim. of a lost baby-word of the *papa* type (cf. Ger. *amme*, nurse, and see *nun*, *pope*). Mod. F. *tante*, found from 13 cent., is due to infantile reduplication *antante* (cf. *papa*, etc.). *Naunt*, for *mine aunt*, was once common (cf. *nuncle*) and is still used in dial. *Aunt Sally*, first recorded for 1861 (*NED.*), has become at F. fairs *âne salé*. An elaboration of the same sport was known c. 1900 as *Emma*.

aura. L., G. αὖρα, breath, breeze.

aureate. L. *aureatus*, from *aurum*, gold.

aurelia. Formerly used for *chrysalis* (q.v.). It., lit. golden, from L. *aurum*.

aureole. Now used for halo and wrongly connected by some writers with *aura*, air, emanation. Prop. the golden disc surrounding holy personages in early pictures. Cf. earlier *aureola* (sc. *corona*), the celestial golden crown of martyrs, virgins, and doctors.

auricula. Plant, "bear's ear," from shape of leaves. L., dim. of *auris*, ear. Cf. *auricular*, earliest in *auricular confession* (16 cent.).

auriferous. From L. *aurum*, gold.

aurochs. Extinct wild ox (*urus* in Caesar). Also wrongly applied to an extant bison (Lithuania). Ger. *auerochs*, OHG. *ûrohso*, whence L. *ûrus*; cf. AS. *ûr*, Sanskrit *usrá*, bull. For second element see *ox*.

Aurora Borealis. Named by Gassendi (1621). For *aurora* see *east*, for *borealis* see *boreal*.

auscultation. From L. *auscultare*, to listen, where *aus-* is for *aur-* (*auris*, ear).

ausgleich [*hist.*]. Austro-Hungarian compromise. Ger., compromise, "levelling out." See *like*.

A serious factor for discussion is the question of the *ausgleich* (*Sunday Times*, June 17, 1917).

auspice. F., L. *auspicium*, from *auspex*, *auspic-*, from *avis*, bird, *-specere*, to behold. Cf. L. *haruspex*, one who inspects entrails.

Aussey [*war slang*]. Australian soldier.

austere. F. *austère*, L., G. αὐστηρός, making the tongue rough, or dry, from αὔειν, to dry. Formerly in lit. sense, of fruits, wines, etc. In ME. often *austern*, the parasite *-n* being partly due to popular connection with *stern*[1].

I dredde thee, for thou art an austerne [*var.* a stern] man (Wyc. *Luke*, xix. 21).

Austin friar. See *August*.

Austral, Australia, Australasian. L. *australis*, from *Auster*, the south wind. Orig. used of the southern hemisphere generally, Polynesia, etc. called collectively *terra australis*.

authentic. F. *authentique*, L., G. αὐθεντικός, from αὐθέντης, one who does things for himself, from αὐτός, self, and *-έντης*, cogn. with L. *sons*, *sont-*, guilty, orig. pres. part., "being," the one it was.

author. ME. *autor*, *autour*, F. *auteur*, L. *auctor-em*, lit. increaser, promoter, from *augêre*, *auct-*, to increase. Mod. spelling seems to be accidental, and it is not known at what date it altered the pronunc. It appears also in *authority*, *authorize*. The first Bible transl. with title *authorized* is the Bishops' Bible (1540).

Dressed in a little brief authority
(*Meas. for Meas.* ii. 2).

auto-. G. αὐτο-, from αὐτός, self.

autochthon. Aborigine. Usu. pl., from G. αὐτόχθονες, of the land, χθών, χθον-, itself.

autocrat. G. αὐτοκρατής, ruling by oneself. Extinct as pol. type exc. in new republics.

auto-da-fé. Port., act of the faith. Judicial sentence of the Inquisition, esp. public burning of heretics.

For once we'll be gay;
A grand Auto-da-fé
Is much better fun than a ball or a play
(*Ingoldsby*).

autograph. F. *autographe*, G. αὐτόγραφος, from γράφειν, to write.

Autolycus. "A snapper-up of unconsidered trifles" (*Winter's Tale*, iv. 3).

A few items which the Autolycus of social history will find acceptable
(*Times Lit. Supp.* May 8, 1919).

automaton. Earlier *automate*, from F. (Rabelais), G. αὐτόματον, self-moving.

automate: anything that goes by a vice, or peise, yet seemes to move of itselfe (Cotg.).

Automedon. Skilled driver. Name of charioteer of Achilles. Cf. *Jehu*.

automobile [*neol.*]. F., from *mobile* (q.v.). Cf. later *autobus*, *autocar*, etc.

autonomy. G. αὐτονομία, self rule, from νόμος, law.

autopsy. G. αὐτοψία, lit. seeing for oneself, its earliest sense also in E. See *optic*.

autumn. F. *automne*, L. *au(c)tumnus*, perh. cogn. with *augêre*, *auct-*, to increase. Has replaced, in sense of season, native *harvest* (q.v.).

auxiliary. From L. *auxilium*, help, from *augêre*, *aux-*, to increase.

avadavat. Indian bird. Prop. *amadavat*. From Ahmadabad (Gujerat), i.e. city of Ahmed.

avail. App. from obs. *vail*, from tonic stem of F. *valoir*, L. *valêre*, to be worth, by analogy with other verbs of double form (*mount*, *amount*, *wake*, *awake*, etc.). There is no corresponding OF. verb recorded, but Godef. has the noun *avail*, advantage, increase, which seems to indicate that such a verb may have existed.

To hym not vailith his preching,
All helpe he other with his teching
(*Romaunt of Rose*, 5763).

avalanche. F., altered, by association with F. *avaler*, to descend (*à val*), from earlier *lavanche*, Prov. *lavanca*; cf. Piedmont *lavanca* (whence by metath. It. *valanga*). With changed suffix from Late L. *labina*, landslide (from *labi*, to glide), whence Swiss F. (Engadine) *lavina*, Ger. *lawine*.

avarice. F., L. *avaritia*, from *avarus*, greedy, from *avēre*, to desire; cf. *avidity*. *Beyond the dreams of avarice* is app. due to Dr Johnson, in ref. to the potentialities of Barclay and Perkins' brewery.

avast. *NED.* suggests a worn down form of Du. *houd vast*, hold fast. More prob. seems Port. *abasta*; cf. It. *basta*, from *bastare*, to suffice, of unknown origin.

abasta: v. imp.: enough, or it is enough (Vieyra).

avatar. Sanskrit *avatarana*, descent, lit., down-passing (of a Hindu deity).

avaunt. F. *avant*, VL. *ab-ante*. Orig. onward (cf. *move on*).

ave. L. imper., from *avēre*, to fare well. Short for *Ave Maria*, *Ave Mary*. Cf. *paternoster*.

Ave Maria gratia plena; Dominus tecum; benedicta tu in mulieribus (*Vulg. Luke*, i. 28).

avenge. OF. *avengier*, from *vengier* (*venger*), L. *vindicare* (cf. *manger* from *manducare*). See *vindicate*. The *avenger of bloude* (Coverd. *Joshua*, xx. 5) is for earlier *blood wreker* (Wyc.).

avens. Plant. OF. *avence*; cf. MedL. *avencia*. Origin unknown.

aventurine. Glass, quartz. F., It. *avventurino*, "la pierre artificielle étant produite par de la limaille jetée *à l'aventure* sur du verre en fusion" (*Dict. Gén.*).

avenue. Orig. an approach. From p.p. fem. of OF. *avenir* (now *advenir*), L. *advenire*. Cf. *alley*[1]. Spec. application to a way bordered, and shadowed, by trees seems to be due to Evelyn.

aver. F. *avérer* (cf. It. *avverare*), VL. **adverare*, from *verus*, true. F. sense is to recognize as true.

average. First appears in E. c. 1500; cf. F. *avarie* (12 cent.), Sp. *averia*, It. *avaria*, Du. *haverij*, Ger. *haverei*, etc. It has passed through the meanings of customs impost, extraordinary expenses, damage at sea (usu. sense of F. *avarie*), equitable distribution of resulting loss, to the modern math. sense, which is peculiar to E. The E. form may be corrupted from a plur. *avarais*, used by the same author (Rich. Arnold) in whom we first find *average*. This would be facilitated by the numerous naut. words in -*age*, e.g. *pilotage*, *primage*, *tonnage*, etc., and by possible association with archaic Sc. *average*, *arrage*, a feudal due, also of unknown origin. The word is naut. and from the Mediterranean, which makes Arab. origin possible, but its etym. is still unsolved,

though "few words have received more etymological investigation" (*NED.*). The ModG. form ἀβαρία suggests possible connection with βάρις, ship, ἀβαρός, unloading. But this, and also Arab. '*awār*, damaged ware, may be from It. or Sp.

Avernus. Bottomless pit. *Lago Averno* in Campania, L. *Avernus*, taken, from its poisonous exhalations, as mouth of Hades (*Aen.* vi. 126). Trad. from G. ἀ-, neg., ὄρνις, bird, because birds flying over the lake were to die from poison.

Facilis descensus Averno;
Noctes atque dies patet atri janua Ditis
(*Aen.* vi. 126).

averroism. Doctrine of mortality of soul. From *Averroes* (Ibn Roshd), Arab. philosopher of Cordova (†1225).

averruncator. Gardening tool. From L. *averruncare*, to ward off, through mistaken connection with L. *eruncare*, to weed out. App. this confusion existed in L.

avert. L. *avertere*, *ab* from, and *vertere*, to turn. Cf. *averse*, turned away, *aversion*.

Avesta. See *Zend*.

aviary. L. *aviarium*, from *avis*, bird.

aviator, aviation. F. *aviateur*, *aviation*, from L. *avis*, bird.

avidity. From L. *aviditas*. See *avarice*.

aviso. Despatch boat. Sp., lit. intelligence, advice.

avizandum, at [*Sc. leg.*]. For private consideration. From MedL. *avizare*, to advise.

avocado. Pear. See *alligator*.

avocation. L. *avocatio-n-*, from *avocare*, from *ad* and *vocare*, to call. Cf. *advowson*.

avocet, avoset. Bird. F. *avocette*, It. *avosetta*. Origin unknown. Derivation from *avis* is unlikely, as this hardly appears in the Rom. langs., being displaced by VL. *avicellus*, *aucellus* (F. *oiseau*).

avoid. OF. *esvuider*, to empty out, with change of prefix, as in *award*. See *void*. Orig. to empty out, eject, get rid of, or intrans. to withdraw. Cf. sense-development of *evacuate*. Mod. sense corresponds to F. *éviter*, with which it may have been confused. ME. *voiden* may be an aphet. form or from the simple *vuidier* (*vider*). Cf. ModF. *vider les lieux*, to "clear out."

He shal lyve with thee and avoide thee out [*Vulg.* evacuabit te, *AV.* make thee bare]
(Wyc. *Ecclesiasticus*, xiii. 6).

Hence, quoth the Lord, hence, hence, accursed race, Out of my garden: quicke, avoyd the place [du Bart. vuidez-moi ce verger]
(Sylv. *The Deceipt*).

avoirdupois. Mod. corrupt. of AF. *averdepeis*, *averdepois*, OF. *aveir* (*avoir*) *de pois*, goods sold by weight, as distinguished from those sold by measure or number. The infin. *aveir* (*avoir*), goods, property, survives in Sc. *avers*, farm beasts. *Pois* is L. *pensum* (*pendere*, to weigh), whence OF. *peis*. ModF. *poids* is due to mistaken association with *pondus*. In ME. and later very often *haber-* (see *haberdasher*).

avouch. Now usu. *vouch*. OF. *avochier*, L. *advocare*. This became regularly *avoer*, *avouer*, whence E. *avow*, OF. *avochier* being a learned form due to the common use of *advocare* in leg. L. Orig. to summon, appeal to, as an authority or warrant.

avow. See *avouch*.

avulsion. From L. *avellere*, to tear away, from *ab* and *vellere*, *vuls-*, to tear.

avuncular. Of an uncle (q.v.).

await. ONF. *awaitier*, OF. *agaitier*, to lie in wait for. See *wait*. Orig. sense as below.

I awayte, I lie in wayte of a person to marke what he dothe or sayeth; je aguayte (Palsg.).

awake, awaken. Two separate verbs are mixed up, viz. AS. *āwæcnan*, earlier *on-* (strong), whence past *awoke*, and *āwacian* (weak), whence *awaked*. The predicative adj. *awake* is for the p.p. *awaken* (cf. *ago*). Both verbs were orig. intrans., the trans. sense being expressed by ME. *awecchen*, AS. *āweccan* (cf. *fall, fell*; Ger. *wachen, wecken*).

He was slapende..., and hi awehton hine
(*AS. Gosp. Mark*, iv. 38).

award. ONF. *eswarder*, or noun *esward*, for OF. *esgarder, esgard* (*égard*), with prefix changed as in *avoid*. The noun is prob. the older word. Orig. a decision after examination. *Agard* is equally common in AF. See *guard, ward*.

esgard: respect, heed, regard, observation; advisement, consideration, reckoning, account; also, a report made, or account given, of (Cotg.).

aware. ME. *iware*, AS. *gewǣr*; cf. Ger. *gewahr*, aware. Also reduced to *ware* (see *beware*).

away. AS. *onweg, āweg*, on the way. Also, as prefix, sometimes reduced to *weg* (see *wayward*); cf. similar use of Ger. *weg*, for earlier *enwec, in wec*, in *wegwerfen*, to throw away, etc. To *give away* in slang sense in US.

awe. ME. had both *eye*, AS. *ege*, fear, and *aw*, ON. *agi*, the latter of which has prevailed. Com. Teut.; cf. Goth. *agis*, OHG. *egiso*. Current sense is due to Bibl. use of the

word. The slang meaning of *awful, awfully* (19 cent.) has numerous parallels in E. and other langs., e.g. *a devilish pretty girl*, or, conversely, a *jolly miserable day*.

awkward. Orig. adv., formed with suffix *-ward* from obs. *awk*, back-handed, "froward," etc., ON. *afug*, turned the wrong way (cf. Sw. *afwug*), a derivative of *af*, away, off. Cogn. forms are found in OHG. & MHG. Cf. *froward*. See also quot. from Palsg. s.v. *backward*.

auke, or angry: contrarius, bilosus, perversus
(*Prompt. Parv.*).
auke, or wronge: sinister (*ib.*).
awkwarde, frowarde: pervers (Palsg.).

awl. AS. *æl*. Com. Teut.; cf. Du. *aal*, Ger. *ahle* (OHG. *āla*), ON. *alr*; ? cogn. with L. *aculeus*, needle. From a lengthened form, OHG. *alansa* (with suffix as in *sense, scythe*), comes F. *alène*, awl (see *anlace*).

awn. Beard (of barley, etc.). ON. *ögn*. Com. Teut.; cf. AS. *egenu*, husk, Ger. *ahne* (OHG. *agana*), Goth. *ahana*; cogn. with L. *acus*, needle, G. ἄκανος, thistle.

awning. First occurs in Capt. John Smith. Origin unknown.

Wee did hang an awning (which is an old saile) to... trees to shadow us from the sunne
(Capt. John Smith, 1624).

awry. Earlier *on wry*. See *wry*.

Owthir all evin, or on wry (Barbour).

axe. AS. *æx*. Com. Teut.; cf. Du. *aaks*, Ger. *axt* (OHG. *acchus*), ON. *öx*, Goth. *aqizi*; cogn. with G. ἀξίνη and perh. with L. *ascia* (? for **acscia*). *Curtle-axe, pickaxe* (q.v.) are unrelated. The expression *axe to grind* is from US. politics (cf. *wire-pulling*) and originated in an experience of childhood related by Franklin. A stranger persuaded him to play truant in order to help grind an axe and then left him in the lurch. For another phrase due to Franklin see *whistle*.

axil [*bot.*]. Angle. L. *axilla*, armpit, whence also *axillary* (med.).

axiom. F. *axiome*, L., G. ἀξίωμα, from ἀξιοῦν, to think fit, require.

axis. L., axle, pivot, from *agere*, to move.

axle. First in compd. *axle-tree*, ON. *öxul-trē*, which in ME. superseded the native *ax-tree*, from AS. *æxe*; cf. Ger. *achse* (OHG. *ahsa*); cogn. with L. *axis*. *Axle* is not found alone till 17 cent.

axolotl. Mexican lizard. Aztec, lit. water-servant.

ay, aye. Ever. ON. *ei.* Com. Teut.; cf. AS. *ā*, Ger. *je* (OHG. *eo, io*), Goth. *aiw*; cogn. with L. *aevum*, G. αἰών. AS. *ā* gave ME. *oo*, which survived some time in the combined *for ay and oo*, equivalent to mod. *for ever and ay*. See also *ever*.

ayah. Port. *aia*, nurse, fem. of *aio*, tutor; cf. Sp. *ayo*, It. *aio*. It came to us from India; cf. *padre, tank*, etc. ? Of Goth. origin, and cogn. with Ger. *hegen*, to cherish.

aye. Yes. In dial. and H. of C. Origin uncertain. Although first recorded for 16 cent., always as *I*, it must, from its extensive dial. use, be much older in colloq. speech. It may be the pronoun *I*; cf. ME. *nic*, no, lit. not I. Another theory is that it is *ay*, ever (v.s.), used as an intens. affirmation, and this theory is supported by its opposite *nay* (q.v.).

Nothing but No and I, and I and No (Drayton).

aye-aye. Lemur (Madagascar). Prob. from cry. The word came through F.

azalea. Named by Linnaeus. Fem. of G. ἀζαλέος, dry.

azarole. Neapolitan medlar. F. *azerole*, Sp. *azarolla*, Arab. *az-zu'rūr*, where *az* is for *al*, def. art. Cf. *assagai*.

azedarac. F. *azédarac*, lilas de Chine, Sp., Arab., Pers. *āzād dirakht*, free tree.

azimuth [*astron.*]. Arc from zenith to horizon. F. *azimut* (cf. It. *azzimutto*), Arab. *as-sumūt*, for *al-sumūt*, pl. of *samt*, way, whence *zenith* (q.v.).

azote. Old name for nitrogen. F., coined by Lavoisier from G. ἀ-, neg., ζωή, life.

Azrael. Angel of Death. Made invisible at entreaty of Mohammed. Heb., help of God.

Aztec. People and native lang. of Mexico. ? From native name, "heron," of an individual clan.

azure. Orig. the precious stone *lapis lazuli*, later, blue in heraldry. F. *azur* (*Chanson de Roland*); cf. It. *azzurro*, Sp. *azul* (OSp. *azur*), from Arab. *lazward*, Pers. *lajward*, a place in Turkestan whence the stone was procured. The *l-* is supposed to have been lost in the Rom. langs. through being taken as the def. art. Cf. *ounce²*. But it may be noted that Arab. for blue is *azraq* (e.g. *Bahr-al-azraq*, the Blue Nile), which may have affected the word.

B. Not to *know a B from a bull's foot* is recorded c. 1400.

baa. Imit. Recorded for 16 cent., but of course a most ancient word. Cf. *bow-wow*.

He spake to them in the cattels language, which was never changed at the confusion of Babel, which was "moath" for oxen and kine and "baa" for sheepe; which language the people understood very well without any interpreter (Purch.).

Baal. Phoenician god. Heb. *ba'al*, lord. Cf. *Beelzebub*.

baas [*SAfr.*]. Boss. Du., uncle. See *boss²*.

babacoote. Lemur. Malagasy *babakoto*.

babble. Imit. of infantile speech; cf. F. *babiller*, to chatter, L. *balbus*, stammerer. Of similar origin are *papa, mamma, babe, baby, pap*, etc.

babe, baby. From 14 cent., earlier *baban* (see *babble*). *Babe* only is used in *AV*. With *baby-farmer* (19 cent.) cf. *baby-killer* (20 cent.).

babel. From *Tower of Babel*, app. understood (*Gen.* xi. 9) as confusion (*babble*), but prob. Assyr. *bāb-ili*, gate of the gods. Cf. *Bab-el-Mandeb*, lit. gate of the devil, commonly called by early sailors 'the Bab.'

Therfor was called the name of it Babel, for ther was confoundid the lippe of all the erthe (Wyc.).

C'est véritablement la tour de Babylone,
Car chacun y babille, et tout du long de l'aune
      (*Tartufe*, i. 1).

babiana. Flower. Du. *babianer*, from *babian*, because fed on by the baboon (q.v.).

babiroussa. Hog-deer. Malay *bābi*, hog, *rūsa*, deer.

baboo, babu. Hind. *bābū*, Sanskrit *vapra*, father. Title corresponding to our Mr or Esquire. In Anglo-Ind. has become slightly disparaging. Cf. *Mossoo, Mynheer*, etc.

baboon. F. *babouin* (also *babion*); cf. It. *babbuino*, Sp. *babuino*, with several MedL. forms (13 cent.). Referred by some to F. *baboue*, grimace, imit. of gibbering (see *babble*). There is also MedL. *papio-n-*, wild dog, whence Du. *baviaan*, Ger. *pavian*, baboon, the baboon having a dog-like snout, but the source of this *papio* is unknown. It is prob. only the F. word latinized. The oldest recorded meaning of OF. *babuin* is *homuncio*, manikin, grotesque figure, a sense found also earliest in ME. The most likely starting-point is the natural base *bab-* (see *babble*). It. *babbuino*, besides meaning baboon, occurs in the sense both of babbler and stammerer.

babouche. Turk. slipper. F., Arab. *bābūsh*,

Pers. *pā*, foot, *push*, covering. For formation cf. *pyjamas*. For interchange of *p-*, *b-* cf. *pacha*, *bashaw*. See also *pump²*.

baby. See *babe*.

Babylon. G. Βαβυλών, for *Babel* (q.v.).

baccalaureat. See *bachelor*.

baccarat. F., also *baccara*, card-game at which the ten is called *baccara*. Origin unknown. There is a small French town called *Baccarat* (Meurthe-et-Moselle) not far from Lunéville. ? Cf. origin of *boston*.

bacchanal. L. *bacchanalis*, from *Bacchus*, G. Βάκχος.

bacharach [*archaic*]. Wine. From name of town on Rhine.

bachelor. OF. *bacheler* (*bachelier*), MedL. *baccalaris*, and later, as academic term, *baccalaureus*, as though from *bacca*, berry, *laurus*, laurel; hence *baccalaureat*. Cf. It. *baccalare*, Sp. *bachiller*. Oldest F. sense (*Chanson de Roland*) appears to be young man aspiring to knighthood, squire. Hence, junior member, of a gild or univ., as still in *Bachelor of Arts*, etc., orig. one who qualified to begin his university course, which is still the meaning of F. *bachelier*. From the "junior" idea is evolved that of young unmarried man. All these meanings occur in Chauc. Few words have provoked more etym. speculation, but the origin is still unknown. Ger. *hagestolz*, bachelor, OHG. *hagustalt*, means lit. hedge-holder (cf. AS. *hagosteald*, ON. *haukstaldr*), in contrast to the holder of the homestead. The younger son held a small enclosure while the elder inherited the estate. Already in OHG. the word also means celibate, as does the corresponding AS. *hagosteald*. This has been thought to point vaguely to *bacca*, berry, as a possible etymon of the F. word. Attempts have also been made to connect it with L. *baculum*, or its dim. *bacillus*, the staff being regarded as symbolical of the grade attained in a gild or univ., or as used, instead of lance or sword, by the young man practising warlike exercises.

Yong, fressh, and strong, in armes desirous
As any bacheler of al his hous (Chauc. F. 23).

At Orliens in studie a book he say
Of magyk natureel, which his felawe,
That was that tyme a bacheler of lawe,—
Al were he ther to lerne another craft,—
Hadde prively upon his desk y-laft (*ib.* F. 1124).

And trewely it sit wel to be so
That bacheleris have often peyne and wo
(*ib.* E. 1277).

bacillus. Late L., dim. of *baculus*, var. of *baculum*, rod; cf. *bacterion*.

back. AS. *bæc*; cf. Du. ON. *bak*. Not found in Ger., which has *rücken*, ridge, in general sense of *back* (but see *bacon*). Adv. *back* is for *aback* (q.v.), earlier *on back*; cf. Ger. *zurück*, from *rücken* (v.s.). From the noun comes the verb *back*, to support. To *back out* is orig. to leave a room backwards, hence to retire from an enterprise not too abruptly. *Backstair*, in the sense of underhand, clandestine, occurs in 17 cent. (Vanbrugh). *Backsword*, orig. sword with one edge only, like a navy cutlass, is also used of single-stick. With *backwoods* cf. *hinterland*. The verb to *backbite* is common in ME. With *backslide*, in rel. sense (16 cent.), cf. *relapse*. To *put* (*get*) *one's back up* suggests the angry cat. With to *back a bill* cf. *endorse*. See also *backward*.

He that bakbitith his brother bakbitith the lawe
(Wyc. *James*, iv. 11).

Willum's sweetheart...has strictly enjoined him not to get his head broke at back-swording
(*Tom Brown's Schooldays*).

back-formation [*ling.*]. A process the reverse of the usual, the formation of a word from a longer word which would appear to be derived from it. See *beggar*, *cadge¹*, *chamfer*, *former*, *fur*, *grovel*, *maffick*, *peddle*, etc.

backgammon. Also (18 cent.) *backgame*. ME. *gamen* (see *gammon¹*). So called because the pieces are sometimes forced to go back. Cf. its Du. name, from *verkeeren*, to turn back, and archaic F. *revertier*. Formerly called *tables*, and in F. *tric-trac*. Urquhart renders Rabelais' *toutes tables* by "the long tables or *verkeering*."

verkeer spel: game of tables, so called (Hexham).

backsheesh, baksheesh. Pers. *bakhshīsh*, present, from *bakhshīdan*, to give, also found in Arab., Turk. and Urdu.

Bacsheese (as they say in the Arabicke tongue) that is gratis freely (Purch.).

backward, backwards. For *abackward* (see *back*). In to *ring the bells backward*, i.e. upwards, beginning with the bass bell, as alarm. *Backwardation*, opposite of *contango*, is a Stock Exchange coinage (c. 1850).

I rynge aukewarde, as men do whan houses be afyre, or whan ennemyes be coming; je sonne a bransle
(Palsg.).

The bells are rung backward, the drums they are beat (*Bonnie Dundee*).

bacon. OF. (now replaced by *lard*, q.v.), MedL. *baco-n-*, OHG. *bahho*, buttock, ham;

cogn. with *back*. Of very early introduction, as Welsh *bacwn* (from E.) is recorded for 13 cent. In to *save one's bacon*, a vulgarism recorded for 17 cent., *bacon* is used for body, hide, etc.

Sorgt ihr nur für eure eigne haut: do but save your own bacon (Ludw.).

Baconian. In ref. both to Roger (†1294) and Francis (†1626).

bacterium. G. βακτήριον, dim. of βάκτρον, staff. From shape. Cf. *bacillus*.

baculine. In *baculine* (forcible) *argument*. From L. *baculum*, staff.

bad. ME. *badde*. Formerly compared *badder*, *baddest* (as late as Defoe). Origin uncertain. ? AS. *bæddel*, hermaphrodite, used contemptuously, with -*l* lost as in *muche* from *micel* (cf. adj. use of *bastard*); ? or AS. *gebæd(e)d*, forced, oppressed (cf. hist. of *caitiff*). It is curious that Pers. *bad* has the same sense (see *badmash*).

Baddeley cake. Cut in Drury Lane greenroom on Twelfth Night. Bequest of *Baddeley*, 18 cent. actor.

badge. ME. *bage, bagge*; cf. MedL. *bagia*, from the E. word. Origin unknown. OF. *bage* is later and prob. from E.

badger. A 16 cent. name for the animal previously called *brock* (Celt.), *bawson* (OF.), or *gray*. Origin much disputed. *NED.* accepts derivation from *badge*, referring to the white mark on the badger's head. But there is no record of *badge*, mark on an animal, and it seems a very unlikely word to be used in this sense. Earlier etymologists, comparing F. *blaireau*, badger, which they took to be a dim. of OF. *blaier*, corndealer (*blé*, corn), regarded *badger* as a nickname taken from archaic *badger* (? from *bag*), a middleman, esp. in the corn and flour trade, often regarded as a furtive and nocturnal individual. The fact that the animal does not store corn is no argument against this etym.; cf. rustic superstitions with regard to various animals, e.g. the *shrew*, *toad*, *slow-worm*, etc., or the inappropriate name *honeysuckle* (q.v.). But F. *blaireau* is perh. rather from LG. *blār*, blaze² (q.v.). Cf. dial. *blairie*, the baldheaded coot, and the origin of *bawson* (v.s.), from Celt. *bal*, white mark on the forehead (see *bald*), which is ult. cogn. with *blār* (v.s.) and with G. φαλαρός, "starred" (of a horse). Verb to *badger* is from the sport of badger baiting.

blaireau: a badger, gray, boason, brocke (Cotg.).

badinage. F., from *badiner*, to jest, *badin*, playful, earlier, foolish, Prov. *badin*, prob. orig. gaper. See *bay*³.

badinage (French): foolery, buffonry, waggishness (Phillips).

badmash, budmash [*Anglo-Ind.*]. Rascal. Urdu, from Pers. *bad*, evil, Arab. *ma'āsh*, means of livelihood.

badminton. Drink and game. From Duke of Beaufort's seat (Glouc.).

baffle. Cf. archaic F. *beffler*, to ridicule, and F. *bafouer*, to hold up to public contempt, both of uncertain origin, but generally referred to a radical *baf*, a natural sound of the *pooh, bah* type. Cf. It. *beffare*, with same meaning, and Ger. *ganz baff machen*, to flabbergast. But the earliest records (16 cent.) are Sc. and refer to the ignominious punishment of a perjured knight. This was Sc. *bauchle*, of unknown origin, and may be a separate word.

He by the heels him hung upon a tree
And bafful'd so, that all which passed by
The picture of his punishment might see
(*Faerie Queene*, VI. vii. 27).

baffoüer: to hoodwinke; also, to deceive; also, to besmeare; also, to baffle, abuse, revile, disgrace, handle basely in termes, give reproachfull words of, or unto (Cotg.).

beffler: to deceive, mocke, or gull, with faire words, etc. (*ib.*).

baffy [*golf*]. From Sc. *baff*, blow; cf. OF. *baffe* and see *buffet*¹.

bag. ME. *bagge*, ON. *baggi*. Cf. archaic F. *bagues*, baggage. Earlier hist. obscure; ? cogn. with *pack*. The earliest *NED.* record for *bags*, trousers, is from the blameless *Smiles*. The whole *bag of tricks*, referred by the *NED.* to the fable of the Fox and the Cat, would seem to come rather from the conjuror's outfit. With to *let the cat out of the bag*, i.e. show the true character of the article for sale, cf. F. *acheter chat en poche* (our *pig in a poke*). To *give the bag*, a mod. variation on to *give the sack*, was orig. used in opposite sense, viz. of a servant decamping without notice. With *bagman*, commercial traveller, cf. *carpet-bagger*. *Bag and baggage* was orig. used of an honourable evacuation or retreat; cf. F. *vie et bagues sauves*, and see quot. s.v. *colour*. It now implies headlong expulsion, esp. with reference to Gladstone's famous speech (v.i.) on the Bulgarian atrocities, in which he hardly anticipated the policy of Ferdinand the Fearless.

bagues sauves: with bag and baggage, safe and sound, scotfree (Cotg.).

The Turks...one and all, bag and baggage, shall, I hope, clear out from the province they have desolated and profaned (1876).

bagatelle. Orig. (17 cent.) a trifle. The game is 19 cent. F., It. *bagattella*. Prob. from L. *baca*, berry, derivatives of which occur in Rom. langs. in sense of valueless object. Cf. *trifle* (q.v.) and obs. *nifle*, prob. F. *nèfle*, medlar. Cf. also the prob. cogn. F. *baguenaude* (v.i.).

bagatelle: a toy, nifle, trifle, thing of small value (Cotg.).

baguenaudes: bladder nuts, S. Anthonies nuts, wild pistachios; also, the cods, or fruit of bastard sene; also (the fruit of red night-shade, or alkakengie) red winter cherries; (all of which being of little, or no value, cause this word to signifie) also, trifles, nifles, toyes, paltry trash (*ib.*).

baggage. F. *bagage*, from *bague* (see *bag*). Now usu. replaced, exc. in US., by *luggage*. Applied also disparagingly to, usu. young, women. Cf. *naughty pack, nice piece of goods*, etc.; also F. *garnement*, in same sense. Perh. influenced by F. *bagasse*, quean (OF. *baiasse*), glossed *baggage* by Cotg. This from It. *bagascia*, glossed *baggage* by Flor., of unknown origin.

bagnio. It. *bagno*, bath, L. *balneum*; later, brothel (cf. *stew*). In sense of convict prison, introduced after abolition of the galleys, from *bagnio*, oriental prison, said to be due to the conversion of an old Roman bath at Constantinople into a prison.

bagpipe. Now chiefly Sc., but once a favourite rural E. instrument.

A baggepipe wel koude he [the miller] blowe and sowne,
And therwithal he broghte us out of toune
(Chauc. A. 565).

bah. Cf. F. *bah!* See *bay*[3,5].

bahadur. Hind., *bahādur*, hero, champion, title of honour orig. conferred by great Mogul and introduced into India by Chinghiz Khan; cf. *Bobs Bahadur*, the late Lord Roberts. Forms are found also in Russ. (*Bogatyr*), Pol., Hung., Manchu, etc. Origin uncertain. Sanskrit *bhaga-dara*, happiness possessing, and Zend *baghaputhra*, son of God, have been suggested.

baignoire. Lowest tier box at theatre. F., orig. dressing-box at bath. See *bagnio*.

bail. Oldest sense, friendly custody (Law L.

ballium), OF. *bail* (now = lease), *baille*, from *bailler*, to give (still dial. F.), L. *bajulare*, to bear, from *bajulus*, porter. This is the accepted etym., though the sense-development is not easy to establish. With *I'll go bail* cf. *I'll be bound*. ME. *bail*, also *bailly*, enclosure, is OF. *bail, baile*, stockade, etc., perh. evolved from the idea of authority contained in *bailler*, to have in power, control, etc., but possibly rather connected with L. *baculum*, staff. The *Old Bailey* (*Vetus Ballium*, Duc.) was the *ballium* of the City wall between Lud Gate and New Gate. The cricket *bails* were orig. a cross-piece about two feet long resting on two stumps. This is dial. F. *bail*, crossbar on two stakes, prob. L. *baculum*. Cf. also the *bail*, or separating-bar, in a stable, and Austral. *bail*, framework for securing head of a cow while milking. Hence to *bail up* (a cow), and prob. the bushrangers' summons. The relative shares of *bajulus* and *baculum* in this group of words are hard to establish. In view of the extraordinary sense-development of the E. *staff*, it seems likely that etymologists have hardly given *baculum* its due.

bail². To scoop up water. See *bale*³.

bailie, bailiff. OF. *bailif* (*bailli*), VL. **bajulivus*, orig. official in charge of castle (see *bail*¹). In OF. the *f* was lost before -*s*, hence ME. *bailie* and the Sc. form. The E. word has gradually descended in meaning, exc. in some spec. titles, while Sc. *bailie*, orig. equivalent to sheriff, has retained more of the earlier sense. For *bailiwick* see *wick*².

bairn. Sc. form introduced into E. literature c. 1700; cf. obs. or dial. E. *bern, barn*, AS. *bearn*. Com. Teut.; cf. obs. Du. *baren*, OHG. ON. Goth. *barn*; cogn. with *bear*².

bait. First as verb. ON. *beita*, to cause to bite, causal of *bita*, to bite; cf. Ger. *beizen*, to etch, lit. to make bite. Hence *bear baiting*, etc., to *bait* (i.e. feed) horses. Cf. *bait* for fish, and see *abet*. Cf. also OF. *beter* (*un ours*), from Teut.

baize. Earlier *bayes*, pl. of *bay*⁴, from its orig. colour; for pl. cf. *chintz*. Du. *baai* has same sense.

baye: the cloth called *bayes* (Cotg.).

bake. AS. *bacan*. Com. Teut.; cf. Du. *bakken*, Ger. *backen*, ON. *baka*; ? cogn. with L. *focus*, hearth. Past tense was orig. *bōc*, and strong p.p. *baken* is usual in *AV*. With *baker legs*, knock-knees, cf. *housemaid's*

knee, painter's colic, clergyman's throat, etc.
Baker's dozen, i.e. thirteen, is due to extra
loaf being supplied, according to law, by
medieval bakers to retail hucksters. With
half-baked, imbecile, cf. synon. dial. *sam-
sodden*, AS. *sāmsoden*, half boiled (see *sand-
blind*).

She...boke therf looves (Wyc. 1 *Sam.* xxviii. 24).

As regrateresces...xiii darrees de payn pur xii
(*Lib. Albus*).

baksheesh. See *backsheesh*.

Balaam. Disappointing prophet (*Numb.* xxii–
xxiv.). In journalism, stock paragraphs
kept for filling up when news is short; app.
first so used by *Blackwood's Magazine*.

balance. F., VL. **bilancia* for *bilanx, bilanc-*,
from *bis*, twice, *lanx*, platter. Confused, in
some fig. senses, with *ballast*. The *balance
of power* is recorded for 1701 (*Lond. Gaz.*),
for earlier *ballance of Europe* (1653).

The centre and characteristic of the old order was
that unstable thing which we used to call the
"balance of power"
(President Wilson, Dec. 28, 1918).

balas [*archaic*]. Ruby. F. *balais* (cf. It.
balascio, Sp. *balaj*), MedL. *balascius*, Arab.
balaksh, from Pers. *Badakhshān*, district
near Samarcand.

balbriggan (**hose**). From *Balbriggan*, Co.
Dublin.

balcony. Earlier *balcóne*, It., from *balco*,
scaffold, OHG. *balcho*, balk, beam. Vulgar
balcóny was usual up to 18 cent., exc. once
in Swift, whose pronunc. made Samuel
Rogers "sick." Swift's was prob. Ir. (cf.
pollis for *police*).

The maids to the doors and the balconies ran
(Swift).

At Edmonton his loving wife
From the balcony spied
Her tender husband, wondering much
To see how he did ride (*John Gilpin*).

bald. Earlier *balled*, from Welsh *bâl*, white
streak on the brow (see *badger*), whence
Ball, name of a horse in Tusser, of a sheep
in the *Prompt. Parv.*, of a dog in *Privy
purse expenses of Henry VIII*, in each
case named from having a *blaze²* (q.v.), a
word which has the same double meaning,
e.g. Hexham explains Du. *blesse* as "a bald
forehead, a white star in the forehead of
a hors." Cf. similar use of *bald* by horse-
dealers, and tavern-sign of *Baldfaced Stag*;
also *baldicoot*. There has prob. been association also with *ball¹*; cf. *bald as a billiard-
ball*. To *go for a thing baldheaded* (US.) may
be a perversion of Du. *balddadig*, audacious,

altered, under influence of *bald*, bold (as
though bold-doing), from *baldadig*, of which
first element is cogn. with *bale¹* (q.v.); cf.
baloorig, stubborn, *balsturig*, perverse.

His heed was balled that shoon as any glas
(Chauc. A. 198).

bald-daedigh: audax, temerarius, praeceps (Kil.).

baldachin, baldaquin [*archaic*]. Rich stuff,
usu. *baudekin* in ME.; later, a canopy, orig.
hung with this material. F. *baldaquin*, It.
baldacchino, MedL. *baldakinus*, from *Bal-
dacco*, It. name of *Baghdad*, place of origin.

balderdash. Orig. (16 cent.) poor mixed
drink, hence jumbled nonsense. MedL. *bal-
ductum*, strained milk, was similarly used.
Origin of both words unknown (cf. *flapdoodle*, *slumgullion*). ? Connected with
Dan. *pladder*, slush, weak tipple, foolish
talk, which is imit. of splashing sound.

balderdash: of drink, *mixta potio*; of other things,
farrago (*Litt.*).

baldric. ME. also *baudrik, baudry*, the latter
from OF. form *baudrei*. Cf. late OHG.
balderich. As the *baldric* was very ornamental, the word may represent the OHG.
name *Baldarīh* or AS. *Bealdrīc*, bold rich,
whence F. surname *Baudry* and our
Badrick, Baldry, etc. For similar cases see
goblet, nickel, tankard, etc.

bale¹ [*poet.*]. Harm. AS. *bealo*, woe, calamity.
Com. Teut.; cf. OSax. *balu*, OHG. *balo*, ON.
böl, also Goth. *balws*, adj. A poet. word
in AS. & ME., often contrasted alliteratively
with *boot*, profit, and *bliss*. Obs. by 1600,
but revived by mod. romantics. Hence
baleful. Balefire, often understood as belonging to the same word and hence
wrongly used, is AS. *bǣlfȳr*, from *bǣl*,
blaze, funeral pile, ON. *bāl*. Its erron. use
as beacon fire is due to Scott.

Her face resigned to bliss or bale (*Christabel*).

Sweet Teviot! on thy silver tide
The glaring bale-fires blaze no more (*Lay*, iv. 1).

The bale-fires of murderous licence and savage
anarchy (Motley).

bale². Of goods. AF. var. of F. *balle*, ball¹,
bale.

bale³. Verb. From archaic *bail*, bucket, F.
baille. MedL. *aquae baiula* points to orig.
sense of water-bearer (see *bail¹*) and sense-
development as in *scullion* (q.v.).

baleen. Whalebone. Orig. whale. F. *baleine*,
L. *balaena*.

balefire [*poet.*]. See *bale¹*.

baleful. See *bale¹*.

balk, baulk. AS. *balca*, ridge. Com. Teut.; cf. Du. *balk*, Ger. *balken*, ON. *bjālki*, all meaning beam, also ON. *bālkr*, hedge, boundary. The *baulk* at billiards is one of the latest developments of the ground-meaning of boundary. Hence verb to *balk*, intrans. to dodge, avoid, trans. to hinder, i.e. interpose a balk; cf. *thwart*. Or it may be a ploughing metaphor, to go off the line (see *delirium*).

Balkanize [*nonce-word*]. To convert into a set of hostile units.

This treaty tends to Balkanize—if we may coin the word—three fourths of Europe
(*Obs.* May 11, 1919).

ball[1]. Sphere. ME. *bal*, ON. *böllr*, cogn. with Ger. *ball*, whence F. *balle*. Senses may have been affected by It. *palla* (see *pallmall*), which is from Teut. The three (golden) balls are supposed to have been taken from the *palle* in the coat-of-arms of the Medici family, the early pawnbrokers having been of It. origin.

It would enable me to bear my share of the Vauxhall bill without a disagreeable reference to the *three blue balls* (Hickey's *Memoirs*, i. 334).

ball[2]. Dance. F. *bal*, from OF. *baler*, to dance, Late L. *ballare*, ? from G. βαλλίζειν, to dance. Cf. *ballad*, *ballet*.

ballad. F. *ballade*, Prov. *balada*, orig. a dancing-song (see *ball[2]*). F. *ballade* is a poem of fixed form, usu. three stanzas and *envoi* with refrain line. In E. it has various meanings and is earlier found as *ballat*, *ballet*, etc. In the High St of Amersham, Bucks, is a notice, dated 1821, to the effect that the constable has orders to apprehend all *ballad-singers*.

I occasioned much mirth by a ballet I brought with me, made from the seamen at sea to their ladies in town [Lord Dorset's "To all you ladies now on land"] (Pepys).

ballast. Second element is *last*, burden (whence F. *lest*, ballast), found in all Teut. langs. (see *last[1]*); first element is doubtful, perhaps *bare*, as oldest form appears to be *barlast* (OSw. & ODan.). Another possibility is that it is a LG. *bal*, worthless, which appears in Du. *balsturig*, cross, perverse. Some earlier E. forms show confusion with *balance*. *Ballast* in road-making (19 cent.) is the same word, from the stones, sand, etc. used as ship's ballast.

Solid and sober natures have more of the ballast then of the saile (Bacon).

ballerina. It., dancing girl. Cf. *ballet*.

ballet. F., It. *balletto*, dim. of *ballo*, ball, dance. See *ball[2]*, *ballad*.

ballista [*hist.*]. Catapult. L., from G. βάλλειν, to cast.

ballium [*hist.*]. Latinized form of *bailey*. See *bail[1]*.

ballon d'essai. F., small balloon sent up to determine direction of wind before ascent was made.

balloon. F. *ballon*, It. *ballone*, "a great ball, a foot-ball" (Flor.), augment. of *balla*, ball, from Teut. Earlier meaning, football. In current sense in ref. to Montgolfier's aerostat (1783).

ballot. It. *ballotta*, dim. of *balla*, ball (cf. *blackball*). Earliest references are to Venice.

ballottare: to choose, to cast or draw lots with bullets, as they use in Venice (Flor.).

Ballplatz [*hist.*]. Austrian Foreign Office. From address. Cf. *Quai d'Orsay*, etc.

bally [*slang*]. From c. 1885 as euph. for *bloody*. Cf. *blooming*, *blinking*, *blighter*. Perh. from music-hall tag *Ballyhooly truth*, suggested as Ir. for *whole bloody truth*.

ballyrag, bullyrag. First in US. *bulrag* (1758) with sense of *haze[2]*. ? Cf. *bulldoze*. Perh. both orig. from bull-baiting. Hence mod. schoolboy *rag*.

balm. ME. also *baume*, F. *baume*, L. *balsamum*. Orig. an aromatic vegetable juice.

balm-cricket. Cicada. Mistransl. of Ger. *baumgrille*, tree cricket.

balmoral. In various trade-names. Sc. residence (Aberdeen) of Queen Victoria.

balmy [*slang*]. For earlier *barmy* (q.v.).

We don't care a damn for Will-i-am,
Because we know he's balmy (T. Atkins)

balsam. It. *balsamo*, L. *balsamum*, G. βάλσαμον, Heb. *baalschamen*, king of oils. See *Baal*. *Balsam* is found in AS., but was replaced, till c. 1600, by *balm*.

baltimore. Black and orange starling (US.). Colours of *Lord Baltimore*, proprietor of Maryland (17 cent.).

baluster, banister. F. *balustre*, It. *balustro*, from *balaustra*, flower of wild pomegranate, L. *balaustium*, G. βαλαύστιον. Orig. the bulging colonets of a balustrade. From shape. *Banister*, formerly regarded as a vulgarism, appears in 17 cent. With corrupt. cf. name *Bannister*, from *balestier*, crossbow man.

balustres: ballisters; little, round, and short pillars, ranked on the outside of cloisters, terraces, galleries etc. (Cotg.).

bam. Humbug. Goes with *bamboozle*.

bambino. It., baby, esp. Infant Jesus. Cf. G. βαμβαίνειν, to stammer. See *babble*.

bamboo. Earlier *bambus*, pl. *bambuses*. In most Europ. langs., earliest in Du. (*bamboes*). Malay. As earliest form is *mambu*, it may be for Malay *samambu*, Malacca cane.

bamboozle. One of the numerous slang words appearing c. 1700. Also in shortened form *bam*. Perh. connected with the onomat. *bab-* (*babble*, *baby*, *baboon*, etc.). Florio uses *embambuinize* to render Montaigne's *embabuiner*, to make a fool (lit. baboon) of; cf. also Catalan *embabiecar*, to deceive.

Certain words invented by some pretty fellows, such as banter, bamboozle (Swift).

Bampton lectures. At St Mary's, Oxford, founded by *Canon Bampton* (†1751).

ban¹. To proclaim, etc. Verb is older in E. AS. *bannan*, to summon by proclamation; later, to curse, excommunicate. Com. Teut.; cf. obs. Du. *bannen*, OHG. *bannan*, ON. *banna*. Senses of noun have been partly influenced by F. *ban* (MedL. *bannum*) of same origin. Cf. *banish*. The proclamation sense survives in *banns of marriage*. See *arrière-ban*, *banal*.

ban². Governor of certain districts in Hungary, Croatia, etc. Pers. *bān*, lord. Hence *banat*, province.

Banagher. To bang. See *beat*.

banal. F., commonplace, orig. for public use of all under the same *ban*, or feudal jurisdiction. See *ban¹*.

bannal: common; which anyone may, and every one (residing within that liberty, or precinct) must, use, and pay for the use of (Cotg.).

banana. Sp. or Port., prob. from native name (Guinea); but "the coincidence of this name with the Arab. *banān*, fingers or toes, and *banāna*, a single finger or toe, can hardly be accidental" (Yule). But, according to Platt, *banana* is a Carib word early transferred to Africa (cf. *yaws*, *cayman*, *papaw*).

Banbury. In Oxf. Famous, since 16 cent., for puritans, cheeses, and cakes. *NED.* does not recognize the *Banbury chair*, familiar to children.

band¹. Ligature. AS. has only *bend* (q.v.), but *band* is found in most Teut. langs. It belongs to the verb to *bind*. Earliest sense, bond, fetter, etc. In sense of flat strip, ribbon, etc., it is F. *bande*, ult. the same word. Hence *bandbox*, orig. (17 cent.) made for bands or ruffs. See also *bandog*.

band². Company. F. *bande*, It. *banda*. Prob. cogn. with *banner* (q.v.) and going back to Goth. *bandwa*, sign, flag. Cf. MedL. *bandum*, banner. It has also been popularly connected with *band¹* (cf. *banded together*), and possibly also with *ban¹*. The common E. meaning, as in *regimental band* (*band of musicians*, 17 cent.), is unknown in F., exc. in archaic *grand'bande*, chamber orchestra of Louis XIV. The *Band of Hope* dates from c. 1847. Perh. the popular association with *band¹* (v.s.) suggested to Dickens the *Infant Bonds of Joy* as the name of one of Mrs Pardiggle's beneficent organisations.

bandanna. Earlier *bandanno*. Hind., prob. through Port. Orig. of a kind of dyeing in which the spotted effect was produced by tying the material in various ways.

bandar log. Nation of monkeys in Kipling's *Jungle Book*. Fig. any collection of irresponsible chatterers and poseurs. Hind. *bandar*, monkey (cf. *wanderoo*), *log*, people.

When our boys get back and begin to ask the Bandar Log what they *did* in the Great War
(Ian Hay, *Carrying on*, ch. xiii).

banderole. F., from archaic *bandière*, banner, It. *bandiera*.

bandicoot. Large Indian rat; Austral. marsupial of similar appearance. Telugu *pandi kokku*, pig rat.

bandit. Earlier *banditto*, It. *bandito*, p.p. of *bandire*, to banish (q.v.). Cf. *outlaw*.

A Roman sworder and banditto slave
(2 *Hen. VI*, iv. 1).

bandog. For *band-dog* (*band¹*). Cf. *leash-hound*, and F. *limier*, from *lien*, bond. So also F. *les limiers de la police* corresponding to our *bandogs of the law*.

bande dog: molosus (*Cath. Angl.*).

bandoleer [*mil.*]. F. *bandoulière*, Sp. *bandolera* or It. *bandoliera*, from *banda*, band, strap.

bandouilleres: a musketiers bandoleers; or charges, like little boxes, hanging at a belt about his neck (Cotg.).

bandoline. For the hair. F., hybrid coinage from *bandeau*, band of hair, and L. *linere*, to anoint.

bandy¹. Verb. From F. *bander* "to bandie, at tennis" (Cotg.), hence to throw (jests, reproaches, etc.) to and fro. Of Teut. origin and cogn. with *bend*. Sense-development of the F. word, orig. to bend a bow, is not quite clear. For final -*y*, cf. *levy*, *parry*.

Had she affections and warm youthful blood,
She'd be as swift in motion as a ball;
My words would bandy her to my sweet love,
And his to me (*Rom. & Jul.* ii. 5).

bandy[2]. Hockey; orig. the curved stick with which it is played. Prob. from *bend*, but influenced by *bandy*[1]. See *hockey*.

a bandy: hama, clava falcata (Litt.).

bandy[3]. Or *bandy-legged*. Common sense suggests *bendy*, perh. associated also with *bandy*[2]. *Bandy-legged*, "valgus, varus" (Litt.), is rather earlier than first *NED.* record.

bane. Orig. killer, murderer. AS. *bana*. Com. Teut.; cf. OSax. OHG. *bano*, ON. *bani*; cogn. with Goth. *banja*, wound, and ult. with G. φόνος, murder. Hence also obs. *bane*, to poison (*Merch. of Ven.* iv. 1). Cf. *henbane*.

bang[1]. To thump, etc. ON. *banga*, to beat; cf. Du. *bangen*. In some senses imit. With *bang up*, smart, cf. *slap up*. *Bang-tail*, a horse's tail cut horizontally, is perh. from the same word, suggesting abruptness; cf. *bang goes saxpence*. Also *bang*, a horizontal fringe across the forehead, orig. US. For to *bang Banagher* see *beat*.

bang[2]. Drug. See *bhang*.

bangle. From Hind. *bangrī*, orig. coloured glass bracelet or anklet.

banian, banyan. Port., Arab. *banyān*, Gujarati *vāniyo*, Sanskrit *vanij*, merchant. Man of trading caste (see *bunya*). Orig. pl. (cf. *Bedouin*). This caste abstains from animal food, hence naut. *banyan day*. The *banian tree*, a gigantic fig tree, obtained its E. name from its being an object of veneration to the *banians*, who built their temples under it (v.i.). App. the name was first given to one at Gombroon, on the Persian Gulf.

The govenour is a Bannyan, one of those kind of people that observe the law of Pythagoras
(Purch. 1609).

The Banian tree is a little beyond the great tanck [of Surat]....This is of an exceedinge bredth, much honoured by the Banians (Peter Mundy, 1629).

He has been ill—and so he banyanned upon lobster salad and chocolate cream, washed down by deluges of champagne (Lady Lyttelton, 1839).

banish. F. *bannir, banniss-*, to proclaim as an outlaw, from *ban*[1] (q.v.). Cf. Ger. *verbannen*.

banister. See *baluster*.

banjo. Negro corrupt. of archaic *bandore*, L. *pandura*, G. πανδοῦρα.

pandura: an instrument called a bandore like a lute; a rebeck; a violin (Litt.).

"What is this, mamma?—It is not a guitar, is it?" "No, my dear, it is called a banjo; it is an African instrument, of which the negroes are particularly fond" (Miss Edgeworth, *Belinda*).

bank[1]. Of earth. Earliest sense, raised shelf or ridge. ME. *banke*; cf. ON. *bakki*; cogn. with *bank*[2] and *bench*. Hence naut. *banker*, boat fishing on Newfoundland bank; cf. *coaster* and 16 cent. *roader*. To *bank*, of an aeroplane, is borrowed from the motor racing-track.

There is a rich fisheing very neere this land [Newfoundland] called the *Banke*, where there doe yearely fish at least 400 French shipps
(R. Hayman to Charles I, 1628).

Practically the whole of the French bankers are laid up in St Malo (*Obs.* Feb. 10, 1918).

bank[2]. Bench, etc. F. *banc*, OHG. *banc*, ult. ident. with *bank*[1]; cf. Du. *bank*. In ME. means bench, as still in some techn. applications. Hence *double-banked*, used of galleys with two tiers of oars, involving two tiers of rowing benches. The financ. *bank* is F. *banque*, It. *banca*, from OHG., orig. money-changers' bench or table. Most of our early financ. words are It. (cf. *bankrupt*). *Bank-holidays* were established by Sir John Lubbock's Act (1871) in order to legalize the closing of banks on certain fixed days. They were not intended as public saturnalia.

Christ overthrew the exchangers bankes
(*NED.* 1567).

bankrupt. Earlier (16 cent.) *bankrout*, F. *banqueroute*, It. *banca rotta*, broken bank. Now remodelled on L. *rupta*. See *bank*[2].

banksia. Austral. shrub. From *Sir Joseph Banks* (†1820), botanist, companion of Captain Cook. Cf. *dahlia, fuchsia*, etc.

banlieue. F., outskirts (of a town). Orig. league (*lieue*) radius under town authority. See *ban*[1].

banner. OF. *banere* (*bannière*); cf. It. *bandiera*, Sp. *bandera*, from MedL. *bannum, bandum*, flag. See *band*[2]. In the Rom. langs. there has been confusion with *ban*[1] (q.v.), and the ult. origin of both groups of words is obscure. The analogy of F. *drapeau*, from *drap*, cloth, suggests that L. *pannus*, cloth, may be involved.

banneret. OF. *baneret*, adj., "bannered," with -*et* from L. -*atus*. Orig. knight whose vassals fought under his own banner. The order was allowed to die out after the institution of *baronets* (1611).

bannock [*Sc. & North*]. Loaf of home-made bread. Gael. *bannach*, prob. a loan-word, from L. *panis*; cf. AS. *bannuc*.

banns. See *ban*[1].

banquet. F., dim. of *banc*, bench, table (see *bank*[2]); cf. It. *banchetto*, dim. of *banco*, table. For sense-development cf. *board*, *table*. Earlier E. sense is a kind of dessert (*Esther*, v, vii).

banquette [*mil.*]. Ledge inside rampart or trench. F., It. *banchetta*, dim. of *banca*, bench, shelf. See *bank*[2].

banshee [*Ir.*]. Ir. *bean sidhe*, woman of the fairies; cf. Gael. *bean*, woman, *sith*, fairy.

> The fatal Ben-shie's boding scream
> (*Lady of Lake*, iii. 7).

bant. See *banting*.

bantam. Place in Java, but the bird was orig. Jap. (cf. *guinea-pig*). Latest use in sense of small, miniature, is in *bantam battalion* (1915), composed of very short men.

banter. One of the words assailed by Swift in the *Tatler* (see *bamboozle*, with which it was earlier synon.). Origin unknown. It occurs in Pepys (Dec. 24, 1667) earlier than *NED*. records.

> He that first brought the word..."banter" in use, put together, as he thought fit, those ideas he made it stand for (Locke).

banting. Name of a London cabinet-maker who published (1864) his method of reducing obesity. With back-formation *bant* cf. *maffick*.

bantling. Prob. corrupted (16 cent.) from archaic Ger. *bänkling*, from *bank*, bench. See *bastard*, with which *bantling* was formerly synon.

Bantu [*ling.*]. Group of SAfr. langs., esp. Zulu. Native name for "people."

banxring. Squirrel-like animal (Java). Native name.

banyan. See *banian*.

banzai. Jap. war-cry, lit. ten thousand years; cf. Chin. *wan*, myriad, *sui*, year.

baobab. Tree. African, but long naturalized in India. Prob. native name (EAfr.).

baptize. F. *baptiser*, L., G. βαπτίζειν, to immerse, from βάπτειν, to dip. *Christen* is much older. The *baptist* sect was orig., and by opponents up to 19 cent., called *ana-baptist* (q.v.). The currency of *baptism of fire* (suggested by *Luke*, iii. 16) is perh. due to F. *baptême de feu* used by Napoleon III

in a despatch to the Empress early in the war of 1870.

bar. F. *barre*; cf. *barra* in other Rom. langs. and in MedL. Origin unknown. Ground-sense, barrier, as in *Temple Bar*, *harbour bar*. A *barrister* practises "at the bar," orig. the rail marking off the judge's seat, after being called "to the bar," the rail separating the benchers from the body of the hall in the Inns of Court. As a King's Counsel he is called "within the bar." In the tavern sense *bar* is 16 cent. *Barman* (19 cent.) is more recent than *barmaid* (1732). To *bar*, cold-shoulder, is univ. slang.

baragouin. Jargon. F., from Bret. *bara*, bread, *gwin*, wine, often heard, but not understood, by Frenchmen among Bretons.

baralipton. See *barbara*.

barb[1]. Of arrow. F. *barbe*, L. *barba*, beard, hook, in various senses. Hence *barbed wire*, "that invention of the devil" (Sir Ian Hamilton).

> *barbelé*: bearded; also, full of snags, snips, jags, notches; whence, *Flesche barbelée*, a bearded, or barbed arrow (Cotg.).

barb[2]. Horse (archaic), pigeon. F. *barbe*, from *Barbary*.

barbara [*logic*]. The words *barbara*, *baralipton*, *bocardo*, *celarent* were used by medieval logicians as mnemonics, the vowels standing for various forms of syllogism. Hence *barbara and baralipton* in ref. to scholastic pedantry.

> Ce n'est pas "barbara et baralipton" qui forment le raisonnement (Pascal).

barbaresque. F., It. *barbaresco*, orig. of *Barbary*, also barbarous, primitive.

barbarian, barbaric, barbarous. All three have been used indifferently in the past, though now differentiated. Earlier is ME. *barbar*, F. *barbare*, L., G. βάρβαρος, with ref. to unintelligible speech (*bar-bar*); cf. *Hottentot*. Hence *barbarism*, orig. the mixing of foreign words with Greek or Latin.

> I schal be to him, to whom I schal speke, a barbar (Wyc. 1 *Cor.* xiv. 11).

Barbary. In ME. heathenism, etc.; now, N. Africa. Hence *barbary ape*, the only ape found wild in Europe (Gibraltar). See *berber*.

barbecue. Sp. *barbacoa*, from lang. of Hayti. Orig. frame-work on posts to sleep on, or to smoke meat on. Hence, an animal roasted whole, jollification, drying floor for coffee.

> His couch or barbecu of sticks (Dampier).
> The barbecu'd sucking-pig's crisp'd to a turn
> (*Ingoldsby*).

barbed [*archaic*]. Of a horse, equipped and caparisoned. Mistake for *barded*, from F. *barde*, horse-armour, also rough saddle, Sp. Port. *albarda*, packsaddle, Arab. *al barda'at*.

A bardit curser stout and bald (Gavin Douglas).

His glittering arms he will condemn to rust,
His barbed steeds to stables (*Rich. II*, iii. 3).

barbel. OF. *barbel* (*barbeau*), VL. **barbellus*, dim. of *barbus*, from its beard.

barber. ME. *barbour*, OF. *barbeor*, VL. **barbator-em*. Mod. form partly due to suffix substitution (cf. *turner* for *turnour*), partly to ModF. *barbier*, It. *barbiere*. The barber was formerly also dentist and surgeon, hence *Company of Barber-Surgeons* (1461–1745). Hence the small metal bowls, orig. for blood-letting, which are still the barber's sign in some countries, while the barber's pole is said to represent the bandage.

My name is Salvation Yeo, born in Clovelly Street, in the year 1526, where my father exercised the mystery of a barber surgeon (*Westward Ho !*).

barberry. OF. *barberis*, with -*s* lost as in *cherry*; cf. It. *berberi*, Sp. *berberis*, MedL. *barbaris*. Origin unknown. The -*berry* is folk-etym.

berberi: sunt fructus cuiusdam arboris, *anglicè* berberynes (*Voc.* 15 cent.).

barbette [*mil.*]. Gun platform for firing over parapet or ship's turret. F., dim. of *barbe*, but sense-development not clear.

barbican [*hist.*]. Outer defence. F. *barbacane* (12 cent.); cf. It. *barbacane*, Sp. *barbacana*. A word that has given rise to very numerous conjectures, the most reasonable being Arab.-Pers. *bāb-khānah*, gate-house (see *Babel*), the regular name in the East for a towered gateway, which is about the meaning of *barbican*. This leaves the -*r*- unaccounted for, unless we assume association with *bar*. There seems to be little doubt that the word comes from the Crusades (Joinville). For its survival as the name of a London street cf. *Old Bailey* (see *bail¹*).

Egyptian rulers, from the Pharaohs to Napoleon and Mehemet Ali, have tried to seize it [Palestine] as the outer barbican of Africa
(*Daily Chron.* Dec. 11, 1917).

barcarolle. F., Venet. *barcarola*, It. *barcaruola*, boatman's song, from *barca*. See *bark²*.

bard¹. Gael. Ir. *bard*, whence G. βάρδος, L. *bardus* (in Lucan). Orig. of Celt. bards only, and, in Lowland Sc., of a vagabond minstrel. Though first recorded by *NED.*

c. 1450, it was a surname by 1297; cf. Sc. *Baird*.

The Schireffe...sal punish sorners, over-lyars, maister-full beggars, fuilles, bairdes, vagaboundes (Skene).

bard². See *barbed*.

bare. AS. *bær*. Com. Teut.; cf. Du. *baar*, Ger. *bar*, ON. *berr*. Orig. uncovered, then unequipped, e.g. *bareback*, without addition of any kind, as in *bare majority* (*subsistence*). *Barefaced* (first in Shaks.) has degenerated from orig. sense of undisguised, without scheming.

barège. Fabric, from *Barèges* (Hautes-Pyrénées).

baresark. See *berserk*.

bargain. OF. *bargagne*; cf. It. *bargagno*, Port. *barganha*. The corresponding verb, OF. *bargagner* (*barguigner*), found also in the other Rom. langs., is Late L. *barcaniare*, to haggle (temp. Charles the Bald). Many forms and derivatives are found in MedL., but the origin is unknown. OHG. *borganjan* to lend, borrow, pledge, has been suggested, but the -*a*- of the Rom. forms is against this. If the word was orig. OF. and borrowed by the other Rom. langs., it may be simply *gagner*, to gain (q.v.), with pejorative prefix *bar*-, or even represent a mixture of *gagner* and the synon. *barater*, to barter. With to *strike a bargain* cf. *swap, tope³*.

barguigner: to chaffer; to bargaine; or (more properly) to wrangle, dodge, haggle, brabble, in the making of a bargaine (Cotg.).

barge. F., Late L. *barga*, var. of *barca*, *bark²*. *Bargee* is used by Pepys. Like most shipnames, has had a variety of senses. *NED.* does not recognize slang to *barge*, rush heavily.

barilla. Plant. Sp. *barrilla*, "saltwort" (Minsh.).

baritone. See *barytone*.

barium [*chem.*]. Isolated and named by Davy (1808), from G. βαρύς, heavy.

bark¹. Of a tree. ON. *börkr*, prob. cogn. with *birch*. Native word is *rind*.

bark², **barque**. Vessel. F. *barque*, It. *barca*, Late L. *barca*, ship of burden, of doubtful origin. ? From G. βᾶρις, boat, from Egypt. Cf. the earlier *barge*. The spelling *barque* is now limited to a spec. rig.

bark³. Verb. AS. *beorcan*, orig. strong, with p.p. *borcen*; cf. ON. *berkja*, ?from *barki*, windpipe. Hence *barker*, pistol, fire-arm.

Chien qui abbaye [*aboie*] *ne mord pas*: the dog that barkes much, bites little; a great prater, a weake performer (Cotg.).

barley. Orig. adj., as still in *barleycorn*. AS. *bærlic*, from *bere*, barley; cf. ON. *barr*, corn, barley, Goth. *barizeins*, of barley; ult. cogn. with L. *far*, corn. *John Barleycorn*, as emblem of malt liquor, occurs in the title of a ballad in the Pepys collection. Cf. the old song of the *barleymow*, where *mow* means heap, stack. *Barley-water* dates from 14 cent. With *barleycorn* as unit of measure cf. *grain* as unit of weight.

Hitt was ordeyned [by the Statute of Winchester] that iii barley-cornes take out of the middes of the ere makith a inch (*Coventry Leet Book*, 1474).

barm. Yeast, froth. AS. *beorma*, with LG. and Scand. cognates; cf. Ger. dial. *bärme*; ult. cogn. with L. *fermentum*. Hence *barmy*, now often spelt *balmy*.

Hope puts that hast into your heid,
Quhilk boyles your barmy brain
                    (Montgomerie, c. 1600).
Why did I join the R.N.A.S.?
Why didn't I join the army?
Why did I come to Salonika?
(*Chorus*) I must have been —— well barmy (Anon.).

Barmecide banquet. Allusion to a tale in the *Arabian Nights* of a prince who offered an imaginary feast to a beggar. The *Barmecides* were a family ruling in Baghdad just before Haroun-al-Raschid. Cf. *Alnaschar dreams*.

barn. ME. *bern*, AS. *bereærn*, barley-place, of which contracted forms also occur in AS. Cf. relation of L. *horreum*, barn, to *hordeum*, barley. *Barn-stormer*, strolling actor, is late 19 cent.

Barnaby. Feast of *St Barnabas* (June 11), considered the longest day under the Old Style.

Barnaby bright,
Longest day and shortest night.

barnacle[1]. For horses. ME. *bernacle*, earlier *bernak*, AF. *bernac*, glossed *camus*, a bit, snaffle. Cf. also OF. *bernicles*, Saracen instrument of torture (Joinville). Origin unknown. In sense of spectacles (16 cent.) *barnacles* seems to be a playful extension of the same word, due to the way in which *barnacles* are fitted to a horse's nose. There may also have been association with F. *besicles*, spectacles, formerly *bericles*. This is rendered *barnacles* in Motteux' transl. of Rabelais (*Pantagruel*, v. 27).

A scourge to an hors, and a bernacle to an asse
                    (Wyc. *Prov.* xxvi. 3).

barnacle[2]. Kind of wild goose; shell-fish. ME. *bernekke*, *bernake*, OF. *bernaque*, MedL. *bernaca*, etc. The connection of the two is

due to a very ancient and wide-spread superstition that the goose was hatched from shell-fish adhering to trees over the water. Of the numerous conjectures that the word has provoked the most reasonable is that which derives it from Gael. *bairneach*, limpet, from *barenn*, rock. But the weak point in this theory is that, although the goose is supposed to spring from the shell-fish, the former is recorded some centuries earlier. Also the Gael. word may be borrowed from E. Cf. also Sp. *bernache*, Port. *bernaca*. The following quot. shows the muddled character of the superstition.

So, slow Bootes underneath him sees
In th'ycie Iles, those goslings hatcht of trees,
Whose fruitfull leaves falling into the water,
Are turn'd (they say) to living fowles soone after.
So, rotten sides of broken shipps doo change
To barnacles; O transformation strange!
'Twas first a greene tree, then a gallant hull,
Lately a mushrum, now a flying gull (Sylv. i. 6).

barnacles. Spectacles. See *barnacle[1]*.

barney [*slang*]. Lark, spree; earlier (c. 1860), humbug. ? From name *Barney* (for *Barnaby*); cf. abstr. sense of *paddy*.

Barnum. US. proprietor of the greatest show on earth (†1891).

His attendant officers, gigantic men selected on the Barnum principle
(S. L. Hughes, M.P., on Kaiser's entry into Jerusalem).

barometer. From G. βάρος, weight. Due to Boyle (17 cent.).

baron. F., Late L. *baro-n-*, used in Salic Law as equivalent to *homo*; cf. double meaning of AS. *mann*, man, warrior, hero, and sense-development of *knight*, *vassal*, etc. Origin unknown, but prob. Teut. According to some it is L. *baro*, simpleton, whence It. *barone*, rogue, which seems unlikely. The *baron of beef*, or double sirloin, is a witticism due to the old story of knighting the loin. *Baronet* is used for sirloin by Fielding (v. i.). The title *baronet* occurs in 14 cent., but its exact meaning is doubtful, though it seems to have been used for *banneret* (q.v.). The present order dates from 1611 and was established to raise money for the settlement of Ulster. Orig. obtainable for £1000, but it is understood that the current price is much higher.

The sight of the roast beef struck him dumb, permitting him only to say grace, and to declare he must pay his respects to the "baronet," for so he called the sirloin (*Tom Jones*, iv. 10).

baroque. Orig. irregularly shaped pearl. F., Port. *barrocco* or Sp. *barrueco*. Origin unknown.

barouche. Earlier (1805) *birutsche*, Ger. dial. *barutsche, birutsche*, It. *baroccio*, for *biroccio*, from L. *birotus*, two-wheeled, from *bis* and *rota*. Cf. F. *brouette*, wheel-barrow, earlier *berouette*, dim. of OF. *beroue*, L. *birota*.

barque. See *bark²*.

barquentine. Differs from a barque in having only the fore-mast square-rigged. Sp. *bergantin*, brigantine, confused with *barque* (see *bark², brig*).

barracan. See *barragan*.

barrack. F. *baraque*, It. *baracca* or Sp. *barraca*; ? cogn. with *bar*. Orig. booth, hut, which is still the meaning of F. *baraque*. Hence *barracoon*, slave pen (Sp.).

barracking. On the cricket field. Said to come from a native Austral. (NSW.) word *borak* meaning derision. It bears a curious resemblance to *barrakin'*, gibberish, formerly used in East End of London. This is F. *baragouin* (q.v.).

barracoon. See *barrack*.

barracuda, barracoota. Large WInd. sea-perch. Origin unknown. ? From Sp. *barrigudo*, big-bellied.

barracoutha: the name of a fish peculiar to some parts of America (Phillips).

barragan. Orig. coarse camlet. Earlier *barracan*. OF. *baracan, baragant* (*bouracan*), Arab. *barrakān*, camlet, from Pers. *barak*, garment of camel's hair. Cf. Du. *barkan*, Ger. *barchent*.

barrage [*hist.*]. Adopted in the Great War for curtain fire, intended to isolate the objective. F., barrier, weir, from *barrer*, to bar.

Keep up a steady potato barrage from the end of March until May (*Daily Chron.*, Feb. 2, 1918).

Field-Marshal Sir Douglas Haig passed into London through a creeping barrage of cheers
(*ib.* Dec. 20, 1918).

barratry [*leg.*]. Formerly traffic in church office, simony; now esp. marine fraud. OF. *baraterie*, from *barate*, fraud, strife; cf. It. *barattare*, to barter (q.v.), Sp. *baratar*, to sell cheap, OIt. *baratta*, strife. All app. from ON. *barátta*, strife, if this is a genuine ON. word, in which case it may have been taken to the South by the Vikings. It. *barataria* occurs in marine laws of Amalfi (11 cent.).

barrel. F. *baril*, with forms in all Rom. langs. ? Connected with *bar*; cf. F. *au-dessus* (*au-dessous*) *de la barre*, of wine regarded as superior (inferior) according as it is drawn from the upper (lower) part of the cask,

the latter being strengthened by an internal bar or stanchion. The *barrel organ* (18 cent.) is so called because the keys are struck by pins on a revolving barrel or cylinder. For gen. sense of cylinder, as in gun-*barrel*, cf. *tunnel*.

barren. Orig. of female. Archaic F. *bréhaigne*, OF. *brehaing, baraing*, etc. Origin obscure. Perh. from OHG. *ham*, mutilated, preceded by the pejorative particle *bar-*. Cf. Ger. *hammel*, castrated ram. See *maim*.

barret [*hist.*]. Cap. F. *barrette*. See *biretta*.

barricade. F., It. *barricata* or Sp. *barricada*, from *barrica*, barrel, used in extempore barriers. Incorr. *barricado* is found earlier; cf. *ambuscado, armado, bastinado*. Hist. esp. in ref. to Parisian émeutes.

barriquade: a barricado; a defence of barrels, timber, pales, earth, or stones, heaped up, or closed together; and serving to stop up a street, or passage, and to keep off shot, etc. (Cotg.).

barrico [*naut.*]. See *breaker*.

barrier. F. *barrière*, from *barre*, bar.

barring-out. Recorded for 1728 (Swift).

Revolts, republics, revolutions, most
No graver than a schoolboys' "barring-out"
(Tennyson, *Princess*).

barrister. Earlier *barrester, barraster*. Mod. formation from *bar*, app. modelled on *chorister, sophister*. Cf. ME. *legistre* (from *lex*) and its MedL. form *legista*. The name originated with the bar of the Inns of Court, but is now associated with the bar of a tribunal. See *bar*.

barrow¹. Funeral mound. Orig. hill, mountain. AS. *beorg*. Com. Teut.; cf. Du. Ger. *berg*, ON. *berg, bjarg*, Goth. *baírgahei*, mountain chain. Prob. also Aryan; cf. Armen. *berj*, OIr. *brig*, etc.

barrow². Vehicle. AS. *bearwe*. Orig. stretcher, bier (q.v.), hand-barrow; cogn. with *bear²*. Later meaning may have been affected by F. dial. *barou*, app. related to *brouette*, wheel-barrow (see *barouche*).

They brought out the sycke...and layed them upon beddes and barowes (Coverd. *Acts*, v. 15).

bart. Abbrev. of *baronet*.

barter [*archaic*]. F. *barater*, to deceive, in OF. to exchange, haggle, from *barat* (see *barratry*); cf. It. *barattare*, Sp. *baratar*. For connection between trading and cheating cf. Ger. *tauschen*, to exchange, *täuschen*, to deceive.

baratar: to sell cheape, to deceive (Percyvall).

barater: to cheat, cousen, beguyle, deceive, lie, cog, foist, in bargaining; also, to trucke, scourse, barter, exchange (Cotg.).

bartizan [*poet.*]. Sc. (16 cent.), of uncertain meaning, but app. corrupt. of *bratticing*, timber-work. Currency is due to Scott. See *brattice*.

bretasynge: propugnaculum (*Cath. Angl.*).

barton [*dial.*]. Enclosure in various senses. AS. *beretūn*. See *barley* and *town*.

barytes [*min.*]. From *barium* (q.v.).

barytone, baritone. F. *baryton* or It. *baritono*, from G. βαρύς, heavy, τόνος, tone.

basalt. L. *basaltes*, said by Pliny to be an Afr. word. Not connected with *salt*.

basan, bazan. Kind of sheep-skin leather. Corruptly *basil, bazil*. F. *basane*, Prov. *bazana*, Sp. *badana*, Arab. *bitānah*, inside, lining.

bascinet. See *basinet*.

bascule [*mech.*]. F., see-saw, for earlier *bacule*, from OF. *baculer*, from *battre*, to beat, *cul*, posterior.

The practice of flying through the Tower Bridge between the high-level foot-ways and the bascules must cease (*Daily Chron.* June 27, 1919).

base[1]. Noun. F., L., G. βάσις, step, also pedestal, from βαίνειν, to step.

base[2]. Adj. F. *bas*, VL. *bassus*, stumpy, common in classical L. as cognomen. For sense-development cf. *low*. *Baseborn* may be for earlier *low-born*, but, as there is no other example of adv. use of *base*, it is perh. connected with OF. *fils de bast*, whence ME. *a bast ibore*, baseborn (see *bastard*).

baseball. Now chiefly US., so-called from the *bases*, or bounds, which mark the circuit, but these *bases* were taken over from *Prisoners' base* (15 cent.), which is for *bars*, the *-r-* being lost as in *bass*[1] (q.v.).

bace pley: barri (*Prompt. Parv.*).

bace playe: jeu aux barres (Palsg.).

barres: the play at bace; or, prison bars (Cotg.).

baseborn. See *base*[2].

basement. Connected by *NED.* with *base*[1], by Skeat with *base*[2]. Cf. F. *soubassement*, with very similar meaning. But Cotg. has, marked as archaic, *soubastement*, app. from *bastir* (*bâtir*), which suits the sense better.

soubastement: a foundation, or ground-work; a low building within the ground for the support of roomes above-ground (Cotg.).

bash [*colloq.*]. Chiefly northern. Origin unknown. ? Cf. Sw. *basa*, Dan. *baske*, to beat, ? or mixture of such words as *bang* and *smash*. Cf. also archaic and dial. *pash*.

bashaw. Earlier E. form of *pasha* (q.v.).

bashful. From *abash* (q.v.). Formerly also

daunted, e.g. Clarendon speaks of a "bashful army." Cf. ME. *bashment*, discomfiture.

bashi-bazouk. Turk. irregular soldier. Turk. *bāshi-bōzuk*, one whose head is turned. App. became familiar at time of Crimean War. Cf. *pasha*, *bimbashi*.

This form of Bashi-bazookism is actually called "nationalization" in the jargon of the Southern Bolsheviks (*Daily Chron.* July 2, 1919).

basil[1]. Plant. OF. *basile*, L., G. βασιλικόν, royal (sovereign remedy). ModF. *basilic* means both the plant and the *basilisk* (q.v.). In the OF. names for both the same confusion appears, no doubt as a result of some belief in the plant as an antidote against the bite of the reptile.

basil[2]. See *basan*.

Basilian. Of *St Basil*, bishop of Caesarea, as in *Basilian liturgy*.

basilica. L., G. βασιλική (sc. οἰκία), royal dwelling. Later, hall of justice, then the same used as a place of worship. In Rome applied spec. to the seven churches established by Constantine.

basilisk. Fabulous monster, cockatrice, whose breath and glance were fatal. Hence *basilisk glance*. G. βασιλίσκος, little king, because of a mark depicted on its head resembling a crown. Cf. L. *regulus*, lit. little king.

Ther [in India] ben the basylicocks which have the sight so venymous that they sle all men
     (Caxton, *Mirror of World*).

The viper and the flying basiliscus [*Vulg.* regulus volans] (*Douay Bible, Is.* xxx. 6).

basin. OF. *bacin* (*bassin*), VL. *bacchinon* (Gregory of Tours), for *baccinum*, from *bacca*, vessel for water (Isidore). Hence also It. *bacino*, Sp. *bacin*, Ger. *becken*. Ult. origin unknown. Perh. a Gaulish word and cogn. with F. *bac*, trough, ferryboat.

basinet, bascinet, basnet. Basin-shaped helmet. OF. *bacinet*, dim. of *bacin*, basin. Cf. synon. Ger. *kesselhut*, lit. kettle hat. Mod. *bowler* belongs to the same class of ideas. Obs. 1600–1800, but revived by Scott.

And a brasun basynet on his heed
     (Wyc. 1 *Sam.* xvii. 5).

bassinet: a little bowle, a small bason; also, the scull, sleight helmet, or head piece, worne, in old time, by the French men of armes (Cotg.).

basis. L. See *base*[1].

bask. ON. *bathask*, whence ModIcel. *bathast*, to bathe oneself, reflex. of *batha*, to bathe. For formation cf. *busk*[1]. See *bath*.

Seynge his brother baskynge in his bloud (Lydgate).

Baskerville. Famous Birmingham printer (†1775). Cf. *aldine, elzevir.*

basket. At one time thought to be Celt., but Gael. *bascaid,* Ir. *basgaod,* Welsh *basged* are from E. A supposed Gaulish word *bascauda* is used by Juvenal and Martial, the latter of whom expressly describes it as British. The *NED.*'s objection that *bascauda* is described as a tub or brazen vessel, and so could not be a basket, is not serious, as the change of meaning could easily be paralleled. Cf. *canister,* now a metal receptacle, from L. *canistrum,* a wicker basket. Moreover *bascauda* gave OF. *baschoe,* a basket. In OF. we also find *basche, basse,* used in the same sense. It would appear that *basket,* found in AF. c. 1200, though not recorded in continental OF., must have been a dim. formation belonging to the same group. This leaves the real origin of *bascauda* unsolved. It may be cogn. with L. *fascia.*

Barbara de pictis veni bascauda Britannis,
Sed me jam mavult dicere Roma suam (Martial).

bachoue: a kind of flat-sided basket, of wicker, close woven, and pitched in the inside; used in times of vintage (Cotg.).

basnet. See *basinet.*

bason [*Bibl.*]. Archaic form of *basin.*

Basque. Race and non-Aryan lang. of western Pyrenees. Late L. *Vasco, Vasconia.* Its only contribution to E. is perh. *jingo.*

basque. Of a dress. F., earlier also *baste.* Origin unknown. Prob. not connected with the national name *Basque,* although from this we have *basquine,* "a Spanish vardingale" (Cotg.).

bas-relief. F., It. *bassorilievo.* See *base²* and *relief.*

bass¹. Fish. Earlier *barse* (still in dial.), AS. *bærs;* cf. Du. *baars,* Ger. *barsch, kaulbars,* perch; cogn. with *bristle.*

bass². Fibre. See *bast.* Hence *bass-broom, bass-wood.*

bass³ [*mus.*]. Formerly *base,* now remodelled on It. *basso, base².*

basset¹. Short-legged dog. OF., dim. of *bas,* low.

basset: a terrier, or earthing beagle (Cotg.).

basset² [*archaic*]. Card-game. F. *bassette,* It. *bassetta,* supposed to be in some way connected with *basso,* low.

bassinet(te). Cradle. First in Thackeray. Supposed to be a dim. of F. *bassin,* basin; but this seems unlikely, and F. *bassinet* is not used in same sense. Perh. corrupted

from F. *bercelonnette,* double dim. of *berceau,* cradle.

bassoon. F. *basson,* augment. of *basse,* bass³.

bast. Inner bark of lime. AS. *bæst.* Com. Teut.; cf. Du. Ger. ON. *bast.* See *bass².*

bastard. OF. *bastard (bâtard)* with corresponding forms in most Europ. langs. In OF. also *fils de bast,* son of a pack-saddle, with pejorative ending *-art,* Ger. *-hart.* Cf. synon. OF. *coitrart,* from *coite,* quilt, Ger. *bankert,* earlier *bankart,* from *bank,* bench, LG. *mantelkind,* mantle child, ON. *hrīsungr,* from *hrīs,* brushwood. See *bantling* and *bat³.* Not always a term of reproach, e.g. the Conqueror is often referred to as *William the Bastard.* Cf. surname *Bastard.*

A bastard, or he that is i-gete of a worthy fader and i-bore of an unworthy moder (Trev. ii. 269).

I begat the whoreson in bast;
It was done all in haste (*Nature,* c. 1475).

banckaerd: spurius, nothus, illegitimus, non in lecto geniali, sed quovis scamno fortuito a matre conceptus (Kil.).

baste¹. To sew. OF. *bastir,* OHG. *bastjan, bestan,* to sew with *bast* (q.v.). Or, the E. word being app. earlier recorded than the F., the verb may be of native formation from *bast.* See also *bastille.*

baastynge of cloth: subsutura (*Prompt. Parv.*).

I baste a garment with threde: je bastys (Palsg.).

baste². Cooking. OF. *basser,* to soak, the mod. form being from the p.p. The OF. word is of unknown origin.

to bast the rost: basser (du Guez).

The fat pygge is baast (Barclay).

baste³. To beat. Jocular application of *baste².* Both occur first as p.p. Cf. Ger. *schmieren,* to drub, lit. to anoint, and F. *frotter.* See also *smite.*

froter: to rub; to chafe; to fret, or grate against; also, to bathe; also, to cudgell, thwack, baste or knocke soundly (Cotg.).

bastille. F., from Prov. *bastida,* from *bastire,* to build. Now only of the historic building in Paris, but in common ME. use (*bastel,* etc.), of a fort. The popular form occurs as late as Butler. The derivation of *bâtir,* OF. *bastir,* MedL. *bastire,* is doubtful, but some authorities derive it from OHG. *bastjan,* to sew with bast, hence construct, a very possible sense-development. See *baste¹.*

Conveys him to enchanted castle,
There shuts him fast in wooden bastile (*Hudibras*).

bastinado. Sp. *bastonada*, beating, from *baston*, cudgel (see *baton*). For ending see *ambuscade, armada*. The limitation of meaning to beating the soles of the feet is comparatively mod. See *drub*.

bastion. F., It. *bastione*, from *bastia*, fort (whence *Bastia* in Corsica), from *bastire*, to build. See *bastille*.

bat¹. Cudgel, etc. AS. *batt*, club, ? from Celt. Some senses perh. from F. *batte*, which is usu. connected with *battre*, to beat. The cricket *bat* is recorded for 1706. To *carry* (*bring out*) *one's bat* goes back to the less luxurious days when the man "out" left the bat for the next comer. *Bat*, lump, clod, is supposed to be the same word, hence *brickbat*. Also *bat*, pace, as in *at a great bat*, from dial. sense of stroke. *Batfowling* (*Temp.* ii. 1) means dazing birds with a light at night and then knocking them down with a bat.

With hym came a grete cumpanye, with swerdis and battis (Wyc. *Matt.* xxvi. 47).

bat². Animal. In ME. usu. *bakke*. Origin obscure, but app. Scand. Cf. Dan. *aftenbakke*, evening bat, Sw. dial. *nattbatta*, night bat. The AS. term was *hrēremus*, from *hrēran*, to shake; cf. Ger. *fledermaus* and E. dial. *flittermouse* (Tennyson).

Moldewarpis and backes [*var.* rere-myis]
(Wyc. *Is.* ii. 20).

bat³ [*mil.*]. Packsaddle. F. *bât*, OF. *bast*, MedL. *bastum*. Relation to G. βαστάζειν, to bear, is unlikely. Now only in mil. use; cf. *bathorse, batman*, the latter used by Washington (1757).

batata. Sweet potato. Sp. and Port., prob. from Hayti. Applied later to another plant in the form *potato* (q.v.).

Batavian. Occ. used of the Dutch. L. *Batavia* and *Batavi*, inhabitants of island of *Betawe* between the Rhine and the Waal. Second element is cogn. with *ait* (q.v.) and appears also in *Scandinavia*.

batch. Orig. a "baking" of bread. ME. *bache*, from *bake* (cf. *match* and *make*). For sense-development cf. F. *fournée*, oven-ful, used of the "batches" in which victims were sent to the guillotine during the Reign of Terror. Mod. *whole boiling* is a similar metaphor.

batche of bredde: fournee de pain (Palsg.).

bate¹. Aphet. for *abate* (q.v.). Esp. in *bated breath*, to *bate a jot*. Hence *bating*, except, barring.

bate². Strife. Aphet. for *debate*. Now only in archaic *makebate*.

bath¹. For washing. AS. *bæth*. Com. Teut.; cf. Du. Ger. *bad*, ON. *bath*. With *bath-bathe* cf. *grass-graze*. The *Order of the Bath*, established temp. Hen. IV and revived temp. George I, takes its name from the purification of the new knight. The town of *Bath* was orig. *æt bathum*, at the baths (cf. Ger. *Baden*), and Horace Walpole still called it "the Bath." Hence *go to Bath*, lunatics being supposed to benefit from the waters. Also *Bath bun, chair, brick* (made at Bridgwater), *stone, Oliver* (from the name of a Bath doctor), *chap*, etc.

At all times of the tide [at Margate] the machines or bathing waggons can drive a proper depth into the sea (J. Ames, c. 1740).

bath². Liquid measure (*Is.* v. 10). Heb.

Bathonian [*geol.*]. From ModL. *Bathonia*, Bath.

bathos. G. βάθος, depth. In literary sense introduced by Pope.

My heart is in the grave with her;
The family went abroad (Alexander Smith).

bating. See *bate¹*.

batiste. F., cambric. Said to be from name of first manufacturer at Cambrai (13 cent.).

batman. See *bat³*.

baton. Earlier *batoon*. F. *bâton*, OF. *baston*, of doubtful origin. See also *batten*. Very general as symbol of authority; hence the *baton* of a Marshal. The *bâton* of the *chef d'orchestre* is of recent F. introduction.

batrachian. From G. βάτραχος, frog.

batta [*mil.*]. Extra allowance for officers serving in India. Earlier, maintenance. Indo-Port., orig. from Canarese *bhatta*, rice. Cf. hist. of *salary*. See *paddy*.

battalion. F. *bataillon*, It. *battaglione*, dim. of *battaglia*. See *battle*. Earlier one of the main divisions of an army.

battaglione: a battalion, a great squadron, the maine battle (Flor.).

battels [*Oxf.*]. College-bill, esp. for provisions from buttery. Prob. connected with obs. *battle*, to grow fat, which is app. a var. of *batten²* (q.v.). Latinized as *batilli, batellae* (16 cent.). Quot. 1 is a century older than *NED.* record.

In battel apud Ripon vidz in vino ijd. ob.
(*Mem. of Fountains Abbey*, 1447).

One of the most infallible marks by which our English grasiers know their battle and feeding grounds (Purch. xvi. 89).

batten[1]. Strip of wood. Var. of *baton* (q.v.). Hence naut. to *batten down* esp. hatches.

batten[2]. To feed gluttonously, now usu. fig. Orig. to thrive, grow fat (see *battels*). ON. *batna*, to improve, grow "better," cogn. with AS. *batian*, to feed, thrive. Cf. Du. *baat*, profit, and, for sense, Norw. Dan. *gjöde*, to fatten cattle, lit. to made good.

My cradle was a corslet, and for milke
I battened was with blood (*Trag. of Tiberius*, 1609).

une fille bien advenuē: well proved, well growne, well come on, well prospered; well batned, or batled (Cotg.).

batter. F. *battre*, VL. **battere*, for *battuere*, to beat, of Celt. origin. Also influenced by the verb to *bat*, from *bat*[1]. Noun *batter*, now only culinary, represents F. *batture* (cf. *fritter* from *friture*). Oldest sense of *battery*, F. *batterie*, is the act of beating, as in *assault and battery*; hence, preparations for "battering" a fortress, arrangement of artillery, etc. The *battering-ram* translates L. *aries* and the head of the instrument was sometimes shaped like that of the animal.

batowr of flowre or mel with watyr: mola
(*Prompt. Parv.*).

aries, bellica machina, muris urbium evertendis apta: a great peece of timber shodde with brasse, in facion like a rammes head (Coop.).

battle. F. *bataille*, VL. *battualia*, neut. pl. of *battualis*, from *battuere*, to beat. Oldest L. sense is "exercitationes militum vel gladiatorum." In ME. and up to 17 cent. the meaning of warlike array, army division, was common. A *pitched battle* was orig. one taking place by mutual arrangement on selected ground. A *battle royal*, in which several combatants engage, is from cockfighting, but perh. orig. meant battle with kings in command (see *royal*). It is characteristic of the revolution in nav. nomenclature that the *NED.* has not *battle-ship* (for older *line-of-battle ship*) or *battle-cruiser* under *battle*.

battledore. Orig. a washing beetle. App. Prov. *batador* or Sp. *batidor*, influenced by dial. *battle*, to beat linen (see *beetle*[2]). Cf. synon. F. *battoir*.

batyldere, or waschynge betyl: feritorium
(*Prompt. Parv.*).

batador: a washing beetle (Minsh.).

battlement. OF. *batillement*, app. irreg. formed from OF. *bataillier*, to furnish a wall with movable defences, or else for *bastillement*, from *bastiller*, to fortify. See *bastille*. Cf. *embattled*.

battology. Needless repetition. From G.

βαττολόγος, stammerer, from personal name Βάττος (Herod. iv. 155).

battue. Fem. p.p. of F. *battre*, to beat (the game).

batty. As *batta* (q.v.).

bauble. Earlier also *bable*. OF. *baubel*, toy, kindred with *babble*, *baby*. Cf. F. *babiole*, from It. *babbola*. A fool's *bauble* parodied the sceptre.

Take away that bauble (Oliver Cromwell).

baudekin, **bawdkin** [*archaic*]. Rich fabric. Obs. exc. in romance. OF. *baudequin*. See *baldachin*.

baulk. See *balk*.

bawbee [*Sc.*]. Halfpenny. Prob. from the *Laird of Sillebawby*, 16 cent. mint-master. Another coin was called an *Atchison*, from a mint-master who is coupled with the above in Treasury records. Similarly *bodle*, *boddle* is referred to a mint-master *Bothwell*, but for this there is no evidence.

bawd. Aphet. for *ribaud*. See *ribald*.

bagos: a man-baud, a ribauld (Cotg.).

ribaud: leno (Holyoak).

bawdry or ribaldry: obscenitas (Litt.).

bawl. Orig. of animals. MedL. *baulare*, to bark. Prob. imit. Cf. *bellow*, Ger. *bellen*, to bark, Icel. *baula*, to low.

bawn [*hist.*]. Enclosure (Ir.). Ir. *bádhun*, from *ba*, cows, *dún*, fortress.

bay[1]. Tree. Short for *bay-tree* (cf. *myrtle*), from archaic *bay*, berry, F. *baie*, L. *baca*. Hence *bay-rum*.

bay[2] [*geog.*]. F. *baie*, Late L. *baia* (Isidore); cf. Span. Port. *bahia*. Of unknown origin, but associated in F. & E. with *bay*[3]. Spec. application to Bay of Biscay, and the name *Bayonne*, supposed to mean good harbour, would seem to indicate Basque origin.

bay[3] [*arch.*]. F. *baie*, from *bayer*, to gape, VL. *batare*, from *ba*, natural sound of astonishment. See *bay*[5] and *abeyance*. Hence *bay-window*, not orig. same shape as *bow-window*; also naut. *sick-bay*.

bay[4]. Colour. F. *bai*, L. *badius*, used by Varro of the colour of a horse.

equus badius: of bay colour, bayarde (Coop.).

bay[5]. Of hounds. Earlier *abay*, OF. *abayer* (*aboyer*), to bark, VL. **ad-batare* (see *bay*[3]). Hence to *stand at bay*, i.e. facing the hounds, F. *être aux abois*.

abbayer: to barke, or bay at (Cotg.).

to keep one at a bay: morari, sistere, tenere (Litt.).

bayadère. Hindu dancing-girl. F., Port. *bailadeira*, from *bailar*, to dance. See *ball*[2].

bayard [*poet.*]. Bay steed, esp. the steed that carried the four sons of Aymon. See *bay*[4]. Formerly as type of blind recklessness.

Bayard. Hero "sans peur et sans reproche." Famous F. soldier (1476–1524).

bayonet. F. *baïonnette*, orig. a dagger, trad., since Tabourot des Accords (1614), derived from *Bayonne*, though proof is lacking. Popularly also *bagonet*, *bagnet*. In E. from 17 cent. Cf. origin of *pistol*.

bayou [*US.*]. Creek. F. *boyau*, gut. See *bowel*.

Have you nowhere encountered my Gabriel's boat on the bayous? (*Evangeline*).

bay-salt. From Bay of Biscay, on the coast of which are extensive salt-marshes. Quot. 1 appears to settle this origin, which *NED.* regards as conjectural only. Similarly we find LG. *die baie* applied to Bourgneuf in Brittany in connection with the 15 cent. salt-trade.

La nief [ship] appelez le Gaynpayn se fist charger de seel en la Bay [of Biscay]
(*John of Gaunt's Reg.* 1372–76).
bay-salt, from Baionne in France: sal Gallicus (Litt.).

bazaar. Earlier *bazarro*. Pers. *bāzār*, market. Prob. via Turk. and It. For mod. use, due to Anglo-Indians, cf. *gymkhana*.

bazan. See *basan*.

bazil. See *basil*.

bdellium. Tree and gum-resin. L. (*Vulg.*), G. βδέλλιον, used to render Heb. *b'dōlakh*, of unknown Eastern origin. See *Gen.* ii. 12.

be. This verb contains three stems, viz. *be*-, cogn. with L. *fu*-, G. φυ- (cf. Ger. *du bist*), *es*-, cogn. with L. *esse* (cf. G. ἔστι), and *wes*- (cf. OHG. *wesan* and Ger. *gewesen*). *Am*, cogn. with Sanskrit *asmi*, is the solitary survival in E. of a -*mi* verb; cf. G. εἰμί (*ἔσμι), L. *sum*, Ger. *bin*. *Art*, *is* are from the *es*- stem (cf. *was*, *were*), so also *are*. *Was*, *were* are from the *wes*- stem (cf. *lose*, *lorn*). The existing paradigm of the verb is an accidental conglomeration from the different Old English dials. The pres. pl. *sind*, *sindon* (cf. L. *sunt*, Ger. *sind*) has entirely disappeared. *Be-all*, usu. with *end-all*, is after *Macb.* i. 5.

be-. Weakened form of AS. *bī*, by (e.g. in *beside*, *beyond*). As verb prefix often intens. See *by*.

beach. Of late appearance (16 cent.), though prob. old in dial. As AS. *bece*, brook, has become -*beach* in many place-names (*Wisbech*, *Waterbeach*, *Holbeach*, etc.), this may be the same word, with transference of meaning from the brook to the pebbly shore. Hence *beach-comber*, long crested wave (Pacific), fig. long-shore wastrel (ib.).

beacon. AS. *bēacn*, sign, portent. Also esp. fire-signal, AS. *bēacn-fȳr*; cf. obs. Du. *boken*, OHG. *bauhhan*, Ger. *bake*, from LG.; cogn. with *beck*[2], *beckon*.

bead. Orig. prayer. AS. *gebed* (see *bid*). Hence *bead-roll*, *beadsman*. Later applied to the device used in telling one's beads, i.e. counting one's prayers. The rosary is regularly called *pair of beads* in ME. From the *bead*, or small metal knob forming front-sight of a rifle, comes to *draw a bead on* (US.).

Of smal coral aboute hire arm she bar
A peire of bedes, gauded al with grene
(Chauc. A. 158).

The Beadsman, after thousand aves told,
For aye unsought-for slept among his ashes cold
(*Eve of Saint Agnes*).

beadle. OF. *bedel* (*bedeau*), OHG. *bidal* messenger of justice, gradually replaced ME. *bidel*, *budel*, from cogn. AS. *bydel*, from AS. *bēodan*, to proclaim (cf. Ger. *bieten*, to bid). The latter survives in surnames *Biddle*, *Buddle*. Archaic *bedell* is still in use at universities. The parish *beadle* is recorded from 16 cent. Hence *beadledom* for *Bumbledom* (q.v.).

beagle. ME. *begle* (15 cent.). Spelt also *begele*. Certainly F., and, the beagle being noted for its loud musical bark, perh. from *bégueule*, gaping throat, used in OF. of a noisy person. See *bay*[5], *gules*.

beak. F. *bec*, L. *beccus* (Suetonius), of Celt. origin. In sense of magistrate (16 cent.) from thieves' slang. Quite mod. in sense of assistant master.

beaker. ME. *biker*, ON. *bikarr*; cf. Sc. *bicker*. In most Europ. langs. Cf. Du. *beker*, Ger. *becher*, It. *bicchiere*, MedL. *bicarium*. ? From G. βῖκος, earthen drinking bowl. See *pitcher*.

beam. AS. *bēam*, tree (as in *hornbeam*, *whitebeam*). WGer.; cf. Du. *boom*, Ger. *baum*; cogn. with ON. *bathmr*, Goth. *bagms*. To *kick* (*strike*) *the beam*, i.e. to prove the lighter, is from the *beam* of a balance. The *beams* of a ship are transverse, the timbers being vertical; hence *abeam*, abreast, *on one's beam-ends*, almost capsized. Also used of the extreme breadth of a ship. Fig. senses from naut. metaphor, e.g. to be *over-engined for one's beam*. A *beam* of light is the same word, AS. *bēam* being used to render *columna* in ref. to the Bibl. pillar of fire. See also *boom²*.

bean. AS. *bēan*. Com. Teut.; cf. Du. *boon*, Ger. *bohne*, ON. *baun*. *Full of beans* is used of a well-fed horse needing exercise. To *give beans* seems to be quite mod. *Bean-feast* (*NED.* 1882), vulgarly *beano*, is perh. to be explained from quot. below.

Mr Day was the possessor of a small estate in Essex, at no great distance from Fairlop Oak. To this venerable tree he used, on the first Friday in July, annually to repair; thither it was his custom to invite a party of his neighbours to accompany him, and, under the shade of its branches and leaves, to dine on beans and bacon....For several years before the death of the benevolent, although humorous, founder of this public bean-feast, the pump and block makers of Wapping went annually to the fair in a...vehicle drawn by six post-horses, the whole adorned with ribands, flags, and streamers
(*Time's Telescope for* 1820, p. 247).

bear¹. Animal. AS. *bera*. WGer.; cf. Du. *beer*, Ger. *bär*; cogn. with ON. *björn*. As a Stock Exchange term it seems to be due to the proverb about selling the bear's skin before killing the bear. At the time of the South Sea Bubble a *bear* was called a *bear-s.in jobber*. The contrasted *bull* appears later and was prob. suggested by *bear*, perh. with a vague idea of "tossing up" contrasted with "pulling down." A *bear-garden* was orig. a place for bear-baiting and other rough sports. *Bear-leader* (18 cent.) is a travelling tutor in charge of a "cub" whom he has to "lick into shape."

A stock-jobber who had some losing bargains of bearskins (*Mist's Journal*, Mar. 28, 1719).

bear². Verb. AS. *beran*. Aryan; cf. OSax. *beran*, Ger. *gebären*, to bring forth, ON. *bera*, Goth. *bairan*, L. *ferre*, G. φέρειν, Sanskrit *bhar-*. For two main groups of senses cf. relationship of cogn. L. *ferre* and *fertilis*. The past *bore* is not found in the *AV.* (*bare*) and the mod. distinction between *born* and *borne* is artificial. Intrans. senses, e.g. to *bear to the left*, are orig. naut. (cf. to *take bearings*). Mechanical *bearings* are so called because intended to bear the friction. *Bearer*, in Anglo-Ind. sense of palanquin-bearer, head-servant, as in Mrs Sherwood's famous *Little Henry and his Bearer*, has perh. been influenced by synon. Bengali *behārā* (cf. *grasscutter*).

bearbine. Convolvulus. From obs. *bear*, barley, round stalks of which it winds. See *barley, bind, bine*.

beard. AS. *beard*. Com. Teut.; cf. Du. *baard*, Ger. *bart*, ON. *barthr* (only in names); ult. cogn. with L. *barba* (cf. *red—ruber*, *word—verbum*). Hence verb to *beard*, a good example of our instinct for ellipt. expression.

à sa barbe: to his teeth, in his presence, before his face; also, mauger his beard, in despight of him
(Cotg.).

beast. OF. *beste* (*bête*), VL. **besta* for *bestia*. In its orig. sense displaced AS. *deōr* (see *deer*) to be later displaced itself by *animal*, exc. in spec. connections, e.g. *beast-market*, *man and beast*.

It is sowun a beestly [*Vulg.* animale] body, it schal ryse a spiritual body (Wyc. 1 *Cor.* xv. 44).

beat. AS. *bēatan*; cf. OHG. *bōzan* (whence Ger. *amboss*, anvil), ON. *bauta*. Var. of p.p. still in *dead-beat*. *Beating the bounds* consists in striking certain points in parish boundaries with rods. In to *beat a retreat*, to *beat up recruits*, etc., there is a suggestion of the drum, with influence of the unrelated F. *battre*. To *beat about the bush* is altered in form and meaning from earlier to *beat the bush*, in order to start the game. Both in E. and US. there are many phrases of the type to *beat creation* (*cock-fighting*, etc.). Cf. Ir. to *bang Banagher*, a village in King's Co. See also *hoof*.

'Ate of the 'art and 'ate of the 'and,
'Ate by water and 'ate by land,
'Oo do we 'ate to beat the band?
England!
(*Hymn of Hate*, trad. T. Atkins).

beatitude. L. *beatitudo*, state of blessedness, from *beatus*, p.p. of *beare*, to bless. Esp. in ref. to Sermon on the Mount. *Beatific vision* is ult. Plato's μακαρία ὄψις (Phaedrus).

Beatrice. Inspiring mistress. From Dante's *Beatrice*. Cf. *Dulcinea, Egeria*.

beau, belle. Mod. introductions (17 cent.). ME. had the masc. form pronounced as in *beauty* (q.v.).

beau ideal. F. *beau idéal*, where *idéal* is the adj., the phrase being often misunderstood, and hence misused, in E.

beaujolais. Burgundy wine. District in the Lyonnais.

beaune. Burgundy wine. From place of origin (Côte-d'Or).

beauty. F. *beauté*, VL. **bellitas, bellitat-*, from *bellus*, beautiful, which is represented, to the exclusion of *pulcher*, in all Rom. langs. *Beauty-spot* is 17 cent., *beauty-sleep*, i.e. sleep before midnight, is 19 cent.

Fine by degrees and beautifully less
(Prior, *Henry and Emma*).

beaver[1]. Animal. AS. *beofor*. Aryan; cf. Du. *bever*, Ger. *biber*, ON. *bjǫrr*, L. *fiber*, Sanskrit *babhrŭ-*, brown; also OF. *bièvre*, OIt. *bevero*, OSp. *befre*, Late L. *beber* (Priscian), all from Teut. Hence *beaver* (hat) and to *cock one's beaver*, i.e. assume a swaggering demeanour.

Upon his heed a Flaundrish bevere hat
(Chauc. A. 272).

beaver[2] [*hist.*]. Lower part of vizor. F. *bavière*, bib, from *baver*, to slobber.

Then saw you not his face?—
O yes, my lord, he wore his beaver up (*Haml.* i. 2).
baviere: a bib; *baviere d'un armet*: the beaver of a helmet (Cotg.).

beaverteen. Fabric. From *beaver*[1], after *velveteen*.

because. Earlier *by cause*.

beccafico. Bird. It., lit. "peck-fig."

bechamel. Sauce. Named after *Marquis de Béchamel*, 17 cent. epicure, steward to Louis XIV.

bêche-de-mer. Sea-slug, also called *trepang*. F. *bêche*, grub, caterpillar, of obscure origin; not ident. with *bêche*, spade, VL. **biseca*, double-cutter.

beck[1] [*north. dial.*]. Stream. ON. *bekkr*. Com. Teut.; cf. OSax. *beki*, Du. *beek* (as in *Zonnebeek*), Ger. *bach*. Hence are derived Norman place-names in *-bec*, e.g. *Caudebec*, i.e. cold beck.

beck[2]. Gesture. Esp. in *beck and call*. From obs. verb *beck* used in ME. for *beckon* (q.v.).

Nods and becks and wreathed smiles (*Allegro*).

becket [*naut.*]. Loop of rope to secure object. Origin unknown.

beckon. AS. *bīcnan*, from *bēacn*, sign, beacon (q.v.). Now usu. of summoning gesture, but orig. wider sense in *Luke*, i. 22.

become. Compd. of *come*, prefix orig. ident. with *by*. For gen. sense cf. synon. F. *devenir*, from *venir*, to come. For sense of suiting, cf. *comely*, *convenient*, F. *avenant*, Ger. *bequem*, convenient (from *bekommen*).

Becquerel rays. Discovered by *Becquerel*, F. physicist (†1891).

bed. AS. *bedd*. Com. Teut.; cf. Du. *bed*, Ger. *bett*, Norw. dial. *bed*, Goth. *badi*. Perh. orig. lair of animal and cogn. with L. *fodere*, to dig. Garden sense, found in AS., is differentiated in Ger. by spelling *beet*. *In the twinkling of a bed-post* is for earlier *bed-staff*, an implement of indefinite function, but app. regarded as a readily extemporized weapon in nocturnal alarms and excursions. *Bedstead* is lit. bed place (see *stead*). *Bed-*

ridden is for earlier *bedrid*, AS. *bedrida*, lit. bed-rider. Cf. ME. *bedlawer* (lier). It has app. been altered on *hag-ridden*. *Bedrock* is US. mining term.

paraliticus: *bedrida* (*Voc.*).
bedrede man or woman: decumbens (*Prompt. Parv.*).
bedlawere: supra in *bedrede* (*ib.*).

In her hand she grasped the bed-staff, a weapon of mickle might (*Ingoldsby*).

bedad [*Anglo-Ir.*]. For "by Gad."

bedeguar. Formerly plant; now, moss-like excrescence on rose-bush. F. *bédegar*, Pers. *bād-āwar*, wind-brought.

bedell [*univ.*]. See *beadle*.

Bedford level. Part of fen country, drained (1634) by *Earl of Bedford*.

bedight. See *dight*.

bedizen. For earlier *dizen*, lit. to put flax on a distaff (q.v.).

I dysyn a dystaffe, I put the flaxe upon it to spynne: je charge la quenouille (Palsg.).

Bedlam. ME. *Bethleem*, etc., hospital of *St Mary of Bethlehem*, founded 1247, received under protection of City of London (1346), and, on dissolution of monasteries, converted into state lunatic asylum (1547). For contr. cf. *maudlin*.

God be his guide,
As he guided the three kings into Bedlam
(*Calisto & Melibaea*, c. 1530).

bedlington. Terrier, from *Bedlington*, Northumb.

Bedouin. F., Arab. *badāwīn* (pl.), desert dwellers, from *badw*, desert. For pl. form cf. *assassin*. Both are Crusade words.

Li Beduyn ne croient point en Mahommet, ainçois (but) croient en la loy Haali, qui fu oncles Mahommet; et aussi y croient li Vieil de la Montaigne, cil qui nourrissent les Assacis (Joinville).

bedridden. See *bed*.

bee. AS. *bēo*. Com. Teut.; cf. Du. *bij*, Ger. *biene*, in which the *n* was orig. inflexional (cf. *birne*, pear), ON. *bȳ*. *Bee*, social gathering for mutual help (*husking bee*, *quilting bee*, *spelling bee*, etc.), supposed to be suggested by the busy and social character of the insect, is US. (1769), as is also *bee-line*, shortest route, taken by bee returning to hive; cf. *as the crow flies*. With *bee in one's bonnet*, earlier (16 cent.) *in one's head*, cf. use of Ger. *grille*, grasshopper.

Der mensch hat wunderliche grillen in seinem kopff: he is a whimsical fellow; he has strange fits, spurts or starts of fancy; he has his head full of caprichios, caprices, figaries, freaks, whimsies, maggets or conumdrums (Ludw.).

beech. AS. *bēce*. Com. Teut.; cf. Du. *beuk*, Ger. *buche*, ON. *bōk*; cogn. with L. *fagus* and prob. with G. φαγεῖν, to eat, from mast. Primitive form, AS. *bōc*, survives in some place-names in *Buck-*. See also *book*, *buckwheat*.

beef. OF. *beuf* (*bœuf*), L. *bos*, *bov-*, ox; cf. G. βοῦς. Still used in Sc. of the live beast. Hence *beef-eater*, servant, over-fed menial, and esp. yeoman of the guard, Tower warder. Cf. AS. *hlāfǣta*, loaf-eater, servant. The old popular explanation from *buffet*, side-board, is nonsense. The first *NED.* record in yeoman of guard sense is 1671, so that the explanation below is almost contemporary.

> If eny person of this citie, beyng no bocher, do kyll eny beiffes, mottons, veiles, porkettes, or lambes within this citie... (*Coventry Leet Book*, 1525).

> C'est ainsi qu'on appelle par dérision les *Yeomen of the Guard* dans la cour d'Angleterre, qui sont des gardes à peu près comme les cent Suisses en France. Et on leur donne ce nom-là, parce qu'à la cour ils ne vivent que de bœuf: par opposition à ces collèges d'Angleterre, où les écoliers ne mangent que du mouton (Miège, *French Dict.* 1688).

> "Who's he, father?"—"He's a beefeater."—"Is that why Lord Rhondda shut him up in the Tower?" (*Punch*, Feb. 6, 1918).

Beelzebub. Orig. god of Ekron. L., G., Heb. *ba'al-z'bub*, fly-lord (2 *Kings*, i. 2). Mod. meaning comes from *NT.* use (*Matt.* xii. 24) in sense of prince of devils, AS. *aldormann-diobla*.

beer. AS. *bēor*. WGer.; cf. Du. Ger. *bier*; ? cogn. with *barley*. Scand. has forms of *ale* (q.v.), which was the more usual word up to 16 cent., *beer* being then applied esp. to hopped malt liquor. It is not in Chauc. or *Piers Plowm.*

> To suckle fools and chronicle small beer (*Oth.* ii. 1).

beeregar [*dial.*]. From *beer*, after *vinegar*; cf. *alegar*.

beestings [*dial.*]. First milk of cow after calving. From synon. AS. *bēost*. Cf. Ger. *biestmilch*, and archaic F. *béton*, OF. *bet*, from OHG. *beost*. Various forms in dial. use.

> A beslings-puddin' an' Adam's wine
> (Tennyson, *Northern Cobbler*).

beet. AS. *bēte*, L. *beta*. Adopted in many Europ. langs. Cf. F. *betterave*, Ger. *beete*.

beetle¹. Mallet. AS. *bīetl*, beater; cf. MHG. *bōzel*, cudgel, LG. *betel*, mallet. Hence *beetle-brained*, *beetle-head* (cf. *blockhead*), *blind*, *deaf as a beetle* (cf. *deaf as a post*), but in such phrases there is usu. association with *beetle²*.

beetle². Insect. AS. *bitel*, prob. "biter." The *black-beetle* (cockroach) is not a beetle. *Blind as a beetle* (cf. *blind as a bat*) is due to the insect's apparently aimless flight in the dark (but see *beetle¹*). *Beetle-browed*, orig. with bushy eye-brows, seems to be due to the tufted antennae of certain species. Early observation of such physical details, as seen in popular names of animals and plants, was very minute and accurate; cf. F. *sourcils de hanneton* (cockchafer's eye-brows), used of a kind of fringe. Hence *beetle*, to overhang, of which mod. use dates from its employment as nonce-word in Shaks. (v.i.). William Finch (1607, in Purch.) describes an African fish *with beetle brows*, so that the phrase was not used only of human beings.

> mordiculus: *bitela* (*Voc.*).

> Bitelbrowed and baberliped
> (*Piers Plowm.* B. v 190).

> The dreadful summit of the cliff
> That beetles o'er his base into the sea (*Haml.* i. 4).

before. AS. *beforan*, from *bi*, by, *foran*, in front. With AS. *fore*, *foran* cf. Ger. *vor*, *vorn*. With *beforehand*, earlier also *before the hand*, cf. *ready to hand*, and L. *prae manu* or *manibus*, used with same meaning in ME.; also Ger. *vor der hand* in somewhat different sense. See *behindhand*.

beg¹, beggar. The verb is evolved from the noun (cf. *cadge*), OF. *begard*, MedL. *begardus*, member of mendicant order founded (early 13 cent.) in Netherlands, in imitation of the earlier *béguines* (see *biggin*), who were of the rule of *Lambert le Bègue* (Liège, 12 cent.). *Begging the question* translates L. *petitio principii*. The *beggar on horseback* is 16 cent.

> *beghardi*: haeretici exorti primum in Alemania, qui vulgariter *Begehardi* quoad viros, et *Beginae* quoad feminas nominantur (Duc.).

> As for her person, It beggared all description
> (*Ant. & Cleop.* ii. 2).

beg². Title. Osmanli *beg*, now *bey* (q.v.).

begad. For *by God*. Cf. *bedad*.

beget. AS. *begitan*, from *get* (q.v.).

beggar. See *beg¹*.

Beghard. See *beg¹*.

begin. AS. *beginnan*, of which the simplex is not found in any Teut. lang. Cf. Du. Ger. *beginnen*, Goth. *duginnan*. The aphet. *gin* once common but now only poet., may also represent the commoner AS. *onginnan*. Scand. forms are from LG.

begone. For *be gone* (imper.). Cf. *beware* and see *woebegone*.

begonia. From WInd. Named by Plumier, F. botanist (17 cent.), after *Michel Begon*, contemporary governor of Saint-Domingo. Cf. *dahlia, fuchsia, magnolia*, etc.

Beguine. Member of still existing lay sisterhood. See *beg*[1].

begum. Princess. Urdu *begam*, Pers., Turk. *bigīm*, fem. of *beg*[2], *bey*.

behalf. Orig. prep. or adv., by (the) side, a common AS. and ME. meaning of *half*. Cf. Ger. *oberhalb*, above, *meinethalben*, as far as I am concerned, etc. Mod. use represents a mixture of *on his halve*, on his side, and *bihalve him*, beside him.

The Jewis seyde that Crist was not on Goddis halfe (Wyc.).

behave. App. formed in ME. as intens. from *have*. Cf. Ger. *sich behaben*, F. *se porter*. *Behaviour*, earlier *behavour*, owes its ending to obs. *havour, haviour*, corrupt. of F. *avoir*, used in very similar sense.

behemoth. Heb. *b'hēmŏth*, pl. of *b'hēmāh*, beast, but prob. adapted from Egypt. *p-ehe-mau*, water-ox, i.e. hippopotamus. Cf. *leviathan*.

Lo! bemoth that I made with thee (Wyc. *Job*, xl. 15).

behest. AS. *behǣs*, vow, promise, from *behātan*, to promise, with excrescent *-t*. Mod. sense due to early confusion with simple *hest*, command. In ME. esp. in *land of behest*.

Bi feith he dwelte in the loond of biheest (Wyc. *Heb.* xi. 9).

behind. AS. *behindan*. Cf. *before*, and see *hind*. *Behindhand* is formed (16 cent.) by analogy with *beforehand* (q.v.). Both seem to have been orig. used in ref. to payments.

behold. AS. *behealdan*, to hold in view. Current E. sense is not found in other Teut. langs. Sense of obligation in *beholden*, though arising naturally from the etym., is confined to p.p. See *hold*[1].

behove, behoof. AS. *behōfian*, to need, require, from *behōf*, advantage; cf. Du. *behoef*, Ger. *behuf*, behoof, MHG. *beheben*, to receive, maintain. Ult. from *heave*, but sense-development is obscure.

beige. F. dial. form of *bis*, yellowish grey, dingy; cf. It. *bigio*. Origin unknown.

bekko-ware. Jap., tortoise-shell.

beknown [*dial.*]. Now usu. in neg. *unbeknown*. From obs. *beknow*; cf. Ger. *bekennen*, to acknowledge.

belabour. From *labour* with intens. prefix.

For sense cf. Ger. *bearbeiten*, to belabour, from *arbeiten*, to work.

belay. Compd. of *lay*[1]. Obs. exc. in naut. sense of making fast a rope, which is prob. borrowed from cogn. Du. *beleggen*. With *belay*, stop it, stow it, cf. *avast*.

een touw aan een' paal beleggen: to fasten a rope to a pile (Sewel).

belch. AS. *bealcan*; cf. Du. *balken*, to bawl.

belcher [*archaic*]. Blue and white spotted handkerchief, "bird's eye wipe." From *Jim Belcher*, pugilist († 1811). The name is Picard form of *bel-sire, beau-sire*. See *beldam*.

beldam. Grandmother; later, great grandmother; hence, hag. Both senses are in Shaks. From F. *belle* and *dame*; cf. *grandam*. In ME. we find also *belsire, belfader*.

Shakes the old beldam earth and topples down Steeples and moss-grown towers. At your birth Our grandam earth, having this distemperature, In passion shook (1 *Hen. IV*, iii. 1).

beleaguer. Du. *belegeren*, from *leger*, camp, leaguer (q.v.). A 16 cent. word from the Flemish wars, which superseded E. *belay*. Spelling perh. influenced by *league*[2]. Cf. Ger. *belagern*, to besiege, and see *laager, lair*.

It was by King Stephen belaied once or twise with sieges (Holland's *Camden*, 1610).

belemnite. Fossil. From G. βέλεμνον, dart. Cf. *ammonite*.

belfry. OF. *berfrei, belfrei* (*beffroi*), OHG. *bergfrid*, guard peace. Hence MedL. *belfredus*. Orig. tower used by besiegers. The *-l-*, due to dissim. (cf. *pilgrim*), has prevailed in E. by popular association with *bell*. For other warlike implements containing the element *berg* cf. *hauberk, scabbard*. Corrupted forms, usu. in orig. warlike sense, are found in other langs., e.g. obs. Du. *belfort*, It. *battifredo*. Some, however, take the first element to be *berg*, mountain, and orig. sense to have been hill-fort.

Belgravian. Of fashionable district round *Belgrave Square*, named from *Belgrave* (Leic.), seat of ground-landlord.

Hearts just as true and fair May beat in Belgrave Square As in the purer air Of Seven Dials (Gilbert).

Belial. Heb. *b'li*, not, *ya'al*, use. Esp. in *sons of Belial*, the name being identified by Milt. with one of the fallen angels.

belie. AS. *belēogan*, to deceive (see *lie*[2]). Current sense from 17 cent. The same transition is seen in F. *démentir*.

believe. ME. *beleven*, from obs. *leven*, AS. *gelīefan*. Com. Teut.; cf. Du. *gelooven*, Ger. *glauben* (OHG. *gilouban*), Goth. *galaubjan*; cogn. with Ger. *erlauben*, to allow, *loben*, to praise, and ult. with E. *love*, ground-sense being approval. Artificial spelling, for *beleeve*, is due to *relieve*.

belike [*archaic*]. For *by like*, according to appearance. See *like*.

belittle. Orig. US., coined by Jefferson. Cf. F. *rapetisser*.

bell¹. Noun. AS. *belle*. A LG. word; cf. Du. *bel*. Perh. cogn. with *bellow*. The naut. *bells* are struck every half-hour of the watch. *By bell, book and candle* (c. 1300) is from a form of excommunication which concluded with "Doe to the book, quench the candle, ring the bell." To *bear, carry away, the bell*, i.e. to be winner, refers to earlier use of silver bell as prize, e.g. the Chester Cup was in 1609 a bell. To *bell the cat* alludes to the fable of the rats and the cat.

La difficulté fut d'attacher le grelot
(La Fontaine, *Fables*, ii. 2).

bell². Verb. See *bellow*.

belladonna. It., lit. fair lady; cf. synon. F. *belle-dame*, "great nightshade; or, a kind of dwale, or sleeping nightshade" (Cotg.). Prob. from its use for dilating the pupil of the eye.

bellarmine [*hist.*]. Drinking-jug designed by Netherland Protestants as caricature of *Cardinal Bellarmine* (17 cent.). Cf. *Toby jug, demijohn, goblet*.

belle. See *beau*.

belletrist [*neol.*]. Ger., coined from F. *belles-lettres*.

bellicose. L. *bellicosus*, from *bellum*, war.

belligerent. Earlier *belligerant* (Johns.), from pres. part. of L. *belligerare*, from *bellum*, war, *gerere*, to wage. See *duel*.

Bellona. L., from *bellum*, war. Goddess of war; hence, formidable lady. Cf. *virago*.

bellow. ME. *belwen*, AS. *bylgan*; cogn. with *bell²*, still used of cry of stag; cf. Ger. *bellen*, to bark.

The wild buck bells from ferny brake (*Marm.* iv. 15).

bellows. Earlier also *bellow* (cf. *gallows*), ME. *bely*, AS. *bylig*, lit. belly, the full AS. name being *blǣst-belg*, from *blāwan*, to blow. Mod. form is northern, ON. *belgr*. Cf. Ger. *balg*, skin, *blasebalg*, bellows. Fig. lungs, as in *bellows to mend*, broken-winded.

The develes bely, with which he bloweth in man the fir of flesshly concupiscence (Chauc. I. 353).

belly. AS. *bylig*. See *bellows*. Cf. AS. *belgan*, Ger. *belgen*, to swell, be angry, ON. *bolgenn*, swollen, angry; ult. cogn. with *bulge*. *Belly-timber*, food, was formerly in serious use.

Rumble thy bellyful. Spit, fire! spout, rain!
(*Lear*, iii. 2).

belong. ME., for earlier *long*, app. to "go along with." See quot. s. v. *derring do*. Cf. Ger. *belang*, importance.

beloved. From obs. verb *belove*; cf. Ger. *beliebt*.

below. For *by low*; cf. *beneath*. A rare word till 16 cent., the usual ME. being *alow*, corresponding to *ahigh*, now replaced by *on high*.

belt. AS. *belt*; cf. OHG. *balz*. Both from L. *balteus*. To *hit below the belt* is from the prize-ring. From the distinctive *belt* of the earl or knight we have *belted earl*.

Belt [*geog.*]. In *Great* (*Little*) *Belt*. Norw. Dan. *bælt*, cogn. with *Baltic*; cf. poet. Ger. *Belt*, "the east-sea, the baltick sea" (Ludw.).

Beltane [*Sc.*]. Old May-Day, celebrated by bonfires. Gael. *bealltuinn*, bright fire, first element cogn. with AS. *bǣl*, as in *bale-fire* (see *bale¹*).

At Beltane game,
Thou ledst the dance with Malcolm Graeme
(*Lady of Lake*, ii. 15).

beluga. Great sturgeon, white whale. Russ., from *bel*, white; cf. *Belgrade, Bielgorod*, white city.

belvedere. F. *belvédère*, It. *belvedere*, "a place of a faire prospect" (Flor.), from L. *bellus*, beautiful, *videre*, to see. The *Apollo Belvedere* stands in the belvedere of the Vatican.

bema [*eccl.*]. Chancel, tribune. G. βῆμα, step, from βαίνειν, to go.

bemean. To lower oneself (see *mean¹*). A vulgarism confusing *demean* and *mean²*.

bemuse. Compd. of *muse²*. Cf. *amuse*.

ben¹ [*Sc.*]. Coupled with *butt*, the inner and outer rooms of a Scotch hut. ME. *binne*, AS. *binnan, bi innan*, within (cf. Du. Ger. *binnen*), and ME. *but*, AS. *būtan, bi ūtan*, without.

Now butt an' ben the change-house fills (Burns).

ben² [*geog.*]. Gael. *beann*, peak, as in *Ben Nevis*.

bench. AS. *benc*; cf. Ger. *bank* and see *bank²*. Hence *bencher*, senior member of Inn of Court, earlier also judge, alderman, etc. The use of the word (from 13 cent.) for judges and bishops points to Spartan customs. App. only the Lord Chancellor had a soft seat, the woolsack.

bend. AS. *bendan*, for **bandjan*, earliest sense, to bind, constrain, by tension, the idea of curvature first appearing in connection with bending a bow (cf. F. *bander un arc*), while orig. sense survives in naut. to *bend a rope* (*sail*). Orig. p.p. *bended* now only with *knee*. With fig. senses, e.g. *bent on*, cf. *intent* and Ger. *gespannt*. Hence nouns *bend* and *bent*, the latter by analogy with *extend, extent*. AS. *bend*, bond, survives only in naut. lang., e.g. *carrick bend*, other senses of *bend* being from the verb, though the her. sense is also represented by cogn. OF. *bende* (*bande*), OHG. *binda*. See *bind*.

bene. Prayer. AS. *bǣn, bēn*; cogn. with ON. *bōn*, whence *boon*. Obs. exc. in allusive *bootless bene* (Wordsworth, *Bolton Abbey*).

beneath. AS. *bineothan*, from *bi*, by, *neothan*, below. See *nether*.

benedicite. Oldest sense, grace before meat, as still in F. Imper. of L. *benedicere*, to bless, from *bene*, well, *dicere*, to say.

Benedick, benedict. Married man. Character in Shaks.

> How dost thou, Benedick, the married man?
> (*Much Ado*, v. 4).

Benedictine. Monk of order of *St Benedict*, founded 529. Also liqueur made by the monks. Cf. *chartreuse*.

Benedictus. Canticle. From init. word of L. version (*Luke*, i. 68), p.p. of L. *benedicere*, to bless.

benefactor. L., well-doer; cf. AS. *wel-dōend.*

benefice. Orig. good deed, L. *beneficium*, hence grant to church, ecclesiastical living. Cf. F. *bénéfice*, profit, perquisite.

benefit. Partial re-construction of ME. AF. *benfet* (F. *bienfait*), L. *benefactum*, well done. *Benefit of clergy*, orig. exemption of clergy from secular jurisdiction, was gradually extended to all "clerks," i.e. those who could read. See *neck-verse*. The first theat. *benefit* was granted to Mrs Barry, Jan. 16, 1687.

benevolent. OF., from L. *bene* and pres. part. of *velle*, to wish. *Benevolence*, in hist. sense of "war-loan," occurs in 1473.

Bengali [*ling*.]. One of the Aryan vernaculars of India.

benighted. From archaic verb *benight*, to cover with darkness. Cf. *beloved*.

benign. Through OF. from L. *benignus*, for **bene-genus* (*gignere*, to beget); cf. *generous*. *Benignant*, not in Johns., though used by Boswell, is modelled on *malignant*.

benison [*archaic*]. OF. *beneïson*, L. *benedic-*

tio-n-. Revived by Scott, Southey, etc. Cf. *malison*.

Benjamin. Beloved youngest son. *Gen.* xlii. 4.

benjamin [*archaic*]. Kind of over-coat. Prob. a playful variation on the earlier *joseph* (q.v.). See also *benzoin*.

bennet, herb bennet. OF. *herbe beneite*, L. *herba benedicta*, from supposed qualities.

bent¹. Grass. AS. *beonot-*, only recorded in place-names, e.g. *Bentley*, and surviving as dial. *bennet*. Cf. Ger. *binse*, rush, OHG. *binuz*. Also, in ME. and mod. poetry, grassy expanse, etc., and esp. battle-field.

> On by holt and headland,
> Over heath and bent (Kingsley).

bent². Inclination, etc. See *bend*. In sense of extreme limit of tension only now in one phrase.

> They fool me to the top of my bent (*Haml.* iii. 2).

Benthamism. "Greatest happiness of the greatest number." *Jeremy Bentham* (†1832).

ben trovato. It., well found, invented (even if not true).

> Se non è vero, è molto ben trovato
> (Giordano Bruno, 1585).

> Such is the local legend related by a truthful Italian resident, Signor Ben Trovato
> (*Westm. Gaz.* May 21, 1919).

benumb. Orig. p.p. *benumen* of *beniman*, to deprive, compd. of *niman*, to take. *Numb* (q.v.) is evolved from it with excrescent *-b*. Cf. F. *perclus*, lit. shut off.

> *benombe of ones lymbes*: perclus (Palsg.).

benzoin. Resinous gum; cf. F. *benjoin*, Sp. *benjui*, It. *benzoi*, from Arab. *lubān jāwī*, frankincense of Java, the *lu-* prob. being taken for def. art. (cf. *azure*). Hence a group of chem. words, *benzoic, benzine, benzoline*, etc. It was popularly called *benjamin*.

> *benjoin*: the aromaticall gumme, called benjamin, or benzoin (Cotg.).

bequeath. AS. *becwethan*, from *cwethan*, to say (see *quoth*). "An ancient word the retention of which is due to the traditional language of wills" (*NED.*). Hence *bequest*, of obscure formation, app. influenced by *request, behest*.

Berber. Race and langs. of N.Afr. Var. of *Barbar* (see *Barbary*) introduced by mod. ethnologists.

bereave. AS. *berēafian*, from *rēafian*, to rob, whence *reave, reive* (q.v.).

beret. Basque cap. See *barret, biretta*.

bergamask, bergomask [*archaic*]. It. *berga-masca*, rustic dance of *Bergamo* (Venice). According to Nares the people of Bergamo were renowned for their clownishness (see *zany*). Cf. *Boeotian*.

bergamot[1]. Tree and essence. Perh. from *Bergamo* (Venice), but by some identified with *bergamot*[2].

bergamot[2]. Pear. F. *bergamotte*, It. *berga-motta*, corrupted from Turk. *beg-armüdi*, prince's pear (see *beg*[2], *bey*). Cf. Ger. *fürstenbirne*.

bergschrund [*geol.*]. Ger., mountain cleft.

beriberi. Disease. Redupl. of Singhalese *beri*, weakness. Recorded in F. for 1752.

Berkeleian. *Bishop Berkeley* (†1753) denied objective existence of material world.

berlin, berline. Carriage. Introduced by an officer of the Elector of Brandenburg (c. 1670). Cf. *landau*.

berm [*fort.*] Ledge. F. *berme*, of Teut. origin; cf. Du. *berm*. Cogn. with *brim*.

Bernardine. Monk. From *St Bernard*, abbot of Clairvaux (12 cent.). See *Cistercian*.

berretta. See *biretta*.

berry. AS. *berie*. Com. Teut.; cf. Du. *bes*, *bezie*, Ger. *beere*, ON. *ber*, Goth. *basi*. This and *apple* are the only native fruit-names.

bersagliere. Italian sharpshooter. Cf. OF. *berser*, to shoot with the bow, *bersail*, target. Of unknown origin.

berserker. Icel. *berserkr*, bear sark, bearskin. Cf. ON. *ûlfhēthinn*, lit. wolf-doublet, in similar sense. Corruptly *baresark*, as though "bare shirt." Introduced, and wrongly explained, by Scott (*Pirate*, Note B). With to *go berserk* cf. to *run amok*.

I will go baresark to-morrow to the war
(Kingsley, *Hereward*).

berth. Oldest sense (16 cent.), convenient sea-room, whence all later meanings are evolved, a good example of our love of naut. metaphor. Prob. from *bear*[2], in naut. sense of direction, and hence ult. ident. with *birth*, the spellings occurring indifferently. To *give a wide* (formerly *good*) *berth* retains the oldest meaning.

bertha, berthe. Kind of lace collar. F., from the trad. modesty of Queen *Berthe*, mother of Charlemagne.

Bertha. Nickname, *die dicke Bertha*, of long-range gun, esp. that used to bombard Paris (1918). From *Bertha Krupp*, of Essen.

Bertillon. System of criminal anthropometry. Name of F. anthropologist (19 cent.).

beryl. F. *béryl*, L. *beryllus*, G. βήρυλλος, of Eastern origin. Cf. Pers. and Arab. *ballûr*, crystal, which is the medieval meaning of *beryl*, whence OF. *bericles* (*besicles*), spectacles, Ger. *brille*.

Beril est en Inde trovee
(*Lapidaire de Marbode*, 12 cent.).

besant, bezant [*hist.*]. F. *besant*, gold coin of *Byzantium*, current in Europe from 9 cent. Cf. *ducat*, *florin*, etc.

Lord, thi besaunt hath wunne ten besauntis
(Wyc. *Luke*, xix. 16).

beseech. ME. compd. of *sechen*, southern form of *seek* (q.v.). Orig. the dir. obj. was the thing sought. The form *biseke* is also common in ME.

But we biseken mercy and socour (Chauc. A. 918).

beseem. From *seem* (q.v.). Cf. *seemly*.

beset. AS. *besettan*, from *set* (q.v.). Oldest sense, to set round, encompass; cf. Ger. *besetzen*. *Besetting sin* (*Heb.* xii. 1) is for *Vulg. circumstans peccatum*.

beshrew. ME. compd. of earlier *shrew*, to curse, formed from noun *shrew* (q.v.).

And first I shrewe myself, bothe blood and bones,
If thou bigyle me any ofter than ones
(Chauc. B. 4617).

beside, besides. AS. *bi sīdan*, dat. of *sīde*, side. The two forms are used indifferently in ME., the *-s* being due to the tendency to regard adverbs as genitives. Also means in ME. outside, hence *beside oneself*, with which cf. F. *hors de soi*, Ger. *ausser sich*.

besiege. With altered prefix from ME. *asege*, F. *assiéger*, VL. **ad-sediare* (*sedēre*), to sit down before. Or formed directly from *siege*. Cf. *beleaguer*, *beset*, which may have brought about change of prefix.

besom. AS. *besema*. Earliest sense, rod, birch; cf. Du. *bezem*, Ger. *besen*, broom; ? ult. cogn. with L. *ferula*, broom-plant, rod. *NED.* regards Sc. *besom*, in *impudent besom*, *old besom*, etc. as a separate word, but it may be noted that Ger. *besen* is also applied to women. Cf. *old faggot*, also Sc. *auld birkie*, perh. from *birk*, birch.

To set up to be sae muckle better than ither folk,
the auld besom (*Old Mortality*).

bespeak. AS. *besprecan*, from *sprecan* (see *speak*). Earlier senses various and loosely connected. Current sense from about 16 cent. *Bespoke* is now used only in trade, e.g. *bespoke bootmaker*, for *bespoke-boot maker*.

besprent [*poet.*]. Besprinkled. From obs. *bespreng*, AS. *besprengan*, from *sprengan*, to sprinkle, causal of *springan*, to spring; cf. Du. Ger. *besprengen*.

Bess. See *brown*. Quot. below suggests that the name for the musket was allusive to some early sense.

She's none of these coy dames, she's as good as Brown Bessie (*Misogonus*, ii. 4, c. 1550).

bessemer, steel, iron. Process invented (1856) by *Sir H. Bessemer* (†1898).

best. AS. *bet(e)st*. See *better*. Com. Teut.; cf. Du. Ger. *best*, ON. *bazt*, Goth. *batist*. *Best man* is Sc. and quite recent in E. Verb to *best* (19 cent.) is almost synon. with much earlier to *worst*. So also, to *do one's best* was earlier equivalent to to *do one's worst* (v.i.).

And if he list to bryng them yn thus he shuld have good thanke, and if not then to kepe them and do his best (*Coventry Leet Book*, 1509).

bestead¹ [*archaic*]. To help. App. 16 cent. compd. for earlier *stead*, to prop, support. See *stead*, *stay¹*.

How little you bested,
Or fill the fixed mind with all your toys!
(*Penseroso*, 3).

bestead², bested. Now only with *ill*, *sore*, *hard*. ME. *bistad*, situated, compd. of *stad*, placed, p.p. of ON. *stethja*, to place, cogn. with *bestead¹*. Cf. *beset*, *bestow*.

bestad, or withholdyne in wele or woo: detentus
(*Prompt. Parv.*).

bestial. L. *bestialis* (see *beast*). In Sc. sense of cattle it is from OF. (*bétail*). Cf. *bestiary*, medieval work on animals.

bestow. ME. compd. of *stow* (q.v.). Etym. to put in a place, as in *well* (*ill*) *bestowed*.

bestride. AS. *bestrīdan*, to sit a horse. See *stride*.

bet. App. aphet. form (16 cent.) of *abet* (q.v.), though the syntactical construction presents difficulty. It has perh. been influenced by Ger. *wetten*, "to bet with one for something" (Ludw.), for which see *wed*.

betake. ME. compd. of *take* (q.v.). Earlier, to hand over, commit. Now only reflex.

bête noire. Pet aversion. F., orig. wild boar or wolf, as distinguished from *bête fauve*, stag, hart, roebuck.

betel. Plant. Port. (16 cent.), Tamil *veṭṭilei*.

tambu: the bastard pepper plant called bettle, or betre, sometimes (but improperly) taken for the Indian leafe (Cotg.).

Bethel. Heb. *bēth-ēl*, house of God (*Gen.* xxviii. 17). Hence nonconformist chapel (19 cent.). Cf. *bethesda*, house of mercy (*John*, v. 2), similarly used, esp. in Wales.

bethink. AS. *bethencan*, to call to mind, from *think* (q.v.). Now usu. reflex. Cf. Du. Ger. *bedenken*.

'Tis well bethought (*Pericles*, v. 1).

betide. ME. *betiden*, from *tiden*, to happen. See *tide*, *tidings*. Now only in 3rd pers. sing. of pres. subjunct. in *whate'er betide*, *woe betide*.

Er ich wedde such a wif wo me bytyde
(*Piers Plowm.* C. iv. 157).

betimes. ME. also *betime*, by time. The -*s* is the adv. genitive. Cf. *beside-s*.

betoken. ME. *bitacnien*; cf. AS. *getācnian*, from *tācn*, token (q.v.). Cf. Du. *beteekenen*, Ger. *bezeichnen*.

beton. Kind of concrete. F. *béton*, from OF. *beter*, to congeal (the *mer betée* of OF. romance renders L. *mare concretum*), unless this is a back-formation from OF. *beton* and the latter from L. *bitumen*.

betony. Plant. F. *bétoine*, L. *betonica*, for *vetonnica*, said by Pliny to have been discovered by a Spanish tribe called *Vettones*. *Betonica* is found in AS.

betray. ME. *betraien*, compd. (perh. suggested by *bewray*) of *traien*, OF. *traïr* (*trahir*), from L. *tradere* (*trans dare*), to hand over. ME. had also *betrais*, *bytrassh*, etc. from F. forms in -*iss*- (cf. *abash*, *flourish*, etc.).

betroth. ME. *bitreuthien*, from *treuthe*, truth. Later form influenced by *troth* (q.v.). Cf. the relation of F. *fiancer* to *fides*, faith, and of *engaged* to *gage*, pledge.

better. AS. *betera*, compar. of a lost **bat*-stem (see *batten²*). Com. Teut.; cf. Du. *beter*, Ger. *besser*, ON. *betri*, Goth. *batiza*. The adv. was earlier *bet* (cf. archaic Ger. *bass*). *Better half* is first recorded in Sidney; cf. F. *chère moitié*, L. *animae dimidium meae* (Hor.). The phrase *we had better*, etc. was earlier *us* (dat.) *were* (subjunct.) *better*, then *we were better*, mod. form being due to *we had liefer*, *rather*. *No better than one should be* is app. quite mod. With the verb cf. Ger. *bessern*, *verbessern*. To *better oneself* (17 cent.) is called by Mary Wollstonecraft a "significant vulgar phrase." *Betterment*, improvement of property, is US. and has replaced early *melioration* (Pepys). *Bettermost* is 18 cent. formation on *uppermost*, etc.

He knew the tavernes well in all the toun
And everich hostiler and tappestere
Bet than a lazar or a beggestere (Chauc. A. 240).

Betty Martin. In *my eye and Betty Martin*. The origin of the phrase is unknown and the identity of the lady is as vague as that of *Tommy* in *like hell and Tommy*.

That's my eye, Betty Martin: an answer to any one that attempts to impose or humbug (Grose).

between, betwixt. ME. *bitwenen*, AS. *betwēonum*, from prep. *be*, by, and dat. plur. of *twēon*, twain, orig. distrib. numeral of *two* (q.v.). In AS. this numeral qualifies the noun now governed by *between*, e.g. *be sǣm twēonum*, by seas twain. *Betwixt* comes, with excrescent *-t* (as in *against*, etc.), from ME. *betwix*, AS. *betweox*, etc., earlier in dat. form (*betweoxn*, King Alfred), from an unrecorded *twisc*, twofold, of which the Ger. cogn. appears in prep. *zwischen*, between, orig. a dat. pl. *Betwixt and between*, middling, is not recorded till 19 cent.

Beulah [*Bibl.*]. Happy land (*Is.* lxii. 4).

Our toilsome but happy progress to the Beulah of victory and peace (*Obs.* Jan. 19, 1919).

beurré. Pear. F., lit. "buttered." In Littleton (1677).

beurée: the name of a very tender, and delicate peare (Cotg.).

bevel. OF. *bevel* (*biveau*), *buveau* in Cotg., prob. related to L. *bis* and to *bias*, *bezel*, all three words being unsolved. Cf. OF. *bever*, to diverge.

bever [*dial.*]. Orig. drink; now, luncheon. OF. *beivre* (*boire*), to drink, L. *bibere*. Cf. *nuncheon*.

beverage. OF. *bevrage* (*breuvage*), from *beivre*, L. *bibere*; or VL. *biberaticum*; cf. It. *beveraggio*.

bevy. In late ME. a company of roes, larks, quails, or ladies. One of the numerous fantastic terms of venery. AF. *bevee*, of unknown origin. It. *beva*, "a beavie" is in Flor., but here *beavie* is prob. a misprint for *beaver* (= *bever*) copied by later dicts.

beware. Prop. a compd., *be ware*, e.g. we cannot say *he bewared*. See *ware*[2]. Survival of compd. is prob. due to frequent imper. use (cf. *begone*). It has partly absorbed the verb *ware*, AS. *warian*, to guard against, which survives in the hunting phrase *ware wire!* if this is not aphet. for *beware*.

They were ware of it, and fled unto Lystra
(*Acts*, xiv. 6).

bewilder. Lit. "to lose in pathless ways" (Johns.). A 17 cent. word, orig. as p.p. (*bewildered*), from obs. *wildern*, wilderness (see *wild*). Cf. *belated*, *benighted*, etc.

bewitch. ME. compd. of *wicchen*, AS. *wiccian*, to enchant. See *witch*. Cf. *beshrew*.

bewray [*archaic*]. ME. *bewreien*, to divulge, orig. to accuse, compd. of *wreien*, AS. *wrēgan*, to accuse; cf. Ger. *rügen*, to accuse. Later sense influenced by *betray*. Used by Tynd. (*Matt.* xxvi. 73) where Wyc. has *makith thee open* (var. *knowen*) for *Vulg. manifestum te facit.*

Ne dorst he nat to hire his wo biwreye
(Chauc. F. 954).

bey. Mod. pronunc. of Turk. *beg*, prince. Formerly also *by*, *beg*. Cf. *begum*. With *beylik*, principality, cf. *pashalik*.

beyond. AS. *begeondan*, *bi geondan*, from AS. *geondan*, beyond. See *yonder*, and cf. Ger. *jenseits*, on yonder side.

bezant. See *besant*.

bezantler [*ven.*]. Second branch of deer's horn. From *antler* (q.v.) and *bes-*, *bis-*, as in F. *bisaïeul*, great grandfather.

Above the "burr" came the brow-antlier now the brow-point; next the bezantlier, now the bay
(Richard Jefferies).

bezel. OF. *bisel* (*biseau*, *béseau*). Cf. *bevel*, *bias*, both of which approach *bezel* in sense.

biseau: a bezle, bezeling, or scuing; such a slopenesse, or slope forme, as in the point of an yron leaver, chizle, etc. (Cotg.).

bezesteen. Eastern market-place. Turk. *bazistān*, from Pers.

bezique. F. *bésique*, also *bésy*. Called a neol. by *Dict. Gén.*, but *basseque* is in Oudin (1660). Cf. It. *bazzica*, card game, ? from Arab. *bazz*, to win booty.

bezoar [*archaic*]. Bezoar-stone, intestinal calculus found in some animals and credited with medicinal powers. Cf. F. *bézoard*, Port. *bezuar*, OF. *bezahard*. From Arab. *bāzahr* or *bādizahr*, Pers. *pād-zahr*, counterpoison.

bezonian [*archaic*]. Earlier also *besonio*. It. *bisogno*, "need, want; also, a fresh needy souldier" (Flor.). Cf. OF. *bisogne*. Origin of F. *besoin*, *besogne*, from Merovingian L. *sonium*, *sonia*, is unknown.

bisongne: a filthie knave, or cloune; a raskall, bisonian, base humored scoundrell (Cotg.).

Great men oft die by vile bezonians
(2 *Hen. VI*, iv. 1).

bhang, bang. Narcotic from hemp. Port. *bangue*, Hind. *bhang*, Sanskrit *banghā*, hemp.

bheesty [*Anglo-Ind.*]. Water-bearer. Urdu *bhīstī*, Pers. *bihishtī*, from *bihisht*, paradise. "Prob. of jocular origin" (*NED.*).

bi-. L. prefix *bi-* for earlier *dui-*, cogn. with G. δι- from δύο, two. Cf. *bin-*, from *bini*, two at a time; also *bis-* for OL. *duis*.

bias. F. *biais*, slant, etc., of unknown origin. Cf. *bevel*, *bezel*. Fig. senses are due to the early use of the word in connection with the game of bowls.

'Twill make me think the world is full of rubs,
And that my fortune runs against the bias
(Rich. II, iii. 4).

bib. ME. *bibben*, to tipple, L. *bibere*. Hence *wine-bibber* (*Luke,* vii. 34) for *Vulg. bibens vinum*. With child's *bib* cf. F. *biberon*, feeding-bottle.

bibelot. Trinket. F., earlier *beubelet*, etc., prob. from infantile redupl. *bel-bel*. Cf. E. *pretty-pretty*.

Bible. F., Late L. *biblia* (f.), orig. neut. pl., G. τὰ βιβλία, the books, βιβλίον being dim. of βίβλος inner bark of the papyrus. In most Europ. langs. Cf. *book*, *code*, *library*. More gen. sense survives in *bibliography*, *bibliophile*, etc. *Bibliomaniac* is first recorded in Scott (*Antiquary*) who applies it to Don Quixote. Chesterfield uses *bibliomanie*, from F.

biblio-. See *Bible*.

bibulous. From L. *bibulus* (see *bib*).

bicameral [*pol.*]. App. coined by Bentham (18 cent.). See *bi-* and *chamber*.

bice. Pigment. Earlier *blewe bis*, F. *bleu bis*, dull blue. F. *bis*, dingy, It. *bigio*, are thought to be from the second syllable of L. *bombyceus*, of cotton (see *bombasine*).

biceps [*anat.*]. L., lit. two-headed, from *bis* and *caput*. Cf. L. *anceps*, doubtful, from *ambo* and *caput*.

bicker¹. Sc. form of *beaker* (q.v.).

bicker². To quarrel. In ME. as noun and verb, skirmish, hence wrangle. Origin obscure. Senses correspond pretty well with those of F. *piquer*. Cf. OHG. *bicken*, to hack, stab, etc. From a base *bic, pic*, found in both Teut. and Rom. (cf. *peck²*, *pick²*).

bicycle. F., from *bi-* and G. κύκλος, wheel. Superseded *velocipede* (q.v.).

Bysicles and trysicles which we saw in the Champs Elysées (*Daily News,* Sep. 7, 1868).

bid. Confusion of two Com. Teut. verbs, viz. AS. *bēodan*, to announce, command, offer, etc. (cf. Du. *bieden*, Ger. *bieten*, ON. *bjótha*, Goth. *biudan*; cogn. with *bode*), and AS. *biddan*, to request (cf. Du. *bidden*, Ger. *bitten*, ON. *bithja*, Goth. *bidjan*; cogn. with *bead*). With the first cf. to *bid at an auction*,

bid good day (*defiance*). The more gen. sense, to command (cf. *forbid*), combines both. To *bid fair* was earlier to *bid fair for*, i.e. to offer with reasonable probability. *Bidding prayer*, now understood as exhorting to prayer, meant orig. praying of prayers. Cf. earlier *bidding beads*, in same sense.

bide. AS. *bīdan*, to remain. Com. Teut.; cf. Du. *beiden*, Ger. dial. *beiten*, ON. *bītha*, Goth. *beidan*. In most senses used indifferently with *abide*, of which it is often an aphet. form. In AS. also trans., to await, now only in to *bide one's time*.

bield [*north. dial.*]. Shelter. ? Ident. with obs. *bield*, courage, assurance, AS. *beldo*, from *bold*, ? or connected with *build*.

He [the fox] tore off for a bield 300 yards away
(*Manch. Guard.* Mar. 13, 1918).

biennial. From L. *biennium*, two years, from *bi-* and *annus*, year.

bier. AS. *bǣr*, bier, litter, from *bear²*. Com. Teut.; cf. Du. *baar*, Ger. *bahre*, ON. *barar* (pl.). Mod. spelling is due to F. *bière*, of Teut. origin. Cf. *barrow²*. Not orig. limited to funeral bier. For poet. sense of tomb cf. *hearse*.

Drop upon Fox's grave a tear,
'Twill trickle to his rival's bier (*Marmion, Introd.*).

biestings. See *beestings*.

biff [*slang*]. To shove, etc. ? Thinned form of *buff¹* (q.v.), *buffet*. Cf. *bilge*.

biffin. Apple (Norf.). ? For *beefing*, from its deep red colour; cf. *golding*, *sweeting*. The old etymologists explained it from F. *beau fin*, which is at least as likely.

bifurcate. From *bi-* and L. *furca*, fork.

big. Northern ME. (end of 13 cent.), but recorded as name, *Bicga*, in 11 cent. This is prob. cogn. with earlier *Bucga*, and with Norw. dial. *bugge*, great man, *bugga*, rich, important, whence E. dial. *buggy*, proud, and pleon. *big bug*.

cheval de trompette: one thats not afraid of shadowes, one whom no big, nor bug words can terrifie
(Cotg.).

bigamy. F. *bigamie*, MedL. *bigamia*, from G. γάμος, marriage.

bigaroon. Cherry. Earlier *bigarreau* (F.), from *bigarré*, variegated, of unknown origin.

bigarreaus: a kinde of cherries, which bee halfe white, halfe red (Cotg.).

biggin¹ [*archaic*]. Cap. F. *béguin*, head-dress of *béguine* nuns. See *beg¹*, *Beguine*.

byggen for a childes heed: beguyne (Palsg.).

biggin[2]. Kind of coffee-pot. From inventor's name (c. 1800).

"Mr Baptist—tea pot!" "Mr Baptist—dust-pan!" "Mr Baptist—flour-dredger!" "Mr Baptist—coffee-biggin" (*Little Dorrit*, ch. xxv.).

bigging [*north. dial.*]. Building. From ME. *biggen*, to build, ON. *byggja*. Cf. place-name *Newbigging*.

bight [*naut.*]. Loop of rope, or of coast. AS. *byht*, from *būgan*, to bow, bend. Cf. Ger. *bucht*, bay, from LG. See *bow*[2].

bignonia. Flower. Named by Tournefort (c. 1700) after the *abbé Bignon*, librarian to Louis XIV. Cf. *begonia, wistaria*, etc.

bigot. In OF. a term of abuse applied to the Normans (Wace). Origin much disputed. Personally I see no improbability in the old theory (derided by *NED.*) that it arose from a Teut. oath "by God." Cf. OF. *goddam*, an Englishman. On the common formation of nicknames from oaths see my *Surnames* (pp. 180–2). The Norman *Bigod*, who came over with the Conqueror and became Earl of Norfolk, may have had a nickname of the same type as *Pardoe, Pardew, Purdy*, etc., which represent F. *par (pour) Dieu*.

bijou. F., Bret. *bizou*, ring with stone; cf. Corn. *bisou*, finger-ring, Bret. *bez*, finger, Welsh *bys*, finger.

bike. Slang perversion of *bicycle*.

bilander [*naut.*]. Coasting vessel. Du. *bijlander*, by lander, whence also F. *bélandre*.

bilberry. Adapted from dial. form of Dan. *böllebær*, prob. ball-berry, from shape. Also called *blaeberry, whortleberry*.

bilbo [*hist.*]. Sword. From *Bilbao*, Spain. Cf. *Toledo*. See *Merry Wives*, iii. 5.

bilbo blade: from Bilboa...in Spain where the best blades are made (Blount).

bilboes [*naut.*]. Shackles. Earlier *bilbowes*. Prob. a sailor's perversion, associated with *bilbo*, of OSc. *boyes*, fetters, later *bowes*, OF. *boie, buie*, fetter, L. *boia*, whence also MHG. *boie*, Du. *boei*, fetter (see *buoy*). The story about *bilboes* brought from *Bilbao* by the Armada is disproved by chronology, the word occurring in 1557 (Hakl. ii. 374).

bile. F., L. *bilis*. One of the four "humours," earlier called *choler*. Hence *bilious*.

bilge. Lowest part of hull, hence, foulness that collects there. "Belly" of cask. Alteration of *bulge* (q.v.). Hence *bilge-keel, bilge-water*, and to *bilge*, stave in

(ship's bottom). Cf. F. *bouge*, bilge, of ship or cask.

bildge, or *buldge*: is the breadth of the floor, whereon the ship rests, when she is a-ground
(*Sea-Dict.* 1708).

A considerable volume [of water] had filled the bilge and orlop (*Daily Chron.* June 23, 1919).

bilious. See *bile*.

bilk. Thinned form of *balk* (q.v.), with which it orig. interchanged as a term at cribbage. Cf. *mister, demnition*, etc., and surname *Binks*, for *Banks*.

bill[1] [*hist.*]. Weapon. AS. *bil*, sword. WGer.; cf. OSax. *bil*, OHG. *bill* (Ger. *bille*, hoe). Perh. cogn. with *bill*[2]. Obs. exc. in *bill-hook* and hist. *brown-bill*.

bill[2]. Of a bird. AS. *bile*. Perh. cogn. with *bill*[1]. *Billing and cooing* was earlier simply *billing*.

Like two silver doves that sit a-billing
(*Venus & Adonis*, 366).

bill[3]. Document, orig. sealed. AF. *bille*, Late L. *billa, bulla*, seal (see *bull*[2], *bulletin*), L. *bulla*, "a bosse; a bullion; great heade of a nayle in doores or gates; sometimes studdes in girdels or like things" (Coop.), orig. bubble. It came to be used in AF. & ME. of any document, e.g. *bill of fare* (*lading, health*, etc.). In the sense of poster it is as old as 15 cent.

And the pope darlaye hath graunted in his byll
That every brother may do what he wyll
(*Cocke Lorelles Bote*).

affiche: a siquis; a bill set up, or pasted, or fastened, on a post, doore, gate, etc. (Cotg.).

billet[1]. Note. ME. *billette*, OF. *billete* (cf. F. *billet, billet doux*), dim. of *bill*[3]. In mil. sense (17 cent.) from written order issued by officer who quarters troops. Hence *every bullet has its billet*, saying attributed by Wesley to William III.

billet[2]. Block of wood. OF. *billete* (cf. F. *billot*), dim. of *bille*, log, MedL. *billa*. Orig. obscure, perh. Celt. (cf. Ir. *bile*, tree, mast).

billiards. F. *bille*, the ball, *billard*, the cue, are from It. *biglia, bigliardo*, of unknown origin. E. in 16 cent.

For iij yardes, iij quarters of greyn clothe to cover the billeyarde borde, xliijs. (*Rutland MSS.* 1603).

Billingsgate. Fishmarket near *Billing's gate*, one of the old gates of London, app. named after some AS. *Billing*. Famous for rhetoric from 17 cent.

billion. Coined (with *trillion, quadrillion*, etc.) in F. (16 cent.) to express second (third, fourth, etc.) power of *million*, but in ModF.

billion is a thousand millions only, *trillion* a thousand billions, and so on. Hence *billionaire*, playful imit. of *millionaire*.

billon. Inferior alloy or coin. Has often been confused with *bullion* (q.v.). F., orig. lump, ingot, from *bille*, log. Cf. *or* (*argent*) *en bille* (*en barre*). See *billet*[2].

Si je montrais une masse de plomb et que je disse: "Ce billon d'or m'a été donné..." (Calvin).

billow. Earlier *bellow*. From 16 cent. Cf. ON. *bylga*, from *belgja*, to swell (see *bellows*). Cf. *swell*, *surge*, the sense in which *billow* is used by Raleigh.

billy. Name *William* in various fig. senses, e.g. fellow, brother (Sc.), bushman's tea-can (Austral.), male goat (cf. *nanny goat*). With *silly Billy* cf. *silly Johnny*. Cf. *bobby*, *dandy*, *jack*, *jemmy*, etc.

billyboy. Barge (east coast). Perh. connected with *buoy*. In Ger. a somewhat similar craft is called *bojer*, from *boje*, buoy.

billycock. Hat. Earlier (1721) *bully-cocked*, i.e. worn in aggressive manner.

biltong [*SAfr.*]. Strip of dried beef. Du. *bil*, buttock, *tong*, tongue, being cut from the buttock and looking like a smoked tongue. Cut from the eland it is called *thigh-tongue*.

bimetallism. F. *bimétallique* was coined (1869) by Cernuschi, addressing Society of Political Economy at Paris.

bimbashee. Colonel (in Egypt. army). Turk. *bing-bāshī*, thousand captain. Cf. *pasha*, *bashi-bazouk*.

bin. AS. *binn*, manger, prob. Celt. Cf. F. *benne*, hamper, cart, Gaulish *benna*, cart.

binary. L. *binarius*, from *bini*, two at a time, from *bis*, twice, OL. *duis*, from *duo*, two.

bind. AS. *bindan*. Com. Teut.; cf. Du. Ger. *binden*, ON. *binda*, Goth. *bindan*. Cogn. with *band*[1], *bend* (q.v.). For fig. senses cf. *oblige*. Old p.p. survives in *bounden duty*. With *I'll be bound* (leg.) cf. *I'll go bail* and archaic *I'll be sworn*. With *bound up with* (*in*) (*Gen.* xliv. 30) cf. *wrapt up in*.

bine. Flexible shoot, orig. of hops. Dial. form of *bind*. Hence *woodbine*, earlier *woodbind*, AS. *wudu-binde*. Also trade-name for a famous cigarette.

bing [*techn. & dial.*]. Heap. ON. *bingr*, heap.

bingo [*slang*]. Brandy. App. coined from *b* (cf. *B. and S.*, brandy and soda) and *stingo* (q.v.).

binnacle [*naut.*]. Earlier *bittacle*, *bitakle* (1485), which survived to 18 cent., mod. form perh. due to *bin*. From OF. *abitacle* (*habitacle*) or

Port. *bitacola* (cf. Sp. *bitácora*, It. *abitacolo*), L. *habitaculum*, a small shelter.

bitacola: the bittacle, a frame of timber in the steerage, where the compass is placed on board a ship (Vieyra, 1794).

binocular. From L. *bini*, two together, *oculus*, eye.

binomial. Of two terms, esp. with *theorem* (Newton). Cf. F. *binôme*, from G. νόμος, law.

bio-. G. βίο-, from βίος, life. For *biogenesis* see *abiogenesis*. Cf. *biography*, *biology*. *Biograph*, *bioscope* were early names for cinematograph.

biped. L. *bipes*, *biped-*, from *bi-* and *pes*, foot.

biplane. See *bi-*, *aeroplane*.

Bipontine [*bibl.*]. Editions of classics printed (18 cent.) at *Zweibrücken* (latinized *Bipontium*) in Bavaria. Cf. *aldine*, *transpontine*.

birch. AS. *birce*, whence *birch*, and *beorc*, ON. *björk*, whence northern *birk* (cf. *Birkenhead*). Aryan; cf. Du. *berk*, Ger. *birke*, Sanskrit *bhūrja-*. Prob. cogn. with *bark*[1]. *Birch-rod* is represented in ME. by *yerde of byrke*. With archaic *birchen* cf. *oaken*.

bird. AS. *bridd*, young bird, chick, used in ME. also for young of other animals. Only found in E., usu. Teut. word being *fowl* (q.v.). Connection with *breed*, *brood* is doubtful. From being applied to small birds it gradually spread to the whole tribe, but *fowl* is still usual in *AV*. With *bird's eye* (*view*) cf. synon. F. *à vol d'oiseau*. *Birdseye* (*tobacco*) is named from the section of the cut leaf-ribs.

Eddris and eddris briddis (Wyc. *Matt.* xxiii. 33).

bireme [*hist.*]. Double-banked galley. L. *biremis*, from *bi-* and *remus*, oar.

biretta. It. *berretta* or Sp. *birreta*, Late L. *birretum*, from *birrus*, *byrrhus*, red, G. πυρρός, flame coloured. Cf. F. *béret*.

birth. App. ON. *byrth*, replacing AS. *gebyrd*, from *beran*, to bear, with which cf. Ger. *geburt*, from *gebären*. *Birthright* is used by Coverd. (*Gen.* xxv. 31) where Wyc. has *the ryghtis of thi fyrst getyng* (begetting). See also *berth*.

bis-. See *bi-*.

biscuit. Restored spelling of Tudor *bisket*, OF. *bescuit* (*biscuit*), L. *bis coctus* (*panis*), twice baked, of which Ger. *zwieback* is a translation. Hence also *biscuit pottery*, though app. this is only baked once.

bysquyt brede: biscoctus (*Prompt. Parv.*).

bisect. From *bi-* and L. *secare*, *sect-*, to cut.

bishop. AS. *biscop*, L., G. ἐπίσκοπος, over-seer, from ἐπί, on, σκοπός, watcher (cf. *scope*). Early loan in all Teut. langs. (cf. Ger. *bischoff*), and at first vaguely used of various church officers. *Bishopric* is a hybrid, from AS. *rīce*, power, realm (cf. Ger. *reich*, and see *rich*). The *bishop* at chess seems to have been due orig. to an accidental mitre-like appearance. It was formerly *alfin*, Arab. *al-fīl*, the elephant. In 16 cent. also *archer*. In F. it is *fou*, perh. also due to the head-dress. The 18 cent. *bowl of bishop* was perh. named from purple colour; cf. Du. *bisschop*, Norw. Dan. *bisp*, used in same sense. The *bishops' Bible* is the version of 1568, published under the direction of Archbishop Parker. A *bishop in partibus*, i.e. not in possession of his diocese, was orig. one expelled from the Holy Land by the Saracens, his see being *in partibus infidelium*. To *bishop* a horse's teeth in order to conceal its age is prob. from the name of a horse-dealer (c. 1700). See also *burke*.

bisk. F. *bisque*, crayfish soup, of unknown origin.

Bismillah. Arab. *bismi-'llāh*, in the name of Allah.

bismuth. Ger. *wismut* (1530), latinized as *bisemutum*. For initial *b*- cf. *bison*. Origin unknown. Our earliest loans from Mod. Ger. are mostly metallurgical (*cobalt, nickel*, etc.).

bison. ME. *bisont*, F. *bison*, L. *bison*, *bisont*- (Martial), from OHG. *wisunt*, the aurochs; cf. AS. *wesend*, ON. *visundr*; prob. of Balto-Slav. origin. The Teut. forms became obs. with the animal and the word was re-introduced from L. and applied to the American bison.

bison: the bison; a kind of hulch-backt, rough-maned, broad-faced, and great-ey'd, wild-oxe, that will not be taken as long as hee can stand, nor tamed after hee is taken (Cotg.).

bisque. At tennis. F., earlier *biscaye*, which suggests some connection with the province of *Biscay*, the inhabitants of which are the great experts at a form of tennis called *la pelote*.

biscaye: a vantage at tennis (Cotg.).

bisque: a fault, at tennis (ib.).

bissextile. Leap-year. L. *bissextilis* (*annus*), the year containing the *bissextus*, twice sixth, the day intercalated every four years in the Julian calendar after the sixth day before the Calends of March.

bistoury. Surgeon's scalpel. F. *bistouri*, OF.

bistorie, dagger (cf. surg. use of *lance*). As it is described as crooked and double-edged, the first element is prob. L. *bis*. Cf. OF. *bisaguë*, double-edged mattock, F. *bis-tourner*, to make crooked.

bistre. Yellowish brown pigment. F., of unknown origin.

bit¹. Morsel. AS. *bita*, morsel, from *bītan*, to bite (cf. F. *morceau*, *mordre*). With US. sense of small coin cf. our *threepenny-bit*.

bit². Of horse. AS. *bite*, bite, cutting (cf. F. *mors*, *mordre*). Also in mech. applications.

bitch¹. Animal. AS. *bicce*; cf. ON. *bikkja*. Origin unknown.

bitch² [*slang*]. To bungle. Thinned form of *botch²* (q.v.). Cf. *bilk*, *bilge*.

bite. AS. *bītan*. Com. Teut.; cf. Du. *bijten*, Ger. *beissen*, ON. *bīta*, Goth. *beitan*. Orig. past tense *bote* (cf. *wrote*); ult. cogn. with L. *findere*, to cleave. *Bitten* (infected) *with* (a mania, etc.) is a mad dog metaphor. George III, being told that Wolfe was mad, expressed a wish that he might bite some of his other generals. *Hardbitten*, tough in fight, inured to bites, app. comes from dog-fighting. Its earliest use refers to animals. The phrase *the biter bit* is from 17 cent. use of *biter* for sharper.

A biter is one who thinks you a fool, because you do not think him a knave (Steele).

bitt [*naut.*]. Usu. pl. Two posts on ship's deck for fastening cables, etc. Forms are found in most Europ. langs. Prob. ON. *biti*, cross-beam (in house or ship). Hence naut. *bitter*, "the turne of a cable about the *bits*" (Capt. John Smith), and *bitter end*, which has acquired fig. sense by association with adj. *bitter*.

The bitter end is that end of the cable within boord at the bitt (Purch.).

When a chain or rope is paid out to the bitter-end, no more remains to be let go (Smyth).

bitter. AS. *biter*. Com. Teut.; cf. Du. Ger. *bitter*, ON. *bitr*, Goth. *baitrs*; cogn. with *bite* (cf. *mordant*). For *bitter end* see *bitt*.

bittern. With excrescent -*n*, from ME. *bitour*, earlier *botour*, F. *butor*. For older form cf. dial. *butterbump* (Tennyson, *Northern Farmer, Old Style*). Earliest is MedL. *butorius*, *bitorius*. Early L. dicts. give *butio*, a bittour, but the L. word is perh. only a var. of *buteo*, buzzard. OF. *bustor* looks like confusion with *bustard*. Everything suggests that the bird was named from its very remarkable cry.

As a bitore bombleth in the myre (Chauc. D. 972).

bitumen. L., orig. mineral pitch from Palestine. Cf. *asphalte*. An Osco-Umbrian word.

bivalve. F., from *bi-*, and *valve* (q.v.).

bivouac. F., Swiss-Ger. *biwacht*, by watch, patrol, its earlier meaning in F. & E. Introduced into F. by Swiss mercenaries during Thirty Years War. Johns. describes it as "not in use."

biz [*slang*]. Late 19 cent. for *business* (see *busy*).

bizarre. F., Sp. *bizarro*, brave, its earlier F. meaning. Formerly also *bigearre* and influenced in sense by F. *bigarré*, motley, variegated (see *bigaroon*). Perh. from Basque *bizar*, beard, the valiant man being "bearded like the pard."

blab. In ME. alternates with *lab*. Imit.; cf. Ger. *plappern* and see *babble*. *John le Blabbere* (*Pat. R.* 13 cent.) is earlier than dict. records.

Blabbe, or labe, or bewryere of counselle
(*Prompt. Parv.*).

black. AS. *blæc*, black, ink, already confused in AS. with *blāc*, white, bright (see *bleach*, *bleak*). The two words are prob. related, the common meaning being lack of colour. Usual Teut. for black is *swart* (q.v.). To *black-ball* is recorded for 18 cent. (see *ballot*), and has been adopted, with other "high-life" words, in F. (*blackbouler*). *Blackbird* is naut. slang for a kidnapped negro or Polynesian. *Black books*, for recording offenders' names, are mentioned in 16 cent. The *Black Country* includes parts of Staffordshire and Warwickshire. The *black guard* (16 cent.) consisted of the lowest menials of a large household, who took charge of pots and pans on journeys, also hangers-on of an army. The *black guard* of the king's kitchen is mentioned in 1535. *Black hole*, lock-up, dates from the notoriety of the *Black Hole* of Calcutta (1756). *Blackleg*, swindler (18 cent.) is perh. a description of the *rook*. *Black sheep*, wastrel, is also 18 cent. (*NED.*), but the nursery rime "Ba! Ba! black sheep" suggests much greater antiquity. *Blackmail*, orig. tribute paid by farmers to freebooters (Sc. & North), is Sc. *mail*, still used of rent (see *mail*³). It was perh. called *black* because often paid in black cattle, rents paid in silver being called *white mail*. The *Black Watch* orig. raised (early 18 cent.) for service in the Highlands, wore a dark uniform, to distinguish them from the red-coats of the old army. Cf. the *black friars*, or Dominicans (13 cent.), whence *Blackfriars* in London. *Black and*

blue was in ME. *blak and bla* (*blo*), *blue* (q.v.) being substituted as cogn. *blo* became obs. *Blackamoor* is a dial. form of *black Moor*. Archaic *Black-a-vised*, swarthy, contains F. *vis*, face, as in *vis-à-vis*.

You need not care a pin, if you ha't in white and black (*Misogonus*, iii. 2, c. 1550).

The boldest of them will never steal a hoof from anyone that pays black-mail to Vich Ian Vohr
(*Waverley*).

bladder. AS. *blæddre*. Com. Teut.; cf. Du. *blaar* (earlier *blader*, Flem. *bladder*), Ger. *blatter*, ON. *blāthra*; cogn. with *blow*¹.

blade. AS. *blæd*, blade (of oar). Com. Teut.; cf. Du. *blad*, Ger. *blatt*, leaf (*schulterblatt*, shoulder-blade), ON. *blath*. The usual plant word in AS. & ME. was *leaf* (q.v.), and it seems likely that *blade*, applied to corn, grass, etc., is partly due to MedL. *bladum*, corn, OF. *bled* (*blé*), of unknown origin, but possibly cogn. with above. As applied to persons, *jovial blade*, *roistering blade*, etc. it is usu. connected with sword-blade, a ME. sense of the word, though the development of meaning is not made out. The first record, *a very good blade* (*Rom. & Jul.* ii. 4), has an approximate F. parallel in *une bonne épée* (*lame*), a noted swordsman, but the usu. half contemptuous use of *blade* suggests Du. *blæt*, foolish talker, braggart. For double sense of *blade* cf. *foil*², with which it is ult. cogn.

blaeberry, bleaberry [*dial.*]. Bilberry. See *bilberry, blue*.

blague. Humbug. F., prob. ident. with *blague*, tobacco pouch, Ger. *balg*, skin. See *belly, bellows*.

blain. AS. *blegen*; cf. Norw. Dan. *blegn*, Du. *blein*, LG. *bleien*; ? cogn. with *blow*¹ (cf. *blister*). Now rare exc. in *chilblain*.

blame. F. *blâmer*, OF. *blasmer*, Late L. *blasphemare*, used in *Vulg.* for G. βλασφη-μεῖν. See *blaspheme*.

blanch. F. *blanchir*, to whiten, or perh. from corresponding adj. *blanch*, in common ME. use. *Blanched almonds* are mentioned in the *Prompt. Parv*. See *blank*.

blancmange. ME. *blancmangere*, a kind of galantine of meat, F. *blanc manger*. See *mange*.

For blankmanger, that made he with the beste
(Chauc. A. 387).

blandish. F. *blandir*, *blandiss-*, from L. *blandiri*, from *blandus*, bland, smooth. Hence *blandishments*, much commoner than the verb, and slang *blandiloquence* (Blount).

blank. F. *blanc*, white, OHG. *blanch* (cf. AS. *blanca*, ON. *blakkr*, steed); prob. cogn. with *bleak*. Adopted by all Rom. langs. Sense of colourless passes into that of empty in to *look blank, blank look-out, blank cartridge*. App. Cuthbert Bede introduced the euph. use of the word (cf. *dash*). *Blank verse* was introduced from It. by the Earl of Surrey (†1547). The It. name is *versi sciolti* (free).

Here's a pretty blank, I don't think! I wouldn't give a blank for such a blank blank. I'm blank if he don't look as though he'd swallered a blank codfish, and had bust out into blank barnacles
(*Verdant Green*, ii. 4).

To talk about a blank cheque is blank nonsense
(D. Lloyd George, Nov. 1918).

blanket. OF. *blanquete*, from *blanc*, white. Orig. a white woollen material; cf. ME. *whitel*, AS. *hwītel*, in similar sense. *Wet blanket* is fig. from extinguishing a fire (cf. *throw cold water on*). To *toss in a blanket* is in Shaks. (2 *Hen. IV*, ii. 4). *Wrong side of the blanket* is in Smollett (*Humphrey Clinker*). *Blanketeer* (hist.) was the name given to the operatives who assembled (1817) in St Peter's Fields, Manchester, provided with blankets in order to march to London and demand redress of their grievances. The attack upon them by the military gave rise to the portmanteau word *Peterloo* (*St Peter's Fields* × *Waterloo*), a very early example of this formation and a curious parallel to *Bakerloo*.

blare. Cf. Du. *blaren*, MHG. *bleren, blerren*, Ger. *plärren*, all of imit. origin. In ME. to bellow, weep, etc. Now only of a trumpet.

The worthies also of Moab bleared for very sorow
(Coverd. *Is.* xv. 4).

blarney. From a stone at *Blarney Castle*, near Cork, the kissing of which, a gymnastic operation, confers magic powers of cajolery. For local origin cf. *bunkum*.

blasé. F. *blaser*, to wear out (17 cent.). Origin unknown.

blason. See *blazon*.

blaspheme. F. *blasphémer*, Church L. *blasphemare*, G. βλασφημεῖν, to speak evil, from φημί, I say, with doubtful first element.

blast. AS. *blǣst*, strong gust of wind; cf. OHG. *blāst* (Ger. *blasen*, to blow), ON. *blöstr*. See *blaze³*. Fig. wind-born plague or infection, hence curse, etc.

blastoderm [*biol.*]. Superficial layer of embryo in early condition. From G. βλαστός, germ, sprout, δέρμα, skin.

They christened him [Aurelian McGoggin] the

": Blastoderm,"—he said he came from a family of that name somewhere in the prehistoric ages
(Kipling).

blatant. Coined by Spenser, in ref. to calumny. He may have had dial. *blate*, to bellow, or L. *blaterare*, to babble, in his mind.

A monster which the blatant beast men call
(*Faerie Queene*, v. xii. 37).

blatherskite. Orig. US. See *blether, bletherskate*.

The attempt of the Censorship to burke the Sinn Fein Assembly's Declaration of Independence has given a gratuitous advertisement to that bit of sublimated blatherskite
(*Sunday Times*, Jan. 26, 1919).

blay. See *bleak²*.

blaze¹. Of fire. AS. *blase, blæse*, torch, fire; cf. MHG. *blas*, torch; prob. cogn. with *blaze²* (q.v.), with orig. sense of shining. In *go to blazes*, etc., it is euph. for hell. *Blazer* was orig. applied at Cambridge (1850–60) to the bright scarlet of St John's College. *Blazing indiscretion* was first used by Lord Morley in ref. to the great Marquis of Salisbury who generally called a spade a spade.

blaze². White mark on horse's face. First recorded in 17 cent., hence prob. from Du. *bles* (see *blesbok*). Cf. synon. ON. *blesi*, Ger. *blässe*, from *blass*, pale (prob. cogn. with *blaze¹*). Later applied to white marks made on trees to indicate track, which, being US., may be an independent introduction from Du.

blaze³. To proclaim, as with a trumpet (*Mark*, i. 45). ON. *blāsa*, to blow. Com. Teut., though the verb does not appear in AS., which has, however, the corresponding noun *blast*; cf. Du. *blazen*, Ger. *blasen*, Goth. *-blēsan*; cogn. with L. *flare*. Later confused with *blazon* (q.v.) as in quot. below.

High was Redmond's youthful name
Blazed in the roll of martial fame (*Rokeby*, iv. 16).

blazon. F. *blason*, heraldry, orig. shield. Later senses are due to decoration of shield. As the "blazing" appearance of arms and armour is constantly emphasized in OF. poetry, it is not impossible that *blazon* is connected with *blaze¹* (cf. *brand*). The use of *blazon* for proclamation (cf. to *blazon forth*) is due to mistaken association with *blaze³*. It arises partly from the sense of description contained in the her. *blazon*.

But this eternal blazon must not be
To ears of flesh and blood (*Haml.* i. 5).

bleaberry. See *blaeberry*.

bleach. AS. *blǣcan*, from *blāc*, pale (see *bleak¹*); cf. Ger. *bleichen*, ON. *bleikja*. In obs. *bleach*, to blacken, we have the confusion indicated s.v. *black*.

noircir: to blacke, blacken; bleach, darken (Cotg.).

bleak¹. Adj. Formerly, and still in dial., pale. Parallel form (ON. *bleikr*) of ME. *bleche*, pale (AS. *blāc*, *blǣc*); cf. Du. *bleek*, colourless, Ger. *bleich*, pale, and see *bleach*.

bleke of colour: pallidus, subalbus (*Prompt. Parv.*).

bleak². Fish. ON. *bleikja*, from its colour (see *bleak¹*); cf. F. *able*, dim. of L. *albus*. Its true E. name is *blay*, AS. *blǣge*, with which cf. Ger. *bleihe*.

able: a blay, or bleak, fish (Cotg.).

bleared, blear-eyed. From ME. *bleren*, to have inflamed eyes, also to dim the eyes, hoodwink. Cf. LG. *blarr-oged*, *bleer-oged*, whence also various Scand. forms. This may be ident. with Prov. *blar*, OF. *bler*, glossed *glaucus*, applied esp. to the eyes, and app. of Teut. origin.

Lya was with blerid eyen (Wyc. *Gen.* xxix. 17).

For thow yt seme gold and schynyth rychely,
Alle ys but sotelte off the fend to blere yowre ye
(Metham, *Amoryus & Cleopes*, 1980).

bleat. AS. *blǣtan*. WGer.; cf. Du. *blaten*, MHG. *blazen*. Imit.

bleb. Small blister or bubble. Imit. of action of forming bubble with lips; cf. *blob*, *blubber*, *bubble*.

blee [*poet.*]. Hue. AS. *blēo*, with LG. cognates, used poet. in ME., esp. in *bright of blee*, and revived by mod. poets.

bleed. AS. *blēdan*, from *blood*.

blemish. F. *blêmir*, *blêmiss-*, to turn pale, OF. *blesmir*, to wound, of obscure origin. ON. *blāmi*, livid bluish colour, with influence of F. *blesser*, to wound, has been suggested.

blench. To flinch, earlier to swerve, and orig. trans., to deceive, elude. AS. *blencan*, to deceive, make to blink (cf. *drench*, *drink*). ME. had a northern form *blenk*. Sense-development has been influenced by obs. *blanch*, to turn pale.

And before his eye, thus, I will hang my net
To blench his sight (*Nature*, c. 1475).

That little foot-page he blenched with fear
(*Ingoldsby*).

blend. ME. *blenden*, ON. *blanda*, to mix (pres. *blend-*); cf. AS. *blandan*, to mix, *gebland*, mixture. Perh. ident. with obs. *blend*, to make blind, confuse, with which cf. Ger. *blenden* (v.i.).

blende [*min.*]. Ger. *blende*, from *blenden*, to blind, deceive, because a deceptive mineral (cf. *cobalt*, *nickel*). Hence *hornblende*, so called from its horny appearance, *pitchblende*.

blenheim orange, spaniel. From Duke of Marlborough's seat (Oxf.). Cf. *ribstone*, *clumber*.

blenny. Fish. L. *blendius* (Pliny), from G. βλέννος, mucus, descriptive of its scales.

blesbok. Antelope. SAfrDu., blaze buck. See *blaze²*.

bless. AS. *blētsian*, *blǣdsian*, to consecrate (with the *blood* of sacrifice). Sense-development is due to the choice of this word to render L. *benedicere*, while some later meanings, "to make happy," are due to mistaken association with *bliss* (q.v.). In fact *bless* may sometimes represent AS. *blithsian*, to gladden. A *penny to bless oneself with* alludes to the cross on some old coins. In *I'm blessed if..., Well I'm blessed, a blessed idiot*, we have mod. euphemisms for another word (cf. F. *sacré*). *Single blessedness* is an ironic application of what Shaks. says of the holiness of celibate life. It may be noted that AS. *blētsian*, in its etym. sense, would explain F. *blesser*, to wound, which has no Rom. cognates.

Earthlier happy is the rose distill'd,
Than that which, withering on the virgin thorn,
Grows, lives, and dies in single blessedness
(*Mids. Night's Dream*, i. 1).

blether, blather [*Sc.*]. ON. *blathra*, to talk stupidly, from *blathr*, nonsense, ? orig. windbag (see *bladder*). Hence US. *bletherskate*, *blatherskite*, orig. Sc. It occurs in the song *Maggie Lauder*, a favourite camp-ditty during Amer. War of Independence.

Jog on your gate, ye bletherskate
(Sempill, *Maggie Lauder*, c. 1650).

bletted [*techn.*]. Of medlar in condition for eating. From F. *blet*, over-ripe, as in *poire blette*; of Teut. origin.

blight. From 17 cent. only. Origin obscure. Cotg. app. regarded it as a kind of growth. Perh. related to obs. *blichening*, blight, from obs. *blikne*, to turn pale (see *bleak¹*). This word is used to render L. *rubigo*, blight, in the ME. version of Palladius (c. 1420).

brulure: blight, brancorne; (an hearbe) (Cotg.).

blighter. Recent (late 19 cent.) euph. for an uglier word. Cf. *blooming*, *blinking*. Perh. suggested by *blithering*.

I've strafed one of the blighters this time
(Destroyer of the Cuffley Zeppelin, Sep. 2, 1916).

blighty. Came into use in the Great War. Urdu *bilati* (adj.), Arab. *wilāyatī*, from *wilāyat*, government, esp. England, from *wali*, governor. *Belait* is used in this sense by Kipling c. 1887. Cf. *vilayet*. With *blighty wound* cf. synon. Ger. *heimatschuss*, lit. home-shot.

Nor do the Sahibs use the *belaitee panee* [soda water] when they are thirsty
(Kipling, *Smith Administration*).

The adj. *bilāyatī* or *wilāyatī* is applied specifically to a variety of exotic articles (*Hobson-Jobson*).

blimp [*neol.*]. Aeroplane converted into dirigible balloon. One of the weird coinages of the airman. Quot. below refers to R. 34, which crossed the Atlantic in July, 1919.

I'd worked hard on the bally blimp
(Mr Stowaway Ballantine).

blimy [*slang*]. For *Gawblimy*, God blind me; cf. *swop me bob*, for *so help me God*.

blind. AS. *blind*. Com. Teut.; cf. Du. Ger. *blind*, ON. *blindr*, Goth. *blinds*. Oldest sense of noun *blind* is mil., for F. *blinde*, obstruction, Ger. *blende*, from *blenden*, to make blind. Fig. sense of *blind alley* (occupation) is mod. *Blindfold* is for *blindfeld*, p.p. of ME. *blind-fellen*, to strike (*fell*) blind, mod. spelling being due to association with *fold*. *Blind-man's-buff*, formerly *blindman-buff, -buffet* (c. 1600), is from obs. *buff*, OF. *bufe*, a blow (see *buffet*[1]), the blind-folded person being buffeted by the other players (see quot. from Wyc. below). Also called earlier *hoodman blind* (see *hood*). The *blind-worm* (see *slow-worm*) is so named from its minute eyes; cf. Ger. *blindschleiche*.

And thei blynfelden hym, and smyten his face
(Wyc. *Luke*, xxii. 64).

blyndfyld: excecatus (*Prompt. Parv.*).

blink. ME. usu. *blenk*, AS. *blencan*, to deceive (dazzle), mod. form perh. due to Du. *blinken*; cf. Ger. *blinken*, to shine; cogn. with *blank*, in sense of bright, dazzling (cf. ON. *blakra*, to blink). Something of etym. sense survives in *ice-blink*, orig. brightness on the horizon due to reflection from ice. This is prob. Du. *ijsblink* or Dan. *isblink*. Sense of failing to see, esp. to *blink* (shut one's eyes to) *the fact* was orig. sporting, of dogs missing their birds. *Blinking* (slang) is quite recent. It is prob. for *blanking*, euph. for *bleeding*, with vowel thinned as in *bilk*. See also *blench*.

bliss. AS. *blīths*, from *blīthe*. Sense-development already in AS. shows association with

bless (q.v.), the two words being even confused in spelling.

Two blessis ben—blesse of the soule and blisse of the bodi (Wyc.).

blister. ME. *blester*, OF. *blestre*, ON. *blāstr* (dat. *blǽstri*), swelling, from *blāsa*, to blow. Cf. Ger. *blase*, blister, from *blasen*, to blow. See *blaze*[3].

blithe. AS. *blīthe*. Com. Teut.; cf. Du. *blijde*, *blij*, OHG. *blīdi*, ON. *blīthr*, Goth. *bleiths*. Cf. *bliss*.

blithering. Usu. with *idiot*. Thinned form of *blather*, *blether*, with vowel perh. suggested by *drivelling*.

blizzard. Came into gen. use in US. & E. in the hard winter of 1880–1. Earlier (US. 1834) in sense of hard blow. Probabilities point to its being an E. dial. word ult. cogn. with *blaze*[3].

bloat. Earliest as adj., soft, flabby, as in *the bloat* (old editions *blowt*) *king* (*Haml.* iii. 4). ON. *blautr*, soft, whence Sw. *blöt*, as in *blöt-fisc*, soaked fish. *Bloater* was earlier (16 cent.) *bloat herring*, formerly (17 cent.) opposed to dried, though also used for smoked, as the process was altered. For sense-development cf. *kipper*. Also puffed up, inflated, as in *bloated armaments* (Disraeli), *bloated aristocrat, capitalist*, or anything else that the speaker disapproves of. With cogn. Ger. *blöde*, feeble, bashful, cf. Sc. *blate* and fig. use of *soft* in E.

fumer: to bloat, besmoake, hang, or drie in the smoake (Cotg.).

blob. Orig. a bubble; cf. *bleb*. In mod. cricket slang, a "duck's egg."

bloc [*pol.*]. F., block (v.i.).

block. F. *bloc*, OHG. *bloch* (*block*), with cogn. forms in Du. Sw. Dan. Hence verb, to stop, as at cricket and in Parliament (cf. *stumbling-block*). In the *block-system* a line is divided into a number of *blocks*, or sections. *Chip of the old block* occurs 17 cent. *Blockade* (17 cent.) is archaic Ger. *blocquada*, formed by analogy with mil. words of It. origin at time of Thirty Years War. Its earlier E. sense was blockhouse, palisade (Fryer's *E. Ind. & Pers.* i. 80), so that it has changed its meaning in the same way as F. *blocus*. *Blockade-running* first occurs at time of Amer. Civil War, when English vessels attempted to trade profitably with Southern ports. *Blockhouse*, a detached fort, later applied in US. to house of squared logs, or blocks (cf. *log-hut*), is prob. Ger. or Du.; cf. F. *blocus*, orig. blockhouse, now blockade, from Ger. *blockhaus*, which occurs on Franco-German frontier in 14 cent.

bloke. 19 cent. thieves' slang. Shelta.

blond. F., MedL. *blundus*. Prob., like most colours, of Teut. origin, and perh. orig. applied esp. to the yellow-haired Germans. Origin unknown; but cf. AS. *blanden-feax*, *blonden-feax*, grizzled hair (cf. *Fairfax*), lit. of mixed ("blended") colour. Colour words, being purely subjective, are of most elusive and changeable meaning (see *auburn*, *black*).

blood. AS. *blōd*. Com. Teut.; cf. Du. *bloed*, Ger. *blut*, ON. Goth. *blōth*. With verb to *blood* (hounds, troops) cf. hist. of F. *acharner*, from L. *ad carnem* (see *flesh*). *Blue blood* is translated from Sp. *sangre azul*, of race not contaminated by Moorish or Jewish mixture, with blue veins showing clearly on white skin. With *blood*, applied to persons, cf. Ger. *ein junges blut*. *Blood and thunder* was orig. an oath. The *bloodhound* (14 cent.) was supposed to scent the blood of the fugitive. *Blood-money* is used by Coverd. (*Matt.* xxvii. 6). *Bloodshot* was earlier *blood-shotten*, shot, i.e. suffused, with blood. The *bloody hand* as armorial device of baronets is derived from O'Neill, Earl of Ulster. The vulgar *bloody* was orig. adv., occurring esp. in the phrase *bloody drunk* (common c. 1700). It is merely an intens. of the same type as *awfully*, *thundering*, etc., and may have been suggested by the use as intens. prefixes of Du. *bloed*, Ger. *blut*; e.g. Ger. *blutarm*, miserably poor, might be rendered *bloody poor* in Shavian E.; cf. *blutdieb*, "an arch thief" (Ludw.). Quot. 1 is much earlier than first *NED*. record and quot. 2 shows that the word was not orig. offensive.

A man cruelly eloquent and bluddily learned
(Marston, *Faun*, i. 2., 1606).

It was bloody hot walking to-day
(Swift to Stella, May 28, 1711).

The Bismarck theory of blood and iron has the great merit of being simple and concise. The German theory of warfare fits it as a bludgeon fits the hand of a footpad (R. Blatchford, Dec. 16, 1909).

bloodwite [*hist.*]. AS. *blōdwīte*, blood penalty. See *twit*.

bloom¹. Flower. ON. *blōm*, whence ME. (northern) *blome*, the southern word being *blossom* (q.v.), both now superseded, exc. in spec. senses, by *flower*. Com. Teut.; cf. Du. *bloem*, Ger. *blume*, Goth. *blōma*; cogn. with *blow²* and ult. with L. *flos*, *florēre*.

bloom² [*techn.*]. Mass of hammered iron. AS. *blōma*. *NED*. finds a gap in the history of the word from AS. to 16 cent., but the surname *Bloomer* (v.i.), i.e. worker in a bloom-smithy, is well attested in ME. records.

bloomer. Costume (US. c. 1850). "After *Mrs Bloomer* (†1894), an American lady who introduced the costume" (*NED*.). "She did not invent it, was not the first to wear it, and protested against its being called by her name" (Thornton).

blooming. Euph. for *bloody* (see *blood*). Cf. *bleeding*, *blinking*.

blossom. AS. *blōstm*; cf. Du. *bloesem*, ON. *blōmstr*; cogn. with *bloom¹*. Both now replaced, exc. in spec. senses, by *flower*.

We generally call those flowers blossoms, which are not much regarded in themselves, but as a token of some following production (Johns.).

blot¹. Blemish, etc. In ME. also *plot*. Earliest sense (14 cent.), blemish. Perh. ident. with *plot* (q.v.); cf. Ger. *fleck*, piece of ground, blot, and various senses of *spot*. There is also an OF. *blote*, clod of earth. Hence *blottesque*, coined on *grotesque*, *picturesque*, etc. *Blotting-paper* (1519) is rather a misnomer, its object being to prevent blots.

blot² [*archaic*]. Exposed piece at backgammon. App. Dan. *blot* or Du. *bloot*, bare (cf. Ger. *bloss*), but the identity has not been established. ? Or same as *blot¹* in sense of "weak spot."

I find them [a committee of enquiry] wise and reserved, and instructed to hit all our blots
(Pepys, Oct. 3, 1666).

blotch. Earliest sense (17 cent.) boil, pustule. OF. *bloche* (also *blost*, *blostre*), clod of earth, also tumour, OHG. *bluster*, cogn. with *blow¹* (cf. *blister*). Partly due also to earlier *botch¹*. MedL. *plustula* suggests mixture of this word with *pustule*.

blouse. 19 cent. from F. (18 cent.), workman's or peasant's smock, of unknown origin. Application to lady's garment is recent.

blow¹. Of wind. AS. *blāwan*; cf. Ger. *blähen*, to inflate; ult. cogn. with *blaze³* and with L. *flare*. To *blow hot and cold* is an allusion to the fable of the traveller who mystified his host by blowing on his fingers to warm them and on his broth to cool it. With to *blow upon* (a secret) cf. similar use of F. *éventer*, from *vent*, wind. See also *gaff²*. *Blowfly* is connected with erron. notion of the insect's methods. Colloq. *blow it* is prob. euph. for *blast*.

blow². Of flowers. AS. *blōwan*. WGer.; cf. Du. *bloeien*, Ger. *blühen*; cogn. with *bloom¹*, *blossom*.

blow³. Noun. 15 cent. (north). Earliest form *blaw*. Cf. Ger. *bläuen*, to beat (OHG. *bliuwan*), Du. *blouwen*, but the E. word only occurs as a noun, while the Du. & Ger. are verbs only. The date is also against connection. It is perh. a peculiar application of *blow¹*. Cf. F. *soufflet*, bellows, box on the ear, from *souffler*, to blow, and OF. *buffet* (related to *puff*), with same two meanings; also ON. *pustr*, box on the ear, cogn. with LG. *puster*, pair of bellows.

blowzy. From obs. *blouze*, beggar's trull, usu. described as red-faced, "a ruddy, fat-faced wench" (Johns.), hence perh. cogn. with Du. *blos*, blush. See *blush*.

Sweet blowse, you are a beauteous blossom sure
(*Tit. Andron.* iv. 2).

blubber. Orig. bubble. Of imit. formation. *Blubber-lipped* was earlier *blabber* (*blobber*) lipped, also *babber-lipped*, all expressing the idea of protruding. See *bleb, blob*. *Bubble* is used in Sc. for *blubber*, to weep.

blober upon water: bouteillis (Palsg.).

blucher. Boot. Named after *Marshal Blücher*. Cf. *wellington*. Non-privileged cabs, admitted to stations after others have been hired, were also called *bluchers*, in allusion to the Prussian arrival at Waterloo. Cf. F. (argot) *grouchy*, late arrival.

bludgeon. From 18 cent. Perh. OF. *bougeon*, *boujon* (OF. *boljon*), dim. of OF. *bolge*, *bouge*, club. This is explained by Cotg. as a bolt with a heavy head and is still used in dial. for rung of a ladder, bar of a chair, etc. Mod. form may be due to association with *blood*.

blue¹. Adj. ME. *blew*, F. *bleu*, Ger. *blau*. This replaced cogn. ME. *blo* (see *blaeberry*), from ON. *blā*, which survived for a time in sense of livid (*black and blue*). *True blue*, due to old association of the colour with constancy, was later used of the Scottish Whigs (17 cent.) and of strong Tories (19 cent.), the application being in both cases from adoption of a party colour. *Blue* was also the garb of recipients of charity, hence *bluecoat* (school), Sc. *bluegown*. University *blues* are 19 cent. The *blues*, depression, is for *blue devils*, appearing to the despondent. The *Blues* (Horse-guards) were so-called (1690) when separated from William III's Dutch guard. *Till all's blue* was orig. used of effect

of drink on the sight. *By all that's blue* may be adapted from F. *parbleu* (euph. for *par Dieu*). *Bluebeard*, wife-killer with secret chamber for the bodies, is F. *Barbe bleue* (Perrault). His original has been sought in the medieval monster Gilles de Retz (†1440). *Bluebottle* was applied to the cornflower much earlier than to the fly. As a contemptuous term for a constable it is used by Shaks. (2 *Hen. IV*. v. 4). *Blue books* (from cover) are mentioned in 1715. *Blue John*, kind of fluor-spar (Derbysh.), may be from F. *bleu jaune*, blue yellow. *Bluenose*, US. nickname for Nova Scotian, alludes to cold climate. The *blue ribbon* was adopted as badge of temperance c. 1878. Earlier it was used vaguely of any high distinction; cf. F. *cordon bleu*. *Blue-stocking* is said to have been applied (c. 1750) to intellectual gatherings at houses of Mrs Montague and other ladies, some of the *gentlemen* frequenting these assemblies having adopted plain blue worsted stockings instead of the fashionable silk. It has been adopted in F. (*bas bleu*) and Ger. (*blaustrumpf*). According to some authorities the name goes back to the Venetian society *della calza* (16 cent.). The *blue-water* school has been applied since c. 1905 to those who pin their faith on the naval offensive as the surest defensive. With *once in a blue moon* cf. *at the Greek calends*, F. *la semaine des quatre jeudis*, Du. *blaauw maandag*.

Yf they say the mone is blewe,
We must beleve that it is true
(*Rede me and be not wrothe*, 1528).

blue² [*slang*]. Verb, to cause to disappear. Cf. synon. F. *faire passer au bleu*, ? orig. to send into the sky. Ger. *schwärzen*, to smuggle, lit. blacken, may also be compared.

bluff¹. Of a countenance or ship. Corresponds to obs. Du. *blaf*, with same meaning. For vowel change cf. US. *slug*, to strike, from Du. *slagen*. US. *bluff*, steep cliff, etc. is the same word.

bluff, or *bluff-headed*: when a ship has a small rake forward on, and so that she is built with her stem too streight up (*Sea-Dict.* 1708).

bluff². Verb. Orig. US., ? from Du. *verbluffen*, "to baffle, to put out of countenance" (Sewel). Cf. E. dial. *bluff*, to blindfold, hoodwink, which may be cogn. with the Du. word.

blunder. ME. *blondren*, to confuse, to flounder; cf. Norw. Sw. dial. *blundra*. Of doubtful origin; ? cogn. with AS. *blandan*, ME. *blonden*, to mix, blend, and with *blind*. With *blunder-head*, for earlier *dunder-head*, cf. *blunderbuss*.

Who has blondred these thynges on this facyon? Qui a perturbé ces choses en ceste sorte? (Palsg.).

blunderbuss. Perversion of Du. *donderbus*, thunder-box. See *bush²* and cf. Ger. *büchse*, gun. The early corruptions are numerous.

blunt. From c. 1200. Earliest sense, dull, esp. of sight. Origin unknown. ? Cogn. with *blind*.

blur. 16 cent., synon. with *blot*. Origin unknown.

blurt. 16 cent., usu. with *out*. Prob. imit. Cf. Sc. *blirt*, gust, sudden weeping.

blush. AS. *blyscan*, to shine, *āblysian*, to blush, from *blyse*, torch, fire; cf. Du. *blozen*, LG. *blüsken*, Norw. Dan. *blusse*, to blush. Oldest sense in ME. is to shine forth, cast a glance; hence *at the first blush*. In quot. below it is app. confused with *flush*.

A young actress in the first blush of success
(S. Weyman).

bluster. 16 cent. Prob. imit., with suggestion of *blow*, *blast*. Gavin Douglas uses pres. part. *blasterand* in same sense. Holthausen gives LG. *blüstern*, to blow. *Blustering* is, since Spenser, stock epithet of Boreas.

Cease rude Boreas, blust'ring railer
(G. A. Stevens, †1784).

bo, boh. Natural exclamation intended to surprise or frighten. Hence *Bo to a goose* (16 cent.). *Bo-peep*, nursery game with children, is still older. See *peep¹*.

Mark how he playeth bo-peep with the scriptures
(Tynd.).

boa. L. (Pliny). Connected by Pliny and other early etymologists, with varied explanations, with L. *bos*, ox, but perh. rather from *bo!* exclamation of terror (v.s.). Hence *boa constrictor*, named by Linnaeus, and often erron. applied to much larger serpents. Fur *boa* is in Dickens (1836).

boanerges. Vociferous preacher. G. βοανεργές (*Mark*, iii. 17), Heb. *b'nēy regesh*, sons of thunder. With first syllable cf. *Ben* in Jewish names, e.g. *Benjamin*, son of the right hand.

boar. AS. *bār*. WGer.; cf. Du. *beer*, OHG. *bēr* (ModGer. dial. *bär*), which also mean bear.

board. AS. *bord*, board, plank, table, side of a ship. Com. Teut.; cf. Du. *boord*, Ger. *bort*, ON. *borth*, Goth. *baurd*. Orig. combining two related words, one meaning

edge. Many E. senses are due to F. *bord* (from Teut.). The meaning is easily traced from *board*, plank, table, via *board* (and lodging) to a mod. *board* (table) *of guardians* or a *school board*. In sense of edge, border, it is usu. F. *bord*. So also the verb to *board* (naut.), orig. to range up alongside, is F. *aborder*. *Board on board* was formerly used for *yard-arm to yard-arm*, i.e. in close combat. To *go by the board* is to fall overboard. To *sweep the board* is from cardplaying (cf. *above-board*). *Bound in boards* dates from the time when book-covers were of wood.

boorder that gothe to borde: commensal (Palsg.).

John Kynge, blowen over the borde into the see
(*Voyage of the Barbara*, 1540).

boast. ME. *bost*, clamour, ostentation, AF. *bost*. Origin unknown, but form suggests F. (cf. *coast*, *roast*, *toast*). Perh. via an unrecorded OF. **boster* from a Teut. root meaning swelling.

Men that boosen her bristis [puff out their breasts]
(*Lantern of Light*, c. 1410).

boat. AS. *bāt*, whence ON. *bātr* and Du. Ger. *boot*. App. E. is the home of the word (Ger. *boot* is from Du.), which has also passed into the Rom. langs. (OF. *bat*, F. *bateau*, etc.). *Boatswain* is late AS. *bātswegen*, the second element being ON. (see *swain*). It is spelt *boson* in 1600 (*Cecil MSS.*).

Have ye pain? So likewise pain have we
For in one boat we both imbarked be
(Hudson, *Judith*, 1584).

bob. The *NED.* recognizes provisionally nine nouns and four verbs, which may be of various origins. The oldest meaning of the noun seems to be a pendent cluster, hence perh. *bob-wig*, *bob-tail*, that of the verb is to mock and strike, the first from OF. *bober*, to mock (cf. Sp. *bobo*, fool). The idea of jerky motion is present in bell-ringing, e.g. *treble bob major*, etc.; also in *cherry-bob*. In *dry-bob*, *wet-bob* (Eton) we have perh. the name *Bob*, with a vague punning allusion to obs. *dry-bob*, a blow which does not draw blood; cf. *light-bob*, light infantry soldier. *Bob*, a shilling (19 cent. slang) is perh. from *Robert* (cf. *joey²*). With naut. *bobstay*, which holds down the bowsprit, cf. the *bob* of a pendulum. For *bobtail* see also *tag*. *Bobsleigh* is US. (19 cent.).

Bobadil [*archaic*]. Braggart. Character in Jonson, *Every Man in his Humour*. From *Boabdil*, last Moorish king of Granada, Sp. corrupt. of *Abū Abd'illāh*, father of the servant of Allah. Cf. *abigail, Bombastes,* etc.

bobbery [*Anglo-Ind.*]. Hind. *bāp re,* O father! Cf. *my aunt!* For change of cry into noun cf. F. *vacarme,* uproar, bobbery, Du. *wacharme,* lit. woe poor (fellow).

bobbin. F. *bobine,* of unknown origin, but prob. connected with some sense of *bob.* With *bobbinet,* cotton net, orig. imitating pillow lace, cf. *stockinet.*

bobbish [*slang*]. Usu. with *pretty.* App. from *bob,* to bounce, etc.

bobby [*slang*]. *Robert Peel* was Home Secretary when Metropolitan Police Act was passed (1828). Cf. *peeler.*

bobolink. NAmer. singing bird. From its cry, app. first (18 cent.) understood as *Bob o' Lincoln.* Cf. *whippoorwill, katydid.* But very possibly adapted from a native name related to word below.

Grene birds, as big as sparrowes, like the catalinkins of West India (Purch.).

bocardo. See *barbara.* Also name of prison at Oxford (suppressed 1771), prob. given as result of some logician's witticism.

Boche, Bosche [*neol.*]. F., for *Alleboche,* argotic perversion of *Allemand,* German, in use long before the War. Perh. suggested by *tête de boche,* from *boche,* bowl[2], of Prov. origin; cf. It. *boccia,* bowl, and our *bullet-headed.* I have heard Germans called *têtes de boche* c. 1890, and *Alboche* is in Villatte's *Parisismen* (1890). But Swiss F. has also *Allemoche.*

bock. F., glass of beer. Ger. *bock,* for earlier *ambock,* beer from *Eimbeck,* Hanover.

bocking. Fabric. From *Bocking,* Essex. Cf. *worsted.*

boddle. See *bodle.*

bode. Usu. with *well. ill.* AS. *bodian,* to announce, from *boda,* messenger. Com. Teut.; cf. Du. *bode,* Ger. *bote,* messenger, ON. *bothi;* cogn. with *bid,* to offer. Hence *forebode.*

bodega. Wine-shop. Sp., L. *apotheca,* G. ἀποθήκη (see *apothecary*); cf. F. *boutique,* shop.

bodge. Var. of *botch*[2] (q.v.).

bodice. For (*pair of*) *bodies;* cf. *pence* for *pennies.* For sense cf. *corset* (q.v.).

A pair of bodice of the cumbrous form in vogue a: the beginning of the last century
(Ainsworth, *Jack Sheppard,* ch. 1).

bodkin. Formerly a piercing instrument. ME. *boidekin, boitequin.* Origin unknown. The ME. form suggests an AF. **boitequin,* little

box, and sense-development as in *tweezers* (q.v.), but this is only my conjecture. To *ride bodkin* is unexplained; ? cf. dial. *pin,* middle horse of a team of three harnessed tandem fashion.

They...provoked themselves with knyves and botkens (Coverd. 1 *Kings,* xviii. 28).

He's too big to travel bodkin between you and me
(*Vanity Fair*).

bodle, boddle [*Sc.*]. Halfpenny. See *bawbee.*

I do not value your favour at a boddle's purchase
(*Kidnapped,* Ch. iii.).

Bodleian library. At Oxford. Restored and enriched (1597) by *Sir Thomas Bodley.*

body. AS. *bodig;* cf. OHG. *botah,* whence Ger. *bottich,* brewing-tub. Fig. uses as those of L. *corpus* and F. *corps.* In ME. also human being (cf. OF. *cors*), as still in *somebody, busibody, a nice body,* etc. *Body-snatcher* is early 19 cent. (see *burke*). To *keep body and soul together* is for earlier *life and soul.*

By my trowthe they ar as good menys bodys as eny leve (*Paston Let.* ii. 387).

Boehmenist [*theol.*]. Follower of *Jacob Boehme* or *Behm* (i.e. Bohemian), Ger. mystic (†1624).

Boeotian. Dull clown. From reputation of *Boeotia,* in ancient Greece. Cf. *Arcadian, solecism.*

boer. Du., peasant, farmer. Cf. *boor, bond*[2], and Ger. *bauer.*

bog. Ir. Gael. *bogach,* from *bog,* soft. In Shaks. (*Hen. V.* iii. 7). With *bogtrotter,* applied to Irish since 17 cent., cf. *moss-trooper.* For *bog-bean* see *buck*[1].

bogey. See *bogie, bogy.*

boggart [*dial.*]. Goblin, bugbear. Origin obscure. See *boggle, bogie, bogle, bug*[1].

boggle. Orig. to start with fright, as though at sight of a spectre. See *bogle.* Now confused with *bungle.*

You boggle shrewdly, every feather starts you
(*All's Well,* v. 3).

A thing their superstition boggles at
(Browning, *Ring and Book,* vi. 282).

It takes up about eighty thousand lines,
A thing imagination boggles at:
And might, odds-bobs, sir! in judicious hands
Extend from here to Mesopotamy
(Calverley, *Cock and Bull*).

bogie. Truck (19 cent.). Origin unknown. App. northern dial. ? Cf. *buggy.* For obscurity of so recent a techn. word cf. *culvert, lorry, sponson, trolley,* etc.

bogle [*archaic*]. Spectre. Sc. (c. 1500). Prob. Celt. Cf. Welsh *bwgwl,* terror. See *bug*[1], also *boggart, boggle, bogy.*

bogus. US. slang. Orig. (1827) apparatus for counterfeit coining. Origin unknown. *Calibogus*, "rum and spruce beer, American beverage" (Grose), suggests a parallel to *balderdash*. ? Connected with F. *bagasse*, sugar-cane refuse, Sp. *bagazo*.

bogy, bogey. App. related to *bogle* (q.v.) and *bug*[1] (q.v.). Earliest (19 cent.) as nickname for Satan. Hence prob. *bogey*, the "colonel," at golf. Perh. ult. cogn. with *Puck*.

bohea. Tea. Chin. *Wu-i*, hills north of Fuhkien, the dial. of which substitutes *b* for *w*.

Bohemian. Adaptation of F. *Bohème, Bohémien*, a gipsy, a name given under a misapprehension (cf. *gipsy*), the tribe having reached Western Europe (15 cent.) through Bohemia (OHG. *Beheim*, home of the Boii). This is the usual explanation, but the name is perh. rather due to some vague association with the Bohemian heretics. Mod. application is esp. due to Henri Murger's *Scènes de la Vie de Bohême* (1845).

boil[1]. Swelling. Orig. *bile* (see quot. s.v. *hound*), as still in dial. AS. *býl*; cf. Ger. *beule*, Goth. *uf-bauljan*, to blow up. For converse sound-change see *rile*.

boil[2]. Verb. OF. *boillir* (*bouillir*), L. *bullire*, to boil, bubble, from *bulla*, bubble (see *bull*[2]). The *whole boiling* is a metaphor of the same type as *batch*.

boisterous. Lengthened from ME. *boistous*, orig. rough, coarse, in gen. sense, AF. *bustous*, rough (of a road), which can hardly be the same as F. *boiteux*, limping. It agrees better in sense with *robustious*, which is however recorded much later. It may be ult. of the same origin as *boast* (q.v.). Cf. hist. of *rude*.

Roboam was buystuouse [*Vulg.* rudis]
(Wyc. 2 *Chron.* xiii. 7).
There Nemproth [Nimrod] the bostuous [Higd. robustus] oppressor of men began to reigne in the cite of Babilon
(15 cent. transl. of Higden's *Polychronicon*).

bolas [*SAmer.*]. Missile lasso loaded with balls to entangle legs of animals. Pl. of Sp. *bola*, ball. Cf. *lasso*.

bold. AS. *bald*. Com. Teut.; cf. Du. *boud*, OHG. *bald*, ON. *ballr*, Goth. *balths*, in compds. To *make bold with* (cf. *make free with*) is in Shaks. (*Merry Wives*, ii. 2).

bole[1]. Of a tree. ON. *bolr*; cf. Ger. *bohle*, plank, and see *bulwark*.

bole[2]. Earthy clay. MedL. *bolus*, G. βῶλος, clod. Hence *bole armeniac* or *Armenian bole* (*boole armonyak* in Chauc.).

bolection [*arch.*]. Raised moulding. Orig. form (? *bol-, bal-, bel-*) and origin unknown.

bolero. Dance. Sp. Cf. *cachucha, fandango*. Also short jacket.

boletus. Fungus. L., G. βωλίτης, mushroom.

bolide. Meteor. F., L. *bolis, bolid-*, G. βολίς, missile, from βάλλειν, to throw.

boll[1]. Rounded pod. Var. of *bowl*[1] (q.v.).

The barley was in the ear, and the flax was bolled
(*Ex.* ix. 31).

That pest of the cotton plant, the boll weevil
(*Daily Chron.* March 30, 1917).

boll[2] [*Sc.*]. Measure. ? ON. *bolli*, *bowl*[1].

Bollandists. Writers continuing *Acta Sanctorum* of *John Bolland*, Flemish Jesuit (17 cent.).

bollard. Strong post for securing hawser. Cf. Norw. *puller*, Dan. *pullert*, LG. *poller*, Du. *polder*, ? all from OF. *poltre* (*poutre*), beam, Late L. *pulletrum*, from *pullus*, foal, young animal.

bolo. Mil. slang for *Bolshevist* (NRuss. campaign, 1918), perh. partly suggested by following.

boloism [*neol.*]. Pacifist propaganda financed from Germany. From *Bolo Pasha*, engaged in similar roguery in France (Sep. 1917) and shot (Apr. 17, 1918).

Look out for boloism in all its shapes and forms. It is the latest and most formidable weapon in Germany's armoury
(D. Lloyd George, Oct. 23, 1917).

Bologna. In Italy. L. *Bononia*. Hence *Bologna sausage*. See *polony*.

Bolshevik, Bolshevist [*Russ.*]. Majority socialist, wrongly rendered *maximalist*. Dates from Russ. Socialist Conference of 1903; cf. Russ. *bolshinstvo*, majority, from *bolshe*, greater. Now (beginning of 1918) adopted as gen. term for pol. upheavalist. Cf. *menshevik*.

What we might call the Bolshewig party—that strange combination led by Lord Lansdowne and Mr Ramsay Macdonald (*Morn. Post*, Aug. 14, 1918).

Those swine whom we call Bolsheviks are mere bloodthirsty cutthroats who murder for the love of it. Their régime has destroyed more peasants and poor people in one year then did the Czars in a hundred (Col. John Ward, the navvy M.P., Nov. 29, 1918).

bolster. AS. *bolster*. Com. Teut.; cf. Du. *bolster*, Ger. *polster*, ON. *bolstr*; from a Teut. root meaning to swell. With to *bolster up* (16 cent.) cf. fig. senses of to *pad*.

bolt[1]. Noun. AS. *bolt*, arrow with heavy head. Com. Teut.; cf. Du. *bout*, Ger. *bolzen*, ON. *bolte*. Hence *bird-bolt*, kind of arrow, *bolt upright* (cf. *straight as a dart*), *thunderbolt*, and verb to *bolt* (cf. to *dart*). *A bolt from the blue* was app. adapted by Carlyle from Ger. *ein blitz aus blauem himmel*. *A fool's bolt is soon shot* dates from early 13 cent. The door-*bolt* is the same word, orig. a bar with a knobbed end, and we still speak of "shooting" it. Ger. *bolzen* also has the double sense. A *bolt* (roll) of canvas is named from its shape.

Long as a mast and uprighte as a bolt
(Chauc. A. 3264).

bolt², **boult** [*archaic*]. To sift (flour, etc.). OF. *buleter* (*bluter*), app. for **bureter*, cogn. with It. *burattare*, from *buratto*, sieve, fine-cloth, perh. dim. of *bura*, for which see *bureau*.

I ne kan nat bulte it to the bren (Chauc. B. 4430).

boltel, **bowtell** [*arch.*]. Round moulding, shaft of clustered pillar. Prob. of OF. origin and ult. related to L. *bulla*, bubble, boss, etc.

embouti: raised, imbossed, or boultled (Cotg.).

boltered [*archaic*]. In *blood-boltered*, sometimes used as echo of Shaks. Midl. dial. *balter*, to clot, tangle, etc. Prob. from ON. Cf. Dan. *baltre*, *boltre*, to wallow.

Blood-bolter'd Banquo smiles upon me
(*Macb.* iv. 1).

bolus. L., G. βῶλος, clod. See *bole²*.

bomb. F. *bombe*, Sp. *bomba*, from L. *bombus*, humming, G. βόμβος, of imit. origin (cf. *boom¹*). Verb to *bomb* became obs. (!) in 18 cent., last *NED.* quot. being from Nelson (1797).

I saw a trial of those devilish murdering mischief-doing engines call'd bombs, shot out of the morter-piece on Blackheath (Evelyn, Mar. 16, 1686).

bombard. Earliest as noun, a deep-toned wind instrument (Gower), an early cannon (Lydgate). F. *bombarde*, in same two senses, augment. of *bombe* (v.s.). In Shaks. (*Temp.* ii. 2) also used of a drinking vessel, prob. from its shape. Hence *bombardier*, now artillery corporal. *Bombardon*, a wind instrument, is of recent introduction, It. *bombardone*.

bombasine [*archaic*]. F. *bombasin*, Late L. *bombasinum*, for *bombycinum*, from *bombyx*, *bombyc-*, silkworm, G. βόμβυξ. Synon. F. *basin* is due to *bombasin* being understood as *bon basin*, and Ger. *baumseide*, lit. tree-silk, is also folk-etym.

bombast. Earlier *bombace*, OF., Late L. *bombax*, *bombac-*, for *bombyx* (v.s.), cotton wool, padding, or fig., boasting, tall talk.

Cf. *fustian*, *padding*, etc. In quot. below we should now use *pad*. *Bombastes Furioso* is a mock epic (1815) by W. B. Rhodes.

He is as well able to bombast out a blank verse as the best of you (Greene, *Groatsworth of Wit*).

Bombay duck. Fish. See *bummalo*. Cf. *Welsh rabbit*.

bombilation, **bombination.** Variations on L. *bombizatio*, buzzing. See *bomb*.

bona-fide. L., in good faith, i.e. genuine, esp. as applied to thirsty Sunday wayfarers.

bonanza. Successful mine, lucky enterprise (US.). Sp. *bonanza*, fair weather, prosperity, from L. *bonus*, good.

bona-roba. "A showy wanton" (Johns.). It. *buonaroba*, "as we say good stuffe, that is a good wholesome plum-cheeked wench" (Flor.).

bonbon. F. baby lang., with the usual redupl. Cf. E. *goody*.

bond¹. Shackle, restraint, etc. Var. of *band¹* (from *bind*), with which it is used indifferently in many senses, though always *bond* as leg. term, e.g. in Shylock's *bond*. The *Afrikander Bond* (SAfr.) is from cogn. Du. *bond*; cf. Ger. *bund*, confederation, etc.

bond² [*archaic*]. Serf. Hence *bondage*, *bondman*, *bondwoman*, *bond and free*. Orig. a farmer, late AS. *bōnda*, ON. *bōndi*, for *būandi*, pres. part. of *būa*, to dwell, till; cogn. with Ger. *bauer*, peasant, and Du. *boer* (q.v.). Change of meaning is due partly to humble position (cf. *churl*, *villain*), and partly to mistaken association with *bond¹*. Orig. sense survives in Norw. Dan. Sw. *bonde*, small freeholder, husbandman, etc.

bone. AS. *bān*. Com. Teut.; cf. Du. *been*, Ger. ON. *bein*, these usu. meaning leg. Differs from other important body-words in having no cognates outside Teut. A *bone of contention* was orig. fought for by two dogs; cf. to *have a bone to pick with*. To *make no bones about* was earlier (15 cent.) to *find no bones in*, i.e. to swallow without difficulty. The verb to *bone* (thieves' slang, 19 cent.) is perh. from the dog making off with a bone. *Bone-lace* was orig. made with bone bobbins.

bonfire. For *bone-fire*, ME. & Sc. *bane-fire*, perh. originating in some heathen rite. "For the annual midsummer banefire or bonfire, old bones were regularly collected and stored up, down to c. 1800" (*NED.*). It is the usual rendering of *rogus* and *pyra* in L. dicts. of 16–17 cents. Cf. synon. F. *feu d'os.*

bane-fyre: ignis ossium (*Cath. Angl.*).

feu de behourdis: a bone-fire (Cotg.).

bone-fire: een been-vier, dat is, als men victorie brandt (Hexham).

bonhomie. F., good-fellowship. Cf. *Jacques Bonhomme*, trad. nickname of F. peasant.

Boniface. Name of innkeeper in Farquhar's *Beaux' Stratagem* (1707). Cf. *abigail.* Much earlier is *Bonifazio* in a similar rôle in Ariosto's *La Scolastica.*

bonito. Fish, kind of tunny. Sp. Port. *bonito.* Cf. F. *bonite* and MedLat. *bonitum.* May be Sp. *bonito,* fine, but the fact that it is commonly coupled with *albacore* (q.v.) suggests Arab. origin.

bonne. Nurse-maid, servant. F., good.

bonne bouche. Misused in E. for dainty morsel. In F. pleasant taste in the mouth, e.g. *garder pour la bonne bouche, rester sur la bonne bouche,* etc.

bonnet. F., for *chapeau de bonnet,* ? some unknown material, MedL. *bonetum.* But earlier is Late L. *abonnis,* cap (7 cent.). Superseded in 17 cent., exc. in Sc., by *cap* in gen. sense, and surviving only in ref. to woman's head-gear. Sc. *bonnet laird* is one who wears a bonnet like the peasants; cf. *bonnet-piece,* gold coin on which James V is represented wearing a bonnet. In sense of accomplice, etc. (thieves' slang 19 cent.) there is perh. a reminiscence of F. *deux têtes dans un bonnet,* hand and glove. Naut. *bonnet,* orig. topsail, is in *Piers Plowm.*

Un chapel ot de bonet en sa teste (*Charoi de Nimes*).

bonny. App. formed, with E. suffix -*y*, from F. *bon,* by analogy with *jolly, pretty,* etc. Cf. Sp. *bonito,* pretty.

bonnyclabber. Clotted milk. Ir. *bainne,* milk, *clabair,* thick. In general US. use.

bonspiel [*Sc.*]. Curling match between two clubs or districts. Du. *spel,* game, with doubtful first element, perh. *bond,* covenant, society, thus a collective encounter, club match.

bontebok [*SAfr.*]. Antelope. Du. *bont,* pied. Cf. *blesbok, springbok,* etc.

bonus. For *bonum,* something good. Stock Exchange Latin.

bonze. Buddhist priest. F., Port. *bonzo,* Jap. *bonzi,* Chin. *fan seng,* religious one.

booby. From Sp. *bobo,* fool, ? from an imit. *bob* (cf. *baby, babble,* etc.), ? or L. *balbus,* stammerer (which comes to the same thing).

For application to a stupid bird cf. *dodo, dotterel, loon,* etc., also *noddy* (q.v.), used of a sea-bird in Purch. With *booby trap* cf. synon. F. *attrape-nigaud,* from *nigaud,* "a fop, nidget, ideot" (Cotg.), prob. familiar form of *Nicodème* (see *noddy*).

boodle [*US.*]. Usu. with *whole,* as in *whole kit and boodle* (Stephen Crane), or in sense of funds (US.). ? Du. *boedel,* estates, effects, cogn. with *booth* and AS. *botl,* house. Cf. *caboodle.*

book. AS. *bōc,* beech-tree, whence *bōcstæf,* beech staff, letter, character; cf. synon. Du. *boekstaf,* Ger. *buchstabe,* ON. *bōkstafr.* It is supposed that runes were scratched on beech bark. Cf. Sanskrit *bhūrja-,* birch, bark for writing, and Late L. *fraxineae tabellae* (Venantius Fortunatus), from *fraxinus,* ash. Cf. also *Bible, code, library, paper.* The suitability of beech-bark for inscriptions is still observed by the tripper. So also Ger. *buch,* Du. *boek,* etc. *Book-muslin* is folded in book-form when sold in the piece. With *good books* cf. *black books* (see *black*). With to *take a leaf out of one's book,* i.e. to adopt his teaching, cf. to *turn over a new leaf.* To *bring to book* was orig. to demand proofs ("chapter and verse") for statement. *Bookworm,* lover of books (Ben Jonson), is from the maggot which destroys books. The railway *booking office* was taken over (with *guard, coach,* etc.) from the old stage-coach days when intending passengers' names were taken down.

bookworm: blatta (Litt.).

Booke callicos and callicos made up in rowles   (Purch. 1613).

There ought to be some means of bringing to book a soldier, in the receipt of money from the State, who speaks of a friendly power as Lord Roberts spoke of Germany (*Nation,* Oct. 26, 1912).

boom[1]. Sound. ME. *bommen,* to hum. Imit., cf. Ger. *bummen,* Du. *bommen,* and see *bomb.* Earliest used of bee, wasp, etc. For business sense (US.), opposite of *slump,* cf. to *make things hum,* but it may have orig. been a naut. metaphor, connected with *boom[2]*; cf. *a ship comes booming,* "she comes with all the sail she can make" (*Sea Dict.* 1708) and the parallel case of *vogue* (q.v.).

boom[2] [*naut.*]. Du. *boom,* beam, tree, cogn. with *beam* (q.v.).

boomerang. Modification of some Austral. native name. *Wo-mur-rang* is given in 1798 in a short vocabulary of Port Jackson words. For its vague hist. cf. *kangaroo.*

Often used fig. of a weapon which recoils on its user.

This weapon [aerial bombing of civilian population] will not only fail, but prove a terrible boomerang to the enemy (Gen. Smuts, Oct. 4, 1917).

boon¹. Favour. ON. *bōn*, petition, prayeɪ to God; cf. AS. *bēn*, whence (bootless) *bene* (q.v.). Mod. sense comes from to *grant* (*have*) *one's boon*, and has perh. been influenced by *boon²*.

boon². Adj. F. *bon*. Now usu. with *companion*. With *boonfellow* (Meredith) cf. surname *Bonfellow*.

A cette époque, être de "bonne compagnie," c'était se montrer avant tout d'une gaîté franche, spirituelle et amusante, d'où est resté le mot de "bon compagnon" (Sainte-Beuve).

boor. Orig. husbandman. Cf. AS. *gebūr* (see *neighbour*). But as the word is very rare before c. 1500, and is esp. applied, as also adj. *boorish*, to the Dutch and Germans, it is prob. LG. *būr* or Du. *boer*, cogn. with above; cf. Ger. *bauer*, peasant. All these words mean dweller, tiller (see *bond²*). For degeneration cf. *churl*, *villain*. See also *bower²*.

Germany hath her boores, like our yeomen (Fuller).

boost. Hoist (US.). Origin unknown.

boot¹. For foot. ME. *bote*, F. *botte*; cf. Sp. Port. *bota*, MedL. *botta*. Of obscure origin; cogn. with Ger. dial. *boss*. Orig. of riding boots only. The *boot* of a coach (so F. *botte*) was orig. named from its shape. *Boot and saddle* is a perversion of F. *boute-selle*, put saddle. It is difficult to account for *sly-boots*, *clumsy boots*, etc., but, as the earliest of the type is *smooth-boots* (c. 1600), the orig. allusion may have been to stealthiness.

boute-selle: to horse (Cotg.).

The word "boot-legger" [provider of alcohol in a "dry" country] hails from the prairie, where they conceal bottles between the knee-boot and the leg (*Daily Mail*, Dec. 2, 1919).

boot². Profit. Now only in *to boot* (cf. *into the bargain*), *bootless*, and as verb. AS. *bōt*, profit, advantage (cf. ON. *bót*), cogn. with *better*. Cf. Ger. *busse*, repentance, expiation, and *batten²*.

Bootes [*astron.*]. G. βοώτης, waggoner, lit. oxdriver, from βοῦς, ox.

booth. ODan. *both*, ON. *būth*, from *būa*, to dwell; cf. Ger. *bude*; cogn. with OIr. *both*, AS. *botl*.

booty. F. *butin*, influenced by *boot²*. Cf. Du. *buit* (see *freebooter*), Ger. *beute*, ON. *býti*,

exchange. The F. word is prob. of Teut. origin, and it is suggested that the origin is a LG. *būten*, to share (q.v.), for **bi-ūtian*, from *ut*, out. To *play booty*, act as confederate with a view to spoil, is 16 cent.

butiner: to prey, get booty, make spoyle of, to bootehale, to live, or gaine, by pillage (Cotg.).

booze [*slang*]. Du. *buizen*, to drink to excess; cf. LG. *būsen*, Ger. *bausen*; see *quaff*. A ME. *bouse* is recorded c. 1300, but the word as we have it is prob. a new introduction (16 cent.). In the old play *Health and Wealth* (c. 1560) a drunken Fleming is called *Hanijkin Bowse*.

And in his hand [Gluttony] did bear a bouzing can,
Of which he supt so oft, that on his seat
His dronken corse he scarse upholden can
(*Faerie Queene*, I. iv. 22).

buysen: to drink great drafts, or to quaf (Hexham).

bo-peep. See *bo*, *peep*, and cf. Du. *kiekeboe speelen*, "to play at boo-peep" (Sewel), also *piepbeu*.

bora. Severe north wind in Adriatic. It. dial. *bora*, for *borea*, north wind (see *boreal*). Cf. Texan *norther*.

To day [on the Isonzo] the icy bora has blown itself out (*Daily Chron.* Feb. 2, 1917).

boracic. See *borax*.

borage. F. *bourrache*; cf. Sp. *borraja*, It. *borragine*, etc., MedL. *borrago*, ? Arab. *abū*, father, *araq*, sweat (see *arrack*), from med. use.

borax. ME. OF. *boras* (*borax*), with many vars. and MedL. forms, Arab. *būraq*, Pers. *būrah*.

border. F. *bordure*, from *border*, to edge, from *bord*, edge, orig. of a ship (see *board*), or from Late L. *bordatura*; cf. It. *bordatura*, Sp. *bordadura*. For ending cf. *batter*, *fritter*, and, for a converse case, *failure*. The *Border*, in hist. sense (16 cent.), is of Sc. origin, the earlier term, both in E. & Sc., being *march*.

bore¹. Verb. AS. *borian*, to pierce. Com. Teut.; cf. Du. *boren*, Ger. *bohren*, ON. *bora*; cogn. with L. *forare*. The sense of wearying (c. 1750) may have started by a punning allusion to *boring the ears*, in token of servitude. Cf. Ger. *drillen*, to drill, bore, plague (see *drill²*). F. *raser*, to bore, lit. shave, and *scie*, a bore, lit. saw, may also be compared.

That old churl, I am sure, would have bored you through nose (*Misogonus*, ii. 1, c. 1550).

His master shall bore his ear through with an aul (*Ex.* xxi. 6).

This is enough for an understanding eare without farther boring it (*NED.* 1622).

bore². Tidal wave. ON. *bāra,* wave, whence also F. *barre,* tidal wave in river. But there is a gap between ME. *bare,* wave, and the first record of *bore* (c. 1600). See *eagre* for another possible origin.

Such a boore (as the seamen terme it) and violent encounter of two tydes coming in (Purch. xvi. 391).

boreal. L. *borealis,* from *Boreas,* north wind, G. βορέας.

borecole. Du. *boerenkool,* peasant's cabbage. See *boor, cole, kale.*

boreen [*Ir.*]. Narrow lane. Ir., from *bóthar,* road, with dim. *-een;* cf. *colleen, squireen,* etc.

born. See *bear².* The connection has almost ceased to be felt.

borough. AS. *burg, burh,* castle, manor-house, with meaning gradually extended as in *town* or F. *ville.* Cogn. with AS. *beorgan,* to protect. Com. Teut.; cf. Du. Ger. *burg,* ON. *borg,* Goth. *baurgs;* also Late L. *burgus,* earliest Teut. loan-word in L., whence forms in Rom. langs. *Burrow* (q.v.) is the same word, and *bury* (*Canterbury,* etc.) is from the AS. dat. *byrig.* Cf. Sc. *burgh* (*Edinburgh,* etc.). Hence *borough English,* system of tenure by which, in some countries, youngest son inherits all lands and tenements, partial transl. of AF. *tenure en burgh engloys. Borough-monger* was coined (18 cent.) to describe one who traded in parliamentary representation; cf. hist. *pocket-borough, rotten borough,* constituency without voters before Reform Bill of 1832.

borrel [*archaic*]. Rude, unlettered. Revived by Scott, imitated by Willam Morris. Ident. with ME. *burel,* rough clothing, also used of the laity. See *bureau* and cf. fig. use of *homespun.*

Religioun hath take up al the corn
Of tredyng, and we borel men been shrympes
(Chauc. B. 3144).

borrow. AS. *borgian,* from *borg, borh,* pledge. Cf. Du. *borg,* pledge, Ger. *borgen,* to borrow, late ON. *borga,* to stand security. Ult. cogn. with *borough,* with ground-sense of security. In AS. and the other Teut. langs. the orig. sense is rather to lend than to borrow.

Borstal system. Established (1902) for dealing with "juvenile adult" offenders at *Borstal* (Kent).

borzoi [*Russ.*]. Hound. Orig. adj., swift; cf. synon. Serbo-Croat. *brzo,* Czech *brzy.*

bosch. Du. for *bush,* whence SAfr. *boschbok,* bush-buck, *boschman,* Bushman, *boschvark,* bush hog. Also used as trade equivalent

for margarine, from its place of manufacture, *'sHertogenbosch* (Bois-le-Duc).

Bosche. See *Boche.*

bosh. Turk., empty, worthless. Popularized by Morier's *Ayesha* (1834).

bosky. For ME. *busky,* from *busk,* northern form of *bush¹,* refashioned (16 cent.) under It. influence (*bosco, boscoso,* etc.). With *boskage* (Tennyson) cf. OF. *boscage.* Also *bosket,* F. *bosquet,* It. *boschetto* (see *bouquet*). *Bosky,* intoxicated (Bailey, 1730), may be perverted from Sp. *boquiseco,* dry mouthed, but adjs. expressive of drunkenness seem to be created spontaneously (cf. *squiffy,* etc.).

bosom. AS. *bōsm.* WGer.; cf. Du. *boezem,* Ger. *busen. Wife of one's bosom* is a Hebraism adopted by *AV.* (*Deut.* xiii. 6; cf. xxviii. 56). So also other fig. senses (*bosom friend, bosom of the Church*) are mostly Bibl., with spec. ref. to *Luke,* xvi. 22.

boss¹. Protuberance (cf. *emboss*). F. *bosse,* hump, with cognates in Rom. langs., but of unknown origin. *Boss-eyed* may be an imit. of obs. *boss-backed,* hump backed, and have given rise to *boss-shot, boss,* to miss, etc.

boss-eyed: a person with one eye, or rather with one eye injured (Hotten).

boss². Master. US., from Du. *baas,* orig. uncle; cf. Ger. *base,* aunt, cousin.

Our baase, for so a Dutch captaine is called
(John Davis, 1598, in Purch.).

boston. Card game (F.). From siege of Boston (1775–6) during Amer. War of Independence, the technicalities of the game corresponding to siege terms. Cf. obs. *portobello* an outdoor game (late 18 cent.).

Boswell. Admiring biographer. From Boswell's *Life of Dr Johnson* (1791).

bot, bott [*dial.*]. Usu. pl., parasitic worm attacking horses and cattle. ? Cf. ME. *bude,* AS. *budda,* weevil, malt-worm. Hence, according to Hotten, *botty,* conceited, orig from stable slang, troubled with the botts.

botany. Formed, by analogy with *astronomy, astronomic,* from *botanic,* F. *botanique,* MedL., G. βοτανικός, from βοτάνη, plant. *Botany Bay* was named by Capt. Cook (18 cent.) from vegetation.

botargo. Kind of caviare, made from roe of mullet or tunny. Obs. It. *botargo* (*bottarga*), Arab. *butarkhah,* Coptic *butarakhon,* from Coptic *bu,* the, and G. ταρίχιον, pickle. Cf. F. *boutarque* (Rabelais).

botargo: a kinde of salt meate made of fish used in Italy in Lent (Flor.).

botch[1] [*archaic*]. Protuberance, ulcer, etc. NF. *boche*, var. of *bosse* (see *boss*[1]). Partly replaced by *blotch*.

botch[2]. Verb. ME. *bocchen*, to patch; later also *bodge*. ? F. *boucher*, to stop up; cf. Ger. *strümpfe stopfen*, to darn stockings. F. *boucher* is of doubtful origin.

both. ME. *bathe*, ON. *bāthar* (m.), *bāthir* (f.), *bāthi* (n.). First element as in AS. *bēgen* (m.), *bā* (f. & n.), with which cf. Goth. *bai*, *ba*. Second represents def. art.; cf. Ger. *beide*, both the. The AS. simplex survived up to 14 cent. as *beyn, ba* or *bo* (cf. *twain, two*). Ult. cogn. with L. *am-bo*, both.

bother. Earlier also *bodder*. First in Anglo-Ir. writers (Sheridan, Swift, etc.). The verb is older and corresponds in meaning to Ir. *bōdhairim*, I deafen (cf. Sc. *deave*, to deafen, bewilder, bother). This would not give *bother* phonetically, Ir. *-dh-* being mute, but might have been corrupted by E. speakers. Cf. *bothy, cateran*.

bothy. Hut. Gael. *bothag*, dim. of *both*, hut, from ON. *būth*, booth. But Gael. *-th-* is silent. Cf. *bother*.

bo-tree. The pipal, allied to the banian. Corrupt., through Singhalese, of Pali *bodhitaru*, perfect-knowledge tree, under which Gautama, founder of Buddhism, meditated.

bottine. F., dim. of *botte*, boot.

bottle[1]. For liquids. F. *bouteille*, Late L. *butticula*, dim. of *buttis*, cask (see *butt*[2]); cf. It. *bottiglia*, Sp. *botella*. See also *butler*. *Bottle-holder*, backer, is from pugilism.

bottle[2]. Bundle (of hay, etc.). OF. *botel*, dim. of *botte*, truss, MHG. *bote*, bundle. Hence *to look for a needle in a bottle of hay*.

bottom. AS. *botm*. WGer.; cf. Du. *bodem*, Ger. *boden*; ult. cogn. with L. *fundus*. Becomes adj. in *bottommost* (neol.), *bottom dollar* (US.). See also *bottomry*. *Bottomless pit* (*Rev.* ix. 1) is in Tynd.

bottomry. Marine contract or speculation. From *bottom*, in the sense of ship (orig. part lying below the wales), after cogn. Du. *bodmerij*, whence also F. *bomerie*.

bodemery: usury, or gain of shipping (Hexham), bottomry (Sewel).

botty [*colloq.*]. See *bot*.

botulism [*neol.*]. Ger. *botulismus*, discovered and named (1896) by Ermengem. From L. *botulus*, sausage, being caused, in Germany, by eating same. See newspapers Apr. 24, 1918.

boucherize [*neol.*]. To treat timber with pro-tective impregnation. From *A. Boucherie*, F. chemist. Cf. *kyanize*.

boudoir. F., lit. sulking-room, from *bouder*, to sulk, "pout," after *dortoir, parloir*. *Bouder* is from the same root (idea of swollen) as *pudding, pout*. Cf. Prov. *pot*, lip.

bouffe. In *opéra bouffe*. F. *bouffe*, It. *buffa*, joke. Cf. *buffoon*.

bougainvillaea. Plant. From *Bougainville*, French navigator (†1811).

bough. AS. *bōg, bōh*, shoulder, arm; bough. Com. Teut. and ident. with *bow*[3] (q.v.), but tree sense is peculiar to E.

bougie. Wax candle; fig. catheter, etc. F., from *Bougie* (Algeria), Arab. *Bijiyah*, where made.

bouillabaisse. Fish soup in Provence. F. (cf. Mod. Prov. *bouiabaisso*), said to be for *bouille-abaisse*, lit. abbess' bowels. Such a fantastic name is not without parallels, e.g. *pet de nonne*, a kind of light pastry.

bouillon. F., soup, from *bouillir*, to boil.

boulder. For *boulder-stone*, ME. *bulderston*, Sw. dial. *bullersten*, noise stone (in stream), as opposed to *klappersten*, rattle stone, pebble, from Sw. *bullra*, to roar. Cf. Dan. *buldre*, to roar, and cogn. Ger. *poltern* (see *poltergeist*).

boule. See *buhl*.

boulevard. F., orig. rampart, "bulwark" (q.v.), disused ramparts being turned into promenades. For final dental cf. F. *gerfaut*, OF. *gerfauc*, gerfalcon.

boult. See *bolt*[2].

boun [*poet.*]. See *bound*[3].

bounce. ME. *bunsen*, to thump. Imit.; cf. Du. *bonsen*, to beat or strike. US. to *get the bounce* is, like so many Americanisms, of Du. origin.

bons: a shog, bounce, thump; *den bons krygen*: to be casheered (Sewel).

A certain man named Adam, whom the cherubim bounced from the orchard (O. Henry).

bound[1]. Boundary. AF. *bounde*, OF. *bodne* (now *borne*), MedL. *bodina*, prob. of Celt. origin. For excrescent *-d* cf. *bound*[3]. See *bourn*[2].

bound[2]. To leap. F. *bondir*, orig. to re-echo, VL. **bombitire*, for *bombitare*, to hum (whence OF. *bonder*). See *bomb*.

bound[3]. Adj. Usu. with *for*, or in *homeward bound*, etc. Earlier *boun*, ready, with excrescent *-d*, ON. *būinn*, p.p. of *būa*, to get ready (see *busk*[2]). In *bound to* it is not to be distinguished from the p.p. of *bind*. Scott revived *boun* as infin. (*Marm.* iv. 22).

She was bown to goon the wey forth right
(Chauc. F. 1503)

bound⁴. As in *bound to go*, etc. See *bind*, *bound³*.

bounden. See *bind*.

bounder. Camb. slang c. 1883. From *bound²*; cf. fig. senses of *bounce*.

bounteous. ME. *bountevous*, from OF. *bontif*, benevolent, with suffix *-ous*. See *bounty*. Altered on *beauteous*, etc.; cf. *righteous*.

bounty. F. *bonté*, L. *bonitas*, *bonitat-*, goodness. *Queen Anne's Bounty* was established (1704), from the confiscated first-fruits, for the augmentation of poor livings (see *annates*). *Lady Bountiful* is a character in Farquhar's *Beaux' Stratagem* (1707).

For she hirself is honour and the roote
Of bountee (Chauc. B. 1655).

bouquet. F., orig. little wood; cf. F. *bosquet*, grove, It. *boschetto*. See *bush¹*. For sense cf. Ger. *strauss*, nosegay, orig. bush.

bourbon [*US.*]. Whisky. From *Bourbon county* (Kentucky), named from F. *Bourbon* (Allier) which gave its name to a line of kings of France.

bourdon. Bass stop in organ. F., see *burden²*.

bourg. F., see *borough*.

Ye think the rustic cackle of your bourg
The murmur of the world! (*Geraint & Enid*).

bourgeois. F., from *bourg*, the ending *-ois* representing L. *-ensis*. Cf. *burgess*. *Bourgeois* type, between long primer and brevier, is said to be from name of a F. printer. Others take it to be from the idea of middle, medium, contained in the word *bourgeois*. From time of F. Revolution, *bourgeois* has undergone the same eclipse as our *middle class*, being contemptuously applied by "intellectuals" to those who pay their way and look after their children. As I write (Dec. 1917) Russ. "citizens" are very busy massacring the *bourgeoisie*. The true sense of this ancient word survives in Rodin's *Bourgeois de Calais*. See also *burgee*.

bourgeon. See *burgeon*.

bourignonism. Form of mysticism. From *Antoinette Bourignon*, Flemish mystic (17 cent.).

bourn¹. Stream. Common in place-names. Orig. ident. with *burn¹* (q.v.), of which it is a southern form.

bourn². Boundary. F. *borne* (see *bound¹*).

Adopted in 17 cent., common in Shaks., and revived by 18–19 cent. romantic poets in imit. of the famous passage below.

The undiscover'd country, from whose bourn
No traveller returns (*Haml.* iii. 1).

Bourse. F., Stock Exchange, esp. at Paris. See *purse*.

bouse¹, **bowse**. See *booze*.

bouse², **bowse** [*naut.*]. To hoist. ? Backformation from *bowsesynge* (see *seize*). In to *bouse one's jib*, get "tight," there is a play on *bouse¹*.

boustrophedon. Written alternately from left to right and right to left, like course of a plough. G., ox-turning. See *bulimy*, *strophe*.

bout. For earlier *bought*, bend, turn (see *bight*), from LG. *bucht*, Du. *bogt*, or Norw. Dan. *bugt*; cogn. with *bow¹*. Influenced in meaning by obs. *bout* for *about* (q.v.), as in *'bout ship!* and perh. also by F. *bout*, end, piece. Cf. *turn*, *round* (in a fight, etc.).

boutade. Outburst. F., from *bouter*, to butt⁵.

bouts-rimés. F., rimed ends. See *butt³*.

bovate [*hist.*]. An oxgang (q.v.). MedL. *bovata*, from L. *bos*, *bov-*, ox. Cf. *carucate*, *virgate*.

bovine. L. *bovinus*, of the ox (v.s.).

bovril. Coined from L. *bos*, *bov-*, ox, and ? *vril*, magic power, the latter (Lytton's *Coming Race*) perh. suggested by L. *vis*, *vires*, or *virilis*.

bow¹. Anything bent. AS. *boga*, cogn. with *būgan*, to bow, bend (see *bow²*). Com. Teut.; cf. Du. *boog*, Ger. *bogen*, ON. *bogi*. Not connected with *bow³*. For main developments from orig. sense cf. *arc*, *arch¹*. The three oldest meanings (c. 1000) are archer's bow, arch (*Beowulf*), rainbow (Ælfric, *Gen.* ix. 14). The *bowstring* as Turk. instrument of execution is recorded c. 1600. A *bow-window* is a spec. type of the earlier *bay-window*. With *bow*, neck-tie, etc., cf. earlier *bow-knot*.

bow². Verb. AS. *būgan*, orig. strong intrans. Com. Teut.; cf. Du. *buigen*, Ger. *biegen*, ON. *bjuga*, Goth. *biugan*. Trans. sense was represented by obs. *bey*, AS. *bīegan*, to cause to bow (cf. Ger. *beugen* and see *buxom*). Noun *bow*, inclination of head, from verb, is of late appearance (17 cent.).

bow³. Of ship. Borrowed (c. 1600) from LG. *būg*, Du. *boeg*, Dan. *boug*, *bov*, or Sw. *bog*, all meaning shoulder, and bow of ship. Not related to *bow¹*, but ult. ident. with *bough* (q.v.). See also *bowline*, *bowsprit*.

Bow-bells. Bells of *St Mary-le-Bow*, or *of the Arches* (see *arch¹*, *bow¹*), used allusively as symbol of City and cockneydom.

bowdlerize. *Dr T. Bowdler* published (1818) a text of Shakespeare which could "with propriety be read aloud in a family." Cf. Ger. *ballhornisieren* or *verballhornen*, to spoil a book by "improvements," from *Ballhorn*, a Lübeck printer of the 16 cent.

bowel. OF. *boel, bouel (boyau)*, L. *botellus*, pudding (Martial), dim. of *botulus*, sausage; cf. It. *budello*, OSp. *budel*. See also *pudding*. With symbolical use, as in *the bowelis of Jhesu Crist* (Wyc. *Phil.* i. 8), cf. fig. sense of F. *entrailles*, and of E. *heart, liver, kidney*.

bower¹. Retreat. AS. *būr*, dwelling. Com. Teut.; cf. OSax. *būr*, Ger. *bauer*, bird-cage, ON. *būr*. In ME. esp. inner room, bed-chamber. Sense of leafy arbour, etc. is later. Cogn. with *boor, neighbour, byre*.

bower² [*naut.*]. For *bower anchor*, suspended at *bow³*.

bower³. Knave at euchre (US.). Ger. *bauer*, peasant, also knave at cards, or perh. cogn. Du. *boer*. Cf. *Bowery*.

> At last he put down a right bower [knave of trumps],
> Which the same Nye had dealt unto me
> *(Heathen Chinee).*

Bowery. Part of New York, orig. a homestead. Du. *bowerij* (see *bower³*). The New York *Bowery* was a farm bought (1631) by Governor Stuyvesant for 6400 guilders (Thornton).

bowie. For *bowie-knife* (US.), popularized by *Colonel James Bowie* (†1836).

> He smiled,—a bitter smile to see,—
> And drew the weapon of Bowie
> *(Bret Harte, A Moral Vindicator).*

bowl¹. Basin. ME. *bolle* (see *boll¹*), AS. *bolle*. Com. Teut.; cf. Du. *bol*, Ger. *bohle* (from LG.), ON. *bolli*. Correct mod. form would be *boll*, but it has been affected by *bowl²*.

bowl². Ball. F. *boule*, L. *bulla*, bubble, round knob (see *bull²*). Hence verb to *bowl* (at cricket), derived from the time when the ball was really "trundled" under-hand as in game of bowls. Fig. to *bowl out* is prob. from cricket, to *bowl over* from skittles. *Longbowls* (naut.), engagement with distant enemy, is from the orig. game of bowls, of which there were two varieties, called long and short. The sound (for *bool*) has been influenced by *bowl¹*, the spelling of which has been assimilated to *bowl²*.

bowler. Hat. From *bowl¹*; a curious mod. parallel to *basinet*.

bowline. Found much earlier (14 cent.) than *bow³*, and prob. from OF. *bouline, bueline* (Wace, 12 cent.). Cf. It. Sp. Port. *bolina*. Of later appearance in Teut. langs., e.g. Dan. *bovline*, Du. *boeglijn*, in which it is felt as *bow-line*. But these may all be folk-etym. from the F. form, and it is quite possible that the first element is not *bow*, from which it differs in pronunciation. Kil. glosses *boech-lijne* by *funis bolidis*, which suggests possible connection with L. *bolis*, plummet, sounding line.

bowse. See *bouse²*.

bowsprit. App. *bow³* and *sprit* (q.v.), AS. *sprēot*, pole; but the late appearance of *bow³* (q.v.) and the many earlier perversions of *bowsprit* suggest that the word may rather have been borrowed whole (14 cent.) from Du. *boegspriet* or LG. *bogspret*.

Bow-street runner [*hist.*]. Police officer (18 cent.), from principal metropolitan police office.

bow-wow. Applied by Max Müller (c. 1860) to the theory that human speech originated in imitation of animal sounds. The earliest record for this word is 1576. It must of course be as old as articulate speech. See *puss.*

box¹. Orig. the tree. AS. *box*, L. *buxus*, G. πύξος (see *pyx*). Hence receptacle made esp. of box-wood, now used in an infinity of senses (cf. F. *boîte*, Ger. *büchse*). Earliest, a small box for drugs, unguents, etc., belonging to lang. of medicine; hence, possibly, the *wrong box*, a mistaken remedy, treatment, etc. A *Christmas-box* was an earthenware receptacle for the tips of servants, apprentices, etc., broken open for sharing after Christmas, but the oldest sense may belong rather to *box²*; cf. Sw. *julklapp*, Christmas-box, lit. Yule-knock (on the door). Hence *Boxing-day*. *Box-cloth* belongs to *box-coat*, a heavy driving-coat worn on the *box* of a vehicle, the coachman's seat being still a lid; but for this sense of *box* cf. Du. *bok*, Ger. *bock*, lit. goat, similarly used. To *box the compass*, i.e. to run through all the points in order, prob. refers to the *box* in which the compass is kept; cf. F. *boussole*, It. *bossola*, compass, lit. little box.

box². A blow. Prob. a playful application of the above, a present (cf. Ger. *ohrfeige*, lit. ear-fig). Or perh. G. πύξ (cf. L. *pugnus*, fist), with clenched fist, as in πὺξ ἀγαθός, good at boxing, if the E. word originated among students or schoolboys.

> He that hath a-boughte his love ful dere,
> Or had in armes many a blody box
> (Chauc. *Leg. Good Women*, 1387).

boxer. Member of Chinese anti-foreign movement (c. 1900). Anglicized from Chin. *I-Ho-Chuan*, lit. righteous-uniting-fist, orig. secret society at Shantung.

boy. ME. *boi*, not found in AS., exc. perh. in personal name *Bofa*; cf. EFris. *boi*, young gentleman, Du. *boef*, knave, MHG. *buobe*, OHG. *Buobo* as personal name, whence Ger. *bube*, Bav. *bua*, lad. Earlier hist. obscure, perh. a baby-word of the *papa, mama* class. As Anglo-Ind. word for servant, which has spread to other parts of the empire, e.g. *Cape-boy*, it has been influenced by Telugu *bōyi*, Tamil *bōvi*, a caste who were usually palankeen bearers, whence Port. *boy, boi* in same sense. Cf. *bearer, grass-cutter*.

boef, boeve: nebulo, tenebrio (Kil.).

boef: puer, adolescens (*ib.*).

boyar, boyard. Russ. title of nobility, abolished by Peter the Great, but often erron. used by E. writers in speaking of landed proprietors, squires. Russ. *bojare*, pl. of *bojarin*, grandee, of doubtful origin, ?from *boj*, fight, title conferred on feudal barons. Cf. contr. *barin*, used (up to 1917) by servants and peasants in addressing squire.

boyau [*mil.*]. Communication trench. F., gut, bowel (q.v.).

boycott. From the treatment (1880) of *Capt. Boycott*, of Lough Mask House, Co. Mayo, by the Ir. Land League. Speedily adopted into most Europ. langs.

Boyle. In *Boyle's law* (phys.), *lectures*, from Hon. R. *Boyle* (†1691). The first Boyle lecturer was Bentley, appointed by Evelyn as one of the trustees. In *Boyle controversy* (Epistles of Phalaris), from Hon. C. *Boyle* (†1731).

Brabançonne. Belgian national song, lit. woman of *Brabant*. Cf. surname *Brabazon*.

brabble [*archaic*]. Orig. to dispute captiously. Perh. VL. *parabolare*, whence F. *parler*, Welsh *parablu*, but in later use affected by *brawl, babble*.

brace. F. *brasse*, L. *brachia* (pl.), two arms, fathom (cf. *embrace*). Hence used of devices for fastening, tightening, etc. Some senses prob. from F. *bras*, L. *brachium* (sing.), used of many mech. devices, e.g. *bras de vergue*

(naut.) corresponds to *brace of a yard*. In sense of pair, orig. of hounds, the *brace* was the leash (cf. history of *couple*).

bracelet. F., dim. of OF. *bracel*, L. *brachiale*, armlet, from *brachium*, arm.

bracer [*archaic*]. Wrist guard, esp. for archers. OF. *brasseure* and F. *brassard*, derivatives of *bras*.

> Upon his arm he baar a gay bracer (Chauc. A. 111).

brach [*archaic*]. Bitch hound (1 *Hen. IV*, iii. 1). Shortened from ME. & OF. *brachet*, dim. of OF. *brac*, hound (cf. It. *bracco*, Sp. *braco*), OHG. *bracco* (*bracke*), sleuth-hound. Cf. F. *braconnier*, poacher, orig. hound-keeper.

brachiopod [*biol.*]. From G. βραχίων, arm, πούς, ποδ-, foot.

brachycephalic [*ethn.*]. Short skulled. From G. βραχύς, short, κεφαλή, head.

bracken. ME. *braken*, prob. ON.; cf. Sw. *bräken*, Dan. *bregne*, fern. See also *brake*[1].

bracket. Earlier *bragget*. Orig. support in building. Dim. of F. *brague*, "a kind of mortaise, or joyning of peeces together" (Cotg.). App. a fig. use of *brague(s)*, breeches, L. *braccae*; cf. *breeching* of a gun, and Sp. *bragueta*, "cod-piece," support. Cf. also F. *bracon*, support. Typ. *bracket* is from resemblance to some double supports in carpentry. With verb to *bracket*, now used of artillery fire against hostile aircraft, cf. to *straddle*. The senses of *bracket* have been affected by association with L. *brachium*, arm (see *brake*[4]).

brackish. From *brack* (Gavin Douglas), Du. *brak, brakwater*, with earlier var. *wrack*. Some connect it ult. with G. βραχός, swamp (only in pl.); cf. cogn. and synon. Welsh *merd-dwfr*, lit. marsh water.

wrack, fland. i. *brack*: acidus et salsus (Kil.).

wrack, brack: brack, or saltish (Hexham).

bracteate. L. *bracteatus*, from *bractea*, thin plate.

brad. ME. *brod*, ON. *broddr*, spike; cf. AS. *brord*, point. Hence *brad-awl*. With AS. *brord* cf. dial. *braird*, to sprout (of corn).

Bradbury [*hist.*]. Treasury note bearing (from 1914) signature of *John Bradbury*, secretary to the Treasury.

Bradshaw. Manchester printer, published first railway time-table (1839) and monthly railway guide (1841).

brae [*dial.*]. ON. *brā*, cogn. with AS. *bræw*, brow[1].

brag. Earliest as adj., valiant, boastful. Also used of the "bray" of the trumpet. Prob.

from a root *brag-*, expressing explosive noise. Cf. similar use of *crack*.

Whanne the voyce of the trompe...in youre eeris braggith (Wyc. *Joshua*, vi. 5).

braggadocio. Orig. personification of vainglory. Coined by Spenser from *brag* by analogy with other It. words in *-occio*. With *braggart*, F. *braguard*, cf. *dastard*, *sluggard*, etc.

bragget [*archaic & dial.*]. Drink made of ale and honey. Welsh *bragod*, from *bragu*, to malt, brew. Cf. L. *bracis*, a kind of grain (Pliny), from Celt., whence F. *brasser*, to brew.

brahma, brahmapootra. Fowl. Said to have been introduced (1846) from Lakhimpur on the river *Brahmaputra*. Cf. *cochin china*, *bantam*, etc.

brahman, brahmin. Sanskrit *brāhmana*, from *brahman*, praise, worship. *Brahmin* represents vernacular Ind. pronunc. Hence adj. *brahminee*, by analogy with *Bengalee* (*bengālī*), etc.

braid. First as verb. AS. *bregdan*, to move quickly, jerk, etc., hence, weave. See *upbraid*, *broider*. Com. Teut.; cf. Du. *breien* (earlier *breiden*), OHG. *brettan*, ON. *bregtha*.

braidism. Hypnotism. Investigated (1842) by Dr *James Braid*.

brail [*naut.*]. OF. *braiel*, usu. breech-girdle, L. *bracale*, but used also in naut. sense. See *breeches*.

Les brails font lier al mast,
Ke li venz par desuz ne past (Wace).

braille. Writing, etc. for blind. Name of F. inventor (c. 1834).

brain. AS. *brægen*, with cognates in LG., but not in HG. & Scand. *Brain-fag, -storm, -wave* are mod., the last from US.

braise. F. *braiser*, from *braise*, hot charcoal (cf. *embraser*, to kindle), with cognates in Rom. & Teut. langs. Of obscure origin, but prob. Teut. See *braze²*, *breeze³*.

brake¹. Fern. Prob. shortened in south from northern *bracken* (q.v.).

brake². Thicket, as in *cane-brake*. Associated already in ME. with *brake¹*, but orig. distinct. Cf. LG. *brake*, as in *busk unde brake*, bush and brake, whence synon. OF. *bracon*. Earliest sense prob. stumps, broken branches; cogn. with *break*.

brake³. Instrument for beating, crushing (flax or hemp). Cf. synon. Du. *braak*, Ger. *breche*; cogn. with *break*.

brake⁴. Retarding instrument (18 cent.). Perh. ident. with archaic *brake*, bridle,

curb (cf. F. *frein*, bridle, brake), lever, pump-handle, etc., ? OF. *brac*, L. *brachium*, arm. The guard's *brake* is for *brake-van*; cf. US. *brakesman*, railway guard. It is uncertain whether a *four-horse brake* (*break*) belongs here or to the use of such a vehicle for "breaking" horses.

bramah press, lock. From *Joseph Bramah*, mechanician (†1814).

bramble. ME. also *bremble, brimble*. AS. *bræmbel*, earlier *bræmel*, from *brōm*, broom. Cf. Du. *braam*, OHG. *brāma*, whence Ger. *brombeere*, blackberry.

bran. F., with cognates in It., Sp., etc. Origin doubtful, prob. Celt.; cf. Welsh *brann*, Breton *brenn*.

brancard. Horse-litter. F., litter, shaft, from *branche*, branch.

branch. F. *branche*, Late L. *branca*, paw (cf. orig. meaning of *bough*), prob. of Teut. origin. *Root and branch*, in Petition for abolition of episcopal government (1640), is a reminiscence of *Malachi*, iv. 1.

branchiopod [*biol.*]. Gill-footed. From G. βράγχια, gills, πούς, ποδ-, foot.

brand. AS. *brand*. Com. Teut.; cf. Du. Ger. *brand*, ON. *brandr*; cogn. with *burn²*. Earliest sense, burning, firebrand, also (poet.), sword (cf. *brandish*). *Brand from the burning* alludes to *Zech*. iii. 2. With *brand-new*, corruptly *bran-new*, fresh from the furnace, cf. earlier *fire-new*, Ger. *funkelnagelneu*, lit. spark nail new. The tradesman's *brand* is later than the *branding* of criminals with a hot iron, whence *branded with infamy*, etc.

brandish. F. *brandir, brandiss-*, to flourish a sword, for which *brand* (q.v.) is the regular word in OF. epic.

brandling [*angling*]. Worm. Dim. of *brand*, from marking.

brandreth [*dial.*]. Gridiron, trivet, various frame-works suggesting same. ON. *brandreith*, burning-carriage; cf. AS. *brandrida*, OHG. *brandreita*. See *brand, ride*.

brandy. Short for *brandewine*. Du. *brandewijn*, burnt wine; cf. Ger. *branntwein*. It is curious that *whisky, gin, rum* are also all shortened forms. *Brandy-pawnee*, Anglo-Ind. for brandy and water, is from Hind. *pānī*, water (see quot. s.v. *blighty*).

branks [*hist.*]. Scold's bridle (Sc. 16 cent.). Orig. bridle for horse improvised from halter by means of two wooden "cheeks," corresponding to the *branches* of a bridle, *branks* representing Norm. form *branques*. Hence Sc. *brank*, to restrain, also, to prance, show off, with which cf. to *bridle*, for both senses.

les branches de la bride: les deux pièces de fer, d'acier, que relie le mors (*Dict. Gén.*).

brankursine. Acanthus, bear's breech. MedL. *branca ursina*, bear's claw. See *branch*.

bran-new. See *brand*.

brant-goose, brent-goose. Cf. Sw. *brandgås*, Ger. *brandgans*, both sometimes used of the sheldrake. Prob. from *brand*, with ref. to marking. So also *brant-fox*, Ger. *brandfuchs*. Cf. obs. *branded*, brindled (see *brindle*).

braqua [*nonce-word*]. "Government ale."

It is derived from *beer* and *aqua*, the Latin name for water, and it is a good description
(*Daily Expr.* June 9, 1919).

brash. Fragments, esp. of ice. F. *brèche*; cf. It. *breccia*. Of Teut. origin (*break*). *Brash*, sickness, vomiting, as in *water-brash*, is perh. the same word; cf. Ger. *brechen*, to vomit, lit. to break.

brasier. See *brazier*.

brass. AS. *bræs*, with no known cognates. As it was orig. an alloy of copper and tin (now *bronze*), connection suggests itself with F. *brasser*, to brew, to stir molten metal (see *brassage*). For slang sense (coin) cf. *tin*. This week (Feb. 11–18, 1917) we are invited to subscribe to the great War Loan by the legend "brass up" printed conspicuously on the Nottingham tram-cars. As emblem of endurance or effrontery (*Is.* xlviii. 4) *brass* is common from 16 cent. onward. With *brass farthing*, which I have heard an Irish politician inevitably alter to *brass sixpence*, cf. *red cent*. The golfer's *brassy* is not in *NED*. (cf. *divot*). *Brass-hat*, staff-officer, dates from SAfr. War (1899).

brassage. Mint-charge for coining. F. *brasser*, to brew, to stir molten metal (? cf. *bullion*). F. *brasser*, MedL. *braciare*, is from Late L. *bracis*, corn from which malt is made, of Gaulish origin (see *bragget*).

brassard. Orig. armour from shoulder to elbow, now, badge, armlet. F. (see *bracer*).

brasserie. F., brewery, tavern. See *brassage*.

brat. From c. 1500, usu. associated with *beggar*. Perh. ident. with dial. *brat*, cloak, pinafore, "skin" on porridge, etc., OIr. *bratt*, cloth. Cf. the somewhat similar use of Ger. *balg* and *haut*, both meaning skin, covering.

Irsche brybour baird, wyle beggar with thy brattis
(Dunbar).

brattice [*archaic*]. Temporary defence, battle-ment, etc.; hence *bratticing* (see *bartisan*),

still used of timber-work in mine, etc. F. *bretèche*. The ME. & OF. forms, usu. glossed *propugnaculum*, are very numerous, also Rom. cognates and MedL. forms. Prob. a derivative of Ger. *brett*, board. The alter-native etym. from *brittisca*, British, would account better for the various forms, but lacks hist. explanation.

bretex of a walle: propinnaculum (*Prompt. Parv.*).

I arme or decke, as a man doth a shyppe: je betresche
(Palsg.).

bravado. Sp. *bravada*, p.p. fem. of *bravar*, to brave (cf. *armada*), with ending altered as in *bastinado*, *salvo*[1], etc.

brave. F., It. *bravo*, and in most Europ. langs. Origin unknown (? cf. Ir. *breagh*, Sc. *braw*, Cornish *bray*, brave, ? or L. *barbarus*, in sense of wild, indomitable). Earliest sense is intrepid, then fine in attire, etc. Red Indian *brave* is due to F. settlers in N. America.

bravo[1]. "A man who murders for hire" (Johns.). It., brave.

His bravoes of Alsatia and pages of Whitehall
(Macaulay, *Battle of Naseby*).

Their name for a cowardly assassin is "a brave man," and for a harlot "a courteous person"
(*Cloister & Hearth*, ch. lvi.).

bravo[2]. It., fine, excellent, used as exclama-tion of approval. To a female singer or actress, *brava*. So also *brava Italia!*

bravura. Brilliancy (esp. mus.). It., bravery, spirit. See *brave*.

brawl[1]. Quarrel. F. *brailler*, to shout noisily, frequent. of *braire*, to bray. Cf. to *brawl in church*, *brawling stream*. The *NED*. thinks this impossible, but cf. *maul* (from *mail*), and possibly *trawl* (q.v.). Ger. *prahlen* and Du. *brallen*, to brag, shout, are comparatively mod. words, prob. of same imit. origin (cf. Welsh *bragaldian*, to jabber, prate).

brawl[2] [*archaic*]. Dance. Formerly also *brangle*. F. *branle*, from *branler*, to shake, totter, for *brandeler*, frequent. of *brandir* (see *brandish*).

bransle: a brawle or daunce, wherein many...move altogether (Cotg.).

brawn. Orig. flesh, muscle, then esp. that of boar. OF. *braon*, fleshy part, esp. buttock, OHG. *brāto*, ham; cf. Prov. *bradon*, brawn. For restriction of sense cf. *bacon*.

bray[1]. Of an ass, but formerly of other animals and of human beings. F. *braire* (cf. Prov. *braire*, MedL. *bragire*), prob. imit. See *brag*.

bray² [*archaic*]. To pulverize. OF. *breier* (*broyer*), OHG. *brekan*, to break (cf. F. *noyer* from L. *necare*). Hence to *bray a fool in a mortar* (*Prov.* xxvii. 22). Cf. *brake³*.

Fyve busshellis of brayid corn
(Wyc. 1 *Sam.* xxv. 18).

braze¹. To cover with, make like, brass. Formed from *brass* by analogy with *grass, graze,* AS. *brasian* not surviving in ME., though *brazier,* brass worker, is common. In its mod. sense, to harden, as in *brazen impudence, brazen-faced,* there may have been contamination with *braze²,* but cf. fig. uses of *brass*.

braze². To fire, solder. F. *braser,* to solder, ON. *brasa,* to harden in the fire; cf. Sw. *brasa,* to flame, Dan. *brase,* to roast (see *braise*). Influenced by *braze¹*.

brazen. AS. *bræsen,* from *bræs,* brass. Hence to *brazen* (*it out*), used by Bishop Latimer. The *brazen age,* the third age in Graeco-L. myth., is the age of war.

brazier¹. Brass-worker. From *brass;* cf. *glazier, grazier*.

brazier². Pan for charcoal. F. *brasier,* from *braise* (q.v.).

brazil. Dye-wood. Sp. Port. *brasil;* cf. It. *brasile,* F. *brésil,* MedL. *brasilium.* Origin unknown, but OIt. *verzino* suggests connection with Arab. *wars,* saffron. Some propose *braise* (q.v.) as etymon. With naming of country (v.i.) cf. *Madeira, Canary*.

Him nedeth nat his colour for to dyen
With brasile, ne with greyn of Portyngale
(Chauc. B. 4648).
Hee [Capralis] named this land of store of that wood called brasill (Purch.).

breach. ME. *breche,* replacing (under influence of cogn. F. *brèche*) ME. *bruche,* AS. *bryce,* breaking (cf. Ger. *bruch*). With *breach of the peace* cf. history of *fray. More honoured in the breach than the observance* is from *Haml.* i. 4. Used as verb by whalers of leap or breaking from water of whale (see *broach*).

Asher continued on the sea-shore and abode in his breaches [*Vulg.* portubus, Wyc. havens]
(*Judges,* v. 17).

bread. AS. *brēad.* Com. Teut.; cf. Du. *brood,* Ger. *brot,* ON. *brauth.* Earliest sense perh. fragment, crumb, the orig. Teut. word being *loaf¹* (q.v.). Cf. Ger. *brosam,* crumb, *brödeln,* to crumble. To *know on which side one's bread is buttered* occurs in 16 cent. *Bread-and-butter miss,* modelled on earlier *bread-and-butter rogue* (*politician*), is prob. due to Byron (v.i.). With slang *bread-basket* (18 cent.) cf. *potato-trap,* naut. for mouth, and the later prize-ring variations, e.g. *the meat-safe, pantry,* etc. The *bread-fruit* is mentioned by Dampier. With *bread-winner,* person or implement, cf. the much earlier F. *gagne-pain*.

The nursery still lisps out in all they utter—
Besides, they always smell of bread and butter
(*Beppo,* xxxix.).

breadth. Substituted (16 cent.) for earlier *brede,* AS. *brǣdu* (cf. Ger. *breite,* Sc. *abrede,* abroad), by analogy with *length.* See *broad*.

break. AS. *brecan.* Com. Teut., though the verb is not found in ON.; cf. Du. *breken,* Ger. *brechen,* Goth. *brikan;* cogn. with L. *frag-* (*frangere*). Past *brake* archaic and poet. *Broke,* for *broken,* in *stony-broke* and in mil. sense (see *cashier², cast²*). To *break ground* is naut., from weighing anchor, but is also in early use for commencing siege operations. To *break the bank* meant earlier (16 cent.) to become bankrupt. With *break, break in,* to tame, etc. cf. F. *rompre.* From this is developed to *break one of a habit,* etc. To *break news* (*a secret,* etc.) had orig. no sense of caution (cf. *broach*). To *break a jest* (*joke*) is modelled on earlier to *break a lance.* To *break the ice* is first used of arctic exploration (c. 1600). A *break* at billiards (or croquet) belongs to *break* in the archaic sense of taking a new direction. In the sense of run of luck it occurs in US. 1827. For *break,* vehicle, see *brake⁴.* With *breakfast* cf. F. *déjeuner,* from L. *dis* and *jejunus,* fasting.

We brake ground out of the sound of Plimmouth on Thursday the 28 of August
(*Drake's last voyage,* Hakl. x. 226).
rompu aux affaires: practised, much exercised, fully beaten in, well acquainted with, the course of businesses (Cotg.).
Who breaks a butterfly upon a wheel? (Pope).

breaker [*naut.*]. Small cask. Perversion of *barrico* (Purch.), from Sp. *barrica,* cask (see *barrel, barricade*). ?For corrupt. cf. *grouper.* In recent accounts (Feb. 1917) of U-boat brutalities *beaker* has sometimes occurred in this sense, a perversion due to ignorance (cf. *broach, brow²*).

bream¹. Fish. F. *brème,* OF. *bresme,* OHG. *brahsema* (*brassen*); cf. Du. *brasem*.

bream² [*naut.*]. To clean a ship's bottom with burning furze, etc. From Du. *brem,* furze, broom (see *bramble, broom*). Cf. It. *bruscare,* to bream, from *brusca,* broom, heath.

viij lode of brome...spent abought the bremyng of the ships sides (*Nav. Accts.* 1495–97).

breast. AS. *brēost.* Com. Teut.; cf. Du. *borst,* Ger. *brust,* ON. *brjōst,* Goth. *brusts.* Orig. dual, with no cognates outside Teut. With to *make a clean breast of* cf. F. *en avoir le cœur net,* Ger. *sich das herz ausschütten,* and orig. meaning of *expectorate* (q.v.).

breastsummer, bressummer [*archaic*]. Horizontal beam over large opening, lintel. From *breast* and dial. *summer,* beam, F. *sommier* (see *sumpter*). Cf. *breastwork, parapet* (q.v.).

breath. AS. *brǣth, brēth,* odour, exhalation (caused by heat or fire); cf. Ger. *brodem,* vapour. Orig. long vowel survives in *breathe.* In mod. sense has replaced (from c. 1300) AS. *ǣthm,* ME. *ethem* (cf. Ger. *atem, odem*), which points to the *br-* of *breath, brodem,* being a worn-down prefix. Wider sense survives in *breath of air* (*wind*).

breccia. Composite rock, pudding stone. It., "gravel or rubbish of broken walls" (Flor.). See *breach, brash.* First occurs in *breccia marble.*

brede. Archaic form of *braid,* used by several mod. poets (Keats, Tennyson, etc.).

breech. Now usu. *breeches,* double pl., *breech* being AS. *brēc,* pl. of *brōc* (as *foot, feet*). Com. Teut.; cf. Du. *broek,* Ger. *bruch,* ON. *brōk* (whence name of *Ragnar Lodbrog,* hairy breeches). Prob. cogn. with L. *braccae,* breeches (see *brogue*). It is uncertain whether anatomical or sartorial sense is earlier, or whether the group of words is orig. Teut. or Celt. Hence archaic *breech,* to flog (*Shrew,* iii. 1). To *wear the breeches* (16 cent.) has foreign parallels. With *breech of a fire-arm* cf. synon. F. *culasse,* from *cul,* posterior. The *Breeches Bible* (Geneva, 1560) was anticipated by Wyc.

They soweden to gidre leeves of a fige tree and maden hem brechis (Wyc. *Gen.* iii. 7).

breed. Orig. to conceive, give birth to, etc. AS. *brēdan;* cf. Ger. *brüten,* to hatch, and see *brood.* The ground-idea is that of warmth; cf. Ger. *brühen,* to boil, make broth, which in dial. means also to hatch, as does also Du. *broeijen.* For archaic *breedbate,* fomenter of quarrels, see *bate².*

The Judge: "What is meant by the word breedbates?" Mr Thomas: "It is a good Shakespearean expression, my lord" (*Pall Mall Gaz.* Apr. 9, 1918).

breeks [*dial.*]. Northern form of *breeches.* ON. *brœkr,* pl. of *brōk.*

breeze¹ [*archaic*]. Gadfly (*Ant. & Cleop.* iii. 10). AS. *brēosa.* Perh. cogn. with synon. *brimse* (obs.), ON. *brims,* Ger. *bremse,* Swiss

bräme, from a root meaning to hum. Cf. Sanskrit *bhramara,* bee.

tahon [*taon*]: a brizze, brimsee, gadbee, dunflie, oxflie (Cotg.).

breeze². Wind. Earlier *brize.* Orig. N. or N.E. wind. F. *brise;* cf. Sp. *brisa.* App. a sailors' alteration of F. *bise,* NE. wind, OHG. *bīsa.* The "ordinary brise" in the Atlantic is described in the Hawkins voyage of 1564 as either N.E. or N.W.

brize for bize: the north-winde (Cotg.)

breeze³. Small coke. F. *braise,* as in *braise de boulanger,* baker's breeze. See *braise.*

brehon [*hist.*]. Ancient Irish judge. Ir. *breathamh,* from *breth,* judgment.

brent-goose. See *brant-goose.*

brer. In *Brer Rabbit.* Negro corrupt. of *brother,* perh. due to Du. *broer,* usual pronunc. of *broeder.*

bressummer. See *breastsummer.*

brethren. See *brother.*

bretwalda [*hist.*]. AS. *bretenwealda,* Britain ruler (wielder), a title applied in the AS. *Chronicle* to Egbert, and retrospectively to seven other AS. rulers, who had real or nominal hegemony. Corresponds to *rector Britanniae* in a charter of Athelstan.

breve [*mus.*]. For *brief,* though it is now the longest note. Also in other techn. senses, prob. sometimes representing It. *breve.*

breve: a briefe in musicke (Flor.).

brevet. Orig. a papal indulgence. F., dim. of *bref,* short (see *brief*). *Brevet* rank does not carry corresponding pay.

breviary. L. *breviarium,* summary, from *brevis,* short. Hence *brevier* type, orig. used in breviaries (cf. *long primer, pica*).

brevier [*typ.*]. See *breviary.*

brevity. AF. *breveté* (cf. F. *brièveté*), L. *brevitas,* from *brevis,* short, brief.

brew. AS. *brēowan.* Com. Teut.; cf. Du. *brouwen,* Ger. *brauen,* ON. *brugga.* See *brewster, broth, imbrue.*

brewis, browis, brose [*dial.*]. Broth, etc. OF. *broez,* pl. of *broet* (whence obs. *browet*); cf. use of *broth, porridge* as pl. in some dials. OF. *broet* is dim. of *bro,* broth (cf. It. *brodo*), OHG. *brod.* Related to *bread* and *brew,* from the essential root of food preparation; cf. AS. *brīwan,* to prepare food. The adoption of the pl. form may have been partly due to association with *cullis* (see *colander*). *Athole brose* is a mixture of whisky and honey.

brewis: ossulae adipatae (Litt.).

Maclaren pressed them to taste..."the wife's brose," reminding them the wife was out of Athole
(*Kidnapped,* ch. xxv).

brewster. Now only in *Brewster Sessions* or as surname. The fem. ending *-ster* is due to the fact that brewing was often a female calling. Cf. *baxter* for *baker*.

briar, brier. Earlier *brere*, AS. *brǣr*, *brēr*, of unknown origin. For change of sound cf. *friar* (q.v.). But in *briar* (*root*) *pipe*, earlier *bruyer* (1868), we have F. *bruyère*, heather, Late L. *brugaria*, prob. Celt.

Briarean. With a hundred hands. From *Briareus*, giant of G. myth.

bribe. Earliest sense (Chauc. A. 4417) app. to steal, extort, or, as noun, plunder, undeserved alms. This is app. F. *bribe*, broken meat, fragment, OF. also *brimbe*, from OF. *briber*, *brimber*, to beg, of unknown origin. Cf. Sp. *bribar*, to be a vagabond, It. *birbare*, "to play the sly knave" (Flor.).

bribe: a peece, lumpe, or cantill of bread, given unto a beggar (Cotg.).

bric-a-brac. Things collected at hazard. F. *à bric et à brac*, *de bric et de broc*, by hook or crook; cf. OF. *en bloc et en blic* (Gringoire). In such formations (*see-saw, zig-zag*) only the fuller vowel as a rule needs explanation. Prob. the starting-point here is OF. *broc*, fork (see *brooch*).

brick. F. *brique* in mod. sense is from E., but the E. word appears to be OF. *brique*, fragment, and this, in its turn, is AS. *bryce*, fragment, cogn. with *break*, or from some related Teut. word. Fig. sense (19 cent.) is perh. due to idea of firmness and steadfastness. The *brickbat*, "the typical ready missile, where stones are scarce" (*NED.*), was known as such to Milton. See *bat*[1].

bricole. "Cushion" stroke at tennis or billiards. Earlier a military catapult. It. *briccola*, prob. of Teut. origin and cogn. with *break*. In 16–17 cents. often perverted to *brick-wall*.

bricole: a bricke-wall, a side-stroake at tennis... also, a kind of engine wherewith, in old time, they beat downe walls (Cotg.).

bridal. AS. *brȳd-eala*, wedding-feast (ale). Mod. form influenced by *espousal, nuptial*, etc.

Church-ales, help-ales, and soul-ales, called also dirge-ales, and heathenish rioting at bride-ales (Harrison, *Description of England*, 1577).

bride[1]. Wife. Earlier also betrothed (as still Ger. *braut*). AS. *brȳd*. Com. Teut.; cf. Du. *bruid*, Ger. *braut* (OHG. *brūt*, whence F. *bru*, daughter-in-law), ON. *brūthr*, Goth. *brūths*. Perh. from same root as *brew, broth, bread*,

etc. (cf. hist. of *lord, lady*). *Bridegroom* was substituted for ME. *bridegome*, as *gome*, man (cogn. with L. *homo*), became obs. This is AS. *brȳd-guma*. Com. Teut.; cf. Du. *bruidegom*, Ger. *bräutigam*, ON. *brūthgumi*, but Goth. *brūthfaths*, bride-lord.

bride[2]. Bonnet-string. F., bridle (q.v.).

bridewell [*hist.*]. Prison. From *Bridewell*, i.e. *St Bride's* (*Bridget's*) *Well*, London, orig. a hospital, later a house of correction.

A special constable was fined for disorderly conduct and assaulting the police at the bridewell [at Liverpool] (*Daily Expr.* Aug. 5, 1919).

bridge[1]. Across water. AS. *brycg*. Com. Teut.; cf. Du. *brug* (as in *Zeebrugge*), Ger. *brücke*, ON. *bryggja*, landing-stage. It is prob. that the most primitive bridge was a wooden causeway over a swamp and that the orig. meaning is rather board, log (cf. Ger. *prügel*, cudgel). With *bridge of gold*, to make enemy's retreat easy, cf. similar use of F. *pont d'or*. The *bridge* of the nose occurs in ME. Mil. *bridge-head* translates F. *tête de pont*.

bridge[2]. Card-game of Russ. origin. For earlier (1886) "*biritch*, or Russian whist." Origin unknown. Its Russ. name is *vint*, screw.

Bridgetine. Member of order of *St Bridget* (14 cent.).

Bridgewater prize. Instituted by *Earl of Bridgewater* (1825). Cf. *Nobel*.

His essay...was highly spoken of, and narrowly escaped obtaining a Bridgewater prize (*Ingoldsby*).

bridle. AS. *brīdel*, for earlier *brigdel*, from *bregdan*, to pull, turn (see *braid*). Cf. Ger. *zügel*, bridle, from *ziehen*, to pull. WGer.; cf. Du. *breidel*, OHG. *brittel*. Hence to *bridle* (*up*), toss the head, with which cf. similar use of Sc. *brank* (q.v.). F. *bride* is from Teut.

How would she have bridled had she known that they only shared his meditations with a pair of breeches! (*Ingoldsby*).

bridoon [*mil.*]. Snaffle. F. *bridon*, from *bride*, bridle (v.s.).

brief. ME. *bref*, OF. *brief* (*bref*), L. *brevis*, short. As in *chief*, the mod. spelling represents the correct OF. form. Orig. missive, esp. papal letter. Cf. Ger. *brief*, letter. As adj. it occurs a little later. A barrister's *brief*, i.e. summary of the case, appears in 17 cent. Found in all Teut. langs., exc. AS., as a loan-word from official L.

brier. See *briar*.

brig. Short for *brigantine* (q.v.), though the rigs are now distinct, the latter being what is called a hermaphrodite brig.

brigade. F., It. *brigata*, "company, crew, rout of good fellows" (Flor.), from *brigare*, to fight, wrangle, from Late L. *briga*, strife, dubiously connected with the Teut. *break* group. Note that F. *brigadier* is not a general, but a cavalry corporal. Application of *brigade* to civil organizations (*fire-, shoeblack-, Church lads*) is 19 cent.

brigand. F., It. *brigante*, from *brigare* (see *brigade*). Orig. light-armed soldier, but bandit sense appears almost as early.

brigandine, brigantine [*archaic*]. Light coat of mail. F., from *brigand* (q.v.). Revived by Scott.

> Furbish the spears, and put on the brigandines
> (*Jer.* xlvi. 4).

brigantine. F. *brigantin*, It. *brigantino*; cf. MedL. *brigantinus*. Perh. orig. a skirmishing or pirate ship (cf. *yacht*). See the preceding words and also *brig, barquentine*. It is a Mediterranean word, and has never been a recognized E. type of ship.

bright. AS. *beorht*, also *breht, bryht*. Com. Teut., but lost in other langs.; cf. OSax. *berht*, OHG. *beraht*, ON. *bjartr*, Goth. *baihrts*. These survive in the *Bert-, -bert* of Teut. names. Ult. cogn. with L. *flagrare*. For fig. senses cf. *dull*.

Bright's disease. Diagnosed (1827) by *Dr R. Bright*. Cf. *Graves' disease*.

brigue. F., intrigue, orig. strife. See *brigade*.

brill. Kind of turbot. Earlier *prill, perl*. ?Cf. Bret. *brill, brezel*, mackerel, Corn. *brilli*, mackerel, for *brithelli* (cf. Welsh *brithyll*), app. from a Celt. root, "spotted," whence also *bret, birt, burt*, obs. names for turbot.

brilliant. F. *brillant*, from *briller*, to shine, It. *brillare*, ?VL. **beryllare* (see *beryl*). For *brilliantine* cf. *bandoline*, etc.

brim. ME. *brymme*, edge of the sea. Cf. ON. *barmr*, brim, MHG. *brem*, whence Ger. *verbrämen*, to border with lace. Cf. *berm*.

brimstone. ME. *bern- (brin-, brim-) ston*, burn stone. Cf. ON. *brenni-steinn* (Du. *barnsteen*, Ger. *bernstein* mean amber). Survival of *brim-* form is perh. due to association with obs. *brim, breme*, fierce, fiery.

brindle, brindled. Also *brinded*, for earlier *brended*, ?orig. marked as though by branding or burning, or from ON. *brandr*, brand, in sense of staff (cf. ON. *stafathr*, striped). But the later *brindle* is due to association with *burnel*, common nickname and sur-

name in ME. This is OF. *brunel*, from *brun*, brown. Similarly *Brindle* (Lanc.) was formerly *burn-hill*.

brine. AS. *brȳne*; cf. Du. *brijn*. Earlier hist. unknown. With a *dip in the briny* cf. Dick Swiveller's use of *the mazy (rosy)*.

bring. AS. *bringan*. Com. Teut., but app. lost early in ON.; cf. Du. *brengen*, Ger. *bringen*, Goth. *briggan*. The *NED*. points out that, in sense, it is the causal of *come*, the opposite idea being expressed by *take*. Thus, to *bring off a catch* is to make it *come off*.

brinjal [*Anglo-Ind.*]. Fruit of egg-plant. Port. *bringella*; cf. Sp. *berengena*, Arab. *bādindjān*, from Pers. *bādīn-gān*. See *aubergine*, which is the same word.

brinjarry [*Anglo-Ind.*]. Travelling merchant. Urdu *banjārā*, ult. from Sanskrit *vanij*, trade. Cf. *banian*.

brink. ME. *brink, brenk*; cf. Du. LG. *brink*, hill-side, Dan. *brink*, precipice; cogn. with ON. *brekka*, hill-side. Now usu. fig., *on the brink, brink of the grave*, but in its hist. parallel with *brim*.

brio [*mus.*]. Vivacity. It., of doubtful origin, but prob. Celt.; ?cf. Ir. *brígh*, power.

briony. See *bryony*.

briquette. F., dim. of *brique*, brick (q.v.).

brisk. F. *brusque*, It. *brusco*, rough, prob. from *brusco*, furze, which may be ult. cogn. with *bristle*. Cf. *brusque*, earlier *brusk*, which appears almost as soon as *brisk*. For change of vowel in latter (*i* for F. or Celt. *u*) cf. *ribbon, whisky*. *Brisk* had earlier the current sense of *brusque*.

> *brusque*: briske, lively, quicke; also,...wilde, fierce, ...harsh (Cotg.).

brisket. Earlier *bruskette*, OF. *bruschet, brischet* (*brechet*). The meaning, and the fact that it is glossed *pectusculum* in ME. (*Voc., Cath. Angl.*), suggest an irregular dim. from Ger. *brust*, breast.

bristle. Orig. of pigs only. ME. *brustel* (cf. Du. *borstel*), dim. of AS. *byrst*; cogn. with Ger. *borste*, ON. *borst*. Cf. also Ger. *bürste*, brush.

Bristol. AS. *brycg-stow*, bridge-place. Associated, like *Bath*, with several products and manufactures. Archaic *Bristol fashion* (naut.), shipshape, is an allusion to its early pre-eminence as seaport.

brit. See *britt*.

Britain. ME. *Bretayne*, OF. *Bretaigne* (*Bretagne*), L. *Brittania* (for *Britannia*), G. Βρεττανία, origin of which is doubtful. The

F word replaced AS. *Breten, Bretenland, Brettland,* but was only in hist. or antiquarian use till Tudor times. James I was proclaimed King of *Great Britain. Little Britain* was applied to Brittany in France, hence also to a street in London once inhabited by Breton immigrants. *Brittany* is also commonly used for *Britain* in 16–17 cents. *Britannia,* as national personification, is first mentioned by Pepys in connection with a medal. *Britannia metal* is early 19 cent. *British,* AS. *bryttisc,* is purely geog. in ME., being first used of the race by Shaks. (*Lear,* iii. 4). *British Schools* were founded (1808) by the *British and Foreign Bible Society. Breton* is F. acc. of OF. *Bret,* Late L. *Britto-n-. Britisher* (US.) is prob. due to Ger. or Du. influence.

britt [*dial.*]. West country (Dev. & Corn.) name for spawn of herring, sprat, etc. Used also by Melville in *Moby Dick* of the spawn on which whales feed. ?A Corn. word, ult. cogn. with *brill.*

brittle. ME. *britel* (also *brotel, brutel*), from AS. *brēotan,* to break. Cf. obs. and synon. *brickle,* from *break,* or L. *fragilis* from *frangere* (*frag*). To *brittle* (ven.), break up (a stag), is a frequent. form of *brēotan.*

britzka. Pol. *bryczka,* dim. of *bryka,* heavy waggon.

Lord Bareacres' chariot, britzka, and fourgon
(*Vanity Fair,* ch. lxii.).

brize. See *breeze¹.*

broach. Spit, and hence, various sharp or tapering objects. Cf. *brooch,* which is the same word. F. *broche,* spit, cogn. with L. *brocchus,* projecting (of teeth), used by Varro, and prob. of Celt. origin; cf. It. *brocca,* Sp. *broca.* Hence to *broach* a cask, and, fig., a subject. Naut. to *broach to* perh. comes from the metaphor of the spit turning back. In quot. below *broach* is app. a mistake for *breach* (q.v.). See *breaker.*

[The damaged submarine] shortly afterwards broached about 500 yards away
(*Amer. Official,* Nov. 24, 1917).

broad. AS. *brād.* Com. Teut.; cf. Du. *breed,* Ger. *breit,* ON. *breithr,* Goth. *braiths.* With the Norfolk *Broads,* i.e. *broad waters,* cf. *narrows* (of water). *Broadcast* was used orig. of seed scattered on the surface instead of in drills or furrows. *Broad Church,* by analogy with *High* and *Low,* was coined by Clough (c. 1850). *Broadcloth* was at first (15 cent.) two yards wide. A *broadsheet,* earlier *broadside,* was printed on one side

only. *Broadside* of a ship is in Shaks. (*2 Hen. IV,* ii. 4); cf. synon. F. *bordée,* from *bord,* side (of ship). *Broadsword* is found in AS. and then not till 16 cent. Archaic *broadpiece* (coin) was first applied, on the introduction of the guinea (1663), to the older Jacobus and Carolus, which were broader and thinner. *Broadway* was once a familiar compd., as still in New York, Hammersmith, etc. (cf. *highway*).

They of the Barbara shotte ther brood syde of ordnyaunce at the Spanysshe shyppe
(*Voyage of the Barbara,* 1540).

Brobdingnagian. Gigantic. From land of *Brobdingnag* (*Gulliver's Travels,* 1726). Coined by Swift. Cf. *Lilliputian.*

brocade. Earlier also *brocado,* Sp. Port.; cf. It. *broccato.* Orig. p.p. of verb corresponding to F. *brocher,* to work with needle. See *broach, brooch, brochure.*

brocard [*archaic*]. Gibe, orig. maxim. F., from *Burchard,* bishop of Worms (11 cent.), author of *Regulae Ecclesiasticae.*

brocatelle. F., It. *broccatello,* dim. of *broccato,* brocade (q.v.).

broccoli. It., pl. of *broccolo,* sprout, dim. of *brocco,* spike (see *broach*). First record in Evelyn.

broccoli: the stalkes, sproutes or tops of coleworts
(Flor.).

broch [*antiq.*]. Prehistoric building (N.E. Scotland). ON. *borg,* fort, borough (q.v.).

broché. F., stitched (v.i.).

brochure. F., from *brocher,* to stitch (sheets together). See *broach, brooch.*

brock [*dial.*]. Badger (q.v.). AS. *brocc,* of Celt. origin; cf. Welsh *broch,* badger, *broc,* of mixed colour, Gael. *broc,* badger. Perh. cogn. with G. φορκός, grey (cf. its other names, *bawson, gray*), or with L. *brocchus* (see *broach*), from its projecting jaw (cf. *pike*).

brocket [*ven.*]. Stag in second year. F. *brocart,* "a two-yeare-old deere, which if he be a red deere, we call a brocket; if a fallow, a pricket" (Cotg.), from *broche,* spike (see *broach*). Cf. *pricket.*

brodrick [*mil. slang*]. Peaked cap introduced into British Army by St John Brodrick, Secretary for War (1900–3).

brogue. Ir. Gael. *brōg,* shoe, ?from ON. *brōk,* breeches (q.v.), OIr. *brōc* occurring in compds. for various nether garments. Cf., for vague meaning, F. *chausses,* breeches (ult. from L. *calx, calc-,* heel). App. *brogue,* Irish accent, is a playful allusion to national attire.

broider [*archaic*]. Lengthened from ME. *browd*, F. *broder*, OF. *brosder* (Prov. *broidar*), from a, prob. Celt., root which appears in MedL. *brosdus*, "opus phrygium acupictum." The -*oi*- is due to ME. *broiden*, AS. *brogden*, p.p. of *bregdan* (see *braid*), which was perh. also associated with the Prov. form (v.s.), and in early use there is confusion in sense between the two words (v.i.). The word is thus of rather complicated origin. The surname *Broster* (*browdster*) preserves an older form.

Of goldsmythrye, of browdynge, and of steel
(Chauc. A. 2498).

I broder, as a brouderer dothe a vestmente; je brode (Palsg.).

I broyde heare, or a lace, or such lyke: je tortille. *Brayde your heare up... (ib.)*.

Not with broided hair, or gold, or pearls, or costly array (1 *Tim.* ii. 9).

broil[1]. Quarrel. From obs. *broil*, to mix up, F. *brouiller*; cf. It. *imbroglio*. The F. and It. forms suggest connection with F. *breuil*, thicket, jungle (whence *the Broyle*, Sussex), from Gaulish *brogilos*.

broil[2]. Orig. to burn, char. F. *brûler*. Earliest ME. form is *brule*. Prob. influenced by *boil*[2]; but E. is fond of *oi* (see *foil*[2], *recoil*). F. *brûler*, OF. *brusler*, is of unknown origin (? L. *ustulare*, from *urere*, *ust-*, to burn, × Ger. *brennen*).

broke [*techn.*]. Short-stapled "broken" wool. Cf. *noil*.

broker. AF. *brokour*, OF. *brocheor*. Supposed to have meant orig. a *broacher*, and seller, of wine (see *broach*). But mod. sense is prob. influenced by some other word of wider meaning. We find also AF. *abrocour*, corresponding to MedL. *abbrocator*, which may have been confused with MedL. *abbocator*, a broker, lit. one who brings buyer and seller mouth to mouth. Cf. It. *abboccatore* and F. *aboucher*, from *bocca*, *bouche*, mouth, VL. *bucca*. A plausible theory connects the word with Sp. *albóroque*, "a gratuity given to one that makes up a bargain between two, in the nature of brokeridge" (Stevens), recorded as early as 1020, and derived from Hebr. *berakah*, present, or cogn. Arab. *baraka*. The medieval brokers were often Jews or Arabs. Cf. Prov. *abrocatge*, brokerage. *Honest broker*, in pol. sense, is Bismarck's *ehrlicher mäkler* (in Reichstag, Feb. 19, 1878).

abboccatore: a broker, a daies-man; such as bring men to speake togither (Flor.).

brolly [*colloq.*]. Perversion of *umbrella*. I do not know the "phonetic" explanation.

bromine [*chem.*]. For earlier *brome*, F., from G. βρῶμος, stink.

bronchitis. ModL. (early 19 cent.), ult. from G. βρόγχος, wind-pipe. See -*itis* and cf. other med. coinages in *broncho-*, *bronchio-*.

bronco. Half-tamed horse (Mexico and California). Sp., rough, of unknown origin. Cf. *mustang*, *lariat*, *quirt*, etc.

bronze. F., It. *bronzo*, from *Brundusium* (Brindisi). Pliny speaks of *aes Brundusium*. Cf. hist. of *copper*.

brooch. Var. of *broach* (q.v.), in sense of pin, differentiation of spelling being quite mod.

brood. AS. *brōd*, cogn. with *breed* (q.v.); cf. Du. *broed*, Ger. *brut*. With verb to *brood* (*over*) cf. fig. senses of Ger. *brüten* and F. *couver* (see *covey*).

brook[1]. Noun. AS. *brōc*; cf. Du. *broek*, marsh, Ger. *bruch*, marsh; prob. cogn. with *break*. In *brooklime*, kind of speedwell, the second element is not *lime*[2], but AS. *hleomoc*, name of the plant.

brook[2]. Verb. AS. *brūcan*, to use. Com. Teut.; cf. Du. *bruiken*, Ger. *brauchen*, to use, Goth. *brukjan*; ult. cogn. with L. *frui*, *fruct-*, to enjoy. With mod. meaning, usu. neg., cf. to *have no use for*. Intermediate sense was to digest, etc. (cf. to *stomach*).

Let us bruik the present hour (*Sc. ballad*).

broom. AS. *brōm*; cf. Du. *braam*, Ger. *bram*. See *bramble*. For application of plant to implement cf. *brush*.

brose. See *brewis*.

broth. AS. *broth*, cogn. with *brew*; cf. OHG. *brod*, ON. *broth*. Widely adopted in Rom. langs. (see *brewis*, *imbrue*). ?Hence *broth of a boy* (Ir.), "the essence of manhood, as broth is the essence of meat" (Joyce).

brothel. ME. *brothel*, vile person of either sex, from AS. *brēothan*, to go to ruin (cf. synon. *losel* from *lose*). Mod. sense springs from a confusion (c. 1600) of *brothel-house* with obs. *bordel*, F. (cf. It. *bordello*), little house, of Teut. origin (*board*).

brother. AS. *brōthor*. Aryan; cf. Du. *broeder*, Ger. *bruder*, ON. *brōthir*, Goth. *brōthar*, L. *frater*, G. φράτηρ, Sanskrit *bhrātṛ*, Gael. Ir. *bráthair*. *Brethren* is a mixture of two pl. forms, *brether* and *brothren*.

brougham. From *Lord Brougham* (c. 1850). Cf. *spencer*, *sandwich*, etc.

brow[1]. Of eye or hill. AS. *brū*, eye-lash, -lid, -brow, unrelated, according to the best authorities, with *brae* (q.v.). In ON. *brūn*, eyebrow, *brā*, eye-lid, and OHG. *brū*, later replaced by MHG. *brā*, *brāw-*, we have similar pairs; cf. Sanskrit *bhrūs*, eye-brow. Poet. sense of forehead is 16 cent. In *brow-beat* (16 cent.) the brow is that of the threatener. This compd. appears also to have been associated in use with *beetle-browed* (q.v.).

Into the same hue doe they [Turkish women] die their eye-breies [?eye-lids, or -lashes] and eye-browes (Sandys, 1615, in Purch.).

brow² [*naut.*]. Landing-plank for horses. Dan. or Sw. *bru*, bridge, ON. *brū*. Used in offic. account of Zeebrugge raid (Apr. 23, 1918). First *NED.* record is from Smyth (1867), but see below. The newspaper accounts of Zeebrugge sometimes substituted *prow*.

A brow [MS. brew] or stage made at the stem of the ship (Phineas Pett, 1609).

browis. See *brewis*.

brown. AS. *brūn*. Com. Teut.; cf. Du. *bruin*, Ger. *braun*, ON. *brūnn*. Also adopted, like so many colour-words, by the Rom. langs. Its earliest meaning contained also the idea of brightness (see *burnish*), hence it is in OF. & ME. a common epithet of the sword. To shoot *into the brown* is to shoot where the birds are so thick that missing is difficult. *Brown Bess* (18 cent.) for earlier *brown musket*, was the old regulation flint-lock with brown walnut stock; it has been suggested that *Bess* is here for Ger. *büchse* (see *arquebus*, *blunderbuss*), but it is more prob. a personal name (see *Bess*). *Brown George* was used in 17 cent. of a coarse loaf (cf. F. *gros-Guillaume* in same sense), in 19 cent. of a brown wig (*Ingoldsby*) and a brown jug (*Tom Brown at Oxford*). *Brownie* (Sc.) is a little brown elf or goblin. With *brown study*, "gloomy meditations" (Johns.), we may perh. compare F. *offusquer*, to overshadow, create melancholy absorption, from L. *fuscus*, brown.

donner la muse à: to amuse, or put into dumpes; to drive into a brown study (Cotg.).

browning. Revolver. From inventor (c. 1900); cf. *derringer*, *bowie*, etc.

Brownist [*hist.*]. Adherent of *Robert Browne* (c. 1581), puritan theologian (Independent).

browse. From obs. noun *browse*, young shoots on which cattle feed. OF. *brouz*, pl. of *broust*, from *brouster* (*brouter*), to browse. App. from a Teut. root meaning to sprout, perh. cogn. with *breast*.

vescae salicum frondes: brouse made for beastes of withie bowes (Coop.).

frondator: a wood-lopper, a browser (ib.).

bruin. Du., brown, name of the bear in the Old Flemish poem *Reineke Vos*, Reynard the Fox. It appears first in Caxton's transl. See *renard*, *chanticleer*, *monkey*.

bruise. Mixed form from AS. *brīesan* (in *tōbrīesan*, to break to pieces) and AF. *bruser*, OF. *bruisier*, var. of *briser*, to break, prob. from the AS. word; ?of Celt. origin. *Bruiser*, pugilist, is used by Horace Walpole.

bruit. Usu. with *about*, *abroad*. From *bruit*, rumour, F., orig. p.p. of *bruire*, to sound, etc., prob. of imit. origin (cf. *bray*¹).

Brummagem. For *Bromwicham* (*Thersites*, 1537), corrupt., under influence of *Bromwich*, of *Brimidgeham*, for *Birming(e)ham*. The orig. allusion is to counterfeit coin made there.

Bromicham, particularly noted a few years ago, for the counterfeit groats made here (*NED.* 1691).

brumous. F. *brumeux*, from *brume*, mist, L. *bruma*.

brunette. F., "a nut-browne girl" (Cotg.), dim. of *brune*, brown (q.v.).

Brunswick. LG. form of Ger. *Braunschweig*, adopted in F. & E. Hence *Brunswick black* (cf. *Prussian blue*), *Black Brunswicker* (hussar), *House of Brunswick*, Hanover having once consisted of the Electorate of Brunswick-Lüneburg.

brunt. Usu. with *to bear*. Orig. (c. 1325) a blow, whence stock phrase *at the first brunt*. ?From ON. *brundr*, sexual heat, as in *brund-līth*, rutting time, cogn. with *burn*²; cf. Ger. *brunst*, ardour, etc. Regular occurrence of *at the first brunt* suggests a sense-development like that of *blush*.

primo impetu: at the first brunt (Coop.).

brush. Orig. loppings of trees, faggots, etc., OF. *brousse*, whence F. *broussailles*, thicket, brushwood, of Teut. origin; cf. Ger. *bürste*, a brush, *borste*, a bristle. The implement *brush* is ult. the same word (cf. *broom*). The fox's *brush* (cf. synon. Ger. *rute*, lit. rod) is recorded c. 1700. To *brush by* (*against*, etc.) is from the idea of frictional contact, but there is an archaic *brush*, to decamp, spec. from archaic F. *brosser*, used of a stag, etc. making off through the brushwood. With *brush*, encounter, cf. F. *se frotter à quelqu'un* and somewhat similar use of *rub*.

brushe to make brushes on: bruyere (Palsg.).

For, that one of their drummers, and one Sergeant Matcham
Had "brush'd with the dibs," and they never could catch 'em (*Ingoldsby*).

brusque. F., see *brisk*.

Brussels. *Lace* (Richardson) and *sprouts* (18 cent.) are recorded earlier than *carpets*.

brute. F., from L. *brutus*, dull, stupid. In earliest occurrences (15–16 cents.) always as adj. qualifying *beast*.

brutus. Wig and style of hair-dressing (19 cent.). Said to be from a style of hair-dressing affected by people of Republican ideas.

bryology [*bot.*]. Study of mosses. From G. βρύον, mossy sea-weed.

bryony. L., G. βρυωνία, from G. βρύειν, to burst forth.

Brythonic [*ethn. & ling.*]. From Welsh *brython*, Briton. Introduced by Rhys in contrast to *Goidelic* (q.v.).

bub¹ [*slang*]. Drink. For *bib*.

bub² [*slang*]. Breast (of woman). For earlier *bubby*; cf. Ger. dial. *bübbi*, teat. From baby lang.

bub³ [*US.*]. Boy, regarded as m. of *siss*, sister, but app. from Ger. *bube*, boy (q.v.). The m. of *siss* is rather *bud*, which may stand for negro *brudder*.

bubble. Earlier *burble*. Of imit. origin; cf. *babble*, *blob*, etc. Hence *bubble*, to cheat, to delude with bubbles, or unrealities. Its very common use in 18 cent. is perh. spec. due to the *South Sea Bubble* (1710–20). *Bubble and squeak*, yesterday's vegetables, etc. fried up, is an allusion to the noise of frying. *Bubble reputation* is from *As You Like It*, ii. 7.

What mortals bubble call and squeak,
When 'midst the frying-pan in accents savage,
The beef so surly quarrels with the cabbage
(*Peter Pindar*).

bubbly-jock [*Sc.*]. Turkey-cock. Imit., cf. *gobbler*. *Jock* is Sc. for *Jack* (q.v.).

bubonic. From Late L. *bubo*, G. βουβών, groin, swelling in groin.

buccaneer. Orig. French hunter in San Domingo who prepared the flesh of wild oxen by means of a *boucan* (v.i.). Later, a freebooter, and finally, a pirate. Cf. F. *boucané*, smoke-dried. *Boucan* is a Tupi (Brazil) word taken to Hayti by early travellers. It is so explained (Purch. xvi. 519) by a Frenchman who was in Brazil 1557–8.

boucan: a woodden-gridiron, whereon the cannibals broile pieces of men, and other flesh (Cotg.).

buccinator [*anat.*]. Cheek-muscle. L., trumpeter, from *buccina*, trumpet.

bucellas. White wine. Village near Lisbon.

bucentaur. State-barge in which, on Ascension Day, the Doge of Venice went to wed the Adriatic by dropping a ring into it. It. *bucentoro*, supposed to allude to the figure-head, ox-centaur. See *bucephalus*, *centaur*.

bucephalus. Horse of Alexander the Great. G. βουκέφαλος, ox-headed, from βοῦς, ox, κεφαλή, head. Cf. *bayard*, *rosinante*, etc.

buck¹. Animal. AS. *bucc*, male deer, *bucca*, he-goat. Com. Teut.; cf. Du. *bok*, Ger. *bock*, ON. *bokkr*, all orig. he-goat; also adopted by Rom. & Celt. langs. Mod. application to a man (from c. 1700) has a curious parallel in ON. *bokki*, my good fellow, old buck (cf. US. *old hoss*). Hence prob. also to *buck up*. *Buckbean* is Du. *bocksboon*, goat's bean, also altered to *bogbean*. *Buckjump*, i.e. to jump like a buck, is Austral. *Buck-shot rule* in Ireland (c. 1880) was popularly associated with W. E. Forster, Secretary for Ireland. With *buckthorn* cf. It. *spino cervino*, from *cervo*, deer.

buck² [*dial.*]. Body of vehicle, as still in US. *buckboard*. AS. *būc*, trunk, belly (cf. Ger. *bauch*).

buck³ [*dial.*]. To wash clothes, whence *buck-basket* (*Merry Wives*, iii. 5). Cf. Sw. *byka*, Ger. *bauchen* (MHG. *büchen*, whence F. *buer*), It. *bucare*; prob. cogn. with AS. *būc*, pitcher, still in dial. use.

bucke to wasshe clothes in: cuvier (Palsg.).

buckeen [*Ir.*]. Squireen of poorer class. From *buck¹*, with dim. suffix; cf. *colleen*, *squireen*, etc.

bucket. AF. *boket*, *buquet*, dim., from AS. *būc*, pitcher (see *buck³*), but prob. associated also with F. *baquet*, bucket. *Bucket-shop* in New York "is a low 'gin-mill' or 'distillery,' where small quantities of spirit are dispensed in pitchers and pails. When the shops dealing with one-share and five-share lots of stocks were opened, these dispensaries of smaller lots than could be got from regular dealers were at once named 'bucket-shops'" (*New York Evening Post*, Oct. 1881). With verb to *bucket*, in riding or rowing, cf. to *pump*. To *kick the bucket* is prob. from dial. *bucket*, beam, yoke (cf. to *kick the beam*), OF. *buquet*, balance, which survives in F. *trébuchet*. This is a separate word of obscure origin.

Swifter than he that gibbets on the brewer's bucket
(2 *Hen. IV*, iii. 2).

buckie [*Sc.*]. Whelk shell. App. from L. *buccinum*, whelk, lit. trumpet.

buckle. F. *boucle*, which in OF. meant cheek, strap of helmet, boss of shield (see *buckler*), L. *buccula*, dim. of *bucca*, mouth. With to *buckle to*, set hard to work, cf. to *gird up one's loins* preparatory to active exertion, and see *fettle*. *Buckle*, to bend, is included here by the *NED.*, but is surely rather connected with Du. *buigen*, to bend, or Ger. *buckel*, hump, cogn. with *bow*[1].

Reason doth buckle and bowe the mind unto the nature of things (Bacon).

boghel, beughel: hemicyclus, semicirculus, curvatura semicircularis (Kil.).

My lady Batten and her daughter look something askew upon my wife because my wife do not buckle to them (Pepys, Aug. 25, 1661).

to buckle to his business: se ad opus accingere (Litt.).

das kleid sitzt puckelicht: this suit of clothes doth pucker (Ludw.).

buckler. F. *bouclier*, VL. **buccularium* (sc. *scutum*), with a boss (see *buckle*).

Trenchet ces hanstes et cez escus buclers
(*Roland*, 1968).

buckra. Master, white man, in negro patois of Surinam. From Calabar *bakra*, master.

buckram. Orig. a fine cotton fabric, later applied to an inferior material used as stiffening. ME. *bukeram, bougeren*, etc., OF. *boquerant* (*bougran*); cf. MedL. *boquerannus* and forms in most Europ. langs. Origin doubtful, perh. from *Bokhara* (cf. *astrakhan*, etc.). Some authorities regard it as a corrupt. of obs. *barracan* (see *barragan*). *Men in buckram* is after 1 *Hen. IV*, ii. 4. For form cf. *grogram*, for vague meaning *camlet*.

He [Kerenski] wasted time in delivering an oration, and the Red Guards scattered his buckram army
(J. Buchan).

buckshee [*mil. slang*]. See *bukshee*.
buckthorn. See *buck*[1].
buckwheat. Du. *boekweit*, first element meaning *beech*, this wheat having grains shaped like those of beech-mast. Cf. Ger. *buchweizen* and It. *fagopiro*, from *fago*, beech. It was introduced from Asia (15 cent.) whence its F. name *sarrasin*.

bucolic. L., G. βουκολικός, from βουκόλος, herdsman, from βοῦς, bull.

bud. ME. *bodde*. Cf. Du. *bot*, Ger. *butten*, in *hagebutten*, hips and haws, lit. hedge-buds. Origin unknown. F. *bouton* is from Teut.

Buddhism. From *Buddha*, lit. the enlightened, awakened, p.p. of Sanskrit *budh*, to awake, perceive, applied to a series of heaven-sent teachers, and spec. to Gautama, also called Sakyamuni and Siddhartha (fl. 5 cent. B.C. in Northern India).

bude light. Invented (19 cent.) by Gurney, who lived at *Bude* (Cornwall).

budge. A "low word" (Johns.). F. *bouger*, to stir, VL. **bullicare*, from *bullire*, to boil. This etym., though rather speculative, is strongly supported by Prov. *bolegar*, to budge.

budgerigar. Austral. parakeet. Native (NSW.) *betcherrygah*, lit. good cockatoo, corrupted in US. to *beauregarde*.

budgerow [*Anglo-Ind.*]. Barge. Hind. *bājrā*.

budget. OF. *bougette*, dim. of *bouge* (whence obs. E. *budge, bouge*), L. *bulga*, of Celt. orig.; cf. OIr. *bolg*, bag; cogn. with Ger. *balg*, skin (see also *bulge*). Orig. a bag, wallet, etc., as in *budget of letters, news*, etc. (v.i.). The Chancellor of the Exchequer, in making his statement, theoretically *opens his budget*.

This bochet with othre lettres conteigned in the same (1512–13).

bulga: a male or bouget of leather, a purse, a bagge
(Coop.).

budmash. See *badmash*.
buff. Colour. Orig. buffalo, then, buffalo-hide (whence *buff-coat*) and its colour. F. *buffle* (see *buffalo*). In to *strip to the buff* it is used for human skin. The *Buffs* (E. Kent Reg.) and *Ross-shire Buffs* (2nd Seaforths) were named from facings (cf. the *Blues*).

buffle: the buffe, buffle, bugle, or wild oxe (Cotg.).

buff, blind man's. See *blind*. The fact that in some other langs. the game is named from an animal, e.g. Ger. *blinde kuh* (blind cow), Port. *cabracega* (blind goat), suggests some connection with *buff* (v.s.), which is supported by *behold the buff*, used (1647) to render It. *ecco la cieca*. On the other hand the game is also called *blind man's buffet* or *blind and buffet*.

buffalo. Port. *búfalo*, L., G. βούβαλος, orig. kind of antelope, from βοῦς, ox, bull. Earlier also *buffle*, from F. Often wrongly applied to Amer. bison. According to a writer in *Notes and Queries* (Oct. 1919), the *Royal and Ancient Order of Buffaloes* grew out of a convivial and friendly club started (18 cent.) at the Harp tavern by Drury Lane actors. The club-room was adorned with a pair of buffalo horns in honour of Nimrod, claimed as one of the founders of the society.

buff-coat. See *buff*.

buffer[1]. Fellow. In ME. stammerer (Wyc. *Is.* xxxii. 4), in Sc. foolish fellow, in obs. slang, suborned witness. Prob. all belong to an imit. *buff*; cf. *puff* and see *buffoon*.

buffer[2]. Of engine, etc. From verb to *buff*, imit. of muffled blow. Cf. synon. Ger. *puffer* and see *buffet*[1]. Hence *buffer state*, rendered in F. by *état tampon* (see *tompion*).

buffet[1]. Blow. OF., dim. of *buffe*; see *buffer*[1], *buffoon*, and cf. Ger. *puffen*, to jostle, hustle.

buffet[2]. Side-board. F., of unknown origin. Cf. It. *buffetto*. The 18 cent. spelling *beaufet*, *beaufait* is artificial and misleading. Perh. the same word as *buffet*[3]. OF. *buffet* is used (13 cent.) in Boileau's *Mestiers de Paris* of a bench for displaying goods. For sense cf. *shamble*[1], also orig. a low stool. Quot. below is from 12 cent.

Duo bancha tornatilia, et una mensa dormiens, et unum buffeth
(Hales' *Domesday of St Paul's*, p. 137).

buffet[3]. Low stool, hassock. Now dial. or in ref. to *Little Miss Muffet*, though *tuffet* is often substituted in mod. versions. OF. (v.s.), of unknown origin.

bofet, iii foted stole: tripes (*Prompt. Parv.*).

buffo. Comic, etc. It. See *buffoon*.

buffoon. F. *bouffon*, It. *buffone*, from *buffa*, jest, from *buffare*, to puff, prob. with allusion to cheeks puffed out in grimacing, etc.; cf. F. *pouffer de rire*.

bug[1]. Spectre. Obs. exc. in *bugbear*, *bugaboo*. ME. *bugge*, Welsh *bwg*, ghost. See *bogy*, *boggle*.

Thou shalt not nede to be afrayed for eny bugges by night (Coverd. *Ps.* xci. 5).

Warwick was a bug that fear'd us all
(3 *Hen. VI*, v. 2).

The German element [in US.] is a bug-a-boo....The police can look after them all right
(Sir H. W. Thornton, Amer. Manager of G.E.R.).

bug[2]. Insect. Orig., as still in dial. and US., beetle, insect, in general. Irreg. corrupt. of AS. *budda*, beetle, whence perh. also *boud*, weevil. Cf. dial. *shornbug* for AS. *scearnbudda*, dung-beetle.

blatta: a shorn-bug, the chafer, or beetle
(Ainsworth, 1736).

bug[3]. In colloq. *big-bug*. See *big*.

bugaboo. Welsh *bwci-bo*, elaboration of *bwg* (see *bug*[1]). Cf. OF. *bugibu*.

bugbear. Formed (16 cent.) from *bug*[1] (q.v.). Second element may be an imit. corrupt. of some other ending. We also find *bull-*

bear, *bullbeggar* (? for *-boggart*) in same sense. Cf. Du. *bullebak* (Kil.).

Maugre such bug-beare, bull-beare bellowings
(Purch.).

bugger. F. *bougre*, L. *Bulgarus*, Bulgarian. Orig. sect of heretics who came from *Bulgaria* in 11 cent.

Ma dame, sachez ke jo.maund verité loyal, e si nul [anyone] vous fet autre chose entendre, il est bugre
(Archbp Peckham to Queen Eleanor, 1283).

buggy. Vehicle. Now US. and colonial. Origin unknown, but prob. facetious. A Camb. undergrad. spells it *bougée* in 1767.

bugle[1]. Plant. F., Late L. *bugula*, whence also It. *bugola*. Perh. related to *bugloss*, with which it is confused by ME. writers.

buglosa: bugle (*Voc.* c. 1265).

bugle[2]. Buffalo or wild ox. OF., L. *buculus*, dim. of *bos*, ox. Hence mus. instrument, for *bugle-horn*.

Oxen, shepe, and gootes, hert, roo, and bugle
(*Bible of* 1551, *Deut.* xiv. 5).

bugle[3]. Bead ornament. Perh. ident. with *bugle*[2], from horny appearance.

Beades, bracelets, chaines, or collers of bewgle
(Hakl. viii. 99).

bugle: kind of glass or black horne (Holyoke, 1649).

bugloss. Plant. F. *buglosse*, L. *buglossa*, from G. βούγλωσσος, ox-tongued. See *bugle*[1], *glossary*.

Buhl. Also *Boule*, F. wood-carver (fl. temp. Louis XIV).

build. Earlier *bild*, *byld*, AS. *byldan*. Not known outside E.

He builded better than he knew:—
The conscious stone to beauty grew
(Emerson, *Problem*).

bukshee [*Anglo-Ind.*]. Paymaster. Pers. *bakhshī*, from *bakhshīdan*, to give. Cf. *backsheesh*.

bulb. L. *bulbus*, G. βολβός, onion, its earlier meaning in E.; cogn. with L. *bulla*, bubble, etc.

bulbul. Eastern song-thrush. Pers. Arab., imit. of note. Cf. *jug*[2] (q.v.).

Bulgarian. A Slav. lang.

bulge. First as noun, hump, protuberance. Prob. ident. with obs. *bulge*, wallet, etc. (see *budget*, *bilge*), and ult. cogn. with *belly*, *bellows*.

bulimy. Unnatural hunger. MedL., G. βουλιμία, from βοῦς, ox, λιμός, hunger.

bulk. Earliest sense, cargo, whence to *break bulk*, begin unloading. Late ON. *bŭlki*, heap, cargo, or Dan. *bulk*, lump, clod. In late

ME., by association with *bouk*, AS. *bŭc*, belly (cf. Ger. *bauch*), it came to mean trunk of body, etc., whence some of its mod. senses and derivatives. Cf. OF. *bouche*, bundle, from Teut.

bulkhead. First element is ME. *bolk* (*Coventry Leet Book*, 1421), ON. *bālkr*, beam, balk, whence Norw. *balk*, *bolk*. Linc. dial. *bulkar*, beams, is in Skinner. Cf. Shaks. *bulk*, shop-front (*Cor.* ii. 1). The oldest sense of *bulkhead* is naut. (in Capt. John Smith, who also calls it a *bulk*). In *Pat. R.* temp. Hen. III occur *William le Balker* and *Gilbert le Bolker*, both of Canterbury.

That no man hold no swyne in hur bolkys
(*Coventry Leet Book*, 1421).

That no other man or bocher kep within the wallys of this cite noo swyne in sties, ne bulkes
(*ib.* 1423).

bull[1]. Animal. ME. *bole*; cf. Du. *bol*, Ger. dial. *bulle*, ON. *boli*. The corresponding word prob. existed in AS. as we have the dim. *bulluc*, whence *bullock*. ?Cogn. with *bellow*. For Stock Exchange use see *bear*. Fig. applications of *bull's eye* are numerous in 18–19 cents. (cf. Dan. *koöie*, Sw. *oxöga*, both used of small round window). The earliest appears to be crown-piece (c. 1690), later shortened to *bull*. With *bullfinch* cf. F. *bouvreuil*, lit. little bull-herd. *Bullfinch*, stiff fence (hunting), is said to be corrupted from *-fence*, but is more likely due to some forgotten witticism. With *bulldog* cf. Ger. *bullenbeisser*, lit. bull-biter. *John Bull* as personification of England dates from Arbuthnot's satire (1712).

Four half-bulls, wot you may call half-crowns
(*Bleak House*, ch. xlvii.).

bull[2]. Papal. Orig. seal attached to document, esp. leaden seal of Pope's edicts. L. *bulla*. See *bill*[3] and *bulletin*.

The Pope sent a general sentence under his bulles of lede unto the archebisshop (Caxton).

bull[3]. Irish. Earlier, jest; not at first associated with Ireland. Cf. rare ME. *bul*, falsehood, and rare 16 cent. *bull*, bubble, both prob. from F. *boule*, bubble, L. *bulla*, whence also perh. Du. *bol*, "garrulitas, loquacitas" (Kil.). Mod. sense of incongruous statement is perh. partly due to *cock and bull story*. See quot. s.v. *mute*.

a bull or incongruous speech: solaecismus (Litt.).

Only on the terms of free choice can we have Irish compulsion (*Daily News*, Apr. 1918).

"If the patients were deprived of tobacco," reported Dr Myles to the committee of the Ballinasloe Lunatic Asylum, "they would 'go mad'"
(*Pall Mall Gaz.* May 17, 1918).

bullace. Wild plum. OF. *beloce*, with many Rom. cognates (mostly dial.), prob. of Gaulish origin.

bellocier: a bullace-tree, or wilde plum tree (Cotg.).

bulldose, bulldoze [*US*.]. To intimidate, orig. negroes, by unmerciful flogging. Said to mean to give a "dose" strong enough for a "bull"; but cf. obs. Du. *doesen*, "pulsare cum impetu et fragore" (Kil.).

The War Department is trying to bulldose the country into conscription
(Speaker of Congress, Apr. 24, 1917).

bullet. F. *boulette*, dim. of *boule* (see *bowl*[2]). In ModF. *balle* = bullet, *boulet* = cannon-shot. E. *bullet* also had the latter meaning in 16–18 cents., as still in *bullet-headed* (cf. *pellet*).

bulletin. Orig. from It. *bullettino*, double dim. from L. *bulla* (see *bull*[2]), meaning warrant, etc., with seal; but usual mod. sense (from 18 cent.) represents that of F. *bulletin*, popularized by Napoleonic wars.

bullion. AF. *bullion*, *boillon* (*Statutes of Realm*, 1336), which would represent exactly F. *bouillon*, a boiling (of precious metal), but there is no evidence that the OF. word had this spec. sense, and the orig. meaning of the E. word is also uncertain. Cf. however *brassage* (q.v.) for similar sense-development. There has been confusion with *billon* (q.v.). *Bullion* lace is etym. the same word, F. *bouillon*, "fil d'or ou d'argent tourné en rond" (Littré), going back to L. *bulla*, bubble, etc.

bouillons: puffes, in a garment (Cotg.).

bullock. See *bull*[1].

bully. Oldest sense is brother, dear fellow, etc. Du. *boel*, lover, brother, etc., from MHG. *buole* (*buhle*), lover, OHG. *Buolo*, as personal name only. Prob. orig. brother. Earliest meaning still in Shaks. and in US. Later meanings have perh. been affected by *bull*[1], or by Du. *bulderen*, LG. *bullern*, to bluster. Obs. *bully-jack*, *bully-rock*, *bully-back*, etc. have parallels in LG. *buller-jaan*, *buller-brook*, *buller-bak*, etc. For *bullyrag* see *ballyrag*. In *bullyrook* (*Merry Wives*, i. 3), later also *-rock*, *-rake*, the second element is of doubtful origin. See also *billy-cock*. The hockey *bully-off* is an imit. of the Eton football *bully*.

buler: an amorist, a paramour, a lover, a wooer, a gallant, a spark (Ludw.).

bully-beef. Orig. naut. For earlier *bull-beef*.

bulrush. ME. also *holrysch*, app. from AS. *hol*, hollow. *Bul-* is prob. *bole*[1], stem. But it may be intens., like *horse-* in *horseradish*, *cow* in *cow-parsley*, etc.

holrysche or *bulrysche*: papirus
(*Prompt. Parv., Harl. MS.*).

bulwark. Orig. rampart (*Deut.* xx. 20); naut. sense only from c. 1800. From *bole*[1] (q.v.) and *work*. Cf. Du. *bolwerk*, Ger. *bollwerk*, whence F. *boulevard*.

bol-werck, block-werc: propugnaculum, agger, etc.
(Kil.).

bum. ME. *bom*, Du. dial. *boem*, for *bodem*, bottom. Cf. obs. *bummery* (Pepys) for *bottomry* (q.v.). With *bumbailiff* (*Twelfth Night*, iii. 4) cf. F. *pousse-cul*. *Bumboat*, orig. (17 cent.) scavenger boat, is sailors' slang.

pousse-cul: a bum-baily (Miège, 1688).

Bumble, Bumbledom. From *Bumble*, the beadle (*Oliver Twist*). The name is AF. *bonbel*, good, beautiful.

bumble-bee. Imit., cf. *humble-bee*. See *bomb*, *boom*[1], etc.

I bomme, as a bombyll bee dothe or any flye: je bruys
(Palsg.).

bumble-puppy. Unscientific whist; orig. outdoor game, nine holes. Obs. *bumble*, to bungle, blunder, and *puppy*, but reason for name unknown.

bumbo. Weak cold punch. Cf. It. *bombo*, baby name for drink, and obs. E. *bum* (v.i.). Prob. suggested partly by *rumbo* (q.v.). Smollett is earliest authority for both.

bum, drinke: potus (*Manip. Voc.*).

bummalo. Fish, "Bombay duck." From Mahratti *bombīla*.

The sailors, by way of joke, call them "Bombay ducks" (Cordiner, *Voyage to India*, 18 cent.).

bummaree. Middleman in Billingsgate fish trade. ?F. *bonne marée*, good sea-fish, as salesman's cry.

bummer [*US.*]. Loafer. Ger. *bummler*, stroller, etc., orig. from student slang.

bump. Imit. of a dull blow and its result. Also influenced, when referring to form, by cogn. *bomb* (q.v.); cf. F. *front bombé*, bulging forehead. Hence *bumper*, full glass (cf. *thumping*, *whopping*, etc.), also in *bumper crop* (*audience*, etc.).

bumpkin. Prob. dim. of Du. *boom*, tree, boom, etc., as in naut. *bumkin*, a short boom. Cf. similar use of Ger. *flegel*, flail.

The first quot. suggests that the word was orig. applied to a Dutchman.

a bunkin, fellow: Batavus, strigo (*Manip. Voc.*).

ein ertzbauer, ein grober flegel: a clownish, boorish, or rusticall fellow; a churl, a clown, an arch-clown, a hoydon, a meer boor, a country-bumkin, a home-spun, a plough-jogger, a kern, a lob, a lobcock
(Ludw.).

bumptious. App. jocular coinage (c. 1800) from *bump*; cf. fig. use of *bounce*.

bun[1]. Cake. ME. *bunne*, small round loaf. Origin unknown. Perh. simply a spec. use of F. *bon*; cf. history of *scone* (q.v.).

bunne, whyt brede: placenta (*Prompt. Parv.*).

bun[2], **bunny.** Pet name for rabbit, squirrel, etc. Perh. F. *bon*, common as personal name in ME., whence surname *Bunn*. Celt. *bun*, stump, has also been suggested, *bun* being commonly used in Sc. for the hare's "scut."

bunch. Orig. hump (on the back). Perh. suggested by obs. *bulch*, the same, and *hunch*.

buncombe. See *bunkum*.

bund [*Anglo-Ind.*]. Embankment. Hind. *band*, from Pers. Hence *Bendemeer*, lit. the Emir's dam.

There's a bower of roses by Bendemeer's stream
(*Lalla Rookh*).

A break in the river [Tigris] bund had been repaired
(*Daily Chron.* March 26, 1917).

Bundesrat [*hist.*]. Federal council of Ger. empire. From *bund*, league (see *bind*), *rat*, council (see *riddle*).

bundle. From *bind*; cf. Ger. *bündel*. With to *bundle off* cf. similar use of *pack*.

bung. Obs. Du. *bonghe*, from F. *bonde*, of Ger. origin; cf. Ger. dial. *punt*, *bunte*, prob. L. *puncta*, and Ger. *spund*, L. *ex-puncta* (see *spontoon*). Hence to *bung up*, and *bung*, publican.

bungalow. Hind. adj. *bangla*, belonging to Bengal. For *-u-* cf. *pundit*.

bungle. ?Combined from *boggle* and obs. *bumble* (see *bumble-puppy*).

bunion. Properly a corn on the ball of the great toe. ?It. *bugnone*, "a push, a bile, a blane, a botch" (Flor.), augment. of *bugno*; cf. OF. *bugne*, swelling, of unknown origin, whence app. ME. *bunny*, watery swelling. But the sense suggests rather F. *bouillon*, "a lump or excrescency of flesh that grows either upon or just by the frush (see *frog*[2])...and makes the horse halt" (*Gent. Dict.* 1705), which was in E. vet. use. The change of *-l-* to *-n-* is easily paralleled (see *banister, mullion*). For the etym. of the F. word see *bullion*.

bunk. Sleeping-berth. Perh. Du. *bank*, bench. For vowel change cf. *bulkhead*. ?Hence to *bunk*, abscond (?by sea).

bunker [*Sc.*]. Orig. seat. Then, earthen outdoor seat, hollow in sand-hills, receptacle for coal. Origin unknown. Norw. Dan. *bunke* means heap, cargo, earlier also hold of ship.

> They sat cosily niched into what you might call a bunker, a little sand-pit (*Redgauntlet*, ch. x.).

bunkum, buncombe. *Buncombe* is a county in N. Carolina, the member for which once insisted, towards the end of a wearisome debate in Congress, on "making a speech for Buncombe," i.e. showing his constituents that he was doing something for them.

> All over America, every place likes to hear of its member of Congress and see their speeches; and if they don't, they send a piece to the paper, inquirin' if their member's died a natural death, or was skivered with a bowie knife, for they hante seen his speeches lately, and his friends are anxious to know his fate. Our free and enlightened citizens don't approbate silent members....So every feller, in bounden duty, talks, and talks big too, and the smaller the state, the louder, bigger, and fiercer its members talk. Well, when a crittur talks for talk sake, jist to have a speech in the paper to send to home, and not for any other airthly puppus but electioneering, our folks call it "Bunkum"
>   (Judge Haliburton).

bunny. See *bun²*. Hence *bunny-hug*, with which cf. *turkey-trot*.

bunsen. Burner, etc. Invented (1855) by *Prof. Bunsen*, of Heidelberg.

bunt. "Belly" of a sail, pouch of a net. ?Corrupt. of Sw. *bugt*, bend, bulge, cogn. with *bow²*.

bunter [*geol.*]. Ger. *bunter sandstein*, variegated sandstone.

bunting¹. Bird. ME. *bountyng*. This was a female font-name in ME. (*Bontyng the brewster*, in the *Coventry plays*) and is one origin of the surname *Bunting*. App. this is for earlier *Bonneton* (*Alice Bunetun*, in the *Hund. R.*, 1273), which is a double dim. of F. *bon*, as in the F. surname *Bonneton*. It may be that this was a pet name for the bird (cf. *robin*), as also for a child in *Baby bunting*. In the old play *Respublica* (1553) Avarice calls his plumply filled purses his *buntings*.

bunting². Flag material. Perh. from obs. *bunt*, to sift. Cf. F. *étamine*, which means both "bunting" and cloth used for sifting or "bolting" flour, etc.

> *étamine*: buntine, the woollen stuff of which the ships colours are made (Lesc.).

bunyip [*Austral.*]. Native name for fabulous water-monster, hence impostor.

buoy. Du. *boei* or OF. *boie* (now replaced by *bouée*), with forms in most Europ. langs., L. *boia*, chain, fetter (by which the buoy was secured), which some would connect with the tribal name *Boii*. See *bilboes*. But some regard the *buoy* word-group as belonging rather to the Teut. root of *beacon*, which is quite possible.

> *boy of an ancre*: boyee (Palsg.).

bur, burr. ME. *borre, burre*; cf. Dan. *borre*, bur, Sw. *kard-borre*, burdock, the latter a compd. of *bur* (see *dock¹*). By some considered Teut., by others connected with F. *bourre*, shaggy substance, bristles on plants, etc., L. *burra*, rough wool (see *burl, burgeon*). In the sense of north country accent it perhaps comes from the idea of a *bur* in the throat, a phrase occurring in *Piers Plowm*. *Burr*, rough edge, as in the dentist's *burr-drill*, and *burr*, whetstone, clinker, etc., may be the same word, from the idea of roughness.

burberry. Overcoat. Maker's name (20 cent.). Cf. *mackintosh*.

> If she [Spring] is a virgin wise as well as beautiful, she will have a burberry over her arm
>   (*Sunday Times*, Mar. 30, 1919).

burble. To confuse, also to babble, talk nonsense. Cf. obs. *burble*, to bubble (with parallels in Rom. langs.), and obs. Sc. *barbulye*, to muddle, F. *barbouiller*, "to jumble, confound, muddle" (Cotg.). All of imit. origin. Cf. Serb. *brbljati*, to chatter.

burbot. Fish. F. *barbote, bourbotte*, from *barboter*, to flounder, from *bourbe*, mud; but the first form is perh. rather connected with *barbe*, beard, the *burbot* being a bearded fish (cf. *barbel*).

burden¹, burthen. AS. *byrthen*, from *bear²*; cf. OSax. *burthinnia*, OHG. *burdin* (*bürde*), ON. *byrthr*, Goth. *baurthei*. For usual mod. form cf. *murder*, which has prevailed, and *furder*, which has not.

burden². Of a song. F. *bourdon*; cf. It. *bordone*, Sp. *bordon*. Prob. imit.; cf. Late L. *burdo*, drone bee. Fanciful attempts have been made to connect these words with F. *bourdon*, It. *bordone*, pilgrim's staff, perh. from Late L. *burdo-n-*, mule.

> *bourdon*: a drone, or dorre-bee; also, the humming, or buzzing of bees; also, the drone of a bag-pipe...; also, a pilgrims staffe (Cotg.).

burdock. See *bur*.

bureau. F., office, the earliest sense (18 cent.) in E. (cf. *bureaucracy*), earlier, desk, and orig. cloth covering desk (cf. *sur le tapis*). OF. *burel*, a coarse cloth, whence ME. *borel, burel*, homespun, is dim. of *bure*, supposed to be from G. πυρρός, fiery, tawny. Cf. L. name *Burrus* for G. Πυρρός. L. *burra*, shaggy wool, has also been suggested (see *burlesque*). *Bureaucracy* is adapted from F. *bureaucratie*, coined by the economist Gournay (†1759).

bureau: a thicke and course cloath, of a browne russet, or darke mingled, colour; also, the table thats within a court of audit, or of audience (belike, because 'tis usually covered with a carpet of that cloath), also, the court it selfe (Cotg.).

burette. Small graduated glass measure. F., cruet bottle, dim. of *buire*, vessel, of doubtful origin.

burgage [*hist.*]. Mode of tenure. MedL. *burgagium*, from *borough* (q.v.).

burgee. Yacht flag, orig. owner's flag. Formed (like *Chinee, marquee*, etc.) from OF. *burgeis* (*bourgeois*), a name once applied to the owner of a vessel. So also we find *burgee's caution* (1653) for F. *caution bourgeoise*, sound security. The word is much older than *NED.* records, being found, with spec. sense of owner's flag, in an Amer. newspaper of 1750. Both uses of *bourgeois* are in Cotg.

bourgeois: the proprietor or owner of a ship (Falc.).

burgeon [*poet.*]. Bud. F. *bourgeon*, of doubtful origin, perh. VL. *burrio-n-*, from *burra*, rough wool. See *bur*.

burgess. Norm. form of F. *bourgeois*, Late L. *burgensis*, from Late L. *burgus* (2 cent.). See *borough*.

burgh. Var. of *borough* (q.v.), preserved in Sc.

burgher. Du. *burger*, citizen (see *borough*). In Shaks. (*Merch. of Ven.* i. 1), but now spec. applied to the Boers, also to descendants of Du. settlers in Ceylon.

burglar. Cf. AL. *burglator* (13 cent.), prob. altered, on L. *latro*, thief (whence OF. *lere, laron*), from *burgator*. Earliest (c. 1200) is AL. *burgaria*, burglary, which looks like an adj. formed from *burg*, dwelling (see *borough*), qualifying some word understood, e.g. *felonia*.

burgomaster. From Du. *burgemeester*, borough master; cf. Ger. *bürgermeister*, earlier *bürgemeister*.

burgonet [*hist.*]. Helmet, as worn by Ironsides. F. *bourguignotte*, of Burgundy. Also adopted in It. and Sp.

borghinetta: a burganet, a skull, a caske (Flor.).

burgoo. Sailors' gruel, etc., loblolly, also *burgle, burgee*. ?Arab. *burghul*, wheat dried and boiled. Earlier than dict. records is *burgoût* (1743), prob. an artificial spelling.

burgrave [*hist.*]. Ger. *burggraf*, castle count. Cf. *landgrave, margrave*, and F. *châtelain*.

burgundy. Wine. The province is MedL. *Burgundia* (whence F. *Bourgogne*), from the *Burgunds*, a German tribe. Cf. *champagne*.

At the Rose on Sunday
I'll treat you with Burgundy (Swift).

burial. False sing. (after *betrothal, espousal*, etc.) from ME. *buriels*, AS. *byrgels*, tomb, formed, with suffix as in OSax. *burgisli*, from *byrgen*, cogn. with *beorgan*, to cover, hide.

Buridan, ass of. An ass equidistant between two bundles of hay as experiment in free will. From *Buridan*, 14 cent. F. philosopher.

burin. Graver. F.; cf. It. *borino*, Sp. *buril*. ?From OHG. *boro*, borer.

In vain had Whistler and Muirhead Bone taken the burin in hand (E. V. Lucas, *Mr Ingleside*).

burke. To stifle. *Burke* (executed at Edinburgh 1829) and Hare killed people in order to sell their bodies for dissection. The verb came into existence the same year. Cf. the less common to *bishop*, from one *Bishop*, who drowned a boy at Bethnal Green (1836) with a similar object.

I burk'd the papa, now I'll bishop the son
(*Ingoldsby*).

burl [*techn.*]. To dress cloth, removing the "burls." OF. *bourle*, dim. of *bourre*. See *bur, burgeon*. Sp. *borla* means both bur and burl.

burlap [*archaic*]. Coarse canvas. Compd. of *lap* (q.v.), clout, flap, etc. First element may be *boor*. Cf. *wraprascal*, a red cloak (Grose).

burlesque. F., It. *burlesco*, from *burla*, jest, mockery, perh. ult. from L. *burra*, flock of wool, and fig. nonsense (Ausonius). Cf. hist. of *bombast, fustian*, etc. But VL. *burrula* should have given -o-, as in Sp. *borla*, tassel.

burletta. Farce. It., dim. of *burla* (v.s.).

burly. Orig. stately, massive, etc. Northern form of ME. *borlich*. Not found in AS. or ON., but cf. OHG. *burlīh*, lofty, from *burjan*, to lift up.

burn¹. Stream. AS. *burne, burna*. Com. Teut.; cf. Du. *born*, Ger. *born* (poet.), *brunnen*, ON. *brunnr*, Goth. *brunna*; prob. cogn. with *burn*[2] (cf. *torrent*).

burn[2]. Verb. AS. *bærnan* (weak trans.), causal of *biernan* (strong intrans.). Com. Teut.; cf. OSax. OHG. ON. Goth. *brinnan* (intrans.), OSax. OHG. *brennian* (*brennen*), ON. *brenna*, Goth. *brannjan* (trans.). To *burn one's boats*, leave oneself no retreat, is an allusion to Cortez, or perh. to earlier adventurers. With *burning shame* (*disgrace*, etc.) cf. *flagrant*.

burnet. Plant. OF. *burnete*, *brunete*, dim. of *brun*, brown.

burnish. F. *brunir*, *bruniss-*, OF. also *burnir*, from *brun*, brown, also bright. See *brown*.

burnous. Arab cloak. F., Arab. *burnus*. Cf. Sp. *albornuz*. Purch. has *barnuche*.

burr. See *bur*.

burro [*US.*]. Donkey. Sp., app. back-formation from *borrico*, L. *burricus*, small shaggy horse, prob. cogn. with *burrus*, reddish-brown (see *bureau* and cf. *Dan Burnel the ass* in Chauc.); cf. F. *bourrique*, donkey.

burrow. Var. of *borough* (q.v.) with differentiated sense.

Foxes han dichis, or borowis (Wyc. *Matt.* viii. 20).

bursar. MedL. *bursarius*, purse-bearer. See *purse*, for which *burse* is still used in certain techn. senses.

burst. AS. *berstan*. In ME. *bresten* is common. Com. Teut.; cf. Du. *berstan*, Ger. *bersten*, ON. *bresta*. Orig. strong with p.p. *bursten*, still in occ. use.

burthen. See *burden*[1].

bury[1]. Verb. AS. *byrgan*. See *burial*.

bury[2]. In place-names. See *borough*.

bus. For *omnibus* (q.v.). Mod. mil. slang for aeroplane.

busby. Hussar fur head-dress (19 cent.), large bushy wig (18 cent.). Prob. from surname *Busby*.

bush[1]. Thicket, etc. ME. *bush*, *busk*, ON. *buskr*; not found in AS.; cf. Du. *bosch*, Ger. *busch*, also Late L. *boscus*, F. *bois*, It. *bosco*. Earlier hist. uncertain, perh. orig. pasture-land, from G. βόσκειν, to feed cattle. In the colonies *bush* is usu. from Du. *bosch*, as applied by early settlers from Holland. So also *Bushman*, SAfr. tribe. The first *bushrangers* (c. 1800) were escaped convicts. *Bushwhacker* (US.) is prob. corrupted from Du. *boschwachter*, forest watcher, woodman. *Good wine needs no bush* alludes to the ivy-bush once used as tavern-sign.

à bon vin il ne faut point d'enseigne: good wine drawes customers without any help of an ivy-bush (Cotg.).

bush[2]. Axle-box. Du. *bus*, box (q.v.). Cf. *arquebus*, *blunderbuss*, which have earlier forms in -*bush*.

bushel. OF. *boissel* (*boisseau*), dim. of *boiste* (*boîte*), VL. **buxida*. See *box*, *pyx*.

No man lightneth a lanterne, and puttith it in hidlis, other undir a boyschel (Wyc. *Luke*, xi. 33).

business. See *busy*.

busk[1], **bust**. These are the same word, a *busk* being a support for the *bust*, the latter orig. meaning a torso, a body *without* a head. Origin uncertain, but the analogy of It. *torso* (q.v.), *fusto*, *tronco*, all used in same sense, "a bodie without a head" (Flor.), suggests identity with Prov. *bust*, tree-trunk, of unknown origin. The form *busk*, with differentiation of sense, is F. *busc*, It. *busco*.

busto: a trunke, a bodie without a head, a trusse. Also a womans buske (Flor.).

busq: a buske; or buste (Cotg.).

busk[2] [*Sc. & north*]. To prepare. ON. *būask*, from *būa*, to prepare, with reflex. pron. *sik* (cf. *bask*). Hence construction below is pleon.

Busk thee, busk thee, my bonnie bride
                          (*Braes of Yarrow*).

buskin. Metath. of *buck-skin* (sc. *shoes*). The various continental words usu. mentioned as possible origins of *buskin* (c. 1500) are quite unconnected. Cf. mod. *buckskins*, breeches, or *cowhide*, whip.

My lord paied to his cordwaner [i.e. shoemaker] for a payr bucskyns xviiid (*NED.* 1481–90).

buss[1]. Vessel, esp. *herring-buss*. Cf. AS. *butse*, in *butsecarl*, sailor, OF. *busse*, Du. *buis*, OHG. *būzo*, ON. *būza*. Origin unknown.

buysse: heering-buss or bark (Hexham).

Out and away aboard a ship among the buscarles
                          (Kingsley, *Hereward*).

buss[2] [*dial.*]. Kiss. Replaces earlier *bass*, F. *baiser*, L. *basiare*. But may be quite a separate word; cf. Ger. dial. *buss*, Sp. *buz*, Gael. *bus*, orig. mouth (cf. L. *osculum*, little mouth, kiss).

Thy knees bussing the stones (*Cor.* iii. 2).

bust[1]. Of body. See *busk*[1].

bust[2]. Vulgar for *burst* (cf. *fust* for *first*), esp. in *bust up* (orig. US.).

bustard. From 15 cent. in *NED.*, but occurs as surname temp. John. OF. has *bistarde*, *oustarde* (*outarde*), both app. from L. *avis* *tarda* (Pliny), with cognates in other Rom. langs. Cf. *ostrich*. But the L. name is prob. folk-etym. for some other name, the bustard being really very swift. ? Ult. from G. ὠτίς, ὠτίδ-, bustard.

bustle¹. Tumult, etc. Prob. altered from obs. *buskle*, to make hurried preparations, frequent. of *busk²* (q.v.).

bustle². Article of dress. Late 18 cent. Prob. Ger. *büschel*, bunch, pad, dim. of *bausch*, pad, bolster, etc. It occurs as *bustler* (US. 1787) and is referred to the visit of a Ger. duchess to London in 1783.

busy. ME. *bisi*, AS. *bysig*. Only known cogn. is Du. *bezig*. Origin unknown. ?From *bee*; cf. Ger. *emsig*, busy, prob. ant-like (see *ant*). Mod. spelling, from 15 cent., seems to be due to AF. *busoignes* (F. *besognes*), regarded by early etymologists as the origin of *business*, and representing it regularly in AF. texts. This AF. *-u-* for F. *-e-* is due to influence of labial *b-*.

Lez assisez, plees, et juggementz hustengals, et autres busoignez de la dite citee
(*Liber Albus*, p. 308).

but. First as prep. AS. *būtan, bi ūtan*, outside. Cf. Sc. *butt the house* (see *ben¹*) and E. *nobody but me* (Ger. *ausser mir*), all *but*. For formation cf. *beyond*, and see *above*.

butcher. F. *boucher*, from *bouc*, goat. Cf. It. *beccaio*, butcher, from *becco*, goat. See *buck¹*.

butler. Norm. form of OF. *bouteillier*, bottler. Cf. *buckler*, both words illustrating two Norm. features, viz. *u* for OF. *o, ou*, and *-er* for *-ier*.

butt¹. Flat fish, as in *halibut* (q.v.), *turbot*. Cf. Sw. *butta*, LG. *butte*, Du. *bot*, "flounder" (Sewel). Origin unknown, perh. thick, stumpy; see *butt³*.

butt². Cask. F. *botte*; cf. It. *botte*, Sp. Port. *bota*. Also in Teut. langs., e.g. OHG. *butin*, AS. *bytt*, whence obs. *bit*, in same senses (cask, wineskin), MedL. *butis, buttis, butina*. Ult. from G. πυτίνη, wine-flask. See also *bottle¹*.

butt³. Thick end. Cf. ON. *būtr*, log, Du. *bot*, blunt, stump, whence F. *pied-bot*, club foot. Prob. not related to F. *bout*, end.

butt⁴. Boundary, target. F. *but*, end, aim, parallel form to *bout*, end. Partly also from fem. form *butte*, mound, as in *butte de Montmartre, rifle butts*. See *abut*. The *NED.* recognizes thirteen nouns *butt*, and, as in the case of many monosyllables (cf. *bob*), their classification and hist. are very complicated.

butt⁵. Verb. F. *bouter*, to thrust, push. Of Teut. origin; cf. OHG. *bōzan*, to beat. To *butt in* is US.

butt⁶ [*Sc.*]. See *ben¹, but*.

butte [*geog.*]. Small *mesa* (q.v.). F., mound. Cf. *butt⁴*.

butter. AS. *butere*, an early L. loan-word, found in other Teut. langs. (cf. *cheese*), L. *butyrum*, G. βούτυρον, regarded as from βοῦς, ox, cow, τυρός, cheese, but prob. folk-etym. for some word borrowed from the Scythians or other nomad tribe. For another case of G. folk-etym. see *squirrel*. The native E. name was *smeoru* (smear). *Buttercup* is for older *butterflower* (cf. Ger. *butterblume*) and *king-cup*.

butterbump. See *bittern*.

butterfly. AS. *buterflēoge*; cf. Du. *botervlieg*, Ger. dial. *butterfliege, buttervogel*, also *milchdieb, molkendieb* (usual Ger. is *schmetterling*, from dial. *schmetten*, cream). These names prob. all go back to some forgotten piece of folk-lore, or they may refer simply to the colour of the commonest varieties.

butterscotch. From 19 cent. Also *butterscot*. ?Of Scotch manufacture.

buttery. ME. *boterie, botelrie*, OF. *boterie, boteillerie*. The first might be from *butt²*, but the second and MedL. *botelleria* point to *bottle¹*. For extension of meaning cf. *larder, pantry*. Cf. *butler*.

buttock. App. dim. of *butt³*, though recorded much earlier. Cf. seniority of *bullock* to *bull¹*. For sense-development cf. Sc. *doup*, end, podex, and E. dial. *end*, podex.

button. F. *bouton*, orig. bud. Prob., like *bout*, end, from *bouter*, to thrust (see *butt⁵*). To *buttonhole*, keep in conversation, is altered from the earlier, and more logical, *buttonhold*.

buttress. OF. *bouterez*, pl. of *bouteret*, a support, from *bouter*, to thrust, prop, etc. Cf. F. *arc-boutant*, flying buttress, lit. propping arch. For pl. form cf. *quince, truce*, etc.

butty [*loc.*]. Middleman in coal-mining. Earlier sense, confederate, sharer. For *booty* (q.v.).

botyfelowe: parsomner [*read* parsonnier, i.e. partner]
(Palsg.).

butyric. Of butter (q.v.).

buxom. Orig. obedient; hence, cheerful, of cheerful aspect, etc. ME. *buhsam*, from AS. *būgan*, to bow; cf. Du. *buigzaam*, Ger. *biegsam*. With application to physique cf. *lusty*.

buxum: clemens, propicius, flexibilis, flexuosus, paciens, obidiens, pronus (*Cath. Angl.*).

buy. ME. *bien*, also *beg-*, *big-*, *bug-*, AS. *bycgan*; cf. OSax. *buggian*, Goth. *bugjan*. Origin unknown. See *abide*.

buzz[1]. Sound. Imit.

buzz[2] [*archaic*]. Wig. Short for *busby* (q.v.).

buzzard. Inferior hawk; hence, dullard. OF. *busard*, from *buse*, L. *buteo* (Pliny).

by. Earliest as adv., as in to *put by, stand by!* AS. *bī* (stressed), *be* (unstressed); cf. Du. *bij*, Ger. *bei*, Goth. *bi*; said to be cogn. with G. ἀμφί, L. *am-bi*. With its force in *by-product, byway, by-election*, etc. cf. Ger. *neben* in *nebenprodukt*, etc. So also a *bye* (golf, tennis, etc.), as opposed to a full game. *By-law, bye-law*, now usu. understood as subsidiary law, orig. meant township-law, from ME. *bi* as in *Derby, Whitby*, etc., ON. *bȳr*. We also find *byrlaw*, where the first syllable represents the ON. gen. With *by and by* cf. Ger. *nach und nach*, gradually, but the changed meaning (cf. *anon, presently*) shows man's procrastinating nature. In *by the by* we have the noun *by, bye*, side-way, subsidiary matter, which has developed from the prep. *By and large*, now often fig., is naut., to the wind and off it.

The end is not by and by [εὐθέως] (*Luke*, xxi. 9).

bye. Noun. In various sporting senses. Subst. use of *by* (q.v.).

bye-bye. Baby redupl.; cf. *lullaby, hushaby, bye baby bunting*. Also playfully for *good-bye* (q.v.).

by-law, bye-land. See *by*.

byre. AS. *bȳre*, cattle-stall, cogn. with *bower*[1] (q.v.). Not from ON. *bȳr*, in which the inflexional *-r* disappeared, giving ME. *bi* (see *by*). Both words are however from the same root, and cogn. with *boor*.

byrnie [*poet.*]. Revived by mod. poets from ME. *brinie*, coat of mail, ON. *brynja*; cf. OF. *bronie, broigne*, the stock name for armour in OF. epic, from Teut. ?Cogn. with *brown*.

byssus. Fine fabric. L., G. βύσσος, Heb. *būts* (rendered "fine linen" in *AV.*), Arab. *būts*, to be very white.

byword. AS. *bī-word*, translating L. *proverbium* or G. παρα-βολή. Cf. *gospel*.

Byzantine. Of *Byzantium*, Constantinople. Formerly used for *besant* (q.v.). As term of art, history, etc., it is mod. Of late (1916) *Byzantinism* has also been used of tyrannical rule by moral degenerates, like some of the later emperors.

c-. Some words of foreign origin not included here may be found under *k-*.

C 3. Lowest physical grading for army purposes (Great War).

You cannot maintain an A 1 empire on a C 3 population (D. Lloyd George, Sep. 12, 1918).

Caaba. Moslem "holy of holies" at Mecca, containing the "black stone." Arab. *ka'abah*, cubical house.

cab[1]. Heb. dry measure (2 *Kings*, vi. 25). Heb. *qab*, hollowed out.

cab[2]. Short for *cabriolet* (q.v.). Not orig. limited to public vehicles.

"You had better take Tom's cab" quoth the squire (*Ingoldsby*).

cab[3] [*school slang*]. To crib. Short for *cabbage*[2] (q.v.).

cabal. Earlier *cabbala*, MedL. (whence F. *cabale*, It. Sp. Port. *cabala*), Heb. *qabbālāh*, tradition. Mystical interpretation of *OT.*, hence, mystery, secret intrigue, etc. Applied by Pepys to the junto of the Privy Council (1665), i.e. some years before the nicknaming of the 1672 ministry (Clifford, Arlington, Buckingham, Ashley, Lauderdale), whose names happened to fit it. *Cabala* occurs 1521, *cabal* 1616, and "Cabala, Mysteries of State" was published in 1654.

caballero. Sp., gentleman, knight. See *cavalier, chevalier*.

cabana. Cigar. Name of Sp. exporters.

cabaret. Southern F., of unknown origin. L. *caput arietis*, ram's head (as sign), has been suggested, and has some sort of parallel in E. *hogshead*.

cabbage[1]. Vegetable. F. *caboche*, head (chump), which also means cabbage in Channel Islands, It. *capocchia*, augment. of *capo*, head, L. *caput*. Cf. Du. *kabuiskool*, cabbage cole. Has almost replaced earlier *cole, kale*.

cabbage[2]. Shreds and remnants appropriated by tailor as perquisite; hence, to pilfer. Cf. OF. *cabasser*, to steal, from *cabas*, theft, lit. *basket*, Prov., ?from L. *capax, capac-*, holding. Cf. to *bag*.

cabbala. See *cabal*.

caber [*Sc.*]. For tossing. Gael. *cabar*, pole, rafter. Not Gael., but from VL. **capro-n-*, rafter (see *chevron*), from *capra*, goat. Cf. *crane, easel*, etc., also Prov. *cabrioun*, joist.

cabin. F. *cabane*, Late L. *capanna*, hut, of doubtful origin (also Late L. *canaba, canapa*). ModF. *cabine* (of ship) is borrowed back from E. To *cabin*, confine, is an echo of *Macb.* iii. 4.

Hoc [tugurium] rustici "capanna" vocant (Isidore).
Thi seetis of rowers...and thi litil cabans
(Wyc. *Ezek.* xxvii. 6).

cabinet. Dim. of *cabin.* Orig. small hut, den, etc. Mod. pol. use (E. only) comes from *cabanett councelles* (Bacon, c. 1610), i.e. the inner group of the Privy Council meeting in a *cabinet*, private room. *Cabinet edition* (*photograph*, etc.) means of style and size fit for a *cabinet*, or room for display of valuable objects. Hence sense of elaborate case, and trade of *cabinet-maker*.

We are never ready for war, and yet we never have a Cabinet that dare tell the people this truth
(Lord Wolseley).

cable. F. *câble*; cf. It. *cappio*, Sp. *cable*; also Du. Ger. *kabel* (from some Rom. lang.). Late L. *capulum, caplum*, halter, app. from *capere*, to seize. With hybrid *cablegram* cf. the still more barbarous *marconigram*.

Charlie Chaplin...has cablegraphically contributed 30,000 pounds sterling to the new war loan
(*Daily Gleaner*, Kingston, Jamaica, Feb. 26, 1917).

cabob. Meat on skewers. Arab. *kabāb.*

caboched [*her.*]. Head (of deer, bull, etc.) cut off close behind the ears. From F. *caboche*, head (see *cabbage*[1]).

cabochon. Precious stone cut without facets, F. (v.s.).

caboodle [*US.*]. Usu. with *whole*. Some writers have *whole kit and boodle* in same sense. Prob. cow-boy word. ? Port. *cabedal*, "a stock, what a man is worth" (Vieyra), ident. with *capital*[3], influenced by *boodle* (q.v.).

caboose. Kitchen of small merchant ship. Du. *kabuis, kombuis*, earlier *cabuse, combuse*, LG. *kabhuse*, which suggests connection with *cabin* and *house* (?cf. *cuddy*); but the hist. is obscure. Falc. and Lesc. both describe it as a kind of cowl, so it may be cogn. with *capote, capuchin*.

coboose: couverture des cheminées des cuisines dans les vaisseaux marchands (Lesc.).

cabotage [*naut.*]. Coasting trade. F., ?from Prov. *cap* or Sp. *cabo*, as going from cape to cape.

cabriolet. F., from *cabriole, capriole*, leap as of a goat, It. *capriola*, from L. *caper*, goat. See *cab*[2].

Cabriolets are about to be established in London as public conveyances at a fare one half the price of hackney-coaches (*Times*, Apr. 15, 1823).

caçador [*mil.*]. Port., lit. hunter, chaser. For mil. use cf. F. *chasseur*, Ger. *jäger*.

ca' canny. To work slowly, so as to leave plenty for others to do. Recent application of Sc. *ca' canny*, drive gently (Galt), from Sc. *ca*, to drive cattle, with which cf. Norw. *kaue*, cry of summons to cattle.

Ca' the yowes to the knowes (*Sc. song*).
Willing workers, free from the blight of ca' canny
(*Daily Chron.* Dec. 23, 1916).

cacao. Earlier and correct form of *cocoa*, still used in F. & G. Sp., orig. a wrong division of Mex. *caca-uatl*, cocoa-tree.

cachalot. Sperm-whale. F., from dial. of Bayonne (17 cent.), and now in most Europ. langs. Perh. "toothed," from Gasc. *cachau*, tooth, with many vars. in dials. of S. France. Another plausible conjecture is L. *cacabus*, pot, which has Rom. derivatives meaning pot, skull, etc. The two characteristics of the sperm-whale are its teeth and cranial reservoir. A third suggestion, supported by synon. Catalan *cap-gros*, connects it with Port. *cachola*, head, "chump."

cache. Hiding-place for treasure, stores, etc. F., from *cacher*, to hide. ? VL. *coacticare*, for *cogere* (*co-agere*), to force together. A 19 cent. word from French Canadian trappers, but used once by Drake.

cachet. F., stamp, "sign manual," from *cacher*, in obs. sense of pressing. See *cache.*

cachexy [*med.*]. Morbid condition. F. *cachexie*, G. καχεξία, from κακός, bad, ἕξις, state, from ἔχειν, to have. Cf. *malady*.

cachinnation. From L. *cachinnare*, to laugh, of imit. origin.

cachou. For smokers. F. form of *catechu* (q.v.).

cachucha. Dance. Sp.

A court where it's thought in a lord or a duke a
Disgrace to fall short in the brawls (their cachouca)
(*Ingoldsby*).

cacique. Sp., "a prince of the Indians" (Percyvall), ? from Haytian word for chief.

cack-handed [*slang*]. Left-handed, clumsy. ? Connected with dial. *cack*, stercorare, L. *cacare*.

cackle. Imit., cf. Du. *kakelen*, Ger. *gackeln*, F. *caqueter*.

Cut the cackle and come to the 'osses (Anon.).

cacoethes. Usu. with *scribendi* (Juvenal, *Sat.* vii. 52). G. κακοήθης, bad habit, itch, from κακός, bad, ἦθος, character. Cf. *ethic*.

cacolet. Horse-litter for wounded. F. dial. word (Pyrenees), first employed in Crimean war. Cf. *ambulance*.

cacophony. G. κακοφωνία. Cf. *euphony*.

cactus. L., G. κάκτος.

cad. Shortened from *caddie, cadee,* pop. forms of *cadet*[1] (q.v.). Mod. sense of *cad* originated (19 cent.) at Eton and Oxf., as *snob* at Camb. Hence quot. 3 is a considerable anachronism. Earlier meaning was that of humble person prepared to run errands, also bus-conductor. *Caddie* (golf) is from Sc.

There is in Edinburgh a society or corporation of errand-boys, called "cawdies" (*Humphrey Clinker*).

cad: an omnibus conductor (Hotten).

These same day-boys were all "caddes," as we had discovered to call it (*Lorna Doone*).

cadastral. Relating to survey and valuation of property for taxation. From F. *cadastre,* It. *catast(r)o,* orig. (12 cent.) a Venet. word, *catastico,* Late G. κατάστιχον, list (see *cata-, acrostic*).

cadaverous. From L. *cadaver,* corpse, cogn. with *cadere,* to fall; cf. synon. G. πτῶμα, from πίπτειν, to fall.

caddie. See *cad.*

caddis, caddice. Larva of may-fly, etc., used esp. as bait in angling. Earliest as *cadisworm* (17 cent.). Perh. from archaic or obs. *caddis, caddice* (15 cent.), a loose material, also worsted yarn. OF. *cadarce,* Prov. *cadarz* (cf. It. *catarzo,* Sp. *cadarzo*), G. ἀκάθαρτος, uncleansed.

caddy. Earlier *catty* (16 cent.), Malay *kāti,* weight slightly over a pound.

cade[1] [*loc.*]. Cask for herrings. F., L. *cadus,* wine-jar, G. κάδος. See *albatross.* With Shakspeare's etym. (2 *Hen. VI,* iv. 2) cf. quot. below.

The rebel Jack Cade was the first that devised to put red herrings in cades, and from him they have their name! (Nashe).

cade[2] [*dial.*]. Or *cade-lamb,* pet, or weak, lamb, reared by hand. Occ. of other animals. ? For *cadel-lamb*; cf. OF. *cadeler,* "to cocker, pamper, feedle, cherish, make much of" (Cotg.), this prob. from L. *catulus,* puppy, kitten.

It's ill bringing up a cade-lamb (*Adam Bede*).

cadence. F., It. *cadenza,* from L. *cadere,* to fall. Mus. sense is in Chauc. Her. *cadency* is app. associated with *cadet*[1].

cadet[1]. Younger son, junior officer. F., Gasc. *capdet,* youth of noble birth, dim. of *cap,* head. Earlier *caddie, cadee.*

Commissions are dear,
Yet I'll buy him one this year;
For he shall serve no longer a cadie
                    (Allan Ramsay).

cadet[2] [*pol.*]. Name of Russ. pol. party (now mostly massacred). An acrostic formation from *konstituciónnaya demokrátya* (K.D.), constitutional democracy. Cf. Russ. *eser,* socialistic reformer (S.R.).

cadge[1], **cadger.** Verb (c. 1607) is back-formation from noun (c. 1450). Cf. *beg, beggar.* Orig. pedlar, itinerant merchant, as still in Sc. and Ir. From F. *cage,* in sense of wicker basket carried on back of *cadger* or his pony. Immediate source prob. Du. (v.i.). See *cage.*

A cadgear, with capill [nag] and with creils [fishbaskets] (Henryson).

cagie: cavea, corbis dossuaria (Kil.).

cagiaerd: qui caveam aut corbem portat (*ib.*).

cadge[2]. Falconers' frame. See *cage.*

cadi. Arab. *qāḍī,* judge. Cf. *alcade, alcalde,* and Nigerian *alkali* (*Daily Chron.* Nov. 7, 1919).

Cadmean. From *Cadmus,* G. Κάδμος, legendary founder of Thebes and inventor of letters. With *Cadmean victory,* destructive to victor, cf. *Pyrrhic victory.*

cadmium [*chem.*]. Metal. Ult. from *Cadmus* (v.s.). See *calamine.*

cadre [*mil.*]. Detachment (orig. corps of officers) forming skeleton of regiment. F., lit. frame, It. *quadro,* L. *quadrus,* foursided. Cf. L. *cadran,* dial.

caduceus. Wand of Hermes (Mercury). L., from Doric form of G. κηρύκειον, from κῆρυξ, herald.

caducity. F. *caducité,* from *caduc,* infirm, L. *caducus,* from *cadere,* to fall.

caecum [*anat.*]. Blind gut. Neut. of L. *caecus,* blind (sc. *intestinum*). Cf. *rectum, duodenum.*

caerulean. See *cerulean.*

Caesar. Cognomen, ? meaning "hairy," of Caius Julius. Earliest L. word adopted in Teut. (see *kaiser, czar*). Hence *Caesarean birth,* by incision, due to fancied connection of name with *caedere, caes-,* to cut. With *Caesarism* cf. *Czarism, Kaiserism.*

caesium [*chem.*]. Metal. L., neut. of *caesius,* bluish-grey.

caestus. See *cestus.*

caesura [*metr.*]. L., from *caedere, caes-,* to cut.

café. F., coffee (q.v.).

caffeine. F. *caféine,* alkaloid from coffee.

Caffre. See *Kaffir.*

cafila. Caravan, in earlier sense. Arab. *qāfilah.*

The "caffolla" as they call them, which is the fleete of friggotts (Jourdain's *Journ.* 1611).

caftan. Garment. Turk. *qaftān*, also used in Pers.

cage. F., L. *cavea*, hollow. In 16 cent. also *cadge* (q.v.). Hence also *cadge*, frame on which hawks were carried, if this is not a ghost-word.

A pair of gerfalcons, in golden hoods, upon a golden cadge (Hewlett, *Song of Renny*).

cahier. F., as *quire* (q.v.).

caid, kaid. Arab. *qa'īd*, leader.

caiman. See *cayman*.

Cain, to raise. Orig. US., app. euph. for to *raise the devil*.

caïque. Boat. F., Turk. *kaik*. The F. form (Byron) has superseded earlier *caik*, etc.

Ça ira [*hist.*]. F., that will go. Refrain of Republican song (c. 1790).

cairn. Gael. *carn*, heap of stones, as in *Cairn-gorm*, blue mountain, whence precious stone.

caisson. F., from *caisse*, case² (q.v.).

caitiff [*archaic*]. ONF. *caitif* (*chétif*, wretched), L. *captivus*, from *capere, capt-*, to take.

Therfor lad caitif is my puple (Wyc. *Is.* v. 13).

cajole. F. *cajoler*, earlier sense of which was to chatter like a jay, from *gajole*, a southern dim. of *geai*, jay. In ModF. this has taken, by some vague association of form and sense, or perh. via the sense of talking over (cf. Ger. *beschwatzen*), the meaning of F. *enjôler*, etym. to *en-gaol*. See *gaol*. In 17 cent. referred to as new, "a low word" (Johns.).

engeoler: to attract, intice, allure, win, inveagle, besot, inthrall (by faire and deceitful lwords); also to incage, or ingaole (Cotg.).

cake. ON. *kaka*, whence Sw. *kaka*, Dan. *kage*; cogn. with Du. *koek*, Ger. *kuchen*, cake, but app. not with L. *coquere*, whence ult. Ger. *küche*, kitchen. Orig. a flat loaf, as in story of Alfred. Hence *Land o' cakes*, Scotland (17 cent.), at first with bantering allusion to oat-cakes. To *take the cake*, win the prize, appears to be earlier than *cake-walk*, a grotesque nigger dance lately introduced from US. The former may be a jocular allusion to G. πυραμοῦς, prize of victory, orig. cake of roasted wheat and honey awarded to person of greatest vigilance in night-watch.

Dost thou think, because thou art virtuous, there shall be no more cakes and ale? (*Twelfth Night*, ii. 3).

For rudeness to the Grand Old Man
Lord Randolph takes the cake
(*Topical Song*, c. 1882).

calabash. F. *calebasse*, Sp. *calabaza*, Pers. *kharbuz* or *kharbuza*, melon, ? cogn. with L. (*cu*)*curbita*, gourd.

calabaça: a gourd, a bottle of a gourd (Percyvall).

calaboose. Prison, esp. at New Orleans. Negro F., from Sp. *calabozo*, dungeon.

calaboço: a kind of prison, or place of execution, where condemned persons were cast downe headlong (Percyvall).

caladium. Plant. Latinized (1750) from Malay *kelādy*.

calamanco. Fabric, with checks on one side. Cf. F. *calmande*, Du. *kalamink*, Ger. *kalmank*. Origin unknown. Yule quotes (1676) s.v. *chintz*, "painted calicuts which they call *calmendar*, i.e. done with a pencil," which suggests Ind. origin.

Then the old man turn'd up, and a fresh bite of Sancho's
Tore out the whole seat of his striped calimancoes
(*Ingoldsby*).

calamander. Wood akin to ebony (India & Ceylon). Singhalese *kalimadīriya*, which is regarded by some as a corrupt. of *Coromandel*. ? Or from *calmendar* (v.s.), from grain.

calamary. Kind of cuttle-fish. L. *calamarius*, from *calamus*, reed, pen, perh. from pen-like internal shell.

calamine. Ore of zinc. F., MedL. *calamina* (cf. Ger. *kalmei*), prob. corrupted by alchemists from L. *cadmea*. See *cadmium*.

calamint. Herb. F. *calament*, L., G. καλαμίνθη, from καλός, beautiful, μίνθη, mint.

calamite. Fossil plant. ModL. *calamites*, from *calamus*, reed.

calamity. F. *calamité*, L. *calamitas*. Derived by early etymologists from *calamus*, stem (v.i.), but now regarded as related to an archaic L. word which appears in *in-columis*, safe.

The word "calamitas" was first derived from "calamus," when the corn could not get out of the stalke (Bacon).

calash [*archaic*]. Vehicle, woman's hood suggesting hood of same. F. *calèche*, Ger. *kalesch*, Bohem. *kolésa*, lit. wheeled carriage. Cf. Russ. *kolesó*, wheel.

Mrs Bute Crawley...in her clogs and calash
(*Vanity Fair*, ch. xxxix.).

calcareous. From L. *calcarius*, from *calx, calc-*, lime.

calceolaria. From L. *calceolus*, little shoe, dim. of *calceus*, from *calx, calc-*, heel. Also called *slipper-flower*.

calcine. MedL. *calcinare*, to reduce to lime, L. *calx*.

And in amalgamyng and calcenyng
Of quyk-silver, y-clept mercurie crude
(Chauc. G. 771).

calcium [*chem.*]. Named by Davy from L. *calx, calc-*, lime.

calculate. Replaced earlier *calcule* (*Piers Plowm.*), F. *calculer*, Late L. *calculare*, from *calculus*, pebble, dim. of *calx, calc-*, lime, used in elementary calculation.

The New Englander calculates, the Westerner reckons (Thornton).

calculus [*med. & math.*]. See *calculate*.

caldron. See *cauldron*.

Caledonia. L. (Tacitus), from Gael. *Dun-Callden*, fort of the Caledonians (cf. *Dunkeld*), from Gael. *coille*, wood.

calefaction. Heating. L. *calefactio-n-*, from *calēre*, to be hot, *facere*, to make.

calendar. OF. *calendier* (*calendrier*), L. *calendarium*, account-book noting the *calends*, first days of the month, prob. from *calare*, to proclaim. In early use also for register, list, esp. of canonized saints. *At the Greek calends*, i.e. never, is L. *ad calendas Graecas*.

calender[1]. To smooth cloth, etc. F. *calandrer*, from MedL. *calendra*, prob. from G. κύλινδρος, cylinder, roller. Hence John Gilpin's "good friend the calender," for *calenderer*.

calender[2]. Mendicant dervish (*Arabian Nights*), described by Mr Pecksniff as a "one-eyed almanack." Pers. *qalandar*, of unknown origin.

calends. See *calendar*.

calenture [*WInd.*]. Fever. F., Sp. *calentura*, fever, from *calentar*, to be hot, from L. *calēre*.

calf. AS. *cealf*. Com. Teut.; cf. Du. *kalf*, Ger. *kalb*, ON. *kálfr*, Goth. *kalbō* (f.). Fig. small island lying near larger, e.g. *Calf of Man*, also detached iceberg, both from ON. use. The *calf of the leg*, ON. *kalfi*, may be related (cf. history of *muscle*).

hic musculus: thè calfe of the lege (*Voc.*).

Caliban. Prob. suggested to Shaks. by *cannibal* or *Carib*, as *Setebos* from the Patagonian devil mentioned by Magellan.

A beastly sort of baptist Caliban (*Daniel Deronda*).

calibre. Also *caliver*, musket (hist.), *calliper*, compasses, used for measuring calibres and projectiles. All three appear in E. in 16 cent. and seem to have been at once differentiated in form and meaning. Cf. F. *calibre*, It. *calibro*, OSp. *calibo*. ? Arab.

qālib, mould for casting metal, which would suggest the OSp. form as earliest in Europe. This etym. dates from Ménage. Cotg. has *qualibre*, suggesting L. *qua libra*, and Jal quotes, without ref., an earlier *équalibre*, which, if genuine, disposes of the Arab. origin and points to MedL. **aequalibrare*, for *aequilibrare*, suiting both sound and sense.

calibro: an instrument that gunners use to measure the height of any piece or bullet. Also the height or bore of any piece, from whence our word caliver is derived; being at first a piece different from others (Flor. 1611).

Caliburn. See *Excalibur*.

calico. Substituted (16 cent.) for *calicut*, from *Calicut* (India), whence shipped. Port. form of Arab. *Qālicūt*.

caligraphy. See *calligraphy*.

calipash, calipee. Orig. upper and lower shell of turtle; now, gelatinous substance contiguous to each. As the words are WInd., *calipash* may be a negro corrupt. of *carapace*, orig. the upper shell, and *calipee* an arbitrary variation. But the odd form below (with which cf. Sp. *galapago*, turtle) is much earlier than dict. records of E. *calipash* and F. *carapace*, and may represent a sailors' perversion of some native original.

The upper part of them is covered with a great shell, which wee call a "galley patch"
(Norwood's *Bermudas*, in Purch. xix. 190).

calipers. See *calibre*.

caliph, calif. F. *calife*, Arab. *khalīfa*, successor, orig. Abu-bekr, after death of Mahomet. Cf. the Sudan *khalifa*, who succeeded the Mahdi.

calisthenics. See *callisthenics*.

caliver. See *calibre*.

calix, calyx. Distinct (but cogn.) words, though now usu. confused by writers on botany. For *calix* see *chalice*. *Calyx* is G. κάλυξ, outer covering pod, from root of καλύπτειν, to conceal (cf. *apocalypse*). The same confusion is found in other langs., e.g. Ger. *kelch*, Norw. *kalk* have both senses.

calk[1]. See *caulk*.

calk[2] [*neol.*]. To trace in drawing. F. *calquer*, It., L. *calcare*, to tread, from *calx*, heel.

calkin. Turned edge of horse-shoes, to prevent slipping. OF. *calcain, cauquain, chauchein*, heel, Late L. *calcaneum*, from *calx*, heel.

call. ME. *callen* (north.), ON. *kalla*, to cry loudly. Com. Teut.; cf. Du. *kallen*, to chatter, OHG. *challōn*, to talk noisily. *Calling*, vocation, starts from 1 Cor. vii. 20. *Call* has replaced native *clipian*, *cleopian* (see *yclept*), e.g. *clepe* in Wyc. is always *call* in Tynd. With to *call out*, challenge, cf. synon. F. *provoquer*.

caller herrin'. App. two words are here confused, viz. earlier *calver* (cf. Sc. *siller* for *silver*), of dubious sense and origin, often applied to salmon, and ON. *kaldr*, cold, fresh, with exceptional retention of inflexional *-r*.

callet [*archaic* or *dial.*]. Scolding drab, etc. (*Oth.* iv. 2, and elsewhere in Shaks., also in Burns, *Jolly Beggars*). ? A gipsy word. It may be noted that there is a ME. female name *Calote* (for *Nicolette*). It was borne by the daughter of Langland, author of *Piers Plowm.* Some female names assume a bad sense, e.g. *jilt*.

callidity. L. *calliditas*, from *callidus*, cunning.

calligraphy. G. καλλιγραφία, from κάλλος, beauty.

callipers. See *calibre*.

callipygian. Epithet of Venus. From G. κάλλος, beauty, πυγή, buttock.

callisthenics. From G. κάλλος, beauty, σθένος, strength. Cf. name *Callisthenes*.

callous. F. *calleux*, L. *callosus*, thick-skinned, from *callus*, hardened skin.

callow. AS. *calu*, *calw-*, bald. WGer.; cf. Du. *kaal*, Ger. *kahl*; early loan from L. *calvus*, bald.

calm. First as noun. F. *calme*, It. *calma*, VL. **calma*, G. καῦμα, heat, from καίειν, to burn. Supposed to have been applied orig. to the mid-day heat, general rest during that period; cf. F. *chômer*, to knock off work, VL. **caumare*. The phonetic change is unusual, but not unparalleled. There may also have been influence of L. *calor*, heat.

Calmuck. See *Kalmuck*.

calomel. F., earlier *calomélas*, coined from G. καλός, beautiful, μέλας, black, "la poudre blanche qui constitue le calomel étant noire pendant la préparation de ce corps" (*Dict. Gén.*).

caloric. F. *calorique*, coined (18 cent.) by Lavoisier, from L. *calor*, heat. Cf. F. *calorie* (current in E. in 1917) for heat-producing unit.

Plain and humble folk...instead of the number of calories want to know the number of tablespoonfuls (*Pall Mall Gaz.* March 8, 1917).

calotte. Skull-cap. F., Prov. *calota*, It.

callotta, G. καλύπτρα, hood, veil (see *apocalypse*). Cf. *caul*.

calotype. Name given (1841) by Fox Talbot to photographic process. From G. καλός, beautiful.

caloyer. Greek monk (*Childe Har.* ii. 49). F., It. *caloiero* (common in Purch.), Late G. καλόγηρος, beautiful in old age, from καλός, beautiful, -γηρος, aged.

calpack. Eastern head-dress (Turkestan). Turki *qālpāk*. Hence F. *colback*, kind of busby.

caltrop, caltrap, calthrop. Name of various spiky plants, and of a spiked ball put on ground to upset cavalry. AS. *calcatrippe* thistle. Also ME. *calketrappe*, from F. *chaussetrape*, ONF. also *cauketrape*. Second element is *trap*[1] (q.v.), first is L. *calx*, heel, or *calcare*, to tread.

calumet. Peace-pipe (*Hiawatha*). Dial. F., dim. of L. *calamus*, stem. "*Calumet* est un mot normand qui veut dire *chalumeau* (reed, pipe), et est proprement le tuyau d'une pipe" (*NED.* 1721). Taken to America by F. settlers. See *shawm*.

calumny. F. *calomnie*, L. *calumnia*, false accusation. See *challenge*.

Calvary. L. *calvaria*, skull, transl. of *Golgotha* (q.v.).

A place that is clepid Golgatha, that is, the place of Calvarie (Wyc. *Matt.* xxvii. 33).

calvered [*archaic*]. Used of salmon. Exact meaning and origin unknown.

Calvinism. Doctrine of *Jean Cauvin* or *Chauvin* (1509–64), latinized as *Calvinus*; esp. that of grace or predestination. See *Arminian*.

O Thou, who in the Heavens does dwell,
Who, as it pleases best Thysel',
Sends ane to heaven an' ten to hell,
   A' for Thy glory!
            (Burns, *Holy Willy's Prayer*).
The bells of hell go ting-a-ling-a-ling,
   For you, but not for me (T. Atkins).

calx. L., lime. Formerly used for *oxide*. Cf. *calcine*.

calycanthus. Shrub. From G. κάλυξ, calyx, ἄνθος, flower.

calyx. See *calix*.

cam [*techn.*]. Toothed rim of wheel, etc. Var. of *comb*. Cf. Ger. *kammrad*, cogged wheel.

camaraderie. F., see *comrade*.

camarilla. Clique, junto. Sp., dim. of *camara*, chamber. Orig. inner group of the *Cámara de Castilla*.

The small, but powerful, pro-German camarilla [in Russia] (*Daily Chron.* March 16, 1917).

camber. To arch slightly, esp. naut. F. *cambrer*, from L. *camurus*, bent.

Lorries swaying perilously along the high-cambered tracks on the edge of greasy ditches
(*Daily Tel.* Nov. 7, 1918).

cambist. Expert in theory of exchange. F. *cambiste*, It. *cambista*, from *cambio*, change (q.v.).

cambium [*bot.*]. Formerly used of "alimentary humours" of the body. Late L. *cambium*, change.

Cambria. Same word as *Cumbria*, latinized from *Cymry*, Welshmen, older *Combroges*, "co-landers"; cf. L. *Allobroges*, "other-landers," from Gaulish.

cambric. From *Kamerijk*, Flem. form of *Cambrai* (Nord). See *batiste* and cf. *arras*.

kamerycks doeck: cambric (Hexham).

camel. AS. *camel* (or ONF. *camel*), L. *camelus*, G. κάμηλος, Heb. *gāmāl*; cogn. with Arab. *jamal*.

These are the ships of Arabia, their seas are the deserts (Purch.).

camellia. Named (18 cent.) by Linnaeus after *Kamel* (latinized *Camellus*), Jesuit who described vegetation of Luzon.

camelopard. L. *camelopardus*, from G. καμηλοπάρδαλις, camel pard, having legs and neck of camel, spots of pard. See *leopard*, by association with which it is commonly pronounced *camel-leopard*.

camembert. Cheese. French village (Orne). Cf. *cheddar*, *gruyère*.

cameo. It. *cammeo*, with various forms in Rom. langs. Earliest are OF. *camehu* (*camaïeu*), MedL. *camahutus*, also occurring in 13 cent. E. Origin unknown.

camera. L., chamber. Hence *camera obscura*, invented (16 cent.) by Giambattista della Porta. Simply *camera* (phot.) since Daguerre.

camerlengo. It., chamberlain (q.v.). Cardinal acting as Pope's chief adviser.

Cameronian [*hist.*]. Follower of *Richard Cameron*, 17 cent. Covenanter. Also 1st Batt. Scottish Rifles, orig. Cameronians who joined William III.

camisado [*hist.*]. Sp. *camisada*, night raid made in shirts, so that attacking party should not mistake each other in darkness. From Sp. *camisa* (see *chemise*).

camisard [*hist.*]. Protestant insurgent in Cevennes (late 17 cent.). From Prov. *camisa*, uniform of rebels (v.s.).

camisole. F., Sp. *camisola* or It. *camiciola*. See *chemise*.

camlet [*archaic*]. F. *camelot*, *chamelot*, with forms in most Europ. langs. Popularly associated with *camel*, and perh. orig. made from camel's hair, later from the hair of the Angora goat. There is also an Arab. *khamlat*, nap of cloth. The word, like so many names of supposed Oriental fabrics, is of obscure origin and varying sense.

camomile. F. *camomille*, L. *chamomilla*, altered from G. χαμαίμηλον, earth apple. See *melon*, *chameleon*.

camorra. It. secret society. Origin obscure. App. from earlier meaning "Irish rugge or mantle, a mariners frocke" (Flor.); cf. *carmagnole*.

The Camorists [? meaning Camarillists] at the War Office (*Sunday Times*, Jan. 20, 1918).

camouflage. A word which was naturalized with amazing rapidity early in 1917. Orig. from Parisian slang, which has *camoufle*, candle, personal description, *camoufler*, to disguise, *camouflet*, chandelier, app. connected in some way with the older *camouflet* (v.i.). Cf. It. *camuffare*, to disguise, ? for *capo muffare*, to muffle the head.

I was in khaki by way of camouflage
(G. B. Shaw in *Daily Chron.* March 5, 1917).
The ermine is simply the little brown stoat in winter camouflage (*ib.* Jan. 7, 1918).
At Hampstead 50 girls, camouflaged for the day as Welsh peasants, presented Mrs Lloyd George with 50 purses (*ib.* March 2, 1918).

camouflet [*mil.*]. Asphyxiating mine. F., orig. of blowing smoke in one's face. Earlier *moflet*, app. from OF. *mofler*, to stuff; also (15 cent.) *chaut* (*chaud*) *mouflet*, which may, however, be folk-etym. The verb *mofler* gave E. *muffle* (q.v.).

camoufflet: a snuft, or cold pye, a smoaky paper held under the nose of a slug, or sleeper (Cotg.).

camp. F., It. *campo*, L. *campus*, field, esp. as in *Campus Martius*, place for athletic contests, parade ground, etc. Cf. ME. *champ*, field, from F., and ME. *camp*, contest, AS. *camp*, early loan from L. *campus*. Cf. Ger. *kampf*, fight, from L., and mil. sense of *field*. See also *champion*. The *Field of the Cloth of Gold* renders F. *camp du Drap-d'Or*.

campagnol. Short-tailed field mouse. F., from *campagne*, country.

campaign. F. *campagne*, It. *campagna*, L. *campania*, from *campus*, field. Orig. open country; cf. archaic *champaign* (*Lear*, i. 1), and F. *Champagne*. Mil. sense arises from contrast between armies in the field and in winter quarters. Cf. Ger. *feldzug*, campaign.

The next campaine is usually taken for the next summers expedition of an army, or its taking the field (Blount).

campanile. Bell-tower. It., from Late L. *campana*, bell. Cf. *campanula*, "the blue-bell-flower or flower called Canterbury bells" (Litt.); *campanology*, science of bells and bell-ringing.

campeachy wood. Logwood, from *Campeachy*, Central America.

camphor. ME. *caumfre*, F. *camphre*, MedL. *camphora* (cf. It. *canfora*, Sp. Port. *alcanfor*), Arab. *kāfūr*, Malay *kāpūr*, chalk. Spelt *camphire* in *Song of Solomon* (i. 14).

campion. Flower. Origin unknown. As it has fantastic names in other langs., it may be from obs. var. of *champion*. Cf. Norw. *kjæmpe*, plantain, lit. champion, because children use the heads to play at "conquers."

campo santo. It., holy field, cemetery.

campshot. Facing of piles to protect the Thames aits against the current. Also -*shed*, -*shoot*, etc. Prob., like many words of the water-course vocabulary, of Du. origin. Second element is Du. *schut*, barrier, protection, first may be *kamp*, enclosed land, field.

camwood. From native WAfr. name *kambi* (Sierra Leone).

can¹. Verb. Pres. of AS. *cunnan*, to know, one of the preterito-present group. Com. Teut.; cf. Du. *kunnen*, Ger. *kennen*, to know, *können*, to be able, ON. *kunna*, Goth. *kunnan*, and see *ken*. Past *could*, for ME. *coude*, is due to *should*, *would*. Past part. *couth* survives in *uncouth* (q.v.). See also *cunning*.

can². Noun. AS. *canne*. Com. Teut. and formerly applied to vessels of any material; cf. Du. *kan*, Ger. *kanne*, ON. *kanna*. Ulterior hist. unknown, derivation from L. *canna*, reed, being unlikely in view of the early and wide existence of the word in Teut. langs. Sense of receptacle, "tin," is US.

Canaanite. Jewish zealot fanatically opposed to Rome. Hence Simon the *Canaanite* (*Matt.* x. 4), *Cananaean* (*RV*.), *Zelotes* (*Luke*, vi. 15).

canaille. F., It. *canaglia*, collect. from L. *canis*, dog.

canal. F., L. *canalis*. See the earlier *channel*, *kennel²*.

canard. F., lit. drake. Adopted in Ger. as *zeitungsente*, newspaper duck. Perh. from phrase *donner un canard à moitié*, to take in, lit. half give a duck, of obscure origin. *Canard* is supposed to come from OF. *cane*, skiff, Ger. *kahn*.

vendeur de canards à moitié: a cousener, guller, cogger, foister, lyer (Cotg.).

Canarese [*ling.*]. Dravidian lang. of *Canara* (S.W. India). Prop. *Kannada*, from *kar*, black, *nādu*, country.

Canary. F. *Canarie*, Sp. *Canaria*, L. *insula Canaria*, from dogs, *canes*, found there (Pliny). Hence wine, bird, dance.

canaster. Tobacco. From basket in which imported. Sp. *canastra* (see *canister*). Cf. Ger. *knaster*.

knaster-toback oder canaster-toback der toback der in canastern oder körben aus Neu-Spanien kommt: Spanish tobacco (Ludw.).

cancan. Dance. F., orig. univ. speech, then pedantic argument, tittle-tattle, etc. L. *quanquam*, although, usual beginning of univ. argument.

De quoi les pédants firent de grands cancans
(Sully, 1602).

cancel. OF. *canceller*, L. *cancellare*, "to make in form of lattise; to cancell or crosse out a thing written" (Coop.). Quot. below, a stock AF. phrase, suggests that the ult. connection with *chancellor* was still felt. See *chancel*.

Il a restituz et susrenduz nos dites lettres en nostre chauncellerie a canceller
(*John of Gaunt's Reg.* 1372–76).

cancer. L., crab, replacing in spec. sense earlier *canker* (q.v.). From eating away (cf. *lupus*). Cf. *Tropic of Cancer*.

candelabrum. L., from *candela*, candle.

candescent. From pres. part. of L. *candescere*, incept. of *candēre*, to shine.

candid. L. *candidus*, white, from *candēre*, to shine. Hence *candidate*, because candidates for office wore the white toga.

Save, save, oh! save me from the candid friend
(Canning).

candle. AS. *candel*, early Church word, L. *candela*. To *hold a candle to* meant orig. to help in subordinate capacity, but in connection with the devil (v.i.), alludes to the advantage of having friends everywhere. *The game is not worth the candle*, i.e. the stakes are not high enough to pay for the lights. The above, and other familiar "candle" phrases have parallels in other langs. *Candlemas*, feast of the purification (Feb. 2), AS. *candelmæsse*, is said to be partly due to the pre-Christian Roman candle-processions in the feast of purification (Feb. 15).

It is a comon proverbe, "A man must sumtyme set a candel before the Devyle" (*Paston Let.* ii. 73).

candour. Orig. brightness, purity. L. *candor.* See *candid.*

candy. From *sugar-candy*, F. *sucre candi*; cf. It. *zucchero candi*, Sp. *azucar cande*, etc. Arab. *qandī*, candied, from *qand*, sugar, from Pers., ult. Sanskrit *khanda*, piece.

candytuft. From *Candy*, obs. form of *Candia*, i.e. Crete.

cane. F. *canne*, L. *canna*, G. κάννα, reed, perh. of Eastern origin; cf. Heb. *quāneh*, Arab. *qānah*.

cangue [*China*]. Wooden frame round neck. F., Port. *cango*; cf. Port. *canga*, yoke. It occurs first as verb, *congoed*, perh. corrupt. of *cangado*, p.p. of *cangare*, to yoke. For non-Chin. origin cf. *joss, junk, mandarin.*

canicular. L. *canicularis*, of the dog-star, *canicula*, L. name of Sirius or Procyon. Cf. F. *canicule*, dog-days, period of great heat.

canine. L. *caninus*, of the dog, *canis.*

canister. L. *canistrum*, bread-basket, G. κάνυστρον, wicker basket, from κάννα, reed. See *canaster, basket.* Current sense of metal receptacle (from c. 1700) is partly due to association with *can²*.

canker. AS. *cancer* or ONF. *cancre*, L. *cancer*, crab. Formerly also in sense of *cancer* (q.v.). Normal F. form is *chancre*, whence E. *shanker*.

canna. Flower. L., reed.

cannel. Coal. Said to be for *candle-coal*, because it burns without smoke like a candle.

cannelure. Grooving. F., from *canneler*, to groove. See *canal, channel¹*.

cannibal. Sp. *canibal*, for *Caribal* (Columbus), Carib, perh. partly by popular association with Sp. *can*, dog. But Columbus believed the *Cannibals* to be so-called as subjects of the Great *Khan* (of Tartary), whose territory he thought he had reached. *Carib* is prob. a native word for valiant. See *Caliban.*

Las islas...se llamaron los Canibales por los muchos Caribes, comedores de carne humana, que truvo en ellas
    (Herrera, *Descripcion de las Indias Occidentales*).
A place called the Kennyballes, in the sayd lande of Brasyle (*Voyage of the Barbara*, 1540).

cannon¹. Gun. F. *canon*, It. *cannone*, augment. of *canna*, tube, L. *canna*, reed (see *cane*). Cf. F. *canon d'un fusil*, barrel of a gun. Collect. sense is in Shaks.

cannon². At billiards. Perversion of earlier *carom, carrom* (still in US.), short for F. *carambole*, Sp. Port. *carambola*, the red ball. This may be Port. *carambola*, a golden yellow fruit from Malabar, Mahratti *karanbal*. Those who have misspent their youth in billiard rooms will think of the parallel "raspberry."

canny [*Sc. & north.*]. App. a fairly mod. formation (17 cent.) from *can¹* (q.v.). Cf. Sw. *kunnig*, knowing, cunning (in etym. sense). See *ca' canny. Canny Scot(chman)* is app. due to Scott (*Antiq.* xxxviii.).

canoe. Orig. *canoa*, Sp., native Haytian word (Columbus).

The boate of one tree called the canoa (Raleigh).

canon¹. Decree of the church, and hence, rule, principle, in various senses. AS. *canon*, L., G. κανών, rule. With *canon* type cf. *primer, brevier*, etc. To *canonize*, make eccl: enactment, has already in Wyc. spec. sense of inscribing on calendar of saints. *Canonicals* are the regulation dress of a duly appointed priest.

A cloak and cassock for my brother...I will have him in a canonical dress (Pepys, Sep. 27, 1666).

canon². Dignitary. AS. *canonic*, Church L. *canonicus*, regular priest (see *canon¹*), was replaced in ME. by *canoun, chanoun*, OF. *chanonie (chanoine)*, L. *canonicus.*

cañon, canyon. Sp. *cañon*, tube, etc., applied to deep river-gorges in NAmer. Thus ident. with *cannon¹*.

canoodle [*slang*]. A dial. word (Somerset) for donkey, "spoony." Perh. in current sense vaguely associated with *cuddle.*

canopy. F. *canapé*, sofa, OF. *conopé*, bed-curtain, MedL. *canapeum*, L. *conopeum*, G. κωνωπεῖον, couch with mosquito curtains, from κώνωψ, gnat, mosquito. E. has thus more of the orig. sense, the Rom. langs. taking that of the (curtained) couch.

canorous. From L. *canorus*, from *canere*, to sing. Cf. *sonorous.*

Canossa, go to [*pol.*]. Used by Bismarck of humiliating surrender. Castle near Reggio, where Emperor Henry IV made submission to Pope Gregory VII (1077).

Mr Lloyd George approaching his Canossa
    (*Westm. Gaz.* Nov. 17, 1920).

cant¹. Corner, edge. ONF. *cant (chant)*, MedL. *cantus* (whence also It. *canto*, Du. *kant*, Ger. *kante*), perh. Late L. *canthus*, corner of the eye, G. κανθός. Now more common as verb, to tilt, set edge-ways. Cf. F. *poser de chant*, often wrongly spelt *de champ*.

cant². Slang, humbug. ONF. *cant* (*chant*), singing; hence, the whining speech of beggars; in 17–18 cents. esp. the secret jargon of the criminal and vagabond classes, "the canting crew." Mod. sense springs from hostile application of the term to phraseology of certain sects and groups. *Canting arms* (her.) are punning or allusive; cf. F. *armes parlantes*.

Their languag—which they term peddelars Frenche or canting—began but within these xxx yeeres
(Harman's *Caveat*, 1567).

Boleyn—or Bullen—had the canting arms of a black bull's head (C. M. Yonge).

Cant is the Englishman's second nature
(Kuno Meyer, late professor at Liverpool).

Cantab. For *Cantabrigian*, MedL. *Cantabrigiensis*, from latinized form of *Cambridge*, orig. *Grantabridge*, later *Gantabridge*, *Cantabridge*.

The Oxonians and Cantabrigians...are the happiest Academians on earth (Howell, 1619).

cantaliver. See *cantilever*.

cantaloup. Melon. F., It. *Cantaloupo*, former estate of the Pope where it is said to have been introduced from Armenia.

cantankerous. Prob. coined, on *cankerous*, *rancorous*, from ME. *contekous*, from ME. & AF. *contak*, *conteke*, strife, *contekour*, disputant. The first *NED*. examples are from Goldsmith and Sheridan, so it may be of Ir. formation. *Contek* is altered from AF. *contet* (= *contest*).

Mortel cuntet cumence a lever en la cite de Nicole [Lincoln] (Mayor of Lincoln, c. 1272).

cantata. It., from *cantare*, to sing.

cantatrice. F., It., L. *cantatrix*, *cantatric-*, fem. of *cantator*, singer.

canteen. F. *cantine*, It. *cantina*, app. cogn. with *cant*¹; cf. Du. *winkel*, shop, lit. corner. Also in F. and E. a case fitted with bottles, knives and forks, etc.

The canteen of cutlery was restored to defendant
(*Ev. News*, May 11, 1917).

canter. Short for *Canterbury pace*, *gallop*, pilgrims' pace on the Old Kent Road. A *preliminary canter* precedes the race itself.

The Pegasus of Pope, like a Kentish post-horse, is always on the Canterbury (J. Dennis, 1729).

canterbury. Music-stand, etc. From c. 1850. Cf. *pembroke*.

Canterbury bell. Fancifully associated with bells on pilgrims' horses. See *canter*.

cantharides. L., pl. of *cantharis*, G. κανθαρίς, blister-fly, Spanish fly.

canticle. L. *canticulum*, dim. from *cantus*, song, from *canere*, to sing.

cantilever [*arch.*]. Bracket. Has been associated with *lever*, but the form *cantlapper* (1611), recorded in Appendix V to Phineas Pett's *Autobiography*, 50 years earlier than *NED*. records, points to something quite different. First element is Sp. *can*, dog.

can: in architecture, the end of timber or stone jutting out of a wall, on which in old buildings the beams us'd to rest, called cantilevers
(Stevens, 1706).

cantle. Piece, corner, etc. ONF. *cantel* (*chanteau*), dim. of *cant*¹ (q.v.).

canto. It., L. *cantus*. First in Spenser.

canton. F., It. *cantone*, augment. of *canto*, corner. See *cant*¹. It has many obs. or archaic meanings. For mil. sense (*cantonments*) cf. *quarters*.

canton: a corner, or crosse-way, in a street; also, a canton, or hundred; a precinct, or circuit of territory, wherein there be divers good townes and villages; (This word is proper to Helvetia, or Switzerland; which, at this day, consists of thirteen such cantons) (Cotg.).

cantoris [*eccl.*]. L., of the singer, i.e. on the side of the *precentor*. Opposite is *decani*, of the *dean*.

cantrip [*Sc.*]. Spell, trick. Orig. in to *cast cantrips*, tell fortunes. Earliest form *cantrape* (Allan Ramsay). Perh. connected with *incantation*.

Cantuar. Signature of archbp of Canterbury. Cf. MedL. *Cantuari*, men of Kent, from AS.

Canuck [*US.*]. French Canadian. App. from *Canada* by analogy with *Chinook* (q.v.).

canvas. F. *canevas* (cf. It. *canavaccio*), from OF. *caneve*, hemp, L. *cannabis*, G. κάνναβις. Prob. of Oriental origin (cf. Pers. *kanab*) and ult. cogn. with *hemp* (q.v.). Hence verb to *canvas*(s), perh. orig. to sift through canvas.

canyon. See *cañon*.

canzonet. It. *canzonetta*, dim. of *canzone*, song, VL. *cantio-n-*; cf. F. *chanson*, *chansonnette*.

caoutchouc. F. (18 cent.), from native SAmer. word (Carib).

cap. AS. *cæppe*, hood, Late L. *cappa*, mantle, of obscure origin, but perh. shortened from *capitulare*, head-dress; cf. Late L. *capa*, cape, cope. Both words have a numerous progeny in the Europ. langs. Mod. sense of *cap* is evolved from that of woman's hood. The *cap of liberty* is the Phrygian cap given to Roman slaves on emancipation. Among fig. meanings is *percussion cap*, put like a cap on the nipple of the gun. To *cap verses* (*anecdotes*, etc.) is to fit one on another. To *set one's cap at* is orig. one of the many naut. metaphors which are no longer felt as such; cf. F. *mettre le cap sur*, to turn the ship's head towards. Here *cap* is Prov. for head, L. *caput*.

capable. F., Late L. *capabilis*, receptive, in early theol. use, from *capere*, to hold.

capacious. For obs. *capace*, L. *capax, capac-*, from *capere*, to take.

cap-à-pie. OF., head to foot. ModF. *de pied en cap. Cap* is Prov. or It. *capo*, L. *caput*, whence also F. *chef*.

caparison. F. *caparaçon*, Sp. *caparazon*, app. from Late L. *capa* (see *cape*¹); cf. MedL. *caparo*, hood (see *chaperon*). Or it may be ult. cogn. with *carapace*, having been orig. applied to armour of warhorse.

cape¹. Garment, orig. hood, "Spanish cloak." F., Sp. *capa*, Late L. *capa*. True F. form is *chape*, cope. See *cap*.

cape². Promontory. F. *cap*, Prov. or It. *capo*, head, L. *caput*. Cf. *headland*. From 17 cent. spec. for Cape of Good Hope, usu. Cape de Bona Speranza in Hakl. and Purch. See also *boy*.

capelin. Fish. F.,? from L. *caput*, head.

caper¹. Plant. F. *câpre*, It. *cappero*, L. *capperis*, G. κάππαρις. Spelt in OF. and ME. with final *-s* which has been taken for pl. sign and dropped. Cf. *pea*.

> The erbe caperis shal be scatered
> (Wyc. *Eccles.* xii. 5).

caper². Gambol. App. short for *capriole* (see *cabriolet*). Cf. to *play the giddy goat*.

> *capriola*: a capriole or caper in dancing (Flor.).

capercailzie. Cock of the woods. The *-z-* is late printer's substitute for obs. palatal better represented by *-y-* (cf. *Dalziell, Mackenzie*, etc.). Gael. *capull-coille*, horse (from L. *caballus*) of the woods. Cf. *Caledonia*.

capias. Writ of arrest. L., thou mayst take. Cf. *habeas corpus*.

capibara. See *capybara*.

capillary. From L. *capillaris*, from *capillus*, hair, cogn. with *caput*, head. *Capillary attraction* dates from Laplace (†1827).

capital¹. Of a column. For *capitel*, L. *capitellum*, dim. of *caput*, head; cf. OF. *chapitel* (*chapiteau*).

capital². Adj. L. *capitalis*, from *caput*, head, etym. sense surviving in *capital punishment* (*offence*). Later senses show the same

tendency as *ripping, awfully*, etc. With *capital*, chief town, cf. synon. AS. *hēafodstōl*, head stool, capital.

capital³. Money. Late L. *capitale*, stock, property, neut. of *capitalis* (v.s.). See *cattle, chattel. Capitalist*, as term of reproach for the provident, is F. *capitaliste*, a Revolution coinage (see *-ist*).

capitan [*hist.*]. Sp., captain (q.v.); esp. in *capitan pasha*, chief admiral of Turk. fleet.

capitation. F., L. *capitatio-n-*. Cf. *poll-tax, head-money*.

> *capitation*: head-silver, pole-money (Cotg.).

Capitol. L. *capitolium*, from *caput*. Orig. Temple of Jupiter on the Tarpeian Hill; later, the citadel. Trad. from a head which was discovered in digging the foundations.

capitular. See *chapter*.

capitulate. From MedL. *capitulare* (from *caput, capit-*, head), to draw up an agreement under "heads." Retains orig. sense in the hist. *capitulations* (1535) between Turkey and France.

caplin. See *capelin*.

capon. AS. *capun*, L. *capo-n-*.

caponier [*fort.*]. Covered passage. F. *caponnière*, Sp. *caponera*, "a coope wherein capons are put to feed" (Minsh.). For sense-development cf. *sentinel*.

caporal. F., tobacco of quality superior to *tabac du soldat* (*de cantine*). See *corporal*.

capot. Winning all tricks at piquet. From *capot*, hood, dim. of *cape*, in *faire capot*, though metaphor not clear. See *domino*.

> Vous allez faire pic, repic et capot tout ce qu'il y a de galant à Paris (Mol. *Précieuses*, 9).

> She would ridicule the pedantry of the terms— such as pique, repique, the capot
> (Lamb, *Mrs Battle*).

capote. F., also *capot* (v.s.), dim. of *cape* (see *cape*¹).

caprice. F., It. *capriccio* (also formerly in E. use), from *capro*, goat, L. *caper* (cf. *caper*²). But It. *capriccio* is connected by some with L. *caput*, head; cf. synon. F. *coup de tête*.

Capricorn. L. *capricornus*, horned goat (v.s.). Cf. G. αἰγόκερως.

capriole. Leap, etc. See *caper*².

capsicum. ModL., perh. from L. *capsa*, case, pod. Cf. *capsule*.

capsize. Replaced (18 cent.) earlier *overset*. Orig. *capacise* (v.i.), an older form than *NED.* records. First element prob. means head; cf. Ger. *koppseisen*, from E., & F. *chavirer*, to capsize, prob. from *caput* and *virer*, to turn. But synon. F. *capoter*, Sp. *capuzar*, suggest some connection with *cape*, hood.

to capacise: renverser ou chavirer quelque chose; c'est une expression vulgaire (Lesc.).

capstan. Prov. *cabestan* (whence F. *cabestan*), for *cabestran* (cf. Sp. *cabestrante*), from *cabestrare*, L. *capistrare*, to fasten with a rope, L. *capistrum*, from *capere*, to take, seize. Sp. *cabrestante* is folk-etym., "standing goat." So also E. *capstern*, as late as Marryat.

cabestan: the capstern or crab of a ship (Falc.).

capsule. F., L. *capsula*, dim. of *capsa*, chest, case.

captain. F. *capitaine*, Late L. *capitaneus*, from *caput*, head. A learned word, perh. influenced by It. *capitano*, Sp. *capitan*. The true OF. word is *chataigne*, *chevetain*, whence E. *chieftain*. The *captain* of a ship orig. commanded the fighting men (see *master*). Also in poet. sense of great commander, as in Kipling's line *The captains and the kings depart*, the deletion of which from a press article, as "likely to convey information to the enemy," gained anonymous immortality for one of the censor's staff. *Led-captain*, hired bully, is associated with F. *capitan*, braggart, ruffler, from Sp. (v.s.).

caption [*neol. from US.*]. Title, of article, etc.

captious. F. *captieux*, L. *captiosus*, from *captio*, sophistical argument, lit. taking hold, from *capere*, to seize.

captive. L. *captivus*. See *caitiff*. With *captivate* cf. *enthral*.

capture. F., L. *captura*, from *capere*, *capt-*, to take. Cf. *caption*, *captor*.

Capua. Place of effeminate influences, from trad. effect on Hannibal's soldiers.

How...skilfully Gainsborough painted, before at Bath he found his Capua (*Athenaeum*, Oct. 29, 1887).

capuchin. F., It. *capuccino*, from *capuccio*, hood, from *capa* (see *cape*[1]). Pointed hood adopted by Franciscans of new rule (1528).

capybara. Largest extant rodent (SAmer.). Native Braz. name. Cf. *cavy*. Purch. has *capivara* (xvi. 288).

car. ONF. *carre*, Late L. **carra* for *carrus*, whence F. *char*, It. Sp. *carro*. Of Celt. origin (cf. Ir. *carr*, ult. cogn. with L. *currus*). First used by Caesar of the Celtic war-chariot. Application to public vehicles is US.

Carabas, marquis of. From title invented for

his master by Puss in Boots (Perrault, 17 cent.).

carabine. See *carbine*. The *Carabineers* are the 6th Dragoon Guards.

caracal. Feline animal, the lynx of the ancients. F., Turk. *qarah-qulaq*, black-ear.

caracole [*equit.*]. Half-turn. F., It. *caracollo* or Sp. Port. *caracol*, spiral shell, staircase, etc. Origin unknown. ? From Celt.; cf. Gael. *car*, turn, twist.

caracul. Fur resembling astrakhan. From *Kara-Kul*, i.e. black lake (near Bokhara).

And on his head he plac'd his sheep-skin cap, Black, glossy, curl'd, the fleece of Kara-Kul
(M. Arnold, *Sohrab & Rustum*).

carafe. F., It. *caraffa*, Pers. *qarābah*, flagon (see *carboy*). Another etym. is from Arab. *gharafa*, to draw water; cf. Sp. Port. *garrafa*.

carambole. See *cannon*[2].

caramel. F., It. Sp. *caramelo*, "marchpane, or such-like delicate confection" (Minsh.). ? Ult. L. *canna mellis* (cf. *sugar-stick*).

carapace. F.; ? cogn. with *caparison*. But see also *calipash*.

carat. F., It. *carato*, Arab. *qīrāt*, G. κεράτιον, little horn, hence fruit of carob tree, small weight. In earlier use confused with obs. *caract*, mark, sign (*character*).

carato: a waight or degree called a caract (Flor.).

caravan. F. *caravane*, a word dating from the Crusades, Pers. *kārwān*, company of merchants or ships travelling together, "also of late corruptly used with us for a kind of waggon to carry passengers to and from London" (Blount, 1674). Hence *caravanserai*, from Pers. *sarāī*, mansion, inn. New sense in E. prob. arose in connection with the wanderings of gipsies.

caravel [*hist.*]. See *carvel*.

caraway, carraway. Cf. F. It. Sp. *carvi* (Sc. *carvy*), OSp. *al-caravea*, Arab. *karawiyā*, prob. from G. κάρον, whence L. *carum*, *careum* (Pliny); cf. Du. *karwij*, Ger. *karbe*. The E. form has parallels in surnames like *Ottoway*, *Hadaway*, etc., where the final syllable is for *-wy*, AS. *-wīg*, as in *Edwy*, from *Eadwīg*.

carbine. Earlier (17 cent.) *carabine*, F. (16 cent.), app. weapon of a *carabin*, light horseman, though the converse may be the case (cf. *dragoon*). Origin unknown. OF. var. *calabrin* and MedL. *calabrinus* have suggested connection with *Calabria*.

carabin: a carbine, or curbeene; an arquebuzier... serving on horsebacke (Cotg.).

carbolic. From *carbon* by analogy with *alcoholic.*

carbon. Coined by Lavoisier (†1794) from L. *carbo-n-*, whence F. *charbon*, charcoal.

carbonado [*archaic*]. Sp. *carbonada*, "a carbonardo on the coals" (Minsh.). Hence, to broil, and fig. to slash. See *carbon.*

> I'll so carbonado your shanks (*Lear*, ii. 2).

Carbonari [*hist.*]. Secret society formed in Naples during Murat's rule (c. 1810). Pl. of *carbonaro*, charcoal-burner (v.s.). Cf. *gueux*, beggars, name assumed by Du. republicans (16 cent.).

carboy. Large wicker-covered vessel for chemicals. Pers. *qarābah*, flagon. See *carafe.*

carbuncle. ME. & OF. usu. *charbucle*, but ONF. *carbuncle*, L. *carbunculus*, little coal. Forms in most Europ. langs., including Ger. *karfunkel*, popularly connected with *funkeln*, to sparkle. For double sense-development, found also in other langs., cf. *anthrax.*

> *carbunculus*: a little cole: a certaine botch comming of inflammation: a precious stone: a carbuncle (Coop.).

carburet. Coined (18 cent.) from *carbon*, by analogy with *sulphuret.*

carcajou. Canad. F. for wolverine. Amer. Ind. name.

carcanet [*antiq.*]. Jewelled collar, fillet. Dim. of F. *carcan*, iron collar as pillory, Merovingian L. *carcannum*. ?Cf. OHG. *cwerca*, throat, ON. *kverk*, angle under chin. Obs. E. *quarken*, to choke, is cogn.

carcase, carcass. ME. *carcays*, AF. *carcois*, OF. *charquois*, represented by MedL. *carcosium*. This was replaced (16 cent.) by mod. form, F. *carcasse*, It. *carcassa*. Earlier sense was skeleton. It is possible that the first form is L. *carchesium*, tall drinking vessel, G. καρχήσιον, whence It. *carcasso*, Sp. *carcaj*, quiver, OF. *carquois*, upper part of skeleton, now also, quiver; but the whole group of words is obscure. Others regard all these words as coming, via MedL. *tarchesium*, from Pers. *tarkash*, quiver, with dissim. like that of Ger. *kartoffel* (see *truffle*). In archaic sense of bomb always spelt *carcass.*

carcel. Lamp. Name of F. inventor (19 cent.).

carcinology. Study of the crab, G. καρκίνος.

card¹. Pasteboard. F. *carte*, It. *carta*, L. *charta*, G. χάρτης, leaf of papyrus. Earliest in playing-card sense. *Carte* is still usual in Sc. See *chart*, with which *card* was once synon., as in to *speak by the card*, i.e. by the compass-card. As applied to a person, *queer card*, *knowing card*, it may be an extension of the metaph. *good card*, *sure card*, etc., or may be an anglicized form of Sc. *caird*, tinker (cf. *artful beggar*, etc.). *On the cards* refers to the possibilities of the game.

> I showed them tricks which they did not know to be on the cards (Smollett's *Gil Blas*).

card². For wool. F. *carde*, teasel, Prov. *carda*, VL. **carda*, for *carduus*, thistle. Earliest as verb.

> To karde and to kembe (*Piers Plowm.* C. x. 80).

cardamine. Plant. Mod. (Linnaeus), G. καρδαμίνη, from κάρδαμον, cress.

cardamom. Spice. OF. *cardemome*, L., G. καρδάμωμον, from κάρδαμον, cress, and ἄμωμον, a spice-plant.

cardiac. F. *cardiaque*, L., G. καρδιακός, from καρδία, heart, cogn. with L. *cor-d-*.

cardigan. Jacket. From seventh *Earl of Cardigan* (Balaclava). Cf. *spencer, wellington*, etc.

cardinal. L. *cardinalis*, essential, as in *cardinal points* (*virtues*), from *cardo, cardin-*, hinge; cf. G. καρδᾶν, to swing. Earliest as noun (12 cent.), from Late L. *episcopus* (or *presbyter*) *cardinalis*, orig. in charge of one of the *cardinal* (or parish) churches of Rome, and, since third Lateran Council (1173), member of council electing the Pope. As name of colour from red hat and robe.

cardio-. See *cardiac.*

cardoon. Kind of artichoke. F., Prov. *cardon*, VL. **cardo-n-*, for *carduus*, thistle. Cf. F. *chardon*, thistle.

care. AS. *caru*, noun, *cearian*, verb. Orig. sorrow; with secondary sense of close attention cf. to *take pains*. Com. Teut.; cf. OSax. *cara*, OHG. *chara*, ON. *kör*, Goth. *kara*. Only surviving outside E. in Ger. *Karfreitag*, Good Friday, with which cf. obs. Sc. *Care-Sunday*, 5th in Lent. See *chary*. *Black care* is Horace's *atra cura.*

> Post equitem sedet atra cura (*Odes*, iii. 1. 40).

careen. To turn a ship on one side for cleaning, etc. F. *caréner*, from *carène*, keel, It. (Genoese) *carena*, L. *carina*. Or perh. rather from Sp., the duties of the "carenero or calker" being described in detail in Hakl. (xi. 447).

career. F. *carrière*, It. *carriera*, from *carro*, chariot (see *car*). Orig. race, race-course; cf. *in full career*, to *come careering down the street*, etc. For later sense cf. *curriculum*.

caress. F. *caresser*, It. *carezzare*, from *carezza*, L. *caritia*, from *carus*, dear.

caret [*typ.*]. Sign of omission (∧). L., from *carēre*, to be lacking. The symbol is the circumflex accent, commonly used as sign of omission.

carfax [*hist.*]. Cross-roads, as still at Oxford and Exeter. ME. *carrefoukes*, *carfox*, pl. of OF. *carrefourc* (*carrefour*), VL. **quadrifurcus*, four-forked.

cargo. Sp. *cargo* or *carga*, from *cargar*, to load; cf. It. *carrica*, F. *charge*. See *charge*, *cark*.

cariatid. See *caryatid*.

Carib [*ling.*]. Used of a large group of WInd. langs. See *cannibal*.

caribou. NAmer. reindeer. Canad. F., from Micmac (Algonkin) *kaleboo*, said to mean "shoveller," because the deer shovels away the snow with its hoofs to get at the moss on which it feeds.

caricature. F., It. *caricatura*. The It. form was in common E. use 17–18 cents. Lit. an over-loading, from *carricare*, to load. See *charge* and cf. F. *charge*, caricature.

carillon. F., chime, VL. **quadrilio-n-*, peal of four. OF. had also *carignon*, VL. **quatrinio-n-*; cf. Prov. *trinho*, *trilho*, chime, from **trinio-n-*. The references are mostly to Flanders, "where the carillons ripple from old spires" (Dowden).

carin- [*biol.*]. From L. *carina*, keel.

cariole. See *carriole*.

carious [*med.*]. From L. *caries*, decay.

cark. AF. *kark*, load, Norm. form of F. *charge*, load, burden. Thus, "load of care," with which it commonly occurs, e.g. *carking care*, for which Spenser has *careful cark*.

carl, carlin [*dial.*]. Man, old woman. ON. *karl* (m.), *kerling* (f.), whence Sw. Dan. *karl*, fellow, cogn. with *churl* (q.v.).

> The carlin claught her by the rump,
> And left poor Maggie scarce a stump
>   (*Tam o' Shanter*).

carline. Thistle. F., Sp. It. MedL. *carlina*, with a legendary ref. to *Charlemagne*.

carling [*naut.*]. Longitudinal timber. Icel. *kerling* suggests identity with *carlin* (q.v.). But F. *carlingue* is app. for older *escarlingue* (Jal), which suggests connection with Du. *schaar*, Ger. *scher*, as in *schaarstokken*, *scherstöcke*, carlings. The second

part may be OF. *leigne*, wood, L. *lignum*. Cf. It. Sp. *carlinga*.

Carliol. Signature of bishop of Carlisle, MedL. *Carliolum*.

Carlist [*hist.*]. Spanish legitimist, supporting claims of Don Carlos, second son of Charles IV of Spain, as opposed to reigning family, sprung from daughter of Ferdinand VII (†1833).

Carlovingian, Carolingian [*hist.*]. F. kings descended from *Charlemagne*, MedL. *Carolus Magnus*. F. *carlovingien* is after *mérovingien*.

carmagnole. Revolutionary song and dance (Paris 1793), from a kind of jacket favoured by the Republicans. ? From *Carmagnola* in Piedmont.

Carmelite. White friar. From monastery on *Mount Carmel* founded by Berthold (12 cent.). Hence also fabric.

carminative. Remedy for flatulency. From L. *carminare*, to card wool, hence fig. to purify.

carmine. F. *carmin* (12 cent.), MedL. *carminus*, from Arab. *qirmazī*, from *qirmiz*, kermes (q.v.). Cf. Sp. *carmín*, *carmesí*, crimson (q.v.). Form has perh. been influenced by association with *minium* (see *miniature*).

carnac [*archaic*]. Elephant-driver, mahout. F. *cornac*, Port. *cornáca*, Singhalese *kūrawanāyaka*, stud keeper. Has been assimilated to surname *Carnac*, a famous Anglo-Ind. name.

carnage. F., It. *carnaggio*, "carnage, slaughter, murther; also all manner of flesh meate" (Flor.), from L. *caro*, *carn-*, flesh. Cf. archaic F. *charnage*, Church season at which flesh may be eaten.

carnal. L. *carnalis*, of the flesh, *caro*, *carn-*. Cf. F. *charnel*.

carnation. Orig. flesh-colour. F., from L. *caro*, *carn-*, flesh, after It. *carnagione*, "the hew or colour of ones skin and flesh" (Flor.). The flower is also called *incarnation* and *coronation* by 16 cent. herbalists, but F. *œillet carné*, flesh-coloured pink, points to *carnation* as the original. For converse sense-development see *pink*[3]. Cf. *cornelian*.

carnelian. See *cornelian*.

carnival. F. *carnaval* or It. *carnevale*, Shrove Tuesday. Cf. MedL. *carnelevarium*, *carnilevamen*, from L. *carnem levare*, to remove meat. Forms have been influenced by fanciful derivations from L. *vale*, farewell (v.i.), or F. *à val*, down (with). In most Europ. langs.

carnevale: shrove-tide, shroving time, when flesh is bidden farewell (Torr.).

This feast is named the Carnival, which being Interpreted, implies "farewell to flesh"
(Byron, *Beppo*, vi.).

carnivorous. From L. *carnivorus*, from *caro, carn-*, flesh, *vorare*, to devour.

carny [*dial.*]. To wheedle. Origin unknown.

carob. Locust bean. Usu. identified with the Prodigal's husks and John the Baptist's locusts. OF. *carobe, carroube*, It. *carrubo*, Sp. *garrobo*, Arab. *kharrūbah*.

carrobe: the carob, carob-beane, or carob beane cod, S. John's bread (Cotg.).

caroche. Obs. form of *carriage* (q.v.), used by Thackeray.

carol. In ME. a round dance (cf. *ballad*), OF. *carole*, Prov. *corola*, L. *corolla*, garland. *Carole* is common in OF. of a ring of people, assembly, circle of pillars, etc. Some connect it rather with *chorus*.

carolle: a kinde of dance wherein many may dance together; also, a carroll, or Christmas song (Cotg.).

Caroline. Belonging to *Charles*, esp. *Charlemagne* (see *Carlovingian*), and *Charles* I and II of England.

Carolingian. See *Carlovingian*.

carolus. Gold coin of *Charles I*, also of *Charles VIII* of France. Cf. *jacobus, louis*, etc.

carom. See *cannon²*.

carotid. G. καρωτίδες (pl.), from καροῦν, to stupefy, because compression of the artery has this effect (Galen).

carousal. From *carouse* (q.v.), but sometimes confused by hist. writers with archaic *carousel, carrousel*, festival with chariot-racing, tilting, etc., "a kind of superb, betailored running at the ring" (Carlyle), F., It. *carosello*, prob. from L. *carrus*, chariot (cf. *career*).

carouse. From the phrase *drink carouse*, to drink bumpers, OF. *carous*, Ger. *gar aus*, quite out. We also find obs. *garous, garaus*, straight from Ger. *All out* was also used; cf. Ger. *all aus*. See also *rouse²*.

Je ne suis de ces importuns lifrelofres, qui, par force, par oultraige, contraignent...les compaignons trinquer, voyre carous et alluz, qui pis est
(*Pantagruel*, iii. *Prol.*).

The queen carouses to thy fortune, Hamlet
(*Haml.* v. 2).

carp¹. ·Fish. F. *carpe*, Late L. *carpa* (cf. It.

Sp. *carpa*), used (6 cent.) of a Danube fish, and hence prob. of Teut. or Slav. origin. Cf. Ger. *karpfen*, Russ. *karpu*, Serb. *krap*, etc.

carp². Verb. ME. to speak, talk, later ME. to talk censoriously. App. ON. *karpa*, to chatter, brag, influenced in meaning by association with L. *carpere*, to pluck, pull to pieces.

Thus conscience of Crist and of the croys carpede
(*Piers Plowm.* C. xxii. 199).

carpal [*anat.*]. Of the wrist, L. *carpus*, G. καρπός.

carpel [*bot.*]. Pistil cell. Dim. from G. καρπός, fruit. Cf. F. *carpelle*.

carpenter. ONF. *carpentier* (*charpentier*), L. *carpentarius*, cart-wright, from *carpentum*, chariot, of Celt. origin; cf. Gael. *carbod*, chariot, OIr. *carpat*, Welsh *cerbyd* (from Ir.); prob. cogn. with L. *corbis*, basket, ground-idea being vehicle of wicker. For Celt. origin cf. *car*.

carpet. OF. *carpite*, a coarse shaggy material; cf. MedL. It. *carpita*, rough patchwork, etc., from VL. **carpire*, for *carpere*, to pluck. Cf. F. *charpie*, lint for wounds, from OF. *charpir*, to pluck to pieces. For sense-development cf. *rug*. *Carpets* covered tables and beds before they were used for floors. Hence *on the carpet*, like F. *sur le tapis*, means on the table, before the council, etc. (see *bureau*). A *carpet-knight* was one knighted at court, kneeling on the carpet before the throne, instead of on the battlefield. A *carpet-bagger* was orig. a pol. adventurer from the northern US., who, after the war (1861–5), threw himself into southern politics to exploit the negro vote. The verb to *carpet*, to reprimand, was first used of servants made to "walk the carpet," i.e. summoned into the "parlour" for a wigging.

This man [Paris] is alwaye descrived of Homere as a more pleasaunt carpet knight then stoute warriour, and more delighting in instrumentes and daliaunce then martial prowesse and chivalrie
(Coop. *Dict. Hist.* 1565).

carpo- [*bot.*]. From G. καρπός, fruit.

carrack [*hist.*]. Large ship, galleon. OF. *caraque*, It. *caraca*, Sp. Port. *carraca*, MedL. *carraca, carrica*, whence also Du. *kraak* and obs. E. *crack*. A Mediterranean word. ? From Arab. *qarāqīr*, pl. of *qurqūr* (whence Port. *coracora*, kind of ship), from Late L. *carricare* (see *charge, carry*). Hence perh.

also naut. *carrick-bend, carrick-bitts*; cf. *karryk anker* (*Nav. Accts.* 1495–97).

And now hath Sathanas, seith he, a tayl,
Brodder than of a carryk is the sayl
(Chauc. D. 1687).

Two greate carracores and twò greate proas
(Jourdain's *Journ.* 1613).

carrageen. Edible sea-weed. From *Carragheen*, near Waterford.

carraway. See *caraway*.

carriage. ONF. *cariage* (*charriage*), from *carier* (see *carry*). The sense of vehicle was evolved from the abstract idea of carrying (cf. *conveyance*), and has, since middle of 18 cent., partly absorbed *caroch*, 16 cent. F. *carroche* (*carrosse*), It. *carroccia, carrozza*, from *carro*, car. F. *voiture*, VL. *vectura*, shows the same transition from the abstract to the concrete. For fig. sense cf. *bearing, deportment*.

carrucha: a carroch, a coche (Percyvall).

David left his carriage [*Vulg.* vasa quae attulerat] in the hand of the keeper of the carriage
(1 *Sam.* xvii. 22).

carrick bend [*naut.*]. See *carrack*.

carriole. F., It. *carriola*, from *carro*, car. Common in Canada (also kind of sleigh) and US., where it is sometimes altered to *carry-all*.

A new brightly-painted carry-all drawn by a slothful gray horse (O. Henry).

carrion. ONF. *caronie, caroigne* (*charogne*), VL. **caronia*, from *caro*, flesh; cf. It. *carogna*, Sp. *caroña*. Orig. (OF. & ME.) dead body.

carronade [*naut.*]. Short heavy naval gun, introduced 1779. From *Carron* iron-works, near Falkirk.

carrot. F. *carrotte*, L. *carota*, G. καρωτόν, prob. from κάρα, head.

carry. ONF. *carier* (*charrier*), from *car* (*char*), vehicle, car. For sense of winning, e.g. to *carry a fortress* (*all before one*), cf. similar use of F. *emporter*. Intrans. to *carry on* (naut.) seems to be evolved from to *carry sail*, F. *charrier de la voile*. For fig. sense cf. to *go on*.

cart. ON. *kartr*, cogn. with AS. *cræt*, chariot. ? Orig. of wicker (see *crate*). Has prob. also absorbed ONF. *carete* (*charrette*), dim. of *car* (*char*). To *cart*, defeat utterly, to be *in the cart*, done for, perh. go back to the cart in which criminals were taken to execution.

carte¹, quarte [*fencing*]. F. *quarte* (sc. *parade*), fem. of *quart*, fourth, L. *quartus*. Cf. *tierce*.

carte². F., in *carte blanche*, blank charter, *carte-de-visite*, small photograph, orig. intended to be used as visiting card. See *card¹*.

cartel. Challenge, written agreement. F., It. *cartello*, from *carta* (see *card¹*). Sense of commercial trust, also *kartel*, is app. via Ger. *kartell*.

Cartesian. Follower of *René Descartes*, F. mathematician and philosopher (1596–1650), latinized *Cartesius*.

Carthusian. MedL. *Cartusianus*, monk of *la Grande-Chartreuse* (Isère). Order founded by St Bruno (1086). See *charter-house*.

cartilage. F., L. *cartilago*.

cartle. See *kartel*.

cartography. See *card¹, chart*.

carton. F., card-board, card-board box (v.i.).

cartoon. F. *carton*, It. *cartone*, augment. of *carta*, card. *Punch* sense is mod.

cartouche. Ornament in scroll form, also figure in Egyptian hieroglyphics. F., It. *cartoccio*, from *carta*, card. Earlier also *cartridge* (v.i.).

cartoche: as cartouche, also, a cartridge, or roll (in architecture) (Cotg.).

cartridge. Corrupt. of *cartouche*, F., It. *cartoccio*, "a coffin of paper" (Flor.), from *carta*, card. *Cartridge-paper* was orig. the stiff, rough paper used for cartridges.

cartouche: a cartouch, or full charge, for a pistoll, put up within a little paper, to be the readier for use (Cotg.).

cartulary, chartulary. Late L. *cartularium*, from Late L. *cartula*, charter, dim. of L. *carta, charta*.

carucate [*hist.*]. Measure of land, prop. as much as could be ploughed with a team of eight in a year. MedL. *carrucata*, from Late L. *carruca*, plough, from *carrus*, car. Cf. *bovate, oxgang*.

caruncle. Fleshy excrescence. F. *caroncule*, L. *caruncula*, dim. from *caro*, flesh.

carve. AS. *ceorfan*. Com. Teut.; cf. Du. *kerven*, Ger. *kerben*, to notch, ON. *kyrfa*; cogn. with G. γράφειν, to write. Orig. strong, as in archaic p.p. *carven*. Replaced by *cut*, exc. in spec. senses.

carvel, caravel [*hist.*]. As I have shown elsewhere in an exhaustive note (*Trans. Phil. Soc.* Feb. 1910) these were orig. separate words. *Carvel-built*, i.e. with planks fitting edge to edge, as opposed to *clinker-built*, with overlapping planks, is of Du. origin. The reference is to the kind of nail used,

Du. *karviel* Sp. *cavilla*, L. *clavicula*, contrasted with *clincher*. *Caravel*, F. *caravelle*,
It. *caravella* (cf. Sp. *carabela*), is from Late
L. *carabus*, coracle, G. κάραβος. The two
words soon became hopelessly confused.

caryatid [*arch.*]. Column in form of female
figure. From L., G. Καρυάτιδες, pl. of
Καρυᾶτις, priestess of Artemis at *Caryae* in
Laconia.

cascabel [*archaic*]. Knob at rear of cannon.
Sp., little round bell, child's rattle, from
Late L. *cascabus*, bell.

cascade. F., It. *cascata*, from *cascare*, to fall,
VL. **casicare*, from *casus*, fall, *case*[1].

cascara. Sp., rind, bark, from *cascar*, to
break, VL. **quassicare*, from *quatere*,
quass-, to break. Cf. *quash*.

case[1]. Orig. what happens or befalls. F. *cas*,
L. *casus*, from *cadere*, *cas-*, to fall. In
gram. sense a transl. of G. πτῶσις, from
πίπτειν, to fall. Hence *casual*, *casualty*.
A much overworked word.

Case and instance are the commonest and the most
dangerous of a number of parasitic growths which
are the dry-rot of syntax
(*Times Lit. Supp.* May 8, 1919).

case[2]. Receptacle. ONF. *casse* (*châsse*), L.
capsa, from *capere*, to take, hold. Hence
case-hardened, of iron hardened on the surface; but, as *case* was used in 16 cent. for
skin or hide, perh. the epithet was orig.
of the same type as *hide-bound* (cf. to *case*,
i.e. skin, *a hare*, Mrs Glasse).

Glosty the fox is fled, there lies his case
(*Look about you*, 1600).

Hide-bound officials and service people of the case
hardened armour-plate type
(*Sunday Times*, July 8, 1917).

casein [*chem.*]. From L. *caseus*, cheese.

casemate. F.; cf. It. *casamatta*, Sp. *casamata*.
Orig. a cavity in the foss of a fortification,
as is shown by the Ger. equivalents *mord-
grube*, *mordkeller*, murder-ditch (-cellar).
First element has been associated with It.
casa, house, hut, and second with Sp.
matar, to slay (cf. *matador*), hence Flor.
has *casamatta*, "a casamat, or a slaughter-
house." But the earliest authority for the
word, Rabelais, has *chasmate*, both in the
mil. sense and in that of chasm, abyss (v.i.).
Hence Ménage was perh. right in deriving
the word from G. χάσμα, χασματ-, which
may very well have been introduced into
mil. lang. by the learned engineers of the
Renaissance, whose theories were chiefly
based on Caesar, Thucydides, etc. The use

of *vuider*, to empty, in quot. 1, shows that
the casemate was a cavity or pit.

Les autres...escuroyent contremines, gabionnoyent
deffenses, ordonnoyent plates formes, vuidoyent
chasmates (*Pantagruel*, iii. *Prol.*).

Bestes nommes neades, à la seule voix desquelles
la terre fondoyt en chasmates et en abysme
(*ib.* iv. 62).

casement. Prob. aphet. for *encasement*; cf.
OF. *enchâssement*, window frame. See
chase[2], *sash*[2].

caseous. See *casein*.

casern [*archaic*]. Barracks. Orig. used, like
barracks, of small huts ? for four men each
(cf. *mess*). F., Prov. *cazerna*, L. *quaterna*;
cf. Prov. *cazern*, quire (q.v.).

cash[1]. Money. F. *caisse* or It. *cassa*, L.
capsa, receptacle (see *case*[2]). Orig. money-
box. Financial terms are largely It. (cf.
bankrupt). In ModF. *caisse* means counting-house.

cassa: a chest,...also, a merchant's cash, or counter
(Flor.).

cash[2]. Various small Eastern coins. Perh.
ult. Tamil *kāsu*, some small coin or weight.
Cf. Port. *caixa*, *caxa*. Spelling has been
influenced by *cash*[1].

cashew. Nut. F., Port. *acajou*, which also
means mahogany, Brazil. *acaju*.

cashier[1]. Of bank. Adapted from F. *caissier*
(see *cash*[1]).

cashier[2] [*mil.*]. To dismiss. Archaic Du. *kas-
seren*, F. *casser*, to break, L. *quassare*, from
quassus (*quatere*). Cf. *roster*, *leaguer*, *furlough* and other war-words from the Low
Countries. Earlier also *cass*, from F. *casser*,
of which the p.p. is still in mil. use, in *cast
stores* (*horses*, etc.).

casser: to casse, cassere, discharge (Cotg.).

But the colonel said he must go, and he [the drum
horse] was cast [i.e. cassed] in due form
(Kipling, *Rout of the White Hussars*).

cashmere. From *Kashmir*, in Western Hima-
layas. Hence corrupt. *kerseymere*. With
archaic *cassimere* cf. F. perversion *casi-
mir*, assimilated to Pol. name.

casino. It., from *casa*, house, L. *casa*, hut.

cask. Sp. *casco*, pot, head, helmet, orig.
potsherd, from *cascare*, to break up, VL.
*quassicare (*quatere*). For sense-development cf. F. *tête*, L. *testa*, potsherd, vessel.
With later sense of helmet cf. once common use of *pot*, *kettle-hat*, etc. in same
sense (see also *bascinet*). *Casque*, from F.,
is thus the same word as *cask*, from which
it did not earlier differ in spelling. The
Elizabethan sailors regularly use *cask* as

collect. or pl. (cf. *cannon* and see quot. s.v. *size*).

casco: a caske or barganet, the sheards of an earthen pot, a tile-sheard, a head, a head-peece (Minsh.).

casket. Corrupted from F. *cassette* (14 cent.), dim. of *casse* (see *case²*). For -*k*- cf. *gasket*.

cassette: a small casket, chest, cabinet, or forcer (Cotg.).

casque. F., Sp. *casco*, replacing OF. *heaume* (OHG. *helm*). See *cask*.

Cassandra. Unheeded prophetess. Priam's daughter, who foretold destruction of Troy.

cassation. F., annulment, as in *cour de cassation*, from F. *casser*, to quash (q.v.).

cassava. Plant. A Haytian word with forms also in F., Sp. Port. See also *manioc*.

casserole. F., from *casse*, bowl, Sp. *cazo*, Arab. *qasa*, dish. Cf. *cassolette*.

cassia. Kind of cinnamon (*Ps.* xlv. 8). G. κασία, from Heb. *qātsa*, to strip off bark.

cassimere. See *cashmere*.

cassock. F. *casaque*, It. *casacca*, "a frocke, a horse-mans cote, a long cote" (Flor.); cf. Sp. *casaca*. Prob. of Slav. origin, ? *Cossack* (coat). Cf. *dalmatic*, *cravat*, and obs. *esclavine*, Slav mantle. *Cossack* is regularly *cassak* in Hakl. Eccl. sense is latest (17 cent.).

cassolette. Pan or box for perfumes. F., see *casserole*.

cassowary. Malay *kasuārī*, prob. via Du. or F.

cast. ON. *kasta*, cogn. with L. *gestare*. In ME. this replaced AS. *weorpan* (see *warp*), and is now itself largely replaced by *throw*. Formerly used in mod. sense of warp, turn, as still in a *cast in the eye*. The oldest sense seems to have been to throw into a heap, give shape to (cf. Norw. *kast*, *kost*, heap, pile). Hence metal *casting*, *cast of mind* (*actors*), *casting* a horoscope. From the last comes *forecast*. Obs. sense of deciding appears in *casting vote*. *Castaway* is oldest as theol. term, reprobate (1 *Cor.* ix. 27), where Wyc. has *reprovable*. So in 2 *Cor.* xiii. 5, Tynd., Coverd., Cranmer have *cast-away* where *AV.* has *reprobate*. Used allusively by Cowper (1799) as title of poem, and hence now associated with the sea. Some of the senses of the p.p. *cast* are from the obs. *cass* (see *cashier²*). Here belongs also partly *cast in damages*.

They all v wher cast for to dee
(Machyn's *Diary*, 1550–63).

Castalian. Of the Muses. From G. Κασταλία, spring on Mount Parnassus.

castanet. F. *castagnette*, Sp. *castañeta*, dim. of *castaña*, chestnut (q.v.), L. *castanea*. From shape.

castaway. See *cast*.

caste. Sp. Port. *casta*, race, orig. fem. of *casto*, pure, chaste, L. *castus*. First from Sp., but in mod. sense from India via Port., the spelling being taken from F. Cf. *padre*, *tank*. Hence to *lose caste*. *Caste* is now (1917–18) much used of any class claiming special privileges and immunities, Junkers, Bolshevists, trade-unionists, etc.

castellan [*archaic*]. ONF. *castellain*. See *châtelaine*.

castigate. From L. *castigare*. See *chastise*.

castle. AS. *castel*, village, L. *castellum*, dim. of *castrum*, fort; ME. *castel*, castle, ONF. *castel* (*château*). Introduced twice, in different senses now amalgamated. With *castle in the air* (16 cent.) cf. the earlier *castle in Spain*, from F. *château en Espagne*, recorded in 13 cent. (*Rom. de la Rose*). The chess *castle* replaced the *rook²* in 17 cent.

Go ye into the castel which is agens you
(Wyc. *Luke*, xix. 30).

castor¹. Beaver, beaver-hat. F., L., G. κάστωρ, an Eastern word. *Castor-oil*, now vegetable, was earlier applied to a drug obtained from the animal, L. *castoreum*, "oil made from the stones of the beaver" (Litt.). *Cold-drawn castor oil* is pressed out of the seeds without use of heat.

castor². As in *pepper-castor*, castor on chair-leg, for earlier *caster*, from *cast*, to throw, also, to turn. Hence *castor-sugar* (neol.), with which cf. Ger. *streuzucker*, lit. strew-sugar.

Castor and Pollux. See *Dioscuri*.

castrametation [*fort.*]. From L. *castra*, camp, *metari*, to measure.

castrate. From L. *castrare*, perh. cogn. with *castus*, pure.

casual. L. *casualis*, from *casus*, chance. Hence *casual labourer* (*pauper*, *ward*). *Casualty* in mil. sense is from earlier sense of mischance, accident.

casuist. F. *casuiste*, Sp. *casuista*, theologian who resolves "cases of conscience" (MedL. *casus conscientiae*), esp. (c. 1600) with ref. to the Jesuits.

cat. ONF. *cat* (*chat*), Late L. *cattus*; cf. Late G. κάττα. In most Europ. langs., but of obscure origin. Hence *cat o' nine tails* (17 cent.), the game of *cat* (16 cent.), *care killed the cat* (in spite of its nine lives). A *catcall* was orig. an instrument. Pepys bought one for theatre purposes. *Catspaw* refers to fable of cat, monkey and chestnuts. To *see which way the cat jumps*, i.e. to await events, appears to be mod.; cf. to *sit on the fence*. The obs. vessel called a *cat* (hence perh. mod. *catboat*) is the same word, though the reason for the name is not known. With *it rains cats and dogs* cf. F. *il pleut des hallebardes*, Ger. *es regnet heugabeln* (*bauernbuben*).

My Lord Bruncker, which I make use of as a monkey do the cat's foot (Pepys, June 6, 1666).

cata-. G. κατά, down, but with many subsidiary senses. Also *cat-, cath-*.

catachresis [*rhet.*]. Improper use of term. G., from καταχρῆσθαι, to misuse.

cataclysm. F. *cataclysme*, G. κατακλυσμός, from κλύζειν, to wash.

catacombs. Mod. sense dates from exploration of subterranean Rome, but the name, Late L. *Catacumbas* (c. 400 A.D.), was orig. applied only to the cemetery of St Sebastian near the Appian way. It is prob. a proper name the origin of which is lost. It occurs in AS. (10 cent.) and has forms in most Europ. langs.

catadromous. Of fish periodically descending river. Opposite of *anadromous*. From G. κατάδρομος, running down. Cf. *hippodrome*.

catafalque. F., It. *catafalco*. See *scaffold*.

Catalan [*ling.*]. Lang. of Catalonia, dial. of Provençal with Sp. affinities.

catalepsy. G. κατάληψις, from λαμβάνειν, to seize.

catalogue. F., Late L., G. κατάλογος, from λέγειν, to choose.

catalpa. Tree. Native NAmer. name (Carolina).

catalysis [*chem.*]. G. κατάλυσις, from λύειν, to loose.

catamaran. Navigable raft. From Tamil *katṭa*, tie, *maram*, wood.

catamount, catamountain. Leopard, panther, now more esp. puma. ME. *cat of mountain* was used to render L. *pardus*.

And the beast which I sawe was lyke a catte off the mountayne (Tynd. *Rev.* xiii. 2).

cataplasm. G. κατάπλασμα, poultice, from πλάσσειν, to plaster.

catapult. L. *catapulta*, G. καταπέλτης, from πάλλειν, to hurl. Orig. warlike engine, current sense from c. 1870.

cataract. F. *cataracte*, L. *cataracta*, G. καταράκτης, ? from ῥηγνύναι, to break, ? or ῥάσσειν, to dash. Oldest ME. sense is portcullis, whence the *cataract* obscuring

the eye. It occurs of the floodgates of heaven earlier than in the waterfall sense.

cataractae caeli apertae sunt (*Vulg. Gen.* vii. 11). *coulisse*: a portcullis; also a web in the eye (Cotg.).

catarrh. F. *catarrhe*, L., G. κατάρρους, from καταρρεῖν, to flow down.

catastrophe. G. καταστροφή, from στρέφειν, to turn. Orig. the fatal turning-point of a drama.

catawampous, catawamptious [*US.*]. Humorous coinage, perh. suggested by *catamount*.

catawba. Grape and wine. River in S. Carolina, named from the *Katahba* Indians.

catch. ONF. *cachier*, Picard form of *chasser*, VL. *captiare* for *captare*. See *chase*[1]. Past *caught*, for *catched*, is app. due to obs. *laught*, from ME. *lacchen*, native synonym of *catch*. This word perh. also accounts for the spec. sense which *catch* has acquired in E. A *catchword* was orig. the initial word of the following page placed to catch the reader's eye before turning over. Cf. the musical *catch*, in which each singer catches the line or melody from the preceding.

Things in motion sooner catch the eye
(*Troil. & Cress.* iii. 3).

catchpole [*hist.*]. MedL. *cacepollus*, OF. *chacepole* (*chasse poule*, hunt hen). See *catch*, *chase*[1], *polecat*. Orig. tax-gatherer, confiscating poultry if money was not forthcoming. Later, lower law officer.

Saul sente catchpollis [*Vulg.* lictores] for to take David (Wyc. 1 *Sam.* xix. 20).

catchup, catsup. Incorr. for *ketchup* (q.v.).

cate [*archaic*]. Aphet. for ME. *acate*, ONF. *acat* (*achat*), from *acheter*, to buy, L. *adcapitare*, to add to one's capital. Orig. purchase, later, dainty, delicacy, etc. Cf. *cater*.

My super-dainty Kate,
For dainties are all Kates, and therefore, Kate,
Take this of me (*Shrew*, ii. 1).

catechize. MedL. *catechizare*, G. κατηχίζειν, from κατηχεῖν, to resound, teach, etc. (*Luke*, i. 4), from κατά, down, ἠχεῖν, to sound. *Catechumen* (*Piers Plowm.*) is G. κατηχούμενος (pres. part. pass.).

catechu. Astringent from bark. Malay *kāchu*. Also in Canarese and Tamil.

category. G. κατηγορία, accusation, assertion, from κατηγορεῖν, to speak against, from ἀγορά, place of assembly. Use of the word is chiefly due to Aristotle. *Categorical imperative*, moral law springing from pure reason, is from Kant.

catenary [*math.*]. From L. *catena*, chain.

cater. First as noun. ME. *acatour, catour*, buyer (see *cate*). For lengthened *caterer* cf. *fruiterer, poulterer, upholsterer*. Hence perh. archaic *cater-cousin*, intimate (cf. *foster-brother, messmate, chum*).

A gentil Maunciple was ther of a temple,
Of which achatours myghte take exemple...
Algate he wayted so in his achaat
That he was ay biforn and in good staat
                    (Chauc. A. 567).

cateran. Highland marauder. Orig. collect. Gael. *ceathairne*, peasantry. The *-th-*, long mute in Celt., should have disappeared, as in the doublet *kern*; but cf. *bother, bothy*.

caterpillar. From OF. *chatepelose*, hairy cat, from L. *pilosus*, hairy. Cf. F. *chenille*, caterpillar, lit. little dog; also E. *woolly bear*, of a special kind (see also *catkin*). The ending has been assimilated to *piller*, one who "pills" the bark from trees, plunders. This connection appears in the frequent use of *caterpillar* for extortioner.

catyrpyllar worme: chatte pelouse (Palsg.).
Covetous persons, extorcioners, oppressours, catir-pillers, usurers (Latimer).

caterwaul. Replaced (c. 1500) older *caterwaw* (Chauc.), *caterwrawle*, etc. The second syllable is imit. of the voice of the amorous cat, the first element suggests Ger. & Du. *kater*, male cat, not otherwise recorded in E. It is perh. for **cata-*, with *-a-* as in *blackamoor, Greenaway*, etc.

catgut. From *cat* and *gut*, though made from intestines of sheep. Cf. synon. Du. *katte-darm*. Earliest ref. (16 cent.) is to fiddle-strings. Cf. *catling*.

cathartic. Purgative. L., G. καθαρτικός, from καθαρός, clean.

Cathay [*poet.*]. Northern China. MedL. *Kitai* (13 cent.) as name of inhabitants, from foreign dynasty, the *Khitan*.

cathedral. Orig. adj., as in *cathedral church*. MedL. *cathedralis*, from G. καθέδρα, seat, from κατά, down, ἑδ-, sit. Cf. *see*[2], and see *chair*. Cf. *ex cathedra*, authoritative pronouncement, as from seat of dignity.

Catherine wheel. Spiked wheel used in legendary martyrdom of *St Catherine* of Alexandria, whose name, Αἰκατερίνα, was altered on καθαρός, pure.

catheter. G., from καθιέναι, to send down.

cathode [*electr.*]. G. κάθοδος, way down. Cf. *anode*.

catholic. F. *catholique*, MedL. *catholicus*, G. καθολικός, universal, from κατά and ὅλος, whole, as applied to the Church "through-

out all the world." The E. word dates, in gen. and spec. sense, from 16 cent. At first applied to the whole Christian Church, it had been assumed by the Western Church after its separation from the Eastern (Orthodox). In E. it tended to become offensive after the Reformation, and was replaced by *Roman Catholic* in the negotiations for the Spanish Match (1618–24). Cf. *catholicon*, panacea.

catkin. Used by Lyte (1578) in his transl. of Dodoens to render Du. *katteken*, lit. kitten. Cf. F. *chaton*, Ger. *kätzchen*, both used in same sense, and synon. derivatives of *cattus* in most Rom. dialects. Earlier called *aglet, tag*.

chattons: the catkins, cattails, aglet-like blowings, or bloomings, of nut-trees, etc. (Cotg.).

catling. Fine cat-gut (*Troil. & Cress.* iii. 3). From *cat*.

catonism. Austerity. From *Cato the Censor*, or *Cato of Utica*.

catoptric. Of reflexion. G. κατοπτρικός, from κατά and ὀπ-, see. Cf. *optics*.

catsup. See *ketchup*. For folk-etym. perversion cf. *Welsh rarebit* for *rabbit*.

cattle. ONF. *catel*, L. *capitale*, stock, capital, from *caput, capit-*, head. In ME. esp. moveable property, beasts (*chattels*), as opposed to lands, etc. (*goods*). Cf. hist. of *fee* and *pecuniary*. See *chattel*. Used of farm-beasts from 13 cent., and of horses from 17 cent.

With all my worldely cathel I the endowe
            (*Sarum Manual*, c. 1400).

catty. Weight (EInd.). Ident. with *caddy*.

caubeen [*Ir.*]. Hat. Ir. *cáibín*, dim. of *cap*. Cf. *colleen, squireen*.

Caucasian. Formerly used (first by Blumenbach, c. 1800) for Indo-European, white races, from supposed place of origin.

Is our civilization a failure?
Or is the Caucasian played out? (*Heathen Chinee*).

caucus. US. (18 cent.). Private political meeting. Applied opprobriously (1878) by Beaconsfield to the Birmingham "Six Hundred," but used much earlier in E. (v.i.). Prob. an Algonkin word for counsellor, found in Capt. John Smith as *Caw-cawaassough*. Cf. *pow-wow, Tammany*.

A selection...similar to that which our Transatlantic brethren would call a "caucus"
         (Lord Strangford, in H. of L., 1831).

caudal, caudate. From L. *cauda*, tail.

Caudine Forks. Pass near Capua where the Romans were defeated (321 B.C.) by the Samnites and were made to pass under the yoke. Hence fig. irretrievable disaster.

caudle. ONF. *caudel* (*chaudeau*), from *chaud*, hot, L. *calidus*.

chaudeau: a caudle; or warme broth (Cotg.).

cauk. See *cawk*.

caul. Orig. close-fitting cap or net. F. *cale*, cap, back-formation from *calotte* (q.v.). For naut. superstition connected with *caul* cf. its Icel. name *sigurcufl*, lit. victory cowl. With•archaic *born with a caul* (i.e. lucky) cf. F. *né coiffé*.

cauldron. ONF. *caudron* (*chauderon*), augment. of *chaudière*, L. *cal(i)daria*, also *cal(i)-darium*, from *calidus*, hot. Cf. It. *calderone*, Sp. *calderón*. The *-l-* has been restored by learned influence. See also *chaldron*, *chowder*.

What shal comune the caudron to the pot?
(Wyc. *Ecclesiasticus*, xiii. 3).

cauliflower. For earlier *cole florie*, with first element latinized (*caulis*, cabbage). Cf. F. *chou-fleur*, earlier *chou-flori*, Sp. *coliflor*, Ger. *blumenkohl*, etc. See *cole*.

choux fleuris: the collyflory, or·Cypres colewort
(Cotg.).

caulk, calk. Late L. *calicare*, to stop up chinks with lime, L. *calx*. This replaced (c. 1500) earlier to *lime*. Cf. F. *calfater*, Port. *calafetar*, from *cal*, lime, *afeitar*, to arrange, L. *affectare*, forms of which exist in this sense in almost every naut. lang. The earliest *caulkers* (Noah and the mother of Moses) used bitumen, still employed for the same purpose in the East (see *goufa*). In MedL. *bituminatus* is regularly used for caulked, and is rendered *i-glewed* by Trevisa. Raleigh caulked his ships with "stone-pitch" from the pitch lake of Trinidad and caulking with lime is described in Hakl. (x. 202).

Lyme it [the ark] with cleye and pitche within and without (Caxton, 1483).

The shippe for to caulke and pyche (*NED.* c. 1500).

In stead of pitch we made lime and did plaster the morter into the seames (Hakl.).

cause. F., L. *causa*, which had the main senses found in F. & E. *Causerie, causeuse*, F., are from *causer*, in secondary sense of talking.

causeway. Folk-etym. for earlier *causey* (still in dial. use), ONF. *caucíée* (*chaussée*), Late L. *calciata* (*via*), which some connect with

L. *calx*, lime, others with *calx*, heel (cf. *trodden* way).

The causey to Hell-gate (*Par. L.* x. 417).

caustic. L., G. καυστικός, from καίειν, to burn.

cautelous [*archaic*]. F. *cauteleux*, from L. *cautela*, caution (q.v.).

The Jews, not undoubtedly resolved of the sciatica-side of Jacob, do cautelously in their diet refrain from the sinew of both (Sir T. Browne).

cauterize. F. *cautériser*, Late L. *cauterizare*, from *cauterium*, hot iron, G. καυτήριον, from καίειν, to burn.

caution. F., L. *cautio-n-*, from *cavēre, caut-*, to beware. Oldest sense, security, as still in *caution-money* (univ.). The US. meaning of extraordinary person, circumstance, etc., perh. springs from such use as that exemplified below. Cf. *example*.

The way I'll lick you will be a caution to the balance of your family (Thornton, 1834).

Our appetite for dinner will be a caution to alligators (*ib.* 1862).

cavalcade. F., Prov. *cavalcada* or It. *cavalcata*, from p.p. fem. of Late L. *caballicare*, to ride, from *caballus*, horse. Cf. F. *chevauchée*, mounted raid, the earliest sense of *cavalcade* in E.

cavalier. Orig. horseman. F., It. *cavaliere*, from *cavallo*, horse, corresponding to F. *chevalier*. Earlier adopted as *cavalero* from OSp. *cavallero* (*caballero*). As applied to the partisans of Charles I it was orig. reproachful (like *Roundhead*). In both E. & F. it has also the sense of off-hand, discourteous, e.g. *cavalier treatment* (*tone*, etc.).

cavally. Fish, "horse-mackerel." Synon. It. *cavallo*, lit. horse.

cavalry. F. *cavalerie*, It. *cavalleria*. See *cavalier, chivalry*, for the latter of which it is often used in 16 cent.

cavatina [*mus.*]. It., dim. of *cavata*, prop. a detached air, from *cavare*, to hollow out, remove, from *cavus*, hollow.

cave. F., L. *cava*, neut. pl. of L. *cavus*, hollow. In ModF. means cellar only. For current pol. sense see *Adullamite*.

cave in. Chiefly US., also with trans. sense. Altered, on *cave*, from earlier E. dial. to *calve in*, with which cf. WFlem. *in-kalven*, to cave in, Du. *af-kalven*, to break away, *uit-kalven*, to fall apart, all "navvy" words. Perh. introduced into EAngl. by Du. drainage experts. So also we have dial. to *colt in*, in same sense, ground-idea being app. separation at birth.

A dyche bank apon the same dyche, the which colted in (*Coventry Leet Book*, 1451).

The way they heav'd those fossils in their anger was a sin,
Till the skull of an old mammoth caved the head of Thompson in (Bret Harte).

caveat [*leg.*]. L., let him beware, from *cavēre*. Init. word of certain legal cautions. Cf. schoolboy *cave* (imper.) and proverb. *caveat emptor*, let the purchaser look out for himself.

cavendish. (1) Tobacco. ?From name of exporter. (2) Treatise on whist (1862), from pen-name of author, H. Jones.

cavern. F. *caverne*, L. *caverna*, from *cavus*, hollow.

cavesson. Nose-band for a horse. F. *caveçon*, It. *cavezzone*, from *cavezza*, halter, prob. connected with L. *capistrum*, halter (see *capstan*).

cavey. See *cavy*.

caviare. Earlier also *cavialy* (16 cent. F. *cavial*, It. *caviale*). F. *caviar*, It. *caviaro*. Turk. *khāvyār* is prob. from It. Though from Russia, it is app. not a Russ. word, the native name being *ikra*. The earlier E. forms are numerous and varied. Hence *caviare to the general*, too subtle for the common herd (*Haml.* ii. 2).

Of ickary or cavery a great quantitie is made upon the river of Volgha (Hakl. iii. 367).

cavil. F. *caviller*, L. *cavillari*, to satirize, argue scoffingly. But dial. *cavil*, to squabble, suggests rather synon. Norw. dial. *kjavla*, to quarrel, ult. cogn. with AS. *ceafl*, jaw.

cavity. F. *cavité*, Late L. *cavitas*, from *cavus*, hollow; cf. It. *cavità*, Sp. *cavidad*.

cavort [*US.*]. To prance. Prob. cowboy perversion of *curvet* (q.v.).

The general sits his cavorting steed (O. Henry).

cavy. Rodent of guinea-pig tribe. *Cabiai*, native name in F. Guiana. Cf. *capybara*.

caw. Imit. Cf. Du. *kaauw*, jackdaw.

cawk [*geol.*]. Loc. name for kind of spar. Northern form of *chalk*.

caxon [*archaic*]. Wig. ? From surname *Caxon*; ? cf. *busby*.

caxton. Book printed by *Caxton* (†1492). Cf. *elzevir*.

cay. See *key*[2].

cayenne. Pepper. Earlier *cayan, kian*, etc., as still pronounced, Tupi (Brazil) *kyynha*, mistakenly associated with the town of *Cayenne* (F. Guiana). Cf. *guinea-pig*.

cayman, caiman. Sp. Port. *caiman*, of Carib origin, but described as a Congo word in 1598. Many early exotic names of animals, plants, etc. wandered from E. to W. and vice-versa, often perh. in connection with the slave-trade (cf. *banana, papaw, yaws*).

A fish called by the Spaniards "lagarto," and by the Indians "caiman," which is indeed a crocodile (Hakl.).

cease. ME. *cessen*, F. *cesser*, L. *cessare*, frequent. of *cedere, cess-*, to give way.

cecity. L. *caecitas*, from *caecus*, blind.

Cecropian. Of *Cecrops*, founder of Athens.

cedar. F. *cèdre*, L., G. κέδρος. Also AS. *ceder*, direct from L.

cede. L. *cedere*, to yield.

cedilla. Sp. *cedilla*, It. *zediglia*, little *z*.

cee-spring, C-spring [*carriage-building*]. From shape. Cf. *S-drain, T-square, Y-bracket*, etc.

ceiling, cieling. From verb to *ceil*, prob. from F. *ciel*, canopy, L. *caelum*, heaven (cf. Ger. *himmel*, heaven, ceiling); but influenced by OF. *cieller*, L. *caelare*, to carve, and by *seal*[2] (q.v.) in its sense of complete enclosure. *Syll-, seel-* are the usual earlier spellings.

celadon [*archaic*]. Pale green. F., name of character in d'Urfé's *Astrée* (1610). Cf. *isabel*.

celandine. Swallow-wort. Earlier *celidony*, OF. *celidoine*, L. *chelidonia*, from G. χελιδόνιον, from χελιδών, swallow.

celarent [*logic*]. Mnemonic word. See *barbara*.

-cele [*med.*]. In *varicocele*, etc. G. κήλη, swelling.

celebrate. From L. *celebrare*, orig. to honour by assembling, from *celeber, celebr-*, populous, renowned. Earliest (17 cent.) in ref. to Eucharist.

celeriac. App. arbitrary formation from *celery* (q.v.).

celerity. F. *célérité*, L. *celeritas*, from *celer*, swift.

celery. F. *céleri*, It. dial. *sellari*, pl. of *sellaro* (It. *sedano*), ult. from G. σέλινον. For pl. form cf. *lettuce*.

celestial. OF. *celestiel*, from *céleste*, L. *caelestis*, from *caelum*, heaven. *Celestial Empire*, for China, is due to the title *T'ien-tsz*, son of heaven, formerly borne by the Emperor.

Celestine. Branch of Benedictines, established by Pope *Celestine V* (13 cent.).

celibate. From L. *caelibatus*, celibacy, from *caelebs*, *caelib-*, unmarried.

cell. ME. & OF. *celle*, L. *cella*, cogn. with *celare*, to hide. Earliest sense is monastic. Biol. sense from 17 cent.

cellar. L. *cellarium*, set of cells. But *salt-cellar* is for earlier *saler*, *seller*, F. *salière*, salt-cellar, whence ME. *saler*, *seler*, so that *salt-* is pleon.

saliere: a salt-seller (Cotg.).

cello. For *violoncello* (q.v.).

celluloid. Invented in US. and patented here in 1871. Orig. adj., cell-like, from F. *cellule*, L. *cellula*, which in F. (and consequently in many E. derivatives) has replaced OF. *celle*, L. *cella*.

Celt, Kelt. F. *Celte*, L. *Celta*, sing. of *Celtae*, G. Κελτοί (Herodotus), used by the Romans esp. of the Gauls, but app. not of the British. Mod. usage in ethnology and philology began in F. (c. 1700). Hence *Celtomaniac*, philologist who finds Celt. traces everywhere. See also *Brythonic*, *Goidelic*.

celt [*antiq.*]. Prehistoric implement. Prob. a ghost-word, occurring only in some MSS. of the Clementine text of the *Vulg.*, where it may be a misprint for *certe*. Adopted (c. 1700) by archaeologists, perh. by a fanciful association with *Celt*.

Stylo ferreo, et plumbi lamina, vel celte sculpantur in silice (*Vulg. Job*, xix. 24).

cembalo. Mus. instrument. It., as *cymbal* (q.v.).

cement. ME. *cyment*, F. *ciment*, L. *caementum*, for *caedimentum*, from *caedere*, to cut, the earliest cement being made from small chippings of stone.

cemetery. L., G. κοιμητήριον, dormitory, from κοιμᾶν, to put to sleep. Adopted in this sense by early Christians and applied at first to the catacombs. Earlier *cymetery* came via F. *cimetière*.

cenacle. Literary coterie. F. *cénacle*, name of first Romantic group (c. 1820), L. *cenaculum*, supper-room, esp. in ref. to Last Supper, from L. *cena*, supper.

cenobite. See *coenobite*.

cenotaph. Monument to person buried elsewhere. G. κενοτάφιον, from κενός, empty, τάφος, tomb. A household word from 1919.

censer. For *incenser*; cf. F. *encensoir*. See *incense*.

censor. L., arbiter of morals, from *censēre*, to judge. *NED.* (1893) finds no example of verb to *censor*. Cf. *censure*, F., L. *censura*.

census. L., from *censēre*, to estimate. Earlier used also of a poll-tax. The offic. census dates from 1790 (US.), 1791 (France), 1801 (Great Britain), 1813 (Ireland).

cent. F., L. *centum*, hundred. *Per cent.* is from It. *per cento* (cf. F. *pour cent*), our financ. and bookkeeping terms being largely It. Adopted (1786) in US. for one-hundredth of dollar. Cf. F. *centime*, one-hundredth of franc (First Republic). *A red cent* may refer to colour of copper (cf. archaic F. *rouge liard* and E. *brass farthing*), or *red* may be a substitution for a more emphatic adj.

cental. Weight of 100 lbs. introduced into Liverpool corn-market 1859, and legalized 1879. From *cent* after *quintal* (q.v.).

centaur. L., G. κένταυρος. Hence the plant *centaury*, G. κενταύρειον, med. qualities of which were fabled to have been discovered by Chiron the centaur.

centenary. L. *centenarius*, numbering a hundred. Cf. *centennial*, formed after *biennial*, etc.

centesimal. From L. *centesimus*, hundredth.

centigrade. Thermometer of Celsius (†1744), with 100 degrees between freezing and boiling point. F., from L. *centum*, hundred, *gradus*, degree.

centipede. F. *centipède*, L. *centipeda*, from *pes*, *ped-*, foot.

cento. Composition from scraps of other authors. L., patchwork; cf. G. κέντρων, patchwork.

centre. F., L. *centrum*, G. κέντρον, goad, stationary point of compasses, from κεντεῖν, to prick. Several of the math. senses appear in Chauc., who also uses *centre* for later *centre of gravity* (17 cent.). In F. politics the *centre* is composed of moderates, the *left* being radical and the *right* reactionary. This is an inheritance from the National Assembly of 1789 in which the nobles took the place of honour on the president's right, while the representatives of the Third Estate (the Commons) were on his left. In Ger. the *centre* is composed of the Catholics or Ultramontanes. *Centrifugal* (L. *fugere*, to flee) and *centripetal* (L. *petere*, to seek) were coined by Newton.

centuple. F., Late L. *centuplus*, for *centuplex*, from *centum*, hundred, *plic-*, fold.

century. L. *centuria*, group of one hundred in various senses. Cf. *centurion*, explained by Tynd. as *hunder-captain*. Usual meaning, peculiar to E., is for earlier *century of years* (17 cent.).

ceorl [*hist.*]. AS. original of *churl* (q.v.). Cf. *carl*.

cephalic. F. *céphalique*, L., G. κεφαλικός, from κεφαλή, head. Cf. *cephalopod*, cuttle-fish, etc., from πούς, ποδ-, foot.

ceramic. G. κεραμικός, from κέραμος, potter's earth.

cerastes. Horned viper. L., G. κεράστης, from κέρας, horn. Cf. biol. terms in *cerato*-.

Cerberus. L., G. Κέρβερος, watch-dog of hell. Hence *sop to Cerberus*.

Cui vates, horrere videns jam colla colubris,
Melle soporatam et medicatis frugibus offam
Obicit (*Aen.* vi. 419).

cereal. L. *cerealis*, from *Ceres*, goddess of agriculture.

cerebral. From L. *cerebrum*, brain (with dim. *cerebellum*), cogn. with G. κάρα, head. *Unconscious cerebration* was coined (1853) by W. B. Carpenter.

cerecloth (*Merch. of Ven.* ii. 7), **cerement** (*Haml.* i. 4). From F. *cirer*, to wax, from L. *cera*, wax, G. κηρός; cf. obs. to *cere*, to wrap corpse in waxed cloth (*Cymb.* i. 1).

ceremony. Also ME. *ceremoyne*, OF. *ceremoine* (*cérémonie*), L. *caerimonia*. With to *stand on ceremony* (*Jul. Caes.* ii. 2) cf. to *insist*, L. *insistere*, to stand on.

ceriph, serif [*typ.*]. Fine horizontal hair-line at termination of (esp. capital) letter. ? Du. *schreef*, line, stroke. Many early printing terms are Du.; but *sanserif* (q.v.) is earlier.

cerise. F., cherry (q.v.).

cerium [*chem.*]. Named after the then (1801) recently discovered planet *Ceres*.

cero-. From L. *cera* or G. κηρός, wax.

cert. Colloq. shortening of *certainty*. App. mod. (not in *NED.*).

certain. F., Late L. **certanus*, from *certus*, orig. p.p. of *cernere*, to decide. Sense-development follows that of L. *certus*. Indef. meaning, app. the opposite of the original, a *certain man*, a *lady of a certain age*, etc., springs from the idea of an ascertained fact the details of which are not necessarily accessible to all.

A very old house, perhaps as old as it claimed to be, and perhaps older, which will sometimes happen with houses of an uncertain, as with ladies of a certain age (*Barnaby Rudge*, ch. i.).

certes [*archaic*]. F., prob. L. *certas*, used as adv.; cf. OSp. *certas*.

certify. F. *certifier*, Late L. *certificare*, from *certus* and *facere*. Cf. *certificate*.

certiorari [*leg.*]. Writ from higher to lower court. L., to be made more certain, occurs in writ. Cf. *habeas corpus*, *caveat*, etc.

certitude. F., Late L. *certitudo*, from *certus*.

cerulean, caerulean. From L. *caeruleus*, blue, blue-green, etc., prob. by dissim. for **caeluleus*, from *caelum*, heaven, sky.

ceruse. White lead. F. *céruse*, L. *cerussa*, perh. from G. κηρός, wax.

cervical. From L. *cervix*, *cervic*-, neck.

cervine. L. *cervinus*, from *cervus*, hart. Cf. *bovine*, *ovine*, etc.

Cesarevitch, -witch. Earlier *Czarevitsch*, *Czarowicz*, etc., son of *czar* (q.v.), was replaced as official title by *Cesarevitsch*, modelled on restored spelling (*Caesar*). The ending is Russ. *vitsch*, Pol. *wicz*, common in patronymics. The race called the *Cesarewitch* (Newmarket, 1839) was named in honour of the Russ. prince, afterwards Alexander II, who was on a state visit to England.

cespitose. From L. *caespis*, *caespit*-, turf.

cess [*Sc. & Ind.*]. Rate, land-tax; also as verb. For *sess*, aphet. for *assess* (q.v.). In Ir. also of military exactions, hence perh. *bad cess to you* (? or for *bad success*). L. *census*, tax, etc., has app. had some influence on this word (cf. *excise*).

census: valued, cessed, taxed (Coop.).

The English garrisons cessed and pillaged the farmers of Meath and Dublin (Froude).

cessation. L. *cessatio-n-*. See *cease*.

cesser [*leg.*]. Termination. F. *cesser*, to cease (q.v.). For use of infin. cf. *misnomer*, *oyer et terminer*, etc.

cession. F., L. *cessio-n-*, from *cedere*, *cess*-, to yield.

cesspool. Earliest form *cesperalle* (16 cent.) suggests perversion of obs. *suspiral*, F. *soupirail*, ventilator, air-shaft, from L. *suspirium*, breath. Further corrupt. to *cesspool* (*suspool*, *sesspool*, *cestpool*) would be quite possible. It. *cesso*, privy, from L. *secessus*, has also been suggested, but it does not seem likely that an It. word would have been introduced to form a hybrid dial. compd. Skeat suggests *recess*, and quotes (1764) "two recesses or pools, as reservoirs of dung and water," but no other record is known of *recess* in this sense.

Cestr. Signature of bishop of Chester. For MedL. *Cestrensis*.

cestus. Girdle, esp. of Aphrodite. L., G. κεστός, lit. stitched. Perh. hence also the

gladiatorial *caestus, cestus*, glove, usu. regarded as irreg. formation from *caedere*, to
strike.

cesura. See *caesura*.

cetacea. ModL. from L. *cetus*, whale, G. κῆτος.

chablis. White wine from *Chablis* (Yonne).

chabouk. See *sjambok*.

Chadband. Sanctimonious humbug (*Bleak
House*). Cf. *Stiggins, Podsnap*, etc.

Chadbands all over the country have shrieked
over the soldier's rum ration
(*Referee*, June 24, 1917).

chafe. Earlier *chaufe*, F. *chauffer*, VL. **cale-
fare* for *calefacere*, to make hot, *calidus*.
Cf. *chafing-dish*. For vowel cf. *safe*. Fig.
senses via that of heat-producing friction.

chafer. Insect. AS. *ceafor*; cf. Du. *kever*, Ger.
käfer. Prob. gnawer (cf. *beetle* and see *jowl*).
The more usual *cockchafer* is comparatively
mod. The prefix may suggest size, but
may be for *cack*, stercus. Cf. synon. *dung-
beetle*, and Ger. *kotkäfer, mistkäfer*, also obs.
kaakkäfer.

chaff. AS. *ceaf*; cf. Du., Ger. dial. *kaf*. In
AS. Bible versions also for straw. With
chaffinch cf. Late L. *furfurio*, chaffinch,
from *furfur*, bran. The verb in its mod.
slang sense is a combination of *chafe*, to
irritate, and of the noun *chaff* in its fig.
sense of nonsense, worthless matter (which
will not catch birds).

His reasons are two grains of wheat hid in two
bushels of chaff (*Merch. of Ven.* i. 1).

chaffer. Now equivalent to *barter, haggle*, but
orig. trade. First as noun, from AS. *cēap*,
price, *faru*, journey, etc.; cf. ON. *kaupför*,
commercial journey, and Ger. *kauffahr-
teischiff*, merchant ship. *Cheapfare* occurs
in ME. See also *chapman, cheap, coper,
cooper²*.

To wite hou myche ech hadde wonne bi chaffaryng
(Wyc. *Luke*, xix. 15).

chagrin. F., from Turk. *saghri*, rump of a
horse, whence *shagreen* (q.v.), a leather of
granulated appearance, is prepared. For
the metaphor cf. *gooseflesh* and F. *chair de
poule*. There are chronological difficulties
in the hist. of the F. word, but the quot.
below points clearly to association with
the leather in E.

Thoughts which...had made their skin run into a
chagrin (*NED.* 1734).

chain. F. *chaîne*, L. *catena*.

chair. F. *chaire*, L. *cathedra*, G. καθέδρα,
from κατά, down, ἑδ-, sit. For F. *chaise*,

which has superseded *chaire*, exc. in spec.
senses (pulpit, professorial chair), see
chaise. Replaced native *stool* as name for
seat suggesting added ease and dignity,
traces of which survive in some mod.
senses (e.g. in *chairman*).

chaise. F., chair (q.v.), taking the sense
of vehicle via that of sedan chair, *chaise
à porteurs*. *Chair* was used in same sense
in 18 cent. See also *chay, shay*. F. *chaise*
is due to an affected Parisian interchange
of *r-s* (15–16 cents.) often satirized by F.
writers.

Les musailles ont deroseilles (Marot).

chalcedony. L. *c(h)alcedonius* (*Rev.* xxi. 19),
G. χαλκηδών. The ME. form was *cassidoine*,
from OF. Vars. such as *carchedonius* occur
in Pliny and Isidore. Hence place of origin
may have been *Chalcedon* (Asia Minor) or
Καρχηδών (Carthage).

Calcedoine est piere jalne
Entre iacint e beril meaine...
De Sithie [Scythia] est enveiee
E de culurs treis est trovee
(*Lapidaire de Marbod*, 12 cent.).

chalcography. Copper engraving. From G.
χαλκός, copper.

Chaldaic, Chaldean, Chaldee. From G. Χαλ-
δαῖος, of *Chaldea*, i.e. Babylonia. Esp. with
ref. to magical and astrological studies.
The lang. (Aramaic) was that of the Jews
after the Captivity and is exemplified in
the few reported sayings of Our Lord
(*ephphatha, talitha cumi*, etc.).

Like the Chaldean, he could watch the stars
(*Childe Harold*, iii. 14).

chaldron. Dry measure (32 bushels, or, if
coal, 36, and, at Newcastle, 53 cwt.). This
and Sc. *chalder* (32 to 64 bushels), earlier
(1497) also *chelder*, are usu. referred to F.
chaudron, cauldron (q.v.). But what a
cauldron! The Sc. forms, with corresponding MedL. *celdra* (in early Sc. statutes)
and AF. *chaldre de carbons* (1416), also do
not favour the "cauldron" etym. ? From
Du. *kelder*, cellar.

A chalder of coles for the merchauntes own house,
meanyng so many coles as ye will spend yearlye
(*York Merch. Advent.* 1562).

chalet. Swiss-F. Origin obscure. ? A dim.
of L. *castellum*; cf. Languedoc *castrun*,
shepherd's hut.

chalice. OF. (*calice*), L. *calix, calic-*, cogn.
with G. κύλιξ, cup. In eccl. sense appears
earlier in AS. *calic*, and *cal-* forms are also
found in ME.

chalk. AS. *cealc*, Lat. *calx, calc-*, lime. F. has *chaux*, lime, and *craie*, L. *creta*, chalk, so also Ger. *kalk*, lime, *kreide*, chalk. The change of sense in E. is no doubt due to the chalk (carbonate of lime) which is such a conspicuous feature of the south of England. *By a long chalk* is from the use of chalk in scoring points in games.

Lo, how they feignen chalk for chese (Gower).

challenge. First as verb. OF. *chalengier, chalongier*, from OF. *chalonge*, L. *calumnia*, false accusation. Orig. to accuse, call to account, a trace of which survives in *challenging* a juryman (sentry).

The King of Spain doth challenge me to be the quarreller, and the beginner of all these wars
(Queen Elizabeth).

challis. Fabric, first made at Norwich (c. 1830). ? From surname *Challis*, which is derived from *Calais*. ? Or from the town itself, pronounced *Ch-* in patois.

chalybeate. Irreg. (*-eate* for *-ate*) from L. *chalybs*, steel, G. χάλυψ. Cf. *roseate*.

Cham [*hist.*]. Obs. form of *Khan¹* (q.v.), applied esp. to the Khan of Tartary (*Much Ado*, ii. 1), and, by Smollett, to Dr Johnson.

chamade [*hist.*]. Drum or trumpet signal for parley. F., Port. *chamada*, from *chamar*, to cry, L. *clamare*.

fazer chamada: to beat a parley (Vieyra).

chamber. F., L. *camera*, G. καμάρα, cogn. with L. *camurus*, arched (see *camber*). *Chamberlain* is one of several OF. forms of *chambellan*, the correct form being *chambrelenc*, OHG. *chamarling*, from Ger. *kammer* (from L.), and Ger. suffix *-ling* (cf. *camerlengo*). For mod. dignity cf. *constable, marshal, steward*. The licensing of plays by the *Lord Chamberlain of the Household* is the last relic of the authority formerly wielded by that functionary over the "royal actors."

chambertin. Wine. From an estate in Burgundy, near Dijon.

chameleon. G. χαμαιλέων, from χαμαί, on the earth, dwarf, λέων, lion. Cf. *caterpillar, hippopotamus, antlion*, etc. Often fig., as fabled to live on air and able to change colour.

The thin chameleon, fed with air, receives
The colour of the thing to which he cleaves
(Dryden).

chamfer [*techn.*]. To groove. Back-formation from *chamfering*, perversion of F. *chan-*

frein, OF. *chanfraint*, p.p. of OF. *chanfraindre*, from *chant*, edge (see *cant¹*) and OF. *fraindre*, to break, L. *frangere*. For corrupt. cf. *fingering*, for back-formation cf. *maffick*.

chanfrain: a chanfering; or, a channell, furrow, hollow gutter, or streake, in stone-worke, etc.
(Cotg.).

chamfrain, chamfron [*hist.*]. Frontlet of barded horse. F. *chanfrein*, perh. from L. *camus*, muzzle, and *frenum*, bridle, but the many early forms, due to folk-etym., make the origin doubtful.

His gallant war-house...with a chamfron, or plaited head-piece upon his head (*Ivanhoe*, ch. ii.).

chamois. F.; cf. It. *camoscio, camozza*, Prov. *camis*, Ger. *gemse* (OHG. *gamiza*). It is uncertain which way the borrowing has taken place, but the earliest known form, Late L. *camox* (5 cent.), suggests connection with F. *camus*, flat-nosed, cogn. with L. *camurus* (see *camber*), a natural description of the animal. But some regard it as a pre-Roman Alp. word. The old form *chamoy, shammoy* (Goldsmith), due to taking *-s* as sign of pl. (cf. *cherry*), survives in *shammy-leather*.

chamomile. See *camomile*.

champ. To chew. Earlier also *cham*. Prob. imit. and ident. with *jam*.

champac. Magnolia. Hind. from Sanskrit *chāmpākā*.

champagne. Wine from that province. Cf. *burgundy*.

champaign [*archaic*]. Open country. Often spelt *champian, champion* by early writers. See *campaign*.

champarty, champerty [*leg.*]. Contributing to legal expenses on condition of sharing spoil. For earlier *champart*, division of produce, from *champ*, field, *part*, share; cf. MedL. *campipars*.

champignon. Mushroom. F., VL. **campinio-n-*, from *campus*, field. Cf. origin of *mushroom*.

champion. F., Late L. *campio-n-*, fighter in the arena (see *camp*); cf. It. *campione*, Sp. *campion*. Borrowed also by the Teutons, e.g. ON. *kempa*, AS. *cempa*, whence surname *Kemp*; cf. Ger. *kämpfen*, to fight.

chance. F. (OF. *cheance*), from *cheoir*, to fall, VL. **cadēre* for *cadere*. Thus a doublet of *cadence*. The orig. F. sense, of the "fall" of the dice, is found in ME. So also the *main chance* belongs orig. to the game of hazard.

See *main*[1,2]. For sense-development cf. *hazard*.

> Sevene is my chaunce, and thyn is cynk and treye
> (Chauc. C. 653).

> To set all on a maine chance (Holinshed).

chancel. F. *cancel*, *chancel*, L. *cancellus*, for *cancelli*, lattice (see *cancel*) separating the choir from the nave; dim. of *cancer*, grating, ? dissim. of *carcer*, prison (see *incarcerate*). Hence *chancellor*, AF. *chanceler*, F. *chancelier*, orig. keeper of the barrier, but introduced as offic. title into E. by Edward the Confessor.

chance-medley [*leg.*]. Orig. homicide intermediate between manslaughter and accident. Lit. mixed chance.

chancery. For *chancellery*, *chancelry*, office of *chancellor* (see *chancel*). Hence pugil. *in chancery*, i.e. not likely to get away without serious damage.

chancre. Venereal ulcer. F., see *cancer*, *canker*.

chandelier. F., candle-stick, etc. (v.i.).

chandler. F. *chandelier*, candle-stick, candle-maker, from *chandelle*, L. *candela*. In first sense, common in ME., now replaced by ModF. *chandelier*. Second sense has been extended (*corn-chandler*, *ship-chandler*); cf. *costermonger*.

change. F. *changer*, Late L. *cambiare*, for *cambire*, from *cambium*, exchange, of Celt. origin (cf. *gombeen man*); cf. It. *cambiare*, Sp. *cambiar* (see *cambist*). Hence *change*, meeting-place of merchants, often erron. *'change*, as though for the later *exchange*. To *ring the changes* was orig. of bells. In sense of swindling there is a punning allusion to *change*, money, i.e. the smaller coins for which a larger is changed. *Changeling* is from OF. *changeon*, with suffix altered on *suckling*, *nursling*.

channel[1]. Water-course. OF. *chanel* (*chenal*), L. *canalis*, whence *canal* (cf. *kennel*[2]). *The Channel* is first in Shaks. (*2 Hen. VI*, iv. 1).

channel[2] [*naut.*]. For *chain-wale*; cf. *gunwale*, and see *wale*.

> *port'-aubans*: chaine-wales: pieces of wood nailed on both the outsides of a ship, to keep them from being worn, or galled by the shrowdes (Cotg.).

> I took my station in the fore-channels
> (*Frank Mildmay*, ch. xi.).

chanson. F., song, VL. *cantio-n-* (v.i.).

chant. F. *chanter*, L. *cantare*, frequent. of *canere*, to sing. Hence *chantry* (Chauc. A. 512), endowment for good of founder's soul. With *horse-chanter*, fraudulent horse-dealer,

cf. F. *chantage*, blackmail. Both are neologisms difficult of explanation.

chantarelle, chanterelle. Cup-shaped fungus. F., dim. from L. *cantharus*, drinking-cup, G. κάνθαρος.

chanticleer. OF. *Chante-cler*, sing-clear, name of the cock in the *Roman de Renart* (13 cent.). Cf. *bruin*, *renard*.

> She hadde a cok, heet Chauntecleer
> (Chauc. B. 4039).

chantry. See *chant*.

chanty. Sailors' song. Earlier *shanty*. ? F. imper. *chantez* (cf. *revelly*). A very early example occurs in the *Complaynt of Scotlande* (1549).

chaos. G. χάος, abyss, empty space, etc.; cf. χάσκειν, to yawn. Its earliest E. use is with ref. to *Luke*, xvi. 26. Cf. *cosmos*.

chap[1]. To crack. Related to *chip*, *chop*[1]. Cf. Du. LG. *kappen*, to chop.

> The ground is chapt, for there was no rain in the earth (*Jer.* xiv. 4).

chap[2]. Jaw, esp. lower. Now usu. *chop*, as in to *lick one's chops*, *chops* (jaws) *of the Channel*, *chopfallen* (*Haml.* v. 1) for *chapfallen*, orig. of the dead. Perh. altered, by association with *chop*[1], from north. dial. *chaft*, of Scand. origin; cf. Sw. *käft*, Dan. *kieft*, cogn. with Ger. *kiefer*, jaw.

chap[3]. Fellow. Short for *chapman* (q.v.). Cf. fig. use of *customer*, and Sc. *callant*, lad, Du. *kalant*, F. *chaland*, customer. So also *chap-book*, coined (19 cent.) on *chapman*, to denote type of book formerly sold by itinerant vendors. Dim. *chappy* was orig. Sc.

chaparral. Thicket. Sp., from *chaparra*, evergreen oak, Basque *zaparra*.

chap-book. See *chap*[3].

chape [*hist.*]. "Cap" of a scabbard. F., cape, cope, used in same sense. See *cape*[1]. OF. used also the dim. *chapel* (*chapeau*, hat), e.g. *chapiax à coutiaux et à espees* are mentioned in 13 cent. *ordonnances* for the sheath-makers, so perh. *chape* in this sense is rather a back-formation from the dim.

chapel. F. *chapelle*. Orig. sanctuary where was deposited the *cappella*, or sacred cloak, of St Martin. In most Europ. langs. See *cape*[1], *cap*, *chaplain*. *Chapel of ease* is 16 cent. Application to place of worship outside the state religion, e.g. *Roman Catholic* (*Nonconformist*, and, in Scotland, *Episcopal*) *chapel*, begins in 17 cent. Sense of printers' workshop association is also 17 cent.

chaperon. F., hood, as in *Le petit Chaperon rouge*, from *chape* (see *cape*[1]). Mod. sense is due to *chaperon* being regarded as a protection. Not orig. always a female.

chaperon: an affected word, of very recent introduction...to denote a gentleman attending a lady in a publick assembly (Todd).

chapiter [*arch.*]. F. *chapitre*, now replaced by *chapiteau*. Etym. ident. with *chapter* (q.v.).

chaplain. F. *chapelain*. The orig. *cappellani* were the custodians of St Martin's cloak. See *chapel*.

chaplet. F. *chapelet*, dim. of OF. *chapel* (*chapeau*), hat, hood, garland. See *cap*, *cape*[1]. For later sense, string of beads, cf. *rosary*.

chapman [*archaic*]. Dealer. AS. *cēapman*; cf. Du. *koopman*, Ger. *kaufmann*. Cf. *chaffer*, *cheap*, (horse) *coper*, etc. See also *chap*[3].

chapter. F. *chapitre*, L. *capitulum*, dim. of *caput*, head. Earlier also *chapiter*, *chapitle*. The *chapter* of a cathedral, order of knights, etc., was orig. the meeting at which a *chapter* was read, a practice instituted (8 cent.) by Bishop Chrodegang of Metz. Hence *chapter-house*. *Chapter of accidents* is 18 cent.

char[1], **chare.** Turn of work, spell. Also *chore* (US.). AS. *cierr*, time, occasion, from *cierran*, to turn; ? cogn. with Ger. *kehren*, to turn. Hence *charwoman* (14 cent.).

char[2]. Verb. Also found as *chark*. Backformation from *charcoal* (q.v.).

char[3]. Fish. Perh. Gael. *ceara*, blood-red, from *cear*, blood. Cf. its Welsh name *torgoch*, red-belly.

char-à-banc. F., car with bench.

character. Restored from ME. *caracter*, F. *caractère*, L., G. χαρακτήρ, tool for stamping, marking, from χαράττειν, to cut grooves, engrave. Earlier also *caract*, OF. *caracte*, VL. **characta*. Sense of fictitious personage (in play, novel), whence *in* (*out of*) *character*, is 18 cent.

In all his dressings, caracts, titles, forms
                    (*Meas. for Meas.* v. 1).

charade. F., Prov. *charrada*, of obscure origin, perh. from *charrare*, to prattle, cogn. with It. *ciarlare*, which may be of imit. origin. See *charlatan*.

charcoal. Perh. from *char*, to turn (see *char*[1]). Cf. "cole-turned wood" (Chapman's *Odyssey*). ? Or a mixed form from *coal*, which in ME. meant charcoal, and F. *charbon*. Mod. verb to *char* is a back-formation.

chard. Of artichoke. Cf. F. *carde*, Sp. *cardo*, in same sense. Ult. from L. *carduus*, thistle.

chare. See *char*[1].

The maid that milks and does the meanest chares
                    (*Ant. & Cleop.* iv. 15).

charge. F. *charger*, to load, burden, VL. *carricare*, from *carrus* (see *car*). From the sense of load is evolved that of task, responsibility, office, custody. In mil. sense the idea is that of using weight, but *charger*, horse, app. meant orig. one for carrying heavy loads, pack-horse, e.g. *our chardger and horsse* (*York Merch. Advent.* 1579). The Bibl. *charger*, bearer (*Matt.* xiv. 8), is in Wyc. *disch*, in Tynd. *platter*. Sense of price, outlay, etc., is evolved from that of burden. For association with firearms cf. *load* (q.v.).

chargé d'affaires. F., entrusted with business.

chariot. F., from *char* (see *car*). ModF. *chariot* means waggon.

charity. F. *charité*, L. *caritas*, from *carus*, dear. *Caritas* in *Vulg.* usu. renders G. ἀγάπη, love (e.g. 1 *Cor.* xiii.), perh. in order to avoid sexual suggestion of *amor*. For spec. sense of almsgiving cf. sense-history of *pity*. *Cold as charity* may be partly due to Wyclif's rendering of *Matt.* xxiv. 12.

charivari. Recorded 1615 (William Browne's *Works*, ii. 293, ed. Hazlitt). F., orig. mock music expressing popular disapproval. At one time also the title of a Parisian satirical paper; hence the sub-title of *Punch*. OF. also *calivali*, *caribari*. Origin unknown. The second element appears in *hourvari*, hullabaloo.

charivaris de poelles: the carting of an infamous person, graced with the harmony of tinging kettles, and frying-pan musicke (Cotg.).

charlatan. F., It. *ciarlatano*, "a mountibanke, pratler, babler" (Flor.), app. altered, by association with *ciarlare*, to chatter, from *ciaratano* (Flor.), for earlier *ceretano* (Flor.), orig. vendor of papal indulgences from *Cerreto* (Spoletum).

Charles's Wain. Also called Ursa Major or the Plough. AS. *Carles-wægn* (see *wain*), the wain of *Arcturus* (q.v.) having first been understood as that of *Arthur*, and then transferred to *Carl*, i.e. Charlemagne, by the legendary association between the two heroes; cf. ME. *Charlemaynes wayne*. *Charles* is Ger. *Karl*, latinized as *Carolus*, and ident. with *churl* (q.v.); cf. Ger. *kerl*, fellow.

charley [*hist.*]. Watchman. Conjecturally explained as due to reorganization of London watch temp. *Charles I* (cf. *bobby*), but chronology is against this.

charlock. Wild mustard. AS. *cerlic*.

charlotte, charlotte russe. F., from the female name.

charm. F. *charme*, L. *carmen*, song, incantation, for **canmen*, from *canere*, to sing (cf. *germ*). For sense-development cf. *bewitching*, etc. *Charmed life* is from *Macb.* v. 8.

Sechith to me a womman havynge a charmynge goost (Wyc. 1 *Kings*, xxviii. 7).

charnel-house. Explanatory for earlier *charnel*, burial place (*Piers Plowm.*), OF., Late L. *carnale*, from *caro, carn-*, flesh. F. has also *charnier*, Late L. *carnarium*, both for larder and cemetery.

Charon. Ferryman. G. Χάρων, ferryman of the Styx.

charpie. Linen unravelled for dressing wounds. F., p.p. fem. of *charpir*, VL. **carpire*, for *carpere*, to pluck, unravel. Cf. *carpet*.

charpoy. Indian bedstead. Urdu *chārpāī*, Pers. *chahārpāī*, four-footed, ult. cogn. with *quadru-ped*.

charqui. Peruv. for dried beef, early corrupted to *jerked beef*.

chart. F. *charte*, L. *charta*, paper, G. χάρτης. Cf. F. *carte*, Ger. *karte*, map, and see *card*[1]. Latest sense in *health-chart*.

charter. OF. *chartre* (*charte*), L. *chartula*, dim. of *charta*, paper. Hence *Chartist*, from the *People's Charter* (1838). *Charter-party*, now only used in connection with ships, is F. *charte partie*, divided document, half of which is retained by each party (cf. *indenture*). With *chartered libertine* (*Hen. V*, i. 1) cf. colloq. use of F. *fieffé*, lit. enfeoffed, e.g. *filou fieffé* (Mol.).

Charterhouse. Carthusian monastery. Folk-etym. for F. *chartreuse* (see *Carthusian* and cf. Ger. *Karthause*). The famous public school and hospital was founded (1611) on the site of a Carthusian monastery.

Children not yet come to, and old men already past, helping of themselves, have in this hospital their souls and bodies provided for (Fuller).

Chartist. See *charter*.

chartreuse. Made by monks of *Chartreuse*. See *Carthusian*, *Charterhouse*.

chartulary. See *cartulary*.

charwoman. See *char*[1], *chare*.

chary. Usu. with *of*. AS. *cearig*, from *care*. Orig. careful, i.e. sorrowful, but now only associated with secondary sense of *care*.

Charybdis. See *Scylla*.

chase[1]. Pursuit. F. *chasse*, from *chasser*, VL. **captiare* for **captare*, frequent. of *capere*, *capt-*, to take (see *catch*); cf. It. *cacciare*, Sp. *cazar*. A *chase* differed from a park in not being enclosed.

chase[2]. To emboss, engrave. Aphet. for *enchase*, F. *enchâsser*, to enshrine, from *châsse*, shrine, L. *capsa* (see *case*[2]).

chase[3]. Hollow, groove, in various senses, esp. cavity of gun-barrel. Also frame in which type is locked. F. *châsse* in various senses, also in some cases from the masc. form *chas*. See *case*[2], *chase*[2].

chaas: the space and length between beame and beame, wall and wall, in building (Cotg.).

chasse d'un trebuchet: the shrine of a paire of gold weights; the hollow wherein the cock, tongue, or tryall playeth (*ib.*).

chasm. G. χάσμα, cogn. with *chaos* (q.v.).

chasse. Liqueur after coffee. For F. *chasse-café*, now usu. *pousse-café*.

chassé-croisé. Dance-step. F., see *chase*[1], *cross*.

chasse-marée. Coasting-vessel. F., chase tide.

chassepot. Obs. F. rifle. Inventor's name. It means "pot hunter," in the sense of seeker after hospitality.

chasseur. F., lit. hunter. Cf. *jäger*.

chassis [*neol.*]. Of a motor-car, etc. F. *châssis*, from *châsse*. See *case*[2], *sash*[2].

chaste. F., L. *castus*, pure.

chastise. Irreg. from OF. *chastier* (*châtier*), L. *castigare*, to make pure, *castus*. In ME. we find also *chaste*, *chasty*, in this sense. *Chasten* is later. All orig. to improve, correct.

Whom the Lorde loveth, him he chasteneth [Wyc. chastisith] (Tynd. *Heb.* xii. 6).

chasuble. F., dubiously connected with L. *casula*, little house (dim. of *casa*), which in Church L. also meant hooded vestment. ME. & OF. *chasible, chesible*, suggest a form **casipula* (cf. *manipulus*, from *manus*); cf. It. *casipola*, hut.

chat. Shortened from *chatter* (q.v.). Also applied, owing to their cry, to various birds, e.g. *stone-chat*, *whin-chat*.

château. F., OF. *chastel*, L. *castellum* (see *castle*). Hence *Château-Margaux*, etc., clarets named from famous vine-growing estates.

châtelaine. F., lady of castle (see *château*). Hence, belt with keys, etc.; cf. secondary sense of *housewife*.

chatoyant. F., pres. part. of *chatoyer*, from *chat*, cat, with ref. to changing colour of its eye.

chattel. OF. *chatel*, Late L. *capitale*, property. See *cattle*, which is the Norman-Picard form of the same word.

She is my goods, my chattels (*Shrew*, iii. 2).

chatter. Imit.; cf. *jabber*, *twitter*, etc. *Chatter-box* (19 cent.), i.e. box full of chatter, is modelled on the much earlier *saucebox* (16 cent.). Cf. obs. *prattle-box*.

chatty [*Anglo-Ind.*]. Porous water-pot. Hind. *chātī*.

chauffeur. F., stoker, from *chauffer*, to heat (see *chafe*). F. nickname for early motorists.

chaussée. F., see *causeway*.

chauvin. F., jingo. From *Nicolas Chauvin*, a veteran of the Grande Armée, who was introduced into several popular F. plays of the early 19 cent. The name was esp. familiarized by the line " Je suis Français, je suis Chauvin," in Cogniard's vaudeville *La Cocarde tricolore* (1832). The name is ident. with *Calvin*, and is a dim. of *chauve*, bald.

chavender. See *chevin*.

chaw. By-form of *chew*. Now dial. (cf. *chaw-bacon*) or US. (e.g. *chawed up*), but a recognized literary form in 16–17 cents.

mascheur: a chawer, chewer (Cotg.).

Some roll tobacco, to smell to and chaw
(Pepys, June 7, 1665).

chawbuck. Obs. form of *chabouk*. See *sjam-bok*.

chay, shay. Vulg. for *chaise* (q.v.). For back-formation cf. *pea*, *cherry*, *Chinee*, etc.

"How shall we go?" "A chay," suggested Mr Joseph Tuggs. "Chaise," whispered Mr Cymon. "I should think one would be enough," said Mr Joseph (Dickens, *The Tuggs's at Ramsgate*).

cheap. Orig. noun, barter, as in *Cheapside*. AS. *cēap*. Com. Teut.; cf. Du. *koop*, Ger. *kauf*, ON. *kaup*, whence Dan. *kjöb*, in *Kjöbnhavn* (Copenhagen). See also *chaffer*, *chapman*. Prob. all from L. *caupo*, huckster, innkeeper. Mod. adj. sense (16 cent.) is short for *good cheap*, good business; cf. F. *bon marché*, "good cheap" (Cotg.). As verb (cf. Ger. *kaufen*, Du. *koopen*, etc.) now obs., but traces of orig. sense still in *cheapen*, to bargain. See also *coper*, *coopering*.

And he, gon out about the thridde hour, say other stondynge ydil in the chepyng (Wyc. *Matt.* xx. 3).

Which do give much offence to the people here at court to see how cheap the King makes himself
(Pepys, Feb. 17, 1669).

cheat. Aphet. for *escheat* (q.v.), regarded as confiscation. Falstaff puns on the double meaning. Sense has also been affected by *cheat*, thing (early thieves' slang), of unknown origin.

chete for the lord: caducum, confiscarium, fisca
(*Prompt. Parv.*).

I will be cheater to them both, and they shall be exchequers to me (*Merry Wives*, i. 3).

check. OF. *eschec* (*échec*), Pers. *shāh*, king (in danger), adopted, through Arab., by most Europ. langs. with the game of *chess* (q.v.). Hence fig. to repulse, attack, put to the test, as in to *check a statement* (*account*), or to pay by *check* (now *cheque*), i.e. in a manner easy to verify. Also of various controlling mechanisms. Much used, esp. in US., of receipts, counters in games, etc., hence to *hand in one's checks*, retire from the game, die (cf. to *peg out*). For *check*(*er*) pattern, etc., see *chequer*, *exchequer*. *Checkmate* is OF. *eschec mat*, Arab. *shāh māt*, the king is dead.

Ther-with Fortune seyde, "Chek heer!"
And "Mate!" in the myd poynt of the chekkere,
With a poune erraunt, allas!
(Chauc. *Blanche the Duchess*, 658).

checker. See *chequer*.

cheddar. Cheese. From village in Somerset.

chee-chee. Eurasian accent in speaking E. Hind. *chhi-chhi*, fie (lit. dirt), exclamation attributed to Eurasians, or perh. imit. of their mincing speech.

cheek. AS. *cēace*, jaw; cf. Du. *kaak*, jaw, cheek, LG. *kake*, *keke*. With to *have the cheek* cf. to *have the face* (*front*). Already in ME. *cheek* is used in phrases of the type to *one's beard* (*teeth*). In earliest use also for jaw, as still in *cheek by jowl*.

We will have owre wille maugre thi chekes
(*Piers Plowm.* B. vi. 158).

cheep. Imit. of cry of small birds, etc.; cf. Ger. *piepen*, F. *pépier*. Hence *cheeper*, young partridge (grouse).

cheer. Orig. face. F. *chère*, Late L. *cara* (whence Prov. Sp. Port. *cara*). Identity with G. κάρα, head, is unlikely, in view of the absence of the word from It. Mod. senses develop from *good cheer*, F. *bonne chère*, as in *be of good cheer* (countenance, bearing), *with good cheer* (cordial manner); hence friendly treatment, resultant satisfaction and approval (*three cheers*). *Cheery*, "a ludicrous word" (Johns.), is much later than *cheerful*.

chere: the face, visage, countenance, favor, look,

aspect of a man; also, cheer, victuals, intertainment for the teeth (Cotg.).

All fancy sick she is, and pale of cheer
(*Mids. Night's Dream*, iii. 2).

We gave them a cheer, as the seamen call it
(Defoe, *Capt. Singleton*).

cheese[1]. Food. AS. *cīese*, L. *caseus*. WGer.; cf. Du. *kaas*, Ger. *käse*. Introduced into WGer. langs. with *butter* (q.v.), while the Rom. langs. preferred **formaticum* (F. *fromage*), expressing the shape. *Caseus* is prob. not orig. L., but borrowed from some nomadic tribe (cf. *butter*). *Cheeseparing* is in Shaks. (2 *Hen. IV*, iii. 2), but fig. sense of niggardly is 19 cent.

rimbeccarsela: to swallowe a cudgeon, to believe that the moone is made of greene cheese (Flor.).

cheese[2] [*Anglo-Ind.*]. The correct thing. Urdu, Pers. *chīz*, thing.

cheese it. Thieves' slang, of unknown origin.

cheetah. Leopard trained for hunting. Hind. *chīta*, Sanskrit *chitraka*, speckled. See *chintz*, *chit*[2].

chef. Cook. For F. *chef de cuisine*.

chego. Monkey. See *jocko*.

cheiro-. From G. χείρ, hand. More usu. *chiro-*.

chela. Buddhist novice, such as Kipling's *Kim*. Hind. *chēlā*, servant, disciple, Sanskrit *chēta*.

chemise. In its ME. usage, of various garments, from AS. *cemes*, Late L. *camisia* (c. 400 A.D.); but in mod. use, as euph. for smock, shift, from F. Late L. *camisia*, first as soldiers' word, is prob. of Gaulish origin and ult. cogn. with Ger. *hemd*, shirt. Also found in Arab. (*qamīç*), in Rum., and in Slav. langs. For vulg. *shimmey* cf. *chay*, *cherry*, etc.

You may do what you please,
You may sell my chemise,
(Mrs P. was too well-bred to mention her smock)
(*Ingoldsby*).

chemist. Earlier *chymist*, F. *chimiste*, ModL. *alchimista*. Orig. synon. with *alchemist* (see *alchemy*).

chenille. F., lit. caterpillar, L. *canicula*, little dog, from *canis*. Cf. *caterpillar*.

cheque. Earlier *check*, as still in US. Orig. counterfoil for *checking* purposes. Mod. spelling due to *exchequer*.

chequer, checker. Aphet. for *exchequer* (q.v.), in orig. sense of chess-board; cf. *checkers*, draughts. With *chequered career*, i.e. one of strong contrasts, cf. mod. mil. to *chessboard* (a road), i.e. excavate it in zigzag fashion to hold up pursuing force. *Exchequer* in mod. sense was once commonly spelt *cheker*, *chequer*, e.g. in Pepys. Hence also *check*, pattern.

He [Hindenburg] "chess-boarded" the ordinary highways and blew up railway stations, watertowers and bridges (J. Buchan).

cherimoya. Fruit. From Quichua lang. of Peru.

cherish. F. *chérir*, *chériss-*, from *cher*, dear, L. *carus*. Cf. *flourish*, *nourish*, etc.

cheroot. Tamil *shuruṭṭu*, roll (of tobacco).

He who wants to purchase a segar in the East, must ask for a sharoot (*NED*. 1807).

cherry. With AS. *ciris*, *cyrs*, found in compds. only, e.g. *cirisbēam*, cherry tree, cf. Du. *kers*, Ger. *kirsche*. The existing word was taken by ME. from ONF. *cherise* (*cerise*), corrupted from L. *cerasum*, G. κεράσιον, trad. brought (c. 100 B.C.) by Lucullus from *Cerasus* in Pontus; but it is possible that the place was named from the tree, G. κέρασος, and that the latter is cogn. with G. κέρας, horn, from its smooth bark (cf. *hornbeam*). For loss of -*s* cf. *chay*, *pea*, *sherry*, etc. So also dial. *merry*, wild cherry, F. *merise*.

By Jingo, I believe he wou'd make three bits of a cherry [troys morceaulx d'une cerise]
(Motteux' *Rabelais*, v. 28).

chersonese. Peninsula, esp. that of Thrace. G. χερσόνησος, peninsula, from χέρσος, dry, νῆσος, island.

chert. Kind of quartz. Perh. for *sherd*, *shard*. Cf. origin of *brescia*, *slate*.

cherub. Back-formation from *cherubim*, *cherubin*, formerly used as sing., L. (*Vulg.*), G. (LXX.) χερουβίμ, Heb. *k'rūbīm*, pl. of *k'rūb*, origin and real meaning of which are unknown. The pl. being more familiar, the earliest form was AS. *cherubin*, -*bim*, in general ME. use for *cherub*, as still in *AV*. and uneducated speech. So also F. *chérubin*, It. *cherubino*, etc. Cf. *assassin*, *Bedouin*, and see *seraph*. Wyc. has both *cherub* and *cherubin*, Shaks. has the latter several times and *cherub* only once.

Still quiring to the young-eyed cherubins
(*Merch. of Ven.* v. 1).

Here lies the body of Martha Gwynn,
Who was so very pure within.
She burst the outer shell of sin
And hatch'd herself a cherubin (*Old Epitaph*).

chervil. Herb. AS. *cærfille*, L., G. χαιρέφυλλον, from φύλλον, leaf, ? and χαῖρε, rejoice. Cf. Du. *kervel*, Ger. *kerbel*, obs. E. *cerfoil*, F. *cerfeuil*.

Cheshire cat. Famed for grinning in 18 cent. (*Peter Pindar*), but reason unknown. US. has *chessy* (*jessy*) *cat*.

chesnut. See *chestnut*.

chess. OF. *esches*, pl. of *eschec* (*échec*). See *check*. In late ME. we find a new pl. *chesses*, and in 16–17 cents. *chests*. *Chess-men* is for ME. *chess-mesne*, where the second element is obs. *meiny*, retinue (see *ménage*). The item *tabeliers et meisne*, i.e. boards and "men," occurs in accts. of Earl of Derby's Expedition (1390–93). See also *chequer*.

Whose deepest projects, and egregious gests,
Are but dull morals of a game at chests (Donne).

chess-trees [*naut.*]. Timber with eye through which passes clew of mainsail. Prob. from *chase*[3]; cf. F. *chas*, eye of needle.

chest. AS. *cest*, L. *cista*, G. κίστη; cf. Du. *kist*, Ger. *kiste*, ON. *kista*. Early pre-Christian loan (see *ark*). In AS. & ME. esp. in sense of coffin. For anat. sense cf. Ger. *brustkasten*, lit. breast-box, of which second element is unrelated.

He [Joseph] dieth, and is chested (*Gen.* l. *heading*).

chesterfield. Overcoat, couch. From a 19 cent. *Earl of Chesterfield*. Cf. *raglan*, *spencer*, *wellington*, etc.

chestnut. For *chesteine-nut*, ME. *chesteine*, OF. *chastaigne* (*châtaigne*), L., G. καστανέα, either ? from *Castanis* (Pontus) or *Castanaea* (Thessaly). But see remark on *cherry*. Armen. *kaskeni*, chestnut tree, may be the true origin. Earlier is AS. *cisten-bēam*, chestnut tree (cf. Ger. *kestenbaum*, now usu. *kastanienbaum*). In ME. *chastein*, *chestein*, etc. is also used of the tree. *Chestnuts out of the fire* is from the fable of the cat and the monkey (cf. *catspaw*). In the sense of venerable tale (US.) perh. from a spec. oft-repeated story in which a chestnut-tree is particularly mentioned.

"When suddenly from the thick boughs of a cork-tree"—"A chestnut, captain, a chestnut." "Bah! booby, I say a cork-tree." "A chestnut," reiterates Pablo; "I should know as well as you, having heard you tell the tale these twenty-seven times" (Hatton's *Reminiscences of Toole*, 1888, quoted by *NED.*).

cheval-de-frise. See *chevaux-de-frise*.

cheval-glass. F. *cheval*, horse. Cf. *chevalet*, easel (q.v.).

chevalier. F., horseman, knight, VL. **caballarius*, from *caballus*, horse. Cf. Ger. *ritter*, knight, lit. rider. F. *chevalier*, knight, *cavalier*, horseman, etc. (from It.) are now differentiated. The ME. form was *chevaler*,

chivaler, etc., the ModF. form being introduced later. Esp. the *Chevalier de Saint-George*, Old Pretender, and the *Young Chevalier*, Young Pretender. *Chevalier of industry*, sharper, is adapted from F. *chevalier d'industrie*. Cf. *chivalry*.

chevaux-de-frise [*fort.*]. Lit. Frisian horses, device adopted by the Netherlanders to make up for their lack of cavalry against the Spaniards. Cf. archaic Ger. *spanische reuter* (*reiter*), in same sense.

vriesse paerden (*balken om den aanval der vyandelike ruyters te stuyten*): chevaux de Frise (Sewel).

chevelure. Head of hair. F., L. *capillatura*, from *capillus*, hair; cf. It. *capillatura*.

chevin. Chub. F. *chevin*, *chevanne*; cf. obs. E. *chavender*. Prob. from L. *caput*, head.

The chub or chavender (Izaak Walton).

cheviot. Cloth from wool of *Cheviot* sheep.

chevrette. Skin for gloves. F., kid, dim. of *chèvre*, goat, L. *capra*.

chevron. Stripe (⌄) of non-commissioned officer. Also in her. (⌃). Earliest sense, rafter. F., VL. **capro-n-*, from *caper*, goat; cf. Sp. *cabriol*, L. *capreolus*, dim. of *caper*, in same sense.

chevron: a kid; a chevron (of timber in building); a rafter or sparre (Cotg.).

capreoli: cross pieces of timber to hold together larger beams and keep them together (Litt.).

chevrotain, chevrotin. Small musk-deer (S.E. Asia). F., double dim. of *chèvre*, she-goat, L. *capra*.

chevy, chivy. To pursue. From hunting-cry *chivy*, from ballad of *Chevy Chase*, on battle of Otterburn (1388) between Douglas and Hotspur. For *Cheviot Chase*, a later version being called the *Cheviot Hunting*.

With a hey, ho, chivy!
Hark forward! hark forward! tantivy
(O'Keefe, *Old Towler*, c. 1785).

chew. AS. *cēowan*; cf. Du. *kauwen*, Ger. *kauen*. See *chaw*.

Britain bit off far more than Napoleon ever tried to chew—and chewed it
(F. W. Wile, *Explaining the Britishers*, Nov. 1918).

chianti. Wine. From place of origin in Tuscany.

chiaroscuro. It. *chiaro*, light, L. *clarus*, *oscuro*, dark, L. *obscurus*. Orig. both of black and white and light and shade.

chiasmus. G. χιασμός, crossing, lit. making shape of letter χ. Order of words as in

Frequentia sustentatur, alitur otio (Cic.).

I cannot dig, to beg I am ashamed (*Luke*, xvi. 3).

Au sublime spectacle un spectateur sublime
(Sainte-Beuve).

chiaus. See *chouse*.

chibouk, chibouque. Long pipe. Turk. *chibūk*, stick, pipe-stem.

chic. F., smartness. Cf. Ger. *schick*, in same sense, found early (14 cent.) in LG. From *schicken*, to send, in secondary sense of arrange appropriately, etc.

chicanery. Pettifogging, quibbling. F. *chicanerie*, from *chicane*. The latter word was applied in Languedoc to a form of golf, and golfers will readily understand how the sense of taking advantage of petty accidents may have been evolved. The F. word is from MedG. τζυκανίζειν, to play polo (q.v.), a game once known all over the Mohammedan world and in Christian Byzantium. This is from Pers. *chaugān*, a crooked stick. The game has given rise to many metaphors in Pers.

chicha. Fermented drink from maize. Native lang. of Hayti.

chick¹. Bird. Shortened from *chicken* (q.v.). Cf. *oft* for *often*.

il n'a enfant ne bremant: hee hath nor childe, nor chicke to care for (Cotg.).

chick² [*Anglo-Ind.*]. Cane blind. Hind. *chik*, perh. a Mongol word.

Old Chinn could no more pass that chick without fiddling with it than....
(Kipling, *Tomb of his Ancestors*).

chick³ [*Anglo-Ind.*]. Short for *chickeen*. See *chicken-hazard*.

chickabiddy. From *chick¹* and *biddy*, obs. child's name for bird (? *birdy*).

Ay, biddy, come with me (*Twelfth Night*, iii. 4).

chicken. AS. *cicen*; cf. Du. *kieken*, Ger. *küchlein*, ON. *kjūklingr*; perh. ult. cogn. with *cock*. In *chicken-pox* app. in sense of small, inconsiderable.

Perrette là-dessus saute aussi, transportée:
Le lait tombe; adieu veau, vache, cochon, couvée
(La Fontaine, *Fables*, vii. 10).

chicken-hazard. For *chickeen*, Anglo-Ind. form of *sequin* (q.v.), *zecchin*.

Billiards, short whist, chicken-hazard, and punting
(*Ingoldsby*).

chickery-pokery. Var. of *jiggery-pokery* (q.v.).

chick-pea. Earlier *ciche pease*, F. *pois chiche* (earlier *ciche*), L. *cicer*, pea. Also called *chickling*, earlier *cichling*.

chickweed. For earlier *chicken-weed*, as still in Sc.

chicory. Earlier *cicory*, OF. *cichoree* (*chicorée*), L. *cichoreum*, from G. κίχορα, endive, succory (q.v.).

chide. AS. *cīdan*, not known in other Teut. langs. Orig. intrans., to brawl, rail, with dat. of person (now disguised as acc.). Construction with prep. *with, against* is intermediate.

The people did chide with Moses (*Ex.* xvii. 2).

chief. ME. *chefe*, F. *chef*, L. *caput*, head. Correct OF. spelling is *chief*, which may have affected mod. form. *In chief* in oldest sense (feud.) represents L. *in capite*. With adj. use cf. native *head* as in *head-master*, or Ger. *haupt* in *hauptmann*, captain. Hence *chieftain*, ME. & OF. *chevetain*, remodelled on *chief*. See *captain*.

chiff-chaff. Bird. Imit. of note.

chiffer-chaffer. Nonce-word, redupl. on *chaffer* (q.v.).

Let the Labour party cease chiffer-chaffering over things it does not understand, like the disposal of Africa, or the state of Russia
(*Daily Chron.* Sep. 27, 1918).

chiffon. F., lit. rag, dim. of F. *chiffe*, perh. for OF. *chipe*, rag, ? from E. *chip*. Hence *chiffonnier*, orig. with drawers for putting away sewing materials, etc. ModF. sense is ragpicker.

chignon. OF. *eschignon*, nape of the neck, from *eschine* (*échine*), backbone (see *chine²*), confused with F. *chaînon*, dim. of *chaîne*, also used of the nape of the neck.

chainon du col: the naupe, or (more properly) the chine-bone of the neck (Cotg.).

chigoe. WInd. burrowing flea, jigger² (q.v.). Prob. negro corrupt. of Sp. *chico*, small, whence also synon. F. *chique*.

chilblain. From *chill* and *blain* (q.v.).

child. AS. *cild* (neut.); ? cf. Goth. *kilthei*, womb. In E. only; in other WGer. langs. represented by *kind*. AS. pl. was *cild*, ME. *child* and *childre*, the latter surviving in dial. *childer*, replaced in south by double pl. *children*, after *brethren*. Earliest sense esp. in connection with birth (*childbed*, *with child*). In ME. and later also spec. youth of gentle birth (cf. *Childe Harold*), also servant, page. In 16 cent. esp. girl. *My child* in Shaks. never refers to son, and mod. usage shows traces of this. With *Childermas*, Feast of the Holy Innocents (Dec. 28), cf. AS. *cyldamæsse* (see *mass¹*).

By the mouth of our fadir Davith, thi child
(Wyc. *Acts*, iv. 25).

A very pretty barne; a boy or a child, I wonder?
(*Winter's Tale*, iii. 3).

chiliad. Thousand. L., G. χιλιάς, χιλιάδ-, from χίλιοι, thousand.

chill. AS. *cele*, *ciele*, cold (noun), in gen. sense. Noun gave way in ME. to *cold*, and, in its mod. sense (*take a chill*, etc.), is from the adj. or verb derived from orig. noun. See also *cold*, *cool*.

chilli. Capsicum pod, used in pickles, etc. Sp., Mex. *chilli*, native name.

Chiltern Hundreds. Former crown manor (Oxford and Bucks), of which stewardship (a sinecure or fictitious office) is taken by M.P.'s as a way of resigning, an office under the crown being (since 1707) a disqualification for membership of Parliament. See *hundred*.

chime[1]. Of bells. ME. & OF. *chimbe*, L. *cymbalum*, G. κύμβαλον, from κύμβη, hollow of a vessel (cf. L. *cymba*). Cymbal (q.v.) was orig. sense of E. *chime*.

> Lovys him in chymys wele sownande
>   (Hampole's *Psalter*, cl. 5).

chime[2], **chimb.** Rim of a cask. In Johns. Cf. Du. *kim*, the same, Ger. *kimme*, edge, AS. *cimbing*, joining. Also incorr. *chine*.

chimer, chimar [*hist.*]. Bishop's robe. OF. *chamarre* (*simarre*); cf. It. *zimarra*, Sp. *zamarra*. Origin unknown.

chimera, chimaera. Fabulous composite monster. L., G. χίμαιρα, she-goat.

chimney. F. *cheminée*, Late L. *caminata*, from *caminus*, furnace, oven, G. κάμινος. Orig. fire-place, as in *chimney corner*, *chimney piece*, the latter orig. a picture. But earliest sense of Late L. *caminata* was room provided with a stove[1] (q.v.).

> The chimney
> Is south the chamber, and the chimney-piece
> Chaste Dian, bathing (*Cymb.* ii. 4).

chimpanzee. Bantu (Angola) *kampenzi*.

chin. AS. *cin*. WGer.; cf. Du. *kin*, Ger. *kinn*; cogn. with G. γένυς, lower jaw, L. *gena*, cheek.

China. Sanskrit *China*, perh. from *Ch'in* or *Ts'in* dynasty (3 cent. B.C.). *Chin* in Marco Polo. Hence, porcelain from *China*, pronounced *cheyney* well into 19 cent., with the consequence that *Cheyne Walk*, Chelsea, was sometimes spelt *China Walk*! With *China orange* cf. Ger. *apfelsine*, orange, lit. apple of China, the fruit having been introduced from China by the Portuguese in 16 cent. The *NED.* quotes "a hundred pounds to a China orange on Eclipse" (1771). A *Chinaman* was, before the 19 cent., a dealer in Chinese ware (cf. *Indiaman*). *Chinese*, OF. *Chineis* (*Chinois*),

was formerly used as noun. For slang *Chinee* cf. *Portugee*, *marquee*, *burgee*, etc.

> Sericana, where Chineses drive,
> With sails and wind, their cany waggons light
>   (*Par. Lost*, iii. 438).

> She [a lady of rank who died, aetat. 104, in 1877] always spoke of her "chaney" and of the balcóny, theáyter, etc. (From a correspondent).

chinch. Bug (US.). Sp. *chinche*, L. *cimex*, *cimic-*.

chinchilla. Small rodent (SAmer.). Sp., perh. from *chinch* (q.v.), from erron. belief that it smelt badly. Cf. OF. *cincele*, *chincele*, bug.

chin-chin [*Anglo-Chin.*]. Chin. *ts'ing-ts'ing*, please-please.

> The mandarin went off in high glee, saying "chin, chin" as he departed, which is the common salutation (Hickey's *Memoirs*, i. 223).

chinchona. See *cinchona*.

chine[1]. Ravine (Hants and I. of Wight). AS. *cinu*, fissure. Cf. Du. *keen*, *chap*[1]. A common ME. word now superseded by *chink*[1] (q.v.). Cogn. with Ger. *keim*, bud (at its opening).

> In the chyne of a ston wal
>   (Wyc. *Song of Solomon*, ii. 14).

chine[2]. Backbone, etc. F. *échine*, OHG. *scina* (*schiene*), splinter, shinbone (cf. history of *spine*), whence also It. *schiena*, Sp. *esquena*. See *shin*.

chine[3]. See *chime*[2].

Chinee, Chinese. See *China*.

chink[1]. Fissure. Replaces (from 16 cent.) *chine*[1], from which it is app. derived. For abnormal formation cf. *Chink*.

chink[2]. Sound. Imit., cf. F. *tinter*, Ger. *klingeln*. Hence, money, earliest sense recorded in *NED*.

> To buie it the cheaper, have chinkes in thy purse
>   (Tusser, 1573).

Chink [*Austral. & US.*]. "Chinee." For formation cf. *chink*[1].

Chinook. "Pidgin" language of Columbia and Oregon; also warm ocean wind. Name of native tribe on Columbia river with which Hudson Bay traders came in contact.

chintz. For *chints*, pl. of *chint*, Hind. *chīnt*. Earlier also *chite*, Mahrati *chīt*, from Sanskrit *chitra*, variegated. Cf. *cheetah*, *chit*[2], and, for pl. form, *baize*. So also Du. *sits*, earlier *chits*, *chitsen*, "chints" (Sewel).

> Bought my wife a chint, that is, a painted Indian callico (Pepys, Sep. 5, 1663).

chip. Prob. thinned form of *chop*¹ (cf. *drip*, *drop*). Cf. *kippen* in various LG. dialects. To *chip in* may be a variation on to *cut in* (orig. at cards) or come from *chip* in slang sense of counter used in card-playing, whence *chips*, money; cf. Du. *splint*, splinter, *spaan*, chip, both used for money. *Chip of the old block* is used by Milton (*Smectymnuus*).

chipmuck, chipmunk. Squirrel (US.). The alternative name *hackle* (J. G. Wood) suggests an E. formation from *chip* and *mink* (q.v.).

chippendale. Name of cabinet-maker (†1779). Cf. *sheraton*.

chippy. Dry as a *chip*; hence, suffering from after-effects of alcohol.

chiro-. Latinized form of *cheiro-* (q.v.), adopted in F. Hence *chirography*, handwriting; *chiromancy*, palmistry; *chiropodist*, from G. πούς, ποδ-, foot.

chirp, chirrup. Imit. For obs. *chirk*, *chirt* (= *cheep*). With later *chirrup* cf. *alarum*. Earliest is AS. *cearcian*, whence ME. *chark*, to creak. To *feel chirpy, chirrupy* is coloured by *cheer-up*.

> [He] chirkith [*var.* chirtith] as a sparwe
> (Chauc. D. 1804).

chirurgeon [*archaic*]. Restored spelling of OF. *cirurgien* (whence ME. *sirurgien*, *surgeon*) corresponding to Sp. *cirujano*, Port. *cirurgião*. From G. χειρουργός, surgeon, from χείρ, hand, ἔργον, work.

chisel. ONF. *chisel* (*ciseau*), VL. **cisellus*, for **caesellus* (whence It. *cesello*), from *caedere*, *caes-*, to cut. See *scissors*. With *chiselled features* cf. *pencilled eyebrows*.

chit¹. Brat. App. var. of *kit* (*kitten*); cf. dial. *chit*, kitten, Sc. *cheet*, puss. Cf. use of *kid*, *cub*, *whelp*, etc. But associated in sense with dial. *chit*, sprout. Cf. *imp*, *scion*, and Ger. *sprössling*. Wyc. has *chittes*, var. *whelpis* (*Is*. xxxiv. 15) for *Vulg. catuli*.

> *murelegus, catus, catulus*: catte, idem est chytte
> (*Voc.*).

chit². chitty [*Anglo-Ind.*]. Document. Mahrati *chittī*, Sanskrit *chitra*, "black and white." See *cheetah*, *chintz* and cf. *pie*¹.

> At last I got his cheet for some [of his debt]
> (Purch. 1608).

chit-chat. Redupl. on *chat* (q.v.). Cf. *chitter* for *chatter*, and *tittle-tattle*.

chitin. Substance forming integuments of insects, etc. F. *chitine*, irreg. from G. χιτών, tunic.

chiton. Tunic. G. χιτών.

chittagong. Breed of fowls, from *Chittagong*, Bengal.

chitterling. Mostly dial., with numerous vars. With secondary (slang) sense of shirt-frill cf. F. *fraise*, mesentery, ruff, and see *tripe*. Origin obscure; ? cf. Ger. *kutteln*, chitterlings, Goth. *qithus*, belly, cogn. with LG. *kiit*, intestine, Du. *kuit*, fish-roe, from a Teut. root applied to soft parts of the body.

> *andouille*: a linke, or chitterling; a big hogges gut stuffed with small guts (Cotg.).
> *fraise*: a ruffe; also, a calves chaldern (*ib.*).

chitty. See *chit*².

chivalry. F. *chevalerie*, collect. from *chevalier* (q.v.). Doublet of *cavalry*, with which it was sometimes synon., though earliest E. sense is bravery, prowess, e.g. *flower of chivalry* (1297).

chive. Herb. ONF. *cive*, L. *cepa*, onion. Cf. AS. *cīpe*, onion, from L.

chivy. See *chevy*.

chlamys. G. χλαμύς, cloak.

chloral. Coined by Liebig from *chlor(ine)* *al(cohol)*.

chlorine. Named (1810) by Davy from its colour. G. χλωρός, yellowish green.

chlorodyne. Artificial trade-name from *chloroform* (q.v.) and *anodyne* (q.v.).

chloroform. F. *chloroforme*, coined (1834) by Dumas. See *chlorine*. Used as anaesthetic by Simpson (1847).

> This new anaesthetic agent was used most successfully last Monday (*Ill. Lond. News*, Dec. 4, 1847).

chlorophyll. Green colouring matter of plants. G. χλωρός, green, φύλλον, leaf.

chlorosis. "Green sickness." Mod., from G. χλωρός, green.

chock, chuck. Block of wood, wedge (chiefly naut.). ONF. *choque*, *chouque* (*souche*, stump). *Chockfull, chokefull*, though now to some extent associated with *chock*, is a much older word (c. 1400) and prob. comes from ME. *choke*, jaw-bone, "chops," ON. *kjálki*, jaw-bone (cf. Sc. *chowk*); thus "full to the chops," with which cf. F. *regorger*, to be chock-full, from *gorge*, throat.

chocolate. F. *chocolat*, Sp. *chocolate*, Mex. *chocolatl*. Orig. (c. 1600) a drink made from cacao seeds, but, according to some, distinct from *cacao* (q.v.).

> To a coffee-house, to drink jocolatte, very good
> (Pepys, Nov. 24, 1664).

choctaw. Name of Red Indian tribe used as fancy skating term. Cf. *mohawk*.

choice. ME. & OF. *chois* (*choix*), from *choisir*, OHG. *kiusjan* (*kiesen*). See *choose*. As adj. *choice* replaced ME. *chis* (AS. *cīs*, fastidious, perh. from *cēosan*, to choose), partly under influence of F. adj. *de choix* (cf. adj. use of *prize*). *Choice spirit* is from Shaks. (1 *Hen. VI*, v. 3; *Jul. Caes.* iii. 1).

choir, quire. ME. *quer*, OF. *cuer* (*chœur*), L. *chorus*, G. χορός, company of dancers or singers. *Quire* (still in *PB.*) was replaced c. 1700 by *choir*, an assimilation to F. & L. forms.

choke. Aphet. for *achoke*, AS. *ācēocian*, prob. cogn. with *cheek* (cf. *throat*, *throttle*, L. *jugulum*, *jugulare*, F. *gorge*, *égorger*). To *choke off* is orig. of dogs. With *choke-pear*, also fig., cf. synon. F. *poire d'angoisse* (*d'étranguillon*). A *choke-bore* diminishes towards the muzzle.

chokee. See *choky*.

chokidar [*Anglo-Ind.*]. Watchman. Urdu *chaukīdar*, from Hind. *chaukī*, watching (v.i.), Pers. *-dar*, possessing, master, as in *sirdar*, etc.

choky, chokee [*slang*]. Prison, quod. Orig. Anglo-Ind., from *chaukī*, station, watch-house, etc. Cf. *chokidar*.

choler. ME. & OF. *colre* (*colère*), L., G. χολέρα, bilious disorder, from χολή, bile. *Choler* assumed the meaning of χολή and became the name of one of the four "humours" (*sanguis*, *cholera*, *melancholia*, *phlegma*).

Certes this dreem, which ye han met to-nyght,
Cometh of the greet superfluytee
Of youre rede colera [*var.* colere colre, coloure]
(Chauc. B. 4116).

cholera. In ME. ident. with *choler* (q.v.), from 16 cent. used of English cholera, and from c. 1800 of Asiatic cholera.

choliambic [*metr.*]. Variation on iambic metre. G. χωλός, lame, and ἴαμβος.

chondro-. From G. χόνδρος, cartilage.

choose. AS. *cēosan*. Com. Teut.; cf. Du. *kiezen*, Ger. *kiesen*, Goth. *kiusan*; also ON. *kör*, choice; cogn. with L. *gustare*, to taste. Usu. *chuse* till Johns. F. *choisir* is from Teut. (see *choice*).

chop¹. To cut. ME. also *chap*, corresponding to Du. *kappen* (see *chap¹*). Its parallelism in use with *cut* suggests influence of OF. *coper* (*couper*), which had a Picard var. *choper*. A mutton *chop* is "chopped" off. In some colloq. senses *chop¹* runs together with *chop²*.

Mesire Robiers...chopa la coife de fier, et li fist
grant plaie en la tieste
(*Le Roi Flore et la Belle Jehanne*).

chop² [*archaic*]. To barter. AS. *cēapian*. See *chap³*, *cheap*. Survives in to *chop and change*, orig. to barter and exchange, but now associated partly with *chop¹*, and applied to sudden movements, esp. of wind. So also to *chop logic*, to "exchange" arguments, is perh. now understood in a "mincing," "hair-splitting" sense.

to *chappe*: mercari, negociari (*Cath. Angl.*).

changer: to exchange, interchange, trucke, scoorse, barter, chop with (Cotg.).

Many...which choppe and chaunge [*Vulg.* adulterantes] with the worde of God (Tynd. 2 *Cor.* ii. 17).

chop³. Jaw, etc., e.g. *chops of the Channel*. See *chap²*. Once literary.

The sommers sweet distilling drops
Upon the meddowes thirsty-yawning chops
(Sylv. *Ark*).

chop⁴. As in *first-chop*. Hind. *chhāp*, seal, impression, stamp. Common in Purch. in sense of authorizing signature. Taken by Europ. traders from India to China.

The Americans (whom the Chinese distinguish by the title of second chop Englishmen) have also a flag (Hickey's *Memoirs*, i. 202).

The chop-mark of the friend or foe may count for years to come in conservative China
(*Pall Mall Gaz.* March 15, 1917).

chop⁵ [*WAfr.*]. Food; to eat. ? Suggested by *chop-sticks*, ? or from obs. *chop*, to devour, from *chop³*.

chopsticks. Sailors' rendering of Chin. *k'wai-tsze*, nimble ones, *chop* being "pidgin" for quick. In Dampier (17 cent.).

choragus. Chorus leader. Master of musical Praxis (Oxf.). L., G. χορηγός, from χορός, chorus, ἄγειν, to lead.

choral-e. In spec. sense of stately hymn sung in unison, adapted from Ger. *choral(gesang)*.

chord. Restored spelling, on G. χορδή, of *cord* (q.v.), in spec. sense. So also (math.) *chord of an arc*, lit. string of a bow. In sense of combination of notes it is for obs. *cord*, aphet. for *accord* (q.v.).

In psawtry of ten cordis
(Hampole's *Psalter*, cxliii. 10).

chore [*US.*]. See *char¹*, *chare*.

chorea [*med.*]. St Vitus' Dance, *chorea Sancti Viti*. G. χορεία, dance (see *chorus*).

choriambus [*metr.*]. G., from χορεῖος, belonging to dancing, ἴαμβος, iambus.

chorister. Altered on *chorus* (see *choir*) from ME. *querister*, AF. *cueristre*, *cueriste*, MedL. *chorista*. Cf. *barrister*.

chorography. Intermediate between geography and topography. F. *chorographie*,

L., G. χωρογραφία, from χώρα, land. Cf. *chorology*, science of distribution of fauna and flora.

chortle. Coined by Lewis Carroll (*Through the Looking-Glass*). Cf. *galumph*, *jabberwock*.

chorus. L., G. χορός, dance, etc. See *choir*. Earliest E. use is in drama (16 cent.).

chouan [*hist.*]. Irregular fighter in West of France on behalf of Bourbons (c. 1793 and 1832). F., screech owl (by folk-etym. *chat huant*), cry of which was used as signal, Late L. *cavannus*, prob. imit. of cry.

chough. Bird of crow tribe, now esp. red-legged crow, *Cornish chough*. Cf. Du. *kauw*, Dan. *kaa*, OHG. *chāha*, etc.; also ME. *co*, *coo*, jackdaw. Prob. imit. of cry. Cf. also F. *choucas*, jack-daw, and see *chouan*.

choquar: a chough; or, Cornish chough (Cotg.).

chouse. Orig. swindler. Earlier (17 cent.) also *cniaus*, etc., Turk. *chāush* (cf. Pers. *chāwush*), messenger. Used several times by Ben Jonson with the implied meaning of swindler (cf. *cozen*). Gifford's story about an individual *chiaus* who did some swindling in London in 1609 dates from 1756 only, and is not mentioned by 17 cent. etymologists who recognized the etym. of *chouse*.

The governor [of Aden] sent a chouse of his owne, which was one of his chiefe men
(Jourdain's *Journ.* 1608).
Chiaus'd by a scholar! (Shirley, c. 1659).

chow [*Austral.*]. Chinaman; dog of Chinese breed. App. from "pidgin" word for food. See *chow-chow*.

chow-chow [*pidgin*]. Mixed pickles or preserves.

A small jar of sacred and imperial chow-chow
(Kipling, *Bread upon the Waters*).

chowder [*Canada & US.*]. Stew, including fish or clams. F. *chaudière*, cauldron (q.v.), introduced into Newfoundland, etc. by Breton fishermen.

chowry [*Anglo-Ind.*]. Fly-whisk, prop. tail of Tibetan yak elaborately mounted. In 17–18 cent. E. usu. called *cow-tail*. Hind. *chaunrī*.

A confidential servant waved the great chowry, or cow-tail (*Surgeon's Daughter*, ch. xiv.).

chrematistic. Concerning money. G. χρηματιστικός, from χρῆμα, money, lit. the "needful."

chrestomathy. Choice of extracts. G. χρηστομάθεια, from χρηστός, useful, -μαθεια, learning.

chrism, chrisom. Consecrated oil in various rites. ME. *crisme*, *crisum*, *creme*, etc., AS. *crisma*, L., G. χρῖσμα, anointing, from χρίειν, to anoint. Hence OF. *cresme* (*crême*); see *cream*. *Chrisom* is for *chrisom-cloth*, *-robe*, etc., white robe of baptism, orig. perh. a head-cloth used to avoid the rubbing away of the *chrism*.

cresme: the crisome, or oyle wherewith a baptized child is annointed (Cotg.).

Christ. L. *Christus*, G. Χριστός, anointed (v.s.), translating *Messiah* (q.v.). Hence *christen*, AS. *crīstenian*, and *Christian*, restored spelling for earlier *cristen*. *Christendom* orig. meant Christianity. In all these words *ch*- is a restored spelling. *Christian science* was established (1866) in US. by Mary B. Eddy.

Et docuerunt turbam multam, ita ut cognominarentur primum Antiochae discipuli, Christiani
(*Vulg. Acts*, xi. 26).

Christadelphian. Sect founded (1847) in US. From G. Χριστός, Christ, ἀδελφός, brother.

He appealed for the certificate [of exemption] granted to a Christadelphian to be cancelled; the latter had been fined for knocking a horse's eye out (*Daily Chron.* Jan. 23, 1918).

christ-cross-row, criss- [*archaic*]. Child's horn-book (q.v.) with cross preceding alphabet.

Infant-conning of the Christ-cross-row
(*Excursion*, viii. 419).

Christmas. AS. *Crīstmæsse* (see *mass*[1]). The *Christmas tree* is a Ger. institution, popularized by its introduction into the royal household temp. Queen Victoria. The institution is not old in Germany, being app. of local origin. See also *box*.

tire-lire: a Christmas box; a box having a cleft on the lid, or on the side, for money to enter it; used in France by begging friers, and here by butlers, and prentices, etc. (Cotg.).

Christy Minstrels. Original troupe of "negro" entertainers, organized (c. 1860) by *George Christy* of New York.

chromatic. G. χρωματικός, from χρῶμα, colour. Earliest, and most usu., in mus. sense.

chrome. F., G. χρῶμα, colour, cogn. with χρώς, skin. Orig. name given (1797) to metal *chromium* by its discoverer, Vauquelin. With *chromograph* cf. *oleograph*.

chronic. F. *chronique*, L., G. χρονικός, from χρόνος, time. Mod. slang sense is evolved from that of *chronic complaint*.

chronicle. ME. also *cronique*, F. *chronique*, Late L., G. χρονικά, annals, from χρόνος, time. For ending cf. *participle*, *principle*, *syllable*. Cf. *chronogram, chronology, chrono-meter*.

chrys-, chryso-. From G. χρυσός, gold.

chrysalis. G. χρυσαλλίς, from χρυσός, gold, owing to usual colour. Cf. Late L. *aurelia* in same sense.

chrysanthemum. G. χρυσάνθεμον, lit. gold flower, ἄνθεμον.

chryselephantine. Of gold and ivory. See *elephant*.

chrysolite. ME. & OF. *crisolite*, G. χρυσό-λιθος, from λίθος, stone.

chrysoprase. ME. & OF. *crisopace*, G. χρυσό-πρασος, from πράσον, leek; from its colour.

The tenth, crisopassus (Wyc. *Rev.* xxi. 20).

chub. Fish. Also, dial., block of wood, dolt. Origin obscure; ? cf. Norw. *kubbe*, log, *kubben*, stumpy. Hence *chubby*.

raccourci: chubby, trust up, short and strong
(Cotg.).

chubb. Lock. From *Charles Chubb*, lock-smith (†1845).

chubby. See *chub*.

chuck[1]. Call to fowls. Imit. and partly suggested by *chick*[1]. Cf. *chuck*, archaic term of endearment, for *chick*.

chuck[2]. To throw. Earlier *chock*. F. *choquer*, of doubtful origin. Earliest E. sense is connected with *chin*.

mantonniere: a chocke, or bob under the chinne
(Cotg.).

chuck[3] [*dial.*]. Lump of wood. See *chock*.

chuckle. Orig. of noisy, now of somewhat suppressed, laughter. Cf. obs. *checkle*, also *cackle*, and *chuck*[1].

chuckle-head. From *chuck*[3]. Cf. *block-head*.

chum. "A chamber-fellow, a term used in the universities" (Johns.). Clipped form of *chamber-fellow*. It is recorded for 1684 and explained thus c. 1690. This was the age of clipped words (*mob, cit, bam*, etc.) and the vowel change is like that of *com-rade* (q.v.), *bungalow, pundit*, etc. See *Pickwick*, ch. xlii.

Come my Bro Richard from schole to [be] my chamber-fellow at the university (Evelyn, 1640).

To my chum, Mr Hody of Wadham College
(*NED.* 1684).

Where he was of Wadham, being chamber-fellow of Humph. Hody (Hearne, 1706).

chump. Log, thick end, vulg. head. Of mod. formation, perh. suggested by *chunk, lump*.

chunk. Chiefly US. App. var. of *chuck*[3]. Cf. dial. *junk*.

chupatty [*hist.*]. Hind. *chapātī*, unleavened cake. Used as "fiery cross" in Ind. Mutiny (1857).

chuprassy [*Anglo-Ind.*]. Attendant, hench-man. Hind. *chaprāsī*, from *chaprās*, official badge.

church. AS. *cirice*, G. κυριακόν (sc. δῶμα), from κύριος, lord; cf. Du. *kerk*, Ger. *kirche*, ON. *kirkia*. See also *kirk*. Not found in Rom. & Celt. langs., which have deriva-tives of *ecclesia* (see *ecclesiastic*), nor in Goth., though most Teut. Church-words came through that lang. The *Church visible* is the Church on earth, as contrasted with the invisible, mystical, Church. *Church of England* is used, in L. form, by Becket (see *Anglican*). *Holy Church* is AS., *Mother Church* is in Wyc. *Churchwarden* is for older *churchward* (still a surname), AS. *ciricweard*. With *poor as a church mouse* cf. F. *gueux comme un rat d'église*, and with *churchyard cough* cf. F. *toux qui sent le sapin* (coffin wood).

churl. AS. *ceorl*, man, used for husband (*John*, iv. 17), later, countryman, peasant, etc. WGer., cf. Du. *kerel*, Ger. *kerl*, fellow. Hence name *Charles*. See *carl*. For de-generation of sense cf. *boor, villain*.

churn. AS. *cyrin*. Com. Teut.; cf. Du. *karn*, Ger. dial. *kirn*, ON. *kirna*. From a.Teut. root meaning cream (cf. Ger. dial. *kern*, cream), prob. cogn. with *corn*[1], *kernel*, from granular appearance assumed by churned cream.

chute. Fall, esp. of water. F., VL. **caduta*, from **cadēre*, to fall (for *cadere*). Confused with *shoot*, as in to *shoot the rapids*, partly due to adoption of *chute* from Canad. F. But cf. to *shoot coals* (*rubbish*), with some-what similar mental picture, and see also *shoot*[1,2].

chutney. Hind. *chatnī*.

chyle, chyme [*physiol.*]. G. χυλός, χυμός, juice, from χεῖν, to pour. Differentiated by Galen.

chymist. See *chemist*.

ciborium. MedL., G. κιβώριον, cup-shaped seed-vessel, cup. Eccl. sense, receptacle for Eucharist, due to fancied connection with L. *cibus*, food.

cicada, cicala. Insect. L. *cicada*. With second form, from It., cf. F. *cigale*, from Prov.

cicatrice. F., L. *cicatrix, -tric-*, scar.

cicerone. It., lit. Cicero, L. *Cicero-n-*, a name prob. derived from *cicer*, small pease. Cf. *Fabius, Lentulus, Piso*.

Cicestr. Signature of bishop of Chichester. Cf. *Cestr.*

cicisbeo. Recognized gallant of married lady. It., of unknown origin.

The widow's eye-glass turned from her cicisbeo's whiskers to the mantling ivy (*Ingoldsby*).

Cid. Sp., hero, Arab. *sayyid*, lord, title given by the Arabs of Spain to the champion of Christianity, Ruy Diaz, Count of Bivar (11 cent.).

Puisque Cid en leur langue est autant que seigneur,
Je ne t'envierai pas ce beau titre d'honneur
(Corneille).

-cide. As in *homicide, regicide.* F., L. *-cidium*, of act, *-cida*, of agent, from *caedere*, to kill.

cider. ME. *sider*, OF. *sidre* (*cidre*), MedL. *sicera*, G. σίκερα, used in *Vulg.* and LXX. for Heb. *shēkār*, strong drink.

He schal not drynke wyn and sydir [*AS. transl.* bēor] (Wyc. *Luke*, i. 15).

ci-devant [*hist.*]. Nickname (French Revolution) for former nobles. F. *ci-devant*, heretofore, formerly, as in *le citoyen Blanc, ci-devant marquis de....* Cf. *sans-culotte. Ci* is for *ici*, VL. *ecce-hic; devant* is VL. *de-ab-ante.*

cieling. See *ceiling.*

cierge. F., wax candle, L. *cereus*, waxen, from *cera*, wax.

cigar. Earlier *segar.* Sp. *cigarro.* ? Explained as from *cigarra*, cicada (q.v.), from shape resembling body of insect, or from puffing suggesting cicada's chirp. *Cigarette* is F.

With one of those bits of white card in your mouth Which gentlemen smoke who have been in the South (Trevelyan, 1866).

ciliary. From L. *cilium*, eyelash.

cilice [*archaic*]. Hair-shirt. F., L. *cilicium*, G. κιλίκιον, cloth made from *Cilician* goat's hair. Also AS. *cilic* (*Matt.* xi. 21).

Cimmerian. From L., G. Κιμμέριοι, a people fabled to live in perpetual darkness (*Odyssey*, xi.).

cinch [*US.*]. Sp. *cincha*, girth, from L. *cingulum.* A cow-boy word occurring in the fig. to *get a cinch on.*

cinchona. Peruvian bark. Named (1742) by Linnaeus in honour of *Countess of Chinchon* (in Castile) who introduced it from Peru (1640).

Cincinnatus. Great man in retirement. Roman general, called from the plough to Dictatorship when Rome was threatened by the Volscians.

cincture. L. *cinctura*, from *cingere*, *cinct-*, to gird.

cinder. AS. *sinder*, dross, slag; cf. Ger. *sinter*, ON. *sintr.* Later associated with, and affected in sense by, F. *cendre*, L. *cinis, ciner-*, ash.

Cinderella. Adapted from F. *cendrillon*, from *cendre* (v.s.); cf. Ger. *Aschenbrödel, -puttel*, etc. Hence *Cinderella dance*, over at midnight.

Artillery had been made the German military hobby; the German infantry in the mass was the Cinderella of the force (*Westm. Gaz.* Aug. 30, 1917).

cinematograph. F. *cinématographe*, invented and named by MM. Lumière, of Paris. Hence *cin-* for E. *kin-* (*kinetics*, etc.). From G. κίνημα, motion, from κινεῖν, to move. The shortened *cinema* is also F. (*cinéma*).

An exhibition of the "cinématographe"...yesterday afternoon (*Daily News*, Feb. 21, 1896).

The Church and the Press combined do not possess nearly so much power (*Cinema*, July 3, 1919).

cineraria. Genus of plants. ModL., from *cinis, ciner-*, ashes, from ashy down on leaves. Cf. *cinerary urn*, for ashes of the cremated.

cinet. Mod. var. of *sennit* (q.v.).

Cingalese, Singhalese, Sinhalese. Sanskrit *siṅhalās*, people of Ceylon (*Siṅhalam*).

cinnabar. Red mercuric sulphide. OF. *cinabre*, L., G. κιννάβαρι, of Oriental origin; cf. Pers. *zanjifrah.*

cinnamon. F. *cinnamome*, L., G. κιννάμωμον, Heb. *qinnāmōn.*

cinquecentist. It. artist of 16 cent. (*mil cinque cento*).

Cinque Ports. Orig. (12 cent.) Hastings, Sandwich, Dover, Romney, Hythe. F. *cinq*, L. *quinque*, five (see *quinary*). Cf. *cinquefoil* (bot. & her.).

cipher, cypher. Arab. *cifr*, nil, lit. empty, rendering Sanskrit *sūnya*, empty. The word penetrated into Europe with the Arab. notation (cf. F. *chiffre*, It. *cifra*, Sp. Port. *cifra*, Du. *cijfer*, Ger. *ziffer*) and kept sense of nil till 16–17 cents. (still in Port.), orig. sense (surviving in *mere cipher*) being supplied by Sp. *cero*, a contracted form, whence *zero.* Sense of secret writing is found in F. & It.

cipolin. Marble. F., It. *cippolino*, from *cippolo*, onion, from its foliated formation. See *chive.*

Circassian circle. Fancy name for dance (19 cent.). Cf. *Lancers, Caledonians.*

Circe. G. Κίρκη, myth. enchantress (*Odyssey*) whose cup changed those who drank into swine.

circle. AS. *circul* (astron.) and F. *cercle* (gen. sense), L. *circulus*, dim. of *circus* (q.v.). *Circular*, in business sense, is short for *circular letter*; cf. *circulation* of newspaper. *Circulation of blood* dates from 1628 (*circulatio sanguinis*, Harvey). Society sense, as in *court, upper, circles*, etc., starts from idea of circle surrounding principal personage. Cf. F. *cercle*, club, and similar use of Ger. *kreis*, circle.

circuit. F., L. *circuitus*, going round, from *circum* and *ire*, to go.

circular, circulation. See *circle*.

circum-. L., around, from *circus*, circle. In mod. spelling often replaces older *circon-*, from F.

circumbendibus. A 17 cent. humorous formation.

The periphrasis, which the moderns call the circumbendibus (Pope).

circumcise. F. *circoncis*, p.p. of *circoncire*, L. *circumcidere*; or perh. back-formation from earlier *circumcision*. Wyc. has *circumcide*.

circumference. F. *circonférence*, L. *circumferentia*, neut. pl. of *circumferens*, bearing round, transl. of G. περιφέρεια, periphery.

circumflex. Lit. bent round. Orig. (ˆ), now usually (ˆ), because easier for type-founders to make.

accent circonflex, ou contourné: the bowed accent (Cotg.).

circumjacent. Cf. *adjacent*.

circumlocution. L. *circumlocutio-n-*, translating G. *periphrasis*, talking round. Hence *Circumlocution Office* (*Little Dorrit*), skilled in the art of "How not to do it."

circumscribe. L. *circumscribere*, to write (draw lines) round.

circumspect. L. *circumspectus*, p.p. of *circumspicere*, to look round. Orig. of things, and illogically applied to persons; cf. *considerate, deliberate, outspoken*, etc.

circumstance. F. *circonstance*, L. *circumstantia*, neut. pl. of *circumstans*, pres. part. of *circumstare*, to stand round. Hence accompaniment, ceremony. *Circumstantial evidence* is in Burton's *Anatomy*.

Pride, pomp, and circumstance of glorious war (*Oth*. iii. 3).

circumvallation [*fort.*]. From L. *circumvallare*, to wall round, from *vallum*, rampart. See *wall*.

circumvent. From p.p. of L. *circumvenire*, to "get round."

circumvolution. L. *circumvolutio-n-*, from *volvere, volut-*, to roll.

circus. L., G. κίρκος, κρίκος, ring, circle. Orig. of the Roman *Circus Maximus*. F. *cirque* is used of natural amphitheatres, esp. in Pyrenees.

cirque. See *circus*.

cirrhosis [*med.*]. Disease of the liver. Named by Laennec, from G. κιρρός, tawny.

cirrus. L., curl, fringe, applied to form of cloud. Hence scient. terms in *cirri-, cirro-*.

cis-. L., on this side of. With *cispontine* cf. *transpontine*, with *cismontane* cf. *ultramontane*.

cissoid. Curve. G. κισσοειδής, ivy-like, from κισσός, ivy.

cist [*antiq.*]. L. *cista*, box, G. κίστη (see *chest*). In sense of pre-historic coffin through Welsh; cf. *kistvaen*.

Cistercian. F. *Cistercien*, order founded at Cîteaux (L. *Cistercium*) near Dijon by Robert, abbot of Molesme. Cf. *Carthusian*.

cistern. L. *cisterna*, from *cista*, chest. For suffix cf. *cavern*.

cistus. Shrub. G. κίστος, κίσθος, whence L. *cisthus* (Pliny).

cit. "A pert low townsman; a pragmatical trader" (Johns.). A 17 cent. clipped form of *citizen*. Cf. *mob*.

citadel. F. *citadelle*, It. *citadella*, dim. of *cittade* (*città*), city (q.v.).

cite. F. *citer*, L. *citare*, frequent. of *ciēre, cit-*, to set in motion.

cither, cithern. F. *cithare*, L. *cithara*, G. κιθάρα. Cf. *guitar* and obs. *gittern*, with excrescent *-n*. *Zither* is the Ger. form.

citizen. AF. *citezein*, etc., for OF. *citeain* (*citoyen*), altered on *denizen* (q.v.). See *city*. *Citizen of the world* (15 cent.) translates *cosmopolitan* (q.v.). Republican sense dates from F. Revolution, hence *American citizen* in contrast with *British subject*.

citole. OF., Prov. *citola*, dim. from L. *cithara*, cither (q.v.).

And angels meeting us shall sing
To their citherns and citoles
(Rossetti, *Blessed Damozel*).

citra-. L., on this side; cogn. with *cis-*.

citric. From *citron*.

citron. F., lemon (the citron is *cédrat*), It. *citrone*, from L. *citrus*, citron-tree. Cf. G. κίτριον, citron-tree, prob. of Oriental origin and cogn. with *cedar*. Hence chem. terms in *citr-, citro-*.

city. F. *cité*, L. *civitas, civitat-*, orig. citizenship, community, from *civis*, citizen; cf.

It. *città*, Sp. *ciudad*. *Civitas* app. replaced *urbs* as Rome lost its prestige. In medieval practice ident. with cathedral town, but now extended. With *the City*, i.e. that part of London within the old boundaries, cf. F. *cité* used of the orig. *ville de Paris* on the two islands.

cive. See *chive*.

civet. Cat. F. *civette*, It. *zibetto*, Arab. *zabād*.

civic. L. *civicus*, of a citizen (v.i.), esp. in *corona civica*, won by saving a Roman citizen's life.

civil. F., L. *civilis*, from *civis*, citizen, ult. cogn. with AS. *hīwan* (pl.), household. Cf. L. *bellum civile*. For sense of polite cf. *urbane*. *Civil Service* was orig. the non-military service of the E. India Company. The *Civil List*, orig. of all administrative charges, is now limited to those representing the royal expenditure and bounty.

Our first task is to teach them that militarism does not pay and that civilism does
(*Shoe and Leather Gazette*, Apr. 1918).

civism. F. *civisme* (v.s.), a Revolution word.

civvies [*mil. slang*]. Mufti. Perh. suggested by similar sense of F., Ger. *civil*.

clachan [*Sc.*]. Highland village. Gael., village, burial place, app. from *clach*, stone. Orig. set of monastic cells.

clack. Imit. Cf. F. *claque*, Du. *klak*.

clad. AS. *clāthod*, p.p. of *clāthian*, to clothe, surviving in stereotyped uses, e.g. *iron-clad*, after poet. *mailclad*.

claim. Tonic stem of OF. *clamer*, L. *clamare*, to shout. Leg. term *claimant* was long associated with the notorious Tichborne impostor (1873). The miner's *claim* is Austral. (19 cent.).

clairvoyant. F., seeing clearly, adopted c. 1850 in spec. sense.

clam. Bivalve. Earlier *clamshell*, as worn by pilgrims, from archaic *clam*, bond, clutch, etc., AS. *clamm*, grasp, bond. Cf. dial. *clem*, to pinch, starve, and see *clamp*.

Mustels, wilks, oisters, clamps, periwinkels
(*Capt. John Smith, 1624*).

clamant. Urgent. Pedantic for *crying* (*need*, etc.). From pres. part. of L. *clamare*, to shout.

clamber. Ger. *sich klammern*, in similar sense, from *klammer*, hook, etc., points to *clam*; cf. F. *s'accrocher* and hist. of *crawl*[1].

clamjamphrie [*Sc.*]. Heterogeneous collection, rabble. By Scott and Galt spelt *clan-*,

as though a derisive parody of *Clan Chattan*, etc.

clammy. Earliest *claymy*. Cf. dial. *clam*, *cleam*, to smear, daub, AS. *clǣman*, from *clām*, mud, cloam. Prob. associated also in meaning with *clam* (q.v.), with which it may be etym. ident. (clinging idea). Cf. Du. *klam*.

klam, klamp: tenax, humidus, lentus, viscosus, *ang.* klammy (Kil.).

clamour. F. *clameur*, L. *clamor-em*. See *claim*.

clamp[1]. Fastening. Du. *klamp*, cogn. with Ger. *klammer* and Ger. dial. *klampfe*. See *clam, clammy*.

clamp[2] [*dial.*]. Heap, esp. rick (Ir.). Cf. Du. *klamp*, heap; not connected with *clamp*[1]. ? Cf. *clump*.

Allowing for the usual storage [of potatoes] in clamps on the farms
(*Capt. Bathurst, M.P., in H. of C., June 5, 1917*).

clan. Gael. *clann*. Prob. from L. *planta*, in sense of *stirps*, stock; cf. Welsh *plant*, OIr. *cland*, the latter revived in *Clan-na-Gael*, a pol. society.

clandestine. L. *clandestinus*, from *clam*, secretly, cogn. with *celare*, to hide.

clang. L. *clangere*, to resound. Imit.; cf. G. κλάζειν.

clank. Combined from earlier *clink* (q.v.) and *clang*. Or from Du. *klank*. In any case imit.

clap[1]. Imit. of sharp sound; cf. Du. Ger. *klappen*, ON. *klappa*; also AS. *clæppettan*, to throb. Later applied to quick action, e.g. to *clap eyes on*, *clap into gaol*, etc.

That anxious exertion at the close of a speech which is called by the comedians a clap-trap
(*Davies, Life of Garrick, 1780*).

clap[2]. Gonorrhoea. Shortened from OF. *clapoir*, perh. from *clapier*, brothel.

clapboard. Overlapping board used in building. Partial transl. of Ger. *klapholz*, LG. *klapholt*, Du. *klaphout*, clap wood; cf. Ger. *klappen*, to fit together. Now chiefly US.

clapperclaw. App. from idea of combined noise and scratching, or *clapper* may have sense of hand (cf. *smeller*, *peeper*, etc.). From c. 1600 (see *Merry Wives*, ii. 3).

claque. F., organized applause at theatre, from *claquer*, to clap, of imit. origin.

clarence. Four-wheeled cab. From *Duke of Clarence*, afterwards William IV. *NED.* has no example after 1864, but an old cabby used the word in giving evidence in a London Police Court (1914). The Dukedom of Clarence was created for Lionel, second son of Edward III, when he married the heiress of Clare (Suff.). Hence *Clarencieux King-of-Arms*, an office still existing.

clarendon [*typ.*]. Thick type. Named by 19 cent. printer.

claret. OF. *vin claret* (*clairet*), prop. applied to light-coloured red wine intermediate between red and white.

cleret, or *claret*, *as wyne*: semiclarus (*Prompt. Parv.*).

clarify. F. *clarifier*, L. *clarificare*, to make clear (v.i.).

clarion. F. *clairon*, OF. *claron*, or rather, the E. word being app. of earlier date, Late L. *clario-n-*, from *clarus*, clear. Dim. *clarionet*, also *clarinet*, the latter from F. *clarinette*.

clarity. Restored spelling of ME. *clartee*, F. *clarté*, L. *claritas*, *-tat-*, from *clarus*, clear.

This [the enemy's fire] in no way interfered with the clarity of their reports
(Sir D. Beatty, June 19, 1916).

clary. Herb. Cf. MedL. *sclarea*, F. *sclarée*. Earlier is AS. *slarige*. Origin unknown.

clash. From c. 1500. Imit.; cf. *clack*, *splash*, etc.; also Du. *klessen*, earlier *kletsen*. Fig. to *clash with* is from the noise of conflicting weapons.

clasp. First as noun, earlier also *clapse*. Prob. imit. of sound; cf. *snap* (of a bracelet), Ger. *schnalle*, clasp, buckle, from *schnallen*, to snap, crack. Has nearly replaced *clip²*, perh. partly from similarity of init.

class. F. *classe*, L. *classis*, one of the six divisions of the Roman people, G. κλῆσις, from καλεῖν, to call, summon. "The evidence for the E. word begins with Blount" (*NED.*). Hence *classic*, L. *classicus*, as in *scriptor classicus*, opposed by Gellius to *proletarius*, but associated in F. with works read in univ. *classes*.

classe: a ship, or navy, an order or distribution of people according to their several degrees. In schools (wherein this word is most used) a form or lecture restrained to a certain company of scholars
(Blount).

Poetic fields encompass me around
And still I seem to tread on classic ground
(Addison).

clatter. Cf. AS. *clatrung*, noise. Imit.; cf. Du. *klateren*, Ger. dial. *klattern*.

Claude Lorraine glass. For viewing landscape. From *Claude of Lorraine*, F. painter (1600–82).

clause. F., L. *clausa*, used in MedL. for *clausula*, end of a period, from *claudere*, *claus-*, to close.

claustral. Of the cloister (q.v.). Cf. *claustromania* (neol.), morbid fear of being shut in.

clavate [*biol.*]. Club-shaped, from L. *clava*, club.

clavecin [*mus.*]. F., harpsichord, MedL. *clavicymbalum*, key cymbal.

clavi-. From L. *clavis*, key, and *clava*, club.

clavichord [*archaic*]. Rudimentary piano. MedL. *clavichordium*, key string. Corruptly *clarichord*.

clavicle. L. *clavicula*, collar-bone, lit. little key, *clavis*, cogn. with *claudere*, to shut.

clavier [*mus.*]. Key-board, piano. F., from L. *clavis*, key. Hence Ger. *klavier*, piano.

claw. AS. *clawu*. Com. Teut.; cf. Du. *klauw*, Ger. *klaue*, ON. *klō*.

clay. AS. *clǣg*; cf. Du. *klei*, Ger. *klei* (from LG.), Dan. *klæg*, Norw. dial. *kli*; cogn. with G. γλία, γλοία, glue, L. *glus*, and ult. with dial. *cleg*, gadfly, from sticking to object.

How should he return to dust
Who daily wets his clay? (Fielding).

claymore. Gael. *claidheamh*, sword, *mor*, great (see *glaive*). An antiquarian word, earlier *glaymore*, familiarized by Scott. Ult. cogn. with L. *clades*, slaughter.

clean. AS. *clǣne*. Com. Teut.; cf. Du. Ger. *klein*, ON. *klēnn*, all meaning small; but orig. Teut. sense, surviving in E., appears also in Ger. *kleinod*, jewel. Largely replaced by *clear*, *pure* in the higher senses. Wyc. still has *clean* where Tynd. uses *pure*. With adv. sense (*clean crazy*) cf. *pure folly*, etc., and similar use of Ger. *rein*, clean. As verb now usual for older *cleanse*, AS. *clǣnsian*, with which cf. Du. *kleinzen*, to strain, filter.

The citee it silf was of cleene gold, lijk to cleene glass (Wyc. *Rev.* xxi. 18).

clear. ME. *clere*, OF. *cler* (*clair*), L. *clarus*; cf. It. *chiaro*, Sp. *claro*. In the sense of free from encumbrance (from c. 1500) it occurs in several naut. metaphors (to *steer clear of*, *stand clear*, *coast is clear*, *clear the decks*, etc.). For *clearstory* see *clerestory*.

cleat [*chiefly naut.*]. Wedge, block. AS. **clēat*. WGer.; cf. Du. *kloot*, Ger. *kloss*; cogn. with *clod*, *clot*.

cleave¹. To split. AS. *clēofan*. Com. Teut.; cf. Du. *klieven*, Ger. *klieben*, ON. *kljūfa*; cogn. with L. *glubere*, to flay, G. γλύφειν, to hollow out. Archaic past *clave* survives in *AV.* (cf. *brake*, *sware*), while new weak p.p. *cleft* (*cleaved*) exists side by side with orig. strong *cloven* (*cleft stick*, *cloven hoof*). Hence *cleavage*, now much used of pol. opinions, etc., a metaphor from geol.

cleave². To adhere. AS. *clifian*. Com. Teut.; cf. Du. *kleven*, Ger. *kleben*, ON. *klīfa*, to clamber. Weak forms much confused with those of strong *cleave¹*. Both verbs are obsolescent, replaced by *split*, *stick*. With *cleavers*, goose-grass, cf. Ger. *klebekraut*.

cleek [*Sc.*]. Orig. hook, from obs. verb *cleek*, to clutch, for past tense of which (*claught*) see quot. s.v. *carl*. ? Cogn. with *clutch¹*.

cleyke, staff: cambusca (*Prompt. Parv.*).

clef [*mus.*]. F., L. *clavis*, key.

cleft. ME. *clift*, from *cleave¹*. Cf. Du. Ger. *kluft*. See *kloof*.

clem [*dial.*]. To endure privations, orig. to pinch with hunger. Cf. Du. Ger. *klemmen*, to pinch. See *clam¹*.

clematis. L., G. κληματίς, from κλῆμα, vine-branch.

clement. L. *clemens*, *clement-*, cogn. with *-clinare*, to lean.

Clementine. Of *Clement*, esp. edition of *Vulg.* due to *Pope Clement V* (1309–14).

clench, clinch. AS. *-clencan*, in *beclencan*, to make to "cling." Cf. Du. *klink*, latch, rivet, Ger. *klinke*, latch. The two mod. forms are to some extent differentiated in use, e.g. to *clench one's fist, teeth*, to *clinch the matter*. See also *clinch, clinker-built*, and *cling*.

clepsydra. Water-clock. G. κλεψύδρα, from κλέπτειν, to steal, ὕδωρ, water.

clerestory [*arch.*]. App. *clear story*, but found much earlier than the simple *story²*.

clergy. Combines F. *clergé*, clergy, Church L. *clericatus*, from *clericus* (see *clerk*), and archaic F. *clergie*, clerkly knowledge, formed in F. from *clerc*.

Gramaire is the fondement and the begynnyng of clergye (Caxton, *Mirror of World*).

clerical. See *clerk*. *Clericalism*, in hostile sense, is a neol. Cf. *militarism, sacerdotalism*, etc.

clerk. AS. *cleric, clerc*, and F. *clerc*, L. *clericus*, G. κληρικός, from κλῆρος, allotment, heritage, used in 2 cent. of the sacerdotal order. Orig. clergyman, then one who could read and write, and (from c. 1500), official, account-keeper, etc. Usu. spelt *clark* in 15–18 cents., as still in surname. The imaginary *Clerk of the Weather* is imitated from the numerous official titles of the same type.

For he was numbered with us, and had obtained part of this ministry [τὸν κλῆρον τῆς διακονίας ταύτης] (*Acts*, i. 17).

clerc: a clarke; a scholler, or learned person; hence,

also, a churchman (who should be learned); also, a clarke in an office; a lawyers clarke; and generally any penman (Cotg.).

cleugh [*dial.*]. Sc. form of *clough* (q.v.), e.g. *Clym o' the Cleugh*, hero of famous ballad.

cleve. Var. of *cliff*, common in place-names.

clever. Recorded once (*cliver*) c. 1220, then not till 16 cent., when it replaces earlier *deliver*. Orig. expert at seizing (cf. *nimble, handy*). Described by Sir T. Browne as EAngl. and as a dial. word by Ray (1674). Prob. EFris. *clüfer*; cf. Dan. dial. *klever*; ? cogn. with ME. *cliver*, claw. But analogy of *skill, discerning*, Ger. *gescheidt*, clever, all containing idea of separation, suggests ult. connection with *cleave¹*.

deliver, redy, quicke to do any thyng: agile, delivré (Palsg.).

clew, clue. AS. *clīwen, cleowen*, ball of thread. WGer.; cf. Du. *kluwen*, Ger. *knäuel*, the latter by dissim. from MHG. *kliuwel*, dim. of OHG. *kliuwi*; cogn. with L. *glomus*. Mod. sense, usu. *clue*, from legend of Theseus and the Cretan Labyrinth. *Clew* is usual in naut. lang.

By a clewe of twyne, as he hath gon,
The same way he may returne anon,
Folwynge alway the threde, as he hath come
(Chauc. *Leg. of Good Women*, 2016).

cliché. Hackneyed phrase. Orig. stereotype. From p.p. of *clicher*, to "click," from sound made in process.

He indulges in invective against the stale phrases and topical allusions which infest our journalism and our oratory....But on the very next page our mentor himself indulges in " the unspeakable Turk," "the mailed fist," "bloated armaments," and "the silver sea" (*Sunday Times*, Aug. 3, 1919).

click. Imit., representing a thinner sound than *clack*. Cf. *clink, clank*, also F. *cliquer*, Du. *klikken*. A *clicker* in the boot trade, now a foreman cutter-out, was orig. a tout (cf. *clique, claque*), ? or for *cleeker*, from obs. *cleek*, to clutch.

clicker: the shoe-maker's journeyman or servant, that cuts out all the work, and stands at or walks before the door, and saies, "What d'ye lack, sir? What d'ye buy, madam?" (*Dict. Canting Crew*).

client. F., L. *cliens, client-*, earlier *cluens*, pres. part. of *cluere*, to listen to, G. κλύειν, to hear. Orig. a dependent, in F. a customer. Some regard *cliens* as earlier form and connect it with *-clinare*, to incline. Cf. *clientèle*, L. *clientela*, common in 16–17 cents., now readopted from F. AF. *client* occurs in 1306 (*Year-books of Ed. I*).

cliff. AS. *clif*; cf. Du. *klip*, Ger. *klippe* (LG.), ON. *klif*. See also *cleve*.

climacteric. Critical period, esp. 63rd year (*grand climacteric*), product of 9 and 7, the two critical numbers. From G. κλιμακτήρ, rung of a ladder. See *climax*.

climate. F. *climat*, Late L. *clima*, *climat-*, G. κλίμα, κλιματ-, slope (from the equator to the poles). Orig. sense of region, zone, survives in poet. *clime*.

climate: a portion of the earth contained between two circles parallel to the equator (Phillips).

climax. L., G. κλῖμαξ, ladder, and (rhet.) series of propositions rising in effectiveness; cf. *anti-climax*, bathos. Current sense, "due to popular ignorance" (*NED.*), is not recognized by Todd.

climb. AS. *climban*. WGer.; cf. Du. Ger. *klimmen*; cogn. with *cleave²* (cf. ON. *klīfa*, ME. *cliven*, to climb, and see *clamber*). A strong verb in AS. but weak by 16 cent., poet. *clomb* being a Spenserian archaism imitated by mod. poets.

clime. See *climate*.

clinch. See *clench*. *Clinch* is esp. common in techn. applications (rivet, etc.), and has a northern form *clink*. Hence *clincher-*, *clinker-built*, of boats, orig. contrasted with *carvel-built* (see *carvel*). Fig. a *clincher* is an argument that rivets, hits the right nail on the head.

cling. AS. *clingan*, of which *clench*, *clinch* is the causal. Orig. to adhere together in a stiff mass; cf. synon. Norw. *klænge*, ON. *klengjask* (reflex., cf. *bask*), to pick a quarrel, lit. to fasten (oneself) on.

clinic. L., G. κλινικός, from κλίνη, a bed, from κλίνειν, to make to lean.

clink¹. Sound. Imit. of a thinner sound than *clang*, *clank*. Cf. Du. *klinken*, Ger. *klingen*, Sw. *klinga*, Dan. *klinge*, etc. With intens. *clinking* cf. *rattling*.

clink² [*slang & mil.*]. Prison. Orig. prison at Southwark. Prob. related to *clench*, *clinch*; cf. Du. *klink*, door-latch, and "under lock and key."

Then art thou clapped in the Flete or Clinke (*NED.* 1515).

clinker. Orig. hard brick, hence, hard mass, slag, etc. Du. *klinker*, earlier *klinkaerd*, from *klinken*, to clink. First in Evelyn (*clincar*, *klincart*), in ref. to aqueduct at Amsterdam.

klinckaerd: later excoctus et durus imprimis q.d. tinniens sive tinnulus, dum pulsatur (Kil.).

clinker-built. See *clinch*, *carvel*.

clinometer. Math. instrument. From G. κλιν-, sloping (see *clinic*).

clip¹. To shear. Northern ME., ON. *klippa*, whence also Dan. *klippe*, Sw. *klippa*; cf. LG. *klippen*. Prob. imit. and representing a thinner sound than *clap* (cf. *snip*, *snap*).

clip² [*archaic*]. To embrace, clutch. AS. *clyppan*; cf. ON. *klȳpa*, to pinch, OFris. *kleppa*, to embrace. Hence noun *clip* in mech. senses, e.g. *clip of cartridges*, *paper-clip*.

clipper. Fast sailing-ship, swift horse. In first sense from *clip¹* (? cf. *cutter*). In second from Ger. or Du. *klepper*, now, sorry nag, but in 16 cent. swift trotter, from LG. *kleppen*, to resound, with ref. to the hoof-beat.

clique. F., set of backers, from *cliquer*, to make a noise; cf. *claque*. The F. word occurs in sense of band, crew, in 14 cent.

clitell- [*zool.*]. From L. *clitellae*, packsaddle.

clitoris [*anat.*]. G. κλειτορίς, from κλείειν, to sheathe.

cloaca. L., sewer, for *clovaca*, from *cluere*, to cleanse.

cloak. Earlier *cloke*. ONF. *cloque* (*cloche*), from its "bell" shape (see *clock*). For fig. sense cf. *palliate*.

Of double worstede was his semycope,
That rounded as a belle (Chauc. A. 262).

cloam [*dial.*]. Earthenware. AS. *clām*, mud, clay. Cf. *clammy*.

clock. ONF. *cloque* (*cloche*), Late L. *clocca*; cf. AS. *clucga*, Du. *klok*, Ger. *glocke*, bell. Also Ir. *clog*, Gael. *clag*, Welsh *cloch*. Orig. bell, in which sense its spread was due to the early Irish missionaries. This sense is not strongly evidenced in ME.; which already had *bell*. Prob. of imit. origin, and found, as Church word, in Teut. & Celt. langs. from 8 cent. Not in Southern Rom. langs., which preserved L. *campana*. Hence prob. also *clock* of a stocking, from shape. It is called in F. *coin*, wedge, and in It. *staffa*, stirrup, the latter being an object of very much the same shape as the conventional bells of heraldry.

clod, clot. Now differentiated (*clod of earth*, *clot of blood*), but synon. up to 18 cent. AS. *clod-* (only in compds.). WGer.; cf. Du. *kloot*, Ger. *klotz*, clod, also in fig. sense of E. word. With *clodhopper*, rustic, cf. *bog-trotter*, Irishman, *mosstrooper*.

His locks with clods of bloud and dust bedight (Fairfax's *Tasso*).

Where ye clottes of the earth are golde (Coverd. *Job*, xxviii. 6).

clodhopper: a ploughman (*Dict. Cant. Crew*).

clog. First as noun (c. 1400), log of wood. Cf. Sc. *yule-clog*. Associated in later senses with dial. *clag*, to bedaub, make sticky. Origin unknown. For application to wooden shoe cf. use of Du. cognate of *clump* (q.v.).

cloisonné. In compartments (of enamels). F., from *cloison*, partition, VL. **clausio-n-*, from *claudere*, *claus-*, to close.

cloister. OF. *cloistre* (*cloître*), VL. **claustrium*, from *claudere*, *claus-*, to close. L. *claustrum* gave AS. *clūster* and OF. *clostre*. Fig. sense (*The Cloister and the Hearth*) as in F. *cloître*. F. has *cloître* for cathedral close, but not in the sense of arcaded walk which has developed from it in E. (cf. *piazza*).

Clootie [*Sc.*]. Satan. From dial. *cloot*, cloven hoof, from ON. *klō*, claw.

> O thou! whatever title suit thee,
> Auld Hornie, Satan, Nick, or Clootie.
> (Burns, *Address to the Deil*).

close. Noun and adj. F. *clos*, p.p. of archaic *clore*, to close, L. *claudere*. Verb from *clos-*, stem of *clore*. Participial origin of the adj. is still apparent in *close-fisted*, opposite of *open-handed*. Secondary sense of "near" arises from that of having all intervals "closed"; cf. mil. to *close up*. The double sense appears in *close quarters*, now understood of proximity, but orig. "closed" space on ship-board where last stand could be made against boarders.

closet. OF., dim. of *clos* (v.s.). In *Matt.* vi. 6 renders L. *cubiculum*, G. ταμιεῖον.

closure. F., L. *clausura*, from *claudere*, *claus-*, to close. Found in several archaic senses in E. Since 1882 esp. in H. of C., at first in competition with F. *clôture*, VL. **clausitura*.

clot. See *clod*.

cloth. AS. *clāth*. WGer.; cf. Du. *kleed*, Ger. *kleid*, garment. The AS. word is not applied to the material, but to a "cloth" (cf. *loin-cloth*) to wrap round one (see *Mark*, xiv. 51), and the pl. is used for "clothes." This is the only sense of the Du. & Ger. words. Earlier hist. obscure. From 17 cent. used as symbol of profession, esp. the Church. The double sense appears in *clothier*, in ME. a cloth-worker, now a tailor.

clôture. See *closure*.

cloud. AS. *clūd*, rock, mass, cogn. with *clod*, and assuming (c. 13 cent.) sense of mass of cloud, *cumulus*. *Under a cloud* is recorded c. 1500. Something of orig. sense survives in *cloud of sail* (*canvas*).

clough [*north*.]. Ravine with river. AS. *clōh* (in place-names); cf. OHG. *clāh*, Sc. *cleugh*. Not related to Du. *kloof*.

> The valley of the Ancre is a steep and narrow clough
> (*Manch. Guard.* Nov. 15, 1916).

clout. Piece, patch. AS. *clūt*; cf. ON. *klūtr*; cogn. with *clod*, *clot*. In sense of blow from c. 1400, though the metaphor is not clear (but cf. *clump*). With archaic *clouted cream* cf. *clotted*.

> I wasted them and so clouted [*Vulg.* confringere] them that they could not arise
> (Tynd. 2 *Sam*. xxii. 39).

clove¹. Of garlic, etc. AS. *clufu*, cogn. with *cleave¹*. Cf. Ger. *knoblauch*, by dissim. from MHG. *klobelouch*, corresponding to ME. *clove-leek*. See *onion*.

clove². Spice, flower. ME. *clou* (later influenced by *clove¹*), F. *clou* (*de girofle*), from shape of bud, L. *clavus*, nail. Cf. Ger. *nelke*, pink (little nail), South Ger. *nägele*, clove spice. See *gillyflower*.

> Ther spryngen herbes grete and smale,
> The lycorys and cetewale,
> And many a clowe-gylofre (Chauc. B. 1950).

clove³. Obs. weight (cheese, wool). F. *clou*, L. *clavus*, nail, MedL. *clavus lanae* (Duc.). Cf. *clove²*.

clove-hitch [*naut*.]. From divided appearance. From *cleave¹*.

cloven. See *cleave¹*. Satan prob. inherited the *cloven hoof* from Pan.

clover. AS. *clāfre*, *clǣfre*; cf. Du. *klaver*, LG. *klever*, Sw. *klöfwer*, Norw. Dan. *klöver* (these from LG.). Prob. an old compd. of which first element appears in Ger. *klee*. Hence *in clover*, i.e. especially good pasture.

clown. From 16 cent., also *cloyn*. App. related to several Scand. dial. and LG. words meaning log, lump, and hence lout, boorish fellow. Cf. fig. use of *clod*, *bumpkin*. The pantomime *clown* represents a blend of the Shaks. rustic with one of the stock types of the It. comedy.

cloy. For obs. *accloy*, from F. *enclouer* (from *clou*, nail), to prick a horse's hoof in shoeing, to spike a gun. Both F. senses are found in 16 cent. E. Mod. meaning is supposed to have developed from the gen. idea of clogging, stopping; but cf. Norw. *klie*, Dan. dial. *klöge*, to feel nausea, ON. *klīgja*.

> [They] stopped and cloied the touch holes of three peeces of the artillerie (Holinshed).
> Our generall would not suffer any man to carry much...away, because they should not cloy themselves with burthens (Purch.).

club. ON. *klubba*, for *klumba*, clump; cf. ON. *klumbu-, klubbu-fôtr*, club-foot. With *club-law* cf. Ger. *faustrecht*, lit. fist-right. The *club* at cards translates Sp. *basto* or It. *bastone*, but we have adopted the F. pattern, *trèfle*, trefoil (cf. *spade*²). In sense of assembly, *club* appears first as verb, to collect in a bunch, etc. Cf. *clump* of trees, spectators, *knot* of lookers-on, etc. But the much older ON. *hjūkolfr*, club house, of which the second element means club, cudgel (see *golf*), has given rise to the theory that a "club" was orig. called together by a club-bearer. F. *club*, from E., is usu. pol. (dating from Revolution) or of sporting clubs also of E. origin (Jockey, Racing, Touring). *Clubbable* was coined by Dr Johnson.

We went to Woods at the Pell-Mell (our old house for clubbing) (Pepys, July 26, 1660).

faustrecht brauchen: to go to club-law with one
(Ludw.).

cluck. Earlier *clock*. AS. *cloccian*. Imit., cf. Ger. *glucken*, F. *glousser*, OF. *glosser*, "to cluck, or clock, as a henne" (Cotg.).

clue. See *clew*.

clumber. Spaniel. From *Clumber*, Duke of Newcastle's estate (Notts). Cf. *blenheim*.

clump. From end of 16 cent. Du. *klomp* or LG. *klump*, esp. in sense of wooden clog; cf. AS. *clympre*, whence dial. *clumper*, lump, clod. See *club*. With *clump on the head* cf. *clout*.

de boer droeg houtene klompen: the clown wore wooden clogs (Sewel).

clumsy. Orig. benumbed or stiff with cold. Not in Shaks. or *AV*. Earlier *clumsed*, p.p. of ME. *clumsen*, to benumb, become numb. App. AS. **clumsian* (cf. *cleanse* from *clænsian*), from a base *clum-*, cogn. with *clam* (q.v.), which appears in many Scand. & LG. words of similar meaning.

Whan thow clomsest for colde or clyngest for drye (*Piers Plowm.* B. xiv. 50).

clunch [*arch.*]. Kind of limestone. A dial. word, lump, lumpy, app. related to *clump* (cf. *hump, hunch; lump, lunch*).

Cluniac, Clunist. Monk of order established at *Cluny* (Saône-et-Loire), which separated (11 cent.) from Benedictines.

cluster. AS. *cluster*; prob. cogn. with *clot, clew*.

clutch¹. Grasp. ME. *cloke*, claw, later *cloche*, influenced by verb *clutch*, for earlier *clitch*, AS. *clyccan*, to clench, curve the fingers, cogn. with noun. Orig. sense survives in *in one's clutches*.

clutch². Of chickens, eggs, etc. Var. of dial. *cletch*, from obs. verb *cleck*, ON. *klekja*, to hatch.

clutter. Coagulation, confused mass, etc. Var. of *clotter*, from *clot*. In sense of noise, confusion, prob. associated with *clatter*.

grumeau de sang: a clot, or clutter, of congealed blood (Cotg.).

clydesdale. Dray-horse, from *vale of Clyde*.

clypeo- [*zool.*]. From L. *clypeus*, shield.

clyster. F. *clystère*, L., G. κλυστήρ, from κλύζειν, to wash out.

co-. Shortened form of L. *com-*, for *cum*, with.

coacervation. Heap. From L. *coacervare*, from *acervus*, heap.

coach. F. *coche*, Ger. *kutsche* (16 cent. *kutschwagen*), Hung. *koszi*, adj., from *Koszi*, place between Raab and Buda. Said to date from the reign of Matthias Corvinus (15 cent.). Montaigne, in his essay "Des Coches," gives an account of a battle in which the Hungarians with their coaches anticipated the tanks. Forms are found in most Europ. langs. Up to early 19 cent. also for *hackney-coach*, the predecessor of the *cab*. The railway *coach* is an inheritance from the stage-*coach* (cf. *driver, guard, booking-office*). In univ. slang, a help to progress (at Oxf. since c. 1830). To *drive a coach and six through an Act of Parliament* is recorded c. 1700, the *coach and six* being used also by Otway as a kind of contrast to the cat that is swung round. The earliest *NED*. record for *slow-coach* (*Pickwick*) is already fig.

coadjutor. L., from *adjuvare, adjut-*, to help.

coagulate. From L. *coagulare*, from *agere*, to drive.

coaita. Monkey. Tupi (Brazil).

coal. AS. *col*. Com. Teut.; cf. Du. *kool*, Ger. *kohle*, ON. *kol*. In ME. both charcoal and earth-coal (see *collier*). To *heap coals of fire* is lit. from G. (v.i.). To *call* (*haul*) *over the coals* was earlier (16 cent.) to *fetch over the coals*, orig. with reference to treatment of heretics. There is no evidence for the statement, periodically repeated from Brewer, that it comes from medieval torture of Jews. "Salt to Dysert (Dysart in Fife), or *colles to Newcastle*" is recorded (c. 1600) as rendering of G. γλαῦκ᾽ εἰς Ἀθήνας, owls to Athens.

ἄνθρακας πυρὸς σωρεύσεις ἐπὶ τὴν κεφαλὴν αὐτοῦ
(*Rom.* xii. 20).

This false chanoun—the foule feend hym fecche!—
Out of his bosom took a bechen cole
(Chauc. G. 1159).

coalesce. L. *coalescere*, to grow together, from incept. of *alere*, to nourish. Hence *coalition*, first used in pol. sense in 1715. Cf. *coalitioneer*, coined (Dec. 1918) on *electioneer* by H. H. Asquith.

coalmouse, colemouse. Dark coloured bird. AS. *colmāse* from *coal* and second element as in *titmouse* (q.v.); cf. Ger. *kohlmeise*.

coalport. China. From *Coalport* (Salop).

coaming [*naut.*]. Erection round hatchway. Origin unknown. Cotg. and Capt. John Smith make it synon. with *carling*.

coarse. ME. *cors*, later *course*. Earliest of cloth. Metath. of AF. *cros*, as in *crospais*, for *grampus* (q.v.), F. *gros* (see *gross*[1]). Cf. also *Le Cros* as E. surname (13 cent.). Lit. and fig. senses of *coarse* run exactly parallel to those of *gross* and of F. *gros*; cf. also Ger. *grob* for sense-development.

coast. OF. *coste* (*côte*), L. *costa*, rib, side, whence It. Sp. *costa*, as in *Costa Rica*. In ref. to toboganning, and hence, letting cycle run down hill, it is the same word in F. sense of hill-side, toboggan track, taken from Canad. F.

> *coste:* a rib; also, a little hill, or descent of land; also, a coast, or land by the sea-side (Cotg.).

coat. F. *cotte* (now, petticoat, overall); cf. It. *cotta*, Prov. Sp. Port. *cota*, MedL. *cotta*. Prob. of Teut. origin; cf. OHG. *chozzo* (*kotze*), shaggy mantle. *Coat of arms* (*mail*) represent F. *cotte d'armes*, orig. coat with her. device worn over armour, and *cotte de mailles* (see *mail*[1]). To *trail one's coat*, i.e. invite anyone who wants trouble to tread on the tail of it, is a reminiscence of Donnybrook Fair. To *turn coat* (16 cent.) was orig. to put one's coat on inside out so as to hide badge.

> Mr Ginnell was again trailing his coat in the House of Commons yesterday
> (*Daily Chron.* Feb. 23, 1917).

coati. Animal of racoon tribe. Tupi (Brazil), from *cua*, cincture, *tim*, nose, from appearance of snout.

coax. A "low word" (Johns.). First as noun (16 cent.) *cokes*, *cox*, etc., a fool; cf. verbs to *fool*, to *gull*, etc. Of obscure origin; perh. connected with obs. *princox*, *princocks* (*Rom. & Jul.* i. 5). Both prob. belong to *cock*[1]. Or, it may be F. *cocasse*, ridiculous (cf. *hoax* from *hocus*), which occurs in E. in 1546.

> *coquard:* a proud gull, peart goose, quaint fop, saucy dolt, malapert coxcomb, rash or forward cokes (Cotg.).

cob[1]. Noun. The *NED.* recognizes eight nouns *cob*, with numerous sub-groups. Like other monosyllables common in dial., its hist. is inextricable. In some senses it may be ident. with *cop*, rounded top, AS. *copp*, summit (cf. *Spion Kop*). The idea of roundness appears in *cob-loaf*, and perh. in *cob* (horse), said to be orig. for horse with *cobs*, testicles. *Cob*, mixture of clay, straw, etc. for building, may go with *cob*, little round heap. *Cob-nut* is prob. from sense of cluster.

> He was one oth' cobbe-knights in the throng,
> When they were dubd in clusters
> (Brome, *Damoiselle*, i. 1).

cob[2] [*slang*]. To beat, in various senses; in ME. to fight. Perh. imit. of blow.

> The rough discipline used by the crew,
> Who, before they let one of the set see the back of them,
> "Cobb'd" the whole party,—ay, "every man Jack of them" (*Ingoldsby*).

cobalt. Ger. *kobalt*, earlier *kobold*, goblin. Named by miners because regarded as useless and harmful (cf. *nickel*, *blende*). *Kobold* is a spec. application of a common Ger. name, from OHG. *Godbald*, lit. God bold (cf. our *Cobbold*, *Godbolt*), conferred in the same way as *Old Nick*, *Will o' the wisp*, etc. (see *goblin*). Another Ger. name for goblin is *Oppold*, formed in the same way from OHG. name *Otbald*, ident. with the common AS. *Ēadbeald*. Like other Ger. mining terms *cobalt* has passed into most Europ. langs.

cobble[1]. Stone. Prob. from *cob*[1]; cf. synon. Norw. dial. *koppul*.

cobble[2]. To mend clumsily. Prob. also from *cob*[1], ? doing up in rough lumps, etc. ? Hence *cobbler*, US. drink (before 1919), as patching up the constitution.

> "This wonderful invention, Sir," said Mark, tenderly patting the empty glass, "is called a cobbler"
> (*Martin Chuzzlewit*, ch. xvii).

Cobdenism. Economic and pol. teaching of *Richard Cobden* (†1865). See *Manchester School*.

coble. Fishing boat. Welsh *ceubal*, ferryboat, skiff, prob. meaning "hollow" (*dugout*); cf. Bret. *caubal*. Hence prob. Late L. *caupulus* (Isidore), whence AS. (Northumb.) *cuopel* (*Matt.* viii. 23).

cobra. Short for *cobra de capello*, Port., hood snake. L. *colubra*, snake. *Capello* is Port. equivalent of F. *chapeau*, Late L. *cappellum* (see *cap*). The word came to us via

India. Native name is *nag*, snake (see Kipling, *Jungle-Book*), whence scient. *naja tripudians*.

coburg loaf. "Was introduced into this country soon after the marriage of the late Queen Victoria, when it was known, particularly in the provinces, as the 'Coronation loaf'" (F. C. Finch, of *Bakers' Record*, in *Daily Chron.* Dec. 5, 1918). Cf. *albert chain*.

cobweb. ME. *coppeweb*, from *coppe*, spider. Cf. dial. *attercop*, spider, AS. *ātorcoppe*, from *ātor*, poison, second element perh. ident. with *cob¹*. Cf. Du. *spinnekop*, spider.

kop, koppe: spider, or a cob (Hexham).

coca. Shrub. Sp., Peruv. *cuca*. Hence *cocaine*.

coccagee. Apple. Ir. *cac a' gheidh*, dung of goose. From colour.

Cocceian. Theol. views of *John Cocceius* (*Koch* or *Koken*), professor at Leyden († 1669). See *Heart of Midlothian*, ch. xii.

coccus. Cochineal insect. G. κόκκος, grain.

coccyx [*anat.*]. Bone ending spine. G. κόκκυξ, cuckoo, because supposed to resemble cuckoo's bill.

cochin-china. Fowl. From place of origin. Cf. *brahmapootra, bantam, orpington*.

cochineal. F. *cochenille*, Sp. *cochinilla*, from L. *coccinus*, scarlet, from *coccum*, scarlet grain, from G. κόκκος, grain. Cf. F. *coccinelle*, lady-bird. The insect was at first taken to be a berry. See *kermes* and cf. *dyed in grain*.

cochlea. Cavity of ear. L., snail, G. κοχλίας. From shape.

cock¹. Bird. AS. *cocc*; cf. F. *coq*, Late L. *coccus*. Prob. imit. of cry; cf. Ger. *gockelhahn, hahn* representing true Teut. name of the bird (see *hen*). In mech. senses (of a gun, water-tap) from fancied resemblance; cf. Ger. *hahn* in both senses. *Cock of the walk* alludes to pugnacious and autocratic character of the bird; hence also *cocky* or *coxy*. Cf. to *cock one's hat* and *cocked hat*. To *knock into a cocked hat*, change shape beyond recognition, is 19 cent. slang. *Cock-eyed* is one of many expressions evolved from the verb to *cock*, to tilt, etc. (see *cockade*). With to *live like fighting cocks*, treated very carefully in comparison with the domestic variety, cf. *in clover*. *Cock and bull story* was earlier represented by obs. *cockalane*, F. *coq à l'âne*, incoherent story muddling one object with another (OF. *saillir du coq en*

l'asne, 14 cent.): *Cockshy* comes from the obs. Shrovetide amusement of throwing at tied cocks. In *ride a cock-horse* we have 16 cent. *cock-horse*, toy horse, perh. with cock's head, as sometimes on roundabouts; but first syllable may be an attempt at the coachman's "click" (cf. baby Ger. *hottpferd* from *hott*, cry to horse).

cockthrowing at Shrovetide: gallicidium (Robertson, 1681).

"And what does the boy mean," added Mr Willet, after he had stared at him for a little time, in a species of stupefaction, "by cocking his hat to such an extent? Are you a-going to kill the wintner, sir?" (*Barnaby Rudge*, ch. xii.).

cock². Of hay. ON. *kökkr*, lump, whence Norw. *kok*, heap.

cockabondy [*angling*]. Fly. Welsh *coch a bondu*, red with black trunk. Cf. names *Couch, Gough* (red), and *Roderick Dhu* (black).

cockade. Earlier *cocard*, F. *cocarde*. Nature of connection with *coq* (*cock¹*) uncertain.

bonnet à la coquarde: a Spanish cap, or fashion of bonnet used by the most substantiall men of yore; (tearmed so, perhaps, because those that wore them grew thereby the prouder, and presumed the most of themselves); also, any bonnet, or cap, worn proudly, or peartly on th' one side (Cotg.).

cock-a-doodle-doo. Imit. Cf. F. *cocorico*, Ger. *kikeriki*, L. *cucurire*.

cock-a-hoop. Earliest (Sir T. More, 1529) in to *set the cock on the hoop*, ? the spigot on the hoop of the cask, as a preliminary to vigorous drinking. But the existence of such tavern-signs as the *Cock* (Swan, Falcon, Crown, Bell, etc.) *on the Hoop*, from 15 cent., points to some earlier allusion. The meaning of the phrase has varied according to fancied origins.

se goguer: to be most frolick, lively, blithe, cranke, merry; to take his pleasure, sport at ease, make good cheere, set cocke-a-hoope, throw the house out at windowes (Cotg.).

Cockaigne, Cockayne [*archaic*]. Imaginary land of ease and luxury. F. *cocagne* (OF. *quoquaigne*, 12 cent.); cf. It. *cuccagna*, "lubber-land" (Flor.), Sp. *cucaña*. So also Ger. *schlaraffenland*, ? from MHG. *slûr-affe*, lazy ape. Usu. supposed to mean "cake land," MedL. *Cocania* being modelled on *Allemania*, etc., from OHG. *kuocho* (*kuchen*), with which cf. Sc. *cooky*. This agrees with the earliest accounts (in E. c. 1300) which describe *Cockaigne* as a land where the roofs and walls are of cake. Often now applied to London by mistaken association with *cockney* (q.v.).

cockaleekie. See *cocky-leeky*.

cockalorum. From *cock*[1]. Perh. Du. and of same type as *cock-a-doodle-doo*. ? Or mock-Latin of the type common in 15 cent.

kockeloeren: to crow like a cock, or a cockril
(Hexham).

cock-and-bull. See *cock*[1].

cock-and-pie [*archaic*]. Oath. *Cock*, euph. for *God, pie*[1] (q.v.), the ordinal of the Cath. Church. *Cokkesbones* is in Chauc.

cockatoo. Du. *kakketoe*, Malay *kakatúa*; cf. F. *cacatoès*. Prob. imit. of cry.

cockatrice. OF. *cocatris*, corrupted (on *coq*) from *calcatris*, Prov. *calcatriz*, It. *calcatrice*, Late L. **calcatrix, calcatric-* (*caucatrix* in Duc.), from *calcare*, to tread (*calx*, heel), as transl. of G. ἰχνεύμων (see *ichneumon*). The fabulous *cockatrice* is identified also in E. with the basilisk (q.v.) and sometimes with the crocodile.

cockboat. Also (15 cent.) *cogboat*, and, from 16 cent., *cock* (*Lear*, iv. 6). Boat towed behind ship. Often as emblem of smallest craft. The oldest form (1420) is *cok* or *cokbote*. ? Cf. OF. *coque*, vessel, ModF. hull, ident. with *coque*, shell of egg, walnut, etc.

cockchafer. See *chafer*.

cocker[1]. Spaniel. Trained to start *wood-cock*.

cocker[2]. Verb. Also *cock* (only in Tusser) and *cockle*. Cf. Du. *kokelen*, "nutrire sive fovere culina" (Kil.), with a (possibly forced) association with *kokene*, kitchen; also OF. *coqueliner*, "to dandle, cocker, fedle, pamper, make a wanton of, a child" (Cotg.). Tusser appears to bring it into connection with *cockney* (q.v.).

Some cockneies with cocking are verie fooles
(*Good Husbandry*).

Cocker, according to. *Edward Cocker*, penman and arithmetician (1631–75). Pepys employed him (*Diary*, Aug. 10, 1664).

cockerel. Dim. of *cock*[1]; cf. *pickerel*.

cocket. Seal (? or certificate) of Custom House. Quot. below suggests that it was orig. of the "score and tally" description, in which case it would be a dim. of F. *coche*, "a nock, notch, nick" (Cotg.).

Item, payd to the klarke and to the kountroller for talying [i.e. cutting] owt of the kokett at Hull, xjs viiid. (*York Merch. Advent. Accts.* 1467).

cockle[1]. Weed. AS. *coccel*, perh. dim. from L. *coccum* (see *cochineal*). Commonly used in ME. for the tares of the Bible.

His enmye came, and sew above dernel, or cokil [1388 *taris*] in the midil of whete
(Wyc. *Matt.* xiii. 25).

cockle[2]. Shell. F. *coquille*, from VL. **coccylium*, L. *conchylium*, G. κογχύλιον, from κόγχη, whence L. *concha*, VL. *cocca*, origin of F. *coque*, shell (of egg). For *cockle-shell*, emblem of pilgrim, see *scallop*. The *cockles of the heart* are explained (1669) as for the related *cochlea* (q.v.), winding cavity. *Hot cockles*, a game in which a blindfolded person has to guess who slaps him, occurs in Sidney's *Arcadia*. It is app. adapted from F. *jeu de la main chaude*, but *cockles* is unexplained.

cockle[3]. Pucker. F. *coquille*, blister on bread, spec. use of *coquille*, shell (see *cockle*[2]). Perh. through Du.

kokelen (kreukelen als dunne zyde stoffen): to cockle
(Sewel).

cockloft. "The room over the garret" (Johns.). Perh. orig. where fowls were kept, but used as contemptuous term for poor dwelling (cf. naut. use of *cockpit*). Ger. *hahnebalken*, roost, Du. *haanebalken*, "the cockloft" (Sewel), suggest that it was orig. the roosting-place for fowls. Cf. orig. sense of *roost*.

cockney. ME. *cokenay*. It is difficult to reconcile the different uses of the word. In *Piers Plowm.*, and occ. up to c. 1600, it appears to mean something to eat (see *collop*), explained by *NED*. as "cock's egg." In the sense of milksop, later townsman, and eventually (c. 1600) Londoner, it is from an Eastern form (OF. -*ei*) of F. *acoquiné*, made into a *coquin*, a word of unknown origin. The *Cockney School* (Leigh Hunt, etc.) was christened by Lockhart (1817). Associated with *cocker*[2] and *Cockaigne* (q.v.).

And when this jape is tald another day,
I sal been halde a daf, a cokenay
(Chauc. A. 4207).

I coker: je mignotte (Palsg.).

I bring up lyke a cocknay: je mignotte (*ib.*).

delicias facere: to dally, to wanton, to play the cockney (Coop.).

acoquiné: made tame, inward, familiar; also, growne as lazie, sloathfull, idle, as a beggar (Cotg.).

cockpit. Place for cock-fights. Hence *cockpit of Europe* (Belgium). Also (naut.), since c. 1700, midshipmen's quarters, used as hospital when in action.

cockroach. Earlier *cacarootch*, etc. Sp. *cucaracha*; cf. Port. *caroucha*, a chafer, or beetle, Creole F. *coquerache*.

A certain Indian bugge called by the Spaniards a *cacaroatch* (Capt. John Smith).

cocksure. Earlier in serious and dignified sense, and used objectively, which makes derivation from *cock*[1] doubtful. Can it be for *God sure*? See *cock-and-pie* and cf. the many strange oaths of the 15 cent. in which *cock* is substituted for *God*.

> Whoso dwelleth under that secret thing, and help of the Lord, shall be cock-sure for evermore (Foxe).

cocktail [*US.*]. ? Obs. Recorded c. 1800. Origin unknown. ? From inspiring effect; cf. to *have one's tail up*, feel confidence.

> Those recondite beverages, cock-tail, stone-fence, and sherry-cobbler (W. Irving).

cocky. See *cock*[1].

cocky-leeky [*Sc.*]. Cock boiled with leeks.

coco-, cocoa-, coker-nut. Sp. *coco*, baby-word for ugly face, bogy-man; from marks at one end of shell. Erron. form *cocoa* dates from mistake in Johns. *Coker* is of old standing and is used in Port of London to avoid confusion with *cocoa*.

> Cokar nuts and berries (Capt. John Smith).
>
> *coco*: the word us'd to fright children, as we say the Bulbeggar (Stevens).

cocoa. Incorr. (since 18 cent.) for *cacao* (q.v.). *Cocoa-nib* is the cotyledon of the seed (see *nib*[1]). Quot. below, allusive to the anti-national tone of newspapers financed by wealthy cocoa-merchants, may one day puzzle historians.

> Since I have thrown myself into the vigorous prosecution of the war, I have been drenched with cocoa slops (D. Lloyd George, May 9, 1918).

cocoon. F. *cocon*, ModProv. *coucoun*, from *coco*, shell. See *cockle*[2].

cocotte. F., orig. hen, of baby formation from *coq*, cock.

cocus. Jamaica ebony, used for flutes and police truncheons. App. from Ger. *kokos*, cocoa(-nut).

cod[1]. Bag, in various archaic senses, e.g. *pease-cod*. AS. *codd*; cf. ON. *kodde*, pillow, Du. *kodde*, bag.

> The coddis whiche the hoggis eeten
>   (Wyc. *Luke*, xv. 6).

cod[2]. Fish. Perh. from *cod*[1]; cf. Du. *bolk*, cod, prob. cogn. with *bulge* (see *budget*). Earliest record in *NED.* is AF. (1357), but *codfish* was in use as a surname earlier (*Hund. R.* 1273). It is even possible that E. fishermen understood obs. Du. *bolick* as *balloc*, testicle, cod. The med. use of *cod-liver oil* is mentioned in 1783 in *Lond. Med. Journal*, but it was not adopted in E. till 1846. The manufacture of the oil is alluded to as early

as c. 1600 (*Stiffkey Papers*). *Cod*, fool, is short for earlier *cods-head*, in same sense, sometimes elaborated into *cod's head and shoulders*. Hence to *cod*, to deceive; cf. to *gull* (q.v.).

coda [*mus.*]. It., lit. tail, L. *cauda*.

coddle. To boil gently, etc. Prob. for *caudle* (q.v.). Hence, perh. by association with *cuddle*, mod. sense of pampering, etc.

>   Will the cold brook,
> Candied with ice, caudle thy morning taste
> To cure thy o'er-night's surfeit? (*Timon*, iv. 3).

code. F., L. *codex*, earlier *caudex*, tree-trunk, ? from *cudere*, to strike (cf. *truncus*, *truncare*); hence wooden tablet, book, manuscript. Cf. *book*, *Bible*, *library*.

codex. See *code*.

codger. "A miser, one who rakes together all he can" (Todd). Var. of *cadger* (q.v.). For sense-development cf. a *rum beggar*, etc. But cf. dial. *codger*, cobbler, for obs. *cozier*, from OF. *couseur*, sewer, from *coudre*, *cous-*, L. *consuere*, to sew together.

codicil. L. *codicillus* (usu. in pl.), dim. of *codex*.

codling, codlin. Apple. The earlier forms *quodling*, *quadling* (16–17 cents.), *querdling*, *qwerdelyng* (15 cent.) correspond exactly with those of the surname *Codlin*. Hence the origin is *cœur-de-lion*, a fancy name for an esteemed apple. Cf. F. *reine-claude*, greengage, from the wife of Francis I, and the pear called *bon-chrétien*, from St Francis of Paula. *Quodling*, *Quadling* are existing EAngl. surnames. *John Querdling*, *Qwerdelyng* lived in Norwich in 15 cent, and *Querdelyon* is fairly common in 14 and 13 cents., *quer* being the usual AF. form of *cœur*.

co-education. Orig. US. (c. 1874).

coefficient. L. *coefficiens*, pres. part. of *co-efficere* (see *effect*), was first used in math. sense by Vieta (†1603).

coehorn [*hist.*]. Mortar. From *Coehorn*, Du. mil. engineer (†1704). The name means "cow-horn."

coeliac [*anat.*]. Abdominal. From G. κοιλία, belly.

coenobite. Contrasted with *anchorite*. From G. κοινόβιον, from κοινός, common, βίος, life.

coerce. L. *coercēre*, from *co-* and *arcēre*, to restrain. Pol. sense of *coercion* is esp. associated with Ireland (*Coercion Acts* of 1833 and later).

coeval. From L. *coaevus*, from *co-* and *aevum*, age.

coffee. Adopted by most Europ. langs. (c. 1600) from Turk. *kahveh*, Arab. *qahwah*, app. first as name of drink. Early forms are very numerous. *Coffee* was soon followed by the *coffee-house* (cf. F. *café*).

Coho, a blacke biterish drinke, made of a berry like a bay berry, brought from Mecca (Purch. 1607).

He [a Greek student at Oxford, 1637] was the first I ever saw drink coffee, which custom came not into England till thirty years after (Evelyn).

cauphe-house: a tavern or inn where they sell cauphe (Blount).

coffer. F. *coffre*, L. *cophinus* (see *coffin*). For ending cf. *order*. Among ME. meanings are strong-box, coffin, ark of bulrushes.

coffin. OF. *cofin*, L. *cophinus*, G. κόφινος, basket. Mod. sense from c. 1500. In ME. and later, basket (Wyc. *Matt.* xiv. 20), piecrust, etc.

Why, thou say'st true; it is a paltry cap,
A custard-coffin, a bauble, a silken pie
(*Shrew*, iv. 3).

cog¹ [*hist.*]. Vessel. It is uncertain whether the word is Teut. (OHG. *coccho*, Du. *cogge*, Icel. *kuggi*, etc.) or Rom. (OF. *cogue*, *coque*, ident. with *coque*, shell, hull, for which see *cockle²*). In E. it has become mixed up with *cockboat* (q.v.) and is used by Chauc. of a skiff.

cogbote: scapha (*Prompt. Parv.*).

cog². On a wheel. ME. *cogge*, of Scand. origin; cf. Sw. *kugge*, Norw. *kug*.

cog³. To cheat with dice (16 cent.). Orig. to control their fall, or substitute false dice. Hence *cogged dice*, now wrongly understood as loaded dice. ? From *cog²*, with idea of mech. device.

cogent. From pres. part. of L. *cogere*, to constrain, from *co-* and *agere*, to drive.

cogitate. From L. *cogitare*, from *co-* and *agitare*, frequent. of *agere*.

cognac. Orig. distilled from wine of *Cognac* (Charente).

cognate. L. *cognatus*, from *co-* and *gnatus*, old form of *natus*, born. Words that are *cognate* have the cousinly, not the parental or filial, relation.

cognition. L. *cognitio-n-*, from *cognoscere*, *cognit-*, to know, from *co-* and *gnoscere*.

cognizance. Half-latinized from ME. *conisaunce*, OF. *conisance*, var. of *conoisance* (*connaissance*), from *conoistre* (*connaître*), L. *cognoscere* (v.s.). Now chiefly leg., in to *take cognizance of*, etc., and in her., badge, mark, by which bearer is known.

cognoistre d'une cause: to take notice of, deale in,

or intermeddle with, a suit, or cause, depending in law (Cotg.).

cognomen. L., *co-* and *gnomen*, old form of *nomen*. See *agnomen*.

cognoscente. Connoisseur (art). Latinized from It. *conoscente*, from pres. part. of L. *cognoscere*.

cognovit [*leg.*]. L. *cognovit actionem*, he has acknowledged the action. Orig. of withdrawing defence.

You gave them a cognovit for the amount of your costs (*Pickwick*, ch. xlvi.).

cohabit. Late L. *cohabitare*, from *habitare*, to dwell, frequent. of *habēre*.

cohere. L. *cohaerēre*, from *haerēre*, *haes-*, to stick. Hence *incoherent*, not hanging together. Cf. *cohesion*.

cohorn. See *coehorn*.

cohort. L. *cohors*, *cohort-*, from *hortus*, garden, enclosure; cogn. with G. χόρτος, E. *yard²*, *garth*, *garden*. See *court*.

coif. F. *coiffe*, Late L. *cofea*, whence It. *cuffia*, Sp. *cofia*, Port. *coifa*, etc. Oldest F. sense is inner part of helmet. Late L. *cofea* is prob. OHG. *chupphā* (MHG. *kupfe*), from L. *cuppa*, cup, vessel (cf. *bascinet*). Orig. sense of *coiffeur* appears in *coiffure*, headdress.

Trenchet la coife entresques a la carn
(*Roland*, 3436).

[He cleaves the coif (of the helmet) right to the flesh.]

coign. Archaic spelling of *coin*, *quoin*, preserved in *coign of vantage* (*Macb.* i. 6), mod. currency of which dates from Scott.

coil¹. Verb. OF. *coildre*, *coillir* (*cueillir*), L. *colligere*, to collect, gather, from *co-* and *legere*, to gather (cf. *cull*). ME. sense survives in northern dial. to *coil hay*, put it in cocks.

coil². Disturbance, fuss, etc. Archaic, exc. in *this mortal coil* (*Haml.* iii. 1). OF. *acueil* (*accueil*), encounter, collision. The earliest E. examples (from 1567) are all *such* (*what*) *a coil*, prob. for *accoil* (cf. *rouse¹*), although this hypothesis is not necessary in accounting for the normal loss of init. *a-* (see *cater*). The OF. meanings of *accueillir* are very numerous and varied. Spenser uses *accoil*, to crowd, throng. For origin of F. *accueillir* see *coil¹*.

About the caudron many cookes accoyled
With hookes and ladles, as need did requyre
(*Faerie Queene*, II. ix 30)

coin. F., wedge (see *quoin*), corner, die for stamping, L. *cuneus*; cf. It. *conio*, Sp. *cuño*. Mod. sense appears in ME. (Chauc.) almost as soon as that of die (*Piers Plowm.*).

coincide. F. *coïncider*, MedL. *co-incidere*, to fall together.

coir. Coco-nut fibre for ropes. Earlier (16 cent.) *cayro*, Port. *cairo*, Malayalam *kāyar*, rope.

coit. See *quoit*.

coition. L. *coitio-n-*, from *coire*, from *co-* and *ire, it-*, to go.

coke. First found (17 cent.) as northern dial. word, and often in pl. (*coaks*). Perh. ident. with northern dial. *colk*, core.

Coke-upon-Littleton. Subtleties of the law. Allusion to the *Institutes of the Law of England* (1628 sqq.), based by *Sir Edward Coke* on the *Tenures* of *Sir Thomas Littleton* (15 cent.).

coker-nut. See *coco-nut*.

col. Mountain pass. F., neck, L. *collum*. Cf. SAfr. *nek*.

cola, kola. Nut. Native WAfr. name (Sierra Leone).

colander. From L. *colare*, to strain; cf. MedL. *colator*, Sp. *colador*, ModProv. *couladou*. Immediate source of E. word unknown. Cf. obs. *cullis*, clear broth.

colendre to strayne with: couleresse (Palsg.).

colchicum. Meadow saffron. L., G. κολχικόν, from *Colchis* (E. of Black Sea), with implied allusion to Medea of Colchis, skilled in poisons.

colcothar. Red peroxide of iron. F., Sp. *colcotar*, Arab. *qalqaṭār*, prob. from G. χάλκανθos, from χαλκός, copper, ἄνθοs, flower.

cold. AS. *ceald*. Com. Teut.; cf. Du. *koud*, Ger. *kalt*, ON. *kaldr*, Goth. *kalds*; cogn. with L. *gelid-us*; cf. *chill, cool*. *Cold comfort* is recorded c. 1325. A *cold chisel* is used on cold iron and is all metal, while the smith's chisel has a wooden grip to prevent conduction from the hot iron; cf. *cold-drawn*. A *cold* (in the head, etc.) replaced (16 cent.) earlier *rheum* (q.v.). *Cold cream* is recorded c. 1700. The *NED.* sees in to *throw cold water on* an allusion to the shock thus given to the naked body; but cf. *wet blanket*.

coldshort [*techn.*]. Brittle (of iron in the cold state). Corrupt. of Norw. Dan. *kuldskjær* or Sw. *kallskör*, in which second element means timid.

cole. Cabbage. Now usu. in compds. (*cole-*

wort, sea-kale). AS. *cawel, cāl*, L. *caulis*, whence also Du. *kool*, Ger. *kohl*, ON. *kāl*, OF. *chol* (*chou*); also in Celt. langs. A characteristic example of the Roman culture in Europe. See also *kale, colza*.

colemouse. See *coalmouse*.

coleoptera. Beetles. From G. κολεός, sheath, πτερόν, wing. Cf. *lepidoptera*.

colibri. Humming-bird. F., Sp., from Carib.

colic. Orig. adj. F. *colique*, L., G. κολικός, belonging to the κόλον, lower intestine.

colyk, sekenesse: colica passio (*Prompt. Parv.*).

coliseum. After Rom. & MedL. forms of L. *colosseum*, amphitheatre of Vespasian at Rome, neut. of adj. *colosseus*, gigantic. See *colossus*.

collaborate. From L. *collaborare*, from *co-* and *laborare*, to work.

collapse. From L. *collabi*, from *co-* and *labi, laps-*, to slip, fall.

collar. ME. & AF. *coler*, F. *collier*, necklace, L. *collare*, from *collum*, neck (whence F. *col*, collar), with mod. spelling assimilated to L. Earliest of armour, jewelled collar, etc., as still in *collar of the Garter*, etc. To *slip the collar, against the collar, collar-work* refer to collar of horse. Earliest sense of verb is in wrestling (16 cent.). *Collared head (brawn)* is so called (17 cent.) from being rolled up like a collar.

collard. Cabbage that does not heart. Said to be corrupt. of *colewort*.

collate. OF. *collater*, from L. *collatus*, p.p. of *conferre*, to bring together, confer. Used for *confer* in spec. sense (eccl.).

collateral. MedL. *collateralis*, from L. *lateralis*, from *latus, later-*, side. In *Piers Plowm.* and Chauc.

collation. Light meal, esp. *cold collation*, "a treat less than a feast" (Johns.). Earlier, light evening meal in monastery, orig. after the reading aloud of *collations*, or Lives of the Fathers, esp. the *Collationes Patrum in Scetica Eremo Commorantium*, by John Cassian (c. 400 A.D.). Cf. hist. of *chapter* (eccl.).

colleague. F. *collègue*, L. *collega*, partner in office, from *legere*, to choose (see *coilege*). Distinct from archaic to *colleague*, co-operate, conspire, OF. *colliguer*, from L. *ligare*, to bind, though sometimes wrongly associated, as in quot. 1. From the latter word comes mod. sense of *collogue* (now Midl. & Ir. dials.), orig. to cajole, prob. from F. *colloque*, dialogue, debate. It is given by Cotg. s.v. *flater*, and is called a "low word" by Johns.

These howses thei usuallie call colleges, beecause they are ther colliged in felawship and ministerie (*Transl. of Polydore Vergil*, c. 1534).

How long have you been so thick with Dunsey that you must "collogue" with him to embezzle my money? (*Silas Marner*).

collect. Prayer. This is oldest sense (*Ancren Riwle*), but Wyc. also uses it for offertory (1 *Cor.* xvi. 1) and congregation (*Neh.* viii. 18). Verb to *collect* is much more recent (16 cent.). Church sense comes from MedL. *collectio* or *collecta*, used in Gallican liturgies of a summary of ideas suggested by the chapters for the day. From L. *colligere*, *collect-*, to gather together (see *coil¹*). To *collect oneself* is to "pull oneself together." *Collectivism, -ist* are from F. (c. 1880).

colleen. Ir. *cailín*, girl, dim. of *caile*, wench. Said to be ult. cogn. with L. *pellex*, G. παλλακή, concubine. Cf. *boreen*, *squireen*, etc.

college. F. *collège*, L. *collegium* (see *colleague*). Earliest E. sense, community, or in ref. to Oxf. and Camb. A *collegiate* church has a chapter (*college*) of canons. *College pudding* ? for earlier *New College* (Oxf.) *pudding* (Landor).

Crist and his colage [the apostles] (Wyc.).

collet. Part of ring in which stone is set. F., dim. of *col*, neck, which has given E. *collet* in various techn. senses. Prob. confused also with *collet*, base of cut diamond, also *culet*, dim. of F. *cul*, bottom, L. *culus*. In F. this is *culasse*.

collide. L. *collidere*, from *co-* and *laedere*, to hurt. Hence *collision*.

collie, colly. Usu. explained as from dial. adj. *colly*, coaly, coal-black, which is also a dial. name for the blackbird. Much more prob. from common Sc. name *Colin*. *Colle*, as proper name for a dog, occurs in Chauc. (v.i.). With *collie dog* cf. *robin redbreast*.

Ran Colle, oure dogge, and Talbot, and Gerland, And Malkyn, with a dystaf in hir hand (B. 4573).

collier. Orig. charcoal-burner, which accounts for its frequency as a surname in parts of England where no coal exists. From *coal* (q.v.).

colligate. From L. *colligare*, to bind together.

collimate. To adjust line of sight, etc. From ghost-word *collimare*, wrong reading in some editions of Cicero for *collineare*, to bring into line. Adopted by earlier as-

tronomers who wrote in L., e.g. Kepler. Cf. *syllabus*.

collision. See *collide*.

collodion. From G. κολλώδης, glue-like, from κόλλα, glue.

collogue [*dial.*]. See *colleague*.

collop. Orig. bacon and eggs. Earliest form *coloppe, colhoppe* (*Piers Plowm.*). But found a century earlier as (still existing) surname, e.g. *Colop* (*Close R.* temp. Henry III), *Colhoppe* (*Feet of Fines*). First element is *coal*, second obscure. Cf. OSw. *kol-huppadher*, roasted on coals, Sw. *glöd-hoppad*, from *glöd*, glowing coal, "glede."

I have no salt bacon,
Ne no cokeneyes, bi Crist, colopus [*var.* colopis, colhoppes] to maken (*Piers Plowm.* A. vii. 272).

colloppe, meate: œuf au lard (Palsg.).

colloquy. L. *colloquium*, from *colloqui*, to speak together. Cf. *colloquial*.

collotype. From G. κόλλα, glue.

collusion. F., L. *collusio-n-*, from *colludere*, *collus-*, to play together, i.e. into one another's hands.

collyrium. Eye-wash, etc. From G. κολλύριον, poultice, from κολλύρα, roll of coarse bread.

collywobbles. Jocular formation ? on *colic* and *wobble*.

colocynth. Drug. Earlier *coloquint*. G. κολοκυνθίς, -θιδ-.

As bitter as coloquintida (*Oth.* i. 3)

Cologne. F. form of Ger. *Köln*, L. *colonia* (*Agrippina*), whence *eau de Cologne*. The *Three Kings of Cologne* were the three Wise Men from the East, Gaspar, Melchior, Balthazar, fabled to be buried there.

colon. G. κῶλον, limb, member of sentence.

colonel. Up to c. 1650 usu. *coronel*, Sp., by dissim. from It. *colonnello*, from *colonna*, column; for dissim. cf. Prov. *coronel*, doorpost. This form persisted in speech and accounts for mod. pronunc. The *colonel*, for *colonel Bogey* (golf), is mod.

colonell: a colonell, or coronell; the commander of a regiment (Cotg.).

colonnade. F., from *colonne*, L. *columna*, after It. *colonnato*.

colony. F. *colonie*, L. *colonia*, from *colonus*, tiller, from *colere*, to till. Current sense from c. 1600.

Philippi, which is the chief city of that part of Macedonia, and a colony (*Acts*, xvi. 12).

Get a map of the world and show me where the d—d places are (Early Victorian statesman).

colophon. Inscription or device at end of book. G. κολοφών, summit, finishing stroke.

colophony. Resin. From *Colophon*, town in Lydia, prob. ident. in etym. with preceding.

coloquintida. It. for *colocynth* (q.v.).

color-. See *colour*.

Colorado beetle. Fatal to potatoes (scare of 1877). From state of *Colorado* (US.), named from *Rio Colorado*, coloured river (Sp.). Cf. *colorado*, dark, *claro* light, on cigar-boxes.

colosseum. See *coliseum*.

colossus. L., G. κολοσσός, orig. applied by Herodotus to gigantic Egypt. statues, but usu. connected with bronze statue of Apollo at entrance to harbour of Rhodes. Punningly applied to Cecil Rhodes (†1902).

colour. F. *couleur*, L. *color-em*, cogn. with *celare*, to hide; replacing as gen. term AS. *hiw* (see *hue*). *Man of colour*, now usu. negro, was orig mixed breed intermediate between black and white. As mil. and nav. term *colour* dates back to age of chivalry (*colours* of a knight). Hence many fig. uses, some naut. (*false colours, nail colours to the mast*), others rather mil. (*with flying colours, stick to one's colours*). In sense of semblance (*under colour of*) it is recorded c. 1300, this use perh. springing from the badge sense (see quot. 1). Cf. *colourable*, specious (Wyc.), and prob. *colour of one's money*, as inspiring confidence. Later are the art metaphors (*true colours, lively colours*). *Colour-blindness* (19 cent.) was earlier *Daltonism* (q.v.). *Local colour(s)* is in Bailey (1721). The rank of *colour-sergeant* was created (1813) by George IV, when Regent, in recognition of the part played by non-commissioned officers in Peninsular War.

Brybers that wold a robbed a ship undyr colar of my Lord of Warwyk (*Paston Lett.*).

They should depart with flying colours, with bag and baggage (Sydenham Poyntz, 1624–36).

colporteur. In E. book (esp. Bible) pedlar. F., pedlar (in gen. sense), from *colporter*, to carry (*porter*) on the neck (*col*); but this is a late substitution, due to folk-etym., for OF. *comporter*, to carry with one.

colt. AS. *colt*, orig. young ass, or camel (*Gen.* xxxii. 15). Origin unknown. Also in ME. for novice, etc., as now in cricket. In sense of "rope's-end" perh. for *colt's-tail*; cf. *cat (o' nine tails)*.

Colt's revolver. See *revolver*.

colubrine. Of the snake, L. *colubra*. Cf. *cobra, culverin*.

columbarium. L., dove-cot, from *columba*, dove; hence, catacomb with cinerary urns in "pigeon-holes."

Columbia. Poet. for US. From *Columbus*; cf. origin of *America*. Hence *columbiad*, heavy gun in Amer. Civil War.

columbine¹. Flower. F., L. *columbina*, from *columba*, dove, shape suggesting cluster of pigeons.

columbine². In pantomime. It. proper name *Colombina* (dove-like), mistress of Harlequin in It. comedy.

column. Restored spelling of *colompne*, OF., L. *colum(p)na*, cogn. with *culmen*, summit. Earliest E. sense in ref. to column of manuscript.

colure [*astron.*]. L. *colurus*, G. κόλουρος, from κόλος, docked, οὐρά, tail, because lower part of circle is never in view.

colza. F., earlier *colzat*, Du. *koolzaad*, coleseed.

com-. L., archaic form of *cum*, with, but sense is sometimes merely intens. Also *co-, col-, con-, cor-*.

coma¹ [*med.*]. G. κῶμα, cogn. with κοιμᾶν, to put to sleep (cf. *cemetery*).

coma² [*bot. & astron.*]. L., G. κόμη, hair of the head. See *comet*.

comb. AS. *camb*. Com. Teut.; cf. Du. *kam*, Ger. *kamm*, ON. *kambr*; cogn. with Sanskrit *qhambas*, tooth. In many fig. senses, e.g. *honeycomb* (AS. *hunigcamb*), *cock's comb* (see *coxcomb*), whence to *cut one's comb* (16 cent.), make one less "cocky." As verb replaces earlier *kemb* (AS. *cemban*), which survives in *unkempt* (q.v.) and surname *Kempster*. To *comb out* (neol.) is a somewhat unsavoury metaphor from the use of a small-toothed comb for certain toilet purposes.

comb(e). See *coomb(e)*.

combat. Earlier also *combate* (cf. *debate*), F. *combattre*, VL. **com-battere*, from *battuere*. In all Rom. langs.

combine. Late L. *combinare*, to put two-and-two, L. *bini*, together. *Combination* (garment) is recorded for 1884. *Combination-room* (Camb.) in sense of *common-room* (Oxf.) is 17 cent.

combustion. F., Late L. *combustio-n-*, from *comburere*, from *comb-* (for *cum*) and *urere, ust-*, to burn.

come. AS. *cuman*. Com. Teut.; cf. Du.

komen, Ger. *kommen*, ON. *koma*, Goth. *qiman*; cogn. with Sanskrit *gam*.

comeatable. Recorded by *NED* for 1687, but must be older (v.i.).

uncomeatable: quod parare quis vel consequi non possit (Litt.).

comedy. F. *comédie*, L., G. κωμῳδία, ? from κῶμος, revel (whence Milton's *Comus*), ? or κώμη, village, and ἀείδειν, to sing (cf. *ode*). First E. sense (Chauc.), narrative poem, from It., as in Dante's *Commedia*. Cf. *tragedy*.

comely. AS. *cymlic*, beautiful, splendid; related to *come*; cf. L. *conveniens*, F. *avenant*, MHG. *komlich*, archaic Du. *komelick*, all in similar sense; cf. also *becoming*.

comely as a garment or atyer is to a person: advenant (Palsg.).

advenant: handsome, proper, comely, decent, neat, gracefull, well-fashioned, well-behaved (Cotg.).

komelick: conveniens, congruens, commodus, aptus (Kil.).

comestible. F., Late L. *comestibilis*, from L. *comedere*, *comes-*, from *com-* and *edere*, to eat.

comet. AS. *cometa* and F. *comète*, L., G. κομήτης, from κόμη, head of hair, tail of comet.

I stood beside the grave of him who blazed
  The comet of a season (Byron, *Churchill's Grave*).

comether [*Anglo-Ir.*]. To *put the comether on*, cajole. *Come hither*, in coaxing horse, etc.

He cud put the comether on any woman that trod the green earth av God (Kipling, *Love o' Women*).

comfit. ME. *confit*, F., p.p. of *confire*, to pickle, etc., L. *conficere*, to put together. Learned form is *confect*. Cf. *discomfit*, to undo.

comfort. Archaic F. *conforter*, Late L. *confortare*, to strengthen, from *fortis*, strong. ModF. *confort* is borrowed back from E. in sense of well-being, etc. As title of Holy Ghost, *comforter* (Wyc.) is for L. *consolator*, rendering G. παράκλητος (*John*, xiv. 16). See *paraclete*. *Comforter*, scarf, is 19 cent.; in US. it means thick quilt.

And the child wexide, and was coumfortid [*Vulg.* confortabatur] (Wyc. *Luke*, i. 80).

comfrey. OF. *confirie* (whence MedL. *cumfiria*), from *firie*, liver (ModF. *foie*), a word derived in a complicated manner from L. (*jecur*) *ficatum*, goose-liver stuffed with figs, a bit of Roman slang (cf. ModG. συκώτι, liver, from σῦκον, fig). The plant was so

called because of its congealing properties esp. in case of wounds (hence bot. name *symphytum officinale*). Cf. its Late L. names *consolida* (whence F. *consoude*, It. *consolida*, Sp. *consuelda*), *conferva*, also MedL. *confirma*, *conserva*. The usual F. for congeal is *figer*, from *ficatum* (v.s.), with which cf. MHG. *liberen*, to congeal, lit. to assume a "liver-like" aspect. Cf. also Norw. *vallsaks*, lit. weld-sedge, Ger. *beinwell*, lit. bone-weld, and other foreign names of the plant.

comic. Orig. belonging to *comedy* (q.v.). L., G. κωμικός.

comitadji. Member of a "committee," i.e., in the Balkans, a gang of patriotic cutthroats. The Turk. suffix makes it likely that the word originated in Greece. It translates Serb. *chetnik*, from *cheta*, band, number.

His name is Feodor, and he is a Bulgar comitadjus, or whatever is the singular of comitadji
  (*Punch*, Jan. 24, 1917).

comitia. L., general assembly, pl. of *comitium*, from *com-* and *ire*, *it-*, to go.

comity. L. *comitas*, from *comis*, courteous. Esp. in *comity* (courteous understanding) *of nations*, now often misused as though from *comes*, *comit-*, companion.

comma. L., G. κόμμα, piece cut off, short clause, from κόπτειν, to cut.

command. F. *commander*, VL. **commandare*, from *mandare*, partly replacing L. *commendare*, which is of same origin (*manus* and *dare*). *Commandeer*, SAfrDu. *kommanderen*, is F. *commander* (cf. *cashier²*); and *commando*, party called out for mil. service, is adopted from Port. (cf. *kraal*, *sjambok*). *Commander of the Faithful* translates title assumed by Caliph Omar I (c. 640). *Ten commandments*, for fingernails of angry woman, is used by mod. writers after 2 *Hen. VI*, i. 3. Also called *ten talents* (*talons*).

commemorate. From L. *commemorare*. See *memory*.

commence. F. *commencer*, VL. **com-initiare*, from *initium*, beginning; cf. It. *cominciare*, Sp. *comenzar*. In univ. lang. translates L. *incipere*, used in same sense in MedL.

commend. L. *commendare*. See *command*. Sense of praising springs from that of presenting as worthy of favourable regard.

commendam. Acc. of MedL. *commenda*, trust, in phrase *in commendam*, used of provisional occupation of office.

commensal. F., MedL. *commensalis*, eating at same table, *mensa*.

commensurate. Late L. *commensuratus*, from *mensurare*, to measure.

comment. OF. *coment* (now only in verb *commenter*), L. *commentus*, p.p. of *comminisci*, *comment-*, to contrive, etc., from same root as *mens*, mind, *memini*, I remember. Verb also represents MedL. *commentare*.

commerce. F., L. *commercium*, from *merx*, *merc-*, merchandise. For fig. sense cf. *dealings*.

commination. F., L. *comminatio-n-*, from *comminari*, to threaten strongly.

comminute. From L. *comminuere*, to reduce to minute portions.

commiserate. From L. *commiserari*, from *miserari*, to bewail, from *miser*, wretched.

commissariat. F., office or duty of a *commissaire*, i.e. commissary, commissioner, one to whom certain duties are "committed." ModE. sense, not found in F. (*approvisionnement*), is due to spec. use of E. *commissary* (from 15 cent.).

commission. F., L. *commissio-n-*, from *committere*, *-miss-*, to entrust. Oldest sense is the written instrument or warrant.

commissionaire. F., in this sense from *commission*, errand. The *Corps of Commissionaires* was established 1859.

commissure [*anat.*]. Line of juncture. F., L. *commissura*, from *committere* (v.i.).

commit. L. *committere*, to entrust, etc., from *mittere*, to send. Sense of perpetrating, ancient in L., seems to arise from the idea of "putting together," contriving. That of compromising, as in *non-committal*, was adopted (c. 1770) from F. *commettre* by author of *Letters of Junius*.

committee. Orig. one person (cf. *payee*, *patentee*), as still in *Court of Committees* of Guy's Hospital. AF. p.p. *committé*, substituted for F. *commis*. Collect. sense from c. 1600. F. *comité* is from E.

commode. Head-dress (obs.), furniture. F., adj., as noun. Cf. *commodious*, OF. *commodieux*, from L. *commodus*, from *modus*, measure. *Commodity* implies goods from which mankind receives advantage.

commodore. Appears as *commandore*, *commadore*, temp. William III, therefore perh. Du. *commandeur*, from F., but the unusual ending suggests Sp. or Port. influence. Falconer's theory that it is corrupted from Sp. *comendador* (also Port.), a commendary,

receives some support from the fact that a *commodore* is an admiral *in commendam* (q.v.).

> A commodore is only an occasional dignity...when the commission ceases, he descends again to the rank of a private captain (*NED.* 1757).

common. F. *commun*, L. *communis*, second element of which is cogn. with E. *mean²*; cf. Ger. *gemein*, common, mean. With *common* (land), orig. opposite of *close*, cf. F. *pré communal*. With *commonal(i)ty*, OF. *comunalté* (*communauté*), cf. MedL. *communalitas*. A *commoner* (Oxf.), not being on the foundation, pays for his *commons*, provisions supplied for the community (whence *short commons*); cf. Camb. *pensioner* (q.v.). *Commonplace* translates L. *locus communis* for G. κοινὸς τόπος, general theme. *Common Prayer* is contrasted with private prayer. *House of Commons* first occurs in a letter of James I (1621). *Common sense* was orig. (14 cent.) the inward power of unifying mentally the impressions conveyed by the five physical senses; cf. L. *communis sensus*, social instinct. *Commonweal* (14 cent.), *commonwealth* (c. 1500), not orig. compds., were used indiscriminately; cf. F. *bien public*, L. *res publica*. For gen. degeneration of the word cf. that of *mean²*. Its ground-sense is about equivalent to *municipal* (q.v.).

commotion. F., L. *commotio-n-*, from *commovēre*, from *movēre*, *mot-*, to move.

commune¹. Noun. Smallest F. administrative division. MedL. *communa*, from *communis*, common. Also title twice assumed by Parisian political desperadoes (Reign of Terror and 1871). *Communism* was prob. coined (1840) by Goodwyn Barmby, founder of London Communist Propaganda Society.

commune². Verb. OF. *comuner*, from adj. *commun* (v.s.).

communicate. From L. *communicare*, to make common. Cf. F. p.p. *communiqué*, now current E.

communion. F., or Church L. *communio-n-*, from *communis*.

> Calix benedictionis, cui benedicimus, nonne communicatio [G. κοινωνία, Wyc. comenynge, Tynd. Cranm. partakynge, *AV.* communion] sanguinis Christi est? (*Vulg.* 1 *Cor.* x. 16).

commute. "To buy off or ransom one obligation by another" (Johns.). L. *commutare*, from *mutare*, to change.

compact¹. Concentrated. From p.p. of L.

compingere, to join together, from *pangere*, *pact-*.

compact². Agreement. From p.p. of L. *compacisci*, to agree together.

compagination. Late L. *compaginatio-n-*, from *compaginare*, to fit together, from *compago*, *compagin-*, joint, from root *pag-* of *pangere*, to fasten.

companion¹, company. F. *compagnon*, VL. **companio-n-*, from *panis*, bread, whence also It. *compagnone*; cf. OHG. *gileibo*, "messmate," from *leib* (*laib*), loaf. *Company* is F. *compagnie*, formed (like It. *compagnia*, Sp. *compañía*, etc.) on same stem. *Companion* was formerly used, as F. *compagnon* still is, contemptuously for fellow.

Scurvy companion! saucy tarpaulin! impertinent fellow (*Roderick Random*).

companion² [*naut.*]. Du. *kampanje*, quarter-deck, earlier *kompanje* (Kil., Sewel), OF. *compagne*, steward's room in galley, It. *compagna*, for *camera della compagna*, store-room, caboose, OCatalan *companya*, provision store, from L. *panis*, bread (see *companion¹*). Meaning has changed and varied between the time of the medieval galley and E. use (first in Falc.). There may also have been confusion with MedL. *capanna* (see *cabin*), in fact some regard this as the true origin.

companion: capot d'échelle dans les bâtimens marchands, dans les yachts, &c. (Lesc.).

compare. F. *comparer*, from L. *comparare*, from *par*, equal. To *compare notes* is recorded from c. 1700. See also *compeer*.

compartment. F. *compartiment*, It. *compartimento*, from Late L. *compartiri*, to divide, from *pars*, *part-*, part. Cf. *apartment*.

compass. F. *compas*, from *compasser*, to go round, VL. **compassare*, from *passus*, step. Cf. MedL. *compassus*, It. *compasso*, Sp. *compas*, pair of compasses, Ger. *kompass*, Du. *kompas*, mariner's compass. In most Europ. langs., math. in Rom. and naut. in Teut., E. having both senses. Fig. senses (*within compass*, to *fetch a compass*) are usu. from the math., and earlier, sense. So also in verb to *compass one's ends* (*an enemy's destruction*, etc.) the idea of design is predominant.

compassion. F., Late L. *compassio-n-*, from *pati*, *pass-*, to suffer. Cf. *fellow-feeling*, *sympathy*, Ger. *mitgefühl*.

compatible. F., MedL. *compatibilis* (from *pati*, to suffer), sharing in suffering, hence mutually tolerant, etc.

compatriot. F. *compatriote*, Late L. *compatriota*. See *patriot*.

compeer. OF. *comper*, *-pair*, equal, L. *compar*, prob. confused, in sense of companion, with F. *compère*, Church L. *compater*, fellow godfather, hence crony, "gossip." Hence *without compare*, associated mentally with cogn. *compare* (q.v.); cf. *peerless* and F. *sans pair*. See *peer¹*.

compel. OF. *compéller*, L. *compellere*, *-puls-*, to drive together. Hence *compulsion*.

compendium. L., what is weighed together. Cf. *compensate*.

compensate. From L. *compensare*, to weigh together, from *pensare*, frequent. of *pendere*, *pens-*, to weigh.

compete. L. *competere*, to seek in common. Rare before 19 cent. *Competition wallah* (Anglo-Ind.), member of Indian Civil Service under competitive system (from 1856), is known in E. chiefly by Trevelyan's *Letters of a Competition-wallah* (1864). See *wallah*. *Competent*, *competence*, *competency* come, through F., from L. *competere* in intrans. sense of coinciding, being convenient.

From the use of the Scotticisms "succumb," "compete,"...he ought to be a Scotchman
(De Quincey, 1824).

compile. F. *compiler*, L. *compilare*, to plunder, orig. in literary sense (see *pillage*). Later sense influenced by *pile²*, as though to heap up. Some regard the latter as the orig. sense.

complacent. See *complaisant*.

complain. Archaic F. *complaindre*, to lament, Late L. *complangere*, from *plangere*, to beat the breast. Hence *complaint*, (chronic) ailment (c. 1700), because regarded as a cause of complaint. *Complainant* is AF. pres. part.

complaisant. F., pres. part. of *complaire*, from L. *complacēre* (see *please*, *pleasure*). *Complacent*, from L., has acquired passive sense.

complement. L. *complementum*, filling up (v.i.).

complete. L. *completus*, p.p. of *complēre*, to fill up, from *plēre*, to fill.

complex. L. *complexus*, from *complectere*, lit. to plait together.

complexion. F., L. *complexio-n-*, from *complexus*, from *complecti*, to embrace, comprise, analysed as "twining, weaving together" (cf. L. *complex*, etc.). In Late L., and in OF. & ME. physiology, the combination of supposed "humours" in man; hence, physical and moral character; later, the colour of face (and hair), supposed to be indicative of temperament. Traces of orig. sense survive, e.g. to *put a fresh complexion on the matter*.

Of his complexioun he was sangwyn
(Chauc. A. 333).

Something of a jealous complexion (*Much Ado*, ii. 1).

My father was of a sanguine complexion, mixed with a dash of choler (Evelyn).

compliant. See *comply*.

complicate. From L. *complicare*, to fold together. Cf. Ger. *verwickeln*.

complicity. From archaic *complice*, now usu. *accomplice* (q.v.).

compliment. F., It. *complimento*, Sp. *cumplimiento*, the "fulfilling" of an act of courtesy. Ident. with *complement* (q.v.), which occurs earlier in same sense, the two forms being for some time used indifferently.

compline. Earlier *complin*. Last service of canonical hours. ME. *cumplie*, OF. *complie* (now *complies* by analogy with *heures*, *vêpres*), p.p. fem. of OF. *complir*, coined on Church L. *completa* (sc. *hora*). Ending *-in*, from 13 cent., perh. by analogy with *matin*.

complot [*archaic*]. F., orig. dense crowd (12 cent.), also OF. *complote*, crowd, mêlée. Perh. from *pelote*, ball, bunch, VL. *pilotta, dim. of *pila*. See *plot*.

Des autres meseaus [lepers] li conplot...
Tot droit vont vers l'enbuschement (*Tristan*).

compluvium [*antiq.*]. Opening in roof of atrium. L., from *pluere*, to rain.

comply. It. *complire*, borrowed from Sp. *cumplir* (cf. *compliment*), which had the spec. sense of satisfying requirements (true It. form from L. *complēre* is *compire*). Adopted in E. c. 1600. Influenced in form by *supply* (q.v.) and in meaning by *ply*, e.g. *compliant* is often understood as pliable, flexible.

compo. Short for *composition*, esp. in sense of stucco.

composant. Corrupt. of *corposant* (q.v.).

component. From pres. part. of L. *componere*, to put together.

comport. L. *comportare*, to bear together, carry with one.

compose. See *pose*. But much influenced in F. & E. by L. *compos-*, from *componere*,

to put together, whence *composite*, *composition*, *compositor*; e.g. a composition with creditors is also called *compounding* (see *compound*[1]). For fig. use of *composed* cf. *collected*. *Compositor* (typ.) is 16 cent.

compos, non (sc. **mentis**). L. *compos*, from *-potis*, capable, whence also L. *posse* (*potis esse*).

compost. OF. (*compôt*, *compote*), L. *compositum*, from *componere*, *compos-*, to put together.

compote. F., see *compost*.

compound[1]. To mix, etc. Earlier also *compoun*, *compone*, OF. *componre*, *compondre* (replaced by *composer*), L. *componere*, to put together. From the etym. sense of composing, settling, comes that of *compounding a felony* (*with one's creditors*). Adj. *compound* was orig. the p.p. *compouned*.

compound[2] [*Anglo-Ind.*]. Enclosure. Malay *kampung*, enclosure, etc.; but this is possibly from Port. *campo*, field. *Hobson-Jobson* quotes from a modern novel—

When the Rebellion broke out...I left our own compost!

comprador. In East, native servant who buys for household, purveyor. Port., L. *comparator-em*, from *comparare*, to buy, from *parare*, to prepare. Cf. *caterer*.

compree [*neol.*]. From mil. slang. See *comprise*.

comprehend. L. *comprehendere*, to grasp, from *com-* and *prehendere*, to seize. Has replaced ME. *comprend*, F. *comprendre*.

comprise. F. *compris*, p.p. of F. *comprendre*, L. *comprehendere*. This very common process, the adoption of a F. p.p. as a finite verb, is curiously exemplified by *compree*, now (1917) current E. in our army.

The Briton had a hand under the Teuton's arm and was encouraging him in the *lingua franca*. "No walkee much further," he said, "Soon there now. Compree, Fritz?" "Ja," groaned Fritz. He compreed.

compromise. Orig. agreement, with no suggestion of concession, or surrender. F. *compromis*, p.p. of *compromettre*, L. *compromittere*, to put before a disinterested arbiter.

That damned word "compromise"—the beastliest word in the English language
(Lord Fisher, *Times*, Sep. 9, 1919).

compter [*hist.*]. Name of various London debtors' prisons. Etymologizing spelling of *counter*[2], office, etc.

comptoir. F., counter².

comptometer [*neol.*]. Calculating machine. From F. *compter*, L. *computare*.

> Six comptometers are kept going with calculations
> (*Ev. Stand.* Apr. 8, 1918).

comptroller. In some official titles for *controller*. Bad spelling, due to mistaken association with F. *compte*, account. See *control*.

compulsion. F., L. *compulsio-n-*. See *compel*.

compunction. OF., L. *compunctio-n-*, used by early Church writers for "prick of conscience," from L. *compungere*, *-punct-*, to prick.

compurgator [*hist.*]. MedL., witness to character, lit. purifier, from *purgare*, to purge.

compute. F. *computer*, L. *computare*, from *putare*, to reckon.

comrade. Earlier *camerade*, F. *camarade*, Sp. *camarada*, orig. room-full (cf. mil. F. *chambrée*), later, chamber-fellow, "chum" (q.v.). Spelt *cumrade* in Shaks. For sense-development cf. Ger. *bursch*, fellow, orig. college hostel, *frauenzimmer*, wench, lit. women's room. Sense of fellow-socialist is a neol.

> *camarada*: a camerade, or cabbin mate (Minsh.)

comtism. System of *Auguste Comte* (†1857), positivism. See *altruism*.

Comus. God of revelry. See *comedy*.

con¹. To examine, learn by heart (a page, lesson, etc.). Earlier *cun*, AS. *cunnian*, to test, examine, secondary form of *cunnan*, to know, learn. See *can¹*, *ken¹*.

con². To guide a ship by directing the helmsman. Earlier *cond*, ME. *condue*, *condy*, to guide, from F. *conduire*, L. *conducere*. Hence *conning-tower*.

con³. For L. *contra*, in *pro and con*.

con-. L., for *cum*, with.

conacre [*Anglo-Ir.*]. Prepared land sub-let to small tenant. For *corn-acre*.

conation [*philos.*]. L. *conatio-n-*, from *conari*, to attempt.

concatenate. From Late L. *concatenare*, to link together, from *catena*, chain.

concave. F., L. *concavus*, from *cavus*, hollow.

conceal. Tonic stem (*conceil-*) of OF *conceler*, L. *concelare*, from *celare*, to hide.

concede. L. *concedere*, from *cedere*, to give way.

conceit. AF., p.p. of *conceive* (q.v.). Orig. sense of opinion in *out of conceit with*. *Conceited* is for earlier *self-conceited*, containing the idea of *wise in one's own conceit*

(15 cent.), whence deterioration of the word. Verbal *conceit* is It. *concetto*, "a conceit or apprehension of the minde" (Flor.).

> At this day ye stand gretly in the countreys conceyte (*Paston Let.* i. 347).

> Be not proude in your awne consaytes
> (Coverd. *Rom.* xii. 16).

> Lord, send us a gude conceit o' oursel' (Burns).

conceive. F. *concevoir*, VL. **concipēre* for *concipere*, from *capere*, to take.

concent [*archaic*]. Harmony. L. *concentus*, from *concinere*, to sing (*canere*) together; cf. It. *concento*. Now absorbed by *consent* (q.v.).

> For government, though high, and low, and lower,
> Put into parts, doth keep in one concent,
> Congreeing in a full and natural close,
> Like music (*Hen. V*, i. 2).

concentrate. For earlier *concentre*, F. *concentrer*, from L. *cum* and *centrum*. Cf. *concentric*, with common centre.

conception. F., L. *conceptio-n-*, from *concipere*, *concept-*, to conceive. First (c. 1300) of the Immaculate Conception. *Concept*, in philos. sense, is 19 cent.

concern. Late L. *concernere*, to sift, separate, used in MedL. as intens. of *cernere*, to perceive, have regard to. To *be concerned about*, i.e. distressed, etc. (orig. interested generally), is evolved from to *be concerned in*, i.e. interested in. The noun has progressed from the idea of a relation or connection to that of a business organization, etc., e.g. a *flourishing concern*. Cf. sense-development of *affair*.

> My Lord Sandwich is well and mightily concerned to hear that I was well (Pepys, Sep. 17, 1665).

concert. F. *concerter*, It. *concertare*, ? L. *concertare*, to strive together. VL. **consertare*, from *conserere*, *-sert-*, to join together, better suits sense and earlier It. form *consertare* (Flor.). Constantly confused, even now, with *consort* (q.v.), esp. in to *act in consort with*. Hence noun *concert*, F., It. *concerto*. The *concertina* was invented by Wheatstone (1829).

concession. F., L. *concessio-n-*, from *concedere*, *-cess-*, to grant. Spec. sense of privilege granted by government, etc., is developed in F.; cf. *concessionaire*. First *NED.* record of this meaning is connected with Suez Canal.

concetto. Usu. in pl. *concetti*. It., verbal "conceit," witticism.

conch. L. *concha*, G. κόγχη, cockle, mussel. Hence *conchology*, science of shells.

conchy [*neol.*]. For *conscientious objector*.

> The majority of the conchies is in reality composed of the "gun-shies"
> (A Quaker Descendant, *Times*, Nov. 30, 1917).

concierge. Doorkeeper. F., earlier also -*serge*, -*sierge*, VL. **conservians*, for *conservans*, pres. part. of *conservare*, to keep.
> *kepar of a kynges or a great lordes place*: consierge
> (Palsg.).

conciliate. From L. *conciliare*, to bring together, convoke. See *council*.

concinnity. Harmony. L. *concinnitas*, from *concinnus*, skilfully adjusted.

concise. From L. *concidere, concis-*, to cut (*caedere*) up.

conclamation. L. *conclamatio-n-*, general cry, from *clamare*, to shout.

conclave. F., L. *conclave*, from *clavis*, key Earliest in ref. to *conclave* of cardinals.

conclude. L. *concludere*, from *claudere*, to close. With to *try conclusions* (*Haml.* iii. 4) cf. to *be at issue*.

concoct. From p.p. of L. *concoquere, -coct-*, to boil together. With fig. senses cf. those of *brew*.

concomitant. From pres. part. of L. *concomitari*, to go with as companion, *comes, comit-*. Thus pleon. (see *count*[1]).

concord. F. *concorde*, L. *concordia*. See *accord*. Hence *concordance*, in Bibl. sense from 14 cent. Cf. *concordat*, F., L. *concordatum*, from *concordare*, to agree, esp. in ref. to agreements between Papal See and French monarchy, e.g. between Pius VIII and Napoleon I (1802).

concourse. F. *concours*, L. *concursus*, from *concurrere, -curs-*, to run together. The most usual F. meaning, competition, has not passed into E.

concrete. L. *concretus*, p.p. of *concrescere*, to grow together. The 19 cent. meaning, conglomeration of stone and cement, is thus fairly logical. As opposite to *abstract* it was applied by early logicians to a quality adherent as opposed to one detached.

concubine. F., L. *concubina*, from *con-*, together, *cubare*, to lie.

concupiscence. L. *concupiscentia* from *concupiscere*, incept. of *concupere*, from *cupere*, to desire.

concur. L. *concurrere*, to run together. In 16–17 cents. often replaced by *condog*, a somewhat feeble witticism.

> *concurrere*: to concur, to condog (Litt.).

concussion. L. *concussio-n-*, from *concutere, -cuss-*, to strike together, from *quatere*, to shake.

condemn. L. *condem(p)nare*, from *dam(p)nare*, to damage.

condense. F. *condenser*, L. *condensare*, to make dense, concentrate.

condescend. F. *condescendre*, Late L. *condescendere*, to come down from one's position; cf. Ger. *sich herablassen*, lit. to let oneself down. Not orig. with any idea of assumed superiority (*Rom.* xii. 16).

condign. L. *condignus*. Now only of making "the punishment fit the crime," but earlier in etym. sense of equally worthy.

> Without giving me leasure to yeeld him condigne thankes, if any thankes could be condigne, for so great and so noble a benefit
> (Sir Anth. Sherley, in Purch.).

condiment. F., L. *condimentum*, from *condire*, to pickle.

condition. L. *condicio-n-*, incorr. *condit-*, lit. discussion, from *dicere*, to speak. ME. sense of temperament, evolved from that of essential circumstance, survives in *ill-conditioned*, and, more vaguely, in gen. sense of state, fettle.

condole. L. *condolere*, to suffer with; cf. *compassion, sympathy*.

condominium. Joint sovereignty. L. *con-* and *dominium*, rule. App. a Ger. coinage (c. 1700).

condone. L. *condonare*, to give up, remit; cf. *pardon*. Chief current sense dates from Divorce Act (1857).

condor. Sp., Peruv. *cuntur*. F. *condore* is in Cotg.

condottiere. Mercenary leader. It., lit. conductor; cf. MedL. *conducterius*, mercenary (12 cent.), for *conducticius*.

conduce. L. *conducere* (v.i.).

conduct. Both noun and verb were in ME. also *conduyt, condute*, etc., from F. *conduit-e*, p.p. of *conduire*, L. *conducere*, from *ducere, duct-*, to lead. Cf. *safe-conduct* from F. *sauf-conduit*. With sense of behaviour cf. to *lead a good* (*bad*) *life*.

conduit. ME. also *condit, cundit*, F. *conduit*, from *conduire*, to lead (v.s.); cf. Ger. *wasserleitung* and archaic E. *lode* (q.v.).

Condy's fluid. Name of patentee (19 cent.).

condyle [*anat.*]. Rounded end of bone fitting socket. F., L., G. κόνδυλος, knuckle.

cone. L. *conus*, G. κῶνος, cone, pine-cone, spinning top.

confab. For *confabulation*, from L. *confabulari*, to chat together. See *fable*.

confarreation [*antiq.*]. L. *confarreatio-n-*, solemnization of marriage by offering of bread. From L. *far, farr-*, grain.

confect. Restored spelling of *comfit* (q.v.).

confection. F., L. *confectio-n-*, from *conficere*, *-fect-*, to make up. For limitation of orig. sense of *confectioner* cf. *stationer, undertaker*, etc. F. *confectionneur* means ready-made clothier, *confectioner* being represented by *confiseur*. See *comfit, confetti*.

confederate. L. *confoederatus*, from *foedus*, *foeder-*, treaty, league. In US. of the eleven southern states which seceded in 1860. Cf. *federal*.

confer. L. *conferre*, to bring together. Sense of taking counsel, whence *conference*, arises from that of comparing opinions. See also *collate*.

confess. OF. *confesser*, L. *confitēri, confess-*, to acknowledge (*fatēri*) together. Hence *confession*, first in rel. sense, and later used by early Reformed Churches of their spec. tenets. Also *confessor*, orig. one who avows his religion in spite of persecution, but does not suffer martyrdom. Hence *Edward the Confessor* (†1066), whose title is often misunderstood as though implying a comparison with the priest who hears confessions, a much later sense of the word in E.

confetti. It., pl. of *confetto*, sweetmeat. As *comfit* (q.v.).

confide. L. *confidere*, from *fidere*, to trust. Cf. *confidante*, app. meant to represent pronunc. of F. *confident-e*, It. *confidente*, a stage type introduced (16 cent.) into F. from It. drama. The *confidence trick* was orig. US.

confine. F. *confiner*, from *confins*, bounds, L. *confinis*, having common frontier (*finis*). Hence *confinement*, 18 cent. euph. for child-bed, from earlier *confined to one's bed* (*by the gout*, etc.). ME. said, much more poetically, *Our Lady's bands* (*bonds*).

confirm. F. *confirmer*, L. *confirmare*, to make firm. In eccl. sense (c. 1300) preceded by to *bishop*.

confiscate. For earlier *confisk*, F. *confisquer*, L. *confiscare*, orig. to appropriate for the treasury, *fiscus*. See *fiscal*.

confiteor. L., I confess.

conflagration. L. *conflagratio-n-*, from *conflagrare*, to burn up. Cf. *flagrant*.

conflation. Fusing together. L. *conflatio-n-*, from *conflare*, to blow together.

conflict. From L. *confligere, -flict-*, to strike together.

confluence. Late L. *confluentia*, from *confluere*, to flow together. Hence *Coblentz*, on Rhine and Moselle.

conform. F. *conformer*, L. *conformare*, orig. trans., mod. sense being for earlier reflex. Eccl. sense from c. 1600.

confound. F. *confondre*, L. *confundere*, to pour together. Earliest E. sense is to overthrow utterly, whence use as imprecation; cf. to *put to confusion*.

confrère. F., MedL. *confrater*, whence also *confraternity*.

confront. F. *confronter*, from *front*.

Confucian. Of *Confucius*, latinized form of Chin. *K'ung Fû tsze*, K'ung the master (†478 B.C.).

confuse. Orig. used as p.p. of *confound*. See *fuse. Confusion worse confounded* is from *Par. L.* ii. 992.

confute. L. *confutare*, orig. a cooking term, cogn. with *fundere*, to pour. Cf. *refute*.
confutare: properly to cool or keel the pot by stirring it when it boils (Litt.).

congeal. F. *congeler* (*congel-*), L. *congelare*, to freeze together. See *jelly*.

congee[1], **congé**. F. *congé*, L. *commeatus*, leave to go, furlough, etc., from *meare*, to pass through. Fully naturalized, also as *congy*, in 14–17 cents., now made F. again. Hence eccl. *congé d'élire*, leave to elect, granted by Crown. The *congee*, or low bow, was orig. at leave-taking.

çongee[2]. See *conjee*.

congener. L., of the same *genus, gener-*.

congenial. ModL. *congenialis*, suiting one's *genius*.

congenital. From L. *congenitus*, born with, from *gignere, genit-*, to beget.

conger. F. *congre*, L. *congrus*, G. γόγγρος.

congeries. L., from *congerere*, to bring together.

congestion. L. *congestio-n-*, from *congerere, -gest-* (v.s.).

conglomerate. See *agglomerate*.

congou. Tea. For Chin. *kung-fu-ch'a*, work tea, tea on which labour has been expended. This is *kang-hu-tê* in Amoy dial.

congratulate. From L. *congratulari*, from *gratus*, pleasing.

congregation. F., L. *congregatio-n-*, from *congregare*, to herd together, from *grex, greg-*, herd. Hence *congregationalism*, system of the Independents, the word *congregation* being much used by the Reformers, after Tynd., as a substitute for *church*, owing to the "sacerdotal" associations of the latter word.

Apon this roocke I wyll bylde my congregacion
(Tynd. *Matt.* xvi. 18).

congress. L. *congressus*, from *congredi, -gress-*, to go together, from *gradi*, to step. The US. *Congress*, as now constituted, first met March 4, 1789.

Congreve rocket. Invented (1808) by *Sir William Congreve*.

congruent. From pres. part. of L. *congruere*, to agree, from *ruere*, to rush.

conic sections [*math.*]. So called because each of the curves may be regarded as section of a cone.

conifer. See *cone* and *-fer(ous)*.

conjecture. L. *conjectura*, from *conicere, conject-*, to cast (*jacere*) together.

conjee, congee [*Anglo-Ind.*]. Rice-water. Tamil *kanjī*, boilings, in Urdu *ganji*. Hence *congee-house*, mil. lock-up.

conjugal. L. *conjugalis*, from *conju(n)x, conjug-*, spouse, lit. joined together. Cf. *conjugation*, lit. joining or yoking together. See *join, yoke*.

conjunctive [*gram.*]. *Modus conjunctivus* and *subjunctivus* are used by L. grammarians of 4 cent. See *subjunctive*.

conjuncture. F. *conjoncture*, from L. *conjungere, -junct-*. App. an astrol. metaphor (*favourable, critical, fatal*), for earlier *conjunction*, proximity of planets, in same sense. The latter word is in Chauc., and Wyc. uses it in the gram. sense.

conjure. F. *conjurer*, L. *conjurare*, to swear together. Mod. sense of producing rabbits from a hat is evolved from ME. meaning of constraining by a spell a demon to do one's bidding. Usu. accented on first syll. in all senses in ME.

conk. Nose. Slang c. 1800. ? F. *conque*, shell, conch.

Est-ce [votre nez] une conque, êtes-vous un triton?
(Rostand, *Cyrano de Bergerac*, i. 4).

connate. L. *connatus*, born together. from *nasci, nat-*, to be born.

connect. L. *connectere*, to fasten together. *Connexion*, with var. *connection*, is a late word (not in *AV.* or Shaks.). Its rel. sense is due to Wesley.

connive. L. *connivēre*, to wink.

connoisseur. OF. (*connaisseur*), from *conoistre* (*connaître*), L. *cognoscere*, to know.

connote. MedL. *connotare*, as term in logic. Mod. use, contrasted with *denote*, dates from Mill. See *note*.

connubial. L. *conubialis*, from *conubium*, marriage, from *nubere*, to wed.

conquer. OF. *conquerre* (*conquérir*), VL. **conquaerere*, from *quaerere, quaesit-*, to seek. *Conquest* represents OF. *conquest* (*conquêt*), what is acquired, and *conqueste* (*conquête*), the act of acquiring. Traces of the former are found in Sc. law.

conquistador [*hist.*]. Sp., conqueror, from *conquistar*, to conquer (see *conquest*). Applied to Sp. conquerors of Mexico and Peru.

consanguinity. F. *consanguinité*, L. *consanguinitas*, blood relationship, from *sanguis*, blood.

conscience. F., L. *conscientia*, knowledge within oneself, superseding E. *inwit*, once used to render it, e.g. in *Ayenbite of Inwite*, i.e. remorse of conscience (cf. Ger. *gewissen*, likewise due to the L. word). *In all conscience* orig. meant in all fairness, justice. *Conscionable, unconscionable* are irreg. *Conscience money* is recorded for 1860, and the practice of paying it for the 18 cent. (but see quot. 1).

Of a Baysler [Bachelor] of Martyn College for a other man whoys concyans dyd gruge hym for his privy tythes, 3d.
(*Accts. of All Saints Church, Oxf.* 1513).

I never heard a man yet begin to prate of his conscience, but I knew that he was about to do something more than ordinarily cruel or false
(*Westward Ho!* ch. vii.).

A conscientious objector, who gave an address at Knutsford, was fined £4 at Warrington for defrauding the railway company
(*Daily Chron.* Apr. 24, 1918).

conscript. The now common verbal use, for correct *conscribe*, L. *conscribere, conscript-*, to write together, originated in Civil War in US. *Conscription*, in sense of compulsory enlistment, appears in F. c. 1789. For sense-development cf. *enroll, enlist*.

Every atom of personality...is conscripted into the task (*Daily Chron.* Jan. 15, 1917).

consecrate. From L. *consecrare*, to make holy, *sacer*.

consecutive. F. *consécutif*, from L. *consequor, -secut-*, to follow.

consensus. L., consent.

consent. F. *consentir*, L. *consentire*, to feel together. Sense as noun has been affected by obs. *concent* (q.v.).

consequence. F. *conséquence*, L. *consequentia* (see *consecutive*). Mod. sense of *consequential*, self-important, springs from that of important, pregnant with consequences or results; cf. *of consequence*.

une matiere de consequence: a matter of importance, moment, or weight (Cotg.).

conservatoire. F., It. *conservatorio*, orig. for "preserving" and rearing of foundlings, etc., to whom a musical education was given. First at Naples (1537).

conserve. F. *conserver*, L. *conservare*, to protect, from *servare*, to preserve. Cf. *conservancy* (of rivers, esp. Thames), a mistake of Johns. for earlier *conservacy*, OF. *conservacie*, MedL. *conservatia* for *conservatio*. *Conservation of energy* (*force*) occurs first in Leibnitz (c. 1692), *la conservation de la force absolue*. *Conservative* was suggested as substitute for *Tory* by J. Wilson Croker. It had previously been used by Canning.

What is called the Tory, and which might with more propriety be called the Conservative, party (Croker, *Quart. Rev.* Jan. 1830).

consider. Orig., as still in F., to view attentively. F. *considérer*, L. *considerare*, perh. orig. astron., from *sidus*, *sider-*, star (cf. *desire*, *contemplate*). Prep. *considering* replaced earlier and logical *considered*; the ellipt. use, as in *pretty well, considering* (all things), is found in Richardson. For *consideration*, regard, payment, cf. *regard*, *reward*. For illogical sense of *considerate* cf. *circumspect*.

consign. Orig. to mark with a sign or seal. F. *consigner*, L. *consignare*.

consist. L. *consistere*, to stand firm. Cf. *consistory*, F. *consistoire*, Late L. *consistorium*, standing-place, waiting room, hence council room of Roman Emperors. Now eccl., Papal, Episcopal, Presbyterian, etc.

consolation. F., L. *consolatio-n-*, from *consolari*, to console, from *solari*, to comfort (see *solace*). *Consolation prize* is from earlier (18 cent.) practice at cards of giving something to the loser.

console [*arch.*]. F., app. from *consoler*, to console, as F. *consolateur* occurs in same sense (1562). ? Idea of support, help.

consolateur: a consolator, solacer, comforter; also, a corbell (in building) or, as *console de bastiment* (Cotg.).

consolidate. From L. *consolidare*, from *solidus*. In current (1915) mil. sense, to *consolidate captured position*, etc., app. adapted from F. *consolider*.

consols. For *consolidated annuities*, various government securities consolidated into one fund in 1751.

consommé. Soup. F., p.p. of *consommer*, in this sense from L. *consumere*, to consume, the nourishment of the meat being completely used up for the soup.

consonant. F., from pres. part. of L. *consonare*, to sound with.

consort. First (c. 1400) as noun, partner, colleague, etc. F., L. *consors*, *consort-*, from *sors*, fate, lot. Constantly confused in form and sense with *concert* (q.v.).

conspectus. L., general view. Cf. *synopsis*.

conspicuous. From L. *conspicuus*, from *conspicere*, to see clearly, from *specere*. *Conspicuous by absence* was coined (1859) by Lord John Russell after Tacitus.

Praefulgebant Cassius atque Brutus eo ipso quod effigies eorum non visebantur (*Annals*, iii. 76).

conspire. F. *conspirer*, L. *conspirare*, lit. to breathe together.

constable. OF. *conestable* (*connétable*), Late L. *comes stabuli* (A.D. 438), count of the stable, translating Teut. *marshal* (q.v.), orig. principal officer of household of Frankish kings. For wide sense-development cf. *marshal*, *steward*, *sergeant*.

outrun the constable: to spend more than is got, or run out of an estate, to run riot (*Dict. Cant. Crew*).

constant. F., from pres. part. of L. *constare*, to stand together, firm.

constantia. Wine from *Constantia Farm*, near Capetown.

They gave us some stuff under the name of Constantia, which to my palate was more like treacle and water than a rich and generous wine (Hickey's *Memoirs*, ii. 106).

constellation. F., L. *constellatio-n-*, cluster of stars (*stella*).

consternation. F., L. *consternatio-n-*, from *consternare*, ? for *consternere*, to bestrew, throw down, from *sternere*, to strew.

constipate. From L. *constipare*, to press together. See *costive*, *stevedore*.

constituency. First (1831) in Macaulay, but app. not his coinage.

constitute. From L. *constituere*, *-stitut-*, to place (*statuere*) together. *Constitution*, in sense of politic system of a state, was gradually evolved between the two great Revolutions (1689–1789). *Constitutional* (walk) was orig. a univ. word, now replaced at Camb. by *grind*.

constrain. OF. *constreindre* (*contraindre*), L. *constringere*, *constrict-*, to tighten, whence also *constrict-*. Cf. *strain*[1].

constriction. L. *constrictio-n-* (v.s.).

construct. See *construe*.

construe. L. *construere*, to pile together, construct, from *struere*, *struct-*, to heap. Esp. as gram. term, to analyse construction of sentence, interpret, etc., in which sense the later *construct* has also been used. With gram. sense goes to *put a good (bad, favourable) construction on*; cf. also *constructive blasphemy (possession, treason,* etc.), i.e. susceptible of being interpreted as such.

consubstantiation [*theol.*]. Formed (16 cent.) on *transubstantiation* (q.v.) to designate controversially the Lutheran conception of the Eucharist; but not accepted by Lutherans. L. *consubstantialis* (Tertullian) was used to translate G. ὁμοούσιος, of common substance.

consuetudinary. From L. *consuetudo*, custom (q.v.).

consul. L., ult. cogn. with *counsel* and *consult.* Mod. diplomatic sense was evolved (16 cent.) from the earlier meaning of a representative chosen by any society of merchants established in a foreign country. In MedL. & ME. the title was vaguely used as equivalent to count. The Roman method of denoting the years by consulships survives in the familiar *Consule Planco* (Hor.), which Byron (*Don Juan,* i. 212) renders "When George the Third was King."

consult. L. *consultare*, frequent. of *consulere*, to take counsel.

consume. L. *consumere*, to use up, from *sumere*, to take hold of. Hence *consumedly*, at first as expression of dislike (cf. *confoundedly*), but now app. felt as for *consummately*.

consummate. From L. *consummare*, from *summus*, highest, *summa*, total, for **supmus*, from *super*.

consumption. See *consume.* Med. sense is common in ME.

contact. From L. *contingere, contact-*, compd. of *tangere*, to touch. Hence also *contagion*, L. *contagio-n-*.

contadino. It. peasant, from *contado*, county.

contagion. See *contact.*

contain. F. *contenir*, VL. **contenire* for *continēre*, from *tenēre*, to hold.

contaminate. From L. *contaminare*, from *contamen*, contagion, for **contagmen*.

contango [*Stock Exchange*]. Percentage paid to postpone transfer, opposite of *backwardation.* ? Sp. *contengo*, I hold back, "contain," ? or arbitrary perversion of *continue.*

contemn. L. *contem(p)nere, contem(p)t-*. Hence *contempt, contemptible*, the latter used (since Sep. 1914) to render Ger. *verächtlich*, an epithet oddly applied by Wilhelm II of Germany to the finest army that ever took the field. Cf. *frightfulness.*

This makes me naturally love a souldier, and honour those tattered and contemptible regiments that will dye at the command of a sergeant
(*Religio Medici*).

contemplate. From L. *contemplari*, orig. used of augurs viewing a *templum* in the sky. Cf. *consider.*

contemporary. In sense of Late L. *contemporalis*, L. *contemporaneus* (whence F. *contemporain*),from *con-* and *tempus, tempor-*, time.

contempt. See *contemn.*

contend. L. *contendere*, intens. of *tendere*, to stretch.

content. F., L. *contentus*, p.p. of *continēre*, to contain. The *contented* man's desires are "bounded" by what he has (cf. adj. *continent*). The etym. sense (as in *cubic content*) and the fig. are combined in *to one's heart's content.*

Such is the fullness of my heart's content
(2 *Hen. VI,* i. 1).

conterminous. From L. *conterminus*, with common boundary.

contest. F. *contester*, L. *contestari*, to call to witness (*testis*), esp. as in *contestari litem*, to open proceedings.

context. L. *contextus*, from *contexere*, to weave together.

contiguous. From L. *contiguus*, from *contingere*, to be in contact.

continent. F., from pres. part. of L. *continēre*, to hold (*tenēre*) together. In geog. sense, for *continent* (i.e. continuous) *land.*

contingent. From pres. part. of L. *contingere*, from *tangere*, to touch. Mil. sense, orig. (18 cent.) proportion of force to be contributed by each contracting power, arises from that of "liable to occur" (cf. *contingency*).

continue. F. *continuer*, L. *continuare*, from *continuus*, from *continēre* (see *continent*).

conto. Million reis. Port., Late L. *computus.*

contort. From L. *contorquēre, contort-*, to twist together.

contour. F., from *contourner*, to follow the outline (see *turn*). It. *contorno* is used in same sense.

contra-. L., against, orig. a compar. formation from *con, cum*, with. Cf. native equivalent *with-*. Cf. *counter-*.

contraband. Sp. *contrabanda*, It. *contrabbando*, against law (see *ban*[1]). Dates in E. from illicit trade (c. 1600) with Sp. possessions in SAmer.

contract. L. *contractus*, a drawing together, from *contrahere*, from *trahere*, *tract-*, to draw. The same idea is seen in to *contract a disease* (*matrimonial alliance*, etc.). For current limited sense of *contractor*, as in *Builders and Contractors*, cf. *undertaker*.

contradict. From L. *contradicere*, *-dict-*, to speak against. *Contradiction in terms* is mod. for earlier *contradiction* (*Par. L.* x. 799).

contralto. It., "a counter treble in musicke" (Flor.). From L. *contra* and *altus*, high. Not orig. limited to female voice. Cf. obs. *contratenor*.

contraption [*dial. & US.*]. App. formed irreg. from *contrive*, on *deceive*, *deception*, etc.

contrapuntal. From It. form of *counterpoint* (q.v.).

contrary. OF. *contrarie* (*contraire*), L. *contrarius*, from *contra*, against. "The accent is invariably placed on the first syllable by all correct speakers, and as constantly removed to the second by the illiterate and vulgar" (Walker). The vulgar pronunc. is, as usual, the older.

Mary, Mary, quite contrary,
How does your garden grow?

contrast. F. *contraster*, Late L. *contrastare*, to stand against.

contravallation [*fort.*]. See *circumvallation*.

contravene. F. *contrevenir*, L. *contravenire*, to come against.

contre-danse. F. corrupt. of *country-dance* (q.v.).

contretemps. F., out of time. In E. first as fencing term.

contribute. From L. *contribuere*, *contribut-*. See *tribute*.

contrite. From L. *conterere*, *contrit-*, to bruise, crush. Cf. *attrition*.

contrive. ME. *contreve*, to invent, etc., esp. of evil devices, OF. *contruev-*, *-treuv-*, tonic stem of OF. *controver* (*controuver*), from *trouver*, of doubtful origin (see *trover*). OF. *ue*, *eu*, regularly become E. *ē*; cf. *retrieve*, *beef*, *people*.

Guy Fawkes, Guy!
He and his companions did contrive
To blow all England up alive.

control. F. *contrôle*, OF. *contre-rolle*, register kept in duplicate for checking purposes, a

sense not preserved in E. Cf. *counterfoil* and see *roll*. Much older than *control* is *controller*, whence corruptly *comptroller*. Now (1918) esp. in *Food Controller*. *Decontrol* is a neol. (1919).

contrerolle: a controlement, or contrarolement; the copy of a role (of accounts &c.), a parallel of the same quality and content, with the originall (Cotg.).

controvert. Back-formation, by analogy with *convert, divert*, etc., from *controversy* (Wyc.), from L. *controversus*, turned against.

contumacy. L. *contumacia*, from *contumax*, *-tumac-*, prob. from *tumēre*, to swell.

contumely. L. *contumelia*, cogn. with above.

contuse. From L. *contundere*, *-tus-*, from *tundere*, to beat.

conundrum. "A cant word" (Johns.). Earliest sense (c. 1600) seems to have been whimsy, oddity, either in speech or appearance. Later, a play on words, "a low jest; a quibble; a mean conceit" (Johns.), and finally (late 18 cent.), a riddle. Prob. univ. slang (associated with Oxf., 1645) originating in a parody of some L. scholastic phrase. Cf. *panjandrum, hocus-pocus*. See quot. s.v. *bee*.

Others weare a dead ratt tyed by the tayle and such like conundrums
(*Travaile into Virginia*, c. 1612).

I begin to have strange conundrums in my head
(Massinger).

convalescent. From pres. part. of L. *convalescere*, to grow strong, from incept. of *valēre*, to be strong.

convection [*phys.*]. L. *convectio-n-*, from *convehere*, from *vehere*, *vect-*, to carry.

convenance. Usu. pl. F., from *convenir*, to agree, be fitting. Cf. *comely*.

convene. F. *convenir*, L. *convenire*, to come together. Mod. trans. sense, to summon, is due to double function of other E. verbs (*assemble, gather, disperse*, etc.).

convenient. F. *convénient*, from pres. part. of L. *convenire*, to come together, agree, suit. Cf. *convenance*.

convent. ME. usually *couvent, covent* (as in *Covent Garden*). F. *couvent*, Church L. *conventus*, assembly. Restored spelling *convent* is also found in OF., but now rejected for *couvent*. In ModE. esp. nunnery.

convent: a covent, cloister, or abbey of monkes, or nunnes (Cotg.).

conventicle. L. *conventiculum*, meeting, place of meeting, from *convenire*, *convent-*, to come together, applied by Roman Christians (4 cent.) to their places of worship.

In Middle Ages assumed disparaging sense, being applied to illicit or heretical assemblies. Hist. sense dates esp. from *Conventicle Act* (1664).

That ye suffer no ryottes, conventiculs, ne congregasions of lewde pepull among you
(*Coventry Leet Book*, 1451).

convention. F., L. *conventio-n-*, meeting, agreement, from *convenire*, to come together. Hence *conventional*, applied (19 cent.) to lang., art, etc.

converge. Late L. *convergere*, to incline together, from *vergere*, to bend.

conversation. Orig. association, frequentation, behaviour, as still in *crim. con.* From L. *conversari*, to dwell (lit. turn about) with; cf. *conversant*. Current sense from 16 cent.

Our conversation [*Vulg.* conversatio, G. πολίτευμα, *RV.* citizenship] is in heaven (*Phil.* iii. 20).

conversazione. It., social gathering, "at home," lit. conversation. From 18 cent.

converse. Opposite. L. *conversus*, p.p. of *convertere*, to turn about.

convert. As noun, substituted under influence of verb *convert* (v.s.) for earlier *converse*.

Conversis fro hethenesse to the lawe of Israel
(Wyc. 1 *Chron.* xxii. 2).

convex. L. *convexus*, from *convehere*, to bring together (two surfaces). Cf. *concave*.

convey. OF. *conveier* (*convoyer*), VL. *conviare*, from *via*, way. Orig. to escort, accompany (cf. *convoy*). In 15–17 cents. euph. for *steal* (cf. current *expropriate*). Hence leg. *conveyance*, transfer of property. For vehicle sense cf. *carriage*. Dr Thompson, Master of Trinity, once suggested that a dispute as to a distinguished contemporary being the son of a lawyer or of a cabman might be settled by the compromise *conveyancer*.

Convey, the wise it call. Steal? foh! a fico for the phrase (*Merry Wives*, i. 3).

convict, convince. L. *convincere, convict-*, from *vincere*, to vanquish. *Convict* as noun dates from 16 cent. Use of *convincing* in "intellectual" jargon is mod. (not in *NED.*).

He that complies against his will
Is of his own opinion still (*Hudibras*, III. iii. 547).

The three-quarters, though more convincing than those of the other side, were given very little scope
(*Daily Tel.* Apr. 17, 1919).

convivial. Late L. *convivialis*, from *convivium*, feast, from *con-* and *vivere*, to live.

convoke. F. *convoquer*, L. *convocare*, to call together. *Convocation*, in eccl. sense, dates from temp. Ed. I, in univ. sense from 15 cent.

convolution. From L. *convolvere, convolut-*, to roll together; cf. *convolvulus*, L., bindweed.

convoy. F. *convoyer* (see *convey*), keeping more of orig. sense, esp. mil. and naut.

The sinking of the great galiasse, the taking of their convoie, which in the East partes is called a carvana [*caravan*] (Camden, 1602).

convulse. From L. *convellere, -vuls-*, to pull violently.

convulsionnaire [*hist.*]. F., fanatic indulging in convulsions at tomb of François de Paris in graveyard of St Médard, Paris, where miracles were reported to take place. The prohibition of these performances led some humorist to fix to the church door the following—

De par le roi, défense à Dieu
De faire miracle en ce lieu.

cony. First in AF. pl. *conys*, from OF, *conil*, L. *cuniculus*; cf. It. *coniglio*, Sp. *conejo*. Orig. rimed with *honey, money*. Now usu. replaced by *rabbit* (q.v.). The animal is of southern origin, as no Celt. or Teut. names for it exist; cf. Ger. *kaninchen*, MHG. *küniklin*, etc., also from L. The L. word is supposed to be Iberian. The *cony* of the Bible is really the *hyrax Syriacus*, a small pachyderm resembling the marmot.

coo. Earlier *croo*. Imit., cf. F. *roucouler*. With double form cf. F. *croasser* (of raven), *coasser* (of frog).

roucoulement: the crooing of doves (Cotg.).

cooee, cooey [*Austral.*]. Adopted from native signal-cry. Cf. *yodel*.

cook. First as noun. AS. *cōc*, L. *coquus*, whence also Du. *kok*, Ger. *koch*, archaic F. *queux*, It. *cuoco*, etc. Verb from noun in ME. Teut. langs. had *bake, roast, seethe*, but no gen. term (cf. *kitchen*). With to *cook one's goose* cf. to *settle one's hash*. To *cook* (*accounts, statements*, etc.) is 17 cent. (cf. *concoct*).

cooky [*Sc.*]. Cake. Du. *koekje*, dim. of *koek*, cake; cogn. with Ger. *kuchen*. For LG. origin cf. *scone*.

cool. AS. *cōl*. WGer.; cf. Du. *koel*, Ger. *kühl*; cogn. with L. *gelidus*. See *cold*. The verb, earlier *kele* (whence Shaks. to *keel the pot*, for which see also quot. s.v. *confute*), has been assimilated to the adj. In application to sums of money perh. from idea of

deliberate counting. To *cool one's heels*, now
iron., was orig. used of a rest on the march.
A *cool hand* appears to be suggested by such
expressions as *skilled (cunning) hand*.

"A cool four thousand, Pip!" I never discovered
from whom Joe derived the conventional temperature of the four thousand pounds, but it appeared
to make the sum of money more to him, and he had
a manifest relish in insisting on its being *cool*
(*Great Expectations*, ch. lvii.).

coolie, cooly. Prob. from *Kulī, Kolī*, name of
aboriginal tribe of Guzerat. So used in
16 cent. Port. Cf. hist. of *slave*.

coomb¹, combe. Hollow, valley, esp. in S.W.
of England. AS. *cumb*, prob. of Celt.
origin. Very common in place-names. Cf.
F. *combe*.

coomb². Obs. dry measure. AS. *cumb*, vessel;
cf. Ger. *kumpf*.

coon [*US.*]. Aphet. for *racoon* (q.v.). Fig.
and prov. uses appear to come esp. from
negro pastime of coon-hunting.

coop. ME. *cupe*, L. *cupa*, vat, cask, etc.,
whence F. *cuve*, vat. Existence of Ger.
kufe, tub, suggests that the word may have
been adopted also in AS. For changed E.
sense cf. *basket*.

cooper¹. Maker of casks. Du. *cuper*, MedL.
cuparius, from L. *cupa*, cask (v.s.). Not
immediately from *coop*, which has never
meant cask in E. Earlier forms *couper*,
cowper survive as surnames. Hence *cooper*,
stout and porter mixed, favourite tap of
brewery cooper (cf. *porter³*).

cooper², coper. Chiefly in *horse-co(o)per*.
From Du. *koopen*, to buy; cf. Ger. *kaufen*
and see *cheap, chapman*. Cf. also *co(o)per*,
Du. ship trading with North Sea fishermen,
"floating grog-shop."

cooperate. From Late L. *cooperari*, to work
together, from *opus, oper-*, work. Hence
cooperation, in econ. sense app. introduced
(1817) by Owen.

co-opt. L. *cooptare*, to choose together.
Earlier *cooptate* (Blount).

coordinate. From MedL. *coordinare*, to arrange together, from *ordo, ordin-*, order.

coot. Applied in ME. to various water-fowl.
ME. *cote, coote*; cf. Du. *koet*. A LG. word
of unknown origin.

What though she be toothless and bald as a coot?
(Heywood, 1562).

cop [*slang*]. To seize. ? Northern pronunc.
of obs. *cap*, OF. *caper*, L. *capere*. Hence a
fair cop, copper, policeman. *No cop* is a
variation on *no catch*.

copaiba [*med.*]. Balsam. Sp. Port., Brazil.
cupauba.

copal. Resin. Sp., Mex. *copalli*, incense.

coparcener [*leg.*]. From obs. *parcener*, partner, OF. *parçonier*, from *parçon*, share, L.
partio-n-.

cope¹. Garment. ME. *cope*, earlier *cape*, Late
L. *capa* (see *cap, cape¹*). Hence verb to
cope, cover (a wall), as in *coping*. Fig. in
cope (i.e. *mantle*) *of night, of heaven*.

Halfe so trewe a man ther nas of love
Under the cope of hevene, that is above .
(Chauc. *Leg. Good Women*, 1526).

cope². Verb. OF. *coper* (*couper*), to strike,
from *coup*, blow, VL. **colapus*, for *colaphus*,
G. κόλαφος, buffet. Influenced in sense by
obs. *cope*, to traffic (see *cooper²*), occurring
commonly in to *cope with* (cf. fig. sense of
to *deal with*). Nor can F. *coupler*, "to
couple, joyne, yoake; also, to coape, or
graple together" (Cotg.), be left out of
account (cf. *buff*, for *buffle*).

copeck. Small Russ. coin. Russ. *kopeika*,
dim. of *kopyé*, lance. Effigy of Ivan IV
with lance was substituted (1535) for that
of his predecessor with sword. Cf. *tester²*.

coper. See *cooper²*.

Copernican. Astron. system of *Copernicus*,
latinized form of *Koppernik*, Pruss. astronomer (1473–1543).

coping. See *cope¹*.

copious. F. *copieux*, L. *copiosus*, from *copia*,
plenty, from *co-* and *ops*, wealth. See
copy.

copper¹. Metal. AS. *coper*, VL. *cuprum*, for
Cyprium aes, Cyprian bronze, from *Cyprus*,
G. Κύπρος, most Europ. langs., e.g. Du.
kobber, Ger. *kupfer*, ON. *kopar*, F. *cuivre*,
etc. In *hot coppers* there is prob. the metaphor of the over-heated vessel, the kitchen
copper dating from 17 cent. Sense of coin
is in Steele, who uses it collect. (cf. *silver*).

copper² [*slang*]. Policeman. See *cop*.

copperas. ME. *coperose*; cf. F. *couperose*, It.
copparosa, Ger. *kupferrose*. Origin uncertain; ? from Late L. adj. *cuprosa*, of copper
(cf. *tuberose*), ? or an imitation of synon.
G. χάλκανθos, flower (rose) of brass.

copperhead [*US. hist.*]. Venomous snake.
Fig. northern sympathizer with Secession
(1862).

coppice, copse. OF. *copeïs*, from *coper* (*couper*), to cut (see *cope²*), with suffix -*eïs*, L.
-*aticius*. Cf. synon. F. *taillis*, from *tailler*,
to cut. With dial. *coppy* cf. *cherry, pea*,
etc.

copra. Dried kernel of coco-nut. Sp. Port. *copra*, Malayalam *koppara* (Hind. *khoprā*), coco-nut.

coprolite [*min.*]. From G. κόπρος, dung, λίθος, stone, from supposed composition.

copse. See *coppice*.

Copt. Native Egypt. Christian. ModL. *Coptus*, earlier *Cophtus*, Arab. *quft, qift*, Coptic *qyptios*, G. Αἰγύπτιος, Egyptian. Coptic lang. ceased to be spoken after 17 cent.

copulate. From L. *copulare*, from *copula*, bond, couple, from *co-* and *apere*, to fit.

copy. F. *copie*, L. *copia*, abundance, whence mod. sense via that of multiplying examples; cf. MedL. *copiare*, to transcribe. Sense of MS. for printer is in Caxton. *Copyhold* is from *copy* in ME. sense of transcript of manorial court-roll. *Copyright* is 18 cent. *Copy-book*, in current sense, is in Shaks. (*Love's Lab. Lost*, v. 2).

coquelicot. F., wild poppy. Imit. of cry of cock, suggested by resemblance of bright red flower to cock's comb.

coquette. Earlier also *coquet*. F. *coquet* (m.), *coquette* (f.), dim. of *coq* (see *cock*[1]).

coquette: a pratling, or proud gossip; a fisking, or fliperous minx; a cocket, or tatling houswife, a titifill, a flebergebit (Cotg.).

coquito. Palm. Sp., dim. of *coco* (q.v.).

cor. Measure (*Ezek.* xlv. 14). Heb. *kor*.

coracle. Welsh *cwrwgl, corwgl*, for *corwg*, trunk, carcase, coracle; cf. Ir. Gael. *curach*.

carabe: a coracle, or little round skiffe, made of ozier twigs woven together, and covered with raw hides (Cotg.).

coracoid [*anat.*]. Beaked. From G. κόραξ, κορακ-, raven, crow. Cf. *coccyx*.

corah. Unbleached or undyed silk. Urdu *kŏrā*.

coral. OF. (*corail*), L. *corallum*, G. κοράλλιον.

coran. See *alcoran*.

cor anglais. F., English horn. L. *cornu*.

coranto [*archaic*]. Dance. F. *courante*, "a curranto" (Cotg.), lit. running (dance), italianized in form.

corban. Offering vowed to God (*Mark*, vii. 11). Heb. *qorbān*, offering. Cf. *taboo*.

corbel [*arch.*]. Bracket. OF. (*corbeau*), raven, dim. of OF. *corb*, VL. **corbus*, for *corvus*, raven, in ref. to beaked shape.

corbie [*Sc.*]. Raven. From OF. *corb* (v.s.). With *corbie-steps*, projections on edges of gable, cf. synon. Ger. *katzentreppe*, cat-stairs.

cord. F. *corde*, L. *chorda*, G. χορδή, gut, string of instrument (see *chord*). Native *rope* is used of thicker type, but *cordage* is applied to ropes also in collect. sense.

Cordelier. Franciscan friar wearing rope girdle. F., from *cordelle*, dim. of *corde*, rope. Hence one of the pol. clubs of the Revolution, housed in former convent of Cordeliers. Cf. *Jacobin*.

cordial. F., MedL. *cordialis*, from *cor, cord-*, heart. Earliest E. use is med.

For gold in phisik is a cordial (Chauc. A. 443).

cordillera [*geog.*]. Sp., from *cordilla*, OSp. dim. of *cuerda*, rope. Hence *las Cordilleras de los Andes*. Cf. *sierra*.

cordilléra: the running a long of a rock or hill in length, as a cord (Minsh.).

cordite. Explosive (1889), from string-like appearance.

cordon. F., dim. of *corde*, in various senses. With *cordon bleu*, highest distinction, orig. ribbon worn by Knights Grand Cross of the French Order of the Holy Ghost, cf. *blue ribbon*. Humorously applied to a distinguished *chef* (*de cuisine*). *Cordon sanitaire* is a precaution against infection.

A sanitary cordon to bar the road to Bolshevism
(*Westm. Gaz.* Mar. 27, 1919).

cordovan. Of *Cordova*, esp. leather. See *cordwainer*.

corduroy, corderoy. Late 18 cent. Origin unknown. It may be a trade-name (*corde du roi*) of the *bovril* type, or from a maker's name, *Corduroy, Corderey*, etc., as surname, being a ME. nickname "king's heart." I have suggested elsewhere (*Trans. Phil. Soc.* 1910) that it may be contracted from the earlier material *colourderoy*, F. *couleur de roi*, orig. purple, but in Cotgrave's time the "bright tawnie."

cordwainer [*archaic*]. Worker in leather, shoemaker. OF. *cordouanier* (*cordonnier*), worker in *cordouan*, i.e. leather from *Córdova* (Sp.). Still in official use. F. *cordonnier* shows the same mistaken association with *cord*(*e*).

core. First c. 1400, replacing in this sense earlier *colk* (see *coke*). Derived by the old etymologists from L. *cor*, heart, and nothing more plausible has been suggested. The final *-e* is not an insuperable difficulty as we find *core* also for *corn*[2], from F. *cor*, "a core in the feet" (Hollyband, 1580).

cuor: a hart or courage. Also a core of any fruit
(Flor.).

corf [*techn. & dial.*]. Basket. Du. or LG. *korf*, L. *corbis*, early adopted in WGer.; cf. Ger. *korb*.

coriaceous. Leathery. From L. *coriaceus*, from *corium*, hide, cogn. with *cortex*, bark.

coriander. Plant. F. *coriandre*, L. *coriandrum*, from G. κορίαννον, prob. not of G. origin.

Corinthian [*archaic*]. Dandy, "toff" (18–19 cents.); earlier, profligate, dissipated, from proverbially licentious manners of Corinth. Cf. similar use of *Ephesian* (*Merry Wives*, iv. 5).

A Corinthian, a lad of mettle (1 *Hen. IV*, ii. 4).

cork. Earliest sense (14 cent.) is shoe, slipper, Sp. *alcorque*, "a corke shooe, a pantofle" (Minsh.), of Arab. origin (cf. Sp. *alcornoque*, cork tree). This was also the earliest sense of Ger. *kork*, and the substance was called *pantoffelholz*, slipper-wood. The above words are connected by some with L. *quercus*, oak, which seems unlikely. Their relation to Sp. *corcha*, cork, and of the latter to L. *cortex*, *cortic-*, bark, is a mystery. With *corker* (app. US.) cf. to *put the lid on*.

cork, bark: cortex (*Prompt. Parv.*).

corking-pin [*archaic*]. "A pin of the largest size" (Johns.). Earlier *calkin*, *cawking*, but relation to *calkin* (q.v.) is obscure.

cormorant. F. *cormoran*, earlier *cormaran*, *-ein*, *-in*, from OF. *marenc*, of the sea, from L. *mare* with Ger. suffix *-ing*, of which fem. survives in F. dial. *pie marenge*, cormorant. Cf. MedL. *corvus marinus*, sea raven, whence Port. *corvomarinho*. For E. *-t* cf. *pheasant*, *tyrant*, etc.

corn¹. Grain. AS. *corn*. Com. Teut.; cf. Du. *koren*, Ger. ON. *korn*, Goth. *kaurn*; cogn. with L. *granum*. For double sense (single seed, as in *peppercorn*, and collect.) cf. *grain*. In US. esp. maize, whence *corn-cob*, *cornflour*. *Cornstalk*, native-born Australian (esp. NSW.), alludes to height and slimness. *Corned beef* is so called because preserved with "corns" (grains) of salt.

corn². On foot. OF. *corn* (*cor*), horn, horny substance, L. *cornu*. See *core*.

cornbrash. Sandstone. From *corn¹* and *brash* (q.v.).

cornea [*anat.*]. Of the eye. For L. *cornea tela*, horny web.

cornel. Tree. In 16 cent. *cornel-tree*, for Ger. *cornel-baum*, from MedL. *cornolius*, from L. *cornus*, cornel tree, named, like the *horn-*

beam, from horny nature. Cf. F. *cornouiller*, cornel tree.

cornelian. Stone. ME. *corneline*, F. *cornaline*; cf. It. *cornalina*, Prov. *cornelina*. ? From L. *cornu*, horn (cf. *onyx*), or from resembling fruit of *cornel tree* (v.s.). The form *carnelian* (cf. Ger. *karneol*) is due to mistaken association with L. *caro*, *carn-*, flesh (v.i.).

cornaline: the cornix, or cornaline; a flesh-coloured stone (Cotg.).

corner. ME. & AF. *corner*, F. *cornier*, VL. **cornarium*, from *cornu*, horn. The verb to *corner* (commodities) arises from earlier sense (also US.) of driving into a corner. *The Corner*, Tattersall's, was formerly at Hyde Park Corner. *Corner-stone* is in Wyc. (*Vulg. lapis angularis*).

cornet¹. Instrument. OF., It. *cornetto*, dim. of *corno*, horn, L. *cornu*.

cornet². Head-dress, standard of troop of cavalry. F. *cornette*, dim. of *corne*, horn, L. *corn(u)a*, neut. pl. taken as fem. sing. With obs. *cornet* (of horse) cf. *ensign* (of foot).

cornice. Earlier also *cornish*, F. *corniche*, It. *cornice*. App. ident. with It. *cornice*, crow, L. *cornix*, *cornic-*. Cf. *corbel*.

Cornish [*ling.*]. Celt. lang. which became extinct in 18 cent.

cornopean. Cornet à piston. ? Arbitrary formation (19 cent.).

cornucopia. For L. *cornu copiae*, horn of plenty. Orig. horn of the she-goat Amalthaea which suckled infant Zeus.

corody. See *corrody*.

corolla. L., dim. of *corona*, crown, garland.

corollary. L. *corollarium*, gratuity, orig. one given for garland (v.s.). Math. sense is in Chauc.

corolaire: a corollaire; a surplusage, overplus, addition to, vantage above measure; also, a small gift, or largesse bestowed on the people at publique feastes, and playes (Cotg.).

coronach [*Sc.*]. Funeral lament. Gael. *corranach*, from *comh-*ł together, *ránach*, outcry.

coronation. OF. *coronacion*, from *coroner* (*couronner*), to crown, from L. *corona*.

coroner. AF. *corouner*, from *coroune*, crown, F. *couronne*, L. *corona*. Orig. (from 1194) *custos placitorum coronae*, an official attending to private rights of crown, his functions being now limited. Also pop. *crowner*.

The crowner hath sat on her, and finds it Christian burial (*Haml.* v. 1).

coronet. OF. *coronete*, dim. of *corone* (*couronne*), crown.

corozo. SAmer. tree, whence vegetable ivory. Native name.

corporal[1] [*eccl.*]. Cloth covering Eucharistic elements. MedL. *corporalis* (sc. *palla*). Cf. *corporas*.

corporal[2]. Adj. L. *corporalis*, from *corpus*, *corpor-*, body.

corporal[3] [*mil.*]. OF. (replaced by *caporal*), MedL. *corporalis*, from *corpus*, *corpor-*, body. F. *caporal*, It. *caporale*, seems to be perverted under influence of It. *capo*, head, VL. *caporalis*, from *caput*, *capit-*, being abnormal.

corporas [*archaic*]. ME. & OF. *corporaus*, pl. of *corporal*, linen vestment, linen cloth used at Eucharist, MedL. *corporalis*, from *corpus*, *corpor-*, body. See *corporal*[1].

corporation. Late L. *corporatio-n-*, from *corporare*, to embody (v.s.). Slang sense, due to association with *corpulent*, dates from 18 cent. (Smollett).

corposant [*naut.*]. "St Elmo's fire." Port. *corpo santo*, holy body.

> *Ariel.*   Now on the beak,
> Now in the waist, the deck, in every cabin,
> I flam'd amazement; sometimes I'd divide
> And burn in many places; on the topmast,
> The yards and bowsprit would I flame distinctly
> (*Temp.* i. 2).

corps [*mil.*]. F., body (v.i.), as in *corps d'-armée, d'élite*, etc.

corpse. Restored spelling (influencing pronunc.) of ME. & OF. *cors*, L. *corpus*. Hence dial. sing. *corp* by back-formation. *Corse* survives in poet. style (*Burial of Sir John Moore*). Earlier also live body (see quot. s.v. *booze*), hence *dead corpse* (2 *Kings*, xix. 35), *lifeless corpse*, not orig. pleon. Cf. Ger. *leiche, leichnam*, corpse, orig. body (see *lich*).

corpulent. F., L. *corpulentus*, from *corpus*, body.

corpus. L., body; esp. in *Corpus Poetarum Latinorum* and other such comprehensive works. Cf. leg. *corpus delicti*, body (of facts forming part) of crime.

Corpus Christi. Thursday after Trinity (cf. F. *fête-Dieu*, Ger. *Fronleichnam*); constantly associated with early rel. drama.

> As clerkes in corpus christi feste singen and reden
> (*Piers Plowm.* B. xv. 381).

corpuscle. L. *corpusculum*, dim. of *corpus*, body. From 17 cent.

corral. Enclosure, pen. Sp., from *correr*, to run, L. *currere*, as in *correr toros*, to hold

a bull-fight. See *kraal*. With to *corral*, secure, cf. to *round up*.

corrasion [*geol.*]. From L. *corradere, -ras-*, to scrape together, after *corrosion*.

correct. From L. *corrigere, correct-*, from *regere*, to rule. *House of Correction* is 16 cent.

corregidor. Sp., magistrate. From *corregir*, to correct (v.s.).

correspond. F. *correspondre*, MedL. *correspondēre*. See *respond* and cf. to *answer to*. In journalistic sense gradually evolved since establishment of periodical literature (c. 1700).

corridor. F., It. *corridore*, from *correre*, to run, L. *currere*; cf. Sp. *corredor*. Replaced OF. *couroir* (see *couloir*).

> The corridor train is so named from a narrow passage which runs from end to end
> (*Daily News*, Mar. 8, 1892).

corrie [*Sc.*]. Circular glen. Gael. *coire*, cauldron.

corrigenda. L., neut. pl. gerund. of *corrigere*, to correct. Cf. *addenda*.

corroborate. From L. *corroborare*, to strengthen, from *robur, robor-*, strength. Cf. *robust*.

corroboree. Dance of Austral. aboriginals. According to *NED.*, from extinct native lang. of Port Jackson (NSW.). Morris gives native *korobra*, to dance.

corrode. L. *corrodere*, from *rodere, ros-*, to gnaw. Hence *corrosive*.

corrody [*hist.*]. Allowance, orig. preparation, outfit. AF. *corodie*, MedL. *corrodium*, for *corredium* (see *curry*[1]).

corrosion. See *corrode*.

corrugated. L. *corrugatus*, from *ruga*, wrinkle, furrow. With *corrugated iron* cf. F. *tôle gaufrée* (see *gopher*), Ger. *welleisen* (from *welle*, wave).

corrupt. From L. *corrumpere, corrupt-*, lit. to break up.

corsage. F., cf. *corset*.

corsair. F. *corsaire*, It. *corsare*, earlier *corsaro*, MedL. *cursarius*, from *cursus*, raid, incursion, from L. *currere, curs-*, to run. See *hussar*.

corse. See *corpse*.

corset. F., dim. of OF. *cors* (*corps*), body (see *corpse*). With mod. pl. *corsets* cf. hist. of *bodice*. *Corslet* is a double dim., *-el-et*.

> *corset*: a paire of bodies (for a woman) (Cotg.).

corslet [*hist.*]. See *corset*.

cortège. F., It. *corteggio*, from *corte*, court, "also a princes whole familie or traine" (Flor.).

Cortes. Legislative assembly. Sp. Port., pl. of *corte*, court.

cortical. Of bark, L. *cortex, cortic-*.

corundum [*min.*]. Tamil *kurundam*, Sanskrit *kuruvinda*, ruby.

coruscate. From L. *coruscare*, to glitter.

corvée. Forced labour. F., OF. *corovee*, p.p. fem. of OF. *cor-rover*, to call together, rendered in MedL. by *corrogata* (*opera*); but OF. *rover*, to ask, summon, is more prob. from OSax. *rōpan* (cf. Ger. *rufen*), to call (cf. Sc. *roop*, auction).

corvette. Small frigate. F., Port. *corveta*, L. *corbita* (sc. *navis*), from *corbis*, basket; reason of name unknown.

corvine. L. *corvinus*, of the crow, *corvus*.

Corybant. Priest of Phrygian worship of Cybele, wild dancer. F. *corybante*, L., G. Κορύβας, Κορυβαντ-.

Corydon. Conventional rustic (*Allegro*, 83). L., G. proper name Κορύδων (Theocritus).

corymb [*bot.*]. G. κόρυμβος, cluster, esp. of ivy-berries.

coryphaeus. Chorus leader (in Attic drama). G. κορυφαῖος, from κορυφή, head.

cos. Lettuce. From Aegean island, G. Κῶς, now Stanchio.

cosher[1]. To cocker, pamper. Ir. *cóisir*, feast.

cosher[2]. See *kosher*.

cosmetic. G. κοσμητικός, from κόσμος, order, adornment.

cosmos. G. κόσμος, order, a name given by Pythagoras to the universe. Often contrasted with *chaos* (q.v.). Cf. *cosmogony*, creation, from -γονια, begetting; *cosmopolite*, citizen of the world, from πολίτης, citizen; *cosmography*, etc.

coss, koss [*Anglo-Ind.*]. Varying measure of length (usu. about 2 miles). Hind. *kōs*, Sanskrit *krosa*, measure, orig. call showing distance.

"The city is many koss wide," the Havildar-Major resumed (Kipling, *In the Presence*).

396 course of India make English miles 551½
(Peter Mundy, 1631).

Cossack. Earlier (16 cent.) *cassacke*, Turki *quzzāq*, adventurer, freebooter, etc.

The Cossacks are a species of Tartars; their name signifies freebooters (Jonas Hanway, 1753).

cosset. To pamper. From *cosset*, spoilt child, young animal brought up by hand, "cade-lamb." Perh. AS. *cotsetla*, cot-dweller (cf. It. *casiccio*, pet lamb, from *casa*, house, and Ger. *hauslamm*, pet); but there is no record of the AS. word between Domesday

and 1579, though the corresponding Ger. compd. survives (*kossat*, cotter).

cost. OF. *coster* (*coûter*), L. *constare*, from *stare*, to stand; cf. It. *costare*, Sp. *costar*. The L. idiom is curiously like ModE., e.g. *Hoc constitit mihi tribus assibus*, "stood me in." See *stand*.

costal [*anat.*]. Of the rib, L. *costa*.

costard. Apple, fig. head. ? From OF. *coste*, L. *costa*, rib, the apple being described as "ribbed"; cf. OF. *poire à cousteau*, app. ribbed pear. Hence *costard-monger*, apple-dealer, for extended sense of which (*coster-monger*) cf. *chandler*. For the opposite cf. *stationer, undertaker*.

costardmonger: fruyctier (Palsg.).

costive. OF. *costevé*, L. *constipatus*. For loss of suffix cf. *signal*[2], *trove*, *defile*[2], etc. See *constipate*.

costmary [*archaic*]. Plant. Earlier also *cost*, L. *costus*, G. κόστος, Arab. *qust*, Sanskrit *kustha*, name of plant found in Cashmere. Second element is *St Mary*; cf. synon. OF. *herbe sainte Marie*, Ger. *Marienblättchen*, etc. Has influenced *rosemary* (q.v.).

costume. F., It., custom, fashion, L. *consuetudo, -tudin-*, custom. Cf. double meaning of *habit*. Introduced as art term, and italicized up to c. 1750. Not in Johns.

cosy. Orig. Sc., comfortable, snug. Earliest (c. 1700) *colsie*. Origin doubtful. ? Norw. *koselig*, snug, cosy, from *kose sig*, to make oneself comfortable; cf. Ger. *kosen*, to chat familiarly, *liebkosen*, to caress, ult. ident. with F. *causer*, to talk.

cot[1], **cote.** Dwelling. AS. *cot*; cf. Du. LG. ON. *kot*; also AS. *cote*, whence *cote* in *sheep-cote*, *dove-cote*, etc. Prob. cogn. with *coat* (q.v.) with ground-idea of covering.

cot[2]. Bed. Hind. *khāṭ*, Sanskrit *khatwā*. From 17 cent. in mil. and naut. use. Child's *cot* first in Todd.

cote. See *cot*[1].

coterie. F., orig. association of peasants holding land from a lord, from OF. *cotier*, cot-dweller; cf. MedL. *coteria*. See *cot*[1].

cothurnus. Tragic buskin. L., G. κόθορνος.

cotillon. F., petticoat, double dim. of *cotte*, skirt, etc. (see *coat*). Reason for application to a dance is obscure.

cotta [*eccl.*]. Surplice. MedL. *cotta*. See *coat*.

cottage. AF. *cotage*, from *cot*[1]; cf. MedL. *cotagium*. Hence *cottage loaf*, easily made without elaborate apparatus.

cotter[1], **cottar, cottier.** Cottager. See *cot*[1].

cotter² [*techn.*]. Peg, wedge, in various senses. Earlier *cotterel*. Prob. fig. use of same words in ME. sense of servile tenant, villein, lit. cot-dweller, MedL. *cottarius*, *cotterellus*. Cf. Ger. *stiefelknecht*, bootjack.

cotton. F. *coton*, Arab. *qutn* (see *acton*). In most Europ. langs. The verb to *cotton*, orig. (16 cent.) to prosper, succeed, appears to be due to a fig. sense of raising a nap on cloth, or of getting materials to combine successfully. See quot. below, in which, however, the association may be forced. *Cottonocracy* is applied in E. to the cotton-lords of Lancashire, in US. to the planters.

It cottens well; it cannot choose but bear a pretty nap (Middleton, 1608).

Cottonian. Library of *Sir R. Cotton* (†1631), nucleus of British Museum.

cotwal [*Anglo-Ind.*]. Head of police. Pers. *kot-wāl*, fort commander.

cotyledon [*bot.*]. Introduced by Linnaeus. G. κοτυληδών, cup-shaped cavity, from κοτύλη, hollow vessel.

couch. First as verb. F. *coucher*, OF. *colchier*, L. *collocare*, to place together; cf. It. *colcare*, Sp. *colgar*. Gen. idea, to lay horizontally, e.g. to *couch a lance*. Etym. sense survives in to *couch in obscure language* (*technical phraseology*, etc.), with which cf. F. *coucher par écrit*, to set down in writing. In med. *couching of cataract*, orig. sense is to lower, depress.

couch-grass. See *quitch*.

cougar. Puma, catamount. F. *couguar*, Buffon's adaptation of an earlier *cuguacu ara*, for Guarani (Brazil) *guazu ara*. Cf. *jaguar*.

cough. Found in AS. only in derivative *cohhetan*. Cf. Du. *kuchen*, to cough, Ger. *keuchen*, to pant, whence *keuchhusten*, whooping-cough. All imit. Synon. AS. *hwōstan* survives in Sc. *hoast*; cf. Ger. *husten*.

could. See *can*.

coulée [*geol.*]. Solidified lava. F., p.p. fem. of *couler*, to flow, L. *colare*.

coulisse. Side-scene on stage, etc. F., fem. form of *coulis*, from *couler*, to flow, slide, L. *colare*. Cf. *portcullis*.

couloir [*Alp.*]. Steep gorge. F., by dissim. for OF. *couroir*, corridor (q.v.).

coulomb. Unit of electricity. From *C. A. de Coulomb*, F. physicist (†1806). Cf. *ampère*, *volt*.

coulter. Of plough. AS. *culter*, from L. See *cutlas*.

council. L. *concilium*, assembly, ? lit. a calling together, L. *calare*. Unconnected with

counsel, F. *conseil*, L. *consilium*, plan, opinion, ? lit. leaping together, from L. *salire*. But the two words were completely confused in E., though vaguely, and often incorrectly, differentiated from 16 cent. *Council* has encroached on *counsel*, while F. still limits *concile* to eccl. sense. So also *councillor* is for older *counsellor*, F. *conseiller*. *Counsel* as applied to individual (K.C.) is evolved from sense of body of counsellors. Cf. Ger. *geheimrat*, privy-councillor, lit. privy-council.

But I do see by how much greater the council, and the number of counsellors is, the more confused the issue is of their councils (Pepys, Jan. 2, 1668).

counsel. See *council*. F. *conseil* had also in OF. the sense of (secret) plan, whence to *keep one's own counsel*.

count¹. Title. OF. *conte* (*comte*), L. *comes*, *comit-*, companion, from *cum* and *ire*, to go; cf. It. *conte*, Sp. *conde*. Used in AF. for *earl*, but not recognized as E. word till 16 cent., though *countess*, *county* are common in ME.

count². Verb. OF. *conter*, L. *computare*, from *putare*, to think, reckon. ModF. has *conter*, to tell (a story), *compter*, to count (cf. double sense of E. *tell*). For restored spelling of F. *compter* cf. E. *accompt*. Archaic to *count*, plead in a court of law, whence the *counts* of an indictment, belongs in sense to ModF. *conter*.

countenance. F. *contenance*, L. *continentia*, manner of holding oneself, bearing, from *continēre*, lit. to hold together. In E. gradually applied esp. to the "behaviour" of the features, e.g. to *change countenance*. Orig. sense of bearing appears in to *keep in* (*put out of*) *countenance*, whence *countenance*, moral support.

counter¹. Adv. Esp. in to *run counter*. See *counter-*. Also with adj. sense, e.g. in *counter revolution*.

counter². Of a shop. Extended use of same word meaning banker's desk, counting-house; cf. F. *comptoir*, MedL. *computatorium*.

counter³. Part of horse's breast. From *counter*¹. Cf. origin of *withers* (q.v.).

counter⁴. Of a ship. Perh. as *counter*³, ? from shape.

counter⁵. In fencing, boxing. For earlier *counter-parade*, *counter-parry* (see *counter-*).

counter⁶. Verb. From adv. *counter*¹, but in some senses aphet. for *encounter* and obs. *accounter*.

counter-. AF. form of F. *contre*, L. *contra*, against.

counterblast. App. from blast blown on trumpet in answer to challenge. Revived in 19 cent. as echo of James I's *Counterblast to Tobacco* (1604).

counterfeit. F. *contrefait*, p.p. of *contrefaire*, from *contre* and *faire*, L. *facere*. Not orig. with suggestion of fraud.

counterfoil. See *foil*¹.

counterfort [*arch.*]. F. *contrefort*, buttress, from *fort*, strong.

countermand. F. *contremander*, from *mander*, L. *mandare*, to order.

counterpane. Earlier *counter-point*, OF. *coutepointe* (now corruptly *courte-pointe*), Late L. *culcita puncta*, stitched quilt, from *pungere*, to prick. The corrupted *contre-pointe* is found in OF., being explained by Cotg. as "wrought with the backe stitch." The altered ending in E. is perh. due to *pane*, *cover-pane*, F. *pan*, cloth (see *panel*), formerly used in similar sense. See also *quilt*.

> In ivory coffers I have stuff'd my crowns;
> In cypress chests my arras, counterpoints,
> Costly apparel, tents and canopies (*Shrew*, ii. 1).

counterpoint [*mus.*]. F. *contrepoint*, It. *contrappunto*, an accompaniment "pricked against" notes of melody. See *puncture*.

countervail. From tonic stem of OF. *contrevaloir*, from L. *contra* and *valēre*, to be worth. Cf. *avail*, *prevail*.

> The enemy could not countervail the king's damage (*Esth*. vii. 4).

counting-house. See *count*². First record in *NED*. is 1440 (*Prompt. Parv.*), but *Nicholas del Countynghouse* is in *Issue Rolls* (1381).

country. F. *contrée*, Late L. *contrata*, (land) spread before one (*contra*). Cf. Ger. *gegend*, district, from *gegen*, against. The oldest E. sense is region, district, as F. *contrée*, and the three main existing meanings are all exemplified in *countryman*. Hence *country-dance*, in F. corrupted to *contredanse*. *Countryside*, orig. Sc., or north., is a neol. in literary E. The Teut. word, in same senses, is *land*, which has prevailed in the other Teut. langs.

> In a country dress, she and others having, it seemed, had a country dance in the play
> (Pepys, May 22, 1667).

county. AF. *counté*, OF. *conté* (*comté*), L. *comitatus* (see *count*¹). The *county court* translates the AS. *shire-moot*, the *county council* dates from 1888.

coup. F. (see *cope*²). Now common in E.,

e.g. *coup d'essai*, *coup d'État* (esp. in ref. to Louis Napoleon, 1851), *coup de grâce*, of mercy (putting opponent out of his misery), *coup de main*, *coup de théâtre*.

> Mr Lloyd George aimed at a *coup d'état*, but he has achieved a *coup de théâtre*
> (*Daily News*, Dec. 3, 1918).

coupé. F., p.p. of *couper*, to cut (in half). See *cope*².

couple. F., L. *copula*, bond. In ME. esp. leash, brace of hounds, as in to *uncouple*, *hunt in couples*, etc.

coupon. F., a "detachable" certificate, from *couper*, to cut (see *cope*²). In travel sense introduced by Cook (1864). Now (1918) one of the most familiar words in the lang. (cf. *control*, *censor*, etc.).

> On no account should voters be fooled by the fact that candidates have been couponed or ticketed by the Coalition (*Daily Mail*, Dec. 9, 1918).

> The election of December, 1918, may not impossibly be known in history as "the coupon election"
> (H. H. Asquith, Apr. 11, 1919).

courage. F., VL. *coraticum*, from *cor*, heart; cf. It. *coraggio*, Sp. *coraje*. In ME., as in F. up to 17 cent., commonly used for heart.

> Ce grand prince calma les courages émus (Bossuet).

courbash. See *kourbash*.

courier. Combined from F. *coureur*, runner, from *courir*, to run (corresponding to Sp. *corredor*, It. *corridore*, Late L. *curritor-em*), and 16 cent. F. *courrier*, courier, It. *corriere* (corresponding to MedL. *currerius*).

course. Combined from F. *cours*, L. *cursus*, whence also It. *corso*, Sp. *curso*, and the later fem. form *course*. Has taken over some senses of native noun *run*. Wyc. uses in etym. sense of race (2 *Tim*. iv. 7, *Vulg. cursus*). Sense of routine order has given *of course*, *matter of course* (see also *cursitor*). Hence verb to *course*, now only hares, rabbits, but formerly also boars, wolves, etc.; cf. F. *courre le cerf*. The sense-development of naut. *course* (*fore-course*, *main-course*) is perh. connected with the "running" of ships under these sails.

court. OF. *court* (*cour*), L. *cohors*, *cohort-*, cogn. with *hortus*, garden, and used by Varro in sense of poultry-yard. It represents partly also L. *curia*, used as its MedL. equivalent in leg. and administrative sense. For double group of meanings cf. Ger. *hof*, yard, court (of prince, etc.). In *courteous* there has been change of suffix, F. *courtois*, ONF. *curteis*, L. *-ensis*, surviving in name *Curtis*. For *courtesy* see *curtsy*. *Courtesan*,

F. *courtisane*, It. *cortigiana*, is euph. (see *bravo*). *Courtier* is from OF. *cortoier*, to frequent court (F. *courtesan* = courtier, F. *courtier* = broker). With verb to *court* cf. F. *faire la cour*. *Court-plaster* was formerly used for "patches" by ladies of the court. *Court hand*, in writing, is that in which leg. enactments are copied. *Court martial* was earlier (16 cent.) *martial court*, the inversion being app. due to association with *provost marshal*, who carried out sentencĕ of *court martial*. It is often spelt *court marshal* in 17 cent., *martial* and *marshal* being quite unconnected. *Court-yard* is pleon., the two words being synon. and ult. ident.

For freend in court ay better is
Than peny in purs certis (*Rom. of Rose*, 5541).

court-card. For earlier *coat-card*, from the pictures; cf. It. *carta di figura*, "a cote carde" (Flor.).

couscous. Afr. dish. F., Arab. *kuskus*, from *kaskasa*, to pound small.

cousin. F.; cf. It. *cugino*, MedL. *cosinus* (7 cent.), with meaning of L. *consanguineus*. *Cosinus* is supposed to be a contr. (? due to infantile speech) of L. *consobrinus*, "cousin germane, sisters sonne" (Coop.), but this seems hardly credible. But one might conjecture that the OL. form *consuesrinus* might have become *consuesinus* and so *cosinus*.

couvade. Custom ascribed to some races of father taking to his bed on birth of a child. F. (see *covey*). Earliest mention of the custom is prob. in the *Argonautica* of *Apollonius* (†186 B.C.).

cove¹. Creek. In AS. chamber, cell, recess, etc., whence mod. sense of concave arch. AS. *cofa*. Com. Teut.; cf. Ger. *kofen*, pigsty (from LG.), *koben*, hut, ON. *kofi*, hut. See *cubby-house*.

cove² [slang]. Earlier (16 cent. thieves' cant) *cofe*. Prob. ident. with Sc. *cofe*, hawker, cogn. with *chapman* (q.v.). Cf. degeneration of *cadger*.

covenant. Pres. part. of OF. *covenir* (*convenir*), to agree, L. *convenire*, to come together. As Bibl. word represents Heb. *berīth*, contract, rendered by διαθήκη in LXX. and in *Vulg.* by *foedus*, *pactum*, *testamentum*. Hence Sc. *Covenanter* (hist.), subscriber to the *National Covenant* (1638) or the *Solemn League and Covenant* (1643).

Coventry, send to. In current sense from 18 cent. Origin unknown.

Bromigham [Birmingham] a town so generally wicked that it had risen upon small parties of the king's and killed or taken them prisoners and sent them to Coventry
(Clarendon, *Hist. of Great Rebellion*).

If Monsᵣ de Foscani be weary of Coventry, where he has been alone I believe these ten months, I know no reason why he may not remove to Lichfield: he desired himself to be sent to Coventry to avoid being with the French
(Marlborough, *Letter to Harley*, 1707).

cover. F. *couvrir*, L. *cooperire*; cf. It. *coprire*, Sp. *cubrir*. The vulgar *kiver* is ME. *kever*, regularly from OF. tonic stem *cuevr-* (cf. ME. *keverchefe*, kerchief). Some of the senses of the noun (*under cover*) are from F. *couvert*, orig. p.p. of *couvrir*, of which the OF. pl. was *coverz*. Hence *covert* for game. The participial sense survives in *covert glance* (*threat*, etc.). *Coverture*, protected state of married woman, *femme couverte*, is from Law F.

coverlet, coverlid. AF. *coverlit* (14 cent.), cover bed, formed like *curfew*, *kerchief* (q.v.). Not from ModF. *couvre-lit*, which is a neol.

covet. OF. *coveiter* (*convoiter*), VL. *cupiditare*, from *cupiditas*, desire; cf. It. *cubitare*, Prov. *cobeitar*.

covey. F. *couvée*, brood, p.p. fem. of *couver*, to brood, incubate, L. *cubare*; cf. It. *covata*, "a covie of partridges, a bevie of phesants, a broode of chickens, an ayrie of haukes" (Flor.).

cow¹. Noun. AS. *cū*. Aryan; cf. Du. *koe*, Ger. *kuh*, ON. *kȳr*, Sanskrit *gāus* (see *nylghau*, *Guicowar*); ult. cogn. with G. βοῦς, βο-, L. *bos*, *bov-*. *Kine* is a southern form (cf. *brethren*) of pl. *kye*, AS. *cȳ* (cf. *mouse*, *mice*), which was usual up to 17 cent. *Cowboy* (US.) was orig. used hist. of sympathizers with England in War of Independence (see Fenimore Cooper's *Spy*). *Cowhide*, whip, is also US. For *cowpox*, first investigated by Jenner (1798), see *pox*.

cow². Verb. ON. *kūga*, to cow, whence Norw. *kue*. First in Shaks. (*Macb.* v. 8). Owing to late appearance it is often felt as back-formation from *coward*.

cowage, cowitch. Plant. Hind. *kawānch*. Corrupted to *cowitch* owing to its stinging properties.

coward. Archaic F. *couard*, from OF. *coue* (*queue*), tail, L. *cauda*, with depreciatory suffix *-ard*, Ger. *-hart*, as in *bastard*, *laggard*, etc.; cf. It. *codardo*. No doubt an allusion to the tail between the legs. *Cowardy custard* seems to be meaningless infantile alliteration.

cower. Prob. of Norse origin; cf. Sw. *kura*, Dan. *kure*, to squat, and Ger. *kauern*, to cower. Influenced in sense by *cow*², ME. meaning being to squat, crouch.

cowitch. See *cowage*.

cowl¹. Garment. AS. *cugele*, Late L. *cuculla*, cowl, for *cucullus*, hood of a cloak; cf. MHG. *kugel*.

cowl² [*archaic*]. Tub. AS. *cūfel*, dim. from L. *cupa*; cf. Ger. *kübel*, tub, bucket, and see *coop*. Hence *cowl-staff*, for carrying a cowl.

cowrie. Hind. *kauṛī*. The use of the *cowrie* as money is mentioned by Chin. writers of 14 cent. B.C.

cowslip. AS. *cū-slyppe*, cow dung. Cf. *oxlip* and dial. *bull-slop*.

cowslope, herbe: herba petri (*Prompt. Parv.*).

cox. See *coxswain*.

coxal [*anat.*]. Of the hip, L. *coxa*.

coxcomb. Cock's comb. Orig. ornamentation of head-dress of professional fool.

If thou follow him, thou must needs wear my coxcomb (*Lear*, i. 4).

coxswain. Earlier *cock-swain*. See *cockboat* and *swain*. Orig. sailor in charge of boat (cf. *boatswain*). Hence, by incorr. separation, *cox* as noun and verb.

coy. F. *coi*, VL. **quetus* for *quietus*. In ME. first in etym. sense and usu. in to *hold* (*keep*) *oneself coy*, for F. *se tenir coi*.

coyote. Prairie wolf. Sp., Mex. *coyotl*.

coz. For *cousin*, which is usu. spelt *cozen* in 17 cent., e.g. in Pepys.

cozen. It. *cozzonare*, "to breake horses, to plaie the horse-courser, or knavish knave" (Flor.), "to have perfect skill in all cosenages" (Torr.), from *cozzone*, "a horse-courser, a horse-breaker, a craftie knave" (Flor.). Cf. to *jockey*. *Cozzone* is L. *coctio-n-* (for *cocio*), whence OF. & ME. *cosson*, horse-dealer. The word was app. brought to England by young nobles who included Italy in the grand tour. Often punningly connected with *cousin*. Earliest recorded in noun *cousoner* (1561).

By gar I am cozened, I ha married oon garsoon, a boy (*Merry Wives*, v. 5).

Cousins, indeed; and by their uncle cozened
Of comfort, kingdom, kindred, freedom, life
(*Rich. III*, iv. 4).

cozy. See *cosy*.

crab¹. Crustacean. AS. *crabba*; cf. Du. *krabbe*, and LG. *krabben*, to scratch, claw. Cogn. with Ger. *krebs* (see *crayfish*) and with *crawl*¹. With *crab*, capstan, orig. with claws, cf. *crane* and other animal names for mech. devices. With to *catch a crab*, as though a crab had got hold of the oar, cf. It. *pigliare un granchio* (crab), used of any kind of blunder. Verb to *crab*, to "pull to pieces," was orig. a term of falconry. Adj. *crabbed* referred orig. to the crooked, wayward gait of the crab, as still in *crabbed handwriting* (*style*, etc.), but has been affected in sense by the idea of sourness associated with *crab*². For formation cf. *dogged*.

crabbyd, awk, or wraw: ceronicus, bilosus, cancerinus (*Prompt. Parv.*).

crab². Apple. Possibly Sc. form *scrab* (Gavin Douglas), Sw. dial. *skrabba*, wild apple, is the older, in which case the E. form may have been assimilated to *crab*¹ as a depreciatory name for the fruit. Cf. double idea contained in *crabbed* (v.s.) and dial. *crabstick*, ill-tempered person, prop. crabtree cudgel. The existence of the common Yorks. surname *Crabtree* shows that the word must be some centuries older than the first *NED.* record (1420).

crack. First as verb, AS. *cracian*; cf. Du. *kraken*, Ger. *krachen*, F. *craquer*; of imit. origin, the name of the sound extending to the break which produces it. The ME. sense of uttering loudly survives in to *crack a joke*, and Sc. *crack*, to talk. That of boasting, praising, in to *crack up*, whence also use of *crack* for person or thing praised (*crack regiment*, etc.). *Crack of doom* is from *Macb.* iv. 1. *Cracksman*, burglar, is from *crack*, breaking open, in thieves' slang, as in to *crack a crib*, words popularized by Dickens (*Oliver Twist*). With *cracker*, thin, hard biscuit (now chiefly US.), cf. *cracknel* and *crackling*.

crackle. Frequent. of *crack*. Hence *crackling* (of roast pork). *Crackle*-china is so called from its fissured appearance; cf. synon. F. *craquelin*.

cracknel. Metath. of F. *craquelin*, from Du. *krakeling*; cf. E. dial. *crackling* and see *crack*.

craquelin: a cracknell; made of the yolks of egges, water, and flower; and fashioned like a hollow trendle (Cotg.).

And take with thee ten loaves, and cracknels [*Vulg. crustula*], and a cruse of honey (1 *Kings*, xiv. 3).

cracksman. See *crack*.

cracovienne [*archaic*]. Dance. F., from *Cracovie*, Cracow; cf. *varsovienne*, *polka*, etc.

-cracy. Earlier *-cratie*, F., MedL., G. *-κρατία*, from *κράτος*, power. Change of spelling is due to F. pronunc. Hence many jocular formations with connecting *-o-* (*mobocracy*, *cottonocracy*, *beerocracy*, etc.).

A democracy, a theocracy, an aristocracy, an autocracy, or any other form of "cracy"
(H. Belloc, *Daily News*, July 24, 1917).

cradle. AS. *cradol*, cogn. with OHG. *chratto*, basket; cf. Du. *krat*, basket. Applied techn. to various frame-works or rocking contrivances. *Cradle-walk* (Evelyn), overarched with trees, is translated from synon. F. *berceau*.

berceau: a cradle; also, an arbor, or bower in a garden (Cotg.).

The hand that rocks the cradle
Is the hand that rules the world
(W. R. Wallace, c. 1866).

craft. AS. *cræft*. Com. Teut. in sense of strength; cf. Du. *kracht*, Ger. *kraft*, ON. *kraptr*. Sense of skill, ingenuity, degenerating early to slyness, is peculiar to E. (cf. *artful*, *cunning*, *knowing*). This survives in *handicraft*, *witchcraft*, *craftsman*, *members of same craft*, etc. Sense of vessel, earlier only small vessel, and orig. (17 cent.) always accompanied by adj. *small*, prob. arose ellipt. from some such phrase as "vessels of small craft," small power and activity. *Aircraft* is, like all our air vocabulary, modelled on naut.

The lyf so short, the craft so long to lerne
(Chauc. *Parl. of Fowls*, 1).
Of his [a hockey-player's] stickcraft there is no question (*Daily Chron.* Nov. 26, 1919).

crag. Celt.; cf. Gael. Ir. *creag*, Welsh *craig*; cogn. with place-name *Carrick*.

crake. In *corn-crake*. Cf. ME. & dial. *crake*, crow, ON. *kråka*, crow, *kråkr*, raven. Imit.; cf. *croak*.

cram. AS. *crammian*, from *crimman* (*cram*, *crummen*), to insert, orig. to squeeze, press; cogn. with *cramp*. With *cram*, lie, cf. to *stuff up*. Locke uses *cram* of undigested learning.

The best fattening of all fowls is, first, to feed them with good meat, secondly, to give it them not continually, as crammers do (*NED.* 1655).

crambo. 16 cent. *crambe*, used of a riming game, capping verses, now usu. *dumb crambo*, and orig. of distasteful repetition. L. *crambe*, cabbage, G. *κράμβη*, with ref.

to *crambe repetita*, cabbage served up again.

Occidit miseros crambe repetita magistros
(Juv. vii. 154).
From thence to the Hague again, playing at crambo in the waggon (Pepys, May 19, 1660).

cramoisy [*archaic*]. F. *cramoisi*, crimson. See *carmine*, *crimson*.

cramp. OF. *crampe*, bent, twisted, of LG. origin (cf. Du. *kramp*), and cogn. with Ger. *krampf*, cramp, orig. adj., bent. Cogn. with *cram*, *crimp*, *crump-le*. In mech. sense (e.g. *cramp-iron*) it is the same word, prob. through obs. Du. *krampe* (*kram*). Both origins unite in some senses of the verb.

cran [*Sc.*]. Measure of fresh herrings (37½ gallons). Gael. *crann*, share, lot.

cranberry. Ger. *kranbeere*, crane berry, taken to NAmer. by emigrants, and introduced, with the fruit, into E. in 17 cent. For the double voyage cf. *boss*[2]. Cf. Sw. *tranbär*, Dan. *tranebær*, from *trana*, *trane*, crane.

Hujus baccas a Nova Anglia usque missas Londini vidimus et gustavimus (Ray, 1686).

crane. AS. *cran*; cf. Du. *kraan*, Ger. *kran-ich*; cogn. with L. *grus*, G. *γέρανος*, Welsh *garan*. The Norse langs. have *tr-*, e.g. ON. *trani*. The mech. application is found also in other langs. Cf. to *crane one's neck*, fig. to hesitate, like a horse "looking before leaping," *craning* at a fence.

grue: a crane; also, the engine so called (Cotg.).

cranium. MedL., G. *κρανίον*, skull.

crank[1]. Instrument, handle. AS. *cranc*, in *cranc-stæf*. Orig. something bent, cogn. with *cringe*, *cringle*, *crinkle*. Hence used, after Milton's *quips and cranks* (*Allegro*, 25), of fanciful twists or turns of speech. Sense of eccentricity is 19 cent., and *crank*, eccentric person, is US. (cf. *crook*). With *cranky*, of mod. formation and representing various senses of *crank*, cf. Ger. *krank*, ill. The verb to *come cranking in* is after Shaks.

See, how this river comes me cranking in,
And cuts me from the best of all my land
A huge half-moon, a monstrous cantle out
(1 *Hen. IV*, iii. 1).

crank[2] [*naut.*]. Easily capsized. Earlier *crank-sided* (Capt. John Smith). From Du. *krengen*, to push over, careen a ship, ult. cogn. with *crank*[1], in sense of turn.

crannog. Celt. lake-dwelling. Ir. *crannóg*, Gael. *crannag*, from *crann*, tree, beam.

cranny. App. from F. *cran*, earlier *cren*, VL. **crennum*. The dim. appears in *crenelate* (q.v.). Cf. It. *crena*, notch, indentation on leaves. L. *crena*, from which these words were formerly derived, is now regarded as a wrong reading in Pliny.

crape. F. *crêpe*, OF. *crespe*, L. *crispa*, curly (sc. *tela*).

crapulous. From L. *crapula*, drunkenness, G. κραιπάλη, drunken head-ache, nausea.

crash¹. Of noise, etc. First as verb in ME. Imit.; related to *crack* as *clash* to *clack*. Cf. Ger. *krach*, crash, commercial disaster, from *krachen*, to crack. Spec. application to fall of aeroplane dates from Great War.

crash². Coarse linen used for towels. From Russ. *krashenina*, coloured linen. Usu. *crasko* in Hakl. and Purch.

crasis [*ling.*]. Running together of vowels, as in κἀγώ for καὶ ἐγώ. G. κρᾶσις, mixture, from κεραννύναι, to mix.

crass. L. *crassus*, fat, thick. In F. only in fem. (*ignorance crasse*), L. *crassus* giving F. *gras*.

-crat. See *-cracy.*

cratch [*dial.*]. Manger. F. *crèche*, OHG. *chrippa* (*krippe*), ident. with *crib* (q.v.). Cf. *match²*, *patch.*

Sche childide her firste born sone, and wlappide him in clothis, and puttide him in a cracche
(Wyc. *Luke*, ii. 7).

crate. Du. *krat*, basket (see *cradle*). Prob. introduced with earthenware from Delft.

crater. L., bowl, G. κρατήρ, mixing-bowl (see *crasis*). Recorded for 1839 in mil. sense, now so familiar, of cavity caused by explosive.

craunch. Earlier used for *crunch* (q.v.). Prob. nasalized form of *crash¹*. *Scraunch* is also found (cf. *scrunch*).

Herke howe he crassheth these grystels bytwene his hethe (Palsg.).

The queen...would craunch the wing of a lark, bones and all, between her teeth (*Gulliver*).

cravat. F. *cravate* (17 cent.), scarf like those worn by Croatian soldiers (Thirty Years War). Cf. F. *Cravate*, Croat, Ger. *Krabate*, Flem. *Crawaat*, Croato-Serbian *Hrvat*. There is at Woodchurch, Kent, an inn called the *Jolly Cravat*, perh. founded by some returned soldier of fortune.

crabbat: ...a new fashionable gorget which women wear (Blount).

crave. AS. *crafian*, to demand as a right; cf. synon. ON. *krefja*; ? cogn. with *craft*, power. Current sense comes via that of

asking very earnestly (*I crave your pardon*), as still in *cravings of hunger*, etc.

craven. ME. *cravant*, *cravand*, vanquished, cowardly, app. confused, esp. in to *cry craven*, with the commoner *creant*, aphet. for *recreant* (q.v.). Related to OF. *craventer*, *crevanter*, to overthrow, VL. **crepantare*, for *crepare* (whence F. *crever*, to burst, etc.). It may be the F. p.p. with suffix lost as in *costive*, *defile²*, *trove*, or a verbal adj. of the same type as *stale*. Sense has been affected by association with *crave* (mercy, pardon, etc.).

craw. Crop of a bird. ME. *crawe*, cogn. with Du. *kraag*, neck, OHG. *chrago*; cf. Ger. *kragen*, collar, Sc. *cra(i)g*, neck. These forms point to an AS. **craga*.

crawfish. See *crayfish.*

crawl¹. Verb. ON. *krafla*, to claw; cf. Norw. *kravle*, to crawl, climb, Sw. *krafla*. Orig. to claw one's way. Cogn. with *crab¹*; cf. Ger. *krabbeln*, to crawl, from LG.

crawl² [*WInd.*]. Pen in water for turtles, etc. Var. of *corral*, *kraal* (q.v.).

crayfish, crawfish. Corrupted from ME. *crevesse*, F. *écrevisse*, OF. also *crevice*, OHG. *krebiz* (*krebs*), crab.

escrevisse: a crevice, or crayfish (Cotg.).

crayon. F., pencil, from *craie*, chalk, L. *creta*. Formerly used for *pencil* (q.v.).

craze. To break, crack, whence *crazed*, *crazy*. Aphet. for OF. *acraser*, var. of *escraser* (*écraser*), from Sw. *krasa*, to break, prob. related to *crash¹*. Orig. sense survives in ref. to china-ware (cf. *crackle*).

With glas
Were al the wyndowes wel y-glased
Ful clere, and nat an hole y-crased
(Chauc. *Blanche the Duchess*, 322).

I was yesterday so crased and sicke, that I kept my bedd all day (*Plumpton Let.* temp. Hen. VII).

creak. First used in ME. of cry of crows, geese, etc. Imit., cf. *crake*, *croak*.

cream. F. *crême*, OF. *cresme*, L. *chrisma* (see *chrism*). Referred by 16 cent. etymologists to L. *cremor lactis*, "creame of milke" (Coop.), which has no doubt influenced the sense-development. *Cream-laid paper* is *laid* (i.e. rolled, not wove) *paper* of *cream* colour and should rather be *cream laid-paper* (cf. *bespoke bootmaker*). *Cream* replaced native *ream* (see *reaming*).

crease¹. Inequality. Earlier (16 cent.) *creaste*, OF. *creste* (*crête*), crest, ridge, Lat. *crista*. Orig. the ridge as opposed to the corresponding depression. F. *crête* means ridge, not peak, e.g. *la crête d'une vague, d'un toit*, etc. Cf. US. *crease*, to stun (a horse, etc.) by a shot through the "crest" or ridge of the neck.

A rough harde stone, full of creastes and gutters
(Lyte's *Dodoens*, 1578).

Creasing consists in sending a bullet through the gristle of the mustang's neck, just above the bone, so as to stun the animal
(Ballantyne, *Dog Crusoe*, ch. xv.).

crease², creese, kris. Dagger. Malay *kirīs, krīs*, of Javanese origin.

Their ordinary weapon is called a crise, it is about two feet in length, the blade being waved, and crooked to and fro, indenture like
(Scot's *Java*, 1602–5).

creator. Church word, occurring earlier than the verb to *create*. F. *créateur*, L. *creator-em*, used in ME. for AS. *scieppend* (cf. Ger. *schöpfer*). *Creature*, in sense of drink, esp. Ir. *cratur*, is a spec. application of the word in the sense of product, thing created for the use of man (cf. *creature comforts*).

Good wine is a good familiar creature (*Oth*. ii. 3).

For, after death, spirits have just such natures
They had, for all the world, when human creatures
(Dryden).

crèche. Late 19 cent. from F., orig. manger in which Christ was born. Ger. *krippe* is used in same sense. See *cratch, crib*.

credence. F. *crédence*, It. *credenza*, VL. *credentia*, from *credere*, to believe. Sense of faith, confidence, is archaic in F., usual meaning being side-board, as in eccl. E. *credence-table* (19 cent.). This arose from the practice of "assaying" meat and drink at the side-board so as to inspire confidence against poison. Cf. *salver*.

credenza: credence, credite, trust, confidence, safe-conduct. Also a cubboarde of plate, a butterie.... Also the taste or assaie of a princes meate and drinke (Flor.).

credentials. From 17 cent., for earlier *letters of credence* (14 cent.).

credit. F. *crédit*, It. *credito*, p.p. of *credere*, to believe, trust. A *creditable* action orig. inspired trust.

credo. L., I believe, first word of Apostles' and Nicene Creeds. So in most Europ. langs. Cf. *angelus, ave, dirge*, etc.

credulous. From L. *credulus*, from *credere*, to believe.

creed. AS. *crēda*, L. *credo* (q.v.). Early Church word. The *Apostles' Creed*, trad. ascribed to the Apostles, dates from 4 cent. (exposition of Rufinus). See *Athanasian, Nicene*.

creek. Cf. F. *crique*, Du. *kreek*. In ME. usually *crike*, from F. ? ON. *kriki*, nook, bend, cogn. with *crook*.

He knew wel alle the havenes, as they were,
From Gootlond to the Cape of Fynystere,
And every cryke in Britaigne and in Spayne
(Chauc. A. 406).

a creek, crook, or nook to unload wares: crepido
(Litt.).

creel. OF. *greille*, grill, sieve, VL. *craticula*, from *crates*, wicker-work, hurdle; cf. OF. *creil*, hurdle. *Creel* is still in techn. and dial. use for various frame-works. See *grill*. Cf. It. *gradella*, creel.

creep. AS. *crēopan*, orig. strong (*crēap, cropen*); cf. Du. *kruipen*, ON. *krjūpa*. Cf. *cripple*.

creese. See *crease²*.

cremation. L. *crematio-n-*, from *cremare*, to burn. Hence *crematorium*, MedL., after *auditorium*, etc.

cremona. Violin from *Cremona*, in Lombardy. Also used wrongly for *cromorne* (q.v.).

crenate [*bot.*]. ModL. *crenatus*, notched (v.i.).

crenelate. To embattle. For earlier *crenel*, F. *créneler*, from OF. *crenel* (*créneau*), battlement, dim. of OF. *cren* (*cran*), notch (see *cranny*). The noun was common in ME. in forms *carnel, kernel*, etc.

creole. F. *créole*, earlier *criole*, Sp. *criollo*, orig. applied to all West Indians (white or black) wholly or partly of foreign parentage; now usu. to those of Europ. ancestry. Perh. corrupt. or dim. of Sp. *criado*, foster-child, L. *creatus*, said to have been orig. applied to the indoor slaves. Cf. OPort. *gallinha crioula*, pet hen.

criollos: those that are borne of the Spaniard and Indians (Minsh.).

creosote. Mod. formation from G. κρέας, flesh, and σώζειν, to save; from antiseptic properties. Discovered (1832) by Reichenbach.

crêpe. F., see *crape*.

crepitate. From L. *crepitare*, frequent. of *crepare, crepit-*, to crack, resound.

crépon. F., from *crêpe*, crape.

crepuscular. From L. *crepusculum*, twilight.

crescendo [*mus.*]. It., from L. *crescere*, to grow. Often fig. as noun, e.g. *a crescendo of admiration*.

crescent. Restored spelling, on L. *crescens, crescent-*, of ME. *cressant*, OF. *creissant* (*croissant*), pres. part. of *creistre* (*croître*), to grow, L. *crescere*. First applied to the growing moon. Often wrongly used, owing to its adoption by the Turk. Sultans, as a symbol of Mohammedanism in general. Russ. churches are often surmounted by the cross standing on the over-turned crescent, and *Red Crescent* is applied to a Turk. organization corresponding to our *Red Cross*.

cress. AS. *cærse, cerse, cresse*. WGer.; cf. Du. *kers*, Ger. *kresse*; also borrowed by Scand. & Rom. langs., e.g. F. *cresson*; perh. cogn. with OHG. *chresan*, to creep. Older form still in place-names, e.g. *Kersey*, cress island, and in *not to care a curse* (see *curse, damn*).

cresset. Portable beacon. OF. *craisset*, lantern, from OF. *craisse* (*graisse*), grease (with which a *cresset* is filled). See *grease*.

crest. OF. *creste* (*crête*), L. *crista*, crest of cock or helmet. *Crestfallen* belongs to cock-fighting. The *crest* of a horse is the neck ridge (see *crease*[1]).

cretaceous. From L. *cretaceus*, from *creta*, chalk, orig. p.p. of *cernere*, to separate (sc. *terra*).

Cretan. Liar (*Tit.* i. 12). Cf. *syncretism*.

An introduction to Dora might inspire some of these modern Cretans with a wholesome respect for the truth (*Pall Mall Gaz.* Jan. 30, 1918).

cretic [*metr.*]. Amphimacer. L. *Creticus*, of *Crete*.

crétin. Deformed idiot, in Alps. F., from Swiss dial. *crestin, creitin*, Christian. Cf. similar use of *innocent, natural*, also F. *benêt*, fool, L. *benedictus*.

cretonne. Made at *Creton* (Eure).

crevasse [*Alp.*]. F., see *crevice*.

crevice. ME. *crevace*, F. *crevasse*, from *crever*, to burst, L. *crepare*.

crew. Earlier (15 cent.) *crue*, also *accrue*, p.p. fem. of F. *croître, accroître*, to grow, OF. *creistre*, L. *crescere*. Orig. reinforcement, mil. or nav.; cf. *recruit*.

The forts thereabouts were not supplied with anie new accrewes of soldiers (Holinshed).

crewel. Earlier (1500–1600), *crule, crewle, croole, croile*, also *crewe, crue*. Origin doubtful ? F. *écru*, unbleached, L. *ex* and *crudus*, raw, as in *fil escru*, unbleached yarn (13 cent.), altered as *scroll* (q.v.). Another suggestion is OF. *escrouelles*, shreds (see *scroll*), which suits the form, but hardly the sense. It is not certain whether the name was orig. applied to the

yarn or to the material on which it was worked.

j fyne counterpoynt [counterpane] of sylk and cruell of Joseph and Mary (*Rutland MSS.* 1543).

crib. AS. *cribb*, ox-stall, etc. WGer.; cf. Du. *krib*, Ger. *krippe* (see also *cratch, crèche*); cf. MHG. *krebe*, basket, a common meaning of *crib* in E. dial., whence *crib*, to steal (cf. *cabbage*[2]), and hence, to cheat in schoolboy sense. The game of *cribbage* is from the *crib*, or store of cards, secured by the dealer. Earliest records refer chiefly to the *crib* in which Christ was born, hence later child's *crib*. The sense of small dwelling, etc., e.g. a *snug crib*, is evolved from that of ox-stall, the latest shade of meaning appearing in the burglar's to *crack a crib*.

Now, my dear, about that crib at Chertsey
(*Oliver Twist*, ch. xix.).

Crichton. All round gifted man. *James Crichton*, called "the Admirable" by Urquhart, soldier, scholar, swordsman, etc., killed in a brawl at Mantua (1585).

crick. Prob. cogn. with *crook*; cf. synon. F. *torticolis*, It. *torcicollo*, lit. twist-neck. Another name was *schote* (in *Prompt. Parv.* with *cryk*), with which cf. Ger. *schuss*, shooting, as in *hexenschuss*, lumbago.

cricket[1]. Insect. F. *criquet*, from *criquer*, "to creak, rattle, crackle" (Cotg.), imit. of sound; cf. Du. *krekel* and F. *cri-cri*. The *cricket on the hearth* is from Dickens after Milton (*Penseroso*, 82). With *merry as a cricket* (1 *Hen. IV*, ii. 4) cf. *grig*.

cricket[2]. Game. First recorded (*creckett*) 1598. App. first used of the wicket; cf. OF. *criquet*, stake used as goal at bowls, from Flem. *krick*, "scipio, baculus" (Kil.), cogn. with *crutch*. Cotg. gives *cricket-staffe* as one meaning of F. *crosse*, and Urquhart (*Rab.* i. 22) renders *la crosse* by *cricket*. The adoption of the word as emblem of fair-play is mod.

Last week a tryal was brought at Guildhall before the Lord Chief Justice Pratt, between two companies of cricket players, the men of Kent plaintiffs, and the men of London defendants, for sixty pounds, played for at cricket, and after a long hearing, my Lord, not understanding the game, ordered them to play it over again
(*Mist's Journal*, Mar. 28, 1719).

crikey [*vulg.*]. Euph. alteration of *Christ*. Cf. *lawks*.

crim. con. [*leg.*]. For *criminal conversation*.

crime. F., L. *crimen, crimin-*, from root of *cernere*, to separate, decide.

We share Dr Topinard's dislike of the term "criminal anthropology," and may adopt the term "criminology" till a better can be found
(*Athenaeum*, Sep. 6, 1890).

criminy, crimine [*colloq.*]. Suggested by *Christ* (cf. *crikey*) and *jiminy* (q.v.).

crimp. Du. *krimpen*, "contrahere, diminuere, arctare, coarctare, extenuare" (Kil.); cogn. with *cramp, crumple.* Fish are *crimped* to make their flesh contract. From the verb comes naut. *crimp*, perh. via an obs. (17 cent.) card-game.

to play crimp: to lay or bet on one side, and (by foul play) to let t'other win, having a share of it
(*Dict. Cant. Crew*).

crimson. Earlier (15 cent.) *cremesyn*, OSp. *cremesin (carmesi)* or OIt. *cremesino (cremesi)*, Arab. *qermazi*; cf. F. *cramoisi.* Ult. source is Arab. *qirmiz*, kermes, cochineal insect. See *kermes, carmine.*

cringe. Orig. trans. ME. *crengen*, causal of AS. *cringan*, to fall in battle, orig. to become bent, "succumb"; cogn. with *crank¹.*

cringle [*naut.*]. Ring. Earlier *creengle* (Capt. John Smith, 1627). From LG. or Du. Cf. Du. Ger. *kring*, circle, etc., ON. *kringja*, to encircle; cogn. with *crank¹, crinkle.*

crinite [*biol.*]. L. *crinitus*, from *crinis*, hair.

crinkle. Earlier also *crenkle*, frequent. from AS. *crincan*, var. of *cringan* (see *cringe*), or from cogn. LG. or Du. *krinkel*, turn, twist; cogn. with *crank¹, cringle.* Cf. *crinkum-crankum*, elaborately intricate, full of "crinks" and "cranks."

The house is crynkled to and fro,
And hath so queynte weyes for to go,
For it is shapen as the mase is wroght
(Chauc. *Leg. Good Women*, 2012).

crinoline. Orig. (c. 1830) stiff fabric with warp of thread and woof of horse-hair. F., 19 cent. coinage from *crin*, horse-hair L. *crinis*, and *lin*, flax, L. *linum.* Cf. *linoleum. Crinolette* is from c. 1880.

cripple. AS. *crypel*, cogn. with *crēopan*, to creep, crawl; cf. Du. *kreupel*, Ger. *krüppel* (from LG.), ON. *cryppill.*

crisis. L., G. κρίσις, decision, from κρίνειν, to judge. Earliest (16 cent.) in medicine.

crisp. AS. *crisp, cyrps*, L. *crispus*, curled. Hence surnames *Crisp, Cripps.* Mod. sense, opposed to flabby, now often fig., is from 16 cent.

crispin [*archaic*]. Shoemaker. From *St Crispin*, patron saint of the craft.

criss-cross. Now regarded as redupl. of *cross*, but orig. suggested by *christ-cross row* (see *Christ*).

la croix de par Dieu: the Christes-crosse-row; or, the hornebooke wherein a child learnes it (Cotg.).

cristate [*biol.*]. L. *cristatus*, from *crista*, crest.

criterion. G. κριτήριον, from κριτής, judge.

critic. L. *criticus* or F. *critique*, G. κριτικός from κρίνειν, to judge (v.s.). *Critique* is restored spelling, after F., of earlier *critick*, criticism.

croak. ME. *crouken, crowken.* Imit., cf. *crake, creak*, Ger. *krächzen*, F. *croasser.* Slang to *croak*, die, is from the sound of the death-rattle. *Croaker*, prophet of evil, alludes to the raven.

I would croak like a raven; I would bode, I would bode (*Troil. & Cress.* v. 2).

Croat [*hist.*]. See *cravat.* The lang. is Serb.

crochet. F., dim. of *croc*, hook·(see *crook*). Cf. Ger. *häkeln*, to crochet, from *haken*, hook.

crocidolite [*min.*]. Named (1831) from G. κροκίς, κροκιδ-, var. of κροκύς, nap of cloth, and λίθος, stone.

crock¹. Vessel. AS. *crocc, crocca*, pot. Com. Teut.; cf. Du. *kruik*, Ger. *krug*, ON. *krukka*; also in Rom. langs., e.g. F. *cruche*, and with cogn. forms in Celt. ? Cogn. with *cruse.*

crock². Duffer. Earlier (16 cent. Sc.) worn-out ewe; hence applied to horse and person. Various words of somewhat similar meaning in *krak-*, found in Scand. & LG., are app. related to *crack*, so that a *crack* and a *crock* may be etym. ident. It may however be noted that F. *cruche*, pitcher, *crock¹*, from OHG., also has the meaning of duffer, simpleton.

kraecke: jumentum coriaginosum (Kil.).

crocket [*arch.*]. AF. from ONF. form of *crochet*, hook. See *crochet, crotchet.*

Crockford. Clergy directory. From compiler of first issue (1865). Cf. *Bradshaw.*

crocodile. Restored spelling of ME. & OF. *cocodrille*, with corresponding forms, now also restored, in other Rom. langs. L., G. κροκόδειλος, lizard, applied by Herodotus to the crocodile of the Nile (cf. history of *alligator*). St Asterius, bishop of Amasia (4 cent.), explains that the crocodile weeps over the head of his victim, after devouring the body, not from repentance or sorrow, but because he regrets that the bony nature of the head makes it unsuitable for food—εἰς βρῶσιν οὐκ ἐπιτήδειον.

crocus. L., G. κρόκος, crocus, saffron; prob. of Semit. origin; cf. Heb. *karkōm*, Arab. *karkam*.

Croesus. King of Lydia (6 cent. B.C.), famed for wealth.

croft [*dial.*]. Small enclosed piece of arable land, and, in Sc., one worked by peasant tenant, *crofter*. Very common, also as *craft*, in place-names and surnames, but unfamiliar in some parts of the south. AS. *croft*, small field; cf. Du. *kroft, krocht*, hillock, land above water-level.

cromlech. Welsh, crooked stone, from *crom* fem. of *crwm*, bent, and *llech*, flat stone. Cf. *crumpet*.

cromorne [*mus.*]. Reed-stop in organ. F., Ger. *krummhorn*, crooked horn. Incorr. *cremona*.

crone. Usu. identified with archaic and dial. *crone*, worn-out ewe (cf. *crock*[2]), archaic Du. *kronje, karonje*, from Picard *carogne* (*charogne*), carrion (q.v.). The sense of hag is, however, much the older (Chauc.); and, though F. *charogne* is used as a term of abuse, the mental picture of a bent or crooked crone suggests a possible connection with Walloon *crôn*, bent, hunchbacked, Du. *krom* (cf. Ger. *krumm* and see *crumpet*).

This olde sowdanesse, cursed krone (Chauc. B. 432).

kronie: adasia, ovis vetula, rejecula; *ang.* crone
(Kil.).

karonie: cadaver, corpus mortuum (*ib*).

an old crone: vieille accroupie (Sherwood).

Marie Stuart avait eu des bontés pour le cron, Rizzio (V. Hugo, *L'Homme qui rit*).

crony. Earlier *chrony*. G. χρόνιος, from χρόνος, time, used in univ. slang for contemporary (v.i.). Skinner (1671) explains it as *vox academica*.

The scholar...content to destroy his body with night labours and everlasting study to overtake his chronyes and contemporaries
(1652, in *Hist. MSS. Various Collections*, ii. 207).

crook. ME. *crok*, ON. *krōkr*; cogn. with obs. Du. *croec*, OHG. *krāko*. The same root is represented in VL. (see *crochet, crocket, croquet, crosier*). US. *crook*, swindler, one who is not "straight," was perh. partly suggested by synon. F. *escroc*.

croon. Orig. Sc. Prob. of LG. origin; cf. Du. *kreunen*, earlier *kronen*, to whimper, groan.

crop. AS. *cropp*, head of herb, bunch of flowers, ear of corn, crop (of bird), kidney. Ground-sense appears to be swelling; cf. Du. *krop*, Ger. *kropf*, crop of bird, ON.

kroppr, hump. Has passed into Rom. langs. (see *group*). Sense of sprout, hence, in ME., product of soil, is E. only. Verb to *crop*, intrans. and trans. (to *crop up*, to *crop the hair*), arises naturally from the agricultural sense. *Crop-ear*, orig. of horses and dogs, was applied by Cavaliers to Roundheads, to suggest loss of ears at hands of executioner; cf. *croppy*, Ir. rebel (1798) wearing short hair as sign of sympathy with F. revolution. Sense of head, top-end, is obs. exc. in *neck and crop*, to *come a cropper* (cf. *header*). *Hunting-crop*, orig. switch, preserves the sense of shoot, slender growth, as in Chauc. (v.i.). See also *croup*[1].

Whan Zephirus eek with his swete breeth
Inspired hath in every holt and heeth
The tendre croppes (Chauc. A. 5).

houssine: a riding rod of holly; a holly wand; a crop of holly (Cotg.).

croquet. Popular in Ireland (c. 1830), introduced into England (c. 1850). Said to be from Brittany and to be etym. ident. with *crochet* (q.v.), ? curved stick used for mallet. But *croquet*, as now used in F., is from E. An earlier game of the type was *pall-mall* (q.v).

croquette. Kind of rissole. F., from *croquer*, to crunch.

crore [*Anglo-Ind.*]. One hundred lakhs (of rupees). Hind. *kror*, Sanskrit *koṭi*.

Words unintelligible to English ears, with lacs and crores, zemindars and aumils
(Macaulay, *Warren Hastings*).

crosier, crozier. For *crosier-staff*, the *crosier* being orig. the bearer (hence surname *Crosier*), ME. *crosier*, OF. *crossier*, from *crosse*, crook, pastoral staff, VL. **croccia*, bent (see *crook*). Not immediately related to *cross*, though often confused with it in ME. and by mod. eccl. writers. The first quot. below shows that the *crosse* was a "crook," not a "cross," while the second is an example of early confusion between the two. Cf. *lacrosse*.

A bisschopes crosse [*var.* croce]
Is hoked in that one ende to halie men fro helle
(*Piers Plowm.* B. viii. 94).

crocer: crociarius, cruciferarius (*Prompt. Parv.*).

cross. The adoption of the Roman gibbet as symbol of Christianity has resulted in a large contribution to the Europ. vocabulary. Lat. *crux, cruc-*, gave F. *croix*, Sp. *cruz*, It. *croce*, Ger. *kreuz*, and late AS. *crūc*, replacing earlier *rōd* (*rood*). From AS *crŭc* comes ME. *cruche, crouche* (whence *Crutched Friars, Crouch End*, etc.), gradually superseded by northern *cross*, late AS. *cros* (in north country place-names), from ON. *kross*. In southern ME. *crois*, from OF., is the usual form. *Crossbow*, contrasted with *longbow*, is 15 cent., but the weapon (*arbalest*) is much older. As adj. applied to persons (from 17 cent.) *cross* is a fig. use of earlier sense of athwart, opposed to; cf. *cross as two sticks*. *Crosspatch* prèserves archaic *patch*, fool, child. *Cross-grained* was first used of "obstinate" timber, and quot. below is much earlier than *NED*. With *on the cross* (slang), i.e. not straight, cf. *queer*. As prefix *cross-* is sometimes aphet. for *across-*, e.g. in *cross-country*, with which cf. *longshore*.

His Majesty [James I] protested very earnestly the cross grain was in the men and not in the timber
(Phineas Pett, 1609).

crosse. See *lacrosse*.

crotalus. Rattle-snake. From G. κρόταλον, rattle.

crotch [*dial. & US.*]. Fork in various senses. F. *croche*, fem. of *croc*, hook, VL. **croccus* (see *crook*); but in some senses for *crutch* (q.v.).

crotchet [*mus.*]. F. *crochet*, little hook (v.s.). It is doubtful, in spite of Cotg. (v.i.), whether *crotchet*, whim (16 cent.), arises from the mus. sense; it seems rather to contain the idea of kink, twist, "crank."

crochüe: a quaver in musicke; whence *il a des crochües en teste* (we say) his head is full of crotches
(Cotg.).

croton. G. κροτών, a tick, dog-louse, and hence the castor-oil plant, named from the shape of its seed.

crouch. Late ME., perh. suggested by combination of *crook, cringe* and *couch*. Cf. *lion couchant* and *crouching lion*. OF. *crochir*, given by some, is a very rare word, and would hardly give *crouch*.

Issachar is a strong ass couching down between two burdens (*Gen.* xlix. 14).

croup[1]. Of a horse. F. *croupe*, of Teut. origin and ident. with *crop* (q.v.), in sense of rounded protuberance. Cf. ON. *kroppr*, hump, protuberance, Norw. Dan. *krop*, body, trunk. See *crupper, group*.

croup[2]. Disease. Sc., orig. verb, to croak hoarsely. Imit.

croupier. F., orig. one who rides behind, *en croupe*, hence one acting as second to gamester, etc. See *croup*[1].

Le cavalier croupier se laissa tomber à terre
(Scarron).

crow[1]. Bird. AS. *crāwe*, imit. of cry, AS. *crāwan*, to crow; cf. Du. *kraai, kraaijen*, Ger. *krähe, krähen*, etc. So also L. *cornix, corvus*, from imit. *cor*! To *have a crow to pluck* (15 cent. *pull*) *with* suggests animals struggling over prey, and has numerous parallels in other langs.

So longe mote ye live, and alle proude,
Til crowes feet be growe under your ye
(Chauc. *Troil.* ii. 402).

crow[2]. Tool, crowbar. Now usu. *crow-bar*. Although early associated with *crow*[1] and fig. use of L. *corvus*, this is a separate word. The oldest examples are always *crows* (*croes*) *of iron*, representing synon. OF. *cros* (pl. of *croc*, hook, crook) *de fer*. In early use we find in same sense *crome, crone*, both ult. from Du. *krom*, bent.

crow[3]. Mesentery, esp. in *liver and crow*. Cf. obs. Du. *kroos*, giblets, Ger. *gekröse*, cogn. with *kraus*, curly, from appearance. See *frill*.

crowd[1]. Multitude. First as verb; noun only from 16 cent., replacing earlier *press*. AS. *crūdan*, to press, push (cf. to *crowd sail*). US. *crowd*, to hustle, bully (*Brer Rabbit*), is prob. from cogn. LG. or Du. form. For sense-development cf. *press, throng*, and F. *foule*, crowd, from *fouler*, to trample, press. See *curd*.

One crowded hour of glorious life
Is worth an age without a name
(quoted by Scott, *Old Mortality*, ch. xxxiv., from
T. O. Mordaunt).

crowd[2] [*archaic & dial.*]. Fiddle (*Ivanhoe*, ch. xli.). Welsh *crwth*. See *rote*[1]. Hence surname *Crowder, Crowther*.

He herde a symphonye and a crowde
(Wyc. *Luke*, xv. 25).

crown. AF. *coroune*, OF. *corone* (*couronne*), L. *corona*, from G. κορωνός, curved. In most Europ. langs., but rendered in AS. by *cyne-helm*, royal helmet, the (royal) crown being orig. Oriental. The *crown of the head* was orig., like F. *couronne*, applied to the tonsure. With *the crown of the causeway*, i.e. the highest and central part of the road, cf. F. *le haut du pavé*, both expressions going back to a time when there were no side-walks and the "weakest went to the wall." The first E. *crown-pieces* were coined (1526) by Henry VIII, the name having been used earlier for various

F. coins marked with the crown. *Crown octavo* had a crown as watermark; cf. *foolscap, crown Derby*. *Crowning mercy* was used by Cromwell in his dispatch after Worcester (1651).

The crowning mercy of Ypres in 1914
(*Daily Tel.* Oct. 31, 1917).

crowner. See *coroner*.

croydon. Gig. From *Croydon* (Surr.); cf. *berlin, landau.*

crozier. See *crosier.*

crucial. Explained by Bacon as from L. *crux*, cross, in sense of finger-post at cross-roads, where decision has to be made as to course, "parting of the ways." In mod. use associated with *crux*, difficulty, from scholastic L. *crux* (martyrdom, torture) *interpretum.*

crucible. MedL. *crucibulum*, as though from *crux*, cross, with suffix as in *thuribulum*, censer; cf. OF. *croiseul, croiset, creuseul*, crucible (now *creuset*). But the first element is prob. MHG. *krŭse*, earthen pot (see *cruse*).

creuset: a crucible, cruzet, or cruet; a little earthen pot, wherein goldsmiths melt their silver, etc.
(Cotg.).

cruciferous [*bot.*]. Plant with flower having four petals arranged cross-wise. See *cross, -ferous.*

crucifix. Orig. the Crucified One. F., L. *crucifixus*, fixed to the cross. *Crucify*, F. *crucifier*, is Late L. **crucificare* for *cruci figere.*

He that swears by the Cross swears by the Holy Crucifix, that is, Jesus crucified thereon
(Jeremy Taylor).

crude. L. *crudus*, raw, cogn. with *cruor*, blood.

cruel. F., L. *crudelis*, from *crudus* (v.s.).

cruet. In E. first of vessel used in Eucharist. AF. dim. of OF. *cruie*, pot, OLG. *krŭga, krŭca* (cf. Ger. *krug*, E. *crock*), whence also F. *cruche*, pitcher.

Waischingis of cuppis and cruetis [Tynd. cruses]
(Wyc. *Mark*, vii. 4).

cruise. Spelt (17 cent.) after Du. *kruisen*, from *kruis*, cross (cf. Ger. *kreuzen* from *kreuz*); but prob. from Sp. Port. *cruzar*, to cruise, or F. *croisière*, a cruise. In any case ult. from L. *crux*, cross, with ref. to varying direction.

crumb. AS. *cruma*; cf. Du. *kruim*, Ger. *krume* (from LG.); cogn. with Ger. *krauen*, to scratch. Hence *crumble.*

crump. A hard hit, from verb *crump*, orig. of "crunching" food. Much used of shells at the front.

Until he's got a crump on his coker-nut, the old Turk doesn't know when he's beat (T. Atkins).

crumpet. App. ME. *crompid*, p.p. of *crump*, to bend, curl up, from archaic adj. *crump*, crooked (still as surname), AS. *crump*, cogn. with *cramp, crimp*; cf. Ger. *krumm*, OHG. *krumpf*. Gael. Ir. *crom*, bent, crooked, whence *Crummie*, "cow with crumpled horn," is prob. cogn. For final *-t* cf. *pouncet-box, stickit minister.*

A crusted cake spreynde with oyle, a crompid cake [*Vulg.* lagenum, *AV.* wafer] (Wyc. *Ex.* xxix. 23).

crumple. From obs. *crump* (v.s.). *Crumpled roseleaf* goes back to the Sybarite mentioned by Seneca (*De Ira*, ii. 25), who felt ill "quod foliis rosae duplicatis incubuisset."

crunch. Mod. var. of *craunch* (q.v.), perh. influenced by *crump.*

crupper. Orig. tail-strap. F. *croupière*; see *croup*[1]. For transference to part of body cf. *saddle* (of mutton).

crural [*anat.*]. L. *cruralis*, from *crus, crur-*, leg.

crusade. Earlier *croisad, croisado, crusada*, etc.; cf. F. *croisade*, replacing (after Sp. *cruzada*) OF. *croisée*, p.p. fem. of *croiser*, to take the cross. A 16 cent. word in E., superseding earlier *croiserie, croisee*, from OF.

The Americans are the greatest crusaders there iver was—for a shorrt distance (*Dooley*, 1919).

crusado. Coin. Port. *cruzado*, marked with cross; cf. Ger. *kreutzer.*

cruse [*archaic*]. Cf. Du. *kroes*, Ger. *krause*, ON. *krūs*. Ult. source unknown, but app. Teut. and cogn. with *crock*[1]. Cf. *crucible.*

kroes: a cup to drink out. *smelt-kroes*: a crucible
(Sewel).

crush. OF. *croissir, cruissir*; cf. It. *crosciare*, Sp. *crujir*; of Teut. origin; cf. Goth. *kriustan*, to gnash the teeth (*Mark*, ix. 18). In E. orig., as in OF., of clash of weapons, its earlier senses now being taken by *crash*. In current sense since Shaks. With archaic to *crush a pot* (*cup*) (*Rom. & Jul.* i. 2) cf. to *crack a bottle* (see 2 *Hen. IV*, v. 3).

crust. OF. *crouste* (*croûte*), L. *crusta*, or, in some senses, immediately from L. Cf. *crustacean*, hard-shelled. *Crusty*, ill-tempered, ? hard and cornery like crust, has perh. been associated with *curst*, peevish, shrewish, used repeatedly of Katherine in the *Taming of the Shrew*.

Thou crusty batch of nature (*Troil. & Cress.* v. 1).

crutch. AS. *crycc*; cf. Du. *kruk*, Ger. *krücke*; cogn. with *crook*, orig. sense being staff with bent handle. AS. *crycc* is also used for crosier. Some connect this group with L. *crux*, *cruc-*, cross, staff with cross-piece.

Crutched Friars. Order of friars carrying, or wearing, a cross, ME. *crouch* (see *cross*). They appeared in E. in 1244 and were suppressed in 1656. Hence street in London; cf. *Blackfriars*, *Whitefriars*, *Austin Friars*.

Fratres dicti cruciferi, dicti sic, quia cruces in baculis efferebant (Matt. Paris, 1259).

crux. L., cross. See *crucial.*

cry. F. *crier*, ? VL. **critare*, L. *quiritare*, to summon to one's help the *Quirites*, citizens; cf. It. *gridare*, Sp. *gritar*. A rival, and more likely, etym. is from Goth. **kreitan*, to cry out, shriek, corresponding to MHG. *krizen*, Ger. *kreischen*. Also it is prob. that *quiritare* is of imit. origin and only connected by folketym. with *Quirites*. Since 16 cent. has replaced *weep* in colloq. E. *Much cry and little wool* is from the proverbial uselessness of shearing hogs (see *wool*). A *crying injustice* (*wrong*, etc.) is one that "cries to heaven" for vengeance (*Gen.* iv. 10). The *crier* became the rival of the beadle c. 1300.

Does ever any man cry stinking fish to be sold?
(Jer. Taylor)

cryo-. From G. κρύος, frost.

crypt. L. *crypta*, G. κρυπτή, vault, etc., from κρύπτειν, to hide. First in sense of grot (q.v.), arch. sense being mod. Cf. *cryptic*, hidden, mysterious; *cryptogram*, hidden writing, cipher, esp. in ref. to Ignatius Donnelly's Bacon-Shakspeare cryptogram (1888); *cryptogamia* (bot.), without stamens or pistils, from G. γάμος, marriage.

crystal. Restored spelling of F. *cristal*, G. κρύσταλλος, clear ice, from κρύος, frost.

cteno-. From G. κτείς, κτεν-, comb.

cub. Orig. young fox (Palsg.), as still in *cub-hunting*; cf. Norw. *kobbe*, Icel. *kobbi*, seal, which, like *cub*, are prob. related to Norw. *kubbe*, *kub*, block, stump, cogn. with *cob*[1], from idea of shapelessness (v.i.). Has replaced *whelp* in some senses. *Unlicked cub* refers to the popular belief that the bear "licks into shape" its young; cf. F. *ours mal léché.*

cubby-house. From archaic and dial. *cub*, crib, partition, etc., with various LG. cognates. Cf. Ger. *koben*, from MHG. *kobe*, sty, cage, cogn. with *cove*[1] (q.v.). *Cobhouse* occurs in ME. (*Cleanness*, 629).

cube. F., L., G. κύβος, orig. a die for play. Hence *cubist* (neol.), eccentric artist.

cubeb. Berry. F. *cubèbe*, MedL. *cubeba* (as in It. & Sp.), Arab. *kabābah.*

cubicle. L. *cubiculum*, from *cubare*, to lie. A ME. word revived in 19 cent.

cubit. L. *cubitus*, arm from elbow to finger tips, from *cubare*, to recline. Cf. *ell, foot*, etc.

cucking-stool [*hist.*]. Instrument for punishing scolds, etc. From obs. verb *cuck*, stercorare, ON. *kûka*. From its orig. form.

That ther be a cookestowle made to punysche skolders and chidders (*Coventry Leet Book*, 1423).

cuckold [*archaic*]. ME. *cukeweld*, *cokewald*, etc., OF. *cucualt*, *coucuol*, formed, with suffix *-ald*, Ger. *-wald*, from *coucou*, cuckoo, from some belief as to the habits of the hen-bird; cf. F. *cocu.*

Who hath no wyf he is no cokewold
(Chauc. A. 3152)

cuckoo. F. *coucou*, imit. of cry. Cf. L. *cuculus*, G. κόκκυξ, Ger. *kuckuck*, etc. The AS. name was *gēac*, cogn. with Ger. *gauch*, now meaning fool, gowk.

cucumber. OF. *cocombre* (*concombre*), L. *cucumis*, *cucumer-*. Spelt and pronounced *cowcumber* in 17–18 cents., as by the author's grandfather (†1876), a country schoolmaster. Cf. *sparrowgrass.*

cud. AS. *cwudu*, *cudu*, cogn. with OHG. *chuti*, *quiti*, glutinous substance (*kitt*, plaster, glue). Cf. *quid*[1]. For fig. sense cf. *ruminate.*

cudbear. Dye from lichen. Coined from his own name by patentee, *Cuthbert Gordon* (18 cent.).

cuddle. Of late appearance (18 cent.). App. a mod. variation (after *mull*, *muddle*, *mell*, *meddle*, etc.) on archaic *cull*, *coll*, to embrace, OF. *acoler*, from *col*, neck.

cuddy[1] [*naut.*]. Du. *kajuit*, earlier *kajute*, F. *cahute*, little hut, perh. from *hutte*, hut, influenced by *cabane*, cabin. In Pepys (May 14, 1660).

kaiute, *kaiwyte*: cubile naucleri, cubiculum navarchi. *Gal.* cahute, casa (Kil.).

cuddy[2] [*dial.*]. Donkey. From name *Cuthbert* (cf. *Cuddy Headrigg* in *Old Mortality*); cf. *dicky*, *neddy*, in same sense.

cudgel. AS. *cycgel*. Earliest sense perh. dart (cf. OF. *boujon*, *garrot*, *materas*, all of which mean heavy-headed dart and also club); cogn. with Ger. *kugel*, ball, *keule*, cudgel. Currency of to *cudgel one's brains* (cf F. *se rompre la tête*, Ger. *sich den kopf zerbrechen*) is revived from Shaks. (*Haml.* v. 1).

I am ready to take up the cudgels in his defence
(T. Brown, c. 1700).

cue¹. Pigtail, billiard cue. F. *queue*, tail (also in both E. senses), L. *cauda*. See *queue*. ? Orig., in billiards, applied to the tapering end of the stick.

cue² [*theat.*]. Earlier *q*, explained in 17 cent. as abbrev. of L. *quando*, when (to come in), in stage-directions. Hence to *take one's cue from*, *be in the cue for*, etc.

> "Deceiving me" is Thisbe's cue; she is to enter, and I am to spy her through the wall
>   (*Mids. N. Dream*, v. 1).

cuff¹. Mitten. ME. *coffe*, *cuffe*. If orig. sense was covering in general, it may be related to *coif* (q.v.); or, if it were possible to fill in the history of *handcuff* (q.v.) between AS. and Defoe, it might be a playful application of that word. L. *manica* means both cuff and handcuff.

cuff². Buffet. First as verb. Cf. synon. LG. *kuffen*, Sw. dial. *kuffa*, to push roughly; ? cogn. with *cow²*.

> *I cuffe one, I pomell hym about the heed:* je torche
>   (Palsg.).

cui bono. L., to whose advantage? Attributed by Cicero to Lucius Cassius. Often wrongly used in E., as though, to what purpose?

> Lucius Cassius ille, quem populus Romanus verissimum et sapientissimum judicem putabat, identidem in causis quaerere solebat, "Cui bono fuisset?"
>   (*Pro Roscio Amer.* cap. xxx.).

cuirass. F. *cuirasse*, from *cuir*, leather, L. *corium*; cf. It. *corazza*, Sp. *coraza*. A backformation *curat* was common in 16–17 cents.

> These arrowes...pierce quilted breast-plates or curates (Purch. xvi. 430).

cuisine. F., VL. *coquina* (from *coquere*, to cook), for *culina*; cf. It. *cucina*, and see *kitchen*.

cuisse, cuish [*hist.*]. Thigh armour (1 *Hen. IV*, iv. 1). ME. pl. *cuissues*, OF. *cuisseaux*, pl. of *cuissel* (from *cuisse*, thigh, L. *coxa*, hip), became *cuisses*, whence new sing.

Culdee [*hist.*]. Scoto-Ir. rel. order (Iona, 8 cent.). OIr. *céle dé*, friend or servant of God. Later form is due to a fancied etym. *cultor Dei*.

cul de lampe, cul de sac. F. *cul*, bottom, L. *culus*.

-cule. L. dim. suffix *-culus*, *-a*, *-um*.

culinary. L. *culinarius*, from *culina*, kitchen. See *kiln*.

cull. F. *cueillir*, from L. *colligere*, to collect. Cf. *coil¹*.

cullender. See *colander*.

culm¹ [*dial.*]. Soot, coal-dust. Also *coom*. ? Cf. Ger. *qualm*, Du. *kwalm*, reek, smoke.

> *colme of a smek*: ffuligo (*Prompt. Parv.*).

culm² [*bot.*]. L. *culmus*, stalk.

culminate. From Late L. *culminare*, from *culmen*, *culmin-*, summit.

culpable. Restored spelling of ME. *coupable*, F., L. *culpabilis*, from *culpa*, fault.

culprit. Prop. only in "Culprit, how will you be tried?" said by Clerk of Crown to prisoner pleading not guilty. Supposed to have arisen from written contr. *cul. prest*, for Law F. *culpable*; *prest à averer nostre bille*, (you are) guilty; (I am) ready to prove our case. *Culprit* occurs first in trial for murder of Earl of Pembroke (1678), but *non cul. prist* is found in a 16 cent. abridgment of Assize records of 13 cent. The above explanation, given by Blackstone, is not altogether satisfactory.

cult. F. *culte*, L. *cultus*, from *colere*, *cult-*, to cultivate, worship, etc. Cf. *culture*.

cultivate. From Late L. *cultivare* from *cultiva* (*terra*), from *colere*, *cult-* (v.s.). Cf. *colony*, *kultur*.

culver [*archaic*]. Dove, pigeon. AS. *culfre*. No cogn. forms known, unless it was in some way altered from L. *columba*.

> He say the Spirit of God cummynge doun as a culver [Tynd. dove] (Wyc. *Matt.* iii. 16).

culverin [*hist.*]. Long cannon. F. *couleuvrine*, from *couleuvre*, snake, from L. *coluber*. Cf. *falconet*, Ger. *feldschlange*, etc.

culvert. From c. 1770. ? Name of some engineer or bridge-builder (cf. *macadam*).

cumber. First as verb (c. 1300), corresponding to F. *encombrer*, from Late L. *combrus*, barrier, weir, of doubtful origin, prob. Celt. Cf. Du. *kommer*, Ger. *kummer*, It. *ingombro*, etc., from Late L.

Cumbria. See *Cambria*.

cumin, cummin. AS. *cymen*, L. *cuminum*, G. κύμινον, Heb. *kammōn* or Arab. *kammūn*. In most Europ. langs., e.g. It. *cumino*, Ger. *kümmel*. Now usu. with ref. to *Matt.* xxiii. 23.

> The false values which our educational authorities attach to the mint and cummin of theology
>   (*Sunday Times*, Mar. 3, 1918).

cummer, kimmer [*Sc. & north.*]. Female friend, gossip. F. *commère*, fellow godmother. See *compeer*, *gossip*.

cummerbund. Urdu *kamar-band*, loin-band, from Pers.

cummin. See *cumin*.

cumulate. From L. *cumulare*, from *cumulus*, heap.

cuneate, cuneiform. From L. *cuneus*, wedge.

cunning. Midl. form of pres. part. of ME. *cunnen*, to know, AS. *cunnan*. Later extended to south. For degeneration cf. *knowing, crafty*, etc. See *can*[1], *con*[1].

The sone of Ysaye Bethlemyte, kunnynge [*Vulg.* sciens] to harpe (Wyc. 1 *Sam.* xvi. 18).

cup. AS. *cuppe*, Late L. *cuppa* for *cupa* (see *coop*); cf. F. *coupe*, Sp. Port. *copa*. Du. *kop*, OHG. *kopf*, beaker (now, head), etc. With *in one's cups* cf. obs. *in one's pots* (Purch.). A *cupboard* was orig. a table, side-board.

The cups that cheer, but not inebriate
(Cowper, *Task*, iv. 39).

A cupboard love is seldom true (*Poor Robin*, 1757).

cupel. Vessel used in assaying. F. *coupelle*, dim. of *coupe*, cup, goblet.

cupid. L. *cupido*, from *cupere*, to desire. Cf. *cupidity*, L. *cupiditas*; *cupidinous* (Meredith).

cupola. It., from L. *cupa*, cask, tun (see *coop*).

cupreous. From L. *cupreus*, from *cuprum*, copper (q.v.).

cur. Earlier (13 cent.) *cur-dog*, prob. from Sw. or Norw. dial. verb *kurre, korre*, from ON. *kurra*, to grumble. This seems confirmed by the same word having been applied to the gurnard (q.v.), and also to a kind of duck with croaking cry.

cuculo: a fish called a gournard or cur (Flor.).

curaçao. From name of island off Venezuela, whence also *curassow*, kind of turkey. Commonly misspelt (cf. *cocoa*).

curare. Indian arrow poison from Guiana. Carib *ourari, ourali*, etc., the *c*- being an attempt at a native init. "click." Cf. *wourali*. Laurence Keymis (1596) gives *ourari* as one of the "poysoned hearbes" of Guiana.

Mason showed some of the curari, or Indian arrow poison (*Nottingham Guard.* Feb. 5, 1917).

curassow. See *curaçao*.

curate. MedL. *curatus*, entrusted with a cure (of souls), whence F. *curé*, from L. *cura*, care, cure (of souls). ModE. sense (about equivalent to F. *vicaire*) is evolved from that of priest put in charge during absence of incumbent. See *vicar*, and cf. *curator* (L.).

curb. F. *courber*, to bend, VL. **curbare* for *curvare*. Hence *curb-stone, kerb*.

curcuma. Arab. *kurkum*, saffron, turmeric.

curd. ME. *crudde*, prob. from AS. *crūdan*, to press (see *crowd*[1]); cf. relation of L. *coagulum*, curd, to *cogere* (*co-agere*), to press; hence *curdle*.

cure[1]. To heal. F., L. *curare*, from *cura*, care. Oldest E. sense, of spiritual care, as in *cure of souls*. Sense of healing, found in Wyc., though *AV*. prefers *heal*, develops from gen. sense of caring for, seeing to (cf. to *cure bacon*). *Curator* is in Lydgate.

cure[2] [*slang*]. Short for *curio* or *curiosity*.

curé. F., see *curate*.

curfew. AF. *covre-fu, cure-fu*, cover (imper.) fire. See *cover* and *focus*. In gen. use in Med. Europe; not introduced by the Conqueror.

curia. Court, esp. Papal; hence *curial-ism*. L., division of orig. Roman tribe; hence, senate, senate-house.

curio. Abbrev. (19 cent.) of *curiosity*.

curious. F. *curieux*, L. *curiosus*, inquisitive, caring for, from *cura*, care. The later objective sense, exciting attention, has many parallels in the hist. of adjectives, e.g. *nauseous* was earlier used in sense of squeamish. For an opposite example see *fastidious*.

curl. First as adj. ME. *crul*; cogn. with Du. *krul*, Ger. *krolle*, curl (from LG.). For metath. cf. *curd, cress*. The game of *curling* is so called from the curving path of the stones, like that of a bowl. Cf. Flem. *krullebol*, bowl[2].

With lokkes crulle as they were leyd in presse
(Chauc. A. 81).

curlew. F. *courlieu, courlis*, with many dial. vars. App. imit. of cry (cf. *peewit*).

curmudgeon. "An avaricious, churlish fellow; a miser; a niggard" (Johns.). Origin unknown. Johns. gave, from an "unknown correspondent," as suggested etym., F. *cœur méchant*, which led Ash in his *Dict.* (1775) to give the derivation from F. *cœur* unknown, and *méchant*, a correspondent. It may be noted, however, that the spelling *curmegient* is found (1626), and that *Curmegan*, occurring as a medieval nickname or surname (*Ramsey Cartulary*), is not impossibly F. *cœur méchant*.

currant. Orig. (14 cent.) AF. *raisins de Coraunte*, Corinth grapes, the small fruit imported dried from the Levant. Applied, from resemblance of clusters, to garden currant (*riba*) introduced in 16 cent. This was called by Lyte (1578) the "beyond sea gooseberry" or "bastard currant."

Both the gooseberry and garden currant are called *groseille* in F.

Pro viij lb. racemorum de Coraunt
(*Earl of Derby's Exped*. 1390–93).

groiselles: gooseberries; thorne-berries; fea-berries; *groiselles noires*: blacke gooseberries, blacke ribes; an ill-tasting kinde of the beyond-sea gooseberrie; *groiselles rouges*: red gooseberries, beyond-sea gooseberries, garden currans, bastard currans (Cotg.).

currency. Former name for Austral. born, from fig. comparison between colonial and imperial (sterling) currency.

You're a regular currency lass...always thinking about horses (Rolf Boldrewood).

current. From pres. part. of L. *currere*, to run, replacing ME. *corant*, *couraunt*, from OF. With *current coin* cf. F. *argent de cours*.

curricle [*archaic*]. L. *curriculum*, race-course, racing chariot, dim. of *currus*. Cf. *curriculum*, academic "course."

curry[1]. To dress (a horse or leather). OF. *correer* (*corroyer, courroyer*), to prepare, VL. *con-red-are, from Teut. root of *ready* (q.v.); see *array*, and cf. It. *corredare*, to fit out. ModF. *courroyer* is partly due to association with *courroie*, strap, L. *corrigia*. For limitation of sense cf. Ger. *gerben*, to tan, lit. to make ready, from *gar*, cogn. with Shaks. *yare* (*Temp*. i. 1). To *curry favour* is folk-etym. for ME. *curry favel* (c. 1400), from *Favel*, OF. *Fauvel*, the name of a fawn coloured horse (see *fallow*) used as type of hypocrisy in a 14 cent. F. allegory. The name is explained for edification as an acrostic from the vices *Flatterie, Avarice, Vilenie, Variété, Envie, Lâcheté*. Hence we have to *curry acquaintance* (*pardon*, etc.).

curryfavell, a flatterar: estrille-fauveau (Palsg.).

curry[2]. Dish. Earlier (16–17 cents.) *carriel, carree* (cf. F. *cari*, Port. *caril*). Tamil *kari*, Canarese *karil*, sauce, relish.

curse. First as noun, late AS. *curs*, of unknown origin. I suggest that it may be F. *courroux*, or rather OF. *coroz* (10 cent.), Norman *curuz* (*Laws of William the Conqueror*). The first example of *curse* is *Goddes curs* (11 cent.) which may very well mean orig. wrath. With the verb, late AS. *cursian*, cf. OF. *corocier* (*courroucer*), *corecier, curcier*, the last form being esp. AF., VL. *corruptiare, with forms in other Rom. langs. Not *to care a curse* is prob. ME. *kers*, cress (*Piers Plowm*.), though there is a gap between that and mod. use (see note on *damn*). The *curse of Scotland*, i.e. nine of

diamonds (recorded from 1710), is prob. from its resemblance to the arms (nine lozenges on a saltire) of Dalrymple, Lord Stair, instigator of the Massacre of Glencoe (1692) and of the Parliamentary union (1707).

Wisdome and witte now is nought worth a carse [*var.* kerse] (*Piers Plowm*. B. x. 17).

cursitor [*hist*.]. AF. *coursetour*, MedL. *cursitor*, clerk of Court of Chancery who made out writs *de cursu*, of common routine. Hence *Cursitor Street*, Chancery Lane (where Mr Snagsby lived).

cursive. MedL. *cursivus*, running, from L. *cursus*, from *currere, curs-*, to run. Cf. *cursory*, L. *cursorius*, from *cursor*, runner.

curt. L. *curtus*, short, cogn. with G. καρτός, from κείρειν, to cut. A mod. word (17 cent.), but appearing much earlier in derived *kirtle* (q.v.).

curtail. Mentally associated with *tail*, or with F. *tailler*, to cut, but evolved as verb from earlier *curtal*, horse with docked tail (or ears), OF. *courtald* (*courtaud*), from *court*, short, L. *curtus*, and suffix -*ald*, Ger. -*wald*; cf. It. *cortaldo*. *Cut-tail*, as in *long and cut-tail*, is prob. the same word.

courtault: a curtall, a horse (Palsg.).

cortaldo: a curtall, a horse without a taile (Flor.).

curtain. ME. *curtine*, F. *courtine*, Late L. *cortina* (*Vulg. Ex*. xxvi. 1), perh. a transl. of G. αὐλαία, curtain, αὐλή, hall, court, being regarded as equivalent to *cohors* (see *court*). *Curtain lecture*, "a reproof given by a wife to her husband in bed" (Johns.), is recorded for 17 cent. *Curtain fire* is now replaced by *barrage* (q.v.). *Curtain-raiser* (theat.) is after F. *lever de rideau*.

curtal-axe, curtle- [*hist*.]. Corrupt. (16 cent. to Scott) of *cutlas* (q.v.). Cf. *pickaxe*.

curtana [*hist*.]. Pointless "sword of mercy" borne before E. monarchs at coronation. Cf. OF. *cortain*, the sword of Ogier le Danois. ? From L. *curtus*, short.

curtilage [*leg*.]. Court-yard, etc. OF. *cortilage*, from *cortil*, court, enclosure, from *cort* (*cour*), court. Cf. *village* from *ville*.

curtle-axe. See *curtal-*.

curtsy. Var. of *courtesy*. Cf. fig. use of *reverence, obeisance*.

curule chair. Of highest Roman magistrates. L. *cur(r)ulis*, supposed to come from *currus*, chariot.

curve. L. *curvare*. A late substitution for ME. *curb* (q.v.). As noun it is for *curve line*; cf. F. *ligne courbe*.

curvet. It. *corvetta,* from archaic *corvo* (*curvo*), bent, L. *curvus*; cf. F. *courbette,* "a curvet, or the curvetting of a horse" (Cotg.). See *cavort.*

cuscus. Indian grass. Urdu *khas khas,* from Pers.

cushat [*dial.*]. Wood-pigeon, ring-dove. AS. *cūsceote,* first element of which is prob. from cry, *cog,* second perh. cogn. with *scēotan,* to shoot. Cf. relationship of *dove* to *dive.*

cushion. F. *coussin,* OF. *coissin,* VL. **coxinum,* from *coxa,* thigh (cf. L. *cubital,* elbow-cushion, from *cubitus,* elbow); cf. It. *cuscino,* Sp. *cojín.* The OF. & ME. forms are very numerous, and more than 400 spellings of the pl. *cushions* have been noted in ME. wills and inventories.

cushy [*neol.*]. Associated with *cushion,* but said to be Hind., from Pers. *khŭsh,* pleasure.

The making of cushy jobs in these days of labour famine is an evident evil
(*Daily Expr.* Feb. 7, 1917).

cusp. L. *cuspis,* point.

cuspidor [*US.*]. Spittoon. Port., from *cuspir,* to spit, L. *conspuere.*

cuss. Colloq. US. for *curse* (cf. *bust* for *burst*). Hence *cussedness.* But a *rum cuss* is prob. rather for *customer*; cf. hist. of *chap,* or Sc. *callant,* from F. *chaland,* customer.

I do not heed their coarse remarks, but, with their playful cusses,
They frighten from our healthful parks the children with their nusses (*Punch*).

custard. Altered from ME. *crustade,* a pie with a crust; cf. It. *crostata,* "a kinde of daintie pye, chewet, or such paste meate" (Flor.). The recipes in a 15 cent. cookery-book for *custard* and *crustade* are ident.

custody. L. *custodia,* from *custos, custod-,* keeper.

custom. OF. *coustume* (*coutume*), L. *consuetudo, -tudin-*; cf. *costume.* In spec. sense of "regular" due has superseded *toll.* With *queer customer,* etc. (from 16 cent.), cf. *chap,* Sc. *callant,* and see *cuss.*

custos rotulorum [*hist.*]. L., keeper of the rolls.

cut. Replaces in many senses, from c. 1300, AS. *ceorfan, snīthan, scieran.* Origin obscure. Some connect it with F. *couteau,* knife (see *cutlas*). It has perh. been affected by F. *écourter,* VL. **ex-curtare,* from *curtus,* short. *Cutty* (*pipe, sark*) corresponds exactly to F. *écourté*; see also *cut-tail* (s.v. *curtail*). To *draw cuts,* i.e. lots, is very suggestive of F. *tirer à la courte paille.* A *cut above* is perh. from *cut,* style, fashion. To *cut and run,* i.e. to cut the cable and sail away, and to *cut out,* are both orig. naut. To have *one's work cut out* perh. refers to a difficult piece of tailoring. To *cut up well,* i.e. leave money, likens the defunct to a joint, and to *cut up rough,* etc. is a variation on the same idea. To *cut one's stick* is to prepare for a journey by providing oneself with a staff. *Cut and dried* was orig. used of herbs ready for use.

Il li ont sun somer de la coue escurté
(*Anglo-Norm. Life of Becket,* 12 cent.).

Anon to drawen every wight bigan,
And, shortly for to tellen as it was,
Were it by aventure, or sort, or cas,
The sothe is this, the cut [i.e. the short straw] fil to the knyght (Chauc. A. 842).

court festu [straw]: drawing of cuts (Cotg.).

Upon all such occasions, thou hast a thousand excuses ready cut and dry'd for the purpose
(T. Brown, c. 1700).

cutaneous. From MedL. *cutaneus,* from *cutis,* skin.

cutcha [*Anglo-Ind.*]. Mud brick. Hind. *kachchā,* raw, crude, etc. Often contrasted with *pucka* (q.v.).

The only objection that could be made [to the house] was its being cutcha, that is, built with mud instead of mortar (Hickey's *Memoirs,* ii. 134).

cutcherry [*Anglo-Ind.*]. Office, administration. Hind. *kachahrī,* audience room.

The prodigious labours of cutcherry
(*Vanity Fair,* ch. lvii.).

cute. Aphet. for *acute.* In Bailey (1731).

Cuthbert. Used of late (early 1917) of "knut" supposed to be escaping mil. service by holding government employ. Perh. suggested by music-hall song on "Cuthbert, Clarence and Claude."

From Whitehall we could raise regiments of Cuthberts (*Ev. News,* Apr. 5, 1917).

Cuthbert duck. From *St Cuthbert,* apostle of Northumbria, because it breeds on the Farne islands (see also *Marmion,* ii. 16).

cuticle. L. *cuticula,* dim. of *cutis,* skin.

cutlas. F. *coutelas,* augment. of OF. *coutel* (*couteau*), L. *cultellus,* dim. of *culter,* ploughshare. Often corrupted into *curtal-axe, cutlash,* etc. Cf. It. *coltellaccio,* "a curtelax, or chopping knife" (Flor.).

cutler. F. *coutelier,* from OF. *coutel* (v.s.).

cutlet. F. *côtelette,* double dim. of *côte,* rib, L. *costa.* No connection with *cut.*

cutter. Vessel. ? From *cut*; cf. *clipper*. Some identify it with *catur*, a vessel used on Malabar coast, perh. from Sanskrit *chatura*, swift. The *NED.* rejects this too readily. *Catur* was adopted by Port., and is used in E. (1643) a century before the first record of *cutter* (1745). There are other examples of Eastern boat-names adopted by the navy (see *dinghy*, *launch*), and we have always been easily familiarized with such exotic words (*junk*, *sampan*, *catamaran*, *kayak*, etc.), and have been expert in corrupting them (*jolly-boat*, *barquentine*).
catur: (an Indian word), a sort of small man-of-war (Vieyra).

cuttle-fish. AS. *cudele*, glossed as *wasescite*, ooze shooter. Found also in OLow Frankish c. 1100. Cogn. with *cod*[1], with allusion to the bag that contains the black fluid. The explanatory *-fish* is added from 16 cent.

cutty. See *cut*.

cwt. For hybrid *centum weight*, for *hundredweight*. Cf. *dwt*.

cyanide [*chem.*]. From G. κύανος, dark blue.

cycad. Palm. ModL.: *cycas*, *cycad-*, from supposed G. κύκας, scribal error for κόϊκας, acc. pl. of κόϊξ, the Egypt. doum-palm.

cyclamen. From G. κυκλάμινος, perh. from κύκλος, circle, in allusion to round roots.

cycle. G. κύκλος, circle. Orig. astron. in E. For *bicycle* since c. 1870. Cf. *Cyclades*, islands lying in a circle round Delos.

cyclo-. See *cycle*.

cyclone. Irreg. (19 cent.) from G. κύκλος, circle.

cyclopaedia. For earlier *encyclopaedia* (q.v.).

Cyclops. L., G. Κύκλωψ, from κύκλος, circle, ὤψ, eye.

cyder. See *cider*.

cygnet. Dim. from F. *cygne*, swan, L. *cygnus*, earlier *cycnus*, G. κύκνος, cogn. with L. *ciconia*, stork.

cylinder. From L., G. κύλινδρος, roller, from κυλίνδειν, to roll.
When it suits the purpose of the military chieftains they [German statesmen] are allowed to let loose peace cylinders...to poison the atmosphere
(D. Lloyd George, May 24, 1918).

cyma [*arch.*]. Moulding. G. κῦμα, anything swollen or waved.

cymar [*hist.*]. F. *simarre*, earlier *cimarre*, It. *cimarra*. Cf. *chimer*.
The purple robe, the cymar, the coronet
(*Ingoldsby*).

cymbal. L., G. κύμβαλον, from κύμβη, hollow of vessel, whence L. *cymba*, boat. See *chime*.

cyme [*bot.*]. F. *cime*, summit. As *cyma* (q.v.).

Cymric. From Welsh *Cymru*, Wales (see *Cambria*).

cynanche [*med.*]. See *quinsy*.

cynic. G. κυνικός, dog-like, from κύων, κυν-, dog. Cf. *hunks*. "In the appellation of the Cynic philosophers there was prob. an original reference to the κυνόσαργες, a gymnasium where Antisthenes taught" (*NED.*). Cf. hist. of *stoic*.

cynocephalus. Dog-headed baboon. From G. κεφαλή, head (v.s.).

cynosure. F., L., G. κυνόσουρα, dog's tail (οὐρά). Constellation of Ursa Minor, in tail of which is pole star. Esp. in *cynosure of neighbouring eyes* (*Allegro*, 77).

cypher. See *cipher*.

cypres [*leg.*]. Law F., for *si près*, as nearly as possible.

cypress[1]. Tree. Restored spelling of ME. & OF. *cipres* (*cyprès*), Late L. *cypressus* for *cupressus*, G. κυπάρισσος.

cypress[2] [*archaic*]. Fabric. Esp. in *cypress-lawn* (*Penseroso*, 35). Used in ME. of various fabrics from *Cyprus*. Earlier *cipre*, from OF.

Cyprian. Of *Cyprus*; hence, licentious. Cf. *Corinthian*.

Cyrenaic. Of *Cyrene*, G. Κυρήνη, G. colony in Afr. Esp. in ref. to hedonistic philosophy of Aristippus of Cyrene (5 cent. B.C.).

Cyrillic. Alphabet used by Slav. nations of Greek church. Attributed to *St Cyril*, apostle of Slavs (9 cent.).

cyst. From G. κύστις, bladder.

Cytherean. Of Aphrodite, or Venus, from her favourite isle of Κύθηρα, now Cerigo.

cytisus. Shrub. G. κύτισος. Cf. F. *cytise*.

czar, tzar, tsar [*hist.*]. Russ. *tsar*, OSlav. *césare*, L. *Caesar*, adopted in various forms by Slav. langs. The spelling *czar* is due to an early Ger. form, our knowledge of Russ. matters having as a rule passed through Germany. The title was used in Russia in 15 cent., but not formally adopted by the Emperor till 1547 (Ivan IV). Cf. *kaiser*. *Czarina*, F. *tsarine*, *czarine*, and corresponding It. Sp. Port. forms in *-ina*, all represent Ger. *zarin*, with the Ger. fem. suffix *-in* (see *vixen*). The correct Russ. word is *czaritza*, *tsaritsa*. *Czarevitch*, *czarevna*, son, daughter, of *czar*, had ceased to be offic. titles before the Revolution of 1917. See also *cesarevitch*.

Czech. Native and lang. (Slav.) of Bohemia. Also *Tschekh*; cf. F. *Tchèque*, Boh. *Chech*, Pol. *Czech*.

D. For 500, in Roman numerals, is an approximate imitation of half the peculiarly shaped Roman CIↃ, i.e. M (for *mille*, thousand).

dab¹. Verb. Perh. imit. of a short quick blow, its ME. sense, and influenced later by F. *dauber* (see *daub*), as in *wattle and dab*. Hence prob. *dab*, small flat fish, likened to a *dab* (of wax, paint, etc.), as *pat* (of butter) from verb to *pat*.

dab². Adept. Also *dabster* (from c. 1700). Slang. Origin obscure. ? Corrupt. of *adept*.

dab: expert, exquisite in roguery (*Dict. Cant. Crew*).

dabble. Obs. Du. *dabbelen*, frequent. of earlier *dabben*. First in Tusser (16 cent.). Perh. related to *dab¹*.

dabben, dabbelen: pulverem sive lutum versare manibus aut pedibus (Kil.).

dabchick. Earlier also *dap-, dip-, dob-*, related to *dip* and *dive*. Cf. synon. *didopper* (q.v.).

daboya. Viper. Hind. *daboyā*, from *dabnā*, to lurk.

dabster. See *dab²*.

da capo [*mus.*]. It., from beginning (head).

dace. In ME. also *darse*, OF. *dars*, nom. of *dard*, dart, dace. The fish is supposed to be named from its darting motion; but the name is prob. of Gaulish origin and unconnected with *dart*. For loss of -*r*- cf. *bass¹*.

dard: a dart, a javeling, a gleave; also, a dace, or dare fish (Cotg.).

dachshund. Ger., badger hound. *Dachs* is OHG. *dahs*, whence Late L. *taxus, taxo*, F. dial. *taisson*, badger, and It. name *Tasso*.

dacoit. Hind. *dakait, dākāyat*, robber belonging to armed band.

dactyl [*metr.*]. L., G. δάκτυλος, finger (– ᴗ ᴗ).

dad, daddy. From infantile speech; cf. *mammy, baby*, etc. Corresponding forms in most langs., e.g. Sanskrit *tata*. Recorded c. 1500, but prob. prehistoric.

dado. It., L. *datum* (see *die²*). Orig. the die-shaped part of pedestal; then, part of wall representing continuous pedestal. Hence *dado round the dining-room*, knitted abdominal belt (T. Atkins, 1914).

daedal. Maze-like, etc. From G. name Δαίδαλος, "the cunning one," constructor of the Cretan labyrinth.

daemonic. See *demon*.

daff. Occasional var. of *doff* (q.v.).

daffodil. For earlier *affodil*, F. *asphodèle* (see *asphodel*). For *d-*, prob. playful elaboration, cf. *dapple-grey*. *Daffadowndilly* is in Spenser.

asphodile: the daffadill, affodill, or asphodill, flower (Cotg.).

Daffy's elixir [*archaic*]. Invented by *Thomas Daffy*, a Leicestershire clergyman (17 cent.).

daft. AS. *gedæfte*, gentle, meek, cogn. with *gedafenian*, to be fitting, becoming, whence the sense preserved in *deft* (q.v.); cf. Goth. *gadaban*, to be fitting. For degeneration of *daft* cf. *silly* (q.v.).

dag¹ [*hist.*]. Short hand-gun. Prob. F. *dague*, dagger (q.v.). Cf. F. *pistolet*, which formerly meant dagger as well as pistol, while, according to Howell (v.i.), both *dag* and *dagger* were used indifferently in the two senses.

a dague: (F.) pistolet; (It.) pistola, daga; (Sp.) pistol, pistolete, daga.

a great horseman's dagger or pistoll: (F.) pistole; (It.) pistola; (Sp.) pistol (Howell, *Lex. Tetraglot*. 1660).

"This shall prove whether thou art human or not," cried Henry, taking deliberate aim at him with his dag (Ainsworth, *Windsor Castle*).

dag² [*ven.*]. Pointed horn of young stag. F. *dague*, "a dagger, also the head of the young deere, called a spitter, or pricket" (Cotg.).

dagger. Cf. F. *dague*, It. Sp. *daga*, Ger. *degen*, sword (from F.). MedL. *daggarius* occurs c. 1200. Origin unknown. Earliest record (12 cent.) is E. With *at daggers drawn*, earlier also *at daggers drawing* (Pepys, Dec. 3, 1665), cf. F. *à couteaux tirés*. With to *look daggers* cf. Shaks. to *speak daggers* (*Haml*. iii. 2). Both above phrases only became common in 19 cent.

daggle. Frequent. of dial. *dag*, in same sense; cf. noun *dag*, tag, clotted lock of wool, etc. Associated in meaning with *dabble, draggle*, and also with dial. *dag*, dew, ON. *dögg*.

I daggyl or I dagge a thing with myer: je crotte (Palsg.).

dago [*US.*]. Orig. Spaniard, now also Italian and Portuguese. Sp. *Diego*, a form of James, taken as typical name (cf. *John Bull, Fritz*). This was anticipated under the Stuarts (v.i.).

The Diego [the Spaniard] was a dapper fellow (Dekker, 1613).

dagoba. Buddhist shrine for relics of saint. Singhalese *dāghaba*, Sanskrit *dhātu-garbha*, relic receptacle.

Dagon. Fish-tailed deity of Philistines (*Judges*, xvi. 23). Heb. *dāgōn*, dim. of *dāg*, fish.

dags, to do. Schoolboy perversion of *dare*. Cf. *fag*[1], *fug*.

daguerreotype. Earliest photograph. From *Daguerre*, F. inventor (1839).

dahabeeyah. Large sailing barge on Nile. Arab. *dhahabīyah*, the golden, from *dhahab*, gold; orig. gilded barge of Moslem rulers.

dahlia. Discovered in Mexico by Humboldt and named (1791) in honour of *Dahl*, Sw. botanist.

Dail Eireann [*neol*.]. Gael. Ir. *dáil*, meeting, and genitive of *Eire*, Ireland (see *Erse*).

The Dail Eireann, or Irish Constituent Assembly, met in the Mansion House at Dublin
(*Daily Mail*, Jan. 22, 1919).

daimio. Obs. title of great Jap. noble. Chin. *dai*, great, *mio*, name.

dainty. First as noun, meaning honour, regard, etc. OF. *deintié*, L. *dignitas*, *-tat-*, from *dignus*, worthy. For development of adj. from noun cf. *choice*, and for wide range of senses cf. *nice*. Sense of pleasing, esp. to the palate, appears early (Wyc., Chauc.). Cf. *deign*, *disdain*.

dairy. ME. & AF. *deierie*, *dayerie*, from ME. *dey*, woman, servant, AS. *dæge*, for which see *lady*. Cf. the similarly formed *pantry*, *laundry*, *buttery*, all of F. origin. The native compd. was *dey-house*, still in dial. use.

Le chat lui mena...en le deyerie (Bozon).
deyerie: vaccaria (*Prompt. Parv.*).

dais. F., L. *discus*, disk, quoit, G. δίσκος; in Late L. table; cf. *desk*, *dish*, *disk*. Orig. raised table, high table, as in OF. In ModF. canopy.

daisy. AS. *dæges ēage*, day's eye, from its opening in the morning and also from its appearance. *Daisy-cutter* (cricket), ball that keeps low, was earlier applied to a horse that kept its feet close to the ground in trotting.

Men by resoun wel it calle may
The dayesie, or elles the ye of day
(Chauc. *Leg. Good Women*, 183).

dak, dawk. Hind. & Mahratti *dāk*, post, orig. transport by relays of men and horses. Hence *dak-bungalow*, rest house in India.

daker. See *dicker*.

Dalai Lama. Mongolian *dalai*, ocean, to indicate the extent of power of the Grand Lama of Tibet. See *lama*.

dale. AS. *dæl*. Com. Teut.; cf. Du. *dal*, Ger. *tal* (see *thaler*), ON. *dalr*, Goth. *dal*. Prevalence in north is due to ON. influence, more gen. term being *dean*[2] (q.v.).

dallastype [*phot*.]. Invented (1875) by *D. C. Dallas*.

dally. OF. *dailler*, *dallier*, to chaff, from OF. *dail*, sickle, blade. Orig. in F. to slash, then used of cut-and-thrust repartee, hence, in E., conversation, and finally, frivolous preoccupation, etc. OF. *dail* is of unknown origin; cf. Norw. *dælje*, Sw. dial. *dalja*, LG. *daljen*, to strike and hew, which may be of Teut. rather than OF. origin. From F. comes Ger. *dahlen*, to trifle.

Patrick de Graham, ke demourt et daille
Del espé furbie [slashes with his bright sword]
(Langtoft).

Pur ceo nous aprent coment devoms dalier [behave, deal judiciously] od gentz qi sont en power de baillye ou de seignurie (Bozon).

Lewd and schrewd dalyauns [i.e. conversation]
(*Paston Let.* i. 514).

dalmatian. Dog from *Dalmatia*. Hence also *dalmatic*, vestment, F. *dalmatique*. Cf. *cravat*.

Dalmatica vestis primum in Dalmatia provincia Graeciae texta est, tunica sacerdotalis candida cum clavis ex purpura (Isidore).

Daltonism. Colour-blindness. *John Dalton* (†1844), famous E. chemist, originator of atomic theory, was colour-blind. Term is of F. introduction, *daltonisme* (Prévost, professor at Geneva).

dam[1]. Barrier. Com. Teut.; cf. Du. *dam* (as in *Amsterdam*), MHG. *tam* (*damm*), ON. *dammr*. Noun not recorded in AS., which has, however, *fordemman*, to obstruct, with which cf. Goth. *faurdammjan*.

dam[2]. Mother. Var. of *dame* (q.v.), from which it is differentiated since 16 cent. In lang. of venery correlative to *sire*. For application to birds see *Deut.* xxii. 6.

Dam Fortone...turnes about ay hir whele
(Hampole, 14 cent.).

damage. OF. (*dommage*), from OF. *dam*, harm, L. *damnum*. Hence leg. *damage feasant*, damage due to trespass of animals, AF. *feasant*, OF. *fesant* (*faisant*). *What's the damage?* is app. a playful variation on earlier *what's the shot?*

damascene, -keen. To ornament with incised patterns as famous armourers of *Damascus*. Cf. *bilbo*, *toledo*.

damask. From *Damascus*, through It. *Damasco*; cf. F. *damas*, damask, and the material called *damassé*. Also *damask rose*, whence fig. rosy, beautiful cheek (*As You Like It*, iii. 5).

rose de Damas: the damaske, or muske rose (Cotg.).

dambrod, damboard [*Sc.*]. Draught-board. Du. *dambord* or Dan. *dambret*, the name coming from F. *jeu des dames*, as distinguished from *jeu des rois* (chess). See *dam²*.

dame. F., L. *domina*; cf. It. *donna*, Sp. *doña, dueña (duenna)*. Orig. used indifferently with *dam²* (q.v.). Gradually extended to women of lower rank (*dame's school*), but still leg. title for wife of knight or baronet. See *damsel*. The weakening of vowel in F. is perh. due to its unemphatic use as title. Cf. *sir* (q.v.), *m'm*.

damn. F. *damner*, L. *dam(p)nare*, to condemn to a penalty. Theol. sense from 14 cent. Coverd. uses it four times in *Joshua*, vi. 18. Pope's *damn with faint praise*, aimed at Addison, is borrowed from the prologue to Wycherley's *Plain Dealer*. As oath recorded from 16 cent., but the English were known in earlier ÔF. as *godons, goddams* (temp. Joan of Arc), from their habitual oath. The *NED.* rejects the suggestion that not to *care a damn* is from Hind. *dām*, a small copper coin. I believe that at any rate the popularity of the expression is of this origin. In all langs. expressions of this kind are from (i) small coins and sums (*twopence, brass farthing*), or (ii) objects of no value (*button, straw*). Such expressions swarm esp. in OF. I know no parallel to *damn* in this sense, for not to *care a curse* (see *curse*) is really an argument in favour of the small coin suggestion. The popularizer in E. of the *twopenny damn*, in which the coin association seems to survive, was a great Anglo-Indian, the Duke of Wellington. With euph. *d—d* cf. Du. *verdijd*, for *verdomd*.

England expects that every tank will do its damnedest
(Admiral of the Tank Fleet, Nov. 20, 1917).

Damnonian. Of Devonshire. From L. *Damnonia*, Roman name for county.

Damocles, sword of. Imminent peril waiting on apparent prosperity. *Damocles*, feasted by Dionysius, tyrant of Syracuse (4 cent. B.C.), suddenly noticed sword suspended by horse-hair above his head.

Damon and Pythias. Types of ardent friendship; cf. *David and Jonathan*. *Damon*, condemned to death by Dionysius (v.s.), left *Pythias* as surety while he returned home to settle his affairs. See Schiller's ballad *die Bürgschaft*.

damp. Prob. a LG. word. Quot. below, referring to coal-mine *damp*, is some centuries older than *NED.* records. Cf. Du. *damp*, Ger. *dampf*, steam, Norw. Dan. *damp* (from LG.); cogn. with Ger. *dumpf*, close, oppressive. Cf. verb to *damp*, choke, smother. Orig. sense of exhalation, vapour, survives in miners' *fire-damp, choke-damp*. Hence *damper*, flour and water cake of Austral. bushmen (1827). To *put a damper on* is from mus. sense of muffling sound.

Ventus qui vocatur "le damp"
(*Wollaton MSS.* 1316).

damsel. ME. & OF. *dameisele (demoiselle)*, VL. **dominicella*, from *domina* (see *dame*); ct. It. *donzella*, Sp. *doncella*. Orig. maiden of gentle birth. Archaic *damosel, -zel*, was revived by romantic poets, esp. Scott. OF. had also masc. form *dameisel (damoiseau)*, young squire.

damson. ME. *damascene, damsin*, etc., plum of *Damascus*. See *damask*.

damaisine: a damascene, or damsen plum (Cotg.).

dan¹ [*archaic*]. OF., lord, L. *dominus*; masc. of *dame* (q.v.). Hence ME. *daun*, common in Chauc., who is also called *Dan Chaucer* by Spenser; cf. It. *donno*, Sp. *don*. For vowel cf. *dame*.

dan² [*naut.*]. Small buoy used by trawlers. ? From name *Daniel*.

Let go your warp and put a dan on the end of it
(Skipper T. Crisp, R.N.R., V.C.).

Danaid. G. Δαναίδες, daughters of *Danaus*, king of Argos, condemned, for the murder of their husbands, to attempt to fill sieves with water. Hence *Danaidean* (endless, hopeless) *task*.

dance. F. *danser*; cf. It. *danzare*, Sp. *danzar*, Ger. *tanzen* (from It.). ? All from OHG. *dansōn*, to draw along, cogn. with OHG. *dinsan* and Goth. *at-thinsan*, to draw towards one (*John*, vi. 44). Hence app. first of choric or processional dancing; but this etym. is prob. wrong. In ME. replaced AS. *sealtian*, L. *saltare*. The *Dance of Death* represented the equality of all men before Death (see *macabre*).

I purpose verrely, with Goddes grace, therafftre to daunce atendaunce most abowt your plesure and ease (*Paston Let.* iii. 130).

dancette [*arch.*], **dancetté** [*her.*]. Cf. OF. *danché*, indented, Late L. *denticatus*, from *dens, dent-*, tooth.

dandelion. F. *dent de lion*, from toothed edge of leaf. Cf. synon. Ger. *löwenzahn*, lit. lion's tooth.

dander [*U.S.*]. Temper, as in to *get one's dander up*. ? Fig. use of WInd. *dander*, fermentation (of sugar), usu. *dunder*, from Sp. *redundar*, to overflow, L. *redundare*.

Dandie Dinmont. See *dandy*.

dandiprat. Insignificant dwarf. Also (16 cent.) small copper coin. For double sense cf. obs. *scuddick*, small coin, dwarf. ? Of the same family as *Jack Sprat*.

> This Jack Prat will go boast
> And say he hath cowed me
>   (*Misogonus*, ii. 1, c. 1550).

dandle. From 16 cent. Cf. It. *dondolare*, F. *dodeliner*, prob. cogn. with F. *dodo*, baby word for *dormir*, as in *faire dodo*, go to by-by. Has been confused with *dangle* (q.v.).

dandruff, dandriff. Second element is ON. *hrufa*, scab (cf. Ger. *rufe*, OHG. *hruf*), whence E. dial. *hurf*; first doubtful. Cf. AS. *hrēofla*, leper.

> *porrigo*: scurfe or scaules in the head, dandraffe
>   (Holyoak).

dandy[1]. Fop. First on Sc. border at end of 18 cent., hence prob. for *Andrew*. Cf. mod. use of *Johnny*. From Scott's *Dandie Dinmont* (*Guy Mannering*) comes name of terrier; cf. *King Charles' spaniel*.

dandy[2] [*Anglo-Ind.*]. Hammock slung on pole for carrying. Hind. *ḍāṇḍi*, from *ḍāṇḍ*, staff.

Dane. From Dan. *Daner*, ON. *Danir*. Hence also (hist.) *Danegeld*, ODan. *Danegjeld* (see *yield*), and *Danelaw, -lagh* (see *law*). With *great dane* (dog), cf. earlier F. *grand danois* (Buffon); cf. also *dalmatian, pomeranian*, etc. The *Dane John* (Canterbury) is supposed to be corrupted from *donjon* (q.v.).

> Within an hour all Canterbury was in commotion....
> From St George's Gate to St Dunstan's suburb, from the Donjon to the borough of Staplegate, all was noise and hubbub (*Ingoldsby*).

Danebrog. See *Dannebrog*.

dane-hole. See *dene-hole*.

dang. Euph. for *damn*; cf. *darn*[2].

danger. F., VL. **dominiarium*, for *dominium*, rule, lordship. Change of vowel (OF. also *dongier*) is due to association with *damnum*. Sense-development took place in OF., earliest meaning surviving in *in danger of*, orig. subject to the·jurisdiction of, e.g. in *Matt.* v. 22, where it represents *Vulg. reus*.

In the *Paston Let.* constantly used in sense of being in debt to.

> Metons nos hors de lor dangier (Wace).

> You stand within his danger, do you not?
>   (*Merch. of Ven.* iv. 1).

dangle. From 16 cent., with cogn. forms in Scand. & NFris. A frequent. verb, related by ablaut to *ding*[1] (q.v.), in sense of setting in motion. Confused in senses with *dandle*.

Daniel. Wise and upright judge (*Merch. of Ven.* iv. 1). From *Daniel* of Apocrypha.

Danish. AS. *Denisc*; cf. ON. *Danskr*. In ME. usu. *densh*, whence surname *Dench*; also *daneis*, from OF., whence *Dennis*. Lang., one of the mod. forms of ON., is almost ident. with Norw., and the hist. Danes also came mostly from Norway.

Danite. Member of supposed murderous organization among early Mormons, taking name from Bibl. *Danites* (*Gen.* xlix. 16).

dank. Now usu. replaced as adj. by *damp* (q.v.). Origin obscure; believed to be cogn. with Ger. *dunkel*, dark. Earliest records refer to dew.

Dannebrog, Danebrog. Dan. national flag. Second element is thought to be ODan. *brog*, breech, clout (see *brogues*); but some regard the word as a perversion of Jutish *danbroget*, red with white "blaze" and fetlocks, perh. from Fris. *dan*, red. This would have a parallel in OF. *bausant*, the Templars' black and white flag (*Ivanhoe*, ch. xii.), prop. a horse with a "blaze," and ident. with E. dial. *bawson*, badger (q.v.).

danseuse. F., see *dance*.

daphne. Laurel. G. δάφνη, derived in myth. from name of nymph changed into laurel to escape pursuit of Apollo.

dapper. Du., brave, sprightly; cf. Ger. *tapfer*, brave, OSlav. *dobli*, strong, doughty. ON. *dapr*, sad, is the same word, the intermediate sense being grim; cf. hist. of *moody*, or relation of Ger. *dreist*, audacious, to L. *tristis*, sad.

> *dapyr, or praty*: elegans (*Prompt. Parv.*).

> The pert fairies and the dapper elves (*Comus*, 118).

dapple. Back-formation from *dapple-grey*, for unrecorded **apple-grey*, the markings being likened to the splashes of colour on an apple; cf. F. *gris pommelé*, It. *pomelato*, Ger. *apfelschimmel*, etc., all rendered *dapple-grey* in early dicts. So also ON. *apalgrār* and Russ. *yablochnyi*, dappled, from *yabloko*, apple. For prefixed *d-* cf. *daffodil*.

> This reve sat upon a ful good stot,
> That was al pomely grey, and highte Scot
> (Chauc. A. 615).
> His steede was al dappull-gray (*ib.* B. 2074).

darbies [*slang*]. Handcuffs. Origin unknown, but earliest records (v.i.), always *Derby's bands* (*bonds*), suggest that *Darby* (from *Derby*) was some noted usurer, or perh. officer of the law.

> To binde such babes in father Derbies bands
> (Gascoyne, *Steel Glass*, 16 cent.).

Darby and Joan. First used of attached old couple in song in *Gentleman's Mag.* (1735), perh. characters from real life.

dare. An old preterite-present verb, as shown by orig. absence of *-s* in third person, *he dare not* (cf. *can, may*, etc.). AS. *dearr*, with past *dorste* (*durst*), cogn. with G. θαρσεῖν, to dare; cf. OSax. *gidar*, OHG. *tar*, Goth. *ga-daursan*. Absent from ON. *Daredevil* is formed like *cutthroat, scapegrace, Shakespear*, etc.

dark. AS. *deorc*, cogn. with OHG. *tarchanjan*, to conceal, but without other parallel forms. Opposite of *light* in lit. and fig. senses. *Dark horse* (racing, politics) is 19 cent. *Dark Continent* appears to have been coined by Stanley. *Dark Ages*, as applied to the Middle Ages, is a mod. impertinence. To *darken one's door* may be one of Benjamin Franklin's coinages. *Darkle* is a back-formation from adv. *darkling* (cf. *grovel*). *Darky*, negro, is US.

darling. AS. *dēorling, dīerling*, double dim., *-l-ing*, of *dear*[1].

darn[1]. To mend. Also earlier *dern, dearn*. Appears c. 1600 and is prob. a spec. use of *dern, darn*, to hide, common in ME. and still in dial. use, from AS. *dierne*, hidden, secret, cogn. with Ger. *tarnkappe*, coat of invisibility in *Nibelungenlied*. Cf. Ger. *strümpfe stopfen*, to darn (lit. stop up) stockings.

darn[2] [*US.*]. Euph. for *damn*. So also *darned, darnation* (*tarnation*).

darnel. Used in early Bible translations indifferently with *tares* and *cockle*. Cf. F. dial. *darnelle*. Second element is F. *nielle*, cockle, L. *nigella*, first is of unknown origin, but app. contains idea of stupefying; cf. F. *ivraie*, tares, from *ivre*, drunk, L. *ebrius*, and the L. name *lolium temulentum*, drunken tare, from stupefying properties; also Du. *dolik*, darnel, from *dol*, mad.

> *yvraie*: the vicious graine called ray, or darnell
> (Cotg.).

dart. F. *dard*, OF. also *dart*; cf. It. Sp. *dardo*. Of Teut. origin; cf. AS. *daroth, -eth*, javelin, found also in OHG., whence prob. the continental forms; also ON. *darrathr*.

dartre. Ulcer. F., for OF. *derte, darte*. ? From Gaulish *derbita*.

Darwinian. Of *Charles Darwin*, the naturalist (†1882), but applied earlier to his grandfather, *Erasmus Darwin*, the poet (†1802).

dash[1]. Of hasty movement, etc. ME. also *dasse, dassch*. Prob. imit., of same type as *bash, smash*, etc.; cf. Sw. *daska*, Dan. *daske*, to beat, slap, etc. Oldest sense as in mod. to *dash in pieces*. Noun, in various senses, from idea of sudden, rapid movement contained in verb. To *cut a dash* is for earlier to *cut a feather* (see *feather*). *Dashed*, euph. for *damned*, contains an allusion to the *dash* in *d—d* (cf. *blank, blankety*).

dash[2] [*WAfr.*]. Present, commission. App. native word of long standing (v.i.).

> When they have bestowed their monie, then we must give them some-what to boot, which they call dache (Purch. *Descript. of Guinea*).

dastard. Formed with depreciatory suffix *-ard* (cf. *sluggard*) from p.p. of *daze*. Orig. dullard and synon. with obs. *dasiberd*, lit. dazy beard. See *daze*. Cf. obs. Du. *dæsærd*, "delirus, insanus, phantasticus, perterritus" (Kil.).

> Daff, or dastard, or he that spekyth not in tyme
> (*Prompt. Parv.*).
> Dastard, or dullard (*ib.*).

dasyure. "Brush-tailed possum," "native cat" (Austral.). From G. δασύς, hairy, οὐρά, tail.

data. L., things given. From *dare, dat-*, to give.

dataller [*dial.*]. Day-taler, day-labourer. From *day* and *tale*. Common in Midlands and north.

date[1]. Fruit. OF. (*datte*), L., G. δάκτυλος, finger; cf. OIt. *dattilo*, whence Ger. *dattel*. From shape; ? cf. *banana*, and also L. *dactylis*, "a long grape like a finger" (Coop.). Some suggest that L. *dactylus* in this sense is merely an imit. form of an Arab. word, but the opposite is more likely (cf. *carat, apricot*, etc.).

date[2]. Time. F., L. *data*, p.p. neut. pl. of *dare*, to give, as in *Data Romae prid. kal. Apr.*, (these) given at Rome March 31, but in MedL. understood as fem. (sc. *epistola*). *Up to date* is orig. from book-keeping.

dative [*gram.*]. L. *dativus*, rendering G. δοτική (πτῶσις), giving (case).

datum. Assumption taken as basis of calculation. Sing. of *data* (q.v.).

datura. Narcotic plant. Hind. *dhatūra*, from Sanskrit.

daub. F. *dauber*, L. *dealbare*, to plaster, from L. *albus*, white. *Daubing* was orig. a handicraft (cf. *wattle and daub*), now replaced by plastering.

daughter. AS. *dohtor*. Aryan; cf. Du. *dochter*, Ger. *tochter*, ON. *dōtter*, Goth. *dauhtar*, G. θυγάτηρ, Sanskrit *duhitar*. ? From Sanskrit root *dugh*, to milk. Found in the same langs. as the cognates of *son*. Normal form *doughter* (Tynd., Coverd.) was replaced by *daughter* (Cranmer).

daunt. OF. *danter*, *donter* (*dompter*), L. *domitare*, frequent. of *domare*, to tame (q.v.). For vowel cf. *dan*[1], *dame*, *danger*.

Dauphin [*hist.*]. Title assumed (1349) by eldest son of king of France. The province of Dauphiné took its name from the *Dauphin* family, lit. dolphin (q.v.), a common early surname in E. & F.

Daulphin de France: the dolphin, or eldest son of France; called so, of Daulphiné, a province given, or (as some report it) sold in the year 1349, by Humbert Earle thereof to Philippe de Valois, partly on condition, that for ever the French Kings eldest sonne should hold it (during his fathers life) of the empire (Cotg.).

davenport. Writing-table (19 cent.). Maker's name. Cf. *chippendale*, *tilbury*, etc.

David and Jonathan. Cf. *Damon and Pythias*.

davit [*naut.*]. Earlier (15 cent.) *daviot*. AF. & OF. *daviet*, *daviot*, dim. of name *David*. Cf. Ger. *jütte*, davit, from *Judith*, and numerous meanings of *jack*. In 17 cent. usu. *david*. ? Allusion to David being let down from a window (1 *Sam*. xix. 12). Some suggest that OF. *daviet* is a naut. perversion of Sp. *gaviéte*, davit, which belongs to *gaff*[1].

davy[1]. Lamp. Invented (1815) by *Sir Humphry Davy*.

davy[2]. Vulgar for *affidavit* (q.v.).

Davy Jones. Spirit of the sea in naut. myth. Reason for choice of name unknown. Cf. *blue Peter*, *round robin*, *Mother Carey's chicken*, all naut. ? Reminiscence of *Jonah*, ii. 5, the prophet, formerly called *Jonas*, being made into *Jones* and supplied with a fitting Welsh christian name. Hence *Davy Jones' locker*, the sea (see *lock*[2] for early quot.).

daw. Now usu. *jackdaw* (cf. *magpie*, *tomtit*, etc.); cf. Sc. *caddow*, from ME. compd. *ca-daw*, of which both parts are prob.

imit. of cry. Ger. *dohle*, earlier *dahle*, MHG. *tahele*, from *tahe*, OHG. *tāhā*, may be related. The F. name *choucas* is from E. *chough*.

chouca: a chough, or Jack Daw (Cotg.).

dawdle. Became popular in 18 cent. Not in Bailey or Johns. Prob. dial. var. of *daddle*, to walk unsteadily, trifle. Cf. *dadder*, *dodder*, *dither*, all with idea of unsteady movement; also obs. or dial. *dade*. There are also LG. parallels, e.g. Hamburg *daudeln*, to waste one's time.

dawk. See *dak*.

dawn. First as verb (c. 1500), replacing earlier *daw*, AS. *dagian* (from *day*). Thus *dawn of day* is pleon. Earliest is *dawning* (c. 1300) app. of Norse origin; cf. Sw. Dan. *dagning*. The *Prompt. Parv.* has both *dawyn* and *dawnyng*.

The cock may craw, the day may daw (Burns).

day. AS. *dæg*. Com. Teut.; cf. Du. *dag*, Ger. *tag*, ON. *dagr*, Goth. *dags*. Orig. time of sunlight, the 24 hours being represented by *night* (q.v.). *Dayspring*, archaic for dawn, usu. after *Luke*, i. 78 (*Vulg. oriens*), is app. from *spring*, ?but cf. Norw. *dagsbryn*, ON. *dagsbrūn*, dawn, lit. day's brow. In *now-a-days*, *twice-a-day*, etc., *a* is for earlier *on*. *One of these days* is used by Coverd. (1 *Sam*. xxvii. 1) for *Vulg. aliquando*. Ger. *der tag*, the day, is said to have been a pre-war toast in the Ger. navy, alluding to the coming encounter with the British fleet.

In the fulness of his heart, he [Mr Brass] invited Mr Swiveller to partake of a bowl of punch with him at that remote and indefinite period which is currently denominated "one of these days"

(*Old Curiosity Shop*, ch. xxxv.).

daysman [*archaic*]. Umpire. Usu. after *Job*, ix. 33. Contains a reminiscence of archaic use of *day*, in sense of time appointed for judgment. Cf. Ger. *tagen*, to hold assembly (as in *Reichstag*, *Landtag*) and see *diet*[2].

daze. ON. **dasa*, as in reflex. *dasask*, to become exhausted (cf. *bask*, *busk*[2]); cf. ON. *dasi*, dullard, whence Norw. *daase*. In ME. to numb, become numbed, dazzled, etc.

dazzle. Frequent. of *daze*. Earliest intrans., of eyes. Hence *dazzle-ship* (1917), camouflaged so as to confuse hostile gunners, invented by Lieut. Commander N. Wilkinson.

de-. L. *de*, from, downward, but often a mere intens. (*demur*, *denigrate*). In words of F. origin usu. for *dé-*, OF. *des-*, L. *dis-*, which largely replaced *de-* in VL. Often in nonce-words or neols. (*decelerate, decode*).

deacon. AS. *dīacon*, L., G. διάκονος, servant. Orig. business helper of the apostles (*Acts*, vi. 1–6). Cf. mod. nonconformist use. Dan. *degn*, Norw. dial. *dekn* mean sexton.

dead. AS. *dēad*. Com. Teut.; cf. Du. *dood*, Ger. *tot*, ON. *dauthr*, Goth. *dauths*; cogn. with *die*[1] (q.v.). In many fig. uses (*dead certainty, shot, dead on the target*) with sense of the inevitable, or to express silence and stagnation (*dead of night*). *Dead as a doornail* is in *Piers Plowm.* From the idea of unrelieved continuity comes *dead wall*. *Deadhead* (US.) was orig. applied to passengers not paying fare, likened to dead head (of cattle), as opposed to live stock. Naut. *deadeye* was earlier (15 cent.) *dead man's eye*. *Dead heat* (19 cent.) was earlier simply *dead*. *Dead-alive*, now used of places, was in 16 cent. applied to people; cf. *living death*. *Dead letter* was applied first to lit., as opposed to spiritual, meaning (2 *Cor.* iii. 6), then to writ or law becoming inoperative, and finally (18 cent.) became a postal term. *Deadlock* is from wrestling, each being afraid to let go. *Dead reckoning* may be from naut. abbrev. *ded.* (= *deduced*) in log-book (cf. F. *route estimée*).

Mammon well follow'd, Cupid bravely led;
Both touchers; equal fortune makes a dead
(Quarles, 1635).

deaf. AS. *dēaf*. Com. Teut.; cf. Du. *doof*, Ger. *taub*, ON. *daufr*, Goth. *daufs*; cogn. with G. τυφλός, blind, common idea being dullness, obtuseness, a sense of *deaf* in ME.; cf. our *blind nettle* with Ger. *taubnessel*, deaf nettle. *Deaf as a post* was earlier *as a doorpost*, or *doornail*. With *deaf nut* (without kernel) cf. Ger. *taube nuss*. Till 18 cent. rimed with *thief*, as still in dial. and US.

Till Death shall bring the kind relief,
We must be patient, or be deaf (Prior, 1717).

deal[1]. Share, quantity. AS. *dǣl*. Com. Teut.; cf. Du. *deel*, Ger. *teil*, Norw. Dan. *del*, Goth. *dails*. See also *dole*[1]. Orig. part, as in *good* (*great*) *deal*. Hence verb to *deal*, distribute (cards, blows, etc.), take a share in business, and finally, have transactions with. Mod. sense of bargain, often with suggestion of dishonesty, is US.

This werke I departe and dele in sevene bookes
(Trev. i. 27).
With the one lamb a tenth deal of flour
(*Ex.* xxix. 40).

deal[2]. Timber. A LG. word, introduced by Baltic trade (c. 1460). Orig. plank, hence kind of tree or timber from which planks were made. Cf. Du. *deel*, Ger. *diele*, plank, also from LG. Cogn. with E. *thill* (q.v.), OHG. *dilli*, ON. *thilja*, rower's bench.

dean[1]. Church dignitary. OF. *deien* (*doyen*), L., Church G. δεκανός, from δέκα, ten. Used in *Vulg.* in sense of *decurio* (v.i.). In eccl. sense (*dean and chapter*) orig. chief of ten monks. In sense of senior (professor, ambassador, etc.) F. *doyen* is sometimes used in E.

Ordeyne thou of hem tribunes, and centurions, and quinquagenaries, and deenys
(Wyc. *Ex.* xviii. 21).

dean[2], **dene**. Valley. AS. *denu*, valley. Esp. in place-names, often alternating with *-den* in Kent. Cogn. with *den*.

dear[1]. Precious, beloved. AS. *dēore, dīere*. Com. Teut.; cf. Du. *duur*, costly, Ger. *teuer*, ON. *dȳrr*. For two groups of meanings cf. F. *cher*. In exclamations, such as *O dear!* it is prob. for *dear Lord*; cf. Ir. *Dear bless you, Dear knows*, etc. This will, however, hardly account for *Dear me*, which has been conjectured to be from some such It. phrase as *Dio mi* (*salvi*).

dear[2] [*archaic*]. AS. *dēor*, bold, fierce, perh. ult. ident. with *dear*[1]. In AS. & ME. poetry, revived by Spenser and used by Shaks. and later poets, by whom it was prob. felt as an oxymoronic application of *dear*[1], as in *dearest foe*.

I, made lame by fortune's dearest spite
(*Sonnet* xxxvii.).

dearth. From *dear*[1] (q.v.). Not found in AS., but cf. corresponding ON. *dȳrth*, glory, OHG. *tiurida*, honour, preciousness, showing the other sense of *dear*[1]. Mod. sense of scarcity appears earliest in ME., but must have been evolved from etym. sense of costliness (cf. synon. Ger. *teuerung*, from *teuer*, dear, costly). In *Prayer in the Time of Dearth and Famine* (PB.) *scarcity and dearth* are contrasted with *plenty and cheapness*.

death. AS. *dēath*. Com. Teut.; cf. Du. *dood*, Ger. *tod*, ON. *dauthi*, Goth. *dauthus*; cogn. with *die*[1], *dead*. Already personified in AS. *Black Death*, for the oriental plague which reached Europe in 14 cent., was app. introduced into E. by Mrs Markham (1823), corresponding descriptions occurring earliest in Sw. & Dan. (16 cent.). It is recorded as MedL. *mala mors* (1358). *In at the death* is from fox-hunting.

debacle. F. *débâcle*, orig. "bust-up" of ice on river; hence, stampede. From *débâcler*, from *bâcler*, to fasten up, Prov. *baclar*, to bar, from L. *baculus*, staff, crossbar. In mil. sense esp. since Zola's novel *La Débâcle* (1892).

debar. App. of E. formation from *bar* (q.v.). F. *débarrer*, OF. *desbarer*, has almost opposite sense, to unbar (door, window).

debark. F. *débarquer*. See *bark*². Now usu. replaced by *disembark*.

debate. F. *débattre*. Orig., in F. & E., to fight (see *combat*). Cf. *daughter of debate* (Mary, Queen of Scots). Hence *debatable ground*, esp. as recognized Tudor name for part of the Border claimed by both countries.

And over that his cote-armour,
As whit as is a lilye flower,
In which he wol debate (Chauc. B. 2056).

debauch. F. *débaucher*, OF. *desbaucher*, orig. to lead astray, as in *debauchee*, from F p.p. Origin unknown. Parallel of *delirium* (q.v.), and of such mod. expressions as to *run off the line*, suggests formation from Teut. *balk*, in gen. sense of line, ridge, boundary (see *balk*). Perh. orig. ploughing metaphor.

debenture. Earlier (15 cent.) *debentur*, they are owing, from L. *debēre*, to owe. Supposed to have been init. word of document. Cf. *affidavit*, *item*, *purview*, etc. Orig. voucher for goods supplied to government, etc. Current sense from middle of 19 cent.

debility. F. *débilité*, L. *debilitas*, from *debilis*, weak.

debit. F. *débit*, L. *debitum*, from *debēre*, to owe. Cf. *credit*.

debonair. OF. *debonaire* (*débonnaire*), for *de bon' aire*, of good race, orig. of hawks (see *aery*, *eyry*), hence "thorough-bred." Very common in ME. for docile, courteously well-bred (hence surname *Bonar*, *Bonner*), but obsolescent after Milton. Mod. sense is somewhat altered. OF. had also the opposite *demalaire*.

E! gentilz hum, chevaliers de bon aire (*Rol.* 2252).
Ahi, culvert [caitiff], malvais hum de put aire
(*ib.* 762).

deboshed. Archaic var. of *debauched*, revived by Scott.

debouch. Mil. word of 18 cent. F. *déboucher*, OF. *desboucher*, from *bouche*, mouth, L.

bucca, lit. cheek, used in VL. for *os*. Cf. It. *sboccare*, "to mouth or fall into the sea as a river" (Flor.). See *disembogue*.

débris. F., from *débriser*, from *briser*, to break. See *bruise*.

debt. Restored spelling of ME. *det*, *dette*, F. *dette*, L. *debita*, p.p. neut. pl. of *debēre*, to owe. *Debt of honour* (17 cent.) is so-called because it cannot be legally enforced. *Debt of nature*, death, is ME. The *National Debt* is the sum of a number of *national debts* from end of 17 cent. onward.

debus [*neol.*]. This and *embus* were officially used (1914) on the model of *debark*, *embark*, *detrain*, *entrain*.

début. F., from *débuter*, to lead off at bowls, etc. From *but*, mark, goal.

deca-. G. δέκα, ten.

decade. F., L., G. δεκάς, δεκάδ-, group of ten, δέκα.

decadent. F. *décadent*, from pres. part. of VL. *decadere (*decidere*), to fall, decay. Applied to themselves (c. 1885) by a group of unwholesome young F. writers, "unpleasant little anthropoids with the sexless little Muse and the dirty little Eros" (G. Du Maurier), who affected admiration for literature of Roman decadence.

decalogue. F., L., G. δεκάλογος (sc. βίβλος), from phrase οἱ δέκα λόγοι, Ten Commandments, in LXX. Used by Wyc.

Decameron. It. *Decamerone*, title of Boccaccio's (†1375) collection of tales, supposed to occupy ten days. From G. δέκα, ten, ἡμέρα, day. Cf. F. *Heptaméron* (seven days), tales of Marguerite de Navarre (16 cent.). Both are formed on MedL. *hexameron*, incorr. contr. of G. ἑξαήμερον.

decamp. F. *décamper*, orig. to break up camp, OF. *descamper*; cf. It. *scampare*, and see *scamper*. A mil. word from 17 cent.

decanal [*eccl.*]. Of a *dean*¹ (q.v.). Hence *ruri-decanal*, of a *rural dean*.

decani [*eccl.*]. Dean's side of choir. Genitive of L. *decanus*, dean. Cf. *cantoris*.

decant. Orig. in alch. F. *décanter*, MedL. *decanthare*, from *canthus*, corner, lip of jug, supposed to be from G. κανθός, corner of eye. See *cant*¹.

decant: from the Lat. Barb. decantare, a word lately found out by more barbarous chymists; which those mighty Zoilus's derive from the Lat. de, and the Gr. κάνθος, a corner
(*Gazophylacium Anglicanum*, 1689)

decapitate. After F. *décapiter*, from Late L. *decapitare*, from *caput*, *capit-*, head.

decay. OF. *decaïr*, dial. form ot *decheeir* (*déchoir*), VL. **decadēre*, for *decidere*, to "fall off"; cf. Sp. *decaer*.

decease. ME. *deces*, F. *décès*, L. *decessus*, lit. "departure," euph. for *mors*. In F. & E. chiefly offic.

> Le Décès, ce spectre bureaucratique qui gère le cimetière comme un arrondissement silencieux
> (Paul de Saint-Victor).

deceit. OF. *deceite*, p.p. fem. of *deceveir* (*décevoir*), VL. **decipēre* for *decipere*, from *capere*, to catch. The normal OF. was *decete* (cf. *recette* from *recepta*), but the vowel has been assimilated to the OF. tonic stem *deceiv-*, whence also E. *deceive*, riming with *save* in 17 cent.

decelerate [*neol*.]. A scient. word. First used in railway sense in offic. notice as to modification of railway service (Jan. 1917). Cf. the *decertification order* (*Nott. Guard.* April 24, 1918) and more recent *decontrol*.

December. F. *décembre*, L. *december*, from *decem*, ten, with suffix *-ber*, of obscure origin. Replaced AS. *ǣrra gēola*, earlier Yule. With *Decembrist*, from abortive Russ. revolution (Dec. 1825), cf. more recent *Octobrist*.

decemvir [*hist*.]. L., sing. of *decem viri*, ten men, appointed (5 cent. B.C.) to draw up the laws of the Twelve Tables. Later, Venet. Council of Ten.

decennial. From L. *decennium*, ten years, from *decem* and *annus*.

decent. F. *décent*, from pres. part. of L. *decēre*, to be fitting. Cf. *decorate*.

deci-. F., abbreviated from L. *decimus*, tenth, in terms of metric system.

decide. F. *décider*, L. *decidere*, *decis-*, from *caedere*, to cut. Cf. F. *trancher la question*, to come to a "decision."

deciduous. From L. *deciduus*, from *decidere*, to fall down, from *cadere*.

decimal. MedL. *decimalis*, from *decem*, ten, applied to the Arab. notation, and later to *decimal fractions*, an extension of the same. Hence *decimal coinage*.

decimate. From L. *decimare*, to put to death every tenth man of unit, as punishment for mutiny, etc. Much misused by mod. journalists ("literally decimated"), as almost equivalent to annihilate. Earliest sense in L. & E. is to take tithe.

> *decimare*: to tieth, to take the tenth part. *decimare legiones*: to punish or put to death the tenth man of every legion (Coop.).

decision. See *decide*.

deck[1]. Of ship. Du. *dek*, covering, roof, cogn. with E. *thatch* (q.v.). Du. has *verdek* in naut. sense; cf. Ger. *verdeck*. Earliest E. sense is covering (15 cent.), and the naut. *deck* was at first regarded rather as a roof than a floor; cf. F. *plafond*, ceiling, lit. floor (*plat fond*, flat bottom). So also verb to *deck*, adorn, meant orig. to cover.

> Ye decke youre selves, but ye are not warme
> (Coverd. *Haggai*, i. 6).

deck[2] [*archaic*]. Pack of cards (3 *Hen. VI*, v. 1); still usual in US. Ident. with *deck*[1]; cf. dial. *deck*, used of things of same shape piled one on another.

> While I had the cards that night, I marked every one in every deck (O. Henry).

deckle-edge. Of paper, rough edge caused by the *deckle*, or covering over the mould, Ger. *deckel*, cover, lid (see *deck*[1]).

declaim. For earlier *declame*, L. *declamare*, altered on *claim* (q.v.).

declare. F. *déclarer*, L. *declarare*, to make clear, *clarus*; hence, to announce, proclaim. With ellipt. *Well, I declare!* cf. archaic use of *protest*, *vow*.

déclassé. F., unclassed, one who has lost class.

declension. F. *déclinaison*, L. *declinatio-n-*, from *declinare*, to decline. Cf. *case* (gram.). Form has been affected by *extension, dimension*, etc.

decline. F. *décliner*, L. *declinare*, to bend away; cf. G. κλίνειν, to bend; cogn. with *lean*[2]. Sense has been affected by interpreting *de-* as downward, e.g. *decline of life*. Trans. meaning, euph. for *refuse*, as in to *decline an invitation*, is evolved from earlier to *decline* (i.e. turn away, avert) *a contest, argument*, etc. Cf. synon. Ger. *ablehnen*, lit. to lean away.

declivity. L. *declivitas*, from *declivis*, sloping down, from *clivus*, slope; cogn. with *decline*.

decoction. OF., from L. *decoquere, decoct-*, to boil down.

decode [*neol*.]. Coined on *decipher*.

decollation. Chiefly in connection with *Feast of Decollation* of St John the Baptist (Aug. 29). From L. *decollare*, to behead, from *collum*, neck.

décolleté. F., lit. uncollared, from *collet*, dim. of *col*, collar, L. *collum*, neck.

decompose. See *compose*. Sense of putrefaction from 18 cent.

decorate. From L. *decorare*, from *decus, decor-*, ornament.

decorticate. From L. *decorticare*, from *cortex, cortic-*, bark.

decorum. L. neut. adj., fitting. Cf. *decent, decorate*.

decoy. Orig. pond into which wild fowl are lured. First (1625) in *decoy-duck*, with which cf. Du. *kooieend* (*eend*, duck). Earlier *coy*, Du. *kooi*, cage, Late L. *cavea* (see *cage*). The *de-* may be Du. def. art., *de kooi*, the cage, or be due to influence of *decoy*, card-game of 16 cent., of unknown origin. Prob. affected in meaning by obs. *coy*, to smooth down, coax, from adj. *coy* (q.v.).

kooyen, endt-vogelen vangen: to catch wild duckes in the quoyes with quoy ducks (Hexham).

decrease. ME. *discrese*, OF. *descreiss-*, stem of *descreistre* (*décroître*), VL. **discrescere* for *decrescere*, from *crescere*, to grow; cf. It. *discrescere*, Sp. *descrecer*.

decree. First as noun. OF. *decré* (*décret*), L. *decretum*, from *decernere*, to decree, from *cernere, cret-*, to separate, etc. *Decree nisi*, "unless" cause to the contrary is shown within six months.

decrement. L. *decrementum*, from *decrescere*, to decrease.

decrepit. F. *décrépit*, L. *decrepitus*, "very olde; at the pittes brinke" (Coop.), from *crepare*, to creak.

decretal. Orig. (14 cent.) papal decree. Cf. MedL. *decretales epistolae*.

decry. F. *décrier*, OF. *descrier*, from *dis* and *crier* (see *cry*), orig. to announce withdrawal of coin from currency. In E. usu. understood as from *de-*, as though to "cry down."

on le descrie comme la vieille monnoye: he hath a very bad report among the people; his credit is wholly crackt, fame blemished, reputation lost (Cotg.).

decuman. Usu. with wave, billow. L. *decumanus*, powerful, orig. of the tenth cohort, and applied to the chief entrance of camp. Already in L. *decumanus fluctus*, associated with the superstition that the tenth wave is the largest. Cf. *decumana ova*, large eggs.

decumbent. From pres. part. of L. *decumbere*, to recline.

decuple. F. *décuple*, L. *decuplus*, ten-fold. Cf. *simple, double*, etc.

decurion [*hist.*]. L. *decurio-n-*, from *decem*, ten. Cf. *centurion*.

decussate [*bot.*]. X-shaped. From L. *decussare*, to divide cross-wise, from *decussis*, the number ten (X), the ten-as piece. Cf. *chiasmus*.

dedal. See *daedal*.

dedicate. From L. *dedicare*, to proclaim, devote in set words, in earliest E. sense to the Deity.

deduce. L. *deducere*, to lead down; *deduce, deduct* were formerly used indifferently. Hence *deductive*, opposed to *inductive*.

dee. D-shaped piece of harness; cf. *cee-spring*.

deed. AS. *dǣd*. Com. Teut.; cf. Du. *daad*, Ger. *tat*, ON. *dáth*, Goth. *dēds*. See *do*[1]. For later sense of document cf. *act*. With *indeed* cf. Ger. *in der tat*, L. *de facto*.

deem. AS. *dēman*. Com. Teut.; cf. Du. *doemen*, OHG. *tuomian*, ON. *dǣma*, Goth. *dōmjan* (see *doom*). Hence *deemster*, judge, etym. a fem. form of *deemer*, still used in I. of Man.

For in what dome ye demen, ye shulen be demyd (Wyc. *Matt.* vii. 2).

deep. AS. *dēop*. Com. Teut.; cf. Du. *diep*, Ger. *tief*, ON. *djupr*, Goth. *diups*; cogn. with *dip*. Most of the fig. senses appear already in AS., e.g. *the deep* (*Luke*, v. 4), orig. as opposed to shallows near shore.

deer. AS. *dēor*, wild animal. Com. Teut.; cf. Du. *dier*, Ger. *tier*, animal, Icel. *dȳr*, Goth. *dius*; prob. cogn. with *dear*[2], but not with G. θήρ. Spec., as well as gen., sense found in AS. Gradually replaced in gen. sense by *beast, animal*.

But mice, and rats, and such small deer, Have been Tom's food for many a year (*Lear*, iii. 4).

deface. OF. *desfacer* (see *face*); cf. It. *sfacciare*.

defalcate. From MedL. *defalcare*, to lop off, from L. *falx, falc-*, sickle, pruning hook; cf. F. *défalquer*, to deduct. E. sense of embezzle is 19 cent. Or perh. borrowed, with other financ. terms, from It. (v.i.), and associated in sense with *default*.

diffalcare: to deduce or deduct in reckonings, to defalke, to abate, to bate (Flor.).

default. Earlier *defaut*. See *fault*.

defeasance [*leg.*]. Annulment, etc. AF. *defesaunce*, OF. *desfesance*, from *desfaire* (*défaire*), to undo (v.i.).

defeat. From *défait*, p.p. of F. *défaire*, to undo, VL. **disfacere* for *deficere*. In ME. to undo, destroy, etc., mil. sense being later, e.g. not in Shaks. *Defeatist* was adopted (1917) from F. *défaitiste*, applied to a man suspected of working against his own country.

defecate. From L. *defaecare*, to clear from dregs, *faex*, *faec-*.

defect. L. *defectus*, from *deficere*, *defect-*, to undo.

defend. L. *defendere*, to ward off (cf. *fend*, *fence*), earlier also in F. sense of prohibit, e.g. *defended fruit* (*Par. Lost*, xi. 84). *Defender of the Faith* is for L. *Fidei Defensor*, title conferred (1521) on Henry VIII by Leo X for writing against Luther. With *defendant*, from F. pres. part., cf. *complainant*.

defer¹. To delay. Etym. ident. with *differ* (q.v.), F. *différer*, from L. *differre*, to set aside, postpone, from *ferre*, to bear. Form has been influenced by *delay*.

My master wyl differ his commynge
(Tynd. *Matt.* xxiv. 48).

defer². To submit. F. *déférer*, from L. *deferre*, to submit (trans.), from *ferre*, to bear. Usual mod. sense comes from reflex. use, to submit oneself.

defervescence. See *effervescence*.

deficient. From pres. part. of L. *deficere*, to fail, etc.

deficit. F. *déficit*, L. *deficit*, there lacks, as introductory word in clauses of inventory. Cf. *item*.

defilade [*mil.*]. To protect from enfilading fire. Coined on *enfilade* (q.v.).

defile¹. Verb. ME. *defoul*, *defoil*, OF. *defouler*, to trample upon (see *fuller*), with sense influenced by E. *foul* and by the corresponding verb *file*, AS. *fȳlan*, to make foul, filthy.

To no thing is it worth over, no bot it be sent out,
and defoulid [AS. fortreden] of men
(Wyc. *Matt.* v. 13).

It's a foul bird that files its ain nest (Galt, *Entail*).

defile². Narrow way. Earlier *defilee*, F. *défilé* (mil.), from *défiler*, to march past, from *file*, *file³* (q.v.). For loss of ending cf. *signal²*, *costive*, etc.

defile or *defilee*: a straight, narrow lane, through which a company of soldiers can pass only in file (Kersey).

define. Orig. to determine the end or limits. OF. *definer*, from *fin*, end, now replaced by *définir*, L. *definire* (see *fine¹*). With *definition* cf. *aphorism* (q.v.).

deflagrate. From L. *deflagrare*, to burn away.

deflate. Mod. coinage on *inflate*; misuse of L. *deflare*, to blow away.

deflect. L. *deflectere*, to bend aside.

deflower [*archaic*]. F. *déflorer*, L. *deflorare*, from *flos*, *flor-*, flower. Orig. to strip of flowers, hence ravish, defile. In ME. often to make extracts from book (cf. *anthology*).

deformation. Acquired deformity. F. *déformation*.

The great word of reformation, or rather deformation, in the worship of God (Nicholas Bacon).

deformity. OF. *deformité*, L. *deformitas*, from *deformis*, ill-formed. ModF. has *difformité*, from *difformis* (*dis-*).

defray. F. *défrayer*, from OF. *frai*, cost (now only in pl. *frais*), OHG. *fridu*, peace (*friede*), whence MedL. *fredum*, fine. For sense-development cf. *pay¹* (q.v.). A rival etym. is from L. *fractum*, broken, with some idea of paying the damage (cf. F. *dédommager*, to defray); but OF. *desfroi*, expense, supports the first. Cf. *affray* (q.v.).

deft. AS. *gedæfte*, mild, gentle; cf. Goth. *gadaban*, to befit. For sense-development cf. *handy*, which partly represents ME. *hende*, courteous. See also *daft*.

That defte meiden, Marie bi name (*NED.* 13 cent.).

defunct. L. *defunctus*, p.p. of *defungi*, to accomplish one's duty.

defy. F. *défier*, VL. **disfidare*, from *fidus*, faithful. Orig. to proclaim breach of alliance. Secondary F. sense, distrust, is due to association with L. *diffidere*, whence *diffident*.

dégagé. F., free, unembarrassed. See *gage¹*.

degenerate. From L. *degenerare*, from *genus*, *gener-*, race. Noun, in sense of unwholesome crank or sexual freak, is a quite mod. use of the adj. as employed in biol.

deglutition. F. *déglutition*, from L. *deglutire*, to swallow down. See *glut*.

degrade. F. *dégrader*, Church L. *degradare*, to reduce in rank, from L. *gradus*, degree, etc.

degree. F. *degré*, VL. **degradus*, from *gradus*, step; cf. Prov. *degrat*. The other Rom. langs. use forms of the simple *gradus*. For fig. senses cf. *scale³*, and mil. to *get one's step*, i.e. promotion. Univ. sense is in Wyc.

dehiscent [*biol.*]. From pres. part. of L. *dehiscere*, from *de* and *hiscere*, incept. of *hiare*, to gape. Cf. *hiatus*.

dehort. L. *dehortari*, to dissuade.

deictic. Directly demonstrative. G. δεικτικός from δεικνύναι, to show.

deify. F. *déifier*, L. *deificare*, to make into a god, from *deus* and *facere*.

deign. OF. *deignier* (*daigner*), VL. *dignare*, for *dignari*, to deem fit, *dignus*. Cf. *disdain, dainty.*

deipnosophist. One skilled in art of dining. From title of work by Athenaeus (3 cent.). From G. δεῖπνον, dinner.

deist. F. *déiste*, from L. *deus*, god. Orig. opposed to *atheist* and interchangeable with *theist* as late as c. 1700 (Locke).

deity. F. *déité*, Late L. *deitas, deitat-*, from *deus*, coined (c. 400) by Augustine on *divinitas*. For cognates of *deus* see *Tuesday*.

deject. From L. *deicere, deject-*, to cast down, from *jacere*.

déjeuner. F., see *dine*.

del. For *delineavit*, he drew, after artist's name.

delaine. Fabric. For *muslin delaine*, F *mousseline de laine*, muslin of wool, L. *lana*.

delate [*chiefly Sc.*]. To accuse, inform against. From *delator*, informer, F. *délateur*, L. *delator-em*, from *deferre, delat-*, to deliver, etc.

delator: a secrete accusour or complayner; a tell tale; a picke thanke (Coop.).

delay. F. *délai*, noun, *dilayer*, verb, the latter remodelled on Late L. *dilatare* (from *differre, dilat-*), whence E. *dilatory*. OF. had also *deleer*, from *dilatare*, but the form *-laier* cannot be of the same origin, as the *i* indicates an orig. *g* (**lagare*). OF. *laier, laiier*, to let, is a common word; cf. Prov. *laihar*. The root is prob. that of E. *lag*, as is seen in OCatalan (v.i.).

E aco deu fer sens tot lagui e sens tot contrast [and this he ought to do without any delay or dispute] (*Costumes de la Mar*, 14 cent.).

del credere. It., of trust, implying that agent guarantees solvency of buyer.

dele [*typ.*]. Imper. of L. *delēre*, to blot out, delete. Or perh. short for *deleatur*, let it be deleted, used (1602) like *imprimatur*.

delectable. L. *delectabilis*, from *delectare*, to delight (q.v.).

delectus. L., selection, from *deligere, delect-*, to choose. Cf. *gradus* (s.v. *grade*).

delegate. From L. *delegare*, from *legare*, to send on a mission. See *legate*.

delete. From L. *delēre, delet-*, to blot out, cogn. with *linere*, to daub.

deleterious. G. δηλητήριος, from δηλητήρ, destroyer, from δηλεῖσθαι, to destroy.

delf(t). Earthenware from *Delft* (Holl.), formerly *Delf*, from Flem. *delf*, canal, as in E. dial. (see *delve*). Cf. *china, coalport*, etc.

Delian. Of *Delos*, G. island, esp. in ref. to Apollo.

deliberate. From L. *deliberare*, to weigh, from *libra*, scales. Cf. *ponder*.

delicate. L. *delicatus*, prob. from *deliciae*, delight. Some senses rather via F. *délicat*. For gen. sense-development cf. *dainty*. Cf. *delicious*, F. *délicieux*, Late L. *deliciosus*. See also *delight*.

delict. L. *delictum*, fault, from *delinquere*, to leave undone. Esp. *in flagrant delict*, L. *in flagrante delicto*, in glaring offence.

delight. ME. & OF. *delit*, from *deliter*, to delight, L. *delectare*, frequent. of *delicere*, to entice, from *lacere*, to ensnare (see *lace*); cf. *dilettante*. For unorig. -*g*- cf. *distraught, sprightly*, etc.

Delilah. Temptress (*Judges*, xvi.).

delineate. From L. *delineare*, from *linea*, line.

delinquent. From pres. part. of L. *delinquere*, from *linquere*, to leave.

deliquesce. L. *deliquescere*, from *liquescere*, incept. of *liquēre*, to be liquid.

delirium. L., from *delirare*, to rave, lit. leave the furrow, *lira*. Thus a ploughing metaphor; ? cf. *debauch*. A more mod. metaphor is to *run off the rails*, with which cf. Ger. *aus dem geleise kommen*, where *geleise* is cogn. with L. *lira*. *Delirium tremens*, trembling delirium, was introduced as med. term by Dr Sutton (1813).

delirare: to go out of the right way, to make a balke in earing [i.e. ploughing]; not to go straight (Coop.).

delitescent. From pres. part. of L. *delitescere*, from *litescere*, incept. of *latēre*, to lie hidden.

deliver. F. *délivrer*, VL. *deliberare*, in sense of *liberare*, to set free, *liber*. ModF. *délivrer, livrer*, represent the two almost opposed senses of E. *deliver*, to set free, to hand over. See *livery*.

dell. AS. *dell*. Related to *dale* as *den* to *dean²*; cf. Du. *del*, Ger. dial. *delle*.

Della Cruscan. From It. *Accademia della Crusca*, Academy of the bran (sifting), formed (1582) at Florence to purify It. lang. It. *crusca* is OHG. *crusc*, bran. Hence applied (c. 1800) to artificial E. school, of which a prominent member, Merry, had been elected to the *A. della C.*

The hall of the Academie de la Crusca [at Florence] is hung about with impresses and devices painted, all of them relating to corne sifted from the brann (Evelyn).

Merry and his Della Cruscans, a set of minor bards and mutual admirers who had infested the magazines and the libraries for some years (Saintsbury, *Nineteenth Cent. Lit.*).

Della Robbia ware. From name of It. sculptor (†1482).

Delphic. Usu. with *utterance*. Of *Delphi*, seat of G. oracle.

delphin [*bibl.*]. Of L. texts edited *in usum Delphini*, i.e. for the son of Louis XIV. See *dauphin, dolphin*.

delphinium. Larkspur. L., G. δελφίνιον, little dolphin, from form of nectary.

delta. G. letter D (Δ), adapted from Phoenician *daleth*, "tent door" (see *alphabet*). Used by Herodotus of the Nile, by Strabo of the Indus. Hence *deltoid* (anat.), delta shaped.

delude. L. *deludere*, to play false, from *ludere, lus-*, to play.

deluge. F. *déluge*, L. *diluvium*, from *diluere*, to wash away. Cf. *antediluvian*.

delve [*archaic*]. AS. *delfan*, orig. strong (v.i.). WGer.; cf. Du. *delven*, OHG. *bitelban*. Now, exc. in dial., usu. fig., e.g. to *delve into the past*. It is the regular word in Wyc. where Tynd. has *dig*.

Thei dolven a diche bifore my face (Wyc. *Ps.* lvi. 7).

demagogue. G. δημαγωγός, from δῆμος, people, ἀγωγός, leader, from ἄγειν, to lead. First, disparagingly, in *Eikon Basilike* (1648).

Setting aside the affrightment of this goblin word [demagogue]; for the king by his leave cannot coin English as well as he could money....
(Milton, *Eikonoklastes*).

demand. F. *demander*, L. *demandare*, to entrust (from *mandare*, to order), which assumed in Late L. sense of request; cf. It. *dimandare*, Sp. *demandar*. Used (econ.) in correlation with *supply* since Adam Smith (1776). The peremptory sense is peculiar to E. (cf. *require*), and of late esp. illustrated by the various ukases issued by privileged organisations.

The railwaymen in conference at Plymouth demanded instant withdrawal of British troops from Russia (*Pall Mall Gaz.* June 19, 1919).

demarcation. Sp. *demarcación*, from *demarcar*, to mark out boundary (see *march¹, mark¹*). First in *linea de demarcacion*, by which Pope Alexander VI divided the New World between the Spaniards and Portuguese (1493).

démarche. F., step (see *march²*), esp. in pol. sense.

deme. G. δῆμος, district, township. Hence, set of cells (biol.).

demean. F. *démener, démèn-* (OF. *demein-*), from *mener*, to lead, VL. *minare*, for *minari*, to threaten, drive with threats, lead. Very common in OF. & ME., now only reflex., to *demean* (behave) *oneself*. Hence *demeanour, misdemeanour*, AF. formations (cf. *behaviour*). To *demean* (lower) *oneself*, in vulgar speech, is prob. the same word, by association with *mean²* and analogy of *debase*.

dement. L. *dementare*, to send out of one's mind, *mens, ment-*. Dementia L., has replaced earlier *demency*; cf. F. *démence*.

démenti. Official denial. F., p.p. of *démentir*, to give the lie, belie. See *mendacious*.

demerit. F. *démérite*, L. *demeritum*, desert, prefix *de-* having been erron. taken as neg. in Late L. & Rom. langs. Orig. sense survives in ME. and Shaks.

demereri: to deserve thanke (Coop.).

My demerits
May speak, unbonneted, to as proud a fortune
As this that I have reached (*Oth.* i. 2).

demesne [*leg.*]. Estate held with full rights. ME. *demein, demayn*, etc., OF. *demeine*, L. *dominium*, now replaced by *domaine*. OF. *demeine* is also an adj., own. The *-s-* of *demesne*, a late spelling, is prob. due to analogy of contrasted *mesne* (q.v.), in which it is also unoriginal, perh. partly to OF. *mesnie*, household (*meiny* in Shaks.). An intrusive *-s-* is very common in OF. & AF., esp. before *-n*. See also *domain*.

demaine, (dominicum) is a French word, otherwise written domaine and signifieth patrimonium domini as Hotoman saith, in verbis feudalibus (Cowel).

demi-. F. prefix, also used in E. See *demy*.

demijohn [*naut.*]. Corrupt. of F. *dame-jeanne*, lit. *lady Jane*; cf. It. *damigiana*, Sp. *damajuana*. It is not certain in which lang. the word arose. Similar fanciful names for vessels are *jack, jug, jorum*, etc. Cf. also *bellarmine, tankard*, and obs. *goddard*. Perh. the wicker-covered bottle suggested a portly lady in the costume of the period.

dame-jane: les matelots appellent ainsi une grosse bouteille de verre, couverte de natte
(Th. Corneille).

dame-jeanne: a demijan, or large bottle, containing about four or five gallons, covered with basket work, and much used in merchant-ships (Falc.).

demi-monde. Coined (1855) by Alexandre Dumas *fils* as title of comedy.

demi-rep. *Rep* for *reputation* is among the abbreviations mentioned in Swift's *Polite Conversation*.

demise. F., p.p. fem. of *démettre*, to put off, *se démettre*, to resign, L. *demittere*. Used first of transfer of property, then, in *demise of the crown*, of transfer by death; hence, fig. death itself.

demiurge. Orig. creator of world in Platonic philosophy. G. δημιουργός, from δῆμος, public, -ἐργος, working.

demob [*slang*]. For *demobilize* (1919).

I beg that we do not demobilize the spirit of patriotism in this country
(D. Lloyd George, in H. of C., July 3, 1919).

democracy. F. *démocratie*, MedL. *democratia*, in 13 cent. transl. of Aristotle, G. δημοκρατία, from δῆμος, people. Defined (1863) by Lincoln as "government of the people, by the people, for the people," a variation on Webster's earlier (1830) definition. Earlier still is Byron's "aristocracy of blackguards." In US. *Democrat* and *Republican* represent earlier *Federal* and *Whig*.

The world must be made safe for democracy
(Pres. Wilson, Apr. 2, 1917).

Democritean. Of *Democritus*, the laughing philosopher of Abdera (5 cent. B.C.). The name means judge of the people.

demogorgon. App. Late L. formation from δαίμων, divinity, demon, and γοργός, terrible (see *gorgon*), but possibly perverted from some Eastern word. First mentioned (5 cent.) as name of deity invoked in magic rites. Introduced into literature by Boccaccio and Ariosto.

demolish. F. *démolir*, *démoliss-*, from L. *demoliri*, from *moles*, heap, building.

demon. L., G. δαίμων, divinity, tutelary genius; but, in usual E. sense, from L. *daemonium*, G. dim. δαιμόνιον, used in LXX. and *Vulg*. in its Jewish sense of god of the heathen and "unclean spirit." Orig. sense survives in *daemonic*. *Demonology* was coined (1597) by James VI of Scotland (James I) as title of his treatise on witchcraft.

That daemonic element—so essential in times of crisis—is not necessarily a turbulent spirit
(Oliver, *Ordeal by Battle*).

demonetize. F. *démonétiser* (see *money*).

demonstrate. From L. *demonstrare*, from *monstrare*, to show. See *monster*, *muster*.

demoralize. F. *démoraliser*, a Revolution coinage, of which Laharpe says, "Si 'démoraliser' pouvait être français, il signifierait 'cesser de parler de morale.'" Cf. *denationalize* and see *moral*.

demos. G. δῆμος, people. From 19 cent.

demotic. G. δημοτικός, plebeian, of the people, δῆμος. In ref. to Egypt. written character, contrasted with *hieratic* (q.v.).

demulcent. From pres. part. of L. *demulcēre*, to soothe.

demur. AF. *demurer*, OF. *demorer* (*demeurer*), VL. **demorare*, for *demorari*, to delay. Orig. sense of tarrying survives in leg. *demurrage*, *demurrer*, the latter an infin. (cf. *attainder*, *misnomer*, etc.).

demure. From AF. *demurer*, to stay (v.s.). Cf. synon. *staid* (q.v.). It possibly represents the p.p.; cf. *costive*, *signal²*, *trove*, for parallels to loss of *-e*. But OF. forms many adjs. from verb stems without suffix (cf. *stale*). The oldest meaning of *demure* is quiet, settled, used of the sea, later it meant sober, sedate (*Penseroso*, 32), and became ironical c. 1700.

demurrage. See *demur*.

demy. Size of paper, sheet folded in half. For *demi*, F., L. *dimidium*, half, from *di-* and *medium*. A *demy* at Magdalen (Oxf.) was so-called because his allowance was half that of a fellow.

den. AS. *denn*, lair of wild beast, cogn. with *dean²*; ? cf. Ger. *tenne*, floor, archaic Du. *denne*, floor, cavern.

denary. L. *denarius*, relating to ten, from *deni*, ten at a time, for **decni*, from *decem*.

denationalize. F. *dénationaliser*, a Revolution coinage. Cf. *demoralize*.

dendrite [*min.*]. G. δενδρίτης, from δένδρον, tree. From markings.

dene. Sandhill. ? F. *dune* (q.v.).

denegation. F. *dénégation*, L. *denegatio-n-*, from *denegare*, to deny.

dene-hole [*antiq.*]. Recorded, as *Dane-hole*, from 18 cent. only, a name prob. due to popular connection with the *Danes*.

dengue. Eruptive fever with pain in joints (EAfr. and WInd.). Agrees in form with Sp. *dengue*, affected contortion, prob. from *denegar*, to refuse (with idea of affectation). But, in this sense, a perversion, assimilated to Sp. *dengue*, of Swahili (Zanzibar) *dinga*, cramp-like seizure. The negro WInd. name is *dandy*, and the disease is also called the *giraffe*, each name alluding to the stiff unnatural holding of neck and shoulders.

denier [*hist.*]. F., L. *denarius*, coin worth ten *asses*; cf. It. *denaro*, Sp. *dinero*, Arab. *dinar*. Applied to various obs. coins in F. & E., and used (*d.*) for penny.

denigrate. From L. *denigrare*, to defame, lit. blacken. Obs. in 18 cent. and now revived in imit. of F. *dénigrer*.

denizen. AF. *deinzein* (*denzein, deinzain*), from *deinz*, within, OF. *denz* (*dans*), L. *de intus*. Orig. native as distinguished from foreigner, and, in City records, esp. citizen (which it has affected in form) as distinguished from outsider. Cf. *foreign*. Quot. below refers to mixed juries deciding on disputes between citizens and non-citizens.

Et enqueste jointe, denzein et forein, soit fait par xii, dont la moitee soit de denzeines et lautre moitee des foreins demurrantz en ville
(*Liber Albus*, p. 292).

denominate. From L. *denominare*, to specify by name, *nomen*. *Denominational* first occurs in sectarian sense in Gladstone's *Church and State* (cf. *disestablishment*).

denote. F. *dénoter*, L. *denotare*, from *nota*, mark, note. As term of logic dates from Mill (cf. *connote*).

dénouement [*theat.*]. F., lit. untying (of plot). F. *nouer* is L. *nodare*, from *nodus*, knot. Cf. F. *nœud*, knot, in sense of plot.

denounce. F. *dénoncer*, L. *denuntiare*, to intimate by messenger, *nuntius*. In earlier use almost equivalent to *announce* (see *fetial*). To *denounce a treaty* is 19 cent., from F.

dense. F., L. *densus*, compact.

dent. Var. of *dint* (q.v.). Mod. sense has been affected by *in-dent-ation*, etc.

dental. MedL. *dentalis*, from *dens, dent-*, tooth. *Dentifrice*, F., L. *dentifricium*, from *fricare*, to rub, dates from 16 cent.

dentist. F. *dentiste*, replacing (18 cent.) native *tooth-drawer* (*Piers Plowm.*).

denude. L. *denudare*, to lay bare, *nudus*.

denunciate. See *denounce*.

deny. F. *dénier*, L. *denegare*, from *negare*.

deodand [*hist.*]. Object which, having caused death, was confiscated to Crown (up to 1846). L. *Deo dandum*, to be given to God.

deodand (*deodandum*): is a thing given or forfeited (as it were) to God for the pacification of his wrath in a case of misadventure, whereby any Christian soule commeth to a violent end, without the fault of any reasonable creature (Cowel).

deodar. Hind. *dēod'ār*, Sanskrit *deva-dāra*, divine tree. In E. from c. 1800, but mentioned by Avicenna (11 cent.).

deodorize. Coined (19 cent.) from *odour*.

deontology [*phil.*]. Ethics. From G. δέον, pres. part. neut. of δεῖ, it behoves.

depart. F. *départir*, VL. **dispartire* for *dispertire*, to divide, from *pars, part-*, part. Orig. trans., to divide, mod. sense springing from reflex. use, as in the case also of F. *partir* (cf. *abscond*). Trans. sense survives in to *depart this life*, whence *the departed*, and in *department*, F. *département* (1790), division, province; also in marriage service "till death us depart," altered (1662) to "do part" at request of Puritan divines. *New departure* is US. (19 cent.).

depend. F. *dépendre*, from L. *dependēre*, to hang from, influenced in form by trans. *pendere*, whence F. *pendre*. *That depends* is an ellipt. expression of the same type as *I daresay*.

depict. From L. *depingere, -pict-*, from *pingere*, to paint.

depilatory. From L. *depilare*, to remove hair, *pilus*.

deplete. From L. *deplēre, -plet-*, to empty, lit. un-fill.

deplore. L. *deplorare*, from *plorare*, to weep.

deploy. F. *déployer*, L. *displicare*, to unfold. Mil. word from 18 cent. Cf. *display*.

deponent. From pres. part. of L. *deponere*, to put down. Used by Late L. grammarians of verbs which were supposed to have "laid down" their passive sense. The so-called deponent verbs were orig. reflexives corresponding to the G. middle voice. Leg. sense appears in Late L. *deponere*. With *deponent*, one who gives evidence, cf. *depositions*.

deport[1]. To behave (reflex.). From OF. *desporter*, from *porter*, to carry. Hence *deportment*.

deport[2]. To expel, transport. From F. *déporter* (18 cent.), L. *deportare*, also from *portare*, to carry, but mentally associated (like *import, export*) with *portus*, harbour (v.i.).

En vertu de cette loi, qu'on appelle *alien-bill*...si je commettais là [en Angleterre] quelque sottise... je serais banni du royaume, ou, pour mieux dire, déporté: cela s'exécute militairement. L'étranger qui se conduit mal ou déplaît, on le prend, on le mène au port le plus proche, on l'embarque sur le premier bâtiment prêt à faire voile, on le jette sur la première côte où il aborde
(P.-L. Courier, 1823).

depose. F. *déposer*, to set down (see *pose*). *Deposition* belongs to L. *deponere*, but the confusion between the two groups of words is complete.

deposit. First as noun. L. *depositum*, what is laid down (v.s.).

depot. F *dépôt*, OF. *depost*, L. *depositum*, from *deponere*. US. sense of railway station occurs earlier in E. of a goods station.

deprave. L. *depravare*, from *pravus*, crooked, wrong.

deprecate. From L. *deprecari*, to pray against.

depreciate. From L. *depretiare*, to lower price, *pretium*.

depredate. From L. *depraedari*, from *praeda*, prey.

depress. From L. *deprimere*, *depress-*, to press down, from *premere*. For fig. sense cf. *deject*.

deprive. OF. *depriver*, Late L. *deprivare for *privare*, to deprive. *Deprivatio* is recorded in Late L.

de profundis. L., out of the depths. First words of *Ps*. cxxx.

depth. Formed in ME. from *deep*, after *length*, *breadth*, etc. AS. has *dēopnes*.

depute. F. *députer*, L. *deputare*, lit. to cut off; cf. *detached for special service*. *Deputy* is F. p.p. *député*. From the sense of acting as agent comes that of substitute and also that of manager of a lodging-house.

deracinate. From F. *déraciner*, from *racine*, root, VL. *radicina*, from *radix*, *radic-*.

derail. F. *dérailler*. Adopted in US. earlier than in E. See *rail*[1].

derange. F. *déranger*, lit. to throw out of rank. See *range*, *arrange*. Not in Johns., who considered it a F. word. For application to insanity, orig. in *deranged mind* (*head*), cf. *disordered mind*. In gen. sense replaced by *disarrange*.

Derby. Race, at Epsom, founded (1780) by twelfth *Earl of Derby*. Parliament always adjourned for it before the carpet-bagging period. *Derby scheme*, *Derby man* date from the *Earl of Derby's* appeal (1915) to Britons to attest as ready for national service.

derelict. L. *derelictus*, p.p. of *derelinquere*, to forsake entirely. Hence *dereliction*, esp. in *dereliction of duty* (mod.).

deride. L. *deridēre*, to laugh at.

derive. F., L. *derivare*, to lead water, from *rivus*, brook. This is also orig. sense in F. & E.

I deryve, or bringe out thynge out of another, as water is brought whan it is brought from the spring: je derive (Palsg.).

derm [*med.*]. F. *derme*, G. δέρμα, skin. Cf. *dermis* (ModL.).

derogate. From L. *derogare*, to repeal partly,

from *rogare*, to ask. Orig. trans., to detract from.

To derogate the honour of the State
(Milton, *Smectymnuus*).

derrick. Gallows-shaped mech. device. From *Derrick*, hangman at Tyburn (c. 1600). A Du. name, *Diederik*, corresponding to Ger. *Theodoric*, *Dietrich*, people mighty, whence F. *Thierry* and our *Terry*. Naut. Du. *dirk*, "lifts," is the same word borrowed back.

I would there were a Derick to hang up him too
(Dekker, 1606).

derring-do [*archaic*]. Used several times by Spenser as an abstract noun, "manhood and chevalrie." He misunderstood a passage in Lydgate, misprinted *derrynge do*, which is imitated from Chauc. (v.i.). Revived by Scott (*Ivanhoe*, ch. xxix.) and hence used by other romantic writers.

And certeinliche in storie it is y-founde
That Troilus was nevere unto no wight,
As in his time, in no degre secounde
In durring don that longeth to a knight
[In daring to do what belongeth]
(Chauc. *Troilus*, v. 834).

derringer. Name of US. gunsmith c. 1850.

derry-down. Meaningless song refrain; cf. *tol-de-rol* and F. jingle *laridondaine*.

dervish. Turk. *dervīsh*, Pers. *darvīsh*, poor, hence religious mendicant; cf. F. *derviche*, It. *dervis*, etc. Equivalent to Arab. *faqīr*. *Dervish* is also loosely applied to Soudanese follower of the Mahdi, "fuzzy-wuzzy."

des-. OF. *des-* (*dés-*, *dé-*), L. *dis-*. See *dis-*.

descant. First as noun, variation on melody. OF. *deschant*, *descant* (*déchant*), MedL. *discantus*, part song. With to *descant on* cf. to *harp on*, *ring the changes on* (a theme).

descend. F. *descendre*, L. *descendere*, to climb (*scandere*) down.

describe. Reconstruction, on L. *describere*, to write down, of earlier *descrive*, OF. *descrire*, *descriv-* (*décrire*). All senses, including math., appear in 16 cent.

descry. OF. *descrier*, to shout, proclaim, equivalent to *escrier* (*écrier*), whence obs. E. *ascry*, *escry*, in same sense (see *cry*). Orig. used of announcing by a shout the presence of enemy, land, game, etc. (cf. *explore*). Occ. confused with obs. *descrive* (v.s.).

Mès le dit James Douglas fut escryé des gueites en l'ost, et se mist a le fuite
(*French Chron. of London*).

desecrate. Formed in E. as opposite of *con-secrate* (q.v.). L. *desecrare* means to make holy.

desert[1]. What is deserved. OF., from *de-servir* (*desservir*), L. *deservire*, to serve well, and, in VL., to merit (cf. Ger. *verdienen*, to merit, from *dienen*, to serve). Now usu. in bad sense, to *get one's deserts*.

desert[2]. Wilderness. F. *désert*, L. *desertum* (wilderness in *Vulg.*), from L. *deserere*, to abandon, lit. to unbind, from *serere*, *sert-*.

desert[3]. Verb. F. *déserter*, from above; cf. Late L. *desertare*, It. *desertare*, Sp. *desertar*. In mil. sense from 17 cent.

deserve. See *desert[1]*.

déshabillé, dishabille. F. *déshabillé*, un-dressed. See *habiliment*.

desiccate. From L. *desiccare*, to make dry, *siccus*.

desiderate. From L. *desiderare*, of which *desideratum* is the p.p. neut. See *desire*.

design. F. *désigner*, L. *designare*, to mark out, from *signum*, mark. Noun was earlier also *desseigne*, after F. *dessein*, It. *disegno*. F. now differentiates *dessein*, project, *dessin*, drawing, but they are the same word. For deterioration of sense cf. *plot*.

Artful and designing 'Tilda! (*Nickleby*, ch. xlii.).

desipience. L. *desipientia*, from *desipere*, to be silly, from *sapere*, to know, be wise.

desire. F. *désirer*, L. *desiderare*, orig. to regret. Prob., like *consider* (q.v.), derived from *sidus*, *sider-*, star. In earlier use often to look back with regret.

He reigned in Jerusalem eight years, and departed without being desired (2 *Chron.* xxi. 20).

desist. F. *désister*, L. *desistere*, to stand back.

desk. It. *desco*, "a deske, a table, a boord, a counting boord" (Flor.), L. *discus*, disk, in Late L. table (cf. Ger. *tisch*, from L.). Hence MedL. *desca* (by analogy with *mensa*, *tabula*), which is the source of ME. *deske* (Chauc.). See *dish*, *dais*.

desm-. G. δεσμός, bond, chain.

desolate. From L. *desolare*, to desert, leave alone, *solus*.

He which that hath no wyf I holde hym shent;
He lyveth helplees and al desolat (Chauc. E. 1320).

despair. First as verb. OF. *desperer*, *despeir-* (replaced by *désespérer*), L. *desperare*, to give up hope, from *sperare*, to hope. As noun has supplanted native *wanhope*, from AS. *wan*, wanting.

despatch. See *dispatch*.

desperado. From c. 1600. OSp., p.p. of *desperar* (replaced by *desesperar*), to despair.

desperate. L. *desperatus*, p.p. of *desperare*, to despair. For intens. sense (*desperate scoun-drel*) cf. *desperado*.

despise. OF. *despire*, *despis-*, L. *despicere*, to look down, from *specere*, to look. Cf. *des-picable*, *despite*.

despite. OF. *despit* (*dépit*), L. *despectus*, from *despicere* (v.s.); cf. It. *dispetto*, "despight" (Flor.). Orig. scorn, as in *in despite of*, F. *en dépit de*, i.e. in contempt of, short-ened to *despite of* or simply *despite*. Often *despight* in 16 cent. (cf. *delight*, *sprightly*). Now replaced in most senses by aphet. *spite* (cf. *sport*, *splay*, etc.).

despoil. OF. *despoilier* (*dépouiller*), L. *des-poliare*, to plunder; cf. It. *dispogliare*, Sp. *despojar*. See *spoil*.

despond. From L. *despondēre* (sc. *animum*), to lose heart, lit. to give away, affiance, from *spondēre*, to promise. As noun only in *slough of despond* (Bunyan).

despot. F. *despote*, L., G. δεσπότης, orig. master of the house, and, in ModG., usual title of bishop. As title of various Balkan princes it appears in F. of 14 cent., whence its usual meaning in other Europ. langs. For sense-development cf. *tyrant*.

desquamation [*med.*]. From L. *desquamare*, to remove scales, *squama*.

dessert. F., from *desservir*, to clear away, from *servir*, to lay the table. OF. also *desserte*, still used of "fragments that re-main."

dessous. F., underneath, L. *de subtus*. In ModF. & E. for underwear, "undies."

destine. F. *destiner*, L. *destinare*, to make fast, cogn. with *stare*, to stand, and with *obstinate*.

destitute. L. *destitutus*, p.p. of *destituere*, to abandon, from *statuere*, to set up.

destrier [*hist.*]. Warhorse. F., MedL. *dex-trarius* (*equus*), because led by squire at knight's right hand.

destroy. OF. *destruire* (*détruire*), VL. **des-trugere* (cf. It. *distruggere*), for *destruere*, from *strues*, pile, building (cf. *demolish*). Hence *destroyer*, for *torpedo-boat destroyer*, replacing (1893) earlier *torpedo catcher*.

destruction. F., L. *destructio-n-* (v.s.).

desuetude. F. *désuétude*, L. *desuetudo*, disuse, from *de* and *suescere*, *suet-*, to be accus-tomed. See *custom*.

desultory. L. *desultorius*, from *desultor*, circus equestrian, lit. leaper down, from *desilire*, from *salire*, to leap.

desultores: horsemen that in bataille had two horses, and quickly would chaunge horses, and leape from one to an other (Coop.).

detach. F. *détacher*. See *attach*.

detail. F. *détail*, from *détailler*, to cut up. First (c. 1600) in phrase *in detail*, F. *en détail*, opposed to *en gros*. For mil. sense cf. *detach*. Oldest F. sense of the noun is replaced in E. by *retail*. See *tally, tailor*.

detain. F. *détenir*, VL. *detenire, for *detinēre*, to hold back. With leg. *detainer*, AF. infin. *detener*, cf. *remainder, disclaimer*, etc.

detect. From L. *detegere, detect-*, to uncover (see *thatch*). Hence *detective*, for *detective policeman, officer* (c. 1850), vulg. *tec'*.

détente [*neol.*]. Slackening of pol. tension. F., from *tendre*, to stretch. Cf. *detent*, in various mech. senses, orig. in OF. of the catch of a cross-bow.

detention. F. *détention*, L. *detentio-n-*, from *detinēre, detent-*, to detain.

deter. L. *deterrēre*, to frighten off.

deterge. L. *detergere*, to wipe off.

deteriorate. From L. *deteriorare*, from *deterior*, compar. of lost adj. *deter, from *de*, down. Cf. *inferior*, etc.

determine. F. *déterminer*, L. *determinare*. Orig. to bring (come) to an end, *terminus*, as still in some spec. senses (cf. *define*). *Self-determination* (of races) renders Ger. *selbstbestimmung*, an idealistic compd. much used early in 1917. *Determinism* as opposed to *freewill* is 19 cent.

detersive. See *deterge*.

detest. F. *détester*, L. *detestari*, to execrate, calling God to witness, *testis*.

detinue, writ of [*leg.*]. ME. *detenewe*, F. *détenu*, p.p. of *détenir*, to detain.

detonate. From L. *detonare*, to thunder down.

détour. F., from *détourner*, to turn aside. See *turn*.

detract. From L. *detrahere, detract-*, to draw away.

detrain [*mil.*]. From c. 1880, after *debark*. Cf. *debus*.

detriment. L. *detrimentum*, from *deterere, detrit-*, to rub away. Hence *detrimental*, younger brother of heir, regarded as ineligible suitor.

detritus [*geol.*]. Incorr. use of L. *detritus*, process of wearing down, from *deterere* (v.s.).

deuce. Two, at cards or dice. F. *deux*, L. *duos*; equal, at tennis, F. *à deux de jeu*.

Hence *the deuce!* dicer's exclamation at making lowest throw (*ambsace*), later adopted as euph. for *devil*. Cf. Ger. *daus*, two at dice, OF. *dous* (*deux*), similarly used. In secondary sense *deuce* may have been associated with ME. *dewes!* God! OF. *Dieus*, nom. & voc. of *Dieu*.

adua, adue, aduo: two by two, two and two togither; a dewce at tennice play (Flor.).
duini: two dewces at dice (*ib.*).

deus ex machina. L., god from a machine. Allusion to intervening deity suspended in air on ancient stage.

Deuteronomy. G. δευτερονόμιον, from δεύτερος, second, νόμος, law, used erron. by LXX. (*Deut.* xvii. 18), where Heb. original means "copy of this law."

deutzia. Flower. From *J. Deutz* (Amsterdam, 1781). Cf. *dahlia, fuchsia*, etc.

devanagari [*ling.*]. Sanskrit script. Sanskrit *deva-nāgarī*, lit. divine-urban.

devastate. From L. *devastare*, to lay waste. See *vast, waste*.

develope. F. *développer*, from OF. *veloper, voloper*, to wrap, from a radical *velop, volep*, of unknown origin, which is found also in Prov. *desvolopar*. Cf. *envelope* and It. *inviluppare*, to wrap up. Perh. from Teut. *wrap*, affected initially by L. *volvere*; cf. *Salop*, from Roman pronunc. of *Shropshire*, scrub shire.

deviate. From L. *deviare*, to depart from the way, *via*.

device. F. *devis* (m.), *devise* (f.), verbal nouns from *deviser*, to divide, arrange, VL. *divisare, for *dividere, divis-*, to divide; cf. It. *diviso, divisa*. The E. senses often confuse the two F. words. *To one's own devices* corresponds to OF. *à son devis*, where *devis* has sense of plan, decision. In her., e.g. *a banner with this strange device*, it was orig. an emblem used as distinctive mark (cf. *cognizance*). See *devise*.

devil. AS. *dēofol*, L. *diabolus*, G. διάβολος, lit. slanderer, from διαβάλλειν, to slander, lit. throw across. Used by the LXX. to render Heb. *Satan* (q.v.). Adopted in all Europ. langs., including OSlav. and Celt., e.g. F. *diable*, Ger. *teufel*, Norw. Dan. *djævel*, Welsh *diawl*, etc. Orig. the archfiend only, but early confused with *demon*. *Printer's devil* is 17 cent. In sense of junior doing work for superior there is prob. a reminiscence of the sorcerer's devil or familiar spirit. Hence perh. *Devil's own* for Inns of Court Volunteers (also 88th

Connaught Rangers). In cookery sense the allusion is to the temperature associated with the devil. For *go to the devil* the *NED.* quotes a chronicle of 1394 which represents Richard II as saying to the Earl of Arundel, "Quod si tu mihi imponas... vadas ad diabolum." For the *devil to pay* see *pay²*. So also *between the devil and the deep* (17 cent. also *Dead*) *sea* has been connected with *devil* in the sense of seam close to the waterline. But in each case the naut. interpretation is prob. secondary. With the last phrase cf. G. ἔμπροσθεν κρημνός, ὄπισθεν λύκοι, a precipice in front, wolves behind. The *devil on two sticks* is the name of a game recently revived as *diabolo*. *Devil's advocate* is for Church L. *advocatus Diaboli*, raising objections to canonization. *Devil-may-care* is first recorded as adj. in *Pickwick*, but the interj. *devil care!* is much older. *Foreign devil*, as opposed to *Celestial* (Chinese), is a misunderstanding of Chin. *yang-kiwei*, ocean ghost, a name given to the Du. sailors, whose fair hair and pale faces appeared ghostly to the Chinese. *What the devil... is* directly from F. *que diable...* (12 cent.).

They report this pagan deity to have beene a woman, yea that she still lives (the divell she doth!) but will not shew her selfe (Purch. 1611).

These boys do in a printing-house commonly black and dawb themselves: whence the workmen do jocosely call them devils (*NED.* 1683).

devious. From L. *devius*, out of the way, *via*.

devise. F. *deviser*, VL. *divisare* (see *device*). In this, as in other words, the mod. distinction between -*s*- and -*c*- is artificial. Orig. to arrange, etym. sense surviving in law, to *devise* being to arrange a "division" of one's property.

devoid. Orig. p.p. of obs. verb *devoid*, to empty out, OF. *desvuidier* (replaced by *dévider*). See *avoid*.

devoir [*archaic*]. Restored from ME. *dever*, OF. *deveir* (*devoir*), L. *debēre*, used as noun. See *endeavour*.

devolve. L. *devolvere*, to roll down. Hence *devolution*, opposed, in biol., to *evolution*, and used pol. for *decentralization*.

Devonian [*geol.*]. Old red sandstone, between carboniferous and Silurian, well exemplified in *Devon*, and adopted as geol. term in F. and other langs.

devote. From L. *devovēre*, *devot*-, to dedicate by vow, *votum*. Hence *devotee*, by analogy with *refugee*, *payee*, etc. (which represent

the F. p.p.), replacing earlier *devote*, F. *dévot-e*, devout.

devour. F. *dévorer*, L. *devorare*, to swallow down, from *vorare*, to swallow. Fire is called the *devouring element* by Spenser.

devout. F. *dévot*, L. *devotus*, p.p. of *devovēre*, to devote. Hence *devoutly*, sincerely, esp. in *consummation devoutly to be wish'd* (*Haml.* iii. 1).

dew. AS. *dēaw*. Com. Teut.; cf. Du. *dauw*, Ger. *tau*, ON. *dögg*. *Mountain dew* is whisky illicitly distilled on mountains. *Dewlap* (14 cent.), *dewclaw* (16 cent.) prob. belong together, as F. *fanon* means both dewlap and the hair of the fetlock. For *dewlap* see *lap¹*. The first element is prob. *dew*, though in the Scand. equivalents the first element (Dan. Norw. *dog*-, Sw. *drög*-) does not mean dew. Both the *dewlap* and *dewclaw* come naturally into contact with the dew. *Dew-pond* is a dial. word (Wilts.) recently adopted.

controngle: the deaw-claw, or water-claw, of dogs, etc. (Cotg.).

dewan. See *divan*.

dewitt [*hist.*]. To murder by mob-violence, the fate of John and Cornelius *de Witt*, opponents of William of Orange (1672). Cf. *burke*, *lynch*, *boycott*. A pamphlet published in 1695 was entitled "The De-Witting of Glencoe."

dexter [*her.*]. L., on the right hand. Cogn. with G. δεξιός, Goth. *taihswa*, OHG. *zeso*, *zesw*-. Hence *dexterous* (with etym. sense surviving in *ambi-dexterous*), *dexterity*.

dextrin [*chem.*]. Named (1833) by Biot and Persoz. Cf. chem. terms in *dextro*-, due to causing plane of ray of polarized light to rotate to the right.

dey [*hist.*]. F., Turk. *dāī*, maternal uncle, applied to commander of janissaries at Algiers, who in 1710 deposed the civil governor and became ruler.

dhoby [*Anglo-Ind.*]. Washerman. Hind. *dhōbi*, from *dhōb*, washing.

dhooly. See *doolie*.

dhourra. See *durra*.

dhow, dow. Vessel, esp. of slavers. ModArab. *dāw*. Origin unknown.

di-. For L. *di-*, *dis-*, apart, or G. δι- for δίς, twice, corresponding to L. *bi-*.

dia-. G. διά, through, cogn. with δίς (v.s.); also *di-*.

diabetes. G., from διαβαίνειν, to pass through. Cf. *diarrhoea*.

diablerie. F., devilry. See *devil*.

diabolical. See *devil*.

diabolo. Fancy name for old game revived c. 1907. App. a mixture of It. *diavolo* and Sp. *diablo*. See *devil*.

diachylon. Orig. ointment of vegetable juices. L. *diachylon*, G. διὰ χυλῶν, by means of juices, from χυλός, juice (see *chyle*).

diaconal. See *deacon*.

diacritic. G. διακριτικός, from διακρίνειν, to separate, distinguish.

diadem. F. *diadème*, L., G. διάδημα, fillet, esp. royal fillet of Pers. kings adopted by Alexander the Great. From G. διαδεῖν, to bind round.

diaeresis. G., from διαιρεῖν, to take apart.

diagnosis. G., from διαγιγνώσκειν, to discern, know apart. *Diagnose* is a back-formation.

diagonal. From G. διαγώνιος, from γωνία, angle.

diagram. F. *diagramme*, G. διάγραμμα, from διαγράφειν, to mark out.

dial. Only in E. App. MedL. *dialis*, from *dies*, used for *diurnalis*. Froissart has *dyal*, explained as *roe journal*, day wheel. First of sun-dial (Lydgate).

diall to knowe the houres by the course of the sonne: quadrant (Palsg.).

dialect. L., G. διάλεκτος, from διαλέγεσθαι, to discourse. Earlier is *dialectic* (Wyc.), art of formal discussion, invented, according to Aristotle, by Zeno of Elea, and perfected by Plato, G. διαλεκτική (sc. τέχνη).

dialogue. F., L., G. διάλογος (v.s.). *Dialogues of St Gregory* are mentioned in *Ancren Riwle* (early 13 cent.). Sometimes felt as limited to two persons, through confusion between *dia-* and *di-*.

dialysis. G. διάλυσις. See *analysis*.

diameter. F. *diamètre*, L., G. διάμετρος, measuring through.

diamond. F. *diamant*, Late L. *diamas, diamant-*, corrupt. of *adamas*. See *adamant*, in sense of which Milton still uses *diamond*. *Diamond* (i.e. smallest) *type* is of Du. origin. Dryden calls Chaucer a *rough diamond*.

Diana. Type of purity, or huntress. L. divinity, later identified with G. Artemis, e.g. *Diana of the Ephesians*. For *Divana*, from *divus*, god.

diapason. L., G. διὰ πασῶν, through all, for ἡ διὰ πασῶν χορδῶν συμφωνία. Cf. *diatessaron*.

diaper. OF. *diaspre* (whence F. *diaprer*, to checker), MedL. *diasprus*, MedG. δίασπρος, ? white in places, from Byzantine G. ἄσπρος,

white. Used in OF. of a precious flowered fabric. The sense-development has been influenced by *jasper*, with which it is confused in MedL., It. & Sp. (cf. F. *marbré*, used of patterns from 12 cent.).

diaphanous. From G. διαφανής, transparent, from φαίνειν, to show.

diaphoretic. G. διαφορητικός, promoting perspiration, from διαφορεῖν, to carry off.

diaphragm. L., G. διάφραγμα, from φράγμα, fence, from φράσσειν, to hedge in, etc. E. word is *midriff* (q.v.).

diarchy. See *dyarchy*.

diarrhoea. L., G. διάρροια, from διαρρεῖν, to flow through.

diary. L. *diarium*, daily allowance, later, daily record, from *dies*, day.

diastole. Dilatation (of heart), opposed to *systole*, contraction. G. διαστολή, from διαστέλλειν, to put asunder. Often fig.

The great respiration, ebb and flood, systole and diastole, of the national intercourse (De Quincey).

diatessaron. Gospel harmony. From title given (2 cent.) by Tatian to his gospel harmony, Εὐαγγέλιον διὰ τεσσάρων, gospel made of four. Cf. *diapason*.

diatonic. G. διατονικός, through the notes, τόνος.

diatribe. F., L., G. διατριβή, wearing away (of time), from διατρίβειν, to rub through. Orig. discourse, etc.; from c. 1800 associated with invective.

dib, dibble. Lighter forms of *dab, dabble*; cf. *dibchick* for *dabchick*. *Dibs*, money, earlier applied to counters used at play (cf. *chips*), is perh. the same word; also *dibstones, dabs*, used of a children's game. *Dibber*, for gardening, is prob. old in dial.

dicast [*hist.*]. G. δικαστής, judge, juryman, from δίκη, justice.

dice. See *die*².

dichotomy. G. διχοτομία, cutting in two, from δίχα, in two, τέμνειν, to cut.

Dick, dick¹. Rimed pet form of *Richard*. Often used, as one of the commonest E. names (cf. *Jack*), as equivalent to fellow, e.g. *dirty Dick; Tom, Dick and Harry*. So also *dicky bird* (cf. *robin redbreast, jack daw*, etc.), *dicky*, a donkey (cf. *neddy*), *dick*, a leather bib, *dicky*, a detachable shirt-front, seat in carriage. Some of these are no doubt old, though early records are naturally hard to find.

dick² [*slang*]. In to *take one's dick*. Short for *declaration* (cf. *davy* for *affidavit*). Hence also *up to dick*, i.e. up to declared quality.

dickens. Euph. for *devil*; cf. *old Nick*. From *Dicken*, *Dickon*, pet form of *Richard*, whence also surname *Dickens*.

I cannot tell what the dickens his name is
     (*Merry Wives*, iii. 2).

dicker [*techn.*]. Ten, esp. ten hides. L. *de-curia*, set of ten. The wide and early extension of this word, which occurs in *Domesday Book* and prob. existed in AS., is supposed to be due to ten hides having been adopted by the Romans as unit of tribute and barter on the frontier. Cf. Du. *daker*, Ger. *decher*, "a dicker of leather, ten hides" (Ludw.), Icel. *dekr*, Norw. Dan. *deger*, Sw. *däcker*, also MedL. *dacra*, OF. *dacre*. It is likely that US. *dicker*, orig. to barter for skins with the Indians on the frontier, is the same word, a curious parallel to its hist. origin.

Husbands will be too scarce to dicker about
  (Gertrude Atherton, *The Living Present*, 1917).

dicky¹. See *dick¹*.

dicky². Inferior, shaky. Slang, from c. 1800. Origin unknown.

dictate. From L. *dictare*, frequent. of *dicere*, to say. Hence *dictator*, orig., in Republican Rome, magistrate invested temporarily with absolute power. Cf. *food dictator*.

diction. F., L. *dictio-n-*, from *dicere*, *dict-*, to say; cogn. with Ger. *zeihen*, to accuse (*verzeihen*, to forgive), AS. *tēon*, to accuse.

dictionary. MedL. *dictionarium* or *dictionarius* (sc. *liber*), a collection of "dictions," usu. arranged under subject-headings and not alphabetically. E. word, as book-title, dates prob. from Sir Thomas Elyot's *Latin Dictionary* (1538), and F. *dictionnaire* from Robert Estienne's *Dictionnaire francois-latin* (1539).

dictum. L., from *dicere*, *dict-*, to say. Hence archaic F. *dit*, saying.

didactic. G. διδακτικός, from διδάσκειν, to teach.

didapper. Dabchick. For *dive-dapper*, from obs. *dive-dap*, AS. *dūfedoppa*, from *dūfan*, to dive, and second element cogn. with *dip*. Cf. synon. F. *plongeon*, Ger. *tauchente*, "diving duck."

diddle. To swindle. Back-formation (cf. *peddle*) from *Jeremy Diddler*, name of swindling character in Kenney's farce *Raising the Wind* (1803). Cf. *burke*, *boycott*, *Mrs Grundy*, etc. But the selection of the name was prob. due to dial. *duddle*, to trick (16 cent.), app. related to dial.

diddle, to totter (cf. sense-history of *swindle*), and ult. with AS. *dyderian*, to fool.

This was their fine device to fray our horses, when our horsemen should come at them. Howbeit, because the riders were no babies, nor their horses any colts, they could neither duddle the one, nor affray the other (W. Patten, 1548).

didymium [*chem.*]. Named (1843) from G. δίδυμος, twin, because of its close association with *lanthanium*.

die¹. Verb. ME. *deghen*, ON. *deyja*, replacing AS. *steorfan* (cf. Ger. *sterben* and see *starve*). Usual ME. form was *dey* (cf. Sc. *dee*). See *dead*. The *Die-hards*, Middlesex regiment (old 57th foot), won the title at Albuera (1811).

die². Sing. of *dice*. ME. also *de*, *dee*, *dey*, F. *dé*, L. *datum*, from *dare*, in sense of throw (cf. Ger. *würfel*, from *werfen*). See *dado*. Chauc. MSS. have pl. *dees*, *deis*, *dys*, *dyse*, *dise*. Pl. *dice* is often used as sing. in 14–17 cents. and the sing. hardly occurs now exc. in fig. phrases. With *true*, *straight*, *as a die* cf. earlier *smooth as a die*. The other senses, cubical block, stamping-die, are much later (17 cent.). *The die is cast* is after L. *jacta est alea*, ascribed to Caesar on crossing the Rubicon.

dies irae. Opening words of L. hymn ascribed to Thomas of Celano (c. 1250).

dies non [*leg.*]. For *dies non juridicus*, day not counting for legal purposes.

diet¹. Rations. F. *diète*, L. *diaeta*, G. δίαιτα, system of life. Cf. It. Sp. *dieta*.

diet². Parliamentary assembly. MedL. *dieta*, whence F. *diète*. In E. used (from 16 cent.) esp. of such Ger. bodies as the Reichstag, Bundestag, Landtag (though the word is foreign to Ger.), and also of Hungary and Poland. MedL. *dieta* meant also a day's journey, work, wage, etc., corresponding thus to F. *journée*. This fact, and the spec. use of *diet* for Ger. -*tag*, day (see *daysman*, *Reichstag*), point to derivation from L. *dies*. It occurs in 15 cent. Sc. both for formal meeting and day's work. The form of the MedL. word was no doubt suggested by association with *diet¹* (q.v.), hence agreement in form of the two words in the Rom. langs. (v.i.).

dieta: a diet or abstinence from meate or prescription when to eate. Also a parliament or generall assembly of estates (Flor.).

differ. F. *différer*, from L. *differre*, from *dis-* and *ferre*, to bear. Ident. with *defer¹* (q.v.), from which it has been differentiated in sense and sound since c. 1500. With *difference*, quarrel, cf. *variance*. The *differential calculus*, dealing with infinitesimal differences, was invented by Leibnitz (1677). Hence *differentiate*, a neol. first used in math.

difficult. Back-formation from *difficulty*, L. *difficultas*, replacing (16 cent.) earlier *difficil*, F. *difficile*, L. *difficilis*, from *dis-* and *facilis*, easy.

Al thinges seme dyfficyle to the dyscyple (Caxton).

diffident. From pres. part. of L. *diffidere*, to distrust. Now usu. of distrusting oneself.

Thou dost shame thy mother
And wound her honour with this diffidence
(*King John*, i. 1).

diffract. From L. *diffringere*, *diffract-*, to break (*frangere*) apart.

diffuse. First as adj., F. *diffus*, L. *diffusus*, p.p. of L. *diffundere*, to pour apart.

dig. F. *diguer*, to prick, spur, orig. to excavate, from *digue*, dike. Of Teut. origin; cf. *dike* and AS. *dīcian*, to dig. Orig. weak (past always *digged* in *AV.*). Replaces (from 14 cent.) native *delve* (q.v.) and *grave*. *Diggings*, abode, is found almost as early (1838) as first record in sense of gold-diggers' camp.

digamma. Sixth letter of orig. G. alphabet, from Semit., with sound *w* or *v*. So called because it (**F**) was the shape of two *gammas* (**Γ**).

digest. Earliest (14 cent.) E. sense is body of Roman Law compiled by order of Justinian. From L. neut. pl. *digesta*, from *digerere*, to put apart, arrange; also *digerere cibum*, to digest food.

dight [*poet.*]. Orig. p.p. of AS. *dihtan*, to compose, L. *dictare*, whence also Ger. *dichten*, to write poetry. Very common in ME., to equip, order, prepare, etc., but obs. after Milton till revived by Scott.

Storied windows richly dight (*Penseroso*, 159).

Why do these steeds stand ready dight? (*Lay*, i. 6).

digit. L. *digitus*, finger. First in math. sense, the Arab. notation being based on the ten fingers. Hence ModL. *digitalis*, fox-glove, named by Fuchs (1542) after Ger. *fingerhut*, fox-glove, lit. thimble, "finger-hat." With *digitigrade*, toe-walking (cats, dogs, etc.), cf. *plantigrade* (bears).

dignity. F. *dignité*, L. *dignitas*, from *dignus*, worthy. See *deign*, *dainty*. *Dignitary* is F. *dignitaire*.

digraph. From G. δι-, two, γραφή, writing. See *diphthong*.

digress. From L. *digredi*, *digress-*, to step aside, from *dis-* and *gradior*, I step.

dike, dyke. AS. *dīc*, excavation, later also mound resulting (cf. *moat* for converse case of double sense, also Du. *dam*, bank, pool). Ident. with *ditch* (q.v.), the EAngl. currency of the word being prob. due to association with cogn. Du. *dijk*, dam. Cf. also Ger. *teich*, pool. The office of *dike-reeve*, surveyor of dams and water-courses, still exists in the fen-country.

dilapidate. From L. *dilapidare*, orig. to throw stones, *lapis*, *lapid-*, apart, as still in geol.

dilate. F. *dilater*, L. *dilatare*, from *latus*, wide. With to *dilate on*, earlier also to *dilate oneself on*, cf. *expatiate* and colloq. to *spread oneself*.

dilatory. Late L. *dilatorius*, from *differre*, *dilat-*, to put off.

dilemma. G. δίλημμα, from δι-, double, λῆμμα, assumption, from λαμβάνειν, to take. The alternatives are commonly called the "horns," as they catch one on both sides.

Either horn of the dilemma impales him
(*Pall Mall Gaz.* Sep. 3, 1917).

dilettante. It., from *dilettare*, to delight (q.v.), L. *delectare*. Cf. *amateur*, ModE. sense of which is now replaced in F. by *dilettante*.

diligent. F., from pres. part. of L. *diligere*, to delight in, orig. to choose (*legere*) between (*dis-*). *Diligence*, stage-coach, F., is for *carrosse de diligence*, coach of dispatch. Hence dial. *dilly* for various vehicles.

dill. Plant. AS. *dile* (*Matt.* xxiii. 23); cf. Du. *dille*, Ger. *dill*. Origin unknown.

dilly[1]. See *diligence*.

dilly[2]. Nursery name for duck, as in "dilly, dilly, come and be killed."

dilly-bag [*Austral.*]. Native *dilli*, bag of rushes (Queensland). See *ditty-bag*.

dilly-dally. Redupl. on *dally*. Cf. *shilly-shally*.

dilute. From L. *diluere*, *dilut-*, from *luere*, to wash. *Dilution* of (skilled) labour is a neol.

The May agreement made provision for dilutees being first taken from the workshops
(*Sunday Times*, Jan. 20, 1918).

diluvial. Resulting from flood. See *deluge*, *antediluvian*.

dim. AS. *dimm*, dark, wicked; cf. ON. *dimmr*, OHG. *timbar*, Swiss. dial. *timmer*. App. cogn. with Ger. *dämmern*, to be twilight (cf. *Götterdämmerung*), and L. *tenebrae*.

dime [*US.*]. F. *dîme*, tenth part, tithe, Church L. *decima* (sc. *pars*), whence ME. *dime* in same sense. Adopted (1786) in US. for tenth of dollar (ten cents). With US. *dime novel* cf. *penny dreadful, shilling shocker*.

dimension. F., L. *dimensio-n-*, from *demetiri*, to measure out, from *metiri, mens-*.

dimidiated. Halved. See *demy*.

diminish. Combined (c. 1400) from earlier *diminue*, F. *diminuer*, L. *diminuere*, and *minish*, F. *menuiser*, VL. **minutiare*, from *minutus*, from *minuere*, cogn. with *minor*, less. See *mince*.

Ye shall not minish ought from your bricks of your daily task (*Ex.* v. 19).

dimissory letters [*eccl.*]. L. *litterae dimissoriae*, valedictory letter, from *dimittere, dimiss-*, to dismiss.

dimity. It. *dimiti*, pl. of *dimito*, MedL. *dimitum*, from G. δίμιτος, of double thread, μίτος. Cf. *twill, samite*.

dimorphous. From G. δίμορφος, from δι-, two, and μορφή, form.

dimple. Cogn. with dial. *dimble, dumble*, ravine (e.g. *Lambley Dumbles* near Nottingham), Ger. *tümpel*, pool, and ult. with *deep, dip*. Cf. synon. F. *fossette*, Ger. *grübchen*.

fossette: a little pit; small hole; narrow ditch, or trench; also, a dimple on the cheeke, or chin (Cotg.).

din. AS. *dyne*, noun, *dynian*, verb; cf. ON. *dynr*, din, MHG. *tünen*, to rumble, Sanskrit *dhūni*, roaring.

dinar. See *denier*.

dine. F. *dîner*, OF. *disner*, VL. **disjunare* for **disjejunare*, to break fast, from *jejunus*, fasting. The two verbs *dîner, déjeuner* are from the atonic and tonic stems respectively, e.g. **disjunare* gave OF. *disner*, **disjunat* gave OF. *desjuene*. *Diner*, for *dining-car*, is US.

ding[1] [*archaic*]. To knock, beat. Cf. ON. *dengja*, to hammer. A strong verb (*dang, dung*) and the origin of *dangle* (q.v.); cf. Ger. *dengeln*. Possibly of imit. origin (v.i.).

ding[2]**, ding-dong.** Imit. Perh. ident. with *ding*[1]. The two ideas run together in a *ding-dong struggle*.

dinghy, dingey. Hind. *dēngī, dīngī*, small boat, dug out from log.

dingle. Of late appearance (17 cent.) in literature and app. cogn. with *dimple* (q.v.). Recorded earlier once (13 cent.) in sense of abyss.

dingo. Austral. wild dog. From obs. native (NSW.) name. Cf. *kangaroo*.

dingy. A dial. (SE.) word of late appearance in literature. Prob. from *dung*. For changed sound of *-g-* cf. *stingy*.

dinky [*neol.*]. Dainty, spruce. Cf. dial. *dink* (Sc. & north). Origin unknown.

My lady's dink, my lady's drest,
The flower and fancy o' the west (Burns).

A dinky little rail-road (O. Henry).

dinner. F. *dîner*, infin. as noun (cf. *supper*). See *dine*.

dinornis. Scient. name for *moa*. Coined (1843) by Owen from G. δεινός, terrible, ὄρνις, bird.

dinosaur. Gigantic fossil lizard. From G. σαῦρος, lizard (v.s.). Coined (1841) by Owen.

dinothere. Gigantic fossil tapir. From G. θηρίον, wild beast (v.s.).

dint. Also *dent* (q.v.) and dial. *dunt*. AS. *dynt*; cf. ON. *dyntr*. Orig. blow of weapon; hence *by dint of* (sword, axe, etc.); cf. *push of pike*.

We have [at Pinkie] overcome the double of our number and strength, in open field, by plain dint of sword (W. Patten, 1548).

diocese. F. *diocèse*, MedL. *diocesis*, governor's (in Church L. bishop's) jurisdiction, G. διοίκησις, orig. house-keeping, from διοικεῖν, to manage, from οἶκος, house. See *parish*.

dioecious [*biol.*]. Sexually separate. Coined by Linnaeus from G. δι-, twice, οἶκος, house.

Diogenic. Of *Diogenes*, cynic philosopher (4 cent. B.C.). Cf. *Socratic*.

dionysiac. Pertaining to *Dionysus* (Bacchus). Cf. *aphrodisiac, bacchanalian*.

Dionysian. As above. Also, in *Dionysian era*, from abbot *Dionysius* (6 cent.) who is supposed to have established chronology from birth of Christ. Also of *Dionysius*, tyrant of Syracuse, and *Dionysius* the Areopagite (*Acts*, xvii. 34).

dioptric. G. διοπτρικός, from διόπτρα, from δι-, δια-, through, ὀπ- as in *optics* (q.v.).

diorama. Coined on *panorama* from G. διορᾶν, to see through.

Dioscuri. Twins. G. Διόσκουροι, Castor and Pollux, twins of Leda. From Διός, genitive of Ζεύς, and κοῦρος, boy.

dip. AS. *dyppan*, cogn. with *deep*; cf. Du. *doopen*, Ger. *taufen*, ON. *deypa*, Goth. *daupjan*, all chiefly in sense of baptize. With to *dip into a book* cf. to *dabble in* *philology*, to *skim a novel*. *Dip*, candle, is for earlier *dip-candle*, made by dipping wick in tallow instead of moulding. Hence *dips*, the purser (Marryat), as *chips*, the carpenter.

> None of your rascally "dips"—but sound,
> Round, tenpenny moulds of four to the pound
> (*Ingoldsby*).

diphtheria. From F. *diphthérie*, substituted (1855) by Bretonneau for his earlier *diphthérite* (1821) coined from G. διφθέρα, skin.

diphthong. F. *diphtongue*, L., G. δίφθογγος, from δι-, twice, φθόγγος, voice, sound. Prop. two vowel sounds in one syllable, as in *rice, found, foil*, but often used for *digraph*, double letter, e.g. *Cæsar*.

diploma. L., G. δίπλωμα, folded paper, from διπλοῦς, double, hence official document, certificate, etc. *Diplomatic* is F. *diplomatique*, having to do with diplomas, and *diplomat* is a back-formation after *aristocrat, democrat*, etc.

dipsomania. Coined (19 cent.) from G. δίψα, thirst.

diptera [*biol.*]. G., neut. pl. of δίπτερος, from δι-, two, πτερόν, wing.

diptych. L. *diptycha* (neut. pl.), Late G. δίπτυχα, pair of writing tablets, from δίπτυχος, double folded, from πτυχή, fold. Cf. *diploma*.

dire. L. *dirus*, terrible, cogn. with G. δεινός.

direct. First as verb. From L. *dirigere, direct-*, to make straight, from *regere*, to rule. For temporal meaning of *directly* cf. *immediately, straightway*. *Direct action* (pol.) is 20 cent. (cf. *Bolshevist, frightfulness*). *Directory* in sense of address-book is recorded (for London) in 1732. In hist. sense it translates F. *Directoire* (1795–99).

dirge. L. *dirige*, in antiphon at Matins in Office for the Dead, beginning "Dirige, Domine, Deus meus, in conspectu tuo viam meam" (*Ps*. v. 8). Cf. *placebo, requiem*.

> *dyryge*: offyce for ded men (*Prompt. Parv.*).

dirigible. From L. *dirigere*, to direct (q.v.). In aeronautics adopted from F. *dirigeable*.

diriment [*leg.*]. From pres. part. of L. *dirimere*, to separate, hence to nullify.

dirk. Earlier also *dork, durk*. The true Gael. word is *biodag*. Prob. from proper name *Dirk, Dirik*, used in Dan. & Sw., like Ger. *Dietrich*, of a picklock, and hence perh. applied to an instrument for "letting daylight into" the human body. Cf. double

meaning of Du. word below. See also *derrick*.

> *opsteeker*: a picklock, a great knife, or a dagger
> (Sewel, 1727).

dirt. ME., ON. *drit*, excrement. AS. has verb *drītan*. For metath. cf. *bird*. Used by Wyc. (*Philip*. iii. 8), var. *toordis*, for *Vulg. stercora* (*AV. dung*); cf. Du. *drijten*, stercorare. *Dirty Half-hundred*, 50th foot (1st bat. Royal West Kent), *Dirty Shirts* 101st foot (1st bat. Munster Fus.). The first name is said to be due to the men becoming smeared with dye from black facings of uniform in Peninsular War, the second to the regiment having fought in shirt-sleeves at Delhi (1857).

dis-. L. prefix cogn. with *bis* (for **dvis* = G. δίς, twice) and with *duo*, two. Hence sometimes E. *de-*, from OF. *des- (dé-)*, now often replaced by reconstruction, e.g: *disarrange, derange; disembark, debark; disinherit* (q.v.).

disaffected. See *affect*. Sense of mutinous from 17 cent.

disappoint. Prop. to break an arrangement, appointment. See *appoint*.

disaster. F. *désastre* or It. *disastro*, orig. evil star, L. *astrum*. Cf. *ill-starred*.

disband. F. *débander*, earlier *desbander*, imitated from It. *sbandare* in mil. sense. See *band²*.

disburse. OF. *desbourser (débourser)*, from *bourse*, purse. Cf. *out-of-pocket*. See *bursar, purse*.

disc. See *disk*.

discard. Earlier also *decard*. OF. *descarter*, to scatter (cf. Sp. Port. *descartar*), for more usual *escarter (écarter)*, VL. **exquartare*, to quarter out, remove portions (cf. It. *scartare*). Though early associated with card play it can hardly be from *card*, as *discard* could only mean to remove from the card (cf. *disburse, disgorge, disfranchise*, etc.). For formation, from L. *quartus*, cf. OF. *entercier*, to put on one side, from *tertius*, third.

discern. L. *discernere*, to separate.

discharge. OF. *descharger (décharger)*, to unload. See *charge*. With leg. sense cf. *exonerate*.

disciple. AS. *discipul* and F. *disciple*, L. *discipulus*, pupil, from **discipere* (contrasted with *praecipere*, to teach), but influenced by *discere*, to learn. E. sense has been determined by Bibl. use. AS. had also *leorningcniht*. *Discipline* is F., L. *disciplina*.

disclaimer. AF. infin. as noun, OF. *des-clamer*, L. *disclamare*. Cf. *attainder, remainder, misnomer*, etc. See *claim*.

discobolus. Statue of quoit-thrower. From G. βάλλειν, to throw. See *disk*.

discomfit. OF. *desconfit*, p.p. of *desconfire* (*déconfire*), VL. **disconficere*, to undo (see *comfit*). First as p.p. in E.

discommon. To expel from community (see *common*). At Oxf. and Camb. (from 16 cent.) to deprive tradesman of liberty to supply undergraduates.

disconcert. Now usu. with personal object, but orig. of deranging, frustrating (plans, etc.). See *concert*.

disconsertare: to bring out of order, frame, tune, or proportion (Flor.).

discord. OF. *descorde*, L. *discordia*. See *accord*.

discount. OF. *desconte, descompte* (*décompte*), from *desconter*, to count off. See *count²*. ModF. now uses rather *escompte*, It. *sconto*.

discourse. F. *discours*, L. *discursus*, orig. running to and fro, from *discurrere*. Etym. sense appears in *discursive*.

Discourse, strictly speaking, is the motion or progress of the mind from one judgment to another (Wesley).

discover. OF. *descovrir* (*découvrir*), to uncover, as in *check by discovery* (chess). See *cover*.

discreet. F. *discret*, L. *discretus*, orig. separated, from *discernere*, but taking act. sense in Late L. Cf. Ger. *gescheidt*, clever, lit. separated. In *to surrender at discretion* the *discretion* is that of the victor. *Years of discretion*, fixed by E. law at fourteen (Littleton's *Tenures*), dates from 14 cent.

The better part of valour is discretion (1 *Hen. IV*. v. 4).

discrepant. From pres. part. of L. *discrepare*, lit. to sound ill, jar, from *crepare*, to sound. Cf. fig. sense of *clash*.

discriminate. From L. *discriminare*, to divide. See *crime*.

discursive. See *discourse*.

discuss. AF. *discusser*, from OF. *descous*, p.p. of *descoure*, L. *discutere*, to agitate, from *quatere*, to shake.

Tieux custumes et usages serront discuz par les mair et aldermans (*Liber Albus*, p. 214).

disdain. OF. *desdain, desdeign* (*dédain*), from *desdeignier* (*dédaigner*), VL. **disdignare* for *dedignari*, from *dignus*, worthy. See *deign*.

disease. OF. *desaise*, discomfort (see *ease*).

For strengthened sense cf. *disgust, disgrace*, all orig. euph. coinages.

The Kinges Majestie was a litle diseased with could [cold] takinge (Wriothesley, *Chron.* 1553).

disembogue [*archaic*]. To come into open sea, now esp. of rivers. Sp. *desembocar*, "to come out of the mouth of a river or haven" (Minsh.), from Sp. *boca*, mouth (see *debouch*). A word from the Spanish Main, earliest examples, var. *disemboque*, being from Drake, Hawkins, Raleigh, usu. of ship emerging from bay or river-mouth. Earlier is the simplex (v.i.), Sp. *embocar*, expressing the opposite. In Hakl. (viii. 412) we also find *disbock*, app. a Norman var. of OF. *desbocher*.

Where they...shall land, travayle, lodge, and ymbucke (*Commission to Sir W. Morgan*, 1577).

disestablish. In ref. to scheme directed against the Church of England first recorded in Gladstone's *Church and State* (1838).

disfigure. For sense cf. *deface, deform*.

disgorge. OF. *desgorger* (*dégorger*). App. from lang. of falconry (see *gorge*). Now usu. fig. Quot. below suggests a curious picture.

People found hoarding oil will be made to disgorge it, as was done in the case of food (*Daily News*, Sep. 26, 1918).

disgrace. Orig. loss of favour (*grace*), as still in F. Cf. *in disgrace*. For strengthened sense cf. *disease, disgust*.

I hear Macduff lives in disgrace (*Macb*. iii. 6).

disgruntled. Now chief US., but 17 cent. E. From *gruntle*, frequent. of *grunt*.

disguise. OF. *desguiser* (*déguiser*), to change costume (see *guise*). Not orig. with sense of concealment. Cf. *disguised in liquor* (Massinger), appearance being changed by intoxication.

He [the prophet] is disguised from the rest in his apparell (Purch.).

disgust. OF. *desgoust* (*dégoût*). See *gusto*. Orig. distaste, now strengthened in meaning.

dish. AS. *disc*, bowl, platter, L. *discus*, quoit, dish (in *Vulg.*). See *disk*. Cf. Ger. *tisch* (from L.), table, and see *dais, desk*. Wyc. uses it also in L. sense of quoit. *Dish of tea* (*coffee*) is common in 17–19 cents. With to *dish*, to baffle, cf. to *do for*, to *cook one's goose, settle one's hash*. Esp. in hist. phrase *dishing the Whigs* (Reform Bill, 1867), perh. due to Disraeli, who often uses the verb.

dishabille [*archaic*]. See *déshabillé*. For loss of final syllable cf. *signal²*, *defile²*, etc. See *habiliment*.

dishevelled. Earlier *dishevely*, *dishevel*, OF. *deschevelé* (*déchevelé*, usu. replaced by *échevelé*), from *dis-* and *chevel* (*cheveu*), hair, L. *capillus*. *Dishevelled hair* is thus pleon.

disinherit. Preserves obs. sense of *inherit* (q.v.), to make heir. For earlier *disherit*, F. *déshériter*.

disjunctive. L. *disjunctivus*. See *join*.

disk, disc. L. *discus*, G. δίσκος, quoit, its earliest sense in E. (Pope's *Iliad*). See *dais, desk, dish*.

dislike. Hybrid, replacing (16 cent.) native *mislike* (q.v.).

dismal. From ME. *in the dismal*, with which cf. mod. *in the dismals*. OF. *dis mal*, L. *dies mali*, unpropitious days of medieval calendar, also called *dies Aegyptiaci*. The word is still esp. used with *day*. Chauc. app. understood it as OF. *dis mals* (*dix maux*), ten plagues.

Ore dirrai des jours denietz [forbidden]
Que vous dismal appeletz
(AF. *Art de Kalender*, 13 cent.).

I trowe hit was in the dismalle,
That was the ten woundes of Egipte
(Chauc. *Blanche the Duchess*, 1205).

dismantle. Earliest (16 cent.) in mil. sense, to raze. OF. *desmanteler* (*démanteler*), to strip. See *mantle*.

dismay. AF. **desmaier*, for OF. *esmaier*, whence ModF. *émoi*, agitation. From *dis-* and Teut. *mag*, power, as in OHG. *magan* (*mögen*), to be able, E. *may*. Cf. It. *sma gare*, Sp. *desmaiar*. For E. preference for *dis-* cf. *discard*, *dishevel*.

dismiss. For earlier *dismit*, OF. *desmetre* (*démettre*), from L. *dimittere, dimiss-*, from *mittere*, to send, with usual change of prefix in VL.

disorder. F. *désordre*. The verb is for earlier *disordain*, OF. *desordener, desordein-* (now *désordonner*). See *order, ordain*.

disoriented [*neol.*]. Adaptation of F. *dés-orienté*, having lost one's bearings. See *orientation*.

The returned soldier, bewildered, disoriented, nerve-wracked (*Times Lit. Sup.* Jan. 19, 1920).

disparage. OF. *desparagier*, orig. to marry unequally (cf. *mésalliance*), also earliest sense in E., from *parage*, rank, "peerage." See *peer¹*.

disparity. See *parity*.

dispart [*mil.*]. Difference between semi-diameters of cannon at base-ring and muzzle. Hence, sight constructed to allow for difference. App. from archaic *dispart*, to separate, OF. *despartir* (*départir*), L. *dispartire, -pertire*, to divide.

dispatch, despatch. Sp. *despachar*, to expedite, opposite of *empachar*, to impede (cf. It. *dispacciare, impacciare*). Has absorbed and superseded obs. *depeach*, F. *dépêcher*; but the two words are not related, F. *-pêcher* representing VL. **pedicare*, to cause to stumble, from *pedica*, fetter (*pes, ped-*, foot), while the radical of the Sp. & It. words is prob. *pact-*, from *pangere*, to fasten. First used by Bp Tunstall, Commissioner to Spain (1516–17). For *happy dispatch* (19 cent.) see *hara-kiri*.

dispel. L. *dispellere*, to drive apart.

dispense. OF. *despenser* (*dépenser*), L. *dispensare*, frequent. of *dispendere*, to weigh out. Hence *dispensary*, place for "weighing out" medicines, first in Garth's mock-heroic poem, *The Dispensary* (1699). In *dispensation*, the sense of ordering, management, e.g. *divine dispensation, Mosaic dispensation*, is due to rendering in *NT*. of G. οἰκονομία, office, method of administration, by L. *dispensatio*, weighing out, stewardship. Sense of exemption, relaxation, springs from MedL. sense of *dispensare*, to act as steward, deal administratively with spec. cases, whence *dispense from, with*. The *dispensing power* (of kings) first occurs temp. Charles I.

disperse. F. *disperser*, L. *dispergere, -spers-*, to scatter (*spargere*) apart.

dispiteous. For archaic *despiteous*, from *de-spite* (q.v.), revived by 19 cent. poets.

display. OF. *despleier* (*déployer*). See *deploy*. No connection with *play*.

disport [*archaic*]. OF. *desporter*, to carry away; cf. sense-development of *distract, divert*. Orig. trans., to amuse, intrans. sense springing from reflex. (cf. *abscond*). Now mostly replaced by aphet. *sport* (q.v.).

dispose. F. *disposer* (see *pose*). Etym. to put apart, hence arrange, etc. *Disposition*, temperament, is from astrol. use of the word (14 cent.) for position of planet as determining influence.

dispute. F., L. *disputare*, to compute, discuss; in *Vulg.* to argue, contend in words.

disquisition. L. *disquisitio-n-*, from *disquirere, -quisit-*, to investigate, from *quaerere*, to seek.

disruption. L. *disruptio-n-*, from *disrumpere*, *-rupt-*, to break apart. Esp. split in Established Church of Scotland (1843).

dissect. L. *dissecare*, *-sect-*, to cut up. Cf. *anatomy*.

disseisin [*leg.*]. OF. *dessaisine*. See *seisin*.

dissel-boom [*SAfr.*]. Waggon-pole. Du., shaft-beam (see *boom²*). First element is cogn. with Ger. *deichsel*, AS. & ON. *thīsl*, waggon-pole.

dissemble. For earlier *dissimule, dissimil*, F. *dissimuler*, L. *dissimulare*. After cogn. *assemble, resemble*. See *similar, simulate*.

He dissymelide [*Vulg.* dissimulabat] hym to here (Wyc. 1 *Sam.* x. 27).

disseminate. From L. *disseminare*, to scatter seed, *semen*.

dissent. L. *dissentire*, to differ in feeling. Hence *dissenter*, in spec. mod. sense from 17 cent. First *NED.* ref. is to Oliver Cromwell as "dissenter from the discipline of the Church of England."

dissertation. L. *dissertatio-n-*, from *disserere*, to discuss, from *serere, sert-*, to join, compose.

dissever. OF. *dessevrer*, Late L. *disseparare*, in which prefix is intens.

dissident. From pres. part. of L. *dissidēre*, to sit (*sedēre*) apart.

dissimilation [*ling.*]. Tendency of like sounds to change or disappear when occurring contiguously, e.g. *pilgrim, oriel, fugleman, prow* (q.v.). Cf. *assimilation*. Affects esp. *r–r, l–l, n–n*.

dissimulate. From L. *dissimulare*. See *dissemble*.

dissipate. L. *dissipare*, to scatter, from OL. *sipare*, to throw. For sense of *dissipated* cf. *dissolute*.

dissociate. From L. *dissociare*, from *socius*, companion. Cf. *associate*.

dissolute. Lit. dissolved, separated (v.i.), hence unrestrained. Intermediate sense is lax. *Dissolution* (of Parliament, monasteries, also of soul from body) is from 16 cent.

Sloathe sendith in slep; and a dissolut soule [*Vulg.* anima dissoluta] shal hungre (Wyc. *Prov.* xix. 15).

dissolve. L. *dissolvere*, to loosen. See *solve*.

dissonant. F., from pres. part. of L. *dissonare*, to sound diversely.

dissuade. L. *dissuadēre*, from *suadēre*, to advise. See *suasion*.

dissyllable. See *disyllable*.

distaff. AS. *distæf*, first element cogn. with LG. *diesse*, bunch of flax, as in *dizen, be-*

dizen (q.v.). Often as emblem of female authority, or the "spindle-side" in genealogy, formerly opposed to the "spear-side." Cf. similar use of F. *quenouille*.

quenouille: a distaffe; also, the feminine line in a succession (Cotg.).

distain [*archaic*]. OF. *desteindre* (*déteindre*), L. *dis* and *tingere*, to colour. Now usu. replaced by aphet. *stain*.

May coward shame distain his name (Burns).

distant. F., from pres. part. of L. *distare*, to stand apart. For fig. sense cf. *stand-offish*.

'Tis distance lends enchantment to the view
(Campbell, *Pleasures of Hope*, i. 7).

distemper. From OF. *destempré, -trempé*, MedL. *distemperatus*, disturbed, immoderate, from L. *temperare*, to mix, temper. Orig. of disturbing the "tempers," or four humours, recognized by medieval physicians. Hence, as noun, disease, now esp. of dogs. *Distemper*, to dilute, mix, paint with mixture, is etym. the same word, OF. *destemprer* (*détremper*). See *temper*.

distend. L. *distendere*, to stretch apart.

distich. L., G. δίστιχον, neut. of δίστιχος, from δι-, two, στίχος, line. Cf. *acrostic*.

distil. Orig. intrans., L. *distillare*, to trickle down. See *still²*.

distingué. F., p.p. of *distinguer* (v.i.).

distinguish. Earlier *distingue* (Chauc. & Wyc.), F. *distinguer*, L. *distinguere*, lit. to "prick off," cogn. with G. στίζειν, to prick. For incorr. *-ish*, also in *extinguish*, cf. *astonish, admonish*.

distort. From L. *distorquēre, -tort-*, to twist apart.

distract. From L. *distrahere, -tract-*, to pull apart. For fig. sense cf. *divert*, and for *distracted*, mad, cf. *distraught*.

distrain. OF. *destreindre, destreign-*, L. *distringere*, to draw asunder, but in Late L. as intens. of *stringere*, to stretch. First in leg. use (13 cent.), to constrain to a course of action, etc. by seizure of goods. Now usu. to *distrain upon*.

distrait. F., absent-minded, p.p. of *distraire*, to distract, draw away, L. *distrahere*. Occurs in ME. in sense of *distraught*, but in current use is a borrowing from ModF.

distraught [*poet.*]. Barbarous spelling of above, perh. due to obs. *straught*, p.p. of *stretch*. Or it may be for the latinized *distract*. The three forms *distract, distrait* (*destrat*), *distraught* were used indifferently in ME.

distress. OF. *destrece* (*détresse*), from *des-trecier*, VL. **districtiare*, from *districtus*, p.p. of *distringere*, to pull asunder, etc. Cf. etym. of *dress*. Orig. pressure, esp. in leg. sense, as *distrain* (q.v.). *Stress* (q.v.) is often its aphet. form.

distribute. From L. *distribuere, -tribut-*. See *tribute*.

district. F., orig. control, then region over which control extends, MedL. *districtus*, from *distringere*, in sense of binding, controlling (see *distrain*). Orig. sense survives in F.

district: a district; the liberties, or precincts of a place; the territorie, or circuit of countrey, within which a lord, or his officers may judge, compell, or call in question, the inhabitants (Cotg.).

disturb. ME. *destourb*, OF. *destorber*, L. *disturbare*, intens. of *turbare*, from *turba*, mob. Now respelt after L.

disyllable. Prefix is G. δι-, twice. Hence *dissyllable* is etym. incorr. See *syllable*.

ditch. AS. *dīc*, of which *dike* (q.v.) is the northern development. To *die in the last ditch* is as old as Burnet (1715). With *dull as ditchwater* (mod.), cf. *light* (i.e. easy) *as ditchwater* (15 cent.), and earlier *digne* (arrogant) *as ditchwater* (cf. stinking with pride).

She was as digne as water in a dich
(Chauc. A. 3964).

dither. To quake. Dial., but now in pretty gen. use. Earlier *didder*, thinned form of *dodder²*.

Several minutes of sheer dithering funk
(*Daily Chron.* Jan. 12, 1918).

dithyramb. L., G. διθύραμβος, choric hymn, orig. in honour of Dionysus, Bacchus.

dittany. From OF. *ditan, ditain*, L. *dictamnus*, from G. δίκταμνον, from *Dicte*, mountain in Crete, where it grew. Cf. It. *dittamo*. Mod. Europ. forms are numerous and much corrupted as in the case of most herbs (*agrimony, marjoram, valerian*, etc.).

ditto. It., for *detto*, said, L. *dictus*, as in *the said* (before mentioned) *month*. Use has been much extended in E. Hence *suit of dittos*, i.e. all alike (18 cent.). Also *dittography*, accidental repetition by copyist, *dittology*, double interpretation.

ditty. OF. *dité, ditié*, composition, poem, L. *dictatus*, p.p. of *dictare*, frequent. of *dicere*, to say.

Ci s'ensieut [Here follows] le dittié de la flour de la margherite (Froissart).

Thán Moyses soong...this ditee [*Vulg.* carmen] to the Lord (Wyc. *Ex.* xv. 1).

ditty-bag, -box [*naut.*]. ? Sailors' corrupt. of Austral. *dilly-bag* (q.v.), ? or from obs. *dutty*, a coarse brown calico (Purch.), ident. with Hind. *dhōtī*, loin-cloth. The latter is more likely (cf. *dinnage* for *dunnage*).

The notes were missing from a ditty-box in the mess (*Ev. Stand.* April 25, 1919).

diuretic. L., G. διουρητικός, from διουρεῖν, to urinate. See *urine*. Occurs c. 1400.

diurnal. L. *diurnalis*, from *dies*, day. In 17 cent. often for *journal*.

In every mercurius, coranto, gazet or diurnal, I met with camizados, pallizados...squadrons, curassiers, etc. (Pref. to Blount's *Glossographia*, 1656).

diva. Distinguished female singer. It., goddess, from L. (cf. *divine*).

divagation. L. *divagatio-n-*, from L. *divagari*, to wander off.

divan. Turk. *divān*, Pers. *dīwān, dīvān*, whence also It. *divano*, Sp. Port. F. *divan*. Orig. bundle of written sheets, collection of poems, e.g. the *Divān i Hāfiz*, collection of documents, register, office of accounts, custom-house, council chamber, cushioned seat, smoking-room, cigar-shop, a curious chain of meanings. From Arab. form come It. *dogana*, F. *douane,* custom-house.

The captaine was received in a coach and caryed before the dawne (Purch.).

divaricate. To diverge. From L. *divaricare*. See *prevaricate*.

dive. Combines sense of AS. *dūfan* (strong intrans.) with forms of its causal *dȳfan* (weak trans.); cogn. with *dip* (q.v.). The *diving-bell* is mentioned by Evelyn (1661).

diverge. From *di-*, apart, and L. *vergere*, to turn.

divers, diverse. Ident. words now differentiated in form and sense. F. *divers*, L. *diversus*, turned different ways, from *divertere*. The difference is expressed in F. by position, e.g. *en divers endroits, dans des endroits divers*.

divert. F. *divertir*, from L. *divertere*, to turn in different directions. For fig. sense cf. *distract, disport*.

dives. L., rich, used in *Vulg.* (*Luke*, xvi.), hence often taken as name of rich man in parable. Cf. *lazar*.

Lazar and Dives lyveden diversly
(Chauc. D. 1877).

divest. Earlier *devest*, OF. *desvestir* (*dévêtir*), VL. **disvestire* for *devestire*, to undress, from *vestis*, garment.

divide. L. *dividere*, to force asunder, with second element prob. cogn. with *vidua*, widow. Cf. *dividend*, F. *dividende*, L. *dividendum*, to be divided.

divine. L. *divinus*, belonging to the gods, from *divus*, *deus*. Earlier *devine*, from F. popular form, as in *devin*, soothsayer, *deviner*, to guess, orig. to interpret, predict, have supernatural knowledge. In ME. *devine*, *divine*, means both sorcerer and priest. The *divine right* (of kings) came into spec. use under Stuarts. See Cowel's article on *king*, which led to the public burning of his *Interpreter* by decree of Parliament. Regularly contrasted with *human*, and thus used tellingly by Milton in *human form divine* (after *Gen.* i. 26).

division. F., L. *divisio-n-*, from *dividere*, *divis-*, to divide. *Division of labour* dates from Adam Smith (1776).

divorce. F., L. *divortium*, from *divortere*, archaic for *divertere*, to turn away. Cf. L. *dorsum*, back, for *divorsum*.

divot [*Sc.*]. Sod. Esp. in *fail and divot* (16 cent.), where *fail* means a thick divot. It is characteristic of the sudden spread of golf that the only sense in which the word is familiar to most Englishmen is not given (1897) in the *NED*. Origin unknown.

Rights of pasturage—fuel—feal and divot
(*Waverley*, ch. xlii.).

divulge. Orig. simply to publish. L. *divulgare*, to spread among the people, *vulgus*. Cf. F. *divulguer*.

divvy [*slang*]. For *divine*. Late 19 cent.

dixie [*mil. slang*]. Mess-tin. Urdu *dīgshī*, vessel, Pers., dim. of *dīg*, cauldron, pot.

Dixie. Happy land of Amer. negroes. Orig. estate on Manhattan Island belonging to one *Dixie* (Bartlett).

dizen [*poet.*]. See *bedizen*, *distaff*.

dizzy. AS. *dysig*, foolish, used of the foolish virgins (*Matt.* xxv.). WGer.; cf. LG. *dusig*, OHG. *tusig*; also Du. *duizelen*, to be giddy. Prob., like *giddy* (q.v.), ult. possessed by a god, from Aryan root *dhwes-*, cogn. with G. θεός.

Dizzy. Nickname of *Benjamin Disraeli*, Earl of Beaconsfield (†1881). Cf. *Pam*.

djereed. See *jereed*.

djinn. See *genie*, *jinnee*.

do¹. Verb. AS. *dōn*. WGer.; cf. Du. *doen*, Ger. *tun*; not found in ON. & Goth. Past *did* is a reduplicated form, AS. *dyde*; cf. Ger. *tat* (OHG. *teta*), Du. *deed* (ODu. *dede*), and G. τέθεικα from τί-θη-μι, of which

root syllable is cogn. with *do*. The use of this verb to form the periphrastic conjugation (*do you know? I do not know*), or to avoid repetition, has no gen. parallel in allied langs., though F. *faire* occurs to some extent in the latter capacity. The periphrastic construction dates from ME. and is now normal in the negative and interrogative constructions, exc. with *be*, *have* and a few other monosyllabic verbs, e.g. *dare*, *need*. In *well to do, how do you do?* the verb has become intrans., to fare. With mod. to *do for*, destroy, cf. archaic to *fordo*. To *do oneself well* is US., after Ger. *sich gütlich tun*.

do² [*mus.*]. Arbitrary substitute for earlier *ut*. See *gamut*.

doab [*geog.*]. Tongue of land between two rivers, esp. between Ganges and Jumna. Pers. *dōāb*, two waters; ult. cogn. with *Twynam* (Hants), between Avon and Stour.

doat. See *dote*.

dobbin. Nickname for horse (*Merch. of Ven.* ii. 2). Dim. of *Dob*, rimed on *Rob*, for *Robert* (cf. *Dick*). See *hobby*. Cf. *robin*, *magpie*, etc.

docile. F., L. *docilis*, from *docēre*, to teach.

dock¹. Plant. AS. *docce*; cf. obs. Du. *docke*, Ger. *dockenblätter*, obs. Dan. *ādokke*, water dock (AS. *ēadocce*); also Gael. *dogha*. Hence *burdock*.

dock². Solid part of tail. Cf. ModIcel. *dockr*, stumpy tail, LG. *dokke*, bundle, Ger. *docke*, bundle, plug. Perh. from *dock¹*, the root of which is suggestive of a rat's tail. Hence verb to *dock*, to shorten, cut off.

A firme full taile, touching the lowly ground,
With dock betweene two faire fat buttocks drownd
(Sylv. *Handicrafts*).

dock³. For ships. First recorded by *NED*. in Gavin Douglas (1513), who uses it to render L. *sulcus*, furrow (v.i.), made in the sand by a vessel when beached. But it occurs passim in *Nav. Accts.* (1495–97), in which also are many details with regard to the royal dock of Portsmouth, the first *dock* in the mod. sense, commenced by Hen. VII in 1495. According to the editor of *Nav. Accts.* the word was applied as early as 1434 to the bed made on the mud by the vessel when drawn up as far as possible at high tide, which was fenced round while repairs were in progress. This agrees with Gavin Douglas' use of the word, and points to identity with LG. *docke*, channel, runnel; ? cf. Norw. *dokk*, hollow, dial. E. *doke*, furrow. *Dock* was known to the Hanse merchants as an E. word as early as 1436 (v.i.) and has been borrowed by most Europ. langs.

> Inimicam findete rostris
> Hanc terram, sulcumque sibi premat ipsa carina
> (*Aen.* x. 295).

> Gegeven deme manne, de dat schip in de docke lade, 6d (*Hanserecesse*, 1436).

> We caused an anchor to be laid right astern as her dock [i.e. the furrow the grounded vessel had made on the mud-bank] directed us
> (Phineas Pett, 1613).

dock⁴. For criminals. Orig. rogues' slang (cf. *jug*). Used by Ben Jonson (*Alchemist*, v. 4). Then unrecorded till revived by Dickens. Flem. *dok, docke*, hutch, pen. Perh. spec. use of *dock³*.

docket. Memorandum, summary, customs certificate. Earlier (15 cent.) *doggette*, obs. It. *doghetta*, bendlet in heraldry (Torr.), dim. of *doga*, cask-stave. The form has been influenced by *cocket* (q.v.) with which it is commonly associated. Cf. hist. of *label, schedule*, etc.

doctor. L. from *docēre*, to teach. Applied esp. to various great schoolmen, e.g. *doctor angelicus* (Aquinas), *invincibilis* (Ockham), *mirabilis* (Bacon), *subtilis* (Duns Scotus). In spec. sense of *doctor of medicine* already in ME. With fig. sense, to *doctor* (wines, statements, etc.), cf. to *cook* (accounts, etc.). *Doctors' Commons* was orig. the common table of the Association of Doctors of Civil Law in London (incorporated 1768, dissolved 1858) in buildings (demolished 1867) in which five courts were held. In literary allusions usu. with ref. to wills or marriage licenses.

> Seynt Austyn, the firste doctour of Englische men
> (Trev. ii. 43).

> Who shall decide, when doctors disagree?
> (Pope, *Moral Essays*, iii. 1).

doctrine. F., L. *doctrina*, from *doctor* (q.v.). *Doctrinaire*, F., was coined c. 1815 and first applied by extremists to supporters of an ideal "doctrine" of compromise in pol. matters; now to unpractical extremists.

> The dictatorship of a small and extreme oligarchy of doctrinaire socialists and syndicalists
> (*Obs.* June 15, 1919).

document. F., L. *documentum*, proof, example, from *docēre*, to teach. Mod. use, as in *human document*, due to F. naturalistic school (the Goncourts, Zola, etc.), goes back to etym. sense.

dodder¹. Plant. ME. also *doder*; cf. Du., Dan. *dodder*, Ger. *dotter*. Not found in AS., but prob. cogn. with *dodder²*, from shaking.

dodder². To quake, quaver. Also dial. *dade, dadder, daddle, doddle*. Cf. Norw. dial. *duddra*.

doddered [*poet.*]. Usu. with *oak*. After Dryden, rendering Virgil's *veteres, jam fracta cacumina, fagos*. For *doddard*, formed, on *pollard*, from obs. *dod*, to poll.

> Onys in the yeer he was doddid, for the heere hevyde hym (Wyc. 2 *Sam.* xiv. 26).

> He passes now the doddered oak (*Rokeby*, vi. 3).

dodecagon. G., from δώδεκα, twelve, γωνία, angle.

dodge. From 16 cent., in sense of shuffle, play fast and loose, lit. and fig. App. cogn. with Ger. *ducken*, to dodge, duck, earlier also *docken* (Hans Sachs). Current sense of noun, esp. with *artful*, is due to Dickens.

dodo. Extinct bird (Mauritius), clumsy and of poor flight. Port. *doudo*, stupid. Cf. *dotterel*, which is prob. related.

> A Portuguese name it is, and has reference to her simpleness (Sir T. Herbert, 1638).

Dodonaean. Of *Dodona* (Epirus), where was oracle of Zeus in oak-grove.

doe. ME. *doo*, AS. *dā*, perh. cogn. with L. *dama*, whence Ger. *damhirsch*, doe. *Doeskin*, cloth, is coined on *buckskin*, first used of leather and then of material for breeches.

Doe, John. See *John*.

doff. "In all its senses obsolete, and rarely used except by rustics" (Johns.). Contr. of *do off*; cf. *don* and rarer *dup* (see *dub up*).

> Hē him of dyde īsern-byrnan [coat of mail]
> (Beowulf).

dog. Late and rare AS. *docga* (usual word is *hound*), adopted in several Europ. langs. in sense of E. dog, mastiff. This spec. sense survives in *dogged*. Origin unknown. With *fire-dog* cf. F. *chenet*, prob. at first in shape of dog. A *dog-cart* had orig. a box under the seat for sportsmen's dogs. For *dog-days, dog-star*, see *canicular*. *Dog's ear*, in books, is 17 cent. *Dogwatch*, short watch (naut.), may spring from earlier *dog-sleep*, short and fitful. It is also explained by naut. humorists as for *cur-tailed* (two hours instead of four), or from its wakeful character (v.i.). Often *dog-* implies inferiority, e.g. *dog-cheap, -latin, -violet*; so also to *go to the dogs* and Ger. *auf den hund kommen*. But *dog-rose* renders MedL. *rosa canina*, for

G. κυνόροδον, perh. because supposed to be efficacious against bite of mad dog.

> But at four o'clock the ship wakes up. No self-respecting naval man sleeps during the dog-watch
> (*Taffrail*).

Dogberrydom. From *Dogberry*, foolish constable in *Much Ado about Nothing*. Cf. *Bumbledom*.

doge. F., Venetian, L. *dux, duc-*, leader, duke.

dogger. North Sea (esp. Du.) fishing-boat, though not now in Du. use. Hence the *Dogger Bank*. Prob. related to *dog*; cf. *cat*, obs. name of a vessel in several langs. and of very old date. Name prob. arose in E. (14 cent.), and was adopted in Icel., Du. & F. (*dogre*).

> *dogghe*: canis molossus, canis magnus. *Gal.* dogue. *Ang.* dogge (Kil.).

> *dogghe-boot*: cymba major (*ib.*).

doggerel. First in Chauc., applied by the host of the Tabard to the *Tale of Sir Thopas*. Prob. from L. *doga*, cask-stave. Cf. 16 cent. *dudgeon verse* (see *dudgeon*[1]), Ger. *stabreim*, stave rime, or *knüttelvers*, cudgel verse, Du. *kluppelvers* (for earlier *knuppel-*, cudgel), E. *packstaff verse* (see *pikestaff*), and metr. sense of Prov. *bastonnet*, little stick; also *rhopalic* (verse) from G. ῥόπαλον, cudgel.

> "Now swich a rym the devel I biteche! This may wel be rym dogerel," quod he (B. 2114).

doggo, to lie. ? Like a cunning dog.

dog-gone [*US.*]. App. a fantastic perversion of *god-damned*.

> He's as treacherous as a doggone Indian
> (Ridgwell Cullum).

dogma. G. δόγμα, opinion, from δοκεῖν, to seem. Usu. treated as G., with pl. *dogmata*, in 17–18 cents.

doily. Orig. name of material, introduced for summer-wear (17 cent.). From *Doily*, who kept a shop in the Strand. The name is of F. origin, from *Ouilly* (Calvados).

> Coarse Doiley-napkins, fringed at each end (Swift).

doit [*archaic*]. Chiefly in *not* (*worth*) *a doit*. Du. *duit*, earlier *doyt*, eighth part of stiver, ON. *thveit*, piece, from *thvīta*, to cut. Cf. Ger. *deut*, from Du. E. *-thwaite* in northern place-names is ident.

doited [*Sc.*]. Crazy. Prob. for *doted*. See *dote*.

dolce far niente. It., sweet do nothing.

doldrums. Slang *doldrum*, dullard, *doldrums*, dumps. Hence naut., state of being becalmed. From *dull*, after *tantrum*.

dole[1]. Share, esp. in charitable distribution (e.g. at funerals), and in to *dole out*. AS. *dāl*, parallel form to *dǣl*, deal[1]. Also in *happy man be his dole*, i.e. lot, a very common Tudor phrase.

> Happy man, happy dole, so say sycke and hole
> (Heywood, 1562).

dole[2] [*poet.*]. Sorrow. Esp. in *doleful*. OF. *duel*, tonic stem of OF. *doloir, duel-*, to grieve, L. *dolēre*. The more correct *dule* survives in Sc. and is used by some mod. poets. ModF. *deuil*, Late L. *dolium*, grief, is not quite the same word.

dolerite [*min.*]. F. *dolérite*, coined from G. δολερός, deceptive, because of difficulty of determining its constituents.

dolichocephalic [*ethn.*]. Longheaded. From G. δολιχός, long. Cf. *brachycephalic*.

doll. Short for *Dorothy*. Cf. Sc. *doroty*, a doll, and synon. F. *marionnette*, double dim. of *Marie*. In earlier use it was stock name for a mistress or pet, and a child's doll was called a *baby*. Cf. also *dolly* in various mech. applications, esp. (in dial.) the three-legged beater for treating clothes in a *dolly-tub*, also called a *peggy* or *maiden*.

> *doll*: a wooden block to make up commodes upon, also a child's baby (*Dict. Cant. Crew*).

dollar. Earlier (16 cent.) also *daler*. LG. & archaic Du. *daler* (*daalder*), Ger. *taler*, for *Joachimstaler*, coin minted at silver mine of *Joachimstal* (Bohemia) from 1519 onward. Cf. Ger. *heller* from *Schwäbisch-Hall*. *Almighty dollar* was coined by Washington Irving (c. 1836).

> His greate god, gold-allmighty, is able to make him deceive the best friend (E. Verney, 1639).

dollop. Orig., in EAngl., a thick-growing tuft or clump (Tusser). Cf. Norw. dial. *dolp*, lump.

dolly varden. Pattern, style of dress. From *Dolly Varden* (*Barnaby Rudge*). For her christian name see *doll*. Her paternal ancestors prob. came from *Verdun*.

dolman. Hussar jacket. F., Pol. *doloman*, Turk. *dōlāmān*.

> *dolyman*: a Turkish gowne, long coat, or upper garment; collarlesse, and closed with long buttons downe to the girdle-stead (Cotg.).

dolmen. Cromlech. Explained as Bret. *tol*, table, *men*, stone. But prob. a misapplication by Latour d'Auvergne (18 cent.) of Corn. *tolmen*, hole of stone. Cf. *menhir*.

dolomite [*geol.*]. Named (1794) from *Dolomieu*, F. geologist.

dolour. OF. *dolour* (*douleur*), L. *dolor-em*, sorrow.

dolphin. ME. also *delfyn, daulphin*, etc., OF. *dalfin* (*dauphin*), VL. **dalfinus*, for *delphinus*, from G. δελφίς, δελφῖν-. Though not app. recorded in AS., it was a common personal name in 11 cent.

dolt. From 16 cent. From *dull*; perh. contr. of *dullard*.

dom. Port., lord, L. *dominus*. Title of royalty, high ecclesiastics, nobles; cf. Sp. *don*. As title of Benedictines and Carthusians shortened from L. *dominus*.

-dom. AS. *-dōm*, cogn. with to *do* and *deem*; cf. Ger. *-tum*. Often used to form playful mod. compds. and nonce-words, e.g. *bumbledom, topsyturvydom, devil-may-care-dom* (J. Galsworthy).

domain. F. *domaine*, L. *dominium*. OF. also *demaine* (see *demesne*).

Domdaniel. Magic submarine hall. From F. continuation (1788–93) of *Arabian Nights*, whence adopted by Southey in *Thalaba*.

dome. F. *dôme*, It. *duomo*, cathedral, L. *domus* (*Dei*), G. δόμος. F. & E. senses are due rather to G. δῶμα, rendered house-top by Tynd.

domesday [*hist.*]. ME. spelling of *doomsday*, preserved in *Domesday Book* (1086).

Hic liber ab indigenis Domesdei nuncupatur, id est, dies judicii per metaphoram
(*Dialogus de Scaccario*, 1178).

domestic. L. *domesticus*, of the house and home, *domus*.

domicile. F., L. *domicilium*, from *domus*, house. Hence *domiciliary visit*, F. *visite domiciliaire*, where *visite* has its F. sense of search.

dominate. From L. *dominari*, from *dominus*, master, from *domus*, home.

domineer. Archaic Du. *domineren*, F. *dominer*, from L. *dominari*, to "lord it" over. First in Shaks. (*Love's Lab. Lost*, iii. 1). Cf. *commandeer, cashier²*.

dominical [*eccl.*]. Pertaining to the Lord or the Lord's Day. MedL. *dominicalis*. Cf. F. *dimanche*, Sunday, OF. *domenche*, L. *dominicus*.

Dominican. Black Friar. From order of *St Dominic*, Domingo de Guzman (†1221). Cf. *Franciscan*.

dominie [*Sc.*]. L. *domine*, voc. of *dominus*, used by schoolboys in addressing master. Cf. Du. *dominee*, Protestant clergyman.

dominion. L. *dominio-n-*, from *dominus*, lord.

domino. Hooded cloak. F., It., orig. worn by priests, and in some way connected with L. *dominus*. The game of *dominoes* comes from the phrase *faire domino*, to put the last piece and win. Cf. *faire capot* (also a hooded cloak) at piquet, but the exact metaphor is not clear.

Utantur...caputio vulgariter ung domino (Duc.).

don¹. Title. Sp., L. *dominus*, orig. title of high rank, but now general. Cf. evolution in use of *sir* and F. *monsieur*. Univ. sense, orig. contemptuous, is from 17 cent.

don². Verb. For *do on*. Cf. *doff*.

donate. From L. *donare*, to give.

doña, dona. Sp. & Port., L. *domina*. Hence slang *dona*(*h*), sweetheart.

Donatist. Christian sect in NAfr. (4 cent.). From *Donatus*, leading member.

donga. Ravine (SAfr.). Native word.

dongola race. Paddling in punts (from c. 1890). ? Arbitrary perversion of *gondola*, ? or from *Dongola* on the Nile.

donjon [*hist.*]. See *dungeon*.

Don Juan. Libertine. The legend is of Sp. origin. Cf. *Lovelace* (from *Clarissa Harlowe*), used in F. for a lady-killer. Cf. also *Lothario*.

donkey. Slang or dial. word of late appearance, as shown by quot. below. ? Cf. dial. *dunnock*, sparrow, from *dun*, brown (cf. *Dan Burnel*, i.e. Sir Brown, applied to the ass in Chauc.). But possibly from name *Duncan* or *Dominic*; cf. *neddy, dicky*, and dial. *cuddy*, used in same sense. Slang *donkey's years*, a long time, is allusive to the length of donkey's *ears*.

These excursions [in neighbourhood of Lisbon, 1782] being made in carriages, on horseback, and donkeys (asses), the latter animals being exclusively for the ladies' use (Hickey's *Memoirs*, ii. 276).

donna. It., L. *domina*. Cf. *dona*.

Donnybrook Fair. Bacchanalia and saturnalia held at *Donnybrook* (co. Dublin) till 1855.

donor. OF. *doneor* (*donneur*), L. *donator-em*, from *donare*, to give.

donzella. It. form of *damsel* (q.v.).

doolie. Hind. *dōlī*, litter, Sanskrit *dōlā*, swing, cradle, litter. Also earlier *dowle, dowly* (Purch.).

A member of the British Legislature, recounting the incidents of one of our Indian fights, informed his countrymen that "the ferocious Duli" rushed from the hills and carried off the wounded soldier
(Herbert Edwardes, *Calcutta Review*, Dec. 1846).

doom. AS. *dōm*, cogn. with *deem*. Com. Teut.; cf. OSax. *dōm*, OHG. *tuom*, ON. *dōmr*, Goth. *doms*. Orig. law, judgment, what is set up (cf. *statute*); cogn. with G. θέμις. Hence *doomsday*, last judgment.

Doomsday Book. See *domesday*.

door. Combines AS. *duru* (fem.) and *dor* (neut.), with which cf. Ger. *tür* (fem.), door, *tor* (neut.), gate. Aryan; cf. Du. *deur*, ON. *dyrr*, Goth. *daur*, G. θύρα, L. *fores*. See also *durbar*. Some of the cognates were orig. plurals, two leaves of door. *Doormat* is now (1917–18) much used in allusion to the fact that a member of the Cabinet who had gone back on his colleagues was asked to wait while they discussed his position. *Dead as a doornail* is in *Piers Plowm.* (A. i. 161).

Frankness...must take the place of doormat condescension (*Sunday Times*, Jan. 20, 1918).

dope. Lubricant (US.). From Du. *doopen*, to dip. Hence *dope*, to drug (neol.).

Doping the fabric that covers the planes, rudders and ailerons (*Daily Chron.* June 1, 1917).

There are two words you will never hear mentioned in West End "dope" circles. One is cocaine and the other is heroin (*Daily Expr.* Dec. 17, 1919).

dopper [*SAfr.*]. Old-fashioned and puritanical boer, orig. Anabaptist. Du. *dooper*, lit. dipper, Baptist. See *dip*.

dor. Insect. AS. *dora*, prob. "buzzer." Also called *watchman* or *clock*, from loud buzz.

Dora. Acrostic of *Defence Of Realm Act* (1914). Cf. *Anzac*.

Even Dora is timid where Ireland is concerned
(*Referee*, June 24, 1917).

dorado. Dolphin. Sp., L. *deauratus*, gilded. See *dory*.

Dorcas society. See *Acts*, ix. 36.

Dorian, Doric. Of *Doris*, division of ancient Greece; cf. *Aeolic, Attic, Ionian. Doric* is often used for broad Scots.

dorking. Fowl. From *Dorking* (Surr.). Cf. *orpington*.

dormant. F., pres. part. of *dormir*, L. *dormire*, to sleep.

dormer. Orig. dormitory, OF. *dormeor* from *dormir* (replaced by *dortoir*, L. *dormitorium*). Hence *dormer-window, -roof*.

dormitory. L. *dormitorium*, sleeping-place (v.s.).

dormouse. ? From northern dial. *dorm*, to doze, F. *dormir*, and *mouse*. Cf. archaic Du. *slæp-muys* (Kil.).

dormy [*golf*]. ? F. *endormi*, asleep, further exertion being unnecessary. ? Or from dial. *dorm* (v.s.).

dorsal. MedL. *dorsalis*, from *dorsum*, back.

dory[1]. Fish. F. *dorée*, p.p. fem. of *dorer*, to gild, L. *deaurare*. Cf. *dorado*. Now often called *John Dory* (cf. *Jack Sprat* and see *John*).

dorée: the doree, or Saint Peters fish; also (though not so properly) the goldfish or golding (Cotg.).

dory[2]. Boat (US. & WInd.). Origin unknown.

dose. F., MedL., G. δόσις, from διδόναι, to give.

doss [*slang*]. Bed in lodging-house. Also (18 cent.) *dorse*. Prob. ident. with obs. *dorse, doss*, back, in various senses, F. *dos*, L. *dorsum*.

dossal, dossel [*eccl.*]. Ornamental hanging at back. MedL. *dossale*. See *dossier*.

dossier. F., bundle of papers, hence record of individual. Cf. obs. E. *dosser*, basket carried on back, from F. *dossier* in earlier sense, from *dos*, back, VL. *dossum* for *dorsum*. F. *dossier* has also the meaning of *dossal* (v.s.).

dot[1]. AS. *dott*, speck, head of boil, not found between AS. and 16 cent. Cf. Du. *dot*, also as endearing name for small child, archaic Du. *dodde*, plug, Ger. dial. *dütte*, nipple of breast. Of obscure origin and hist. *Dotty*, shaky, is perh. rather connected with *dodder*[2], or with *dote* and *doited*. Cf. obs. *doddy-poll*, earlier (c. 1400) *dotty-poll*. *Dot and go* (*carry*) *one*, to go limpingly, is from child's halting method of calculation, putting down dot as reminder to carry one.

The official Fremdenblatt dots Count Czernin's i's and crosses his t's for him
(*Daily Chron.* Apr. 4, 1917).

dot[2]. F., dowry, L. *dos, dot-*, cogn. with *dare*, to give.

dote, doat. AF. *doter* for F. *radoter*. First (12 cent.) as p.p., enfeebled by age. Of Teut. origin. Cf. obs. Du. *doten*, to dote, Du. *dut*, dotage, Ger. *verdutzt*, flabbergasted. With to *dote on*, cf. to *be fond of*, F. *raffoler de*.

dottel. See *dottle*.

dotterel. Species of plover, fool (dial.). From *dote* (cf. *dodo*).

dotrel, byrd: ffrugus (*Prompt. Parv.*).

dotrel, ffole: idem quod dotorde (*ib.*).

dottle. Plug of unconsumed tobacco in pipe. Dim. of *dot*, of which orig. meaning was perh. clot.

Ortheris shot out the red-hot dottel of his pipe on the back of his hairy fist (Kipling, *Black Jack*).

dotty. See *dot*.

douane. F., custom-house. See *divan*.

Douay bible. E. version of *Vulg.* made at College of Douai (1584–1609).

double. F., L. *duplus,* from *duo* and root of *plēre,* to fill. Fig., e.g. in *double-dealing,* opposed to *simple. Double or quit* is in Sidney's *Arcadia.* With *double-dyed* cf. *engrained habit. Double entendre* is in ModF. *double entente.*

doublet. F., prob. from *doubler* in sense of lining. The F. word is obs. in sense of garment, but is used of double words of ident. origin, e.g. *caitiff, captive; dish, disk; papa, pope; pursue, prosecute,* etc.

doubloon [*hist.*]. Orig. double pistole. F. *doublon,* Sp. *doblón.*

doubt. ME. *dout,* F. *douter,* L. *dubitare;* ult. from *duo,* two, as *dubious* (q.v.); cf. G. δοιάζειν, to doubt, from δοιοί, in two ways. For restored *-b-* cf. *debt.* In OF. & archaic E. also to fear (see *doughty*), as in Bruce's "I doubt I've slain Comyn, "and in dial., e.g. "I doubt (= I don't doubt) he's lost the train."

I do doubt that the Duke of Buckingham will be so flushed that he will not stop at any thing
(Pepys, Mar. 4, 1669).

douce [*Sc.*]. F. *doux,* L. *dulcis.* Cf. *dour.* Hence *douceur,* naturalized in ME., but in later senses of pleasant speech, gratuity, now treated as foreign.

douceur. Gratuity. F., lit. sweetness (v.s.).

douche. F., It. *doccia,* water-pipe, jet, Late L. **ductia* for *ductio,* from *ducere, duct-,* to lead (cf. *conduit*).

dough. AS. *dāg.* Com. Teut.; cf. Du. *deeg,* Ger. *teig,* ON. *deig,* Goth. *daigs.* Ground-idea kneading (see *lady*); cogn. with G. τεῖχος, wall. Cf. *duff. Doughboy,* US. infantry soldier, is said to be a nickname from the shape of the buttons orig. worn by the regular army suggesting the kind of biscuit called a *doughboy* in US. and in 17 cent. E.

doughty. AS. *dyhtig,* altered to *dohtig* by influence of *dohte,* past of cogn. *dugan,* to be fit, to avail; cf. Ger. *tüchtig,* doughty, *taugen,* to be fit. Pronunc. is abnormal and app. affected by F. *douté,* in its OF. sense of redoubtable, dread, as epithet. In 1371 the citizens of Berwick address Edward III as "nostre tres puissant et tres douté sire." See *doubt.*

Le plus fort et le plus doubté homme qui oncques fust ne jamais sera (*Livre du Chevalier de la Tour*).

Doukhobor. New sect. Russ. *dukhobor,* from *dukh,* spirit, *borot'sya* (reflex.), to fight.

doum, dom. Palm. Arab. *daum, dūm.*

dour [*Sc.*]. Opposite of *douce.* F. *dur* or L. *durus,* but the vowel is exceptional.

douse, dowse. To strike (e.g. a *douse on the chops*), beat down, plunge in water, etc. Of LG. origin; cf. archaic Du. *doesen,* "pulsare cum impetu et fragore" (Kil.). With to *douse the glim* (naut.) cf. earlier to *douse topsails.* In the former expression there is association with dial. *dout,* do out, with which cf. *don, doff.*

dove. Com. Teut., though not recorded in AS. (see *culver*); cf. Du. *duif,* Ger. *taube,* ON. *dufa,* Goth. *dūbo;* prob. cogn. with *dive,* from dipping flight (see *cushat*). With *dove-tail* cf. F. *queue d'aronde,* swallow's tail, similarly used.

If you have writ your annals true, 'tis there
That like an eagle in a dove-cote, I
Fluttered your Volscians in Corioli (*Cor.* v. 5).

dow. See *dhow.*

dowager. OF. *douagere,* from *douage,* dower (q.v.).

dowdy. Orig. a shabby woman, from ME. *dowd.* Origin unknown. ? Cogn. with *dud*[1].

Dido, a dowdy; Cleopatra, a gipsy
(*Rom. & Jul.* ii. 4).

dowel. Headless peg for connecting pieces of wood or stone. ? F. *douille,* socket, L. *ductile,* ? or related to synon. Norw. Dan. *dyvel, dybel,* Ger. *döbel,* app. from same root as *dub,* to strike.

The spokis and dowlis [*var.* felijs, *Vulg.* modioli] of the wheelis (Wyc. 1 *Kings,* vii. 33).

An importer of wooden-work, dowels, etc., appealed for exemption (*Lloyd's Weekly News,* Jan. 21, 1917).

dower, dowry. F. *douaire,* Late L. *dotarium,* from L. *dos, dot-,* dower, gift. *Dowry* represents AF. *douairie;* cf. *history, glory.*

dowlas [*archaic*]. Coarse linen (1 *Hen. IV,* iii. 3), from *Daoulas* (Finistère). Cf. *lockram.*

down[1]. Hill, esp. chalk-hills of south; hence roadstead facing the North Downs. AS. *dūn;* cf. Du. *duin,* F. *dune,* sand-hill. Of Celt. origin and found in very old place-names, e.g. *Dumbarton,* hill-fortress of the Britons, *Autun,* L. *Augusti dunum,* etc.; ult. cogn. with *town.* Hence adv. & prep. *down,* for earlier *adown,* AS. *of dūne,* off the hill. Thus *downhill* means etym. hill-hill. To *down tools* is a good example of the E. power of forming verbs from preps.; cf. to *out* (an opponent), to *up* (and speak), etc.

The waiters immediately declared a strike and downed aprons (*Daily Chron.* Mar. 3, 1920)

down² [*prep. & adv.*]. See *down¹*. With *down-cast* cf. *dejected*. For fig. sense of *downright* (13 cent.) cf. *upright, straight-forward, out and out*.

down³. Of birds. ON. *dūnn*, whence also Ger. *daune*. *Downy*, artful, is associated with this in *downy bird*, but is from adv. *down* in slang sense of being "down on" (a situation), practically the same as being "up to" (snuff).

dowse¹. See *douse*.

dowse². To divine presence of water or minerals. *Deusing-rod* is in Locke (1691). Said to have been introduced into Devon and Cornwall by Ger. miners, temp. Elizabeth, and app. connected in some way with Ger. *deuten*, to declare, interpret, also dial. *dauten*.

doxology. F. *doxologie*, MedL., G. δοξολογία, from δόξα, glory.

doxy¹ [*archaic slang*]. Beggars' wench. Prob. from archaic Du. *docke*, doll, OHG. *tocka*, of unknown origin. See *doll*.

-doxy². Opinion. Playful for *orthodoxy*, etc. Cf. *-ology, -ism*.

> Orthodoxy is my doxy and heterodoxy is your doxy (J. Quincey Adams, 1778).

doyen. Senior (ambassador, professor, etc.). F. form of *dean¹* (q.v.).

doyley. See *doily*.

doze. Orig. trans., to stupefy (17 cent.). Cf. Dan. *döse*, to make dull, Sw. dial. *dūsa*, to sleep, Ger. *dusel*, doze, LG. *dös*, sleepiness; ? ult. cogn. with AS. *dwǣs*, stupid. The E. word came from Scand.

dozen. OF. *dozeine* (*douzaine*), from *douze*, twelve, VL. **dodece* for *duodecim*, with suffix from L. *-ena* as in *centena*, etc.

drab¹. Colour. Orig. cloth; then, colour of undyed cloth, earlier *drap-coloured, drab colour*. F. *drap*, cloth, Late L. *drappus*, of unknown origin. See *trappings*. Sense of colourless persists in mod. fig. use.

drab². Slut. Perh. the same word as *drab¹*. Cf. Sp. Port. *trapo*, rag, and Ger. *lump*, rogue, orig. rag. Defoe (*Mem. Cav.* ch. iv) uses *rag* in sense of wench following camp. But analogy of *trapes* (q.v.) suggests possible connection with LG. *draben*, Ger. *traben*, to trot.

drabble. To trail, esp. in water or dirt. Hence sail called *drabler*. LG. *drabbeln*, to paddle in water.

drachm. Coin, weight, dram (solid or fluid). F. *drachme*, earlier *dragme*, L., G. δραχμή, orig. handful, from δράσσεσθαι, to grasp.

Draconic. From *Draco*, archon of Athens (621 B.C.), severe lawgiver.

draff. Dregs, esp. of malt. ON. *draf*, offal; cogn. with Du. *draf*, Ger. *treber* (orig. pl.); cf. AS. *drēfan*, to make turbid, Ger. *trübe*, turbid.

draft. Var. of *draught* (q.v.) from which it is now differentiated in some spec. senses.

drag. Northern dial. form of *draw* (q.v.). AS. *dragan* or cogn. ON. *draga*. In sense of vehicle *drag* is a doublet of *dray* and was orig. applied to a wheelless cart hauled by hand, a sledge. In the *drag-hunt* a red herring (see *herring*) is gen. used. Frequent. *draggle* has been affected in sense by *drabble*, as in *draggle-tail*.

dragoman. F., MedL. *dragumannus*, Late G. δραγούμενος, OArab. *targumān*, from *targama*, to interpret; cf. Chaldee *targēm* (see *targum*). Numerous early forms and vars. in E. and other langs., e.g. obs. E. *truchman*, F. *truchement*, *drogman*, OF. *drugement* (12 cent.). Brought early from Byzantium by Crusaders.

dragon. F., L. *draco-n-*, G. δράκων, δράκοντ-. To *sow dragon's teeth* alludes to armed soldiers who sprang from dragon's teeth sown by Cadmus.

dragonnade [*hist.*]. F., intimidation of Protestants, temp. Louis XIV, by quartering dragoons on them. Cf. to *dragoon*, which is allusive to bullying of Sc. Covenanters by the military.

> Les dragons ont été de très bons missionaires jusques ici; les prédicateurs qu'on envoie présentement rendront l'ouvrage parfait
>   (Mme de Sévigné, Oct. 28, 1685).

dragoon. F. *dragon*, from end of 16 cent. for mounted infantry earlier called *carabins* or *arquebusiers à cheval*. In early 18 cent. soldiers are classed as "horse, foot, or dragoons." F. *dragon*, orig. kind of musket; cf. *falconet, culverin*, etc.

> *dragoons*: musketeers mounted, who serve sometimes a foot, and sometimes a horseback
>   (*Mil. Dict.* 1708).

drain. AS. *drēahnian*, to strain a liquid; cogn. with *dry*. Not found by *NED.* between AS. and 16 cent., but it occurs in surnames, e.g. *John atte Drene* (Somerset, 13 cent.), *Simon Draneland* (Cambridgeshire, 1273).

drake¹ [*archaic*]. Dragon. AS. *draca*, dragon, from L. (see *dragon*). Survives in *fire-drake*, and as anglers' name for species of ephemera used in fly-fishing. WGer.; cf.

Du. *draak*, Ger. *drache*. Perh. an early Church-word.

drake². Bird. First in 13 cent. Cf. Sw. *anddrake*, Ger. dial. *draak*, for OHG. *antrahho* (*enterich*), from *anut*, duck, with doubtful second element, perh. ident. with ON. *-reki*, ruler, as in *landreki*, king; cf. Ger. *gänserich*, gander.

dram. Popular form of *drachm* (q.v.). Sense of liquid measure, as in *dram of poison* (*Rom. & Jul.* v. 1), is later.

drama. Late L., G. δρᾶμα, action, from δρᾶν, to do, act. Cf. theat. sense of *act*. Hence *dramaturge*, F., G. δραματουργός, from ἔργειν, to work; *dramatis personae*, L., characters of the play.

drape. Orig. to weave cloth (see *drab¹*). Current sense first in Tennyson. Cf. *draper*, orig. cloth weaver, F. *drapier*.

drastic. G. δραστικός, active, from δρᾶν, to act. Cf. *drama*.

drat. Earlier *'od rot*, disguising *God rot*; cf. *zounds*. For change of vowel cf. *Gad! stap my vitals!*

"What are they fear'd on? fools! 'od rot 'em!"
Were the last words of Higginbottom
　　　　　　　　　(*Rejected Addresses*).

draught. From *draw* in all senses, with specialized spelling *draft* in some. For very wide range of meanings cf. those of F. *trait*, from *traire*, or Ger. *zug*, from *ziehen*, to draw, one of the two words which Mark Twain regarded as constituting the real Ger. lang. The game of *draughts* (F. *dames*, whence Sc. *dams*) is from ME. sense of move.

Atte ches with me she gan to pleye;
With hir false draughtes dyvers
She stal on me and took my fers [bishop]
　　　　(Chauc. *Blanche the Duchess*, 651).

Dravidian [*ling.*]. Group of ancient agglutinative langs. in Southern India (Tamil, Telugu, Canarese, Malayalam). Name given by Bishop Caldwell (†1891) from Sanskrit *Drāvida*, a geog. term, perh. etym. ident. with *Tamil*.

draw. AS. *dragan*. Com. Teut.; cf. OSax. *dragan*, to carry, Ger. *tragen*, to carry, ON. *draga*, to draw, drag, Goth. *gadragan*, to carry. Ground-idea, to pull, covers all senses (cf. *draught, draft*), a line being "drawn" by "drawing" a pencil across paper. Cf. endless meanings of F. *tirer*, to draw (whence *tiroir*, a drawer). To *draw* (*out*) a person is a metaphor from "drawing the badger." In *hanged, drawn,*

and quartered, *draw* has the sense of disembowel. A *drawn* game is prob. for *withdrawn*, the stakes being "withdrawn" in absence of decision; cf. *drawing-room* for earlier *withdrawing-room*. *Drawers*, garment, is described as thieves' slang in 16 cent. With *drawback* (com.) cf. *backwardation*.

My lord saluted me kindly and took me into the withdrawing-room (Pepys, Dec. 21, 1663).

It was not so much for myself as for that vulgar child—
And I said, "A pint of double X, and please to draw it mild" (*Ingoldsby*).

drawcansir [*archaic*]. Braggart, swashbuckler. Character in Villiers' *Rehearsal* (1672), parodying *Almanzor*, Arab., the victorious, in Dryden's *Conquest of Granada*. Cf. *Bombastes*.

drawer, drawing-room. See *draw*.

drawl. Du. *dralen*, cogn. with *draw*. Orig. to lag, loiter; cf. F. *traîner*, to lag, *voix traînante*, drawling voice.

draelen: cunctari, morari, cessare, tardare; trahere moram, nectere moram (Kil.).

trainer sa parole: to speak draylingly, draw-latch like (Cotg.).

dray. Orig. without wheels. Cogn. with *drag, draw* (q.v.). Cf. Sw. *drög*, sledge, dray.

dread. First as verb. ME. *dreden*, aphet. for *adreden*, AS. *ādrǣdan*, which was formed by wrong separation of synon. *ond-rǣdan*, of which second element is cogn. with ON. *hrǣda*, to be frightened; cf. OHG. *intratan*. Thus the *d-* is artificial. *Dreadnought* was used from c. 1800 of thick material or garment (also *fearnought*). It is also an old naval ship-name, revived (1906) for all-big-gun battle-ship, first of its type. The *Dread-naught* was a Queen's ship in 1596 (Purch.). For adoption as name of type cf. *monitor* (q.v.).

dream. Com. Teut.; cf. Du. *droom*, Ger. *traum*, ON. *draumr*. Must have existed as *drēam in AS., but the fact that there was another *drēam*, joy, music, seems to have led to its disuse, in favour of *swefn*, until ME. period.

Y seig a sweven [*later var.* dreem]
　　　　　　　　(Wyc. *Gen.* xli. 22).

dreary. AS. *drēorig*, dreary, bloody, from *drēor*, gore, shed blood, from *drēosan*, to drip. Cf. cogn. and synon. Ger. *traurig*. *Drear* (Milt.) is a back-formation. The orig. figure was prob. not from gore, but from "drooping" idea.

dredge¹. To remove mud. First in *dreg-boat* (15 cent.). Cf. Du. *dreg*, earlier *dregghe*, "harpago, verriculum" (Kil.); cogn. with *drag*.

dredge². To sprinkle with flour, earlier with spice, etc. From obs. *dredge*, sweetmeat, ME. *dragie*, F. *dragée*, ult., like obs. It. *treggea*, from G. τραγήματα (neut. pl.), sweetmeats. Also used, like F. *dragée*, "the coarse graine called bolymong" (Cotg.), of a mixture of cereals.

The Food Controller has made a dredge corn order (*Morn. Post*, Nov. 21, 1917).

dree [*archaic*]. To endure, perform, in to *dree one's weird*. AS. *drēogan*; cf. ON. *drȳgja*, to perform, Goth. *driugan*, to serve as soldier; also AS. *dryhtin*, lord, the Lord, OHG. *truhtin*. Surviving in Sc. and north, and revived as literary word by Scott.

Were it not bet at ones for to dye
Than evere more in languor thus to drye?
(Chauc. *Troil.* v. 41).

A young gentleman who had spent his substance too freely at Oxford, and was now dreeing his weird in the backwoods (Buchan, *No-man's-land*).

dreg. ON. *dregg*, usu. in pl.

dreibund [*hist.*]. Ger., three-bond, alliance between Germany, Austria, Italy (1883), also called the *triplice* (It.).

drench. Orig. to make to drink, as still in vet. practice. AS. *drencan*, causal of *drink*; cf. Ger. *tränken*, from *trinken*. Common in ME. in sense of *drown* (q.v.), e.g. the *drenching of Pharaoh*.

And thei camen, and filliden bothe litle bootis, so that thei weren al moost drenchid (Wyc. *Luke*, v. 7).

Dresden china. Manufactured at Meissen (Saxony) and named from capital. Hence *Dresden shepherdess*.

dress. F. *dresser*, VL. *directiare*, to make straight (cf. to *dress the ranks*), hence make ready, put in order; cf. It. *d(i)rizzare*, OSp. *derezar*. All mod. senses spring naturally from primitive, e.g. a *dressing (down)* is a "setting to-rights"; cf. *hair-dresser*, *leather-dresser*. As noun, costume, first in Shaks. Food was orig. "dressed" on the *dresser*.

For to dresse oure feet in to the wey of pees (Wyc. *Luke*, i. 79).

dribble. Frequent. of obs. *drib*, cogn. with *drip*, *drop*. Hence *driblet*, small instalment, etc.

Lyke drunkards that dribbes (Skelton).

drift. From *drive* (q.v.). Fig. what one is "driving" at. In fishing, *drifting* (with a net allowed to "drive" with the tide) is contrasted with *trawling*.

Tilly his drift was to have kept the kings army and Saxons asunder (Sydenham Poyntz, 1624–36).

drill¹. Tool. Du. *dril*, cogn. with E. *thrill* (q.v.); cf. *nostril*. Also Du. *drillen*, to pierce. Hence (17 cent.) E. *drill*, Ger. *drillen*, to exercise soldiers, usu. explained as from the idea of moving them round, but more prob. from that of vexing, tormenting (cf. *bore¹*). See examples below. Du. *drillen* also means to drill (soldiers), to fool, deride.

drillen: to drill, or thrill (Ludw.).

ich bin recht mit dem kerl getrillet: that man is a very plague to me (*ib*.).

ein bauren-triller: a driller, vexer or plague, of poor country-people (*ib*.).

drill². Furrow in which seed is sown. From obs. *drill*, rivulet, rill; cf. obs. *drill*, to flow, trickle, earlier *trill*, used of winding course. Cogn. Ger. dial. forms suggest ult. connection with *drill¹*, from idea of sinuous course, percolation.

drill³ [*mil.*]. See *drill¹*.

drill⁴. Fabric. Earlier *drilling*, corrupt. of Ger. *drillich*, OHG. *drilich*, adaptation of L. *trilix*, *trilic-*, three thread, from *licium*, thread. Cf. *twill*, *samite*, *dimity*.

drink. AS. *drincan*. Com. Teut.; cf. Du. *drinken*, Ger. *trinken*, ON. *drekka*, Goth. *drigkan*. The noun, AS. *drinc*, would normally have given southern *drinch* (cf. *drench*), but has been influenced by the verb. *Slave of drink* is in Shaks. (*Macb.* iii. 6). With adj. use of p.p. *drunk*, earlier *drunken*, as still when used attrib. (*a drunken man*, *frolic*, etc.), cf. Ger. *betrunken*, *trunken*. In each case the passive participle has acquired semi-active meaning (cf. *obese*). *Drunkard* (16 cent.) is perh. Du. *dronkaard*.

drip. Scand. form of AS. *drēopan*, whence dial. *dreep*; cf. Norw. Dan. *dryppe*. Cogn. with *drop*, but expressing a lighter movement; cf. Ger. *triefen*.

drive. AS. *drīfan*. Com. Teut.; cf. Du. *drijven*, Ger. *treiben*, ON. *drīfa*, Goth. *drei-ban*. All senses, trans. and intrans., spring from ground-idea of active movement. Latest development is seen in to *drive a roaring trade (hard bargain)*. Orig. past *drave* still in *AV*. and absurdly used by Hood. Noun *drove*, whence *drover*, is AS. *drāf*. See also *drift*.

To a level mead they came, and there
They drave the wickets in (*Eugene Aram*).

drivel. Earlier *drevel*, AS. *dreflian*, to slobber, hence to behave like child or idiot. Ult. cogn., but not ident., with *dribble*.

drizzle. Frequent. of obs. *drese*, AS. *drēosan*, to fall in drops. See *dreary*.

drogher [*naut.*]. Du. *drooger*, lit. drier, earlier *drogher*, ship that caught and dried herring and mackerel. Now only of WInd. coasting cargo-boat. Prob. taken there by French, as Jal has *navire drogueur* (1525) much earlier than first E. record (18 cent.).

drogue [*naut.*]. Drag attached to harpoon or boat. For *drug*, dial. form of *drag*.

droit [*leg.*]. F., right, law, L. *directus*, straight, right. Cf. *tort*.

Lord Phillimore said that droits of the Crown went to the Navy, and droits of the Admiralty to the Exchequer (*Westm. Gaz.* Dec. 17, 1918).

droll. F. *drôle*, earlier (16 cent.) *drolle*, amusing rascal. Perh. MHG. *trolle*, clown, ult. ON. *troll*, legendary giant.

drome. For *aerodrome* (see *hippodrome*).

They commandeered an aeroplane at an adjacent 'drome (*John Bull*, Aug. 31, 1918).

dromedary. F. *dromadaire*, Late L. *dromedarius* (sc. *camelus*), from G. δρομάς, δρομάδ-, runner, from δραμεῖν, to run.

dromas: a kinde of camelles with two bunches on the backe, marveylous swift, and may abyde three dayes journeying without drinke (Coop.).

dromond [*hist.*]. OF. *dromon(t)*, swift ship, Late L., Byzantine G. δρόμων, from δρόμος, racing (see *dromedary*). Very common in OF. epic and hence in ME. romance. Obs. from 1600, revived by Scott.

drone. Male of honey-bee; hence, idler. AS. *drān*, with LG. cognates, whence Ger. *drohne*, replacing HG. *trene* (still in Saxony and Austria). Orig. imit.; cf. Laconian θρῶναξ, a drone. As verb, and in *drone* of bagpipe, from buzz of insect.

droop. ON. *drūpa*, cogn. with *drop*.

drop. AS. *dropa* and verb *dropian*. Cf. Du. *drop*, Ger. *tropfen*, ON. *dropi*; cogn. with *drip*. Orig. globule of liquid falling, then applied to other substances. The very wide extension of senses is curious, nor is there any gen. F. or Ger. equivalent to the verb.

Lo! Jentiles as a drope of a boket [*Vulg.* quasi stilla situlae], and as moment of a balaunce ben holden (Wyc. *Is.* xl. 15).

dropsy. Aphet. for ME. *ydropsie*, OF. *idropisie* (*hydropisie*), from G. ὕδρωψ, dropsy, from ὕδωρ, water. Wyc. (*Luke*, xiv. 2) has *ydropesie*, later var. *dropesie*.

droshky. Russ. *drozhki*, dim. of *drogi*, waggon, pl. of *droga*, shaft. Hence also Ger. *droschke*, cab, through Pol.

dross. AS. *drōs*, *drōsna*; cf. Du. *droesem*, Ger. *drusen*, dregs, husks. Ult. cogn. with *dreg*.

drought. AS. *drūgoth*, dryness, from root of *drȳge*, dry. In ME. also of thirst.

drove, drover. See *drive*. Persistence of *drover* for earlier *driver* is due to desire to differentiate from coachman, etc.

drown. AS. *druncnian*, to be drunk, to get drowned, from p.p. of *drincan*; cf. Ger. *ertrinken* (intrans.), *ertränken* (trans.), to drown. See *drink*, *drench*. With vulgar *drownd* cf. educated *astound*, *sound*[1]. In early use also of ships (v.i.).

xx li to Peter Paule [an Italian diver] towardes recovering of thordynance of the Mary Rose, drowned at Portesmouth

(*Privy Council Acts*, 1549).

drowsy. From verb *drowse*, to be sleepy, sluggish. Cf. AS. *drūsian*, to become sluggish, orig. to fall, decline (see *dreary*). But, as there is no record between AS. and 16 cent., it is likely that the E. word was borrowed from cogn. obs. Du. *droosen*, "dormitare, dormiscere" (Kil.).

drub. Earliest records (17 cent.) are from Eastern travellers and refer to bastinado. Turk. *durb*, from Arab. *daraba*, to beat.

drudge. App. connected with AS. *drēogan*, to perform, endure (see *dree*), but first found in 15 cent.

drug, drugget. That these words belong together is shown by the fact that F. *c'est du droguet* (earlier also *c'est une drogue*) corresponds to E. *a drug in the market* (formerly *drug* alone). Drug, F. *drogue*, found in most Europ. langs., is prob. from Du. *droog*, dry (cf. origin of *cut and dried*); and *drugget*, F. *droguet* (16 cent.), may have been applied to material manufactured without moisture, or perh. playful allusion to *droogh-doeck*, *droogh-kleed*, dishclout (v.i. and cf. *torchon*). Earliest record in *NED.* for *drug* is AF. *drogges de spicerie* (1327), app. dried spices. Another theory is that F. *drogue* represents Arab. *tiryāq*, from G., as *treacle* (q.v.), and a third connects it with Arab. *durāwa*, chaff, refuse.

droogh: torridus, aridus, siccus, exsuccus (Kil.).

droogh-doeck: sudarium, linteum (*ib.*).

droogh-kleed: linteum quo vasa terguntur (*ib.*).

droogh-scheren [to dry-shear]: tondere pannum, tondere pannum siccum: panni villos laneos bene siccos tondere (*ib.*).

droogherȳe, drooghe wære, droogh kruyd: pharmaca,

aromata, *vulgo.* droga *q.d.* arida, exiccantia. Pharmaca enim violenter corpus exiccant & extergunt, alimenti verò adferunt nihil (*ib.*).

Druid. Earliest (16 cent.) always in pl. L. *druidae, druides* (Caes.). Cf. OIr. *drui,* Gael. *draoi,* the source of L. word. Also Welsh *derwyddon,* soothsayers, from *derw,* true, cogn. with E. *true.*

drum. From 16 cent., replacing in mil. sense earlier *taber, naker.* Rather earlier is obs. *drumslade,* corrupt. of Du. *trommelslag* or Ger. *trommelschlag,* drum-beat. Cf. MHG. *trumbe, trumme,* trumpet, drum. Of imit. origin. In 18 cent. a tea-fight, etc., "not unaptly styled a drum, from the noise and emptiness of the entertainment" (Smollett). In a *drum-head court-martial* the drum is used as extempore table for court. *Drum-fire* (neol.) is for Ger. *trommelfeuer. Drummer,* commercial traveller (chiefly US.), contains a reminiscence of the cheap-jack's drum, as means of attracting customers; cf. to *drum up recruits.*

Drummond light. Limelight. Invented (c. 1821) by *Capt. Drummond.*

drunk, drunken. See *drink.*

drupe [*bot.*]. Stone-fruit. L. *drupa* (sc. *oliva*), G. δρύππα, over-ripe olive.

Druse. Tribe and sect in region of Lebanon. Arab. *Durūz* (pl.), from founder, *Ismail al-darazi,* i.e. the tailor (11 cent.), with whose name cf. *Darzee* the tailor-bird in the *Jungle Book.*

druse [*min.*]. Ger. *druse;* cf. Czech *druza.* But app. of Ger. origin and ident. with *drüse,* gland, tumour.

dry. AS. *drȳge;* cf. Du. *droog,* Ger. *trocken;* also ON. *draugr,* dry stump. *Dry humour* is etym. a contradiction in terms (see *humour*). *Dry wine* is so-called from effect on palate. *Dry* in sense of teetotal is US. *Dry light,* untinged by prejudice (Bacon), is derived from a doubtful passage in Heraclitus. *Dry goods,* orig. dealt with by *dry* (not *liquid*) *measure,* is now US. for drapery, etc. A *drysalter* dealt in drugs, dyes, etc., later pickles, preserved meats, etc. To *dry up* (slang), from the figure of a "babbling" fountain, is US.

We could desire that Mr Philip James Bailey would dry up (*Knickerbocker Mag.* 1856).

dryad. L., G. Δρυάς, Δρυάδ-, from δρῦς, δρυ-, tree, oak.

Dryasdust. Fictitious antiquary to whom some of Scott's novels are dedicated.

duad. For *dyad.* G. δυάς, δυάδ-, influenced by L. *duo.* Cf. *monad.*

dual. L. *dualis,* from *duo,* two. Esp. as gram. term, and (hist.) in the *Dual Monarchy,* Austro-Hungary.

duan. Gael., song, canto. Introduced in Macpherson's *Ossian* (1765).

dub. Late AS. *dubbian,* to dub (a knight); cf. F. *adouber,* It. *addobbare,* ON. *dubba.* The chronological relation of these words has not been cleared up, but *adouber* still means to strike, tap, in Walloon. Prob. the origin is a Teut. radical imit. of a light blow (cf. *dab, dib,* and *dub,* to poke, thrust). Later senses of *dub* follow those of F. *adouber,* to trim, put in order, etc. Hence *dubbing* (*dubbin*), for preparing leather. See also *adobe.*

dubious. L. *dubiosus,* from *dubium,* doubt, from *duo,* two; cf. Ger. *zweifel,* doubt, from *zwei,* two; also AS. *twēo,* doubt, cogn. with *two.*

dub up [*slang*]. To pay, "fork out." Archaic *dub, dup,* to open, from *do up.* Cf. *doff, don.*

ducat. F., It. *ducato,* orig. struck (1140) by Roger II of Sicily, ruler of the *ducato,* duchy, of Apulia. Later associated with Venice and the *doges.*

duchess. F. *duchesse,* Late L. *ducissa* (v.i.).

duchy. F. *duché,* L. *ducatus,* from *dux, duc-.* See *duke.*

duck[1]. Bird. AS. *dūce,* diver, from **dūcan,* to duck, dive; cf. Du. *duiken,* Ger. *tauchen.* Com. Teut. name is represented by AS. *ened* (see *drake*). As term of endearment in Shaks. (*Dream,* v. 1). *Ducks and drakes,* as game and fig., is 16 cent. *Lame duck,* defaulter, is 18 cent. With *duckling,* double dim., cf. *gosling.* The *ugly duckling,* which turned out to be a swan, is from Hans Andersen. For *Bombay duck* see *bummalo,* and cf. *Welsh rabbit.*

Do you know what a bull, and a bear, and a lame duck are? (Horace Walpole).

duck[2]. Verb. See *duck*[1].

duck[3]. Fabric. Du. *doek,* linen, cogn. with Ger. *tuch,* cloth. Also in Scand. langs. Origin unknown.

duct. L. *ductus,* from *ducere, duct-,* to lead. Cf. *ductile,* L. *ductilis.*

dud[1]. Garment. Usu. pl. and now slang, in ME. rough cloak, etc. Origin unknown.

dud[2] [*slang*]. Failure, esp. (mil.) shell that

does not burst, from US. sense of sham article, etc. ? Du. *dood*, dead.

The Boches fire a lot of duds now
(*Lloyd's Weekly News*, April 29, 1917).

dude. US. slang c. 1883. ? Ger. dial. *dude*, fool; cf. hist. of *fop*.

dudeen [*Ir.*]. Short clay pipe. Ir. dim. of *dúd*, pipe. Cf. *caubeen, colleen*, etc.

dudgeon¹ [*archaic*]. Kind of wood used for knife-handles, etc. Hence haft of dagger (*Macb.* ii. 1). Usu. contemptuous, the wooden handle being contrasted with metal, ivory, etc. Cf. *dudgeon verse* (16 cent.) for doggerel (q.v.). Nashe uses *dudgeon* repeatedly as contemptuous adj. Earliest is AF. *digeon*, but prevailing ME. form is *dogeon*. Prob. from MedL. *doga*, cask-stave (see *docket*). Jamieson quotes *dugeon*, app. in sense of cask-staves, for 1551, and connects it with Du. *duig*, ident. with *doga*.

daguë à roëlles: a scottish dagger, or dudgeon haft dagger (Cotg.).

dudgeon². Resentment. In 16 cent. always to *take in dudgeon*; also found as *endugine*. Prob. from It. *aduggiare*, to overshadow, from *uggia*, shadow, of doubtful origin. Cf. to *take umbrage*.

aduggiare: obscurcir par son ombre; donner ombrage, donner de l'enuie ou de la jalousie, estre en haine, ou estre odieux (Duez).

aduggioso: ombrageux, jaloux, & odieux (*ib.*).

due. ME. *dewe*, OF. *deu* (*dû*), owed, VL. *debutum* for *debitum*, from *debēre*, to owe. Mod. sense, as in *the train is due*, is evolved from *due time*, proper time (Chauc.). To *give the devil his due* is in Shaks. (1 *Hen. IV*, i. 2).

duel. F., It. *duello*, L. *duellum*, archaic form of *bellum*, from *duo*, two.

duenna. Sp. *dueña*, mistress, governess, L. *domina*.

duet. Earlier *duetto*, It., dim. of *duo*, two.

duff. Var. of *dough* (q.v.).

duffadar. Urdu, Pers. *dafadār*, cavalry non-commissioned officer.

duffel. Fabric. From *Duffel* (Brabant).

And let it be of duffil gray (Wordsworth, *Alice Fell*).

duffer. Sc. *dowfart*, from *dowf*, deaf, stupid. In some senses affected by *duff*, to fake up, cheat, etc., thieves' slang of unknown origin.

dug [*archaic*]. From 16 cent. Origin obscure. ? Ult. cogn. with Sw. *dägga*, Dan. *dægge*, to suckle.

dugong. Cetaceous mammal. Mal. *dūyung*,

which is *dugung* in Philippines. Adopted by Buffon as *dugon* (1765).

dug-out. US. for canoe hollowed from tree-trunk, underground dwelling. Since 1914 for retired officer rejoining army.

duke. F. *duc*, L. *dux, duc-*, leader. For sense of spec. rank cf. Ger. *herzog*, "army leader," of which the Rom. derivatives of *dux* are usu. transls. This accounts also for the (semi-learned) form, which, if the word had passed through the normal OF. process, would have been *dois, doix* (cf. *croix* from *cruc-em*). The first E. titular *duke* was the Black Prince, created Duke of Cornwall (1337), but the word was in much earlier use in gen. sense. In slang sense of fist, e.g. *put up your dukes*, it may be a different word. The *Dukeries* (Notts) is for *Dukery* (1829).

A duk shal gon out that shal governe my peple of Yrael (Wyc. *Matt.* ii. 6).

dulcet. Respelt, on It. *dolcetto*, for ME. *doucet*, F., dim. of *doux*, sweet, L. *dulcis*.

dulcimer. OF. *doulcemer*, usu. *doucemel*, for L. *dulce melos*, sweet tune. Orig. a stringed instrument and wrongly used (*Dan.* iii. 5, etc.) for bagpipe.

Dulcinea. Don Quixote's idealized mistress. Cf. *Egeria, Beatrice*, etc.

dull. AS. *dol*, foolish; cf. Du. *dol*, Ger. *toll*, mad. See *dwell*.

dulse. Edible seaweed. Ir. & Gael. *duileasg*. ? For *duille uisge*, water leaf. Cf. *whisky*.

duma. Russ., orig. thought, idea, from *dumat'*, to think, reflect. Occurs in ORuss. compds., e.g. *bojarskaja-duma*, council of boyars, i.e. nobles, *gorodskaja-duma*, town-council, from *gorod*, town (cf. *Novogorod, Belgrade*, etc.). The hist. *Duma*, first summoned 1906, suppressed 1917, is short for *gosudárstvennaya-duma*, imperial council. Some authorities hold *duma* to be cogn. with *doom*.

dumb. AS. *dumb*. Com. Teut.; cf. Du. *dom*, Ger. *dumm* (OHG. *tump*), stupid (cf. E. *dummy*, dolt), ON. *dumbr*, Goth. *dumbs*, dumb. Ult. cogn. with *deaf*, with which it is occ. synon. in Teut., and perh. with G. τυφλός, blind. The orig. *dumb-bell* was a rope apparatus, also used to teach bell-ringers. *Dumbfound* appears to be formed by analogy with *confound*.

dum-dum [*mil.*]. From *Dumdum*, mil. cantonment near Calcutta, formerly headquarters of Bengal artillery. Hind. *dam-dama*, mound.

dummy. In various senses, from *dumb*. *Dummy whist* is as old as Swift.

dump[1]. Usu. *the dumps*. Cf. Du. *domp*, haze, etc., Ger. *dumpf*, oppressive, gloomy; cogn. with *damp*.

> For Witherington needs must I wail,
> As one in doleful dumps;
> For, when his legs were smitten off,
> He fought upon the stumps (*Chevy Chase*, c. 1600).

dump[2]. ME. *domp*, to fall heavily (cf. *thump*). In mod. use (chiefly US.) to throw down; hence *dump*, refuse heap, and verb to *dump*, unload commodities on another nation (neol.). Here belongs prob. also *dump* used of various small or "dumpy" objects (cf. *dab* of paint, *pat* of butter). *Dumpling*, orig. from Norfolk, is a double dim.

> The Anti-Dumping Bill is in print, and the second reading will probably be taken next week
> (*Obs.* Nov. 23, 1919).

dumpling. See *dump*[2].

dun[1]. Colour. AS. *dunn*, from Celt.; cf. Gael. Ir. *donn*, Welsh *dwn*.

dun[2]. To demand payment. First in Bacon (c. 1626), who quotes from a "plain old man at Buxton that sold besoms." Origin unknown. Quot. 1, from a letter (c. 1488) dealing app. with extortionate demands in connection with subsidies, suggests that it may have been a stock name of the *John Doe, Richard Roe, Tommy Atkins* type; ? cf. *darbies*.

> I moste pray you for the reverens of Jesu to help hym for your tenauntes and myn, or els John Dyn will owver rewle them (*Paston Let.* iii. 337).

> To dun, is a word lately taken up by fancy, and signifies to demand earnestly, or press a man to pay for commodities taken up on trust, or other debt (Blount).

dunce. Earlier *dunsman*. From *John Duns Scotus* († c. 1308), the Doctor Subtilis, whose disciples were regarded by the Renaissance humanists and reformers as opponents of the new learning and enlightenment. He is supposed to have been born at *Duns* in Berwickshire.

> The old barkyng curres, Dunces disciples and lyke draffe called Scotists, the children of darkness
> (Tynd.).

dunderhead. Cf. Sc. *donnered*, stupefied. But hist. of *blunderbuss* (q.v.) suggests possible association with *blunder*.

Dundreary whiskers. Long flowing side-whiskers (Piccadilly weepers) as worn by *Lord Dundreary* in Tom Taylor's *Our American Cousins* (1858).

dune. F., Du. *duin*, earlier *dune*. See *down*[1].

Dunelm. Signature of Bishop of Durham. MedL. *Dunelmensis*, from *Dunelm* or *Dunholm*, earlier forms of Durham.

dung. AS. *dung*; cf. Ger. *dung*, Sw. *dynga*, Norw. *dyngja*, dung-heap. Thought to be cogn. with ON. *dyngja*, underground dwelling, ? orig. winter lair of the old Teutons covered with dung for heating purposes.

dungaree. Fabric. Hind. *dungrī*, coarse calico.

dungeon, donjon. F. *donjon*, Late L. *dominio-n-*. Orig. central tower, keep, of castle, vaults under which were used as prisons. In OF. also *danjon* (cf. *danger*), ? whence the *Dane John* at Canterbury (see *Dane*).

duniwassal [*hist.*]. Highland gentleman of secondary rank. Gael. *duine*, man, *uasal*, noble. In *Bonnie Dundee*.

dunlin. Bird. From *dun*[1].

Dunmow flitch. Reward for harmonious married life. Established (1244) at *Dunmow* (Ess.) by Robert Fitzwalter.

dunnage [*naut.*]. Matting, brushwood, etc., used in packing cargo. Fig. sailor's kit. Earlier also *dinnage*, the uncertainty of the vowel making conjectures useless.

> cccc et dimidia bordarum...pro calfettacione et dennagio dicte navis (1336).

> xxxvj shegge shevys [sheaves of sedge] layed alow in John Millers crayer for donage under the cordage ladyn in here [her] at Lynne
> (*Nav. Accts.* 1495–97).

dunnock [*dial.*]. Hedge-sparrow. From *dun*[1] with dim. suffix *-ock*. Cf. dial. *ruddock*, red-breast.

dunstable [*archaic*]. Plain, straightforward, etc. Orig. allusion to road to *Dunstable* (Edgware Road), part of Watling Street, famous for straight and even character.

> That's the plain dunstable of the matter, Miss
> (*Clarissa Harlowe*).

duo. It., duet, L. *duo*, two. Cf. *trio*.

duodecimo. For L. *in duodecimo*, (folded) in twelve; cf. *quarto, folio*, etc.

duodenum [*anat.*]. Intestine. So called by medieval anatomists because twelve (*duodeni*) inches long.

duologue. From L. *duo*, two, after *monologue*.

duomo. It., cathedral. See *dome*.

dupe. F., ident. with *dupe*, dial. form of *huppe*, the *hoopoe*, L. *upupa*, regarded as a stupid bird. First in thieves' argot (1426).

duplicate. From L. *duplicare*, to double, from *duo*, two, *plicare*, to fold. Cf. *duplicity*, from *duplex*, double.

durable. F., L. *durabilis*, from *durare*, to last, endure.

dura mater [*anat.*]. Envelope of brain and spinal cord. MedL., for Arab. *umm aldumāgh*, mother of the brain. *Dura* is app. as contrast with *pia* (*mater*).

durance. Esp. *in durance vile* (Burns), for earlier *base durance* (Shaks.). Rather a corrupt. of earlier *duress* (q.v.) than a spec. use of archaic *durance*, continuance, lasting quality, etc.

duration. Late L. *duratio-n-*, from *durare*, to last. Now (1914...) esp. in *for the duration* (of the war).

durbar. Urdu, Pers. *darbār*, court, first element cogn. with E. *door*.

dure [*archaic*]. F. *durer*, L. *durare*. Usu. replaced by *endure*. Hence prep. *during*, orig. pres. part. in absolute construction; cf. Ger. *während des krieges* (gen. absolute), the war lasting, F. *pendant la guerre*, corresponding to L. *bello pendente*.

duresco [*neol.*]. Trade name from L. *durescere*, to grow hard.

duress. OF. *duresse*, L. *duritia* (*durities*), from *durus*, hard. Usu. in *under duress*, constrainedly (leg.). In sense of imprisonment replaced by *durance* (q.v.).

durian. Fruit. Malay *durian*, from *dūrī*, thorn.

during. See *dure*.

durmast oak. Prob. due to a mistake (1791) for *dun mast oak*, i.e. dark acorn oak.

durn. Var. of *darn*[2].

durra, dhurra. Grain. Arab. *durrah*.

durst. See *dare*.

dusk. Orig. adj. AS. *dox*, for **dosc*, dark-coloured. Cf. Norw. *dusk*, mist. Prob. cogn. with L. *fuscus*.

dust. AS. *dūst*; cf. ON. & LG. *dust*, dust, Du. *duist*, bran, Ger. *dunst*, fine vapour, the *-n-* having been lost in other langs. In slang sense of money, e.g. *down with your dust* (c. 1600), orig. with ref. to the worthlessness of riches. US. to *dust out*, make off, is app. after Ger. *sich aus dem staube machen*. Slang *dusty* in *not so dusty* is app. a variation on *mouldy*, erron. associated with *mould*[1].

Il jettera à tous les autres la pouldre aux yeux: he will outstrip all his competitors (metaphorically from the swiftest runner in a sandy race, who to make his fellowes follow aloofe, casteth dust with his heeles into their envious eyes) (Cotg.).

duster. Naut. slang for red ensign. Cf. *coach-whip* for navy pennant.

Dutch. Du. *duitsch* (earlier *dutsch*), German, Ger. *deutsch*, OHG. *diut-isc*, orig. of lang., the vulgar tongue (*theodisca lingua*, c. 788) and applied in that sense to Teut. in gen. The word was prob. coined (8 cent.) by the E. missionaries who, under Boniface, converted the Germans. From OHG. *diot*, people; cf. AS. *thēod*, ON. *thjōth*, Goth. *thiuda*; cogn. with OIr. *tuath*. See *Teuton*. In 15 cent. E., and later, equivalent to German in gen. (*Low Dutch*, *High Dutch*), but from c. 1600 tending to be restricted to Holland, e.g. in Pepys. Often used with ref. to drinking habits of Hollanders and Germans, e.g. *Dutch comfort* (*courage*), to their figures, e.g. *Dutch-built*, or to their unintelligible speech, e.g. *double Dutch*. A German is still a *Dutchman* among sailors and in US. The phantom ship called the *Flying Dutchman* appears to be first mentioned in Scott's note to *Rokeby*, ii. 11. I am unable to trace the genealogy of the *Dutch uncle*. Can it be due to the spec. sense of Du. *baas* (see *boss*[2])?

In Denmark...theyr speche is douche
(Andrew Boorde, 1547).

The Dutch their wine and all their brandy lose,
Disarmed of that by which their courage grows
(Waller, 1665).

In the Dutch wars it had been observed that the captain of the Hollander's men-of-war, when they were about to engage with our ships, usually set a hogshead of brandy abroach afore the mast, and bid the men drink *sustick* that they might fight *lustick* (*Lond. & Country Brewer*, 1738).

dutch [*slang*]. In *old dutch*, coster's wife. For *duchess*.

duty. AF. *dueté*, what is *due* (q.v.) or owing; not recorded in continental OF. Hence what one *ought* (q.v.) to do.

Yf our credytours demaund theyr duety,
To confesse poverte than we do pretend
(*Hye Way to the Spyttel Hous*).

duumvir. L., orig. man of the two. One of two co-equal magistrates or officials.

dwarf. AS. *dweorg*, *dweorh*. Com. Teut.; cf. Du. *dwerg*, Ger. *zwerg*, ON. *dvergr*.

dwell. AS. *dwellan*, orig. trans., to lead astray, hinder, make "dull" (cf. AS. *gedwolen*, perverse); then, linger, tarry (cf. to *dwell upon* a subject), hence, to live. Usual intrans. sense comes from cogn. ON. *dvelja*. Cogn. with obs. Du. *dwellen*, to stun,

OHG. *gitwelan*, to be torpid. Sense-development of *tarry* is somewhat similar.

Whanne thei turneden agen, the child dwelte in Jerusalem (Wyc. *Luke*, ii. 43).

dwindle. From earlier (now Sc.) *dwine*, AS. *dwīnan*, to waste away; cf. Du. *verdwijnen*, to vanish, ON. *dvīna*. First in Shaks. (1 *Hen. IV*, iii. 3).

dwt. Hybrid abbrev., *d* for L. *denarius*, *wt* for weight. Cf. *cwt*, and see *L. s. d.*

dyad. Correct form of *duad* (q.v.).

dyarchy. Double government. From G. δύο, two. Cf. *monarchy*. Earlier is *diarchy*, from G. δι-, twice.

dye. AS. *dēag* (noun), *dēagian* (verb), of unknown origin. Mod. spelling *dye* (*die* in Johns.) is for convenience. With fig. uses, e.g. *double dyed villain, of the blackest (deepest) dye*, cf. *engrained*.

dyke. See *dike*.

dynamic. F. *dynamique*, perh. coined by Leibnitz, G. δυναμικός, from δύναμις, power.

dynamite. Coined (1867) by Alfred Nobel, Sw. inventor (v.s.).

dynamo. Shortened (1882) from *dynamo-electric machine* (Siemens, 1867).

dynasty. F. *dynastie*, Late L., G. δυναστεία, lordship, from δυνάστης, prince, from δύνασθαι, to be powerful (v.s.).

dysentery. OF., L., G. δυσεντερία, from δυσ-έντερος, sick in the bowels, from δυσ-, pejorative, and ἔντερα, bowels. Cf. *enteric*.

dyspepsia. L., G. δυσπεψία, indigestion, from πεπτός, cooked, digested (v.s.).

e-. L., for *ex-*, out of.

each. AS. *ǣlc*, for *ā gelīc*, ever alike. See *ay* and cf. Ger. *jeglich*, MHG. *ie-gelīh*, of similar formation. The -*l*-, lost in E. as in *which*, survives in Sc. *ilk* (cf. Du. *elk*). Earlier equivalent to *every* (q.v.).

Ebreus clepen ech water a see (Wyc.).

eager. F. *aigre*, sour, L. *acer*, *acr*-, sharp, keen, cogn. with *acid*. Cf. *vinegar*. Froissart uses *aigre chevalier* for keen warrior.

It is a nipping and an eager air (*Haml.* i. 4).

eagle. F. *aigle*, L. *aquila*, orig. black eagle, from *aquilus*, dark, whence also *aquilo*, the north wind (darkening the sky). Replaced AS. *earn*, whence poet. *erne* (q.v.).

eagre. Tidal wave, esp. on Humber, Severn (see *John Halifax*, ch. iv.). Recorded as MedL. *higra*, c. 1125, and then not till

c. 1600. AS. *ēagor*, flood, tide, suits the sense, but the -*g*- would have given -*y*-. ON. **ēa-gār*, water-borer, has been suggested (cf. *auger*). If this is right *bore²* may belong to *bore¹*.

ean. See *yean*.

ear¹. Organ of hearing. AS. *ēare*. WAryan; cf. Du. *oor*, Ger. *ohr*, ON. *eyra*, Goth. *ausō*, L. *auris*, G. οὖς, OIr. *ó*. To *set by the ears* is from fighting of animals (cf. F. *un chien hargneux a toujours l'oreille déchirée*). To *ear-mark* was orig. used of sheep and cattle, but fig. sense dates from 16 cent. Within (out of) *earshot* is formed on *pistol shot*, etc.

It toke no sojour[n] in myne hede,
For all yede oute at [that] oon ere
That in that other she dide lere [= teach]
(*Rom. of Rose*, 5150).

ear². Of corn. AS. *ēar*. Com. Teut.; cf. Du. *aar*, Ger. *ähre* (orig. pl.), ON. *ax*, Goth. *ahs*. From an Aryan root *ak*, pointed, as in L. *acus*, needle.

ear³. To plough. Obs., but occurs several times in *AV*. and Shaks. AS. *erian*. WAryan; cf. ODu. *erien*, OHG. *erran*, ON. *erja*, Goth. *arjan*, L. *arare*, G. ἀροῦν, Ir. *airim*. Cogn. with *earth* and L. *arvum*.

The oxen likewise and the young asses that ear the ground (*Is.* xxx. 24).

earing [*naut.*]. Small rope fastening corner of sail to yard. Prob. for *ear-ring*, its earlier spelling. Cotg. gives it s.v. *collier*, lit. necklace.

earl. AS. *eorl*, nobleman, warrior, later spec. sense, under Cnut, being due to association with cogn. *jarl* (q.v.). After Conquest adopted as equivalent to *count¹*. See also *alderman*.

early. AS. *ǣrlīce* (adv.). See *ere* and *like, -ly*. Norw. Dan. *aarle* has also become an adj. The transition is via such phrases as *early riser*.

earn. AS. *earnian*; cf. OHG. *arnōn*, to earn, Ger. *ernte*, harvest.

earnest¹. Serious. AS. *eornost*, eagerness, fierceness; cf. obs. Du. *ernst*, OHG. *ernust* (*ernst*). The adj. is evolved from the noun, which survives only in *in earnest*.

earnest². Pledge, orig. small payment to ratify bargain. ME. *ernes*, altered by natural association with *earnest¹*, the two words being often quibbled on (v.i.). *Ernes* is a corrupt. of *arles, erles*, still in dial. use, a dim. formation from F. *arrhes*, L. *arra*, "an earnest penny, earnest money" (Coop.), cogn. with G. ἀρραβών, of Heb. origin.

Now your jest is earnest:
Upon what bargain do you give it me?
(*Com. of Errors*, ii. 2).

argentum Dei: God's penny, earnest money...In Lincolnshire called "erles," or "arles" (Blount, *Law Dict.*).

earth. AS. *eorthe.* Com. Teut.; cf. Du. *aarde*, Ger. *erde*, ON. *jörth*, Goth. *airtha*; ? ult. cogn. with L. *arvum.* *What on earth? what earthly use?* are app. so mod. that they may be euph. substitutions for stronger expressions. Cf. *what in the world?* To *run to earth* is from fox-hunting.

After a cross-Channel flight one notes a marked difference between the French and British earth-scapes (*An Airman's Outings*).

earwig. AS. *ēarwicga*, ear beetle, from the widespread belief that it creeps into the ear. Cf. synon. Ger. *ohrwurm*, F. *perce-oreille*, "the worme, or insect called an earewig" (Cotg.).

ease. F. *aise*, back-formation from *aisance*, comfortable circumstances, in OF. convenience of situation, L. *adjacentia*, neut. pl. of *adjacens*, lying near. A trace of the origin survives in *easement*, used in Sc. of conveniences about a house, such as sheds, farm-buildings, etc., and corresponding to MedL. *adjacentiae* in same sense; cf. also *chapel of ease.*

easel. Du. *ezel*, ass, Ger. *esel*, L. *asinus.* For change of consonant cf. *kettle.* For other Du. art-words cf. *landscape*, *sketch*, *lay-figure.* For sense cf. F. *chevalet*, easel, lit. little horse.

east. AS. *ēaste* (noun), as adj. *ēast-*, only in compds., e.g. *ēast-seaxe*, East Saxons, Essex. Aryan; cf. Du. *oost*, Ger. *osten*, ON. *austr*, L. *aurora* (for **ausōsa*), Sanskrit *ushas*, dawn. Adopted, with the other cardinal points, as naut. term by the Rom. langs., e.g. F. *est.* *Near* (*far*) *East, Eastern question* are late 19 cent.

Easter. AS. *Ēastre*, usu. in pl. *Ēastron* (cf. Ger. *Ostern*), heathen festival at the vernal equinox in April (q.v.) in honour of Teut. goddess of dawn (see *east*). As this coincided more or less with the Christian Paschal festival, the name was adopted as its WGer. transl. after the conversion. Forms of *pascha* are found in LG. and in Goth. *pāska.* Wyc. always uses *Paske*, Tynd. *Easter.* *Easter-eggs*, a mod. revival from Ger. (cf. *Christmas-tree*), were in ME. *pace-eggs*, still in dial.

Easterling [*hist.*]. Native of Eastern Germany, Baltic coast, a region known collectively as *Eastland*; also erron. used by early antiquaries for *sterling* (q.v.). From obs. adj. *easter*, after Du. *ooster*, *oosterling*.

easy. See *ease.* *Easy-going* was orig. used of horses.

eat. AS. *etan.* Aryan; cf. Du. *eten*, Ger. *essen*, ON. *eta*, Goth. *itan*, L. *edere*, G. ἐδ-, Welsh *ysu*, to devour, OIr. *ithe*, devouring, Sanskrit *ādin*, eating. See *fret*[1], *tooth.* To *eat one's terms* (*dinners*) is colloq. for to keep terms at one of the Inns of Court.

eaves. AS. *efes*; cf. ON. *ups*, dial. Ger. *obsen*, church porch; prob. cogn. with *over.* Orig. sing. (cf. *alms*). Hence *eavesdrop*, for earlier *eavesdrip*, AS. *yfesdrype*, space round house liable to receive roof-water, hence used of listening at doors or windows.

Juratores dicunt quod Henricus Rowley est communis evys-dropper et vagator in noctibus (*Nottingham Bor. Rec.* 1487).

ebb. AS. *ebba*; cf. Du. *eb*, *ebbe*, Ger. *ebbe* (from LG.); prob. cogn. with Goth. *ibuks*, backward. Fig. esp. in *low*(*est*) *ebb.*

Ebenezer. Nonconformist chapel. Heb. *eben ha ēzer*, the stone of help (1 *Sam.* vii. 12). Cf. *Bethel.*

Eblis. Arab. *iblis*, chief of spirits expelled from Paradise. See Beckford's *Vathek.*

ebon, ebony. L. *hebenus*, *ebenus*, G. ἔβενος, prob. from Heb. *hobnīm* (*Ezek.* xxvii. 15); cf. F. *ébène*, Ger. *ebenholz.* The formation of the E. words is not clear. Hence *ebonite*, trade-name for vulcanite.

Ebor. Signature of archbp of York, Late L. *Eboracum*, AS. *Eoforwīc.*

ebriety. F. *ébriété*, L. *ebrietas*, from *ebrius*, drunk.

ebullition. L. *ebullitio-n-*, from *ebullire*, to boil out. Now usu. fig.

écarté. F., p.p. of *écarter*, to discard, put aside, because player may discard certain cards, VL. **exquartare*, to divide into four. Though associated with *card*, it is not etym. connected with it. See *discard.*

Ecce Homo. Picture of Christ wearing crown of thorns. L., behold the man (*John*, xix. 5).

eccentric. Orig. math., opposed to *concentric.* From G. ἔκκεντρος, out of centre. See *centre.* For sense-hist. cf. *delirium.*

ecclesiastic. F. *ecclésiastique*, L., G. ἐκκλησιαστικός, from ἐκκλησία, church, orig. assembly of Athenians, from ἐκκαλεῖν, to call out. The LXX. used ἐκκλησιαστής to render Heb. *qōheleth*, one who addresses an assembly (Solomon). The *Ecclesiastical Commission* dates from 1836.

echelon [*mil.*]. F. *échelon*, rung of ladder, dim. of *échelle*, ladder, OF. *eschiele*, L. *scala*. This is the usual explanation, but there is an archaic F. *échelle*, body of troops, OF. *eschiele*, *eschiere*, OHG. *scăr* (*schar*), band, cogn. with *share*.

echinus. Sea-urchin. L., G. ἐχῖνος, hedgehog. Cogn. with AS. *igl*, Ger. *igel*, hedgehog.

echo. L., G. ἠχώ, personified as nymph, from ἠχή, sound.

éclair. F., flash, from *éclairer*, to light up (v.i.), app. from the lightness of the confectionary. Cf. *vol-au-vent*.

éclaircissement. F., from *éclaircir*, to clear up, OF. *esclarcir*, from L. *clarus*, clear, representing a VL. **exclarescire*. Very common in 18 cent. E.

éclat. F., from *éclater*, to burst out, perh. from a VL. **exclappitare*, from the imit. *clap*.

eclectic. G. ἐκλεκτικός, selective, from ἐκλέγειν, to pick out.

eclipse. F. *éclipse*, L., G. ἔκλειψις, from ἐκλείπειν, to fail. In Chauc. and *Piers Plowm.* Hence *ecliptic*, apparent orbit of sun, so called because eclipses can only occur when moon is near this line.

That stroke of [Garrick's] death which has eclipsed the gaiety of nations (Johns.).

eclogue. L., G. ἐκλογή, from ἐκλέγειν, to select. Spenser's spelling *aeglogue* (*Shepherd's Calendar*) is due to a mistaken etym. from αἴξ, αἰγ-, goat, as though "goatherd's song."

ecod. See *egad*.

economy. L., G. οἰκονομία, house management, oldest sense in E., from οἶκος, house, νέμειν, to manage, rendered in Church L. by *dispensatio*. *Political economy* (18 cent.) translates F. *économie politique*.

écru. F., unbleached, OF. *escru*, from L. *ex* and *crudus*, raw.

ecstasy. ME. *extasie*, OF. *extasie* (*extase*), MedL., G. ἔκστασις, from ἐκ, out of, ἱστάναι, to put, esp. in ἐξιστάναι φρενῶν, to drive out of wits. Cf. to *be beside oneself*.

Thei weren fulfillid with wondryng and extasie (Wyc. *Acts*, iii. 10).

ecto-. From G. ἐκτός, outside.

ecumenical. See *oecumenical*.

eczema. G. ἔκζεμα, from ἐκ, out, ζεῖν, to boil.

edacious. From L. *edax*, *edac-*, voracious. A favourite word of Carlyle.

Edda. Ancient Icel. poems. Younger, or prose, *Edda*, compiled (c. 1230) partly by Snorre Sturluson. Elder, or poetic, *Edda* (c. 1200). *Edda* is the name of the great-grandmother in one of the ON. poems, but can hardly be the origin of the word, which appears to be connected with ON. *ōthr*, mind, poetry.

eddish [*dial.*]. Aftergrowth of grass, stubble. Also *errish*, *arrish*. AS. *edisc*, park, pasture. For variation of consonant cf. *park*, *paddock*. Cf. synon. dial. *edgrow*, AS. *edgrōwung*, and see *eddy*.

eddy. ME. *ydy*; cf. ON. *itha*, whirlpool. Prob. cogn. with obs. prefix *ed-*, again, backwards (cf. OHG. *it-*, ON. *ith-*, Goth. *id-*), and ult. with L. *iterum*.

edelweiss. Ger., noble white.

Eden. Heb. *ēden*, pleasure, delight.

edentata [*biol.*]. Order of mammals without front teeth. From L. *edentare*, to remove teeth.

edge. AS. *ecg*. Com. Teut.; cf. Du. *egge*, Ger. *ecke*, corner, ON. *egg*; cogn. with L. *acies*, G. ἀκίς, point. Oldest sense, edge of sword. *Not to put too fine an edge* (*point*) *on it* is to express oneself "bluntly." With *to set teeth on edge* cf. OF. *aacier* (now replaced by *agacer*), VL. **ad-aciare*. See *egg*[2]. *Edge*(*d*) *tools* is 14 cent., fig. 16 cent. In *to edge in* (*off*, *out*) it is sometimes for *hedge* (q.v.).

agacer: to egge, urge, provoke, anger, vex, exasperate; also, to set the teeth on edge (Cotg.).

edible. Late L. *edibilis*, from *edere*, to eat.

edict. Restored spelling of ME. *edit*, F. *édit*, L. *edictum*, from *edicere*, to proclaim. Cf. *verdict*.

edifice. F. *édifice*, L. *aedificium*, from *aedes*, building (cf. *aedile*). Cf. *edify*, F. *édifier*, L. *aedificare*, to build. For fig. sense cf. *instruct*.

edition. F. *édition*, L. *editio-n-*, from *ēdere*, to give out, from *ex* and *dare*. *Edit* is a back-formation from *editor*.

educate. From L. *educare*, cogn. with *educere*, to lead out, whence *educe*, *eduction*, etc.

edulcorate. From Late L. *edulcorare*, from *dulcor*, sweetness.

-ee. Prop. from F. p.p. ending *-é*, L. *-atus*, as in *debauchee*, *refugee*, *payee*, *committee* (q.v.). Hence extended to *bargee*, *devotee*, *dilutee*, etc. *Chinee*, *Portugee*, *marquee*, etc.

are false singulars from -ese, OF. -eis (-ais, -ois), L. -ensis; cf. pea, cherry, burgee.

eel. AS. ǣl. Com. Teut.; cf. Du. Ger. aal, ON. āll. Earlier hist. unknown.

e'en. See eve, even.

-eer. F. -ier, L. -arius, agent-suffix. Now often jocular (profiteer, munitioneer).

e'er. See ever.

eerie, eery. Northern dial. word recently popularized in literature. ME. eri, from argh, timid, AS. earg, cowardly. Com. Teut.; cf. Du. arg, roguish, OHG. arg, cowardly, worthless (in ModGer. vexatious), ON. argr, cowardly. For mod. meaning, inspiring fear, cf. double sense of fearful.

efface. F. effacer, from é-, L. ex, and face. Cf. deface.

effect. AF. for F. effet, L. effectus, p.p. of efficere, to bring about, from ex and facere. The ground-idea is result, hence mod. sense of personal property as manifestation of means. In mil. sense effective is collect. use of earlier effective soldier. With effectual, Late L. effectualis, cf. actual; also effectuate, after actuate.

effeminate. From L. effeminare, from femina, woman.

effendi. Turk. efendi, corrupt. of G. αὐθέντης, lord, master. See authentic.

> Their aphendis written also by the later Greeks ἀφένδης is corrupted from αὐθέντης, i. lord
> (Selden, 1614).

efferent [anat.]. L. efferens, efferent-, pres. part. of efferre, from ex and ferre, to carry.

effervesce. L. effervescere, from ex and fervescere, incept. of fervēre, to be hot.

effete. L. effetus, exhausted by breeding, fetus, hence incapable of producing.

efficacious. From L. efficax, efficac-. Cf. efficient, from pres. part. of efficere. See effect.

effigy. Due to misunderstanding of L. in effigie, abl. of effigies, from effingere, from ex and fingere, to form.

> Mine eye doth his effigies witness
> Most truly limn'd and living in your face
> (As You Like It, ii. 7).
> The pompous funerall of the Duke of Richmond, who was carried in effigie in an open charriot thro London (Evelyn).

effloresce. L. efflorescere, from ex and florescere, incept. of florēre, to bloom, from flos, flor-, flower.

effluent. From pres. part. of L. effluere, from ex and fluere, to flow.

effluvium. Late L., from effluere (v.s.).

Earlier used, like F. effluve, of any kind of radiation, now only of smells, the pl. effluvia being sometimes ignorantly used as sing. For similar blunder cf. animalcule.

> The putrid effluviae (!) in prisons (NED. 1826).

effort. F., back-formation from efforcer, from forcer. See force.

effrontery. F. effronterie, from effronté, lit. without brow (for blushing), from L. ex and frons, front-. Cf. unblushing.

effulgent. See fulgent.

effusion. L. effusio-n-, from effundere, from ex and fundere, fus-, to pour out. Hence effusive, "gushing."

efreet. Var. of afreet (q.v.).

eft. Also dial. efet, evet. Older form of newt (q.v.).

eftsoons [poet.]. Obs. eft, compar. of aft, and soon, with -s added by analogy with other adverbs formed from genitive.

egad. Prob. for ah God. Jonas Chuzzlewit's var. is ecod.

Egeria. Nymph who dictated the laws of Rome to King Numa.

> Il y a peu d'espoir qu'un jour un Numa français rencontre...une autre nymphe Égérie qui lui dicte des lois sages (Anatole France).

egg¹. Noun. ON. egg, replacing in ME. cogn. native ey, AS. ǣg. WAryan; cf. Du. Ger. ei, L. ovum, G. ᾠόν, Ir. og. Egg-nog contains EAngl. nog, strong beer, of unknown origin.

> Bacoun and somtyme an ey or tweye
> (Chauc. B. 4035).

egg². Verb. Usu. with on. ON. eggja, replacing cogn. native edge (q.v.), in same sense.

> Cassius did edge him on the more, for a private quarrell he had conceived against Caesar
> (North's Plutarch).

eglantine. F. églantine, flower of the églantier, wild-rose tree, OF. aiglentier, VL. *aculentarius, thorny, from aculeus, prickle, from acus, needle. Tennyson uses archaic eglatere.

ego. L., I (q.v.). Introduced in 18 cent. to connote the "conscious, thinking subject." Hence egoism, egoist, orig. philos. terms, from F., and the incorr. egotism, egotist (by analogy with such words as nepotism dramatist), to express selfishness. Cf. Ger. ichsucht lit. I disease, F. le culte du moi. See also altruism.

> Man is too thoroughly an egoist not to be also an egotist (O. Henry).

egregious. From L. *egregius*, from *ex*, out of, *grex, greg-*, flock. Not orig. disparaging.

An egregious [*Vulg.* egregius, *AV.* cunning] artificer in wood (Douay Bible, *Ex.* xxxviii. 23).

egress. L. *egressus*, from *egredi*, to go out, from *ex* and *gradior*, I step.

egret. Lesser white heron. F. *aigrette*, dim. from OHG. *heigir*, heron. See *aigrette, heron*.

Egyptian. In various Bibl. allusions, e.g. *bondage, darkness* (*Ex.* x. 22), *spoiling* (xii. 36), *flesh-pots* (xvi. 3); also *corn in Egypt* (*Gen.* xlii. 1). See also *gipsy, dismal*.

eh. ME. *ey*; cf. F. *eh*, Ger. *ei*. Natural exclamation.

eider-down. ON. *æthar-dūnn*, in which first element is gen. of *æthr*, eider-duck. Hence, by wrong separation, *eider* and *eider-duck*; cf. Sw. *ejderdun*, Norw. *ederdun*, whence F. *édredon*. See *down*[3].

eidolon. Spectre. G. εἴδωλον. See *idol*.

eight. AS. *eahta*. Aryan; cf. Du. Ger. *acht*, ON. *ātta*, Goth. *ahtau*, L. *octo*, G. ὀκτώ, OIr. *ocht*, Sanskrit *ashtau*. Orig. a dual. *Piece of eight* (*Treasure Island*) translates Sp. *pieza de ocho* (sc. reals). *Eight days*, week, became common in the Great War, owing to lit. transl. of *huit jours* in F. despatches.

eikon. See *icon*.

eirenicon. Offer of peace. Neut. of G. εἰρηνικός, from εἰρήνη, peace.

eisteddfod. Gathering of Welsh bards. From Welsh *eistedd*, to sit.

either. Orig. adj., each of two, both. AS. *ǣgther*, for *ǣghwæther*, from *ā ge hwæther*, for which see *ay, y-, whether*. Cf. MHG. *jegeweder*, OHG. *eo-gi-wedar*, now replaced by *jedweder*.

On either side one, and Jesus in the midst (*John*, xix. 18).

ejaculate. From L. *ejaculari*, to shoot forth, from *jaculum*, javelin, from *jacere*, to throw. Orig. in lit. sense, esp. med.

eject. From L. *eicere, eject-*, from *ex* and *jacere*, to throw. Cf. to *chuck out*. Hence noun *eject*, coined (1878) by Clifford to express ideas and sensations which cannot be classed as *subjects* or *objects*.

eke. To augment. Usu. with *out*. Has replaced (under influence of obs. noun *eke*, addition) ME. *eche*, AS. *ēcan*. Com. Teut.; cf. OSax. *ōkian*, OHG. *ouhhōn*, ON. *auka*, Goth. *aukan*; cogn. with L. *augēre*, G. αὐξάνειν, to increase. The adv. *eke*, AS. *ēac*

(cf. Du. *ook*, Ger. *auch*), was perh. orig. an imperative, "add."

Delyte not in wo thy wo to seche, As don thise fooles that hir sorwes eche With sorwe (Chauc. *Troilus*, i. 704).

elaborate. From L. *elaborare*, to work out, from *ex* and *laborare*.

elaeo-. From G. ἔλαιον, oil.

élan. F., false sing. from *élans*, from *élancer*, to launch out. See *launch*[1].

eland. SAfr. antelope. Du., elk, Ger. *elend* (now *elentier*), OLithuanian *ellenis*, cogn. with G. ἐλλός, fawn, Welsh *elain*, hind, fawn, and ult. with *elk*. The elk is still found in East Prussia. Earlier E. forms, from Ger. or from F. *élan*, are *ellan, ellend*, applied to the elk proper. Some of its folk-lore attributes are due to mistaken association with Ger. *elend*, wretched.

elan: a certaine wild beast; as *ellend* (Cotg.).

ellend: th'elke; a most fearefull, melancholike, strong, swift, short-neckt, and sharp-hooved, wild beast (*ib.*).

elapse. From L. *elabi, elaps-*, from *ex* and *labi*, to glide.

elastic. Late G. ἐλαστικός, from ἐλαύνειν, to propel. With noun sense cf. F. *gomme élastique*, india-rubber.

elate. Orig. adj., exalted. From L. *efferre, elat-*, from *ex* and *ferre*, to bear.

elbow. AS. *elnboga*, for which see *ell* and *bow*[1]. The compd. is Com. Teut.; cf. Du. *elleboog*, Ger. *ellenbogen*, ON. *ölnbogi*. With *elbow-room* cf. F. *franches coudées*, from *coude*, elbow. *Out at elbow* is in Shaks. (*Meas. for Meas.* ii. 1).

Elchi, Eltchee, Eltchi [*hist.*]. Turk. *ilchī*, ambassador, from *il*, tribe. Applied by Turks esp. to Sir Stratford Canning, Lord Stratford de Redcliffe (†1880).

eld [*poet.*]. Old age. AS. *eldo*, from *eald*, old; cf. OHG. *altī*. Replaced by *age*.

elder[1], **eldest.** Mercian compar. and superl. of *old* (q.v.). The only E. survival of umlaut in comparison. Usu. replaced by *older, oldest*, exc. in spec. senses. The compar. was also used in AS. & ME. for parents (cf. Ger. *eltern*). In eccl. sense *elder* is a lit. rendering of G. πρεσβύτερος (see *presbyter, priest*).

They called the elders of him that had receaved his sight (Coverd. *John*, ix. 18).

elder[2]. Tree. With intrusive *-d-* for earlier *eller*, AS. *ellen, ellern*. Older form survives in place-names, e.g. *Ellerdale, Ellershaw*, etc. For form cf. unrelated *alder*.

eldorado. Sp., the golden (sc. king of a golden realm), supposed by Spaniards and Elizabethan adventurers to exist in SAmer.

This Martinez was he that christened the city of Manoa by the name of El Dorado (Raleigh).

eldritch [*Sc.*]. Earlier *elrish*, app. from *elf*; cf. synon. Sc. *elphrish*. See quot. s.v. *weird*.

Ye fright the nightly wanderer's way
    Wi' eldritch croon (Burns, *Address to Deil*).

elecampane. Plant. OF. *enule-campane*, MedL. *enula campana*, from L. *inula*, whence, by metath., AS. *eolone, elene*; or this may be due to G., as L. *inula* is cogn. with G. ἐλένιον; *campana* is prob. for *campestris*, of the fields.

inula: the herbe called *enula campana*, elicampane
(Coop.).

elect. From L. *eligere, elect-*, from *ex* and *legere*, to pick. Orig. adj., chosen, esp. in theol. sense. Pol. sense dates from temp. Charles I. *Electioneer* is US. *Elector* (e.g. of the Rhine) translates Ger. *kurfürst*, choose prince, i.e. prince formerly having a vote in choice of Emperor.

electric. ModL. *electricus*, from G. ἤλεκτρον, amber, whence also ME. *electre* (Wyc.), an alloy of gold and silver. Amber exercises attraction when rubbed. "The mod. L. word appears to have been first used by W. Gilbert in his treatise *De Magnete*, 1600" (*NED.*). Hence *electrocution*, barbarously coined (1901) in US. after *execution*, with back-formation *electrocute*. *Electrolier*, like *gaselier*, is after *chandelier*.

electuary. Restored spelling, after F. *électuaire*, of ME. *lectuary* (cf. *alembic, limbeck*), Late L. *electuarium*, perverted from G. ἐκλεικτόν, drug dissolved in mouth, from ἐκλείχειν, to lick out; cf. Ger. *latwerge*, It. *lattovaro*.

eleemosynary. MedL. *eleemosynarius*. See *alms*.

elegant. F. *élégant*, L. *elegans, elegant-*, pres. part. of early L. **elegare* (= *eligere*, to pick out), hence orig. dainty, fastidious. Etym. sense survives in *elegant extracts*. US. use of *elegant* (lunch, landscape, pig, etc.) is app. from Ir.

elegans in cibo: fine and picked in his meate
(Coop.).

I haven't the janius for work,
    For 'twas never the gift of the Bradys;
But I'd make a most elegant Turk,
    For I'm fond of tobacco and ladies (Lever).

elegy. F. *élégie*, L., G. ἐλεγεία, orig. neut.

pl., from ἔλεγος, mournful poem. Also applied to anything written in *elegiac* verse, i.e. alternate hexameters and pentameters.

La plaintive élégie en longs habits de deuil
(Boileau).

element. F. *élément*, L. *elementum*, with ground-sense of matter in its simplest form (cf. *rudiment*). Hence the *four elements* (earth, air, fire, water) and *out of one's element*, e.g. like a fish out of water. It has been suggested that L. *elementum* was orig. a term of gram. and may represent a schoolboy formation from *l, m, n* (cf. *abc*, to mind one's *p*'s and *q*'s).

elemi. Resin. Cf. F. *élémi*, Sp. It. *elemi*. Origin doubtful, prob. Arab.

elenchus. Logical refutation. L., G. ἔλεγχος, cross-examination.

elephant. Restored form of ME. & OF. *olifant*, whence name of Roland's horn and our surname *Oliphant*. Change of vowel of L. *elephas, elephant-*, G. ἐλέφας, whence also app. AS. *olfend*, OHG. *olbanta*, Goth. *ulbandus*, camel, is unexplained. The word was prob. introduced by the Phoenicians; *el-* is the Semitic def. art., and the second element is ident. with Heb. *ibah*, cogn. with L. *ebur*, ivory. *White elephant*, burdensome possession, is said to be due to the custom of the kings of Siam of handing over one of the sacred white elephants to a courtier who would be ruined by the cost of maintaining it. The disease *elephantiasis* gives the appearance of elephant-hide to the skin.

Eleusinian. Of *Eleusis*, in Attica, where mysteries of Demeter were celebrated.

eleutherism. Zeal for freedom. From G. ἐλεύθερος, free.

elevate. From L. *elevare*, from *ex* and *levare*, to raise, from *levis*, light. For fig. sense cf. *uplift*. *Elevator*, lift, is US.

eleven. AS. *endlufan*. Com. Teut.; cf. Du. *elf* (earlier *elleven*), Ger. *elf* (OHG. *einlif*), ON. *ellifu*, Goth. *ainlif*. First element is *one* (cf. L. *undecim*), second, found also in *twelve*, is ult. cogn. with Lithuanian *-lika*, similarly used, and perh. with L. *linquere*, to leave, thus "one left over from ten." The cricket *eleven* is recorded (in Hants) for 1751. *Eleventh hour*, last possible time, is from *Matt.* xx.

The hour when the Armistice came into force, the eleventh hour of the eleventh day of the eleventh month (King George V, Nov. 1919).

elf. AS. *ælf*; cf. Ger. *alp* (now nightmare, v.i.), ON. *álfr*. See also *oaf*. Now equivalent to fairy, but orig. rather used of hostile powers. Very common as element in names, e.g. Alfred, Alberic, Auberon (Oberon), etc. Ger. *elf*, from E., dates from Wieland's transl. (1764) of *Midsummer Night's Dream*. *Elfin*, first in Spenser's *elfin knight*, is perh. due to ME. genitive in *elvene land* (cf. hist. of *fairy*). *Elf-locks* are tangles caused by fairies, esp. Queen Mab; cf. synon. Norw. Dan. *marelok*, with first element as in *nightmare*. See also *erl-king*.

> This is that very Mab
> That plats the manes of horses in the night,
> And bakes the elf-locks in foul sluttish hairs,
> Which, once untangled, much misfortune bodes
>   (*Rom. & Jul.* i. 4).

> Like an Alp (!) a frightful feeling of powerlessness has been lying upon us for three and a half years
>   (*Vorwärts*, as translated by *Daily Chron.*
>   Jan. 23, 1918).

Elgin marbles. From Parthenon at Athens. Brought to England (1812) by Earl of Elgin to prevent destruction by the Turks.

elicit. From L. *elicere*, *elicit-*, from *ex* and *lacere*, to entice.

elide. L. *elidere*, from *ex* and *laedere*, to dash. Hence *elision*. Cf. *collide*.

eligible. Late L. *eligibilis*, from *eligere*. See *elect*.

eliminate. From L. *eliminare*, to put out of doors, from *ex* and *limen*, *limin-*, threshold.

elision. See *elide*.

élite. F., from *élire*, L. *eligere*, to pick out.

elixir. MedL., Arab. *al-iksīr*, from Late G. ξήριον, drying powder for wounds, from ξηρός, dry. Used in ME. both of "philosopher's stone" and "elixir of life."

> The philosophres stoon,
> Elixer clept, we sechen faste echoon
>   (Chauc. G. 862).

elk. AS. *eolh*; cf. Ger. *elch*, ON. *elgr*; ult. cogn. with *eland*. L. *alces* (Caesar) is from Teut. Form of word is to be ascribed to AF. treatment of final *-h*, our lang. of ven. being almost entirely F.

ell. AS. *eln*. Com. Teut.; cf. Du. *el*, Ger. *elle* (OHG. *elina*), ON. *öln*, Goth. *aleina*. From Teut. comes MedL. *alena*, whence F. *aune*, ell. Orig. length of fore-arm (cf. *cubit*, *foot*, etc.) and cogn. with L. *ulna*. See *elbow*. Now only in fig. allusions to the *inch* and the *ell*.

ellipse. Back-formation from *ellipses*, pl. of *ellipsis*, from which it is now sometimes differentiated. L., G. ἔλλειψις, from ἐλλείπειν,

to come short, from λείπειν, to leave. In conic sections "the inclination of the cutting plane to the base 'comes short of,' as in the case of the hyperbola it exceeds, the inclination of the side of the cone" (*NED.*).

ellipsis. See *ellipse*.

elm. AS. *elm*; cf. ON. *álmr*, OHG. *elm*, MHG. *ilme* (as in *Ilmenau*); now replaced by *ulme*, L. *ulmus*, whence also Du. *olm*, OF. *olme* (*orme*). But *elm* and *ulmus* are ult. cogn.

Elmo. In *Saint Elmo's fire*, corposant. It. *fuoco di santelmo* or Sp. *fuego de santelmo*; cf. Ger. *Helenenfeuer*. The saint, whether *Elmo* or *Helen*, is prob. as apocryphal as *Vitus*, and the phrase goes back to G. ἑλένη, torch.

elocution. L. *elocutio-n-*, from *eloqui*, to speak out. Orig. used of literary style in gen.

éloge. F., praise, esp. Academy speech. L. *elogium*, G. ἐλεγεῖον, in sense of elegiac inscription on tomb.

Elohist. Author of those parts of the Hexateuch which are characterized by the use of *Elohim* (Heb. pl.), gods, instead of *Yah-veh*, Jehovah.

eloi(g)n [*leg.*]. To remove. F. *éloigner*, from *é-*, L. *ex*, and *loin*, distant, L. *longe*; cf. *purloin*. *Elongate*, from Late L. *elongare*, had formerly the same sense.

> *elongate*: to remove afar off, to defer or prolong
>   (Blount).

elope. AF. *aloper*, app. from ME. & dial. *lope*, *loup* (q.v.), to run, ON. *hlaupa*, cogn. with *leap*, and with Du. *loopen*, Ger. *laufen*, to run. Cf. *interloper* (q.v.). Neither word is found in E. till c. 1600, and influence of Du. *loopen* seems likely in both. Cf. also obs. *outlope* (Florio's *Montaigne*), from Du. *uitloop*.

eloquence. F. *éloquence*, L. *eloquentia*, from *eloqui*, to speak out.

else. AS. *elles* (adv.), otherwise, genitive of lost Teut. adj. cogn. with L. *alius*; cf. AS. *eleland*, foreign country, and Ger. *elend*, misery, orig. banishment; also Ger. *Elsass* (Alsace), seat of strangers.

Eltchee. See *Elchi*.

elucidate. From Late L. *elucidare*, to clear up, from *lucidus*, bright, from *lux*, *luc-*, light. Cf. F. *éclaircir*.

elude. L. *eludere*, *elus-*, from *ex* and *ludus*, play. Hence *elusive*.

elvan. Igneous rock. Corn. *elven*, spark.

elver. Young eel. For *eel-fare*, passage of young eels up a river.

Elysium. L., G. Ἠλύσιον (sc. πεδίον, plain), abode of happy dead. Homer places it on the W. border of the earth, Pindar and Hesiod in the "Islands of the Blest."

elytron [*biol.*]. Wing case. G. ἔλυτρον, sheath, from ἐλύειν, to roll round.

elzevir. Prop. *elzevier*, name of famous family of Du. printers (1592–1680). Cf. *aldine*.

'em. Unstressed form of ME. *hem*, AS. *him*, dat. pl. of pers. pron., 3rd pers., which supplanted acc. *hīe*, and was itself early superseded by *them* (q.v.). No longer literary, but regularly used by the late Dr Furnivall.

em-. F., assimilation of *en-* to following labial. Cf. L. *im-*, *in-*

emaciate. From L. *emaciare*, from *macies*, leanness.

emanate. From L. *ēmanare*, from *ex* and *manare*, to flow. Hence *emanation* (theol.), relation of Son and Holy Ghost to Father.

emancipate. From L. *emancipare*, to release from the power of the *paterfamilias*, from *ex* and *manceps*, *mancip-*, one who acquires property, from *manu capere*, to take by hand. Hence *emancipationist*, used of supporter of Catholic Emancipation Bill(1829), and later of opponents of slavery.

emasculate. From L. *emasculare*, to castrate, from *ex* and *masculus*, male.

embalm. Altered spelling of ME. *embaume* (Chauc.), from *baume*, balm.

embargo. Sp., from *embargar*, to impede, restrain (esp. ship or goods from leaving port), VL. *imbarricare. Cf. *bar*, *embarrass*.

embark. F. *embarquer*; cf. It. *imbarcare*, Sp. *embarcar*; see *bark²*. Orig. trans., to put on board. Fig. sense, e.g. to *embark on an enterprise*, appears early; cf. to *launch a scheme, float a company*, etc.

embarrass. F. *embarrasser*, It. *imbarazzare* or Sp. *embarazar*, to put within "bars."

embassy. Earlier also *ambassy*. See *ambassador*.

embattled. See *battlement*. Confused also with archaic *embattle*, to prepare for battle, OF. *embatailler*.

embay [*naut.*]. To detain within a *bay²* (q.v.).

embellish. F. *embellir*, *embelliss-*, from *en*, and *bel* (*beau*), L. *bellus*. Cf., for formation, F. *enrichir*.

ember. Usu. pl. ME. *emer*, *aymer*, with intrusive *-b-*, AS. *ǣmerge*, *ǣmerye*; cf. OHG. *eimuria*, ON. *eimyrja*. First element is cogn. with ON. *eimr*, steam, vapour, and second with Norw. *mörje*, mass of glowing ashes; cf. Norw. *ildmörje*, embers, of which first element is cogn. with *ann-eal* (q.v.).

ember-day. Usu. pl. AS. *ymbren-dæg, ymbrig-dæg*, from *ymb-ryne*, revolution, from *ymbe*, around, from prep. *ymb* (cf. Ger. *um*), *ryne*, running; cf. ON. *imbrudagar* (from AS.), whence Norw. *imbredage*, last week in Advent. Fixed by Council of Placentia (1095) for Wed. Fri. Sat. following First Sunday in Lent, Whitsunday, Holy Cross Day (Sep. 14), St Lucia's Day (Dec. 13). But synon. Ger. *quatember*, MedL. *quatuor tempora*, suggests possible influence of folk-etym. in E. word also, and, as a fast, it has prob. been associated with *ember¹*.

embry day: angarium, vel dies 4ᵒʳ temporum
                    (*Prompt. Parv.*).

ember-goose. Also *imber*. Norw. *imbre*, prob. because usu. appearing on the coast during the Advent ember-days (v.s.); cf. its Ger. name *Adventsvogel*.

embezzle. AF. *enbesiler*, to damage, waste, steal, from OF. *besillier*, from *besil*, ill-treatment. *Bezzle* was formerly used in same sense. In 16–18 cents. often associated in form and sense with *imbecile* and used for weaken, impair. OF. *besil* is of unknown origin. It may be ident. with *bezel* (q.v.), with idea of slicing-pieces off; cf. F. *écorner* (knock the corners off) *sa fortune* (*ses revenus*).

He hath embeazld his estate ˎBurton).

embezzle: this word seems corrupted by an ignorant pronunciation from imbecil (Johns.).

emblem. F. *emblème*, L., G. ἔμβλημα, inlaid work, from ἐμβάλλειν, to throw in. But fig. sense is oldest in E.

emblem: is properly any fine work cunningly set in wood or other substance, as we see in chess-boards and tables, notwithstanding it is commonly taken for a sweet moral symbol, consisting of picture and words, by which some weighty matter is declared (Blount).

emblement [*leg.*]. Profit of sown land. OF. *emblaement*, from *emblaer* (*emblaver*), to sow with corn, *blé*, MedL. *bladum*. The latter is perh. L. *ablatum*, what is carried off; cf. Ger. *getreide*, corn, MHG. *getregede*, what is carried (*tragen*). But it may be Celt. (cf. Welsh *blawd*, flour).

embody. Hybrid, from F. *en* and E. *body*, coined (16 cent.) to render L. *incorporare*. Cf. *embolden*, replacing earlier *enhardy*, F. *enhardir*.

embolism [*med.*]. Stoppage of artery; formerly also, day intercalated in calendar. L., G. ἐμβολισμός, from ἐμβάλλειν, to throw in.

embonpoint. F., from *en bon point*, in good condition.

> Plump and (as the French has it) *en bon point* (Evelyn).

emboss. OF. *embosser*. See *boss*[1]. For obs. *emboss*, to take refuge in a thicket, see *embusqué*.

embouchure. River-mouth, mouth of wind-instrument. F., from *en* and *bouche*, mouth, L. *bucca*, cheek.

embowel. In archaic sense of *disembowel* (*All's Well*, i. 3), from OF. *esboeler* with change of prefix. See *bowel* and cf. *eviscerate*.

embrace. F. *embrasser*, from *en* and *brasse*, in OF. the two arms, F. fem. sing. from L. neut. pl. *brachia*; cf. It. *imbracciare*.

> Li reis ad pris Tierri entre sa brace (*Rol.* 3939).

embrangle [*archaic*]. To entangle. From obs. *brangle*, F. *branler*, to shake, confuse, for *brandeler*, frequent. of *brandir*. See *brandish*.

embrasure. F., from *embraser*, "to skue, or chamfret off, the jaumbes of a doore, or window" (Cotg.). Also *ébraser*. Prob. from *bras*, arm, with idea of opening out to receive.

embrocation. From G. ἐμβροχή, lotion, from ἐμβρέχειν, from ἐν, in, βρέχειν, to wet.

embroider. See *broider* and cf. OF. *embroder*.

embroil. Orig. to confuse, entangle. F. *embrouiller*. See *broil*[1], *imbroglio*.

embryo. MedL., G. ἔμβρυον, neut. of pres. part., from ἐν and βρύειν, to swell. The incorr. *in embryo* suggests a MedL. **embryum*.

embusqué [*F. slang*]. In sense of one avoiding the front this is a neol. from F. *s'embusquer*, to lie in wait. See *ambush* and cf. obs. *emboss*, to take refuge in a thicket.

> The hert hadde upon lengthe
> So moche embosed (Chauc. *Blanche*, 352).

emend. L. *emendare*, to free from fault, or corresponding OF. *esmender*. See *amend*, *mend*. Hence *emendation*, now only of textual corrections.

emerald. F. *émeraude*, OF. *esmeraude*, L., G. σμάραγδος, Sanskrit *asmā*, stone, *marakata*, emerald. ModE. form prob. due to Sp. Port. *esmeralda*. *Emerald Isle* was

prob. first used by Drennan in song *Erin* (1795).

emerge. L. *emergere*, from *ex* and *mergere*, to dip. An *emergency* is something that "bobs up." Now only of urgency, "a sense not proper" (Johns.), with preps. *in, on*. Also in *emergency man*, called on to assist in Ir. evictions (c. 1880).

> Emergencies such as that in Austria will not wait for the emergence of a League of Nations (Sir W. Goode, Dec. 5, 1919).

emeritus. L., for earlier *emerit*, *emerited*, from L. *emerēri*, to earn one's discharge, lit. to earn out.

emerod [*archaic*]. Popular form (1 *Sam.* v. 6) of *hemorrhoid* (q.v.).

emery. F. *émeri*, OF. *esmeril* (cf. Sp. *esmeril*, It. *smeriglio*), Late L. *smericulum*, *smyriculum*, from G. σμῆρις, σμύρις.

emetic. L., G. ἐμετικός, from ἐμεῖν, to vomit.

émeute. F., VL. **exmota*, p.p. fem. of **exmovēre* (*emovēre*), to stir.

emigrate. From L. *emigrare* (see *migrate*). This and *emigrant* are 18 cent. words. *Émigré*, F. noble leaving France at Revolution, was admitted by Academy in 1798.

eminent. F. *éminent*, from pres. part. of L. *eminēre*, to project, cogn. with *minari*, to threaten. As title of cardinal, conferred (1630) by Urban VIII.

emir. Arab. *amīr*, commander. Esp. title of descendants of Mohammed, wearing the Prophet's colour. See *ameer*, *admiral*.

> The foremost of the band is seen,
> An emir by his garb of green (*Giaour*).

emit. L. *emittere*, from *ex* and *mittere*, to send. Hence *emissary*, usu. with suggestion of spy. Cf. also F. *bouc émissaire*, scapegoat.

emmet [*dial.*]. See *ant*.

emollient. From pres. part. of L. *emollire*, to soften, from *mollis*, soft.

emolument. OF., L. *emolumentum*, perh. orig. the miller's profit, from *emolere*, to grind out. Cf. *grist to the mill*.

emotion. L. *emotio-n-*, from *emovēre*, to stir.

emperor. F. *empereur*, L. *imperator-em*, from *imperare*, to command, from *in* and *parare*, to set in order. Orig. title conferred by vote of Roman army on successful general, later by Senate on Julius and Augustus Caesar, and hence adopted by their successors, exc. Tiberius and Claudius. Conferred by the Pope on Charlemagne on the revival of the Western Empire (800), it remained title of head of Holy Roman

Empire till its dissolution (1806). This is the only meaning of "the Emperor" in medieval hist., though the title has often been used vaguely of monarchs ruling large and distant territories (China, India, Peru, etc.). In 1876 Queen Victoria was proclaimed *Empress of India*. Cf. *empery* (poet.), now replaced by *empire* (q.v.).

emphasis. L., G. ἔμφασις, from ἐμφαίνειν, from ἐν and φαίνειν, to show.

empire. F., L. *imperium* (see *emperor*). In E. since 13 cent. in sense of imperial dignity or territory.

The word carried the implication of reactionary oppression in Russia, of government by massacre in Turkey, of the vast pretentions and corruptions of the fallen empire of Napoleon, and the military rule of that which was rising in Germany (J. R. Green, on assumption of title *Empress of India* by Queen Victoria, 1876).

This great commonwealth of nations known as the British Empire
(D. Lloyd George, in H. of C., July 3, 1919).

empiric. L., G. ἐμπειρικός, experienced, from ἐν and πεῖρα, trial, experiment. Prop. physician working from experience, as opposed to dogmatist; hence, quack.

emplacement. F., site, from *en* and *placer*, to put.

employ. F. *employer*, L. *implicare*, from *in* and *plicare*, to fold, bend; cf. It. *impiegare*, Sp. *emplear*. "The senses are derived from the Late L. sense of *implicare*, 'to bend or direct upon something'; the classioal senses 'enfold, involve' are represented by *imply*" (*NED*). *Employé*, F., clerk, esp. in government, is 19 cent.

emporium. Prop. a mart. L., G. ἐμπόριον, from ἔμπορος, merchant, lit. farer in, ἐν; cf. πορεύεσθαι, to travel.

Paris, London, small cottages in Caesars time, now most noble emporiums (Burton).

empress. OF. *emperesse* (replaced by *impératrice*). Recorded in E. earlier than *emperor* (q.v.).

empressement. F., eagerness, from *s'empresser*, to hasten, be eager. See *press*[1].

emprise [*archaic*]. OF. *emprise*, p.p. fem. of *emprendre*, VL. *imprendere*, from *in* and *prehendere*; cf. *enterprise*, *impresario*. Now only poet., esp. in *high* (*bold*) *emprise*.

emption. Obs. exc. in compds. (*preemption*). L. *emptio-n-*, from *emere*, *empt-*, to buy, orig. to take (cf. sense-hist. of *purchase*).

empty. AS. *ǣmettig*, from *ǣmetta*, leisure, opposite of *gemōt*, meeting, discussion (see *moot*). The *ǣ-* is neg. Cf. *vacant*.

empyrean. Earlier is adj. *empyreal*, used with *heaven*. From G. ἔμπυρος, fiery, from ἐν and πῦρ, fire. By early writers confused with *imperial*, e.g. *heven imperyall* (Caxton).

empyreumatical. Having burnt taste. From G. ἐμπυρεύειν, to set on fire (v.s.).

emu. Prob. from Port. *ema*, crane, ostrich, applied to exotic birds of ostrich-like appearance. Origin unknown.

The bird [cassowary] called emia or eme (Purch.).

ema: a sort of ostrich first found in the islands called Moluccas, and particularly in that of Banda
(Vieyra).

emulate. From L. *aemulari*, to rival.

emulsion. From L. *emulgēre*, *emuls-*, from *ex* and *mulgēre*, to milk.

emunctory. From L. *emungere*, *emunct-*, to blow the nose.

en-. F. *en*, L. *in*, in. See also *in-*. *En-* also represents cogn. G. ἐν and is substituted for AS. *in* in *enlighten*, *enliven*; cf. *embody*, *embolden*.

enact. To put into form of an act. Theat. sense is oldest in E.

I·did enact Julius Caesar (*Haml.* iii. 2).

enallage [*gram.*]. Substitution of one form for another. G. ἐναλλαγή, from ἐναλλάσσειν, to change. The use of *Elohim* as sing. is an example (see *Elohist*).

enamel. Orig. verb. From *en-*, in, and obs. *amel*, enamel, F. *émail*, OF. *esmail*, OLG. *smalt* (Ger. *schmelz*), whence also It. Sp. *smalto*. Cogr with *smelt*. For formation cf. *enamour*. For E. *a-* replacing OF. *es-* cf. *abash*.

ammell for gold smythes: esmael (Palsg.).

enamour. F. *enamourer*, from *en* and *amour*. Usu. in p.p. Cf. Sp. *enamorar*, It. *innamorare*, whence *innamorata* (q.v.).

encaustic. F. *encaustique*, L., G. ἐγκαυστικός, from ἐγκαίειν, from ἐν and καίειν, to burn. See *ink*.

enceinte [*fort.*]. F., p.p. fem. of *enceindre*, to gird round, L. *incingere*. Cf. *precinct*. *Enceinte*, pregnant, is L. *incincta*, to which Isidore (6 cent.) gives late sense of ungirt, but precise meaning is doubtful. Cf. It. *incinta*, Sp. *encinta*.

enchant. F. *enchanter*, L. *incantare*, from *cantare*, to sing. Cf. hist. of *charm*, *spell*.

enchase. F. *enchâsser*, to enshrine; now usu. replaced by *chase*[2] (q.v.).

enchiridion. Handbook. G. ἐγχειρίδιον, from ἐν and χείρ, hand, with dim. suffix.

enchorial. Indigenous. From G. ἐγχώριος, from ἐν and χώρα, country. Formerly used for *demotic* (q.v.) after ἐγχώρια γράμματα (on Rosetta stone).

enclave. Territory surrounded by foreign territory. Common in mod. use in ref. to Afr. coast colonies. F., from *enclaver*, to shut in, Late L. *inclavare*, from *clavis*, key.

enclave: a mortaise, or inlocking; any entry into, or within, another thing; a lying one within another; also, a march, bound, or limit of territory, or jurisdiction; a precinct, or liberty (Cotg.).

enclitic [*gram.*]. L., G. ἐγκλιτικός, from ἐν and κλίνειν, to lean, because an *enclitic* word leans its accent on the preceding word. See *incline*.

enclose. F. *enclore*, *enclos-*, VL. **inclaudere*, for *includere*. See *close*.

encomium. L., G. ἐγκώμιον (sc. ἔπος), eulogy (of victor in Bacchic festival), from ἐν and κῶμος, revelry. See *comic*.

encore. F., ? L. *hanc ad horam*; cf. It. *ancora*. Its E. use is typical of our treatment of foreign words. F. & It. both use *bis*.

Mr Froth cried out "ancora" (Addison).

encounter. Archaic F. *encontrer*, Late L. *incontrare*, from *in* and *contra*; cf. It. *incontrare*, Sp. *encontrar*.

encrinus [*geol.*]. Fossil, "stone lily." Coined (1729) by Harenberg, from G. ἐν and κρίνον, lily.

encroach. OF. *encrochier*, to hook in, from *croc*, hook. See *crook*. Now usu. with *on*, but trans. in ME. Or possibly from the much commoner F. *accrocher*, with prefix change as in *inveigle*. It seems to have been esp. used of fencing in land, not necessarily to the prejudice of others. *Encroachment* and *improvement* occur indifferently in this sense in *Survey of Manor of Penwortham* (1570).

The mighty men accroche ever upon their poore neyghbours: les puissans accrochent tousjours sur leurs povres voisins (Palsg.).

encumber See *cumber*. With *without encumbrance* (children) cf. earlier use in ref. to younger sons, who, from the point of view of the heir, were *encumbrances* on the estate.

encyclical. From Late L. *encyclicus*, for *encyclius*, G. ἐγκύκλιος, from ἐν and κύκλος, circle. Cf. *circular* (letter). Now only of Papal epistles.

encyclopaedia. Late L., pseudo-G. ἐγκυκλο-παιδεία, for ἐγκύκλιος παιδεία, all round

education. See *encyclical*, *pedagogue*. Esp. the F. *Encyclopédie*, edited by Diderot (1751–65).

end. AS. *ende*. Com. Teut.; cf. Du. *einde*, Ger. *ende*, ON. *ender*, *ende*, Goth. *andeis*; cogn. with Sanskrit *anta*, edge, L. *ante*, before, G. ἀντί. With sense of small piece, as still in *odds and ends*, *wax-end*, cf. F. use of *bout*, end, e.g. *bout de ficelle*, piece of string. With to *make ends meet* cf. F. *joindre les deux bouts (de l'an)*. *At a loose end* is naut., of an unattached rope. To *keep one's end up* is from cricket.

endeavour. From F. phrase *se mettre en devoir*, to set to work, make it one's duty. *Devoir* is L. *debēre*, to owe.

I shall put me in dever to fulfill your entent
(*Plumpton Let.* 1487–88).

I have endeavoured [Rab. je me suis en devoir mis] to moderate his tyrannical choler
(Urquhart's *Rabelais*).

endemic. From G. ἐν, in, δῆμος, people. Cf. *epidemic*.

endive. F., Late L. **intybia*, from L. *intybus*, *intubus*; cf. It. Sp. *endivia*. Prob. of Eastern origin.

endo-. G. ἔνδον, within.

endorse. Altered from earlier *endosse*, F. *endosser*, from *en* and *dos*, back, VL. **dossum* for *dorsum*.

Her name on every tree I will endosse
(Spenser, *Colin Clout*).

endow. OF. *endouer*, from *en* and *douer*, L. *dotare*, from *dos*, *dot-*, dower. Later senses influenced by *endue* (q.v.).

endue. F. *enduire*, L. *inducere*, in which sense of cover, invest, is due to influence of L. *induere*, to clothe; cf. G. ἐνδύειν, to put on. Quite confused with *endow*.

indotatus: not indued with anye giftes; that hath no dowerie (Coop.).

With all my worldly goods I thee endow
(*Marriage Service*).

Endue him plenteously with heavenly gifts
(*Prayer for the King's Majesty*).

endure. F. *endurer*, L. *indurare*, from *durus*, hard. See *dure*.

enema [*med.*]. Injection. G. ἔνεμα, from ἐνιέναι, to send in. Usu. mispronounced.

enemy. F. *ennemi*, L. *inimicus*, from *in-*, neg. and *amicus*, friend. Has supplanted, exc. poet., native *foe*. *How goes the enemy?* is first recorded in Dickens.

Wee commonly say of a prodigall man, that hee is no mans foe but his owne (John King, 1594).

energumen. Demoniac. G. ἐνεργούμενος, pass. part. of ἐνεργεῖν, to work upon (v.i.).

energy. F. *énergie*, Late L., G. ἐνέργεια, from ἐν and ἔργον, work. Earliest in rhet. sense, from Aristotle. In phys. first used (1807) by Young.

enervate. From L. *enervare*, to deprive of sinew, *nervus*; replacing earlier *enerve*, F. *énerver*.

enfant terrible. F., terrible child. See *infant*.

enfeoff. AF. *enfeoffer*, OF. *enfieffer*, to endow with a fief (q.v.).

Enfield. Rifle. From small-arms works at *Enfield*, Middlesex.

enfilade [*mil.*]. Orig. noun, in F. *prendre d'en-filade*, from *enfiler*, to arrange on a thread, *fil* (see *file*²). Earlier used of a series of apartments, vista of trees.

enforce. OF. *enforcier*, to strengthen (cf. *reinforce*). Current sense due to phrase to *put in force*, into active operation.

engage. F. *engager*, from *gage*, pledge. Hence adj. *engaging*, from idea of winning to one's side. Mil. sense springs from that of "committing" troops to combat. *Engaged*, for native *betrothed*, is 19 cent. and not found in F. See *gage*¹, *wage*.

engender. F. *engendrer*, L. *ingenerare*, from *genus*, *gener-*, race.

engine. F. *engin*, L. *ingenium*, wit, skill; cf. It. *ingegno*, Sp. *ingenio*. In ME. wit, skill, craft, etc., as well as any mech. device (see *gin*¹). In 19 cent. chiefly for *steam-engine*. Hence *engineer*, for ME. *enginour*, OF. *engigneor*, esp. maker of mil. engines.

Right as a man hath sapiences three,
Memorie, engyn, and intellect also
                       (Chauc. G. 338).

England, English. AS. *Engla-land*, *Englisc*. Earliest sense of *England* is territory of Angles, as distinct from Saxons; but *English* is used without distinction. The above are the only E. words in which *en* has become *in* without ult. change of spelling (*ink*, *string*, etc.). A *Little Englander* prefers a little England to an empire. *Old English* is now often used for *Anglo-Saxon* (up to c. 1150); cf. *Middle English* (c. 1150–1500). *Plain English* is the opposite of *double Dutch*. The *King's English* is in Shaks. (*Merry Wives*, i. 4). To *English*, translate, is used by Wyc.

Heares [here's] a stammerer taken clipping the Kings English, and the constable hath brought him to you to be examin'd (*Look about you*, 1600).

englut. F. *engloutir*. See *glut*.

engrailed [*her.*]. Indented with curved notches. F. *engrêlé*, lit. pitted with hail, *grêle*, OF. *gresle*, from verb *gresler*, ? OHG. *grisilon*, to drizzle.

Armes de France a une bordeure de gueules, en-greslee (14 cent.).

engrain. In *engrained rogue*, *habit*, etc., orig. dyed *in grain* (cf. *double-dyed*), i.e. in cochineal (q.v.), and, by extension, fast-dyed.

All in a robe of darkest grain (*Penseroso*).

engrave. Archaic F. *engraver*. In mod. sense from 17 cent. See *grave*².

engross¹. To copy. AF. *engrosser* (cf. MedL. *ingrossare*), to write large, from F. *grosse*, large letter, fem. of *gros* (see *gross*).

engross². To monopolize. From F. *en gros*, in the bulk, wholesale, as compared with *en détail*, retail; hence *engrosser* (hist.), monopolist, profiteer, whence mod. sense of absorb. See *grocer*.

enhance. AF. *enhauncer*, altered from OF. *enhausser* (replaced by *exhausser*), from *hausser*, to raise, VL. **altiare*. The *h*- of F. *haut*, high, is due to contamination with OHG. *hôh* (*hoch*). The *-n-* may be accounted for by influence of *avancer* or of Prov. *enansar*, to bring forward, VL. **inantiare*; but an intrusive nasal is not uncommon in AF. and we find also the simple *hauncer* for *hausser*.

Si sayly sus, haunça l'espee, si ly fery qe la teste vola en my la place (*Foulques FitzWarin*).
He that shal meeke hym self shal ben enhaunsid
                       (Wyc. *Matt.* xxiii. 12).
subductarius: that wheer with any thing is haunsed up (Coop.).

enharmonic. Lit. in harmony (q.v.).

enigma. L., G. αἴνιγμα, from αἰνίσσεσθαι, to speak obscurely, from αἶνος, apologue.

enjambement [*metr.*]. Continuation of sense of metrical line into next line. F., from *enjamber*, to stride over, from *jambe*, leg (see *gammon*²).

Les stances avec grâce apprirent à tomber,
Et le vers sur le vers n'osa plus enjamber
                       (Boileau, *Art Poét.* i. 137).

enjoin. F. *enjoindre*, L. *injungere*, to join on. Orig. to impose (penalty, etc.).

Penaunce that the prest enjoigneth
                       (*Piers Plowm.* B. xiii. 412).

enjoy. OF. *enjoïr*, from *joïr* (*jouir*), VL. **gaudire* for *gaudēre*. See *joy*. Mod. meanings represent rather F. *jouir* (*de*) and *se réjouir*.

enlarge. See *large*. With fig. to *enlarge upon* cf. *amplify*. With archaic sense of releasing, setting at large, cf. F. *élargir*.

Mr E. N. Buxton enlarged them [roe deer] between Chingford and Loughton
(*Daily Chron.* Feb. 6, 1918).

enlighten. From *light*[1]. Cf. *embolden*, *enliven*. For current fig. sense cf. F. *éclairer*.

To break open a window...which will enlighten the room mightily (Pepys, Aug. 27, 1666).

enlist. To put on a list; cf. *enroll*. Prob. from Du. *inlijsten*, for earlier *list* in same sense. It belongs to the period of Du. mil. words (*furlough*, *roster*, etc.).

King Charles the Second listed himself there [in the Honourable Artillery Company] when he was Prince of Wales
(Chamberlayne, *Present State of England*, 1692).

enmity. AF. *enimité*, F. *inimitié*, VL. **inimicitas*, *-tat-*. See *enemy*.

ennead. Set of nine. G. ἐννεάς, ἐννεάδ-, from ἐννέα, nine. Cf. *chiliad*, *triad*, etc.

ennui. See *annoy*. F. sense was orig. much stronger.

Si d'une mère en pleurs vous plaignez les ennuis
(Racine).

enormous. From earlier *enorm*, F. *énorme*, L. *enormis*, from *ex* and *norma*, rule, pattern. For current sense cf. *monstrous*, *prodigious*, *tremendous*. Etym. sense persists more clearly in *enormity*.

enough. AS. *genōg*, whence *enow; genōh*, whence *enough*. Com. Teut.; cf. Du. *genoeg*, Ger. *genug*, ON. *gnōgr*, Goth. *ganōhs*. Orig. adj., from AS. *genēah*, it suffices, cogn. with L. *nancisci*, *nact-*, to obtain. Cf. Ger. *vergnügen*, to content, please.

enounce. F. *enoncer*, L. *enuntiare*, from *ex* and *nuntiare*, to proclaim. See *nuncio*.

enow [*archaic*]. See *enough*. In Sc. phrases (*friends enow*) it is usu. a survival of the AS. pl. adj.

enrage. From *rage* (q.v.). Hardly from F. *enrager*, which is intrans. only.

enroll. F. *enrôler*, from *rôle*, list, roll (q.v.). Cf. *enlist*.

ensample [*archaic*]. For earlier *asample*, OF. *esemple* (*exemple*), with prefix change as in *encroach*, *ensure*, *inveigle*. See *example*, *sample*.

ensconce. Orig. to place in a *sconce*[2] (q.v.), small fortification.

ensemble. F., together, L. *in simul*.

ensign. F. *enseigne*, L. *insignia*, neut. pl. of *insignis*, conspicuous, from *signum*, sign; cf. It. *insegna*. Orig. signal, watchword;

then, badge, banner (esp. nav. flag), and officer carrying the banner, now obs. in E., but still in US. & F. navies (*enseigne de vaisseau*). In both main senses corrupted in Tudor E. into *ancient*, e.g. *ancient Pistol*.

ensilage. F., from *ensiler* (neol.), adapted from Sp. *ensilar*, to put into a silo (q.v.).

ensue. From OF. *enseu*, p.p. of *ensuivre*, Late L. *insequere* for *insequi*, to follow up. Orig. trans. sense is archaic.

Seek peace and ensue [*AV.* pursue] it
(*Ps.* xxxiv. 14, *PB.*).

ensure. AF. *ensurer*, altered from F. *assurer*. Now differentiated in sense from *insure* (q.v.). See also *assure*.

entablature [*arch.*]. Through F. from It. *intavolatura*, from *intavolare*, from *tavola*, L. *tabula*, board, tablet. The older F. term is *entablement* (12 cent.).

entail. To determine succession so that no possessor may bequeath at pleasure. F. *entailler*, to cut into (cf. MedL. *intaliare* and see *tailor*), whence also obs. *entail*, carving, now replaced by *intaglio*. Sense-development is not clear. Fig. meaning, e.g. to *entail serious consequences*, is from idea of inseparable connection.

entellus. EInd. monkey. Named (1797) by Dufresne from *Entellus* (*Aen.* v. 437 sqq.). Cf. *rhesus*.

entente cordiale. F., friendly understanding, a relation mid-way between a *rapprochement* and an alliance. Now simply *entente*, as in the *Entente Powers*. The phrase is much older in F. in gen. sense, and has been current in E. at various times in the 19 cent.

entente cordiale: témoignages de bon vouloir qu'échangent entre eux les chefs de deux États: locution qui date de l'adresse de la Chambre des Députés de 1840-1 (Littré).

enter. F. *entrer*, L. *intrare*, from *in* and **trare* (cf. *penetrate*); cf. It. *intrare*, Sp. *entrar*. In F. only intrans., *entrer dans*, whence our *enter into*. Practically all senses of *entrance*, *entrée* (q.v.) were formerly expressed by the earlier *entry*. See *trans-*.

enteric. G. ἐντερικός, from ἔντερον, intestine, "inward."

enterprise. F., p.p. fem. of *entreprendre*, from *entre*, L. *inter*, and *prendre*, L. *prendere* for *prehendere*, to take, seize. L. *inter* is ult. cogn. with E. *under*; cf. *undertake*, lit. equivalent of *entreprendre*. Also used as verb, hence adj. *enterprising*.

entertain. F. *entretenir*. Cf. *attain, maintain,* etc. Orig. to maintain, support, take into service. For gen. senses cf. Ger. *unterhalten.* Mod. use of *entertainment,* "dramatick performance, the lower comedy" (Johns.), is 18 cent.

I will entertain Bardolph; he shall draw, he shall tap (*Merry Wives,* i. 3).

enthral. See *thrall.*

enthusiasm. Late L., G. ἐνθουσιασμός, ult. from ἔνθεος, possessed by a god, θεός; cf. *dizzy, giddy.* The back-formation *enthuse* is US.

enthymeme [*log.*]. L., G. ἐνθύμημα, from ἐνθυμεῖσθαι, to infer. Used by Aristotle as an argument on grounds of probability, and in mod. logic of a syllogism with one premiss suppressed.

entice. OF. *enticier,* to provoke, VL. **intitiare,* from *titio,* firebrand. Cf. obs. *attice,* F. *attiser,* to poke the fire. The aphet. *tice,* now used at cricket and croquet, is older than either (13 cent.).

entire. F. *entier,* L. *integer, integr-,* with accent shifted (*intégr-*) in VL.; lit. untouched, from root *tag* of *tangere;* cf. It. *intero,* Sp. *entero.* As a drink, *entire,* replacing what had previously been a mixture ("three threads") of ale, beer, and twopenny, is recorded for 1715.

entity. Scholastic L. *entitas,* from *ens, ent-,* Late L. pres. part. of *esse,* coined on *absens, praesens.* Cf. *nonentity.*

entomology. F. *entomologie,* from G. ἔντομον, insect, from ἐντέμνειν, to cut into. Cf. *insect* (q.v.).

entourage. F., from *entourer,* to surround, from *en* and *tour* (q.v.).

entozoon [*biol.*]. Parasitic animal within another. Mod. coinage from *ento-,* G. ἐντός, within, and ζῷον, animal.

entrail(s). F. *entraille(s),* Late L. *intralia,* neut. pl., inwards, from *intra.* Both F. & E., now only pl., were orig. used as collect. sing. OF. had also *entraigne,* Late L. *intrania* (cf. Sp. *entrañas*).

entrain¹. To involve. F. *entraîner,* to draw along with. See *train.*

entrain² [*mil.*]. Coined, on *embark,* from *train.* Cf. *embus.*

entreat. OF. *entraiter,* from *traiter,* to treat (q.v.). The sense-development is to handle, deal with (cf. Bibl. use), enter into negotiations (cf. to *be in treaty for*), make a request. Mod. sense, to implore, is thus a long way from orig. meaning. See *treat.*

entrechat [*dancing*]. F., earlier *entrechas, entrechasse,* later spelling being due to supposed connection with It. *intrecciato,* intricate. App. from *chasser* (cf. *chassé-croisé*).

entrechasse: a crosse caper (Cotg.).

entrée. F., p.p. fem. of *entrer,* to enter. Applied to dish which is introductory to the roast.

entremets. F., lit. between courses, i.e. between roast and dessert. See *mess.* ME. had *entremess,* from correct OF. *entremes.*

entrench. Coined from *trench* (q.v.) to express sense of F. *retrancher.*

entrepôt. F., from *entreposer,* to deposit provisionally. Cf. *depot.*

entrepreneur. F., lit. undertaker, contractor. Cf. *impresario.*

entresol. F., apartment between ground floor and first floor. Altered on *sol,* ground, from earlier *entresole,* from OF. *sole,* beam, flooring, L. *solum.*

enucleate. From L. *enucleare,* to remove the kernel, *nucleus.* Until recently in fig. sense only.

enumerate. From L. *enumerare,* to number off. See *number.*

enunciate. See *enounce.*

envelop. F. *envelopper.* See *develop.*

environ. F., orig. adv. & prep., from *en* and OF. *viron,* circuit, from *virer* (see *veer²*). *Environment* in scient. sense (Spencer, etc.) appears to be an E. formation unconnected with OF. *environnement.*

envisage. F. *envisager.* See *visage.*

envoy¹. "Sending" of a poem, now usu. concluding stanza of a ballade (as in Chauc.). F. *envoi,* verbal noun from *envoyer* (v.i.).

envoy: a message, or sending; also, the envoy, or conclusion of a ballet or sonnet; in a short stanza by it selfe, and serving, oftentimes, as a dedication of the whole (Cotg.).

envoy². Emissary. Altered (late 17 cent.) from *envoyee,* F. *envoyé,* one sent, from *en* and *voie,* way, L. *via.* Cf. *defile², signal²,* (treasure) *trove,* etc.

envy. F. *envie,* L. *invidia,* from *invidēre,* lit. to look upon (grudgingly); cf. It. *invidia,* Sp. *envidia.*

eocene [*geol.*]. Lowest division of tertiary strata. From G. ἠώς, dawn, καινός, new Cf. *eolithic,* of earliest Stone Age.

epact. Excess (in days) of solar over lunar year; age (in days) of moon on New Year's

Day. From G. ἐπακτός, from ἐπάγειν, to intercalate, from ἐπί, on, ἄγειν, to bring.

eparch [*hist.*]. Governor, bishop. G. ἔπαρχος, ruler over.

epaulement [*mil.*]. F. *épaulement*, from *épaule*, shoulder (v.i.).

epaulet(te). F. *épaulette*, dim. of *épaule*, shoulder, OF. *espale*, Late L. *spatula*, used for *scapula*, shoulder-blade; cf. It. *spalla*, shoulder. See *spatula, espalier*.

epenthesis [*ling.*]. Insertion of sound, e.g. *b* of 'F. *nombre*, L. *numerus*. G. ἐπένθεσις, from ἐπί, upon, ἐν, in, τιθέναι, to place.

epergne. From 18 cent., app. at first to hold pickles. Prob. from F. *épargner*, to spare (q.v.), but connection is not obvious. It may be from character of ornamentation, as *épargne* is used of a varnish intended to "spare" those parts of an ornament which are not to be gilt.

epexegesis. Additional explanation. G., see *epi-* and *exegesis*.

ephah. Dry measure ident. with *bath*[2]. Heb., from Egypt.

ephebe. Greek of 18 to 20. G. ἔφηβος, from ἐπί, upon, ἥβη, early manhood.

ephemera. G. neut. pl. ἐφήμερα (sc. ζῷα), from ἐπί, upon, ἡμέρα, day. Often now taken as fem. sing. (sc. *musca*).

ephod. Heb. *ēphōd*, from *āphad*, to put on.

ephor. Spartan magistrate. G. ἔφορος, overseer, from ἐπί and ὁρᾶν, to see.

epi-. G. ἐπί, on, besides. Also *ep-, eph-*.

epic. L., G. ἐπικός, from ἔπος, word, narrative, poem. Cf. F. *épique*, adj. only, noun sense being expressed by *épopée*, G. ἐποποιία, making of epics.

epicedium. Funeral ode. L., G. ἐπικήδειον, from κῆδος, care, mourning.

epicene. Of common gender, or sex. L., G. ἐπίκοινος, from κοινός, common.

epicure. From *Epicurus*, G. Ἐπίκουρος, Athenian philosopher (c. 300 B.C.), whose doctrine was the opposite of stoicism. Reproachful sense is due to the stoics.

These lascivious friars are the very epicures or offscourings of the earth (Lithgow, *Travels*, ii.).

Who can but pitty the vertuous Epicurus, who is commonly conceived to have placed his chief felicity in pleasure and sensual delyghts and hath therefore left an infamous name behind him?
(Sir T. Browne).

epicycle [*astron.*]. Small circle having centre on circumference of larger circle. L., G., from ἐπί and κύκλος, circle. In Chauc.

epidemic. F. *épidémique*, from *épidémie*, Late

L. *epidemia*, from G. ἐπί and δῆμος, people. Cf. *endemic*.

epidermis. G. ἐπιδερμίς, from δέρμα, skin.

epigastrium [*anat.*]. G. ἐπιγάστριον, from γαστήρ, stomach.

epigenesis [*biol.*]. Theory that germ is brought into existence by successive accretions. From *epi-* and *genesis* (q.v.).

epiglottis [*anat.*]. G. ἐπιγλωττίς, from γλῶττα, tongue.

epigone. Usu. in pl., less distinguished successors of great generation. In common use in Ger. G. ἐπίγονοι, those born after, esp. sons of the Seven against Thebes.

epigram. F. *épigramme*, L., G. ἐπίγραμμα, from ἐπιγράφειν, to write upon. Earlier used indifferently with *epigraph*, G. ἐπιγραφή.

epilepsy. F. *épilepsie*, L., G. ἐπιληψία, from ἐπιλαμβάνειν, to take hold of. Began to replace (16 cent.) earlier *falling sickness*.

epilogue. F., L., G. ἐπίλογος, peroration of speech. Earliest E. sense, speech or poem recited by actor at end of performance. Cf. *prologue*.

epiphany. F. *épiphanie*, L., Late G. ἐπιφάνια, manifestation, from φαίνειν, to show. OF. & ME. also used derivatives of θεοφάνια (see *tiffany*).

epiphyte [*bot.*]. Plant growing on another. From G. φυτόν, plant.

episcopal. See *bishop*.

episode. G. ἐπεισόδιον, coming in besides, from ἐπί, on, εἰς, into, ὁδός, way. Orig. part of G. tragedy interpolated between two choric songs.

epistemology. Theory of knowledge. From G. ἐπιστήμη, knowledge.

epistle. OF. *epistle* (*épître*), L., G. ἐπιστολή, from ἐπιστέλλειν, from στέλλειν, to send. The aphet. *pistell* is common in ME.

epistrophe [*rhet.*]. Repetition of same word at end of successive phrases. G. ἐπιστροφή, from στρέφειν, to turn.

epistyle [*arch.*]. Architrave. G. ἐπιστύλιον, from στῦλος, pillar.

epitaph. F. *épitaphe*, L., G. ἐπιτάφιον, from τάφος, tomb.

epithalamium. L., G. ἐπιθαλάμιον, from θάλαμος, bride-chamber. First in Spenser.

epithet. L., G. ἐπίθετον, from ἐπιτιθέναι, to put on.

epitome. L., G. ἐπιτομή, from ἐπιτέμνειν, to cut into.

epoch. Late L., G. ἐποχή, stoppage, station, from ἐπέχειν, to hold up. Now usu. period, but orig. point of time, as in *epoch-making*. This is for earlier *epoch-forming*, app. adapted by Coleridge from Ger.

epode. L., G. ἐπῳδός, after-song. See *ode*.

eponymous. G. ἐπώνυμος, giving name to, from Aeolic ὄνυμα, name, G. ὄνομα.

epopee, epos. See *epic*.

Epsom salts. Said to have been first obtained in 1675 from spring at *Epsom* (Surrey).

epulary. Of banquets. From L. *epularis*, from *epulum*, feast.

equable. L. *aequabilis*, from *aequare*, to make level.

equal. L. *aequalis*, from *aequus*, level, just. *Egal*, F. *égal*, also existed up to c. 1600.

Deth...maketh egal and evene the heygheste to the loweste (Chauc. *Boethius*, 575).

equanimity. F. *équanimité*, L. *aequanimitas*, from *aequus* and *animus*.

equate. From L. *aequare*, to make equal. Hence *equation, equator*, Late L. (*circulus*) *aequator diei et noctis*. Both are in Chauc., but the Elizabethan sailors usu. say *equinoctial* (*line*). The *personal equation* was orig. astron., with ref. to degree of accuracy of individual observer.

equerry. F. *écurie*, stable, associated in E. with *écuyer*, equerry, orig. esquire, squire. *Écurie*, OF. *escuerie*, may be from OF. *escuyer* (cf. formation of *scullery*), but some authorities connect it with OHG. *scūra* (*scheuer*), barn, whence MedL. *scuria*, stable. The mod. *equerry* is due to association with L. *equus*, horse, the usual early forms being *querry, quirry*, for AF. *esquire de quyrie*, OF. *escuyer d'escuyrie*, "a querry, in a princes stable; the gentleman of a lords horse" (Cotg.).

equestrian. From L. *equestris*, from *eques*, horseman, knight, from *equus*, horse. *Équestrienne*, female circus-rider, is app. intended for F.

equi-. F. *équi-*, L. *aequi-*, from *aequus*, equal.

equilibrium. L. *aequilibrium*, from *libra*, scales.

equine. L. *equinus*, from *equus*, horse, or borrowed from much earlier F. *équin*.

equinox. F. *équinoxe*, L. *aequinoctium*, from *nox, noct-*, night. In Chauc.

equip. F. *équiper*, ONF. *esquiper*, for *eschiper*, from ON. *skip*, or AS. *scip*, ship. Orig. naut.; cf. ON. *skipa*, to arrange, "make ship-shape," MedL. *eschipare*, to man a ship, and F. *équipage*, ship's crew. Some

senses perh. partly influenced by some mental association with *equus*.

equipollent. F. *équipollent*, Late L. *aequipollens, -pollent-*, from *pollēre*, to be powerful.

equitation. L. *equitatio-n-*, from *eques, equit-*, horseman, from *equus*, horse.

equity. F. *équité*, L. *aequitas*, from *aequus*, in sense of fair.

equivalent. F. *équivalent*, from pres. part. of Late L. *aequivalēre*, to be of equal value.

equivocation. Late L. *aequivocatio-n-*, from Late *aequivocare*, to call alike.

era. Earlier (17 cent.) also *aera*, L., orig. pl. of *aes*, brass, in sense of counters for calculation. The word arose in Spain, hence *aera Hispanica*, on which *Christian era* was coined during Renaissance.

eradicate. From L. *eradicare*, from *radix, radic-*, root.

The third affirmeth the roots of mandrakes do make a noise or give a shriek upon eradication
(Sir T. Browne).

erase. From L. *eradere*, from *radere, ras-*, to scrape.

Erastian [*theol.*]. Opponent of Calvinist tyranny. From *Erastus*, G. ἐραστός, lovely, "hellenization" of *Liebler*, Heidelberg physician (16 cent.).

ere. AS. *ǣr*, adj. adv. prep. conj. Orig. a compar.; cf. Du. *eer*, Ger. *eher, ehe*, ON. *ār*, Goth. *air*, early, *airis*, earlier; a by-form *or*, from ON., survives in Bibl. *or ever*. See also *early, erst*.

The lions...brake all their bones in pieces or ever they came at the bottom of the den (*Dan.* vi. 24).

Erebus. G. Ἔρεβος, place of darkness between earth and Hades.

erect. L. *erectus*, from *erigere*, from *regere, rect-*, to direct.

eremite [*poet.*]. Learned form of *hermit* (q.v.).

Nature's patient, sleepless eremite
(Keats, *Last Sonnet*).

erethism. Morbid excitation. F. *éréthisme*, from G. ἐρεθίζειν, to irritate.

War causes a general erethism
(*Daily Chron.* May 9, 1919).

erg [*phys.*]. Also *ergon*. Unit of work. G. ἔργον, work.

ergo. L., therefore.

ergot. Disease of corn. F., cock's spur, from form of noxious fungus.

Erin. Early Ir. *Erenn*, gen. of *Eriu*; cf. Gael. *Eireann*. Cogn. with *Hibernia* and *Ireland*.

Erinnyes [*myth.*]. Pl. of G. Ἐρινύς, fury.

eristic. G. ἐριστικός, disputatious, from ἔρις, strife.

erl-king. Ger. *erlkönig*, as though king of the alders, due to Herder (1779) mistaking Dan. *elle(r)konge*, i.e. *elve(r)konge*, king of the elves, for a compd. of Dan. *elle*, alder (q.v.).

ermine. OF. *(h)ermine*, L. *Armenius*, the animal, also called *mus Ponticus*, being found in *Armenia*. But cf. OHG. *harmo*, weasel, AS. *hearma*, ? shrew mouse (Sweet), weasel (Kluge), cogn. with Lithuanian *szermu*, weasel, ermine. There may thus have been a mixture of two quite separate words.

erne [*archaic*]. AS. *earn*, eagle; cogn. with Du. *arend*, Ger. *aar*, ON. *örn*, Goth. *ara*, and prob. with G. *ὄρνις*, bird. It has helped to form several Teut. names, e.g. *Arnold*, *Arthur*.

erode. F. *éroder*, L. *erodere*, from *rodere*, *ros-*, to gnaw.

erotic. G. *ἐρωτικός*, from *ἔρως*, *ἐρωτ-*, sexual love, personified as *Eros*. Cf. *Cupid*.

err. F. *errer*, L. *errare*, to wander; cogn. with Goth. *airzeis*, led astray, and Ger. *irren*.

errand. AS. *ǣrende*, message, mission; cf. OHG. *ārunti*, ON. *eyrindi*; perh. cogn. with Goth. *airus*, AS. *ār*, messenger. Orig. in dignified sense, e.g. AS. *ǣrendgāst*, angel, ME. *erendes-man*, ambassador. Current sense from 17 cent.

errant. F., pres. part. of *errer*, which, as an OF. verb, has two separate sources, viz. VL. **iterare*, from *iter*, journey, and L. *errare*, to stray. To the former belongs *eyre* (q.v.), while *chevalier errant*, *Juif errant* contain both ideas. See *arrant*.

Donc vint edrant dreitement a la mer
               (*Vie de S. Alexis*, 11 cent.).

erratic, erratum, erroneous, error. See *err*. The occ. use of *error* in lit. sense (from 16 cent.) is a latinism.

The damsel's headlong error through the wood
          (Tennyson, *Gareth & Lynette*).

ersatz [*neol.*]. Ger., replacement, from *ersetzen*, from *setzen*, to set, place.

There will be [in Germany] much ersatz democracy to admire (*Daily Chron.* Sep. 23, 1918).

Erse [*ling.*]. Early Sc. *erische*, AS. *Irisc* or ON. *Irskr*, Irish. Orig. (14 cent.) equivalent to Gaelic.

All the Erischry...of Argyle and the Ilis (Barbour).

erst [*poet.*]. AS. *ǣrest*, superl. of *ǣr* (see *ere*); cf. Du. *eerst*, Ger. *erst*, first. Replaced in gen. sense by *first*.

erubescent. From pres. part. of L. *erubescere*, to blush, from *ruber*, red.

eructate. From L. *eructare*, from *ructare*, to belch; cogn. with G. *ἐρεύγεσθαι*.

erudite. L. *eruditus*, p.p. of *erudire*, from *ex* and *rudis*, rough, untrained.

eruption. L. *eruptio-n-*, from *erumpere*, from *rumpere*, *rupt-*, to break.

Diseased nature oftentimes breaks forth
In strange eruptions (1 *Hen. IV*, iii. 1).

eryngo. Candied root of sea-holly (*Merry Wives*, v. 5). It. or Sp. *eringio*, L., G. *ἠρύγγιον*, dim. of *ἤρυγγος*, name of the plant.

erysipelas. G. *ἐρυσίπελας*, cogn. with *ἐρυθρός*, red, *πέλλα*, skin. Cf. *erythema*, skin inflammation, G. *ἐρύθημα*.

escalade. F., Sp. *escalada*, from *escalar*, to climb, scale; cf. It. *scalata*. See *scale*[3]. Cf. *escalator* (US.).

scalata: a skalado given to any towne or wall (Flor.).

An escalator in a department store (O. Henry).

escallonia. Shrub. From *Escallon*, Sp. discoverer.

escallop. Occ. for earlier *scallop* (q.v.).

escape. ME. also *eschape*, OF. *eschapper* (*échapper*), ONF. *escaper* (cf. It. *scappare*, Sp. *escapar*), from *ex* and *cappa*, cloak (see *cape*[1]). For sense cf. G. *ἐκδύεσθαι*, to put off one's clothes, escape, the idea being that of leaving one's cloak in the clutch of the pursuer, as in *Mark*, xiv. 52. Earlier is the aphet. *scape* (q.v.). *Escapade* is F., from Prov. or Sp. *escapada*. The *escapement* (F. *échappement*) of a watch alternately checks and releases.

escarp [*fort.*]. More usu. *scarp*, F. *escarpe*, It. *scarpa*, "a counter scarfe or curtein of a wall" (Flor.), from OHG. *scarpf*, sharp. Some authorities connect it rather with L. *excarpere*, to pluck out, make smooth; cf. synon. Ger. *böschung*, from *bosch*, sward, cogn. with *bush*.

eschalot. Occ. for *shallot* (q.v.).

eschatology. Science of four last things, viz. death, judgment, heaven, hell. From G. *ἔσχατος*, last.

escheat [*hist.*]. ME. *eschete*, OF. *escheoite*, succession, from *escheoir* (*échoir*), to fall due, VL. **excadēre*, from *ex* and *cadere*, to fall. In AF. applied to the spec. case of property lapsing to crown on owner dying intestate. Hence confiscation, fraud (see *cheat*).

eschew. OF. *eschuer*, var. of *eschiver*, to avoid, OHG. *sciuhen* (*scheuen*), cogn. with *shy*[1]; cf. to *fight shy of*. See *skew*. The OF.

vars. of *eschiver* are numerous. ModF. *esquiver*, to dodge, is from cogn. It. *schivare* or Sp. *esquivar*.

> We went about to eschewe a trackt of sand
> (Peter Mundy, 1633).

eschscholtzia. Plant. Named (1821) by Chamisso from *Eschscholtz* (Ashwood), his colleague in Romanzoff exploration.

escort. F. *escorte*, It. *scorta*, from *scorgere*, to conduct, Late L. *excorrigere*, from *corrigere*, to put in order, from *cum* and *regere*.

escritoire. OF. (*écritoire*), L *scriptorium*, from *scribere*, *script-*, to write.

Esculapian. See *Aesculapian*.

esculent. L. *esculentus*, from *esca*, food, cogn. with *edere*, to eat.

escutcheon. Also *scutcheon*, esp. in *blot on the scutcheon*. ONF. *escuchon* (*écusson*), dim. of *escu* (*écu*), L. *scutum*, shield.

-ese. OF. *-eis*, representing both L. *-ensis* and Teut. *-iscus*.

esker, eskar [*geog.*]. Mound of post-glacial gravel. Ir. *eiscir* (cf. *Esker*, Galway).

Eskimo, Esquimau. Said to mean eater of raw flesh in lang. of Labrador Indians.

esophagus. See *oesophagus*.

esoteric. G. ἐσωτερικός, from ἐσωτέρω, compar. of ἔσω, within. Esp. of doctrines of Pythagoras taught only to most intimate disciples, and, later, of *esoteric Buddhism*. Cf. *exoteric*.

espagnolette. Fastening of French window. F., from *espagnol*, Spanish. See *spaniel*.

espalier. F., It. *spalliere*, from *spalla*, shoulder, support. See *epaulet*.

> *spalliera*: a pouldron, or shoulder-piece. Used also for any roses, trees, vines, flours, or rosemary set and growing up alongst and against any wall (Torr.).

esparto. Sp., L. *spartum*, G. σπάρτον, rope made of σπάρτος, name of plant.

especial, special. F. *spécial*, OF. also *especiel*, L. *specialis*, from *species*, kind; cf. *espouse*, *spouse*, *esquire*, *squire*, etc. The prefixing of *e-* to initial *sc-*, *sp-*, *st-* is regular in OF. We have often double forms, usu. with differentiated meaning.

esperanto. Artificial universal lang., invented (c. 1900) by Dr Zamenhof of Warsaw, and named ? from F. *espérer*, to hope, ? or Sp. *esperanza*, hope, both from L. *sperare*. Cf. *volapük, ido*.

espiègle. F., roguish, arch. According to Oudin (1642) from *Till Eulenspiegel*, hero of popular Ger. stories (mentioned 1515).

espionage. F. *espionnage*, from *espion*, spy, It. *spione*. See *espy, spy*.

esplanade. F., Sp. *esplanada*; cf. It. *spianata*, from *spianare*, to level, L. *explanare*, to level out. Orig. in fort. For transition to sense of open space, promenade, cf. *boulevard*.

espouse. OF. *espouser* (*épouser*), L. *sponsare*, from *spondēre*, *spons-*, to betroth; cf. It. *sposare*, Sp. *esposar*. For orig. sense see *Matt*. i. 18. *Spouse* (q.v.) was used as verb up to c. 1600, when it was replaced by *espouse*. *Espousal, spousal*, was formerly used in pl. only, OF. *espousailles* (*épousailles*), L. *sponsalia*.

esprit. F., L. *spiritus*, adopted in E. in spec. sense of wit; also in *esprit de corps, esprit fort*, free-thinker.

espy. OF. *espier*, whence also *spy*, from which *espy* is now differentiated in meaning (see *especial*). Romanic **spiare* (cf. It. *spiare*, Sp. *espiar*), OHG. *spehōn* (*spähen*), cogn. with L. *specere*, to look.

-esque. F. suffix, It. *-esco*, Late L. *-iscus*, OHG. *-isc*, cogn. with E. *-ish*. Often in neols. and nonce-formations.

> Mr Harvey's "The Beast with Five Fingers" is tinged with the Poesque
> (*Times Lit. Supp.* June 19, 1919).

Esquimau. F. form of *Eskimo* (q.v.).

esquire. OF. *escuyer* (*écuyer*), L. *scutarius*, shield-bearer, from *scutum*, shield; cf. It. *scudiere*, Sp. *escudero*. The doublet *squire* is much earlier. The two words were used indifferently of chief attendant on knight, landed proprietor, while *esquire*, as title of address, formerly limited to certain ranks, is now extended by courtesy to the educated class in gen. It was once as correct to write to *Mr John Smith, Esquire*, as to *Sir John Smith, Bart*.

> There was also one [letter] for me from Mr Blackburne, who with his own hand superscribes it to S. P. Esq., of which God knows I was not a little proud (Pepys, May 25, 1660).

ess. S-shaped, e.g. *ess-pipe* (in drain), *collar of esses*.

-ess. F. *-esse*, Late L. *-issa*, G. *-ισσα*, only in βασίλισσα, queen.

essart. For *assart* (q.v.).

essay. F. *essayer*, VL. **exagiare*, from Late L. *exagium*, weighing (cf. *examen*), from *ex* and *agere*; cf. It. *assaggiare*, Sp. *asayar*. For development from orig. sense, preserved in *assay*, cf. hist. of *try*. Mod. sense of noun is from Montaigne (1580) imitated by Bacon (1597).

> The word [essay] is late, but the thing is ancient
> (Bacon).

esse. In MedL. phrase *in esse*, opposed to *in posse*.

essence. F., L. *essentia*, from **essens, essent-*, fictitious pres. part. of *esse*, to be. The noun imitates G. οὐσία, from stem of pres. part. of εἶναι, to be. Hence *essential*. Sense of extract, common to the Rom. langs., whence that of scent, etc., is prob. due to *Paracelsus* (cf. *quintessence*).

Essene. Ascetic Jewish sect. L., G. Ἐσσηνοί, of uncertain origin.

essential. See *essence*.

establish. OF. *establir, establiss-* (*établir*), L. *stabilire*, from *stabilis*, stable, from *stare*, to stand. Aphet. *stablish* is earlier and more usual in ME. *Established Church* is recorded for 1660 (Declaration of Charles II). Cf. *establishment*, used (from 17 cent.) of the Church, and also of organized mil. forces. We have even coined *establishmentarianism*.

estafette [*mil.*]. F., It. *staffetta*, "a running poste or currier" (Flor.), from *staffa*, stirrup, of Teut. origin and cogn. with *step*.

estaminet. F., Walloon *staminet*, café with smoking-room. Origin unknown. ? Cf. Ger. *stammgast*, regular customer (at café), *stammtisch*, table reserved for such.

estancia. Cattle-farm (Sp. Amer.). Sp., lit. standing; cf. *stance, stanza*.

The champaine which they have chosen to place their stancies and ingenios upon (Purch. xvi. 90).

estate. OF. *estat* (*état*), L. *status*, from *stare*, to stand. Cf. *state*, earlier used indifferently with *estate*. Oldest sense, rank, condition, "standing," as in *men of low (high) estate*, three *Estates of the Realm*, orig. clergy, barons and knights, commons, *Estates-(States-) General*, F. *États-généraux*, representing the three Estates (v.s.). Sense of landed property, now commonest in E., is unknown in F. and is evolved from earlier sense of one's interest or "standing" with regard to any property.

esteem. F. *estimer*, L. *aestimare*. The spelling has followed the sound (see *oblige*). For sense-development cf. *appreciate, value*. The learned form *estimate* has replaced *esteem* in its orig. sense. The *estimates* (parl.) appear in early 18 cent.

What do you esteem it at? (*Cymb.* i. 4).

estop [*leg.*]. To preclude by one's own previous action. Archaic form of *stop* (q.v.).

Greece's default to the Serbian treaty estops her from claiming any sanctity for the Bucharest arrangement (*Daily Chron.* June 12, 1917).

estovers [*leg.*]. "Necessaries allowed by law" (Johns.), esp. right of taking wood. OF. *estoveir*, to be necessary, whence also obs. *stover*, fodder. The Rom. cognates point to L. *stupēre*, to be stunned, rigid, ? hence used of the inevitable. The more reasonable suggestion that the verb is evolved from L. *est opus*, it is needful, presents phonetic difficulties.

estrade. F., Sp. *estrado*, carpeted part of room, L. *stratum*, p.p. of *sternere*, to strew.

estrange. OF. *estrangier*, to make strange (q.v.).

estray. Archaic form of *stray* (q.v.).

estreat. Orig. true copy. OF. *estraite*, p.p. fem. of *estraire* (*extraire*), L. *extrahere*, to extract. Now usu. in to *estreat bail*, by procuring copy thereof for purposes of prosecution.

strete: cacchepole boke to gedyr by mercymentis (*Prompt. Parv.*).

estuary. L. *aestuarium*, lit. tidal, from *aestus*, tide, cogn. with *aestas*, summer, and G. αἴθειν, to burn. Cf. *torrent*.

esurient. From pres. part. of L. *esurire*, desiderative of *edere, es-*, to eat. Chiefly used allusively to Juvenal's *Graeculus esuriens* (iii. 78).

et cetera. L., and the others; cf. G. καὶ τὰ λοιπά.

etch. Du. *etsen*, Ger. *ätzen*, causal of *essen*, to eat. Cf. *easel, lay-figure, landscape*.

etsen, in koper bijten: to eat into copper with strong water [i.e. aqua fortis], or otherwise (Hexham).

eternal. F. *éternel*, VL. *aeternalis*, from *aeternus*, for **aeviternus*, from *aevum*, age. Preceded in ME. by *eterne*.

The dores were al of adamant eterne.
                     (Chauc. A. 1990).

etesian. Regularly occurring winds in Mediterranean; hence also, trade-winds. From G. ἐτήσιος, annual, from ἔτος, year.

Ethanim. Seventh Jewish month (1 *Kings*, viii. 2). Heb. (*yérah hā-)ēthānīm*, month of swollen streams.

ether. Also *aether*, L., G. αἰθήρ, from αἴθειν, to burn, shine. Orig. the clear sky, or the subtle fluid supposed to permeate universe. Later adopted in phys. and chem. Orig. sense survives in *ethereal*.

ethics. After G. τὰ ἠθικά, esp. in ref. to Aristotle's work; G. ἠθικός, from ἦθος, character. But earlier sing. from F. *éthique*.

Ethik that is the sciens of thewes (Trev. iii. 363).

Ethiopian. Earlier *Ethiop*, L., G. Αἰθίοψ, Αἰθίοπ-, as though from αἴθειν, to burn, and ὤψ, face, but perh. corrupt. of some native Afr. word.

ethnic. L., G. ἐθνικός, from ἔθνος, nation. Hence *ethnology, ethnography*.

ethology. Science of ethics (q.v.). Revived by J. S. Mill.

ethos. G. ἦθος. See *ethics*.

etiolate. To make white and sickly, orig. of plants. From F. *étioler*, from Norm. *étieuler*, to turn to stubble, from *éteule* (earlier *esteule*), stubble, OHG. *stupfala*, early agricultural loan-word from L. *stipula*. See *stubble*.

etiology. See *aetiology*.

etiquette. F. *étiquette* (OF. *estiquette*), whence earlier E. *ticket* (cf. Ger. *etikette*, label). Earliest F. sense is label, note, etc. "stuck" on a post. From root of Ger. *stecken*, to put, causal of *stechen*, to stick, pierce. First in Lord Chesterfield (1750). Cf. *that's the ticket*, i.e. quite correct.

> *etiqueter*: to note, marke, or title a booke, bag, or bill, on the outside, the better to remember, or conceive on a sudden, the subject of it (Cotg.).

etna. For heating liquids. From *Etna*, volcano in Sicily. Cf. *geyser*.

Etrurian, Etruscan. Of *Etruria*, ancient country of Italy.

ette. F., VL. -*itta*, dim. suffix, prob. of Celt. origin. Now often jocular, e.g. *suffragette, munitionette*.

etui. Earlier also *etwee*. F. *étui*, case, OF. *estui*, from *estuier, estoier*, to put away, AS. *stōwigan*, from *stow*, place. This does not, however, suit all the app. related words in the Rom. langs. See *tweezers*.

etymology. F. *étymologie*, L., G. ἐτυμολογία, from ἔτυμον, neut. of ἔτυμος, true (whence E. *etymon*). Orig. used of the true, literal sense of a word according to its derivation.

eu-. G. εὖ-, well, from ἐΰς, good. Opposite of *caco-* and *dys-*.

eucalyptus. Coined (1788) by L'Héritier from G. καλυπτός, covered, the flower, before opening, being protected by a cap (v.s.).

eucharis. SAmer. plant. G. εὔχαρις, pleasing, from χάρις, grace.

eucharist. OF. *eucariste* (*eucharistie*), Church L., G. εὐχαριστία, thanksgiving, from χαρίζεσθαι, to offer willingly, from χάρις (v.s.).

euchre [*US.*]. Earlier (1846) *uker, yuker*. ? Du. *jocker*, player, "joker." Cf. *bower*[3], *joker*, and, for init. *eu-*, naut. *euphroe*, dead-eye, from Du. *juffrouw*, maiden.

> It was euchre; the same
> He did not understand (*Heathen Chinee*).

Euclid. G. Εὐκλείδης, Alexandrian mathematician (c. 300 B.C.).

eud(a)emonism. From G. εὐδαίμων, happy, lit. with a good demon (q.v.).

eudiometer. For testing purity of air. From G. εὔδιος, from εὖ- and stem Δι- of Ζεύς, god of the sky.

eugenics. Coined, app. by Galton (1883), on *ethics, politics*, etc., from G. εὖ- and root γεν-, to bring forth. Cf. name *Eugene*, G. εὐγενής, well-born.

euhemerism. Interpretation of mythology, as sprung from human history. From *Euhemerus*, G. Εὐήμερος, Sicilian writer (c. 316 B.C.).

eulogy. G. εὐλογία, praise. Cf. *eulogium*, a MedL. word app. due to confusion between above and L. *elogium* (see *éloge*).

Eumenides. The Furies. G., the gracious ones, a propitiatory name, from εὐμενής, kind, gracious.

eunuch. L., G. εὐνοῦχος, orig. bed-guard, from εὐνή, bed, ἔχειν, to have, keep. Hence, castrated man. Also fig.

> Only a moral eunuch could be neutral
> (Prof. Thayer, of Harvard, Jan. 26, 1917).

euonymus. Plant. L. (Pliny), G. εὐώνυμος, of good name, lucky, perh. a propitiatory name, as the flowering of the plant was supposed to presage pestilence. Cf. *Eumenides*.

eupatrid. Athenian aristocrat. G. εὐπατρίδης, of a good father, πατήρ.

eupeptic. Opposite of *dyspeptic* (q.v.).

euphemism. G. εὐφημισμός, from εὐφημίζειν, to speak fair. In G. applied to words of good omen.

euphonium. Mus. instrument. Coined (19 cent.) after *euphony*.

euphony. F. *euphonie*, G. εὐφωνία, from εὖ- and φωνή, voice, sound.

euphorbia. Genus of plants. L. *euphorbea*, from *Euphorbus*, physician to Juba, king of Mauritania.

euphrasy. Plant eyebright. MedL., G. εὐφρασία, cheerfulness, from εὐφραίνειν, to cheer, from εὖ- and φρήν, mind.

euphroe. See *uphroe*.

Euphuism. Style of Lyly's *Euphues* (1578–80). The name, G. εὐφυής, of good nature, φυή, growth, was suggested to Lyly by a passage in Ascham's *Scholemaster* (1570). Cf. F. *gongorisme* (Gongora), *marinisme* (Marini), similarly used c. 1600, and *marivaudage* (Marivaux) in 18 cent. Sir Piercie

Shafton (*Monastery*) is a caricature of a Euphuist.

euraquilo. See *euroclydon*.

Eurasian. "Modern name for persons of mixt European and Indian blood [Eur(opean)-Asian], devised as being more euphemistic than *half-caste* and more precise than *East Indian*" (Yule).

eureka. For *heureka*, G. εὑρηκα, perf. of εὑρίσκειν, to find, exclamation attributed to Archimedes when, in his bath, he realized that specific gravity would enable him to test Hiero's golden crown.

euroclydon [*Bibl.*]. Only in *Acts*, xxvii. 14 (*A V.*). App. G. εὖρος, east wind, κλύδων, billow; but better reading is εὐρακύλων, *Euroaquilo* (*Vulg.*), from *Aquilo*, north wind, whence *euraquilo* (*RV.*).

Eusebian [*theol.*]. Of *Eusebius*, name of several early Church fathers.

Euskarian [*ethn.*]. Pre-Aryan. From Basque *euskara*, the Basque lang., the Basques being regarded by some ethnologists as relic of a pre-Aryan race.

Eustachian [*anat.*]. From *Eustachius*, It. anatomist (†1574).

Euterpean. From *Euterpe*, muse of music, G. εὐ- and τέρπειν, to please. Cf. *Terpsichorean.*

euthanasia. Gentle and easy death. G. εὐθανασία, from θάνατος, death. Earlier (17 cent.) *euthanasy.*

evacuate. From L. *evacuare*, from *vacuus*, empty.

evade. F. *évader*, L. *evadere*, from *vadere*, to go. First in orig. sense, to escape, as also *evasion.* Cf. sense of F. *évasion.*

evanescent. F. *évanescent*, from pres. part. of L. *evanescere*, from *vanescere*, from *vanus*, vain.

evangel. F. *évangile*, Church L. *evangelium*, G. εὐαγγέλιον, good tidings, from ἀγγέλλειν, to announce; cf. It. Sp. *evangelio.* See *angel, gospel.* Hence *evangelist, evangelical*, the latter adopted by various Protestant sects, and in E. esp. applied, since Wesley, to the Low Church party.

evanish [*poet.*]. OF. *esvanir, esvaniss-* (*évanouir*). See *vanish.*

evaporate. From L. *evaporare*, from *vapor*, vapour.

evasion. See *evade.*

eve, even, evening. *Eve* is shortened from *even*, still in *evensong, eventide* (cf. *morrow* for *morn*), AS. *æfen.* Both are in Chauc. WGer.; cf. Du. *avond*, Ger. *abend*, ON.

aptann (Goth. has *andanahti*, before night). With *eve*, day before, cf. Ger. *Christabend*, Christmas eve, *Sonnabend*, Saturday. With *evening*, AS. *æfnung*, from *æfnian*, to grow towards evening, cf. *morning. Even* also becomes *e'en*, esp. in *Hallow-e'en.*

evection [*astron.*]. L. *evectio-n-*, from *evehere*, from *ex* and *vehere, vect-*, to carry. Cf. *convection.*

even. AS. *efen, efn*, level, equal (cf. double senses of L. *aequus*). Com. Teut.; cf. Du. *even*, Ger. *eben*, ON. *iafn*, Goth. *ibns.* See *anent.* The usual mod. meaning of the adv. seems to have arisen (16 cent.) from earlier sense of emphasizing identity as in Bibl. style; cf. F. *même*, same, self, even, and adv. use of *just.*

> Who? The most exquisite Claudio?
> Even he [F. *lui-même*] (*Much Ado*, i. 3).

> Truth will out, even in an affidavit (Lord Bowen).

evening. See *eve.*

event. OF., L. *eventus*, from *evenire*, from *venire, vent-*, to come. Cf. *outcome.* Coloured in sense by F. *événement*, e.g. *at all events = à tout événement.* With *eventual* cf. *actual. Eventuate* is US. (18 cent.). With *wise after the event* cf. MedL. *sapere post factum.*

> In the upshot, this conclusion eventuated (to speak Yankeeishly) (De Quincey).

ever. AS. *æfre*, prob. related to *ā*, ever (see *ay*). There is no corresponding compd. in any Teut. lang. With ellipt. *did you ever?* cf. *well, I never!*

everglade [*US.*]. Marsh, esp. the *Everglades* (Florida). As the compd. makes no sense, and swamps are not glades, it is prob. a corrupt. of some native name.

everlasting. ME. coinage to render *eternal.*

evert. L. *evertere*, from *vertere*, to turn.

every. AS. *æfre ælc* (or *ylc*), i.e. ever each. Not orig. distinguished in meaning from *each* (q.v.). *Everywhere* represents two distinct formations, viz. *ever ywhere*, AS. *gehwær*, and *every where.*

> Everich of you shal brynge an hundred knyghtes
>   (Chauc. A. 1851).

evict. From L. *evincere, evict-*, to prove, from *vincere*, to conquer. Orig. to recover property, etc., spec. mod. sense being 19 cent.

evident. From pres. part. of L. *evidēre*, from *vidēre*, to see (cf. Late L. *evideri*, to appear). For passive sense, what is clearly seen, cf. F. *couleur voyante.* Leg. *evidence* tends to displace *witness* from c. 1500. To *turn King's evidence* was formerly to *turn evidence* (Defoe).

evil. AS. *yfel*; cf. Du. *euvel*, Ger. *übel*, Goth. *ubils*. Prob. related to *up, over*, as exceeding bounds. Mod. form represents Kentish *evel* (cf. *weevil*). In gen. sense replaced by *bad*. *Evil eye* (Wyc. *Mark*, vii. 22) is in AS.

Deliver us from the evil one (*Matt.* vi. 13, *RV.*).

evince. See *evict*, which it has replaced in sense of giving proof.

evirate. From L. *evirare*, from *ex* and *vir*, man; cf. synon. *emasculate*.

eviscerate. From L. *eviscerare*, to deprive of *viscera*, bowels.

evoke. F. *évoquer*, L. *evocare*, from *vocare*, to call.

evolution. L. *evolutio-n-*, from *evolvere*, from *volvere, volut-*, to roll. The *doctrine* (*theory*) *of evolution* is 19 cent., esp. Herbert Spencer, but the word was used in a somewhat similar sense (*epigenesis*) by Bonnet in 1762.

evulsion. L. *evulsio-n-*, from *evellere*, from *vellere, vuls-*, to pluck.

ewe. AS. *ēowu*, fem. of *ēow*, sheep. Aryan; cf. Du. *ooi*, Ger. dial. *au(lamm)*, ON. *ær*, L. *ovis*, G. *ois*, OIr. *ui*, Sanskrit *avi*; Goth. form only in compds., e.g. *awēthi*, flock. *Ewe-lamb*, sole treasure, is from 2 *Sam.* xii.

ewer. OF. *euwier*, from *eau*, water, L. *aqua*. Cf. F. *évier*, sink, L. *aquarium*, and southern *aiguière*, ewer, L. *aquaria*.

ex-¹. L. *ex*, out of; cf. *e-*.

ex-². As in *ex-chancellor*, an extended use of such L. phrases as *ex consule, ex magistro equitum*, (one who) from being consul, master of the knights (now holds a different position). Later such phrases were replaced by *exconsul, exmagister*; cf. *proconsul*, for *pro consule*.

exacerbate. From L. *exacerbare*, from *acerbus*, from *acer*, sharp, keen.

exact. Adj. L. *exactus*, from *exigere*, to weigh, prove, from *ex* and *agere* (cf. *examine*). The verb represents L. *exigere, exact-*, in its lit. sense to force out.

exaggerate. From L. *exaggerare*, to heap up, from *agger*, mound. Cf. to *make mountains out of mole-hills*.

exalt. L. *exaltare*, from *altus*, high. Cf. *enhance*.

examine. F. *examiner*, L. *examinare*, to weigh accurately, test, etc., from *examen, examin-*, orig. "the needle or tongue in a

balance" (Coop.), for **exagmen*, from *exigere* (see *exact*).

Juppiter ipse duas aequato examine lances
Sustinet, et fata imponit diversa duorum
(*Aen.* xii. 725).

example. Partially restored from earlier *ensample, sample* (q.v.), F. *exemple*, L. *exemplum*, from *eximere, exempt-*, to take out, from *ex* and *emere*, to procure, buy. Oldest E. senses (Wyc.) are pattern of conduct (*good example*) and instance of punishment as deterrent (cf. *exemplary*).

I thought it a good occasion to make an example of him, for he is a proud, idle fellow
(Pepys, Jan. 29, 1669).

exarch. Governor of distant province (Byzantine Empire), bishop (Eastern Church). L., G. ἔξαρχος, from ἐξάρχειν, to take the lead. See *arch²*.

exasperate. From L. *exasperare*, from *asper*, rough, harsh.

Excalibur. OF. *Escalibor*, with numerous vars., from MedL. *Caliburnus* (Geoffrey of Monmouth, c. 1140). There is in Ir. legend a sword *Caladbolg*, app. hard-belly, i.e. the devourer.

ex cathedra. L., from the (teacher's) chair.

excavate. From L. *excavare*, from *cavus*, hollow.

exceed. F. *excéder*, L. *excedere*, to go beyond. For archaic adv. use of *exceeding* cf. archaic *surpassing*.

excel. F. *exceller*, L. *excellere*, to rise above, cogn. with *celsus*, lofty. Hence *excellent, excellence*. For use of latter as title cf. *eminence* (*majesty, worship*, etc.). *Par excellence*, replacing earlier *by excellence*, is after L. *per excellentiam*, on account of pre-eminent fitness.

excelsior. L., compar. of *excelsus*, lofty (v.s.), adopted, app. under the impression that it was an adv., as motto for seal of New York (1778), and popularized by Longfellow.

except. First as adj., passing in ME. into prep. L. *exceptus*, p.p. of *excipere*, to take out, from *capere*; cf. Ger. *ausgenommen*, F. *excepté, hormis*, of which the former still commonly agrees, e.g. *ces dames exceptées*, while OF. has *hors mise la reine*. To *take exception*, i.e. object, is from use in Roman law of *excipere* (*adversus aliquem*), to deny that the opponent's declaration covers the case. *Exception proves the rule* is abbreviated, with alteration of meaning, from *exceptio probat regulam in casibus non exceptis.*

Excepte [*var.* out-taken] oneliche of eche kynde a couple (*Piers Plowm.* B. ix. 141).

excerpt. From L. *excerpere*, from *carpere*, *carpt-*, to pluck.

excess. F. *excès*, L. *excessus*, from *excedere*, from *cedere*, *cess-*, to go. For fig. senses, which are earliest in E., cf. *trespass*.

exchange. Restored from ME. *eschaunge*, OF. *eschanger* (*échanger*), Late L. *excambiare*. See *change*.

exchequer. ME. *escheker*, *cheker*, OF. *eschequier* (*échiquier*), chess-board; cf. MedL. *scaccarium*, It. *scaccario*. Orig. the table marked out in squares on which the revenue accounts were kept by means of counters. Cf. *check*, *chequer*, *chess*.

Discipulus. Quid est *scaccarium*?
Magister. *Scaccarium* tabula est....Superponitur autem *scaccario* superiori pannus in termino Paschae emptus, non quilibet, sed niger virgis distinctus, distantibus a se virgis vel pedis vel palmae extentae spatio. In spatiis autem calculi sunt juxta ordines suos de quibus alias dicetur....
Discipulus. Quae est ratio hujus nominis?
Magister. Nulla mihi verior ad praesens occurrit, quam quod *scaccarii lusilis* similem habet formam (*Dialogus de Scaccario*, temp. Hen. II).

excise¹. "A hateful tax levied on commodities, and adjudged not by the common judges of property, but wretches hired by those to whom excise is paid" (Johns.). First adopted (1643) in imit. of Holland. Earlier also *accise*. Archaic Du. *accijs* (Hexham), OF. *aceis*, VL. **accensus*, from *accensare*, to tax (cf. *cess*); confused at various times with *excise²* (cf. *tallage* and see quot. from Spenser below), and *assize*, in early sense of tax. ModDu. *accijns* is a reversion to supposed L. original, or is influenced by *cijns*, tax, interest. L. *census* (cf. Ger. *zins*). Cf. F. *accise*, MedL. *accisia*, *excisia*.

All the townes of the Lowe-Countreyes doe cutt upon themselves an excise of all thinges towarde the mayntenaunce of the warre
(Spenser, *State of Ireland*).

excise². To cut out. From L. *excidere*, *excis-*, from *caedere*, to cut.

excite. L. *excitare*, frequent. from *ciēre*, *cit-*, to set in motion. Colloq. use of *exciting* is 19 cent.

exclaim. F. *exclamer*, L. *exclamare*. See *claim*.

exclude. L. *excludere*, from *claudere*, to shut. The hist. *exclusionists* aimed at excluding the Duke of York (James II) from the succession.

excommunicate. From Church L. *excommunicare*, to expel from communion (q.v.). F. *excommunier* is much earlier.

They shall excommunicat [*Vulg.* absque synagogis facient] you (Tynd. *John*, xvi. 2).

The Rev. Gerald Dennehy...told about 300 men who received the sacrament in his chapel that any Catholic policemen who assisted in putting conscription in force would be excommunicated and cursed; that the curse of God would follow them in every land, and he asked his hearers to kill them at sight (*Daily Chron.* June 28, 1918).

excoriate. From L. *excoriare*, to flay, from *corium*, hide.

excrement, excrete, excretion. From L. *excernere*, from *cernere*, *cret-*, to separate, sift.

excrescent. From pres. part. of L. *excrescere*, to grow out. See *crescent*.

excruciate. From L. *excruciare*, from *crux*, *cruc-*, cross, as instrument of torture.

exculpate. From L. *ex* and *culpa*, fault; cf. It. *scolpare*, MedL. *exculpare*.

excursion. L. *excursio-n-*, from *excurrere*, from *currere*, *curs-*, to run. Cf. *excursus*, *digression*. *Excursion train* is recorded for 1850.

excuse. F. *excuser*, L. *excusare*, from *ex* and *causa*; cf. *accuse*.

exeat [*univ.*]. L., let him go out, from *exire*; cf. theat. *exit*, *exeunt*, for earlier *exeat*, *exeant*.

execrate. From L. *execrari* for *ex-secrari*, from *sacrare*, to devote (to good or ill), from *sacer*, *sacr-*, holy. Wyc. has *execrable*, *execration*, following L. of *Vulg.*

execution. F. *exécution*, L. *executio-n-*, for *exsecutio-n-*, from *exsequi*, to follow out, from *sequi*, *secut-*, to follow. The *executioner* executes the sentence of the law, as the *executor* does the provisions of a will, but the words were formerly used indifferently.

Delivering o'er to executors pale
The lazy yawning drone (*Hen. V*, i. 2).

exegesis. G. ἐξήγησις, from ἐξηγεῖσθαι, to interpret, from ἡγεῖσθαι, to lead.

exemplar. Respelt, on L. *exemplar* (from neut. of adj. *exemplaris*), for ME. & OF. *exemplaire*. Cf. *sampler*.

exempt. F., L. *exemptus*, p.p. of *eximere*, to take out, from *emere*, to buy, obtain. In F. title of cavalry officer exempted from certain duties (cf. Ger. *gefreiter*, lance-corporal), later applied to police-officer. In E. officer of Yeomen of the Guard, also *exon*, an attempt at the F. pronunc.

exenterate. From L. *exenterare*, to disembowel. From G. (see *enteric*).

exequatur. Formal permission. L. *ex(s)equatur*, let him perform, execute.

exequies. OF., L. *ex(s)equiae*, "the trayne of a funerall pompe" (Coop.), from *ex-(s)equi*, to follow. See *execute* and cf. *obsequies*.

exercise. F. *exercice*, L. *exercitium*, from *exercēre*, to keep at work, orig. to let farm-beasts out to work, from *arcēre*, to shut up.

exergue [*numism.*]. Small space left for inscription on coin or medal. F., coined from G. ἐξ ἔργου, to represent F. *hors d'œuvre* (q.v.).

exert. From L. *exserere, exsert-*, to put forth, from *serere*, to knit. To *exert oneself* is evolved from to *exert one's powers*, etc.

exeunt. L., they go out.

exhale. F. *exhaler*, L. *exhalare*, from *halare*, to breathe.

exhaust. From L. *exhaurire*, from *haurire, haust-*, to draw, drain. Cf. synon. F. *épuiser*, from *puits*, well.

exhibit. From L. *exhibēre, exhibit-*, from *habēre*, to have, hold. *Exhibition*, scholarship, preserves obs. sense, to furnish, provide, which *exhibēre* had in Roman law.

> What maintenance he from his friends receives,
> Like exhibition thou shalt have from me
>   (*Two Gent.* i. 3).

exhilarate. From L. *exhilarare*, from *hilaris*, cheerful. Cf. *hilarious*.

exhort. L. *exhortari*, from *hortari*, to encourage, for *horit-*, from synon. *horiri*; cogn. with G. χαίρειν, to rejoice, and ult. with *yearn*.

exhume. F. *exhumer*, MedL. *exhumare*, from *humus*, ground.

exigent. From pres. part. of L. *exigere*, from *ex* and *agere*. Hence *exigency*, urgency. Cf. F. *exigeant*, exacting, now often used in E. See *exact*.

exiguous. From L. *exiguus*, scanty, from *exigere*, to weigh out. See *exact*.

exile. F. *exil*, L. *exsilium*, from *ex* and root of *salire*, to leap. As applied to a person app. from F. *exilé*, influenced by L. *exsul*, but it may be a transferred use of the abstract; cf. *message, prison*, which in OF. & ME. also mean messenger, prisoner.

exility. Slenderness. L. *exilitas*, from *exilis*, thin, for **exagilis*, cogn. with *exiguous*.

eximious. Select. From L. *eximius*, from *eximere*, to take out. See *exempt*.

exist. F. *exister*, L. *ex(s)istere*, from *sistere*, redupl. form of *stare*, to stand.

exit. Sometimes L. *exitus*, going forth, from *exire* (cf. *adit*), but usu. a verb. See *exeat*.

ex libris. L., from the books. Adopted as book-plate from Ger.

exo-. G. ἔξω, outside.

exodus. L., G. ἔξοδος, way out, from ὁδός, way. Adopted by *Vulg.* from G. translators.

ex officio. L., in virtue of one's office.

exon. See *exempt*.

Exon. Signature of bishop of Exeter, AS. *Exanceaster*.

exonerate. From L. *exonerare*, to unburden, from *onus, oner-*, burden. Orig. in lit. sense, e.g. of a ship. For fig. sense cf. *discharge*.

exorbitant. From pres. part. of L. *exorbitare*, to depart from one's orbit (q.v.). Cf. *delirium*.

> Exorbitant from the milde course of law and justice (*NED.* 1599).

exorcize. Late L. *exorcizare*, G. ἐξορκίζειν, from ἐξ, out, ὅρκος, oath. Cf. *conjure*.

exordium. L., from *exordiri*, from *ordiri*, to begin, orig. to start weaving.

exoteric. G. ἐξωτερικός, from ἔξω, without. Cf. *esoteric*.

exotic. L., G. ἐξωτικός, from ἔξω, without.

expand. L. *expandere*, from *pandere, pans-*, to spread.

ex parte. L., from (one) side (only).

expatiate. From L. *ex(s)patiari*, to walk about, from *spatium*, space, whence also It. *spaziare*, Ger. *spazieren*, to walk. Still occ. in orig. sense. For fig. sense cf. *dilate*.

> Milton, when he has expatiated in the sky, may be allowed sometimes to revisit earth (Johns.).

expatriate. Mod. formation on L. *patria*, country. Cf. earlier F. *expatrier*. See *repair²*.

expect. L. *ex(s)pectare*, to look out for, from *spectare*, frequent. of *specere*, to look.

expectorate. Euph. for *spit²* (chiefly US.). From L. *expectorare*, to ease the mind, make a "clean breast," from *pectus, pector-*, breast.

expedite. From L. *expedire, expedit-*, orig. to free the foot, *pes, ped-*, from fetters (cf. opposite *impede*). Hence *expedient*, helping on; *expediency*, now usu. in bad sense; *expedition*, rapid setting forth.

expel, expulsion. L. *expellere*, from *pellere, puls-*, to drive.

expend, expense. L. *expendere*, from *pendere, pens-*, to weigh. Reconstructed from earlier *spend* (q.v.). *Expenditure* is MedL. *expenditura.*

experience. F. *expérience*, L. *experientia*, from *experiri, expert-*, from *perire*, to go through. In ME. also used, like F. *expérience*, for *experiment*. With *experimentalist* cf. *empiric*. *Expert* as noun is 19 cent.

expiate. From L. *expiare*, from *piare*, "to purge sinne; to please God by sacrifice" (Coop.), from *pius*.

expire. F. *expirer*, L. *ex(s)pirare*, from *spirare*, to breathe. Earliest E. sense is connected with death, but the verb was orig. trans., e.g. to *expire one's soul* (*life, last breath*, etc.).

explain. Earlier (16 cent.) *explane*, L. *explanare*, to make smooth, *planus*. Altered on *plain*. Cf. *esplanade*.

expletive. L. *expletivus*, filling out, from *explēre*, from *plēre, plet-*, to fill (see *plenty*). Current sense of rhetorical "padding" is 19 cent.

He is a sort of expletive at the breakfast-table, serving to stop gaps (O. W. Holmes).

explicate, explicit. From L. *explicare*, from *plicare, plicit-*, to fold. For *explicit faith* cf. *implicit*. *Explicit* at end of medieval books was usu. taken as third person sing., here ends, and sometimes replaced by *expliciunt*, but it was orig. short for *explicitus est liber*, the book is unrolled (Duc. 949).

explode. L. *explodere, explos-*, opposite of *applaud*, from *plaudere*, to clap (at the theatre). Current sense (17 cent.) from that of expulsive noise. Etym. sense still in *exploded theory*.

explodere: to dryve out with noyse and rebuke, or with clapping of handes (Coop.).

For it seems to me to be rather incongruous to write *musick* from *musica*, especially as the *k* has been exploded by general consent from the derivatives *musician* and *musical*
　　　　　　　　　(Ash, *Pref. to Dict.* 1775).

Congreve and Farquhar show their heads once in seven years only, to be exploded and put down instantly (Lamb, *On Comedy*).

exploit. Earlier *esploit*, OF. *esploit, espleit*, L. *explicitus*, unfolded (see *explicate*). The verb is very common in OF. with gen. sense of progress, achievement, its earliest meaning in ME. Current sense of verb, e.g. to *exploit a mine*, is from ModF., pre-

serving exactly the orig. sense (cf. *develope*).

Mult bien espleitet cui Damnes Deus aiuet
　　　　　　　　　　　　　　(*Rol.* 3657).
[He progresses very well whom the Lord God helps]

explore. F. *explorer*, L. *explorare*, from orig. sense, cry, shout, of *plorare*, to weep (cf. *descry*).

Speculator ab exploratore hoc differt, quod speculator hostilia silentio perspicit, explorator pacata clamore cognoscit (Festus).

exponent. From pres. part. of L. *exponere*. See *expound*.

export. L. *exportare*, from *portare*, to carry.

expose. F. *exposer*. See *pose*. *Exposé*, F. p.p., explanation, showing up, is 19 cent. *Exposition* is sometimes used, after F., for *exhibition*. Some senses of *expose* run parallel with those of *expound* (q.v.).

ex post facto. For MedL. *ex postfacto*, from what is done afterwards.

expostulate. From L. *expostulare*, intens. of *postulare*, to demand, used like F. *demander raison*, to seek satisfaction.

expound. ME. also *expoun*, OF. *esponre, espondre*, L. *exponere*, to put forth. The OF. verb has been replaced by *exposer*. See *compound*[1], *propound*. For excrescent -*d* cf. *sound*[1], *bound*[3] and vulgar *drownd*.

Forsothe he expounyde [Tynd. expounded] to his disciplis alle thingis (Wyc. *Mark*, iv. 34).

express. First as adj. F. *exprès*, L. *expressus*, lit. squeezed out, fig. clearly stated, from *exprimere*, from *premere, press-*. For sense-development cf. Ger. *ausdruck*, expression, lit. out-press, *ausdrücklich*, expressly. An *express* train orig. ran "expressly" to a certain station.

exprobration. Reproach. L. *exprobratio-n-*, from *exprobrare*. See *opprobrium*.

expropriate. From L. *expropriare*, to deprive of one's own (see *proper*). Current sense of organized theft appears to have arisen among Ger. socialists.

Three among us do not agree that any compensation whatever should be paid to the present mineral owners for the mineral rights to be acquired by the State (*Report of Coal Commission*, June 23, 1919).

expulsion. See *expel*.

expunge. L. *expungere*, to mark for deletion by dots, from *pungere*, to prick; cf. synon. F. *exponctuer*. In mod. use popularly associated with "passing the 'sponge' over."

expurgate. From L. *expurgare*, to make pure. See *purge*. *Expurgatory index*, list of books of which certain passages are forbidden by Roman Church, is now usu. *index expurgatorius*.

exquisite. L. *exquisitus*, p.p. of *exquirere*, to seek out, from *quaerere*. Cf. F. *recherché*. As noun, fop, from c. 1800.

The olde Zeno in all his exquisite tourmentes never made any lamentable crye (Elyot, *Governour*, ii. 279).

exscind. L. *exscindere*, to cut out.

exsequies. See *exequies*.

exsert [*biol.*]. Var. of *exert* (q.v.) in etym. sense. Cf. *insert*.

exsiccate. From L. *ex(s)iccare*, to make dry, *siccus*.

extant. From pres. part. of L. *ex(s)tare*, to stand forth.

extempore. L. *ex tempore*, out of the time, *tempus*. Cf. *on the spur of the moment*. Hence *extemporize* (17 cent.).

Extempore will he dities compose
(*Ralph Roister Doister*).

extend. L. *extendere*, from *tendere*, to stretch. In ME. also *estend*, OF. *estendre* (*étendre*). Senses run parallel with those of native *stretch*, e.g. *University Extensionists*, who began to attend Summer Meetings at Oxf. in 1888, were sometimes known as *stretchers*.

extenuate. From L. *extenuare*, to make thin, *tenuis*. Orig. to emaciate (cf. F. *exténuer*). Now chiefly in *extenuating circumstances*, for which F. has *circonstances atténuantes*.

exterior. L., compar. of *exterus*, from *extra*, outside.

exterminate. From L. *exterminare*, to drive over the boundary, *terminus*. For strengthened mod. sense, which appears in *Vulg.*, cf. *decimate*. Quot. below shows a curious reversion to etym. sense.

Are you in favour of exterminating every German out of this country?
(Heckler at Dumfries, Dec. 9, 1918).

external. For earlier *externe*, L. *externus*, from *exterus*. See *exterior*.

extinguish, **extinct**. From L. *ex(s)tinguere*, *ex(s)tinct-*. See *distinguish*.

extirpate. Earlier *extirp*, from L. *ex(s)tirpare*, from *stirps*, stem, trunk. Cf. *root out*.

After the old plants be extirped and destroied
(Holland's *Pliny*).

extol. L. *extollere*, from *tollere*, to raise. Cf. *elate*, *exalt*.

extort. From L. *extorquere*, from *torquere*, *tort-*, to twist. Much earlier is *extortion*, prob. through OF.

extra-. L. *extra*, outside, orig. compar. formation from *ex*.

extra. Usu. short for *extraordinary*. Cf. *super*.

extract. From L. *extrahere*, from *trahere*, *tract-*, to draw.

extradition. F. (18 cent.), L. *extraditio-n-*, from *tradere*, to hand over, from *trans* and *dare*, to give. See *traitor*, *tradition*.

extrados [*arch.*]. Upper or outer curve of arch. F., from *dos*, back; cf. *intrados*, *parados*.

extraneous. From L. *extraneus*, from *extra*, outside. See *strange*.

extraordinary. L. *extraordinarius*, from *extra ordinem*, outside (the usual) order, *ordo*, *ordin-*.

extravagant. Earlier is *stravagant*. From pres. part. of Late L. *extravagari*, to wander beyond bounds, from *vagari*; cf. F. *extravagant*. Orig. in lit. sense, e.g. the *extravagant and erring spirit*, i.e. the ghost (*Haml.* i. 1). *Extravaganza* is after It. *stravaganza*.

extravasate [*med.*]. From L. *vas*, vessel; cf. F. *extravaser*.

extreme. F. *extrême*, L. *extremus*, superl. of *exterus*. See *exterior*. Rarely used in etym. sense (cf. *utmost*).

extricate. From L. *extricare*, to disentangle, from *tricae*, perplexities. Cf. *intricate*.

extrinsic. F. *extrinsèque*, from L. adv. *extrinsecus*, from **extrim* (cf. *interim*) and *secus*, beside, cogn. with *sequi*, to follow. Cf. *intrinsic*.

extrude. L. *extrudere*, from *trudere*, to thrust.

exuberant. From pres. part. of L. *exuberare*, from *uber*, fertile; cf. *uber*, udder.

exude. L. *ex(s)udare*, from *sudare*, to sweat.

exult. F. *exulter*, L. *ex(s)ultare*, frequent. of *exsilire*, from *salire*, *salt-*, to leap. Thus, to *exult over* (a vanquished enemy) is etym. to execute a joy-dance over his prostrate body. Cf. *insult*.

exuviae. L., garments stripped off, from *exuere*, to divest. Cf. *endue*.

ex voto. L., introductory words of dedication, *ex voto suscepto*, according to the vow taken.

eyas [*archaic*]. Young falcon. For obs. *nyas*, F. *faucon niais*, VL. **nidax*, *nidac-*, from *nidus*, nest. Ident. with F. *niais*, silly; cf. It. *nidiace*. For loss of *n-* cf. *adder*, *apron*, *auger*. The spelling of *eyas* has been chiefly determined by mistaken association with *eyry* (see *aery*).

nies, as niais: also, a nias hawke (Cotg.).

An eyry of children, little eyases (*Haml.* ii. 2).

eye. AS. *ēage*. Aryan (exc. Celt.); cf. Du. *oog*, Ger. *auge*, ON. *auga*, L. *oculus* (dim.),

Sanskrit *akshi*. With to *make eyes at* cf. *ogle*. *Eyebright* (*euphrasia officinalis*) was formerly a remedy for weak eyes; cf. synon. Du. *oogenklaar*. *Eyebrow* (16 cent.) is for earlier *eye-bree*, AS. *ēag-brǣw* (see *brow*[1]). *Eyelash* is a late compd. (18 cent.) and connection with *lash*[1] is obscure. With *eyelid* cf. Ger. *augenlid*, the only surviving Ger. cognate of E. *lid*, cover. With *eyesore*, orig. soreness of the eyes, cf. *a sight for sore eyes*. *Eyewash* in mod. slang sense is US. *Mind's eye* is first in Shaks. (*Haml.* i. 2). For *eye to eye* (*Is*. lii. 8) Wyc. has *with eye to eye*. *Eye-service* (*Col.* iii. 22) is due to Tynd. (Wyc. *serving at eye*).

eyelet-hole. Altered on *eye* from ME. *oilet*, F. *œillet*, dim. of *œil*, L. *oculus*.

The curtyn shal have fifti oiletis [*AV*. loops] in either parti (Wyc. *Ex*. xxvi. 5).

eyot. See *ait*.

eyre [*hist*.]. From AF. *justices en eyre*, established 1176, also called *justices errauntz*. OF. *eire*, journey, from *eirer*, Late L. **iterare*, from *iter*, journey, from *ire*, *it-*, to go. See *errant*.

eyry. See *aery*.

fa [*mus*.]. See *gamut*.

Fabian. Cautious tactics of *Quintus Fabius Maximus*, nicknamed the *Cunctator*, i.e. delayer, against Hannibal in second Punic War. Hence *Fabian Society*, founded 1884 for gradual introduction of socialism.

fable. F., L. *fabula*, from *fari*, to speak, cogn. with G. φημί, I say; cf. It. *favola*, fable, Sp. *habla*, speech. Orig. sense survives in to *be the fable of*. Sense of animal story was first associated with Aesop's works.

Israel schal be into a proverbe [Coverd. by-worde] and into a fable [*Vulg.* in fabulam]
(Wyc. 1 *Kings*, ix. 7).
Un prince sera la fable de toute l'Europe, et lui seul n'en saura rien (Pascal).

fabliau, fableau. OF. comic story in verse. Dim. of *fable*.

fabric. F. *fabrique*, L. *fabrica*, from *faber*, *fabr-*, smith. In E. first (Caxton) of building, esp. church. Sense of textile from 18 cent. With mod. sense of *fabricate* cf. cogn. *forge*[1]. *Fabricated ships* (1917–18) are usu. of concrete.

God fabricated the earth (*NED*. 1678).

façade. F., It. *facciata*, from *faccia*, face.

face. F., VL. *facia* for *facies*; cf. It. *faccia*, but Sp. *haz* (also *faz*) is from *facies*. Replaced ME. *anleth*, AS. *andwlita* (cf. Ger. *antlitz*). The analogy of this (AS. *wlite*, brightness) suggests that L. *facies* is connected with *fax*, *fac-*, torch. To *lose* (*save*) *one's face* (neol.) is translated from Chin. (see chapter on "Face" in Arthur Smith's *Chinese Characteristics*). To *face the music* is theat., not to be nervous when in front of the orchestra. With to *put through one's facings* (mil., from *right face*, etc.) cf. to *put through one's paces* (equit.).

facet. F. *facette*, dim. of *face*.

facetiae. In booksellers' catalogues now usu. of obscene books, a long way removed from "merie wordes or deedes without dishonestie; merie conceites with a pleasant grace" (Coop.), from *facetus*, graceful, urbane, whence obs. *facete*, now replaced by *facetious*.

Cheerful, facete, jovial (*Tristram Shandy*).

facia. In *sign and facia writer*. See *fascia*.

facile. F., L. *facilis*, from *facere*, to do.

facile princeps. L., easily chief.

facsimile. L. *fac simile*, make (imper.) like. Cf. *factotum* (q.v.).

fact. L. *factum*, thing done, from *facere*, *fact-*. Has replaced native *deed* in some senses; cf. *indeed* and *in fact*. See *feat*.

I think she means that there was more than one confederate in the fact (*Tit. Andr.* iv. 1).

faction. F., L. *factio-n-*, lit. making, from *facere*, *fact-*. Mod. sense is found in L. See *fashion*.

factitious. From L. *factitius*, made by art, from *facere*. See *fetish*. Cf. *factitive* (gram.), ModL. *factitivus*, making to be done.

factor. ME. & OF. *factour* (*facteur*), L. *factor-em*, from *facere*. Orig. agent, as in *corn-factor*, and Sc. *factor*, land-agent. Fig. sense, e.g. *an important factor*, is from math. *Factory* in its oldest sense (16 cent.) is adapted from Port. *feitoria*, "factory, a house or district inhabited by traders in a distant country" (Vieyra), MedL. *fac toria*. Cf. *hacienda*.

factotum. MedL. *fac* (imper.) *totum*, do everything. Cf. F. surname *Faitout* or contrasted E. *Doolittle*. See my *Surnames*, ch. xii.

Being an absolute Johannes fac totum [he, Shakespeare] is in his own conceit the only Shake-scene in a country (Greene).

factum. Statement. From F. leg. use. See *fact*.

faculty. F. *faculté*, L. *facultas* (for *facilitas*), power, opportunity, resources. See *facile*. Oldest E. sense (14 cent.) is branch of learning, department of univ. (Theology, Law, Medicine, Arts), from MedL. *facultas*, translating G. δύναμις, used by Aristotle for a branch of learning. Hence esp. *the Faculty*, i.e. the med. profession (cf. *the Profession, the Trade*).

fad. Of recent adoption from Midl. dial. Cf. *fiddle-faddle*. Perh. connected with F. *fadaise*, foolish trifle, Prov. *fadeza*, from *fad*, L. *fatuus*. Cf. sense-development of *fond*.

fade. OF. *fader* (replaced by *faner*), from *fade*, insipid, colourless, L. *vapidus*, stale, perh. influenced by *fatuus*. For init. cf. F. *fois*, time, L. *vicem*. It is curious that no *v*- forms are recorded in OF., though common in E.

faeces. L., pl. of *faex, faec-*, dregs. Cf. *defecate*.

faerie [*poet.*]. Fairy-land, esp. with ref. to Spenser. See *fairy*.

fag¹. Drudge, weariness. Prob. schoolboy perversion of *fatigue*, as in mil. sense; cf. *fug*. Quot. below suggests a similar arbitrary formation.

Such as went abroad were subject, through weaknesse, to bee suddenly surprized with a disease we called the "feages," which was neither paine nor sickness, but as it were the highest degree of weaknesse, depriving us of power and abilitie for the execution of any bodily exercise (Purch. xix. 182).

fag², **fag-end.** Orig. loose end, last part, esp. of cloth. Much earlier than *fag¹*. Origin unknown. ? Hence *fag*, cigarette (mil.).

The fag-end of a leg of mutton (*NED.* 1613).

faggot. F. *fagot*, It. *fagotto*, ? ult. from G. φάκελος, bundle.

Fahrenheit. Thermometer, name of Pruss. inventor (†1736). An abstract surname, "experience," like our *Peace, Wisdom, Verity*, etc.

faïence. F., for *poterie de Faïence*, from *Faenza* (Italy). Cf. *china, delf, crown Derby*, etc.

fail. F. *faillir* and *falloir*, to be lacking, both representing, with change of conjugation, L. *fallere*, orig. to deceive. Cf. It. *fallire*, Ger. *fehlen* (from F.). Orig. F. sense survives in *failing this* (with which cf. *during the war*), and in noun *failing*, fault, defect, for earlier *fail*, the latter now only in *without fail* (13 cent. for OF. *sanz faille*). *Failure* is also infin., AF. *failer*, for *faillir*,

as leg. term; cf. *misnomer, disclaimer*, etc., and, for alteration of form, *pleasure, leisure*.

fain. AS. *fægen*, glad; cf. ON. *feginn*, OHG. *gi-fehan*, to rejoice. For sense-development cf. *glad*, e.g. the Prodigal Son "would fain (i.e. gladly) have filled his belly" (*Luke*, xv. 16). App. influenced also by OF. *avoir fain* (*faim*), to hunger, used of any eager desire.

I lyste, I have a great wyll or desyre to do a thynge: jay fayn (Palsg.).

My lips will be fain when I sing unto thee
(*Ps.* lxxi. 21, *PB.*).

faineant [*hist.*]. Sluggard, esp. as epithet of later Merovingian kings. OF. *faignant*, pres. part. of *faindre, feindre* (see *faint*), respelt as though "do nothing" (*néant*).

fains. Schoolboy formula, opposite of *bágs*. Prob. *feign*, in ME. sense of shirk, excuse oneself; cf. *faint*.

If I may helpe you in ought
I shall not feyne (*Rom. of Rose*, 2995).

faint. First as adj. F. *feint*, p.p. of *feindre*, to feign (q.v.), in sense of to be sluggish, shirk. This survives in *faint-hearted*.

De tost corre pas ne se faint (*Fableau des Perdrix*).
[He is not sluggish in running at once]

fair¹. Adj. AS. *fæger*. Com. Teut.; cf. OSax. OHG. *fagar*, ON. *fagr*, Goth. *fagrs*, suitable; cogn. with Ger. *fegen*, to clean, sweep. Orig. beautiful (hence, from 14 cent., esp. of women), without blemish, opposed to *foul*, as still in *fair means or foul, fair play* and *foul play*. The later application to hair, etc. reflects the medieval opinion that a brown complexion was *foul*. Harald Harfager, also called Pulchricomus, had beautiful hair, as *fair hair* in mod. sense would not be remarkable in Norway. With *fairly sober* cf. *pretty drunk*. The spec. sense which the word has acquired in *fair play*, etc. is no small testimony to the national character. *Fair trade* was orig. contrasted with contraband. *Fairway* (naut.) appears to be for *fair way*, but has been associated with *fare* (q.v.); cf. synon. ON. *farvegr*, also Ger. *fahrwasser*, navigable river, *fahrweg*, highway. For *fair-maid* see *fumade*.

They were fighting for something for which there is a good word in the English language. I have not been able to discover an equivalent for it in any other tongue. It is "fair-play"
(D. Lloyd George, Sep. 17, 1919).

fair[2]. Noun. OF. *feire* (*foire*), L. *feria*, holiday (orig. rel.); cf. It. *fiera*, Sp. *feria*. *A day after the fair* has been prov. since 16 cent.

It was throughout a dismal confession that we were always a day behind the fair
           (*Nat. News*, Nov. 18, 1917).

fairy. OF. *faierie* (*féerie*), land, or race, of fays (q.v.). For transferred use cf. that of *youth*. Spenser's *Faerie* is deliberately archaic.

faith. OF. *feid* (pronounced *feith*), later *fei* (*foi*), L. *fides*; cf. It. *fede*, Sp. *fe*. The survival of the -*th* sound, due to association with *truth*, *sooth*, etc., is unique, exc. in a few surnames, e.g. *Dainteth* (*Dainty*). *Fay* is also found in ME. As theol. word *faith* translates G. πίστις. *Faithful*, as applied to Mohammedans, translates Arab. *al-mūminūn*. For *faith-cure*, *faith-healing* (c. 1885) see *James*, v. 16.

fake [*slang*]. For earlier *feake*, *feague*, prob. Ger. *fegen*, to sweep, in fig. slang use. Much of our early thieves' slang is Ger. or Du., and dates from the Thirty Years' War.

einem den beutel fegen: to fleece one (Ebers, 1796).
to feague a horse: to make him lively and carry his tail well (Grose).

fakir, **faquir**. Arab. *faqīr*, poor. Cf. *dervish*.

falbala. F., It., also Sp. Port. Origin unknown, but prob. connected with *fold*[1]. In E. usu. corrupted to *furbelow*. Cf. *fal-lal*.

falcate. Sickle-shaped. L. *falcatus*, from *falx*, *falc-*, sickle.

falchion [*hist.*]. ME. *fauchoun*, ONF. *fauchon*, for OF. *fauçon*, VL. **falcio-n-*, from *falx*, *falc-*, sickle. Cf. It. *falcione*, on which E. word has been remade.

falcon. ME. *faucoun, facon*, etc., F. *faucon*, Late L. *falco-n-*, from *falx*, sickle (v.s.). Cf. Du. *valk*, Ger. *falke*. Usu. explained from shape of beak or claws, but perh. rather from the sword-like wings; cf. G. ἅρπη, vulture, lit. sickle, and see *accipitral*. Some regard the word as Teut. and cogn. with Upper Ger. *falch* (*fahl*), fallow; cf. Ger. *falke*, fallow ox, horse, etc. The fact that *Falco* is a prehistoric Teut. personal name (cf. E. *Fawkes*) is an argument for Teut. origin of *falcon*.

falconet [*hist.*]. Light gun. It. *falconetto* (v.s.). Cf. *musket, saker*.

falderal. Cf. *falbala, fal-lal*.

faldstool, fauldstool [*eccl.*]. Late L. *faldestolium* (cf. AS. *fealde-stōl*, OHG. *fald-stuol*), fold-stool, whence F. *fauteuil*, arm-chair.

Orig. chair of bishop when away from his throne in another church.

Falernian. Wine. From the *ager Falernus* in Campania.

fall. AS. *feallan*. Com. Teut.; cf. Du. *vallen*, Ger. *fallen*, ON. *falla*. To *fall foul of* is naut. (see *foul*). To *fall out*, in sense of result, goes back to casting of lots or dice. *The Fall* (of man) is Puritan (16 cent.). *Fall* (*of the leaf*), now US., was ordinary 16 cent. E. for autumn. With archaic *falling sickness*, epilepsy, cf. L. *morbus caducus*.

The hole yere is devided into iiii partes. Spring tyme, somer, faule of the leafe and winter
           (Ascham, *Toxophilus*).

That strain again, it had a dying fall [= cadence]
           (*Twelfth Night*, i. 1).

fallacy. L. *fallacia*, from *fallax, fallac-*, from *fallere*, to deceive.

fal-lal. Of same date as *falbala*, of which it may be a var.

fallible. Late L. *fallibilis*, from *fallere*, to deceive.

fallow[1]. Orig. ploughed land, now land uncropped for the year. ME. *falghe, falwe*, from AS. *fealg*, harrow; cf. MHG. *valgen*, to till, dig. But app. associated with *fallow*[2], from colour of upturned earth, as we find AS. *fealo* in same sense.

fallow[2]. Colour, esp. of deer. AS. *fealo, fealw-*; cf. Du. *vaal*, Ger. *fahl, falb*, ON. *fölr*. Perh. cogn. with L. *pallidus*. Cf. F. *fauve*, It. *falbo*, from Teut.

false. OF. *fals* (*faux*), L. *falsus*, deceived, mistaken, p.p. of *fallere*, to deceive. Orig pass. sense survives in *false step* (*notion*), etc.

falsetto. It., dim. of *falso*, false.

falter. Orig. of the limbs, to give way stumble, as still with *footsteps, knees*. App. formed irreg. from ME. *falden*, to fold, used in same sense; perh. with orig. idea of "doubling up" under stress. Form may have been influenced by *fault*.

I feel my wits to fail and tongue to fold (Spenser).

O rotten props of the craz'd multitude,
How you stil double, faulter, under the lightest chance
That straines your vaines [veins, sinews]
           (Marston, *Ant. & Mellida*, iv.).

When our sceanes falter, or invention halts,
Your favour will give crutches to our faults
           (*ib.* Part II, *Prol.*).

fame. Archaic F., L. *fama*, report, from *fari*, to speak. Orig. in etym. sense of report, common talk,, as still in *common fame, house of ill fame*. Cf. *fable*.

family. Orig. servants of a household. L. *familia*, from *famulus*, servant. The AS. equivalent was *hīwscipe*. *Familiar spirit* was earlier (15 cent.) *familiar angel* (*devil*). *Familiar* (of the Inquisition) is an extended use of earlier sense of confidential servant of Pope or bishop. Current sense of *family way* (18 cent. = *sans cérémonie*) is 19 cent.

Parit enim conversatio contemptum (Apuleius).

famine. F., Late L. **famina*, from *fames*, hunger.

famish. For earlier *fame* (cf. *astonish*), aphet. from F. *affamer*, to starve, VL. **affamare*, to bring to hunger, *ad famem*.

famulus. Sorcerer's attendant. L., servant. Via Ger., in which *famulus* was used of a poor student serving others. Cf. earlier E. univ. sense of *servitor*.

fan. AS. *fann*, L. *vannus*, winnowing-fan; cf. F. *van*, winnowing basket. A *fan-light* has the shape of a lady's fan. The latter is a 16 cent. introduction.

His fann ys on his handa
(*AS. Gospels, Luke*, iii. 17).

fanatic. L. *fanaticus*, "ravished with a propheticall spirite" (Coop.), from *fanum*, temple. Sense-development has been coloured by spec. application of F. *fanatique* to the Camisards (q.v.).

fancy. Contr. of *fantasy, phantasy*, F. *fantaisie*, L., G. φαντασία, used in Late G. of spectral apparition. See *phantom*. Now differentiated from *imagination*, with which it was orig. synon. Sense of the unreal survives in *fantast, fantastic*. Mod. sense of inclination, e.g. to *take one's fancy, pigeon-fancier*, arises from that of whim. Hence the *Fancy*, pugilism, earlier applied to any class spec. interested in a pursuit, e.g. books, pigeons. With adj. *fancy* (only attrib.) cf. *choice, prize*.

I never yet beheld that special face
Which I could fancy more than any other
(*Shrew*, ii. 1).
In maiden meditation, fancy-free (*Dream*, ii. 1).

fandangle. Arbitrary formation (late 19 cent.), perh. suggested by *fandango*.

fandango. Dance. Sp., of negro origin.

fane. L. *fanum*, temple, for **fasnom*, cogn. with *feriae* (OL. *fesiae*), *festus* (see *fair*[2]).

fanfare. Flourish of trumpets. F., of imit. origin. With *fanfaron, fanfaronnade*, F.,

Sp. *fanfarrón*, braggart, cf. to *blow one's own trumpet*.

They wore huge whiskers and walked with a fanfaronading air
(Borrow, *Bible in Spain*, ch. xxvi.).

fang. AS. *fang*, booty, from p.p. *gefangen* of *fōn*, to seize. A Com. Teut. verb; cf. Du. *vangen*, Ger. *fangen* (OHG. *fāhan*), ON. *fā*, Goth. *fāhan*; ult. cogn. with L. *pax, pac-*, peace, orig. thing fixed. Usual senses of noun are comparatively mod., but the verb *fang*, to seize, take, etc. is common in ME.

fan-tan. Game. Chin. *fan t'an*, repeated division.

Fan-tan, for which Chinamen were heavily fined in London this week (*Daily Chron.* June 27, 1917).

fantasia. It., see *fancy*.

fantast-ic, fantasy. See *fancy*.

fanteague, fantigue [*colloq.*]. Earlier *fantique*. Perh. for *frantic* (v.i.). For loss of -*r*- cf. *Fanny* for *Frances*.

He began to enter into such a frantike, as hee regarded not the salute of his friends
(Greene's *Vision*).

fanti, fantee, to go. WAfr. for to run amok. Name of country and tribe on Gold Coast.

Is he likely to "go Fanti,"
Or becoming shrewd and canty?
(*Punch*, Feb. 28, 1917).

fantoccini. It., pl. of *fantoccino*, dim. of *fantoccio*, puppet, from *fante*, boy, L. *infans, infant-*.

faquir. See *fakir*.

far. Orig. adv. AS. *feorr*. Com. Teut.; cf. Du. *ver*, Ger. *fern*, ON. *fiarre*, Goth. *fairra*; cogn. with G. πέραν, Sanskrit *paras*, beyond. Prop. of forward measurement, hence *far and wide*, the latter word expressing lateral extension. Dial. *fur* is a natural var., ME. *fer*.

farad. Electr. unit. Adopted at Electrical Congress at Paris (1881) in memory of *Faraday*, E. electrician (†1867).

farce. F., VL. **farsa*, from *farcire*, to stuff viands. Cf. *force-meat*. A *farce* was orig. an impromptu interlude "stuffed in" between the parts of a more serious play.

farcy. Disease of horses, allied to glanders. F. *farcin*, L. *farciminum*, from *farcire*, to stuff (v.s.).

fardel [*archaic*]. OF. (*fardeau*), dim. of OF. *farde*, burden, Sp. *fardo*, Arab. *fardah*, package.

fare. AS. *faran*, to go, travel. Com. Teut.; cf. Du. *varen*, Ger. *fahren*, ON. *fara*, Goth. *faran*; cogn. with G. πόρος, passage, L.

portare, to carry, and with adv. *far*. Orig. sense obs. exc. in compds., e.g. *wayfarer*, *sea-faring*. Hence noun *fare* (cf. *thorough-fare*, *welfare*), now usu. payment for passage (*Jonah*, i. 3), or even used for passenger, e.g. "a cabman with a drunken fare." *Farewell*, imper., was orig. said to departing person, who replied *good-bye*.

farina. L., from *far*, corn, cogn. with AS. *bere*, barley. Cf. F. *farine*, flour.

farm. F. *ferme*, MedL. *firma*, fixed payment, from *firmare*, to fix, from *firmus*, firm. Earliest use (Chauc.) in connection with *farming* the taxes. With *Farmer-General*, translating F. *fermier-général*, tax-farmer, cf. *baby-farmer* (19 cent.). For spec. agricultural application cf. Ger. *pächter*, farmer, from L. *pactus*, agreement. Cf. also F. *métayer*, VL. **medietarius*, one who manages land on half profit system (see *moiety*). In ordinary speech *farmer* has replaced *churl*, *husbandman*.

A certayne man planted a vyneyarde, and lett it forthe to fermers [Wyc. settide it to ferme to tilieris] (Tynd. *Luke*, xx. 9).

faro. Card-game. Formerly *pharaoh* (H. Walpole), after F. *pharaon*. Reason for name doubtful.

farouche. F., shy, VL. **feroticus*, from *ferox*, fierce.

farrago. L., lit. mixed fodder, from *far*, *farr-*, corn.

farrier. OF. *ferrier* (replaced by *maréchal-ferrant*), L. *ferrarius*, from *ferrum*, iron, horse-shoe.

farrow. Orig. young pig. AS. *fearh*; cf. Du. dim. *varken*, Ger. dim. *ferkel*, hog; cogn. with L. *porcus*.

fart. AS. *feortan*. Aryan; cf. Ger. *farzen*, ON. *freta*, G. πέρδειν, Sanskrit *pard*.

farther, farthest. ME. *ferther*, var. of *further* (q.v.), gradually replacing regular *farrer*, from *far*, which survived till 17 cent.

farthing. AS. *feorthung*, from *feortha*, fourth; cf. ON. *fiörthungr*. In *AV.* used for both L. *as* and *quadrans*. For suffix cf. *penny*, *shilling*.

farthingale [*archaic*]. Corrupt. of OF. *vertugalle*, var. of archaic *vertugade* (*vertugadin*), Sp. *verdugado*, from *verdugo*, green switch (later replaced by whalebone or steel), VL. **viriducus*, from *viridis*, green.

verdugado: a fardingall in Spaine, they are below at the feete (Minsh.).

fasces. L., pl. of *fascis*, bundle (of rods carried by the lictor).

fascia. L., band, fillet, flat surface forming part of architrave; cogn. with *fascis*. Cf. *facia*, *fesse*.

fascicle [*bot.*]. L. *fasciculus*, dim. of *fascis*, bundle.

fascinate. From L. *fascinare*, from *fascinum*, charm, spell.

fascine [*mil.*]. F., L. *fascina*, faggot, from *fascis*, bundle. Often coupled with *gabion*.

fash [*Sc. & dial.*]. F. *fâcher*, OF. *faschier*, ? VL. **fastidicare*, from *fastidium*, disgust.

fashion. F. *façon*, L. *factio-n-*, make, from *facere*; cf. It. *fazione*. *Man of fashion* meant orig. (15 cent.) of high rank and breeding. The *glass of fashion* is after *Haml*. iii. 1, where *fashion* prob. means face. For current sense, with adj. understood, cf. *rank*, *quality*, *style*. Orig. neutral sense in *after a fashion*.

Ye can skyll of the fassion [*Vulg.* facies] of the erth, and of the skye (Tynd. *Luke*, xii. 56).

fast¹. Adj. AS. *fæst*, firm. Com. Teut.; cf. Du. *vast*, Ger. *fest*, ON. *fastr*. With *fast-ness*, fortress, cf. Ger. *festung*. With *to run fast*, app. incongruous with *to stick* (*stand*) *fast*, cf. similar intens. use of *hard*, e.g. *hold hard*, *run hard*. Hence *fast*, of conduct, now opposed to *steady*, with which it is etym. almost synon. *Fast and loose* is an old cheating game with a string or strap.

Juglers play of fast and loose [passe-passe] F.
(Florio's *Montaigne*, iii. 8).

jouer de la navette [shuttle]: to play fast and loosse
(Cotg.).

fast². To abstain. AS. *fæstan*. Com. Teut.; cf. Du. *vasten*, Ger. *fasten*, ON. *fasta*, Goth. *fastan*. Prob. cogn. with *fast¹*, with orig. idea of firm control of oneself. In pre-Christian use, but early associated with the Church.

fasten AS. *fæstnian*, from *fast¹*. With *to fasten on*, of dogs, cf. more expressive US. *to freeze to*, and see ON. parallel s.v. *cling*.

fasti. Calendar. L., pl. of *fastus* (*dies*), lawful (day), from *fas*, right, orig. announcement, cogn. with *fari*, to speak.

fastidious. F. *fastidieux*, L. *fastidiosus*, from *fastidium*, loathing. Earlier used, like many adjs. of this type (*fearful*, *nauseous*, etc.), in both act. and pass. sense.

The thing for the which children be oftentimes beaten is to them ever after fastidious
(Sir T. Elyot).

fat¹ [*Bibl.*]. Vessel (*Joel*, iii. 13), also *winefat*. Replaced by *vat* (q.v.).

fat². AS. *fǣtt*, contracted p.p. of *fǣttian*, to make fat; cf. *fatted calf*, and Ger. *feist*, fat, p.p. of OHG. *feizzen*, to fatten. Ger. *fett* is from LG. The *fat of the land* is after *Gen.* xlv. 18, where *Vulg.* has *medulla terrae*.

> Faith, Doricus, thy braine boiles; keele [cool] it, or all the fatt's in the fire
> (Marston, *What you will, Induction*).

Fata Morgana. Mirage in Strait of Messina It., fairy Morgana, sister of King Arthur, *Morgan le Fey* in AF. poetry, located in Calabria by Norman settlers. See *fay*. The name *Morgan* is Welsh, sea-dweller (cf. *Pelagian*).

fate. L. *fatum*, thing spoken, decree of the gods, from *fari*, to speak. In all Rom. langs. Its first E. use, in Chaucer's *Troilus*, may be from It. *fato*.

father. AS. *fæder*. Aryan; cf. Du. *vader*, *vaar*, Ger. *vater*, ON. *father*, Goth. *fadar* (but Goth. has usu. *atta*), L. *pater*, G. πατήρ, Gael. Ir. *athair*, Sanskrit *pitr*, all prob. orig. from baby-syllable *pa*. With *father-land* cf. *mother-country*, but the word is often allusive to Du. *vaderland* or Ger. *vaterland*. For eccl. sense cf. *abbot*, *pope*.

fathom. AS. *fæthm*, the two arms outstretched (cf. F. *brasse*, fathom, L. *brachia*, arms); cogn. with Du. *vadem*, Ger. *faden*, measure of six feet, thread, and ult. with G. πεταννύναι, to spread out (see *petal*). For fig. sense of verb cf. to *sound⁴*.

fatidic. L. *fatidicus*, fate-telling, from *fatum* and *dicere*.

fatigue. F. *fatiguer*, L. *fatigare*, prob. cogn. with L. *fatiscere*, to gape, yawn, *adfatim*, enough; cf. It. *faticare*, Sp. *fatigar*. Mil. sense from 18 cent.

fatuous. From L. *fatuus*, foolish. Cf. *infatuate*.

faubourg. F., earlier *fauxbourg*, corrupted, as though false town (MedL. *falsus burgus*), from OF. *forsbourg*, from *fors* (*hors*), outside, L. *foris*, and *bourg*, borough.

faucet. Spigot, tap. Obs. in E., exc. dial., but usual word for tap in US. F. *fausset*, ? dim. from L. *faux*, *fauc-*, throat; cf. *goulot*, "the pipe of a sinke, or gutter" (Cotg.), dim. of OF. *goule* (*gueule*), throat, "gullet."

faugh. Earlier (16 cent.) *foh*, *fah*. Natural exclamation, imit. of repelling unpleasant smell. Cf. Ger. *pfui*.

fauldstool. See *faldstool*.

fault. Restored spelling of ME. *faut*, F. *faute*,

VL. **fallita*, coming short, from *fallere*, to deceive; cf. It. Sp. *falta*. In some phrases, e.g. *at fault* (hunting) = F. *en défaut*, aphet. for *default*. The *-l-* was silent up to 18 cent. With *to a fault* cf. synon., but etym. opposite, *to excess*. *Fault* at tennis is recorded 1526.

> Yet he was kind, or if severe in aught,
> The love he bore to learning was in fault
> (*Deserted Village*).

faun. L. *Faunus*, name of rural god or demi-god, identified with Pan.

fauna. L. *Fauna*, sister of *Faunus* (v.s.). Adopted (1746) by Linnaeus as companion-word to *flora* (q.v.).

fauteuil. F., see *faldstool*.

fautor [*leg.*]. Partisan. OF. *fautour*, L. *fautor-em*, from *favēre*, to favour.

faux pas. F., false step.

Favonian. L. *Favonianus*, from *Favonius*, the west wind, cogn. with *favour*.

favour. F. *faveur*, L. *favor-em*, from *favēre*, to regard with goodwill. *Favourite* is OF. *favorit* (*favori*), from It. *favorito*, p.p. of *favorire*, to favour. It is recorded in racing from c. 1800. A *favour*, worn as a distinguishing mark, was orig. conferred as a sign of favour by a prince, lady, etc. *Without fear or favour* is a leg. formula. To *favour* (one's father, mother) is to show (facially) an inclination towards; hence *well-(ill-)favoured*. See also *curry¹*.

fawn¹. Noun. F. *faon*, orig. young of any animal, VL. **feto-n-*, from *fetus*, offspring. For spelling and sound cf. *lawn²*.

> The lyonnesse hath the first yere fyve fawnes
> (Caxton, *Mirror of World*).

fawn². Verb. AS. *fahnian*, to rejoice, be pleased fawn, parallel form of *fægnian*, from *fægen*, glad (see *fain*). The AS. compd. *on-fægnian* is used of dogs.

> *ffawnyn, as houndys*: applaudo, blandior
> (*Prompt. Parv.*).

fay. F. *fée*, fem., L. *fata*, neut. pl., the Fates; cf. It. *fata*, Sp. *hada*. Cf. *Fata Morgana*, *fairy*, and see *fate*.

feal [*archaic*]. OF. *feal*, *feeil*, L. *fidelis*, faithful. Hence *fealty*.

fear. AS. *fǣr*, sudden peril; cf. Du. *gevaar*, Ger. *gefahr*, danger; also Goth. *fērja*, one who lies in wait; cogn. with *fare*. The verb was orig. trans., AS. *fǣran*, to terrify, as still in archaic *I fear me* (see quot. s.v. *bug¹*).

fearnought [*naut.*]. Stout cloth. Cf. *dreadnought*.

feasible. Archaic F. *faisible* (now *faisable*), from *fais-*, stem of *faire*, to do, L. *facere*.

feast. OF. *feste* (*fête*), L. *festa*, neut. pl. of adj. *festus*, joyful, cogn. with *feria* (*fair*[2]); cf. It. *festa*, Sp. *fiesta*. Now replaced, in sense of ceremonial meal, by *banquet*.

feat. AF. *fet*, F. *fait*, deed, L. *factum*, from *facere*. The archaic and dial. adj. *feat*, fit, becoming, dexterous, etc., has same origin, L. *factus*.

feather. AS. *fether* Com. Teut.; cf. Du. *veder*, Ger. *feder*, ON. *fiöthr*; cogn. with G. πτερόν, wing, Sanskrit *pat*, to fly. Sometimes collect. in sense, e.g. *birds of a feather*, *in fine feather*. *Featherbed* is AS. The allusive uses belong esp. to cock-fighting, e.g. a *white feather* in the tail is supposed to indicate a cowardly bird. With *fur and feather* cf. F. *plume et poil*. To *cut a feather* is naut. (v.i.); cf. to *cut a dash*. *Feathering*, in rowing, is to offer a "feather-edge" to the air.

cut a feather: if a ship has too broad a bow, 'tis common to say, she will not "cut a feather"; that is, she will not pass thro' the water, so swift, as to make it foam, or froth (*Gent. Dict.* 1705).

And now is the time come to feather my nest
(*Respublica*, c. 1553).

feature. OF. *feture, faiture*, shape, build, L. *factura*, from *facere*, to make. For mod. limitation of sense cf. *countenance*. The idiotic use of *feature* in "film-land" is quite new.

She was well fietured all but hir face
(Raymond's *Autob.* 17 cent.).

febrifuge. See *fever*.

febrile. F. *fébrile*, Late L. *febrilis*, from *febris*, fever.

February. L. *Februarius*, from *februa*, feast of purification (Feb. 15), of Sabine origin. In most Europ. langs. The E. form is learned, for ME. *feverer, feveryere*, etc. Replaced AS. *sōl-mōnath*, mud month.

fecal. See *faeces*.

fecial. See *fetial*.

feckless [*Sc. & north.*]. For *effectless* (Shaks.). Popularized by Carlyle, to whom quot. 2 alludes.

A fecklesse arrogant conceit of their greatnes and power (James I, *Basilicon Doron*).

The philosophers and economists thought, with Saunders McBullock, the Baron's bagpiper, that "a feckless monk more or less was nae great subject for a clamjamphry" (*Ingoldsby*).

feculent. F. *féculent*, L. *faeculentus*, from *faeces*, dregs.

fecundity. L. *fecunditas*, from *fecundus*, fruitful, ult. cogn. with *femina, felix*.

federal. F. *fédéral*, from L. *foedus, foeder-*, treaty, alliance, cogn. with *fides*, faith. Sense of pol. unity is esp. US. Cf. *confederate*.

fee. AS. *feoh*, cattle, money. Aryan; cf. Du. *vee*, Ger. *vieh*, cattle, ON. *fē*, cattle, money, Goth. *faihu*, property, money, L. *pecu*, cattle, *pecunia*, money, Sanskrit *paçu*, cattle. Cf. hist. of *cattle, chattel*. *Fee-house* in ME. means both cattle-shed and treasury. Related are *fief, feud*[2] (q.v.), and from an AF. form of *fief* comes *fee*, in to *hold in fee*, MedL. *in feodo*, as a fief, feudal tenure. *Fee*, payment, also *feodum* in MedL., is a mixture of the two main groups of senses. *Fee-simple*, MedL. *feodum simplex* or *purum*, is absolute ownership, as opposed to *fee-tail*, entailed or restricted. Chauc. uses it allusively.

Of fees and robes hadde he [the Sergeant of the Law] many oon...
Al was fee symple to hym in effect (A. 317).

feeble. OF. *feble* (*faible*), L. *flebilis*, pitiable, from *flēre*, to weep, the first *-l-* being lost by dissim. as in *fugleman*; cf. It. *fievole*, Sp. *feble*. See *foible*.

feed. AS. *fēdan*, to supply with *food* (q.v.). Hence to supply a machine, to toss balls at rounders, formerly also at cricket. With mod. sense of *feed up*, to fatten, hence (in mil. slang) to over-satiate, cf. F. *j'en ai soupé*, I am fed up with it. *Off one's feed* (*oats*) is from the stable.

We're all getting pretty well fed up with this place by now (Steevens, *Kitchener to Khartum*, ch. xxiii.).

fee-faw-fum. From *Jack the Giant-killer*. Cf. *mumbo-jumbo*.

His word was still, "Fie, foh, and fum,
I smell the blood of a British man" (*Lear*, iii. 4).

feel. AS. *fēlan*. WGer.; cf. Du. *voelen*, Ger. *fühlen*. Orig. of touch; cogn. with AS. *folm*, palm, L. *palma*, G. παλάμη; cf. ON. *falma*, to grope. For fig. senses cf. *touch*.

feign. F. *feindre, feign-*, L. *fingere*, to shape, invent. *Feint* is F. *feinte*, orig. p.p. fem.

feldspar, felspar. Altered, on *spar*[2], from Ger. *feldspat*, field spar. *Felspar* is due to mistaken association by Kirwan (1794) with Ger. *fels*, rock.

felicity. F. *félicité*, L. *felicitas*, from *felix, felic-*, happy. With *felicitous phrase* cf. *happy thought*.

feline. L. *felinus*, from *feles*, cat. Hence

feline amenities, women's veiled spite, used by Du Maurier in *Punch*.

fell[1]. Hide. Chiefly in *fell-monger*. AS. *fell*. Com. Teut.; cf. Du. *vel*, Ger. *fell*, ON. *fiall*, Goth. *fill*; cogn. with L. *pellis*, G. πέλλα, and *film*.

fell[2]. Verb. AS. *f(i)ellan*, causal of *fall* (q.v.). Cf. Ger. *fällen*. In sewing sense from causing seam to fall.

fell[3] [*north*.]. Hill, as in *Scawfell*. ON. *fiall*, cogn. with Ger. *fels*, rock.

fell[4]. Adj. OF. *fel*, nom. of *felon* (q.v.). Esp. in *at one fell swoop* (*Macb*. iv. 1).

Fell, Doctor. Person instinctively disliked. *John Fell*, Dean of Christ-Church (†1686), subject of adaptation by Thomas Brown (†1704), as an undergraduate, of Martial's epigram. There are many versions, that below being from 1719 ed. of Brown's works (iv. 113). There are also F. renderings by Marot and Bussy-Rabutin.

I do not love you, Doctor Fell, But why I cannot tell;
But this I know full well: I do not love you, Doctor Fell.

Non amo te, Sabidi, nec possum dicere quare;
Hoc tantum possum dicere, non amo te (Mart. i. 33).

fellah. Arab. *fellāh*, husbandman, from *falaha*, to till the soil. With pl. *fellaheen* cf. *Bedouin*, *cherubin*, etc.

felloe, felly. Rim of wheel. AS. *felge*; cf. Du. *velge*, Ger. *felge*; also OHG. *felahan*, to fit (wood) together.

fellow. Orig. partner. Late AS. *fēolaga*, ON. *fēlage*, partner, associate; cf. ON. *fēlag*, partnership, lit. fee lay. With *fellow-feeling* cf. *compassion*, *sympathy*. In univ. sense translates L. *socius*. For vaguer senses cf. *companion* and US. *pardner*. *Hail fellow well met* is found in 16 cent. The contemptuous use arises from the orig. kindly manner of addressing servants in ME.

A individual in company has called me a feller
(Sam Weller).

felly. See *felloe*.

felo de se. MedL., felon with regard to himself (v.i.).

felon. F., Carolingian L. *fello-n-*; cf. It. *fellone*, Sp. *felón*, and *fell*[4]. Oldest E. sense is criminal. *Fel*, *felon*, adj., grim, treacherous, terrible, is very common in OF., but is of unknown origin. A plausible suggestion is that from L. *fellare*, to suck, also sensu obsceno, was formed a noun **fello-n-*, used as gen. term of abuse. Cf. *glutton* from *glutto-n-*, also a common term of abuse in

OF. *Felon*, whitlow (dial. & US.), is the same word; cf. L. *tagax*, thievish, whitlow, and *furuncle* (q.v.), also Du. *nijdnagel*, lit. envy-nail.

I've been visiting to Bath because I had a felon on my thumb (*Far from the Madding Crowd*).

felspar. See *feldspar*.

felt. AS. *felt*. WGer.; cf. Du. *vilt*, Ger. *filz*; prob. cogn. with the second element (to beat, hammer) of *anvil* (q.v.). Cf. MedL. *filtrum* (from Teut.), whence F. *feutre*. See *filter*.

felucca [*naut*.]. It., Arab. *falūkah*, cogn. with *folk*, ship; cf. F. *felouque*, Sp. *faluca*. Dozy regards Arab. *falūkah* as a mod. word borrowed from Europ. He derives It. *feluca* from Sp., and the latter from Arab. *harrāca*, small galley, whence OSp. *haloque*. Being a Mediterranean rig, Arab. origin is likely.

falouque: a barge, or a kind of barge-like boat, that hath some five or six oares on a side (Cotg.).

female. F. *femelle*, L. *femella*, dim. of *femina*, woman. Altered on *male* (q.v.). Cf. Ger. *weibchen*, female of animals, lit. little woman.

Maal and femaal he made hem (Wyc. *Gen*. i. 27).

feme [*leg*.]. OF. (*femme*), woman, in *feme covert*, protected, i.e. married, woman, *feme sole*, single woman (v.i.).

feminine. F. *féminin*, L. *femininus*, from *femina*, woman; cogn. with *fellare*, to suckle, and with *filius*, *filia*. *Feminism*, in new sense of "women's rights," is not in *NED*. *The eternal feminine* comes, via F., from Goethe's *ewig-weibliche* (last lines of *Faust* ii.).

femoral [*anat*.]. Late L. *femoralis*, from *femur*, *femor-*, thigh.

fen. AS. *fenn*. Com. Teut.; cf. Du. *veen*, LG. *fenne*, ON. *fen*, Goth. *fani*. Orig. mud. Hence prob. F. *fange*, It. *fango*.

fence. Aphet. for *defence*, F. *défense*, from *défendre*, VL. **disfendere* for *defendere*, to ward off, etc. Hence *fencible*, capable of, or liable for, making defence. With US. to *sit on the fence* cf. Ir. *the best hurlers* (hockey-players) *are on the ditch* (bank), as critical spectators out of danger. Verb to *fence* (with swords) is first in Shaks. (*Merry Wives*, ii. 3).

fence: a receiver and securer of stolen goods
(*Dict. Cant. Crew*).

Charles Seaforth, lieutenant in the Hon. East India Company's second regiment of Bombay Fencibles
(*Ingoldsby*).

fend. Aphet. for *defend* (v.s.). Hence *fender*, protector. To *fend for oneself* is to attend to one's own defence.

fenestella [*arch.*]. L., dim. of *fenestra*, window.

Fenian [*hist.*]. Of uncertain origin. As used by Scott in ref. to *Ossian* (*Antiquary*, ch. xxx.) it is for Macpherson's *Fingalians*, followers of *Fionnghal*, a name adopted by him for a mythical Gaelic hero, but really meaning Norseman, "fair stranger" (cf. *Dougal*, dark stranger). In pol. sense (from c. 1860) it is a mixture of OIr. *fiann*, band of heroes, and OIr. *féne*, one of the names of the ancient population of Ireland.

fennel. AS. *finol*, *finugl*, VL. **fenuculum*, for *feniculum*, dim. of *fenum*, hay; cf. F. *fenouil*.

fent [*archaic & dial.*]. Slit, crack. F. *fente*, from *fendre*, L. *findere*, to split. Cf. *vent*[1].

fenugreek. Plant. F. *fenugrec*, L. *fenum Graecum*, Greek hay. Found also in L. form in AS.

feoffee [*hist.*]. AF. p.p. of *feoffer*, F. *fieffer*, to enfeoff. See *fief*.

-fer, -ferous. From L. *-fer*, from *ferre*, to bear, often via F. *-fère*.

feracious. From L. *ferax*, *ferac-*, prolific, from *ferre*, to bear. Used by Carlyle.

ferae naturae. L., of wild nature.

feral[1]. Deadly. L. *feralis*, funeral; cf. *feralia*, sacrifices for the dead.

feral[2]. Savage. From L. *fera*, wild beast; cf. *ferus*, fierce; cogn. with G. θήρ, wild beast.

fer-de-lance. Viper (Martinique). F., lance-blade, from shape of head.

feretory [*eccl.*]. Shrine, bier. Perversion of ME. *fertre*, OF. *fiertre*, L., G. φέρετρον, from φέρειν, to bear.

ferial. Of ordinary days. Late L. *ferialis*, from *feria*, older *fesia*, cogn. with *festum*, feast. See *fair*[2]. Present sense is opposite of etym. (cf. Port. *feira*, in week-day sense).

ferine. L. *ferinus*, as *feral*[2].

Feringhee. Pers. *farangī*, Arab. *faranjī*, Oriental adaptation of *Frank*, used since 10 cent. for European, with ethnic suffix *-ī*. For init. cf. Kim's *terain* for *train*.

ferio. Mnemonic word in logic. Cf. *barbara*.

ferment. F., L. *fermentum*, from *fervēre*, to boil.

fern. AS. *fearn*; cf. Du. *varen-kruid*, Ger. *farn-kraut*; cogn. with Sanskrit *parna*, wing, feather; cf. G. πτερόν, wing, πτερίς, fern. The connection between fern-seed and invisibility is due to the old belief

that the plant was propagated by invisible seeds.

ferocious. From L. *ferox*, *feroc-*, from *ferus*, wild.

-ferous. See *-fer*.

ferreous. From L. *ferreus*, from *ferrum*, iron.

ferret[1]. Animal. F. *furet*, dim. of OF. *furon*, Late L. *furo-n-*, lit. thief, from *fur*; cf. It. *furetto*, Ger. *frettchen*, from F. or It.

ferret[2]. Silk tape. It. *fioretti*, "a kind of course silke called f[l]oret or ferret silke" (Flor.), pl. of *fioretto*, little flower.

> 'Twas so fram'd and express'd, no tribunal could shake it,
> And firm as red wax and black ferret could make it (*Ingoldsby*).

ferruginous. From L. *ferrugo*, *ferrugin-*, iron rust, from *ferrum*, iron.

ferrule. Altered, as though from *ferrum*, iron, from earlier *verrel*, *virrel*, OF. *virelle*, *virol* (*virole*), prob. from *virer*, to turn (see *veer*[2]); cf. synon. F. *tourillon*, double dim. of *tour*, turn.

> *verelle* (or *vyrelle*) *of a knyffe*: spirula, vel virula secundum quosdam (*Cath. Angl.*).
> *tourillon*: an inner verrill; the round plate of iron whereby a piece of wood, often turned on, is preserved from wearing (Cotg.).

ferry. AS. *ferian*, to carry, make to fare. Com. Teut.; cf. Du. *veer*, Ger. *fähre*, ferry-boat, ON. *ferja*, Goth. *farjan*, to travel; cogn. with *fare*.

fertile. F., L. *fertilis*, from *ferre*, to bear.

ferula, ferule. L. *ferula*, giant fennel, rod, ? from *ferire*, to strike.

fervent. F., from pres. part. of L. *fervēre*, to boil, glow.

fescennine. From *Fescennia* (Etruria), famous for scurrilous verse dialogues. Cf. *vaudeville*.

fescue [*bot. & dial.*]. Grass. Earlier *festu*, OF. (*fétu*), straw, VL. **festucum* for *festuca*. Formerly used of small pointer used in teaching children to read.

> A festu [*Vulg.* festuca], or a litil mote (Wyc. *Matt.* vii. 3).

fesse [*her.*]. OF. *faisse* (*fasce*), L. *fascia*, band. See *fascia*.

festal. OF., from L. *festum*, feast.

fester. OF. *festre*, L. *fistula* (cf. OF. *chartre* from L. *cartula*). See *fistula*.

festino. Mnemonic word in logic. Cf. *barbara*.

festive. L. *festivus*, from *festum*, feast. *Festival*, orig. adj., is OF., now reintroduced (Acad. 1878) into F. from E.

festoon. F. *feston*, It. *festone*, app. connected with L. *festum*, feast.

fetch[1]. Verb. AS. *fetian, feccan,* ? ult. cogn. with *foot.* As archaic noun, dodge, something in the nature of a sought out contrivance; cf. *far fetched. Fet* ran parallel with *fetch* up to 17 cent. and is still in dial. use. It occurs in orig. text of *A V.*, e.g. *Acts,* xxviii. 13. Colloq. sense of *fetching* is late 19 cent.

ascitus: strange, far fet, usurped (Litt.).

She hath more qualities than a water-spaniel... Imprimis: she can fetch and carry
                              (*Two Gent.* iii. 1).

fetch[2]. Wraith. Perh. short for *fetch-life,* messenger fetching soul of dying, or *fetch-light,* corpse-candle, both obs.

The very fetch and ghost of Mrs Gamp
                              (*Chuzzlewit,* ch. xix.).

fête. F., L. *festa,* for *festum* (see *feast*). Hence *fête-champêtre,* L. *campestris,* from *campus,* field.

fetial, fecial. L. *fetialis, fecialis,* "an officer at armes to denounce warre or peace; an ambassadour for that purpose; an harraude" (Coop.).

fetid. L. *fetidus,* from *fetēre,* to stink.

fetish. F. *fétiche,* Port. *feitiço,* "sorcery, charm" (Vieyra), L. *facticius,* made by art, applied by early Port. travellers to native amulets, etc., on Guinea coast (cf. *joss, palaver*). Cf. OF. *faitis,* well-formed, elegant, whence ME. *fetous* (Chauc. A. 273).

Strawen rings called fatissos or gods (Purch.).

The aforesaid king...on whom alone the fitezzas of the Baccaraus [= whites, "buckras"] had no power (Roberts, *Voyages,* 1726).

fetlock. ME. *fetlak, fytlok.* Now associated with *lock*[1], tuft of hair, but earlier prob. with *lock*[2], fastening; cf. hist. of the almost synon. *pastern* (q.v.), and Ger. *fessel,* fetter, fetlock. Cf. LG. *fitlock,* Ger. dial. *fissloch.* First element is *foot,* second is usu. explained as formative suffix, but may very well be *lock*[1].

fetter. AS. *feter;* cf. Du. *veter,* lace, earlier, chain, MHG. *fesser* (replaced by *fessel*), ON. *fiöturr.* From *foot;* cf. L. *pedica* and *compes,* fetter, from *pes,* foot.

fettle. As in *fine fettle.* From dial. verb *fettle,* to make ready, etc. Perh. from AS. *fetel,* belt, as the verb is used reflex. in ME. with sense like to *gird oneself* (cf. to *buckle to*). AS. *fetel* is ult. cogn. with *vat* and Ger. *fassen,* to grasp, embrace.

fetus. Incorr. *foetus.* L., offspring; cogn. with *felix,* happy.

feu [*leg.*]. Sc. form of *fee* (q.v.), OF. *fiu,* fief. See *Bride of Lammermoor,* ch. xii.

Demi Espaigne vus voelt en fiu duner (*Rol.* 432).
Lord Leverhulme does not intend charging any feu duty for the sites
                              (*Sund. Times,* Jan. 26, 1919).

feud[1]. Vendetta. Early Sc. *fede* (14–15 cent.), OF. *faide,* OHG. *fēhida* (*fehde*); cf. AS. *fǣhth,* enmity (see *foe*). Adopted in E. in 16 cent., with unexplained alteration to *feud.* This can hardly be due to association with *feud*[2], a later and learned word never in popular use.

feud[2]. Fief. MedL. *feudum, feodum* (10 cent.). See *fee, feu, fief.* The ending may be OHG. *ōd,* wealth, property, as in *allodial* (q.v.), a word belonging to the same region of ideas. With *feudal* cf. F. *féodal.* This group of words is of fairly late appearance in E., having been introduced from MedL. by the jurists and antiquaries of the 16–17 cents.

feu de joie. F., fire of joy, orig. bonfire.

feuille-morte. F., dead leaf.

feuilleton. F., dim. of *feuille,* leaf. Esp. applied in F. to the short story or serial with which newspapers filled up after the fall of Napoleon left them short of war news. This was the beginning of Dumas' and Eugène Sue's long novels.

fever. AS. *fēfer,* L. *febris.* Adopted by most Europ. langs., e.g. F. *fièvre,* It. *febbre,* Ger. *fieber,* etc. Hence *feverfew,* AF. *fewerfue,* Late L. *febrifugia,* febrifuge (*fugare,* to put to flight), from med. use; cf. AS. *fēferfūge.*

few. AS. *fēawe* (pl.). Com. Teut.; cf. OSax. *fāh,* OHG. *fāo,* ON. *fār,* Goth. *fawai* (pl.); cogn. with L. *paucus.* With jocular *a few,* now gen. US., perh. after F. *un peu,* cf. US. *some.*

fey [*Sc.*]. Of excitement supposed to presage death. AS. *fǣge,* doomed, timid. Com. Teut.; cf. Du. *veeg,* OHG. *feigi* (Ger. *feig,* cowardly), ON. *feigr;* perh. cogn. with L. *piger,* sluggish.

I was but thinkin' you're fey, McRimmon
                              (Kipling, *Bread upon the Waters*).

fez. F., Turk. *fes,* from *Fez* in Morocco.

fiancé. F., p.p. of *fiancer,* to betroth, from OF. *fiance,* pledge, from *fier,* to trust, L. *fidere,* from *fides,* faith. This F. word, variously "pronounced," has practically expelled *betrothed.*

fianchetto [*chess*]. It., little flank (attack).

fiasco. F., It., lit. *bottle* (see *flask*), in phrase *far fiasco,* said to be from slang of Venet.

glass-workers. Orig. sense doubtful; cf. F. *ramasser une pelle*, to come a cropper (in bicycling), lit. to pick up a shovel.

fiat. L., let it be done, in MedL. proclamations and commands, from *fieri*, used as pass. of *facere*. The L. verb is ult. cogn. with *be*.

fib¹. Lie. Perh. for earlier *fible-fable*, redupl. on *fable*. It may however be a thinned form of *fob¹* (q.v.); cf. *bilk*, *bitch²*. Urquhart uses it to render Rabelais' *fourby*.

baye: a lye, fib, foist, gull, rapper (Cotg.).

fib² [*pugil.*]. To strike. Thieves' slang, of unknown origin.

fib: to beat; also a little lie (*Dict. Cant. Crew*).

fibre. F., L. *fibra*; cf. It. Sp. *fibra*.

fibula. L., clasp, buckle, from *fivere*, by-form of *figere*, to fix.

ficelle. F., string, VL. **filicella*, from *filum*, thread.

fichu. F., fig. use of *fichu*, done for, mod. substitution for a coarser word. Cf. *négligé*.

fickle. AS. *ficol*, tricky; cf. *gefic*, deceit, *befician*, to deceive. Perh. orig. of quick movement and cogn. with *fidget*.

fiction. F., L. *fictio-n-*, from *fingere*, *fict-*, to shape, fashion. Cf. *fictile*, of pottery. A *legal fiction* is a feigned statement allowed by the court in order to bring a case within the scope of the law.

fid [*naut.*]. Peg, pin, plug, in various senses. Origin doubtful. ? It. *fitto*, from *figgere*, to drive in, fix, L. *figere*.

épissoire: marling spike, or splicing fid (Lesc.).

fiddle. AS. *fithele* (in *fithelere*); cf. Du. *vedel*, Ger. *fiedel* (OHG. *fidula*), ON. *fithla*, MedL. *vidula*, *vitula*, whence also It. *viola*, F. *viole*, etc. Ult. source unknown. The contemptuous phraseology connected with the *fiddle*, e.g. *fiddlesticks*, to *fiddle about*, *fiddle-de-dee*, etc., is partly due to association with *fiddle-faddle*, redupl. on obs. *faddle*, to trifle. *Fiddler's Green* is the good sailors' Elysium. The verb to *fiddle*, fidget with the hands, may belong rather to ON. *fitla*, to touch with the fingers.

With tymbrels, with myrth, and with fyddels [*Vulg.* sistra] (Coverd. 1 *Sam.* xviii. 6).

fiddley [*naut.*]. Framework round opening to stoke-hole. Perh. from *fiddle*, a favourite word with mariners; cf. the *fiddles* on the saloon table, the *fiddle-head*, carved scrollwork at bow, etc. Or it may be a remini-

scence of sailing-ship days when the ship's fiddler sat on a rail by the mainmast; cf. *fife-rail*.

fidelity. F. *fidélité*, L. *fidelitas*, from *fidelis*, faithful, from *fides*, faith, cogn. with G. πείθεσθαι, to trust.

fidget. Earlier *fidge*, synon. with obs. *fike*, *fig*, ME. *fiken*, to hasten; cf. Ger. *ficken*, to move restlessly; but the relation of these words is obscure. See *fickle*.

Wha can do nought but fike an' fumble (Burns).

fidibus. Paper spill. Ger. student slang (17 cent.), perh. allusive to Horace (v.i.). Another conjecture is that the invitations to students' gatherings, addressed *Fid. Fbus.* (*fidelibus fratribus*), were used as pipe-lights. For a similar formation cf. *circumbendibus*.

Et thure et fidibus juvat
   Placare, et vituli sanguine debito,
Custodes Numidae deos (Hor. *Odes*, i. 36).

fiduciary [*leg.*]. L. *fiduciarius*, from *fiducia*, trust, from *fides*.

fie. Imit. of disgust at smell. Cf. F. *fi*, L. *fi*, *phu*, ON. *fȳ*, Ger. *pfui*. *Fie on*, earlier also *of*, reproduces F. *fi de*.

fief. F., Carolingian L. *fevum*, OHG. *fehu*. See *fee*, *feud²*.

field. AS. *feld*; cf. Du. *veld*, Ger. *feld*; cogn. with AS. *folde*, earth, ON. *fold*, grass-land. Orig. open land, esp. when tilled. Extended meanings agree with those of Ger. *feld*, F. *champ*. Fig. senses usu. in connection with *battle-field*. Collect. use for all engaged in a sport, or, in racing, all horses bar the favourite, is 18 cent. A *fair field and no favour* is mod. and app. also from sport. For *field-cornet* (SAfrDu.) see *cornet²*. *Field-grey*, German soldier, translates Ger. *feldgrau*, colour of uniform, "service grey" (cf. *red-coat*, *blue-jacket*). For some mil. senses cf. *campaign*. See also *camp*.

fieldfare. ME. *feldefare* (3 sylls.), AS. **feldefare* (miswritten *feldewar* in *Voc.*). Associated with *field* and *fare*, to travel, but real origin very doubtful. AS. *fealafor* is app. from *fealo*, fallow, alluding to colour, or to fallow land; cf. AS. *clodhamer*, another name for the fieldfare. Though *fealafor* is not applied in AS. to the fieldfare, but to other birds, it may have changed its meaning, as bird-names are often very vague (cf. *albatross*, *penguin*, *grouse*).

grive: the great thrush called a fieldfare, or feldifare (Cotg.).

fiend. AS. *fēond*. Com. Teut.; cf. Du. *vijand*, Ger. *feind*, ON. *fjǎnde*, Goth. *fijands*. Orig. pres. part. of *fēogan*, to hate. For formation cf. *friend*. Already in AS. applied to Satan, the gen. sense, preserved in Ger. *feind*, being taken by cogn. *foe* and borrowed *enemy*.

fierce. OF. *fiers*, nom. of *fier*, proud, valiant, L. *ferus*, wild (see *feral²*). The unusual survival of the nom. is due to its common use as an epithet of the subject.

fieri facias [*leg.*]. L., cause it to be done, in sheriff's writ. Cf. *habeas corpus*, *venire facias*.

fiery. See *fire*.

fife. Ger. *pfeife*. See *pipe*, and cf. F. *fifre*, piper, Ger. *pfeifer*. Many Ger. musicians are found at E. court in 15–16 cents. Hence *fife-rail* (naut.); see *fiddley*.

Forthwith came a French man being a phipher, in a litle boate, playing on his phiph the tune of the Prince of Orenge his song (Hakl. x. 129).

Fifteen [*hist.*]. Jacobite rising of 1715. Cf. *Forty-five*.

fifth monarchy. Last of five empires prophesied by Daniel (ii. 44). In 17 cent. associated with millennium, hence *fifth-monarchy-man*, anarchist zealot.

fig¹. Fruit. F. *figue*, Prov. *figa*, VL. **fica*, for *ficus*. From latter come AS. *fīc*, OF. *fi*, It. *fico*, Sp. *higo*. Cf. Ger. *feige*, Du. *vijg*, from Prov. or It. *A fig for* is imitated from similar use of It. *fico*, the word being used in its secondary (and obscene) sense. Spec. use of *fig-leaf* dates from Garden of Eden.

A fico for the phrase (*Merry Wives*, i. 3).

fig² [*slang*]. Dress. For obs. *feague* (see *fake*). Hence to *fig out*, *full fig*, the latter prob. also associated with *figure*.

fight. AS. *feohtan*; cf. Du. *vechten*, Ger. *fechten*. To *show fight*, *fight shy*, are both prob. from the prize-ring or cock-fighting. To *fight aloof* was formerly used for the latter.

figment. L. *figmentum*, from *fig-*, root of *fingere*, to fashion. Cf. *fiction*.

figurant. F., It. *figurante*. See *figure*.

figure. F., L. *figura*, form, shape, from *fig-*, root of *fingere*, to fashion; cf. It. Sp. *figura*. Philos. & scient. senses are due to L. *figura* being used to render G. σχῆμα; but sense of numerical symbol is esp. E. To *cut* (earlier *make*) *a figure* is after F. *faire figure*. Fig. use of naut. *figure-head* is late 19 cent.

figurine. F., It. *figurina*, dim. of *figura*.

figwort. Supposed to cure the *fig*, pop. name for piles, from *fig¹*; cf. *pile-wort*.

filacer [*leg.*]. Filer of writs, from obs. *filace*, *file²* (q.v.).

filament. F., Late L. *filamentum*, from *filum*, thread.

filbert. AF. *philbert*, ME. *philliberd* (Gower), because ripe about *St Philibert's Day* (Aug. 22). Cf. Ger. *Lambertsnuss*, filbert, prob. Lombardy nut (cf. *walnut*), but associated with *St Lambert* (Sep. 17); cf. also Ger. *Johannisbeere*, red currant (*St John's Day*, June 24), and see *jenneting*. *Noix de filbert* is the Norm. name. The Saint's name is OHG. *Filu-berht*, very bright.

filch. Thieves' slang (16 cent.). *File* occurs in same sense; ? cf. F. *filou*, pickpocket, *filouter*, to filch.

file¹. Tool. Mercian form *fīl* of AS. *fēol*; cf. Du. *vijl*, Ger. *feile*.

file². For papers. F. *fil*, thread, L. *filum*. Cf. AF. *afiler*, to file.

file: is a threed or wyer, whereon writs...are fastened for the more safe keeping of them (Cowel).

file³. Of soldiers. F., from *filer*, to spin out, arrange one behind another, L. *filare*, from *filum* (v.s.). Hence *rank and file*, body of men measured lengthways and depthways, *Indian file*, one treading in the footsteps of the other.

file: the strait line soldiers make that stand one before another, which is the depth of the batallion or squadron, and thus distinguish'd from the *rank*, where the men stand side by side, and make the length of the batalion or squadron (*Mil. Dict.* 1708).

file⁴ [*archaic*]. Defile¹ (q.v.). Echo of *Macb.* iii. 1.

file⁵. As used by the Artful Dodger (*Oliver Twist*, ch. xliii.), may be ME. *file*, fellow, wench, F. *fille*. For double sex cf. *harlot*. See also *filch*.

filemot, philamot. Colour. Corrupt. of *feuille-morte* (q.v.).

filial. Late L. *filialis*, from *filius*, son; cf. *filiation*. See also *feminine*.

filibeg, philibeg. Highland kilt. Gael. *feileadh*, fold, *beagh*, small. First element perh. from L. *velum*, second appears in names *Begg*, *Baugh*, and cogn. Welsh *Bach*, *Vaughan*.

filibuster. Ult. Du. *vrijbuiter*, freebooter (q.v.), the relation of E. *filibuster*, earlier *flibutor*, F. *flibustier*, earlier *fribustier*, and Sp. *filibustero* being uncertain. For unoriginal -s- cf. *roister*. In US. obstructionist politician, much used Feb. 1917.

flibustiers: West Indian pirates, or buccaneers, freebooters (*Dict. Cant. Crew*).

filic-. From L. *filix, filic-*, fern.

filigrane, filigree. Earlier *filigreen*, F. *filigrane*, It. *filigrana*, from L. *filum*, thread, *granum*, grain, bead.

filioque [*theol.*]. L., and from the Son. Clause in Nicene Creed which separates Eastern Church from Western.

fill. AS. *fyllan*. Aryan (see *full*). Noun *fill*, AS. *fyllo* (cf. Ger. *fülle*), occurs from earliest period only in to *drink* (*have*, etc.) *one's fill*; cf. a *fill* of tobacco. To *fill the bill* is orig. theat., allusive to large letters for the star performer.

fillet. F. *filet*, dim. of *fil*, thread, L. *filum*; cf. It. *filetto*, Sp. *filete*. First E. sense is head-band, partly due to association with *phylactery* (v.i.); then, narrow strip, e.g. of meat.

philett: vitta, phylatorium (*Prompt. Parv.*).

fillibeg. See *filibeg*.

fillip. Imit. of sound and movement. Lengthened form of *flip* (cf. *chirp, chirrup*). Lighter than *flap, flop*.

chiquenaude: a fillip, flirt, or bob given with the finger or naile (Cotg.).

filly. ON. *fylja*, fem. of *foli*, foal (q.v.).

film. AS. *filmen*, membrane, prepuce, cogn. with *fell*[1]; cf. AS. *æger-felma*, skin of egg. Present use (cinema) is from photography.

filoselle. F., It. *filosello*, corrupted, after *filo*, thread, from VL. **follicellus*, for *folliculus*, cocoon, dim. of *follis*, bag. Cf. Mod. Prov. *fousel*, cocoon.

filisello: a kinde of course silke which we call filosetta or flouret silke (Flor.).

filter. F. *filtre*, It. *filtro*, MedL. *filtrum*, felt (q.v.).

feutre: felt; also, a filter; a piece of felt, or thick woollen cloth to distill, or straine things through (Cotg.).

filth. AS. *fÿlth*, from *foul* (q.v.).

fimbria. L., fringe (q.v.).

fin. AS. *finn*; cf. Du. *vin*; cogn. with L. *pinna*, feather, fin.

final. F., L. *finalis*, from *finis*, end. Cf. *finale*, It. adj., orig. of music.

finance. F., from OF. *finer*, to end, settle, from *fin*, L. *finis*. In OF. & ME. esp. ransom, levy (cf. *fine*[1]). Mod. sense also arose first in F. (17–18 cents.), esp. in connection with the tax-farmers or *financiers*.

finch. AS. *finc*. Com. Teut., though not recorded in ON. & Goth.; cf. Du. *vink*, Ger. *fink*, Sw. *fink*, Dan. *finke*. Cogn. with F. *pinson*, It. *pincione*, Welsh *pink*, G. σπίγγος; cf. E. dial. *pink, spink*.

find. AS. *findan*. Com. Teut.; cf. Du. *vinden*, Ger. *finden*, ON. *finna*, Goth. *finthan*. Sense of supply, as in *well-found*, to *find one in*, etc., is very old (v.i.), perh. imitated from AF. use of *trouver*.

Pur povres escolers a l'escole trover et sustenir
(*Will of Lady Clare*, 1355).

And ever mo, un-to that day I dye,
Eterne fir I wol biforn thee fynde
(Chauc. A. 2412, *Arcite's vow to Mars*).

fin de siècle. F., end of century. Much used in the last decade of the 19th century. App. first in title of comedy, *Paris fin de siècle*, produced at the Gymnase, Feb. 1890.

fine[1]. Noun. F. *fin*, end, L. *finis*; cf. It. *fine*, Sp. *fin*. Orig. sense only in *in fine* (cf. F. *enfin*). In MedL. & ME. also final agreement, settlement by payment, etc., whence mod. sense.

fine[2]. Adj. F. *fin*, VL. **finus*, back-formation from *finire*, to finish; cf. It. Sp. *fino*. Borrowed also by all Teut. langs. (e.g. Du. *vijn*, Ger. *fein*). F. has kept orig. sense of delicate, subtle (cf. *finesse*), which survives in our *fine distinction, too fine a point* (see *edge*), *fine-drawn*, lit. invisibly mended, etc. The expression *one of these fine days*, in which the adj. is now purely expletive, has parallels in most Europ. langs.

finesse. F., delicacy, subtlety. See *fine*[2].

finger. AS. *finger*. Com. Teut.; cf. Du. *vinger*, Ger. *finger*, ON. *fingr*, Goth. *figgrs*. To *have a finger in* implies a less active participation than to *have a hand in*. *Finger-print* in crim. sense is not in *NED*. For *finger-stall* see *stall*[1]. *At one's fingers' ends* is allusive to elementary methods of calculation (cf. synon. F. *sur le bout du doigt*).

fyngyr stalle: digitale (*Cath. Angl.*).

fingering. Wool for stockings. Earlier *fingram*, F. *fin grain*. Cf. *grogram, chamfer*.

finial [*arch.*]. E. var. of *final*, suggested by numerous words in *-ial*.

finical. Recorded (1592) earlier than *finikin* (1661), which suggests obs. Du. *fynkens*, "perfectè, exactè ad unguem, concinnè, bellè" (Kil.). In any case ult. from *fine*[2]. *Finick* is back formation.

finis. L., end.

finish. ME. *feniss*, OF. *fenir, feniss-*, L. *finire*, on which it is now respelt, like F. *finir*. Cf. *finite*, L. p.p. *finitus*.

Finn. AS. *Finnas* (pl.); cf. ON. *Finnr*, Sw. Dan. Ger. *Finne*, L. *Fenni* (Tac.), G.

Φίννοι (Ptol.). App. name given by Norsemen to the Suomi (cf. *Lapp*). The lang., non-Aryan, is of the Ural-Altaic, or Finno-Ugrian, group, the latter word, orig. the name of a Baltic tribe, being cogn. with *Hungarian*.

finnan. Haddock. Also *findon*. ? Orig. from river *Findhorn*.

A pile of Findhorn haddocks, that is, haddocks smoked with green wood (*Antiquary*, ch. xxvi.).

fiord. Norw., ON. *fjörthr*. See *firth*. ? Cogn. with *ford*.

fir. ON. *fyra*, usu. *fura*; cf. AS. *furh(-wudu)*, Dan. *fyr*, Ger. *föhre*; cogn. with L. *quercus*, oak.

fire. AS. *fȳr*. WGer.; cf. Du. *vuur*, Ger. *feuer*; cogn. with G. πῦρ and perh. with *pure*. With *fire-dog* cf. F. *chenet*, dim. of *chien*. With *fire and sword* cf. F. *fer et flamme*, "yron and fyre" in Grafton's *Chron*. *Fiery cross* was earlier *fire-cross*, rendering Gael. *cros-t'araidh*, cross of gathering, burnt at one end and dipped in blood at the other as symbol of fire and sword. The *firelock* (wheel-lock, flintlock) superseded (16 cent.) the *matchlock* (see *lock²*). *Firework* was formerly a mil. term, hence the rank of *lieutenant fire-worker* (Kipling, *Tomb of his Ancestors*). To *fire*, dismiss, is a US. witticism for *discharge*. *Firebrand*, incendiary, trouble-raiser, is 16 cent.

firkin. Fourth part of barrel (*John*, ii. 6). Earlier (15 cent.) *ferdekyn*, app. an E. formation on Du. *vierde*, fourth, after earlier *kilderkin* (q.v.). Cf. F. *frequin*, quarter-barrel (of oil, sugar), from Du. or E.

firm. Restored from ME. *ferm*, F. *ferme*, L. *firmus*. As noun, orig. signature; then, title of business. This is Sp. It. *firma*, from L. *firmare*, to confirm, ratify (see *farm*). A *long firm* is prob. so called from choosing its victims at a distance.

firma: a firme of the hand; signatio (Percyvall).

firmament. L. *firmamentum*, from *firmare*, to make firm, used in *Vulg.* to render G. στερέωμα, from στερεός, firm, solid, by which the LXX. translated the Heb. original, prob. meaning expanse.

firman. Pers. *fermān*, command, edict; cf. Sanskrit *pramāna*. By early voyagers app. confused with *firma* (see *firm*).

firn [*Alp.*]. Last year's snow, névé. Ger.; cf. OHG. *firni*, old, cogn. with AS. *fyrn* (in ME. of last year), Goth. *fairneis*.

first. AS. *fyrest*, superl. of *fore* (q.v.); cf. Du.

vorst, Ger. *fürst*, prince (OHG. *furisto*, first), ON. *fyrstr*. See *former*, *foremost*. *First-class* is from the universities via the railways, *first-rate* is from the navy. For hist. *first-fruits*, translating L. *primitiae*, see *annates*.

firth, frith. ON. *fjörthr* (see *fiord*). Introduced into E. from Sc. c. 1600, prob. because associated by scholars with the unrelated L. *fretum*.

The strait or freat of Magellan (Purch.).

fiscal. F., Late L. *fiscalis*, from *fiscus*, fisc, imperial treasury, orig. rush-basket, purse; cf. hist. of *budget*.

fish¹. Noun. AS. *fisc*. Com. Teut.; cf. Du. *visch*, Ger. *fisch*, ON. *fiskr* (whence name *Fisk*), Goth. *fisks*; cogn. with L. *piscis*, OIr. *iasc*. The word belongs to the same Aryan race-groups as L. *mare*, sea, "mere." Use for person, with adj. (*cool, odd, queer*, etc.), no doubt arose among anglers. *Neither fish, flesh, nor good red herring*, with vars., occurs in 16 cent (see 1 *Hen. IV*, iii. 3), and corresponding phrases are found in F., Ger., Scand. *A pretty kettle of fish* (Richardson, Fielding) may allude to Sc. *kettle of fish*, used of a picnic; cf. ironical use of *picnic* almost in same sense, e.g. *here's a pretty picnic, I don't think*. Or perhaps it is merely an elaboration of *pretty mess* (q.v.). *Fishy*, dubious, shady, alludes to intrusive taste or smell from fish. With *fishwife*, famed for rhetoric, cf. similar use of F. *harengère*, herring woman, and see *Billingsgate*.

fish² [*naut.*]. Piece of wood used to strengthen mast; cf. to *fish* a mast, *fish-plate* (railway). Perh. ident. with *fish¹* and due to some mysterious naut. metaphor. But cf. F. *fiche*, a rag-bolt (Lesc.), from *ficher*, to fix, which may have been adopted by E. sailors in an altered sense (cf. *painter, tack*, etc.). To *fish the anchor*, first quoted by *NED.* from Falc., is 15 cent. (v.i.). In sense of peg the same word has given archaic *fish*, counter at cards, often with punning allusion to the *pool²* (q.v.).

Hokes of yron to fysshe ankers with
  (*Nav. Accts.* 1495–97).

Fisher [*neol.*]. Treasury note signed by *Sir Warren Fisher*, replacing (Oct. 1919) the earlier *Bradbury*.

fishgig. See *fizgig*.

fissure. F., L. *fissura*, from *findere*, *fiss-*, to split, ult. cogn. with *bite*.

fist. AS. *fȳst*. WGer.; cf. Du. *vuist*, Ger. *faust*. *Fisticuff*, from *cuff²*, is for earlier *handicuff*, the latter suggested by *handiwork*. Quot. 1 is an early example of the slang sense of handwriting.

A fair hand!
Yea, it is a good running fist (*Mankind*, c. 1475).

And witness'd their divine perfections
By handy-cuffs and maledictions
(Ward, *Hudibras Rediv.* 1715).

fistula. L., pipe, flute, replacing earlier *fistle*; cf. *fester*.

fit¹ [*archaic*]. Division of poem. AS. *fitt*. Cf. latinized OSax. *vittea* in preface to the *Heliand*. Perh. cogn. with Ger. *fitze*, OHG. *fizza*, fixed numbers of threads of yarn, counted and made into skein.

The Hunting of the Snark; an agony in ten fits
(Lewis Carroll).

fit². Paroxysm. AS. *fitt*, conflict (only in Caedmon). In ME. position of hardship, fanciful experience. From 16 cent. paroxysm, etc. Hence *by fits* (*and starts*), etc. *Fitful*, a favourite word with 19 cent. poets, is due to solitary occurrence in Shaks., *life's fitful fever* (*Macb.* iii. 2).

fit³. Suitable, etc. First found 1440 (v.i.). Hence verb (16 cent.), and later noun, e.g. *a good fit*. ME. *fit*, to array troops, only in *Morte Arthure* (c. 1400), may be the same word. In ref. to clothes, etc., partly due to common misprinting of *sit* (*ſit*), to become, as in *the coat sits well*. Origin obscure, main sense app. due to ME. *fete*, adapted (see *feat*), e.g. *Fit for treasons, stratagems and spoils* (*Merch. of Ven.* v.) exactly represents L. *factus ad*. For *-it* cf. *benefit*.

ffytte, or *mete*: equus, congruus (*Prompt. Parv.*).

My garments sit upon me much feater than before
(*Temp.* ii. 1).

fitch¹. For *vetch* (*Is.* xxviii. 25).

fitch², fitchew. Polecat, its hair, etc. OF. *fissel, fissau*, dim. of word found in obs. Du. as *fisse, visse*, prob. from ON. *físa*, to stink.

fissau: a fitch, or fulmart (Cotg.).

fitful. See *fit²*.

Fitz. AF. *fiz*, F. *fils*, L. *filius*. Used regularly in all offic. rolls compiled in AF., its survival in mod. names being a matter of chance.

five. AS. *fif*. Aryan; cf. Du. *vijf*, Ger. *fünf* (OHG. *finf*), ON. *fimm*, Goth. *fimf*, L. *quinque*, G. πέντε, πέμπε, Sanskrit *pañca*, OWelsh *pimp*, etc. E. has lost the nasal before the spirant as in *other*. With game

of *fives* cf. pugil. *bunch of fives*, fist, and F. *jeu de paume* (palm), orig. hand-tennis; but the game is app. much older than the pugil. witticism.

fix. From L. *figere, fix-*; cf. F. *fixer*, It. *fissare*. Much used in US., esp. *fixings*, adjuncts of any kind. *Fix*, predicament, is also US. *Fixture*, for *fixure*, L. *fixura*, is due to *mixture*.

fizgig. In various senses, from *fizz* and *gig¹* (q.v.). In sense of harpoon, corruptly *fishgig*, from Sp. Port. *fisga*, from *fisgar*, "to catch fish with a speare" (Minsh.), ? VL. **fixicare*; cf. *gig²*.

fizz. Imit., cf. *fizzle*.

fizzle. Orig. sine fragore pedere; cf. ON. *físa*, pedere, whence obs. E. *fise, fist*, in same sense. To *fizzle out* is orig. of a wet firework, etc. ? Cf. to *peter out*.

flabbergast. Quoted as new slang word in *Annual Register* (1772). Arbitrary formation on *flap* or *flabby* and *aghast*; cf. dial. *boldacious* (bold × audacious).

flabby. For earlier *flappy*, with suggestion of increased languor.

impassire: to grow flappy, withered, or wrimpled
(Flor.).

flabell-. From VL. **flabellum*, fan, from *flare*, to blow.

flaccid. L. *flaccidus*, from *flaccus*, flabby, "having hanging eares" (Coop.). Hence Horace's cognomen.

flacon. F., see *flagon*.

flag¹. Plant. ME. *flagge, flegge*; cf. Dan. *flæg*, Du. *flag*. Perh. connected with *flay* (q.v.), to cut; cf. L. *gladiolus*, Ger. *schwertlilie*, sword lily, and hist. of *sedge* (q.v.).

fflegge: idem quod *segge* (*Prompt. Parv.*).

flag². Banner, to droop. Both appear in 16 cent. and are prob. of imit. origin; cf. *flap, flacker*, etc. There has also been association with *fag²*, e.g. "the flagg or the fagg federis (of a hawk)" (*Book of St Albans*, 1486), and, in the case of the verb, with OF. *flaque*, flaccid. *Flag*, banner, esp. naut., has been adopted into all Teut. langs., but is app. of E. origin.

flag³. Stone. Orig. slice of turf, etc., as still in EAngl. ON. *flag*, spot where a turf has been cut, *flaga*, slab of stone; cf. *flake*, *flaw, flay*, and *flag¹*.

fflagge off the erth: terricidium, cespes
(*Prompt. Parv.*).

flagellant. From pres. part. of L. *flagellare*, from *flagellum*, dim. of *flagrum*, scourge. The sect of *Flagellants* appeared in 13 cent.

flageolet[1]. Musical instrument. F., dim. of OF. *flageol, flajol*, Prov. *flaujol*. Origin unknown, but ult. connection with *flute* and L. *flare*, to blow, seems likely.

flageolet[2]. Kidney-bean. Corrupted F. dim. of *faséole*, L. *phaseolus*, from *phaselus*, G. φάσηλος; cf. It. *fagiolo*.

faseoles: fasels, long peason, kidney beanes (Cotg.).

flagitate. From L. *flagitare*, to demand urgently, prob. cogn. with next word, though the connection is obscure.

flagitious. L. *flagitiosus*, from *flagitium*, crime.

flagon. ME. *flakon*, F. *flacon*, OF. *flascon*; cf. Late L. *flasco-n-*. See *flask*.

flagrant. From pres. part. of L. *flagrare*, to burn. With *flagrant offence*, "flaming into notice" (Johns.), cf. *burning shame*. See also *delict*.

flail. OF. *flaiel* (*fléau*), L. *flagellum*, scourge; cf. It. *fragello*, Sp. *flagelo*. Replaced AS. *fligel*, from L.; cf. Du. *vlegel*, Ger. *flegel*, also from L. It seems curious that the Teut. races should have borrowed so simple an instrument from Rome, but app. they trod their corn (see *thrash*) before they learnt from the Romans.

flair. F., scent (of hound), from *flairer*, to scent, VL. **flagrare*, by dissim. from *fragrare*. See *fragrant*.

flake. First of snow (Chauc.). Cf. ON. *floke*, flock of wool, Ger. *flocke* (OHG. *flohho*), flock of wool, flake of snow, both prob. from L. *floccus* (see *flock*[2]); so also F. *floc*, flock of wool, *flocon*, snow-flake. This early loan of the Teut. langs. from L. is prob. due to the importation of feathers, down and geese from the north under the Roman Empire; cf. *pillow* and Ger. *flaum*, down, L. *pluma*. Other senses of *flake* suggest connection with *flay* (q.v.) or with Du. *vlak*, flat. Prob. several distinct words are represented.

The old woman's plucking her geese
And selling the feathers a penny a piece
(Child's snow-storm rime).

flam, flim-flam. Humbug. Prob. *flam* is the older; cf. *fible-fable* in same sense, and see *reduplication*. *Flam* may be short for *flamfew* (Sc.), trifle, gew-gaw, OF. *fanfelue* (*fanfreluche*), MedL. *fanfaluca*, bubble, G. πομφόλυξ.

riote: a flimflam, idle discourse, tale of a tub (Cotg.).

flam: a trick, or sham-story (*Dict. Cant. Crew*).

flambeau. F., dim. of *flambe*, flame. Cf.

flamboyant, orig. arch., with flame-like tracery.

flame. OF. (*flambe, flamme*), L. *flamma*, ? cogn. with *flagrare*, to burn, ? or with *flare*, to blow. Early applied to love, but mod. half-jocular use (*an old flame*) is prob. direct from 17 cent. F., *flamme* and *âme* riming in the F. classics almost as regularly as *herz* and *schmerz* in Ger. lyric. The adoption of the word in Teut. (Du. *vlam*, Ger. *flamme*) is curious. The Teut. name is represented by AS. *līeg*, Ger. *lohe*, cogn. with L. *lux, luc-*, light.

flamen. L., priest, of obscure origin.

flamingo. Sp. *flamenco* or Port. *flamengo*, lit. Fleming, the choice of the name being due either to a kind of pun on *flame* or to the medieval reputation of the Flemings for bright dress and florid complexion (Cervantes); cf. Prov. *flamenc*, F. *flamant*, the latter with suffix substitution as in *Flamand*, Fleming.

Un phœnicoptere qui en Languedoc est appelé flammant (Rab. i. 37).

flamenco: a fleming, a kinde of birde like a shoveler; Belga (Percyvall).

flammenwerfer [*hist.*]. Ger., flame-thrower, a Kultur-word from 1915. See *flame, warp*.

flanconnade [*fenc.*]. F., side-thrust, from *flanc*, flank.

flange. Also *flanch*. App. connected with OF. *flanche*, fem. form of *flanc*, side. ? Or from OF. *flangir*, mod. dial. *flancher*, to bend, turn, which is of Teut. origin and ult. cogn. with *flank*.

Creeping along rocky flanges that overlooked awful precipices (O. Henry).

flank. F. *flanc*, OHG. *hlancha*, hip, cogn. with AS. *hlanc*, lank, slender. For change of init. *h-* to *f-* cf. *frock* (q.v.) and OF. epic hero *Floovent*, OHG. *Hlodowing*. In E. chiefly mil.

flannel. Earlier (16 cent.) also *flannen*, which is prob. the orig. form. Welsh *gwlanen*, from *gwlân*, wool. Adopted in most Europ. langs. For *flannelette* cf. *velveteen, satinette*, etc.

flap. Imit., a sound or motion half-way between the lighter *flip* and the heavier *flop*. Hence pendant portion of any object. Mod. sense of *flapper* is perh. due to earlier application to young wild-duck or partridge. Cf. Ger. *backfisch* in same sense. With *flapdoodle*, arbitrary coinage, cf. obs. *fadoodle* (17 cent.).

Looking through the cookery-book, under the

heading "game," I found flappers. I hadn't the least little bit of an idea what sort of game they were. So I inquired of a shooting-man, who told me that flappers were "little ducks"

(Ellen Terry, *Sunday Evening Telegram*, Nov. 11, 1917).

flare. Earlier (16 cent.) *flear*. Orig. to flutter, flicker, later sense influenced by *glare*, ? or by Prov. *flar*, large, flickering flame, from L. *flagrare*. App. a cant word and hence prob. Du. or LG. Cf. Ger. *flattern, fladdern*, Du. *vlederen*, the latter perh. the source of our word, with loss of *-d-*, common in Du. words. Cogn. with *flitter, flutter*.

Ribands pendant, flaring 'bout her head
(*Merry Wives*, iv. 6).

flare: to shine or glare like a comet or beacon
(*Dict. Cant. Crew*).

das fladdern eines lichtes: the flaring of a candle
(Ludw.).

flash. Orig. (14 cent.) to dash, splash, etc., later application to light being partly due to association with *flame*. Of imit. origin, combining the *fl-* of rapid motion with the *-sh* of sound; cf. *flush*[1,2]. Slang uses, e.g. *flash cove*, etc., may spring from 17 cent. sense of show, ostentation. Cf. the *flash* of the Royal Welsh Fusiliers, said to replace the tie-bow of the pig-tail, which they were the last regiment to wear. *Flash in the pan* is from old-fashioned firearm in which the priming sometimes flashed in the "pan" without igniting the charge; cf. F. *coup raté*, lit. and fig.

flask. Adapted (16–17 cent.) from archaic F. *flasque*, for powder, It. *fiasco*, for wine. Also in Teut. langs., e.g. AS. *flasce*, Du. *flesch*, Ger. *flasche*, but in E. early replaced by *bottle*. Earliest forms are Late L. *flasco-n-* (see *flagon*) and *flasca*. An early loan-word in Teut. connected with Roman wine trade. Origin unknown.

Vasa lignea quae vulgo "flascones" vocantur
(Gregory of Tours, c. 600).

flat. ON. *flatr*, smooth, level, whence Sw. *flat*, Dan. *flad*; cogn. with OHG. *flaz*, whence *flazza*, flat of the hand. Said to be unrelated to *plate* (q.v.), which, considering its correspondence in sense with F. *plat*, is hard to believe. Fig. senses via that of smooth, plain, monotonous. *Flat*, floor, dwelling, is of recent introduction from Sc., and was spelt *flet* up to 18 cent. It is AS. *flett*, floor, dwelling, cogn. with above; cf. OSax. *fletti*, OHG. *flazzi*, in same sense. Slang *flat*, greenhorn, is a punning contrast with *sharp*.

flatter. From F. *flatter*, orig. to smooth, from Teut. (v.s.), combining prob. with an E. formation of the *flitter, flutter* type, meaning to caress.

flatulent. F., ModL. *flatulentus*, from *flatus*, from *flare*, to blow.

flaunt. Very common in late 16 cent. in ref. to waving plumes, flags, etc., esp. in phrase *flaunt-a-flaunt*. Origin obscure; ? nasalized from Ger. *flattern* (see *flare*).

flaunting: tearing-fine: to flaunt it: to spark it, or gallant it (*Dict. Cant. Crew*).

flautist. It. *flautista*, from *flauto*, flute.

Flavian amphitheatre. The Coliseum, built by Vespasian, first of the Flavian Emperors.

flavine. New antiseptic, discovered and named (1917) by Dr C. Browning. From *flavin*, yellow dye belonging to acridine series, from L. *flavus*, yellow.

flavour. In ME. smell. OF. *flaor, fleor* (cf. early Sc. *fleore, fleure*, etc.), with *-v-* inserted, perh. by analogy with *savour*, its later synonym. Or perh. from early OF. *flathor, with change of consonant as in *gyve, savory*. App. Late L. *flator-em, from *flare*, to blow, whence obs. It. *fiatore*, stench. Cf. F. *fleurer*, to smell.

The flewer of the fresh herring (Henryson).

Il fleurait bien plus fort, mais non pas mieux que roses (Regnier).

flaw. In ME. flake, with which it is cogn.; later, fissure, imperfection. Prob. Scand.; cf. Sw., Norw. dial. *flaga* in similar senses. See *flag*[3]. *Flaw*, gust of wind or rain, is app. of same origin; cf. Sw. *flaga*, Du. *vlaag*.

vlage: sudden flash of raine (Hexham).

flawn [*archaic*]. Pancake, etc. F. *flan* (OF. *flaon*), MedL. *flado-n-*, OHG. *flado* (*fladen*), flat cake, whence also It. *fiadone*. Ult. cogn. with *flat*. Also Du. *vlade* and ME. *flathe*, whence surname *Flather*.

fiadone: a kind of flawne, egge-pie, doucet or custard (Flor.).

flax. AS. *fleax*. WGer.; cf. Du. *vlas*, Ger. *flachs*; ? cogn. with L. *plectere*, to weave, G. πλέκειν.

flay. AS. *flēan*; cf. obs. Du. *vlaen, vlaeghen*, ON. *flā*; cogn. with *flag*[3], *flaw*, and (some senses of) *flake*.

vlaeghen, vlaen: deglubere (Kil.).

flea. AS. *flēa*. Com. Teut.; cf. Du. *vloo*, Ger. *floh*, ON. *flō*; cogn. with *flee*. *Flea-bitten*, "white spotted all over with sad reddish spots" (*Dict. Rust.* 1717), is 16 cent. *Flea* *in the ear* is found also in F. & Ger., but in somewhat different sense.

> He standeth now as he had a flea in his ear
> (Heywood, *Proverbs*, 1562).

fleam. Vet.'s lancet. OF. *flieme* (*flamme*), Late L. *flebotomum* (see *phlebotomy*); cf. Du. *vlijm*, Ger. *fliete* (OHG. *flietuma*). An early med. word found in most Europ. langs.

flèche. Term in fort., spire. F. *flèche*, arrow, prob. Celt.

fleck. First in p.p. *flecked*, parti-coloured (*Piers Plowm.* and Chauc.). ON. *flekkr*, spot; cf. Du. *vlek*, Ger. *fleck*, spot; these also topogr., place, hamlet.

fledge. Orig. adj., ready to fly. Kentish form of AS. *flycge*, only recorded in *unfligge*, unfledged. WGer.; cf. Du. *vlug*, Ger. *flügge*, a LG. form for HG. *flick, flück*; cogn. with *fly*.

flee. AS. *flēon*. Com. Teut.; cf. Du. *vlieden* (earlier *vlieen*), Ger. *fliehen*, ON. *flȳa*, Goth. *thliuhan*. The Goth. init. points to Teut. *thl-* and hence an origin quite distinct from *fly* (q.v.), but the verbs were already confused in AS. The strong inflexions (cf. Ger. *floh, geflohen*) were replaced in ME. by the weak *fled*.

fleece. AS. *flēos*. WGer.; cf. Du. *vlies*, Ger. *vliess*; prob. cogn. with L. *pluma*. The *Golden Fleece* (Austria & Spain) was instituted at Bruges (1430) by Philip the Good, Duke of Burgundy. Verb to *fleece* does not appear to have ever been used in other than fig. sense.

fleer. To deride, etc. Gen. associated in use with *jeer, leer, sneer*. ? Scand.; cf. Norw. *flire*, to grin. ? Or ident. with Du. *fleer*, blow on the face (cf. sense-development of *gird* [2]).

> She has spat on the ancient chivalries of battle; she has fleered at the decent amenities of diplomacy (S. Coleridge in *Sat. Rev.* Dec. 8, 1917).

fleet[1] [*naut.*]. AS. *flēot*, ship, cogn. with *fleet*[4]; cf. Ger. *floss*, raft. For collect. sense cf. converse case of F. *navire*, ship, in OF. fleet. In 16 cent. usu. *flote*, after F. *flotte*, from Teut.

fleet[2]. Creek, brook. Common in place-names. AS. *flēot*, cogn. with *fleet*[4]; cf. Du. *vliet*. Hence the *Fleet* prison, standing near the *Fleet* brook or ditch, which flows into Thames near Ludgate Hill. In 18 cent. this was frequented by disreputable parsons prepared to marry people without inquiry. Hence *Fleet marriage*.

> *flete a prisone for gentylmen*: consergerie (Palsg.).

fleet[3]. Adj. ON. *fljōtr*, swift, cogn. with *fleet*[4].

fleet[4]. Verb. AS. *flēotan*, to float, drift. Com. Teut.; cf. Du. *vlieten*, Ger. *fliessen*, to flow, ON. *fliōta*; cogn. with L. *pluere*, to rain, G. πλεῖν, to sail. Hardly in mod. use exc. in adj. *fleeting*.

Flemish. Du. *vlaamsch* (earlier *vlaemisch*), of Flanders. In several naut. terms, e.g. *flemish coil*. The lang. is Du.

flench, flense, flinch. To strip blubber from dead whale. Dan. *flense*.

> A dog-toothed laugh laughed Reuben Paine, and bared his flenching-knife
> (Kipling, *Three Sealers*).

flesh. AS. *flǣsc*. WGer.; cf. Du. *vleesch*, Ger. *fleisch*. ON. *flesk* is swine's flesh only, which may have been orig. meaning; ? cf. *flitch*. In food sense, replaced, exc. in dial., by *meat*. With to *flesh one's sword* cf. earlier to *flesh* (also to *blood*) *hounds, hawks*, used like F. *acharner* (from L. *ad carnem*). *Fleshpot*, as emblem of physical well-being, is after *Ex.* xvi. 3.

> *He his fleshed and accustomed to kyll men lyke shepe*: il est aschayrné... (Palsg.).

fletcher [*hist.*]. Arrow-smith. OF. *flechier* (see *flèche*). The *Fletchers* are still one of the City Livery Companies.

fleur-de-lis. Earlier *flower de luce*. Sing. of F. *fleurs de lis*, flowers of lilies, where *lis* is OF. pl. of *lil*, L. *lilium*. As emblem in royal arms of France perh. orig. a spear or sceptre-head.

fleury, flory [*her.*]. F. *fleuré*, tipped with *fleurs-de-lis*.

flews. Hanging chaps of hound. Origin unknown.

flex [*neol.*]. Covered wire connecting electric lamp. L. *flexus* (v.i.).

flexible. F., L. *flexibilis*, from *flectere, flex-*, to bend.

flibbertigibbet. ? Imit. of chattering. Earlier also *flibbergib* (Latimer). According to Harsnet (1603) *Fraleretto, Fliberdigibet, Hoberdidance, Tocobatto* were four devils of the morris-dance (see *Lear*, iv. 1). The name may contain an allusion to *gibbet* and be of the *gallows-bird* type.

flick. Imit.; cf. F. *flic, flicflac*.

flicker. AS. *flicerian*, imit. of a lighter movement than dial. *flacker*. Orig. of birds, to flutter, mod. sense being rare before 19 cent.

> Above hir heed hir dowves flikerynge
> (Chauc. A. 1962).

flight. AS. *flyht*, from *fly* (q.v.), also from *flee* (q.v.), early confused. Cf. Du. *vlugt* in both senses, while Ger. distinguishes *flug* (fly) and *flucht* (flee). With *flighty* cf. *volatile*.

flimsy. ? From *flimflam*, with ending as in *tipsy*. Later senses suggest association with *film*. App. a cant word. But Spurrell has Welsh *llymsi* in same sense, app. a genuine old Welsh word (cf. *flummery* for init. *fl-*). Example below is a little earlier than *NED*.

flimsy: flabby, not firm, sound, or solid
(*Dict. Cant. Crew*).

flinch[1]. To give way. Earlier *flench*, nasalized form of ME. *flecche*, OF. *fleschier* (replaced by *fléchir*), ? VL. **flexicare*, from L. *flectere*, *flex-*, to bend.

flinch[2]. See *flench*.

flinders. Splinters. Also *flitters*. Cf. Norw. dial. *flinter*, Du. *flenter*, Ger. *flinder*, *flitter*; perh. cogn. with *flint*, used of splinter of stone. Almost always with *fly*.

The tough ash spear, so stout and true,
Into a thousand flinders flew (*Lay*, iii. 7).

fling. Cf. ON. *flengja*; but, as this is weak only, the E. verb supposes a strong **flinga*, of which *flengja* would be the regular causal. The ME. intrans. sense appears in to *fling out* (in a passion), also in *Highland fling*, to *have* (earlier *take*) *one's fling*. *Far-flung* is due to Kipling's *far-flung battle-line* (*Recessional*).

flint. AS. *flint*; cf. obs. Du. *vlint*, OHG. *flins*, Du. *flint*, Sw. *flinta*; ? cogn. with G. πλίνθος, tile, and ult. with *splint*. With Ger. *flinte*, musket, flintlock (from Du.), cf. *petronel*.

flip[1]. Light blow. See *fillip*, *flap*, *flop*. Of these *flap* is prob. the first in date. With *flipper*, of seal, cf. *flapper*, of turtle. Also in redupl. *flip-flap*, *flipperty-flapperty*.

flip[2]. As in *egg-flip*. App. a sailors' word. Perh. for *Philip*. The example below suggests a curious parallel to *grog*.

flip: sea drink, of small beer (chiefly) and brandy, sweetnd and spiced upon occasion: a kan of Sir Clously [Admiral Sir Cloudesley Shovel †1707], is among the tars, a kan of choice flip, with a lemon squeez'd in, and the pill hung round
(*Dict. Cant. Crew*).

flippant. Orig. nimble, alert, as still in dial. App. from verb to *flip*, with suffix perh. adopted from the *-ant* of heraldry (*couchant*, *trippant*, etc.). Cf. *blatant*.

flirt. In 16–17 cents. used of a slight blow, jerk (cf. to *flirt a fan*); hence, jest, gibe.

App. of imit. origin, with LG. parallels. Applied to a person, often spelt *flurt*, it had a much stronger sense than now. In its latest development (18 cent. in *NED*.) influenced by OF. *fleureter*, "slightly to run, lightly to passe over; only to touch a thing in going by it (metaphorically from the little bees nimble skipping from flower to flower as she feeds)" (Cotg.). For the phonetics cf. *flurt*, obs. form of *floret* (*ferret*[2]), and *cross flurt* for *croix fleuretée* (her.). Quot. 5 is much earlier than *NED*. records of the verb in current sense.

Diogenes flurting at [Mont. hochant du nez] Alexander (Florio's *Montaigne*).

hocher du nez: disdainfully to snuffe at (Cotg.).

bagasse: a baggage, queane, jyll, punke, flirt (Cotg.).

Do not flirt, or fly from one thing to another
(*NED*. 1707).

I am sure he will come up to[o] with her, and the riding, flawning [? = flaunting], roysting and flortting by the way will be sutche as every ostelor will talk of it (*Wollaton MSS*, c. 1615).

flit. ON. *flytja*, cogn. with *fleet*[4]. Orig. also trans., to remove. *Moonlight flitting* is from spec. Sc. use of *flit*, which is, however, old in E.

I will flitt at this next Mighelmas
(*Plumpton Let.* 1504).

flitch. AS. *flicce*; cf. ON. *flikke*, whence F. *flèche*. See also *Dunmow*, whose famous *flitch* is mentioned in *Piers Plowm*.

flitter. See *flinders*.

flittermouse [*dial.*]. Bat. Cf. Du. *vledermuis*, *vleermuis*, Ger. *fledermaus*; cogn. with *flit*, *flutter*, *flare*.

float. AS. *flotian*, cogn. with *fleet*[4] and ON. *flota*; cf. Du. *vlot*, Ger. *floss*, raft. Influenced by synon. F. *flotter*, which is L. *fluctuare*, from *fluctus*, wave, affected by ON. *flota*. With to *float a company* cf. to *launch an enterprise*.

flocculent. See *flock*[2].

flock[1]. Of sheep. AS. *flocc*, herd, body of men; cf. ON. *flokkr*. Not found in other Teut. langs. ? Cogn. with Teut. *folk*, whence OF. *folc*, *fouc*, herd, multitude, etc.

flock[2]. Of wool. F. *floc*, L. *floccus*. See *flake*.

floe. First used by Arctic explorers c. 1800. App. connected with ON. *flō*, layer, expanse, whence Norw. *flo*, layer, stratum, but exact source doubtful. Dan. *flage*, floe, should give *flaw*. The early voyagers use *flake* (? Ger. *fläche*, flat expanse) or *land of ice*.

flog. Cant word. ? Arbitrary perversion of L. *flagellare*. Cf. *tund*.

flogging-cove: the beadle, or whipper in Bridewell, or in any such place (*Dict. Cant. Crew*).

flood. AS. *flōd*, flowing, river, sea, flood. Com. Teut.; cf. Du. *vloed*, Ger. *flut*, ON. *flōth*, Goth. *flōdus*; cogn. with *flow*. *Flood and field*, water and land, is after *Oth*. i. 3.

floor. AS. *flōr*; cf. Du. *vloer*, Ger. *flur*, plain, field, ON. *flōr*, of a cow-stall.

flop. Imit. of heavier movement than *flap*.

flora. Roman goddess of flowers, from *flos*, *flor-*. Adopted (17 cent.) as title for bot. works and popularized by Linnaeus (1745). Cf. *fauna*.

Florentine. L. *Florentinus*, from *Florentia*, Florence. Hence kind of meat-pie (archaic).

A huge grouse pie and a fine florentine (*Ingoldsby*).

florescence. From L. *florescere*, to begin to flower, from *flos*, *flor-*.

floret [*bot*.]. OF. *florette* (*fleurette*), dim. of *fleur*, L. *flos*, *flor-*.

florid. L. *floridus*, from *flos*, *flor-*, flower. For fig. senses cf. *flowery*, *blooming*, *rosy*.

florilegium. ModL. rendering of *anthology* (q.v.).

florin. F., coin of *Florence* (1252) with the flower as emblem of the city; cf. It. *fiorino*, Sp. *florin*. Partly a back-formation from ME. *florens*, for *florence*, another name of the coin.

florist. From L. *flos*, *flor-*. Cf. F. *fleuriste*.

floruit. L., he flourished, from *florēre*. Cf. *habitat*.

flory. See *fleury*.

floss-silk. Cf. F. *soie floche*, It. *seta floscia*. App. related to *flock²* (q.v.), though the *-s* suggests rather connection with *fleece*; cf. ModIcel. *flos*, nap, Dan. *flos*, plush.

flotation. For *floatation*, after F. *flottaison*. Cf. *flotsam*.

flotilla. Sp., dim. of *flota*, fleet. The latter has affected F. *flotte*, which in OF. meant army only. Both are app. of Teut. origin and cogn. with *flood*.

flotsam. Earlier *flotson*, AF. *floteson*, F. *flottaison*, from *flotter*, to float. Cf. *jetsam*.

Flotson, alias *flotzam*, is a word proper to the seas, signifying any goods that by shipw[r]acke be lost, and lye floting, or swimming upon the top of the water, which with *jetson* and *lagan* be given to the Lord Admirall, by his letters patent. *Jetson* is a thing cast out of the ship being in danger of wrecke, or cast on the shore by the marriners. *Lagan*, alias *lagam* vel *ligan*, is that which lyeth in the bottome of the sea (Cowel).

flounce¹. To plunge. Perh. formed (16 cent.) on *bounce*, *flop*; cf. *flounder²*.

flounce². On dress. For earlier *frounce*, wrinkle, pleat, etc., OF. *fronce* (whence *froncer les sourcils*, to knit the brows, frown), OHG. **hrunza*, *runza* (cf. ON. *hrukka*), whence Ger. *runzel*, wrinkle (q.v.). For initial *f-* cf. *flank*, *frock*.

Not trick'd and frounc'd, as she was wont
With the Attic boy to hunt (*Penseroso*, 123).

flounder¹. Fish. AF. *floundre*, OF. *flondre*, from Teut.; cf. ON. *flythra*, Sw., Norw. *flundra*, Dan. *flynder*; ult. cogn. with *flat*.

flounder². Verb. Orig. to stumble (of a horse). Prob. for *founder¹* (q.v.), by association with *blunder* and dial. *flodder*, to flounder.

flour. Orig. *flower of wheat*, after F. *fleur de farine*, "flower, or the finest meale" (Cotg.). Mod. spelling (from 18 cent.) for convenience.

flourish. OF. *florir* (*fleurir*), *floriss-*, VL. **florire*, for *florēre*, to bloom, etc. Trans. use, e.g. to *flourish a weapon* (Wyc.), is curious. *Flourish of trumpets* springs from sense of florid ornamentation, etc.

flout. ? ME. *flouten*, to play the flute; cf. Du. *fluiten*, to humbug. Very doubtful, as *flout* expresses a much stronger idea.

fluyten: fistula canere, tibiis canere, *et metaph.* mentiri, blandè dicere (Kil.).

flow¹. Verb. AS. *flōwan*, cogn. with ON. *flōa*, to flood, Du. *vloeien*, to flow, and *flood*; also with L. *pluere*, to rain. Has been associated in sense with unrelated L. *fluere*. Orig. strong with p.p. *flown*, as still in *high-flown* (q.v.).

Flown with insolence and wine (*Par. Lost*, i. 501).

flow² [*Sc*.]. Morass, quicksand. ON. *flōi*, cogn. with *flow¹*. ? Hence *Scapa Flow*. Stevenson has *floe* (*Pavilion on Links*).

flower. OF. *flour* (*fleur*), L. *flos*, *flor-*; cogn. with *blow²* and *bloom*; cf. It. *fiore*, Sp. *flor*. For *flower de luce* see *fleur-de-lis*.

flowers [*med*.]. F. *fleurs*, earlier *flueurs*, L. *fluor*, from *fluere*, to flow.

flu [*neol*.]. Influenza. For choice of middle syllable cf. *tec*, *scrip*.

Coroner. "Had the child had influenza?" Witness. "No sir, but she'd had the flu" (June, 1919).

fluctuate. From L. *fluctuare*, from *fluctus*, wave, from *fluere*, to flow.

flue¹. Fishing net. Cf. obs. Du. *vluwe*, now *flouw*, snipe-net. Perh. of F. origin.

flue². Passage, chimney. ? Due to some extraordinary confusion with *flue³* (q.v.) and the connection of both words with *cuniculus*. The words are of about same date (late 16 cent.).

flue³. Fluff. Orig. of rabbit, hare, etc. Cf. Flem. *vluwe*, prob. connected with F. *velu*, woolly, etc. (see *velvet*).

flue of a rabbet: cuniculi vellus (Litt.).

cuniculus: a coney: a coney-burrow; a hole or passage under ground; a long pipe of a still or furnace (*ib.*).

fluent. From pres. part. of L. *fluere*, to flow; cf. *fluid*, L. *fluidus*. The two were not always distinguished.

The most fluid preacher in the age of Queen Elizabeth (Wood, *Athenae Oxon.*).

fluff. First in 18 cent. (Grose). App. on *flue³* and *puff*, imitating sound of blowing away.

fluid. See *fluent*.

fluke¹. Flat fish. AS. *flōc*; cf. ON. *flōke*; ult. cogn. with Ger. *flach*, flat.

fluke². Of anchor, hence of whale's tail. Said to be from *fluke¹*, from shape; but cf. Ger. *flunke*, which Kluge regards as a common LG. word for *flügel*, wing. Ger. *ankerflügel* is used in same sense.

die flügel an einem ancker: the flooks of an anchor (Ludw.).

fluke³. Lucky stroke, ? orig. at billiards. First c. 1850, but found c. 1800 in slang sense of *flat*, one easily taken in, fig. from *fluke¹* (cf. *gudgeon*).

flummery. Welsh *llymru*, sour oatmeal boiled and jellied. Cf. *Fluellen*, *Floyd* (*Lloyd*). Fig. sense from 18 cent.

flummox [*slang*]. First in *Pickwick*. Given as cant word by Hotten (v.i.).

Flummuxed...signifies that the only thing they would be likely to get...would be a month in quod (*Slang Dict.*).

flump. Imit., combining suggestions of *flop* and *thump*.

flunkey. Orig. Sc. Perh. for *flanker*, side attendant, with favourite Sc. dim. suffix. Cf. *sidesman*.

fluor [*chem.*]. L. *fluor*, from *fluere*, to flow. First used by G. Agricola (1546) for Ger. mining word *flusse*, from *fliessen*, to flow.

flurry. Orig. sudden squall. Imit., with reminiscence of *flutter*, *flaw*, *hurry*, and obs. *flurr*, to scatter, whirr. With quot. below cf. the *flurry*, death-struggle, of the whale.

The breaking up of the munsoons, which is the last flory this season makes (Fryer's *E. Ind. and Pers.*).

flush¹. To put up birds. In ME. intrans., to fly up suddenly. ? Imit., with idea of *fly*, *flutter*, *rush*.

flush². To flood. Earlier (16 cent.), to rush, spurt out. Perh. ident. with *flush¹*, but has absorbed earlier senses of *flash* (q.v.). In sense of blood rushing to face it has been influenced by *blush*. In *flushed with victory*, etc. (see quot. s.v. *doubt*), it has been associated with to *flesh* (v.i.). *Flush of* (money) prob. belongs here (but see *flush³*). *Flush*, level with, is doubtful; earliest in *flush deck* (Capt. John Smith). A very puzzling word, both origin and filiation of senses being conjectural.

Flesh'd with slaughter and with conquest crown'd (Dryden).

flush³. Series of cards of same suit. F. *flux*, L. *fluxus*, flow; cf. obs. Du. *fluys*, obs. It. *flusso*, both prob. from F. Urquhart renders Rabelais' *flux* by *flusse*.

flusso: a flix. Also a flush in play at cards (Flor.).

passe sans flux: passe, I am not flush (Cotg.).

flushing [*archaic*]. Fabric for sailor's coat. From *Flushing* (*Vlissingen*), ? place of manufacture, ? or from being worn by Flushing pilots.

fluster. Orig. to excite with drink. Cf. ModIcel. *flaustra*, to bustle.

flute. F. *flûte*, OF. *flaüte*, *flahute*; cf. It. *flauto*, Sp. *flauta*, prob. from F., also Du. *fluit*, Ger. *flöte*, also from F. Origin unknown. The OF. form suggests a VL. **flatuta*, from *flare*, to blow. For extended senses, e.g. *fluted column*, cf. those of *pipe*.

flutter. AS. *floterian*, from *flēotan*, to fleet. Cf. *flitter*, *flicker*. Used in AS. also of motion of sea. For *fluttering of dovecotes* see *dove*. Sense of venture (betting, speculation, etc.) is 19 cent. slang.

fluvial. L. *fluvialis*, from *fluvius*, river, from *fluere*, to flow.

flux. F., L. *fluxus*, from *fluere*, to flow. *Fluxion*, in math. sense, was first used by Newton.

fly. AS. *flēogan*. Com. Teut.; cf. Du. *vliegen*, Ger. *fliegen*, ON. *fliūga*, Goth. **fliugan* (inferred from causal *flaugjan*); cogn. with L. *pluma*. Early confused with unrelated *flee*. Also noun, AS. *flēoge*; but most of the extended senses are through the verb, e.g. *fly*, orig. (18 cent.) quick carriage, or anything loosely attached, e.g. of trousers, tent, space over proscenium, *fly-leaf*, etc. With *fly-sheet*, earlier *flying-sheet*, pamphlet, cf. F. *feuille volante*, Ger. *flugschrift*. With slang *fly*, wide awake, cf. *no flies* (Hotten), but the word is perh. rather connected with *fledge* (v.i.). The study of *flying diseases* was mentioned in H. of C., Feb. 21, 1918; cf. *housemaid's knee, painter's colic*, etc.

vlug[1]: fledge;—volatil, quick, nimble.

vlug[2]: quick, sharp, lively, smart (Sewel, 1766).

flyboat [*hist.*]. Du. *vlieboot*, from the *Vlie*, channel leading to Zuyder Zee. Sense altered on *fly*.

We have burned one hundred and sixty ships of the enemy within the Fly (Pepys, Aug. 15, 1666).

foal. AS. *fola*. Com. Teut.; cf. Du. *veulen*, Ger. *fohlen* (usu. *füllen*), ON. *foli*, Goth. *fula*; cogn. with L. *pullus*, G. πῶλος. Cf. *filly*.

foam. AS. *fām*; cf. Ger. *feim*, scum; cogn. with Sanskrit *phena*, foam, and perh. with L. *s-puma*.

fob[1]. In to *fob off*. ME. *fob*, impostor (*Piers Plowm.*). Prob. OF. *forbe* (*fourbe*), cheat. For loss of *-r-* cf. *filemot*. *Fib*[1] may be partly a thinned form; cf. *bilk, bitch*[2]. But see also *fop*.

fourbe: a fib, jeast, fitton, gudgeon, mockerie, gullery, etc. (Cotg.).

fob[2]. Pocket. Ger. dial. (EPruss.) *fuppe*, of LG. origin; app. an early Ger. loan-word from period of Thirty Years' War.

focus. L., hearth. In math. sense first used (1604) by Kepler, the *focus* of a curve being likened to the burning-point of a lens.

fodder. AS. *fōdor*. Com. Teut.; cf. Du. *voeder*, Ger. *futter*, ON. *fōthr*; cogn. with *food*. See *forage*.

foe. AS. *fāh*, adj., and *gefā*, noun; cogn. with *feud*[1] (q.v.) and *fiend*. The adj. persists in *foeman*, AS. *fāhmann*.

foetus. See *fetus*.

fog. Rank grass (14 cent.). Origin unknown. Hence *foggy*, boggy, spongy, thick, murky, whence by back-formation *fog*, mist (16 cent.). This seems rather fantastic, but is paralleled by prob. identity of E. *mist* (q.v.) with Ger. *mist*, dung. Cf. however, Dan. *fog*, spray, storm, esp. in *snefog*, driving snow.

fogger [*archaic*]. See *pettifogger*.

fogle [*slang*]. Handkerchief. Ger. *vogel*, bird, has been suggested, via "bird's eye wipe." See *belcher*.

The bird's eye fogle round their necks has vanished from the costume of innkeepers (Trollope).

fogy. Usu. with *old*. Also *fogram, foggie*. App. adj. *foggy*, in obs. sense of fat. See *fog*.

a foggy man: een zwaar vet man (Sewel, 1766).

föhn. Hot south wind in Alps. Swiss-Ger., L. *Favonius* (q.v.); cf. Rumansh *favougn, favoign*.

foible. Weak point. OF. (*faible*). See *feeble*. Orig. from fencing, the lower part of the foil being called the *foible*. Cf. *forte*.

foil[1]. Noun. OF. *foil, foille* (*feuille*), leaf, L. *folium, folia* (neut. pl.); cogn. with G. φύλλον. The pl., treated as fem. collect., has superseded sing., exc. in It. *foglio*, leaf of a book. From thin leaf of metal placed under gem to set off its brilliancy springs fig. sense of contrast. Fencing *foil*, orig. a rough sword-blade with blunted *edge*, is the same word, F. *feuille* being still used for blade of saw; cf. Ger. *blatt*, leaf, blade, and obs. Du. *folie*, from F.

fueille: a leafe; also, the foyle of precious stones; or looking-glasses; *fueille d'un[e] espee*: the blade of a sword (Cotg.).

folie: bractea, bracteola, metalli lamella tenuis; *folie, breedswerd*: spatha (Kil.).

foil[2]. Verb. Combined from F. *fouler*, to trample (see *fuller*), and *affoler*, to befool, baffle (see *fool*). For E. love of *-oi-* cf. *recoil, soil*[1]. See also *defile*[1].

fouler: to tread, stampe, or trample on; to presse, oppresse, foyle, overcharge, extreamely (Cotg.).

affoler: to foyle, wound, bruise; also, to besot, gull, befoole (*ib.*).

foin [*archaic*]. To thrust, orig. to prick, pierce. ? Altered in some way from earlier obs. *poin*, to prick, thrust. See *poignant*. F. *feindre* has a dial. var. *foindre*, which may be connected (cf. fenc. use of *feint*).

pungere: poindre de quelque chose que ce soit, piquer (Est.).

pungere: to pricke, to foine, to sting (Coop.).

foison [*archaic*]. Abundance. F., L. *fusio-n-*, from *fundere, fus-*, to pour.

foist. Orig. in dicing. App. from Du. *vuist*, fist. With to *foist on* cf. to *palm off*.

Fokker. Ger. aeroplane. Du. inventor's name. Cf. *pettifogger*.

fold[1]. Verb. AS. *fealdan*. Com. Teut.; cf. Du. *vouwen* (earlier *vouden*), Ger. *falten*, ON. *falda*, Goth. *falthan*; cogn. with G. δι-πλάσιος, two-*fold*, L. *du-plex*, etc., the orig. metaphor being that of plaiting strands.

fold[2]. For sheep. AS. *falod*; cf. LG. *valt*, Du *vaalt*, Dan. *fold*.

oliage. F. *feuillage*, from *feuille*, leaf, L. *folia*, neut. pl.

folio. L. *in folio*, from *folium*, leaf; cf. *quarto, duodecimo*, etc. In book-keeping prob. via It. *foglio*; cf. *bankrupt, ditto, cash*[1], etc.

folk. AS. *folc*; cf. Du. Ger. *volk*, people, ON. *folk*, division of army, perh. orig. sense. *Folk-lore*, suggested (1846) by W. J. Thoms in the *Athenaeum*, is now adopted in several Europ. langs.; cf. *folk-etymology*, as exemplified in *sparrowgrass* (see *asparagus*), *grass-cutter* (q.v.), "*Plug Street*," etc. *Folk-song* is after Ger. *volkslied* (q.v.).

Nous sommes ici en présence d'un thème essentiellement folk-lorique (G. Huet).

follicle [*biol.*]. L. *folliculus*, dim. of *follis*, bag, etc. See *fool*.

follow. AS. *folgian*, also *fylgan*. Com. Teut.; cf. Du. *volgen*, Ger. *folgen*, ON. *fylga*. Perh. ult. a compd. of *full* and *go*. To *follow the sea* is after to *follow the plough* (*drum*). In *as follows*, in ref. to sing. or pl., the construction is impers., perh. after F. *ainsi qu'il suit*.

folly. F. *folie*, from *fol* (*fou*). See *fool*. The sense of structure beyond owner's means is partly due to spec. OF. use of *folie* for country pleasure-house. Thus Roger Wendover applies the name *stultitia Huberti* to Hubert de Burgh's castle on the Welsh Border, destroyed by the Welsh (1228), and no doubt called by its owner *Folie Hubert*. There has also been confusion with OF. *fuellie, foillie*, leafy retreat, summer-house, etc., which is usu. the origin of the surname *Folley*.

foment. F. *fomenter*, Late L. *fomentare*, to warm, cherish, from *fovēre*.

Those who are fermenting (sic) disorder in Ireland
(*Times*, Oct. 24, 1917).
Outwardly calm, but inwardly a foment (sic) of conflicting emotions
(Kyne, *Webster, Man's Man*, ch. xiv.).

fond. ME. *fonned*, p.p. of obs. *fon*, to be foolish, befool, of which *fondle* is frequent.; cf. ME. *fon*, fool, and mod. *fun*. Orig. sense appears in *fond hopes*; cf. *dote, infatuate. Fond-hardy* is common in Florio's *Montaigne*.

fondant. F., from *fondre*, to melt, L. *fundere*.

font. AS. *font*, L. *fons, font-*, fountain, adopted with spec. sense in Church L.

fontanelle [*anat.*]. Space between parietal bones of infant. F., dim. of *fontaine*, fountain.

food. AS. *fōda*; cogn. with ON. *fœthe*, Goth. *fōdeins*, L. *pabulum*, G. πατέομαι, I feed. See *fodder*. With *food for powder* (1 *Hen. IV*, iv. 2) cf. F. *chair à canon*, Ger. *kanonenfutter*. For fig. senses (*food for thought*) cf. *pabulum*.

fool[1]. Foolish person. F. *fol* (*fou*), L. *follis*, bellows, wind-bag, but prob. here in the spec. sense of scrotum; cf. It. *coglione*, "a noddie, a foole, a patch, a dolt, a meacock" (Flor.), lit. testicle; also L. *gerro*, fool, from a Sicilian name for pudendum. *Foolscap* paper formerly had a fool's cap as watermark. *Fool's paradise* is in the *Paston Letters* (15 cent.). For *foolhardy*, OF. *fol hardi*, see *hardy*.

fool[2]. Of gooseberries, etc. Perh. playful application of *fool*[1]; cf. *trifle, sillabub* (q.v.).

ravioli: a kinde of clouted creame called a foole or a trifle (Flor.).

foot. AS. *fōt*. Aryan; cf. Du. *voet*, Ger. *fuss*, ON. *fōtr*, Goth. *fōtus*, L. *pes, ped-*, G. πούς, ποδ-, Sanskrit *pād*. See *charpoy, teapoy*. The extended senses are common to the Europ. langs. A *footman* orig. ran on foot by the side of his master's horse or carriage. With to *know the length of one's foot* cf. to *take one's measure*, phrases alluding to the impossibility of disguising the truth from the shoemaker and tailor. *Footbal* is forbidden in a Sc. statute of 1424.

Foote balle, wherin is nothinge but beastly furie and exstreme violence,…is to be put in perpetuall silence (Elyot, *Governour*, i. 295).

footle. Mod. variation on dial. *footer*, to trifle, potter, F. *foutre*. See *footy*.

footpad. Robber on foot. Earlier *pad*, short for *padder*, from Du. *pad*, path, way. A cant word. Cf. *highwayman*.

Such as robbe on horse-backe were called highlawyers, and those who robbed on foote he called padders (*NED.* 1610).

footy [*archaic*]. Paltry. F. *foutu*, p.p. of *foutre*, common as term of contempt (2 *Hen. IV*, v. 3).

Their footy little ordnance
(*Westward Ho!* ch. xx.).

foozle. To bungle. Cf. dial. Ger. *fuseln*, to bungle, app. cogn. with Ger. *pfuschen, fuschen*, orig. to work as a blackleg, now very common in non-golf senses of E. *foozle*. See *poach, fusel*.

fop. Orig. fool. Cf. Ger. *foppen*, to fool, beguile, from rogues' cant, and orig. used of beggars shamming disease. This can hardly be the origin of the E. word, found in ME., but they are no doubt related. Cf. also *fob*[1].

foppe: supra, idem quod *folet* (*Prompt. Parv.*).

foppen: to fop, baffle, fool, jeer, banter, rally, or lampoon one; to make a fool, fop, or fop-doddle of him (Ludw.).

for. AS. *for*; as prep. not distinguished from cogn. *fore* in AS., but differentiated in ME.; cogn. with Du. *voor*, Ger. *vor*, *für* (as prefix *ver-*), ON. *fyrer*, Goth. *faur*, L. *pro*, G. περί, πρό, παρά. As prefix it implies doing away with, spoiling, etc., like cogn. Ger. *ver-*. Also confused as prefix with *fore-*. The two have separate sense and sound, though the latter is not indicated in spelling as in Ger. *ver-*, *vor-*. With *forasmuch as* cf. *inasmuch as*, and almost synon. F. *d'autant que*.

forage. F. *fourrage*, from *feurre*, fodder, of Teut. origin. See *fodder*.

foramin-. From L. *foramen*, *foramin-*, orifice, from *forare*, to bore.

foray. Back-formation from *forayer*, OF. *forreor*, forager, from *forrer*, to forage, from *feurre*, fodder, forage. Cf. ModF. *fourrier*, harbinger, quartermaster.

fourrager: to fodder; also, to forage, prey, forray, go a foraging; to ransacke, ravage, boot-hale it (Cotg.).

forbear[1]. Ancestor. Orig. Sc. *fore be-er*, one existing before.

forbear[2]. Abstain. AS. *forberan*, to bear privation of, treat with patience.

entbären oder entbehren: to bear the want of a thing; to forbear it (Ludw.).

forbid. AS. *forbēodan*. See *bid*. Cf. Ger. *verbieten*, with its once sacred p.p. *verboten*. Current sense of adj. *forbidding* is from c. 1700. *Forbidden fruit* is 17 cent.

In Deutschland wird keine Revolution stattfinden, weil da Revolutionen verboten sind (Heine).

forby [*Sc.*]. Moreover, not to mention. From *for* and *by*; cf. Ger. *vorbei*, past.

force[1]. Vigour. F., VL. **fortia*, from *fortis*, strong; cf. It. *forza*, Sp. *fuerza*. For VL. formation cf. *grease*, *marvel*. Has assumed certain senses of native *might*, *strength*, e.g. a *military force* was up to 16 cent. a *strength*. With *the* (police) *Force* (c. 1850), cf. *the Trade*, *the Profession*. To *force one's hand* is from whist.

force[2], **foss** [*north.*]. Waterfall. ON. *fors*, whence Sw. *fors*, Dan. *fos*. Cf. *fell*[3], *gill*[2].

force-meat. From archaic *force*, to stuff, for *farce* (q.v.).

forceps. L., pincers, tongs. Orig. smiths'

implement, from *formus*, hot, *capere*, to take.

ford. AS. *ford*; cf. archaic Du. *vord*, Ger. *furt*; cogn. with *fare*, *firth*, also with L. *portus*, harbour, G. πόρος, ford (*Bosporus* = *Oxford*).

fordo, fordone [*archaic*]. AS. *fordōn*, compd. of *do*. Now replaced by *do for*, *done for*. See *do*.

fore. Cogn. with *for* (q.v.). Adj. and noun use, e.g. *fore horse*, *to the fore*, is back-formation from old compds. in which the prefix appears to have adj. force, e.g. *foreman*. Golfers' *fore* is for *before*. In naut. lang. regularly opposed to *aft*, *fore-and-aft* being used of sails that follow the length of the ship, instead of its breadth (*square-rigged*). As prefix *fore-* has meaning of previous, before, but is sometimes confused with *for-*. In a few compds. the first element may have been originally *afore*, *before*, e.g. *foremast hand* (naut.).

forearm. Verb. Only in proverb, with *fore-warn*.

forecast. Orig. to contrive beforehand. For sense-development cf. *conjecture*.

He fell to explaining to me his manner of casting the draught of water which a ship will draw beforehand (Pepys, May 19, 1666).

forecastle. Orig. a castle-like structure at fore-end of vessel.

foreclose. Better *forclose*, F. *forclore*, from *fors*, L. *foris*, outside, and *clore*, *clos-*, L. *claudere*, to shut; cf. *forfeit*. Now usu. of mortgages, to bar right of redemption.

forefather. Perh. formed on L. *progenitor*. The compd. is not found in AS.

forefront. Now chiefly fig., after the *fore-front of the battle* (2 Sam. xi. 15); but orig. used in sense of façade.

foregather. See *forgather*.

forego. To precede. Chiefly in participles, the *foregoing*, *foregone*, the latter esp. with *conclusion*, after Shaks., but used with mistaken sense. See also *forgo*.

But this denoted a foregone conclusion (*Oth.* iii. 3).

forehead. AS. *forhēafod*, with *for-* for *fore-*.

foreign. ME. *foren*, *forein*, etc., F. *forain*, from *fors*, outside, L. *foris*. In dial. still used in earlier sense of outside the town, district, etc. Cf. *forest*, and It. *forestiere*, alien, foreigner. See also *denizen*.

forejudge. Cf. *prejudice*. See also *forjudge*.

forel. Parchment (bookbind.). Orig. case, cover, OF. *forel* (*fourreau*, sheath), dim. from Ger. *futter*, case.

forelock, take Time by the. Adapted from F. *prendre l'occasion aux cheveux*, with *Time* substituted for L. *Occasio*.

Cursu volucri, pendens in novacula,
Calvus, comosa fronte, nudo corpore,
Quem si occuparis, teneas; elapsum semel
Non ipse possit Iuppiter reprehendere...
(Phaedrus, v. 8).

foreman. Orig. leader in gen. sense. *Foreman of jury* is recorded earlier than *foreman*, head workman.

foremost. AS. *formest*, superl. of *forma*, which is itself a superl. from same root as *fore*, with -*m*- suffix as in L. *primus*, etc. Confused with *most* (cf. *utmost*). *Former* is a back-formation from *formest*.

forensic. From L. *forensis*, from *forum* (q.v.).

fore-reach. Orig. naut., to shoot ahead of, hence fig. to get the better of.

You have forereached on Davy [Jones] this time, sir (*Tom Cringle's Log*, ch. x.).

forerunner. First in ME. as rendering of L. *praecursor*, in ref. to John the Baptist.

fore-shorten. As term of art from c. 1600.

foresight. Earliest (c. 1300) in ref. to God's *foresight*, rendering L. *providentia*.

foreskin. Coined (16 cent.) for earlier *prepuce*. Perh. suggested by synon. Ger. *vorhaut*, due to Luther.

forest. OF. (*forêt*), MedL. *forestis* (sc. *sylva*), unenclosed land, from *foris*, outside. In OF. & ME. often opposed to *park*, enclosed land. Cf. *foreign*. In earliest E. use *forest* is esp. associated with the crown and hunting. *Foresters*, benefit society, is 19 cent.

forestall. From AS. *foresteall*, an ambush, waylaying, etc., from *fore* and *stall*. In ME. esp. in sense of intercepting supplies, profiteering, food-hoarding.

forethought. Orig. in evil sense; cf. *malice aforethought*.

foreword. Neol. (19 cent.) after Ger. *vorwort*, preface. Cf. *wordbook*.

Stupid neologisms, such as "foreword," which some Germanizing fool found himself saying, and a hundred light-hearted parrots repeated it
(J. S. Phillimore).

forfeit. F. *forfait*, wrong, crime, p.p. of *forfaire*, to do wrong, MedL. *foris facere*, to transgress, from *foris*, outside. Mod. sense from confiscation following crime.

forfend. Now usu. optative, e.g. *Heaven forfend*. Formed from *fend* (q.v.), to ward off, on model of synon. *forbid*.

And the prestis be forfendid to eny more takyn monee of the puple (Wyc. 2 *Kings*, xii. 8).

forgather [*Sc.*]. From *for* and *gather*; or perh. directly from Du. *vergaderen*, to assemble. For force of prefix cf. synon. Ger. *versammeln*.

forge[1]. Of smith. First as verb. F. *forger*, L. *fabricare*. For sense of counterfeiting, found very early, cf. *fabricate* (q.v.).

Who forgide [*Vulg.* fabricatus est] the dowmbe and the deef, the seer and the blynde?
(Wyc. *Ex*. iv. 11).

forge[2] [*naut.*]. Usu. with *ahead*. Naut. corrupt. of *force*; cf. Mrs Gamp's "Jonadge's belly."

to forge over (corrompu de to force): passe[r] en faisant force de voiles sur un banc de sable, ou à travers les glaces; on dit aussi en françois forcer
(Lesc.).

franchir un banc: to force over a bank (*ib.*).

franchir une roche: to pass over, or forge off from a rock (Falc.).

forget. AS. *forgietan*, from *get*; cf. Du. *vergeten*, Ger. *vergessen*. Orig. idea must have been to lose, but this is not recorded in any Teut. lang. With *forget-me-not* cf. Ger. *vergissmeinnicht*, OF. *ne m'oubliez mye*.

forgive. AS. *forgiefan*, from *give*. Com. Teut. compd.; cf. Du. *vergeven*, Ger. *vergeben*, ON. *fyrirgefa*, Goth. *fragiban*, to grant. See *pardon*.

forgo. To dispense with. AS. *forgān*, to pass over. See *go*. Cf. Ger. *vergehen*. Often wrongly spelt *forego* (q.v.).

forjudge [*leg.*]. To exclude, dispossess by judgment. OF. *forjuger*; cf. *forclose*, *forfeit*, and see *judge*. Incorr. *forejudge* (v.i.).

Forejudged of life and lands (*NED*. 1883).

fork. AS. *force*, L. *furca*. Partly from ONF. *forque* (F. *fourche*); cf. It. *furca*, Sp. *horca*; also Du. *vork*, Ger. *furke*. Orig. pitchfork, etc., an early Roman agricultural loan-word, replacing AS. *gafol* (cf. Ger. *gabel*). The table fork, one for each, is not recorded till 15 cent. With to *fork out* cf. to *stump up*. See also *carfax*.

My silvir forke for grene gyngour
(*Bury Wills*, 1463).

forlorn. ME. p.p. of obs. *forlese*, to abandon, AS. *forlēosan*, to lose utterly; cf. Du. *verliezen*, Ger. *verlieren*, Goth. *fraliusan*. See *lose*, *lorn*. *Forlorn hope* (mil.) is obs. Du. *verloren hoop*, lost "heap"; cf. obs. Ger. *verlorener haufe* and F. *enfants perdus*, "the forlorne hope of a camp" (Cotg.). In Purch. (xvi. 41) used for **vanguard**. Often misused by mod. writers as though connected with E. *hope* (see quot. 2). This has coloured sense of *forlorn*, as in quot. 3.

verloren hoop: emissarii milites, qui precedunt aciem ad lacessendum hostem, et temerè in mortem ruunt (Kil.).

She had had a forlorn hope of a letter (*NED.* 1885).

Commander Goodhart thoroughly realized the forlorn nature of his act. His last remark to the commanding officer was: "If I don't get up, the tin cylinder will"
(*Offic. award of Albert Gold Medal*, Apr. 23, 1918).

form. F. *forme*, L. *forma*, shape; prob. cogn. with *ferire*, to strike (cf. *type*). In all Rom. & Teut. langs. The school sense (6th *form*, etc.), peculiar to E., is from Late L. *forma*, used of orders of clergy, associated also with *form*, bench, OF. *forme*, from phrase *s'asseoir en forme*, to sit in order. The germ of *good* (*bad*) *form* is in Chauc. (v.i.). *Formal* was orig. a scholastic term opposed to *material* (form and matter).

Noght o word spak he moore than was neede,
And that was seyd in forme and reverence
(Chauc. A. 304).

format. F., L. *formatus* (sc. *liber*).

forme¹. Of a hare. Ident. with *form¹*, F. *forme*, mould, being used of the impression left on the ground by the hare.

Un homme entendu à la chasse peut juger à la forme (c'est-à-dire au giste où le lievre a passé la nuict) quel lievre c'est
(Gauchet, *Plaisir des Champs*, 1583).

forme². [*typ.*]. As *form* (q.v.).

former. See *foremost*.

formic. Of ants. For *formicic*, from L. *formica*, ant.

formidable. F., L. *formidabilis*, from *formido*, dread.

formula. L., dim. of *forma*. Mod. sense of conventionality, etc., after Carlyle, is due to that writer's misunderstanding of a remark made by Mirabeau père.

fornication. F., L. *fornicatio-n-*, from *fornicari*, from *fornix*, *fornic-*, brothel, orig. vault, arch.

forsake. AS. *forsacan*, to relinquish, renounce, opposite of *sacan*, to fight, claim; cf. Du. *verzaken*, OHG. *firsahhan*. See *sake*.

forsooth. AS. *forsōth*, for truth. See *sooth*. With mod. ironic use, from c. 1800, cf. *I daresay*, *very likely*, etc.

forspent. From archaic *forspend*, AS. *forspendan*, to squander. See *spend*.

forswear. AS. *forswerian*, to renounce an oath (cf. *abjure*), reflex. to perjure oneself, the only sense of mod. p.p. *forsworn*. For

formation cf. Ger. *verschwören*, to conspire. See *swear*.

fort. F., L. *fortis*, strong; perh. with *château* understood.

fortalice [*archaic*]. MedL. *fortalitia*, from *fortis*, strong; cf. OF. *fortelece*, It. *fortilizio*, Sp. *fortaleza*. See *fortress*.

forte. Strong point. Orig. from fenc. F. *fort*, upper half of sword-blade. See *foible*.

Les hommes...savent tous le fort et le foible les uns des autres (La Bruyère).

forth. AS. *forth*, forward, onward; cogn. with *fore*; cf. Du. *voort*, Ger. *fort*. See *further*. Gray criticized Beattie's use of this "obsolete" word in *The Minstrel* (1771). *Forthcome*, AS. *forthcuman*, is practically obs. exc. in pres. part. With archaic *forthright*, straight forward, cf. *downright*, *upright*. It is often used as noun after *Temp.* iii. 3. *Forthwith*, orig. along with, replaced earlier *forth mid* (see *midwife*).

fortify. F. *fortifier*, Late L. *fortificare*, from *fortis*, strong, *facere*, to make.

fortissimo. It., superl. of *forte*, strong, L. *fortis*.

fortitude. F., L. *fortitudo*, from *fortis*, strong.

fortnight. For *fourteen night*, a combination found in AS.; cf. *sennight*, for *seven night*. See *night*.

fortress. F. *forteresse*, from *fort*, strong, parallel form to OF. *fortalece*; see *fortalice*.

fortuitous. From L. *fortuitus*, from *forte*, by chance, abl. of *fors*, *fort-*, chance, lot.

fortune. F., L. *fortuna*, from *fors* (v.s.). Oldest sense in to *tell fortunes*, and in *fortunate* (cf. *happy*). Sense of owned wealth first in Spenser. *Soldier of fortune*, free lance, a 17 cent. type, does not correspond in meaning with F. *soldat* (*officier*) *de fortune*, one risen from the ranks.

forty. *Roaring forties* (naut.), between 40° and 50° N. latitude. *Forty-five*, Jacobite rising of 1745; cf. *Fifteen*. *Forty-niner* (US.), settler in California at time (1849) of gold-fever.

A miner, forty-niner, and his daughter Clementine.

forum. L., market-place, place of assembly for public business; cogn. with *fores*, doors, *foris*, outside, and ult. with *durbar*.

forward. AS. *foreweard*. See *fore* and *-ward*. With *forwards*, usu. coupled with *backwards*, cf. Ger. *vorwärts*; the *-s* is adv. gen. With verb to *forward* cf. to *further*.

forweary, forworn [*archaic*]. Cf. *forspent*.

fosse. F., L. *fossa*, from *fodere, foss-*, to dig. Cf. *dike*.

fossick [*Austral.*]. To rummage for particles of gold in abandoned workings. E. dial. *fossick*, troublesome person; perh. from *fuss*; cf. *finick*.

A dozen Chinamen fossicking after gold amidst the dirt of the river (Trollope).

fossil. F. *fossile*, L. *fossilis*, from *fodere, foss-*, to dig.

foster. AS. *fóstor, fóster*, feeding, food; cf. ON. *fóstr*, nursing; from root of *food*, with instrument. suffix. The compds. *foster-father, -child*, etc., all occur in AS Verb is now usu. fig.

fother[1]. Load, measure. AS. *fóther*. WGer.; cf. Du. *voer* (earlier *voeder*), Ger. *fuder*, cartload; cogn. with *fathom*.

fother[2], **fodder** [*naut.*]. To choke a leak with oakum. Du. *voeren* (earlier *voederen*), to line; cf. Ger. *füttern*. See *fur*. Or it may be simply to "feed."

foudroyant. F., thunder-smiting, from *foudroyer*, from *foudre*, lightning, L. *fulgur*.

foul. AS. *fúl*. Com. Teut.; cf. Du. *vuil*, Ger. *faul*, ON. *fúll*, Goth. *fúls*; cogn. with L. *putēre*, to stink, G. πύον, pus, Sanskrit *pū*, to stink. The fig. senses are mostly found in AS., the opposites being *clean* and *fair*, and, in naut. lang., *clear*. From naut. to *fall foul of*, become entangled, etc., comes mod. mech. sense, e.g. to *foul the points* (railway).

foulard. Fabric. F., of unknown origin. ? From *fouler*, to trample (? cf. *fichu*).

foumart. Polecat. ME. *fulmard*, AS. *fúl*, foul, *mearth*, marten. Cf. F. *putois*, polecat, from *puer*, to stink.

found[1]. To establish. F. *fonder*, L. *fundare*, from *fundus*, bottom.

found[2]. To cast metal. F. *fondre*, L. *fundere*, to pour.

founder[1]. Of a horse (Chauc.). ME. also *afounder*, F. *effondrer*, to knock out the bottom, *s'effondrer*, to collapse, from L. *ex* and VL. **fundor-*, from *fundus*, bottom; cf. MedL. *fundora*, for *fundus*, and F. *fondrière*, quagmire.

founder[2]. Of a ship. OF. *enfondrir*, to engulf, sink, from L. *fundus*, bottom (v.s.). Much later than *founder*[1], of which it is partly a fig. application.

Then, like a founder'd horse, she [the ship] cannot go (*Sea-Dict.* 1708).

foundling. From *find*; cf. Du. *vondeling*, MHG. *fundelinc* (replaced by *findling* via *fündling*).

foundry. F. *fonderie*. See *found*[2].

fount[1], **fountain.** F. *font*, L. *fons, font-*, now replaced, exc. in *fonts baptismaux*, by *fontaine*, Late L. *fontana*, whence *fountain*. Or E. *fount*, poet. word of late appearance (first in Shaks.), may be a back-formation on *mount-ain*. *Fountain* was orig. synon. with *spring*; cf. *fountain-head*, now usu. fig. A French *fountain-pen* is described in 1658 and Miss Burney used one in 1789.

Portable fountain pens to carry ink and write well, made and sold by E. T. Williams, No. 13, Strand (*Morn. Chron.* June 11, 1788).

fount[2] [*typ.*]. F. *fonte*, casting, from *fondre*. See *found*[2].

four. AS. *féower*. Aryan; cf. Du. Ger. *vier*, ON. *fiórer*, Goth. *fidwōr*, L. *quattuor*, G. τέσσαρες, τέττ-, Sanskrit *katur*, OIr. *cethir*, Welsh *pedwar*. See *charpoy*. *On all fours*, for earlier *on all four* (*Lev.* xi. 42), has fig. sense of fair, evenly, not like a limping dog. A *four in hand* is a team entirely controlled by the driver, i.e. without a postilion for the leaders. In the card-game of *all fours* "the all four are high, low, Jack, and the game" (Johns.). *Foursome* (Sc.), four together, is in Gavin Douglas (16 cent.).

Then of all foure he makes him lightly bound (*Sylv. Handicrafts*).

fourgon. F., baggage-waggon. Perh. ult. cogn. with *fork*, from shape of shafts.

Fourierism. System of *Charles Fourier*, F. socialist (†1837). See *phalanstery*.

fourteen points [*hist.*]. Enunciated (Jan. 8, 1918) by President Wilson.

Le président Wilson est un homme remarquable. Il a quatorze commandements. Le bon Dieu lui-même n'en a que dix (? G. Clemenceau, Apr. 1919).

fourth. Latrine (Camb.). Perh. orig. from number of staircase. Hotten derives it from the "fourth court" of Trinity, but there is no court so named. Also explained as the "fourth" human necessity. *Fourth estate*, the press, is prob. due to Burke, but the phrase had been previously used in various senses, e.g., of the mob (Fielding). The theory of the *fourth dimension* (math.) was originated (1831) by Gauss.

fowl. AS. *fugol*. Com. Teut.; cf. Du. Ger. *vogel*, ON. *fugl*, Goth. *fugls*. Perh. for an earlier **flugl* (cf. Ger. *flügel*, wing), cogn. with *fly*, with early dissim. of one *-l-*; cf. AS. *flugol*, flying, and relation of Sanskrit *pakshin*, fowl, to *paksha*, wing. Usual for *bird* (q.v.) in ME. and later; cf. *fowls of the air*, *wild-fowl*. Mod. limitation from c. 1600. See *flesh*.

fox. AS. *fox*. Com. Teut.; cf. Du. *vos*, Ger. *fuchs*, in which -*s* is masc. suffix; cf. ON. *fóa*, Goth. *fauhō*, vixen. With *foxglove*, AS. *foxes glōfe*, cf. synon. Norw. *ræv-bjelde*, lit. fox-bell. Its F. name is *doigtier*, *doigt de la Vierge* (see *digitalis*). *Foxed*, in book-sellers' catalogues, means stained with fox-coloured marks.

foyer [*theat.*]. F., orig. green-room, lit. hearth, home, VL. **focarium*, from *focus*.

fracas. F., from *fracasser*, to shatter, It. *fracassare*, perh. combined from L. *quassare*, to shatter, and *frag-*, as in *fragment*. See *cashier²*.

fraction. F., Church L. *fractio-n-*, from *frangere*, *fract-*, to break. Math. sense is oldest (Chauc.).

fractious. App. coined (18 cent.) as mixture of *factious* and *refractory*.

fracture. F., L. *fractura*, as *fraction*.

fragile. F., L. *fragilis*, from *frag-*, root of *frangere*, to break.

fragment. L. *fragmentum*, from *frangere* (v.s.).

fragrant. F., from pres. part. of L. *fragrare*, to smell. See *flair*.

frail¹. Adj. OF. *fraile* (*frêle*), L. *fragilis*, fragile (q.v.). Oldest E. sense is fig., unchaste.

frail². Basket for figs, etc. OF. *frael*, *freel*, VL. *fragellum*, for *flagellum*, young shoot of vine (Virg.), hence withe for basket-making.

One fraiel [*Vulg.* calathus] hadde good figus
                       (Wyc. *Jer.* xxiv. 2).

fraise [*fort.*]. Palisade. F., ruff, earlier, mesentery of calf. Perh. cogn. with *frieze¹*; cf. *frill*, *tripe*.

framboesia [*med.*]. The yaws. From F. *framboise*, raspberry, from appearance of swellings.

frame. AS. *framian*, to avail, profit, from *fram*, vigorous, etc., orig. going forward (*from*), cogn. with Ger. *fromm*, pious. Some senses from cogn. ON. *fremja*, to further, execute. Mod. meanings of verb and noun are chiefly from ME. sense of preparing timber for use. The picture sense is first in Shaks. *Frame of mind* (*soul*, *spirit*) is esp. common in 17 cent.

He could not frame to pronounce it right
                       (*Judges*, xii. 6).

franc. F. coin first struck (1360) temp. Jean le Bon with legend *Francorum Rex*. See *frank*.

franchise. F., freedom, from *franc*, free, frank. Hence liberty, privilege, etc. ModE. sense arises accidentally from contextual application of *elective franchise*, freedom to vote.

Franciscan. Of order of *St Francis of Assisi*, founded 1209. Grey friar.

Franco-. From MedL. *Francus*. See *frank¹*.

francolin. Bird. F., It. *francolino*, "a daintye birde called a goodwit" (Flor.); according to a 17 cent. ornithologist from *franco*, free, because a privileged bird which the commons were forbidden to kill. Cf. *franklin*.

franc-tireur [*hist.*]. F., free-shooter. Coined (? in 1870) on older *franc-archer*; cf. Ger. *freischütz*. The accusation that the Belgians had adopted "franc-tireur tactics" was the pretext for the massacres of civilians at Dinant, Aerschot, etc. (1914).

frangible. Late L. *frangibilis*, from *frangere*, to break.

frangipane. Perfume. F., said to have been introduced into France (temp. Catherine de Médicis) by one of the famous It. family *Frangipani*, lit. break-bread, a name earned, according to tradition, by benevolence.

frank¹. Adj. F. *franc* or L. *Francus*, OHG. *Franko*; cf. AS. *Franca*, ON. *Frakki*. A name applied esp. to Ger. tribes which conquered Gaul (6 cent.) and called it *France*; hence member of ruling race, free, open, etc. Cf. hist. of *slave*. Also applied by Orientals to Europeans (see *feringhee*). The ethnic name is sometimes said to be derived from the national weapon, the javelin (AS. *franca*, ON. *frakka*), but the opposite may be the case; cf. F. *francisque*, battle-axe, lit. Frankish. See also *almoign*, *frankpledge*.

frank². Verb. To "free" the carriage of a letter, etc. From *frank¹*. Cf. F. *affranchir*, to set free, to stamp a letter.

Frankenstein. Student who, in story (1818) by Mrs Shelley, created a monster which he could not control. Commonly misused for the monster itself.

The Germans, having created a Frankenstein for their own purposes, seem to be considerably perplexed by its antics (*Daily Chron.* Jan. 7, 1918).

frankincense. OF. *franc encens*, the adj. app. meaning noble, frank¹; cf. Ger. *edelstein*, gem, *edeltanne*, white pine, and see *free-stone* (s.v. *free*).

franklin [*hist.*]. Freeman, freeholder (*Ivanhoe*, ch. i.). AF. *fraunkelain*, MedL. *Franchelanus*, from *Francus*, frank[1], prob. with orig. Teut. suffix -*ling*. Cf. *chamberlain*.

frankpledge [*hist.*]. AF. mistransl. of AS. *frithborh*, peace pledge, *frith* being confused with *free*. See *frank*[1], *frith*[1].

frantic. ME. also *frenetik*, F. *frénétique*, L., G. φρενιτικός. See *frenzy*.

frap [*naut.*]. To bind tightly. F. *frapper*, to strike, in same sense, perh. ult. cogn. with *flap*.

frapper une manœuvre: to fix or seize or lash a rope in its proper place (Lesc.).

frass [*bot.*]. Refuse left by boring insects. Ger., from *fressen*, to devour. See *fret*[1].

frate. It., friar, brother, L. *frater*. Cf. shortened *Fra* in *Fra Angelico*, etc.

frater, fratry [*archaic*]. Refectory. AF. *fraitur*, for *refraitur*, corrupt. of MedL. *refectorium*.

fraternal. From L. *fraternus*, from *frater*, brother. Cf. *fraternize*, F. *fraterniser*, much used at time of F. Revolution, and lately (1917) in ref. to the Russo-Ger. front. *Fraternity* also, though common in ME. of a rel. brotherhood, took a new lease of life at the Revolution, *Liberté, Égalité, Fraternité* being adopted as motto of Republic in 1791.

Sois mon frère, ou je te tue (Anon. 18 cent.).

fratricide. L. *fratricida*, agent, *fratricidium*, act, from *caedere*, to kill. AS. has *bróthorbana* (see *bane*) and -*cwealm* (see *kill*).

fratry. See *frater*.

frau. Ger., woman, orig. lady, fem. of OHG. *fró*, lord, ult. cogn. with *Friday*. Hence dim. *fräulein*.

fraud. F. *fraude*, L. *fraus, fraud-*. *Pious fraud* is in Foxe.

fraught. Now only as p.p., and usu. fig., *fraught with*. Noun and verb *fraught*, replaced by *freight* (q.v.), is Du. or LG. *vracht*, orig. cost of transport; cf. OHG. *fréht*, for *fer-éht*, from *éht*, possession, cogn. with *owe, own*. But some connect *fraught, freight* with L. *fractum* (see *defray*); cf. *what's the damage?*

fraxinella [*bot.*]. ModL. dim. from *fraxinus*, ash.

fray[1]. Fight, quarrel. For *affray* (q.v.). Cf. archaic *fray*, to frighten.

And none shall fray them away (*Jer.* vii. 33).

fray[2]. To rub. F. *frayer*, L. *fricare*. Earliest of deer rubbing horns against trees.

frazzle [*dial. & US.*]. To unravel, etc. App. formed on *fray*[2] and obs. *fasel*, in same sense, cogn. with AS. *fæs*, fringe, Ger. *faser*, fringe, fibre.

The Allies have to beat Germany to a frazzle
          (*Referee*, May 27, 1917).

freak. Caprice. First in 16 cent., *fortune's freaks*. In sense of *lusus naturae* it is US. Perh. a dial. word cogn. with AS. *frícian*, to dance; cf. hist. of *caprice*. But Littleton's gloss (v.i.) suggests rather connection with obs. *freck*, eager, arrogant, which has given surname *Freake*. This is a Com. Teut. word, AS. *frec*; cf. Du. *vrek*, eager, Ger. *frech*, insolent, ON. *frekr*, greedy, Goth. *friks*, greedy.

freak: protervia, petulantia (Litt.).

freaked. App. coined by Milton, who may have had *freckle* and *streak* vaguely in mind.

The pansy freaked with jet (*Lycidas*, 144).

freckle. Earlier *frecken*, ON. *freknur* (pl.), perh. ult. cogn. with G. περκνός, spotted.

A fewe frakenes in his face y-spreynd
          (Chauc. A. 2169).

free. AS. *fréo*, not in bondage, also poet. noble, joyful. Com. Teut.; cf. Du. *vrij*, Ger. *frei*, ON. *frír* (only in compds.), Goth. *freis*; cogn. with Sanskrit *priya*, dear, the orig. sense. See *friend* and cf. Ger. *freien*, to woo. L. *liberi*, children, lit. the free, shows converse sense-development. Fig. senses correspond with those of F. *libre*. *Freeboard* (naut.) was prob. suggested by earlier sense of strip of land outside fence of park. For *freebooter*, Du. *vrijbuiter* (cogn. with *free* and *booty*), cf. *filibuster*. *Free Church* has been lately assumed by Nonconformists. *Freedom of the Seas*, a phrase of doubtful meaning, suggested by Grotius' tract *Mare Liberum* (1608), was much in vogue in Germany at the period of the submarine massacres. *Freehand drawing* is done without math. instruments. *Freehold* translates AF. *fraunc tenement*. *Free lance*, medieval mercenary, is mod., perh. coined by Scott (*Ivanhoe*, ch. xxxiv.). *Freemasons* (cf. Ger. *freimaurer*, F. *franc maçon*) were orig. (14 cent.) a travelling gild of skilled stone-masons with a secret code. *Freestone* translates F. *pierre franche*, "the soft white freestone" (Cotg.); cf. *frankincense*. *Freethinker* (c. 1700) has been adopted as F. *libre penseur*, Ger. *frei-denker* (1715). *Free trade* orig. meant un-restricted trade, but Adam Smith has *free-dom of trade* (1776) in mod. sense. *Free will* is used by Chauc. (*Boeth.*) in associa-tion with *predestination*.

We term it [the Club] *Free-and-Easy*, and yet we Find it no easy matter to be free
(Crabbe, *Borough*).

freemartin. Imperfect heifer. Cf. Ir. Gael. *mart*, heifer.

freesia. Plant. From Cape of Good Hope. ? From *Frees*, a common Du. surname, the Frisian; cf. *fuchsia, dahlia*, etc.

freeze. AS. *frēosan*. Com. Teut.; cf. Du. *friezen*, Ger. *frieren* (OHG. *friesan*), ON. *friōsa*, Goth. **friusan* (inferred from *frius*, frost); cogn. with L. *pruina*, hoar-frost, Sanskrit *prushvā*, ice. Archaic p.p. *frore(n)* (cf. *was, were, lose, lorn*) occ. in poetry after Milton. To *freeze on* (*to, out*) is US.

Snow-fed streams now seen athwart frore vapours (Shelley).

freight. For earlier *fraught* (q.v.), influenced by F. *fret*, of same origin. Much used in US. railway lang., perh. after ModDu. *vragt*.

fret: the fraught, or fraight of a ship; also, the hire that's payed for a ship, or for the fraught thereof (Cotg.).

French. AS. *frencisc*, from *franca* (see *frank*). For contr. cf. surname *Dench*, AS. *denisc*, Danish. To *take French leave* (cf. F. *filer à l'anglaise*) orig. alluded to 18 cent. custom of leaving reception without bid-ding farewell to host and hostess. *French polish* is early 19 cent. Colloquial *Frenchy* may be a back-formation from obs. pl. *Frenches*, for *Frenchmen*; cf. *Portugee*, etc. With *Frenchman*, two words in ME., cf. *Dutchman*. These are the only applica-tions to continental races of the formation exemplified in *Englishman, Welshman*, etc.

Monsieur Fastidious Brisk, otherwise called the fresh Frenchified courtier
(Jonson, *Every Man out of his Hum.* i. 1).

frenzy. F. *frénésie*, from Late L. *phrenesis*, from G. φρήν, mind, reason.

frequent. Adj. is from L. *frequens, frequent-*, whence verb *frequentare*, "to go in great number or many togither" (Coop.). Cf. earlier sense of adj., esp. in *full and frequent*. Hence *frequentative* (gram.), de-rivative verb expressing frequent repeti-tion of action indicated by simple verb,

e.g. L. *cantare*, from *canere*, E. *flutter*, from *flit*.

Apart they sate,
And full and frequent, form'd a dire debate
(Pope, *Odyssey*).

fresco. Painting. Orig. executed *in fresco* (It.), i.e. on mortar or plaster still fresh and moist. Cf. *al fresco*.

fresh. AS. *fersc*, fresh, not salt; combined (from 13 cent.) with cogn. F. *frais*, fresh in gen. sense, OHG. *frisc* (*frisch*). Cf. Du. *versh*, ON. *ferskr*, and forms in Rom. langs. from Teut. *As fresh as paint* may have been orig. ironic for *as fresh as a rose* (daisy); cf. *clear as mud*. US. *fresh*, im-pudent, is Ger. *frech* (see *freak*[1]).

The fresh country ladies had to be warned against spoiling their natural roses with paint
(Mrs Oliphant).

freshet. Rush of water, etc. From *fresh*, in same sense, from adj. *fresh*, perh. orig. of current of fresh water at river-mouth. ? For *fresh shot* (v.i.).

The saide river of Plate is so full of sands and dangers, and the fresh so fierce sometimes, that no shipping dares to deale with it (Hakl. xi. 38).

fresh shot: courant d'eau douce à l'embouchure d'une grande rivière ou d'un fleuve (Lesc.).

fret[1]**.** Verb. AS. *fretan*, for *for-etan* (see *eat*); cf. Du. *vreten*, Ger. *fressen*, Goth. *fraitan*. In ME. to eat, devour, esp. of animals, like Ger. *fressen*. With fig. sense cf. to *eat one's heart out*.

Like a moth fretting a garment (*Ps.* xxxix. 12, *PB.*).

fret[2]**.** Separate words seem to be here con-fused—(1) ornamental interlaced work, esp. as head-dress in ME.; (2) two "bends" intersecting (her.); (3) carved ornament (arch.), cf. *fret-work*; (4) bar or ridge on finger-board of stringed instrument. Pos-sible origins are OF. *frette*, lattice-work, of doubtful origin; F. *fretté*, fretty (her.), which is perh. from AS. *frætwian*, to adorn, though the adoption of an AS. word in OF. her. seems incredible; OF. *frait*, broken, L. *fractus* (cf. Ger. *durchbrochene arbeit*, fret-work); the verb *fret* (cf. hist. of *etch*); and F. *frette*, metal band, etc., by metath. from Frankish *feter*, fetter. It does not seem possible to separate them. In quot. 2 there is a play on words.

This majestical roof fretted with golden fire
(*Haml.* ii. 3).

Though you can fret me, yet you cannot play upon me (*ib.* iii. 2).

friable. F., L. *friabilis*, from *friare*, to crumble.

friar. ME. *frere*, F. *frère*, L. *frater*, *fratr-*, brother. Orig. the mendicant orders (see *Austin, Carmelite, Dominican, Franciscan*) who reached England early in 13 cent.; cf., in this sense, It. *frate, Fra*, Sp. *fraile* (earlier *fraire*), Fray, Port. *frade, Frei*.

fribble. Orig. to falter, stammer. ? Imit. Later associated with *frivol* and *fritter²*.

fricandeau. F., app. related to *fricassee*.

fricandeaux: short, skinlesse, and daintie puddings, or quelkchoses (Cotg.).

fricassee. F. *fricassée*, p.p. fem. of *fricasser*, "to frie" (Cotg.), of doubtful origin. ? From *fracasser* (see *fracas*), influenced by *frire*, to fry. Cf. *concasser*, to pulverize, pound in a mortar.

fricassée: any meat fried in a panne; also, a kind of charge for a morter, or murdering peece, of stones, bullets, nailes, and peeces of old yron closed together with grease, and gunpowder (Cotg.).

fricative [*ling.*]. Consonant produced by obstruction (v.i.). Cf. Ger. *reibelaut*, from *reiben*, to rub.

friction. F., L. *frictio-n-*, from *fricare, frict-*, to rub.

Friday. AS. *frígedæg*, WGer. transl. of L. *Veneris dies* (whence F. *vendredi*), from OFris. *Frīg* (cf. ON. *Frigg*, wife of Odin, Woden, orig. ident. with *Freyja*, the Norse goddess of love); cf. Du. *vrijdag*, Ger. *freitag*. See *frau, free, friend*. ON. *frjādagr* is from AS. With *Good Friday* cf. obs. *good tide*, Christmas, Shrovetide.

friend. AS. *frēond*, orig. pres. part. of a Teut. verb, to love; cf. *free* and Ger. *freien*, to woo. Com. Teut.; cf. Du. *vriend*, Ger. *freund*, ON. *frændi*, Goth. *frijonds*. Assumed as title (17 cent.) by *Society of Friends*, vulg. Quakers. *Friendly Society* was orig. (c. 1700) the name of a fire-insurance company.

frieze¹. Cloth. OF. *drap de Frise*, cloth from *Friesland* (ModF. *toile de Frise* is a different material). The verbs to *frieze* (F. *friser*), *frizz, frizzle*, may have sprung from the curly nap of the material, but there are difficulties of chronology. Some authorities invoke the curly heads of the *Frisians*, others AS. *frīs*, curly, which may be from the race. Connection with F. *fraise*, ruff, etc., is also possible. If the earliest application of F. *friser* is to the hair, one might invoke Du. *vrees*, fright (cf. *horrid* and to *make one's hair curl*).

Pro ix bras panni lanei de Frise
(*Earl of Derby's Exped.* 1390–93).

vreesen: timere, metuere, pavere, formidare, horrere (Kil.).

frieze² [*arch.*]. F. *frise*, app. related to It. *fregio*. Origin doubtful, the accepted etym. from *Phrygium* (*opus*) being an unlikely guess.

frigate. F. *frégate*, It. *fregata*; cf. Sp. Port. *fragata*. Like many other ship-names, of obscure origin and doubtful earlier meaning. The forms are curiously parallel to those of *regatta*. Hence *frigate-bird* (18 cent.) for earlier *man-of-war bird*.

fregata: a kinde of ship called a frigat, a pinace, a barge, a fliebote, a brigandine, or spiall ship (Flor.).

fright. Northumb. *fryhto*, metath. of AS. *fyrhto*. Also verb *fyrhtan*; cf. obs. Du. *vruchten*, Ger. *fürchten*, Goth. *faurhtjan*, to fear. Causal sense is peculiar to E. *Frighten* (not in Shaks. or *AV.*) is a late formation of 17 cent. *Frightful* was orig. timid (cf. *dreadful, fearful*). *Frightfulness* has a spec. sense as rendering of Ger. *schrecklichkeit*, applied officially (Aug. 27, 1914) to the intimidation of a neutral civilian population by outrage, massacre and the destruction of historic buildings and artistic treasures.

Louvain will remain, perhaps, the classic instance of *Schrecklichkeit*....But it was not the worst (Brand-Whitlock, *Belg. under Ger. Occup.* i. 129).

frigid. L. *frigidus*, from *frigēre*, to be cold.

frijoles. Beans. Mex. Sp., perh. cogn. with *flageolet²*.

frill. Prob. the sense of animal's mesentery is the orig., though not recorded early; cf. F. *fraise*, mesentery, ruff, *petite oie*, goose giblets, frills and furbelows, Ger. *gekröse*, mesentery, giblets, plaited ruff, and our own *chitterling* (q.v.), *tripe* (q.v.), and "boiled leg of mutton with the usual trimmings" (*Pickwick*). Origin unknown. To *put on frills* is US.

fringe. ME. & OF. *frenge* (*frange*), L. *fimbria*, edge, plait, etc. Also applied to hair, e.g. *Piccadilly fringe, Newgate fringe* (*frill*).

fringillaceous. From L. *fringilla*, finch.

frippery. Earlier *freperie*, OF. (*friperie*), old clothes, from *friper*, "to wear unto rags by often rubbing" (Cotg.), OF. *freper*, from *frepe, ferpe, felpe*, rag, of obscure origin. For mod. sense cf. *chiffon*.

friseur. F., see *frieze¹*.

Frisian [*ling.*]. Of *Friesland*, Du. and Ger. islands in North Sea. The lang. is the nearest relative of E., and there was prob.

a Fris. element in the various "Anglo-Saxon" expeditions to Britain.

frisk. Orig. adj., fresh, lively. OF. *frisque*, dial. form of *frais*, OHG. *frisc*, fresh.

galante or fresshe in apparayle: frisque (Palsg.).

frisket [*typ.*]. Frame to keep sheet in position. F. *frisquette*, a kind of stencil.

frit. Mixture of sand, etc., prepared for glass-making. F. *fritte*, p.p. fem. of *frire*, to fry, or through It.

frith[1] [*hist. & dial.*]. Forest, waste, esp. in poet. *frith and fell*. Prob. at first enclosure, used by Layamon for park; cf. Ger. *friedhof*, cemetery, *einfriedigen*, to fence in, E. dial. *frith*, hedge. Ident. with AS. *frithu*, peace. Com. Teut.; cf. Du. *vrede*, Ger. *frieden*, ON. *frithr*, Goth. **frithus* (in *Frithareiks*, Frederick); cogn. with *free*, *friend*. Cf. AS. *deorfrith*, deer frith, *frithgeard*, frith yard. See also *frankpledge*.

frith[2]. See *firth*, also quot. s.v. *gale*[2].

fritillary. Plant, butterfly. From L. *fritillus*, dice-box, from markings.

fritter[1]. Pancake. F. *friture*, from *frire*, to fry. Cf. *batter*, *tenter*.

fritter[2]. Verb, usu. with *away*. From *fritter*, fragment, OF. *freture*, *fraiture*, L. *fractura*, from *frangere*, *fract-*, to break, combining with obs. *fitter*, fragment (? cogn. with Ger. *fetzen*, rag).

Fritz. German soldier. Pet form of *Friedrich*, lit. peace powerful. Cf. *dago*, *pandy*[2].

frivolous. For earlier *frivol*, F. *frivole*, L. *frivolus*. Verb to *frivol* is mod. back-formation.

frizz[1], **frizzle.** Curl, etc. See *frieze*[1].

frizz[2], **frizzle.** In frying pan, etc. Imit. extension of *fry*; cf. *sizzle*.

fro. Dial. and in *to and fro*. ON. *frā*, cogn. with *from*; cf. Sc. *frae*. See *froward*.

frock. F. *froc*, OHG. *hroc*, whence MedL. *hroccus*, which Kluge regards as distinct from Ger. *rock*, coat (see *rochet*). For init. cf. *flank*. Orig. garment of monk, whence verb to *unfrock*. For wide variation of sense cf. *gown*.

jetter le froc aux orties: a monke to abandon his order, and profession (Cotg.).

Froebelian. Of *Froebel*, German educationist (†1852), founder of *kindergarten* system.

frog[1]. Reptile. AS. *frogga*, without the suffix which appears in AS. *frox*, for **forsc*; cf. Du. *vorsch*, Ger. *frosch*, ON. *froskr*. *Frosh* is still common in dial. *Frog-march* appears to be a police metaphor. With *froggy* (*frog-eater*), Frenchman, cf. *toady*.

frog[2]. In horse's hoof. Also called *frush*. App. from *frog*[1], as G. βάτραχος also has both meanings; cf. F. *souris*, lit. mouse, cartilage in horse's nostril. The resemblance to F. *fourchette*, little fork, used (vet.) in same sense, is curious, but may be accidental; also It. *forchetta* (v.i.). These may be ult. from OHG. *frosk*, frog, whence OF. *frois*.

The French men call it "furchette," which word our ferrers...do make it a monasillable, and pronounce it "the frush"
(Topsell, *Hist. Four-footed Beasts*, 1607).

forchetta: a disease in a horse called the running frush (Torr.).

frush, or *frug of a horse*: is a sort of tender horn... in the form of a fork (*Gentleman's Dict.*).

frog[3]. On mil. coat. ? Port. *froco*, "a sort of ribband, or label, hanging down on garlands and garments" (Vieyra), L. *floccus* (see *flock*[2]).

frolic. Orig. adj. Du. *vrolijk*, from *vro*, merry; cf. Ger. *froh*, *fröhlich*.

The frolic wind that breathes the spring
(*Allegro*, 18).

from. AS. *fram*, orig. forward (see *frame*); cf. OHG. ON. *fram*, Goth. *framis* (compar.).

frond. L. *frons*, *frond-*, leaf, adopted by Linnaeus in spec. sense distinct from *folium*.

Fronde [*hist.*]. Malcontent party. After F. *fronde*, party of nobles against Mazarin, temp. minority of Louis XIV. F., sling, used of a child's game, OF. *fonde*, L. *funda*, with unexplained *-r-*.

front. F., L. *frons*, *front-*, forehead, orig. sense in E., as still in *head and front*, after *Oth.* i. 3. Mod. mil. sense, developed from more restricted sense of forward line, whence *change of front*, is now borrowed back by F. *Frontage* was orig. land abutting on water; cf. *sea-front*. With *frontier*, F. *frontière*, cf. It. *frontiera*, Sp. *frontera*. *Fronton* (arch.) is F., It. *frontone*.

Frontignac. Wine. Altered, on *cognac*, from *Frontignan* (Hérault).

frontispiece. Altered, perh. on *chimney-piece* (q.v.), from *frontispice*, F., MedL. *frontispicium*, façade of building, from *frons*, front, *specere*, to behold.

frore [*archaic*]. See *freeze*.

frost. AS. *frost*. Com. Teut.; cf. Du. *vorst*, Ger. *frost*, ON. *frost*; cogn. with *freeze*. *Frost*, failure (theat.), is prob. after Wolsey's *killing frost* (*Hen. VIII*, iii. 2). With *frost-bitten* cf. *weather-beaten* (q.v.).

froth. ON. *frotha* or *frauth*; cf. AS. *āfrēothan*, to froth.

frou-frou. F., imit. of rustling sound.

frounce. See *flounce*².

frow. Du. *vrouw.* See *frau.*

froward. From *fro* (q.v.), *-ward* (q.v.). ME. had also *fromward.* Only fig., app. to render L. *perversus* (*Ps.* xviii. 26). Cf. *toward.*

frown. OF. *froignier*, to frown, look disdainful, replaced by *re*(*n*)*frogner*, usu. in p.p., forbidding, surly. ? From Gaulish *frogna*, nostril, with idea of haughty grimace.

frowzy. ? For earlier *frowy*, rank, perh. from AS. *thrōh*, rancid, with init. change common in dial. speech (*I don't fink*). *Froust* is a mod. schoolboy formation.

> Or like not of the frowie fede
> (Spenser, *Shepherd's Cal.* July, 111).

fructify. F. *fructifier*, L. *fructificare*, from *fructus*, fruit, and *facere*. In Chauc.

frugal. F., L. *frugalis*, from *frux*, *frug-*, profit, usu. in pl. *fruges*, fruits; cogn. with *fruit.* For double sense (persons and things) cf. its opposite *luxurious.*

fruit. F., L. *fructus*, from *frui*, *fruct-*, to enjoy (v.s.); cogn. with *brook*². Orig. of all vegetable products, *fruits of the earth.* *Fruiterer* is extended from earlier *fruiter*; cf. *caterer, poulterer*, etc. *Fruitless* occurs first in fig. sense. *Fruitarian* is a bad formation on *vegetarian.* Cf. *fruition.*

frumenty. See *furmety.*

frump. Mod. sense from c. 1800. Earlier (16 cent.), flout, jeer, and app. derisive snort; also as verb, to jeer at. Perh. shortened from earlier *frumple*, to wrinkle, crumple, archaic Du. *frompelen* (*verrompelen*), from *rompelen*, to rumple. Cf. etym. suggested for *frown.*

> *to frumpe or mocke*: jocor, illudo (Holyoak).

frustrate. From L. *frustrari*, from *frustra*, in vain.

frustum. L., piece broken off.

frutescent. Shrublike. Incorr. from L. *frutex, frutic-*, shrub.

fry¹. Verb. F. *frire*, from L. *frigere*, to roast, fry, cogn. with G. φρύγειν; cf. It. *friggere*, Sp. *freir.*

> As Achab whom friede [*Vulg.* frixit] the king of Babiloyne (Wyc. *Jer.* xxix. 22).

> *saulter de la poile, et se jetter dedans les braises*: from ill to worse, from the frying-pan into the fire (Cotg.).

fry². Young fish from spawn. F. *frai*, from *frayer*, OF. *froi-, fri-*, L. *fricare*, to rub, in spec. sense. The form of the E. word may be due to association with ON. *friō*, seed;

cf. Goth. *fraiw*, seed, offspring. With small *fry* cf. F. *menu fretin* (dim. of *frai*).

> Les poissons frient en ycellui temps et laissent leur froiz (14 cent.).

> *fretin*: the frie of any fish; *le menu fretin*: the least size, and worst sort, of cod; of people, the meanest commoners, rascall vulgar, base rout (Cotg.).

fubsy [*colloq.*]. Squat. From obs. *fubs*, small chubby person, app. from baby lang. Applied by Charles II to Duchess of Portsmouth.

fuchsia. From *Fuchs*, Ger. botanist (16 cent.).

fucus. Seaweed. In 17 cent. cosmetic. L., rock-lichen, G. φῦκος.

fuddle. To make drunk; cf. obs. *fuzzle*, in same sense. Very common in Pepys, with alternative *foxed*, of which *fuzzled* may be a playful var.

fudge. As interj. first used by Mr Burchell (*Vic. of Wakef.* ch. xi.). This may be Ger. *futsch*, no good, corrupted from F. *foutu* (see *footy*), ? a reminiscence of Goldsmith's wanderings in Germany. The verb to *fudge* was in my schoolboy days the regular corrupt. of *forge*¹, e.g. a *fudge* for a forged stamp; for loss of *-r-* cf. obs. *fouch*, hindquarters of deer, F. *fourche.* The noun *fudge* may also owe something to Captain *Fudge*, a 17 cent. mariner, known in his day as *Lying Fudge.* His name is ult. ident. with that of Marshal Foch, from one of the Teut. names in *Folc-*, people.

fuel. ME. *fewel*, OF. *fouaille*, Late L. *focalia* (neut. pl.), from *focus*, fire, hearth.

fug [*slang*]. Prob. schoolboy perversion of *fusty.* Cf. *fag*¹.

-fuge, -fugal. From L. *-fugus*, from *fugere*, to flee, with some senses derived from *fugare*, to put to flight.

fugitive. F. *fugitif*, L. *fugitivus*, from *fugere*, *fugit-*, to flee; cogn. with G. φεύγειν. For fig. senses cf. *fleeting.*

fugleman. By dissim. from *flugleman* (c. 1800), Ger. *flügelmann*, wing man, a soldier going through the exercises as a model for recruits. For dissim. cf. *feeble.* *Fugle*, verb (Carlyle), is a back-formation. Cf. *right hand man.*

fugue [*mus.*]. F., It. *fuga*, flight, from L. *fugere*, to flee. Now (Feb. 1919) also of loss of memory, "mental fugue."

-ful. Most adjs. with this suffix have, or had, a double meaning, active and passive, e.g. *fearful, pitiful*, etc.

fulcrum. L., "a stay or proppe" (Coop.), from *fulcire*, to support.

fulfil. AS. *fullfyllan*, a pleon. compd. (*full* and *fill*). For fig. sense cf. F. *remplir*, Ger. *vollbringen*.

A greate mountayne which fulfylleth the whole earth (Coverd. *Dan.* ii. 35).

fulgent. From pres. part. of L. *fulgēre*, to shine; cf. L. *fulgur*, lightning, whence *fulgurite*, explosive.

fuliginous. From L. *fuligo, fuligin-*, soot.

full. AS. *full*. Com. Teut.; cf. Du. *vol*, Ger. *voll*, ON. *fullr*, Goth. *fulls*; cogn. with L. *plēre*, G. πιμπλάναι, to fill. For fig. sense cf. *complete*. Adv. sense, very common in ME., now only in archaic *full well, full many* (after Gray's *Elegy*, 53).

fuller. AS. *fullere*, from L. *fullo*, a fuller of cloth, the verb (cf. F. *fouler*, to trample) being a back-formation.

fulmar. Sea-bird. Orig. from dial. of Hebrides. ON. *fūl*, foul, *mār*, mew, from odour.

fulminate. From L. *fulminare*, from *fulmen, fulmin-*, thunderbolt, cogn. with *fulgur*. Fig. sense orig. in papal condemnations; cf. to *thunder against*.

fulsome. From *full* and *-some*. Orig. overflowing, but associated later in sense with ME. *ful*, foul.

So fulsome a disease (Burton).

fulvous. From L. *fulvus*, tawny.

fumade. Smoked pilchard. Port. *fumado*, from *fumar*, to smoke. Hence, by folk-etym., Corn. *fair-maid*.

fumarole. Vent in volcano. F. *fumerole*, It. *fumarola*, from *fumare*, to smoke.

fumble. Cf. Du. *fommelen*, Ger. *fummeln* (from LG.), also Norw. *fomle*, Dan. *fumle*, and earlier E. *famble*, app. cogn. with AS. *folm*, palm of hand; but partly due to dial. *thumble*, from *thumb*.

fume. F. *fumer*, L. *fumare*, to smoke; cf. It. *fumare*, Sp. *humar*. In fig. sense usu. with *fret* or *chafe*. Cf. *fumigate*, from L. *fumigare*.

fumitory. Plant, also called *earth-smoke*. F. *fumeterre*, MedL. *fumus terrae*; cf. Ger. *erdrauch*.

Lawriol, centaure and fumetere (Chauc. B. 4153).

fun. Orig. hoax, cheat, etc., "a low cant word" (Johns.). From obs. verb *fon* (see *fond*). Orig. sense survives in to *make fun of*. *Funny*, racing skiff (Camb.), is recorded for 1799. The *funny-bone* is so called from its sensitiveness. *Funniment* is mod. after *merriment*.

he put the fun upon the cull: he sharpd the fellow (*Dict. Cant. Crew*).

funambulist. Earlier *funambulo* (Sp.), L. *funambulus*, from *funis*, rope, *ambulare*, to walk.

function. L. *functio-n-*, from *fungi, funct-*, to perform. Math. sense is due to Leibnitz. Mod. sense of gathering is evolved from It. *funzione*, ceremony, orig. of rel. character. As verb (neol.) after F. *fonctionner*. *Functionary* is after F. *fonctionnaire*, coined under the Revolution to replace offic. titles savouring of the royal régime.

fund. L. *fundus*, bottom, whence also F. *fonds*, stock, provision, etc., now differentiated from *fond*, bottom, foundation, etc.

fundament. F. *fondement*, L. *fundamentum*, from *fundare*, to found[1], from *fundus* (v.s.). Formerly in gen. sense (cf. *fundamental*), but anat. sense is equally early (13 cent.).

Whan he heeng up the foundemens of the erthe (Wyc. *Prov.* viii. 29).

funebrial. From L. *funebris*; cf. *funereal*, from L. *funereus*; *funerary*, L. *funerarius* (v.i.).

funeral. First as adj. OF., MedL. *funeralis*. Noun from F. *funeraille*, now only in pl., from L. *funeralia*, neut. pl. of *funeralis*, from *funus, funer-*, burial, etc.

fungible [*leg.*]. Interchangeable, legally substituted. MedL. *fungibilis*; cf. L. *fungi vice*, to act in place of.

fungus. L., cogn. with G. σφόγγος, sponge.

funicular. From L. *funiculus*, dim. of *funis*, rope. Now familiar in connection with Alp. railways.

funk. Oxf. slang, to *be in a funk* (18 cent.). Of Flem. origin (v.i.), prob ident. with obs. *funk*, smoke, stink, which may be ult. from L. *fumigare* (cf. fig. sense of *fume*).

fonck (vetus fland.): turbatio. In de fonck zijn: in perturbatione esse (Kil.).

Where funcking chaps in throngs,
Through clouds arising from tobacco, joke
(*Vademecum for Maltworms*, c. 1720).

funnel. ME. *fonel*, Prov. *founhil, enfounhil*, L. *infundibulum*, from *fundere*, to pour; cf. Sp. *fonil*, Port. *funil*. A word from the southern wine-trade, the F. term being *entonnoir* (see *tun*). *Tunnel* is used in same sense in dial.

entonnoir: a funnell, or tunning-dish (Cotg.).

funny. Racing-skiff. See *fun*.

fur. Noun from verb to *fur*, orig. to cover, line, etc., F. *fourrer*, from OF. *fourre*, sheath, cover (replaced by dim. *fourreau*), OHG. *fuotar*, sheath, fodder, perh. two separate words, but quite possibly ident. (*fodder, fother*). Cf. Goth. *fodr*, scabbard, ON. *fothr*, lining. *Furring*, casing, is still in techn. use.

füttern: to fodder...feed...fother...line a garment... furr a coat (Ludw.).

Her voice, for want of use, is so furred, that it do not at present please me (Pepys, Oct. 12, 1666).

furbelow. See *falbala*.

furbish. F. *fourbir, fourbiss-*, OHG. *furban* (**furbjan*). Orig. of armour, weapons (*Ezek.* xxi. 9).

furcate. MedL. *furcatus*, from *furca*, fork.

furious. F. *furieux*, L. *furiosus* (see *fury*). *Furiously* is often used in gallicism (v.i.) after F. *donner furieusement à penser*, which is from common intens. use of *furieux* (cf. *awful*).

This latest German defeat...must give the German people furiously to think
(Sir F. Maurice, *Daily Chron.* Aug. 13, 1918).

furl. Cf. F. *ferler*, earlier *frêler*. The usual explanation, from *furdle*, for *fardle*, to pack up (see *fardel*), is prob. wrong. There has evidently been confusion with these words, but *furl* is the oldest recorded form. F. *ferler* cannot be from E. if the earlier *fresler* (*Dict. Gén.*) is genuine.

to furl: frêler les voiles (Lesc.).

furlong. AS. *furlang*, from *furh*, furrow. Orig. length of furrow in common field of (theoretically) ten acres.

furlough. Earlier (17 cent.) *furloff*, etc. Du. *verlof*, formed on archaic Ger. *verlaub*, permission, "for leave." The stress is prob. due to synon. Du. *oorlof*, Ger. *urlaub* (the mod. Ger. term). See *leave, believe*.

A Low-Countrey vorloffe (Ben Jonson).

furmety. Earlier *frumenty*, OF. *frumentée, fourmentée*, from *frument, fourment* (*froment*), wheat, L. *frumentum*, cogn. with *frugal, fruit*.

furnace. F. *fournaise*, from L. *fornax, fornac-*, from *fornus*, oven; cf. It. *fornace*, Sp. *hornaza*. First record (c. 1225) refers to *Dan.* iii.

furnish. F. *fournir, fourniss-*, OHG. *frummen* (**frumjan*), to further, accomplish, cogn. with *frame* (q.v.); cf. It. *fornire*, Sp. *fornir*. *Furniture*, F. *fourniture*, has developed in E. a spec. sense (household stuff) unknown to the Rom. langs. In

16–17 centuries it is a gen. term for (war-like) equipment.

Exercises, apt to the furniture of a gentilemannes personage (Sir T. Elyot).

He hath taken into his cabin certain furniture, as swords, caleevers, and musquets (Hakl. xi. 385).

furore. It., craze, L. *furor-em*.

furrow. AS. *furh*. Com. Teut.; cf. Du. *voor*, Ger. *furche*, ON. *for*, drain; cogn. with L. *porca*, "a ridge lying betweene two furrowes" (Coop.).

further. AS. *furthra* (adv. *furthor*), ? from *fore*, with suffix as in *other*, ? or from *forth*. Cf. Ger. *vorder, fürder*. With verb to *further* cf. hist. of *frame, furnish*, and Ger. *fördern*. *Furthest* is a later formation. See *far*.

furtive. F. *furtif*, L. *furtivus*, from *fur*, thief; cogn. with G. φώρ, thief.

furuncle [*med.*]. Boil. F. *furoncle*, L. *furunculus*, lit. little thief (v.s.). Cf. *felon*.

froncle: the hot, and hard bumpe, or swelling, tearmed, a fellon, or uncome (Cotg.).

fury. F. *furie*, L. *furia*, from *furere*, to rage. In sense of virago from L. *Furiae*, used to render G. Ἐρινύες, Εὐμενίδες.

furze. AS. *fyrs*, of unknown origin.

fuscous. From L. *fuscus*, dusky.

fuse[1]. Verb. From L. *fundere, fus-*, to pour. Of much more recent introduction than some of its derivatives.

fuse[2]. Of bomb, etc. It. *fuso*, L. *fusus*, spindle, from orig. shape.

fusee[1]. Of a watch. F. *fusée*, spindleful (v.s.). Also used earlier for *fuse*[2], *fusil*[2].

fusee[2]. Match. App. coined (19 cent.) from F. *fusée*, rocket, orig. spindleful, from L. *fusus*, spindle. See *fuse*[2], *fusee*[1].

fusel. Oil. Ger., bad brandy, formerly, in LG. dial., bad tobacco, from *fuseln*, to bungle. See *foozle*.

fuselage. Body of aeroplane. F., ? from *fuseau*, spindle. See *fuse*[2], *fusil*[1].

fusil[1] [*her.*]. Lozenge, said to have represented orig. a spindle covered with tow. OF. *fusel* (*fuseau*), dim. from L. *fusus*, spindle.

fusil: a spindle, also a term in heraldry, being the representation of a spindle in a coat of arms
(Phillips).

fusil[2] [*hist.*]. Light musket. F., musket, now usual word for rifle, orig. steel for striking sparks, VL. **focile*, whence It. *focile*, from *focus*, hearth, fire; cf. Ger. *flinte*, musket. Hence *fusilier*, orig. armed with *fusil*, and *fusillade* (F.). Spelling *fusee*, *fuzee* is common in 17–18 cents.

fuseleers: are foot soldiers armed with fusees. There are four regiments in our army, which have always been called *Fuseleers*, and go by the name of the *English*, *Scotch*, *Irish* and *Welch Fuseleers*
(*Gent. Dict.*).

fuss. From c. 1700. Origin obscure. It may be Norw. Dan. *fjas*, foolery, nonsense, cogn. with *fise*, pedere. To *make a fuss* was earlier to *keep* (*be in*) *a fuss*.

fustanella. Dim. of Albanian *fustan*, kilt, from It. *fustagno*, fustian.

fustian. OF. *fustaigne* (*futaine*), MedL. *fustaneus*, prob. from *Fostat* (Cairo); cf. It. *fustagno*, Sp. *fustán*. For fig. sense cf. *bombast*.

Of fustian he wered a gypon (Chauc. A. 75).
God forgive me, he speaks Dutch fustian
(Marlowe, *Faustus*).

fustic. Wood and dye. Sp. *fustoc*, Arab. *fustuq*, G. πιστάκη, pistachio.

fustigate. From Late L. *fustigare*, from *fustis*, cudgel.

fusty. OF. *fusté*, "fusty; tasting of the caske" (Cotg.), from *fust* (*fût*), tree trunk, cask, L. *fustis* (v.s.).

futile. F., L. *fut(t)ilis*, easily poured out, leaky, cogn. with *fundere*, to pour.

futtocks [*naut.*]. Also (16–17 cents.) *foot-hooks*, *foot-oaks*, *foot-stocks*. Perh. *foot hooks*, but possibly dim. from F. *fût*, OF. *fust*, L. *fustis*, staff, cudgel, used in many techn. senses. *Futtock-shrouds* is a perversion of earlier *puttock* (q.v.).

cour-baston: a truncheon, or short cudgell; also (in a ship) a crooked peece of timber, termed a knee, or futtocke (Cotg.).

future. F. *futur*, L. *futurus*, fut. part. of *esse*, to be; cf. perf. *fui*, and see *be*. Hence *futurist* (theol.), one who believes that prophecies, esp. of Apocalypse, are not yet fulfilled. In sense of artist determined to save art from "agonizing beneath the ignominious yoke of Michael Angelo" it is quite mod.

fuzz. Imit. of blowing away light particles; cf. *faugh*, *buzz*. Hence *fuzz-ball*, puff-ball, *fuzzy*, fluffy, *fuzzy-wuzzy*, fighting Soudanese dervish with "'ayrick 'ead of 'air" (Kipling).

fylfot. Used by mod. antiquaries for the *gammadion*, *swastika* (q.v.). Misunderstanding of a passage in Lansdowne MS. (c. 1500) where it means ornament used to *fill* the *foot* of a coloured window. For mistake cf. *celt*.

gab, gabble. Imit.; cf. *gaggle*, *gobble*, etc., and obs. Du. *gabbelen*. Prob. distinct from ME. *gab*, to boast, OF. *gaber*, common in OF. epic. Confused also with Sc. *gob*, mouth, Gael. *gob*, beak, e.g. *gift of the gob* is found earlier than *gift of the gab*, and *stop your gab* is for earlier Sc. *steek* (shut up) *your gob*.

gob: the mouth; *gift of the gob*: a wide, open mouth; also a good songster, or singing-master
(*Dict. Cant. Crew*).

gabelle [*hist.*]. F., tax, esp. salt-tax. Arab. *alkabāla*, the word being first recorded (1129) in a proclamation of Roger II of Sicily. For another early Arab. word from the same region see *admiral*.

gaberdine. Cf. OF. *galvardine*, It. *gavardina*, Sp. *gabardina*. It may represent a mixture of Sp. *gabán*, "a gabardine" (Minsh.), and *tabardina* (see *tabard*). Sp. *gabán* is prob. of Pers. origin and cogn. with *caftan*. Now used of a fabric.

Nearly 2,000,000 yards of gabardine have been released for civilian use
(*Daily Chron.* Dec. 13, 1919).

gabion [*mil.*]. Basket of earth. F., It. *gabbione*, from *gabbia*, cage, L. *cavea*, from *cavus*, hollow. Often coupled with *fascine*.

gable. OF., OHG. *gabala* (*gabel*), fork; cf. Ger. *giebel*, gable, Sc. *gavel* from cogn. ON. *gafl*, perh. from Y-shaped timber supporting roof at gable-end. Some authorities connect with OHG. *gibilla*, head, skull, cogn. with G. κεφαλή, head, regarded as ult. cogn. with above.

gaby. Cf. Sc. *gaup*, to gape, *gaupus*, simpleton. Associated with *baby*.

gad[1]. Spike. ON. *gaddr*, spike, nail, associated with unrelated AS. *gād*, goad. Hence *gad-fly*. With quot. (v.i.) cf. *spur of the moment*.

All this was done
Upon the gad (*Lear*, i. 2).

gad[2] [*archaic*]. For *God*, in *egad*, *gadzooks*, etc. The last, sometimes explained as *God's hooks*, may even be for *God's hocks* or *houghs*; cf. the fantastic OF. oath *par les trumeaux de Dieu*.

trumeau de bœuf: a knuckle, hough, or leg, of beefe
(Cotg.).

gad[3]. To wander aimlessly. Back-formation from obs. *gadling*, AS. *gædeling*, comrade, cogn. with *gather*. In ME. this meant base fellow and in 16 cent. vagabond. For *gad-about* cf. earlier *gadder about* (*NED.* 1568).

gadfly. See *gad*[1].

gadgets [*neol.*]. Accessories. From slang of airmen and others associated with machinery, and used like *jigger*. ? From *gadge*, early Sc. form of *gauge*.

The Prussian assessor [state lawyer] with his monocle and ornamental gadgets
(*Daily Chron.* Aug. 3, 1917).

Gadhelic, Goidelic [*ethn. & ling.*]. Mod. formation from Ir. *Gaedheal*, OIr. *Gáidel, Góidel*, Gael. See *Brythonic, Goidelic*.

gadroon [*arch.*]. Opposite of fluting. F. *godron*, of unknown origin.

goderon: a fashion of imbossement used by goldsmiths, etc. and tearmed knurling (Cotg.).

gadzooks. See *gad*[2].

Gael. Sc. Gael. *Gaidheal*. Includes Ir. Celts, but the word was introduced into literature by Scott (*Lady of Lake*).

gaff[1]. Fishing spear, hook. F. *gaffe*; cf. Prov. *gaf*, Sp. Port. *gafa*. Prob. Teut. and cogn. with AS. *gafol*, fork; cf. the naut. *gaff*, boom with forked end to fit against mast.

gaff[2]. Public fair (obs.). Hence, low-class entertainment, *penny-gaff*. To *blow the gaff*, for earlier *blow the gab*, appears to be due to this; cf. to *give away the show*.

gaffer. Perh. for *grandfather*, but analogy of F. *compère*, Ger. *gevatter*, used in same sense, suggests rather *godfather*, dial. *godfer, gatfer*. Cf. fem. *gammer*.

gag[1]. To silence, orig. to strangle. Imit. of sound made by victim; cf. *gaggle*.

gaggyn, or streyn by the throte: suffoco
(*Prompt. Parv.*).

gag[2] [*theat.*]. App. from slang *gag*, to make up a tale, hoax, which may be Sc. *gegg*, in same sense, from *geck*, simpleton, of Du. or LG. origin; cf. Ger. *geck*, fool, etc.

The most notorious geck and gull
(*Twelfth Night*, v. 1).

gage[1]. Pledge. F., of Teut. origin, cogn. with AS. *wedd*, pledge, Goth. *wadi*. It supposes a Late L. *wadium*. Cf. *wage*.

gage[2]. Plum. Now only in *greengage*, but *Sir William Gage*, of Norfolk, popularized (c. 1725) not only the *reine-claude*, named in honour of the wife of Francis I, but also the *blue* and *purple gage*.

gage[3] [*naut.*]. In *weather-gage* (Raleigh), position of advantage. For *gauge*.

gaggle. Cry, company, of geese. Imit.; cf. *cackle, gobble*.

gaikwar, guicowar. Hind. *gāekwar*, cowherd, title of Mahratta kings of Guzerat.

gain. First as noun, in late ME. F., from

gagner, OF. *gaaignier*, OHG. *weidenen* (*waidanjan), from *weida*, pasture, hunting, fishing, cogn. with AS. *wath*, ON. *veithr*, hunting; cf. It. *guadagnare*, to gain, OSp. *guadañar*, to mow. Fig. sense springs from the most ancient human occupations. Owing to late introduction, most of the phrases connected with it are also from F., e.g. to *gain over* is combined from to *win over* and F. *gagner*, so also to *gain time* (*ground, the shore*), to *gain on*, are lit. translations from F. The unnecessary adoption of the word, the senses of which were already provided for by *win*, was perh. due to its resemblance in form and meaning to ME. *gein* (v.i.), advantage, ON. *gagn*, cogn. with *gainly* (v.i.).

But when she saw that hir ne gat no geyn
(Chauc. *Anelida*, 206).

gainly. Now rare exc. in *ungainly*. From dial. adj. *gain*, straight, direct, ON. *gegn*, cogn. with E. *again*(*st*), Ger. *gegen*, against, with idea of direct movement. Cf. *gainsay*, and see *gain*.

gainsay. Solitary survival of a once common prefix, AS. *gegn-, gēan-*, against, or cogn. ON. *gegn* (v.s.). See *again*. Cf. *contradict*.

Gainsborough hat. As in women's portraits by *Gainsborough* (†1788).

gairfowl. See *garefowl*.

gait. Formerly *gate*. See *gate*[2], from which it is now differentiated in form and sense.

gaiter. F. *guêtre*, earlier (15 cent.) *guietre*, the circumflex app. not denoting an orig. -*s*-; cf. Walloon *guetl*, ModProv. *gueto*. Orig. belonging to peasant attire. The most plausible etymon is Ger. *waten*, to wade; cf. E. *waders*, high boots for fishing. But, if the -*s*- is orig., it may represent OHG. *wrist*, ankle, cogn. with E. *wrist*.

guestres: startups; high shoes, or gamashes for countrey folkes (Cotg.).

gala. F., It., cogn. with *gallant*.

galact-. See *galaxy*.

Galahad. Virtuous knight, son of Lancelot. Added by Walter Map to the Arthurian legends.

galantine. F., earlier *galatine* (*Wollaton Papers*, 1304–5), orig. a fish-sauce; cf. It. *galatina*. Mod. sense perh. affected by *gelatine*. ? Connected with G. γάλα, milk (see *galaxy*); but cf. Ger. *gallerte*, MHG. *galrede*, in same sense.

Nas never pyk walwed in galauntyne
As I in love am walwed and y-wounde
(Chauc. *Ballad to Rosamund*, 17).

galanty show. Shadow pantomime (19 cent.).
App. connected with It. *galante*, gallant;
cf. *raree-show*. It is written *galanté* in 1847.

"Well—damn—my eyes!" said Private Dormer in
an awed whisper. "This 'ere is like a bloomin'
gallantry-show" (Kipling, *Only a Subaltern*).

galaxy. F. *galaxie*, L., G. γαλαξίας, from
γάλα, γαλακτ-, milk. In fig. sense from 16
cent.

See yonder, lo, the galaxye,
The which men clepe the Milky Wey
(Chauc. *House of Fame*, ii. 428).

galbanum. Resin. L., G. χαλβάνη, prob.
Oriental; cf. Heb. *ḥelbnāh*, the origin of
the *Vulg.* & LXX. words.

gale¹. Bog-myrtle, also called *sweet-gale*.
AS. *gagel*; cf. Du. Ger. *gagel*.

gale². Of wind. From 16 cent. only. App.
connected with ON. *gol*, breeze, whence
ModIcel. *gola* and other Scand. forms. The
etym. usu. given, from Dan. *gal*, short for
archaic *galen*, mad, furious, as applied to
weather, does not suit earliest use or sound,
pleasant (happy) gale, riming with *sail*. The
vowel may have been affected by obs. *galern*
(15 cent.), F. *galerne*, N.W. wind (cf. Sp.
Port. *galerno*).

We saw our ships, with a good gale and fair order
sailing into their frith, which is a great arm of the
sea (W. Patten, 1548).

With gentle gales [du Bartas, *calme vent*], good
guide, on quiet seas (Sylv. *Furies*).

gale³ [*leg.*]. Arrears of rent, mining-licence,
etc., in Forest of Dean, etc. Contr. of
gavel (q.v.). Cf. *gaveller*, "in the Forest of
Dean, an officer of the Crown who grants
gales to miners" (*NED.*).

galeated [*biol.*]. From L. *galea*, helmet.

galeeny [*dial.*]. Guinea-fowl. Sp. *gallina
morisca*, Moorish hen, L. *gallina*.

Galen. Physician of Pergamos (2 cent.). Cf.
Aesculapius.

What says my Esculapius? my Galen
(*Merry Wives*, ii. 3).

He swallowed, at the least, two pounds...of
chemicals and galenicals (*Ingoldsby*).

galena [*min.*]. Lead ore. L., used by Pliny of
a certain stage in process of melting, ? G.
γαλήνη, a calm.

Galilean. Telescope. From *Galileo*, It. astronomer (†1642).

galilee [*arch.*]. Porch. Cf. MedL. *galilaea*.
Perh. after *Matt.* iv. 15.

Those they pursued had taken refuge in the
galilee of the church (*Fair Maid of Perth*, ch. ix.).

galimatias. Jumbled nonsense. F., perh. ult.

L. *grammatica* (see *grammar, gramarye*),
whence also Basque *kalamatica*, noisy conversation. Cf. synon. *gallimaufrey*.

galingale. Aromatic root. OF. *galingal*,
Arab. *khaulinjān*, ? through Pers., from
Chin. *ko-liang-kiang*, mild ginger from *Ko*
(in Canton); cf. OF. *galangue*, Sp. *galanga*,
Du. *galigaan*, Ger. *galgant*. If the above
is correct, this must have been about the
first Chin. word to reach E. (c. 1000 A.D.).

galiot. See *galliot*.

gall¹. Bile. Now usu. fig., bitterness, venom.
AS. *gealla*; cf. Du. *gal*, Ger. *galle*, ON. *gall*;
cogn. with G. χολή, and perh. ult. with
yellow. *Gall*, sore, orig. swelling on horse,
AS. *gealla*, is prob. the same word, perh.
influenced by F. *gale*, itch, scurf, and also
by *gall²*, in sense of excrescence (cf. *wind-
gall*, tumour on fetlock). The verb to *gall*
is a back-formation from *galled* (found in
AS.), afflicted with *galls*, as in *galled jade*
(*Haml.* iii. 2). In ME. *on the gall* (Chauc.
D. 940) was used like mod. *on the raw*.

gall². Excrescence on oak. F. *galle*, L. *galla*,
"a fruite called galles" (Coop.).

gallant. F. *galant*, pres. part. of OF. *galer*,
to make merry (cf. *gala*). Some of the
F. & E. senses are from cogn. It. *galante*,
courtly, honourable, Sp. *galante*, gaily
dressed, sprightly. Origin obscure. ? From
AS. *gāl*, gay, wanton, proud, also as noun,
levity, lust, etc., cogn. with Goth. *gailjan*,
to cheer, ? and ult. with L. *hilaris*.

galleass. See *galliass*.

galleon. Sp. *galeón*, augment. of obs. *galea*.

gallery. F. *galerie*; cf. It. *galleria*, Sp. *galéria*,
MedL. *galeria* (9 cent.). Origin obscure,
perh. ult. from G. κᾶλον, wood; cf. origin
of *balcony*. The *gallery* is contrasted with
the "gentlemen of the pit" by Lovelace
(1649). To *play to the gallery* is 19 cent.,
but quot. below, of politician talking to
the press, is much earlier than the E.
phrase.

Bien souvent quand il [Lamartine] fait ses haran-
gues à la Chambre, ce n'est pas à elle qu'il s'adresse,
c'est à la galerie, c'est aux gens qui le liront
demain (Sainte-Beuve, 1846).

galley. OF. *galee, galie* (replaced by *galère*).
Origin obscure; cf. Late G. γαλέα, MedL.
galea (in Asser's *Life of Alfred*, 9 cent.),
It. *galea*, obs. Sp. *galea*. Synon. It. *galeara*
(whence F. *galère*), Sp. Port. *galera*, point
to ult. connection with *gallery*; cf. also
MedL. *galeida*, whence MHG. *galeide*.
Perh. ult. from G. κᾶλον, wood, as the

earliest record is G. (cf. *gallery*). The cook's *galley* (naut.) was perh. orig. a joke. The printer's *galley* is the same word; cf. corresponding use of F. *galée*, Sp. *galera*. The *galley* rowers were generally slaves and criminals, whence many allusive uses. *In that galley* is after Molière's *Que diable allait-il faire à* (*dans*) *cette galère?* (*Scapin*, ii. 11). The *galleyworm*, millipede, is named from its legs suggesting the oars.

La Rochefoucauld may seem to come strangely into this gallery (sic)
(*Sunday Times*, June 9, 1918).

galliambic [*metr.*]. From L. *galliambus*, *iambus* of the *galli*, priests of Cybele.

galliard [*archaic*]. F. *gaillard*; cf. It. *gagliardo*, Sp. *gallardo*. App. OHG. *gail*, *geil*, fierce, arrogant (cf. AS. *gāl*, wanton, proud, and see *gallant*), with suffix *-hart*. *Gaillard* is a common personal name in OF. & ME. (cf. mod. *Gaylard*) and occurs as such in E. long before first dict. records of word.

galliass, galleass [*hist.*]. F. *galeasse*, It. *galeazza*, augment. of *galea* (see *galley*).

Gallic. L. *Gallicus*, of Gaul. Playfully for French; cf. *gallicism*, e.g. "the window gave onto (*donnait sur*) a pretty garden"; *gallicè*, in F. parlance; and compds. of *Gallo-*, e.g. *gallophobia*, *-mania*. For *Gallican* (Church) see *Anglican*.

galligaskins [*dial.*]. Leggings, but in 16 cent. breeches. Partly corrupted from 16 cent. F. *greguesques*, *garguesques*, Venetian breeches, *chausses à la garguesque*, It. *alla grechesca*, in the Greek fashion (cf. ModF. *grègues*, breeches); but *gaskins*, *gascoynes*, found equally early, were associated with *Gascony*; *galley-gaskins* are often described in 16 cent. as shipmen's hose, and Nashe even speaks of "a pair of Switzers omnipotent galeasse breeches" (see *galliass*); so also we find *gally-breeches* (*-hose*, *-slops*) all at about the same date. Nashe also has *gallic-gascoynes*. Possibly all three (*greguesques*, *Gascony*, *galley*) have contributed.

gregues: wide slops, gregs, gallogascoins, Venitians; great Gascon, or Spanish, hose (Cotg.).

greguesques: slops, gregs, gallogascoines, Venitians (*ib.*).

gallimaufry. Hotchpotch. F. *galimafrée*. App. related to synon. *galimatias*. An early etymologist has an anecdotic explanation of a lawyer who, disputing in court as to the ownership of a cock claimed by his client *Mathias*, said *galli Mathias*

by mistake for *gallus Mathiae*. This is prob. apocryphal, but it may be noted that *Maufré*, *Maufroi*, etc., is also a common F. name, from OG. *mathal-frid*, council peace.

gallinaceous. From L. *gallinaceus*, from *gallina*, hen, from *gallus*, cock.

gallinazo. Vulture. For Sp. *gallinaza*, augment. of *gallina*, hen.

Gallio. Indifferentist (*Acts*, xviii. 17).

galliot, galiot. F. *galiote*, It. *galeotta*, dim. of *galea*. See *galley*, *jolly-boat*.

gallipot. For *galley pot*, because this earthenware, used esp. by apothecaries, was orig. brought from Italy in galleys; cf. obs. *galley-tile* (c. 1600), *galley-halfpenny* (c. 1400), silver coin from Genoa. Cf. also obs. Du. *kraaksporselein*, majolica, lit. carrack porcelain.

kraak-porcelyn: the oldest and finest porcelain, so called because it was brought with those caracols out of the East Indies (Sewel).

The wavering apprentice [Keats] has been confirmed in his desire to quit the gallipots
(*Blackwood*, 1817).

gallium [*chem.*]. From L. *gallus*, cock, in allusion to name of discoverer, *Lecoq de Boisbaudran* (1875).

gallivant. Playful elaboration of *gallant*.

The witches are in the practice of gallanting over field and flood (Galt).

Gallo-. See *Gallic*.

galloglass, gallowglass [*hist.*]. Retainer of Irish chief. Orig. pl., from Ir. & Gael. *gall*, foreigner, *óglách*, youth, warrior.

Men in those quarters hable to have the conduit of a band of kerne and gallowglasses
(*Privy Council Acts*, 1545).

gallon. Used in ME. for vessel (Wyc. *Mark*, xiv. 13). ONF. *galon*, OF. *jalon*; cf. F. *jale*, bowl. App. connected with Late L. *galleta*, vessel for fluids, of unknown origin, whence also AS. *gellet*, bowl, Ger. *gelte*, pail.

galloon. Braid. F. *galon*, from *galonner*, to braid the hair. Origin unknown.

gallop. F. *galoper*. Replaced (c. 1500), earlier *wallop* (q.v.); cf. It. *galoppare*, Sp. *galopar*, and, for the *w-* forms, MHG. *walop*, *walopiren*, pointing to OF. **waloper*, of Teut. origin, and prob. containing Goth. *hlaupan*, or ON. *hlaupa*, to run (leap), with an obscure first element, perh. cogn. with E. *well* (adv.), the compd. thus representing *well-leap*. See also *pot-walloper*.

To *gallop*, boil rapidly, is half-imit. *Galloping consumption* is 17 cent.

to *gallop*: fundere gradus.

to *wallop*: idem, cursitare (*Manip. Voc.*).

galloway. Horse from *Galloway*, SW. Scotland. Adj. *Gallovidian* is not a playful coinage (like *Liverpudlian*), but comes from MedL. *Gallovidia,* said to mean foreign Gaels. *Galwegian* is on analogy of *Norway, Norwegian*.

gallowglass. See *galloglass*.

gallows. ME. *galwes* (pl.), AS. *gealga* (sing.). Com. Teut.; cf. Du. *galg*, Ger. *galgen*, ON. *galge*, Goth. *galga*. In all Teut. langs. used early of cross of Christ. With *a gallows* cf. *a shambles*.

gally [*dial. & whaling*]. To frighten. Earlier *gallow* (*Lear*, iii. 2), AS. *āgǽlwan*, to astonish.

galoche. See *galosh*.

galoot [*US.*]. Fellow. Earlier raw recruit, green hand, etc. (E. slang). ? Du. *gelubt*, eunuch.

geeloot: a recruit, or awkward soldier (Hotten).

galop. Dance. F., see *gallop*.

galore. Ir. *go leór*, in sufficiency.

galosh, golosh. F. *galoche*, VL. **galopia*, from G. καλόπους, shoemaker's last, from κᾶλον, wood, πούς, foot. Usu. in pl., with many vars., e.g. *golo-shoes*. "It is curious to find *galoshes*, now suggestive of a valetudinarian curate, thus [in *Piers Plowm.*] an essential part of a medieval knight's equipment" (Smythe-Palmer).

gallozza: a kinde of wooden patins, startops, gallages (Flor.).

galumph. Coined by Lewis Carroll, ? on *gallop*, *triumph*; cf. *chortle*.

He left it dead, and with its head,
He went galumphing back
          (*Through the Looking-Glass*).

galvanism. From *Galvani*, It. physicist, who described it (1792). Cf. *mesmerism, voltaism*. *Galvanized iron* is not galvanized.

Galwegian. See *Galloway*.

gamash [*archaic*]. Gaiter. F. *gamache* (dial.), Prov. *galamacha, garamacha*, Sp. *guadamecí*, Arab. *ghadāmasi*, from *Ghadamas* (Tripoli), famous for leather. Hence Ger. *gamaschen*, gaiters.

gamba. In *viola da gamba*. It., leg. See *gammon²*.

gambado¹ [*dial.*]. Legging, orig. fixed to saddle. E. formation from It. *gamba*, leg. See *gammon²*.

gambado². Caper, etc. From Sp. *gambada*, term of horsemanship. Also *gambade*, from F. Cf. *gambit, gambol*.

gambeson [*hist.*]. Wadded mil. tunic. Also *wambeson*. OF. *gambeson, wambeson*, from *gambeis, wambeis*, from OHG. *wamba*, belly, cogn. with *womb*. From OF. *wambeis* comes ModGer. *wamms*, doublet. Cf. Ger. *panzer*, cuirass, lit. *pauncher*. Prob. Scott's choice of the name *Wamba* (*Ivanhoe*) was suggested by *Sancho Panza* (*Don Quixote*).

gambier. Astringent used in tanning. Malay *gambir*, plant from which obtained.

gambit [*chess*]. OF. *gambet* (*gambit*), Sp. *gambito* (Ruy Lopez, 1561), It. *gambetto*, wrestler's trip, from *gamba*, leg. See *gammon²*.

gamble. Orig. (18 cent.) with sense of cheat. Cf. *gamester*, with orig. fem. suffix. Prob. dial. var. of ME. *gamenen*, partly suggested by *gambol*. See *game, gammon¹*.

gamboge. ModL. *gambogium*, ult. from *Cambodia* (Annam), whence obtained. Cf. *indigo*.

gambol. From F. *gambade*, It. *gambata*, from *gamba*, leg. Orig. term of horsemanship. Ending was confused with *-aud*, *-auld*, and *-d* dropped as in obs. *curtal* (see *curtail*). In sense associated with *game¹*.

gambrel [*techn.*]. Wooden bar for hanging carcases. OF. *gamberel*, from Celt. *cam*, bent. Cf. Welsh *cambren*.

game¹. Sport, etc. AS. *gamen*. Teut., but only surviving in E. & Scand. (Sw. *gamman*, Dan. *gamen*). Supposed to be ident. with Goth. *gaman*, participation, from *ga-*, collective prefix, and root of *man*. Orig. amusement, delight, etc. With later sense-development cf. *sport*. In *fair game* (*sport*), legitimate object of attack, there is some association with *fair play*. To *fly at higher game* is from falconry. The number of phrases connected with the word is characteristic of the nation. Cf. *play*. As adj., esp. in to *die game*, it is a back-formation from *game-cock*, cock of the game (cockfighting). As verb now only for *gamble*.

Play up, play up! and play the game
          (Sir H. Newbolt).

game² [*colloq.*]. Of leg. Also *gammy*. OF. *gambi*, "bent, crooked, bowed" (Cotg.), still in F. dial. use in same sense. Prob. cogn. with F. *jambe*, ONF. *gambe*, leg. See *gammon²*.

gamin. F., street arab. ? Ger. *gemein*, common, mean.

gamma. Third letter (γ) of G. alphabet. Heb. *gimel*, the camel. Used of gamma-shaped objects, e.g. the *gamma moth* or "silver Y"; *gammadion*, G. cross with gamma-shaped (Γ) arms (see *fylfot*).

gammer. See *gaffer*. First *NED.* record is *Gammer Gurton's Needle* (1575).

gammon¹. Nonsense, etc. ME. *gamen*, game, as in *backgammon*. But, as it appears to be a cant word, there may be some obscure jocular allusion to *gammon²*. See *game¹, gamble*.

gammon². Of bacon. ONF. *gambon* (*jambon*), ham, from *jambe*, leg, VL. *camba, gamba*, ham, etc. of animal, G. καμπή, bend, from κάμπτειν. In most Rom. langs., but usual Sp. word for leg is *pierna*, L. *perna*, ham, gammon.

gambone: a hanche, or gammon of bacon, a great leg (Flor.).

gammoning [*naut.*]. Of bowsprit. From verb *gammon*, to lash. Perh. cogn. with *gammon²*; cf. F. *gambe de hune*, puttock shroud.

gammy. See *game²*.

gamogenesis [*biol.*]. Sexual reproduction. See *bigamy, genesis*.

gamp. From *Sarah Gamp*.

Mrs Gamp had a large bundle with her, a pair of pattens, and a species of gig umbrella
　　　　　　　　(*Martin Chuzzlewit*, ch. xix.).

gamut. OF. *gamaut*, MedL. *gamma ut*, from *gamma* (q.v.), indicating note below A, and *ut*, first of a series of syllables used to indicate notes of scale. These syllables, *ut, re, mi, fa, sol, la, si*, the first now replaced in E. by *do*, are said to have been adopted by Guy of Arezzo (early 11 cent.) from L. hymn for St John the Baptist's Day (v.i.).

Ut queant laxis *re*sonare fibris
*Mi*ra gestorum *fa*muli tuorum
*Sol*ve polluti *la*bii reatum,
Sancte *J*ohannes.

gander. AS. *gan(d)ra*; cf. Du. LG. *gander*, earlier *ganre*. See *goose, gannet*.

gang. AS. *gang*, going, way, from *gangan*, to go, as in *gang your ain gait*. Com. Teut.; cf. obs. Du. *gangen*, Ger. *gehen* (p.p. *gegangen*), ON. *ganga*, Goth. *gaggan*. Etym. sense survives in *gangway*, orig. in gen. sense, then naut., and now in House of Commons and theatre. For sense of "crew," people going together (orig. naut.), cf. cogn. AS. *genge*, troop (whence obs. naut. *ging*, regularly used for crew of boat in Hakl. and Purch.), and *gegenga*, asso-

ciate (so also Ger. *gefährte*, companion, from *fahren*, to fare). *Gang*, set, is in gen. dial. use.

A gang of white hammock-cloths
　　　　　　　　(Marryat, *Frank Mildmay*).

Gangetic. L. *Gangeticus*, of the *Ganges*, G. Γάγγης.

ganglion. G. γάγγλιον, tumour, used by Galen for nerve-centre.

gangrene. F. *gangrène*, L., G. γάγγραινα; cf. Sanskrit *jarjara*, decayed.

gangue [*min.*]. Matrix. F., Ger. *gang*, lode of metal, cogn. with E. *gang*.

gangway. AS. *gangweg*. See *gang*.

ganja. Preparation of hemp. Hind. *gānjhā*.

gannet. Sea-fowl. AS. *ganot*; cogn. with Du. *gent*, OHG. *ganazzo*, gander. See *goose*. In dial. also *gaunt*.

The great white fowle, called of some a gaunt
　　　　　　　　(Hakl. viii. 59).

ganoid. Of fish scales. F. *ganoïde*, from G. γάνος, brightness.

gantry, gauntry [*dial.*]. Four-footed stand for barrels; now engineering term. ONF. *gantier* (*chantier*), L. *cantherius*, rafter, transom, orig. pack-horse, G. κανθήλιος, pack-ass. Cf. hist. of *chevron, clothes-horse*, etc. Mod. form perh. due to *pantry*, while Sc. *gawntree* is after *gawn*, gallon, and *tree* as in *rooftree*.

chantier: a gauntry, or stilling, for hogsheads &c., to stand on (Cotg.).

Ganymede. Waiter. G. Γανυμήδης, cup-bearer of Zeus. Cf. *Hebe*.

gaol, jail. ONF. *gaole* (*geôle*), VL. *caveola*, dim. of *cavea*, cage. The *g-* was orig. hard (cf. names *Gale, Galer*), but ME. had also *jaole*, from Central F., the sound of which has prevailed. See *cage, cajole*. *Jail-bird* seems to allude to orig. sense (cage), but is prob. after *gallows-bird*. *Jail-delivery* is the clearing out of all prisoners at the assize, when they must be either condemned or acquitted.

gap. ON. *gap*, chasm, cogn. with *gape*. Orig. breach in wall, hedge (*Ezek.* xiii. 5). Esp. with *fill, stop*.

gape. ON. *gapa*, to open the mouth; cf. Du. *gapen*, Ger. *gaffen*. With to *gape after* cf. *abeyance*.

gar. See *garfish*.

garage. F., from *garer*, to make safe. Mod. use from railway sense, to shunt. See *garrison, ware²*.

James Alban, the detective taximan, said he garaged in the mews (*Daily Chron.* Nov. 7, 1919).

garance. Yellow dye. F., madder. OF. *warance* (12 cent.), AF. *warenge*, point to Teut. origin. ? From OHG. *weren* (*währen*), to endure (cf. *fast dye*).

There is no small free-board to Janet McPhee, nor is garance any subdued tint
(Kipling, *Bread upon the Waters*).

garb. Orig. elegance, behaviour, style, e.g. *in the garb of*. OF. *garbe* (*galbe*), contour, It. *garbo*, elegance, from OHG. *garawī*, preparation, whence Ger. *gerben*, to tan. Cf. *gear*, obs. *yare* (*Temp*. v. 1), Ger. *gar*, quite, and Sc. *gar*, to perform, cause.

garbo: grace, handsomnes, finenes, neatenes; also a garbe, a propernes, a comelines (Flor.).

garbage. Orig. (15 cent.) giblets of a fowl; later confused with *garble*, siftings, refuse, from verb *garble* (q.v.). Of obscure origin, but perh. ult. connected with *garb* (q.v.), as OHG. *garawen* had the gen. sense of prepare, also cook. But analogy of *pluck* (q.v.) and dial. *gather* suggests possible connection with *grab*.

garble. Orig. to sift and select spices. Hence to select dishonestly in statements, accounts, etc. OF. *garbeler*, *grabeler*, It. *garbellare*, Arab. *gharbala*, from *ghirbāl*, sieve, Late L. *cribellum*, dim. of *cribrum*, sieve, cogn. with *cernere*, *cret-*, to separate. For wanderings cf. *apricot*, *carat*, etc.

That his spyces be good and clene garbelid
(*Coventry Leet Book*, 1474).

Hee [Richelieu] also had a privat place in Paris call'd *l'Académie de beaux esprits* where 40 of the choicest wits of France used to meet every Munday to refine and garble the French language of all pedantic, and old words (Howell, 1650).

garboard [*naut.*]. Usu. with *strake*. Range of planks next keel. Du. *gaarboord*, with *gaar* for *gader*, gather; cf. F. *gabord*, from Du.

The garbar streeke in the sterne shuttes
(Jourdain's *Journal*, 1612).

garboil [*archaic*]. Hubbub, commotion. OF. *garbouil*, It. *garbuglio*, from *garbugliare*, "to garboile, to hurlie-burlie" (Flor.); second element cogn. with *boil*[1], first doubtful.

garçon. Now only of F. waiter, but a common word (*garsoun*) in ME. Origin unknown.

garden. ONF. *gardin* (*jardin*), from OF. *gard*, *gart*, of Teut. origin; cf. *garth*, *yard*[2]; cogn. with L. *hortus*, G. χόρτος. *Common or garden* (slang) is for scient. L. *communis vel hortensis*, applied to widely diffused plants and insects.

gardenia. From *Dr A. Garden*, Vice-president of Royal Society (†1791).

gare-fowl, **gairfowl**. Great auk. ON. *geirfugl*. First element perh. ON. *geirr*, spear; cf. *geirhvalr*, kind of whale.

garfish. From obs. *gare*, spear, AS. *gār*. Com. Teut.; cf. OHG. *gēr*, ON. *geirr* (v.s.), Goth. *gais* (only in personal names); also L. *gaesum*, G. γαῖσον, javelin, from Teut.; also OIr. *gái*. For fish-name cf. *pike*.

Gargantuan. From *Gargantua*, voracious giant, father of Pantagruel (Rabelais), prob. suggested by OF. *gargate*, throat (v.i.).

garget. Throat-disease of cattle, poultry, etc. Earlier also *gargil*. See *gargle*.

gargle. F. *gargouiller*. Imit.; cf. *gurgle*, L. *gurgulio*, wind-pipe, also G. γαργαρίζειν, to gargle, whence archaic *gargarize*.

gargouiller: to gargle, or gargarize; also, to ratle in the throat (Cotg.).

gargoyle. F. *gargouille*, "the weasle, or weason of the throat; also, the mouth of a spowt, representing a serpent, or the anticke face of some other ugly creature" (Cotg.). As above.

garial. Crocodile. See *gavial*.

garibaldi. Red blouse, like shirts worn by followers of *Garibaldi*, liberator of Italy (†1882). The name is Teut., OHG. *gērbald*, spear bold (see *garfish*).

garish. ? From obs. *gaure*, to stare, perh. cogn. with *gaze* and Sc. *gaw*, to stare. Cf. *staring colour*; also *gazing-stock*, obs. *gauring* (*garing*)*-stock*.

The neighebores, bothe smale and grete,
In ronnen for to gauren on this man
(Chauc. A. 3827).

garland. OF. *garlande* (replaced by *guirlande* from It.); cf. It. *ghirlanda*, Sp. *guirnalda*, and obs. Rom. forms in *gar-*. ? Ult. from MHG. *wieren*, to adorn, OHG. *wiara*, (gold) wire. First meaning was prob. metal circlet, etc. Cf. F. *couronne*, crown, garland.

Coronula aurea, quae vulgariter "garlanda" dicitur
(Matthew Paris, 1247).

garlic. AS. *gārlēac*, spear leek. Earlier also called *clove-leek*; cf. Ger. *knoblauch*, by dissim. from MHG. *klobelouch* (*clove*[1]). See *garfish*, *leek*.

garment. ME. *garnement*, F. (now only in sense of "baggage," bad lot, etc.), from *garnir*. See *garnish*. Cf. *raiment*.

garner. OF. *gernier* (*grenier*), L. *granarium*, granary, from *granum*, grain. Now usu. poet.

garnet[1]. Gem. ME. also *grenat*, F., L. *granatum* (sc. *malum*), pomegranate, from resembling seeds of same. In most Europ. langs.

garnet[2] [*naut.*]. Hoisting tackle. Prob. slightly altered in sense and form from F. *garant*, fall-tackle, Breton *garan*, lit. crane (bird and apparatus). Cf. the almost synon. *burton*, earlier (15 cent.) *brytton*, *breton*, pointing to a Breton contrivance. Howell (*Tetr.*) has *clew garent*, but this may be a misprint.

garnish. F. *garnir*, *garniss-*, OHG. *warnēn* (*warnjan*), reflex. in sense, to protect oneself; cf. AS. *warnian*, to take warning. See *warn*. Orig. chiefly of warlike preparation; cf. F. *garnison*, garrison. Etym. sense survives in leg. sense of warning (bank, etc.) in attaching funds of debtor. Hence *garnishee*. For *garniture* cf. *furniture*.

garotte. See *garrotte*.

garret. In ME. a turret, watch-tower. OF. *garite*, refuge, sanctuary (F. *guérite*, sentry-box), from *garir*, to protect (F. *guérir*, to cure), OHG. *werian* (*warjan*), now *wehren*, to protect; cf. AS. *werian*, to defend. See *ware*[2], *weir*. The hist. of this word is the clue to the origin of *sentry* (q.v.).

garite: a place of refuge; also, a sentrie, or little lodge for a sentinell, built on high (Cotg.).

garrison. OF. *garison*, *warison* (F. *guérison*, cure), whence obs. E. *warison*, misunderstood by Scott (*Lay*, iv. 21) as "war sound." From *garir*, to protect (v.s.). Orig. defence, safety; in mod. sense substituted (c. 1500) for ME. *garnison* (Chauc.), F. *garnison*, from *garnir* (see *garnish*). Henry VII writes *garysson of Frenshmen*, *garnison of Frenshemen*, in the same letter (*Paston Let.* iii. 357).

garron [*Sc.*]. Nag. Gael. *gearran*, gelding, from *gearr*, to cut.

garrotte, **garotte**. Sp. *garrote*, "a cudgell to winde a cord, as carriers do to packe with" (Percyvall). Hence Sp. method of capital punishment by strangulation. Cf. F. *garrot*, cudgel, tourniquet. By some supposed to be Celt. and cogn. with F. *jarret*, hock (see *garter*). *Garrotting* was popular in London (c. 1850–60) till cured by the cat.

garrulous. From L. *garrulus*, from *garrire*, to prattle.

garter. ONF. *gartier*, *garetier* (*jarretière*), from *garet* (*jarret*), bend of the knee, hock, dim. of dial. *garre*, *jarre*, of Celt. origin;

cf. Welsh *gar*, thigh, ham, *garan*, shank. The story of the institution of the *Order of the Garter* (1344) rests on Froissart's authority.

garth [*dial.*]. Paddock, etc. ON. *garthr*, cogn. with *yard*[2] (q.v.). Usual in east and north, where Norse influence is strong.

gas. Coined by Van Helmont, Du. chemist (†1644), with vague reminiscence of *chaos* as used by Paracelsus. The success of this artificial word is unique. With slang *gas*, *gasbag*, cf. *windbag*. The verb to *gas*, used before 1914 in factories, has received an extended sense from Kultur. Hence *poison gas*, fig. for meanness and treachery (see *cylinder*). *Gaselier* is a portmanteau word for earlier *gas-chandelier*.

gasconnade. Boastful talk. F., from reputation of inhabitants of *Gascony*, e.g. d'Artagnan, Cyrano de Bergerac.

gash. Earlier *garshe*, for ME. *garse*, from F. *gercer*, to chap, fissure, ? Late L. *caraxare*, G. χαράσσειν, to cut, incise. Form and sense perh. influenced by *slash*.

incisura: a cutte or garse (Coop.), a cut or gash (Holyoak).

gasket [*naut.*]. Short rope securing furled sail. Earlier *gassit* (Capt. John Smith), F. *garcette*, rope's end, dim. of *garce*, wench; cf. *grummet* (q.v.), with which it is commonly coupled. Cf. also *uphroe* (q.v.) and various naut. senses of Du. *juffer*, Ger. *jungfer*. For -*k*- cf. *casket*, and naut. *lasket*, F. *lacet*. The *NED.* is mistaken in supposing *garcette* to be a mod. word. It is recorded 1634 (Jal).

gasket: garcette, ou raban de frelage (Lesc.).

gasp. ME. also *gaisp*, ON. *geispa*, to yawn, for *geipsa*, cogn. with *gape*. Cf. *wasp*. Hence *gasper*, cigarette (army slang).

au dernier souspir: at the last gaspe (Cotg.).

gasteropod. Mollusc. From G. γαστήρ, belly, πούς, ποδ-, foot. Cf. *gastric*, of the stomach; *gastronomy*, F. *gastronomie*, coined by Berchoux (1800) as title of poem on good living, after G. γαστρολογία, title of poem quoted by Athenaeus.

gate[1]. On hinges. AS. *geat*, pl. *gatu*; cf. ON. *gat*, Du. *gat*, opening. Also ME. & dial. *yate*, normal development of *geat*, common in place-names and as surname (*Yates*, *Yeats*). The *ivory and horn gates* were, in G. legend, those by which false and true dreams came.

gate[2] [*loc.*]. Street, way, in Midlands and north. ON. *gata*; cf. Ger. *gasse*, lane, street, Goth. *gatwō*. Altered to *gait* (q.v.) in spec. sense.

gather. AS. *gadrian*; cf. Du. *gaderen*. Ger. dial. *gattern*; prob. cogn. with AS. *gœdeling*, companion (*gad*[3]), Ger. *gatte*, husband, and ult. with *good*. See *together*. To *gather* (of a sore) refers to the "collection" of pus, hence fig. use of *gather to a head* (of plan, plot, etc.), perh. after *Temp.* v. 1. To *gather*, conclude, infer, is from the idea of collected observations or evidence.

gatling. Obsolete machine gun. Invented by *Dr R. J. Gatling* and first used in Amer. Civil War (1861–5). Cf. *maxim*[2].

gauche. F., awkward, left-handed, replacing, in latter sense, OF. *senestre* (L. *sinister*). Origin doubtful. See *gawk*.

gaucho. SAmer. half-breed. Sp., from Araucanian lang. of Chile. Incorr. *guacho*.

gaud. Orig. prank, trick. App. from F. *se gaudir*, to make merry, scoff, VL. **gaudire* for *gaudēre*. Later sense influenced by obs. *gaud*, large ornamental bead of rosary, app. from L. *gaudium*, joy. *Gaudy* is also used in both senses. Cf. *gaudy* (c. 1500), college festival, esp. at Oxf., and *gaudeamus* (15 cent. F.) from student song *Gaudeamus igitur, juvenes dum sumus*. Cf. also Ger. dial. *gaudi*, rejoicing, perh., like *gaudy* in some senses, from L. imper. *gaude*, rejoice.

> By this gaude have I wonne, yeer by yeer,
> An hundred mark sith I was pardoner
> (Chauc. C. 389).

> My peir bedys of calcidenys gaudied with silver and gilt (*Paston Let.* iii. 287).

gauge, gage. ONF. *gauge* (*jauge*), ? MHG. *galge*, gallows, orig. stake, rod, whence also perh. F. *jalon*, measuring stake. Cf. hist. of *rood*. See also *gage*[3]. Hence *gauger*, exciseman.

Gaul, Gaulish, etc. F. *Gaule*, L. *Gallia*. Facet. for French; cf. *Gallic*. In ling. of extinct Celt. langs. of Gaul.

gault [*geol.*]. Clay. ? ON. *gald*, hard snow, whence Norw. *gald*, hard ground, rocky way.

gaunt. App. an EAngl. word. It is much older than *NED.* records, and occurs commonly as a surname, *le Gant*, temp. John and Hen. III. It may be dial. *gant, gaunt* (cogn. with *goose*), used of various waterfowl, with sense-development like that of *haggard*. See *gannet*.

gauntlet[1]. Glove. F. *gantelet*, dim. of *gant*,

glove, OF. also *guant, want* (cf. *gambeson*), of Teut. origin; cf. Ger. *gewand*, garment, ON. *vöttr*, glove. As gage of battle, etc., F. gen. uses *gant*.

gauntlet[2], **to run**. Orig. mil. punishment. Corrupt. of *gantlope*, Sw. *gatlopp*, "gate run," in sense of *gate*[2], a word from Thirty Years' War. Cf. Ger. *gassenlaufen*, adapted from Sw., for native *spiessruten*, spear rods. In E. fig. sense appears as early (17 cent.) as lit.

> *durch die spiess-ruthen lauffen*: to run the gantlope
> (Ludw.).

gauntry. See *gantry*.

gauze. F. *gaze*, perh. from *Gaza* (Palestine); cf. *damask, muslin*, etc.

gavel[1] [*hist.*]. Now chiefly in *gavel-kind*, system (Kent) by which property is divided equally instead of going to eldest son, but orig. a form of tenure. AS. *gafol*, tribute, and *kind* (q.v.).

> In Gavelkind, though the father be hanged, the sonne shall inherit, for their custom is, "The father to the bough, and the son to the plow"
> (Leigh, *Philologicall Commentary*).

gavel[2] [*US.*]. President's mallet, orig. mason's. Origin unknown. ? Connected with Ger. dial. (lower Rhine) *gaffel*, brotherhood, friendly society, cogn. with *give*.

> He was president of the Reichstag since 1912, unfailingly wielding the gavel in autocracy's interests
> (*Daily Mail*, May 27, 1918).

gavial. Sharp-nosed crocodile of Ganges. F., mistake for *garial*, Hind. *ghaṛiyāl*.

gavotte. F., Prov. *gavoto*, dance of the *Gavots*, Provençal name for inhabitants of Alps. ? Cf. Sp. *gavacho*, contemptuous name for people of Pyrenees or Frenchmen.

gawk, gawky. Meanings correspond with F. *gauche*, clumsy, left-handed. *Gawk* is for older *gallock*, still in dial. use, e.g. *gallock-handed*, which may very well be the origin of F. *gauche*, a word of late appearance (15 cent.), without cognates in Rom. langs., and explained only by very dubious conjectures.

gay. F. *gai*; cf. It. *gaio*, OSp. *gayo*. Of obscure origin, possibly ident. with *jay*, a bright-coloured and chatty bird.

> One night he went to bed betimes, for he had caught a fever,
> Says he, I am a handsome man, but I'm a gay deceiver
> (G. Colman, *Unfortunate Miss Bailey*, 1805).

gaze. Orig. to stare in wonder, etc. Cf. Norw. Sw. dial. *gasa*, to gape, stare, and see *garish*. *At gaze* was orig. used of deer, and later in her. (= *guardant*).

gazebo. Turret on roof or wall. ? Jocular "Latin" coinage on *gaze* (cf. *lavabo*). It has replaced obs. *gazing-room* (17 cent.).

gazelle. F., Arab. *ghazāl*; cf. It. *gazzella*, Sp. *gacela*.

gazette. F., It. *gazzetta*, first published at Venice (c. 1550) and supposed to come from *gazzetta*, small Venetian coin, prob. paid for privilege of reading the news-sheet; but some authorities identify it with It. *gazzetta*, magpie, regarded as typical of false chatter. "The Gazette," with offic. announcement of mil. appointments, bankruptcies, etc., was first issued (1665) at Oxf., whither the Court had fled from the Plague. *Gazetteer*, journalist, was used (1693) by Eachard in the title of his geog. dictionary, *The Gazetteer's, or Newsman's, Interpreter*, second ed. called simply *The Gazetteer*.

gazzette: running reports, daily newes, idle intelligences, or flim-flam tales that are daily written from Italie, namely [i.e. especially] from Rome and Venice (Flor. 1611).

This day the first of the Oxford gazettes came out, which is very pretty, full of newes
(Pepys, Nov. 22, 1665).

gazogene. F. *gazogène*, from *gaz*, gas.

gear. Orig. any equipment, esp. armour. ME. *gere*, ON. *gervi*, *görvi*, cogn. with AS. *gearwe*, clothing, armour, and *gearwian*, to make ready. See *garb*. Perh. the hardest-worked word in early ModE., now largely replaced by *stuff*, *tackle*. Senses have received spec. extension with progress of machinery, but mod. *out of gear* corresponds curiously with ME. *not right in his gere*, i.e. badly harnessed.

The [railway] men at Liverpool are working at slow gear [cf. ca' canny]
(*Pall Mall Gaz.* Nov. 28, 1917).

gecko. Lizard. Malay *gēkoq*, imit. of cry.

ged¹. Pikefish. ON. *gedda*, from *gaddr*, spike. See *gad¹*.

ged². For *gad*, i.e. *God*. Cf. *demme*, *demnition*.

Sir Arthur blew his nose and said, "Good Ged! This is worse than Assaye!"
(Kipling, *Marklake Witches*).

gee-gee. From command to horse, with meaning varying according to locality. With *gee ho* cf. F. *dia*, *hue*, etc., also of unfixed meaning.

L'un tire à dia, l'autre à hurhau
(Mol. *Dép. Am.* iv. 2).

geezer [*slang*]. Dial. form of obs. *guiser*, mummer. See *guise*.

Nice old geezer with a nasty cough
(Albert Chevalier).

Gehenna. Church L., Late G. γέεννα, Late Heb. *gē-hinnōm*, valley of *Hinnom*, near Jerusalem, where children were sacrificed to Baal and Moloch (*Jer.* xix. 5, 6). Cf. *jehannum* and see *Tophet*. Hence F. *gêner*, to incommode, orig. to torture.

geisha. Jap., dancing-girl.

gelatine. F. *gélatine*, It. *gelatina*, from *gelata*, jelly (q.v.). See also *galantine*.

geld¹, gelt, gild [*hist.*]. In *Danegelt*, *wergild*. MedL. *geldum*, from AS. *gield*, payment, tribute. Com. Teut.; cf. Du. Ger. *geld*, money, ON. *giald*, payment, Goth. *gild*, tribute. See *yield*.

geld². Verb. Earlier as adj. ON. *geldr*, barren. Cf. Ger. dial. *gelten*, to geld, *gelze*, castrated swine. Hence *gelding*.

Putiphar, the geldyng [*Vulg.* eunuchus] of Pharao
(Wyc. *Gen.* xxxviii. 36).

gelid. L. *gelidus*, from *gelu*, frost.

gelignite. Explosive. Coined from *gelatine* and *ignite*.

gelt. See *geld¹*.

gem. AS. *gim*, L. *gemma*, orig. bud, cogn. with *genus* (q.v.); respelt on F. *gemme*.

Gemara. Latter part of Talmud, commentary on earlier part, *Mishna* (q.v.). Aramaic *gemārā*, completion.

gemini. L., the twins, constellation; hence *geminate*, arranged in pairs. As exclamation for *jiminy* (q.v.).

gemsbok. SAfr. antelope. Du., chamois, from Ger. *gemse*; for application cf. *eland*. Cf. *gemshorn*, organ stop, from Ger.

-gen. F. *-gène*, G. *-γενής*, cogn. with γίγνεσθαι, to be born.

genappe. Yarn. From *Genappe* (Belgium). Cf. *cambric*.

gendarme. F., back-formation from *gens d'armes*, men at arms, later applied to mil. police. *Not* F. for policeman.

gender. OF. *gendre* (*genre*), L. *genus*, *gener-*, kind, translating as gram. term G. γένος, used by Aristotle. See *genus*.

genealogy. F. *généalogie*, Late L., G. γενεαλογία, from γενεά, race (v.s.). In Wyc.

general. F. *général*, L. *generalis*, from *genus*, *gener-*, kind. Contrasted with *special* (see *genus*, *species*). As mil., earlier also nav., title orig. adj. (cf. *governor general*, *attorney general*) qualifying *captain*, as still in *lieutenant general, major general.* The latter title, dating roughly in E. from Cromwell's division of the country into twelve mil. districts, is for earlier *sergeant-major general.* *Captain* (*colonel*) *general* are obs. in E. exc. hist.; cf. Ger. *general-oberst.* *Generalissimo* is It., superl. of *generale.*

Upon these conditions that the Emperour should make him [Wallenstein] absolute generall, that is generalissimo (Sydenham Poyntz, 1624–36).

generate. From L. *generare,* to procreate, from *genus, gener-,* race. Hence *generation,* first in E. (14 cent.) in sense of period of time. Cf. *generic.* See *genus.*

generous. F. *généreux,* L. *generosus,* of high birth, from *genus, gener-,* race. Fig. senses also in F. & L. Etym. sense still in *generous old port.*

genesis. L., G. γένεσις, from γίγνεσθαι, to be born. See *genus.* Adopted, as title of first Mosaic Book, by *Vulg.* from LXX. Also in mod. scient. terms.

genet, gennet, jennet. (Fur of) civet cat. F. *genette,* Sp. *gineta,* Arab. *jarnait.*

geneva [*archaic*]. Gin. Corrupt. of F. *genièvre.* See *gin².*

Geneva. In Switzerland. Head-quarters of Calvinism (16–17 cents.). Hence *Geneva bands* (*gown, hat*), affected by Puritans; *Geneva Bible,* E. transl. of 1560. For *Geneva Cross* see *Red Cross.*

genial. L. *genialis,* from *genius* (q.v.). Orig. relating to generation, growth, whence mod. fig. sense. Sense of conducive to growth survives in *genial climate* (*temperature*).

genie. Of the lamp, etc. F. *génie,* adopted by translator of *Arab. Nights* as rendering of Arab. word which it accidentally resembled. See *jinn.*

genista. Broom plant. L., see *Plantagenet.*

genital. L. *genitalis,* from *gignere, gen-,* to beget. In Wyc.

genitive. F. *génitif,* L. *genetivus* (v.s.), misused by L. grammarians to render G. γενική (πτῶσις), which means properly "generic" (case).

genius. L., from *gignere, gen-,* to beget. Orig. spirit watching over each person from birth; cf. *good* (*evil*) *genius.* Sense of natural ability, etc., found in all Rom. langs., is partly due to confusion with L. *ingenium* (see *gin¹, engine*). Mod. sense of exceptional creative power (not in Johns.) is partly a throw-back to the orig. meaning.

gennet. See *genet, jennet.*

Genoa. Cake, velvet, etc. *Genoa paste* is recorded 1615 (*NED.*). Traffic between Genoa and England was very active; cf. *gallipot.* See also *jean.*

-genous. From L. *-genus,* from root of *gignere, gen-,* to beget.

genre. Esp. in painting. F., kind (see *gender*). In F., of independent style, as compared with historical, landscape, etc.

gent. Short for *gentleman,* as in offic. descriptions and on old tombstones. Now vulgar (see *pants*).

A Norfolk man and of birth no gent. as I can understand (*Plumpton Let.* 1464).

One Mr Newton, a learned and most religious gent. (Evelyn).

genteel. Earlier (c. 1600) *gentile,* F. *gentil,* in orig. sense of *gentle* (q.v.). Now usu. half-contemptuous; cf. *shabby-genteel* (Thackeray). The form *jaunty* (q.v.) shows a still more serious attempt at the F. pronunc.

gentian. L. *gentiana,* from *Gentius,* king of Illyria (2 cent. B.C.), who discovered its properties (so Pliny). In Wyc. (*Jer.* xvii. 6) and early in most Europ. langs.

gentile. F. *gentil,* L. *gentilis,* from *gens, gent-,* race, etc. In Church L. used (e.g. in *Vulg.*) to render G. τὰ ἔθνη, the nations, for Heb. *goyim.*

gentle¹. Adj. ME., F. *gentil,* L. *gentilis,* in class. sense of belonging to a *gens*; but sense of noble, found in Rom. langs., is not in L. The *gentle craft,* prop. one suited to those of *gentle* birth, is applied facet. (16 cent.) both to shoe-making and fishing. Hence mod. *gentle art* (e.g. *of making enemies*). Latest E. sense, mild, is a further development from courteous. *Gentleman* is now a universal title, but *gentlewoman, gentlefolk,* have preserved more of the exclusiveness of F. *gentilhomme,* nobleman. In its highest sense *gentleman,* already in Chauc. (v.i.), has been adopted in F. & Ger. The *Old Gentleman* (*in black*) is in Dryden.

He sholde nat be called a gentil man that...ne dooth his diligence and bisynesse to kepen his good name (Chauc. B. 2830–35).

Coroner. "Did the driver stick to his brakes?"— Witness. "Yes, sir, he did; like a gentleman" (Aug. 1919).

gentle². Maggot. Ident. with *gentle¹,* from softness (*NED.*).

gentry. Altered from archaic *gentrice,* OF. *genterice,* var. of *gentillesse* (cf. *fortalice, fortress*), from *gentil* (see *gentle*). Orig.

rank, and in ME. courtesy, breeding. For collect. sense cf. *nobility*.

genuflexion. MedL. *genuflexio-n-*, from L. *genu*, knee, *flectere, flex-*, to bend.

genuine. L. *genuinus*, native; cf. *ingenuous*. Cogn. with *genus* (q.v.).

genus. L., cogn. with G. γένος, race, γίγνεσθαι, to be born, Sanskrit *janas*, E. *kin* (q.v.). *Genus* and *species* were adopted in L. as renderings of G. γένος and εἶδος, as used by Aristotle.

-geny. See *-gen*.

geo-. G. γεω-, from γῆ, earth, as in *geode*, concretionary stone, G. γεώδης, earthy; *geodesy*, G. δαίειν, to divide; *geognosy*, G. γιγνώσκειν, to know; *geography, geology*, from MedL.; *geomancy*, divination by means of handfuls of earth (cf. *chiromancy*); *geometry*, G. μετρεῖν, to measure; *geopony*, agriculture, G. πένεσθαι, to labour, and many less familiar scient. terms. The oldest in E. use is *geometry*, used at first in connection with arch.

Geordie [*dial.*]. Collier (man or boat), safety lamp. From *George* (q.v.), last sense with ref. to *George Stephenson*.

George. L., G. Γεώργιος (see *Georgic*), Cappadocian prince supposed to have been martyred temp. Diocletian; patron saint of England since Edward III. Hence jewel of Garter, guinea (slang). *By George* is in Ben Jonson. With *Georgian* cf. *Jacobean, Caroline*, and with *Georgia* (US.) cf. *Carolina, Virginia*.

Georgic. L., G. γεωργικός, of a husbandman, γεώργιος, from γῆ, earth, ἔργον, work, adopted by Virgil as title of poems on rural life. Sainte-Beuve calls George Sand's *Mare au diable*, etc. *les géorgiques de la France du centre*.

geranium. "Crane's bill, stork's bill." L., G. γεράνιον, from γέρανος, crane (q.v.). Cf. *pelargonium*.

gérant. F., manager, from *gérer*, to direct, L. *gerere*.

gerbe [*her.*]. Wheatsheaf. Also, a firework. F., Ger. *garbe*, sheaf.

gerfalcon, gyrfalcon. OF. *gerfaucon*, acc. of *gerfauc* (*gerfaut*), compd. of *falcon* (q.v.); cf. It. *girfalco*, Sp. Port. *gerifalte*, Du. *giervalk*, Ger. *gerfalke, gierfalke*, ON. *geirfālki*, all from F. First element is Teut., as shown by occurrence of *Wirfauc* as ME. surname (William Wirfauc, *Yorks. Fines*, temp. John), much earlier than first *NED*. record of *gerfauk* as common noun. This

rules out Ger. *geier*, vulture, hawk, which could not give *w-*, and suggests ON. *verthr*, worthy, Iceland being the home of the best breeds; cf. Ger. *edelfalke* (noble hawk). The form *gyrfalcon*, MedL. *gyrofalco*, is due to a wrong etymology (*gyrate*) found as early as Giraldus Cambrensis (12 cent.).

germ. F. *germe*, L. *germen*, seed (*Macb.* iv. 1), ? for **genmen*, from *gignere*, to beget.

german. F. *germain*, L. *germanus*, fully akin; cogn. with *germ*. Hence *brother german*, with same parents, *cousin german*, with same grandparents. Mod. use of *germane*, akin (to the matter, subject), is after fig. use of *german* in Shaks. (v.i.).

The phrase would be more german [1 Fol. *germaine*, 1 Quart. *cosingerman*] to the matter, if we could carry cannon by our sides (*Haml.* v. 2).

German. L. *Germanus*, used by Romans and Celts, but not by Teutons (see *Dutch*). Prob. orig. name of particular tribe; cf. F. *allemand*, from the *Alemanni* (now Swabians and Swiss). Replaced (16 cent.) earlier *Almain, Dutch*. Also of things not genuine (*measles, silver*, the latter from Hildburghausen). *German Ocean* is Ptolemy's Γερμανικὸς Ὠκεανός. *High German* (whence the literary lang.) belongs to the south, *Low German* (cf. *plattdeutsch*) to the plains bordering North Sea and Baltic, and includes (ling.) E. & Du. *Old High German, Middle High German* cover periods roughly corresponding with Anglo-Saxon and Middle English. *Germanic* is applied to all Teut. langs., viz. *West Germanic*, High and Low German, *East Germanic*, Gothic. Scandinavian is called *North Germanic*, but sometimes included under *West Germanic*. Etymologies proposed for the name (e.g. OIr. *gair*, neighbour, *gairm*, war-cry, OHG. *gēr*, spear) are pure conjectures.

He called me a German and other filthy names (Defendant in Middlesex Police Court, 1915).

germander. MedL. *germandra* (cf. F. *germandrée*), for *gamandrea*, corrupted from Late G. χαμανδρυά, for χαμαίδρυς, ground oak. See *camomile, Druid*. Cf. Ger. *gamander*.

germane. See *german*.

germinate. From L. *germinare*, from *germen, germin-*, germ.

Gerry. Mil. slang for *German* (1917). See *Jerry*.

gerrymander. System of "faking" electoral districts, originated by *Elbridge Gerry*, Governor of Massachusetts. The shape of one district on the map suggested to a painter a *salamander*, improved by a journalist to *gerrymander*. For full details see Thornton. Though attributed to 1812, the term did not become current till after 1840.

That term of current coinage, so well known in America, "gerrymandering"
(Elihu Burritt, *Walk from London to Land's End*).

Vain attempts to gerrymander afresh the parliamentary representation of the ramshackle empire
(*Daily Chron.* Apr. 14, 1917).

gerund [*gram.*]. L. *gerundium*, from *gerere*, to carry on.

gesso. Plaster of Paris. It., L. *gypsum* (q.v.).

gest [*archaic*]. Exploit, epic. See *jest*.

gestation [*med.*]. L. *gestatio-n-*, from *gestare*, from *gerere*, *gest-*, to bear. Cf. *gestion*, carrying on, management, F., L. *gestio-n-*.

gesticulate. From L. *gesticulari, gesticulat-*, from *gesticulus*, dim. of *gestus*, action, gesture, from *gerere*, *gest-*, to perform. Cf. *gesture*, orig. deportment, MedL. *gestura*.

get. ON. *geta*, to obtain, beget, cogn. with AS. *gietan* (in *forget, beget*). Cognates, only in compds., also in Du. Ger. Goth. Orig. past *gat* (*A V.*), p.p. *gotten* (now chiefly US. or in *ill-gotten*). This verb and *take* (also ON.) have supplanted in many senses AS. *niman* (see *nimble*) and *gewinnan*. Its sense-development is extraordinary, the intrans. senses springing chiefly from reflex., e.g. *get you gone*, to *get* (*oneself*) *disliked*.

Whatever payment is made [for coal-mines] should not be dependent upon the tonnage gotten
(*Report of Coal Commission*, June 23, 1919).

geum. Plant. L., "the herbe called avens" (Coop.).

gew-gaw. ? Adaptation or imit. of F. *joujou*, toy, baby word from *jouer*, to play, L. *jocare*. Cf. *juju*.

gey [*Sc.*]. Considerably, as in *gey sharp*. Sc. form of *gay*; cf. *pretty sharp*.

geyser. Icel. *Geysir*, proper name of a special hot spring, from ON. *göysa*, to gush. See *gush, ingot*.

gharry [*Anglo-Ind.*]. Hind. *gārī*, cart.

ghastly. From obs. *gast*, to terrify. See *aghast, ghost*.

ghaut. River-stairs (India). Hind. *ghāt*. The *Ghauts*, mountains, are so-called (by Europeans) from *ghāt* in sense of mountain pass.

ghazal, gazel. Oriental verse-form. Pers., Arab. *ghazal*, love-song.

ghazi. Arab. *ghāzi*, pres. part. of *ghazā*, to fight.

The fifty were ghazis, half-maddened with drugs and wholly mad with religious fanaticism
(Kipling, *Drums of Fore and Aft*).

ghee. Clarified butter. Hind. *ghī*, from Sanskrit *ghṛ*, to sprinkle.

gherkin. Early Du. dim. (now *gurkje*) of *gurk*, for *agurk*, cucumber. Of Slav. origin; cf. Pol. *ogurek*, Czech *okurka*, cucumber. Hence also Late G. ἀγγούριον, obs. It. *anguria*, OF. *angourie*, etc. Ger. *gurke*, earlier *ajurke*, is from eastern LG. But, according to some, the Late G. word is the original, from OG. ἄωρος, unripe.

ghetto. It., "a place appointed for the Jewes to dwell-in in Venice, and other citties of Italie" (Flor.), L. *Aegyptus*, Egypt. Cf. *gitano*.

Ghibelline [*hist.*]. Of imperial (Hohenstaufen) faction in Italy (12 cent.). It. *ghibellino*, from Ger. *Waiblingen*, seat of Hohenstaufens. Cf. *Guelph*.

ghost. AS. *gāst*. WGer.; cf. Du. *geest*, Ger. *geist*. For unoriginal -*h*- cf. cogn. *aghast*, and Flem. *gheest*, which may have influenced Caxton's spelling. Orig. soul, spirit, as in *ghostly*, to *give up the ghost*, *Holy Ghost*, all in AS. The *ghost doesn't walk* (theat.), i.e. there is no money for the actors, so it's no use waiting about, contains an allusion to *Haml.* i. 1. *Ghost-word*, unreal word persisting from orig. mistake, was coined by Skeat. Good examples are *abacot, collimate, syllabus*.

ghoul. "Body-snatching" demon. Arab. *ghūl*, from verbal root meaning to seize. First in Beckford's *Vathek* (1786). Cf. *afreet*.

Ghurka. See *Goorkha*.

ghyll. See *gill*[2].

giallo antico. Marble. It., antique yellow.

giant. F. *géant*, L. *gigas, gigant-*, G. γίγας. Replaced AS. *gīgant*, from L.

giaour. Turk. term of contempt for non-Mussulmans. Pers. *gaur, gabr*, fire-worshippers. Cf. *Guebre*.

Calling them cafars and gawars, which is, infidels or misbeleevers (Hakl. iii. 145, 1568).

Who falls in battle 'gainst a giaour
Is worthiest an immortal bower (Byron).

gib [*archaic*]. Cat. Abbrev. of name *Gilbert*, AS. *Gislbeorht*, bright hostage (see *gibbon*). Cf. *tom-cat*, and *Tibert* (Theodobert), the cat in the *Roman de Renart*.

gibber. Imit.; cf. *jabber*.

gibberish. Appears earlier (c. 1550) than *gibber* (*Haml.* i. 1). Connection of the two is doubtful. Early used in ref. to lang. of rogues and gipsies.

jargonnois: fustian, gibridge, pedlers French
(Cotg.).

gibbet. F. *gibet*, in OF. cross-handled stick, dim. of OF. *gibe*, staff. Cf. F. *potence*, gallows, orig. bracket, support, L. *potentia*.

gibbon. Ape. F. (Buffon), said to be an Indian word. Skeat suggests that this "Indian word" is E. *Gibbon*, dim. of *Gilbert* (see *gib*). The *NED.* does not record *gibbon* in sense of ape before Buffon, but the tombs of the *Gybbon* family at Rolvenden (Kent), dating from c. 1700, are surmounted by an ape's head, the family crest. King John had a falcon named *Gibbon*.

gibbous. Humped, esp. of moon. From L. *gibbus*, hump, cogn. with G. κυφός, bent.

gibe¹, jibe. To jest. From 16 cent. Cf. LG. *gibeln*, Ger. dial. *geifelen*, to laugh mockingly.

gibe² [*naut.*]. See *gybe*.

Gibeonite. Drudge. See *Josh.* ix. 23.

giblets. Cf. OF. *gibelet*, some sort of dish, F. *gibelotte*, rabbit stew, Walloon *giblé d'awe*, goose giblets. Oldest sense in E. is frivolous additions (perh. from cooking metaphor; cf. F. *petite oie*, trimmings, etc.). In the *Prompt. Parv.* explained as *garbage* (q.v.). The analogy of *haslets* (q.v.) suggests connection with OF. *gibe*, staff (see *gibbet*).

gibus. Opera hat. Name of inventor (19 cent.).

giddy. AS. *gydig*, insane, orig. possessed by a *god*; cf. G. ἔνθεος (see *enthusiasm*), and AS. *ylfig*, raving, ? possessed by an *elf*. See *dizzy*.

gier eagle [*archaic*]. Du. *gier*, vulture; cf. Ger. *geier*, cogn. with *gier*, greed (see *yearn*).

The gier eagle and the cormorant (*Deut.* xiv. 17).

giff-gaff [*Sc. & north.*]. Mutual. Redupl. on *give*; cf. synon. F. *donnant donnant*.

gift. AS. *gift*, from *give* (q.v.); cf. Ger. *gift*, poison, *mitgift*, dowry. To *look a gift-horse in the mouth*, i.e. judge its age by teeth, also occurs in F. & Ger.

gig¹. In ME. spinning-top (cf. *whirligig*), giddy girl (cf. *giglet*); app. cogn. with *jig*. Sense of light vehicle and boat is mod. (late 18 cent.), and identity of these with ME. *gigge* is doubtful. *Gigmanity*, respectability, was coined by Carlyle on the state-

ment of a witness in a murder case (1823) that *Thurtell*, the murderer, "always maintained an appearance of respectability, and kept his horse and gig."

gig². Fish-spear. For *fizgig* (q.v.).

gigantic. Coined from L. *gigas, gigant-*; or G. γιγαντικός.

giggle. Imit., representing a thinner sound than *gaggle*; cf. Du. *giegelen*, Ger. *gickeln, kichern*, etc.

giglet [*archaic*]. From *gig¹*, but now associated with *giggle*.

gadrouillette: a minx, gigle, flirt, callet, gixie (a feigned word, applyable to any such cattle)
(Cotg.).

gigot. Sleeve. F., leg of mutton. Cf. *mutton-chop whiskers*.

Gilbertian. Esp. with *situation*. From *W. S. Gilbert*, author of the *Mikado*, etc.

Gilbertine. Monastic order founded by *Gilbert of Sempringham* (c. 1140).

gild¹. Verb. AS. *gyldan*, from *gold* (q.v.). *Gilt* is its p.p., first in phrase *silver gilt*. *Gilt-edged* was orig. used of books and paper. To *gild the pill* alludes to practice of gilding bitter pill to disguise taste. *Gilded youth* renders F. *jeunesse dorée*. Cf. *gilded chamber*, House of Lords (? due to Disraeli).

To gild refined gold, to paint the lily
(*K. John*, iv. 2).

Be not deluded with golden pills wherein is hidden most deadly poison (Adm. Monson, 1624).

gild². See *guild*.

Giles. Stock name for farmer (cf. *Hodge*). Cf. F. *Gilles*, clown or buffoon. From L. *Egidius*, from *aegis* (q.v.).

gill¹. Of fish. ? Cogn. with synon. Sw. *gäl*, Dan. *gjælle*. ? Cf. Sp. *agalla*.

gill². Deep glen with stream. ON. *gil*, whence Norw. *geil*, passage between hedges. False spelling *ghyll* is due to Wordsworth.

gill³. Measure. Cf. OF. *gille, gelle*, MedL. *gillo, gellus*, measure for wine. Perh. from proper name *Gille-s*, Giles, or from *Gill, Jill*; cf. *jack, jug*, etc., and ME. *gylle*, apron. In dial. *gill* is half a pint, *jack* a quarter.

Gill. See *Jill*.

gillaroo [*angl.*]. Trout. Ir., from *giolla*, lad (v.i.), *ruadh*, red.

gillie. Gael. *gille*, servant (v.s.), as in names *Gilchrist, Gilmour* (Mary), *Gillies* (Jesus), etc.

gillyflower. Corrupt. by folk-etym. of F. *giroflée*, from *girofle*, VL. **garophyllon*, G. καρυόφυλλον, nut leaf, from κάρυον, nut. The flower was named from scent (see *clove*²). Early and dial. perversions are very numerous (cf. *jenneting*).

gelowe floure: oyllet (Palsg.).

The "julyflower" as they are most properly called, though vulgarly "gilliflower" and "gilofer"
(*NED.* 1688).

gilt¹ [*dial*.]. Boar. ON. *gyltr*, young sow, cogn. with dial. *galt*, in same sense.

Keep all the gilts for breeding purposes
(*Times*, March 1, 1918).

gilt². See *gild*¹.

gimbals [*naut*.]. Also (archaic) *gimmal*, ring bit (*Hen. V*, iv. 2). OF. *gemel* (*jumeau*), twin, L. *gemellus*, dim. of *geminus*. Cf. *jumble*².

gimbals: the brass rings by which a sea-compass is suspended in its box (Falc.).

gimcrack. Orig. clever device, dodge. Earlier also *jimcrack*, altered, on name *Jim*, from ME. *gibecrake*, app. inlaid wood-work.

gimlet, gimblet. OF. *guimbelet* (*gibelet*), dim. from ODu. *wimpel*. See *wimble*.

gimmal [*archaic*]. See *gimbals*.

gimp. Cf. Du. *gimp*, Ger. *gimpf*, app. from F. *guimpe*, wimple, of Teut. origin (see *wimple*), but with the sense of F. *guipure* (q.v.).

gin¹. Trap. ME. also, skill, cunning, mech device. Aphet. for *engin*, F., L. *ingenium*. Cf. names *Ginner*, *Jenner*, i.e. engineer.

The amount [of cotton] ginned since the last report is 509000 bales (*Manch. Guard.* Jan. 10, 1919).

gin². Spirit. Short for *geneva* (q.v.), F. *genièvre*, L. *juniperus*, juniper, because flavoured with its berries. Cf. Du. *genever*, which may be immediate origin of *geneva*. For shortening, pointing to frequent use, cf. *brandy*, *rum*, *whisky*. *Geneva* and *gin* were used indifferently c. 1700.

gin³. Aboriginal Austral. woman. Native word. Cf. *squaw*.

gin⁴ [*poet*.]. Verb. Aphet. for *begin* (q.v.).

gingall, jingall [*Anglo-Ind*.]. Musket on swivel. Hind. *janjāl*, corrupt. of Arab. *jaza'il*, pl. of *jazīl*, big, used of Afghan musket fired from rest. Cf. *jezail*.

ginger. AS. *gingiber* & F. *gingembre*, Late L. *gingiber*, Late G. ζιγγίβερις, ult. cogn. with Malayalam *inchiver*, from *inchi*, root; cf. Du. *gember*, Ger. *ingwer*, and forms in most Europ. langs. To *ginger up*, fig. was used by Disraeli (1849). *Gingerbread* (c. 1300), formerly adorned, esp. at country-fairs, with *gilt*, is folk-etym. for OF. *gingimbrat*, MedL. *gingimbratus* (p.p.), gingered.

gingerly. Orig. (c. 1500) of walking "delicately." App. formed from OF. *gensour*, compar. of *gent*, dainty, delicate, etc., L. *genitus*, (well) born.

gentement: neatly...also, gently, easily, softly, gingerly (Cotg.).

He came to him with a soft pace, treading gingerly (as we speak) after a nice and delicate manner
(Bp Patrick, 17 cent., on Agag, 1 *Sam.* xv. 32).

gingham. F. *guingan*; cf. It. *gingano*, Sp. *guingon*, Du. *gingang*, etc.; ult. Malay *ginggang*, striped. For *-am* cf. *grogram*. Prob. Du. was the intermediary.

gingival [*med*.]. Of the gum, L. *gingiva*.

gingko. Tree. Jap., from Chin. *yinhing*, silver apricot.

gingly- [*anat*.]. From G. γίγγλυμος, hinge.

ginseng. Plant. Chin. *jĕn shĕn*, perh. image of man (*jĕn*), from forked root.

giottesque [*art*]. Suggesting *Giotto*, Tuscan painter (13–14 cents.). Cf. *dantesque*, *turneresque*, etc.

gipsy, gypsy. Earlier (16 cent.) *gypcian* for *Egyptian*, because they were supposed to come thence. See *Bohemian*, *Gitano*, *Romany*, *Zingari*. Cf. *gippy* (mil.) for Egypt. soldier. ? Also *Gip*, as name for (? orig. swarthy) dog. The *gipsies* seem doomed to be associated with countries with which they have nothing to do; cf. archaic Sp. *germano*, *flamenco*, both used for gipsy.

Letters were written to...avoyde [rid] the contrey off a certeyne nombre off vagabondes going upp and downe in the name of Egiptians
(*Privy Council Acts*, 1542–3).

giraffe. F. *girafe*, ult. Arab. *zarāfah*. In most Europ. langs. Earlier E. forms (from c. 1600) vary according to immediate source.

girandole. Orig. kind of firework; then, fountain jet (Evelyn). It. *girandola*, from *girare*, to gyrate (q.v.).

girasol. Sunflower (obs.), opal. It. *girasole*, from *girare*, to turn, *sole*, sun. Cf. *heliotrope*. See also *artichoke*.

gird¹. To encircle. AS. *gyrdan*. Com. Teut.; cf. Du. *gorden*, Ger. *gürten*, ON. *gyrtha*, Goth. *-gairdan* (in compds.). Prob. cogn. with *garth* (q.v.). Cf. *girdle*, AS. *gyrdel*; *girth*, ON. *gjörth*. *Girder* is a later formation. From AS. times *gird* is usu. rhet. or Bibl., e.g. to *gird up one's loins*, *gird on sword*, etc. The *Girdlers' Company* still exists.

gird². To assail verbally; usu. with *at*. Orig. (c. 1200) to strike (cf. to *have a hit at*), and ident. with *gird*¹. Cf. F. *cingler*, to beat, lash, from L. *cingulum*, horse-girth, thong, ON. *gyrtha*, to lash, and E. to *strap*, *leather*, etc.

girder. See *gird*[1].

girdle[1]. Belt. See *gird*[1].

girdle[2]. For cakes. Northern var. of *griddle* (q.v.).

girl. ME. *gurle* (13 cent.). Dim. of some unknown word; cf. LG. *gœre* (17 cent.), boy, girl; ? cogn. with ON. *gaurr*, clumsy, stupid person. For obscure hist. cf. *boy*, *lad*, *lass*, and their Scand. synonyms. "Probably most of them arose as jocular transferred uses of words that had originally a different meaning" (*NED*.). Orig. used of both sexes (see *bairn*, *child*). ? Limitation of sex due to association with *Gill*. Girl is little used in dial. (*maid*, *lass*, *wench*, q.v.) and occurs only twice in *AV*. (*maiden*, *damsel*).

Ye [Margaret Paston] are a goode gille
(*Paston Let.* ii. 238).
Come out, thou skittish gill
(*Jacob and Esau*, v. 6, 1568).

giron. See *gyron*.

Girondist [*hist.*]. Moderate party in France (1791–93), led by deputies from the *Gironde*.

girt, girth. See *gird*[1].

gist. OF., 3rd pers. sing. pres. of *gésir*, to lie, L. *jacēre*; cf. *ci-gît*, here lies, on old tombstones. The noun is evolved partly from AF. *l'action gist*, "the action lies," as leg. phrase. See also *agist*.

je sçay bien ou gist le lievre: I know well which is the very point, or knot of the matter (Cotg.).

git [*US.*]. For "*git*" out.

He...told them to get, and they got
(*Graceville Transcript*, Aug. 25, 1884).

Gitano. Gipsy. Sp., MedL. **Egyptianus*. Cf. *ghetto*.

gittern [*archaic*]. OF. *guiterne*. See *cither*, *guitar*, *zither*.

give. Northern form of AS. *giefan* (whence normally ME. *yeve*), influenced by ON. *gefa*. Com. Teut.; cf. Du. *geven*, Ger. *geben*, Goth. *giban*. *Give you joy* is for *God give you joy*; hence to *give Merry Christmas*, etc. Colloq. uses of to *give away* (now US.) are from leg. sense, to sacrifice, renounce. With to *give way* cf. to *give ground*. *Give and take* is orig. from racing, in which weights went according to size of horses.

Now you're married, we give you joy;
First a girl and then a boy.

gizzard. ME. *giser* (cf. "*scholard*"), F. *gésier*,

L. *gigerium* (only in pl.), entrails of fowl, ? ult. cogn. with L. *jecur*, liver.

All in pretty good humour, though I find my wife hath something in her gizzard, that only waits an opportunity (Pepys, June 17, 1668).

glabrous. Hairless. From L. *glaber*. See *glad*.

glacé. F., lit. iced (v.i.), but associated with *glass*, *gloss*[1].

glacial. In geol. sense app. coined (1846) by Forbes. See *glacier*.

glacier. F., from *glace*, ice, VL. **glacia* for *glacies*. From dial. of Savoy, whence also Ger. *gletscher*.

glacis [*fort.*]. Sloping bank. F., from F. *glacer*, to freeze, make slippery (v.s.).

glad. AS. *glæd*. Com. Teut.; cf. Du. *glad*, smooth, Ger. *glatt*, smooth, ON. *glathr*, glad; ult. cogn. with L. *glaber*, smooth (cf. E. *red*, L. *ruber*). Intermediate sense was bright, shining, which still survives in the *glad eye*.

glade. Open (bright) space among trees. Cogn. with *glad*, bright (v.s.); cf. synon. Ger. *lichtung*, from *licht*, light, F. *clairière* and *éclaircie*, from *clair*.

gladiator. L., from *gladius*, sword.

gladiolus. L., dim. of *gladius* (v.s.). Hence F. *glaïeul*. Cf. Ger. *schwertlilie*.

gladstone. Bag, claret. Latter from cheap wine of which importation increased after reduction of duty by *Gladstone* (†1898) when at the Exchequer (1860). *Bismarck* was once in Ger. dial. use for a bad vintage. *Gladstonian* (hist.) was coined at the splitting of the Liberal party (1886) on Gladstone's Home-Rule project.

glair. White of egg. F. *glaire*, VL. **claria*, from *clarus*, clear (cf. F. *glas*, bell-ringing, from L. *classicum*, flourish of trumpets). OF. *glaire d'ou* is recorded for 12 cent.

chiara del' vuouo: the white of an egge (Flor.)

glaive. F., in OF. usu. lance; hence E. dial. *gleave*, fish-spear. L. *gladius* (whence OF. *glai*) mixed with Gaulish *cladebo* (cf. Ir. *claideb*, Gael. *claidheamh*, and see *claymore*).

On a dit spirituellement de "glaive" que dans ce mot "se croisent encore les épées de Vercingétorix et de César" (Nyrop, *Gram. hist.* i. 462).

glamour. Corrupt. of *grammar*, in sense of *gramarye* (q.v.), esp. in Sc. to *cast the glamour* (spell). Cf. obs. *master of glomery* (Camb.). A Scott word.

glance. First as verb. Orig. of blow (to *glance off*, etc.), in which sense it is nasalized from F. *glacer*, which in OF. had meaning of *glisser*, to slide, glance off (*un* *coup qui glisse*). For current sense of noun cf. F. *coup d'œil*. Sense of shining, flashing (from 16 cent.) is influenced by Du. *glanz* (from Ger.), cogn. with *glint*.

glantsen: splendere, fulgere, nitere (Kil.).

gland. F. *glande*, OF. *glandre*, L. *glandula*, dim. of *glans*, *gland-*, acorn. *Glanders*, disease, preserves OF. form. For sense-development cf. similar use of *almond*, *kernel*.

glare. ME. *glaren*; cogn. with early Du. & LG. *glaren*, to gleam, glare, and ult. with *glass*. Cf. AS. *glær*, amber. Sense of fierce look from c. 1600.

> Hit is not al gold that glareth
> (Chauc. *House of Fame*, i. 272).

glass. AS. *glæs*. Com. Teut.; cf. Du. Ger. *glas*, ON. *gler*, also Late L. *glesum*, amber (from Teut.); cogn. with *glare*. The alternation of *-s-*, *-r-*, shows true Teut. origin (cf. *was*, *were*), but some influence may have been exerted by L. *glacies*, ice; cf. F. *glace*, ice, large mirror, and hist. of *crystal*. Possibly the Celt. *glas*, grey, blue, green, is related; cf. AS. *glæsenēage*, grey-eyed, and synon. early Du. *glaer-ooghigh*.

> Who that hath a hed of verre
> For cast of stones war him in the werre
> (Chauc. *Troil.* ii. 867).

Glastonbury. Chair, thorn. First in imit. of *Abbot of Glastonbury's chair* in bishop's palace at Wells; second from famous thorn fabled to have been planted at *Glastonbury* (Somerset) by Joseph of Arimathea.

Glaswegian. Of *Glasgow*. ? Coined on *Galwegian, Norwegian*.

glauber's salts. Sulphate of soda. First made by *Glauber*, Ger. chemist (†1668).

glaucoma. Form of blindness. G. γλαύκωμα, from γλαύξ, γλαυκ-, owl, named from its bright staring eyes (v.i.).

glaucous. From L., G. γλαυκός, sea-coloured.

glaze, glazier. From *glass* (cf. *grass, graze, grazier*).

gleam. First as noun. AS. *glǣm*; cf. OSax. *glīmo*, splendour, OHG. *glīmo*, glow-worm; cogn. with *glimmer, glimpse*. Orig. very bright light, e.g. of the sun.

glean. OF. *glener* (*glaner*), Late L. *glenare* (6 cent.), ? from Celt. *glan*, clean, pure (Gael. Ir. Bret. Welsh *glan*).

glebe. F. *glèbe*, L. *gleba*, clod, lump, ult. cogn. with *globe*. Eccl. sense of land forming part of clergyman's benefice is earliest in E. (Wyc.).

glede, gled [*archaic*]. Kite (*Deut.* xiv. 13). AS. *glida*, the glider; cf. synon. Sw. *glada*.

glee. AS. *glīw, glēo*, minstrelsy, merriment; cf. ON. *glȳ*. Practically obs. c. 1500–1700, and revived late in 18 cent. "It is not now used, except in ludicrous writing, or with some mixture of irony and contempt" (Johns.).

gleek [*archaic*]. Card game. OF. *glic, ghelique*, Ger. *glück* (MHG. *gelücke*), luck (q.v.), which in many parts of Germany is pronounced to rime with *kick*. Cf. *hazard, fortune, chance, bonheur*, all used of card-games.

gleet [*med.*]. F. *glette*, viscous matter, of unknown origin.

glen. Gael. Ir. *gleann*; cf. Welsh, Corn. *glyn*. App. introduced into E. by Spenser in ref. to Ireland.

glendoveer. Sprite. Imitated by Southey from *grandouver* (Sonnerat, *Voyage aux Indes*, 1782), Sanskrit *gandharva*. Cf. *afreet, ghoul, genie*, all due to 18 cent. interest in Orientalism.

glengarry. Bonnet. Place (Inverness). Cf. *glenlivet*, whisky (Banff).

> Had ta mixture been Only half glenlivet (Aytoun).

glib. From c. 1600; also *glibbery*. Orig. smooth, slippery. Cf. Du. *glibberig*, LG. *glibbrig*, slippery; prob. ult. cogn. with *glide*; cf. dial. *gliddery* in same sense.

> I want that glib and oily art
> To speak and purpose not (*Lear*, i. 1).
> Soothing her grief with a smaller allowance of the same glib liquid [rum punch]
> (*Old Curiosity Shop*, ch. xlix

glide. AS. *glīdan*. WGer.; cf. Du. *glijden*, Ger. *gleiten*. Perh. ult. cogn. with *glad* (q.v.).

glim. Usu. in *douse the glim*. Related to *glimmer*. Immediate source perh. OF. *glimpe*, "a light made of the staulke or stemme of an herb dried, and afterward greased over" (Cotg.), which is of Du. or Ger. origin. Cf. *glimpse*.

glimmer. Frequent. from same root as *gleam*; cf. Ger. *glimmen*. Mod. sense (Shaks.) has weakened from ME. sense of shining brightly.

glimpse. First as verb, from root of *gleam, glimmer*; cf. MHG. *glimsen*.

> Ye han som glymsyng and no parfit sighte
> (Chauc. E. 2383).

glint. ME. *glent*, prob. Scand.; cf. Ger. *glänzen*, to glance, shine. Introduced into E. literary use from Sc. (Burns).

glissade [*Alp.*]. Slide. F., from *glisser*, app. due to mixture of OF. *glacier* (see *glance*) and synon. *glier*, of Teut. origin (see *glide*).

glisten, glister. *Glisten* is AS. *glisnian*, to glitter; with *glister* cf. obs. Du. *glisteren* (*glinsteren*). Both have same sense as ME. *glise*, AS. *glīsian*, ult. cogn. with *glitter*.

glitter. ON. *glitra*, from *glit*, brightness; cf. Ger. *glitzern*. These are frequent. verbs cogn. with AS. *glitenian*, to shine.

gloaming. AS. *glōmung*, from *glōm*, twilight, cogn. with *glow*, but not with *gloom*. In literary E. a 19 cent. introduction from Sc. (Burns).

gloat. Usu. with *over*. From 16 cent. Cf. Ger. *glotzen*, to stare, ON. *glotta*, to grin scornfully. Not known to Johns., who conceived it (in Rowe's *Jane Shore*) "to be ignorantly written for 'gloar' (glower)." It is, however, in Wycherley, Otway, Dryden.

globe. F., L. *globus*, round mass, etc., cogn. with *glomus*, lump. A Renaissance word, of much later appearance than *sphere*.

glomerate. See *agglomerate*.

gloom. Back-formation from earlier *gloomy*, from verb *gloom*, to look sullen (14 cent.). Sense of darkness appears to be chiefly due to Milton, who took it from secondary sense of verb as applied to weather (cf. *threatening, lowering, sullen sky*). Cogn. with *glum*, but not with *gloaming*.

It wil be foule wedder to daye for the szkye is reed and gloometh (Coverd. *Matt* xvi. 3).

gloria. L., for *gloria* (*patri, tibi, in excelsis*).

glory. OF. *glorie* (*gloire*), L. *gloria*. *Hand of glory*, severed hand from gallows supposed to point to hidden treasure, translates F. *main de gloire*, corrupt. of *mandragore* (q.v.), whose forked roots were supposed to have the same property. See Ingoldsby, *Hand of Glory*. *Glory-hole*, cell for prisoners, also, untidy receptacle, is perh. from F. *gloriette*, cell in Châtelet, also (dial.) recess behind baker's oven. *Glorious uncertainty* (e.g. of cricket) is from *glorious uncertainty of the law*, proposed as toast at an 18 cent. law dinner. The wording was suggested by the *glorious memory of William III*, stock toast, but aimed at Lord Mansfield, the new Lord Chief Justice.

gloss[1]. Lustre. From 16 cent. Cf. obs. Du. *gloos*, gleaming, MHG. *glos*. Prob. cogn. with *glare, glass*, the latter of which is used indifferently with *gloss* in 16–17 cents. See *gloss*[2].

lustro: a lustre, a glasse, a shining (Flor.).

gloss[2]. Interpretation. Orig. marginal explanation. Earlier *glose, gloze* (q.v.), F., L., G. γλῶσσα, tongue, language. Hence *glossary*. But ME. sense, flattery, deceit, points to early association with the root of *gloss*[1]. Cf. to *gloze over*, explain speciously.

Whan that Fortune list to glose,
Thanne wayteth she hir man to overthrowe
(Chauc. B. 3330).

glossary, glosso-. See *gloss*[2].

glottis [*anat.*]. G. γλωττίς, from γλῶττα, var. of γλῶσσα, tongue (v.s.).

Gloucester, double. Cheese. Made of richer cream than *single Gloucester*.

glove. AS. *glōf*; cf. ON. *glōfe*; ? cogn. with ON. *lōfe*, hand (Sc. *loof*). In many symbolical uses, e.g. as gage of battle (much earlier than *gauntlet*), also as forfeit or present, e.g. *white gloves* (to judge). Some later metaphors from boxing. *Hand and glove* expresses the same close contact as to *fit like a glove*.

glow. AS. *glōwan*, or, as this is a strong verb, perh. rather from cogn. ON. *glōa*; cf. Du. *gloeien*, Ger. *glühen*, obs. E. *gleed*, live coal, and *gloaming*. With *glow-worm* cf. F. *luciole*, It. *lucciola*, from L. *lux*, light.

lucciole: glow wormes, or glaze wormes (Flor.).

glower. Introduced (18 cent.) from Sc., to stare. App. obs. *glore*, to stare, cogn. with *glare*, influenced in sound and sense by *lower*. Cf. Du. *gloren, gluren*, to peep, leer, Sw. dial. *glora*, to shine, stare.

gloxinia. Plant. From *Gloxin*, F. botanist (18 cent.).

gloy. Trade-name for paste. From G. γλοιός, sticky oil.

gloze. F. *gloser*, to interpret, comment on. See *gloss*[2]. When used with *over*, it is associated with *gloss*[1].

For in pleyn tixt it nedyth nat to glose
(Chauc. *Leg. Good Women, Prol.* 254).

glucose. From G. γλυκύς, sweet. Cf. *glycerine, liquorice*.

glue. F. *glu*, bird-lime, glue, Late L. *glus, glut-*; cogn. with L. *gluten*, glue.

glum. First as verb, to look sullen (see *gloom*); cf. Ger. dial. *glum*, turbid, from LG.

glume [*bot.*]. F., L. *gluma*, husk.

glumpy. From *glum*; cf. *grumpy*.

glut. Cf. OF. *gloutir*, to swallow, L. *gluttire*; but E. sense is to cause to swallow, cram; cf. *glut in the market*.

gluten. L., glue. Cf. *agglutinate*.

glutton[1]. Greedy eater. F. *glouton*, L.

glutto-n-, from *gluttire*, to swallow; cf. It. *ghiottone*, Sp. *glotón*.

glutton². Animal. Translated from Ger. *vielfrass* (from *viel*, much, *fressen*, to devour), applied to Scand. variety. This is, however, folk-etym. for Norw. *fjeld-fross*, mountain cat or bear (cf. *catamount*). The animal is called by the L. name *gulo* by Olaus Magnus (1539).

*vielfrass*¹: a greedy, or unsatiable eater; a great glutton; he that progs only for his belly; one that feeds like a farmer.

*vielfrass*²: the hyena; a beast like a wolf with a mane and long hairs, accounted the subtilest of beasts, often changing sex and counterfeiting mans voice (Ludw.).

glycerine. F. *glycérine*, coined (19 cent.) from G. γλυκερός, sweet. Cf. *glucose*.

glyconic [*metr.*]. From Γλύκων, G. lyric poet.

glyptic. Pertaining to carving. G. γλυπτικός, from γλύφειν, to carve. Cf. *glyph*, as in *hieroglyph*.

gnarled. From solitary occurrence, *gnarled oak*, in *Meas. for Meas.* ii. 2 (only in Fol. of 1623), where it is a var. of *knurled*, from *knurl*, dim. of *knur*, *knar*, lump, swelling (see *knur*), cogn. with Ger. *knorren*, knot in wood. Early Ger. vars. and dial. forms with -*s*- for -*r*- point to ult. connection with MHG. *knüsen*, to strike, bang, and AS. *cnossian*, to dash against.

bruscum: a bunche or knurre in a tree (Coop.).

gnash. Substituted (c. 1500) for earlier *gnast* (Wyc.), cogn. with ON. *gnīsta*, to gnash the teeth, Ger. *knirschen*, to gnash, *knistern*, to crackle. Of imit. origin.

I gnaste with the tethe: je grinse des dens (Palsg.).

I gnasshe with the tethe. Loke in *I gnast* (*ib.*).

gnat. AS. *gnæt*; ? cogn. with *gnīdan*, to rub. Cf. Ger. *gnätze*, scurf, from OHG. *gnitan*, to rub.

gnathic [*anat.*]. From G. γνάθος, jaw.

Gnathonic. Sycophantic. From *Gnatho*, parasite in Terence's *Eunuchus* (v.s.).

gnaw. AS. *gnagan*; cf. Du. *knagen*, Ger. *nagen* (OHG. *gnagan*). See *nag²*.

gneiss [*min.*]. Ger., from *gneist*, spark, cogn. with AS. *gnāst*.

gnome. F., ModL. *gnomus*, used by Paracelsus (16 cent.) of pygmies whose natural element is earth. Perh. for a G. *γηνόμος, earth-dweller, imitated from G. θαλασσονόμος, sea-dweller. Cf. *sylph*.

gnomic. Dealing in axioms. From G. γνώμη, thought, judgment, from γιγνώσκειν, to know.

gnomon. Indicator, esp. on sun-dial. G. γνώμων, inspector, indicator, also carpenter's square, from γιγνώσκειν, to know. The *gnomon* of a parallelogram has the form of a carpenter's square.

gnostic. G. γνωστικός, pertaining to knowledge (v.s.). Applied esp. to various early Christian sects which claimed mystical knowledge.

gnu. SAfr. antelope. Kafir *nqu*. Also *wildebeest* (Du.).

go. AS. *gān*. Com. Teut.; cf. Du. *gaan*, Ger. *gehen*, ON. *gā*. Related to *gang* as root *sta*- (cf. Ger. *stehen*) to *stand*. Past sense now replaced from *wend*, Sc. *gaed* being a new formation on *gae*.

Bonnie Kilmeny gede up the glen (Hogg).

goa. Antelope. Native name (Tibet).

goad. AS. *gād*; cogn. with OHG. (Lombardic) *gaida*, spear-head, and ult. with *gar*, in *garfish*. Used indifferently in ME. with unrelated *gad*¹ (q.v.). Fig. sense, from 16 cent., is perh. due to new familiarity with Bible (see *prick*).

goal. ME. *gol*, limit, boundary, occurring once only (c. 1315), may be AS. *gāl*, whence app. AS. *gǣlan*, to hinder, impede. For sense cf. L. *meta*, "the ende or bounde of anything; a butte or pricke to shoote at; a marke or goale in the fielde, where unto men or horses doe runne" (Coop.).

In rennynge, passynge the gole is accounted but rasshenesse (Sir T. Elyot).

goat. AS. *gāt*. Com. Teut.; cf. Du. *geit*, Ger. *geiss*, ON. *geit*, Goth. *gaits*; cogn. with L. *haedus*, kid. US. *goatee*, chin-beard, was perh. suggested by synon. Du. *sik*, lit. goat.

gob. Lump, clot, etc., with dim. *gobbet*. Cf. OF. *gobe*, F. *gobet*, and *gober*, to swallow, gobble. App. of Celt. origin; cf. Gael. *gob*, beak (see *gab*), Ir. *gob*, beak, mouth.

Samuel hewide hym into gobbetis [*Vulg.* frusta] before the Lord (Wyc. 1 Sam. xv. 33).

gobang. Game. Jap. *goban*, Chin. *k'i pan*, chessboard.

gobble. Of turkey-cock. Imit., cf. *gabble*, *cackle*, etc. For swallowing sense see *gob*.

gobelin. Tapestry. From state factory, Paris, founded by *Gobelin* (16 cent.).

gobemouche. Credulous person. F. *gobe-mouches*, swallow-flies, kind of sparrow. For fig. use cf. *gull*.

goblet. OF. *gobelet*, dim. of *gobel*, *gobeau*. All these words are common F. surnames, OHG. *God-bald*, god-bold (cf. E. *Godbolt*), and the vessel is no doubt of same origin. Cf. E. dial. *goddard*, goblet, OF. *godart*, OG. *Gott-hart*, god-strong, named in same way. See *goblin*, and cf. *demijohn, jack, gill*³, *jug, tankard*, ME. *jubbe* (Job) in Chauc., etc.

goblin. F. *gobelin*, dim. of name *Gobel* (v.s.); cf. *kobold* (q.v.), *harlequin, jack o' lantern, will o' the wisp*, etc. *Gobelin* (q.v.) is a common F. surname. Cf. also Ger. *heinzel-männchen*, gnome, from *Heinz*, pet form of *Heinrich*, Henry, with var. *hänsel-männchen*, from *Hans*, Johnny.

A gobelyn goynge in derknessis (Wyc. *Ps.* xc. 6).

goby. Fish. L. *gobius*. See *gudgeon*.

god. AS. *god*. Com. Teut.; cf. Du. *god*, Ger. *gott*, ON. *goth*, Goth. *guth*. Orig. a neuter, as in MHG. *abgott*, idol, change of gender coming about with monotheism. Ult. origin unknown. Often oddly disguised in oaths, e.g. *swop me bob*, for *so help me God!* With *godfather*, and other such AS. compds., cf. *gossip*. F. *goddam*, Englishman, is from national oath, recorded in OF. as *godon*. *Godsend* is for earlier *God's send*, where *send* (Sc.) is an abstr. noun. With *the gods* (theat.) cf. F. *paradis*, the gallery.

Let's carve him as a dish fit for the gods
(*Jul. Caes.* ii. 1).

Les Anglais en vérité ajoutent par-ci, par-là, quelques autres mots en conversant; mais il est bien aisé de voir que goddam est le fond de la langue (*Mariage de Figaro*).

godetia. Flower. From *Godet*, Swiss botanist.

godhead. This and *maidenhead* are the only survivors of ME. suffix *-hede*, cogn. with *-hood* and Ger. *-heit*.

godown. Warehouse in East. Earlier *gadong*, Malay, from Telugu or Tamil.

godwit. Bird. ? From cry; cf. *pewit*. But cf. synon. Norw. Dan. *rödvitte*, with second element as in *musvit*, titmouse. This is perh. archaic Dan. *vitte*, small thing, used like E. *tit*.

goffer, gauffer, gopher. F. *gaufrer*, to stamp with honeycomb pattern, from *gaufre*, thin cake with this pattern, LG. *wafel*, honeycomb (see *wafer, waffle*).

goggle, -eyed. From *goggle*, to move uncertainly here and there, app. cogn. with *jog, joggle*. In Wyc. (*Mark*, ix. 46). Hence *goggles*, spectacles.

œil de bœuf: an outstrouting, or great gogle eye
(Cotg.).

goglet [*Anglo-Ind.*]. Earlier (17 cent.) *gurgulet*, etc., Port. *gorgoleta*, "an earthen and narrow mouthed vessel, out of which the water runs, and guggles" (Vieyra). Cf. *gargle*.

Half-clad men went back and forth with leaf-platters and water-goglets
(Kipling, *In the Presence*).

Goidelic, Gadhelic [*ethn. & ling.*]. From OIr. *goidel*, a Gael. Introduced by Rhys to denote Gaelic (Irish and Scotch) as distinguished from Brythonic (Welsh, Cornish, Breton). Cf. *Gadhelic*.

goitre. F. *goître*, back-formation from *goitreux*, Prov. *goitros*, VL. **gutturiosus*, from *guttur*, throat. Cf. OF. *goitron*, throat.

golconda. Old name of Hyderabad, famous for diamonds. Cf. *eldorado*.

An editor of new letters or diaries is provided with a golconda of illustration
(*Times Lit. Supp.* May 29, 1919).

gold. AS. *gold*. Com. Teut.; cf. Du. *goud*, Ger. *gold*, ON. *goll*, Goth. *gulth*; prob. cogn. with *yellow*. *Goldbeater's skin* is an animal membrane used by *goldbeaters* to separate leaves of gold-foil. The *Golden Age* translates L. *aurea aetas* (Ovid, *Met.* i. 89), period of ideal innocence and prosperity; cf. *golden mean*, L. *aurea mediocritas* (Hor. *Odes*, II. x. 5).

golf. From 15 cent. Du. *kolf*, club, cogn. with Ger. *kolben*, club, musket-butt, and ult. with L. *globus*. Mentioned (1457), with *fut-bal*, in a Sc. statute dealing with forbidden games.

kolf, kolve: clava, ang. clubbe; *kolf-bal, slagh-bal*: pila clavaria (Kil.).

golgotha. G. γολγοθᾶ, Aramaic *gogolthā*, Heb. *gulgōleth*, skull. Cf. *calvary*.

goliardic. Poetry. From the *goliards*, medieval buffoons (12–13 cents.), OF. *goliard*, glutton, from OF. *gole* (*gueule*), mouth, maw, L. *gula*.

golliwog. Created in US. by Miss Florence Upton. Perh. on *golly* (v.i.) with suggestion of dial. *polliwog*, tadpole, which is still common in US. Cf. *teddy-bear*.

golly. Negro perversion of *God*.

golosh. See *galosh*.

goluptious. Facet. perversion (19 cent.) of *voluptuous*; cf. rustic *boldacious* (bold × audacious).

gombeen-man [*Ir.*]. Usurer. From Ir. *gaimbín*, cogn. with MedL. *cambium*. See *change*.

gom(b)roon. Persian pottery. From town on Persian Gulf. See *banian*.

-gon [*math.*]. G. -γωνος, from γωνία, angle. Used for the plane figures with more angles than a *quadrangle*.

gondola. It. "a kinde of small boates like our wherries used in Venice" (Flor.). Perh. a Venet. formation from *dondolare*, to see-saw, an imit. word (cf. *dandle*). For sense of car of air-ship cf. *nacelle*. *Gundel*, ship's long-boat, is common in Purch. and occurs (*gondale*) in the *Voyage of the Barbara* (1540).

gonfalon [*hist.*]. It. *gonfalone*, banner used in Church processions. Earlier is *gonfanon*, knight's pennon (c. 1300), OF. (*gonfalon*), OHG. *guntfano*, battle flag (Ger. *fahne*); cf. AS. *gūthfana*, and see *vane*. Change of -*n*- to -*l*- is due to dissim. (cf. F. *orphelin*, OF. *orfenin*, dim. from L. *orphanus*).

gong. Malay. Imit. of sound. Cf. *tom-tom*.

Gongorism. Affected literary style of *Góngora y Argote*, Sp. poet (†1627). Cf. *Euphuism*.

goniometer. Instrument for measuring angle, G. γωνία.

gonoph [*slang*]. Pickpocket (*Bleak House*, ch. xix.). Jewish Du. *gannef*, Heb. *gannābh*, thief. But the author's father, a Suffolk man (†1920 aetat. 85), used it in the sense of stupid lout, ME. *gnof*, cogn. with EFris. *knufe*, lump.

A riche gnof, that gestes heeld to bord
(Chauc. A. 3188).

gonorrhoea [*med.*]. G., from γόνος, seed, ῥοία, flux; cf. *diarrhoea*.

-gony. G. -γονία, generation, from γίγνεσθαι, to become. Cf. -*geny*.

good. AS. *gōd*. Com. Teut.; cf. Du. *good*, Ger. *gut*, ON. *gōthr*, Goth. *gōths*. With *the good people*, propitiatory name for the fairies, cf. G. Εὐμενίδες, the Furies, lit. the gracious ones, used for the ill-omened Ἐρινύες. In *good gracious* substituted for *God*; cf. *good-bye* (v.i.) and *goodness gracious, for goodness sake*, with orig. ref. to goodness of God. With *goods and chattels*, formerly also in sing., cf. Ger. *hab' und gut*, havings and property, *gut*, an estate. This use goes back to AS. To *make good*, in current sense, is US.

My wife is resolved to go to London for good and all this day (Pepys, Dec. 1, 1665).

good-bye. Earlier (16 cent.) *godbwye*, etc. For *God be with you* (*ye*), altered on *good day*, etc.; cf. F. *adieu*.

Are you resolved upon't? If not, God bw'y'
(Brome, *Jovial Crew*, ii.).

goody[1]. Old country woman. For *goodwife*, fem. of *goodman*, master of the house (*Luke*, xii. 39); cf. *hussy*.

goody[2]. Sweet. Earlier *goody-goody*; cf. F. *bonbon*, from baby-lang.

googly [*cricket*]. From c. 1908. ? Arbitrary formation (*goggle* × *wiggly*), ? or of SAfr. origin, from Du. *goochelen*, to juggle.

gooroo, guru. Hind. *gurū*, teacher, priest, Sanskrit *guru*, grave, dignified.

Guru Har Gobind, sixth of the great Sikh gurus
(Kipling, *In the Presence*).

Goorkha, Gurkha. Nepaulese soldier in British service. Hind. *gurkhā*, prob. cowkeeper. See *gaikwar*.

goosander. Bird. Perh. formed from *goose* after obs. *bergander*, sheldrake. For second element cf. ON. *önd* (pl. *ander*) and see *duck*.

goose. AS. *gōs*. Aryan; cf. Du. Ger. *gans*, ON. *gās*, Sp. *ganso* pointing to Goth. *gans-*; cogn. with L. *anser*, G. χήν, OIr. *geis*, swan, Sanskrit *hamsa*, goose. One of the few bird-names common to Aryan. The -*s* was orig. a suffix (cf. *fox*) and from same root come *gander*, *gannet*, Prov. *ganta*, OF. *jante*, wild goose, Late L. *ganta*. The tailor's *goose* is named from its *goose-neck* handle. With *game of goose* cf. F. *jeu de l'oie*. With *goose-flesh*, resulting from cold or fright, cf. F. *chair de poule*. *Goose-step* is mod. (c. 1800). The game called *goose* in the Midlands, corresponding to the London urchin's *cat*, is perh. a separate word, Fr. dial. (northern) *guisse*.

gooseberry. The *goose* is no doubt for *groose*; cf. dial. *groser*, *grozet*, *grozell*, gooseberry, the third of which is F. *groseille*, from Ger. *kraus*, curly, as in *krausbeere*, *kräuselbeere*, from minute hairs on some varieties. Cf. Du. corrupt. *kruisbes*, lit. cross-berry, with *kruis*, cross, for *kroes*, curly. Cf. MedL. *uva crispa* (curly grape), gooseberry. In sense of chaperon (19 cent.) perh. from affecting to be engaged in picking gooseberries while keeping an eye on the young people.

gopher[1]. Wood (*Gen.* vi. 14). Heb. *gōpher*.

gopher[2]. See *goffer*.

gorcrow [*archaic*]. From *gore*[1], in orig. sense. Cf. *carrion crow*.

Gordian knot. Tied by *Gordius*, king of Gordium (Phrygia), with prophecy that he who untied it should rule the world. Alexander cut it through with his sword. In Shaks. (*Cymb.* ii. 2).

Proverbialiter nodus Gordius de re difficili atque perplexa dicitur (?).

gore[1]. Blood. Orig. filth. AS. *gor*, dung; cogn. with Du. *goor*, mud, MHG. *gor*, dung of animals, still in Swiss *gur*, ? and ult. with Ger. *gären*, to ferment. Earlier sense in archaic *gorbelly*, fat paunch, *gorcrow*. Poet. use, for L. *cruor*, from 16 cent.

gore[2]. Of dress (umbrella, balloon). AS. *gára*, cogn. with *gár*, spear (see *garfish*); formerly used also of triangular piece of ground (*Kensington Gore*). Cf. Du. *geer*, Ger. *gehren*, and similar use of F. *pointe*.

goore of a smocke: poynte de chemise (Palsg.).

gore[3]. Verb. ? From obs. *gore*, *gare*, spear (v.s.). This is very doubtful in view of early Sc. *gorre* and obs. E. *jurre*. Cf. also OF. *gorrette*, "a justle, jurr, thumpe, or thwacke" (Cotg.).

corniller: to jurre, or butt with the hornes (Cotg.).

gorge. F., throat, neck, VL. *gurga, for *gurges*, whirlpool, raging abyss, supposed to have been L. slang for *guttur*. Cf. *testa*, tile, whence F. *tête*, head, and our *bread-basket*, *potato-trap*, etc. In all Rom. langs. In OF. & ME. used esp. of crop of falcon, whence *full-gorged*, to *disgorge*, *make one's gorge rise*, etc. With fig. senses (ravine, etc.) cf. those of *neck*. With *gorget*, OF. *gorgete*, cf. *corset*.

gorga, *gorgia*: the throte, gullet, or weason pipe, the gorge or pannell of a hauke (Flor.).

gorgeous. Earlier *gorgyas*, etc., OF. *gorgias*, elegant, swaggering, also a noun, elaborate neck garment, which must have been first sense (cf. *tawdry*). App. from *gorge* (q.v.). Cf. F. *se rengorger*, to "throw out one's chest" like a peacock, and our fig. use of *swell*.

gorget [*hist.*]. See *gorge*.

gorgio. Romany name for non-gipsy. Bad transliteration (Borrow) of Sp. gipsy *gacho*; cf. Ger. gipsy *gatscho*. Origin unknown.

gorgon. G. Γοργώ, as if for *Γοργών, from γοργός, terrible. Head of Medusa on Athene's shield. Hence *gorgonize*, to petrify (*Maud*, i. xiii. 21).

gorgonzola. Name of village near Milan.

gorilla. Occurs in G. version of voyage of Hanno the Carthaginian (c. 500 B.C.) in sense of hairy savage. Adopted (1847) for giant ape first described by Savage, US. missionary.

gormandize. See *gourmand*.

gorse. AS. *gorst* (still as surname); cogn. with Ger. *gerste*, barley, and L. *hordeum*. The

bush of *Mark*, xii. 26 is rendered by AS. *gorstbēam*.

gosh. For *God*; cf. *gad*, *golly*.

Each man snatch for himself, by gosse
                    (*Respublica*, i. 3, c. 1553).

goshawk. AS. *gōs-hafoc*, goose hawk; cf. ON. *gás-haukr*.

Goshen. Land of light and plenty. Heb. (*Gen.* xlvii. 27).

gosling. Dim. of *goose*.

gospel. AS. *godspel*, for *gōd spel*, good tidings (see *spell*[1]), translating L. *evangelium* (see *evangel*). Associated with *God* also in ON. & OHG.

euuangelium, id est, bonum nuntium: godspel (*Voc.*).

goss [*archaic slang*]. Hat. Short for *gossamer hat*, a light felt popular c. 1830–40.

Wentilation gossamer, I calls it (*Pickwick*, ch. xii.).

gossamer. ME. *gosesomer*, app. for *goose summer*, applied to the period (St Martin's summer) when geese are eaten and *gossamer* is chiefly seen. The substance and season have fantastic names in most Europ. langs., e.g. F. *fils de la Vierge*, Ger. *mädchensommer* (these perh. associated with the Assumption, Aug. 15), Du. *kraanzomer* (crane), etc.

gossip. AS. *godsibb*, God akin, used of those who contracted spiritual affinity by acting as sponsors. With later senses, crony, chatterer, well exemplified in Shaks., cf. hist. of synon. F. *compère*, *commère* (see *compeer*, *cummer*), or of Ger. *gevatter*, formed on Church L. *compater*. With second element cf. Ger. *sippe*, affinity.

Sec. The money, most honourable compere, shal without faile observe your appointed howre. Pet. Thankes, my deere gossip
                    (*Eastward Hoe*, iii. 2).

commerage: gossiping; the acquaintance, affinity, or league that growes betweene women by christning a child together, or one for another (Cotg.).

gossoon [*Anglo-Ir.*]. From ME. *garsoun*, F. *garçon*.

Goth. AS. *Gota*, Late L. pl. *Gothi*, G. Γόθοι, adapted from first element of Goth. *gut-thiuda*, Gothic people (see *Dutch*). Often used of savage spoiler; cf. *Vandal*, *Hun*. The lang. (EGer.) is preserved in the Bible transl. of Ulfila (little wolf), bishop of the Moeso-Goths (4 cent.), and a form of it was spoken in the Crimea during the Middle Ages. As term of art and literature *Gothic* was contrasted with *classic*, and often implied barbarism. Cf. *gothic type*, as opposed to roman, *Gothic* being used

by early scholars for mod. *Germanic,
Teutonic.* See also *Teutonic.*

Gotham. Home of "wise men." Village near
Nottingham. Cf. Ger. *Schildbürger,* similarly used.

The wise men of Gotham are risen again!
(*Misogonus,* ii. 3, c. 1550).

Götterdämmerung. See *twilight.*

gouache [*paint.*]. F., It. *guazzo,* "a water or
washed colour" (Flor.), ? ult. cogn. with
Ger. *wasser,* water, ? or for It. *acquazzo,*
L. *aquat-,* from *aqua,* water.

goufa. Boat on Tigris. See *kuphar.*

They [the goufas] are coated inside and outside
with bitumen (*Daily Chron.* March 30, 1917).

gouge. Chisel. F., Late L. *gubia, gulbia;* cf.
It. *gubbia,* Sp. *gubia.* Of Celt. origin; cf.
OIr. *gulban,* Welsh *gylfin,* beak. For verb
to *gouge,* once very popular in US., see
Thornton.

Claw your eyes right out, like a Carolina gouger
(*Sam Slick*).

goulard. Lotion. From name of F. surgeon.

Opodeldoc, joint-oil, and goulard (*Ingoldsby*).

goulash [*cook.*]. Kind of stew (*Daily Chron.*
Dec. 1, 1919). Ger. *gulasch,* from Hung.

gourd. F. *gourde,* L. *cucurbita,* whence also
Ger. *kürbiss.* For sense of water-bottle
cf. *calabash.*

gourmand. F., connected by some with
gourmet, epicure, wine-taster, and this with
OF. *gromet,* lad, esp. taverner's assistant,
from E. *groom.* But, apart from difficulties
of sense, the chronology of *groom* and
gromet is uncertain.

gout. F. *goutte,* L. *gutta,* drop, from early
med. view as to the "humour" causing it.
In Chauc. Cf. archaic *gout* (of blood), in
mod. use after *Macb.* ii. 1.

govern. F. *gouverner,* L. *gubernare,* G. κυ-
βερνᾶν, to steer a ship (see *James,* iii. 4);
cf. It. *governare,* Sp. *gobernar.* An early
example of naut. metaphor. *Governance*
(Wyc.) is much older than *government* (16
cent.).

gowan [*Sc. & north.*]. Daisy, etc. Cf. earlier
golland, ult. cogn. with *gold* and *yellow.*

gowk [*Sc. & north.*]. Fool. ON. *gaukr,*
cuckoo; cogn. with AS. *gēac.* Cf. Ger.
gauch, cuckoo, fool.

gown. OF. *gonne;* cf. MedL. *gunna,* It.
gonna, OSp. *gona.* App. orig. a fur garment. Ult. origin unknown. For wide
senses cf. *coat, robe, frock.* Often as emblem of office or status, e.g. *gownsman,
town and gown.*

grab. Cf. early Du. & LG. *grabben;* cogn. with
grape, gripe. Cf. *grabble,* to grope, Du.
grabbelen.

grace. F. *grâce,* L. *gratia,* pleasing quality,
favour (cf. orig. sense of *disgrace*), from
gratus, pleasing; cf. It. *grazia,* Sp. *gracia.*
Two groups of senses, as those of *gracious,*
follow L. Oldest E. meaning (c. 1200) is
rel., *God's grace;* cf. *graceless,* reprobate.
Grace after meat, till 16 cent. usu. *graces,*
is adopted from F. *rendre grâces,* L. *gratias
agere.* Hence *grace-cup,* now esp. at universities. French sense of pardon now
chiefly in *act of grace.* For *my gracious!*
etc. see *good. There but for the grace of God
goes...* was prob. said by John Bradford,
Protestant martyr (†1555). With use as
title, of archbishops, dukes, formerly also
of sovereigns, cf. Ger. *Euer Gnaden,* from
gnade, favour.

grackle. Bird. ModL. *gracula,* for L. *gra-
culus,* daw, chough, etc.

grade. F., rank, order, L. *gradus,* step. On
the *up* (*down*) *grade* is US. railway lang.;
cf. *gradient. Gradual* is MedL. *gradualis;*
cf. *graduate,* from MedL. *graduare,* to take
a "degree." The *gradual,* antiphon between epistle and gospel at Eucharist, was
so called because sung at steps of altar.
Gradus, L. school-book, was orig. *Gradus
ad Parnassum* (17 cent.) for help in L.
verse; cf. *delectus* (*sententiarum Graecarum*).

Gradgrind. One who recognizes nothing but
"business." Character in Dickens' *Hard
Times.*

gradin-e [*arch.*]. Tier. F. *gradin,* It. *gradino,*
from L. *gradus,* step, grade.

gradus. See *grade.*

graffito [*art*]. It., from *graffio,* claw, scratch.
Applied to wall inscriptions at Pompeii,
etc. Cogn. with *agrafe* (q.v.).

graft[1]. In gardening. Earlier *graffe* (*Piers
Plowm.*), F. *greffe,* L., G. γραφίον, stylus,
from γράφειν, to write, from pencil-shaped
shoot used in grafting. Cf. *imp.*

greffe: a graffe; a slip, or young shoot fit to be
graffed (Cotg.).

graft[2] [*US.*]. Perh. ident. with E. slang *graft,*
work, from obs. *grave,* to dig. Cf. *I think
I can work it.*

Wherever you have had a democracy, you have
seen it attended by the twin nymphs, Graft and
Boodle (*Blackwood,* May, 1917).

Grahamize [*hist.*]. From *Sir James Graham*, who was Home Secretary when Mazzini's letters were opened in post (1844).

grail [*eccl.*]. Book of Mass-music. OF. *grael*, MedL. *graduale*. See *grade*.

grail, holy. Cup used at Last Supper. OF. *graal*, *grael*, in *saint graal* (ME. *sangreal*), MedL. *sanctus gradalis*, perh. ult. from L. *crater*, bowl. Confused with *sang* and interpreted as bowl in which Joseph of Arimathea caught the blood of the Saviour.

grain[1]. F. *grain*, grain, corn, L. *granum*, and *graine*, seed, L. *grana*, neut. pl. used as collect. Cogn. with *corn*[1], kernel. For *dyed in grain*, i.e. with *kermes*, once believed to be a seed, cf. *engrained*. With *grain*, texture, surface appearance, cf. *granite*. *Against the grain* is from carpentering. See also *cross*. With *grain*, smallest unit of weight, cf. hist. of *carat*, *scruple*, also *barley-corn* as unit of length.

grain[2], **grainse**. Fishspear. ON. *grein*, division, branch, whence dial. E. *grain*, prong.

grallatorial [*ornith.*]. Herons, etc. From L. *grallator*, stilt-walker, from *grallae*, stilts, for **gradlae*, from *gradior*, I step; cf. F. *échassier*, in same sense, from *échasse*, stilt (see *skate*[2]).

gralloch [*ven.*]. To disembowel (deer). From Gael. *grealach*, intestines.

gram[1]. Chick-pea. Port. *grāo*, L. *granum*.

gram[2]. Unit of weight. See *gramme*.

-gram. G. γράμμα, letter, from γράφειν, to write.

gramarye [*archaic*]. ME., grammar, magic. Re-introduced by Scott. See *grammar*, *glamour*.

gramercy [*archaic*]. OF. *grant merci*, great thanks. See *mercy*.

gramineous. From L. *gramen*, *gramin-*, grass.

grammalogue [*shorthand*]. Incorr. for *logogram*. App. coined by Pitman. For inversion of elements cf. *gramophone*.

grammar. F. *grammaire*, L. *grammatica* (sc. *ars*), G. γραμματική (sc. τέχνη), from γράμμα, letter, from γράφειν, to write. For -*r*- cf. OF. *mire*, physician, L. *medicus*. In L. & G. used of philology and literature in widest sense, in Middle Ages esp. of L. grammar (hence *grammar school*, 14 cent.), and also of occult sciences popularly connected with the learned (hence *gramarye*, *glamour*). Most of the L. grammatical terms were translated from G. (see *case*, *genitive*, etc.). "The first school grammar ever written in Europe was the Greek grammar of Dionysius Thrax, a pupil of Aristarchus, which he published at Rome in the time of Pompey" (Whitney). The first English Grammar was written (c. 1600) by Ben Jonson.

gramme, gram. F. *gramme*, Late L. *gramma*, G. γράμμα, letter, also small weight. Adopted as unit in metric system by law of 19 frimaire, year VIII (1799).

gramophone. An atrocity formed by reversing *phonogram*.

grampus. Earlier (16 cent.) *graundepose*, altered, on F. *grand*, from ME. *grapeys*, OF. *grapois*, *graspeis*, *craspois*, L. *crassus piscis*, fat fish; cf. *porpoise*. In ME. also *crospais* (see *coarse*).

granadilla, grenadilla. Flower. Sp., dim. of *granada*, pomegranate.

granary. L. *granarium*, from *granum*, corn. Cf. *garner*.

grand. F., L. *grandis*, which supplanted *magnus* (exc. in *Charlemagne*) in Rom. langs. E. has chiefly adopted spec. sense (cf. *grandeur*), exc. in titles or expressions which imitate foreign usage, e.g. *Grand Duke* (*Inquisitor*), *Grand Junction Canal*, *grand tour*, etc. With *grandfather*, etc., archaic *grandsire*, *grandam*, etc., after F. *grand-père*, etc. (replacing AS. *ealdefæder*), cf. Ger. *grossvater*, etc. The much later *grandson* corresponds to more logical F. *petit-fils*.

grandee. Earlier *grande*, *grandy*, Sp. *grande*, L. *grandis* (v.s.).

grandiloquent. From L. *grandiloquus*, from *loqui*, to speak; after *eloquent*.

grandiose. F., It. *grandioso*.

Grandisonian. Like *Sir Charles Grandison*, faultless hero of Richardson's novel (1753).

grange. Orig. granary, barn. F., VL. **granica*, from *granum*, corn. Later, outlying farm (Chauc.). Cf. Du. *spijker*, Ger. *speicher*, loft, orig. granary, from L. *spica*, ear of corn, the sense having changed as in F. *grenier*, loft.

grangerize. From *James Granger*, who published (1769) a *Biographical History of England* with blank pages for insertion of illustrative engravings, etc. Cf. *bowdlerize*.

> Being an inveterate Graingerizer, I cut out your paragraph to stick in my volume
>
> (*Daily Chron.* Jan. 31, 1917).

granite. It. *granito*, grained; adopted by most Europ. langs. Cf. *granophyre*, coined (1872) by Vogelsang, from Ger. *gran*(*it*)-(*por*)*phyr*.

granny. For *grannam*, colloq. for *grandam*.

grant. AF. *graanter*, *graunter*, OF. *creanter*, from *creant*, pres. part. of *creire* (*croire*), L. *credere*, to believe, entrust (cf. *credit*). Possibly AF. *graunter* may also partly represent F. *garantir* (see *guarantee*).

granulate. From Late L. *granulum*, dim. of *granum*, grain.

grape. F. *grappe* (*de raisin*), bunch (of grapes), cogn. with *grab*, *grapple*, etc. Cf. *grape-shot* (17 cent.). Replaced AS. *winberige*.

graph [*math.*]. For *graphic formula*. Cf. *graphic*, L., G. γραφικός, from γραφή, writing, drawing, from γράφειν, to write, orig. to scratch. *Graphology*, F. *graphologie*, was coined by Abbé Michon (1869).

-graph, -grapher, -graphy. See *graph*.

graphite. Black lead, etc Ger. *graphit*, or F. *graphite* (c. 1800), because used for pencils (v.s.).

grapnel. Orig. naut. (Chauc.). Dim. from F. *grappin*, dim. of OF. *grappe*, hook, of Teut. origin and cogn. with *agrafe*, *grab*, *gripe*, etc.

grapple. Orig. naut. (Palsg.). Cogn. with above. With fig. to *grapple with* cf. to *come to grips*.

grasp. ME. *grasp* (often synon. with *grope*), for *graps*, cogn. with *grab*, *grope*, etc. Cf. *clasp*, *wasp*. For fig. senses cf. *comprehend*.

Thou shalt graasp [*var.* grope, *Vulg.* palpare] in mydday, as is woned a blynd man to graasp in derknisses (Wyc. *Deut.* xxviii. 29).

grass. AS. *gærs*, *græs*. Com. Teut.; cf. Du. Ger. ON. Goth. *gras*; ult. cogn. with *grow*, *green*, and L. *gramen*. Hence *grasshopper*, earlier *grasshop*, AS. *gærs-hoppa* (for Bibl. locust).

grass-cutter [*Anglo-Ind.*]. Corrupt. of Urdu *ghāskatā*. Cf. *boy*, *compound*², *godown*, etc.

grass-widow. Orig. (16 cent.) woman who has cohabited, discarded mistress. Cf. obs. LG. *graswedewe*, in same sense, also Du. *grasweduwe*, Ger. *strohwittwe* (straw), in mod. sense. Orig. allusion prob. to bed of straw or grass (cf. *bastard*). Ger. practice of strewing chopped straw (*häckerling*) before door of unchaste may be connected. Another theory is that the bride who had anticipated conjugal life wore a wreath of straw instead of one of flowers. Current sense, esp. Anglo-Ind., from c. 1850.

Then had wyvys ben in his [St Paul's] time lytel better than grasse wydowes be now (Sir T. More).

Gott verzeih's meinem lieben mann,
Er hat an mir nicht wohl getan!
Geht da stracks in die welt hinein,
Und lässt mich auf dem stroh allein.
       (Goethe, *Faust*, 2865).

grate¹. Bars. MedL., It. *grata*, from L. *cratis*, hurdle. Cf. *grill*.

grate². Verb. F. *gratter*, to scratch, of Teut. origin; cf. Dan. *kratte*, Ger. *kratzen*, E. *s-cratch*. For fig. sense cf. to *set teeth on edge*.

grateful. From obs. adj. *grate*, L. *gratus*, pleasing (cf. *ingrate*). A most unusual formation. *Grateful and comforting* preserves older sense. Cf. *gratitude*, *gratuity*, through F.

gratify. F. *gratifier*, from L. *gratificari*, from *gratus*, pleasing.

gratin [*cook.*]. F., from *gratter*, to grate.

gratis. L., contr. of *gratiis*, abl. pl. of *gratia*, favour. Cf. *gratuitous*, from cogn. L. *gratuitus*, freely bestowed.

gratitude, gratuity. See *grateful*, *gratis*.

gratulate. See *congratulate*.

gravamen. MedL., grievance. See *grave*³, *grief*.

grave¹. Noun. AS. *græf*, cogn. with *grafan*, to dig (v.i.). In dial. also pit.

grave². Verb. AS. *grafan*, to dig. Com. Teut.; cf. Du. *graven*, Ger. *graben*, ON. *grafa*, Goth. *graban*. *Engrave* has nearly supplanted *grave* in spec. sense, but *graven image* survives.

He hath graven and digged up a pit
       (*Ps.* vii. 16, *PB.*).

grave³. Adj. L. *gravis*, heavy, serious. Cf. *gravity*, opposite of *levity*. Scient. sense of *gravitate*, *gravity*, and of their F. equivalents, appears in 17 cent.

grave⁴ [*naut.*]. Chiefly in *graving-dock*, where ship's bottom is cleaned by burning and tarring. From F. *grève*, beach, where ship was careened for the purpose. *Graving-beach* also occurs; cf. to *beach a ship*, and, for simpler ancient naut. methods, see *dock*³. See *gravel*.

graving: (du françois grave, rivage). Action d'échouer un bâtiment à marée basse, pour le caréner ou l'espalmer: on dit en françois "Œuvres de marée" (Lesc.).

gravel. F. *gravelle*, dim. of OF. *grave* (*grève*), shingle, etc. Of Celt. origin; cf. Welsh *gro*, gravel, pebbly beach. To *be gravelled*, in perplexity, is a naut. metaphor; cf. *stranded* and see *grave*⁴. But perh. influenced by *grovel* (v.i.).

When we were fallen into a place betwene two seas, they graveled the ship
       (*Acts*, xxvii. 41. *Rheims version*, 1582).

It strooke him from the place where hee sate, and groveled him (Purch. xix. 10).

gravel-blind. Used by Shaks. (*Merch. of Ven.* ii. 2) as jocular variation on misunderstood *sand-blind* (q.v.). Understood by later writers as halfway between *sand-blind* and *stone-blind*.

graveolent. Fetid. From L. *grave*, heavily, *olēre*, to smell.

graves. See *greaves*².

Graves's disease. Ophthalmic goitre. Diagnosed (1835) by *Dr Graves*, of Dublin. Cf. *Bright's disease*.

gravid. L. *gravidus*, from *gravis*, heavy.

gravitate, gravity. See *grave*³.

gravy. App. originated as cooking-term (14 cent.) from misreading of OF. *grané*, from *grain*, used in OF., as gen. name for cooking ingredients. This conjecture, unlikely as it appears, is confirmed by the fact that ME. recipes for *gravy* and OF. recipes for *grané* are practically ident. (cf. *custard*).

gray. See *grey*. *Grayling*, fish, butterfly; from colour.

graze¹. Of cattle. AS. *grasian*, from *grass* (cf. *glaze*, *glass*). *Grazier*, feeder of cattle, is partly OF. *graissier*, fattener (see *grease*).

graissier: one that loves fat things; also, a grasier, or fattener of cattell (Cotg.).

graze². To touch lightly. Of doubtful origin. It appears to contain suggestions of *rase* (cf. *abrasion*), of obs. *glace*, to glance (q.v.), and of skimming the surface of the *grass* (cf. F. *effleurer*). Prob. associated with *graze¹*.

He caused a souldier to shoote at him with his caleever which grased before his face
(Hakl. vii. 223, 1557).

radere: to flye levell to the ground as some birds do; also to graze on the ground as an arow or a bullet (Flor.).

grease. F. *graisse*, VL. *crassia* for *crassa*, neut. pl., from *crassus*, fat. Cf. *force, marvel*. *Greaser* (US.), Mexican, is said to be due to greasy appearance.

great. AS. *grēat*. WGer.; cf. Du. *groot*, Ger. *gross*. Use in relationships (*great uncle*, etc.) is later than that of *grand*. With Oxf. *Greats* (*Verdant Green*), for earlier *Great Go*, cf. *Smalls*.

greaves¹ [*hist.*]. Armour for legs. OF. *greve*, shin; cf. Ger. *schiene*, shin, greave. Origin unknown; but quot. below, last line of which means "that with which one covers calf and shin," suggests it meant the hard part as opposed to the soft part (F. *mollet*,

calf), and so may be ult. ident. with *greaves*².

Item, je donne à maistre Jaques
Raguyer le grand godet de Grève,
Pourveu qu'il payera quatre plaques,
Deust-il vendre, quoy qu'il luy griefve,
Ce dont on ceuvre mol et grève
(Villon, *Grand Test.* xci.).

greaves², graves. Fibrous refuse of tallow. LG. *greven*, cogn. with OHG. *griubo* (*griebe*), which some connect with Ger. *grob*, coarse, as applied to the solid constituents. Orig. a whaleman's word, borrowed also in Dan. *grever*.

grebe. F. *grèbe*, of unknown origin.

Grecian. In *AV.* (*Acts*, vi. 1) for Greek-speaking Jew. Cf. sense of Greek scholar, hellenist, as still at Christ's Hospital.

Grecian bend. Affected carriage of body (c. 1870). Recorded 1821.

greed. Orig. Sc., back-formation from *greedy*, AS. *grǣdig*. Com. Teut.; cf. OSax. *grādag*, OHG. *grātag*, ON. *grāthugr*, Goth. *grēdags*; also ON. *grāthr*, hunger, Goth. *grēdus*; cogn. with Sanskrit *gṛdh*, to be hungry.

Greek. AS. *Grēcas*, *Crēcas* (pl.); cf. OHG. *Chriech*, Goth. *Krēks*, an early loan from L. *Graeci*, G. Γραικοί (cf. L. *Graii*). In sense of card-sharper from F. *grec* in same sense (? cf. *Corinthian*). The *Greek Church* renounced communion with the Roman Church in 9 cent. (cf. *Greek, Latin, cross*). *Greek fire* (*wildfire*) was first used by the Greeks of Constantinople. In ME. it is called *Greekish fire*, prob. adapted from F. *feu grégeois*. *Greek gift* refers to the wooden horse.

But, for mine own part, it was Greek to me
(*Jul. Caes.* i. 2).

When Greeks joyn'd Greeks, then was the tug of war (Nathaniel Lee, *Rival Queens*, iv. 2).

green. AS. *grēne*. Com. Teut.; cf. Du. *groen*, Ger. *grün*, ON. *grönn*; cogn. with *grass*, *grow*. As emblem of jealousy, after Shaks. *green-eyed monster* (*Oth.* iii. 3), of vitality in *green old age*, of immaturity in *greenhorn*, orig. young horned animal (cf. synon. F. *bec-jaune*, yellow beak), *green hand* (orig. naut.). The first *NED*. record for (village) *green* is 1477, but *atte grene, de la grene*, whence surname *Green*, are abundantly recorded from c. 1200. *Green sickness* (*chlorosis*) is a form of anaemia which gives a greenish tinge to the complexion. The *Board of Green Cloth* (royal household) is recorded from 16 cent. For *greengage* see *gage²*. For *green goose* see *wayzgoose*.

Greenland, ON. *Grönland*, was so named in 986, in order to attract settlers, though "certainly there is no place in the world that is lesse greene" (Purch.). The sign of the *Green Man and Still* was suggested by the arms of the Distillers' Company, the supporters of which were two Indians, "wild men of the woods"; cf. the Ger. sign *zum wilden mann*. The *greenroom* was perh. orig. that of some spec. theatre, decorated in green. Pepys mentions more than once the King's *Greenroom* at Whitehall.

greet[1]. To salute. AS. *grǣtan*. WGer.; cf. Du. *groeten*, Ger. *grüssen*. Orig. sense prob. to come in contact with, as it meant both to salute and attack. "An old word" (Kersey, 1706).

greet[2] [*Sc. & north.*]. To weep. AS. *grǣtan*; cf. MHG. *grazen*, ON. *grāta*, Goth. *grētan*.

greffier. F., notary, etc. From *greffe*, stylus. See *graft*[1].

gregarious. From L. *gregarius*, from *grex*, *greg*-, herd; cf. *congregate*.

Gregorian. Music, from *Pope Gregory I* (590–600). Calendar (1582), from *Pope Gregory XIII*, adopted here in 1752.

Gregory-powder. From *James Gregory*, Sc. physician (†1821). Cf. *Daffy's elixir*.

gremial. Of the lap or bosom, L. *gremium*.

grenade. F., orig. pomegranate (q.v.). Also earlier *grenado*, *granado*, after Sp. *granada*. Orig. of an artillery missile (cf. Ger. *granat*, shell). "Though 'grenades' went out of general use in the 18 cent. (!), the name of 'grenadiers' was retained for a company of the tallest and finest men in the regiment" (*NED.*). The *Grenadier Guards* (first regiment of Foot Guards) received their mod. name "in commemoration of their having defeated the Grenadiers of the French Imperial Guards upon this memorable occasion" (*Gazette*, July 29, 1815).

grenade: a pomegranet; also, a ball of wild-fire, made like a pomegranet (Cotg.).

Now [1678] were brought into service a new sort of soldiers call'd granadiers, who were dexterous in flinging hand-granados (Evelyn).

grenadilla. As *granadilla*.

grenadine. Fabric. F., from *grenade*, orig. spotted with "grains."

Gresham's law [*econ.*]. That bad money drives out good, as explained (1558) by Sir T. Gresham to Queen Elizabeth.

Gretna Green. In Dumfriesshire, just over Sc. border, hence first spot at which runaway marriage could be conveniently celebrated with simplifications allowed by Sc. law.

"He has taken her to a Green." "A Goose Green?" asked Clarinda. "A Gretna Green"
         (J. H. Ewing, *Jackanapes*).

grey, gray. AS. *grǣg*. Com. Teut.; cf. Du. *grauw*, Ger. *grau*, ON. *grār*. For *grey-friar* see *Franciscan* and *friar*. The *grey mare* (better horse) is recorded for 1536. The *Scots Greys* (1681) were orig. named from grey uniform, not from chargers. *Greybeard* is used in Sc. for a large stone (whisky) jug. In *greyhound*, AS. *grīghund*, ON. *greyhundr*, the first element means bitch (cf. Ger. *windhund*, greyhound, from OHG. *wint*, hound), and the compd. has prob. changed its meaning. The ME. *grew-hound*, still in north. dial., results from an etymologizing attempt to connect with OF. *Grieu*, ME. *Grew*, Greek; cf. Sp. *galgo*, greyhound, L. *Gallicus* (*canis*). The first *Atlantic greyhound* was the S.S. *Alaska* (1882). *Greylag* (goose) is supposed to be named from late migration. Quot. below is a nonce-variation on *into the brown* (q.v.). See *field*.

Our machine gunners got fairly into the grey of them (*Daily Mail*, Dec. 5, 1917).

griddle, gridiron. AF. *gridil* (cf. Norm. dial. *gredil*), whence ME. *gredile*. Found also in Gael. Ir. Welsh, from L., so that the immediate source may have been partly Celt. *Gridiron* is folk-etym. for ME. *gredire*, var. of *gredile* (cf. *andiron*). The confusion of *-l-*, *-r-* is common in Norman dial., e.g. *Basire* for *Basile* (cf. also F. *navire*, VL. *navilium). *Grid* is a backformation (19 cent.). See *grill*.

gride [*poet.*]. To pierce, etc. Metath. of *gird*[2], adopted by Spenser from Lydgate.

grief. F., wrong, grievance, from *grever*, to afflict. See *grieve*. In ME. also damage, hurt, as in to *come to grief*.

To implor forgifnes of all greif (Gavin Douglas).

grieve. From tonic stem (*griev-*) of OF. *grever*, to weigh down, afflict, etc., VL. *grevare, from *grevis, altered from *gravis*, heavy, by association with its opposite *levis*, light (see *render*). Cf. fig. use of *heavy*.

Forsothe her eyen weren greved [*Vulg.* gravati]
         (Wyc. *Matt.* xxvi. 43).

griffin[1], **griffon, gryphon**. F. *griffon*, from L. *gryphus*, from G. γρύψ, γρυπ-; cf. G. γρυπός, curved, hook-beaked.

griffin² [*Anglo-Ind.*]. New arrival in India, green hand. Prob. corrupted from some native word (cf. *blighty*).

griffon. Dog. F., see *griffin¹*.

grig. Orig. used of various undersized animals (cf. *tit*), now esp. (in dial.) of a small eel. It is uncertain what *merry grig* orig. meant, as *grig*, grasshopper, cricket, seems to be a mod. assumption from the phrase by analogy with *merry as a cricket*. In earliest records (16 cent.) it means boon companion and is found also as *merry Greek*. Quite possibly it is the pet form of *Gregory* (cf. surname *Grigg*), and *merry Grig* may go with *merry Andrew, zany*, etc. On the other hand Cotg. equates it with F. *gringalet*, undersized man, used in OF. of a small horse.

gringalet: a merry grig, pleasant rogue, sportfull knave (Cotg.).

pantagrueliste: a pantagruelist, a merry Greeke, faithfull drunkard, good fellow (*ib.*).

grill. F. *gril*, gridiron; cf. fem. form *grille*, grating, as in ladies' gallery of House of Commons (removed Aug. 1917). OF. *greil, greille*, L. *craticulum, craticula*, from *crates*, hurdle, grating. Cf. *creel, griddle*.

craticula: ung gril (Est.).

grilse. Young salmon on first return from sea. ? OF. *grisle*, grey; cf. Sw. *grålax*, lit. grey salmon. See *grizzled*.

grim. AS. *grimm*, fierce. Com. Teut.; cf. Du. *grim*, Ger. *grimm*, ON. *grimmr*; cogn. with ME. *grame* and Ger. *gram*, whence OF. *grain*, surly. Esp. in *grim death*, app. after Shaks., but locus classicus is *Par. L.* ii. 804.

Grim Death, how foul and loathsome is thine image
(*Shrew, Induction*, i. 35).

grimace. F., prob. from OHG. *grimmiza*, cogn. with *grim* (v.s.); cf. F. *grincer*, to gnash the teeth, OHG. **grimmizōn*.

grimalkin [*archaic*]. For *gray malkin*, the latter, dim. of *Matilda* and *Mary*, being name for she-cat (cf. *tom-cat*).

I come, Gray-Malkin (*Macb.* i. 1).

grime. First as verb (15 cent.). Of LG. origin; cf. ModFlem. *grijm*, obs. Du. *begremen*, "denigrare, maculis inficere, maculare, angl.* grime" (Kil.); ? cogn. with AS. *grīma*, mask, orig. blackened face, which is still sense of Norw. *grime*.

Grimm's law [*ling.*]. Regular mutation of consonants in Aryan languages. Stated by *Jakob Grimm*, Ger. philologist (†1863).

grimthorpe. To "restore" an ancient building. From restoration (late 19 cent.) of St Albans Abbey by *Lord Grimthorpe*. Coined by the *Athenaeum* (July 23, 1892).

grin. AS. *grennian*; cf. Ger. *greinen, grinsen*; cogn. with *groan*. Orig. to make a wry mouth, expressive of pain or anger.

Y-frounced foule was hir visage
And grennyng for dispitous rage
(*Rom. of Rose*, 156).

grind. AS. *grindan*; ? cogn. with L. *frendere*, to gnash the teeth; cf. Du. *grenden* (rare). Other Teut. langs. have a verb cogn. with L. *molere* (see *meal¹*). Often of hard or monotonous work; hence *grind* (univ.), walk taken for exercise, constitutional. To *grind the faces of the poor* (Wyc.) is a Hebraism (*Is.* iii. 15). A *grindstone* was orig. a millstone. To *keep* (*hold*) *one's nose to the grindstone* meant earlier (c. 1500) to torture.

gringo. Mexican name for Englishman or AS. American. SAmer. Sp., ? corrupt. of *Griego*, Greek.

The Mexicans...finally became friendly with the hated gringoes (*Daily Chron.* March 2, 1917).

grip¹. AS. *gripa*, handful, *gripe*, clutch; cogn. with *gripe*. In earlier use chiefly Sc. With fig. sense cf. *grasp*. US. *grip*, handbag, for *gripsack*, is prob. of Du. origin.

grip² [*dial.*]. Trench, hollow. AS. *grēpe, grȳpe*.

gripe. AS. *grīpan*. Com. Teut.; cf. Du. *grijpen*, Ger. *greifen*, ON. *gripa*, Goth. *greipan*; cogn. with *grope*. With *gripes*, clutching pains, cf. F. *grippe* (v.i.).

grippe. Influenza. F., seizure, from *gripper*, to clutch, of LG. origin (v.s.); ? or Russ. *chrip*, hoarseness.

grisaille [*paint.*]. F., from *gris*, grey, MHG. *grīs*; cf. Ger. *greis*, old man. See *grizzled*.

grisette. F., work-girl, from *gris*, grey (v.s.), from former dress. Cf. Du. *grauw*, populace, lit. grey.

griskin. Dim. of dial. *grice*, pig, ON. *grīss*.

gryse, swyn, or pygge: porcellus (*Prompt. Parv.*).

grisly. AS. *grislic*, terrible, cogn. with *gryche*, terror; cf. ME. *grisen*, to shudder, MHG. *grisenlich*, grisly.

grist. AS. *grīst*, from *grind*; cf. F. *mouture*, grist, *moudre*, to grind. Proverb. use (*grist to the mill*) occurs in ME.

gristle. AS. *gristle*, cartilage of the nose, *næsgristle*. Analogy of Du. *knarsbeen*, gristle, from *knarsen*, to gnash, suggests connection with *grist*, from idea of crunching.

grit. AS. *grēot*, sand, etc. The fact that Ger. *griess*, groats, grits, is from OHG. *grioz*, sand, points to relationship of *grits*, oatmeal, AS. *grytta* (cf. Ger. *grütze*), with *grit*. The vowel of *grit* (for *greet*) is due to association with *grits*. Fig. (US.) for pluck, character, orig. *clear* (*hard*) *grit*, from quality of stone. Synon. US. *sand* (*Huckleberry Finn*) is a further variation on the same idea.

sablonneux: sandy, greetie (Cotg.).

grizzle. To sulk, fret. ? Ironic allusion to *patient Grizel*, Chaucer's *Griseldis*.

Enough to make a grizzle fret (*NED.* 1797).

grizzled, grizzly. From archaic *grizzle*, grey-haired, ME. *grisel*, old man, OF. dim. of *gris*. See *grisaille*. The *grizzly bear* (ursus horribilis) belongs rather to *grisly*.

groan. AS. *grānian*; cogn. with *grin*.

groat. Orig. Du. coin. Du. *groot*, great, in sense of thick; cf. Ger. *groschen*, F. *gros sou*.

I have found the groate which I had loost
(Tynd. *Luke*, xv. 9).

groats. Crushed grain. AS. *grot*, particle, cogn. with *grit*; cf. Du. *grutte*, Ger. *grütze*. See *grout, gruel*.

Grobian. Churl. Ger., facet. latinization (*Grobianus*), from *grob*, coarse, surly, cogn. with *gruff*.

grocer. Orig. dealer "in the gross," wholesale. OF. *grossier*. See *gross, engross*[2]. The Company of Grocers, incorporated 1344, were wholesale dealers in spices and foreign produce. For limitation cf. *stationer*, for converse cf. *costermonger*.

grog. Nickname of Admiral Vernon, who wore usually a *grogram* cloak, and who first (Aug. 1740) ordered dilution of sailors' rum. Hence *groggy*, unsteady.

grogram. Earlier (16 cent.) *grograin, grogeran*, etc., F. *gros grain*, coarse grain; cf. *fingering*. Restored form is used in trade and US. A Ger. perversion is *grobgrün*, lit. coarse green (see *gruff*).

Item paid for xxj yardes iij quarters of grow-graine chamblet iij li. xijs (*Rutland MSS.* 1558).

A grosgrain carpet lay on the asphalt to the edge of the side-walk (O. Henry).

groin. Earlier *grine*, ME. *grynde*; cf. AS. *grynde*, abyss, cogn. with *ground*, and dial. *grindle*, runnel. For change of vowel cf. *boil*[2]. Arch. sense is later than anat.

aines: the grine, or groyne of man or woman (Cotg.).

Grolier [*bibl.*]. From *Jean Grolier*, F. bibliophile (†1565).

gromwell. Plant. Altered, perh. on *speedwell*, from ME. *gromil, gromel*, OF. *gromil* (*grémil*). OF. has also *grenil*, due to influence of *grain*, but the first element is prob. OF. *grume*, pip of grape, also grain in gen., ? L. *grumus*, hillock, clod, clot. The plant (*lithospermum*) is noted for its hard seeds. The var. *graymill* is ModF. *grémil* (v.s.).

groom. Orig. (c. 1200), boy, male child; cf. OF. *gromet*, lad (see *grummet*). Both are of obscure origin (see remark s.v. *girl*). Mod. spec. sense has developed from gen. sense of servant as in *horse-groom, stable-groom*.

groove. Du. *groefe*, trench, cogn. with *grave*[1]; cf. Ger. *grube*, ON. *grōf*, pit, Goth. *grōba*. For fig. sense cf. *rut*.

grope. AS. *grāpian*; cogn. with *grasp* (q.v.), *grip*[1].

grosbeak. Bird. F. *grosbec*. See *gross* and *beak*.

groschen. Coin. Ger., dim. of *gross*, great. Cf. *groat*.

gross. F. *gros*, Late L. *grossus*, of obscure origin, said to be unconnected with Ger. *gross*, great. Many of the E. senses are not found in F., while others are represented by the derived *grossier*, rude, vulgar, etc. For noun sense, bulk, cf. *grocer, engross*[2]. Spec. sense of duodecimal hundred is F. *grosse* (= It. *grossa*, Sp. *gruesa*). Cf. *great hundred, long hundred*, Ger. *grosshundert* (120).

grot, grotto. Earlier *grotta*. F. *grotte*, It. *grotta*, L., G. κρυπτή, from κρύπτειν, to hide (see *crypt*). OF. had *crute, crote*, now superseded by the It. word. The London street *grotto* (Aug. 5) is said to have been orig. in honour of St James the Greater, whose shrine at Compostella was one of the holy places of Europe.

grotesque. F., It. *grottesca* (sc. *opera*), fem. of *grottesco*, from *grotta* (v.s.), because imitated from crude designs found in old buildings excavated.

grottesca: a kinde of rugged unpolished painters worke, anticke worke (Flor.).

ground. AS. *grund*. Com. Teut.; cf. Du. *grond*, Ger. *grund*, ON. *grunnr*, Goth. *grundus* (in compds.). Orig. bottom, esp. of the sea; cf. *groundling, ground-swell*, and Ger. *zu grunde gehen*, to founder. Orig. sense also appears in *grounds*, sediment, for which Ger. uses *boden*, bottom. Later, base, surface. With *down to the ground* cf. F. *à fond*. ME. used *all to ground* in similar sense. Often in mil. metaphor (like F. *terrain*), e.g. to *gain* (*lose, yield, shift one's*) *ground*. To *get in on the ground-floor*, i.e. on a level with the promoters, is US.

groundsel, grunsel. Plant. AS. *grundeswelge* (10 cent.), lit. earth-swallower, appears to be an early gardener's perversion of *gundeswelge* (7 cent.), pus swallower, from use of chopped leaves in poultices. Cf. hist. of *saxifrage, feverfew*. Or both forms may be due to folk-etym. It is uncertain whether the AS. name was applied to the plant which we now call *groundsel*, and Ger. *günsel*, comfrey (q.v.), OHG. *cunsele*, L. *consolida*, suggest a similar origin for our word. There is also a techn. *groundsel*, foundation, etc. (v.i.), app. for "ground sill," to which spelling of the plant-name has been assimilated.

On th' holy groundsill of sweet Edens earth
                  (Sylv. *Handicrafts*).

group. F. *groupe*, It. *groppo*, "a knot, an entangling, a node, a knob, a bunch" (Flor.), of Teut. origin; cf. *crop, crupper*. In E. orig. (17 cent.) term of art (cf. *attitude, costume*).

grouper. Fish. Port. *garupa*, ? from some SAmer. native name, or ? ident. with *garupa*, buttock. For perversion cf. *breaker*. But quot. below, 70 years earlier than *NED.*, suggests that the word may be of E. formation (? from *grope* ? or *group*) and that the Port. word may be from E.

There is great store and varietie of fish, which being for the most part unknowne to us, each man gave them names as they best liked: as one kind they called rocke fish, another "groopers"
    (Norwood's *Bermudas*, 1622, in Purch. xix. 189).

grouse¹. Bird. Orig. pl. used collectively. Perh. F. *grue* or Port. *grou*, crane, from L. *grus, gru-*, crane, used in wrong sense. Bird-names are very vague (see *albatross, heron, penguin*), and *grouse* is explained by Littleton (v.i.) as a young bustard, a bird akin to the crane (Newton), while other early dicts. confuse it with the godwit. The earliest *NED.* records for *grouse* (*grows*, 1531, *grewes*, 1547) may equally well stand for ME. *grew*, crane. My quot., a double pl. perpetrated by a servant, is a little earlier. *Grew* was in common use as a 13 cent. nickname (hence surname *Grew*). MedL. *gruta*, gallina campestris,

may be a latinization of F. *grue* (VL. *grua for *grus*).

A brase of grewyses (*Wollaton Papers*, 1523).

grous, young heath fowl: tetraonum pulli (Litt.).

tetrao: a bustard or bistard (*ib.*).

grouse² [*mil.*]. To grumble. OF. *groucier* (whence *grudge*) has same sense and is still used in Norm. dial., but it hardly seems possible to establish connection. The first *NED.* example is from Kipling (1892), but I have heard the word used by an old soldier of the Indian Mutiny period. Cf. US. *grouch*.

This is BUTTER!
Come on, you grousers
(*Inscription in London Shop*, Mar. 1918).

grout¹. Sediment. Orig. coarse meal. AS. *grūt*; cogn. with *grit, groats. Grout*, thin mortar, is perh. the same word.

grout², groot. To dig with the snout. App. coined from *rout², root²*, under influence of *grunt*.

grove. AS. *grāf*. Cf. ME. *greve*, thicket, AS. *grǣfa*.

grovel. First in Shaks. Back-formation from adj. *grovelling*, orig. adv., face downward; cf. ME. *groof*, ON. *grūfa*, usu. in *ā grūfu*, whence ME. *on grufe*, grovelling. Prob. cogn. with *grub*. For back-formation cf. *sidle*.

Now dounward groff and now upright
              (*Rom. of Rose*, 2561).

grow. AS. *grōwan*; cf. Du. *groeien*, OHG. *gruoan*, ON. *grōa*; cogn. with *grass, green*. Has almost supplanted *wax²* (q.v.).

growl. In mod. sense from 18 cent.; cf. ME. *groll, gurl*, to rumble, OF. *grouiller*, to scold, Du. Ger. *grollen*, to grumble, sulk. All of imit. origin. With *growlery* (*Bleak House*, ch. viii.) cf. *boudoir, den. Growler*, four-wheeler, is 19 cent.

groyne. Structure to check washing up of sand. F. *groin*, snout of pig, back-formation from *grogner*, to grunt, from L. *grunnire*; used in OF. of a promontory. Sailors formerly called Corunna, Sp. la Coruña, the *groyne of Spain* (*Rob. Crusoe*, i. 19).

Vocatur le Groyne; est in mare ut rostrum porci
              (*NED.* 1367).

grub. ME. *grobben, gruben*, etc., to dig, cogn. with *grave¹*; cf. Ger. *grübeln*, to brood over, OHG. *grubilōn*, to bore into. Hence *grub*, digging insect, worm, etc. (see *mulligrubs*). Fig. as in *Grub Street*, now Milton St., Moorfields, inhabited by literary "grubs" in 17 cent. In slang sense of provender (17 cent.) often linked with *bub*, drink.

grudge. Earlier *grutch*, to murmur, grumble, OF. *groucier*, *groucher* (see *grouse*²), of obscure origin, perh. imit.; cf. *growl*, *murmur*.

And the Farisees and scribis grutchiden [*Vulg.* murmurare] (Wyc. *Luke*, xv. 2).

Let them...grudge [*Vulg.* murmurare] if they be not satisfied (*Ps.* lix. 15).

gruel. OF. (*gruau*), crushed grain, groats, dim. of archaic *gru*, of LG. origin; see *groats*. For pugil. to *give one his gruel* see origin of to *serve out* (s.v. *serve*), and cf. Sc. to *give one his kale through the reek* (*Old Mort.* ch. xiv.).

gruesome. From ME. and dial. *grue*, to shudder; cf. Dan. *gru*, horror, Ger. *grauen*, to shudder, *grausam*, cruel, *gräulich*, horrible, etc. Ult. cogn. with *grisly*.

I begin to grue at the sound of it (*Catriona*).

gruff. Orig. (16 cent.) coarse in quality, etc. Du. *grof*, "crassus, spissus, densus, impolitus, rudis" (Kil.); cogn. with Ger. *grob* (OHG. *girob*, perh. a compd. of OHG. *riob*, rough), which means coarse (tobacco, material, etc.) and surly. See *Grobian*.

grumble. Cf. F. *grommeler*, LG. *grummeln*. Imit., or perh. allied to *grim*. Hence *Grumbletonian* (17 cent.), orig. applied to the "Country party" as opposed to the "Court party." Coined on *Muggletonian*.

grume [*med.*]. Clot. OF. (replaced by *grumeau*), L. *grumus*. See *gromwell*.

grummet [*naut.*]. Fig. use of obs. *gromet*, *grummet*, ship's boy, common in F. & E., 13–18 cents., also Sp. *grumete* (see *groom*). Cf. *gasket*, with which it is associated in earliest quotations.

grommets: are little rings which...have no other use but to tie and make fast the casketts [gaskets] (Manwayring, *Seaman's Dict.* 1644).

grumete: garçon ou esclave de galère (Oudin).

gourmette: a ship-boy, servant or apprentice, in the dialect of Province (Falc.).

grump. Suggested by *grumble*, *grunt*, *dump*.

Grundy, Mrs. Character in Morton's *Speed the Plough* (1798). Several times referred to in the play in the now familiar phrase *What will Mrs Grundy say?* It is curious that to this forgotten author is also due the usu. misquoted *Approbation from Sir Hubert Stanley is praise indeed.*

grunsel. See *groundsel*.

grunt. AS. *grunnettan*, frequent. of *grunnian*;

cf. Ger. *grunzen*, from MHG. *grunnen*; also F. *grogner*, L. *grunnire*. Of imit. origin.

gruyère. Cheese. From name of Swiss town (Fribourg).

gryphon. See *griffin*¹.

grysbok. SAfr. antelope. Du. *grijs*, grey; cf. *springbok*, etc.

guacho. See *gaucho*.

guaiacum. Resin. Sp. *guayaco*, *guayacan*, from native lang. of Hayti.

guana. Var. of *iguana* (q.v.).

guanaco. Kind of *llama*. Sp., Peruv. *huanacu*.

guano. Sp., Peruv. *huanu*, dung.

Guarani. Native lang. of Brazil.

guarantee. Also *guaranty*. First as noun (= *warranty*), p.p. fem. of F. *garantir*, to protect, etc., from OF. *garant*, protection, OHG. *werend*, pres. part. of *weren*, to protect. Cf. *weir*, *landwehr*, *warrant*. The verb was orig. used (18 cent.) in pol. sense, e.g. of powers guaranteeing by treaty the independence of smaller countries, such as Belgium.

guard, guardian. F. *garde*, *gardien*. Late (15 cent.) substitutions for *ward*, *warden* (q.v.); cf. the correlation of *guardian* and *ward*. The noun was orig. abstract or collect., as in *on one's guard*, *bodyguard*, etc. The *guard* of a stage-coach was armed for the defence of travellers. He has been taken over with the *driver*, *coach*, and *booking office*, by the railways.

guava. Sp. *guayaba*, from WInd. name of tree.

guabas: a sort of tree in the West Indies of no value (Stevens).

gubernatorial [*US.*]. Of a governor (q.v.).

gudgeon¹. Fish. F. *goujon*, L. *gobio-n-*, from *gobius*; cf. *goby*. Fig. senses from readiness to swallow any bait; cf. *gull*.

gudgeon² [*techn.*]. Pivot of hinge, socket of rudder pintle (naut.). OF. *gojon*, ? from F. *gouge*, wench, prostitute, with an obscene allusion. Cf. synon. F. *femelot* (*de gouvernail*); also E. *male*, *female screw*, *grummet*, *gasket*. See *pintle*, *pivot*.

Guebre. Fire-worshipper. F. *guèbre*, Pers. *gabr*. Cf. *giaour*.

Guelder rose. From *Guelders* (Prussia), old capital of Guelderland (Holland), formerly Pruss. province.

Guelph [*hist.*]. It. *Guelfo*, OHG. *Welf* (whelp), name of a Ger. princely family, used as war-cry of the anti-imperialists at the battle of Weinsberg (1140), as *Waiblingen* was by their opponents. See *Ghibelline*.

Hence ducal house of Brunswick and formerly royal house of Britain (*Windsor*).

guerdon. F., OF. *guedredon*, a mixture of L. *donum*, gift, with OHG. *widarlōn*, return payment, cogn. with AS. *witherlēan*, requital. Cf. It. *guiderdone*. See *with-*, *withers*, *widdershins*, *loan*.

guerilla. Sp., dim. of *guerra*, war, OHG. *werra* (see *war*). Often wrongly used for *guerillero*, guerilla fighter.

guernsey. Seaman's vest, orig. knitted at *Guernsey*. Cf. *jersey*.

guess[1]. Verb. ME. *gessen*, to estimate, appraise, very common in Wyc. for *AV.* *think*; cf. Sw. *gissa*, Dan. *gisse*, Du. *gissen*. Prob. of Norse origin. Used in US. with orig. sense (cf. *calculate*, *reckon*).

guess[2] [*dial.*]. In *another-guess*. Corrupt. of *gates*, genitive of *gate*[2], of another way, kind. See *other*.

My method will be found another gates business than this (Pepys, Sep. 6, 1668).

guest. AS. *giest*, mod. *g-* for *y-* being app. due to cogn. ON. *gestr*. Com. Teut.; cf. Du. Ger. *gast*, Goth. *gasts*; cogn. with L. *hostis*, enemy, common idea being that of stranger.

Gueux [*hist.*]. Name assumed by patriots of Netherlands who rose against Spain (16 cent.). F., beggar, of unknown origin. Cf. *Carbonari*.

guffaw. Orig. Sc. Imit.

guggle. See *goglet*, *gurgle*.

guicowar. See *gaikwar*.

guide. F. *guider*, Prov. *guidar* or It. *guidare* (replacing OF. *guier*, whence ME. *gyen*, to guide), Goth. *witan*, cogn. with Ger. *weisen*, to show, and with E. *wit*.

guidon. Pennon. F., It. *guidone*, from *guidare*, to guide. Replaced OF. *guion* (v.s.).

guild, gild. AS. *gield*, payment, *gegield*, association; cf. *gield-heall*, guild-hall. Orig. idea is contribution to semi-rel., later, to trade or craft, association. Init. *g-* may be due to cogn. ON. *gildi*, guild, guild-feast, or to early adoption by AF. & MedL.; but *y-* forms also occur. Cf. Du. Ger. *geld*, money, Goth. *gild*, tribute, Du. *gild*, guild. See *yield*.

Wel semed ech of hem a fair burgeys
To sitten in a yeldehalle on a deys
(Chauc. A. 369).

guilder. Du. coin. Corrupt. of Du. *gulden* (q.v.).

guile. OF.; cf. AS. *wīl*, trick. See *wile*.

guillemot. Bird. F., dim. of *Guillaume*; cf. *robin*, etc. In Hakl. *wilmot* is often used in same sense. But it may be partly altered from Welsh *gwylog* (see *gull*), which is app. the origin of the word below, similarly associated with *William*.

Sea-fowles which we call willockes (Purch.).

guilloche [*arch.*]. From F. *guillochis*, "a kind of flourishing in masonrie, or carpentrie" (Cotg.), perh. from surname *Guilloche*, derivative of *Guillaume*; cf. *mansard*, *guillotine*, and F. *guillemets*, inverted commas, from printer named *Guillemet*.

guillotine. F., from *Guillotin*, name of physician (†1814) who, from humanitarian motives, suggested its use (1789) instead of the old clumsy method of beheading with a sword. The name is a double dim. of *Guillaume*.

guilt. AS. *gylt*. *NED.* rejects connection with AS. *gieldan*, to pay for, requite (see *guild*, *yield*), although *ys gyltig* renders L. *debet* in AS. version of *Matt.* xxiii. 18, and Ger. *schuld* means both debt and guilt.

guimp. See *gimp*.

guinea. First coined (1663) from *Guinea* gold and for the purposes of the *Guinea* trade. Cf. *guinea-fowl*, imported from *Guinea* in 16 cent., formerly used also of the turkey. The *guinea-pig* comes from Brazil, and quot. below gives an earlier, and more natural, name for the animal. It was, I imagine, so called because brought home by the "Guineamen," slave-ships, at the end of their triangular voyage (England to Guinea with trade-goods, Guinea to WInd. and SAmer. with slaves, the "middle passage," WInd. to England with New World produce). Its F. name *cochon d'Inde* is equally vague. Cf. *gallipot* and hist. of *turkey*. So also maize is often called *Guinea wheat* or *Turkey wheat* in Hakl. and Purch. In sense of company director or jobbing clergyman *guinea-pig* is a 19 cent. witticism.

Item for a cage for the Gwynney coney sent to Belvoyre, iijs. (*Rutland MSS.* 1609).

guipure. F., from *guiper*, of Teut. origin and cogn. with *whip*; cf. Ger. *weifen*, "to wind thread into a skain" (Ludw.).

Half an ounce of whypped lace xd.
(*Wollaton Papers*, 1551).

guipure: a grosse black thread (covered or whipt about with silke) wherof corded hat-bands be made (Cotg.).

guise. F., OHG. *wīsa* (*weise*), manner, whence also It. *guisa*. See *wise*¹. Sense of style, costume, survives in *disguise*, *in the guise of*, etc., and dial. *guiser*, mummer, whence *geezer*.

In their ragged and beggarly guise
(Bunyan, *Mansoul*).

guitar. F. *guitare*, Sp. *guitarra*, G. κιθάρα; cf. *cither*, *citole*, *gittern*, *kit*², *zither*.

gulch [*US.*]. ? From obs. *gulch*, to devour, swallow (of imit. origin) on analogy of *gorge*; or perh. corrupt. of latter.

gulden. Coin. Orig. applied to various gold coins in Holland and Germany. MHG. *guldin* and Du. *gulden*, golden.

gules [*her.*]. Red. F. *gueules*, pl. of *gueule*, maw, throat, L. *gula*, ? from open throat of her. beast. But some derive it from Pers. *gul*, rose.

gulf. F. *golfe*, of the sea, *gouffre*, abyss in gen., Late G. κόλφος, for κόλπος, bosom, used as L. *sinus*, bosom, in same sense; cf. Sp. It. *golfo*, whence F. *golfe*; also Ger. *busen*, gulf. The *Gulf Stream* is named from the *Gulf of Mexico*.

gull¹. Bird. Celt.; cf. Welsh *gwylan*, Corn. *guilan*, Bret. *goelann*, whence F. *goéland*, gull.

gull². Dupe, etc. ? Obs. *gull*, immature fish, also kind of gudgeon, cogn. with Du. *gul*, small cod; cf. *gudgeon* (q.v.) and verb to *cod*. ? Or from *gull*¹, from the bird's ready swallowing of anything thrown to it.

gullet. F. *goulet*, dim. of *gueule*, throat, L. *gula*.

gully. F. *goulet*, in sense of passage, "gorge" (v.s.).

gulp. Imit.; cf. Du. *gulpen*, to gulp, Dan. *gylpe*, to belch, vomit.

gum¹. Of the teeth. AS. *gōma*; cf. Ger. *gaumen*, gum, palate, ON. *gōmr*, palate.

gum². Sticky substance. F. *gomme*, VL. *gumma*, for *gummi*, G. κόμμι, prob. of Egypt. origin. In US. for india-rubber and chewing-gum, gum for sticking being called *mucilage*. For the antiquity of chewing-gum see *masticate*. *Up a gum-tree* refers to the 'possum in difficulties. *Gum arabic* (ME.) is exuded by a kind of acacia.

Whose subdu'd eyes...
Drop tears as fast as the Arabian trees
Their medicinable gum (*Oth.* v. 2).

gumption. Orig. Sc. (c. 1700), of unknown origin.

gun. First recorded 1339, "instrumenta de latone, vocitata *gonnes*." Perh. from female

name *Gunhild*, recorded as applied to a mangonel, "una magna balista de cornu quae vocatur *Domina Gunilda*" (1330–1). *Gunhild*, an ON. name of which both elements mean war (cf. *gonfalon*), was a common name, with pet-form *Gunna*, in ME., and there are many hist. guns which have names of the same type, e.g. the famous 15 cent. *Mons Meg* of Edinburgh. Cf. *Brown Bess*, *Long Tom*, Ger. *die faule Grete* (Brandenburg, 1414) and contemp. Ger. *Bertha* (Krupp), from the proprietress of the gun factory at Essen. A 6-inch howitzer now (Oct. 1918) collecting war-loan subscriptions in Bethnal Green is called *Hungry Liz*. Connection with ON. *gunnr*, war, was even suggested by Lye (1743). Another, and less fanciful, suggestion is that *gun* is for OF. *engon*, var. of *engan*, device (cf. *gin*¹ for *engin*), a form recorded in the region (Mons) whence the first gun constructors came to England; cf. *Mons Meg* (v.s.), prob. made at Mons. Perh. both sources have contributed, the latter having helped to fix the already existing nickname. *Engan* is from OF. *enganner*, to trick, of unknown origin. It has a var. *engaigne*, missile, engine, whence early Sc. *ganyie*, missile, regularly used in association with *gun*. To *stick to one's guns*, *son of a gun*, are both naut. The *gunroom* was formerly used by the gunner and his mates. *Gunpowder tea* is so named from its granular appearance. *Gun-runner*, late 19 cent., was coined on *blockade-runner*.

gunny. Coarse sacking. Hind. *gōnī*, Sanskrit *goṇa*, sack. Cf. Du. *gonje*, from Hind.

gunter. Chain, scale, etc. From *Edmund Gunter*, mathematician (†1626).

gunwale, **gunnel**. From *gun* and *wale* (q.v.). Cf. *channel*². Now usu. of boats, but orig. of bulwarks of ship. Cf. synon. Du. *bosbank*, of which first element is *bus*, gun (see *blunderbuss*).

gunyah. Austral. hut. Native word.

gurgitation. From Late L. *gurgitare*, to engulf, from *gurges*, *gurgit-*, abyss.

gurgle. Cf. *gargle*, Ger. *gurgeln*, It. *gorgogliare*, L. *gurgulio*, gullet. All of imit. origin. Cf. colloq. *guggle* (Johns.).

gurjun. EInd. tree. Native name.

Gurkha. See *Goorkha*.

gurnard, **gurnet**. Fish. OF. *gornard*, from *grogner*, to grunt (v.i.), from L. *grunnire*; because the fish makes a grunting sound when caught. So also in other langs., e.g.

Du. *knorhaan*, from *knorren*, to grumble, Ger. *knurrfisch*, from *knurren*, to growl. See *cur*.

cuculus: a gornart, a curre (A. Junius).

guru. See *gooroo*.

gush. Ult. cogn. with Du. *gutsen*, Ger. *giessen*, ON. *giōsa*, to pour. See *ingot*. With mod. fig. sense cf. *effusive* and F. *épanchement*, lit. pouring forth.

gusset. F. *gousset*, orig. flexible armour joining plates under armpit, perh. from *gousse*, shell of pod.

gust¹. Of wind. ON. *gustr*, cogn. with *giōsa*, to gush. First in Shaks.

gust². See *gusto*.

gusto. It., L. *gustus*, taste; cf. F. *goût*, OF. *goust*, and *disgust*.

He [Evelyn] read me, though with too much gusto, some little poems of his own (Pepys, Nov. 5, 1665).

gut. AS. *guttas* (pl.), from *gēotan*, to pour (see *ingot*). Fishing-*gut* is made from intestines of silkworms; cf. *catgut*. With *gut*, channel, passage, cf. *bayou* (q.v.). With *guts*, stamina, courage, cf. *pluck* (q.v.).

gutta percha. Malay *getah*, gum, *percha*, tree producing it. Assimilated to L. *gutta*, drop.

gutta serena. Amaurosis. L., clear drop.

So thick a drop serene hath quencht their orb
                           (*Par. L.* iii. 25).

gutter. F. *gouttière*, roof gutter, from *goutte*, drop, L. *gutta*. With *guttersnipe* cf. F. *saute-ruisseau*, jump-gutter. The verb to *gutter*, of a candle, refers to its becoming "channelled" on one side.

guttle. To eat greedily. After *gut* and *guzzle*.

guttural. From L. *guttur*, throat.

gutty [*golf*]. For *gutta percha*.

guy¹. In *guy-rope* (naut.). Usu. referred to ME. *gyen*, to guide (q.v.). But cf. Norw. Dan. *gie*, *give*, Sw. *giga*, LG. *giken*, Du. *gijken*, all naut. verbs from a LG. name for the sailyard (Du. *gei*). Cf. Ger. *geie*, guy-rope, *aufgeien*, to guy up (from LG.).

guy². *Guy Fawkes* was executed 1605. The name is found in most Europ. langs., F. *Gui*, It. *Guido*, Ger. *Veit*, etc. See *Vitus*. Verb to *guy* is theat., and, if orig. US., may be rather from Du. *de guig aansteken*, to make fun, where *guig* is prob. connected with *giechelen*, to giggle.

guzzle. From 16 cent., also in sense of gutter, drain. Perh. connected with F.

gosier, throat, or it may be imit. (cf. *gulp*, *gurgle*).

gwyniad. Fish, esp. in Lake Bala. Welsh, from *gwyn*, white.

gybe [*naut.*]. To alter course of vessel so that boom of sail *gybes*, i.e. swings from side to side. Du. *gijpen*, cogn. with *jib²*.

gyle. Beer brewed at one brewing. Du. *gijl*, cogn. with *gijlen*, to ferment.

gymkhana [*Anglo-Ind.*]. Altered, after *gymnastic*, etc., from Urdu *gend-khāna*, racquet court, lit. ball house.

gymnasium. L., G. γυμνάσιον, from γυμνός, naked. Introduced into Ger. as name for high-school by 15 cent. humanists. Cf. *gymnosophist*, Hindu ascetic philosopher (see *sophist*); *gymnotus*, electric eel, coined (1748) by Linnaeus from G. νῶτον, back, because of absence of dorsal fins.

gynaeceum. L., G. γυναικεῖον, apartment for women, from γυνή, γυναικ-, woman. Cf. *gynaecology*, study of women's diseases; *gynocracy*, rule by women. See *queen*.

-gynous. G. -γυνος, from γυνή (v.s.).

gyp. College servant (Camb.). ? Cf. obs. *gippo*, varlet, from obs. *gippo*, short jacket, from F. *jupe* (see *jibbah*). For transference of sense cf. *buttons*.

gypsum. L., from G. γύψος, chalk, gypsum, prob. of Oriental origin.

gypsy. See *gipsy*.

gyrate. From L. *gyrare*, from *gyrus*, circuit, G. γῦρος, ring. Cf. *gyroscope*, invented and named (1852) by Foucault (†1868).

gyrfalcon. See *gerfalcon*.

gyron, giron [*her.*]. Shape of right-angled triangle. F. *giron*, earlier *geron*, from OHG. *gēro*, spear-head. See *gore²*, *garfish*.

gyve. AF. *give*, fetter, also bundle, *gyves de draps* (*Lib. Albus*). Perh. from *withe* (q.v.), used for halter, fetter in ME., with F. *g-* as usual for Teut. *w-*, and corrupt. of *-th-* unpronounceable by Normans. Confusion of *-th-* with *-f-*, *-v-*, is not uncommon (v.i.), e.g. Pepys writes *Queenhive* for *Queenhythe* (see also *savory*). Another possible etymon is OHG. *bewifan*, to swathe, fetter (see *guipure*). Earliest *NED.* record (Layamon) and quot. below show that Eugene Aram wore gyves in the wrong place.

Fiergés [ironed] de deus fort peire gives et manicles
                   (*French Chron. of London*, 1342).

Neither mother, brother, kiffe, nor kinne
                          (*Sylv. Babylon*).

h-. Now unphonetically in restored spelling of many words of F. origin (cf. *able*, *habilitate*). As criterion of educated speech from 19 cent. only.

The *h* and other points of etiquette
(Thackeray, 1848).

ha. Natural exclamation, found in L. & G. and most Europ. langs.

Habeas Corpus. From words of writ, "have thou the body (of so-and-so produced in court)." Hence *Habeas Corpus Act* (1679).

haberdasher. Dealer in *haberdash*, small-wares. First element is perh. ult. that of *avoirdupois* (q.v.); the second may be F. & Prov. *ais*, board, on which the dealer in small wares would display his goods. This is a conjecture only, and, in the absence of any such OF. compd., a very dubious one. Franck-Van Wijk (s.v. *haberdoedas*) inclines to the old wheeze of some such Ger. phrase as *habt ihr das?* have you that? This is not impossible, but supposes the word to have reached us at a very early date from the North Sea or Baltic.

mercerot: a pedler, a paltrie haberdasher (Cotg.).

habergeon [*hist.*]. Coat of mail (2 *Chron.* xxvi. 14). F. *haubergeon*, dim. of *hauberk* (q.v.).

habiliment. F. *habillement*, from *habiller*, to dress, orig. to make ready. Mod. sense has developed under influence of *habit*, but it is quite possible that OF. *abillier* is a formation of the same type as synon. *accoutrer*, and quite unconnected with L. *habēre*.

habilitate. From Med. L. *habilitare*, to make fit, from *habilis*. See *able*.

habit. F., L. *habitus*, from *habēre*. For sense-development cf. (*be*)*haviour* and *costume*. Earliest E. meaning (13 cent.) is fashion of dress. In sense of custom it is taken (16 cent.) directly from L. *Habit of body* is also a latinism. *Habitation* is esp. used in *fit for human habitation*. Its Primrose League sense (1885) is an imitation of the Masonic "lodge."

habitant. Native of Canada of F. descent. F., inhabitant, the usual word for colonial planter in 18 cent., e.g. in *Paul et Virginie*.

habitat. Third pers. sing. pres. of L. *habitare*, to inhabit. Init. word of description in old Faunas and Floras written in L. Cf. *floruit*.

habitué. F., p.p. of *habituer*, to accustom.

hachish. See *hashish*.

hachure. Shading, esp. of maps. F., from *hacher*, to chop, from *hache*, axe, because orig. done on wood-block. Cf. *hatch*[3].

hacienda. Estate, plantation. Sp., from L. *facienda*, things to be done, from *facere*. Cf. spec. use of *factory* (q.v.).

hack[1]. To cut. AS. *haccian*, in compds. only. WGer.; cf. Du. *hakken*, Ger. *hacken* (also noun *hacke*, hoe).

hack[2]. Board on which falcon's meat is put. Var. of *hatch*[1] (q.v.). Hence archaic *at hack and manger*, in clover.

hack[3]. Short for *hackney* (q.v.).

hackbut, hagbut [*hist.*]. Gun. OF. *haquebute*, corrupted from obs. Du. *hakebus*, *haakbus*, hook gun. Cf. *arquebus*, *blunderbuss*. Early vars. are numerous and fantastic, sometimes compromising with *arquebus*, e.g. *arquebut*, *hakkebus*, etc.

hackery [*Anglo-Ind.*]. Bullock-cart. Perh. early (17 cent.) perversion of Hind. *chhakra*, two-wheeled cart; cf. Sanskrit *ṣakaṭa*, waggon.

hackle. Flax-comb (see *heckle*). Also applied, app. from some resemblance, to neck-feathers of cock; hence *cock of a different hackle*, the *red hackle* worn by the Black Watch, and the angler's *hackle-fly*.

hackmatack. Amer. larch. Amer. Ind. name.

hackney. Cf. F. *haquenée*, Sp. *hacanea*, OSp. Port. *facanea*, It. *acchinea*. Prob. E., from *Hackney* (Middlesex), AS. *Hacan īeg*, isle of Haca. Earliest recorded form is AL. *hakeneius* (12 cent.). Skeat suggests that nags were raised on the pasture-land there and taken to Smithfield horse-market via Mare St. It is quite natural for a horse name to originate in E. (cf. *hobby*[1]). In early use for hired horse (cf. *hackney-carriage*), hence fig. senses of *hackney* and shortened *hack*[3].

Having no choice, as he [Fielding] said himself, but to be a hackney writer or a hackney coachman (Lady M. Montague, 1755).

haddock. Prob. ident. with OF. *hadot* (13 cent.) for which Francisque Michel gives also *hadoc*. The *NED.* is mistaken in supposing this to be a rare word. Its prob. meaning was not species of fish, but fish salted in a special way (see quot. from Cotg., and cf. hist. of *bloater*). App. (*h*)*adot* is evolved from pl. (*h*)*adoux*, (*h*)*adoz*, which may be pl. of OF. *adoub*, from *adouber*, to prepare (see *adobe*); cf. It. *adobbo*, "souse or pickle to keep meat or fish in" (Torr.). In OF. *adot* occurs in association with *salloison* (salting) and *parerie* (preparation). With regard to initial *h-* it may be noted that *ânon*, small cod (cf. L. *asellus*), is also usu. spelt with *h-* in OF. Cf. also archaic *haberdine*, *stockfish*, *torsk*, all app. used of prepared fish rather than of species. This is a series of conjectures. For final cf. *havoc*.

hadot, hadou: a salt haddocke (Cotg.).

Hades. G. ᾅδης, in Homer name of god of lower world, later transferred to his kingdom. Adopted by LXX. to render Heb. *sheōl*, abode of departed spirits, and introduced into E. (c. 1600) in connection with controversy on fifth article of Apostles' Creed.

hadji. Arab. *hājī*, pilgrim (to Mecca).

haematite, hematite [*min.*]. L., G. αἱματίτης (sc. λίθος), from αἷμα, blood.

haemorrhage, hemorrhage. Earlier *-hagy*, F. *hémorragie*, L., G. αἱμορραγία, from ῥηγνύναι, to break, burst (v.s.).

haemorrhoid. L., G. αἱμορροΐς, αἱμορροΐδ-, from ῥεῖν, to flow (v.s.). Has replaced *emerod* (14 cent.) from OF.

haft. AS. *hæft*, handle, cogn. with *have*; cf. Ger. *heft* and *handhabe* in same sense.

hag¹. Witch. Shortened from AS. *hægtesse*, witch, fury, from *haga*, hedge, "haw"; cf. synon. OHG. *hagazussa* (*hexe*), also ON. *tūnritha*, OHG. *zûnrita*, lit. hedge rider (see *town*). The suffix is cogn. with Norw. dial. *tysja*, crone. With *hagridden*, oppressed by nightmare, cf. *priestridden*. These words have affected *bedridden* (q.v.).

hag² [*Sc. & north.*]. As in *moss-hag*. ON. *högg*, ravine, orig. blow, cut (see *haggle*).

haggard. F. *hagard*, orig. used (v.i.) of hawk incapable of being tamed. App. from OHG. *hag*, hedge, "haw," whence F. *haie*. As adj. first applied to the eyes, later sense of gaunt, scraggy, being due to association with *hag¹*.

Esprevier hagard est celluy qui est de mue de hayes (*Ménagier de Paris*, 14 cent.).

And, like the haggard, check at every feather
That comes before his eye (*Twelfth Night*, iii. 1).

haggis. Now esp. Sc., but a common word in ME. App. by some strange metaphor from F. *agasse*, *agace*, magpie, OHG. *agalstra*, which usu. has initial *h-* in LG. dials. Cf. the two senses of *pie*, and also obs. *chewet*, daw, meat-pie, F. *chouette*, daw, etc. It has been associated with *hack¹*, and F. *hacher*, to chop (v.i.).

wurstgehäcke: haggass, hotch-potch, or hatched meat (Ludw.).

haggle. Orig. to mangle. Frequent. of dial. *hag*, to chop, hack, ON. *höggva*, cogn. with *hew*, *hack¹*. Fig. sense perh. partly due to association with *chop²* (q.v.).

hagiography, hagiology. From G. ἅγιος, holy. Cf. *hagioscope*, a "squint" in church arch.

ha-ha, haw-haw. Sunk fence. F. *haha*. The suggestion that this is from the exclamation of surprise caused by the obstacle is not very convincing; but it may be from the OF. hunting-cry *hahai*, to rally the dogs. A playful elaboration of *haie*, hedge, seems more likely than either.

hai(c)k. Eastern wrap. Arab. *hayk*, from *hāk*, to weave.

haiduk. See *heyduck*.

hail¹. Frozen rain. AS. *hagol*. Com. Teut.; cf. Du. Ger. *hagel*, ON. *hagl*; cogn. with G. κάχληξ, small stone.

hail². To call. Now chiefly naut., as in to *hail from*. Orig. from noun *hail*, health, safety, used in greeting, as in *hail, fellow, well met*, ON. *heill*, cogn. with AS. *hǣlu*, or from corresponding adj. (see *hale¹*, *wassail*). Cf. Ger. *heil*, used for L. *ave*, *salve*. For cognates see *whole*.

Hail [*Vulg.* ave], thou that art highly favoured (*Luke*, i. 28).

to *hail a ship*: is to call to her, to know whence she is, or whither bound (*Sea-Dict.* 1708).

hair. AS. *hǣr*. Com. Teut.; cf. Du. Ger. *haar*, ON. *hār*. Normal *hear*, *heer*, has been altered under influence of F. *haire*, hairshirt, OHG. *harra* (**harja*), which is common in ME. Mod. collect. has replaced older pl. (*Gen.* xliv. 29). *Hairbreadth escape* is after Shaks. (*Oth.* i. 3). *Not to turn a hair* was used orig. of horses. To *keep one's hair on* is mod., app. playful advice not to *tear one's hair*. *Hair of the dog that bit you*, as homoeopathic remedy, is in Pliny (*Nat. Hist.* xxix. 5). To *split hairs* is 18 cent. for earlier to *cut* (*divide*) *the hair*.

Machiavel cut the hair, when he advised, not absolutely to disavow conscience, but etc. (Sancroft, 1652).

hake¹. Fish. Prob. cogn. with ON. *haki*, hook, from shape of jaw; cf. *pike*, Norw. *hakefisk*, trout, and Ger. *hecht*, pike, cogn. with AS. *hacod*, pike.

hake². Frame-work in various senses. Also *heck*. Var. of *hatch¹* (q.v.).

hakeem, hakim. Eastern physician. Arab. *hakīm*, wise, learned, from *hakama*, to exercise authority.

halberd, halbert [*hist.*]. F. *hallebarde*, MHG. *helmbarde*. Second element is OHG. *barta*, broad-axe, first is either *helm*, shaft, handle, also in E. (v.i.), or *helm*, helmet. A similar doubt exists as to first element of synon. *pole-axe* (q.v.), but the shaft origin seems more natural. *Barta* is cogn. with *beard*; cf. ON. *skeggja*, halberd, from *skegg*, beard, also hist. of *barb*[1].

Like mattokes were here wepens wroght,
With long helmes of yren stoute (*NED.* c. 1430).

halcyon. L., kingfisher, altered from G. ἀλκυών, as though from ἅλς, sea, κύων, conceiving, from the belief that the bird hatched its young in a floating nest during the *halcyon days*. Really cogn. with L. *alcedo*, kingfisher, and prob. with *auk*. Cf. L. *alcedonia*, calm weather.

hale[1]. Adj. Northern form of AS. *hāl*, whole (q.v.). It has coalesced with ME. *hail*, cogn. ON. *heill* (see *hail*[2]).

hale[2]. Verb. F. *haler*, to pull, haul, OHG. *halōn* (*holen*); cf. synon. Du. *halen*; perh. cogn. with G. καλεῖν, to call. *Haul* is a later borrowing of the same F. verb, *hale* surviving in such phrases as *haled to execution*.

half. AS. *healf*. Com. Teut.; cf. Du. *half*, Ger. *halb*, ON. *halfr*, Goth. *halbs*. Oldest sense of noun is side, as in *behalf*, Ger. *innerhalb*, inside, *meinethalben*, on my account, etc. *Half-seas-over*, "almost drunk" (*Dict. Cant. Crew*), meant orig. (16 cent.) halfway across the sea. *Not half*, orig. a long way lacking (cf. *too clever by half*), has reversed its meaning in mod. slang, a good example of meiosis. The *half-butt* and *long-butt* (billiards) have a thick butt end to make up for their length.

Seie that these two my sonys sitten, oon at thi righthalf, and oon at thi lefthalf, in thi kyngdam
(Wyc. *Matt.* xx. 21).

A quart...for a pene and a pynte for a hapeney
(*Nott. Bor. Records*, 1579).

The half hearted and half witted people, which made much the major part of both Houses
(Clarendon).

halibut. From ME. *haly*, holy, and *butt*[1], perh. because eaten on holy days; cf. F. *héllebut*, Du. *heilbot*, Sw. *helgeflundra* (flounder), etc. Capt. John Smith writes it *holybut*.

halidom [*archaic*]. AS. *hāligdōm*, holiness, relic, sanctuary. See *-dom*. Cf. Du. *heiligdom*, Ger. *heiligtum*. In ME. often *-dam*, *-dame*, by association with Our Lady.

hall. AS. *heall*, spacious room or building, cogn. with *helan*, to cover, hide, and ult. with L. *celare*. Com. Teut.; cf. Du. *hal*, Ger. *halle*, ON. *höll*. F. *halle*, covered market, is from Ger. Sense of entry, vestibule, comes from the time when the entrance hall was the chief living-room. *Liberty Hall* is an 18 cent. imit. of earlier *Cutpurse Hall*, *Ruffians Hall*. *Hall-marked* means stamped at *Goldsmiths' Hall*, London.

hallelujah. See *alleluia*.

halliard. See *halyard*.

hallo. Also *hello*, *hillo*, *hollo*, *hullo*, *halloo*, *holla*, etc. Cf. F. *holà!* and our *hi there!* also OHG. *hala*, imper. of *halōn* (see *hale*[2]), as summons to ferryman; but the whole group is mainly natural interjection. In hunting (*view halloo*) perh. OF. *ha lou!* for *loup*, wolf.

hallow. AS. *hālgian*, from *hālig*, holy (q.v.), used to render L. *sanctificare*. Noun *hallow*, AS. *hālga*, saint, survives in *Hallowmass*, *Hallowe'en*, *All Hallows*.

hallucinate. From L. *hallucinari*, for *alucinari*, to wander in mind, coined, on *vaticinari*, from G. ἀλύειν, to be distraught, cogn. with G. ἠλεός, mad.

halm. See *haulm*.

halma. Game. G. ἅλμα, leap, from ἅλλεσθαι, to leap, cogn. with L. *salire*.

halo. From L. *halos*, G. ἅλως, threshing-floor, round disk; cf. F. *halo*, It. *alone*, Sp. *halón*, which point to VL. **halo-n-*. First (16 cent.) in astron.

haloid [*chem.*]. From G. ἅλς, salt.

halt[1] [*archaic*]. Lame. AS. *healt*. Com. Teut.; cf. obs. Du. *halt*, MHG. *halz*, ON. *haltr*, Goth. *halts*. Hence to *halt* (L. *claudicare*) *between two opinions* (1 *Kings*, xviii. 21), *halting delivery*, etc., perh. sometimes felt as belonging to *halt*[2].

halt[2] [*mil.*]. Orig. in to *make halt*, F. *faire halte* (earlier *halt*), Ger. *halt machen*, from *halten*, to hold, stop; cf. It. *fare alto*, Sp. *alto hacer*, also from Ger.

halter. AS. *hælfter*, halter for horses. WGer.; cf. Du. Ger. *halfter*. Orig. sense that by which something is held; cf. *helve*, *helm*, and L. *capistrum*, halter, from *capere*.

halyard, halliard. Corrupt. of *halier* (14 cent.), from *hale*[2]. For *-yard* cf. *lanyard*.

ham. AS. *hamm*; cf. Du. *ham*, Ger. dial. *hamme*, ON. *höm*. Orig. sense prob. crooked, bent. AS. meaning, bend at back of knee, appears in *hamstring*, tendon of hock, now usu. as verb.

hamadryad. L., G. Ἀμαδρυάς, wood-nymph, fabled to die with tree, usu. in pl., from ἅμα, together with, δρῦς, tree. In Chauc. In 19 cent. applied to Indian serpent (*opheophagus*) and Abyssinian baboon.

hame [*dial.*]. Of horse-collar. Of obscure origin. Cf. Du. *haam*, Ger. dial. *hamen*, which, with obs. Ger. *hame*, shackle for horses and cattle, are perh. cogn. with L. *hamus*, hook.

Hamitic [*ling.*]. Of descendants of Ham (*Gen.* ix. 22). Applied esp. to group of ancient Afr. langs., including Egypt. Cf. *Japhetic, Semitic.*

hamlet. OF. *hamelet*, dim. of *hamel* (*hameau*), dim. from LG. *ham*, home (q.v.).

hammam, hummaum. Turkish bath. Arab. *hammām*, bath. In Purch. (1625).

hammer. AS. *hamor*. Com. Teut.; cf. Du. *hamer*, Ger. *hammer*, ON. *hamarr*. The ON. meaning, stone, crag, common in place-names, suggests that orig. sense was weapon of stone. *Hammer and tongs* is from the ardent blacksmith. *Hammerbeam* (arch.) is from shape. The origin of *hammercloth*, cover of driver's box, is obscure. It occurs in 15 cent. as name of a material, perh. for *hammered cloth*; ? or cf. Dan. *hammel*, swingle-bar of vehicle, MHG. *hamel*, pole. With *under the* (*auctioneer's*) *hammer* cf. L. *sub hasta.*

hammock. F. *hamac* or Sp. *hamaca*, a Carib word. Du. *hangmat*, Ger. *hängematte*, hang mat, are late corrupts. due to folk-etym.

> *hamáca*: L. *lectus pensilis*. A. a hanging bed: Brasil beds, made to hang up against a tree or wall, like a cabin bed in a ship (Minsheu).

Hampden, village. Protector of popular rights. From Gray's *Elegy.*

hamper[1]. Verb. In ME. also to fetter, bind. App. cogn. with ON. *hemja*, to restrain, *hemell*, shackle; cf. Ger. *hemmen* (MHG. *hamen*). Analogy of *pastern* (q.v.) suggests ult. connection with *ham*; cf. archaic *ham-shackle.*

hamper[2]. Basket. ME. *hanaper*, OF. *hana-pier*, case to hold *hanaps*, goblets, OHG. *hnapf* (*napf*), cogn. with AS. *hnæpp*, cup, bowl. The name was later applied to a receptacle for documents, hence the *hanaper* or *hamper* of Chancery. For F. *hanap*, due to inability to pronounce *hn-*, cf. *harangue.*

hamster. Rodent. Ger., OHG. *hamustra*, corn-weevil, field-mouse. Of obscure origin, prob. non-Aryan (cf. *rat*). The Lithuanian name is *staras.*

hanaper [*archaic*]. See *hamper*[2].

hand. AS. *hand*. Com. Teut.; cf. Du. Ger. *hand*, ON. *hönd*, Goth. *handus*. For some extended meanings, e.g. that of writing, cf. L. *manus* and F. *main*. With *all hands* (naut.) cf. *hand*, workman, sailor, also *green hand, old hand, to be a good hand at*, etc. To *play into the hands of, show one's hand*, are from cards. *Hand over hand*, now varied to *hand over fist*, refers to rapidly pulling on a rope (naut.). To *wash one's hands of* alludes to Pilate. *Handbook*, AS. *handbōc*, was used to render L. *manuale* or Graeco-L. *enchiridion*, but in current sense is from Ger. *handbuch*. *Handcuff* is app. from *hand* and *cuff*[1], as AS. *handcops*, manacle, is not found in ME. Archaic *handfast*, to betroth, alludes to the clasping of hands. With *hand-canter* (*-gallop*), controlled by rider, cf. *four-in-hand* and *out of hand. Handiwork*, AS. *handgeweorc* (see *aware*), has affected *handicraft*, AS. *hand-cræft*; AS. has also *handweorc*, labour. With verb to *handle* cf. Ger. *handeln*, to deal, and F. *manier*, from *main*, hand. A *handmaid* serves her mistress "ready to hand"; cf. AS. *handthegn*, attendant. *Handsome* meant orig. easy to handle; cf. *toothsome*. In *handsome is that handsome does*, "a proverb frequently cited by ugly women" (Grose), the second *handsome* is an adv. *Handspike* is Du. *handspaak*, of which second element, cogn. with *spoke*, is altered on E. *spike*; cf. F. *anspect*, also from Du. For *handkerchief* see *kerchief.*

> I will venture to recommend them, as an old Parliamentary hand, to do the same
> (Gladstone, in H. of C. Jan. 21, 1886).

handicap. From *hand in cap*, a kind of lottery game at which winners were penalized to the profit of the pool; later applied to method of arranging stakes and weights for horse-race.

> Among the pleasures some of us fell to handycapp, a sport that I never knew before
> (Pepys, Sep. 19, 1660).

handicraft, handiwork. See *hand.*

handle. Noun. AS. *handle*, from *hand. Handle to one's name* is first recorded in Marryat. With *give a handle* cf. F. *donner prise.*

handsaw. See *heron.*

handsel, hansel [*archaic*]. New Year's gift, earnest money, etc. ON. *handsal*, hand sale, used of shaking hands in concluding bargain. But early senses suggest also connection with *hanse* (q.v.); cf. archaic

Dan. *hænse*, to pay one's footing n a gild.

œstreine: a New-Yeares gift, or present; also, a handsell (Cotg.).

handsome. See *hand*.

handy. From *hand*, replacing (16 cent.) ME. *hend, hende, hendy*, ready to hand, skilled, AS. *gehende, hendig*, from *hand* (with umlaut). Cf. Ger. *behende*, handy, from *bei*, by, and old dat. of *hand*. Some regard the old adj. (cf. ON. *höndugr*, capable, Goth. *handugs*, wise) as connected rather with a Teut. verb, to grasp (see *hint*). *Handy-man*, in sense of sailor, is from Kipling.

hang. Mixture of three verbs, viz. AS. *hōn* (cf. OHG. Goth. *hāhan*), strong trans., AS. *hangian*, weak intrans., ON. *hengja*, causal of *hanga*. Cf. Ger. *hangen*, intrans., *hängen*, trans., *henken*, trans. (of execution only). *Hanged* is now usu. limited to death by the rope, or fig., e.g. *I'll be hanged*. To *hang out* refers to old custom of hanging out a sign. With to *hang up*, put out of immediate use, cf. *on the shelf*. To *hang fire* was orig. used of guns. To *hang in the wind* is naut. metaphor. *Hanger*, short sword to hang at belt, may be from cogn. Du. *hangher*, "pugio de zona pendens" (Kil.); in *pothooks and hangers* it is from the kitchen device to which the pots were suspended by hooks. Orig. the *pothook* was ɩ or ꞁ and the *hanger* was ꝝ. *Hangdog*, one fit only to hang dogs, is a formation of the *cutthroat, pickpocket* type. To *get the hang of* is US. *Hanger-on* is 16 cent.

The boat was tossed over the rocks and Long with two others escaped (the rest drowned); one of the three being demanded what he thought in the present peril, answered, hee said nothing, but "Gallowes claime thy right," which within halfe a yeere fell out accordingly (Capt. John Smith).

His [a quack's] flag hangs out in town here, i' the Cross Inn,
With admirable cures of all conditions
(Middleton, *Widow*, iv. 1).

hangar [*neol.*]. F., shed. ? Cf. MedL. *angarium*, shoeing forge, ? or of Teut. origin and cogn. with *hang* (cf. *penthouse*).

angar: an open shed, or hovell, wherein husbandmen set their ploughes, &c. out of the sun, and weather (Cotg.).

hanger. Wood on hill-side. AS. *hangra*, from *hang*.

hank. ON. *hönk*, hank, skein. If dial. *hank*, handle of a jug, is the same word (which is likely, cf. *hasp*), it belongs ult. to *hang*;

cf. Ger. *henkel, hengel*, jug-handle, cogn. with *henken, hängen*, to hang. Cf. also dial. *hank*, propensity, exactly answering to Ger. *hang* (v.i.).

hanker. "Scarcely used but in familiar language" (Johns.). From c. 1600. Cf. dial. *hank* and Du. *hunkeren*, in same sense. Prob. contains idea of *hang* and *hunger*. See *hank*.

a hank or fondness: animi inclinatio sive propensio
(Litt.).

hanky-panky. ? Arbitrary formation, after *hocus-pocus*; cf. *jiggery-pokery* in same sense. Perh. altered from *hokey-pokey* by association with *sleight of hand*. Richard Cocks (in Purch.) uses *legerdy maine* exactly in current sense of *hanky-panky*.

Hansard. Offic. reports of Parliament, published by Messrs *Hansard*, from 1774.

Hanse, Hanseatic [*hist.*]. OHG. *hansa*, used by Tatian for L. *cohors* (*Matt.* xxvii. 27), cogn. with AS. *hōs*, troop, and adopted in MHG. as name of a guild or confederation of traders powerful in various Ger. ports (Hamburg, Bremen, Lübeck), and established in London as early as 12 cent. See *steelyard*.

hansel. See *handsel*.

hansom. From name of patentee (1834).

hap. ON. *happ*, luck, chance, cogn. with AS. *gehæp*, convenient. Hence verb *hap, happen*, and adj. *happy*, orig. lucky, a sense which survives in *happy-go-lucky* and *happily*. For *happy dispatch* see *hara-kiri*. It is possible that in *haphazard* the first element was orig. obs. *hap*, to seize, snatch, F. *happer*, Du. *happen*. This would be a normal formation of the *cutthroat, catchpenny* type, while the collocation of the two nouns *hap* and *hazard* seems unnatural. Synon. Ger. *geratewohl* is a similar formation.

happer: to hap, or catch; to snatch, or graspe at
(Cotg.).

I doubt few will be pleased with his [Prince Rupert's] going [in command of the fleet], being accounted an unhappy man (Pepys, Aug. 31, 1664).

That action is best, which accomplishes the greatest happiness of the greatest numbers
(Francis Hutcheson, 1725).

haplography. Writing only once what should be written twice. From G. ἁπλοῦς, simple. Cf. *dittography*.

hara-kiri, hari-kari. Jap., belly cut. Englished as *happy dispatch*, perh. by some misunderstanding.

harangue. F., earlier *harengue*, OHG. *hring* (*ring*), circle of audience; cf. It. *aringa*. See *rank*[2], *ranch*. For init. *ha-* see *hamper*[2].

arringa: an arange; an oration, a declamation
(Flor.).

arringo: a pulpit; a riding or careering place, a liste for horses, or feates of armes (*ib.*).

haras. Stud-farm. Adopted in ME., but now treated as foreign word. F., prob. connected with Arab. *faras*, horse, whence OF. *haraz*, stallion, via some unrecorded Sp. form.

harass. F. *harasser*, ? from OF. *harer*, to set a dog on.

harbinger. ME. & OF. *herbergeour*, from *herbergier* (*héberger*), to provide "harbourage," lodgings, OF. *herberge*, OHG. *heriberga*, army-shelter. See *harbour*, *belfry*, *scabbard*. Orig. host, entertainer; later, official preceding monarch, etc., to arrange for his quarters, whence fig. sense of forerunner. For *-n-* cf. *passenger*, *messenger*, etc. Office of *knight harbinger* to royal household was abolished in 1846.

Gayus, my herborgere [*var.* oost, *Vulg.* hospes], greetith you wel (Wyc. *Rom.* xvi. 23).

harbour. ME. *herberwe*, AS. **hereborg*, army shelter, or cogn. ON. *herbergi*. Cf. *harbinger*, *harry*, *borough*, *scabbard*. Orig. lodging, shelter, in gen., but naut. sense appears early (Chauc. A. 403). Hence verb to *harbour*, now usu. in bad sense, e.g. to *harbour a constable* (*evil designs*, etc.).

I was herbroulesse, and ye lodged me
(Tynd. *Matt.* xxv. 35).

hard. AS. *heard*. Com. Teut.; cf. Du. *hard*, Ger. *hart*, ON. *harthr*, Goth. *hardus*; cogn. with G. κρατύς, strong. Ground sense, unyielding, opposed to *soft*. Subjective use of *hard*, difficult, now only in *hard of hearing*. ME. sense of firm ground survives in *Portsmouth Hard*. Some adv. uses are parallel with those of *fast*, e.g. to *run* (*follow*) *hard*; cf. *hard and fast* (naut.). For *hardbitten* see *bite*. *Hard up* was orig. naut. (steering). With *hard cash*, opposed to paper money, cf. F. *pièces sonnantes*. *Hardshell*, uncompromising, is US., e.g. *hardshell Baptist*. *Hard labour* occurs in an act of 1853.

hardy. F. *hardi*, p.p. of OF. *hardir*, OHG. *hartjan* (*härten*), to make hard. Orig. bold, reckless, as in *foolhardy*, *hardihood*.

Nether eny man was hardy fro that day, for to axe hym more (Wyc. *Matt.* xxii. 46).

hare. AS. *hara*. Com. Teut.; cf. Du. *haas*, Ger. *hase*, ON. *here*; ? cogn. with AS. *hasu*, grey, and ult. with L. *canus*, hoary (for **casnos*). Heywood (1562) has to *holde with the hare and run with the hounde*. *Harebrained* and the *March Hare* go together (see *hatter*). The *harebell* was in ME. the wild hyacinth or blue-bell. Mod. sense is Sc. and is partly due to *hair*, in allusion to very slender stem. *First catch your hare* is *not* from Mrs Glasse's *Cookery Book*. With *hare-lip* cf. Du. *hazenlip*, L. *labium leporinum*.

harem. Arab. *haram*, from *harama*, to prohibit.

haricot. F., OF. *hericoq*, a stew, ? from *harigoter*, *haligoter*, to cut up. Hence applied to the bean, earlier *fève de haricot*. A recent suggestion that *haricot* is Mex. *ayacotli* is negatived by the fact that the word is much older than the discovery of Amer.

hotchepotte of many meates: haricot (Palsg.).

hari-kari. See *hara-kiri*.

hark. ME. *herkien*, intens. of *hear*; cogn. with Ger. *horchen*; cf. *hearken*, altered, on *hear*, from earlier *harken*, AS. *heorcnian*. *Hark* is almost obs. exc. in imper. As hunting term, e.g. *hark away*, to *hark back* (*forward*), it may be a separate word. Earliest hunting sense, to incite, urge on (*Temp.* iv. 1), suggests connection with OF. *harer*, "to hound a dog at, or set a dog on, a beast" (Cotg.), or F. *haro*, hue and cry (cf. *tally-ho*, *yoicks*).

Harleian. Of books and MSS. collected by *Harley*, Earl of Oxford (†1724) and his son, the MSS. being acquired (1753) by the British Museum.

harlequin. OF. *hierlequin*, *hellequin*, *hennequin*, etc., name of a demon or "wild huntsman," accompanied by a "meiny" like that of Herne the Hunter, who is perh. the same person. OF. *la maisnie Hierlekin* is represented by ME. *Hurlewayne's meyne* (Langland); cf. also the It. demon *Alichino* (Dante). It is a Flem. dim. of some personal name, perh. of *Han*, John, though this cannot be settled without knowledge of orig. form. For the use of personal names for demons cf. *hobgoblin*, *will o' the wisp*, etc. (F. *arlequin* is used for will o' the wisp in Champagne), and for similar application to buffoons cf. *merry andrew*, *jack-pudding*, F. *pierrot*, Ger. *hanswurst*, etc. *Hennequin*, corresponding to E. *Hankin*, is a common F.

surname. The ModE. form is via F. *arlequin*, earlier also *harlequin*, It. *arlecchino*, one of the stock characters of It. comedy (cf. *pantaloon, columbine, scaramouch*).

harlot. Orig. rogue, fellow; mod. sense from 15 cent. Used as euph. for earlier *whore* (Wyc.) in 16 cent. Bible transls. For restriction of sex cf. *hoyden, witch*. OF. *harlot, herlot*, fellow, vagabond; cf. It. *arlotto*, "the name of a merie priest, a lack-latine or hedge-priest" (Flor.). If, as seems possible, the earliest sense was camp-follower, the first element is OHG. *hari*, army (see *harbour, harness*), and the second may be connected with Ger. *lotter*, as in *lotterbube*, synon. with *harlot* in its earliest sense, cogn. with AS. *loddere*, beggar, wastrel.

harm. AS. *hearm*, grief, harm; cf. Ger. *harm*, ON. *harmr*, grief. Has practically ousted *scathe*.

harmattan. Hot wind (Guinea). Native (Fanti) name. Cf. *simoom, sirocco*.

harmony. F. *harmonie*, L., G. ἁρμονία, from ἁρμόζειν, to fit together. Cf. *harmonica*, name of various instruments, and *harmonium*, invented by Debain (c. 1840).

harness. F. *harnais*, whence also It. *arnese*, Sp. *arnés*, Ger. *harnisch*, etc. Orig. equipment, gear, of any kind, esp. armour. ? From ON. *herr*, army, and *nest*, provision, supply (for expedition). To *die in harness*, now understood as in mod. sense of the word, is prob. after Shaks. (v.i.). *Harness-cask* (naut.), containing beef for immediate use, may orig. have held weapons for use in case of piratical attack. It is recorded by the *NED*. for 1818, but see quot. 1.

j harnes barrel that he had kasstyn [i.e. jettisoned]
(*York Merch. Advent.* 1457).

At least we'll die with harness on our back
(*Macb.* v. 5).

harp. AS. *hearpe*. Com. Teut.; cf. Du. *harp*, Ger. *harfe*, ON. *harpa*. MedL. *harpa* (6 cent.), from Teut., has given the Rom. forms, F. *harpe*, etc. To *harp on* (*the same string*) is in Sir T. More. *Harpsichord*, with unexplained -*s*-, comes via F. from It. *arpicordo*, "an instrument like clarigols" (Flor.).

harpings [*naut.*]. Strongest side-timbers near stem. Prob. from F. *harpe*, used of various clamping devices in wall-building, cogn. with *harpoon*.

harpoon. F. *harpon*, from *harpe*, cramp-iron. ? Cogn. with *harpy*, ? or with OHG. *harpa*,

instrument of torture. Earlier (16 cent.) in E. is *harping-iron*. Spec. sense seems to have been given by the Basques, the first whalers, some of whom were usu. taken on the early E. & Du. whaling voyages to the Arctic. Or it may be via Du. *harpoen*, the Dutch having also been early whalers.

The admirall had in her six Biscayners, expert men for the killing of the whale (Purch.).

harpsichord. See *harp*.

harpy. F. *harpie*, L. *harpyia*, usu. pl., G. ἅρπυιαι, winged and clawed monsters with female body, from ἁρπάζειν, to snatch. In fig. sense from 16 cent.

harquebus. See *arquebus*.

harridan. Corrupt. of F. *haridelle*, "a poore tit, or leane ill-favored jade" (Cotg.). Origin obscure. Possibly a fantastic formation on F. dial. (Norm.) *harousse*, jade, ON. *hross*, horse (q.v.). Cf. ModF. *rosse*, jade (lit. & fig.), from Ger.

harrier. The bird, *hen-harrier*, etc., is from *harry*. The hound, though associated with *hare*, is perh. the same word.

harrow. ME. *harwe*, cogn. with ON. *herfi*, ? and with Du. *hark*, rake. For fig. use as verb (*Haml.* i. 5) cf. *toad under the harrow*. It has been associated with obs. *harrow*, by-form of *harry*, used esp. in AS. & ME. of the *harrowing of hell* by Christ.

Cristene men may seye, as...the frogge seide to the harwe, cursid be so many lordis
(Wyc. *Sermons*).

harry. AS. *hergian*, to make war, from *here*, army; cf. Ger. *verheeren*, to harry, also Norw. *herje*, Dan. *hærge*, Swed. *härja* (ON. *herja*) in same sense. For AS. *here* cf. *harbinger, harbour, Hereford*, etc.

Harry. Also ME. *Herry*, F. *Henri*, Ger. *Heinrich*, OHG. *heimi-rīh*, home ruler. With *Old Harry, by the lord Harry*, cf. *Old Nick*. See also '*Arry*. That *Harry*, not *Henry*, was the regular ME. pronunc. is shown by the overwhelming superiority of the surnames *Harris, Harrison*.

harsh. Orig. of texture. ME. *harsk*; cf. Sw. *härsk*, Dan. *harsk*, rancid, rusty, of bacon; also Ger. *harsch* (from LG.); ? ult. cogn. with *hard*.

harslet. See *haslet*.

hart. AS. *heort, heorot*. Com. Teut.; cf. Du. *hert*, Ger. *hirsch* (OHG. *hiruz*), ON. *hjörtr*; ult. cogn. with L. *cervus* and G. κέρας, horn. The calcined horns of the animal were once the chief source of ammonia, hence *hartshorn* as medicament in AS. With *hartstongue* (fern) cf. synon. F. *langue de cerf*.

hartebeest. Antelope. SAfrDu., from *hert* (v.s.) and *beest*, beast.

Hartleian. Of *David Hartley*, psychologist (†1757). Cf. *Berkeleian*.

harum-scarum. Cf. obs. *hare*, to harass (q.v.), frighten, and *scare*. Perh. orig. *hare 'em, scare 'em*.

> To hare and rate them thus at every turn is not to teach them (Locke, *Education*).

haruspex. L., soothsayer by means of entrails of victims. Cf. *auspices*. First element is cogn. with Sanskrit *hirā*, entrails.

harvest. AS. *hærfest*, autumn. WGer.; cf. Du. *herfst*, Ger. *herbst*, autumn; prob. cogn. with ON. *haust*, autumn, and ult. with L. *carpere*, to pluck, G. καρπός, fruit. Goth. has *asans*, work season. Gradual limitation of sense (from 14 cent.) is due to borrowing of *autumn* and competition of *fall* (*of the leaf*). Sense of crop first in Tynd. (*Matt.* ix. 38). *Harvest home*, time at which the crop has been brought home, is first in Tusser.

> *harvest season*: autumpne (Palsg.).

harveyized steel. Process patented (1888) in England by *H. A. Harvey*, of New Jersey. Cf. *macadamize*.

hash. Earlier *hachy, hashee*, F. *hachis*, from *hacher*, to chop (see *hatchet*). To *make a hash of* is perh. a variation on to *make a mess of*. With to *settle one's hash* cf. to *cook one's goose*.

> *hachis*: a hachey, or hachee; a sliced gallimaufrey, or minced meat (Cotg.).

hashish, hachish. Narcotic. Arab. *hashīsh*, dry herb. See *assassin*.

haslet, harslet [*dial.*]. OF. *hastelet* (*hâtelet*), small spit, double dim. of OF. *haste*, spear, L. *hasta*, influenced by OHG. *harst*, gridiron. For -r- of *harslet* cf. *parsnip*.

> *hastilles*: th' inwards of a beast; as a hogs haslet, calves gather, sheeps pluck, &c. (Cotg.).

hasp. AS. *hæpse, hæsp*; cf. obs. Du. *haspe*, Ger. *haspe*, ON. *hespa*. The foreign words also mean skein; cf. *hank*, which has also a double sense.

hassock. Orig. tussock of sedge used as rudimentary kneeling cushion. AS. *hassuc*, coarse grass; ? cf. Welsh *hesg*, cogn. with *sedge*, and obs. Welsh *hesor*, hassock.

hastate. Spear-shaped. L. *hastatus*, from *hasta*.

haste. OF. (*hâte*), of Teut. origin; cf. Goth. *haifsts*, conflict, AS. *hæst*, violent. Du. *haast*, Ger. *hast*, are also from F. Hence verb *haste*, which, since 16 cent., tends to be ousted by *hasten*. *Hastener*, Dutch oven, may be rather connected with obs. *hasteler*, cook, turnspit, and other ME. derivatives of OF. *haster*, to roast (see *haslet*).

> Of fule haist cummis no speid (Barbour).

hat. AS. *hætt*; cf. ON. *höttr*, hood; ult. cogn. with *hood*, Ger. *hut*, hat, and *heed*. It is uncertain whether *hat-trick* refers to a collection or a new hat for the successful professional bowler. The form of the expression is allusive to the conjurer producing articles from a hat. To *eat one's hat* was earlier, according to *NED.*, to eat *Old Rowley's* (Charles II's) *hat*.

hatch[1]. Grating, etc. Now chiefly naut. (*hatchway*), or univ. (*buttery-hatch*). AS. *hæc*, whence also dial. *heck, hack*; cf. Du. *hek*. In gen. senses of gate once much commoner, as is shown by frequent occurrence in place-names (*Colney Hatch* was one of the entrances to Enfield Chase).

hatch[2]. Of birds. ME. *hacchen*; cogn. with Ger. dial. *hecken*, Sw. *hacka*, Dan. *hække*. It may be related in some way to *hatch*[1], the earlier hist. of both words being quite obscure.

hatch[3]. To engrave, shade with fine lines. F. *hacher*, to cut; see *hachure*.

hatchel. See *hackle, heckle*.

hatchet. F. *hachette*, dim. of *hache*, axe, OHG. **hapja* (*hippe*), scythe. F. *hache* could also be Ger. *hacke*, hoe, but this would not account for Prov. *apcha*. With to *bury the hatchet* (NAmer. Ind.) cf. the *pipe of peace*. With *hatchet-faced* cf. *lantern-jawed*. To *throw the hatchet* (mod.) is app. a variation on to *draw the longbow*.

hatchment [*hist.*]. Archaic F. *hachement*, crested helmet, etc. above shield in armorial bearings, app. for *acesmement*, from *acesmer*, to adorn, a very common OF. verb, of doubtful origin. Cf. obs. E. *atcheament*, often confused with *achievement*.

> No trophy, sword, nor hatchment o'er his bones
>   (*Haml.* iv. 5).

hate. AS. *hete*, noun, *hatian*, verb. Com. Teut.; cf. Du. *haat*, Ger. *hass*, ON. *hatr*, Goth. *hatis*. *Hatred* is of ME. formation, with rare suffix -*red*, AS. *ræden*, condition;

cf. *kindred*. Mod. use of *hate* for bombard-
ment, etc., is an allusion to the *Hymn of
Hate*, perpetrated (Aug. 1914) by one
Lissauer. See *beat*.

hatter, mad as a. The association of the
March Hare and the *hatter* is due to Lewis
Carroll. The wildness of the hare during
March is well known, and *mad as a March
hare* is used by Sir T. More (1529). *Mad as
a hatter* is mod. US. (*Sam Slick*, 1837), and
mad has here its US. sense of angry. The
hatter may have orig. been *adder*, or Ger.
otter, which means both adder and otter.
Attercop, spider, has also been suggested,
and has some support in *mad as a bed-bug*,
which I have come across in US. literature.

hauberk [*hist.*]. OF. *hauberc* (*haubert*), OHG.
halsberg, neck protection; cf. AS. *heals-
beorg*, hauberk, which did not survive. See
hawse, scabbard, habergeon.

haugh [*Sc. & north.*]. AS. *healh*, corner, nook.
In Sc. and north used of flat alluvial land beside river, but meaning in E., as of *heal, hale*,
from AS. dat., varies according to locality.
Common in place-names, *-hale, -hall*.

haughty. From earlier *haught*, F. *haut* (see
hauteur). For unoriginal *-g-* cf. *sprightly,
delight*, etc. Perh. really back-formation
from ME. *hauteness*, from F. *hautain*, by
analogy with *naughtiness, naughty*, etc.

No lord of thine, thou haught insulting man
(*Rich. II*, iv. 1).

haul. See *hale²*. In 16 cent. often *hall* (cf.
maul). Noun, as in *fine haul*, is from
metaphor of hauling in a fishing-net.

haulm, halm. "Little used" (Skeat); but
that was before we all became potato
growers. AS. *healm*, stalk. Com. Teut.;
cf. Du. Ger. *halm*, stem of grass, ON.
hālmr, straw; cogn. with L. *calamus*, G.
κάλαμος, reed.

haunch. Earlier *hanch*, F. *hanche*, LG. *hanka*,
? cogn. with Ger. *hinken*, to limp; cf. obs.
Du. *hancke*, hip. OHG. *ancha*, joint (see
ankle), whence Ger. dial. *anke*, nape of
neck, does not account for *h-*.

haunt. F. *hanter*, to frequent, ? from Teut.
ham, home (see *hamlet*), via Late L. *hami-
tare*. Ghost sense, first in Shaks. (*Dream*,
iii. 1), is developed in E.

Hausa [*ling.*]. Bantu lang. spoken on coast
of WAfr. Cf. *Swahili*.

haussmannize [*hist.*]. From *Baron Hauss-
mann*, prefect of Paris (1853–70), who reconstructed a great part of the town. Cf.
grimthorpe.

hautboy. F. *hautbois*, lit. high wood, whence
It. *oboe*.

hauteur. F., from *haut*, high, L. *altus*, influenced by synon. OHG. *hōh* (*hoch*).

havana. Cigar from *Havana* (*Habana*) in
Cuba.

have. AS. *habban*. Com. Teut.; cf. Du.
hebben, Ger. *haben*, ON. *hafa*, Goth. *haban*.
It is uncertain whether L. cognate is *habēre*
or *capere*. Mod. *he had better*, etc., replaces
AS. *him* (dat.) *wēre betere*, etc. In Shaks.
the old and mod. constructions are confused.

Me rather had, my heart might feel your love,
Than my unpleas'ed eye see your courtesy
(*Rich. II*, iii. 3).

haven. AS. *hæfen*, cogn. with *have*; cf. Du.
haven, Ger. *hafen* (from LG. for MHG.
habene), ON. *höfn*, whence Dan. *havn*, corrupted in E. *Copenhagen*. Practically obs.
exc. in fig. sense.

haversack. F. *havresac*, LG. *hafersack* (cf.
Ger. *habersack*), oat sack, orig. trooper's
bag for horse provender; cf. northern dial.
haver, oats, ON. *hafre*. This is the Com.
Teut. word for oats; cf. Du. *haver*.

havildar. Sepoy non-commissioned officer.
Pers. *hawāldār*, from Arab. *hawālah*, charge,
and Pers. agential *-dār* (cf. *sirdar, ressaldar*, etc.).

havoc. Usu. with *make, play*. Orig. only in to
cry havoc, give signal for pillage, OF. *havot,
havo* (12 cent.). Origin unknown, but
prob. Teut. Cf. F. *haro*, also Teut. (Norman), in OF. always in *crier haro* or *clameur
de haro*.

Cry havoc and let slip the dogs of war
(*Jul. Caes.* iii. 1).

haw¹. Berry. AS. *haga*, fruit of *hawthorn*,
AS. *haguthorn*, from *haga*, hedge, enclosure
(see *hag¹*), whence archaic *haw*, as in obs.
church-haw, churchyard. *Hawbuck*, bumpkin, churl (c. 1800), as in *Hawbuck Grange*
(Surtees), is prob. from *haw*, hedge, and
buck, in 18 cent. sense of dandy, etc. (cf.
hedge-priest).

haw². In eye of horse or dog. ? From *haw¹*,
from shape. Cf. F. *orgelet*, sty (in eye),
dim. of OF. *orgeol*, Late L. *hordeolum*,
barley-corn, sty.

unguis: a disease in the eye called an haw (Coop.).

haw³. In *hem and ha(h), haw-haw*, etc. See
hum.

hawk¹. Bird. AS. *hafoc*. Com. Teut.; cf. Du.
havik, Ger. *habicht* (OHG. *habech*), ON.

haukr. ? Ult. cogn. with *have*, in sense of grasp, seize. *Hawkweed* is translated from G. ἱεράκιον, from ἱέραξ, hawk.

hawk². To clear the throat. Imit.

hawk³. Plasterer's "palette." Prob. from *hawk¹*. Cf. F. *oiseau*, hod, lit. bird.

hawker. Kind of pedlar. The form of this word, LG. *höker* or Du. *heuker*, huckster (q.v.), is due to E. *hawker*, which in ME. not only meant falconer, but also itinerant dealer in foreign hawks travelling from castle to castle. Verb to *hawk* is a back-formation (cf. *cadge, peddle*).

hawse [*naut.*]. Earlier *halse*, AS. *heals*, neck, prow of ship. Com. Teut.; cf. Du. Ger. ON. Goth. *hals*; cogn. with L. *collum*. *Halse*, neck, to embrace, is still in dial. use. See also *athwart*.

hawser [*naut.*]. AF. *hauceour* (14 cent.), from OF. *haucier* (*hausser*), to raise, hoist (see *enhance*). Has been associated in form and sense with *hawse* (v.s.). F. *haussière*, hawser, is borrowed back from E. But some connect *hawser* with L. *helciarius*, barge-tower, from G. ἕλκειν, to drag, and this view finds some support in OF. *hausseree*, towing-path.

Laying yourself atwart my harser (Otway).

hawthorn. See *haw¹*.

hay¹. Dried grass. AS. *hīeg*, cogn. with *hew*. Com. Teut.; cf. Du. *hooi*, Ger. *heu*, ON. *hey*, Goth. *hawi*. *Hay-fever* (*hay-asthma, summer catarrh*) is irritation caused by grass pollen.

Whan the sunne shinth make hay
(Heywood, 1546).

hay² [*hist.*]. Hedge, enclosure. AS. *hege*, hedge, enclosure, cogn. with *hag¹, haw¹*; but the ME. word more often represents cogn. F. *haie*, OHG. *haga*. Hence *hayward*, who protected enclosures against cattle and trespassers, common now as surname.

haysel [*dial.*]. Hay season (EAng.). ME. *sele*, season.

The great seasonal occupations, like haysel and harvest (Sir A. Geddes, Oct. 9, 1917).

hazard. F. *hasard* (12 cent.), a dicing game (cf. *chance*); cf. Sp. Port. *azar*. Of Oriental origin. The statement of William of Tyre, a contemporary of the Crusades, that the game was named from the castle of *Asart* (Ain Zarba) in Palestine, has a curious parallel in the hist. of *boston* (q.v.). Vulgar Arab. *az-zahr*, for *al-zahr*, the die (cf. *azimuth*), is a less fanciful etymon, but

this is a word of doubtful authority which may have been borrowed from Sp. or from It. *zara*, "a game at dice called hazard" (Flor.). Cf. *apricot, carat*, etc.

haze¹. Mist. Back-formation from *hazy* (1592), orig. naut. App. connected by some mysterious piece of folklore with Ger. *hase*, hare, an animal which plays an important part in Ger. folklore. Ger. *der hase brauet*, LG. *de hase brouet*, lit. the hare is brewing (in his subterranean kitchen), is used of a ground-mist. Cf. synon. *der fuchs badet sich*, lit. the fox is bathing.

a haze or thick fog: nebula (Litt.).

Siehe, da brauet der hase im weisslichen dampf auf der wiese (Voss).

de hase brouet: sagt man in Niedersachsen, wenn an sommer-abenden sich plötzlich ein nebel über den erdboden zieht. *Eng.* haze
(Berghaus, *Sprachschatz der Sassen*).

haze² [*naut. & US.*]. To bully. E. dial. *haze*, to frighten, ill-treat. App. connected, though reason is quite obscure, with *haze¹*. Cf. F. *brimer*, to bully, haze, dial. form of *brumer*, from *brume*, mist, haze.

to haze or hawze one: perterrefacio, clamore obtundo (Litt.).

hazel. AS. *hæsel*. Com. Teut.; cf. Du. *hazel(aar)*, Ger. *hasel*, ON. *hasl*; cogn. with L. *corulus* (**cosulus*), hazel.

Thou wilt quarrel with a man for cracking nuts, having no other reason but because thou hast hazel eyes (*Rom. & Jul.* iii. 1).

he. AS. *hē*. From the same base, orig. demonstr., as *here, hence*, etc., cogn. with L. *ci-tra*. Ger. *er*, Goth. *is*, represent another base, cogn. with L. *is*, but the *h*- base appears in Ger. advs. *her, hin*, and *heute*, to-day (cf. AS. *hēo-dæg*).

he, he-he. Natural interj.; cf. *ha, hi, ho*, in E. and other langs. *Ha-ha, he-he* are in Aelfric's *Grammar* (c. 1000).

head. AS. *hēafod*. Com. Teut.; cf. Du. *hoofd*, Ger. *haupt*, ON. *höfuth*, Goth. *haubith*; ult. cogn. with L. *caput*. With *head*, unit, cf. *poll-tax, capitation*. For *to come to a head* see *gather*, but there is also association with F. *venir à chef* (see *achieve*). With geog. sense cf. *cape²*; with sense of commander cf. *chief*. *Head and front* is after Shaks. (*Oth.* i. 3). *Head over heels* is a curious perversion of earlier *heels over head*, used in ME. description of Jonah's descent into the whale; cf. *over head and ears, by the head and ears* (*shoulders*). To *make head or tail of* is to disentangle beginning and end. With to *make head against* cf. F. *tenir tête à*. With *headstrong*, *heady*, cf. *testy* (q.v.). *Headway* is naut.; cf. *leeway*, and to *head for* (F. *mettre le cap sur*). To *head off* is to force to change of direction by getting in front.

The water-foules han her hedes leyd
Togedre (Chauc. *Parl. Fowls*, 554).

All the current of a heady fight (1 *Hen. IV*, ii. 3).

-head. ME. suffix *-hede*, cogn. with *-hood*. Only in *godhead*, *maidenhead*.

headborough [*hist.*]. Orig. head officer of a *frithborh* (see *frankpledge*).

headlong. For earlier *headling*, with adv. suffix as in *grovelling*. Cf. *sidelong*.

Al the drove wente heedlynge [*Vulg.* praeceps] in to the see (Wyc. *Matt.* viii. 32).

heal. AS. *hǣlan*, from *hāl*, whole. Com. Teut.; cf. Du. *heelen*, Ger. *heilen*, ON. *heila*, Goth. *haljan*. Cf. Sc. *heal*, health. See *hale*¹, whole, holy. Gradually restricted in sense by adoption of *cure*.

health. AS. *hǣlth*, from *hāl*, whole (v.s.). In ME. also in sense of deliverance, salvation. Cf. *wealth*.

Myn yghen han seyn thin helthe
(Wyc. *Luke*, ii. 30).

heap. AS. *hēap*. WGer.; cf. Du. *hoop*, Ger. *haufen*. See *forlorn hope*. *All of a heap* is for earlier *all on a heap* (Shaks.), for AS. *on heape*. Cf. OF. *cheoir à tas*, to fall all of a heap.

hear. AS. *hīeran*. Com. Teut.; cf. Du. *hooren*, Ger. *hören*, ON. *heyra*, Goth. *hausjan*; prob. cogn. with G. ἀ-κούειν, to hear, and ult. with *ear*¹. Rustic *year* is AS. *gehīeran*, much commoner than simple verb, whence ME. *yhere*. With *hearsay* cf. to *hear say*, now considered vulgar, and F. *entendre dire*.

Then cried a wise woman out of the city, Hear, hear (2 *Sam.* xx. 16).

hearken. See *hark*.

hearse. F. *herse*, harrow, portcullis, L. *hirpex*, *hirpic-*, large rake. In ME. an elaborate framework to hold candles over bier or coffin. Afterwards applied to a canopy, the bier itself, and poet. to the tomb. Mod. use from 17 cent. Cf. *rehearse*.

Underneath this sable hearse
Lies the subject of all verse (W. Browne).

heart. AS. *heorte*. WAryan; cf. Du. *hart*, Ger. *herz*, ON. *hjarta*, Goth. *hairtō*, L. *cor*, *cord-*, G. καρδία, OIr. *cride*, Welsh *craidd*, Russ. *serdtse*, etc. The more elementary fig. senses are found in AS., including that

of seat of intellect, memory, now only in *by heart* (cf. F. *par cœur*). *Searchings of heart* is after *Judges*, v. 16. To *wear one's heart upon one's sleeve* is after Shaks. (*Oth.* i. 1). To *take heart of grace* is a mysterious pun on *hart of grease* (earlier *herte of gresse*), a fat hart (? likened to *stout heart*), simplified by the fact that both words were usu. spelt *herte* in 16 cent.

I take herte a gresse, as one doth that taketh a sodayne courage upon hym: je prens cueur en panse (Palsg.).
Heart of oak are our ships, heart of oak are our men
(*Song*, 1760).

hearth. AS. *heorth*. WGer.; cf. Du. *haard*, Ger. *herd*. For fig. senses, *hearth and home*, etc., cf. F. *foyer*.

heat. AS. *hǣte*, from *hāt*, hot; cogn. with Du. *hitte*, Ger. *hitze*, ON. *hite*, Goth. *heitō*, fever. Sporting sense is from ME. meaning of single intense effort. *Heat-wave* is US.

heath. AS. *hǣth*, heathland, heather. It is uncertain which is orig. sense. Com. Teut.; cf. Du. Ger. *heide*, ON. *heithr*, Goth. *haithi*. With *heathen*, AS. *hǣthen*, cf. Ger. *heide*; but the choice of the word may have been determined by superficial resemblance to G. ἔθνη, nations, gentiles. Some think the Goths took it from Armen. *hethanos*, a loan-word from G. ἔθνος. *Pagan* (q.v.) is not a parallel case. *Heathenesse*, obs. exc. in romantic style, which looks like a formation on F. *largesse*, *noblesse*, is AS. *hǣthennes* (see *-ness*).

heathen. See *heath*.

heather. From 18 cent. only (orig. Sc.), earlier *hathir*, *hadder*. Connection with *heath* is uncertain, though Ger. *heidekraut*, heather, lit. heath-plant, makes it likely (cf. also OHG. *heidahi*, heather). To *set the heather on fire*, start a disturbance, is Sc.

heave. AS. *hebban*. Com. Teut.; cf. Du. *heffen*, Ger. *heben* (OHG. *heffan*), ON. *hefja*, Goth. *hafjan*; cogn. with L. *capere*. Orig. to lift, raise, as in to *heave a sigh*, to *heave the gorge* (*Oth.* ii. 1), whence mod. sense of retching. Cf. also *heave-offering* (*Ex.* xxix. 27). Also intrans., to rise, hence to *heave in sight*. Now chiefly naut., with correct past *hove*.

heaven. AS. *heofon*, heaven, sky, with LG. cognates. App. unconnected with Du. *hemel*, Ger. *himmel*, ON. *himinn*, Goth. *himins*, which are perh. cogn. with *home* (of the gods). Common in pl., after L. *caeli*, G. οὐρανοί, Heb. *shāmayim*, in early

Bibl. lang., but pl. is now restricted to the sky.

heavy. AS. *hefig*, from *heave*. For fig. senses, already in AS., cf. *grave*. To *lie heavy* (fig.) appears to be an improvement on to *sit heavy* (*Rich. III*, v. 3).

She is a hevy [i.e. mournful] gentlewoman; wherfore I cannot say (*Plumpton Let.* temp. Hen. VIII).

hebdomadal. From *hebdomad*, the number seven (cf. *triad*), L., G. ἑβδομάς, ἑβδομάδ-, number seven, seven days. Esp. in ref. to Oxf. (*Hebdomadal Council*). Cf. *heptarchy*.

Hebe. Daughter of Zeus and Hera, cup-bearer of Olympus. G. ἥβη, youthful prime. Cf. *Ganymede*.

hebetate. From L. *hebetare*, from *hebes, hebet-*, dull; cf. F. *hébéter*.

Hebrew. ME. & OF. *ebreu* (*hébreu*), MedL. *Ebreus*, for *Hebraeus*, G. Ἑβραῖος, from Aramaic form of Heb. '*ibri*, one from the other side (of the river Euphrates). With *Hebraic*, Late L., G. Ἑβραϊκός, cf. F. *hébraïque*, fem. only. As vernacular lang. Hebrew became extinct three or four cents. B.C., being replaced by kindred Aramaic or Syriac. It survived, like Sanskrit, as liturgical lang.

Hecate. G. deity identified with Artemis. Fem. of ἕκατος, far-darting, epithet of Apollo. Since Shaks. associated with sorcery.

hecatomb. L., G. ἑκατόμβη, offering of a hundred oxen, from ἑκατόν, hundred, βοῦς, ox. Cf. *holocaust*.

heck. Grating, in various senses. Northern form of *hatch*[1].

heckle, hackle, hatchell. Instrument for combing hemp. Cogn. with *hack*[1] and *hook*. Cf. Du. *hekel*, Ger. *hechel*. With mod. fig. sense of *heckle*, orig. Sc. (Gladstone's Midlothian campaign), cf. hist. of *tease*. Cf. also Ger. *durchhecheln*, to censure, carp at.

hectare. F., see *hecto-* and *are*[2].

hectic. G. ἑκτικός, habitual, consumptive, from ἕξις, habit of body, from ἔχειν, to have. Replaced ME. *etik*, F. *étique*.

hecto-. Adapted in F. metric system from G. ἑκατόν, hundred, to form the multiples.

hector. From *Hector*, bullying braggart of popular drama, G. Ἕκτωρ, from ἔχειν, to hold, as being the prop of Troy. Cf. to *out-herod* Herod.

hedge. AS. *hecg*, cogn. with *haw*[1], *hay*[2], *hag*[1]; cf. Du. *heg*, Ger. *hecke*. Now usu. of living (*quick-set*) growth, but, in earlier

(and loc.) use, of any fence (*Mark*, xii. 1). *Hedgerow* (see *row*[1]) occurs in AS., *hedgehog* in ME., replacing AS. *igl*. In compds. often disparaging, vagabond, found by the wayside, e.g. *hedge-priest*, *hedge-school*, the latter esp. Ir. Cf. Du. *haagpreek*, earlier *-predicant*, and obs. *haeghpape* (Kil.), priest without parish. Sporting sense of verb in betting is for earlier to *hedge in* (*off*), to secure by a hedge (see also *edge*).

Like a rook, I have hedg'd in my bet
    (Buckingham, *Rehearsal*).

hedonism. Cyrenaic school of philosophy. From G. ἡδονή, pleasure.

-hedron [*math.*]. From G. ἕδρα, seat, base.

heed. AS. *hēdan*. WGer.; cf. Du. *hoeden*, Ger. *hüten*, from *hut*, care, heed. Prob. cogn. with *hat*, *hood*, common idea being that of protection. Noun now only as obj. of verb (*give*, *take*, etc.).

hee-haw. Imit., cf. OF. *hinham* (v.i.).

In fine Missae sacerdos versus ad populum vice, Ite Missa est, ter hinhannabit: populus vero vice, Deo gratias, ter respondebit, Hinham, Hinham, Hinham (*Festum Asinorum*, Beauvais, 13 cent.).

heel[1]. Of foot. AS. *hēla*; cf. Du. *hiel*, ON. *hæll*. App. dim. of AS. *hōh*, heel (see *hough*). The gen. Aryan name appears in Ger. *ferse*, heel. *Heeltap* (cf. *supernaculum*) was orig. a shoemakers' term for one of the layers of which the heel of a boot is composed. A *clean* (earlier *fair*) *pair of heels* describes the view offered to the pursuer. To *lay by the heels* is an allusion to the stocks. For *vulnerable heel* see *Achilles*.

heel[2] [*naut.*]. Now usu. with *over*. For earlier *hield*, *heald* (still in dial.), AS. *hieldan*, to incline, from *hylde*, a slope, *heald*, bent; cogn. with AS. *hold*, gracious, loyal; cf. Ger. *halde*, slope, very common in place-names. Ger. *hielen* (naut.) is from E.

I hylde, I leane on the one syde, as a bote or shyp or any other vessell: je enclyne de cousté (Palsg.).

hefty. Subjective use of US. *hefty*, convenient to *heft* (lift), which is app. from Du. *heffen* (see *heave*). US. sense is also affected by Ger. *heftig*, violent. Cf. Du. *hevig*, violent, orig. heavy.

Hegelian. Of *Hegel*, Ger. philosopher (†1831).

hegemony. G. ἡγεμονία, from ἡγεμών, leader, cogn. with ἄγειν, to lead. Orig. of predominance of individual state in G. hist.

hegira. Flight of Mohammed from Mecca to Medina (622 A.D.), from which Moslem chronology reckons. MedL., Arab. *hijrah*, departure, from *hajara*, to depart, cogn. with name *Hagar*.

heifer. AS. *hēahfore, -fre, -fru*, ME. *hayfare*, suggest that this may be for *high-farer* (goer). Another theory connects it with Ger. dial. *hagen, hegel*, bull, and AS. *fearr*, bull.

heigh. Natural ejaculation (interrogative); with addition of *ho* indicates weariness, etc.

heighday. See *heyday*.

height. AS. *hīehthu*, from *high*; cf. *heighten*. Mod. pronunc. (v.i.) was not fixed till 18 cent., and *-th* is still common colloq.

> The highth and depth of thy eternal ways
> (*Par. L.* viii. 413).

Heine [*hist.*]. Ger., for *Heinrich* (see *Harry*).

> The Canadians call their enemy Heine and not Fritz (*Daily Chron.* Aug. 25, 1917).

heinous. F. *haineux* (OF. *haïnos*), from *haine* hatred, from *haïr*, to hate, of LG. origin (cf. Goth. *hatjan*).

heir. Altered from ME. *eir*, OF. (*hoir*), L. *heres* (VL. acc. **herem*, for *heredem*), cogn. with G. χῆρος, bereft. ME. form survives in surnames *Ayre, Eyre*. For *heirloom*, hereditary tool, chattel, see *loom¹*.

> This is the eire; cume ye, slea we hym
> (Wyc. *Matt.* xxi. 38).

helianthus. Sunflower. From G. ἥλιος, sun, ἄνθος, flower.

helichrysm. Immortelle. From G. ἕλιξ, spiral, χρυσός, gold.

Helicon. G. Ἑλικών, mountain in Boeotia, sacred to Muses. Cf. *Parnassus*.

helicopter [*neol.*]. Device for enabling aeroplanes to rise perpendicularly. From G. ἕλιξ (v.s.), πτερόν, wing.

> With the development of a helicopter, machines could land and rise from any flat-roofed house (*Daily Mail*, Mar. 21, 1919).

heliograph. From G. ἥλιος, sun. Orig. of photography.

heliotrope. Orig. kind of sunflower (v.s.). From G. τρέπειν, to turn.

helium [*chem.*]. Isolated (1895) by Ramsay. From G. ἥλιος, sun, after *selenium, tellurium*.

helix. L., G. ἕλιξ, spiral; cf. F. *hélice*, screw (of steamer).

hell. AS. *hell*, abode of dead, place of torment, cogn. with *helan*, to hide, whence dial. *hele*, to cover up, and surnames *Hellier, Hillyar*, etc., tiler. Com. Teut.; cf. Du. *hel*, Ger. *hölle* (OHG. *hella*), ON. *hel*, Goth. *halja*. In *AV.* for *Sheol* (*OT.*), *Hades* and *Gehenna* (*NT.*). For expletive

and fig. uses cf. *devil*. *Gambling-hell* is after 18 cent. F. *enfer*, in same sense. First *NED.* record for *hell-for-leather* is from Kipling, but my memory of it goes back nearly fifty years. Can it be for *all of a lather* (q.v.) with secondary allusion to *leather* in sporting sense of skin as affected by riding? *Hell-cat*, Sc. *hellicat*, are prob. suggested by *Hecate* (*Macb.* iii. 5).

hellebore. Earlier *ellebore*, F. *ellébore*, L., G. ἑλλέβορος.

Hellene. G. Ἕλλην, first as pl., in Homer, of a Thessalian tribe named from its chief. *Hellenistic* is now used of later G.

hello. See *hallo*.

helm¹. Helmet. AS. *helm*. Com. Teut.; cf. Du. Ger. *helm*, ON. *hjalmr*, Goth. *hilms*; cogn. with *hele*, to cover (see *hell*), L. *celare*, G. καλύπτειν. Also in Rom. langs., from OHG. Replaced, exc. poet., by dim. *helmet*, from OF. With *helm-cloud* (lake-country), whence *helm-wind*, cf. the "hat" of Mount Pilatus in Switzerland.

> Hat Pilatus seinen hut, so wird das wetter bleiben gut.

> The helm wind which...blew in the Lake Country last week (*Manch. Guard.* Mar. 13, 1918).

helm². Tiller. AS. *helma*; cf. ON. *hjálm*, helm, MHG. *helm*, handle (see *halbert*); cogn. with *helve*.

helminthology. Study of intestinal worms. From G. ἕλμινς, ἑλμινθ-, maw-worm.

helot. G. Εἵλωτες (pl.), of Ἕλος, Laconian town whose inhabitants were enslaved and, according to Plutarch, made to act as awful examples ("drunken helots") to young Spartans. Sense of ill-used "outlander" (v.i.) dates from Lord Milner's famous speech on SAfr. (c. 1898).

> No Rumanian government could have intervened except for the purpose of redeeming the Rumanian helots in Hungary (*Daily Chron.* Nov. 6, 1916).

help. AS. *helpan*. Com. Teut.; cf. Du. *helpen*, Ger. *helfen*, ON. *hjálpa*, Goth. *hilpan*. Orig. strong, as in Bibl. *holpen*. Spec. sense of serving at table (*second helping*, etc.) prob. began (17 cent.) as transl. of F. *servir*, "to help, stead, availe" (Cotg.). *Help*, servant, is recorded (US.) for 1645; cf. Bibl. *help*, as in *an help meet for him* (*Gen.* ii. 18), for *Vulg. adjutorium simile sibi*, whence ghost-word *helpmeet*, becoming later *helpmate*. In sense of remedy (*can't help, no help*) always with neg. expressed or suggested. Applied in US. to person, so as to avoid the "humiliating" *servant*.

helter-skelter. Cf. *hurry-scurry, harum-scarum*; but both elements are obscure. Can it be formed on obs. Du. *hieltje*, little heel, used, according to Sewel, of the winged heels of Mercury? In Shaks. (2 *Hen. IV*, v. 3) it is used of a messenger's utmost haste.

helve. AS. *hielf*, cogn. with *helm²*, *halter*, and forms in obs. Du., LG. & HG.

jetter le manche apres la coignée: to throw the helve after the hatchet (Cotg.).

Helvetian, Helvetic. From L. *Helvetia* (sc. *terra*), Switzerland.

hem¹. Border. AS. *hem(m)*, cogn. with *ham*, enclosure (see *home*), and with Ger. *hemmen*, to constrain, obstruct; cf. to *hem in*.

hem², h'm. Interj., sound of clearing throat; cf. *ahem, hem and ha(w), hum* (q.v.).

hematite, etc. See *haem-.*

hemisphere. Late L., G. ἡμισφαίριον, from ἡμι-, half, cogn. with L. *semi-*, Sanskrit *sāmi-*, and σφαῖρα, sphere. Cf. *hemistich* (see *distich*).

hemlock. Kentish form of AS. *hymlīce*. No cognates known. For vowel cf. *left*.

hemp. AS. *henep*; cf. Du. *hennep*, Ger. *hanf*, ON. *hampr*. Though widely diffused in Aryan (L. *cannabis*, G. κάνναβις, OSlav. *konoplja*, Pers. *kanab*), it is prob. a non-Aryan word borrowed early from Scythian. The Teut. forms are not from L. *cannabis*, but independent acquisitions from a common source.

hen. AS. *henn*, fem. of *hana*, cock. WGer.; cf. Du. *hen*, Ger. *henne*. Masc. form, Com. Teut., is cogn. with L. *canere*, to sing. For *henbane* see *bane. Henpeck* is 17 cent.

hence. ME. *hennes*, with adv. -*s*, for earlier *henne* (cf. *thence*), from demonstr. stem of *he*; cf. Ger. *hin, hinnen*.

henchman. ME. *henxt-man*, groom (cf. MedL. *hengestmannus*), from AS. *hengest*, horse. Com. Teut.; cf. Du. Ger. *hengst*, ON. *hestr*, horse, stallion, etc., and the war-name of the reputed Jutish conqueror of Kent. For change of sense cf. *constable, marshal.* The word became obs. in 17 cent., and in mod. use may be one of Scott's ghost-words (cf. *bartizan, warison*). He found *hanchman* in Burt's *Letters from North Scotland* (1730), explained as one who is always at his master's *haunch* (cf. *flunkey*), which is either a blunder or an invention. Its introduction into the *Lady of the Lake* (ii. 35) and *Waverley* (see ch. xvi.) made it a mod. literary word. There may thus be no real connection with the ME. word.

hendecagon. From G. ἕνδεκα, eleven, γωνία, angle.

hendiadys [*gram*.]. Late L., for G. ἐν διὰ δυοῖν, one through two, e.g. *pocula et aurum* for *aurea pocula*, golden goblets.

henna. Shrub and dye. Arab. *hinnā*.

henotheism. Dilution of *monotheism.* From G. εἶς, ἐν-, one.

hepatic. L., G. ἡπατικός, from ἡπαρ, liver.

heptad. The number seven. G. ἑπτάς, ἑπταδ-, from ἑπτά, seven, cogn. with L. *septem*. Cf. *heptagon. Heptarchy* was coined, on *monarchy, tetrarchy*, by 16 cent. historians, as name for the supposed seven AS. kingdoms. For *Heptameron* see *Decameron.*

her¹. Objective case. AS. *hire*, dat. of *hēo*, she, which early replaced also acc. *hīe*. See *he.* Hence *herself*; cf. *himself, myself* (for *meself*).

her². Possessive case. AS. *hire*, genitive of *hēo*, she, used as possess. adj. and developing pronoun forms *hers, hern*; cf. Ger. *ihr*, her, orig. genitive of *sie*, she.

Restore thou to hir alle thingis that ben hern [*var.* hyres*]* (Wyc. 2 *Kings*, viii. 6).

herald. OF. *heralt* (cf. It. *araldo*, Sp. *heraldo*), OHG. **hari-walt*, army-wielder (see *harbour*), found as personal name (*Chariovalda*) in Tacitus. Cf. E. *Harold*, AS. *Hereweald*, and first element of *Ariovistus* (Caesar). I see no difficulty in supposing that the herald's functions had changed in pre-documentary times.

herb. F. *herbe* (OF. *erbe*), L. *herba*, grass, etc. The *h-* was correctly mute till 19 cent. *Herbal*, book on herbs, is after *manual, missal*, etc.; hence *herbalist. Herborize*, F. *herboriser*, shows the same confusion with *arbor*, tree, as E. *arbour* (q.v.). *Herb of grace* (*Haml.* iv. 5), also called *herb of repentance*, is a play on double meaning of *rue* (q.v.). See also *bennet.*

Hercules. L., G. Ἡρακλῆς, trad. glory (κλέος) of Hera, at whose command he performed his twelve labours. Hence *Pillars of Hercules*, Calpe and Abyla (now Gibraltar and Ceuta), regarded by ancients as supporting western boundary of the world.

herd. AS. *heord.* Com. Teut.; cf. obs. Du. *herde*, Ger. *herde*, ON. *hjörth*, Goth. *hairda*; cogn. with G. κόρθυς, troop. Cf. *herd*, for *herdsman*, usu. in compds. (*shepherd*, etc.), AS. *hierde*, also Com. Teut. (Ger. *hirt*, etc.). The *common herd* is after Shaks. (*Jul. Caes.* i. 2).

here. AS. *hĕr*, cogn. with *he*. Com. Teut.; cf. Du. Ger. *hier*, ON. Goth. *hĕr*. *Heretofore* preserves otherwise obs. *tofore*, AS. *tōforan* (cf. *before*).

hereditary. L. *hereditarius*, from *heres, hered-*, heir. *Heredity* (biol.), F. *hérédité*, appears to have been introduced by Herbert Spencer. Cf. *heritage, heritor*, F. *héritage, héritier*.

heresy. F. *hérésie*, from L., G. αἵρεσις, selection, school of thought, sect, from αἱρεῖν, to take. The G. word is rendered *sect* in transls. of *NT*.

Surrexerunt autem quidam de haeresi pharisaeorum (*Vulg. Acts*, xv. 5).

heriot [*leg.*]. Gift to lord on death of tenant of latter's best live beast or dead chattel; orig. restoration of mil. equipment. AS. *here-geatwe* (pl.), army gear. Second element is *getāwe*, trappings, etc., from *tāwian*, to prepare (see *taw*[1]). Cf. Du. *verheergewaden*, "to renew fealty and homage to the lord paramount" (Sewel, 1766), from MHG. *hergewǣte*, warlike equipment, from OHG. *giwāti* (*gewand*), attire.

heritage, heritor. See *hereditary*.

hermaphrodite. L., G. Ἑρμαφρόδιτος, son of *Hermes* and *Aphrodite*, who became one with the nymph Salmacis.

'Ee's a kind of a giddy harumfrodite—soldier and sailor too (Kipling).

hermeneutic [*theol.*]. Of interpretation. From G. ἑρμηνεύειν, to interpret, prob. from Ἑρμῆς (v.i.).

Hermes. L., G. Ἑρμῆς, son of Zeus and Maia, identified by Romans with Mercury. Applied as title Ἑρμῆς τρὶς μέγιστος, Hermes thrice greatest, by early mystics and alchemists to Egypt. deity Thoth. Hence *hermetic*, dealing with occult science, and with air-tight sealing of vessels, etc. used by alchemists.

hermetic. See *Hermes*.

hermit. ME. also *ermit, armit*, F. *ermite*, L., G. ἐρημίτης, from ἐρημία, desert (cf. *eremite*). Cf. name *Armitage*. Unoriginal *h-* also in OF. The famous *Hermitage* wine is from a hill near Valence with a ruin at the top.

A solitary churchyard called the Hermitage, or more commonly Armitage
(*Bride of Lammermoor*, ch. xxiii.).

hern. Archaic for *heron* (q.v.).

I come from haunts of coot and hern
(Tennyson, *Brook*).

hernia [*anat.*]. L.; cf. F. *hernie*, replacing OF. *hargne*. In Chauc.

hero. Back-formation from *heroes*, L. *heroës*, pl. of *heros*, G. ἥρως, hero, demi-god; cf. F. *héros*, It. *eroe*, Sp. *héroe*. For back-formation cf. *satellite*. *Heroi-comic(al)*, first as title of Pope's *Rape of the Lock* (1712), is from F. *héroi-comique*, for *héroïco-comique*, with one *-co-* lost by dissim. (cf. *idolatry*). *Heroic verse*, decasyllabic iambic, is from It.

And you beside the honourable band
Of great heroës do in order stand (Spenser).

Herodian. Jewish partisan of *Herod* family, esp. of *Herod Antipas* (B.C. 4–A.D. 39). In AS. gospels (*Mark*, xii. 13). The name is derived from *hero* (v.s.). See also *outherod*.

heroin. Drug. Ger. trade-name disguising connection with morphium.

heron. F. *héron*, OF. *hairon, haigron, hegron*, from latinized form of OHG. *heigir*, with Scand. cognates; cf. It. *aghirone*, Sp. *airón*, and see *aigrette, egret*. OHG. *heigir* is app. connected with MHG. *reiger* (*reiher*), heron, Du. *reiger*, AS. *hrāgra*, while the immediate AS. cognate of *heron* is *higora*, magpie, wood-pecker. *Hern* (archaic & poet.) is very common in place-names and surnames. Archaic and dial. *heronsew, hernshaw*, etc., is OF. dim. *heronceau, heroncel*. Hence, according to Hanmer, to *know a hawk from a handsaw* (*Haml.* ii. 2), but this phrase (not otherwise known) may be of the type to *know a great A from a bull's foot*.

herpes. Skin disease. L., G., from ἕρπειν, to creep, cogn. with *serpent*. Cf. *herpetology*, study of snakes.

Herr. Ger., sir, Mr. Orig. compar. of *hehr*, noble, venerable, cogn. with *hoar* (q.v.).

herring. AS. *hǣring*. WGer.; cf. Du. *haring*, Ger. *häring*; also F. *hareng*, from Du. ? From AS. *hār*, hoar, white; cf. *whiting*. Fig. sense of *red-herring across the track*, in order to throw hounds off the scent (see *drag*), is app. quite mod. *Herring-pond* for Atlantic is recorded 1686.

Herrnhuter. Moravian (q.v.). From first Ger. settlement at *Herrnhut*, Lord's keeping, in Saxony. See *Herr* and *heed*.

hers. See *her*[2]. *Herself*, see *her*[1].

herse [*archaic*]. Portcullis, phalanx. See *hearse*.

Hertzian waves [*phys.*]. Discovered by *Hertz*, Ger. physicist (†1894).

hesitate. From L. *haesitare*, frequent. of *haerēre*, *haes-*, to stick fast.

Hesper, Hesperus. L., G. ἕσπερος, of the evening, western; cogn. with *vesper* (q.v.). Hence the *Hesperides*, daughters of the west, who guarded the golden apples in the isle of the blest; also *hesperid-* in bot. terms dealing with the orange.

Hessian boots. Worn (18 cent.) by *Hessian* troops, from *Hessen*, Germany. The *Hessian fly*, destructive to wheat, was so called because supposed to have been taken to America by *Hessian* troops hired to fight against the colonists during War of Independence (cf. *Hanover rat*).

hest [*archaic*]. AS. *hǣs*, command, with excrescent *-t* as in *amidst*, etc. See *behest*, *hight*.

hetaira. Courtesan. G. ἑταίρα, female companion.

heteroclite [*gram.*]. F. *hétéroclite*, L., G. ἑτερόκλιτος, irregularly inflected, from ἕτερος, other, different, κλίνειν, to bend. Cf. *heterodox*, from δόξα, opinion; *heterogeneous*, from γένος, kind.

hetman. Earlier also *ataman*, of the Cossacks. Pol., from Ger. *hauptmann*, head man, captain. The first *hetman* known to Western Europe was Mazeppa (†1709).

General Kaledin has been elected superior Ataman of Ukraine (*Daily Chron.* Sep. 29, 1917).

heuristic. Irreg. formation from G. εὑρίσκειν, to find.

hew. AS. *hēawan*. Com. Teut.; cf. Du. *houwen*, Ger. *hauen*, ON. *höggva*; cogn. with *hay*[1], and ult. with L. *-cudere*.

hexad. The number six. G. ἑξάς, ἑξαδ-, from ἕξ, six, cogn. with L. *sex*. Cf. *hexagon*, from γωνία, angle; *hexameter*, from μέτρον, measure; *hexapla*, six-fold parallel text of *OT.*, made by Origen, neut. pl. of ἑξαπλοῦς, six-fold; *hexateuch*, pentateuch (q.v.) with Book of Joshua.

heyday. Interj. ? From *heigh*, *hey*, natural ejaculation, with second element as in Ger. *heida*, from which it may have been imitated. This is lit. *hi there*, but the *da* may also be interjectional; cf. F. *oui-da*. The *heyday* (*of youth*, etc.) is now understood as *high day*, but the earlier sense of excitement, etc., e.g. *hey-day in the blood* (*Haml.* iii. 4), seems to have some association with the interj. It is not impossible that the exclamation itself is sometimes for *high day*; cf. F. *jour de Dieu!* *Hey* is a common ME.

spelling of *high*, and the surname *Heyday*, *Hayday* is certainly for *high day* (cf. names *Holiday*, *Christmas*, etc.).

heyday! O festum diem (Litt.).

heyduck, heyduke. Polish servant. Cf. Pol. *hajduk*, also in Boh., Magyar, etc. Said to be name of a Hung. tribe (cf. *slave*, *coolie*, etc.).

hey-ho. Orig. naut. (see *rumbelow*).

hi. Interj. Cf. *hey*, *heigh*, *ho*, etc.

hiatus. L., from *hiare*, to gape. Cf. *dehiscent*, *chasm*.

hibernate. From L. *hibernare*, from *hibernus*, from *hiems*, winter.

Hibernian. From L. *Hibernia*, for *Iverna*, G. Ἰέρνη, from OCelt. form of *Erin*, whence also AS. *Īraland*.

hibiscus. L., G. ἱβίσκος, kind of mallow.

hiccough. Late spelling, associated with *cough*, of earlier *hiccup*, *hicket*, imit. of sound; cf. F. *hiquet*, "the hickock, or yexing" (Cotg.), Du. *hikken*, to sob.

hickory. For *pohickery*, native Virginian name (17 cent.).

hidalgo. Sp., formerly also *hijo dalgo* (*de algo*), son (L. *filius*) of some-one (L. *aliquis*). Cf. OSp. Port. *fidalgo*. This formation, unknown to other Rom. langs., may be an imit. of Arab. *ibn-nās*, son of people, used as complimentary title.

hide[1]. Skin. AS. *hȳd*. Com. Teut.; cf. Du. *huid*, Ger. *haut*, ON. *hūth*; cogn. with L. *cutis*, G. κύτος, and perh. with *hide*[3]. Hence *hide*, to flog. *Hidebound* was orig. (16 cent.) used of cattle, then of trees, but fig. use is very early (cf. *case-hardened*).

hide-bound: a distemper in horses, when the skin sticks so fast to their back and ribbs, that you cannot pull it from the flesh with your hand. In husbandry, trees are likewise said to be hide-bound, when the bark sticks too close
(*Dict. Rust.* 1717).

hide[2] [*hist.*]. Measure of land. AS. *hīd*, earlier *hīgid*, from *hīw-*, family, as in *hīwisc*, *hīwscipe*, family, household, hide of land, cogn. with *hind*[2] and with Ger. *heirat*, marriage. The old popular etym. from *hide*[1] prob. originated from Virgil's account of foundation of Carthage.

Mercatique solum, facti de nomine Byrsam,
Taurino quantum possent circumdare tergo
(*Aen.* i. 367).

hide[3]. Verb. AS. *hȳdan*, with cognates in LG. & obs. Du.; ? cogn. with *hide*[1], ? or with G. κεύθειν, to hide.

hideous. F. *hideux*, OF. *hisdos*, from *hisde*, ? L. *hispidus*, bristly, ult. from *hircus*, goat. Cf. *horrid.*

hie [*archaic*]. AS. *hīgian*, to be intent on, strive, whence ME. *hien*, also reflex., to hasten, gradually becoming a verb of motion (cf. *hasten*); cf. Du. *hijgen*, to pant, Dan. *hige*, to strive after.

Abraham hyede [*var.* hastide, *Vulg.* festinavit] into the tabernacle (Wyc. *Gen.* xviii. 6).

hierarchy. ME. *ierarchie* (Wyc.), OF., L., G. ἱεραρχία, rule of a *hierarch*, high-priest, from ἱερός, holy. Cf. *hieratica* (sc. *charta*), finest papyrus, used in sacred writings.

hieroglyphic. G. ἱερογλυφικός, from γλύφειν, to carve (v.s.). First used of Egypt. picture-writing. Cf. *hierophant*, expounder of sacred mysteries, from G. φαίνειν, to reveal, as in *sycophant.*

higgle. Thinned form of *haggle* (cf. *flip, flap*), representing a less noisy dispute. Hence *higgler*, itinerant dealer.

higgledy-piggledy. Earlier also *higly-pigly.* Prob. reduplicated jingle on *pig*, with ref. to huddling together. To *pig* (*in*) occurs in this sense in 17 cent.

They ly higgledy piggledy, master, mistress, children, men and maid-servants alltogether (*NED.* 1674).

high. AS. *hēah*. Com. Teut.; cf. Du. *hoog*, Ger. *hoch*, ON. *hār*, Goth. *hauhs*; cogn. with Ger. *hügel*, hill, and northern dial. *how.* Fig. senses as in F. *haut*, L. *altus.* Latest application as intens. perh. is *high tea.* *High and dry* is naut. *High and mighty* was orig. epithet of dignity; cf. *highness*, and Du. *Hoogenmoogendheiden*, "High Mightinesses," offic. title of States-General. *Highbrow*, "intellectual," is US. (cf. *supercilious*). *High Churchman*, adopted in mod. sense by Newman and Pusey, was in 17 cent. equivalent to Tory, High-flier. For *high-flown, -falutin'* see below. A *high-low* (boot) is a compromise between a high boot and a low shoe. *High road* is a late formation on *high street, highway*, both AS. compds. With *king's highway* cf. F. *chemin royal.* *High-strung* is orig. from music. *High-toned*, of lofty principle, etc. (now US.), is used by Scott. With *high-handed* cf. F. *haut à la main*, "proud, stately, surly, sullen, stubborne, a striker, like enough to lay about him" (Cotg.).

high-falutin' [*US.*]. Fantastic variation on *high-flown* (? *floating*). See examples in Thornton, app. often quite serious, of which quot. 1 is hardly a caricature. Is this type of oratory due to Red Indian influence? But, as quot. 2 shows, we can do a little in the same line in this country.

He is a true-born child of this free hemisphere! Verdant as the mountains of our country; bright and flowing as our mineral licks; unspiled by withering conventionalities as air our broad and boundless perearers! Rough he may be. So air our barrs. Wild he may be. So air our buffalers. But he is a child of natur' and a child of freedom; and his boastful answer to the despot and the tyrant is that his bright home is in the settin' sun (*Chuzzlewit*, ch. xxxiv.).

They recognized it wasn't frothy turgid rhetoric which has been served up to them for years, it was the dynamite of facts booming like a minute gun awakening the dormant mental splendours of those imaginative industrious sons of toil, revealing to them the sophistical cogwheels of political vote-catching chicanery (*Hull Daily News*, 1919).

high-flown. Associated in sense with *high-flying* (cf. *outspoken* for *out-speaking*), but really from *flown*, swollen, tumid, p.p. of *flow* (q.v.). Cf. synon. Ger. *geschwülstig*, swollen, earlier also *schwülstig*, from *schwellen*, to swell. Formerly used also for drunk (see quot. from Milton s.v. *flow*).

The young gentleman is come in, Madam, as you foresaw very high flowne, but not so drunke as to forget your promise (Brome, *Mad Couple*, iii. 2).

eine schwülstige rede oder schreib-art: a high strain; a bombast; a tumid, high, high-flown, high-strained, bombastick, swelling, swoln or swollen, speech or stile (Ludw.).

hight [*archaic*]. Only as p.p., named, called. Represents the past tense of passive (or middle) voice of AS. *hātan*, to command, and is the only Teut. example of that voice. Com. Teut.; cf. Du. *heeten*, to bid, be named, Ger. *heissen*, ON. *heita*, Goth. *haitan.* It is used as a facetious archaism by Shaks.

This grisly beast, which lion hight by name (*Dream*, v. 140).

highty-tighty. See *hoity-toity.*

hilarity. F. *hilarité*, L. *hilaritas*, from *hilaris*, cheerful, G. ἱλαρός.

Hilary. Session of High Court; term at Oxford and Dublin. From *St Hilary*, Hilarius, bishop of Poitiers (†367), whose day is Jan. 13.

hill. AS. *hyll*, with cognates in LG. & obs. Du.; ult. cogn. with L. *collis*, hill, *celsus*, high. *Hill-top*, describing a pretentious type of novel, is a neol.

hillo. See *hallo.*

hilt. AS. *hilt*; cf. obs. Du. *helt*, OHG. *helza*, ON. *hjalt*; also OF. *helte, heute*, from Teut. Origin unknown. *Up to the hilt* suggests a home thrust.

him. AS. *him*, dat. sing. of *hē* and *hit*, replacing in ME. acc. *hine*, which survives in southern dial., e.g. *have you seed un?* Cf. Ger. *ihn* (acc.), *ihm* (dat.). Hence *himself*, often in ME. *his self, self* being taken as noun; cf. *myself*, etc., and *his own self*.

hind¹. Female deer, fem. of *hart*. AS. *hind*. Com. Teut.; cf. Du. Ger. *hinde*, ON. *hind*. Origin unknown. Perh. orig. the hornless, as opposed to *hart* (q.v.).

hind² [*archaic & dial.*]. Foreman or bailiff of a farm. ME. *hine*, peasant, AS. *hīna*, gen. pl., as in *hīna fæder*, paterfamilias; cogn. with *hide²* (q.v.), orig. sense being member of household. The *-d* is excrescent, as in *sound¹*, *hine* being still in dial. use. Quot. 2 shows confusion between this very respectable word and *hind¹*. App. it was not known in the speaker's country, though it is in common use as far apart as Scotland and Cornwall.

A certain swain or hyne-boy [valet de labourage] (Florio's *Montaigne*, ii. 2).

Something which dropped from the learned and right honourable Lord Advocate last night somewhat grieved me. When he was speaking of the labourers of Scotland I think he called them "hinds."...I think honourable gentlemen on the other side of the House would feel very much annoyed if we were to call them aristocratic "goats" (Joseph Arch, Jan. 26, 1886).

hind³. As in *hindleg, behind*. Earlier *hinder*, as in *hindermost* and dial. *hinder-end*. AS. *hinder*; cf. Ger. *hinter*, as in *hinterbein*, hindleg, *hinterland*. *Hindmost* is after *foremost* (q.v.).

hinder. AS. *hindrian*, to keep back, from above; cf. Ger. *hindern*.

Hindi [*ling.*]. Urdu *hindī*, from Pers. *hind*, India, Sanskrit *sindhu*, river, hence region of Indus and Sindh. Used of a vernacular Aryan lang. of northern India, akin to Sanskrit, and, in this Dict., of such vernaculars in gen. Cf. *Hindu*, Urdu *hindū*, from Pers. *Hindustani*, used for Urdu, from *Hindustān* (*stān*, country, as in *Afghanistan*, etc.), is best avoided as a ling. term owing to possible confusion with *Hindi*. See *Urdu*.

hinge. ME. *heng*, not found in AS., but clearly cogn. with *hang*; cf. F. *penture*, "the hindge of a doore" (Cotg.), from

pendre, to hang. For fig. senses cf. *cardinal*. See also *hook*.

hinny¹. Offspring of stallion and she-ass. L. *hinnus*; cf. G. ἵννος, γίννος.

hinny². To neigh, whinny. ME. *henny*, F. *hennir*, L. *hinnire*.

hinny³ [*Sc. & north.*]. Darling. See *honey*.

hint. First in Shaks., in sense of opportunity, chance, as in Othello's great speech (i. 3). From obs. *hent*, to grasp, AS. *hentan*, to pursue, ? cogn. with *hunt*, ? or with *hand*. With *to take a hint* cf. earlier *to catch hold of a handle* (Sir T. More).

hinterland. Ger., see *hind* and *land*. Due to Ger. colonial expansion.

The very modern theory of the Hinterland (*Daily News*, 1891).

hip¹. Of body. AS. *hype*; cf. Du. *heup*, Ger. *hüfte* (OHG. *huf*), Goth. *hups*. Hence also arch. *hip*. *On the hip* is from wrestling ? or football. *Hip and thigh* (Bibl.) seems to be a Hebraism.

With their knees to catch him upon the hip [at football] (Stubbes, *Anat. of Abuses*).

hip². Of wild rose. ME. *hepe*, AS. *hēope*; cf. OHG. *hiufo*, thorn-bush.

hip³. As in *hip-hip-hurrah*. Earlier also *hep*. Cf. Ger. *hepp*, cry to animals, signal for attack on Jews.

hipped. Depressed. From archaic *hip, hyp* (c. 1700), usu. pl., short for *hypochondria*; cf. *mob, cit*, etc. Cf. Du. *hiep*, melancholy, for *hypochonder*. Perh. influenced by obs. *hip*, to dislocate the hip, or by wrestling *hip*, to throw (see *hip¹*).

escuisser: to hip; to put the hip, or thigh out of joynt (Cotg.).

hippocampus. Fish. G., from ἵππος, horse (cogn. with L. *equus*), and κάμπος, sea-monster.

hippocras [*archaic*]. Spiced wine. ME. *ypocras*, OF., from *Hippocrates*, G. physician (5 cent. B.C.), originator of a filter called Hippocrates' sleeve (bag). The form prob. aims at *hypocras*, as though submixture (see *crasis*).

hippocrene. L., G., fountain on Helicon, from ἵππου κρήνη, fountain of the horse, because made by hoof of Pegasus. See Keats, *Ode to Nightingale*.

hippodrome. F., L., G. ἱππόδρομος, racecourse for chariots, from δρόμος, race. For *hippogryph*, fabulous monster, It. *ippogrifo* (Ariosto), see *griffin¹*.

hippopotamus. Late L., Late G. ἱπποπόταμος,

from πόταμος, river (cf. *Mesopotamia*).
Also called *river-horse* (Longfellow, *Slave's Dream*), and in Ger. *Nilpferd*, Nile horse. Has replaced ME. *ypotame*, etc., from OF.

hircine. Of the goat, L. *hircus*.

hire. AS. *hȳr*, hire, wages, with LG. cognates; cf. Du. *huur*. Not known in HG., ON., or Goth. Ger. *heuer* is from LG. *Hireling* is a late formation (16 cent.), not from AS. *hȳrling*, servant. In *John*, x. 12, Tynd. and Coverd. have *hired servant*.

hirsute. L. *hirsutus*, shaggy, from *hirtus*, in same sense; ? cogn. with *horrid*, ? or with *hircus*, goat.

his. AS. genitive of *hē* and *hit*; cf. OHG. *is*, *es*, genitive of *er*, he, now replaced by *sein*, genitive of reflex. pron. In ref. to neuters *his* is replaced by *its* from c. 1600, but is still usual in *AV*. and Shaks. With ME. *hisen* cf. *hern* (see *her*[2]).

He that takes what isn't hisen,
When he's caught must go to prison.

Hispanic. Of Spain, L. *Hispania*.

hispid [*biol.*]. Bristling. L. *hispidus*. See *hideous*.

hiss. Imit.; cf. Ger. *zischen*, F. *siffler*, to hiss, whistle, L. *sibilare*. Wyc. uses it (var. *whistle*) in both mod. senses.

Pour qui sont ces serpents qui sifflent sur vos têtes?
(Racine, *Andromaque*, v. 5).

hist. Natural ejaculation, better represented by *'st*; cf. *whisht*. Milton uses it as verb, to summon silently.

And the mute silence hist along (*Penseroso*, 55).

histology. Science of organic tissues. From G. ἱστός, web, tissue.

history. Learned form of *story*[1] (q.v.), L. *historia*, G. ἱστορία, from ἵστωρ, ἱστορ-, wise, learned, from root of εἰδέναι, to know. In ME. not differentiated in sense from earlier *story*.

histrionic. From L. *histrio-n-*, actor, of Etruscan origin.

hit. ON. *hitta*, to hit upon, meet with, as in mod. to *hit on*; later, to reach with a blow, etc.; ? cogn. with Goth. *hinthan*, to catch. Has assumed one sense of AS. *slēan* (see *slay*), but there are many traces of orig. sense, e.g. to *make a hit*, to *hit it* (now to *hit it off*), agree, with suggestion of common aim. To *hit the mark, the nail on the head*, are both from archery, the *nail*, earlier *pin*, marking the centre of target. For double sense cf. Ger. *treffen*, to meet, to hit (the mark).

hitch. To raise with a jerk, esp. trousers. First in late ME., which has also *hatch*, *hotch*, in same sense. If the last is the orig., it is F. *hocher* (12 cent.), in same sense (see *hodge-podge*), used esp. in *hocher la tête*. For vowel change cf. *bilk*, *bitch*[2]. Sense of fastening (esp. US.) is orig. naut. (Capt. John Smith). Hence also *hitch*, obstruction, orig. made by quick jerk of rope round object; cf. *clove-hitch* for a special knot (see *cleave*[1]). To *hitch one's waggon to a star* is from Emerson.

hithe, hythe [*hist.*]. AS. *hȳth*, landing-place. Very common in place-names (*Hythe*, *Rotherhithe*, *Lambeth*, *Erith*, etc.).

hither. AS. *hider*, from demonstr. root of *he*, with ending as in cogn. L. *ci-tra*. Cf. *here*, *thither*.

hive. AS. *hȳf*; ? cogn. with ON. *hūfr*, hull of ship, and ult. with L. *cupa*, tub.

ho. Natural exclamation; cf. *ha, hi, oh*, etc. Esp. naut., e.g. *heave ho! westward ho!*

hoar. AS. *hār*, white with age, venerable; cf. Ger. *hehr* (see *Herr*), ON. *hárr*, and cogn. Goth. *hais*, torch. Now chiefly poet. and in *hoarfrost*.

hoard. AS. *hord*, treasure. Com. Teut.; cf. OSax. *hord*, Ger. *hort* (poet.), ON. *hodd*, Goth. *huzd*. Formerly used in connection with treasure, money, etc. (hence surname *Horder*, treasurer); now (1916) of sugar, matches, etc.

hoarding. From archaic *hoard*, fence, barrier, archaic F. *hourd*, palisade, from LG. form of OHG. *hurt* (*hürde*), hurdle (q.v.). Cf. sense-development of *grill* (q.v.).

hoarhound. See *horehound*.

hoarse. ME. *hors*, *hoos*, etc., AS. *hās*. Com. Teut.; cf. obs. Du. *heersch*, *heesch*, Ger. *heiser* (OHG. *heis*), ON. *háss*. The *-r-* is unexplained.

hoos: raucus (*Prompt. Parv.*).

hoax. Contr. (c. 1800) of *hocus* (q.v.).

hob[1]. Clown, goblin. Pet-name of *Robert*. With *hobgoblin* cf. *Robin Goodfellow*. *Hick* is used for Richard II in *Richard the Redeless*, as *Hob* is for Robert Bruce in a song, temp. Ed. I. See also *Hodge*. *Robin Goodfellow* is also called in dial. *Dobby* and *Master Dobbs*, likewise from *Robert*.

From elves, hobs and fairies,
That trouble our dairies (Beaumont and Fletcher).

hob[2]. Side of fire-place. Earlier *hub* (q.v.). Also in various dial. senses. Hence *hobnail*, associated also with *hob*[1].

Hobbesian. Of *Thomas Hobbes*, philosopher (†1679).

hobble. App. cogn. with *hop*[1]; cf. Du. *hobbeln*, LG. *hoppeln*. In sense of shackle for horse, whence *hobble-skirt*, it was formerly *hopple*.

hobbledehoy. Also *hober-*, *hobbard-*, etc. Has been associated with *hobble*, but first element is prob. *hob*[1], in sense of clown. Cf. obs. *hobbinoll*, rustic (Spenser), *hoball*, clown (*Ralph Royster-Doyster*), *hobbidi-dance* (see *flibberdegibbet*). Cf. Ger. *flegel-jahre*, hobbledehoy-hood, from *flegel*, clown (q.v.). It is impossible to say what the ending may have been, the tendency of numerous early forms being to give it a F. appearance, ? as though *hobet de haie*, hedge hawk, with which cf. *mwer* (mewer) *de haye*, worthless hawk (*Paston Let.* iii. 68). F. *hobereau*, hobby hawk (see *hobby*[2]), hawbuck (see *haw*[1]), has also been suggested as etymon, and the two words may at any rate have been associated. *Hobble-* appears in earliest record (v.i.), but a word of this type may exist for centuries before being written down.

Theyr hobledehoye tyme...the yeres that one is neyther a man nor a boye (Palsg. 1540).

The first seven yeeres bring up as a childe,
The next to learning, for waxing too wilde,
The next keepe under sir hobbard de hoy,
The next a man, no longer a boy (Tusser).

hobby[1]. Orig. small horse. ME. & OF. *hobin*, *hobi*, from *hob*[1] (q.v.); cf. *dobbin* (q.v.). Hence obs. *hobler*, light horseman, and *hobby-horse*, small horse, later used of sham horse in morris-dances, etc., toy-horse, favourite amusement. With final sense cf. F. *dada*, gee-gee, also used of a favourite *hobby*, and Ger. *steckenpferd*, stick-horse. So also, to *ride a hobby to death*.

ubino: a hobbie horse, such as Ireland breedeth (Flor.).

ein knäblein so auf einem stecken reitet: a little boy riding on his hobby-horse (Ludw.).

hobby[2] [*archaic*]. Inferior hawk. OF. *hobet*, whence F. *hobereau*. See *hobbledehoy*. Origin unknown, perh. as *hob*[1].

hobgoblin. See *hob*[1].

Robin Goodfellow and Hob goblin
(Scot, *Discovery of Witches*, 1584).

hobnail. See *hob*[2].

hob-nob. Orig. to drink together clinking glasses. Partly associated with earlier *hab-nab*, hit or miss, ult. from AS. *habban*, to have, *nabban*, not to have. But in spec.

sense of intimacy perh. partly a redupl. of familiar name *Hob* (see *hob*[1]).

hobo. Tramp. US., late 19 cent. Origin unknown.

Masters of casual wards are reporting a plentiful crop of hoboes (*Daily Chron.* Jan. 13, 1920).

Hobson's choice. Recorded for 1660 and trad. explained as from *Thomas Hobson*, the Camb. carrier and livery-stable keeper, immortalized by Milton, who refused to let out his horses exc. in strict rotation. But quot. below, written in Japan thirteen years before Hobson's death, makes this very doubtful.

We are put to Hodgson's choise to take such privilesge as they will geve us, or else goe without
(Richard Cocks, 1617).

hock[1]. Of leg. Southern by-form of *hough* (q.v.).

hock[2]. Wine. Short for Ger. *hochheimer*, from *Hochheim*, on the Main. Extended in E. to German white wines in gen. *Hock-amore* is also found.

hock[3]. As in *hockday* (12 cent.), *hock-Tuesday*, second Tuesday after Easter Sunday. Hence later *hock-Monday*, *hocktide*. Orig. disyllabic (cf. surname *Hockaday*, *Hocker-day*). Lambarde's derivation from AS. *hōcor*, derision, deserves consideration, as MHG. *goychkentag*, in same sense, may very well be from *gouchen*, to play the fool, from *gouch*, cuckoo (see *gowk*). Although earliest recorded sense is that of date, rent-day, this must have been fixed by some popular feast. The chief feature of the *hocktide* sports was horse-play, esp. the binding of men by women on Monday and of women by men on Tuesday, release being obtained by payment. The Christian, or heathen, origin of the practice, is as obscure as that of the April fool.

hockey. App. OF. *hoquet*, bent stick, shepherd's crook; cogn. with *hook*; cf. *bandy*[2]. Or it may be simply *hooky* (stick); cf. Sc. *cammock*, hockey stick, lit. bent. Not recorded till c. 1800 exc. in quot. below (from *NED.*), which also supplies an early example of *hurley* (q.v.).

The horlinge of the litill balle with hockie stickes or staves (*Galway Statutes*, 1527).

hocktide. See *hock*[3].

hocus. For *hocus-pocus*, conjuror. Sham L. of quack, perh. suggested by *hotch-pot* or *hotch-potch*; cf. obs. *hicius docius* (? *hicce est doctus*) in same sense. Ger. *taschenspieler* suggests possible connection with *poke*, *pouch.* But the fact that *hokuspokus-filiokus* is still used in Norw. & Sw. suggests that there may be something in the old theory of a blasphemous perversion of the sacramental blessing, *hoc est corpus* (*filii*). Hence *hocus*, to hoax (q.v.); later, to drug one's liquor for swindling purposes.

These jugglers hocus the vulgar and incautelous of the present age (*NED.* 1686).

taschen-spieler: a juggler, a hocus-pocus (Ludw.).

hod. Earlier (13 cent.) *hot*, F. *hotte*, "a scuttle, dosser, basket, to carry on the back" (Cotg.), of Teut. origin; cf. obs. Du. *hodde*, Ger. *hotte*, "a vintager's dorser made of wood" (Ludw.).

hodden grey. Used by Ramsay, for rime, instead of *grey hodden* (cf. *hawthorn green*, etc.), hence by Burns, Scott, and later poets. Origin of *hodden*, cloth made by using one black fleece with twelve white, is doubtful; ? northern p.p. of to *hold*, thus wool "holding" natural hue.

But Meg, poor Meg! maun wi' the shepherds stay,
An' tak' what God will send in hodden gray
(*Gentle Sheph.* v. 2).

Hodge. Yokel. Pet-form of *Roger* (cf. *hob*[1]). See Chauc. A. 4336, 4345, where the Cook is called *Hogge* and *Roger.*

Piano-tuners of doubtful fitness will prove poor substitutes for Hodge (*Obs.* Jan. 21, 1917).

hodge-podge. Earlier *hotch-potch*, which is altered from earlier *hotchpot*, F. *hochepot*, from *hocher*, to shake. Earliest E. sense (c. 1300) is fig., of lumping property before division (? by shaking up names in a pot). Mod. *hot-pot* is partly suggested by it. For F. *hocher* cf. Du. *hutsen, hotsen,* MHG. *hutzen* (see *hustle*).

hodometer, odometer. Pedometer. From G. ὁδός, way. Cf. 18 cent. F. *odomètre.*

hoe. F. *houe,* OHG. *houwā* (*haue*); cogn. with *hew. A hard row to hoe* is US.

hog. AS. *hogg.* In E. a castrated swine reared for slaughter, in Sc. a sheep up to first shearing, also used in dial. of other yearling animals. Perh. cogn. with *hag*, to cut (see *hag*[2]); cf. *gelding*, and Ger. *hammel*, "a ram that is gelded" (Ludw.), from OHG. *hamalōn*, to mutilate. Hence to *hog* a horse's mane, make it bristle. The *whole hog* is perh. connected with the story told by Cowper (v.i.), which is much older than first occurrence of to *go the whole hog*; we may compare Lamb's essay on Roast Pig.

Thus says the prophet of the Turk,
"Good Mussulman, abstain from pork;
There is a part in every swine
No friend or follower of mine
May taste."...
But for one piece they thought it hard
From the whole hog to be debarred....
(*Love of the World reproved,* or, *Hypocrisy detected*).

hogmanay [*Sc. & north.*]. New Year's Eve, etc. Earlier (17 cent.) *hogmynae, hagmane.* Corresponds in sense with OF. *aguillanneuf,* of unknown origin, with innumerable vars. and existing dial. forms, due to folk-etym., such as *hoguinané, hoc in anno,* etc., none of which will explain *hogmanay.*

au-guy-l'an-neuf [lit. to the mistletoe the new year]: the voice of countrey people begging small presents, or new-yeares-gifts, in Christmas; an ancient tearme of rejoicing, derived from the Druides....
(Cotg.).

hogshead. From *hog's head* (14 cent.), a fantastic name which can only be conjecturally explained. Cf. LG. *bullenkop*, a beer measure, lit. bull's head. Hence Du. *okshoofd* (earlier *hockshoot*), Ger. *oxhoft* (from LG.), Sw. *oxhufvud,* Dan. *oxehoved,* altered on *ox.*

hoicks. Var. of *yoicks.*

hoiden. See *hoyden.*

hoist. For *hoise,* earlier (15 cent.) *hysse.* A naut. word found in most Europ. langs.; cf. F. *hisser,* It. *issare,* Sp. *izar,* Norw. Sw. *hissa,* Ger. *hissen* (from LG.), Du. *hijschen,* etc. Our word is from Du., but ult. source is unknown, prob. LG.

They...loosed the rudder bands, and hoised up the mainsail (*Acts,* xxvii. 40).

hoity-toity. Vars. *highty-tighty, heighty-teighty,* and the earliest record, *upon the hoyty-toyty* (1668), suggest the *high ropes* and *tight rope,* or simply a jingle on *high.*

hokey-pokey. For *hocus-pocus.* The suggestion that *hokey-pokey,* ice-cream, is It. *o che poco!* O how little! is ingenious.

hold[1]. AS. *healdan.* Com. Teut.; cf. Du. *houden,* Ger. *halten,* ON. *halda,* Goth. *haldan.* Old p.p. *holden* still in some leg. formulae. Orig. sense prob. to guard cattle. Fig. senses as those of F. *tenir,* which has replaced it in many compds. (*-tain*); cf. also *-hold, holding,* in ref. to property, with *tenancy, tenure.* To *hold with* was orig. to side with. To *hold water* (fig.) is after *Jer.* ii. 13; to *hold forth* is after *Philip.* ii. 16, where orig. sense is to hold out, proffer. *Hold hard* was orig. a hunting phrase. With US. to *hold up,* from order to victims to hold up hands, cf. Austral. to *stick up*. From verb comes noun *hold*, prison, fortress, etc., but not interior of ship (v.i.).

hold² [*naut.*]. For earlier *hol, hole* (q.v.); cf. Du. *hol*, from which E. sense may be borrowed. Howell (*Tetragl.*) has *howl*. For converse change cf. to *buttonhole*.

hole of a schyppe: carina (*Prompt. Parv.*).

hole. AS. *hol*, orig. adj., hollow. Com. Teut.; cf. Du. *hol*, Ger. *hohl*, ON. *hol*; Goth. *hulundi*, cave. Also represents inflected forms of AS. *holh*, a hollow. To *pick holes in* was early to *find holes*, i.e. flaws. The relation between the *peg* and the *hole* appears in obs. to *take a hole lower* (16 cent.) and mod. *tophole*, perh. from some method of scoring; but see *peg, pin*. *Hole-and-corner* is mod., but Coverd. has *not in corners and holes* (*Vulg.* in fossis), *but openly* (*Jer.* ii. 34). The *better 'ole* of Bairnsfather's sketch seems likely to become a permanent addition to the lang.

If I find a hole in his coat, I will tell him my mind (*Hen. V*, iii. 6).

holiday. AS. *hāligdæg*, holy day, with differentiation of sound and meaning since 16 cent. See *hallow, holy, hollyhock*.

holla. F. *holà*; cf. *hi there, houp-là*, and see *hallo*.

Holland. Prob. ODu. *holt lant*, wood land, and not hollow land. Hence *holland* (*cloth*), *hollands* (*gin*), the latter representing Du. adj. *hollandsch* (cf. *Scots*).

hollo, holloa. See *hallo*. Hence verb *hollo(w)*, to shout.

hollow¹. Orig. noun. AS. *holh*. By association with *hol*, adj. and noun (see *hole*), it became an adj. in ME. For to *beat hollow*, etc., earliest to *carry it hollow* (cf. *hollow victory*), Skinner suggests corrupt. of *wholly*. That such corrupt. is possible appears from the names *Hollowbread, Hollowman*, in which first element was orig. *hali, holy*.

hollow². Verb. See *hollo*.

holly. Earlier *hollin* (as in names *Hollins, Hollingshead*, etc.), AS. *holegn*; cogn. with Du. Ger. *hulst* (OHG. *huls*), whence F. *houx*, and prob. with Welsh *celyn*, Ir. *cuillean*, Gael. *cuilionn*. See also *holm-oak*.

hollyhock. For *holy hock*, AS. *hocc*, mallow; cf. synon. Welsh *hocys bendigaid*, which is a mixture of E. & L. (*benedicta*). Cf. *herb bennet, samphire*, etc.

holm [*geog.*]. Small island, esp. in river. Very common in place-names. ON. *holmr*, as in *Isle of Axholme*; cf. LG. *holm*; cogn. with L. *culmen*, E. *hill*. Hence *holmgang*, in mod. romantic novels, of duel on an islet.

holm-oak. Evergreen oak. From dial. *holm*, holly, ME. *hollin*; see *holly*.

Against the feast of Christmas every man's house, as also the parish churches, were decked with holm, ivy, bays (Stow, *Survey of London*, 1603).

holocaust. F. *holocauste* (12 cent.), Late L., G., from ὅλος, whole, καυστός, burnt, from καίειν. An early Bible word. Cf. *holograph*, wholly written; *holophotal*, from φῶς, φωτ-, light.

holothurian. Sea-slug. From L. *holothuria* (Pliny), pl. of G. ὁλοθούριον, kind of zoophyte.

holster. Du. *holster*, "a holster for a pistoll" (Hexham); cf. Sw. *hölster*, Dan. *hylster*; app. cogn. with ON. *hulstr*, case, sheath, AS. *heolstor*, hiding-place. But the sudden appearance in 17 cent. of E. & Du. *holster* in this spec. sense points to association with Ger. *holfter*, "a holster" (Ludw.), from OHG. *huluft*, case, sheath. The etym. relation of the two is obscure. For a similar case cf. Du. *halfter, halster*, halter.

holt [*archaic*]. Wood. Very common in place-names. AS. *holt*. Com. Teut.; cf. Du. *hout*, Ger. *holz*, ON. *holt*; cogn. with G. κλάδος, twig, Gael. *coille*, wood.

holus-bolus. At a gulp. Facet. "latinization" of the *whole bolus*, or as though G. ὅλος βῶλος.

holy. AS. *hālig*, from *hāl*, whole. Com. Teut.; cf. Du. Ger. *heilig*, ON. *heilagr*, Goth. *hailag* (on inscription only; Ulfila has *weihs*). Adopted at conversion to render L. *sacer, sanctus*. *Holy of holies* is a Hebraism, preserved by LXX. and *Vulg.* Cf. *hallow*.

holystone [*naut.*]. Soft sandstone for scrubbing decks. ? For *holey* or *hollow*.

hom. Sacred palm of ancient Persians. Pers. *hōm*, Sanskrit *sōma*.

homage. OF. (*hommage*), from *homme* (OF. *ome, home*), mai., L. *homo, homin-*. Cf. ME. *manred*, homage, AS. *mann-rǣden* (see *hatred*).

home. AS. *hām*. Com. Teut.; cf. Du. *heem*, Ger. *heim*, ON. *heimr*, Goth. *hāims*. In to *go home* we have acc. of direction (cf. L. *domum*), and the dat. was earlier used as locative (cf. L. *domi*). The regular omission of the art., e.g. *there is no place like home, nearer home*, etc., is partly due to this. With to *bring a charge home* cf. *home thrust*. *Home Rule*, for earlier *Repeal*, is first recorded for 1860. For *homestead* see *stead*. *Homely*, plain, ugly (US.), preserves a sense once common in E. For fig. sense of *homespun* cf. quot. 2. *Homesickness* renders Ger. *heimweh*, a Swiss compd., expressing the longing of the mountaineer for his native hills, and introduced into other langs. by Swiss mercenaries in 17 cent.

It is for homely features to keep home
(*Comus*, 748).

Henceforth my wooing mind shall be express'd
In russet yeas and honest kersey noes
(*Love's Lab. Lost*, v. 2).

homer. Measure (*Is.* v. 10). Heb. *khōmer*, heap.

Homeric. Laughter, combat, as of Homer's heroes.

The battle is of a truly Homeric order
(*Pall Mall Gaz.* April 28, 1917).

homicide. F., L. *homicida*, slayer, *homicidium*, slaying, from *caedere*. Cf. *manslaughter*.

homily. F. *homélie* (OF. & ME. *omelie*), Church L. *homilia*, G. ὁμιλία, converse, from ὅμιλος, crowd, from ὁμοῦ, together, ἴλη, crowd. Hence *homilectic*.

hominy. Shortened from Algonkin (Virginia) *rockahomonie*, of which first element means maize.

homoeopathy. Coined (c. 1800) by Hahnemann, Ger. physician, from G. ὅμοιος, of the same kind, πάθος, suffering. Cf. *allopathy*.

homogeneous. For earlier *homogene*, G. ὁμογενής, of the same kind, from ὁμός and γένος. See *same*. Cf. *homologous*, from λόγος, ratio; *homonym*, from ὄνομα, name; *homophone*, from φωνή, sound.

homoiousian, homoousian [*theol.*]. Holding Christ to be of like (ὅμοιος) essence, or same (ὁμός) essence (οὐσία) as the Father.

homunculus. L., dim. of *homo*, man.

hone. Whetstone. AS. *hān*, stone, rock; cf. ON. *hein*, whence Norw. *hein*, whetstone.

honest. OF. (*h*)*oneste* (*honnête*), L. *honestus*, cogn. with *honos*, honour. In ME. as in F., with wider sense of honourable; cf. to *make an honest woman of*. For decline in sense cf. *respectable*.

The membris that ben unhonest han more honestè
(Wyc. 1 *Cor.* xii. 23).

honey. AS. *hunig*; cf. Du. Ger. *honig*, ON. *hunang*. Goth. has *milith*, for which see *mildew, mealy-mouthed*. For Sc. *hinny, hinnie*, as term of endearment, cf. *mither, brither*. *Honeycomb* is an AS. compd., though the resemblance to a comb is not obvious. *Honeydew* was formerly synon. with *mildew* (q.v.). With *honeymoon*, allusive to waning of affection, cf. F. *lune de miel*, Ger. *flitterwochen* (pl.), from *flitter*, tinsel. *Honeysuckle*, earlier *honeysuck*, AS. *hunigsūge*, privet, is a misnomer, as the flower is useless to the bee.

Mi hony, mi hert al hol thou me makest
(*NED.* c. 1350).

honk. Imit. of cry of wild goose or hoot of motor-car.

honorarium. Late L., gift made on appointment to post of honour. Cf. *honorary*, conferring honour without payment; *honorific*, making honour, L. *honorificus*.

honour. OF. (*h*)*onour* (*honneur*), L. *honos, honor-*; cf. It. *onore*, Sp. *honor*. For sense of courtesy, as in to *do the honours, pay the last honours*, etc., cf. sense-development of *curtsy*. *Honour bright* is Anglo-Ir. *Honourable* as "courtesy" title sometimes leads to a bull (v.i.).

The honourable gentleman [Joseph Chamberlain] is a damned liar
(J. Dillon, M.P., in H. of C., c. 1900).

honved. Hung. landwehr; orig. national army of 1848, recognized by constitution of 1868 as *landwehr*, from which it was prob. translated. Hung. *hon*, native land, *ved*, defence.

hood. AS. *hōd*; cf. Du. *hoed*, Ger. *hut*, hat, ON. *höttr*; cogn. with *hat* and ult. with *heed*. Hence *hoodman-blind*, blind man's buff (*Haml.* iii. 4). With *hoodwink* cf. *blinkers*.

-hood. AS. *hād*, condition, orig. person; cogn. with Ger. -*heit*, Goth. *haidus*, manner; cf. -*head*.

hoodlum [*US.*]. San Francisco hooligan (c. 1870). ? Perverted back-spelling (cf. *slop*[3]) of *Muldoon*. Cf. *hooligan, larrikin*.

hoodoo [*US.*]. Opposite of mascot. Said to be for *voodoo* (q.v.), and, according to Sir R. Burton, an Afr. word from Dahomey.

They [the German troops] now look on him [the Kaiser] as their "hoodoo"
(*Sund. Ev. Telegr.* May 26, 1918).

hoof. AS. *hōf*. Com. Teut.; cf. Du. *hoef*, Ger. *huf*, ON. *hōfr*. To *pad the hoof*, for earlier to *beat the hoof*, is perh. altered by association with *pad* in *footpad*. Cf. F. *battre la semelle* (foot-sole), and our policeman's *beat*.

hoof it, or beat it on the hoof: to walk on foot
                         (*Dict. Cant. Crew*).

hook. AS. *hōc*; cf. Du. *hoek*; cogn. with Ger. *haken*, ON. *haki*. To *take* (earlier *sling*) *one's hook* is naut. slang for weighing anchor (the *mudhook*). With *off the hooks* (now used of death) cf. *unhinged* (v.i.). *By hook or crook* (ME. *with hook or with crook*) prob. alludes to instruments used by professional thieves (v.i.). Cf. description of Panurge's equipment (Rabelais, ii. 16).

The hokes [*Vulg.* cardines] of yᵉ dores
                    (Coverd. 1 *Kings*, vii. 50).

Touchant le Jargon [poems in thieves' slang attributed to Villon], je le laisse à corriger et exposer aux successeurs de Villon en l'art de la pinse et du crocq
              (Marot, *Pref. to Villon's Works*, 1532).

To the Duke of Albemarle, whom I found mightily off the hooks (Pepys, May 26, 1664).

hookah. Arab. *huqqah*, vessel (through which the smoke is drawn).

hooker [*naut.*]. Earlier also *howker*, *hawker*. Du. *hoeker*, ? from *hoek*, hook, or connected with *hoeker*, huckster, because a small trading ship, according to Faesch much used on canals. *Hoekboot* is recorded 1262.

hoeck-boot: navis piscatoria, ab hamis dicta (Kil.).

hoecker-schip: a dogger-boat (Hexham).

hooligan. From lively Ir. family of that name in the Borough. This information was given to the author (c. 1896) by a house-surgeon at Guy's who spent some of his time in patching up the results. Hence Russ. *khuligan'* (pl.).

hoop¹. Ring. AS. *hōp*; cf. Du. *hoep*.

hoop². To whoop. F. *houper* (12 cent.), from cry *houp*, to dogs or horses, as in *houp-là*. Hence *hooping-cough*. *Whoop* is a later spelling; cf. 17 cent. *whoot* for *hoot* (see quot. s.v. *reclaim*).

hoopoe. Bird. Earlier *hoop*, *hoopoop*, F. *huppe*, L. *upupa*, from cry.

hoot. From 12 cent. Prob. imit.; cf. *hoop²*, *toot*, *hue²*, Sc. *hoots*, interj. of disapproval.

hop¹. Verb. AS. *hoppian*; cf. Du. *hoppen*, Ger. *hopfen* (usu. *hüpfen*), ON. *hoppa*. In ME. to dance, without any ludicrous suggestion. To *hop the twig* suggests the departing bird. *On the hop*, at a disadvantage, appears to be for *on the hip¹* (q.v.).

With *Hop o' my thumb*, earlier *hoppe upon my thombe* (Palsg.), cf. *Tom Thumb*.

Why hop ye so, ye high hills? (*Ps.* lxviii. 16, *PB.*).

fretillon: a little nimble dwarfe, or hop-on-my-thumb (Cotg.).

hop². Plant. Du. *hop*; cf. Ger. *hopfen*. Origin doubtful, but prob. cogn. with F. *houppe*, tuft, tassel. F. *houblon*, hops, earlier *houbillon*, is of Teut. origin. Another group of names for the same plant is represented by AS. *hymele*, ON. *humall*, Late L. *humulus*, Magyar *komlo*, supposed to be of Finno-Ugrian origin. The cultivation of hops was introduced from Flanders in 16 cent., though the occurrence of the word in the *Prompt. Parv.* shows that they were known earlier as a commodity.

Warrant for cxl. li. for charges in bringing over certein hopsetters (*Privy Council Acts*, 1549–50).

Hops and turkies, carps and beer,
Came into England all in a year
           (Quoted in the *Compleat Angler*, ch. ix.
               from Baker's *Chronicle*, 1643).

hope¹. Verb. AS. *hopian*; cf. Du. *hopen*. App. a LG. word, which appears later in Scand. & HG. (*hoffen*). In ME. often merely to expect, as still in *hoping against hope*. *Young hopeful* has always been ironic.

Yit houp hings by ane hair
Houping aganes all houp
              (*Luvesang on Houp*, 16 cent.).

hope². See *forlorn*.

hoplite. Heavily armed soldier. G. ὁπλίτης, from ὅπλον, armour, etc. See *panoply*.

hopscotch. Earlier *Scotch hoppers* (17 cent.), *hop-score*, *hop-scot*. From the *scotch* (q.v.), scratch, incision, which has to be hopped.

horary. Of hours. MedL. *horarius*, from *hora*. Cf. F. *horaire*, time-table.

horde. Orig. applied to Tatars and other Asiatic nomads. Turki *orda*, *urdu*, camp, which reached Western Europe (16 cent.) via Russ. & Pol., the *h-* appearing first in the latter. In most Europ. langs. See *Urdu*.

horehound. For *hoarhound*, ME. *horehoune*, AS. *hārehūne*, *hūne* being a plant-name of unknown origin. For excrescent *-d* cf. *bound³*, *sound¹*. Named from white down on leaves.

horizon. F. (OF. & ME. *orizont*), Late L., G. ὁρίζων, ὁρίζοντ- (sc. κύκλος), bounding (circle), from ὅρος, boundary. In most Europ. langs.

horn. AS. *horn*. Com. Teut.; cf. Du. *hoorn*, Ger. *horn*, ON. *horn*, Goth. *haurn*; cogn. with L. *cornu*, G. κέρας, Welsh *corn*, etc. Connected with betrayed husband in most Europ. langs., perh. from practice of grafting spurs of capon on the bird's comb, where they became horns; cf. Byz. G. κερασφόρος, cuckold, lit. horn-bearer. Bibl. *horn of salvation, lift up the horn*, is a figure common to Semit. langs., app. taken from horned head-dress. Senses of mus. instrument, drinking-cup, appear in AS. With former cf. *hornpipe*, orig. the instrument to which the dance was performed. With to *draw in one's horns* (like a snail) cf. to *retire into one's shell*. For *hornbeam* see *beam*, and cf. Scand. tree-names in *ben-*, bone; for *hornblende* see *blende*. A *hornbook* is a child's alphabet-sheet, mounted on wood and covered by a thin sheet of transparent horn. For *horn of plenty* see *cornucopia*.

> He was tho glad his hornes in to shrinke
>   (Chauc. *Troil.* i. 300).

hornet. AS. *hyrnet*; cf. OSax. *hornobero*, lit. horn-bearer, Du. *horzel*, Ger. *hornisse*; app. all from *horn*, from shape of antennae; cf. Norw. Dan. *gjedehams*, hornet, lit. goat-wasp; also L. *crabro*, hornet, ult. cogn. with G. κέρας, horn.

hornito [*geog.*]. Volcanic mound (US.). Sp., dim. of *horno*, oven, L. *furnus*.

horologe. OF. (*horloge*), L., G. ὡρολόγιον, hour telling, from ὥρα, hour, time.

> The shadewe of lynes bi the whiche it hadde go doun in the oriloge of Acath (Wyc. *Is.* xxxviii. 8).

horoscope. F., L., G. ὡροσκόπος, nativity, time observer, from σκοπεῖν, to look (v.s.). Cf. *ascendant*.

horrible. F., L. *horribilis*, from *horrēre*, to bristle, shudder, whence also later *horrid*, L. *horridus*, bristling, and poet. *horrent*. *Horrify* is a late coinage (c. 1800). *Horror*, like *horrible*, comes via OF., and both are usu. without *h-* in ME.

> In a deseert loond, in place of orrour
>   (Wyc. *Deut.* xxxii. 10).

horripilation. Late L. *horripilatio-n-*, from *horripilare* (Apuleius), from *pilus*, hair (v.s.).

hors de combat. F., out of fight. Cf. *hors d'œuvre*, lit. outside the work, accessory (cf. *exergue*). *Hors* is supposed to be L. *foris*, outside, but the init. is hard to explain.

horse. AS. *hors*; cf. Du. *ros*, Ger. *ross* (OHG. *hros*), ON. *hross*. Goth. has *aihwa*, cogn. with L. *equus*, G. ἵππος, AS. *eoh*. See also *walrus*. For mech. applications cf. *easel*. The *high* (or *great*) *horse*, orig. distinguished from the palfrey, roadster, etc., is now fig. only, in E. as in other Europ. langs. The *White Horse* (Berks and elsewhere), mentioned 1171, is supposed to be the emblem of Hengist (see *henchman*) and Horsa. The *horse-chestnut* is said to have been used as food for horses; cf. Ger. *ross-kastanie* and Turk. *at kastan*, from *at*, horse. In *horse-laugh, horse-play*, the sense of *horse* seems to be disparaging; cf. *horse-radish*, and even US. *horse-sense*, which has a suggestion of crudeness. The *Horse-guards*, Whitehall, is alluded to as a place of meeting for principal officers in 1659. For *daughters of the horse-leech* see *Prov.* xxx. 15. *Horse-power* was introduced by Watt. The *horse-latitudes* are perh. adapted from Sp. *golfo de las yeguas*, "the gulph of mares, so the Spaniards call the great ocean, betwixt Spain and the Canary Islands" (Stevens), supposed to be from contrast with the *golfo de las damas* (of ladies), from Canaries to West Indies, usu. smooth and with favourable winds. Jocular *horse-marine* may have been suggested by obs. *horse-marine*, sea-horse (her.).

> Hors flesche is of suche a price here that my purce is schant able to bye one hors (*Paston Let.* iii. 376).

hortatory. Late L. *hortatorius*, from *hortari*, to exhort.

horticulture. Coined (17 cent.) from L. *hortus*, garden, after *agriculture*.

hosanna. Late L., G., Heb. *hōsha'nnā*, for *hōshi'āh-nnā*, save, pray! as in *Ps.* cxviii. 25. A Passover cry of the Jews.

hose. AS. *hosa*. Com. Teut.; cf. Du. *hoos*, stocking, Ger. *hose*, trousers, ON. *hosa*, stocking. Also adopted by Rom. langs. (e.g. *Curthose* is OF. *courte heuse*) for various leg-coverings. Now usu. of stockings, but breeches sense survives in *trunk-hose, doublet and hose*. *Hose*, flexible tube, is the same word.

> They tarryed ij days to bye necessaryes for the shype, as hoose for the pumpes
>   (*Voyage of the Barbara*, 1540).

hospice. F., L. *hospitium* (v.i.).

hospital. OF. (*hôpital*), learned form of *hostel*, MedL. *hospitale*, neut. of *hospitalis*, from *hospes, hospit-*, host, guest. In ME. usu. *spital, spittle*, as in *Spitalfields*. See also *hostel, hotel*. Current sense is the latest, older meaning of hospice, charitable foundation, surviving in *Greenwich Hospital, Christ's Hospital*, etc., and in hist. *Knight Hospitaller*, member of Order springing from hospice founded (c. 1048) at Jerusalem for entertainment of poor pilgrims, later *Knight of St John* (*Rhodes, Malta*).

The 23 of November [1552] the poore children of the City of London were taken into Christes Hospitall, late the house of the Grey Fryers
(Wriothesley, *Chron.*).

hospodar. Ottoman governor in Rumania. Rum. *hospodár*, from Russ. *gospod'*, lord, cogn. with L. *hospes* (see *host²*). Or the Rum. word may be direct from L.

host¹. Army. ME. also *ost*, OF. (*h*)*ost*, L. *hostis*, enemy (cogn. with *guest*), treated in Rom. langs. as collect.; cf. It. *oste*, Sp. *hueste*. Replaced AS. *here*, and was replaced, exc. poet. and fig., by *army*. In *Lord of Hosts* (Jehovah Sabaoth) the ref. is to the heavenly hosts of angels.

He was a host of debaters in himself (Burke).

host². Landlord. ME. also *ost*, OF. (*h*)*oste* (*hôte*), host or guest, L. *hospes, hospit-*, host, guest, ? for *hosti-potis, guest lord; cf. Sp. *huésped*, and see *hospodar*. Archaic *mine host* is chiefly after *mine host of the Garter* (*Merry Wives*).

compter sans son hoste: to reckon without his host; to make himself sure of things, which are wholly at the disposition of others (Cotg.).

host³. Consecrated bread. ME. also *oist, ost*, OF. (*h*)*oiste* (replaced by *hostie*), L. *hostia*, sacrificial victim, applied in Church L. to Christ.

hostage. ME. & OF. *ostage* (*otage*), VL. *hospitaticum, which supposes as sense-development the reception and guaranteeing of the stranger (*hospes*). This seems better than an attempt to connect *hostage* and its cognates with L. *obses*, hostage. Cf. Prov. *ostatge*, OIt. *ostaggio, statico*.

ostaggio: an hostage, a pledge, a paune (Flor.).

hostel. OF. (*hôtel*), Late L. *hospitale*. See *hospital*. Both this and *hostelry* were revived by Scott. For *hostler*, OF. *hostelier*, see *ostler*.

hostile. L. *hostilis*, from *hostis*, enemy. First in Shaks., but *hostility* is earlier.

hostler. See *hostel, ostler*.

hot. AS. *hāt*. Com. Teut.; cf. Du. *heet*, Ger. *heiss*, ON. *heitr*. *Hot* and *cold*, in parlour

games, are from hunting (scent). *Hotspur*, usu. associated with Henry Percy (†1403), is much older as a nickname. *In hot water* suggests a medieval torture, but origin is unknown. Fig. sense of *hot-bed* is 18 cent.

hotchkiss. Machine-gun. From inventor's name, which is a var. of *Hodgkins*, son of little Roger. Cf. *gatling, maxim*.

hotch-pot, hotch-potch. See *hodge-podge*.

hotel. F. *hôtel*, hostelry, mansion (cf. *hôtel-Dieu*, hospital, *hôtel-de-ville*, town hall), OF. *hostel*. In 18 cent. E. for inn, hostel (q.v.).

I took up my abode at the new hotel! a term then [1781] little known in England, though now in general use (Hickey's *Memoirs*, ii. 365).

Hottentot. SAfrDu., imit. of clucking speech. So explained 1670. Cf. *barbarian*.

houdah. See *howdah*.

hough [*Bibl.*]. Archaic for *hock¹*. AS. *hōh*, heel, change of sense being due to *hough sinew*, AS. *hōhsinu*, connecting heel and hock. Hence *hough*, to hamstring (*Josh.* xi. 6).

hound¹. AS. *hund*. Com. Teut.; cf. Du. *hond*, Ger. *hund*, ON. *hundr*, Goth. *hunds*; cogn. with G. κύων, κυν-, L. *canis*, Sanskrit *şvan*, and with *hunt*. The true Teut. word, replaced in E., exc. in spec. senses, by later *dog*. To *hound on* is for earlier to *hound*.

Houndis camen and lickiden his bylis
(Wyc. *Luke*, xvi. 21).

houp-là. F., see *hoop²*.

hour. ME. also *ure, oure*, OF. (*h*)*oure* (*heure*), L. *hora*, whence also Ger. *uhr*, hour, clock. Replaced AS. *tīd* and *stund*, e.g. the (seven) *Canonical hours* are in AS. *seofon tīda*.

houri. F., Pers. *hūrī*, nymph of Mohammedan paradise, from Arab. *hawira*, to be dark-eyed (like a gazelle).

house. AS. *hūs*. Com. Teut.; cf. Du. *huis*, Ger. *haus*, ON. *hūs*, Goth. *-hūs*, in *gudhūs*, temple. Usual Goth. is *razn* (see *ransack*). Spec. senses correspond largely with those of F. *maison*. *Housecarl* (hist.) is ON. *hūskarl*; see *carl*, and cf. *household troops*, F. *maison du roi*. With *household* cf. Ger. *haushalt(ung)* (see *hold¹*). To *bring down the house* is theat. With *housewarming* (16 cent.) cf. F. *pendre la crémaillère*, lit. to hang up the pot-hook. With *housewife*, sewing-case, cf. *châtelaine* (see also *hussif*). The *houseleek* is so named from being grown on roof as protection against lightning; cf. its AS. name *thunor-wyrt*, thunder-wort, and F. *joubarbe*, L. *Jovis barba*, beard of Jupiter.

Familiar in his mouth as household words
(*Hen. V*, iv. 3).

housel [*archaic*]. Eucharist. AS. *hūsl*; cf. ON. *hūsl*, Goth. *hunsl*, sacrifice, offering.

Unhousel'd, disappointed, unanel'd (*Haml.* i. 5).

housings. Of horse. Earlier *house*, F. *housse* (13 cent.), "a foot-cloth for a horse" (Cotg.), Arab. *ghūshiah*, saddle-cloth. A crusaders' word.

howse of a horse: sandalum, sudaria (*Cath. Angl.*).

houyhnhnm. Coined by Swift (third voyage of Gulliver). Cf. *Yahoo*.

Hova. Member of ruling class in Madagascar. Native word.

hovel. Orig. shed, cattle-shelter. OF. *huvelet*, pent house, suggests OF. **huvel*. Cf. OF. *hobe*, cabin, hut, perh. from OHG. *hoube* (*haube*), hood, which is cogn. with E. *hive*, L. *cupa*, tub. Cf. fig. uses of *hood*, e.g. of a carriage, hatchway, chimney, etc.

hoveller. Also *hobbler*, *huffler*. Unlicensed pilot, predatory boatman, esp. on Kent coast. ? From *hovel*, as inhabiting cabins on the shore.

hover. From c. 1400, for earlier *hove*. Origin unknown. At first chiefly naut., of ships standing on and off coast.

how[1]. Adv. AS. *hū*, from stem of interrog. *who* (q.v.); cf. Du. *hoe*, and, with different suffix, Ger. *wie* (OHG. *hweo*), Goth. *hwaiwa*. *Howsomever* was once a literary word, and *howbeit* (cf. *albeit*) could be used in past (*how were it*).

how[2] [*north.*]. Hill. ON. *haugr*, lit. high, cogn. with Ger. *hügel* (dim.), hill. Cf. *Hoogh* (near Ypres), from Du., and Cape *La Hogue*, from ON.

howdah, houdah. Pers. & Urdu *haudah*, Arab. *haudaj*, orig. litter carried by camel.

howitzer. Earlier *howitz*, *howbitz*, Ger. *haubitze*, earlier *haufnitz*, Boh. *houfnice*, engine for hurling stones. Introduced into Ger. during Hussite wars (14 cent.). From Ger. come also F. *obus*, shell, *obusier*, howitzer.

howl. ME. *houlen*; cf. Du. *hiulen*, Ger. *heulen*. Imit., like L. *ululare*, whence, influenced by Ger. *heulen*, comes F. *hurler* (OF. *uller*, *urler*). *Howling wilderness* is after *Deut.* xxxii. 10. Colloq. *howler* is for *howling blunder* (cf. *crying shame*, etc.).

howlet [*dial.*]. Owl. Associated with *owl*, but really a dim. of the name *Hugh*. Cf. F. *hulotte* in same sense, and dial. *houchin*,

hob-howchin, owl. The surnames *Howitt Howlitt, Hullett, Hewlett, Houchin, Hutchin* similarly represent OF. dims. of *Hugh* Cf. *robin, jackdaw, dicky (bird)*, etc.

hoy. From 15 cent. Obs. Du. *hoei*. Origin unknown. The "Margate hoy" is in Pepys (June 16, 1661).

hoya. Plant. From *Hoy*, E. gardener (†1821).

hoyden, hoiden. First applied (c. 1600) to boor, clown. Prob. Du. *heiden*, heathen, etc. For vowel change cf. 16 cent. interj. *hoida*, Ger. *heida*.

heyden: homo agrestis et incultus (Kil.).

badault: a foole, dolt, sot, fop, asse, coxcombe; gaping hoydon (Cotg.).

Hoyle, according to [*US.*]. From *Edmond Hoyle* (1672–1769), writer on card-games and chess. Cf. *according to Cocker*.

hub. Prob. ident. with *hob*[2], of which it shares some senses. A dial. word of which mod. use is largely due to O. W. Holmes.

Boston State-house is the hub of the solar system
(*Autocrat of Breakfast-Table*).

hubble-bubble. Imit. name, redupl. on *bubble*, for *hookah*, which is recorded much later.

hubbub. In 16 cent. usu. associated with Ireland. Cf. *abu*, war-cry of ancient Irish, and Gael. *ub! ubub!* interj. of contempt.

The Irish hubbabowe, which theyr kerne use at theyr first encounter (Spenser).

They began to rayse a confused shoute after the manner of the Irish hubbub (*China Voyage*, 1637).

hubby. For *husband*, from 17 cent.

huckaback. Fabric for towels. Among many early vars. *hagabag* (Sc.) suggests redupl. on *bag*.

huckleberry [*US.*]. App. corrupt. of *hurtle-berry, whortleberry* (q.v.).

hucklebone. Hip-bone, also astragalus. Corruptly *knucklebone*. Earlier *huck-bone*, from which dial. *huck*, hip, haunch, is a back-formation. Prob. cogn. with *hook*, in sense of bend, ? or with *hough, hock*[1].

astragalus: the play at dice; tables; huckle-bone (Coop.).

huckster. Obs. Du. *hoekster*, fem. of *hoeker*, "caupo, propola, *Ang.* houkester, hucster" (Kil.). Prob. from Du. *hoek*, corner. Cf. Ger. *krämer*, huckster, from *kram*, booth, and see *canteen*. Dial. *huck*, to higgle, bargain, is back-formation like *beg, cadge, hawk, peddle*. See *hawker*. It may be assumed that the name was orig. applied to a woman keeping a small stall (cf. *baxter, brewster*, orig. of female bakers and brewers).

huddle. Orig. (16 cent.) to pack hastily out of sight. Cf. ME. *hoder*, in similar sense, and obs. *hudder-mudder*, now replaced by *hugger-mugger*. It may be cogn. with *hide*[3]; cf. AS. *hȳdels*, hiding-place. Later sense of hurried, careless work app. influenced by archaic Du. *hoetelen*, "ignaviter aliquid agere" (Kil.).

Hudibrastic. In style of *Hudibras*, mock-heroic poem (1663–78) by Samuel Butler.

hue[1]. AS. *hīw*, form, appearance, colour; cf. Goth. *hiwi*, form, Sanskrit *khavi*, skin, complexion, etc. Squeezed out, from c. 1600, by *colour*, and now only poet.

hue[2] **and cry.** AF. *hu e cri* (13 cent.). The first element is usu. associated with F. *huer*, to hoot, shout, but F. *à cor et à cri* suggests that it may have meant hunting-horn. It was prob. at first a hunting expression. Until 1838 it was also the sub-title of the offic. Police Gazette (*Oliver Twist*, ch. xv.).

Dunc recumencent e li hus e li cris (*Rol.* 2064).

huff. From 16 cent., to blow, puff, play the braggart, etc. Hence *huff*, temper. Perh. imit., but cf. Ger. *hauchen* (MHG. *huchen*), to breathe. At draughts it was once usual to blow on the piece that was "huffed."

to huff a man at draughts: einen stein im damenspiel wegblasen; souffler un pion au jeu des dames (Ludw.).

hug. From 16 cent. Origin obscure. As orig. sense was affectionate, it may be Norw. dial. *hygge*, to care for, love, which belongs ult. to ON. *hugr*, courage, mood, etc.; cf. AS. *hycgan*, to think.

huge. OF. *ahuge*, *ahoge*, in same sense. Origin unknown.

hugger-mugger. Orig. concealment, secrecy, developing new senses as *huddle*. Earlier (16 cent.) *hucker-mucker*, replacing *hudder-mudder* (see *huddle*). Perh. partly suggested by ME. *huke*, *hukel*, cloak, OF. *huque*. With later sense of muddle, confusion, cf. Walloon *hagemag*, in same sense.

He and hys wyf and other have blaveryd here of my kynred in hedermoder (*Paston Let.* ii. 28).

Not by subtill sleights or hugger-mugger [en cachette] (Florio's *Montaigne*).

Huguenot. Double dim. of F. *Hugues*, Hugh, perverted from earliest form *eiguenot* (1550), dial. form of Ger. *eidgenoss*, oath companion, confederate. *Eidgenossen* is still the regular form of address to the Swiss people. The name was given to the

men of Geneva when they joined the Swiss Confederation (1518) and thus was at first of pol. character. *Huguenot* was a French surname long before the Reformation, though less common than *Huguenet* (whence E. *Hignett*), and the unfamiliar foreign word would be readily assimilated to it. ModProv. *aganau* keeps rather nearer the orig. See *oath*, *neat*[1].

hulk. AS. *hulc*, ship. In ME. usu. associated with heavy, unwieldy vessel (hence *hulking*); cf. Du. *hulk*, Ger. *holk*; also OF. *houlque*, *hourque*, etc., Sp. It. *urca*, ? from Teut. In view of the early prevalence of the word in WGer., derivation from G. ὁλκάς, towed ship, from ἕλκειν, to drag, is very doubtful. Connection with *hull* seems more likely; cf. obs. *hulk*, hovel, AS. *hulc*, cogn. with *hull*. The *hulks* were old ships used as prisons (*Great Expectations*, ch. ii.). See also *sheer-hulk*.

hull. AS. *hulu*, husk, shell, cogn. with *helan*, to hide; cf. Ger. *hülle*, covering, *hülse*, husk. For later sense cf. F. *coque*, shell, hull of ship; also L. *carina*, ship, orig. nut-shell.

hullaballoo. Orig. Sc. & north. Prob. with vague suggestion of *howl*, *bellow*, *halloo*, etc. It has many early vars., e.g. *hurley bolloo* (1751).

hullo. See *hallo*.

Hulsean lectures. Established at Camb. by bequest of *Rev. John Hulse* (†1790).

hum. Imit. of bee, fly, etc.; cf. Ger. dial. *hummen*, Ger. *summen*, and see *humble-bee*. In *hum and ha* it is rather for hesitating *hem* (cf. *ahem*). To *make things hum* (US.) contains suggestion of the *hum* of activity, business, etc.; ? cf. *boom*[1]. In *humming ale* it appears to be merely intens.

He wold have gotyn it aweye by humys and by hays, but I wold not so be answeryd (*Paston Let.* ii. 347).

human. Earlier *humain*, F., L. *humanus*, cogn. with *homo*, man. Differentiated from *humane* since c. 1700, the noun *humanity* keeping both senses (cf. also *inhuman*). *Humane studies*, *humanist*, *humanism*, etc., date from Renaissance, reaching E. from It. via F., and imitating L. use of *humanitas* in the sense of education befitting a cultivated man. *Humanitarian* is 19 cent. For *human-e* cf. *urban-e*.

humble. F., L. *humilis*, from *humus*, ground; with silent *h*- till 19 cent. Cf. *lowly*.

humble-bee. Commonly *bumble-bee*. Not found in AS., but probably a native word;

cf. Du. *hommel*, Ger. *hummel* (OHG. *humbal, humpal*); cogn. with *hum* as *bumble-bee* is with *boom*[1].

humble-pie. For *umble-pie*, from *umbles*, earlier *numbles*, entrails, etc. of deer, OF. *nombles*, by dissim. for *lombles*, from L. *lumbulus*, dim. of *lumbus*, loin. For loss of *n-* cf. *apron*, *umpire*, etc. To *eat humble-pie* was orig. a pun; cf. dial. to *eat rue-pie* (see *rue*[1, 2]).

noumbles of a dere or beest: entrailles (Palsg.).

humbug. Recorded as noun and verb c. 1750. Origin unknown. Perh. associated by some obscure metaphor with *humming* and *bug*, insect; cf. Sp. *zumbar*, to hum, to jest, and possible connection of OF. *bourde*, humbug, with *bourdon*, drone-bee; also similar use of Sp. *abejón*, drone (v.i.).

abejon: a bee that has lost his sting, a drone. *Abejon juego*: a sort of play among children, at which one cries *buz*, and if the other is not watchful to pull away his head, he gives him a cuff on the ear. Thence *jugar con uno al abejon* is to make sport of, or make a jest of a man (Stevens).

humdrum. Imit. of monotony. Redupl. on *hum*, with reminiscence of *drum*.

humectate. From L. *humectare*, from *(h)umidus*, damp.

humeral [*anat.*]. From L. *humerus*, shoulder, cogn. with G. ὦμος, whence *omoplate*.

humid. F. *humide*, L. *(h)umidus*, from *umēre*, to be moist. The *h-* is due to association with *humus*, ground.

humiliate. From L. *humiliare*, from *humilis*, humble. *Humiliation, humility* are much older words (Chauc.).

Humism [*phil.*]. Of *David Hume* (†1776).

hummock. Orig. naut. (16 cent.) and written indifferently *ham-, hom-*, later *hum-*, and also *hommaco*, as though Sp. App. cogn. with much later *hump*; cf. LG. *hümmel, hümpel*, Norw. *humpe*, hillock, etc.

hummaum. See *hammam*.

humour. F. *humeur*, L. *(h)umor-em*, moisture. In ancient and medieval physiology, one of the four fluids, "cardinal humours" (v.i.), which determined the individual temperament. Later applied to "temper" or mood caused by such "humours," and, in E. only, from c. 1700, to a spec. aspect of the ludicrous or jocose. The same series of meanings appears in its derivatives, e.g. *humorous* in Shaks. means damp (*Rom. & Jul.* ii. 1), capricious, moody (*As You Like It*, i. 2); and Addison uses *humorist* for faddist.

In every human body
The choler, melancholy, phlegm and blood,
By reason that they flow continually
In some one part, and are not continent,
Receive the name of humours. Now thus far
It may, by metaphor, apply itself
Unto the general disposition;
As when some one peculiar quality
Doth so possess a man, that it doth draw
All his affects, his spirits and his powers,
In his confluctions, all to run one way,
This may be truly said to be a humour
(Jonson, *Every Man out of his Humour, Induction*).

The murmuring and mutinie of such rebellious and turbulent humorists (Purch. xix. 46).

hump. First in *hump-backed* (17 cent.), app. due to mixture of earlier *crump-backed* (see *crumpet*) and *hunch-backed* (see *hunch*); but cf. LG. *humpel, hümpel*, hillock, knob, hump of camel. *Hump*, despondency, may be a playful alteration of *hip*[2] suggested by *dump, grump*.

humph. Grunt of disapproval. Better represented by *mph*.

Humphrey, dine with Duke. Orig. to spend dinner-hour near supposed tomb of *Humphrey of Gloucester* in Old Saint Paul's. Cf. Sc. to *dine with St Giles and the Earl of Murray* (buried in St Giles' Church).

humpty-dumpty. Small "dumpy" person (18 cent.). App. redupl. on *dump*[2] (q.v.). But the antiquity of nursery-rimes suggests that it may orig. have been a proper name, from *Humphrey*.

humus. L., ground, mould, cogn. with G. χθών (for *χθώμ).

Hun. "A reckless or wilful destroyer of the beauties of nature or art; an uncultured devastator; cf. *Vandal, Goth*" (*NED.*). AS. *Húne, Húnas*; cf. ON. *Húnar*, Ger. *Hünen*, MedL. *Hunni, Chunni*, app. from native name of race, which overran Europe in 4–5 cents., known to Chin. as *Hiong-nu* or *Han*. Application to Germans dates from Kaiser's speech (1900) in which he held up to his troops the Hun ideal.

Les Huns ont passé là, Tout est ruine et deuil
(Victor Hugo).

The majority of good Huns all over the world being old soldiers, the Huns will be particularly well placed at the day of Armageddon
(*Ole Luk-oie*, 1907).

hunch. First in *hunch-backed* (*Rich. III*, iv. 4; 2 Quart.), for more usual *bunch-backed* (Folios and 1 Quart.). Cotgrave has *hulch-backed*; and *huck-backed, huckle-backed, hutch-backed*, also occur in 17 cent. Cf. also *hump-backed*. With *hunch* (of bread) and 19 cent. *hunk* cf. WFlem. *hunke*, in same sense. The relation of this series of words is quite obscure.

hundred. AS. *hundred*, from *hund*, the Aryan name (cf. OSax. *hund*, OHG. *hunt*, Goth. *hund*, and cogn. L. *centum*, G. ἐ-κατόν, Welsh *cant*, Sanskrit *satam*), with suffix *-red*, reckoning, as in Du. *hondert*, Ger. *hundert*, ON. *hundrath*; cf. Goth. *rathjan*, to reckon, *rathjo*, number, an early loan from L. *ratio*. The ON. hundred was 120 (see *gross*). Hist. the *hundred* is a sub-division of a county, variously explained, but certainly in some cases representing a hundred hides of land. Cf. *Chiltern Hundreds*. The *Hundred Days* renders F. *Cent Jours*, between Napoleon's return from Elba and his second abdication. The *Old Hundredth* is the metr. version of *Ps.* c.

hunger. AS. *hungor*. Com. Teut.; cf. Du. *honger*, Ger. *hunger*, ·ON. *hungr*, Goth. *huggrjan*, to hunger. *Hunger-strike*, orig. devised by imprisoned suffragettes, is now a normal practice of the incarcerated.

Among the prisoners who have gone on hunger strike in Ireland are prisoners convicted of burglary (*Daily Mail*, Mar. 8, 1918).

hunk. From c. 1800. See *hunch*.

hunker. Orig. Sc. (18 cent.). App. connected with Du. *huiken*, Ger. *hocken*, ON. *hūka*, to squat on one's hams or "hunkers," also ON. *hokra*, to crouch. ? Nasalized under influence of *haunch*.

hunks. From c. 1600. Also *hunx*. Dan. *hundsk*, stingy, lit. doggish. For metath. of consonants cf. *Manx, minx*. Du. *hondsch*, Ger. *hündisch*, occur in same sense.

sordidus: hündisch; honts (A. Junius).

hunt. AS. *huntian*, cogn. with *hound*, and perh. also with *hand*, and Goth. *hinthan*, to seize. From AS. *hunta*, hunter, comes name *Hunt*, still much commoner than later *Hunter*. *Happy hunting ground* app. translates some NAmer. Ind. name for heaven.

Hunterian. Of *William* († 1783) or *John Hunter* († 1793), brothers, anatomists.

hurdle. AS. *hyrdel*, dim. cogn. with Du. *horde*, Ger. *hürde*; cf. ON. *hurth*, Goth. *haurds*, door; cogn. with L. *cratis*, hurdle, G. κυρτία, wicker-work. Much used in ME. of defensive works (cf. *hoarding*). Being *drawn on a hurdle* to execution for high treason was not formally abolished till 1870.

hurdy-gurdy. Imit. of sound. Cf. earlier *hirdy-girdy*, uproar, and *hurlyburly*.

hurl. From 13 cent. Cf. LG. *hurreln*, to hurl, push, etc. Prob. connected with *hurr*, imit. of vibration, "whirring," and influenced also by *hurtle* and *whirl*, as in obs. *hurlpool*, *hirlwind*. Hence *hurley*, Ir. name for hockey (q.v.), hockey-stick, and perh. *hurlyburly*. But with latter cf. F. *hurluberlu*, reckless person, perh. connected with *hurler*, to howl; also Ger. *hurliburli*, precipitately.

hurrah. Later than *huzza*. App. a cry picked up in Thirty Years' War; cf. Norw. Sw. Dan. *hurra*, Ger. *hurrah*, Russ. *ura*, etc.; orig. Ger., perh. from *hurren*, to move quickly,

hurricane. Sp. *huracán*, from Carib, whence also Port. *furacão*. From Sp. come F. *ouragan*, Ger. *orkan*. Some of the numerous early E. forms (from 16 cent.), e.g. *haurachana*, *furicano*, *hurlecano*, are due to folk-etym., and it is possible that the accepted spelling owes something to the early theory that the storm was named from its destruction of sugar plantations (q.d. *hurry cane!*).

hurry. First in Shaks. Cogn. with *hurl* (q.v.), with some earlier meanings of which it coincides. *Hurry-scurry* is a redupl. suggested by *scurry* (q.v.).

In this hurlie and uprore (Holland's *Livy*).

The multitude was all up on a hurrey (*ib.*).

hurst [*dial.*]. Hillock, also grove. Very common in place-names. AS. *hyrst*; cf. obs. Du. *horst*, thicket, Ger. *horst*, esp. in *adlerhorst*, eagle's aery, ON. *hrjōstr*, rough, barren place.

hurt. OF. *hurter* (*heurter*), to collide, dash against; cf. Prov. *urtar*, It. *urtare*. Origin uncertain, but prob. Celt.

If ony man schal wandre in the day, he hirtith not [*Vulg.* non offendit] (Wyc. *John*, xi. 9).

hurtle. From *hurt*. Orig. to strike against. Later senses associated with *hurl* (q.v.), with which it sometimes varies in early MSS.

Whanne we felden into a place of gravel...thei hurtliden [*vars.* hurten, hurliden, *Vulg.* impegerunt] the schipp (Wyc. *Acts*, xxvii. 41).

hurtleberry. Now usu. *whortleberry*. App. from AS. *heorot-berge*, hart berry used of the buckthorn; cf. Ger. *himbeere*, raspberry, lit. hind berry. See also *whortleberry*, *huckleberry*.

husband. AS. *hūsbonda*, master of the house, from ON. *bōndi*, peasant, freeholder (see *bond*[2]). Cf. *housewife*. Senses of tiller of soil (replaced by *husbandman*), spouse, are later. Orig. sense appears in verb to *husband* (one's resources, etc.) and *husbandry*, with which cf. *economy*.

Gif the housbonde man [*Vulg.* paterfamilias] wiste in what houre the theef were to cumme
(Wyc. *Matt.* xxiv. 43).

This day, not for want, but for good husbandry, I sent my father, by his desire, six pair of my old shoes, which fit him, and are good
(Pepys, Dec. 5, 1667).

hush. Earliest is *husht*, adj. (c. 1400), which appears to be ident. with interj. *hust* (Chauc.). In 15 cent. texts varies with *huist*, *whist*, etc., natural exclamations enjoining silence; cf. *hist*. Verb and noun *hush* are back-formations from *husht* regarded as p.p. Cf. also Norw. Dan. *hysse*, to silence, from interj. *hys*. For *hushaby* cf. LG. *hüssen*, to lull. With to *hush up* (17 cent.) cf. *hush-money*, and *hush-ship*, used during the Great War of new ships of secret design and purpose (cf. *Q-boat*).

husk. Late ME. App. a dim. of *house*, perh. from Du.; cf. early sense of Du. *huisken* (v.i.). Approximate parallels are found in Ger. & LG., but some regard it as cogn. with *hose*, in orig. sense of covering. Hence *husky*, dry-throated, or as though choked with husks; cf. *bur*. For US. *husking*, jollification accompanying corn-husking, see *bee*.

huysken: siliqua, gluma, calyx, theca seminis (Kil.).

husky. Eskimo dog. ? Corrupt. of *Eskimo*. A Scotsman resident in Canada suggests to me that it may be the personal name *Husky* (? for Hugh), as in *Huskisson*, given by early Sc. immigrants. Cf. *collie*.

hussar. Hung. *huszar*, freebooter, OSerb. *gusar*, *kursar*, etc., Late G. κουρσάριος, Late L. *cursar us*, whence also *corsair* (q.v.). Applied in 15 cent. to Hung. light horse and adopted by several West Europ. langs. Cf. *cossack*, *pandour*, *uhlan*. The hussar uniform still bears traces of Oriental origin.

The horsemen of Hongary are commonly called hussares, an exceadyng ravenous and cruell kynde of men (*NED*. 1560).

hussars: are horsemen, cloathed in tygers and other skins, and adorn'd with plumes of feathers (*News-reader's Pocket-book*, 1759).

hussif. *Housewife* (q.v.), in sense of needle-case, etc. Cf. *hussy*.

Hussite [*hist.*]. Follower of *John Hus*, Bohemian reformer (15 cent.), burnt at Constance, 1415.

hussy. For *housewife*; cf. *goody* for *goodwife*. For mod. depreciation of sense, due to association with adjs. such as *light*, *saucy*, etc., cf. hist. of *wench*, *quean*, and growing dislike of the vulgar for the word *woman*.

Huswife, Ile have you whipt for slaundring me
(*Look about you*, 1600).

Being so good a hussy of what money I had left her (Defoe, *Colonel Jack*).

husting. AS. *hūsting*, ON. *hūs-thing*, house thing, orig. an assembly of the immediate followers of a king or noble, as distinguished from the general *thing* or *folkmoot*; cf. the London *Court of Hustings*, presided over by the Lord Mayor, and held on a platform in the Guildhall, whence election *hustings* (18 cent.). See *storthing*, *thing*.

hustle. From 17 cent. Orig. to shake up coins (lots) in a hat for gambling. Du. *hutselen*, in same sense, frequent. of *hutsen*, to shake (see *hodge-podge*). The sense of jostling, ill-treating, esp. in connection with robbery, is E. only, which points to confusion with ME. and dial. *huspil*, F. *houspiller*, "to shake, or towse" (Cotg.), OF. *houssepigner*, lit. to comb (*peigner*) one's jacket (see *housing*). With US. sense of *hustler* cf. *push*. The offic. Tube hustler started work at Victoria, Jan. 1920.

huspylyn, or spoylyn: spolio, dispolio (*Prompt. Parv.*).

A "hustler" started work at Tottenham Court Road tube-station yesterday
(*Daily Chron.* Jan. 20, 1920).

hut. F. *hutte*, Ger. *hütte*, cogn. with *hide*[3]. First as mil. word.

hutch. Orig. chest, coffer. F. *huche* (13 cent.); cf. MedL. *hutica*. Perh. from Ger. *hut*, keeping.

Huttonian [*geol.*]. Plutonic theory of rocks. From *James Hutton* (†1796).

hutty [*Anglo-Ind.*]. Elephant (Kipling, *Road to Mandalay*). Hind. *hāthī*, Sanskrit *hastī*, from *hasta*, hand, elephant's trunk (cf. Pliny, *Hist. Nat.* viii. 10. 29).

Hattee, which is likewise elephant in their language (Jourdain's *Journ.* 1612).

huzoor. Eastern formula of respectful address. Arab. *huzūr*, presence.

huzza. Orig. sailors' shout, so perh. for hauling-cry *hissa*, from F. *hisser*, to hoist (q.v.). But cf. Ger. *hussa*.

hyacinth. Now differentiated from earlier *jacinth* (q.v.). F., L., G. ὑάκινθος, flower fabled to have sprung from the blood of *Hyacinthus*, youth beloved by Apollo.

hyacinthe: the blew, or purple jacint, or hyacinth flower (Cotg.).

Hyades [*astron.*]. Group of stars near Pleiades. G. ὑάδες, popularly connected with ὕειν, to rain, but perh. from ὗς, swine, L. name being *suculae*, little pigs. Cf. *hyena*.

hyaena. See *hyena*.

hyaloid. From G. ὕαλος, glass.

hybrid. L. *hybrida, hibrida*, offspring of tame sow and wild boar. ? From G. ὗς, ὑ-, sow, with second element cogn. with L. *aper*, boar.

hydra. L., G. ὕδρα, water-snake. Fig. allusion to the numerous and indestructible heads of the Lernaean Hydra, killed by Hercules, is in Chauc. See *otter*.

hydrangea. Coined by Linnaeus from G. ὕδωρ, water, ἄγγος, vessel, in allusion to form of seed-capsule.

hydrant. Orig. US. Irreg. formation from G. ὕδωρ, water.

hydraulic. L., G. ὑδραυλικός, from ὕδωρ, water, αὐλός, pipe.

hydro. Short for *hydropathic establishment*.

hydrogen. F. *hydrogène*, coined (1787) by G. de Morveau, from G. ὕδωρ, water, and γέν-, to produce. Cf. *hydrography*, study of water distribution; *hydromel*, mead, G. μέλι, honey; *hydropathy*, water cure (cf. *homoeopathy*); *hydrophobia*, G. φόβος, fear, because human sufferers show aversion to water; *hydroplane*, coined on *aeroplane*; *hydropsy*, learned form of *dropsy* (q.v.); *hydrostatic*, etc.

hyena. L. *hyaena*, G. ὕαινα, swine (fem.), from ὗς, ὑ-, pig.

hygiene. F. *hygiène*, G. ὑγιεινή (sc. τέχνη), from ὑγιής, healthy, whence also *Hygiea*, goddess of health.

hygrometer. From G. ὑγρός, wet, fluid.

hylic. Material. G. ὑλικός, from ὕλη, wood, timber, used by Aristotle for matter. Cf. *hylozoism*, theory that matter has life.

Hymen. L., G. Ὑμήν, god of marriage, from ὑμήν, membrane (vaginal). ? Cf. Sanskrit *syūman*, suture. Hence *hymenoptera* (Linnaeus), insects with membranous wings.

hymn. L., G. ὕμνος, song of praise, adopted by LXX. to render various Heb. words.

Cf. AS. *ymen*, ME. *ymne*, now restored on G. form.

Salmes and ymnes and spiritual songis
(Wyc. *Col.* iii. 16).

hyoid [*anat.*]. Shape of G. letter *v*. See -*oid*.

hyoscine. Poison (used by Crippen). From *hyoscyamus*, G., from ὑοσκύαμος, pig's bean, whence F. *jusquiame*.

hypaethral. Open to the sky. From G. ὑπό, under, αἰθήρ, air.

hypallage [*gram.*]. Change of natural order in figure of speech, e.g. *dare classibus austros* (*Aen.* iii. 61) for *dare classes austris*. G., exchange, from ὑπό, under, ἀλλάσσειν, to exchange.

hyperbaton [*gram.*]. Inversion of natural order. G., from ὑπέρ, over (cogn. with L. *super*), βαίνειν, to step. Cf. *hyperbola, hyperbole*, G. βάλλειν, to throw; *hyperborean*, G. βορέας, north (wind); *hypersthene* (min.), F. *hypersthène*, named by Haüy (1803) from G. σθένος, strength, because harder than hornblende; *hypertrophy*, G. τροφή, nourishment (cf. *atrophy*).

hyphen. G. ὑφέν (adv.), together, from ὑπό, under, ἕν, one. Hence *hyphenated American* (1915), of Ger. origin and preserving Ger. sympathies.

hypnotism. Coined (1842) by Dr J. Braid from *hypnotic* (17 cent.), from G. ὕπνος, sleep. Cf. *braidism*.

hypocaust. Heating-chamber of Roman house or bath. G. ὑπόκαυστον, from ὑπό, under (cogn. with L. *sub*), καίειν, to burn. Cf. *hypochondria*, orig. soft part of body, and organs, below costal cartilages, from G. χόνδρος, gristle, hence, in E., melancholy supposed to be situated in liver or spleen; *hypocoristic*, of pet-names, G. κόρος, child; *hypocrite*, G. ὑποκριτής, actor, lit. one who answers back, ult. from κρίνειν, to judge, decide; *hypodermic*, G. δέρμα, skin; *hypostasis*, essence, personality, G. ἱστάναι, to set; *hypotenuse*, G. ὑποτείνουσα, pres. part. fem., from τείνειν, to stretch, because "subtending" the right-angle; *hypothesis*, putting under, "supposition," from G. τιθέναι, to place (cf. *hypothecate*, to mortgage, from F.).

hypso-. From G. ὕψος, height.

hyrax. The "cony" of the Bible. G. ὕραξ, shrew-mouse.

hyson. Cantonese form of Chin. *hei-ch'un*, bright spring.

hyssop. L., G. ὕσσωπος, of Oriental origin; cf. Heb. *ēzōb*. Hence AS. *ysope*.

hysteria. Mod. formation from *hysteric*, F. *hystérique*, L., G. ὑστερικός, from ὑστέρα, womb. Cf. *mother*, in same sense.

O, how this mother swells up toward my heart!
Hysterica passio!—down, thou climbing sorrow
(*Lear*, ii. 4).

hysteron-proteron [*gram.*]. Inversion. G. ὕστερον, latter, πρότερον, former. Cf. *preposterous*.

hythe. See *hithe*.

I. AS. *ic*. Com. Teut.; cf. Du. *ik*, Ger. *ich*, ON. *ek*, Goth. *ik*; cogn. with L. *ego*, G. ἐγώ, Sanskrit *aham*. *Me* (q.v.) is Aryan.

iambic. L., G., from ἴαμβος, ? from ἰάπτειν, to assail, because trad. first used, by Archilochus (7 cent. B.C.), in invective verse. ? Or from root of ἰέναι, to go, with suffix as in διθύραμβος, θρίαμβος. Cf. *trochaic*.

iatric. From G. ἰατρός, healer, physician.

ib., ibid. For L. *ibidem*, in the same place.

Iberian [*ling.*]. Prehistoric race preceding Celts in Western Europe, esp. in Spain. From G. Ἴβηρες, the Spaniards (and Portuguese).

ibex. L., kind of goat.

ibis. L., G. ἴβις, prob. of Egypt. origin.

Ibsenity. Of *Ibsen*, Norw. author (†1914). Jocular (*Punch*), after *obscenity*.

Icarian. Of *Icarus*, son of Daedalus. The earliest airman.

ice. AS. *īs*. Com. Teut.; cf. Du. *ijs*, Ger. *eis*, ON. *īss*. *Iceberg*, ice mountain, may be Du. *ijsberg* or Dan. *isbjerg*.

Icelandic [*ling.*]. Mod. form of Old Norse, from which, owing to centuries of isolation, it differs much less than the cogn. Scand. langs.

Ichabod, to write. See 1 *Sam.* iv. 21.

ichneumon. L., G. ἰχνεύμων, from ἰχνεύειν, to track, from ἴχνος, footstep, because it finds and destroys the eggs of the crocodile. See *cockatrice*.

ichnography [*arch.*]. Ground-plan. From G. ἰχνεύειν, to trace (v.s.).

ichor. F., G. ἰχώρ, fluid replacing blood in veins of the gods.

ichthyosaurus. Fossil monster. From G. ἰχθύς, fish, σαῦρος, lizard. Cf. *ichthyology*, *ichthyophagy*, etc.

icicle. For ice *ickle*. From AS. *īs*, ice, *gicel*, icicle; cf. archaic Dan. *isegel*, Norw. dial. *isjökul*, from ON. *jökull*, icicle. *Ickle* alone is still used in dial.

Be she constant, be she fickle,
Be she fire, or be she ickle (*NED.* 1687).

icon. Image, esp. picture, etc. of saint as object of veneration in Eastern Church. G. εἰκών, likeness.

iconoclast. Late L., Late G. εἰκονοκλάστης, from εἰκών (v.s.), κλάειν, to break. Orig. applied (8–9 cents.) to image-breakers in Eastern Church.

icosahedron. G., from εἴκοσι, twenty, ἕδρα, seat, base.

-ics. Adopted from L., G. neut. pl. -ικά of adjs. in -ικός. F. treats the ending as fem. sing. (*dynamique*, *tactique*, etc.) exc. in *mathématiques*.

ictus. L., stroke, p.p. of archaic *icere*, to strike, used as p.p. of *ferire*.

id [*biol.*]. Unit of germ-plasm. Coined (1891) by Weismann on *idioplasm*.

idea. L., G. ἰδέα, look, semblance, from ἰδεῖν, to see. Earlier is dial. *idee*, via F. Earliest sense in mod. langs. is archetype, as in Platonic philos., something of which survives in *ideal-ist*. Image, conception, are later developments.

Withal, I did infer your lineaments,
Being the right idea of your father,
Both in your form and nobleness of mind
(*Rich. III*, iii. 7).

identity. F. *identité*, Late L. *identitas* (5 cent.), from *idem*, same.

ideology. Science of ideas (q.v.).

ides. F., L. *idus* (pl.).

idiom. F. *idiome*, language, dialect, L., G. ἰδίωμα, peculiarity, from ἴδιος, own, peculiar.

idiosyncrasy. G. ἰδιοσυγκρασία, from ἴδιος (v.s.), σύγκρασις, mixture, from σύν, together (see *crasis*).

idiot. F., L. *idiota*, uncultivated person, G. ἰδιώτης, private person, "layman," from ἴδιος (v.s.). Mod. sense is oldest in E., though theologians, from Wyc. onward, have used the word in L. & G. meaning.

idle. AS. *īdel*, empty, useless. WGer.; cf. Du. *ijdel*, worthless, Ger. *eitel*, vain. Orig. sense still in *idle words* (mind, etc.). Cf. sense-development of *vain* and L. *vacuus*. *Idlesse* is one of Spenser's sham antiques revived by Scott.

The erthe was idel [*var.* veyn with ynne, *Vulg.* inanis] and voide (Wyc. *Gen.* i. 2).

ido. Artificial language, simplified (1907) from *esperanto*. Esperantist suffix -*ido*, son, offspring of.

idol. F. *idole*, Late L., G. εἴδωλον, image, likeness, from εἶδος, form, cogn. with ἰδεῖν, to see. Used by LXX. in mod. sense.

In *idolater, idolatry* (whence *mariolatry, babyolatry,* etc.), second element is from λατρεύειν, to serve. Correctly *idololater,* one -*ol*- being lost by dissim. (cf. *heroi-comic*).

idyll. L., G. εἰδύλλιον, dim. of εῖδος, form, picture. Orig. short descriptive poem of rustic or pastoral type.

.e. For L. *id est,* that is.

-ier. F. agent. suffix, L. -*arius*.

if. AS. *gif.* Com. Teut.; cf. Du. *of* (earlier *jof*), Ger. *ob* (OHG. *oba, ibu*), ON. *ef*, Goth. *ibai.* Supposed to be oblique case of a Teut. noun meaning doubt.

igloe, igloo. Eskimo, house.

igneous. From L. *igneus,* from *ignis,* fire.

ignis fatuus. MedL., foolish fire; cf. F. *feu follet,* will o' the wisp.

ignominy. F. *ignominie,* L. *ignominia,* from *in*-, neg., **gnomen* (*nomen*), name. Cf. *ignoble.*

ignoramus. L., we do not know. Orig. leg. (v.i.), *ignore* still being used of throwing out an indictment. Mod. sense from Ruggle's play (1615), intended to expose the ignorance of the "common lawyers," with *Ignoramus* as title-rôle.

ignoramus: is a word properly used by the grand enquest...and written upon the bill...when as they mislike their evidence, as defective, or too weake to make good the presentment (Cowel).

ignore. Orig. not to know (v.s.), still the only sense of F. *ignorer* (cf. *ignorance*). L. *ignorare,* from *in*-, neg., **gnorare,* to know (cf. *ignarus*). Current sense is quite mod. (v.i.).

They began by reviling me, they now "ignore" me, as the phrase goes (*NED.* 1850).

iguana. Sp., from Carib name *iwana, yuana,* etc. Hence *iguanodon,* fossil dinosaur, coined from G. ὀδούς, ὀδοντ-, tooth, after *mastodon.*

IHS. G. ΙΗΣ, abbrev. of ΙΗΣΟΥΣ, Jesus, transliterated into L. characters with erron. preservation of G. H (instead of E), and hence popularly explained as acrostic for *Iesus Hominum Salvator* or *In Hoc Signo* (*vinces*), *In Hac* (*cruce*) *Salus.*

Dixit autem ihs ad eos
            (*Codex Bezae, Luke,* vi. 5, 7 cent.).

ilex. L., holm-oak, evergreen oak.

iliac. Of the loins. F. *iliaque,* Late L. *iliacus,* from *ilia,* loins, entrails, confused, in *passio iliaca,* with G. ἰλεός, εἰλεός, colic, from εἴλειν, to roll.

Iliad. L. *Ilias, Iliad*-, G. Ἰλιάς (sc. ποίησις), poem of Ἴλιον, Troy.

ilk [*Sc.*]. Same. AS. *ilca,* from pronoun stem (cf. L. *is*) and suffix -*līc* (see *like*). *Of that ilk* implies coincidence of name with estate, e.g. *Lundie of Lundie.* Not ident. with *ilk* in *ilka lassie* (*ilk a lassie*), which is northern form of *each* (q.v.); cf. Sc. *whilk,* for *which.*

ill. ON. *illr,* replacing in early ME. some senses of unrelated *evil.* Apart from current mod. sense, for *sick,* it is chiefly used as adj. and adv. in real or virtual compds. (*ill blood, will; ill-bred, ill-gotten,* etc.).

illaqueate. To snare. From L. *illaqueare,* from *laqueus,* noose, snare. See *lace.*

illative. Inferential. From L. *inferre, illat-.*

illegitimate. Current sense of born out of wedlock is oldest in E. (16 cent.).

illth. Coined by Ruskin on *wealth.* Cf. *coolth.*

illuminate. For earlier *illumine,* L. *illuminare,* to throw into light, *lumen, lumin-.* See *luminary, limn.* Hence *Illuminati,* orig. Sp. sect of 16 cent., later Ger. secret society of 18 cent.; now often used of groups claiming spec. wisdom.

illusion. F., L. *illusio-n*-, from *illudere,* to mock, deceive, from *ludere, lus*-, to play. Cf. *ludicrous.*

illustrate. From L. *illustrare,* to throw into lustre (q.v.); hence, to elucidate by means of pictures, examples, etc. *Illustrious* is for earlier *illustre,* F., L. *illustris.*

im-. See *in*-[1], *in*-[2].

image. F., L. *imago, imagin-,* cogn. with *imitate.* Orig. effigy, likeness (*Gen.* i. 27), as in *the very image of.* Cf. *imagine,* to form a mental image, "picture" to oneself. *Imago,* perfect stage of insect, is due to Linnaeus.

imam, imaum. Mohammedan priest. Arab. *imām,* leader, from *amma,* to go before.

imbecile. F. *imbécile,* L. *imbecillus,* weak in body or mind, for **imbacillus,* "quasi sine baculo," i.e. tottering for lack of support. This etym., long regarded as an early myth, is now accepted by competent authorities.

imbibe. L. *imbibere,* to drink in, lit. and fig.

imbricate [*bot.*]. Overlapping like tiles. From L. *imbricare,* from *imbrex, imbric*-, gutter-tile, from *imber, imbr*-, rain.

imbroglio. It., confusion, tangle, from *broglio.* See *broil*[1].

imbrue. Now usu. with blood, but orig. of bedabblement in gen., earliest records referring to table-manners (v.i.). OF. *embrouer, embruer,* to bedaub, from the same root as *broth* (q.v.); cf. It. *imbrodolare*, "to fowle with broth or dish-wash" (Flor.). Early examples show confusion with *imbue* and *brew*. No connection with OF. *embreuver*, to saturate, which would have given E. *imbreve* (cf. *retrieve*).

> With mouth enbrowide thi coppe thou not take
> (*NED*. c. 1430).

> *s'embruer*: to imbrue, or bedable himselfe with
> (Cotg.).

imbue. L. *imbuere*, to cause to drink in. Earliest as p.p., partly due to F. *imbu*, L. *imbutus*.

imburse [*archaic*]. F. *embourser*, from *en* and *bourse*, purse (q.v.). Hence *reimburse*.

imitate. From L. *imitari*, cogn. with *image*. *Imitative* (ling.) is a convenient term to include *onomatopoeic* and *echoic*.

immaculate. L. *immaculatus*, unspotted, from *macula*, spot (see *mail¹*). Earliest in ref. to the Holy Virgin.

immanent. Contrasted with *transcendent*, *transient*. F., from pres. part. of L. *immanēre*, from *manēre*, to dwell (see *manor*).

immediate. F. *immédiat*, MedL. *immediatus*, without anything between; cf. *medium*, *intermediate*. The adv. *immediately* is much older (15 cent.).

immemorial. See *memory*. Esp. in *time immemorial*, time out of mind; cf. F. *temps immémorial*.

immense. F., L. *immensus*, unmeasured, from *metiri*, *mens-*, to measure.

immerse. From L. *immergere*, *immers-*, to plunge into. Also occ. *immerge* (as *emerge*). See *merge*. *Immersion* first occurs (17 cent.) in ref. to baptism.

immigrant. From L. *immigrare* after earlier *emigrant*. See *migrate*.

imminent. F., from pres. part. of L. *imminēre*, to overhang, from *minēre*, to jut out. Cf. *eminent*.

immolate. From L. *immolare*, orig. to sprinkle with sacrificial meal, *mola*.

immortelle. F. (sc. *fleur*). Cf. synon. *everlasting*. Cf. F. *immortel*, member of Academy.

immunity. F. *immunité*, L. *immunitas*, exemption from public service, etc., from *munus*, service, duty. Med. sense of *immune*, obs. c. 1660–1880, is a reintroduction from F. or G.

immure. F. *emmurer*, to wall in, from *en* and *mur*. See *mural*.

imp. AS. *impa*, shoot, graft, from *impian*, to graft. Like F. *enter*, Ger. *impfen*, an early loan from a L. verb which may be-

long to *putare*, to cut (**im-putare*), or to G. ἔμφυτος, implanted, grafted. The verb, which was also applied to inserting feathers into hawk's wing, is still in dial. use. The noun acquired the sense of human offshoot, child (cf. *scion*), and then, from common use in *imp of Satan* (*hell*, *wickedness*, etc.) reached its current meaning. Cf. *hussy*, *wench*, etc.

> Heav'ns sacred impe, faire goddesse [Peace] that renuest
> Th' old golden age (Sylv. *Handicrafts*).

impact. From L. *impingere*, *impact-*, to dash against.

impair. OF. *empeirier* (*empirer*), to make worse, VL. **in-pejorare*, from *pejor*, worse, or of F. formation from *pire*, OF. *peire*, L. *pejor*.

impale. F. *empaler*, from *pal*, stake, L. *palus*.

impart. OF. *empartir* (replaced by *faire part de*), L. *impartire*, *impertire*, to give a share of, from *pars*, *part-*, part.

impasse. F., from *in-*, neg. and *passer*. Coined by Voltaire as euph. for *cul de sac*.

impassible. F., Church L. *impassibilis*, incapable of suffering, from *pati*, *pass-*, to suffer; cf. *impassive*, not suffering.

impassion. It. *impassionare*. See *passion*.

impasto. It., thick laying-on of colour. See *paste*.

impeach. Orig. to hinder, but Wyc. also has it in sense of accusation. F. *empêcher*, to prevent, Late L. *impedicare*, from *pedica*, fetter, from *pes*, *ped-*, foot. Current E. sense represents rather OF. *empacher*, to accuse, for which see *dispatch*. *Impeach* replaced earlier *appeach* (see *peach²*). *Soft impeachment* is after Sheridan, from hist. *impeachment*, accusation and trial before House of Lords at instance of House of Commons.

> I own the soft impeachment—spare my blushes—
> I am Delia (*Rivals*, v. 3).

impeccable. F., L. *impeccabilis*. See *peccant*.

impecunious. From L. *in-*, neg. and *pecuniosus*, rich. See *pecuniary*.

impede. First in Shaks. L. *impedire*, lit. to shackle, from *pes*, *ped-*, foot. Much earlier is *impediment* (14 cent.).

impel. L. *impellere*, from *pellere*, *puls-*, to drive, force. Cf. *impulse*.

impend. L. *impendēre*, to hang over, from *pendēre*, to hang. Cf. *depend*.

imperative. L. *imperativus*, from *imperare*, to command, from *parare*, to make ready. First (16 cent.) as gram. term.

imperator. See *emperor.*

imperial. F. *impérial*, L. *imperialis*, from *imperium*, rule, empire. *Imperial federation*, *preference*, *imperialism*, in connection with British empire, are quite mod. (c. 1900). As applied to measures *imperial* indicates fixed by statute as contrasted with local usage. Sense of tuft of hair on lower lip is from Emperor Napoleon III. In sense of roof of coach, trunk to fit roof, F. *impériale*, app. jocular application of sense of height and dignity.

imperious. L. *imperiosus*, from *imperium*, rule, empire (q.v.).

imperscriptible. Unrecorded, without written authority. Only with *right*. From L. *in-*, neg. and *perscribere*, to write down.

impertinent. Orig. not to the point. See *pertinent*. Current sense, as also in F., from 17 cent.

impetrate [*theol.*]. To obtain by request. From L. *impetrare*, to wangle, from *patrare*, to bring to pass.

impetuous. F. *impétueux*, L. *impetuosus*, from *impetus*, attack, from *impetere*, to assail, from *petere*, to seek, strive towards.

impi. Zulu army. Native word for company of people, esp. armed.

impinge. L. *impingere*, from *in* and *pangere*, to fix, drive in.

implead [*leg.*]. To sue. OF. *emplaidier*. See *plead*.

implement. Orig. household goods in gen. Late L. *implementum*, from *implēre*, to fill up. Cf. *implement*, fulfilment, in Sc. law. For restriction of sense cf. *utensil*.

implicate. From L. *implicare*, to entangle, involve, from *plicare*, to fold, twist. Cf. *imply*, with which it is often synon., e.g. in *by implication*. Cf. *implicit*, orig. involved; then, implied, but not expressed or *explicit*.

implore. F. *implorer*, L. *implorare*, from *plorare*, to weep, wail.

impluvium [*arch.*]. Basin for rain-water in Roman atrium. L., from *pluere*, to rain.

imply. OF. *emplier*, L. *implicare*. See *implicate*. Hence also *employ*, representing the tonic stem, OF. *emplei-*, *emploi-*, of same verb. Cf. F. *plier* or *ployer*, to bend.

import. F. *importer*, L. *importare*, to bring in, from *portare*, to carry (see *port*¹). Secondary sense from MedL. *importare*, to carry (consequences, etc.) within it.

importunate. For earlier *importune*, F. *importun*, L. *importunus*, unfit, inconvenient, opposite of *opportunus*, cogn. with L. *portus*, harbour, with idea of accessibility or the reverse. Cf. L. *Portunus*, god of harbours, ? formed on *Neptunus*.

impose. F. *imposer*. See *pose*. Earlier is *imposition*, used by Wyc. of laying on of hands. Cf. *imposition*, something put upon one, *impost*, OF. (*impôt*), tax, *impostor*, which belong more directly to L. *imponere*, *impos-*, to lay on. For sense of adj. *imposing* cf. *impressive*.

impostume. Abscess. Altered from earlier *apostume* (q.v.). For prefix-change cf. *inveigle*.

impound. Now usu. of documents. See *pound*².

impoverish. OF. *empovrir*, *empovriss-* (replaced by *appauvrir*), from *en* and *povre* (*pauvre*). See *poor*.

imprecation. F. *imprécation*, L. *imprecatio-n-*, from *imprecari*, to invoke by prayer, from *precari*, to pray. Current limited sense is characteristic of human nature (v.i.); cf. F. *en vouloir à*, to bear ill-will to.

> I wish and imprecate to your Imperial Majestie all happiness (*NED.* 1664).

impregnable. Earlier *imprenable*, F., from *prendre*, *pren-*, to take, L. *prehendere*. For intrusive *-g-* cf. *delight*, *sovereign*, etc.

impregnate. Orig. adj. Late L. *impraegnatus*. See *pregnant*.

impresario. It., operatic manager, from *impresa*, undertaking, "emprise."

imprescriptible. Inalienable, not subject to prescription; usu. with *right*. F. (see *prescribe*).

impress¹. To press into. L. *imprimere*, *impress-*, from *in* and *premere*, *press-*, to press. See *press*¹, *print*. *Impressionism*, in art, dates from c. 1880.

impress². To force to serve, commandeer. See *press*². Early associated with *press*¹.

> Who can impress the forest, bid the tree
> Unfix his earth-bound root? (*Macb.* iv. 1).

imprest. Advance of money. For earlier *prest*. See *press*². Cf. It. *impresto*, OF. *emprest*.

imprimatur. L., let it be printed, from *imprimere*, to impress. Orig. of state licence to print book, now only of R. C. Church.

imprimis. L., for *in primis*, among the first (things).

imprint. Older form of *print* (q.v.).

impromptu. F., L. *in promptu*, from *promptus*, readiness, from *promere*, *prompt-*, to bring forward, from *pro* and *emere*, to obtain.

impropriate [*eccl.*]. To annex profits of benefice to corporation or individual; esp. of
tithes. From MedL. *inpropriare*. Cf. *appropriate*, *expropriate*, and see *proper*.

improve. Earlier *improw*, AF. *emprower*, to
turn to profit, from *en* and OF. *prou*, profit, for which see *prowess*. Earliest E. use
is connected with enclosing land (see *encroach*). Altered by influence of *prove* and
its compds. Etym. sense survives in to
improve the shining hour (Dr Watts), *the
occasion*, etc. *Approw*, *approve*, OF. *ap-
rouer*, was also used in same sense.

improvise. F. *improviser*, It. *improv(v)isare*,
"to say or sing extempore" (Flor.), from
improviso, unprepared, unprovided; cf. L.
adv. *improviso*, *de improviso*. See *provide*.

impudent. F., L. *impudens*, *impudent-*, neg.
of *pudens*, pres. part. of *pudēre*, to be
ashamed. In Chauc. Cf. *shameless*.

impugn. F. *impugner*, L. *impugnare*, to
assail, from *pugnare*, to fight. In lit. sense
in Wyc. (*Judges*, ix. 44).

impulse. See *impel*.

impunity. F. *impunité*, L. *impunitas*, from
impunis, unpunished. See *punish*.

impute. F. *imputer*, L. *imputare*, from *in* and
putare, to reckon.

in. AS. *in*. Com. Teut.; cf. Du. Ger. *in*, ON.
ī, Goth. *in*; cogn. with L. *in*, G. ἐν, Welsh
yn, etc. As adv. it is AS. *inne* (cf. Ger.
innen), whence compar. *inner*. *Inmost* is
a double superl. (see *foremost*, *-most*), and
innermost is a further corrupt. (cf. *utmost*,
uttermost). Hence also verb to *in*, esp. of
reclaiming land, AS. *innian*, *geinnian*.
With *inly*, thoroughly, from the heart, AS.
inlīce, cf. Ger. *innig*, in same sense.

in¹-. L. *in-*, neg., cogn. with Teut. *un-*, G.
ἀν-, ἀ-. Becomes *im-* before labial. Sometimes assumes, e.g. in *infamous*, *impious*,
more than mere neg. force (cf. *dis-*).

in²-. L. *in*, in, into. Becomes *im-* before
labial. Often restored from earlier *en-*, from
F.; cf. *inquire*, *enquire*, *injunction*, *enjoin*.
See also *en-*.

inadvertent. From obs. *advertent*. See *advert*.

inamorato, **-ta**. It., p.p. of *in(n)amorare*, "to
enamour, to fall in love" (Flor.). A 16
cent. word from the Grand Tour.

inane. L. *inanis*, empty. Earlier are *inani-
tion*, emptiness, *inanity*.

inasmuch (**as**). For *in as much*; cf. F. *en tant
que*.

inaugurate. See *augur*.

inca. Peruv., lord, king.

incandescent. From pres. part. of L. *in-
candescere*, from *in* and *candescere*, to begin
to glow, incept. of *candēre*, to glow.

incantation. F., L. *incantatio-n-*, from *incantare*, to sing spells, "enchant."

incarcerate. From L. *in* and *carcerare*, from
carcer, prison, ? cogn. with AS. *hearg*, heathen temple, whence *Harrow*.

incarnadine. Orig. flesh-coloured (cf. *carnation*). F. *incarnadin*, It. *incarnadino*, var.
of *incarnatino*, from *incarnato*, incarnate.
In mod. poet. use as verb after *Macb*. ii. 2.

incarnate. From L. *incarnare*, to make flesh,
caro, *carn-*. Earlier is *incarnation*, OF.,
Church L. *incarnatio-n-*, in Christian sense.
With *fiend incarnate*, etc., cf. fig. senses of
embodiment.

incendiary. L. *incendiarius*, from *incendium*,
conflagration (v.i.).

incense¹. Noun. ME. *encens*, F., L. *incensus*,
p.p. of *incendere*, to set on fire, cogn. with
candēre, to glow (see *incandescent*).

incense². Verb. OF. *incenser*, from L. *incendere*, *incens-*, as above. For current sense
cf. to *inflame*.

incentive. L. *incentivus*, setting the tune,
from *incinere*, **incent-*, to strike up, from
canere to sing. Sense influenced by association with *incendere*, to kindle (v.s.).

inception. L. *inceptio-n-*, beginning, from
incipere, *incept-*, from *capere*, to take. Cf.
Ger. *anfangen*, to begin, from *fangen*, to
take, catch. *Inceptive* is applied to L.
verbs in *-sco*, *-scere*, indicating beginning
of action.

incessant. F., Late L., *incessans*, *incessant-*,
from *cessare*, to cease (q.v.).

incest. L. *incestus*, impure, from *castus*,
chaste.

inch¹. Measure. AS. *ynce*, L. *uncia*, inch,
ounce. Early loan, not found in other Teut.
langs. *Every inch* (15 cent.) is now usu.
after Shaks.

> Ay, every inch a king (*Lear*, iv. 6).

inch². Small island (*Macb*. i. 2). Gael. *innis*;
cf. Ir. *inis*, Welsh *ynys*, Corn. *enys*, all
common in place-names; cogn. with L.
insula.

inchoate. From L. *inchoare*, for *incohare*, to
begin. Hence *inchoative*, sometimes used
for *inceptive*, as name for L. verbs in *-sco*,
-scere.

incident. F., orig. adj., from pres. part. of
L. *incidere*, to fall in, from *cadere*, to fall.
Sense of untoward happening, pol. contre-
temps, etc., is mod.

incinerate. From MedL. *incinerare*, to reduce to ashes. See *cinerary*.

incipient. From pres. part. of L. *incipere*, to begin, from *capere*, to take. Cf. *incipit*, (here) begins.

incision. F., L. *incisio-n-*, from *incidere*, *incis-*, to cut into, from *caedere*, to cut. For fig. sense of *incisive* cf. *trenchant*.

incite. F. *inciter*, L. *incitare*. See *cite*.

incivism. F. *incivisme*, a Revolution coinage. See *civism*.

inclement. F. *inclément*. See *clement*. Limitation to weather is curious.

incline. ME. *encline*, OF. *encliner* (*incliner*), as *decline* (q.v.). For fig. senses cf. to *lean*.

include. L. *includere*, to shut in, from *claudere*, to close.

incognito. It., unknown, esp. in connection with travelling, L. *incognitus*, from *cognoscere*, *cognit-*, to know. Hence *incog.* (c. 1700).

> We set out incog., as he called it (Defoe, *Roxana*).

incoherent. See *cohere*.

income. What "comes in." Cf. Ger. *einkommen*, *einkunft*, F. *revenu*, and opposite "out-goings." The *income-tax*, once assessed at "pence" in the pound, was first levied as a war-tax (1799).

incomprehensible. See *comprehend*. Lit. sense in Athanasian Creed.

incongruous. Not *congruous*. See *congruent*.

incorporate. See *corporate*. Cf. *incarnate* and hybrid *embody*.

incorrigible. F., L. *incorrigibilis*, from *corrigere*, to correct (q.v.).

incrassate [*biol.*]. Thickened. From L. *incrassare*. See *crass*.

increase. ME. *encresse*, AF. *encresser*, OF. *encreistre*, *encreiss-*, later *encroistre* (replaced by *accroître*), L. *increscere*, from *crescere*, to grow. Cf. *crescent*. Prob. influenced also by OF. *encraissier*, to augment, from L. *crassus*, fat.

increment. L. *incrementum*, from *increscere* (v.s.). Esp. in *unearned increment* (J. S. Mill).

incriminate. From MedL. *incriminare*, from *crimen*, *crimin-*, crime.

incubate. From L. *incubare*, to sit on eggs. See *covey*, *cubicle*.

incubus. Orig. night fiend seeking carnal intercourse with women. Late L., for *incubo*, nightmare, from *incubare* (v.s.). Cf. *succubus*.

> Thise spyrites do women schame;
> Incuby demones ys cald ther name (*NED.* c. 1330).

inculcate. From L. *inculcare*, to stamp in, from *calcare*, to tread, from *calx*, *calc-*, heel.

inculpate. From L. *culpa*, fault, as *incriminate*.

incumbent. From pres. part. of L. *incumbere*, to lie upon, apply oneself to, cogn. with *incubate*. Earliest (15 cent.) as noun in Church sense, app. from MedL. sense of obtaining, holding.

incunabula. L., pl., swaddling-clothes, from *cunae*, cradle. Fig. infancy, hence books produced during infancy of printing (before 1500). This sense dates from Van Beughem's *Incunabula Typographiae* (Amsterdam, 1688).

incur. L. *incurrere*, to run into, from *currere*, to run. Lit. sense survives in *incursion*.

indeed. Orig. two words. Cf. *in fact* and Ger. *in der tat*.

indefatigable. OF., L. *indefatigabilis*, from *defatigare*, to tire out.

indefeasible. See *defeasance*.

indelible. Earlier *indeleble*, "that cannot be put, or raced out" (Blount), from L. *delēre*, to wipe out.

indemnity. Orig. security against contingent loss. F. *indemnité*, Late L. *indemnitas*, from *indemnis*, unharmed, from *damnum*, harm, damage. Cf. synon. F. *dédommagement*, lit. dis-damage-ment. *War-indemnity* dates from Germany's extortion of five milliards from France in 1871.

indent. F. *endenter*, to give a serrated edge to, from *dent*, tooth, L. *dens*, *dent-*; cf. MedL. & It. *indentare*. Esp. to separate two halves of document in such a way that their genuineness may be verified by juxtaposition (cf. *tally*, *charter-party*). Hence *indenture*, agreement, esp. in apprenticeship, and to *indent upon* (orig. Anglo-Ind.), to write a formal order with counterfoil; cf. MedL. *carta indentata*, indenture. This verb has absorbed earlier native *indent*, from *dent*, *dint*, opposite to *emboss*.

independent. F. *indépendant* (see *dependent*). As name of rel. sect (17 cent.) equivalent to *Congregational*.

index. L., fore-finger, anything that points out, "indicates." In book sense from 16 cent. Also short for *index librorum prohibitorum*, first published by authority of Pius IV (1564), or *index expurgatorius*, first published by authority of Philip II of Spain (1571), both compilations being due to the Council of Trent (1545–63).

India. L., G. Ἰνδία, from Ἰνδός, the Indus, Pers. *hind*, Sanskrit *sindhu*, river. Also poet. *Ind*, F. *Inde*, and ME. *Indie*, still in pl. *Indies*. Orig. of Indus region only (see *Hindi*), later extended to whole peninsula, and vaguely used for East, e.g. *India paper*, *Indian ink* both come from China. So also the early explorers thought America the back-door of India, whence *West Indies*, *Red Indian*, *Indian corn*, *india-rubber*, etc. *Indian summer*, US. for *All Hallows' summer* (1 *Hen. IV*, i. 2), is first recorded 1798 and "is now a literary convention in three continents" (A. Matthews). Volney (1803) renders it *été sauvage* and compares F. *été de la Saint-Martin*. The popular form *Injun* was commonly written c. 1800 and survives in *honest Injun*, "the [American] boy's equivalent to a Bible oath" (A. Matthews).

indicate. From L. *indicare*, from *dicare*, to make known. Hence *indicative*, first as gram. term, F. *indicatif*.

indict. ME. *endite*, AF. *enditer*, with spec. sense of accusing, which does not appear in OF. *enditer*, from L. *in* and *dictare*, to proclaim. For latinized spelling cf. *interdict*, *verdict*. Cf. *indiction*, fiscal period of fifteen years established by Constantine (313), also assessment, etc., L. *indictio-n-*, from *indicere*, to appoint.

You cannot indict a nation (Burke).

For once we can, and do, indict a whole nation
(*Pall Mall Gaz.* Dec. 6, 1917).

Indies. See *India*.

indifferent. See *different*. Orig. without inclination to either side. From idea of neutrality came sense of fairly good (17–18 cent.), which has now degenerated to rather bad. *Indifferentism* (rel.) is via F.

That they may truly and indifferently minister justice (*Prayer for Church Militant*).

I am indifferent honest (*Haml.* iii. 1).

indigenous. Earlier *indigene*, F. *indigène*, L. *indigena*, from a prefix cogn. with G. ἔνδον, within, and *gignere*, *gen-*, to beget. Cf. *industry*.

indigent. F., from pres. part. of L. *indigēre*, to lack, from *egēre*, to want, with prefix as above.

indign [*archaic*]. F. *indigne*, L. *indignus*, unworthy.

indignation. F., L. *indignatio-n-*, anger at what is regarded as unworthy (v.s.), from *indignari*, to be angry. In Chauc. and Wyc. Cf. *indignity*, unworthy treatment.

indigo. Earlier (16 cent.) *indico*, Sp. *índico*, L. *Indicum*, of India. Earlier name was *anil* (see *aniline*).

indisposed. Orig. not in order. With mod. sense (from c. 1600) cf. *out of sorts*.

indite. ME. *endite*, OF. *enditer*, from L. *dictare*, to dictate. Cf. *indict*.

individual. MedL. *individualis*, from L. *individuus* (whence F. *individu*), from *in-*, neg., *dividere*, to divide. Cf. *atom*. *Individualism*, *individualist* are via F.

Indo-European, Indo-Germanic [*ling.*]. The second is after Ger. *indogermanisch*, coined by Schlegel (1808) and regularly used by Ger. philologists for *Aryan* (q.v.).

indolent. F., Late L. *indolens*, *indolent-*, from *dolēre*, to grieve. Cf. *to take no pains*.

indomitable. After F. *indomptable*, from L. *domitare*, frequent. of *domare*, to tame. See *daunt*.

indoor(s). For earlier *within door(s)*.

indubitable. L. *indubitabilis*, from *dubitare*, to doubt (q.v.).

induce. L. *inducere*, to lead in. Cf. *induct*, to lead in formally, introduce, L. *induct-*; also *induction*, opposed in log. to *deduction*, L. *inductio-n-* being used by Cicero for G. ἐπαγωγή, leading to (Aristotle).

indulge. L. *indulgēre*, to be courteous, complaisant. Much earlier is *indulgence* in gen. and spec. sense of remission of sin obtained by payment.

And purchace al the pardoun of Pampiloun and Rome
And indulgences ynowe
(*Piers Plowm.* B. xvii. 253).

induna. Zulu or Matabele chief. Zulu.

indurate. From L. *indurare*, from *durus*, hard.

indusium [*bot.*]. L., tunic, from *induere*, to put on.

industry. F. *industrie*, L. *industria*, ? for **indu-struua*, from *struere*, to build, with prefix as in *indigenous*. *Industrial-ism* in current sense is mod. via F.

inebriate. From L. *inebriare*, from *ebrius*, drunk.

ineffable. F., L. *ineffabilis*, unutterable, from *effari*, from *ex* and *fari*, to speak. Cf. *fable*.

ineluctable. That cannot be escaped from. F. *inéluctable*, L. *ineluctabilis*, from *eluctari*, to struggle out, from *ex* and *luctari*, to struggle. Cf. *reluctant*.

inept. F. *inepte*, L. *ineptus*, from *aptus*. See *apt*.

inert. F. *inerte*, L. *iners*, *inert-*, sluggish, orig. unskilled, from *in-*, neg. and *ars*, *art-*, art.

Hence *inertia*, introduced into phys. by Kepler.

inevitable. F. *inévitable*, L. *inevitabilis*, from *evitare*, to avoid, from *ex* and *vitare*, to shun.

inexorable. F., L. *inexorabilis*, from *exorare*, to entreat, from *orare*, to pray.

inexpressibles. Trousers (18 cent.). Cf. *un-mentionables*.

inexpugnable. F., L. *inexpugnabilis*, from *expugnare*, to take by attack, from *pugnare*, to fight.

infamous, infamy. See *fame*. For strengthened sense cf. some compds. of *dis-*.

infant. ME. *enfaunt*, F. *enfant*, L. *infans*, *infant-*, unable to speak, *fari*. Aphet. *fant*, *faunt*, common in ME., survive as surnames. Earliest sense of baby is extended to young child (*infant school*) and minor (leg.). Cf. It. Sp. *infante*, child, youth, whence It. *infanteria*, infantry, force composed of those too inexperienced or low in rank for cavalry service, whence E. *infantry* through F. Also Sp. *infanta*, princess, spec. eldest daughter who is not heir to the throne.

infatuate. From L. *infatuare*, from *fatuus*, foolish. Cf. *dote*, *fond*, and F. *affoler*, *assoter*, to infatuate.

infect. From L. *inficere*, *infect-*, to dip in, impregnate, from *facere*, to make. ME. had also adj. *infect*, F. *infecte*, tainted, etc., which may be the source of the verb. Cf. *addict*.

infer. L. *inferre*, to bring in.

inferior. L., compar. of *inferus*, from *infra*, below.

infernal. F., L. *infernalis*, from *infernus*, lower (v.s.). Cf. It. *inferno*, hell, esp. with ref. to Dante's *Divine Comedy*.

infest. F. *infester*, L. *infestare*, from *infestus*, unsafe, hostile.

infidel. F. *infidèle*, L. *infidelis*, from *fides*, faith. Earliest of Saracens.

infiltration. Now much used, after F., in mil. and pol. sense. See *filter*.

infinite. See *finish*. *Infinitive* is L. *infinitivus* (Quintilian and Priscian). *Infinitesimal* is mod. coinage after *centesimal*, etc.

infirmary. Replaces (from 16 cent.) ME. *fermery*, *farmery*, aphet. forms from OF. *enfermerie* (*infirmerie*), place for the infirm, OF. *enferme* (*infirme*).

inflammable. F., from L. *inflammare*, to set on fire, inflame. See *flame*.

inflate. From L. *inflare*, *inflat-*, from *flare*, to blow.

inflect. L. *inflectere*, from *flectere*, *flex-*, to bend; cf. *inflexible*, *inflexion*. With gram. sense of latter cf. hist. of *case*, *declension*. An *inflexional* lang. (Aryan) is one in which orig. *agglutination* (q.v.) is disguised by phonetic decay.

inflict. From L. *infligere*, *inflict-*. See *afflict*.

influence. F., Late L. *influentia*, flowing in, from *fluere*, to flow. Orig. astrol. (Chauc.); cf. Late L. (4 cent.) *influxus* (*stellarum*), astral influence.

influence: a flowing in, (and particularly) an influence, or influent course, of the planets (Cotg.).

influenza. It., influence (v.s.), but also applied to epidemic outbreak, and in 1743 spec. to *la grippe*, which was then raging in Europe and has made periodic visits since. Perh. quot. below records an earlier visit. Also applied in 19 cent., before the real thing arrived, to a bad cold. For specialization cf. *plague*.

I got an extreme cold, such as was afterwards so epidemical, as not only to afflict us in this island, but was rife over all Europe, like a plague
(Evelyn, 1675).

influx. F., Late L. *influxus*, from *fluere*, to flow.

inform. ME. *enforme*, OF. *enformer* (*informer*), L. *informare*, to give form to. Mod. sense springs from that of informing the mind. To *inform*, bring accusation, appears first in the nouns *information*, *informer* (15 cent.), techn. *common informer*, employed with the object of dispensing with the grand jury. The constable usu. begins his evidence in court with *Acting on information received....*

infraction. See *infringe*.

infra dig. L. *infra dignitatem*, a phrase of unknown origin.

infrangible. F., unbreakable, from L. *frangere*, to break.

infringe. L. *infringere*, *infract-*, from *frangere*, to break.

infuse. See *fuse*.

infusoria. ModL. (sc. *animalcula*). First used (c. 1760) by Ledermuller, of Nürnberg.

ingeminate. From L. *ingeminare*, to repeat, from *geminus*, twin. In mod. use after Clarendon.

[Falkland] often, after a deep silence and frequent sighs, would...ingeminate the word, Peace, Peace
(Clarendon, *Hist. of Rebellion*, 1647).

It is no good (in Clarendon's famous phrase) to ingeminate the word "peace"
(H. H. Asquith, Sep. 26, 1917).

ingenio. Sugar-mill (see quot. s.v. *estancia*). Sp., L. *ingenium*. See *engine*.

ingenious. F. *ingénieux*, L. *ingeniosus*, from *ingenium*, natural ability (v.i.).

ingénue. F., artless girl (v.s.), esp. on stage.

ingenuous. From L. *ingenuus*, inborn, free-born, frank, etc., whence F. *ingénu*, art-less. Constantly confused in 17 cent. with above, *ingenuity*, which belongs to *in-genuous*, being used as expressing both qualities, and now definitely assigned to *ingenious*.

I find that men are angry at my ingenuity and openness of discourse (Jeremy Taylor).

ingle. Sc., fire burning on hearth. Gael. *aingeal*, fire, light, cogn. with L. *ignis*.

ingot. Used by Chauc. (G. 1209) of mould into which metal is poured. App. from AS. *gēotan*, to pour; cf. Ger. *einguss*, in-pouring, ingot, from cogn. *giessen*, to pour. F. *lingot* is from E., with agglutination of def. art. as in *lierre*, ivy (OF. *l'ierre*), etc. Mod. form, for normal **inyot*, may be a spelling-pronunc. of a rare techn. word not recorded between Chauc. and late 16 cent.

ingrained. Of habits, prejudices, etc. Lit. *dyed in grain*. See *grain*, *engrain*, and cf. fig. use of *deep-(double-)dyed*.

ingratiate. Coined in 16 cent. from It. *in-graziare* (earlier *ingratiare*), from phrase *in gratia* (*grazia*), L. *in gratiam*, into favour, grace.

ingratiarsi: to engrace, or insinuate himself into favour (Flor.).

ingredient. From pres. part. of L. *ingredi*, to step in. Cf. *grade*.

ingress. As *egress* (v.s.).

inguinal [*anat*.]. L. *inguinalis*, from *inguen*, *inguin-*, groin.

ingurgitate. From L. *ingurgitare*, from *gurges*, *gurgit-*, whirlpool, gulf.

inhabit. ME. *enhabit*, OF. *enhabiter*, L. *in-habitare*, to dwell in, from *habitare*, to dwell. See *habit*. ModF. has *habiter*, while *inhabité* means *uninhabited*.

inhale. L. *inhalare*. Cf. *exhale*.

inhere. L. *inhaerēre*. Cf. *adhere*.

inherit. ME. *enherite*, OF. *enheriter*, to put in possession as heir, from Late L. *heredi-tare*, from *heres*, *hered-*, heir. Orig. sense in *disinherit*. Both senses are in Shaks.

inhibit. In Church law for *prohibit*. From L. *inhibēre*, *inhibit-*, to hold in, from *habēre*, to hold.

inhuman. Opposite of *humane* (q.v.).

Man's inhumanity to man
Makes countless thousands mourn (Burns).

inhume. See *exhume*.

inimical. Late L. *inimicalis*, from *inimicus*, enemy, not friend, *amicus*.

iniquity. F. *iniquité*, L. *iniquitas*, from *iniquus*, from *aequus*, fair, even, etc.

initial. F., L. *initialis*, from *initium*, be-ginning, lit. going in, from *ire*, *it-*, to go. *Initiation* occurs first (16 cent.) of formal introduction to office, society, etc. To *take the initiative* is from F. *prendre l'ini-tiative*; for mil. sense cf. *offensive*, *defensive*. The abuse of initials, for purposes of con-ciseness, has during the War become such as to necessitate a dict. for this new lang.

Deux amis se rencontrent et ce dialogue s'engage: "Où es-tu? Que fais-tu?" "R.A.T. D'abord em-ployé comme G.V.C., je suis maintenant dans une S.H.R., C.A., au B.C.R." L'autre a compris! Il reprend: "Moi, je suis du S.M. de l'A.L.G.P.; mais je vais partir dans la D.C.A. du C.E.O."... Ce jargon signifie que le premier des deux camarades, appartenant à la réserve de l'armée territoriale, après avoir gardé les voies de com-munication, fait partie d'une section hors rang et qu'il est commis d'administration au bureau de centralisation des renseignements. L'autre compte à une section de munitions dans l'artillerie lourde à grande puissance et entrevoit son prochain départ pour la Grèce, où il sera employé à la dé-fense contre les avions au corps expéditionnaire d'Orient (*Temps*).

inject. From L. *inicere*, *inject-*, from *jacere*, to throw.

Injun. Colloq. US. for (*Red*) *Indian*. See *India*.

injunction. Late L. *injunctio-n-*. See *enjoin*.

injury. AF. *injurie*, L. *injuria*, from *in-jurius*, wrongful, from *in-*, neg. and *jus*, *jur-*, right, law. Usual sense of F. *injure*, offensive speech, survives in *injurious words* (*language*). Verb to *injure* is back-formation.

ink. ME. *enke*, OF. *enque* (*encre*), Late L. *encaustum*, with accent shifted to prefix, G. ἔγκαυστος, burnt in (see *encaustic*), from ἐν and καίειν, to burn; cf. It. *inchiostro*, Du. *inkt*, latter from F. Orig. purple ink used in signatures by Roman emperors. Archaic *inkhorn* (i.e. bookish) *term* is 16 cent.

inkle. Narrow tape. Perh. Du. *enkel* (earlier *inckel*), single. Hence *as thick* (*close*) *as inkle-weavers*, from narrowness of loom.

inkling. From ME. *inkle*, recorded once only, to whisper, communicate (the truth), of unknown origin. At first usu. to *hear an inkling*.

inlet. Creek. From *in* and *let*[1], but recorded only from 16 cent. and prob. representing also *yenlet*, a common place-name in Thames Estuary, AS. *gēan-, gegn-*, against, and *lād*, way, "lode."

inmate. From *in* and *mate*[2] (q.v.).

inmost. See *in* and *-most*.

inn. AS. *inn*, from adv. *inn, inne*, within. See *in*. Formerly used also, like *hostel*, of univ. boarding-houses; cf. the *Inns of Court* (orig. Inner and Middle Temple, Lincoln's, Gray's), belonging to leg. societies which have the right of preparing for, and admitting to, the bar.

innate. L. *innatus*, inborn, from *nasci, nat-*, to be born.

inner. Compar. of *in*. *Inner man*, spiritual man, is AS., jocular use being 19 cent.

innermost. See *in* and *-most*.

innings. Recorded only in pl. form (1746) used as sing. For formation, from *in*, cf. *outing*.

innocent. F., L. *innocens, innocent-*, from *nocēre*, to harm. Esp. in ref. to the *Holy Innocents*, massacred by Herod, whence *Innocents' Day* (Dec. 28), formerly *Childermas*.

innocuous. From L. *innocuus*, from *nocēre* (v.s.).

innovate. From L. *innovare*, from *novus*, new.

innuendo. L., by nodding to, abl. gerund of *innuere*, from *nuere*, to nod. Orig. in MedL. leg. phraseology in sense of *to wit*.

innuendo: ...the office of this word is onely to declare and design the person or thing which was named incertain before; as to say, he (*innuendo* the plaintiff) is a theef (Blount).

inoculate. Orig. to bud, graft, from L. *inoculare*, from *oculus*, eye, bud. Cf. Ger. *impfen* (see *imp*), to graft, vaccinate. In med. sense of earlier and cruder form of vaccination, first tried on felons (v.i.).

On Wednesday the seven persons who had the small pox inoculated upon them for an experiment were discharged out of Newgate, all in a perfect state of health (*Applebee's Journal*, Sep. 9, 1721).

inordinate. L. *inordinatus*, unordered. See *order*.

inquest. ME. & OF. *enqueste* (*enquête*), inquiry, VL. **inquesta* (for *inquisita*), from **inquerere* (for *inquirere*), from *quaerere*, to seek. Orig. accented on second syllable, whence *crowner's 'quest*, and used of any offic. investigation. See *coroner*.

inquire. Restored spelling of ME. *enquere*, OF. *enquerre, enquérir, enquier-*, VL. **inquerere* (v.s.).

Whatever sceptick could inquere for,
For every "why" he had a "wherefore"
                    (*Hudibras*, I. i. 131).

inquisition. F., L., *inquisitio-n-*, from *inquirere, inquisit-* (v.s.). Used by Wyc. for *inquiry*; cf. *inquisitive*. In R.C. sense established (13 cent.) by Innocent III, under the Congregation of the Holy Office, and reorganized 1478–83. The office still exists, but occupies itself chiefly with heretical literature. *Inquisitor* is much older, as *inquisitores ad conquirendos et eruendos hereticos* were appointed temp. Theodosius I (4 cent.).

inroad. Preserves etym. sense of *road*, riding. Cf. *raid, incursion*.

insane. L. *insanus*, "madde, peevishe, doting" (Coop.), lit. sense of unhealthy having already in L. given way to spec. sense.

inscribe. L. *inscribere*, replacing ME. *inscrive*, F. *inscrire, inscriv-*. Cf. *describe*.

inscrutable. Late L. *inscrutabilis*. See *scrutiny*.

insect. L. *insectum* (sc. *animal*), from *insecare*, to cut into, from *secare, sect-*, to cut, translating synon. G. ἔντομον (see *entomology*). From sectional aspect of body and limbs.

insert. From L. *inserere, insert-*, from *serere*, to join. Cf. *series*.

insessores [*ornith.*]. Perching birds. From L. *insidēre, insess-*, to sit on, from *sedēre*, to sit.

inside running. Advantage, the inside track of a curved race-course being shorter than the outside.

insidious. L. *insidiosus*, from *insidiae*, ambush, from *insidēre*, to lie in wait. See *insessores*.

insignia. L., neut. pl. of *insignis*, distinguished, from *signum*, sign. Cf. *ensign*.

insinuate. From L. *insinuare*, to introduce tortuously, from *sinuare*, to wind, bend, from *sinus*, curve. Cf. to *worm oneself in*.

insipid. F. *insipide*, L. *insipidus*, from *sapidus*, tasteful. See *savour*.

insist. F. *insister*, L. *insistere*, from *sistere*, to stand. Cf. to *stand on one's rights*.

insolation. Exposure to sun, sunstroke. L. *insolatio-n-*, from *insolare*, from *sol*, sun.

insolent. F., L. *insolens, insolent-*, orig. unaccustomed, from *solēre*, to be accustomed.

For ditty and amorous ode I find Sir Walter Raleigh's vein most lofty, insolent, and passionate (Puttenham, *Art of Eng. Poesy*).

insomnia. L., from *insomnis*, sleepless, from *somnus*, sleep.

insouciant. F., from *se soucier,* to care, L. *sollicitare*, to agitate. Cf. *nonchalant.*

inspan [*SAfr.*]. Du. *inspannen*, to yoke oxen, etc., from *spannen*, to stretch, span.

inspection. F., L. *inspectio-n-*, from *inspicere, inspect-,* to look into. Cf. *aspect*, etc.

inspeximus [*hist.*]. L., we have inspected (v.s.). Used of charters confirmed after examination. Cf. *visa.*

inspire. F. *inspirer*, L. *inspirare*, from *spirare,* to breathe; cf. *spirit*. First (*inspiration,* c. 1300) in rel. sense, which is adapted from G. πνεῖν, to breathe, πνεῦμα, breath, inspiration; e.g. θεόπνευστος, inspired by God (2 *Tim.* iii. 16).

inspissate. To thicken. From L. *inspissare*, from *spissus*, dense.

install. F. *installer*, to put in a *stall* (q.v.). In E. orig. (16 cent.) of enthroning a Church dignitary, etc.

instalment. Payment. Altered from earlier *estallment*, from OF. *estaler*, to fix, from OHG. *stal*, stall. See *stall*.

Nous avons de nostre grace especiale a ly grantez de estaller la dite somme de payer a nous checun an cynk marcz (*John of Gaunt's Reg.* 1372-6).

instance. Orig. urgency, as in *at the instance of.* F., L. *instantia*, from *instare*, to be present, urge one's case. Mod. sense from that of scholastic argument brought forward in proof or disproof, as in *for instance.* Cf. *instant*, orig. urgent, also used of point of present time (*the 5th instant*). *Instantaneous* is coined on *simultaneous.*

They were instant [*Vulg.* instabant] with loud voyces, and required that he might be crucified
(*Luke,* xxiii. 23, Geneva, 1560).

instauration. L. *instauratio-n-*, from *instaurare*, to restore (q.v.). Chiefly allusive to Bacon's *Instauratio Magna* (1620).

instead. *In stead* as two words up to 17 cent., as still in *in his stead*, etc. Cf. F. *au lieu*, Ger. *anstatt*. See *stead*.

instep. App. from *in* and *step*, though this hardly makes sense. In 17 cent. also *instop, instup.* ? Rather from *stoop*[1], bend.

instigate. From L. *instigare*, cogn. with G. στίζειν, to prick. Cf. *stigma.*

instil. L. *instillare*, from *stillare*, to drop. Cf. *distill, still*[2].

instinct. L. *instinctus*, from *instinguere*, to urge, incite, cogn. with *instigate.* Mod. sense of adj., as in *instinct with life*, from c. 1800 only.

institute. First as verb. L. *instituere, institut-*, to set up, from *statuere* (see *statute*). As noun, in jurisprudence, esp. in ref. to *Institutes of Justinian* (533). In sense of society, etc., imitated from F. *Institut national des Sciences et des Arts,* established (1795) to replace the royal academies. In this sense *institution* is earlier (c. 1700).

instruct. From L. *instruere, instruct-*, to build. See *structure*. In E. only in fig. sense (cf. *edify*).

instrument. F., L. *instrumentum*, from *instruere* (v.s.).

insufflation. F., L. *insufflatio-n-*, from *insufflare*, to blow into, from *sufflare*, from *sub* and *flare*, to blow. Esp. in rite of exorcism.

insular. L. *insularis*, from *insula*, island. See *isle.*

insult. F., L. *insultare*, to jump at, assail frequent. of *insilire, insult-*, from *salire, salt-*, to leap. To *add insult to injury* is a latinism, *injuriae contumeliam addere* (Phaedrus, v. iii. 5).

insuperable. L. *insuperabilis*, from *superare*, to overcome, from *super*, over, above.

insure. Differentiated in commerc. sense from *ensure*, and partly replacing earlier *assure*, which was used of all forms of insurance in 16 cent.

insurrection. F., L. *insurrectio-n-*, from *insurgere*, from *surgere, surrect-*, to rise. *Insurgent*, obs. F. (replaced by *insurgé*), is later (18 cent.).

intact. L. *intactus*, from *in-*, neg. and *tangere, tact-*, to touch.

intaglio. It., from *intagliare*, from *tagliare*, to cut. See *tailor.*

integer. L., untouched, "intact," from *in-*, neg. and root of *tangere*, to touch. Hence *integral, integrity.*

integument. L. *integumentum*, from *tegere*, to cover.

intellect. F., L. *intellectus*, from *intellegere, intellect-*, to understand, from *inter*, between, *legere*, to pick, choose. Cf. *intelligence, intellectual.* The use of the latter word for "a person possessing or supposed to possess superior powers of intellect" (*NED.*) dates from c. 1880. In F. it is not yet contemptuous. Cf. *intelligenzia*, used collectively for Russian "intellectuals," app. from L. *intelligentia*.

Ce grand intellectuel [Renan] a donné un très considérable exemple (Faguet).

The self-styled "intellectuals"—if the war sweeps

the ineffable term into oblivion, it will have done some good (Locke, *Red Planet*).

intend. F. *entendre*, L. *intendere, intens-, intent-*, to bend the mind on, from *tendere*, to stretch. Cf. *intendant*, administrator, *intense, intent*, the latter, as noun, from F. *entente*, in obs. sense of intention, purpose, etc., as in *good* (*malicious*) *intent*, etc. *To all intents and purposes* is for earlier (16 cent.) *to all intents, constructions and purposes*. *Intentions* in matrimonial sense is in *Peregrine Pickle* (ch. xxviii.).

inter. ME. *enter*, F. *enterrer*, from *terre*, earth, L. *terra*.

inter-. L., between, cogn. with *under*. In some words represents obs. *entre-*, from F.

intercalate. From L. *intercalare*, to proclaim insertion (of day) in calendar, from *calare*, to proclaim. Cf. *calends*.

intercede. L. *intercedere*, to go between, from *cedere, cess-*, to go.

intercept. From L. *intercipere, intercept-*, to take between, from *capere*, to take.

intercession. See *intercede*.

intercourse. Earlier *entercourse*, F. *entrecours*, from OF. *entrecourre*, to run between, from L. *currere*, to run.

interdict. ME. *entredit*, OF. (*interdit*), L. *interdictum*, from *interdicere*, to decree, from *dicere, dict-*, to proclaim, order. First (c. 1300) in Papal sense. For restored spelling cf. *indict, verdict*.

interest. ME. & AF. *interesse*, L. infin., to be a concern to, used as noun; cf. It. *interesse*, Sp. *interés*, Ger. *interesse*. Altered under influence of OF. *interest* (*intérêt*), L. *interest*, it concerns, used as noun, the change being also partly due to the fact that the obs. verb to *interess* was chiefly used as p.p. *interess'd*. The OF. word usu. meant loss, as still in *dommages et intérêts*. *Interesting condition* occurs in the last chapter of *Roderick Random*.

interessé: interested, or touched in; dishonoured, hurt, or hindered by (Cotg.).

interfere. OF. *entreferir*, from *férir*, to strike, L. *ferire*. Orig. in E. (16 cent.) of horse knocking feet together in trotting, as still in US.

No; not at any price. He interferes; and he's wind-broken (O. Henry, *Gentle Grafter*).

interim. L. adv., meanwhile. From *inter*, between, with adv. suffix *-im*.

interior. L. compar. of *interus*, from *intra*, within; cf. *inferior*. *Interior lines* (mil.) are

an advantage in concentrating on any particular point.

interjection. F., L. *interjectio-n-*, from *intericere, interject-*, to throw between, from *jacere*, to throw.

interlard. Orig. (16 cent.) to mix fat with lean. F. *entrelarder*. See *lard*.

interloper. Orig. (16 cent.) unauthorized trader (by sea) trespassing on privileges and monopolies of chartered company. App. from *lope*, dial. form of *leap*. Cf. *landloper*, vagabond, *elope* (q.v.). *Interlope* occurs esp. in ref. to disputes as to "spheres of influence" between E. and Du. merchant venturers.

interlude. MedL. *interludium*, from *ludus*, play. Orig. farcical episode introduced between acts of mystery play.

intermediate. MedL. *intermediatus*, from *intermedius*. Cf. *immediate*.

intermezzo. It., from *mezzo*, middle, L. *medius*. Cf. *interlude*.

intermit. L. *intermittere*, to leave off, lit. send, put, between, from *mittere*.

intern. F. *interner*, from *interne*, resident within, L. *internus*, from *intra*, within. Cf. *internal*.

international. App. first used (1780) by Bentham in ref. to "law of nations." Cf. *internationalist*, which dates from foundation (1864) in London of International Working Men's Association; also F. *internationale* (sc. *chanson*), revolutionary song.

internecine. L. *internecinus*, deadly, from *necare*, to kill, *inter-* having intens. force. First used by Butler to render L. *bellum internecinum*. Mod. sense is due to erron. explanation of mutually destructive in Johns.

Th' Egyptians worship'd dogs, and for
Their faith made internecine war
               (*Hudibras*, i. i. 174).

interpellation. In mod. sense of interrupting the order of the day from F., L. *interpellatio-n-*, from *interpellare*, to interrupt, lit. drive between, from *pellere*, to drive. But Wyc. uses the verb *enterpele*.

interpolate. From L. *interpolare*, to furbish up, from *polire*, to polish.

interpose. See *pose*.

interpret. F. *interpréter*, L. *interpretari*, from *interpres, interpret-*, agent, translator, "stickler between two at variance" (Coop.), ? orig. helper in bargain-making, with second element cogn. with *pretium*, price.

interregnum. L., between reign.

interrogate. From L. *interrogare*, from *rogare*, to ask.

interrupt. From L. *interrumpere*, from *rumpere*, *rupt-*, to break.

intersect. From L. *intersecare*, from *secare*, *sect-*, to cut.

intersperse. From L. *interspergere*, *interspers-*, from *spargere*, *spars-*, to scatter.

interstice. F., L. *interstitium*, from *intersistere*, to stand between.

interval. ME. *enterval*, OF. *entreval* (*intervalle*), L. *intervallum*, orig. space between ramparts, *vallum*.

intervene. F. *intervenir*, L. *intervenire*, from *venire*, to come.

interview. Earlier *entrevue*, F., p.p. fem. of *entrevoir*, from *entre*, L. *inter*, and *voir*, to see, L. *vidēre*. The journalistic *interview*, whence F. *interviewer*, is US. (c. 1870).

intestate. L. *intestatus*, from *testatus*, p.p. of *testari*, to make will. See *testament*.

intestine. L. *intestinus*, from *intus*, within. Cf. *inn'ards*, *entrails*.

intimate. L. *intimatus*, p.p. of *intimare*, from *intimus* (from *intus*, within), used as superl. of *interior*. From the same verb, with sense of driving in, comes verb to *intimate*.

intimidate. From Late L. *intimidare*, from *timidus*, timid.

intitule. F. *intituler*, Late L. *intitulare*, from *titulus*, title (q.v.).

into. For *in to*.

intone. Church L. *intonare*, from *tonus*, tone (q.v.).

intoxicate. MedL. *intoxicare*, from L. *toxicare*, from *toxicum*, poison, G. τοξικόν, poison for arrows, from τόξον, a bow.

I intoxycat, I poyson with venyme: je entoxyque (Palsg.).

intra-. L., within.

intrados. Inner curve of arch. As *extrados* (q.v.).

intransigent. F. *intransigeant*, adapted from Sp. *los intransigentes*, extreme Left, or Republican, party, from L. *transigere*, to come to an understanding, compromise. See *transaction*.

intrepid. L. *intrepidus*, from *trepidus*, alarmed.

intricate. L. *intricatus*, from *intricare*, to entangle. Cf. *extricate*.

intrigue. F. *intriguer*, It. *intrigare*, "to intricate, entrap" (Flor.), L. *intricare* (v.s.). First E. sense (c. 1600), to perplex, puzzle, has recently been re-introduced as a gallicism.

intrinsic. F. *intrinsèque*, MedL. adj. *intrinsecus*, from L. adv. *intrinsecus*, inwardly. Cf. *extrinsic* (q.v.).

introduce. L. *introducere*, from *intro*, within, *ducere*, to lead.

introit. Antiphon and psalm sung as priest approaches altar. F. *introït*, L. *introitus*, entry, from *ire*, *it-*, to go (v.s.).

intromit. To interfere, etc. L. *intromittere*, from *mittere*, to send, put. Partly refashioned from obs. *entermet*, F. *entremettre*.

introspect. From L. *introspicere*, *introspect-*, look within, from *specere*, to look.

intrude. L. *intrudere*, from *trudere*, *trus-*, to thrust. Orig. trans., current sense being from reflex., to *intrude oneself upon*.

intuition. F., MedL. *intuitio-n-*, from *intueri*, to look upon, from *tueri*, to behold.

inundate. From L. *inundare*, from *unda*, wave.

inure, enure. From *in-*, *en-*, into, and obs. *ure*, work, OF. *uevre* (*œuvre*), L. *opera*, pl. of *opus*. Cf. *manure*. For formation of verb from adv. phrase cf. *endeavour*.

I bring in ure: je habitue (Palsg.).

brought in ure, or accustomed: assuefactus (Litt.).

invade. L. *invadere*, from *vadere*, *vas-*, to go.

invalid. Infirm, sick. Spec. use of *invdlid*, L. *invalidus*, from *validus*, strong, valid, differentiated after F. pronunc. from 18 cent.

invecked, invected [*her.*]. Jagged. From L. *invehere*, *invect-*, to bring in.

invective. Late L. *invectivus*, from *invehere*, *invect-* (v.i.).

inveigh. Earlier *invey*, *invehe*. From pass. of L. *invehere*, from *vehere*, to bring. The sense is to be borne on, carried away (in words) against (v.s.).

invehi: to rebuke one vehemently; to rate; to rayle; with violent and sore wordes to inveigh against (Coop.).

inveigle. Earlier *envegle*, AF. *enveogler*, for F. *aveugler*, from *aveugle*, blind, VL. **aboculus*, for **alboculus*, white eye. *Albus oculus*, blind, occurs in the *Cassel Glossary* (8 cent.). For vowel cf. *people*, *beef*, *retrieve*, etc. For changed prefix cf. *impostume*. But the older etym., **aboculus*, is also possible, as *ab oculis*, modelled on G. ἀπ' ὀμμάτων, is recorded in Late L.

ciecare: to blinde, to enveagle (Flor.).

invent. From L. *invenire*, to come upon, discover, from *venire*, *vent-*, to come. Etym.

sense survives in *inventory*, MedL. *inventorium*, orig. list of chattels "found" in person's possession at his death.

inverness. For *Inverness cape*. Cf. *ulster*.

inverse. L. *inversus* (v.i.).

invert. L. *invertere*, lit. to turn in, hence, to turn inside out, etc., from *vertere*, to turn.

invest. L. *investire*, to clothe, from *vestis*, garment. For mil. sense cf. *envelope*. In ref. to money via It. *investire*, "to laie out or emploie ones money upon anie bargaine for advantage" (Flor.), a sense found in 14 cent. It., and first adopted in E. by East India Company (c. 1600).

investigate. From L. *investigare*, from *vestigare*, to track; cf. *vestigium*, foot-print, vestige.

inveterate. From L. *inveterare*, to make old, from *vetus, veter-*, old.

invidious. L. *invidiosus*, from *invidia*, envy (q.v.).

invigilate. From L. *invigilare*, from *vigil* (q.v.). Almost obs. till revived in connection with examinations.

invincible. F., L. *invincibilis*, from *vincere*, to conquer.

invite. F. *inviter*, L. *invitare*, to invite, allure.

invocation. As *invoke* (q.v.).

invoice. Pl. of obs. *invoy*, F. *envoi*, sending, as in *lettre d'envoi*, invoice. Cf. *bodice*. For F. *envoyer* see *envoy*. The form may have been affected by *advice*, in business sense.

invoke. F. *invoquer*, L. *invocare*, from *vocare*, to call.

involve. L. *involvere*, to envelope, entangle, from *volvere*, to roll. For sense-development cf. *imply*.

inward. AS. *innanweard*, from adv. *innan*; see *-ward*. *Inwardness* is a late 19 cent. revival of a 17 cent. word.

inyala. SAfr. antelope. Native name.

iodine. Named (1814) by Davy from F. *iode*, coined by Gay-Lussac (1812) from ἰώδης, violet coloured, from ἴον, the violet, because of colour of its vapour. Hence *iodoform*, coined on *chloroform*.

Ionian, Ionic. Of *Ionia*, G. Ἰωνία. Cf. *Attic*, *Doric*.

iota. G. ἰῶτα, name of letter ι, corresponding to Heb. *jod, yod*. Cf. *jot*.

Donec transeat caelum et terra, iota unum, aut unus apex non praeteribit a lege
(*Vulg. Matt.* v. 18).

I.O.U. Recorded 1618. Now understood as *I owe you*, but perh. orig. for *I owe unto*, followed by name of creditor.

ipecacuanha. Port., Tupi-Guarani (Brazil), *ipe-kaa-guaña*, lit. small plant causing vomit.

ipomoea. Creeping plant. Coined by Linnaeus from G. ἴψ, ἰπ-, worm, ὅμοιος, like.

ipse dixit. L., he (the master) himself said it, translating G. αὐτὸς ἔφα, used by the disciples of Pythagoras.

ir-. For *in-*, before *r-*.

iracund. L. *iracundus*, from *ira*, wrath, with suffix as in *jucundus, fecundus*, etc.

irade. Written decree of Sultan of Turkey. Turk. *irādah*, will, desire, from Arab.

Iranian [*ling.*]. From Pers. *īrān*, Persia. Includes Zend (q.v.) and Old Persian, with their mod. descendants, forming one of the two Asiatic groups of the Aryan langs.

ire. Archaic F., L. *ira*; cf. *irascible, irate*, from *irasci, irat-*, to get angry.

irenicon. See *eirenicon*.

iridescent. Coined from L. *iris, irid-* (v.i.).

iridium [*chem.*]. Named (1803) by *Tennant* from *iris* (v.i.).

iris. G. ἶρις, rainbow, also personified as messenger of the gods.

Irish. From stem *Īr-* of AS. *Īras* (pl.), cogn. with *Erse*; cf. ON. *Īrar* (noun), *Īrskr* (adj.). *Irish stew* is first recorded in Byron.

irk. Now chiefly in *irksome*. ME. *irken*, to weary, disgust, still used impersonally, is prob. from adj. *irk*, weary, troubled; app. cogn. with AS. *earg*, inert, cowardly; cf. cogn. Ger. *arg, ärgern*, with same sense-development.

das ding ärgert mich: I cannot away with it; it irkes me; it's irksom, tedious, or unsupportable to me (Ludw.).

iron. AS. *īsen, īsern, īren*. The *-s-* forms survive in the name *Icemonger, Isemonger*, for iron-monger. Cf. Du. *ijzer*, Ger. *eisen* (OHG. *īsarn*), ON. *īsarn* (later *earn, jarn*, whence Sw. *järn*, Dan. *jern*), Goth. *eisarn*. With the *-r-* forms cf. Ir. *iarann*, Gael. *iarunn*, Welsh *haearn*, Corn. *hoern*, etc. Perh. borrowed by Teut. from Celt., the Celts having known the use of iron earlier than the Teutons. The *iron age*, the fourth age of Græco-L. mythology, connotes cruelty and oppression. *The iron entered into his soul* (*Ps.* cv. 18, *PB.*) is *Vulg. ferrum pertransiit animam ejus*, a mistransl. of the Heb. which means "his person entered into the iron, i.e. fetters"; cf. *he was laid in iron* (*AV. ib.*). *Ironclad* first came into gen. use during American Civil War (1862–65); cf. *monitor*. *Ironsides* was a nickname for Cromwell before being applied to his men, and is stated (1644) to have been first used by Prince Rupert. It is common as an E. nickname, from Edmund II onward, and is still a surname. *Iron-mould* is for earlier *iron-mole* (16 cent.), from *mole*[1] (q.v.); cf. Du. *ijzermaal. Iron ration* is adapted from Ger. *eiserne portion*, used (1870–1) of a reserve ration enclosed in metal case.

> One yron mole defaceth the whole peece of lawne
> (*Euphues*).
> The cold comfort of iron rations
> (*Daily Chron.* Nov. 5, 1917).

irony. F. *ironie*, L. *ironia*, G. εἰρωνεία, dissimulation, affected ignorance, esp. that of Socrates.

irredentist [*hist.*]. It. *irredentista*, (since 1878) one aiming at the liberation of *Italia irredenta*, unredeemed Italy, the Italian-speaking provinces of Austria. See *redeem*.

irrefragable. F. *irréfragable*, Late L. *irrefragabilis*, from *refragari*, to oppose, contest.

irrigate. From L. *irrigare*, from *rigare*, to moisten.

irrision. Mockery. L. *irrisio-n-*. See *deride*.

irritate. From L. *irritare*, replacing earlier *irrite*, F. *irriter*.

irruption. L. *irruptio-n-*, from *in* and *rumpere*, *rupt-*, to break.

Irvingite. Sect, "Catholic Apostolic," founded (1829) by *Edward Irving*, a minister of the Church of Scotland.

is. See *be*.

isabel, isabella. Colour (pale buff). From name, ult. ident. with *Jezebel* and *Elizabeth*. Trad. from the colour of under-linen of the archduchess *Isabella*, daughter of Philip II of Spain, who vowed not to change her more intimate garments till Ostend fell (1604), but the *NED.* finds it recorded in E. the year (1600) before the siege began. Hence *isabelline bear*.

isagogic. Introductory. G., from εἰς, into, ἄγειν, to lead.

Iscariot. Heb. *īsh-q'rīyōth*, man of *Kerioth*, in Palestine. Cf. *Judas*.

ischiatic. Pertaining to the hip, L. *ischium*, G. ἰσχίον. Altered, on *rheumatic*, etc., from correct *ischiadic*.

-ise. See *-ize*.

-ish. AS. *-isc*, as in *Englisc*; cf. Du. Ger. *-isch*.

Ishmaelite. From Arab claim to be descended from *Ishmael*, Heb., God will hear, outcast son of Abraham (*Gen.* xvi. 12).

Isidorian. Of *Isidore*, archbishop of Seville (7 cent.).

isinglass. Perverted (16 cent.) from obs. Du. *huysenblas*, *huysblas*, "ichthyocolla, gluten piscium" (Kil.), now *huisblad*, lit. sturgeon bladder; cf. Ger. *hausen*, sturgeon, OHG. *hūsō*, of unknown origin, used esp. of the great sturgeon of Black and Caspian Seas.

isinglass: vischlym, huyzenblas (Sewel).

Islam. Arab. *islām*, resignation, from *aslama*, he surrendered himself (to God). Cogn. with *salaam, Moslem, Mussulman*.

island. Mod. spelling, due to unrelated *isle*, of *iland* (up to 17 cent.), AS. *īegland*, pleon. for *īeg*, island, orig. watery land, cogn. with Ger. *aue*, wet land, etc., and L. *aqua*. AS. had also *ēaland*, from cogn. *ēa*, river, stream, which became ME. *eland*, absorbed by *iland*; cf. Du. Ger. *eiland*, ON. *eyland*, and E. *ey* in *Anglesey, Bardsey, Ely*, etc. See *ait, aisle*.

isle. ME. *ile* (cf. surname *Iles*), OF. *ile*, *ille* (cf. *Lille*, for *l'ille*), L. *insula*. OF. had also *isle* (*île*), which tended to prevail from Renaissance onward and was adopted in E. by Spenser. See *island, aisle*.

-ism. L. *-ismus*, G. -ισμός; cf. *-ology*.

> He was the great hieroglyphick of Jesuitism, Puritanism, Quaquerism, and all isms from schism
> (*NED.* 1680).
>
> Un marxisme aggravé de léninisme menace de l'emporter sur le socialisme démocratique de l'Occident (*Civilisation française*, May, 1919).

isobar. Line showing equal atmospheric pressure. From G. ἴσος, equal, βάρος, weight (see *barometer*). Cf. *isothermal*.

isolate. First (18 cent.) in p.p. *isolated*, "a most affected word" (Todd), It. *isolato*, detached, from *isola*, island, L. *insula*. *Splendid isolation* was first used in a speech in the Canadian Parliament, Jan. 1896.

isonomy. It. *isonomia*, G. ἰσονομία, from ἴσος, equal, νόμος, law.

isosceles. G. ἰσοσκελής, from σκέλος, leg (v.s.).

isothermal. See *isobar, thermometer*.

Israel. L., G., Heb. *yisrāēl*, he that striveth with God (*Gen.* xxxii. 28).

issue. F., p.p. fem. (VL. **exuta* for *exita*) of OF. *eissir, issir*, to go out, L. *exire*. Cf. *value, interview*. Appears first as AF. law term, result of plea, whence mod. *at issue*, to *join issue*. With fig. senses cf. *outcome*.

> The Lord kepe thin entre [*Vulg.* introitus] and thi issu [*Vulg.* exitus] (*Wyc. Ps.* cxxi. 8).

-ist. F. *-iste*, L., G. -ίστης, used to form agent. nouns from verbs in -ίζειν. Mod.

formations, often jocular, are innumerable, and the sense is often pejorative.

The treaty is a capitalist, militarist, and imperialist imposition (Ind. Lab. Party, May, 1919).

There are among the Labour party very moderate men, but there are socialists, there are syndicalists, there are direct actionists, there are sovietists, there are bolshevists
(D. Lloyd George, Dec. 6, 1919).

isthmus. L., G. ἰσθμός, neck of land, spec. Isthmus of Corinth, where also the *Isthmian games* were celebrated. Cf. *Olympic.*

it. AS. *hit*, neut. of same demonstr. stem as *he* (q.v.). Cf. Du. *het*, Goth. *hita*, this. Goth. *ita*, Ger. *es*, represent the parallel *i*-stem. Loss of *h*- was due to unemphatic position; cf. *him*, *her*, in such phrases as *give him the book*, *ask her the time*, in which *h*- is only heard in the careful speech of the partially educated. Neut. genitive *his* survived till c. 1600, and *its* does not occur in orig. *A V.*, which has *his*, *her* (according to gram. gender), *thereof*, and once *it* (*Lev.* xxv. 5). Nor is *its* found in editions of Shaks. printed during his life-time. Colloq. use of *it* for the consummate is US.

We say in acclaiming the Atlantic flight made by Alcock and Brown, "This is it"
(W. Churchill, June 20, 1919).

italic. L., G. Ἰταλικός, from Ἰταλία, Italy. Type introduced by Aldus Manutius of Venice (see *Aldine*) and first used (1501) in edition of Virgil dedicated to Italy. Cf. *Italiot*, member of Greek colonies, Magna Graecia, in Italy, *Italian hand*, plain sloping writing as opposed to Gothic.

itch. ME. also *yeke*, *yitch*, etc. AS. *giccan*; cf. Du. *jeuken*, Ger. *jucken*, Goth. *jukjan*. In Sc. still *youk*, *yuke*.

item. L. adv., in like manner, from stem of *is* and adv. suffix *-tem*. Used in ME. inventories, etc., as introductory word.

iterate. From L. *iterare*, from *iterum*, again, orig. compar. formation from same stem as *item*.

ithyphallic. L., G., from ἰθύς, straight, φαλλός, phallus (see *phallic*). Esp. of Bacchic hymns.

itinerant. From pres. part. of Late L. *itinerari*, to journey, from *iter*, *itiner-*, way, journey, from *ire*, *it-*, to go.

-itis [*med.*]. G. -ῖτις, forming fem. of adjs. in -ίτης, and qualifying νόσος, disease, expressed or understood.

Brighton is suffering acutely from jazzitis
(*Daily Express*, Aug. 4, 1919).

its. See *it*. *Itself* was orig. *it self* (see *self*).

ivory. OF. *ivorie* (*ivoire*), L. adj. *eboreus*, from *ebur*, *ebor-*, ivory; cf. Sanskrit *ibha*, elephant.

ivy. AS. *īfig*; cogn. with Ger. *epheu*, OHG. *eba-hewi*. The same first element appears in Du. *eiloof*, ivy leaf. Origin unknown.

iwis, ywis [*archaic*]. AS. *gewis*, certain, of which neut. was used as adv. in ME., being usu. misunderstood by mod. poets as *I wis*, I know; cf. Du. *gewis*, Ger. *gewiss*, and see *aware*. See also *wit*, *wot*, *wist*.

ixia. Plant. L., G. ἰξία.

izard. Pyrenean chamois. F. *isard*, Gasc. *isart*.

-ize, -ise. F. *-iser*, Late L. *-izare*, G. *-ίζειν*.

izzard, izard [*archaic*]. Letter *z*. Earlier (16 cent.) *ezod*; Prov. *izedo*, *izeto* (whence OF. *ézed*), from G. ζῆτα.

It was bad luck to Francis Kearney from A to izard (O. Henry).

jab. Sc. form of *job*[1] (q.v.).

jabber. Imit. Cf. *gab*, *gabble*, *gibber*, etc.

Jabberwock. Weird monster. Coined by Lewis Carroll (*Through the Looking-glass*). Cf. *chortle*.

This super-Jabberwock (*Globe*, Aug. 25, 1917).

jabers, by [*Ir.*]. ? Arbitrary alteration of *Jasus*, Jesus. Cf. *jiminy*.

jabiru. SAmer. bird. Tupi-Guarani (Brazil).

jabot. Shirt-frill, etc. F., wattle of turkey. Origin unknown.

jacana. SAmer. bird. Port. *jaçaná*, Tupi-Guarani (Brazil) *jasaná*.

jacinth. F. *jacinthe*, L. *hyacinthus*; cf. It. *giacinto*, Sp. *jacinto*. See *hyacinth*.

jack[1]. Personal name used in E. as pet-form of *John*, via dim. *Jankin*, *Jackin*, but also representing F. *Jacques*, L. *Jacobus* (see *Jacob*). Used in an infinite number of transferred senses, (1) as comprehensive, usu. contemptuous, name for man, e.g. *Jack and Jill*, *every man jack*, *jack of all trades*, *jack in office*, *cheap-jack* (cf. *chapman*), etc., (2) applied to contrivances replacing servant, e.g. *bootjack* (cf. Ger. *stiefelknecht*, boot knave), *roasting-jack*, (3) in familiar names of animals, indicating male sex, e.g. *jackass*, or smallness, e.g. *jack-snipe*, (4) prefixed to word indicating personality, e.g. *Jack Frost*, *Jack Sprat*. Spec. compds. are *jack o' lantern*, ignis fatuus (cf. *will o' the wisp*), *jack-in-the-green*, a Mayday survival, *jack-in-the-box,* in 16 cent. a sharper, *Jack Ketch*, 17 cent. executioner, whose name was introduced into the early Punch and Judy show, *Jack Pudding*, quack's clown (cf. F. *Jean Potage*, Ger. *Hanswurst*, Du. *Hanssop*), *jack-straws*, game of spelicans, with reminiscence of 14 cent. rebel *Jack Straw*. Also applied to many animals and plants, usu. with implication of smallness, inferiority. Transferred uses of F. *Jean*, *Jacques*, and of Ger. *Hans* are also very numerous. See also below. *Jacked up*, exhausted, is an obscure fig. use of the same phrase meaning hoisted by mech. contrivance called a *jack*.

jack² [*hist.*]. Leather jerkin, coat of mail, leather drinking vessel. F. *jacque*, OF. also *jacques*, from name *Jacques*. Cf. It. *giacco*, Ger. *jacke*, in same senses. An obs. word revived by Scott. Some authorities trace it through Sp. to Arab. *shakk*, but the Europ. association has in any case been with the name.

jack³ [*naut.*]. Orig. small flag at bow. From *jack¹*, used in naut. phrases to indicate smaller size. Also improp. used in *union jack* for *union flag*.

jack⁴. Fruit. Port. *jaca*, Malayalam *chakka*.

jackal. Turk. *chakāl*, Pers. *shagāl*, cogn. with Sanskrit *s'rgāla*, jackal; cf. E. gipsy *jukel*, dog. In most Europ. langs. In fig. sense (17 cent.) from the jackal's relation to the lion, but earlier often *jack-call*, as though a servant at the lion's call.

jackanapes. First recorded as nickname of William de la Pole, Duke of Suffolk, murdered at sea (1450), whose badge was a clog and chain such as were worn by tame apes. But the word must obviously have existed earlier. Perh. orig. for *Jack of Napes*, name for monkey brought from Italy (cf. *fustian-a-napes* for Naples fustian), associated naturally with *ape*. A song of 1432 mentions among imports from Italy "Apes and japes, and marmusettes taylede."

Jac Napes wolde one the see a maryner to ben
With his cloge and his cheyn (*Pol. Song*, 1450).

jackaroo [*Austral.*]. Green hand, new chum. From *jack¹*, after *kangaroo*.

jackboot. Perh. connected with *jack²*, the boot suggesting the vessel. Hence *jack-bootery* (neol.) for bullying form of militarism.

jackdaw. See *daw* and *jack¹*. Cf. *dicky bird*, *magpie*, etc.

jacked up [*slang*]. See *jack¹*.

jacket. F. *jaquette*, dim. of OF. *jacque*. See *jack²*. ? Cf. *jerkin*.

Jack Johnson. Large Ger. shell (1914). From contemp. negro pugilist of large dimensions.

jack-knife. Orig. US. Perh. for obs. *jackleg*, corrupt. of Sc. *jockteleg*, large clasp-knife, said (1776) to be for *Jacques de Liège*, a cutler. This may be a myth, but has a parallel in F. *eustache*, knife carried by an apache, from *Eustache Dubois*, cutler at Saint-Étienne.

jacko. See *jocko*.

Jack Robinson, before you can say. "From a very volatile gentleman of that appellation, who would call on his neighbours, and be gone before his name could be announced" (Grose). Another "explanation" is that the name is corrupted from *Jack! robys on!* in an "old play." Both are of course nonsense.

Jacob. L. *Jacobus*, G., Heb. *ya-'aqōb*, one that takes by the heel (*Gen.* xxv. 26). Hence *Jacob's ladder* (bot. & naut.), with ref. to *Gen.* xxviii. 12; *Jacob's staff*, formerly used for taking altitude of sun; *Jacobean*, of James (king, apostle, etc.); *jacobus*, gold coin of James I. Cf. *Caroline*, *carolus*.

Jacobin. Dominican friar. From church of *Saint-Jacques* (Paris), near which the order built its first convent. The *jacobin* pigeon is named from neck feathers resembling a cowl. The Revolutionary *Jacobins*, extremists, were so called because they took up their quarters (1789) in the old convent of the friars.

Jacobite. Of *Jacob* or *James*, and esp. partisan of James II after his deposition (1688), at which date the word was coined.

jaconet. Fabric. From *Jagganāth* in Cutch (India).

jacquard [*techn.*]. Loom for lace. From inventor, *Jacquard*, of Lyons (c. 1800).

jacquerie [*hist.*]. F. peasant revolt, esp. that of 1357–8. From *Jacques Bonhomme*, nickname of F. peasant. Cf. *Hodge*.

Lenin's agrarian decrees have provoked a new outbreak of jacquerie (*Daily Chron.* Dec. 6, 1917).

jactation. L. *jactatio-n-*, from *jactare*, to throw about, reflex. to brag, frequent. of *jacere*, *jact-*, to throw. Cf. *jactitation* (med.), restlessness, MedL. *jactitatio-n-*.

jade¹. Sorry nag. Hence verb to *jade*, weary out. ? Cf. Sc. *yaud*, ON. *jalda*, mare. For application to woman cf. *harridan*.

jade². Stone. F. *le jade*, for OF. *l'ejade*, Sp.

ijada, in *piedra de ijada*, colic stone, from *ijada*, from L. *ilia*, flanks. It was supposed to cure pain in side, etc. Cf. its other name *nephrite* (see *nephritis*).

A kinde of greene stones, which the Spanyards call *piedras hijadas*, and we use for spleene stones
(Raleigh).

jaeger. Underclothing. Name of inventor.

jag. As noun and verb from c. 1400. Orig. of "jagged" or "dagged" edge of garment. Origin unknown.

jagge or dagge of a garment: fractillus
(*Prompt. Parv.*).

jäger [*mil.*]. Ger., hunter, also rifleman (cf. F. *chasseur*, It. *bersagliere*). In E. also *yager*.

jaggery. Coarse brown sugar. Indo-Port., from Canarese *sharkare*, Sanskrit *ṣarkara*. See *saccharine*, *sugar*.

jaguar. Tupi-Guarani (Brazil) *yaguara*, *jaguara*, class-name for carnivorous beasts.

The Indians call the leopard *jawaryle* and the lions [pumas] *jawarosou*
(Anthony Knivet, in Purch. xvi. 256).

Jah. Heb., shortened form of *Jehovah*.

jail. See *gaol*.

Jain. East Indian sect. Hind. *jaina*, from Sanskrit *gina*, a Buddha, saint, lit. overcomer.

jalap. F., Sp. *jalapa*, for *purga de Jalapa*, from *Jalapa*, Mexico, formerly *Xalapa*, Aztec *Xalapan*.

jalousie. F., lit. *jealousy*; cf. It. *gelosia*, Sp. *celosía*, in same sense. See *jealous*.

gelosia: jealousie, also a window lid (Percyvall).

jam¹. Orig. (18 cent.) verb (naut.) meaning to squeeze, block, tighten, etc. Hence perh. sense of squeezed fruit. ? From *jamb* (q.v.) with idea of being caught in door. Some identify it with *cham*, *champ*, to chew, but this seems unlikely. With *not all jam* cf. *beer and skittles*.

jam². Prince in some parts of India. Of unknown origin.

jamb. F. *jambe*, leg, formerly used for jamb of door (*jambage*), Late L. *gamba*. Cf. *gambol*, *gammon²*.

jambo. Indian fruit, rose-apple. Sanskrit *ǥambu*.

jamboree [*US.*]. Spree. Origin unknown. ? Cf. obs. *boree*, dance, F. *bourrée*.

A Boy Scout 'jamboree' is to be held at Olympia (*Daily News*, Apr. 29, 1920).

james [*slang*]. Burglar's implement. See *jemmy*.

jangle. OF. *jangler*, to babble harshly, dispute, etc. In later senses associated with *jingle*. ? Nasalized from L. *jaculari*, to dart, sling, from *jaculum*, javelin. For sense cf. *dally*, for nasal cf. F. *jongleur*, minstrel, juggler (q.v.).

janissary, janizary. Orig. household troops of Sultan, recruited from Christian youths (14 cent.), massacred and abolished in 1826. Turk. *yeni cheri*, new soldiery. E. form is F. *janissaire* or It. *giannizzero*. Cf. *mameluke*. For fig. sense cf. *alguazil*, *myrmidon*, etc.

Rather than surrender one jot or tittle of their importance...they [the politicians] encourage their journalistic janizaries to seek scapegoats for their own failings among the soldiers
(*Nat. Rev.* Feb. 1918).

janitor. L., doorkeeper, from *janua*, door.

Jansenist [*theol.*]. Follower of *Cornelius Jansen*, bishop of Ypres (†1638), who maintained inability for good of human will.

January. Restored spelling of ME. *Janivere*, *Genever*, etc., F. *janvier*, L. *januarius* (sc. *mensis*), month of *Janus* (q.v.). Replaced AS. *gēola se æfterra*, later Yule.

The dullest month in all the year
Is the month of Janiveer.

Janus. Ancient Roman deity, presiding over doors (see *janitor*), and represented with face back and front, whose temple was only closed in times of peace.

japan. Varnish, lacquer, from *Japan*, Du. *Japan* or Port. *Japão*, Malay *Japang*, Chin. *Jih-pün*, sun rise, corresponding to Jap. *Ni-pon*. Marco Polo (†1323) has *Chipangu*.

jape. As noun and verb from 14 cent. Obs. c. 1600, revived by Scott and other 19 cent. romantics. Earlier sense also obscene, which may be the original. Origin unknown.

Japhetic. From third son of Noah. Sometimes used (ling. & ethn.) for *Aryan*. Cf. *Hamitic*, *Semitic*.

japonica. ModL. *pyrus japonica*, Jap. pear tree.

jar¹. To grate, sound discordantly, vibrate unpleasantly. From 16 cent. App. imit.; cf. obs. vars. *charre*, *gerre*, *chirr*, etc.

jar². Vessel. F. *jarre*, Sp. *jarro*, *jarra*, Arab. *jarrah*, earthen vessel; cf. It. *giara*.

jar³. See *ajar*.

jardinière. F., lit. gardener's wife.

jargon. F., orig., as in E., of the warbling or chatter of birds, a sense revived by mod.

poets (e.g. *Ancient Mariner*, v. 16). Cf. It. *gergone*, Sp. *gerigonza*. App. from same imit. root as *gargle*; cf. obs. *jargle*, to warble, etc., OF. *jargouiller*.

Ful of jargon [*var.* girgoun] as a flekked pye
(Chauc. E. 1848).

jargonelle. Pear. F., orig. applied to an inferior and gritty variety, which Evelyn advises nobody to plant. From *jargon*, kind of stone (v.i.).

jargoon [*min.*]. F. *jargon*, Port. *zarcão*, Arab. *zarqūn*, from Pers. *zar*, gold (? or *āzar*, fire), *qūn*, colour; cf. It. *giargone*.

jarl [*hist.*]. ON., earl (q.v.). Applied by mod. historians to the nobles of Scandinavia, Orkney, Shetland, and the Western Isles.

jarrah [*Austral.*]. Mahogany gum-tree. From native *jerrhyl* (West Austral.).

jarvey, jarvie [*slang*]. Coachman. From name *Jarvis* (*Gervase, Jervis*), perh. in allusion to *St Gervase*, whose attribute is a whip or scourge.

jarvis: a hackney coachman (Grose).

jasey, jazy [*archaic*]. Wig made of worsted. Said to be a corrupt. of *Jersey*, because made of Jersey wool.

He looked at the wig; it had once been a comely jasey enough (*Ingoldsby*).

jasmine, jessamine. F. *jasmin*, OF. also *jessemin*, with forms in most Europ. langs., all from Arab. *yās(a)mīn*, Pers. *yāsmīn*, *yāsman*; cf. G. ἰάσιμον μύρον, a perfume, prob. oil of jasmine.

jasper. OF. *jaspre* (*jaspe*), L. *jaspis, jaspid-*, G. ἴασπις, an Oriental word; cf. Heb. *yashpeh*, Pers. & Arab. *yashp*. Confused with *diaper* in MedL., *diasprus* being used for both, whence It. Sp. *diaspro*, jasper.

jaundice. With intrusive -*d*- from ME. *jaunes*, F. *jaunisse*, from *jaune*, yellow, OF. *jalne*, L. *galbinus*, from *galbus*, ult. cogn. with *yellow*. In early use often treated as pl., *jandies, janders*, by analogy with *measles, glanders*, etc.

jaunt. Orig. to exercise a horse, make him prance, take fatiguing exercise. ? OF. *jambeter*, to kick the legs about, from *jambe*, leg. Sylvester uses it of the prancing of a horse in a passage in which *la jambette* occurs in the orig. We find also *jaunce*, for which Cotg. gives *jancer un cheval*, "to stirre a horse in the stable till hee sweat withall; or (as our) to jaunt," but this is not otherwise recorded in F., and is prob. an error due to E. *jaunce*. The latter seems

to be a corrupt. of *jaunt* due to E. fondness for this ending; cf. *enhance, snaphaunce*, and Skelton's *cormoraunce* for *cormorant*. See also *jounce*.

El fossé les unt fait ruër,
Chevals e humes jambeter (Wace, *Roman de Rou*).

Spur-gall'd and tir'd by jauncing Bolingbroke
(*Rich. II*, v. 5).

jaunt: a tedious, fatiguing walk (Bailey).

jaunty. Earlier (17 cent.) *genty, jentee, janty*, etc., adapted from F. *gentil* (see *genteel*). *Genty* is still used in Sc.

With a jantee pair of canvass trowzers
(Motteux' *Rabelais*, iv. 48).

javelin. F. *javeline*, for more usual *javelot*, AS. *gafeluc*, Welsh *gaflach*, fork, dart. By some connected with the gen. Celt. word for fork (Gael. *gobhal*, Ir. *gabhal*, Welsh *gafl*).

jaw. ME. *jowe*. App. related to *jowl* (q.v.), but of obscure origin and hist. Form due to association with F. *joue*, cheek (for vowel, cf. *paw*). Prob. an earlier form was *chaw*, though this is only recorded later.

My tong shall speak out of my chaws
(Tynd. *Job*, xxxiii. 2).

jay¹. Bird. F. *geai*; cf. ONF. *gai*, Prov. *gai*, Sp. *gayo*. Origin unknown. The analogy of *robin, jackdaw*, etc., suggests that it may be L. *Gaius*, a name which was used very much as *Jack* is in E. to designate persons familiarly. In F. the *jay* is also called *jacques, richard, cola* (*Nicolas*), and in Du. *wouter* (*Walter*).

jay² [*slang*]. Fool. Orig. US., from *jay¹*, but associated in E. c. 1890 with *J* for *Juggins*.

jazz. "A number of niggers surrounded by noise," kind of ragtime dance introduced from US. (Nov. 1918). From negro jargon.

jealous. OF. *jelous* (*jaloux*), Prov. *gelos*, L. *zelosus* (see *zeal*); cf. It. *geloso*, Sp. *celoso*.

I have been very jealous [*Vulg.* zelo zelatus sum for the Lord God of hosts (1 *Kings*, xix. 10).

Jeames. Footman. From Thackeray's *Jeames de la Pluche* (1846), representing a mincing pronunc. of *James*.

jean. Fabric. Earlier also *jenes, geanes*, etc., F. *Gênes*, Genoa, place of origin. In US. *jeans*. Cf. *cambric, muslin*, etc.

Jeddart justice [*hist.*]. Hanging first and trying afterwards, said to have been the practice at *Jedburgh* (Roxburghshire), also called *Jedworth, Jedwood, Jeddart*. See *law¹*.

jeer. From 16 cent. Perh. corrupt. of Du. *scheren*, in *den gek* (fool) *scheeren*, "to make a fool of one, to fool one, to jeer, jest" (Sewel), whence the ModDu. compd. *gekscheren*, in same sense. This is prob. not Du. *scheren*, to shear, but obs. *scheeren*, "to gibe or to jest" (Hexham), cogn. with OHG. *skerōn*, to jest, and Ger. *scherzen*, in same sense.

jehad, jihad. Mohammedan holy war. Arab. *jihād*, contest. Hence fig. crusade.

Jehannum. Arab. form of *Gehenna* (q.v.).

Jehovah. Heb. *Jahveh* or *Yahweh*, the "ineffable" name, written without vowels and read as *ădōnāi* (see *Adonis*), the vowels of which were later inserted in it. Hence *Jehovist, Jahvist*, a name applied to the authors of those parts of the Hexateuch in which this name of the Deity is used. Cf. *Elohist*.

Jehu. Driver (2 *Kings*, ix. 20).

jejune. L. *jejunus*, fasting, transferred to unsatisfying nourishment or pabulum.

jelly. ME. *gelye*, F. *gelée*, p.p. fem. of *geler*, to freeze, L. *gelare*, from *gelu*, frost. To *jell* (US.) is a back-formation.

jemadar [*Anglo-Ind.*]. Native officer. Urdu *jama'dār*, from Pers. *jamā'at*, body of men, with suffix -*dar* as in *sirdar, ressaldar*, etc.

jemimas. Elastic-side boots (*Concise Oxf. Dict.*). From name *Jemima*, Heb., dove.

jemmy. In various slang senses (cf. *jack*), now esp. of burglar's implement, called in 17 cent. *bess, betty, jenny*; cf. synon. Ger. *peterchen, klaus, dietrich*, i.e. little Peter, Nicholas, Theodoric, also Du. *peterken, dierken*, in same sense.

jennet [*archaic*]. Orig. (15 cent.) small Spanish horse. F. *genet* (14 cent.), Sp. *ginete*, short-stirruped rider, ? from a Berber tribe called *Zenetes*. App. still in Ir. use.

Ploughs drawn by every available type of animal— hunters, carriage-horses, mules, jennets
(*Daily Chron.* March 13, 1917).

jenneting. Early apple. Connected with F. *pomme de Saint-Jean*, dial. *pomme de Jeannet*, because ripe about St John's day (June 21); cf. Ger. *Johannisapfel*. Sometimes "explained" as June-eating. The ending has been assimilated to *codlin, sweeting*, etc. *Pome genete* occurs in OF. (13 cent.).

jenny. From *Jane*, fem. of *John* (*Jack*). Applied to animals, e.g. *jenny-ass, jenny wren*; plants, e.g. *creeping jenny*; mech. devices,

e.g. *spinning jenny* (patented by Hargreaves, 1770), and to a stroke at billiards. Cf. *jack*.

jeopardy. "A word not now in use" (Johns.). ME. *juparti*, F. *jeu parti*, divided or even game (result of which cannot be foreseen); cf. MedL. *jocus partitus*. Earliest E. sense (13 cent.) is chess problem, hence dilemma. *Jeopard* (*Judges*, v. 18) is a back-formation.

Il me distrent: "Sire, le jeu nous est mal parti; car vous estes à cheval, si vous enfuirés; et nous sommes à pié, si nous occiront les sarrazins"
(Joinville).

For myn estate lith now in a jupartye,
And ek myn emes [uncle's] lyf is in balaunce
(Chauc. *Troil.* ii. 465).

jerboa. Jumping rodent. Arab. *yarbū'*, loin muscle, from its jumping powers.

jereed. Eastern javelin of wood used in exercises. Arab. *jarīd*, middle-rib of palm-leaf. Also *djereed, tzirid*, etc.

jeremiad. F. *jérémiade*, lamentation like that of the prophet *Jeremiah*.

jerfalcon. See *gerfalcon*.

Jericho, go to. Perh. orig. with allusion to 2 *Sam.* x. 5. The *rose of Jericho* (*Ecclesiasticus*, xxiv. 14) "is properly no rose, but a small thorny shrub or kinde of heath" (Sir T. Browne).

Bid such young boyes to stay in Jericho
Untill their beards were growne (*NED.* 1635).

jerk. Earliest sense (16 cent.) to whip, lash, in which sense it varies with archaic *yerk*. For current meaning cf. to *whip a thing away*. Origin unknown.

jerked beef. From SAmer. Sp. *charquear*, from Peruv. *echarqui*, meat dried in long strips. First as *jerkin beef* (Capt. John Smith), ? suggested by leather *jerkin* (v.i.).

Certeine dried porke cut like leather jerkins along
(Hakl.).

jerkin. From c. 1500. Perh. from *George* (cf. *jacket*), of which the popular OF. form was *Joire, Jour*, preserved in name *Jorkins*. Cf. Ger. dial. *jürken*, jacket, app. from *Jürg*, popular form of *Georg*, and OF. *georget*, in similar sense. There is also OF. *jargot*, doublet, with vars. *jergot, jergault*, etc. A sale of surplus army *jerkins* was announced Jan. 27, 1920.

jeroboam. Large wine-bottle. Prob. suggested by earlier *jack, jordan*. Cf. *jorum*.

They are piled high on the deck, each looking like a double jeroboam of champagne
(*Daily Chron.* Mar. 3, 1918).

jerry. Familiar form of *Jeremiah*, exalted of the Lord. Some of its slang applications, *jerry-hat*, *jerry-shop*, may be connected with the Tom and Jerry of Egan's *Life in London* (1821), which enjoyed great popularity. Earlier is *jerry-sneak* (name of character in Foote's *Mayor of Garratt*, 1763). For sense of chamber-pot cf. *jordan* (q.v.). I conjecture that *jerry-built* may be for *jury-built*, the naut. *jury*, as in *jury-mast*, being used of all sorts of makeshifts and inferior objects, e.g. *jury-leg*, wooden leg, *jury-rigged*, *jury meal*, etc. Its early connection with Liverpool, where *jerry-building* is recorded in a local paper for 1861, makes naut. origin likely.

Jerry. German. Army slang.

Smudges of flame showed where Archie was talking to Jerry (*Daily Chron.* July 13, 1918).

jerrymander. See *gerrymander.*

jersey. Orig. knitted at *Jersey*. Cf. *guernsey.*

jerusalem [*slang*]. For *Jerusalem pony*, facet. for donkey, in allusion to entry into Jerusalem. See also *artichoke.*

jess. Of hawk. ME. *ges*, OF. *gez*, *jez*, pl. of *jet*, cast, from *jeter*, abnormally from L. *jactare*, frequent. of *jacere*, *jact-*, to throw. With double pl. *jesses* cf. *bodices*, *lettuces*, *quinces*, etc.

jesses for a hauke: get (Palsg.).

jessamine, jessamy. See *jasmine.*

Jesse window [*arch.*]. Adorned with the *Jesse tree*, genealogical tree showing descent of Christ from *Jesse* (*Is.* xi. 1).

jest. F. *geste*, as in *chanson de geste*, song of exploits, L. *gesta*, neut. pl., from *gerere*, *gest-*, to perform, carry out. Sense of epic narrative developed into that of mocking tale, joke, etc. To *break a jest* was suggested by *breaking a lance*. Cf. to *crack a joke.*

Item, to Wallass that tellis the geistis to the King, xviijs. (*Sc. Treas. Accts.* 1491).

Settyng furth the jestes, actes and deedes of the nobilitie (*NED.* 1548).

Jesuit. Member of *Society of Jesus*, founded (1533) by Ignatius Loyola to combat protestantism. Fig. sense of *jesuitical* is due to casuistry approved by some of the order.

Jesus. L., G. Ἰησοῦς, Aramaic *Jeshua*, *Joshua*, Jah is salvation. See also *I.H.S. Jesu* is the OF. obj. case.

jet[1]. Black substance. OF. *jaiet* (*jais*), L., G. γαγάτης, from river *Gages*, in Lycia. Cf. *agate.*

The geat or gagates carrieth the name of a river in Lycia (Holland's *Pliny*).

jet[2]. Of water, etc. F., from *jeter*, to throw (see *jess*).

jetsam. OF. *jetaison*, from *jeter*, to throw (see *jess*). Earlier *jettison*, now usu. as verb (see *Jonah*), to throw overboard, also fig. See *flotsam.*

jettison. See *jetsam.*

jetty. F. *jetée*, p.p. fem. of *jeter*, to throw (see *jess*).

jeu. F., L. *jocus*, game. In *jeu de mots* (*d'esprit*).

Jew. OF. *jueu*, *giu* (*juif*), L. *judaeus*, G. Ἰουδαῖος, from Heb. *y'hūdah*, Judah, lit. celebrated. *Worth a Jew's eye* alludes to medieval extortion practised on Jews, while verb to *Jew* suggests extortion the other way round. With *Jewry*, district allotted to Jews, OF. *juerie*, cf. *ghetto. Jew's ear*, fungus, is a mistaken rendering of MedL. *auricula Judae*, Judas' ear, so called because commonly found on the elder (Judas tree), the tree on which Judas Iscariot trad. hanged himself. *Jew's harp* (Hakl.) was earlier *jew's trump*, the reason for the name being unknown.

jewel. AF. *juel*, OF. *joel*, *joiel* (*joyau*), VL. **jocellus*, from *jocus*, game, etc.; cf. It. *gioiello*, Sp. *joyel*. Derivation from *gaudium*, joy (cf. *gaud*), is less likely owing to phonetic difficulties. The regular MedL. is *jocale*, *jocalia*, and the etym. of *fuel* (q.v.) furnishes a parallel.

jezail. Afghan musket. As *gingall* (q.v.).

Jezebel. Harridan, esp. with painted face. From the wife of Ahab (2 *Kings*, ix.). The name means "oath of Baal" and is the source of *Isabel*, *Elizabeth.*

jheel [*Anglo-Ind.*]. Pool left by flood. Hind. *jhīl.*

jib[1]. Sail. Perh. from *jib[2]*, it being a sail which fills from side to side according to wind. Hence *cut of one's jib*, orig. sailor's impression of "strange sail" at sea.

jib[2]. To swing (yard, sail) from side to side. Var. of *gybe* (q.v.). The jibbing of a horse is prob. a naut. metaphor. The word is not found in this sense till 19 cent., so can hardly be OF. *giber*, to kick (cf. F. *regimber*).

jibbah, jubbah. Eastern mantle. Arab. *jubbah*, whence also F. *jupe*, *jupon*, ME. *gipoun*, It. *giubba*. See *jump[2]*.

jibe. Var. of *gibe*, *gybe* (q.v.).

jiffy. From 18 cent. Origin unknown.

jig. Cf. F. *gigue*, dance, OF. *gigue*, fiddle, It. *giga*, fiddle. Of Teut. origin; cf. Ger. *geige*, fiddle, ON. *gigja*, prob. cogn. with *gig*[1] (q.v.). Hence *jigger*, of many small mech. devices, in some cases, e.g. at billiards and golf, app. equivalent to *thingumbob, thingamjig*, etc.

jigger[1]. Implement. See *jig*. Cf. *jig-saw*.

jigger[2]. Corrupt. of *chigoe* (q.v.). Hence perh. *I'm jiggered*, first in Marryat. But this may be rather a fantastic euph. perversion of an uglier word.

jiggery-pokery, jackery-pokery. Sc. *joukery-paukry*, etc., from *jouk*, trick. Cf. *hanky-panky, hocus-pocus*, and obs. *hickery-puckery*.

jig-saw [*US.*]. From verb *jig*, in sense of rapid varying motion.

In machinery, the narrow band-saw that works up and down, cutting tracery and fret-work out of wood, is known as a jigger
(*Notes & Queries*, Nov. 17, 1894).

Jill. Companion of Jack. ME. *Gille*, short for *Gillian*, popular form of *Juliana*, a favourite ME. name, which became practically equivalent to girl, woman. Also in many rustic plant-names.

For Jok nor for Gyll will I turne my face
(*Towneley Myst.* c. 1460).

Our wooing doth not end like an old play: Jack hath not Gill (*Love's Lab. Lost*, v. 2).

jilt. Earlier *gillet, jillet*, dim. of *Jill* (v.s.). Also *jill-flirt, gillian-flirt*, etc. The sense has become softened like that of *flirt*.

Hee hathe apuynted to meete this gyllot that is at your house (Harman, *Caveat*, 1567).

bagasse: a baggage, queane, jyll, punke, flirt (Cotg.).

Jim-crow [*US.*]. Negro. From popular negro song with refrain " Jump, Jim-crow."

jiminy. Disguised oath; cf. Ger. *jemine*, Du. *jemenie*, prob. for *Jesu Domine*, as Ger. *ach je* is for *ach Jesu*. See *gemini, criminy*.

Crimini, jimini!
Did you ever hear such a nimminy-pimminy
Story as Leigh Hunt's Rimini? (Byron).

jim-jams [*slang*]. Delirium tremens. Arbitrary formation.

jimmy. From *James*. In many slang senses of *jemmy*.

jingle. Imit.; cf. *tinkle, chink*, etc. Associated with *jangle* in redupl. *jingle-jangle*, but not orig. connected with that word, though now felt as expressing a lighter form of same sound; cf. *flip, flap*.

jingo. From 17 cent. Perh. Basque *Jinko, Jainko*, God. It may have been picked up from Basque sailors, who were always employed as harpooners by the early whalers

(see *harpoon*). The *Ingoldsby* derivation, from St Gengulphus, "sometimes styled 'the living Jingo,' from the great tenaciousness of vitality exhibited by his severed members," is a joke. Pol. sense (first in *Daily News*, March 11, 1878, and fixed by George Jacob Holyoake's letter, March 13) is from music-hall song (v.i.) popular with Russophobes in 1878. Cf. *chauvin*.

"By Jingo" [Rab. par Dieu], quoth Panurge, "the man talks somewhat like"
(Motteux' *Rabelais*, iv. 56).

We don't want to fight, But by Jingo! if we do, We've got the ships, we've got the men, We've got the money too (G. W. Hunt).

He who appeals to his countrymen to arm in their own defence is not a Jingo
(R. Blatchford, Dec. 23, 1909).

He [Lord Roberts] is a mere jingo in opinion and character, and he interprets the life and interests of this nation and Empire by the crude lusts and fears which haunt the unimaginative soldier's brain
(*Nation*, Oct. 26, 1912).

I am, if you like, a Jingo, a word which, by the way, I was the first person ever to write—at the dictation of my late uncle, George Jacob Holyoake
(H. Bottomley, *John Bull*, Nov. 10, 1917).

jinks, high. According to *NED.* orig. Sc., of frolic at drinking-party, and app. connected with verb to *jink*, dance, dodge, etc. But the verb is much later, and quot. below suggests that the *high* may have been orig. an adv., and the whole phrase a parallel to mod. *up Jenkins!*

The noble and ancient recreation of Round-Robin, Hey-Jinks, and Whipping the Snake, in great request with our merry sailors in Wapping
(T. Brown, c. 1700).

jinn. Arab., pl. of *jinnī*, whence *jinnee* and the *genie* (q.v.) of the *Arabian Nights*.

jinricksha. Jap. *jin-riki-sha*, man-strength-vehicle, which has been facetiously compared with *Pull-man car* (Yule). Now usu. *rickshaw*.

jirgah [*Anglo-Ind.*]. Council of elders. Afghan, from Pers., circle of men.

jiu-jitsu. See *ju-jutsu*.

job[1]. Verb. To peck, etc. Now usu. *jab*. "Expressing the sound or effect of an abruptly arrested stab" (*NED.*).

job[2]. Piece of work. From 17 cent., orig. contrasted with what is continuous. Perh. ident. with obs. *job*, lump, cartload (cf. *job lot*), which may be ult. related to *gob, gobbet*. Suggestion of dishonesty, undue influence, as in *jobbery*, is already in Pepys. With *good* (*bad*) *job* cf. similar use of *business*.

Job. Type of patience (*Job*, i. 22), or poverty (*ib.* i. 21). Cf. *Job's comforter* (*ib.* xvi. 2). Cf. Ger. *Hiobspost*, bad news.

jobation [*slang*]. Lecture like those addressed to *Job* by his "comforters" (v.s.). In dial. corrupted to *jawbation*.

jobbernowl [*archaic*]. Blockhead. From ME. *jobard*, fool, and *noll*, head. *Jobard* is F., from OF. *jobe*, patient fool, prob. from *Job*.

Jock. Highland soldier, esp. of Argyll and Sutherland regiment. Sc. form of *Jack* (v.i.). *Jocky*, Scotsman, occurs repeatedly in *Rump Songs* (1639–61).

jockey. Dim. of *Jock*, northern form of *Jack* (v.s.). Orig. horse-dealer as well as professional rider, "a cheat, a trickish fellow" (Johns.). Hence verb to *jockey*, to swindle, with which cf. *cozen*. Pepys (Dec. 11, 1668) speaks of "the knaveries and tricks of jockeys," i.e. horse-dealers.

Jockey of Norfolk, be not so bold,
For Dickon, thy master, is bought and sold
(*Rich. III*, v. 3).

jockeys: rank horse-coursers, race-riders; also hucksters or sellers of horses, very slippery fellows to deal with (*Dict. Cant. Crew*).

jocko, jacko. Chimpanzee. Made by Buffon (1766) from native WAfr. *ncheko, nschiego*, whence also *chego*.

jockteleg [*Sc.*]. See *jack-knife*.

jocose, jocular. L. *jocosus, jocularis*, from *jocus*, game.

jocund. OF. *jocond*, Late L. *jocundus*, altered, on *jocus*, from *jucundus*, pleasant, from *juvare*, to please, help; cf. It. *giocondo*, Sp. *jocunde*.

The herte of Nabal was jocounde, for he was drunkun greetli (Wyc. 1 *Sam.* xxv. 36).

jodel. See *yodel*.

joe [*archaic*]. Port. coin. From *Joannes V* (†1750); cf. *louis, carolus*, etc.

Joe Manton. Gun by gunsmith of that name, (†1835).

Joe Miller. Stale jest, chestnut. From *Joe Miller's jests, or the Wit's Vade-mecum* (1739), named after, but not compiled by, *Joseph Miller*, actor and wit (†1738).

joey¹. Fourpenny-piece. From *Joe*, for *Joseph*.

joey² [*Austral.*]. Young kangaroo. Native *joè*.

jog. App. imit. of movement, but partly suggested by earlier *shog*, which is cogn. with OHG. *scoc*, swing, oscillation.

Will you shog off? (*Hen. V*, ii. 1).

While he [Hobson the carrier] might still jog on and keep his trot (Milt.).

Johannine. Of *John* (apostle or Baptist).

johannisberger. Wine from *Johannisberg*, vineyard near Wiesbaden.

John. L. *Joannes, Johannes*, G. Ἰωάννης, Heb. *yōchānān*, Jah is gracious. Cf. F. *Jean*, OF. *Jehan*, It. *Giovanni*, Sp. *Juan*, Ger. *Johann*, etc. The fem. is *Joan*, or, through F., *Jane*. Used, with *Johnny*, in many stock epithets (cf. *Jack*), e.g. *John Barleycorn, John Chinaman, Johnny Raw, silly johnny*, etc. With *John Doe* and *Richard Roe*, fictitious plaintiff and defendant in ejection action (abolished 1852), cf. *John a' Nokes* and *John a' Stiles*, i.e. John of the oaks and John of the stiles, also fictitious leg. parties. *John Bull* appears first (1712), with Lewis Baboon, etc., in Arbuthnot's satire. *John Company* is from Du. *Jan Kompanie*, name by which the Du. East India Company and government are known in the East to natives, who cannot conceive an impersonal body. *John Dory*, fish, for earlier *dory* (q.v.), was perh. suggested by a popular song (printed 1609) on a famous privateer.

They [the goods] were taken out of the said galeon by one John Dorye of Dertmouth
(*Privy Council Acts*, 1546).

Johnian. Of *St John's College*, Camb.; also *Johnian hog* (Grose).

John o' Groats. Supposed site of house on Duncansby Head, regarded as extreme north of Scotland.

join. F. *joindre, joign-*, L. *jungere*, cogn. with *jugum*, yoke. *Joint* is the p.p., L. *junctus*. *Joint-stool* is for *joined stool*, made in parts by a joiner; cf. *joyned stockes* (Purch.), for joint stock. With hist. to *join battle* cf. *attack* (q.v.). To *join up* dates from the Great War.

And middle natures, how they long to join,
Yet never pass the insuperable line
(Pope, *Essay on Man*, i. 228).

jointure [*leg.*]. Now limited to wife's or widow's estate, but orig. holding of property for joint use of married couple.

joist. ME. & OF. *giste* (*gîte*), from *gésir*, to lie, L. *jacēre*. For sense-development cf. *sleeper* (railway), for sound-change cf. *boil²*. See *gist*. F. *gîte* is still used of the main beam of a loft.

Also every giste tre of square xij. ynche and more
(*Contract for Newark Bridge*, 1485).

joke. From 17 cent. Prob. It. *gioco*, L. *jocus*; cf. Du. *jok*. It can hardly have been taken straight from L., unless it was univ. slang. *Joker* appears to have been used by thimble-riggers before being applied to a card.

jokul, jökull [*geog.*]. Snow-mountain in Iceland. See *icicle*.

jolly. ME. also *jolif*, OF. (*joli*); cf. It. *giulivo*. Supposed to be from ON. *jól*, Yule, but this is very doubtful. The OF. & ME. meanings are very wide, and intens. senses, e.g. *jolly good hiding, jolly well mistaken*, can be paralleled in ModF. Older form survives in name *Joliffe*. *Jolly*, marine, occurs first in Marryat.

joli: jollie; gay, trim, fine, gallant, neat, handsome, feat, well-fashioned, minion, compt, polite; also, lively, merry, buxom, jocund (Cotg.).

Here we took fishes...of a jolly thickenesse, but not past a foote long (*Hawkins' Voyage*, 1564).

jolly-boat. Prob. a naut. corrupt. of earlier *jolywat* (15 cent.), *gellywat*, used app. in same sense. This may be EInd. *gallivat*, Port. *galeota*, galliot, dim. of *galley*. The objection that *gallivat* is a ship-name, not a boat-name, is hardly serious in view of the whimsicality of naut. nomenclature. The same objection might be urged against *galley* in the sense of rowing-boat on the Thames and elsewhere, or against *frigate*, which for the Elizabethans was a rowing-boat, pinnace; cf. also *skiff*, ult. ident. with *ship*.

The Soveraigne with her grete bote and jolywatt
(*Nav. Accts.* 1495–97).

That day the Pegasus jolly was going on shore for water (Hakl. x. 241).

Having tryed the currant sundrie tymes with our jolly boate (Peter Mundy, 1634).

jolt. App. corrupt. of earlier *jot, jut*, an imit. word, like *jog*. It may have been affected by obs. *joll, jowl*, to bump.

What nedest thou to jotte me with thyne elbowe? a quoi est il besoing de me heurter de ton coulde?
(Palsg.).

heurter: to knock, push, jurre, joult (Cotg.).

jolterhead [*archaic*]. Earlier *jolthead*, an older word than *jolt*, which it may have influenced. "Evidently in some way related to *jowl*, the form *cholt-headed* esp. recalling the *cholle* forms of the latter" (*NED.*).

teste de bœuf: a jolthead, jobernoll, codshead, grout-head, loger-head (Cotg.).

Jonah. Bringer of ill-luck (*Jonah*, i. 7). Hence to *Jonah*, throw overboard (Meredith).

Rather he is the Jonah whose jettisoning would do more than anything else to save their ship
(*Daily Chron.* Jan. 16, 1917).

Jonathan, brother. Said to have been orig. applied (after 2 *Sam.* i. 26) by Washington to *Jonathan Trumbull*, Governor of Connecticut.

jongleur. F., minstrel, juggler. Nasalized from OF. *jogleor*, acc. of *joglere*, L. *joculator*, jester, from *jocus*, jest.

jonquil. F. *jonquille*, Sp. *junquillo*, dim. of *junco*, L. *juncus*, rush. From its rush-like leaves.

jordan. Chamber-pot, in ME. also alchemist's vessel. Prob. an application of the baptismal name *Jordan*, very common in ME. (hence surnames *Jordan*, *Judd*, *Judkins*, etc.), and also in F. (*Jourdain*), It. (*Giordano*), and other langs. Cf. *jack, jug, jerry, jorum*.

Jordan almond. Folk-etym. for ME. *jardyne almaunde* (*Prompt. Parv.*), from F. *jardin*, garden.

jorum. Large drinking-bowl, esp. bowl of punch. From name *Joram* (2 *Sam.* viii. 10). *Jeroboam* (q.v.) is used in similar sense. Both prob. suggested by *jack, jordan, jug*, etc.

joseph [*archaic*]. Ladies' 18 cent. ridingcloak. From name *Joseph*, Heb. *yōsēph*, perh. with obscure allusion to *Gen.* xxxix. 12. Cf. *benjamin*.

joskin [*dial.*]. Bumpkin, yokel. ? Dim. of *Joseph* (cf. *Hodge*), ? or playful variation on *bumpkin* suggested by dial. *joss*, to "bump." Hence perh. *josser*, fellow.

joss. Chinese god, etc. Javanese *jos*, from OPort. *deos* (*deus*), god, taken to China by sailors. For application to China cf. *mandarin*, for travels cf. *assagai*.

jostle, justle. Frequent. of *joust* (q.v.).

s'entr'essayer à la jouste: to trye one an other at justling (Hollyband, *Treas. of Fr. Tongue*, 1580).

jot. L. *iota* (read as *jota*), G. ἰῶτα, name of smallest letter (ι); cf. It. *iota*, Sp. *jota*. Esp. in *jot or tittle* (*Matt.* v. 18) and *not a jot*. Hence verb to *jot down*, with small abbrevs. orig. Sc. See *iota*.

Oon i [Tynd. iott] or titil (Wyc. *Matt.* v. 18).

jounce [*archaic*]. To bump, jolt, etc. Var. of obs. *jaunce*, for which see *jaunt*.

joyuncinge, or grette ongentyl mevynge: strepitus
(*Prompt. Parv.*).

journal. F. (sc. *livre, registre*, etc.), L. *diurnalis*, from *diurnus*, from *dies*, day. Cf. *diary, diurnal*, the latter formerly also as noun (v.i.). *Journalism* was not adopted from F. *journalisme* till 1833. *Journalese* (late 19 cent.) is after *Chinese, Portuguese,* etc.

In every Mercurius, Coranto, Gazet or Diurnal
(Blount).
By "journalism" we mean writing for pay upon matters of which we are ignorant (Leslie Stephen).

journey. F. *journée,* day, esp. day's happenings (work, march, etc.), VL. **diurnata* (v.s.); cf. It. *giornata,* Sp. *jornada.* Etym. sense survives in *journeyman,* one who works by the day; cf. synon. F. *journalier,* Ger. *tagelöhner.* The OF. senses are all found in ME., but the earliest (13 cent.) is that now current.

All the lordes that dyed at the jorney [battle of St Albans] are beryed at seynt Albones
(*Paston Let.* i. 336).

joust. OF. *jouster (jouter),* VL. **juxtare,* from *juxta,* against, close to; cf. It. *giostrare,* Sp. *justar.* The normal E. form is the earlier *just,* which survives in name *Juster.* See *adjust.*

jovial. F., It. *gioviale,* "borne under the planet Jove" (Flor.), L. *jovialis,* from OL. *Jovis, Diovis;* cogn. with L. *deus,* G. Ζεύς (see *Jupiter*). Cf. *mercurial, saturnine.*

The load-stone, the very seed and ingendring stone of discoverie, whose soever Joviall brain first conceived that Minerva (Purch.).

jowl. Jaw. Of obscure origin. In gen. sense equivalent to ME. *chawl,* AS. *ceafl,* jaw, cogn. with Ger. *kiefer.* In sense of fat pendulous throat it appears to be ME. *cheole, chel,* throat, cogn. with Ger. *kehle* (cf. *jollop,* dewlap, in her.). Now chiefly in ref. to aggressive under-jaw, whence dog-name *Jowler,* and in *cheek by jowl.*

chawylbone: mandibula (*Prompt. Parv.*).

jolle, or heed: caput (*ib.*).

Bee thou [Elijah] my coach-man, and now cheeke by joule
With Phoebus chariot let my chariot roule
(Sylv. iv. 1).

joy. F. *joie,* L. *gaudia,* neut. pl. taken as fem. sing., from *gaudēre,* to rejoice; cf. It. *gioia,* Sp. *joya.* *Joy-riding* is US. (1909). Cf. *joy-stick* (aeron.).

To control one [war-machine] the pilot has to manipulate but a single lever, which we call the "joy stick" (Bishop, *Winged Warfare*).

jubbah. See *jibbah.*

jubilation. L. *jubilatio-n-,* from *jubilare,* to shout, as in *jubilate Deo,* init. words of *Ps. c.*

jubilee. F. *jubilé,* Late L. *jubilaeus* (sc. *annus*), G. ἰωβηλαῖος, from ἰώβηλος, jubi-

lee, Heb. *jōbēl,* orig. ram, hence, ram's horn used as trumpet. The form, *ju-* for *jo-,* is due to early association with L. *jubilare* (v.s.). Orig. applied to the Jewish *year of Jubilee* (*Lev.* xxv.), but in early use for other celebrations, usu. in connection with fifty years.

Our sexteyn and oure fermerer,
That han been trewe freres fifty yeer,—
They may now, God be thanked of his loone!
Maken hir jubilee (Chauc. D. 1859).

Judaism. L., G. ἰουδαισμός. See *Jew.*

Judas. L., G. Ἰούδας, Heb. *y'hūdāh,* Judah, a common name among the Jews. Now usu. reserved for the traitor. Hence *judas,* small grating through which one can watch without being seen; also *judas tree* (see *jew's ear*).

judge. F. *juge,* L. *judex, judic-,* from *jus,* law, *dicare,* to proclaim; cf. It. *judice,* Sp. *juez.* *Judgmatic-al,* chiefly US., is coined on *dogmatic.* *Day of judgment* is used by Wyc. alternately with *day of doom.*

judicature. F., MedL. *judicatura,* from *judicare,* to judge (v.s.). Cf. *judicial, judiciary, judicious.* *Judicial murder* is 19 cent.

The judicial murder of Captain Fryatt
(A. J. Balfour, Aug. 4, 1916).

judy. Pet-form of *Judith.* As applied to woman of ridiculous appearance it refers to the wife of Punch. She appears to be of E. origin and not from the It. puppet-play.

jug¹. Vessel. Pet-form of *Joan,* also of *Judith.* Cf. *jack²,* goblet, etc. So also ME. *jobbe, jubbe,* used by Chauc. for a drinking vessel, is prob. from *Job,* often *Jubbe, Juppe* in ME., whence mod. names *Jubb, Jupp.* It is even possible that *jug* is altered on the female name from the earlier *jub.* The *jug,* or *stone-jug,* i.e. gaol, is from thieves' cant.

Pro j pare jobbes de iiij galonibus
(*Earl of Derby's Exped.* 1390–93).

jug². Note of nightingale. Imit.; cf. *bulbul.* It was also used for the bird (v.i.), perh. by association with female name (see *jug¹*).

jug, a nightingale: philomela (Litt.).

juggernaut. Hind. *Jagganáth,* Sanskrit *ga-gan-nātha,* from *gagat,* world, *nātha,* lord, title of Krishna, eighth avatar of Vishnu, and esp. his idol at Puri (Orissa), annually dragged in procession in enormous car under which devotees are supposed formerly to have thrown themselves. Hence used, like *Moloch*, of any institution or movement of which the speaker disapproves. First Europ. account dates from early 14 cent.

juggins [*slang*]. Either surname *Juggins*, from *Jug*, Joan (see *jug*¹), felt as suitable for a simpleton (cf. *Lushington*), or a playful variation on *muggins* (q.v.).

juggler. OF. *joglere* (nom.), *jogleor* (acc.), L. *joculator-em*, from *joculari*, to jest, from *jocus*. See *jongleur*. Cf. It. *giocolatore*, "a jugler, jester, or mountibanke, or tumbler" (Flor.). The word is early (c. 1100) and *juggle* (*Piers Plowm.*) is prob. a back-formation (cf. *peddle*).

Jugo-Slav. Also *Yugo-* (q.v.).

jugular [*anat.*]. MedL. *jugularis*, from *jugulum*, collar-bone, dim. of *jugum*, yoke.

juice. F. *jus*, L., "pottage, liquour, broth, gruell" (Coop.).

ju-ju. WAfr. magic, fetish. Perh. F. *joujou*, toy, infantile redupl. on *jouet*, from *jouer*, to play, L. *jocare*. Cf. hist. of *fetish*, *joss*.

jujube. Fruit. F., MedL. *jujuba*, neut. pl., from *zizyphum*, G. ζίζυφον, of Pers. origin.

ju-jutsu. Chino-Jap., also *jiu-jitsu*, muscle science.

julep. F., MedL. *julapium*, Arab. *julāb*, Pers. *gul-āb*, rose-water (see *attar*); cf. It. *giulebbe*, "a julep, a kinde of potion" (Flor.), Sp. *julepe*. An Arab. med. word (cf. *sirup*).

Julian. Of *Julius Caesar*, esp. in ref. to his reformed calendar (B.C. 46). Cf. *Gregorian*.

julienne. Soup. F. *potage à la julienne*, from name *Julien*.

July. AF. *Julie*, L. *Julius*, from *Julius Caesar*, whose birth-month it was. Replaced AS. *lītha se æfterra* (from *līthe*, mild). Earlier L. name was *Quintilis*, fifth of Rom. calendar. F. *juillet* is a mixture from OF. *juil* (*Julius*) and *juignet*, little June (cf. archaic Ger. *Hornung*, February, son of *Horn*, January). The abnormal accent of *July*, which is mod. (v.i.), is due to instinctive attempt to avoid confusion with *June*. For a similar reason It. prefers *Luglio*, with agglutination of art., to the correct *Giulio*. In ME. we find *Jul*, *Juil*, from OF. (v.s.).

In the month of May, I tell you truly,
Which neither was in June nor July,
The Dutch began to be unruly
(*Rump Song*, c. 1653).

jumble¹. To confuse. Orig. (16 cent.) intrans., to move confusedly. Prob. imit. (cf. *fumble*, *stumble*, etc.) with reminiscence

of *jump*¹. Chauc. has *jumper* in similar sense.

They jumble, tumble, rumble, rage and rave (Sylv.).

jumble². Cake, formerly made in rings. Prob. OF. *jumel* (*jumeau*), twin. See *gimbal*.

stortelli: winding simnels, wreathed jumbals (Torr.).

jumbo. Big, clumsy person. Cf. *mumbo-jumbo*. Chiefly in allusion to famous elephant at Zoo (†1885).

jump¹. Verb. From 16 cent. Of It. origin; cf. NIt. *tzumpa*, Neapolitan *dzumbá*, Sardinian *jumpai*, all dial. words, to jump; also Sp. *jopo*, spring, F. dial. (Morvan) *zhopé*, to jump with feet together. Prob. all imit. of sound of two feet coming down together. Has largely replaced older *leap* and *bound*. From earlier sense (v.i.) is evolved to *jump with*, coincide or tally exactly.

I jumpe, as one dothe that holdeth bothe his fete togyther, and leape upon a thyng: je saulte (Palsg.).

jump². Short coat. Prob. nasalized from earlier *jup*, F. *jupe*, skirt, of Arab. origin, whence also Ger. *juppe*, *joppe*. See *jibbah*. Cf. ME. *gipoun*, knight's surcoat, F. *jupon*, petticoat. Hence naut. *jumper*, jacket.

juppe: a jupo, jacket, or jump (Ludw.).

jumper¹. Garment. See *jump*².

jumper². Welsh Methodist of 18 cent. Cf. *quaker*, *shaker*.

Turks, Infidels, Heretics, Jumpers, and Jews
(*Ingoldsby*).

junction. L. *junctio-n-*, from *jungere*, *junct-*, to join.

juncture. L. *junctura* (v.s.). Current sense, as in *at this juncture*, is astrol. (cf. *conjuncture*).

June. F. *juin*, L. *Junius*, gens from which the month was named; cf. It. *Giugno*, Sp. *Junio*, Ger. *Juni*. Replaced AS. *lītha se ærra* (see *July*).

jungle. Hind. *jangal*, Sanskrit *gaṅgala*, dry, desert; cf. sense-development of *forest*.

junior. L., compar. of *juvenis*, young (q.v.).

juniper. L. *juniperus*. See *geneva*, *gin*².

junk¹ [*naut.*]. Orig. (15 cent.) old or inferior cable. Hence old material, oakum, etc., and fig. lump, e.g. of salt meat. Origin unknown.

junk². Vessel. Port. *junco*, Javanese *djong* or Malay *adjong*. In most Europ. langs. Not orig. applied to Chinese ship (cf. *joss*, *mandarin*). *Jonge* "a shippe" is one of the "wordes of the naturall language of Java" in *Drake's Circumnavigation* (Hakl. xi. 133). ? Is it possible that this "worde of the naturall language" is simply Port. *junco*, reed, rush (see *junket*), used attributively of the reed sails (v.i.).

jonks, or jonques: are vessels very common in the East-Indies. Their sails, often-times, are only of reeds and of matts (*Gent. Dict.*).

junker. Ger., young lord, MHG. *junc-herre* (see *herr*). Cf. *jungfer*, maiden (*jungfrau*). See also *younker*. The offensive sense of *junker*, *junkerism*, dates chiefly from Bismarck's bullying methods, but the *Junkers* had qualities worthy of respect.

The Prussian Junkers have proved themselves more fit for rule than any class in all history. Their virtues are Spartan, their minds narrow but incorruptible, and their bravery and patriotism undoubted (Gerard, *Four Years in Germany*).

junket. Orig. rush-basket, from L. *juncus*, rush. Later, preparation of cream, etc., served in rush-basket (v.i.). Sense of feast, picnic party, etc., seems to be due to association with obs. *junkery*, perh. from F. *joncher*, to spread, orig. to strew rushes.

He tok a jonket of resshen...and putte the litil faunt with ynne (Wyc. *Ex.* ii. 3).

Pertrych and his felaw bere gret visage and kepe gret junkeryes and dyneres (*Paston Let. Supp.* p. 24).

giuncata: a kinde of fresh cheese and creame, so called bicause it is brought to market upon rushes. Also a junket. Also a prettie worke made of bents or rushes (Flor.).

junta. Sp., assembly, council, L. *juncta*, p.p. fem. of *jungere*, to join. Esp. in connection with council formed (1808) to resist Napoleon. For incorr. *junto*, implying intrigue (as *camarilla*), cf. *salvo*, *bastinado*, etc.

jupe [*Sc. & north.*]. See *jibbah*, *jump²*.

Jupiter. L., orig. voc., Father Jove; cf. G. Ζεῦ πάτερ. *Jupiter pluvius* is mod. and jocular after *Jupiter tonans*.

jurassic [*geol.*]. Of oolitic limestone as *Jura* mountains.

jurat. Official in Cinque Ports and Channel Islands. OF., MedL. *juratus*, as *jury*.

juridical. From L. *juridicus*. Cf. *judge*, *jurisdiction*.

jurisdiction. Reconstructed from ME. *juridicioun*, F. *juridiction*, L. *jurisdictio-n-*, lit. declaration of law, *jus*, *jur-*. See *judge*. Cf. *jurisprudence*, science of law; *jurisconsult*, learned in law; *jurist*, law practitioner.

jury. OF. *jurée*, p.p. fem. of *jurer*, to swear, L. *jurare*, from *jus*, *jur-*, right, law. Cf. *juror*, OF. *jureor*, L. *jurator-em*, one who takes oath. Orig. the jurors were rather

of the character of witnesses, selected on account of their special knowledge of local events, character, etc.

jury-mast. An obscure naut. witticism. Cf. synon. F. *mât de fortune*.

I was left all alone, and let me drive in the sea five days before I could make my jury-mast
(Capt. Thompson, 1592).

jusquauboutiste. F., neol. coined from *jusqu'au bout*, up to the end.

For my own part I am a Jusqu'auboutist
(G. B. Shaw, *Daily Chron.* Jan. 12, 1918).

jussive [*gram.*]. From L. *jubēre*, *juss-*, to order. Cf. *imperative*.

just. F. *juste*, L. *justus*, from *jus*, right, law. Adv. sense, precisely, exactly, springs from adj., but in such phrases as *just against* (*by*, *behind*, etc.), it may partly represent OF. *joste*, L. *juxta* (see *joust*).

justice. F., L. *justitia*, from *justus* (v.s.). Use as title, *justice of the peace*, is very early (12 cent.). The *Lord Chief Justice* took over in 13 cent. the functions of the earlier *justiciar-y*, MedL. *justitiarius*.

justify. F. *justifier*, Church L. *justificare*, to make just. *Justification* is in Wyc. (*Rom.* v. 16).

justle. See *jostle*.

jut. Corrupt. of archaic *jet*, to project (see *jetty*). Perh. affected by obs. *jut*, to push (see *jolt*).

Piers, jutties, walles or banckes against the rages of the sea (*NED.* 1547).

porgere: to jut, to jettie, or butte foorth (Flor.).

Jute [*hist.*]. Late L. *Juti*, *Jutae* (Bede), inhabitants of *Jutland*; cf. AS. *Ēotas*, *Gēatas*, ON. *Iōtar*.

jute. Fibre from bark of Indian tree. Bengali *jhōto*, *jhuto*.

juvenile. L. *juvenilis*, from *juvenis*, young (q.v.).

juxtaposition. F., coined from L. *juxta*, beside, and *position*.

k-. Many words, esp. of foreign origin, are spelt both with *k-* and *c-*, and some not included here may be found under the latter initial.

kaama. Hottentot name for *hartebeest*.

Kabyle. F., Arab. *qabāil*, pl. of *qabīla*, tribe.

kadi. See *cadi*.

Kaffir. Arab. *kāfir*, infidel, name given to Bantu tribes by Arab traders and raiders.

They [the Arabs] call the conquered Caffars, misbeleevers or if you will heretikes (Purch.).

kaftan. See *caftan*.

kaid. See *caid*.

kail. See *kale*.

kaimakam. Turk., Arab. *qā'im maqām*, standing (in the) place. Cf. *lieutenant*.

The Turks...their Kaimakams and their Pashas, one and all, bag and baggage (Gladstone, 1876).

kainite [*min.*]. Named (1865) by Zincken, from G. καινός, new, in ref. to its recent formation.

kaiser. OHG. *keisar*; cf. AS. *cāsere*, ON. *keisari*, Goth. *kaisar*. L. *Caesar*, cognomen of Gaius Julius, adopted as title by Teut. & Slav. langs. (cf. *czar, tsar*), as *imperator* was by Rom. langs. Cf. Lithuanian *karalius*, king, Ukranian *korola*, from *Carolus* (*Magnus*), Charlemagne. *Kaiser* is the earliest L. loan-word in Teut. (temp. Augustus).

kajawah [*Anglo-Ind.*]. Camel-litter for women. Urdu, Pers.

kaka. New Zeal. parrot. Maori name. Cf. *kakapo*, owl-parrot, Maori *kaka*, parrot, *po*, night.

kakemono. Wall-picture. Jap. *kake-mono*, hang-thing.

kale, kail. Northern form of *cole*, cabbage. Often used in Sc. for soup, food (e.g. to *give one his kail through the reek*, make it hot for him). The *kailyard school* of literature dates from Ian Maclaren's *Beside the Bonnie Brier Bush* (1894), the title of which comes from old song, "There grows a bonnie brier bush in our kail-yard."

kaleidoscope. Coined (1817) by inventor, Sir David Brewster, from G. καλός, beautiful, εἶδος, shape.

kali. See *alkali*.

kalian, kalioun. Persian hookah. Arab. *qalyān, qalyūn*.

kalmia. Amer. shrub. From *Kalm*, pupil of Linnaeus.

kalmuck. Tatar *khalimik*, apostate (from Buddhism).

kamerad [*mil.*]. To surrender. From Ger. cry of *kamerad*, comrade.

It was only some minutes before Ludendorff's newest division was kamerading itself out of danger (*Daily Chron.* Nov. 15, 1916).

kampong. See *compound*[2].

kamptulicon. Obs. name for floor-cloth. Trade-name coined from G. καμπτός, flexible, οὖλος, thick. App. ousted by *linoleum*.

kamsin. See *khamsin*.

Kanaka. South Sea islander hired as plantation hand. Hawaiian, for Samoan (also Tongan, Maori) *tangata*, man.

kangaroo. Ascribed by Capt. Cook (1770) to natives of Queensland, but not known now in any Austral. lang. (cf. *boomerang*). It prob. originated in a misunderstanding of question and answer. Hence *kangaroo closure* (parl.), which progresses by leaps.

kanoon. Kind of harp. Pers. or Arab. *qānūn*.

Kantian [*philos.*]. Of *Immanuel Kant*, Ger. philosopher (†1804).

kaolin. China clay. F., Chin. *kao-ling*, high hill, name of mountain whence orig. obtained.

kaput. Ger., done for, F. *capot* (q.v.).

Karaite. Jewish sect (8 cent.) which rejects Rabbinical tradition. From Heb. *qārā*, to read (cf. *Koran*).

karaka. New Zeal. tree. Maori name.

karma. Fate, in theosophical jargon. Sanskrit *karman*, action.

kaross. SAfr. skin mantle. According to some authorities neither a Bantu or Hottentot word, but possibly a corrupt. of Du. *kuras* or Port. *couraça*, cuirass (q.v.). Cf. *assagai*, *kraal*. It is described as a corrupt. Du. word in 1673.

karri. Tree and timber. WAustral. native name.

karroo. Barren plateau of SAfr. Hottentot.

kartel, cartle [*SAfr.*]. Bed in ox-waggon. SAfrDu., Port. *catel*, "a sort of bed in Malabar" (Vieyra), Tamil *kaṭṭil*, bedstead. Cf. *sjambok*.

In this after part was a hide cartle or bed (*King Solomon's Mines*).

katabolism [*biol.*]. Destructive metabolism. From G. καταβάλλειν, to throw down.

katydid [*US.*]. Insect. From sound suggesting *Katy did*. Cf. *bobolink*, *whippoor-will*.

kauri. New Zeal. tree. Maori name.

kava. Intoxicating drink (Polynesia). From native name of plant from root of which it is made.

kavass. Armed servant, etc. Turk., Arab. *qawwās*, bowmaker, from *qaws*, bow.

kayak. Eskimo, man's boat; cf. *oomiak*. Recorded 17 cent.

kea. New Zeal. parrot. Maori, from cry.

kedge [*naut.*]. Earlier *cadging-cable, cagger*, the latter passim in *Nav. Accts.* 1495–97, point to ME. *caggen*, to fasten, secure, app. var. of *catch* (cf. *grudge*).

kedgeree. Orig. vegetable curry. Hind. *khichri*, Sanskrit *k'rsara*, dish of rice and sesamum. Earlier (17 cent.) *kercheere, kitsery, cutchery*, etc.

keel[1]. Of ship. ON. *kjölr* (whence Norw. Dan. *kjöl*, Sw. *köl*). Du. & Ger. *kiel* are prob. from E. Hence *keelson*, *kelson*, inside timber bolted to keel; cf. Du. *kolsem* (for *kolzwijn*), Ger. *kielschwein*, Sw. *kölsvin*, in which second element is *swine*, the use of animal names being common in naut. lang.; but some authorities regard Norw. dial. *kjölsvill* as orig. form, with second element, cogn. with E. *sill*, meaning foundation beam. To *keelhaul* (Capt. John Smith, 1626) is adapted from Du. *kielhalen*, to haul under the keel, whence also Ger. *kielholen*.

einen matroos kielhaalen: to pull a marriner up from under the keel, (a seaman's punishment)
(Sewel).

keel[2]. Flat-bottomed lighter, esp. on Tyne and Wear. Du. *kiel*; cogn. with Ger. *kiel*, AS. *cēol*, ON. *kjöll*, all earlier meaning ship, but Du. & Ger. forms have now changed sense under influence of *keel*[1]. Authorities are agreed that the resemblance of the two words is accidental and that, in spite of the parallel double meaning of L. *carina*, there can be no connection between ON. *kjölr* and *kjöll*. Ger. *kiel*, keel, from LG. or Du., dates only from 17 cent., while obs. *kiel*, ship, is OTeut.

keelson [*naut.*]. See *keel*[1].

keen[1]. Adj. AS. *cēne*. Com. Teut.; cf. Du. *koen*, Ger. *kühn*, ON. *kœnn*; prob. cogn. with *can*[1], *ken*[1]. Orig. brave, fierce, application to sight, scent, etc., being latest sense. With mod. *keen on* cf. F. *âpre à*, of which the E. is perh. a transl. For application to edge cf. origin of *whet*.

keen[2]. Irish lament. Ir. *caoine*, from *cáinim*, I weep.

keep. Late AS. *cēpan*, with no known cognates. Orig. trans., to seize, hold, observe, etc., intrans. senses being from earlier reflex., e.g. to *keep* (*oneself*) *silent*, etc. Camb. sense of residing is recorded in ME. With *keep* of a castle cf. It. *tenazza*, "a little hould or keepe" (Flor.), from *tenere*, to hold, keep. The first *NED*. example is from Sidney's *Arcadia*, but it occurs earlier (Leland's *Itinerary*, c. 1540), and the surname *Keep* app. carries it much farther back. *William atte Kep* is recorded in the *Close Rolls*, temp. Ed. I.

kef, kief. Somnolence induced by bhang. Arab. *kaif, kef*, well-being, enjoyment.

keffiyeh. Bedouin head-dress. Arab. *kaffīyah*, perh. of L. origin. See *coif*.

keg. ME. *cagge*, ON. *kaggi*, cask. ? Hence also F. *caque*, herring barrel.

caque: a cag; or, the fourth part of a *muid*; (a barrell, or vessell, wherein sault-meats, pitch, rosen, etc., are usually carried, or kept) (Cotg.).

kelp. Seaweed. ME. *cülp, culp*, later *kilp*. Origin unknown.

kelpie [*Sc.*]. Fabulous water-horse. ? Gael. *colpach*, heifer, steer, colt, prob. from ON. *kálfr*, calf.

kelson. See *keel*[1].

Kemble pipe. From *Kemble*, executed (1679) at Hereford (Oates plot), who smoked and chatted on his way to execution.

kempt. Playful back-formation from *unkempt* (q.v.).

ken[1]. Verb. AS. *cennan*. Com. Teut.; cf. Du. *kennen*, Ger. *kennen, können*, ON. *kenna*, Goth. *kannjan*. Orig. causal of *can*, with sense of making to know; hence used in ME. of guiding, directing. Noun *ken*, usu. with prep., or as echo of Keats (*Sonnet on Chapman's Homer*), is a naut. abbrev. of earlier *kenning*.

Long before Prussia swam into the ken of civilized nations (*Daily Tel.* Nov. 9, 1917).

ken[2] [*thieves' slang*]. ? Short for *kennel*[1].

kennedya. Austral. plant. From *Kennedy*, Hammersmith gardener (c. 1800).

kennel[1]. For dogs. Northern form of F. *chenil*, Late L. *canile*, whence It. *canile*, from *canis*, dog. Cf. obs. *kennet*, small hound, OF. *chenet*, dim. of *chien*.

kennel[2] [*archaic*]. Gutter. Earlier *cannel*, AF. *canel*, ONF. form of *channel* (q.v.).

kenosis [*theol.*]. Renunciation by Christ of Divine character. G., emptying, from κενός, empty.

kenspeck-le [*chiefly dial.*]. Recognizable. From ON. *kennispeki*, power of recognizing, from *kenni*, mark (cf. *ken*[1]), *speki*, wisdom. Change of sense from active to passive is prob. due to association with *conspicuous*.

Kentish fire. Prolonged applause (or dissent). Said to have originated at Kentish meetings (1828–9) in opposition to Catholic Relief Bill.

kentledge [*naut.*]. Pig-iron ballast. Earlier (17 cent.) *kintledge*. ? From *quintal*, with *-age* as in *dunnage*.

kepi. F. *képi*, Ger.-Swiss *käppi*, dim. of *kappe*, cap.

ker-. In US. slang words such as *kerchunk, kerflop, kerwhallop*, etc. ? Influence of Ger.

or Du. *ge-* of p.p. in such phrases as *die glocke kam gewackelt* (Goethe).

keratitis [*med.*]. Form of ophthalmia. From G. κέρας, κερατ-, horn.

kerb. Mod. spelling of *curb* (q.v.) in spec. sense. Orig. of coping round a well.

kerchief. F. *couvrechef*, cover head; cf. *curfew*. See *chief*. ME. and later vars. are very numerous. Shortened *kerch, curch,* is still in dial. use. *Pocket-handkerchief* dates from 18 cent.

> And with my coverchief covered my visage
> (Chauc. D. 590).

kermes. Cochineal insect. Arab. & Pers. *qirmiz,* Sanskrit *kr'mis,* worm, whence also *carmine, crimson.* In most Europ. langs. For sense-development cf. *vermilion.*

kermis. Fair. Du., earlier *kerc-misse,* church mass. Cf. Ger. *kirchmesse, kermis, messe,* fair. See *kirk, mass*[1].

> *kermisse*: the dedication of a church, or parochiall feasts in towns, or villages (Hexham).

kern [*hist.*]. Orig. (14 cent.) light-armed Irish soldier. Ir. *ceithearn,* orig. band of soldiers (see *hubbub*). Cf. *cateran.*

> Murderous Irish rebels and savage kerns
> (*John Inglesant,* ch. xii.).

kernel. AS. *cyrnel,* dim. of *corn*[1] (q.v.).

kerosene. Irreg. formation from G. κηρός, wax. Cf. *cerecloth.*

kersey. Fabric. Earlier also *carsey,* etc. ? From *Kersey* (Suffolk); cf. *worsted,* ? *linsey-woolsey.* But OF. *cresee* suggests *croisé,* and the E. word may be a corrupt., like *kerseymere.* Cf. F. *carisel,* Du. *karsaai,* from E.

kerseymere. Corrupt. of *cassimere, cashmere* (q.v.), due to association with *kersey* (v.s.).

kestrel. F. *crécerelle,* dim. of *crécelle,* both used for kestrel. Orig. a noisy bell or leper's clicket, VL. **crepicella,* from *crepare,* to resound, from the old belief (Columella) that their noise frightened away other hawks (v.i.). Cf. the L. name *tinnunculus,* from *tinnire,* to jingle, re-echo.

> *tinnunculus*: a kinde of haukes; a kistrell or a kastrell; a steyngall. They use to set them in pigeon houses, to make doves to love the place, because they feare away other haukes with their ringing voice (Coop.).

> *quercelle*: a kastrell (Cotg.).

> *crecerelle*: a rattle, or clack, for children; also a kestrell, stanniell (*ib.*).

ketch. Earlier also *catch* (15 cent.), which may be from verb to *catch,* ONF. *cachier,*

to hunt (cf. *yacht*). Du. *kits,* F. *caiche, quaiche,* are from E. But oldest form is app. *kegge,* occurring (1475), with *cogg, kele* (see *keel*[2]), in *York Merch. Advent. Accts.,* p. 73, while *keill, catche,* or *barke* (*ib.* 1603) suggests a later form.

Ketch, Jack. Executioner (†1686). As popular nickname for common hangman by c. 1700.

ketchup. Malay *kĕchap,* ? from Chin. *ke-tsiap,* brine of pickled fish. With incorr. *catsup* cf. *Welsh rarebit.*

kettle. AS. *citel.* Com. Teut.; cf. Du. *ketel,* Ger. *kessel,* ON. *ketill,* Goth. *katils,* all from L. *catinus,* vessel for food (for form cf. *easel*). An early loan due to superiority of Roman cookery (cf. *kitchen*).

keuper [*geol.*]. Upper member of triassic system. Ger. miners' name for kind of sandstone; cf. Bavarian *kiefer,* sand, gravel.

kevel [*naut.*]. Peg, cleat. ONF. *keville,* F. *cheville,* peg, ankle, from L. *clavicula,* dim. of *clavis,* key. For loss of first -*l*- by dissim. cf. *fugleman.*

kex [*dial.*]. Hollow dry stem, hemlock. Cf. *kecksy* (*Hen. V,* v. 2), back-formation from pl. *kexes.* ? Cogn. with L. *cicuta,* hemlock, whence F. *ciguë.* Cf. Welsh *cecys.*

key[1]. AS. *cǣg,* with no cognate exc. in OFris. For abnormal pronunc. cf. *Caius College* (Camb.), refounded (1557) by *John Kay* or *Key,* and also *quay, key*[2]. Mus. sense is due to Guy d'Arezzo's use of L. *clavis* (see *gamut*), but the further extension to mechanism of instrument is E. only. With fig. to *key up* cf. *highly strung.* The *House of Keys* (Isle of Man), consisting of twenty-four elected members, is L. *claves* in 15 cent., but reason for name is unknown.

> When things are safe as old wives say,
> We have them under lock and key
> (*Blacksmith,* 17 cent.)

key[2]. WInd. islet. Earlier *cay,* Sp. *caio,* barrier reef, etc., OF. *cai,* sand-bank, of same origin as *quay* (q.v.).

> *caies*: a ridge of rocks, or sandbanks; called in the West Indies, keys (Falc.).

khaki. Urdu, Pers. *khākī,* dusty, from *khāk,* dust. First worn, before the Mutiny, by the Guides.

khalifa. See *caliph.*

khamsin, kamsin. Hot wind from desert in Egypt. Colloq. Arab. *khamsīn,* orig. oblique case of *khamsūn,* fifty, because blowing for about fifty days.

khan¹. Potentate. Earlier also *cham* (q.v.). Turki *khān*, lord, prince, Tatar *qā'ān*, adopted also in Arab. & Pers. The word became known to Europeans esp. in connection with *Chingīz (Genghiz) khān*, the Mongol invader of India, and occurs in Marco Polo (1298). *Chingīz khān*, lit. great khan, was also corrupted into *Cambuscan*, as in Chaucer's "half-told" story. Now esp. in *Agha Khan*, hereditary title of head of Moslems in India, descendant of Ali and Fatima.

This noble kyng was cleped Cambyuskan
(Chauc. F. 12).

khan². Caravanserai. Arab. *khān*, inn.

khanjar. Also *handjar, cangiar*. Eastern dagger. Pers. *khanjar*, also in Urdu, Turk., Arab.

kheda, keddah. Corral for wild elephants. Hind. *khēdā*.

khedive. Viceroy of Egypt, title granted to Ismail Pasha by Turk. government (1867) and abolished by British government (1914). F. *khédive*, Turk., Pers. *khidīv*, prince.

khidmutgar, kitmudhgar [*Anglo-Ind.*]. Attendant at table. Urdu, Pers. *khidmaɩgār*, from *khidmat*, service, and agent. suffix -*gār*.

khor. Watercourse, nullah. Arab. *khurr, khorr*.

khud. Chasm, ravine. Hind. *khud*.

khus-khus. See *cus-cus*.

kibble. Small coal. ? Thinned form of *cobble*. Cf. surname *Kibble*, for *Cobbold*.

kibe [*archaic*]. Welsh *cibwst*, chilblains, esp. on heel, from *gwst*, pain; hence to *tread on one's kibes*, after *Haml.* v. 1.

kibitka. Tartar tent, Russ. tilt-cart. Russ., from Tatar *kibits*; cf. Arab. *qubbat*, tent of skins.

kiblah. Also *kebla*. Point to which Moslems turn to pray; hence, temple at Mecca. Arab. *qiblah*, from *qabala*, to be opposite.

kibob. Incorr. for *cabob* (q.v.).

kibosh. Orig. in to *put the kibosh on*, dispose of, settle. Perh. Yiddish. Later sense, nonsense, by association with *bosh*.

kick¹. Of foot. ME. *kiken, kyken*. Origin unknown. It occurs first in *kicking against* (*the spur*, etc.), and, if orig. used of a convulsive movement (cf. *alive and kicking*), may be connected with *kink* (q.v.).

It is hard to thee for to kyke agens the pricke
(Wyc. Acts, ix. 5).

kick². Indentation in bottom of bottle. ? Cf. *kink*.

kickshaw. False sing. from *kickshaws, quelk-chose*, etc., F. *quelque chose*, something, L. *qualis quam causa*. See *fricandeau*.

Art thou good at these kickshawses, knight?
(*Twelfth Night*, i. 3).

kid¹. Young of goat. ON. *kith*, whence Norw. Dan. Sw. *kid*, cogn. with Ger. *kitze*. Tirolese *kittele* points to an unrecorded Goth. cognate. Slang sense of child, whence verb to *kid* (cf. to *coax, fool, gull*), and *kidnap* (q.v.), is partly due to Ger. Du. *kind*, child (see *kin*).

kid² [*naut.*]. Tub. ? Var. of *kit¹*.

kidnap. Back-formation from earlier (1678) *kidnapper*, child stealer, from *kid¹* and obs. *nap*, to nab. Orig. sense of decoying children in order to sell them as slaves in NAmer. is preserved in title of Stevenson's novel.

kidney. Earliest (c. 1325) *kidenei*, perh. a compd. of ME. *ei*, egg, AS. *ǣg* (cf. vulgar Ger. *eier*, testicles, lit. eggs). Later ME. *kidneer*, etc. shows assimilation to ME. *nere*, kidney, ON. *nȳra*, cogn. with Ger. *niere*, but is prob. back-formation from pl. *kidneyren, eyren* being ME. pl. of *ei*. First element doubtful, perh. ident. with *cud, quid¹* (see also *chitterling*). The AS. name was *cropp*. *Kidney* was used, like *heart, liver*, of temperament, hence *of that kidney*, etc.

Think of that; a man of my kidney, that am as subject to heat as butter (*Merry Wives*, iii. 5).

kief. See *kef*.

kie-kie. New Zeal. climbing plant. Maori name.

kier. Vat, esp. for bleaching. ? Norw. *kar*, ON. *ker*, tub, cogn. with OHG. *char*, Goth. *kas*.

kilderkin. Obs. Du. *kindeken, kinneken*, fourth part of tun (now *kinnetje*, firkin), dim. from Ger. dial. *kindel*, quintal (q.v.). The early Du. & Ger. forms are associated by folk-etym. with *kind*, child.

Pro iij kynerkynes de salmone salso
(*Earl of Derby's Exped.* 1390-93).
Pro j kilderkyn di. de storgon (*ib.*).
kinnetjen: firkin, or the fourth part of a barrel
(Hexham).

Kilkenny cats. Reported to have fought till only their tails were left. App. originated in a Munchausen story of Curran's.

kill. ME. usu. *cullen, cüllen*, also *kellen*. Earliest sense app. to strike; cf. *slay*, which it has supplanted in ordinary speech. Of obscure origin, but prob. cogn. with *quell. Kilt*, p.p., now regarded as Irishism, was once regular (cf. *spilt*).

killcrop. Changeling. Ger. *kielkropf*. Second element is *kropf*, crop (as of bird). Usual Ger. word is *wechselbalg*, change skin.

kiln. AS. *cylen*, L. *culina*, kitchen, whence also ON. *kylna*. Cf. *mill, kitchen*.

kilo-. Adapted (1799) from G. χίλιοι, thousand, into F. metric system. Hence *kilogram, kilometer*, etc.

kilt. Orig. verb, to tuck up. Dan. *kilte*, also *kilte op*, perh. cogn. with ON. *kilting*, skirt. As name for *philibeg* only from 18 cent. Gavin Douglas describes Venus as with "hir skirt kiltit till hir bair kne" (*Aen.* i. 320).

kimono. Jap. Peter Mundy, at Macao (1637), speaks of "*kimaones*, or Japan coates."

kin. AS. *cynn*. Com. Teut.; cf. Du. *kunne*, OHG. *chunni*, ON. *kyn*, Goth. *kuni*; cogn. with Ger. *kind*, child, L. *genus*, G. γένος. Cf. *kind¹, kindred*. Very common as suffix (= kind) in AS., a dial. survival of which is Sc. *siccan*, such, lit. *such-kin*.

One touch of nature makes the whole world kin
(*Troil. & Cress.* iii. 3).

-kin. Obs. Du. dim. suffix, cogn. with Ger. *-chen*, and now replaced in Du. by *-je, -ke*, (see *kilderkin, schipperke*). It appears first (c. 1200) in personal names, e.g. *Jenkin, Watkin*, which are still commonest in the region of early Flem. settlements, esp. in Wales. The only current word of undoubted E. origin which preserves the suffix is *lambkin*.

kinchin [*slang*]. Small child, as explained by Fagin to Mr Claypole (*Oliver Twist*, ch. xlii.). Ger. *kindchen* or obs. Du. *kindeken*. See *kin, kid¹*.

kincob. Fabric. Urdu, Pers. *kimkhāb*.

kind¹. Noun. AS. *gecynd*, birth, origin, nature, cogn. with *kin*. Roughly equivalent to L. *genus, species*, e.g. *communion in both kinds* is MedL. *utraque specie*, and *payment in kind* is translated from *in specie*. With *a kind of* cf. *a sort of* (mod. *of sorts*), both phrases being colloq. used as advs., e.g. *kind of* (somewhat) *puzzled*.

kind². Adj. AS. *gecynde*, from *kind¹*. Orig. native, natural, etc., as still in *kindly Scot*, *the kindly fruits of the earth* (*Litany*). Current sense springs from that of well-born, as in ME. *kind* (unmixed) *blood* (cf. *generous*).

Neither by lot of destiny,
Nor yet by kindly [L. *merita, Aen.* iv. 696] death
she perished (Surrey).

kindergarten. Ger., children's garden. Coined (1840) by Friedrich Froebel.

kindle. Frequent. from ON. *kynda*, to set on fire. Now usu. fig. exc. in US.

kindred. With intrusive *-d-* for *kin-red*, second element from AS. *rǣden*, condition, reckoning. Cf. *hatred*.

kine. Double pl., after *oxen*, from *kye*, AS. *cȳ*, pl. of *cū*, cow; cf. *mouse-mice*. Or it may represent AS. gen. pl. *cȳna*.

The kye stood rowtin' i' the loan
(Burns, *Twa Dogs*).

kinematic, kinetic. From G. κινεῖν, to move. See *cinema*.

king. AS. *cyning*. Com. Teut.; cf. Du. *koning*, Ger. *könig*, ON. *konungr*. Orig. the head of a "kin," or tribe; cf. AS. *dryhten*, lord, from *dryht*, army, people, ON. *fylkir*, king, from *folk*, Goth. *thiudans*, king, from *thiuda*, nation (see *Dutch*). *Kingfisher* was earlier *king's fisher* (*Prompt. Parv.*), but the reason for the name is not known. In F. it is *martin-pêcheur*. *King's evil*, scrofula, translates MedL. *regius morbus*, supposed to be cured by royal touch. With the *king's highway* cf. Norw. Dan. *kongevei*, F. *chemin royal*.

kink. Orig. naut. Du., cf. LG. *kink*. Prob. of Scand. origin; cf. ON. *kika*, to bend at the knee, *keikr*, bent backward; cogn. with Norw. dial. *kank*, kink in string. Example below, considerably earlier than *NED.* record, occurs in a transl. from Du.

They bid one good morrow and kincke fingers together (Purch.).

kinkajou. Racoon-like animal. F. *quincajou*, from Algonkin (NAmer. Ind.) name for wolverine, carcajou (q.v.), wrongly transferred by Buffon.

kino. Medicinal gum resembling catechu. WAfr. name; cf. Mandingo *cano*.

kiosk. F. *kiosque*, Turk. *kiūshk*, pavilion, Pers. *kūshk*, palace, portico. In Purch. (1625).

kip¹. Hide of small animal, also (earlier) bundle of hides. Obs. Du. *kip, kijp*, bundle, esp. of hides.

kip² [*slang*]. Common lodging-house. Dan. *kippe*, mean hut, alehouse.

kipper. For *kippered herring*, cured in special way, from verb to *kipper*, earlier used of curing salmon, app. from *kipper*, male salmon during spawning season, AS. *cypera*, kind of salmon, exact meaning and origin being doubtful.

Qe null salmon soit pris en Tamise entre Graves-hend et le pount de Henlee sur Tamise en temps q'il soit kiper (*NED.* 1376).

kirk. Northern form of *church* (q.v.). Cf. ON. *kirkja.*

kirschwasser. Ger., cherry water.

kirtle [*archaic*]. AS. *cyrtel*; cf. ON. *kyrtill,* tunic. An early loan from L. *curtus,* short. Cf. *shirt.*

kismet. Turk., Pers. Arab. *qismat,* portion, destiny, from *qasama,* to divide.

kiss. Verb. AS. *cyssan.* Com. Teut. exc. Goth. (*kukjan*); cf. Du. *kussen,* Ger. *küssen,* ON. *kyssa.* The noun, AS. *coss,* has been assimilated to the verb. With *kissing-crust,* where two loaves have kissed, like billiard-balls, cf. synon. F. *baisure.* To *kiss the book* is in Shaks. (*Temp.* ii. 2).

> Kisse he me with the cos of his mowth
> (Wyc. *Song of Sol.* i. 1).

kistvaen [*antiq.*]. Welsh *cist,* chest, *faen,* mutated form of *maen,* stone.

kit[1]. Orig. tub. Cf. obs. Du. *kitte, keet,* Du. *kit,* tankard, perh. cogn. with *kettle.* In sense of outfit from 18 cent. Here belongs US. *whole kit and caboodle.*

kit[2]. Small fiddle (*Bleak House,* ch. xiv.). Short for obs. *gittern* (see *guitar*), of which Norm. dial. form is *quiterne.*

> *mandore:* a kitt, small gitterne (Cotg.).

> *kit:* a dancing-master, so called from his kit or cittern (Grose).

kit-cat. Portrait less than half-length, fig. reduced version. From portraits of *Kit Cat Club,* said to have been painted this size to fit dining-room of club at Barn Elms.

> *kit-cat club:* a society of gentlemen, eminent for wit and learning, who in the reign of Queen Anne and George I met at a house kept by one Christopher Cat [keeper of pie-house near Temple Bar where club orig. met temp. James II]. The portraits of most of the members of this society were painted by Sir Godfrey Kneller, of one size; thence still called the kit-cat size (Grose).

kitchen. AS. *cycene,* VL. *coquina,* from *coquere,* to cook, used for *culina* (see *kiln*); cf. F. *cuisine,* It. *cucina,* Sp. *cozina,* Du. *keuken,* Ger. *küche,* Welsh *cegin,* OIr. *cucenn.* The spread of the word testifies to superiority of Roman cookery. *Kitchener,* cooking stove, may have been partly suggested by the name of *William Kitchiner,* author of *Apicius Redivivus or the Cook's Oracle* (1817).

kite. AS. *cȳta,* with no known cognates. The toy (cf. Ger. *drachen,* F. *cerf-volant*) is named from the bird. With to *fly a kite,*

see which way the wind blows, cf. F. *ballon d'essai.* Hence also *kite-flying* in sense of issuing accommodation bills.

kith. Chiefly in *kith and kin,* lit. acquaintance and relatives. AS. *cȳththu,* cogn. with *cūth,* known, p.p. of *cunnan,* to know (see *uncouth*); cf. OHG. *chundida,* acquaintance.

kitmudhgar. See *khidmutgar.*

kitool. Fibre used for ropes. Singhalese *kitūl,* kind of palm.

kitten. AF. var. of F. *chaton,* dim. of *chat,* cat (q.v.), with vowel app. affected by synon. and cogn. *kitling,* ON. *ketlingr,* dim. of *köttr,* cat.

> Dan, keetlyng [*Vulg.* catulus] of a lyon
> (Wyc. *Deut.* xxxiii. 22).

kittiwake. Gull. From cry. Cf. *bobolink, katydid,* etc.

kittle. Chiefly in *kittle* (ticklish) *cattle* (*to shoe*). Orig. Sc., from obs. *kittle,* to tickle, AS. *citelian,* cogn. with Du. *kittelen,* Ger. *kitzeln,* and ult. ident. with *tickle.*

kiwi. Apteryx. Maori name, from cry.

klepht. Greek partisan fighter, brigand. ModG. κλέφτης, thief (v.i.).

kleptomania. From G. κλέπτης, thief (v.s.).

klipspringer. SAfr. antelope. Du., cliff springer.

kloof. Ravine. Du., cleft, cogn. with *cleave*[1], *clove*[1].

kn-. An initial combination common to the Teut. langs., though silent (since 17 cent.) in standard E. Of late there has been a slang tendency to reintroduce the *k-* sound in *knut, Knightsbridge.*

knack. Trick. Perh. ident. with imit. *knack,* a short sharp blow, less than a *knock.* Cf. F. *tour de main,* knack, lit. turn of hand. Later sense of gewgaw, trifle, now usu. in redupl. *knick-knack.*

> She ne used no such knakkes smale
> (Chauc. *Blanche,* 1032).
> Why, 'tis a cockle or a walnut-shell,
> A knack, a toy, a trick, a baby's cap (*Shrew,* iv. 3).
> You, by the advantage of some knick-knacks, have got the ascendant over them (Marvell, 1673).

knacker. Of horses, now also of houses and ships (cf. extension of *chandler*). App. ident. with 16 cent. *knacker,* harness-maker, who may have been named from *knack* in the sense of contrivance.

> *knacker:* restio [rope-maker] (Litt.).

knap[1] [*dial.*]. Hill. AS. *cnæpp,* mountain-top; cogn. with *knob.*

knap². To break, as in *flint-knapping*. Imit.; cf. Du. Ger. *knappen*.

He knappeth the spear in sunder (*Ps.* xlvi. 9, *PB.*).

knapsack. Du. *knapzak*, from *knappen* (v.s.) in sense of crunch, eat. Earlier also *snap-sack*, with which cf. E. dial. *snap*, provender.

As lying a gossip...as ever knapped ginger (*Merch. of Ven.* iii. 1).

A snapsacke made of rindes of trees to carry his provant (Purch. 1607).

knapweed. Earlier *knopweed*, from knob-like head.

knar. Knot in wood. Also *gnar* (cf. *gnarled*); cogn. with Ger. *knorren*, MHG. also *knure*. See *knur*.

knave. Orig. male-child, boy. AS. *cnafa*; cf. Ger. *knabe*, boy, *knappe*, youth, squire. For later sense-development cf. Ger. *bube*, boy, rogue.

Oon is a knave childe and the other a mayde childe (Trev. ii. 197).

knead. AS. *cnedan*; cf. Du. *kneden*, Ger. *kneten*; cogn. with ON. *knotha*.

knee. AS. *cnēow*. Com. Teut.; cf. Du. Ger. *knie*, ON. *knē*, Goth. *kniu*; cogn. with L. *genu*, G. γόνυ, Sanskrit *gānu*. *On the knees of the gods* is G. θεῶν ἐν γούνασι (Hom.). With *kneel*, AS. *cnēowlian*, cf. Du. *knielen*. Past *knelt*, for earlier *kneeled*, is 19 cent.

knell. AS. *cnyll*, also verb *cnyllan*, to ring, orig. to strike; cf. archaic to *knoll*. Prob. imit.; cf. MHG. *erknellen*, to resound, Ger. *knall*, report of gun, crack of whip.

And so his knell is knoll'd (*Macb.* v. 8).

knickerbocker. From *Diedrich Knickerbocker*, pretended author of Washington Irving's *History of New York* (1809), a later edition of which was illustrated by Cruikshank with pictures of the Du. settlers in knee-breeches. Cf. *Dolly Varden*, from illustrations to *Barnaby Rudge*. Also applied to New Yorkers of Du. descent. The surname *Knickerbacker* is found in New York State from c. 1700 and app. means a baker of "knickers," clay marbles.

knick-knack. See *knack*.

knife. Late AS. *cnīf*, perh. from ON. *knīfr*; cf. Du. *knijf*; cogn. with Ger. *kneip*, shoemaker's knife. F. *canif* is from Teut. *War to the knife* suggests continuance of struggle after chief weapons are broken or made useless (see quot. s.v. *utterance*).

knight. AS. *cniht*, youth, servant. WGer.; cf. Du. Ger. *knecht*. In E. the word has

risen as *knave* has fallen, while Ger. *knecht*, formerly soldier (see *lansquenet*), has now reverted to orig. servile sense. For sense of spec. rank, early evolved from that of soldier, cf. L. *eques* and F. *chevalier*. The usu. MedL. equivalent is *-miles*. *Knightly* in mod. sense is in Wyc.

And sudenly ther is maad with the aungel a multitude of hevenly knyghthod (Wyc. *Luke*, ii. 13).

knit. AS. *cnyttan*, cogn. with *knot¹* (q.v.). To *knit the brows* is in Chauc. (A. 1128).

knob. Cf. Ger. *knobbe*, *knubbe*, and see *knop*. In SAfr. *knobkerie*, bludgeon, first element is Du. and second is from Hottentot or Bushman lang. *Knobstick* is used in various senses in labour parlance, but the metaphor is obscure.

knock. AS. *cnucian*, *cnocian*; cf. ON. *knoka*. Prob. imit. Mod. slang sense of surprising, etc. was popularized by Chevalier's song *Knock'd 'em in the Old Kent Road*. To *knock out* (*of time*) is from pugilism. Hence the *knock-out blow*.

knoll¹. Hill. AS. *cnoll*, hill-top, etc.; cf. Du. *knol*, clod, ball, Ger. *knollen*, lump, etc.

knoll². See *knell*.

knop. Cogn. with *knap*, *knob*; cf. Ger. *knopf*, button, ON. *knappr*, knob, button.

knot¹. AS. *cnotta*; cogn. with Du. *knot*, Ger. *knoten*, ON. *knūtr*, knot, *knöttr*, ball. Naut. *knot* is from practice of attaching knotted string to log-line to indicate naut. mile. A *porter's knot* was a double shoulder-pad.

knot². Bird. Linnaean name *Canutus* is due to Camden's baseless conjecture that the bird was named from *Cnut* or *Canute*, king of Denmark. Origin unknown.

knout. Russ. *knut*, perh. from Sw. *knut*, knot.

know. AS. *cnāwan*, chiefly in compds. Aryan, though lost in other Teut. langs., which use the cognates of *wit* and *ken*; cf. OHG. *-chnāan*, ON. *knā* (pres. tense), L. *gno-scere*, G. γι-γνώ-σκειν, Sanskrit *gnā*, OIr. *gnāth*, known, Russ. *znat'* to know, etc. *In the know* is quite mod., though Shaks. uses *know* as abstract noun (*Haml.* v. 2). For degeneration of *knowing* cf. that of *crafty*, *cunning*.

There has also been a knowing being from eternity (Locke).

knowledge. Orig. (c. 1300), acknowledgement, confession, from earlier verb *cnaw-lechien* (c. 1220), to acknowledge, regularly used by Wyc. to render L. *confiteri*. The second element is unexplained. Skeat regards it as cogn. with AS. *-lāc* as in *wed-lock* (q.v.). See *acknowledge*.

> And he knowelechide, and denyede not
> (Wyc. *John*, i. 20).

knub, knubble. Cf. *nub, nubble*; cogn. with *knob*.

knuckle. ME. *knokel*, not recorded in AS.; cogn. with Du. *kneukel*, knuckle, Ger. *knöchel*, ankle, lit. little bone (Ger. *knochen*, bone). Orig. any joint, current sense being ellipt. for *finger-knuckles*. To *knuckle under* appears to be for earlier to *knock under* (17 cent.), influenced by to *truckle under*. *Knuckle-duster* is US.

knur. Knot. ME. *knorre, knurre*; cf. *knar, gnarl*. Hence the wooden ball used in the north country game of *knur and spell*.

> A truly respectable house where there were skittles and knurr and spell
> (de Morgan, *When Ghost meets Ghost*, ch. v.).

knurl. Projection, ridge. Dim. of *knur*.

knut [*slang*]. See *nut*.

kobold. Ger., "a familiar spirit in mines and houses" (Ludw.). Spec. application of the personal name *Kobold*. See *cobalt, goblin*.

kodak. Trade-name coined arbitrarily (c. 1890) by G. Eastman.

koel. Indian cuckoo. Hind. *koīl*, Sanskrit *kokila*, cogn. with *cuckoo* (q.v.).

koepenick [*neol.*]. Military impostor. The "Captain of Koepenick," a Berlin cobbler named Voight, succeeded (1906), with the help of a second-hand uniform, in persuading the local military to help him raid the bank. A good example of the docility of the Prussian soldier.

> "This young man," said Mr Wild, "is indeed a sort of miniature Koepenick" (*Ev. News*, May 28, 1917).

koh-i-noor. Pers. *kŭh-i-nūr*, mountain of light. Added to E. Crown jewels on conquest of Punjaub (1849).

kohl. Powdered antimony for darkening eyelids. Arab. *kuh'l, koh'l*. See *alcohol*.

kohl-rabi. Turnip-cabbage. Ger., It. *cavoli rape*, pl. of *cavolo rapa*, cole rape. Cf. F. *chou-rave* and see *cole, rape*[1].

kola. See *cola*.

koodoo, kudu. SAfr. antelope. Native (Kaffir) name.

kookri. See *kukri*.

koolah. Austral. marsupial, "Australian bear." Native name.

kopje [*geog.*]. Du., dim. of *kop*, head, as in *Spion Kop*. Du. *kop*, Ger. *kopf*, are from L. *cupa, cuppa*, bowl, "cup" (cf. F. *tête*

from L. *testa*, tile, potsherd). For the true Teut. name see *head*.

koran. Arab. *qorān*, reading. Cf. *alcoran*.

koromiko. New Zeal. shrub. Maori name.

kosher. Food prepared according to Jewish law. Heb. *kāshēr*, right.

kotal [*Anglo-Ind.*]. Mountain pass. Pushto (Afghan) *kōtal*.

kotow, kow-tow. Chin. *k'o-t'ou*, knock head (as sign of submission). See Doyle's *Private of the Buffs*.

kotwal. See *cotwal*.

koumiss. Fermented liquor from mares' milk. Tatar *kumiz*.

kourbash, courbash. Arab. *qurbāsh*, Turk. *qirbāch*, whip. Hence also, via Ger. Slav. Turk., F. *cravache*, riding-whip.

kowhai. New Zeal. plant. Maori name.

kraal. SAfrDu., Port. *curral*; cf. Sp. *corral* (q.v.). Cf. *assagai, sjambok*.

krait, karait. Snake. Hind. *karait*.

kraken. Myth. sea-monster. Norw., first in Pontoppidan's *Naturlige Historie* (1752).

krantz [*SAfr.*]. Over-hanging rock-wall, etc. Du. *krans*, garland, coronet.

Kremlin. At Moscow. Spec. application of Russ. *kreml'*, citadel, of Tatar origin.

kreutzer. Ger. *kreuzer*, from *kreuz*, cross, with which the coin was orig. stamped.

kriegspiel. Ger., war game, second element cogn. with AS. *spilian*, to play. From *krieg* (cf. Du. *krijg*) comes Ger. *kriegen*, to get.

kris. See *crease*[2].

Krishnaism. Worship of *Krishna*, later incarnation of Vishnu.

krone. Coin (cf. *crown*). Usu. in pl. *kroner* (Dan.).

Kroo, Kru. WAfr. name for negro race skilled as sailors, *Kroomen*.

krypton [*chem.*]. Discovered and named (1898) by Ramsay. G. κρυπτόν, hidden.

kudos. G. κῦδος, praise, renown, used in univ. slang.

Ku-klux-klan [*hist.*]. Secret society in Southern States after Amer. Civil War (see Conan Doyle, *Five Orange-pips*). ? G. κύκλος, circle, and *clan*.

kukri, kookri. Goorkha knife. Hind. *kukrī*.

kultur. Ger. (18 cent.). Ident. in origin, but not in sense, with *culture* (q.v.). The latter is expressed by Ger. *bildung*. The *Kulturkampf* was the struggle of Bismarck against the Papacy.

> The vast distance between civilisation and kultur was clearly revealed (Freytag-Loringhoven).

kümmel. Ger., from L., as *cumin* (q.v.).

kunkur. Also *conk-*. Indian limestone. Hind. *kankar*, Prakrit *kakkaram*, Sanskrit *karkaram*. Cf. the *Karakoram Mountains*.

kuphar. Coracle on Euphrates. Arab. *quffah*, circular basket. Cf. *goufa*.

kursaal. Ger., cure hall. See *cure*[1], *saloon*.

kvass. Fermented drink. Russ. *kvas*, leaven.

Their drinke is like our peny ale, and is called quass (Chancellor, 1553).

kyanize. To impregnate timber with preservative. Process patented (1832) by *J. H. Kyan*.

kylin. Porcelain monster. Chin. *ch'i-lin*, male-female.

kyloe. Small West Highland cattle. ? From Sc. *kyle*, narrow strait in West of Scotland, Gael. *caoil*, from *caol*, narrow.

kyrie eleison. G. Κύριε ἐλέησον, Lord, have mercy. Cf. *dirge*, *paternoster*, etc. See *alms*, *church*.

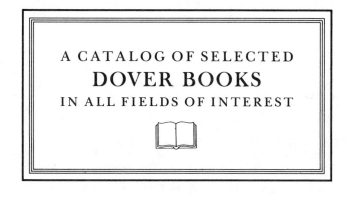

A CATALOG OF SELECTED
DOVER BOOKS
IN ALL FIELDS OF INTEREST

A CATALOG OF SELECTED DOVER
BOOKS IN ALL FIELDS OF INTEREST

CONCERNING THE SPIRITUAL IN ART, Wassily Kandinsky. Pioneering work by father of abstract art. Thoughts on color theory, nature of art. Analysis of earlier masters. 12 illustrations. 80pp. of text. 5⅜ × 8½.   23411-8 Pa. $3.95

ANIMALS: 1,419 Copyright-Free Illustrations of Mammals, Birds, Fish, Insects, etc., Jim Harter (ed.). Clear wood engravings present, in extremely lifelike poses, over 1,000 species of animals. One of the most extensive pictorial sourcebooks of its kind. Captions. Index. 284pp. 9 × 12.   23766-4 Pa. $12.95

CELTIC ART: The Methods of Construction, George Bain. Simple geometric techniques for making Celtic interlacements, spirals, Kells-type initials, animals, humans, etc. Over 500 illustrations. 160pp. 9 × 12. (USO)   22923-8 Pa. $9.95

AN ATLAS OF ANATOMY FOR ARTISTS, Fritz Schider. Most thorough reference work on art anatomy in the world. Hundreds of illustrations, including selections from works by Vesalius, Leonardo, Goya, Ingres, Michelangelo, others. 593 illustrations. 192pp. 7⅞ × 10¼.   20241-0 Pa. $9.95

CELTIC HAND STROKE-BY-STROKE (Irish Half-Uncial from "The Book of Kells"): An Arthur Baker Calligraphy Manual, Arthur Baker. Complete guide to creating each letter of the alphabet in distinctive Celtic manner. Covers hand position, strokes, pens, inks, paper, more. Illustrated. 48pp. 8¼ × 11.
24336-2 Pa. $3.95

EASY ORIGAMI, John Montroll. Charming collection of 32 projects (hat, cup, pelican, piano, swan, many more) specially designed for the novice origami hobbyist. Clearly illustrated easy-to-follow instructions insure that even beginning papercrafters will achieve successful results. 48pp. 8¼ × 11.   27298-2 Pa. $2.95

THE COMPLETE BOOK OF BIRDHOUSE CONSTRUCTION FOR WOOD-WORKERS, Scott D. Campbell. Detailed instructions, illustrations, tables. Also data on bird habitat and instinct patterns. Bibliography. 3 tables. 63 illustrations in 15 figures. 48pp. 5¼ × 8½.   24407-5 Pa. $1.95

BLOOMINGDALE'S ILLUSTRATED 1886 CATALOG: Fashions, Dry Goods and Housewares, Bloomingdale Brothers. Famed merchants' extremely rare catalog depicting about 1,700 products: clothing, housewares, firearms, dry goods, jewelry, more. Invaluable for dating, identifying vintage items. Also, copyright-free graphics for artists, designers. Co-published with Henry Ford Museum & Green-field Village. 160pp. 8¼ × 11.   25780-0 Pa. $9.95

HISTORIC COSTUME IN PICTURES, Braun & Schneider. Over 1,450 costumed figures in clearly detailed engravings—from dawn of civilization to end of 19th century. Captions. Many folk costumes. 256pp. 8⅜ × 11¾.   23150-X Pa. $11.95

STICKLEY CRAFTSMAN FURNITURE CATALOGS, Gustav Stickley and L. & J. G. Stickley. Beautiful, functional furniture in two authentic catalogs from 1910. 594 illustrations, including 277 photos, show settles, rockers, armchairs, reclining chairs, bookcases, desks, tables. 183pp. 6½ × 9¼.   23838-5 Pa. $9.95

AMERICAN LOCOMOTIVES IN HISTORIC PHOTOGRAPHS: 1858 to 1949, Ron Ziel (ed.). A rare collection of 126 meticulously detailed official photographs, called "builder portraits," of American locomotives that majestically chronicle the rise of steam locomotive power in America. Introduction. Detailed captions. xi + 129pp. 9 × 12.   27393-8 Pa. $12.95

AMERICA'S LIGHTHOUSES: An Illustrated History, Francis Ross Holland, Jr. Delightfully written, profusely illustrated fact-filled survey of over 200 American lighthouses since 1716. History, anecdotes, technological advances, more. 240pp. 8 × 10¾.   25576-X Pa. $11.95

TOWARDS A NEW ARCHITECTURE, Le Corbusier. Pioneering manifesto by founder of "International School." Technical and aesthetic theories, views of industry, economics, relation of form to function, "mass-production split" and much more. Profusely illustrated. 320pp. 6⅛ × 9¼. (USO)   25023-7 Pa. $9.95

HOW THE OTHER HALF LIVES, Jacob Riis. Famous journalistic record, exposing poverty and degradation of New York slums around 1900, by major social reformer. 100 striking and influential photographs. 233pp. 10 × 7⅞.

     22012-5 Pa $10.95

FRUIT KEY AND TWIG KEY TO TREES AND SHRUBS, William M. Harlow. One of the handiest and most widely used identification aids. Fruit key covers 120 deciduous and evergreen species; twig key 160 deciduous species. Easily used. Over 300 photographs. 126pp. 5⅜ × 8½.   20511-8 Pa. $3.95

COMMON BIRD SONGS, Dr. Donald J. Borror. Songs of 60 most common U.S. birds: robins, sparrows, cardinals, bluejays, finches, more—arranged in order of increasing complexity. Up to 9 variations of songs of each species.

     Cassette and manual 99911-4 $8.95

ORCHIDS AS HOUSE PLANTS, Rebecca Tyson Northen. Grow cattleyas and many other kinds of orchids—in a window, in a case, or under artificial light. 63 illustrations. 148pp. 5⅜ × 8½.   23261-1 Pa. $4.95

MONSTER MAZES, Dave Phillips. Masterful mazes at four levels of difficulty. Avoid deadly perils and evil creatures to find magical treasures. Solutions for all 32 exciting illustrated puzzles. 48pp. 8¼ × 11.   26005-4 Pa. $2.95

MOZART'S DON GIOVANNI (DOVER OPERA LIBRETTO SERIES), Wolfgang Amadeus Mozart. Introduced and translated by Ellen H. Bleiler. Standard Italian libretto, with complete English translation. Convenient and thoroughly portable—an ideal companion for reading along with a recording or the performance itself. Introduction. List of characters. Plot summary. 121pp. 5¼ × 8½.

     24944-1 Pa. $2.95

TECHNICAL MANUAL AND DICTIONARY OF CLASSICAL BALLET, Gail Grant. Defines, explains, comments on steps, movements, poses and concepts. 15-page pictorial section. Basic book for student, viewer. 127pp. 5⅜ × 8½.

     21843-0 Pa. $4.95

BRASS INSTRUMENTS: Their History and Development, Anthony Baines. Authoritative, updated survey of the evolution of trumpets, trombones, bugles, cornets, French horns, tubas and other brass wind instruments. Over 140 illustrations and 48 music examples. Corrected and updated by author. New preface. Bibliography. 320pp. 5⅜ × 8½. 27574-4 Pa. $9.95

HOLLYWOOD GLAMOR PORTRAITS, John Kobal (ed.). 145 photos from 1926–49. Harlow, Gable, Bogart, Bacall; 94 stars in all. Full background on photographers, technical aspects. 160pp. 8⅜ × 11¼. 23352-9 Pa. $11.95

MAX AND MORITZ, Wilhelm Busch. Great humor classic in both German and English. Also 10 other works: "Cat and Mouse," "Plisch and Plumm," etc. 216pp. 5⅜ × 8½. 20181-3 Pa. $5.95

THE RAVEN AND OTHER FAVORITE POEMS, Edgar Allan Poe. Over 40 of the author's most memorable poems: "The Bells," "Ulalume," "Israfel," "To Helen," "The Conqueror Worm," "Eldorado," "Annabel Lee," many more. Alphabetic lists of titles and first lines. 64pp. 5³⁄₁₆ × 8¼. 26685-0 Pa. $1.00

SEVEN SCIENCE FICTION NOVELS, H. G. Wells. The standard collection of the great novels. Complete, unabridged. First Men in the Moon, Island of Dr. Moreau, War of the Worlds, Food of the Gods, Invisible Man, Time Machine, In the Days of the Comet. Total of 1,015pp. 5⅜ × 8½. (USO) 20264-X Clothbd. $29.95

AMULETS AND SUPERSTITIONS, E. A. Wallis Budge. Comprehensive discourse on origin, powers of amulets in many ancient cultures: Arab, Persian, Babylonian, Assyrian, Egyptian, Gnostic, Hebrew, Phoenician, Syriac, etc. Covers cross, swastika, crucifix, seals, rings, stones, etc. 584pp. 5⅜ × 8½. 23573-4 Pa. $12.95

RUSSIAN STORIES/PYCCKNE PACCKA3bl: A Dual-Language Book, edited by Gleb Struve. Twelve tales by such masters as Chekhov, Tolstoy, Dostoevsky, Pushkin, others. Excellent word-for-word English translations on facing pages, plus teaching and study aids, Russian/English vocabulary, biographical/critical introductions, more. 416pp. 5⅜ × 8½. 26244-8 Pa. $8.95

PHILADELPHIA THEN AND NOW: 60 Sites Photographed in the Past and Present, Kenneth Finkel and Susan Oyama. Rare photographs of City Hall, Logan Square, Independence Hall, Betsy Ross House, other landmarks juxtaposed with contemporary views. Captures changing face of historic city. Introduction. Captions. 128pp. 8¼ × 11. 25790-8 Pa. $9.95

AIA ARCHITECTURAL GUIDE TO NASSAU AND SUFFOLK COUNTIES, LONG ISLAND, The American Institute of Architects, Long Island Chapter, and the Society for the Preservation of Long Island Antiquities. Comprehensive, well-researched and generously illustrated volume brings to life over three centuries of Long Island's great architectural heritage. More than 240 photographs with authoritative, extensively detailed captions. 176pp. 8¼ × 11. 26946-9 Pa. $14.95

NORTH AMERICAN INDIAN LIFE: Customs and Traditions of 23 Tribes, Elsie Clews Parsons (ed.). 27 fictionalized essays by noted anthropologists examine religion, customs, government, additional facets of life among the Winnebago, Crow, Zuni, Eskimo, other tribes. 480pp. 6⅛ × 9¼. 27377-6 Pa. $10.95

FRANK LLOYD WRIGHT'S HOLLYHOCK HOUSE, Donald Hoffmann. Lavishly illustrated, carefully documented study of one of Wright's most controversial residential designs. Over 120 photographs, floor plans, elevations, etc. Detailed perceptive text by noted Wright scholar. Index. 128pp. 9¼ × 10¾.
27133-1 Pa. $11.95

THE MALE AND FEMALE FIGURE IN MOTION: 60 Classic Photographic Sequences, Eadweard Muybridge. 60 true-action photographs of men and women walking, running, climbing, bending, turning, etc., reproduced from rare 19th-century masterpiece. vi + 121pp. 9 × 12.
24745-7 Pa. $10.95

1001 QUESTIONS ANSWERED ABOUT THE SEASHORE, N. J. Berrill and Jacquelyn Berrill. Queries answered about dolphins, sea snails, sponges, starfish, fishes, shore birds, many others. Covers appearance, breeding, growth, feeding, much more. 305pp. 5¼ × 8¼.
23366-9 Pa. $7.95

GUIDE TO OWL WATCHING IN NORTH AMERICA, Donald S. Heintzelman. Superb guide offers complete data and descriptions of 19 species: barn owl, screech owl, snowy owl, many more. Expert coverage of owl-watching equipment, conservation, migrations and invasions, etc. Guide to observing sites. 84 illustrations. xiii + 193pp. 5⅜ × 8½.
27344-X Pa. $8.95

MEDICINAL AND OTHER USES OF NORTH AMERICAN PLANTS: A Historical Survey with Special Reference to the Eastern Indian Tribes, Charlotte Erichsen-Brown. Chronological historical citations document 500 years of usage of plants, trees, shrubs native to eastern Canada, northeastern U.S. Also complete identifying information. 343 illustrations. 544pp. 6½ × 9¼. 25951-X Pa. $12.95

STORYBOOK MAZES, Dave Phillips. 23 stories and mazes on two-page spreads: Wizard of Oz, Treasure Island, Robin Hood, etc. Solutions. 64pp. 8¼ × 11.
23628-5 Pa. $2.95

NEGRO FOLK MUSIC, U.S.A., Harold Courlander. Noted folklorist's scholarly yet readable analysis of rich and varied musical tradition. Includes authentic versions of over 40 folk songs. Valuable bibliography and discography. xi + 324pp. 5⅜ × 8½.
27350-4 Pa. $7.95

MOVIE-STAR PORTRAITS OF THE FORTIES, John Kobal (ed.). 163 glamor, studio photos of 106 stars of the 1940s: Rita Hayworth, Ava Gardner, Marlon Brando, Clark Gable, many more. 176pp. 8⅜ × 11¼. 23546-7 Pa. $11.95

BENCHLEY LOST AND FOUND, Robert Benchley. Finest humor from early 30s, about pet peeves, child psychologists, post office and others. Mostly unavailable elsewhere. 73 illustrations by Peter Arno and others. 183pp. 5⅜ × 8½.
22410-4 Pa. $5.95

YEKL and THE IMPORTED BRIDEGROOM AND OTHER STORIES OF YIDDISH NEW YORK, Abraham Cahan. Film Hester Street based on Yekl (1896). Novel, other stories among first about Jewish immigrants on N.Y.'s East Side. 240pp. 5⅜ × 8½. 22427-9 Pa. $6.95

SELECTED POEMS, Walt Whitman. Generous sampling from *Leaves of Grass*. Twenty-four poems include "I Hear America Singing," "Song of the Open Road," "I Sing the Body Electric," "When Lilacs Last in the Dooryard Bloom'd," "O Captain! My Captain!"—all reprinted from an authoritative edition. Lists of titles and first lines. 128pp. 5³⁄₁₆ × 8¼. 26878-0 Pa. $1.00

THE BEST TALES OF HOFFMANN, E. T. A. Hoffmann. 10 of Hoffmann's most important stories: "Nutcracker and the King of Mice," "The Golden Flowerpot," etc. 458pp. 5⅜ × 8½. 21793-0 Pa. $8.95

FROM FETISH TO GOD IN ANCIENT EGYPT, E. A. Wallis Budge. Rich detailed survey of Egyptian conception of "God" and gods, magic, cult of animals, Osiris, more. Also, superb English translations of hymns and legends. 240 illustrations. 545pp. 5⅜ × 8½. 25803-3 Pa. $11.95

FRENCH STORIES/CONTES FRANÇAIS: A Dual-Language Book, Wallace Fowlie. Ten stories by French masters, Voltaire to Camus: "Micromegas" by Voltaire; "The Atheist's Mass" by Balzac; "Minuet" by de Maupassant; "The Guest" by Camus, six more. Excellent English translations on facing pages. Also French-English vocabulary list, exercises, more. 352pp. 5⅜ × 8½. 26443-2 Pa. $8.95

CHICAGO AT THE TURN OF THE CENTURY IN PHOTOGRAPHS: 122 Historic Views from the Collections of the Chicago Historical Society, Larry A. Viskochil. Rare large-format prints offer detailed views of City Hall, State Street, the Loop, Hull House, Union Station, many other landmarks, circa 1904–1913. Introduction. Captions. Maps. 144pp. 9⅜ × 12¼. 24656-6 Pa. $12.95

OLD BROOKLYN IN EARLY PHOTOGRAPHS, 1865–1929, William Lee Younger. Luna Park, Gravesend race track, construction of Grand Army Plaza, moving of Hotel Brighton, etc. 157 previously unpublished photographs. 165pp. 8⅞ × 11¾. 23587-4 Pa. $13.95

THE MYTHS OF THE NORTH AMERICAN INDIANS, Lewis Spence. Rich anthology of the myths and legends of the Algonquins, Iroquois, Pawnees and Sioux, prefaced by an extensive historical and ethnological commentary. 36 illustrations. 480pp. 5⅜ × 8½. 25967-6 Pa. $8.95

AN ENCYCLOPEDIA OF BATTLES: Accounts of Over 1,560 Battles from 1479 B.C. to the Present, David Eggenberger. Essential details of every major battle in recorded history from the first battle of Megiddo in 1479 B.C. to Grenada in 1984. List of Battle Maps. New Appendix covering the years 1967–1984. Index. 99 illustrations. 544pp. 6½ × 9¼. 24913-1 Pa. $14.95

SAILING ALONE AROUND THE WORLD, Captain Joshua Slocum. First man to sail around the world, alone, in small boat. One of great feats of seamanship told in delightful manner. 67 illustrations. 294pp. 5⅜ × 8½. 20326-3 Pa. $5.95

ANARCHISM AND OTHER ESSAYS, Emma Goldman. Powerful, penetrating, prophetic essays on direct action, role of minorities, prison reform, puritan hypocrisy, violence, etc. 271pp. 5⅜ × 8½. 22484-8 Pa. $5.95

MYTHS OF THE HINDUS AND BUDDHISTS, Ananda K. Coomaraswamy and Sister Nivedita. Great stories of the epics; deeds of Krishna, Shiva, taken from puranas, Vedas, folk tales; etc. 32 illustrations. 400pp. 5⅜ × 8½. 21759-0 Pa. $9.95

BEYOND PSYCHOLOGY, Otto Rank. Fear of death, desire of immortality, nature of sexuality, social organization, creativity, according to Rankian system. 291pp. 5⅜ × 8½. 20485-5 Pa. $8.95

A THEOLOGICO-POLITICAL TREATISE, Benedict Spinoza. Also contains unfinished Political Treatise. Great classic on religious liberty, theory of government on common consent. R. Elwes translation. Total of 421pp. 5⅜ × 8½. 20249-6 Pa. $8.95

MY BONDAGE AND MY FREEDOM, Frederick Douglass. Born a slave, Douglass became outspoken force in antislavery movement. The best of Douglass' autobiographies. Graphic description of slave life. 464pp. 5⅜ × 8½. 22457-0 Pa. $8.95

FOLLOWING THE EQUATOR: A Journey Around the World, Mark Twain. Fascinating humorous account of 1897 voyage to Hawaii, Australia, India, New Zealand, etc. Ironic, bemused reports on peoples, customs, climate, flora and fauna, politics, much more. 197 illustrations. 720pp. 5⅜ × 8½. 26113-1 Pa. $15.95

THE PEOPLE CALLED SHAKERS, Edward D. Andrews. Definitive study of Shakers: origins, beliefs, practices, dances, social organization, furniture and crafts, etc. 33 illustrations. 351pp. 5⅜ × 8½. 21081-2 Pa. $8.95

THE MYTHS OF GREECE AND ROME, H. A. Guerber. A classic of mythology, generously illustrated, long prized for its simple, graphic, accurate retelling of the principal myths of Greece and Rome, and for its commentary on their origins and significance. With 64 illustrations by Michelangelo, Raphael, Titian, Rubens, Canova, Bernini and others. 480pp. 5⅜ × 8½. 27584-1 Pa. $9.95

PSYCHOLOGY OF MUSIC, Carl E. Seashore. Classic work discusses music as a medium from psychological viewpoint. Clear treatment of physical acoustics, auditory apparatus, sound perception, development of musical skills, nature of musical feeling, host of other topics. 88 figures. 408pp. 5⅜ × 8½. 21851-1 Pa. $9.95

THE PHILOSOPHY OF HISTORY, Georg W. Hegel. Great classic of Western thought develops concept that history is not chance but rational process, the evolution of freedom. 457pp. 5⅜ × 8½. 20112-0 Pa. $9.95

THE BOOK OF TEA, Kakuzo Okakura. Minor classic of the Orient: entertaining, charming explanation, interpretation of traditional Japanese culture in terms of tea ceremony. 94pp. 5⅜ × 8½. 20070-1 Pa. $3.95

LIFE IN ANCIENT EGYPT, Adolf Erman. Fullest, most thorough, detailed older account with much not in more recent books, domestic life, religion, magic, medicine, commerce, much more. Many illustrations reproduce tomb paintings, carvings, hieroglyphs, etc. 597pp. 5⅜ × 8½. 22632-8 Pa. $10.95

SUNDIALS, Their Theory and Construction, Albert Waugh. Far and away the best, most thorough coverage of ideas, mathematics concerned, types, construction, adjusting anywhere. Simple, nontechnical treatment allows even children to build several of these dials. Over 100 illustrations. 230pp. 5⅜ × 8½. 22947-5 Pa. $7.95

DYNAMICS OF FLUIDS IN POROUS MEDIA, Jacob Bear. For advanced students of ground water hydrology, soil mechanics and physics, drainage and irrigation engineering, and more. 335 illustrations. Exercises, with answers. 784pp. 6⅛ × 9¼. 65675-6 Pa. $19.95

SONGS OF EXPERIENCE: Facsimile Reproduction with 26 Plates in Full Color, William Blake. 26 full-color plates from a rare 1826 edition. Includes "The Tyger," "London," "Holy Thursday," and other poems. Printed text of poems. 48pp. 5¼ × 7. 24636-1 Pa. $4.95

OLD-TIME VIGNETTES IN FULL COLOR, Carol Belanger Grafton (ed.). Over 390 charming, often sentimental illustrations, selected from archives of Victorian graphics—pretty women posing, children playing, food, flowers, kittens and puppies, smiling cherubs, birds and butterflies, much more. All copyright-free. 48pp. 9¼ × 12¼. 27269-9 Pa. $5.95

CATALOG OF DOVER BOOKS

PERSPECTIVE FOR ARTISTS, Rex Vicat Cole. Depth, perspective of sky and sea, shadows, much more, not usually covered. 391 diagrams, 81 reproductions of drawings and paintings. 279pp. 5⅜ × 8½. 22487-2 Pa. $6.95

DRAWING THE LIVING FIGURE, Joseph Sheppard. Innovative approach to artistic anatomy focuses on specifics of surface anatomy, rather than muscles and bones. Over 170 drawings of live models in front, back and side views, and in widely varying poses. Accompanying diagrams. 177 illustrations. Introduction. Index. 144pp. 8⅜ × 11¼. 26723-7 Pa. $8.95

GOTHIC AND OLD ENGLISH ALPHABETS: 100 Complete Fonts, Dan X. Solo. Add power, elegance to posters, signs, other graphics with 100 stunning copyright-free alphabets: Blackstone, Dolbey, Germania, 97 more—including many lower-case, numerals, punctuation marks. 104pp. 8⅛ × 11. 24695-7 Pa. $8.95

HOW TO DO BEADWORK, Mary White. Fundamental book on craft from simple projects to five-bead chains and woven works. 106 illustrations. 142pp. 5⅜ × 8. 20697-1 Pa. $4.95

THE BOOK OF WOOD CARVING, Charles Marshall Sayers. Finest book for beginners discusses fundamentals and offers 34 designs. "Absolutely first rate . . . well thought out and well executed."—E. J. Tangerman. 118pp. 7¾ × 10⅝. 23654-4 Pa. $5.95

ILLUSTRATED CATALOG OF CIVIL WAR MILITARY GOODS: Union Army Weapons, Insignia, Uniform Accessories, and Other Equipment, Schuyler, Hartley, and Graham. Rare, profusely illustrated 1846 catalog includes Union Army uniform and dress regulations, arms and ammunition, coats, insignia, flags, swords, rifles, etc. 226 illustrations. 160pp. 9 × 12. 24939-5 Pa. $10.95

WOMEN'S FASHIONS OF THE EARLY 1900s: An Unabridged Republication of "New York Fashions, 1909," National Cloak & Suit Co. Rare catalog of mail-order fashions documents women's and children's clothing styles shortly after the turn of the century. Captions offer full descriptions, prices. Invaluable resource for fashion, costume historians. Approximately 725 illustrations. 128pp. 8⅜ × 11¼. 27276-1 Pa. $11.95

THE 1912 AND 1915 GUSTAV STICKLEY FURNITURE CATALOGS, Gustav Stickley. With over 200 detailed illustrations and descriptions, these two catalogs are essential reading and reference materials and identification guides for Stickley furniture. Captions cite materials, dimensions and prices. 112pp. 6½ × 9¼. 26676-1 Pa. $9.95

EARLY AMERICAN LOCOMOTIVES, John H. White, Jr. Finest locomotive engravings from early 19th century: historical (1804–74), main-line (after 1870), special, foreign, etc. 147 plates. 142pp. 11⅜ × 8¼. 22772-3 Pa. $10.95

THE TALL SHIPS OF TODAY IN PHOTOGRAPHS, Frank O. Braynard. Lavishly illustrated tribute to nearly 100 majestic contemporary sailing vessels: Amerigo Vespucci, Clearwater, Constitution, Eagle, Mayflower, Sea Cloud, Victory, many more. Authoritative captions provide statistics, background on each ship. 190 black-and-white photographs and illustrations. Introduction. 128pp. 8⅞ × 11¾. 27163-3 Pa. $13.95

EARLY NINETEENTH-CENTURY CRAFTS AND TRADES, Peter Stockham (ed.). Extremely rare 1807 volume describes to youngsters the crafts and trades of the day: brickmaker, weaver, dressmaker, bookbinder, ropemaker, saddler, many more. Quaint prose, charming illustrations for each craft. 20 black-and-white line illustrations. 192pp. 4⅜ × 6. 27293-1 Pa. $4.95

VICTORIAN FASHIONS AND COSTUMES FROM HARPER'S BAZAR, 1867–1898, Stella Blum (ed.). Day costumes, evening wear, sports clothes, shoes, hats, other accessories in over 1,000 detailed engravings. 320pp. 9⅜ × 12¼. 22990-4 Pa. $13.95

GUSTAV STICKLEY, THE CRAFTSMAN, Mary Ann Smith. Superb study surveys broad scope of Stickley's achievement, especially in architecture. Design philosophy, rise and fall of the Craftsman empire, descriptions and floor plans for many Craftsman houses, more. 86 black-and-white halftones. 31 line illustrations. Introduction. 208pp. 6½ × 9¼. 27210-9 Pa. $9.95

THE LONG ISLAND RAIL ROAD IN EARLY PHOTOGRAPHS, Ron Ziel. Over 220 rare photos, informative text document origin (1844) and development of rail service on Long Island. Vintage views of early trains, locomotives, stations, passengers, crews, much more. Captions. 8⅞ × 11¾. 26301-0 Pa. $13.95

THE BOOK OF OLD SHIPS: From Egyptian Galleys to Clipper Ships, Henry B. Culver. Superb, authoritative history of sailing vessels, with 80 magnificent line illustrations. Galley, bark, caravel, longship, whaler, many more. Detailed, informative text on each vessel by noted naval historian. Introduction. 256pp. 5⅜ × 8½. 27332-6 Pa. $6.95

TEN BOOKS ON ARCHITECTURE, Vitruvius. The most important book ever written on architecture. Early Roman aesthetics, technology, classical orders, site selection, all other aspects. Morgan translation. 331pp. 5⅜ × 8½. 20645-9 Pa. $8.95

THE HUMAN FIGURE IN MOTION, Eadweard Muybridge. More than 4,500 stopped-action photos, in action series, showing undraped men, women, children jumping, lying down, throwing, sitting, wrestling, carrying, etc. 390pp. 7⅞ × 10⅝. 20204-6 Clothbd. $24.95

TREES OF THE EASTERN AND CENTRAL UNITED STATES AND CANADA, William M. Harlow. Best one-volume guide to 140 trees. Full descriptions, woodlore, range, etc. Over 600 illustrations. Handy size. 288pp. 4½ × 6⅜. 20395-6 Pa. $5.95

SONGS OF WESTERN BIRDS, Dr. Donald J. Borror. Complete song and call repertoire of 60 western species, including flycatchers, juncoes, cactus wrens, many more—includes fully illustrated booklet. Cassette and manual 99913-0 $8.95

GROWING AND USING HERBS AND SPICES, Milo Miloradovich. Versatile handbook provides all the information needed for cultivation and use of all the herbs and spices available in North America. 4 illustrations. Index. Glossary. 236pp. 5⅜ × 8½. 25058-X Pa. $6.95

BIG BOOK OF MAZES AND LABYRINTHS, Walter Shepherd. 50 mazes and labyrinths in all—classical, solid, ripple, and more—in one great volume. Perfect inexpensive puzzler for clever youngsters. Full solutions. 112pp. 8⅛ × 11. 22951-3 Pa. $4.95

PIANO TUNING, J. Cree Fischer. Clearest, best book for beginner, amateur. Simple repairs, raising dropped notes, tuning by easy method of flattened fifths. No previous skills needed. 4 illustrations. 201pp. 5⅜ × 8½.   23267-0 Pa. $5.95

A SOURCE BOOK IN THEATRICAL HISTORY, A. M. Nagler. Contemporary observers on acting, directing, make-up, costuming, stage props, machinery, scene design, from Ancient Greece to Chekhov. 611pp. 5⅜ × 8½.   20515-0 Pa. $11.95

THE COMPLETE NONSENSE OF EDWARD LEAR, Edward Lear. All nonsense limericks, zany alphabets, Owl and Pussycat, songs, nonsense botany, etc., illustrated by Lear. Total of 320pp. 5⅜ × 8½. (USO)   20167-8 Pa. $6.95

VICTORIAN PARLOUR POETRY: An Annotated Anthology, Michael R. Turner. 117 gems by Longfellow, Tennyson, Browning, many lesser-known poets. "The Village Blacksmith," "Curfew Must Not Ring Tonight," "Only a Baby Small," dozens more, often difficult to find elsewhere. Index of poets, titles, first lines. xxiii + 325pp. 5⅜ × 8¼.   27044-0 Pa. $8.95

DUBLINERS, James Joyce. Fifteen stories offer vivid, tightly focused observations of the lives of Dublin's poorer classes. At least one, "The Dead," is considered a masterpiece. Reprinted complete and unabridged from standard edition. 160pp. 5³⁄₁₆ × 8¼.   26870-5 Pa. $1.00

THE HAUNTED MONASTERY and THE CHINESE MAZE MURDERS, Robert van Gulik. Two full novels by van Gulik, set in 7th-century China, continue adventures of Judge Dee and his companions. An evil Taoist monastery, seemingly supernatural events; overgrown topiary maze hides strange crimes. 27 illustrations. 328pp. 5⅜ × 8½.   23502-5 Pa. $7.95

THE BOOK OF THE SACRED MAGIC OF ABRAMELIN THE MAGE, translated by S. MacGregor Mathers. Medieval manuscript of ceremonial magic. Basic document in Aleister Crowley, Golden Dawn groups. 268pp. 5⅜ × 8½.
23211-5 Pa. $8.95

NEW RUSSIAN-ENGLISH AND ENGLISH-RUSSIAN DICTIONARY, M. A. O'Brien. This is a remarkably handy Russian dictionary, containing a surprising amount of information, including over 70,000 entries. 366pp. 4½ × 6⅛.
20208-9 Pa. $9.95

HISTORIC HOMES OF THE AMERICAN PRESIDENTS, Second, Revised Edition, Irvin Haas. A traveler's guide to American Presidential homes, most open to the public, depicting and describing homes occupied by every American President from George Washington to George Bush. With visiting hours, admission charges, travel routes. 175 photographs. Index. 160pp. 8¼ × 11. 26751-2 Pa. $10.95

NEW YORK IN THE FORTIES, Andreas Feininger. 162 brilliant photographs by the well-known photographer, formerly with *Life* magazine. Commuters, shoppers, Times Square at night, much else from city at its peak. Captions by John von Hartz. 181pp. 9¼ × 10¾.   23585-8 Pa. $12.95

INDIAN SIGN LANGUAGE, William Tomkins. Over 525 signs developed by Sioux and other tribes. Written instructions and diagrams. Also 290 pictographs. 111pp. 6⅛ × 9¼.   22029-X Pa. $3.50

ANATOMY: A Complete Guide for Artists, Joseph Sheppard. A master of figure drawing shows artists how to render human anatomy convincingly. Over 460 illustrations. 224pp. 8⅜ × 11¼.   27279-6 Pa. $10.95

MEDIEVAL CALLIGRAPHY: Its History and Technique, Marc Drogin. Spirited history, comprehensive instruction manual covers 13 styles (ca. 4th century thru 15th). Excellent photographs; directions for duplicating medieval techniques with modern tools. 224pp. 8⅜ × 11¼.   26142-5 Pa. $11.95

DRIED FLOWERS: How to Prepare Them, Sarah Whitlock and Martha Rankin. Complete instructions on how to use silica gel, meal and borax, perlite aggregate, sand and borax, glycerine and water to create attractive permanent flower arrangements. 12 illustrations. 32pp. 5⅜ × 8½.   21802-3 Pa. $1.00

EASY-TO-MAKE BIRD FEEDERS FOR WOODWORKERS, Scott D. Campbell. Detailed, simple-to-use guide for designing, constructing, caring for and using feeders. Text, illustrations for 12 classic and contemporary designs. 96pp. 5⅜ × 8½.
25847-5 Pa. $2.95

OLD-TIME CRAFTS AND TRADES, Peter Stockham. An 1807 book created to teach children about crafts and trades open to them as future careers. It describes in detailed, nontechnical terms 24 different occupations, among them coachmaker, gardener, hairdresser, lacemaker, shoemaker, wheelwright, copper-plate printer, milliner, trunkmaker, merchant and brewer. Finely detailed engravings illustrate each occupation. 192pp. 4⅝ × 6.   27398-9 Pa. $4.95

THE HISTORY OF UNDERCLOTHES, C. Willett Cunnington and Phyllis Cunnington. Fascinating, well-documented survey covering six centuries of English undergarments, enhanced with over 100 illustrations: 12th-century laced-up bodice, footed long drawers (1795), 19th-century bustles, 19th-century corsets for men, Victorian "bust improvers," much more. 272pp. 5⅜ × 8¼.   27124-2 Pa. $9.95

ARTS AND CRAFTS FURNITURE: The Complete Brooks Catalog of 1912, Brooks Manufacturing Co. Photos and detailed descriptions of more than 150 now very collectible furniture designs from the Arts and Crafts movement depict davenports, settees, buffets, desks, tables, chairs, bedsteads, dressers and more, all built of solid, quarter-sawed oak. Invaluable for students and enthusiasts of antiques, Americana and the decorative arts. 80pp. 6½ × 9¼.   27471-3 Pa. $7.95

HOW WE INVENTED THE AIRPLANE: An Illustrated History, Orville Wright. Fascinating firsthand account covers early experiments, construction of planes and motors, first flights, much more. Introduction and commentary by Fred C. Kelly. 76 photographs. 96pp. 8¼ × 11.   25662-6 Pa. $8.95

THE ARTS OF THE SAILOR: Knotting, Splicing and Ropework, Hervey Garrett Smith. Indispensable shipboard reference covers tools, basic knots and useful hitches; handsewing and canvas work, more. Over 100 illustrations. Delightful reading for sea lovers. 256pp. 5⅜ × 8½.   26440-8 Pa. $7.95

FRANK LLOYD WRIGHT'S FALLINGWATER: The House and Its History, Second, Revised Edition, Donald Hoffmann. A total revision—both in text and illustrations—of the standard document on Fallingwater, the boldest, most personal architectural statement of Wright's mature years, updated with valuable new material from the recently opened Frank Lloyd Wright Archives. "Fascinating"—*The New York Times*. 116 illustrations. 128pp. 9¼ × 10¾.
27430-6 Pa. $10.95

PHOTOGRAPHIC SKETCHBOOK OF THE CIVIL WAR, Alexander Gardner. 100 photos taken on field during the Civil War. Famous shots of Manassas, Harper's Ferry, Lincoln, Richmond, slave pens, etc. 244pp. 10⅝ × 8¼.
22731-6 Pa. $9.95

FIVE ACRES AND INDEPENDENCE, Maurice G. Kains. Great back-to-the-land classic explains basics of self-sufficient farming. The one book to get. 95 illustrations. 397pp. 5⅜ × 8½.
20974-1 Pa. $7.95

SONGS OF EASTERN BIRDS, Dr. Donald J. Borror. Songs and calls of 60 species most common to eastern U.S.: warblers, woodpeckers, flycatchers, thrushes, larks, many more in high-quality recording.
Cassette and manual 99912-2 $8.95

A MODERN HERBAL, Margaret Grieve. Much the fullest, most exact, most useful compilation of herbal material. Gigantic alphabetical encyclopedia, from aconite to zedoary, gives botanical information, medical properties, folklore, economic uses, much else. Indispensable to serious reader. 161 illustrations. 888pp. 6½ × 9¼. 2-vol. set. (USO)
Vol. I: 22798-7 Pa. $9.95
Vol. II: 22799-5 Pa. $9.95

HIDDEN TREASURE MAZE BOOK, Dave Phillips. Solve 34 challenging mazes accompanied by heroic tales of adventure. Evil dragons, people-eating plants, bloodthirsty giants, many more dangerous adversaries lurk at every twist and turn. 34 mazes, stories, solutions. 48pp. 8¼ × 11.
24566-7 Pa. $2.95

LETTERS OF W. A. MOZART, Wolfgang A. Mozart. Remarkable letters show bawdy wit, humor, imagination, musical insights, contemporary musical world; includes some letters from Leopold Mozart. 276pp. 5⅜ × 8½.
22859-2 Pa. $7.95

BASIC PRINCIPLES OF CLASSICAL BALLET, Agrippina Vaganova. Great Russian theoretician, teacher explains methods for teaching classical ballet. 118 illustrations. 175pp. 5⅜ × 8½.
22036-2 Pa. $4.95

THE JUMPING FROG, Mark Twain. Revenge edition. The original story of The Celebrated Jumping Frog of Calaveras County, a hapless French translation, and Twain's hilarious "retranslation" from the French. 12 illustrations. 66pp. 5⅜ × 8½.
22686-7 Pa. $3.95

BEST REMEMBERED POEMS, Martin Gardner (ed.). The 126 poems in this superb collection of 19th- and 20th-century British and American verse range from Shelley's "To a Skylark" to the impassioned "Renascence" of Edna St. Vincent Millay and to Edward Lear's whimsical "The Owl and the Pussycat." 224pp. 5⅜ × 8½.
27165-X Pa. $4.95

COMPLETE SONNETS, William Shakespeare. Over 150 exquisite poems deal with love, friendship, the tyranny of time, beauty's evanescence, death and other themes in language of remarkable power, precision and beauty. Glossary of archaic terms. 80pp. 5³⁄₁₆ × 8¼.
26686-9 Pa. $1.00

BODIES IN A BOOKSHOP, R. T. Campbell. Challenging mystery of blackmail and murder with ingenious plot and superbly drawn characters. In the best tradition of British suspense fiction. 192pp. 5⅜ × 8½.
24720-1 Pa. $5.95

CATALOG OF DOVER BOOKS

THE INFLUENCE OF SEA POWER UPON HISTORY, 1660–1783, A. T. Mahan. Influential classic of naval history and tactics still used as text in war colleges. First paperback edition. 4 maps. 24 battle plans. 640pp. 5⅜ × 8½.
25509-3 Pa. $12.95

THE STORY OF THE TITANIC AS TOLD BY ITS SURVIVORS, Jack Winocour (ed.). What it was really like. Panic, despair, shocking inefficiency, and a little heroism. More thrilling than any fictional account. 26 illustrations. 320pp. 5⅜ × 8½. 20610-6 Pa. $8.95

FAIRY AND FOLK TALES OF THE IRISH PEASANTRY, William Butler Yeats (ed.). Treasury of 64 tales from the twilight world of Celtic myth and legend: "The Soul Cages," "The Kildare Pooka," "King O'Toole and his Goose," many more. Introduction and Notes by W. B. Yeats. 352pp. 5⅜ × 8½. 26941-8 Pa. $8.95

BUDDHIST MAHAYANA TEXTS, E. B. Cowell and Others (eds.). Superb, accurate translations of basic documents in Mahayana Buddhism, highly important in history of religions. The Buddha-karita of Asvaghosha, Larger Sukhavativyuha, more. 448pp. 5⅜ × 8½. 25552-2 Pa. $9.95

ONE TWO THREE . . . INFINITY: Facts and Speculations of Science, George Gamow. Great physicist's fascinating, readable overview of contemporary science: number theory, relativity, fourth dimension, entropy, genes, atomic structure, much more. 128 illustrations. Index. 352pp. 5⅜ × 8½. 25664-2 Pa. $8.95

ENGINEERING IN HISTORY, Richard Shelton Kirby, et al. Broad, nontechnical survey of history's major technological advances: birth of Greek science, industrial revolution, electricity and applied science, 20th-century automation, much more. 181 illustrations. ". . . excellent . . ."—Isis. Bibliography. vii + 530pp. 5⅜ × 8¼.
26412-2 Pa. $14.95

Prices subject to change without notice.

Available at your book dealer or write for free catalog to Dept. GI, Dover Publications, Inc., 31 East 2nd St., Mineola, N.Y. 11501. Dover publishes more than 500 books each year on science, elementary and advanced mathematics, biology, music, art, literary history, social sciences and other areas.